The Encyclopedia

of

Organic Gardening

THE ENCYCLOPEDIA OF ORGANIC GARDENING

By the staff of ORGANIC GARDENING AND FARMING MAGAZINE

J. I. RODALE, *Editor-in-Chief*

ROBERT RODALE, *Editor*

JEROME OLDS, *Executive Editor*

M. C. GOLDMAN, *Managing Editor*

MAURICE FRANZ, *Managing Editor*

JERRY MINNICH, *Associate Editor*

Compilation Supervised by

JEROME OLDS

RODALE BOOKS, INC., EMMAUS, PENNA. 18049

RODALE

WE **INSPIRE** AND **ENABLE** PEOPLE TO IMPROVE
THEIR LIVES AND THE WORLD AROUND THEM

Rodale Garden Books

Executive Editor: Ellen Phillips

Executive Creative Director: Christin Gangi

Designer: Nancy Smola Biltcliff

Associate Copy Manager: Jennifer Hornsby

Manufacturing Manager: Mark Krahforst

We're always happy to hear from you. For questions or comments concerning the editorial content of this book, please write to:
Rodale Inc.
Book Readers' Service
33 East Minor Street
Emmaus, PA 18098
Look for other Rodale books wherever books are sold. Or call us at (800) 848-4735.

For more information about Rodale and the books and magazines we publish, visit our World Wide Web site at:

www.rodale.com

SB453.5.E5   1959
635'.04'8   59—1173"r852

Previous ISBN 0–87596–061–8
ISBN 0–87596–841–4

Introduction

THIRTY YEARS AGO, Sir Albert Howard, the British agricultural scientist, began to express in his writings a natural and whole concept of plant and animal husbandry. Town wastes, he said, should be returned to the soil as compost. Artificial fertilizers and poisonous insecticides became suspect to him as improper tools of sound agriculture. The slow but devastating erosion of good lands everywhere could be stopped, said Sir Albert, if we would let nature be our teacher. The seed of the organic idea had been planted, and it took root on every continent.

In the early years of what came to be known as the organic movement, growth was slow. Here and there a few conservation-minded people were impressed with Sir Albert's reasoning and began trying to teach his ideas to others. Soon, though, garden and farm magazines headed by "organic" editors were being published in the United States, England, Australia, New Zealand, and Germany. These magazines became the principal method of communication in the organic field. Because the usual government channels of education and science were largely closed to those with organic leanings, the magazines became clearing houses of organic activity.

Magazines, though, are not the most efficient tool for permanent reference. They are cumbersome to store and to refer to. Today, there is a tremendous demand for the basic facts about organic methods in a permanent reference book. The ENCYCLOPEDIA OF ORGANIC GARDENING has been created to meet that demand.

This book, though, is broader in scope than you may think when first reading the title. It is actually an encyclopedia covering the whole field of horticulture, from the organic point of view. Even people who are unacquainted with the organic idea will find it a useful reference work. The ENCYCLOPEDIA OF ORGANIC GARDENING will tell you how to plant, how to cultivate, how to fertilize and how to harvest. It will help you identify plants, cure plant disease and prevent insect attack. In short, it will help you solve your garden problems.

It has been many months since the first editorial meeting on the ENCYCLOPEDIA OF ORGANIC GARDENING took place. And, in fact, the idea for a complete reference book about the organic method goes back many more years.

Our editorial objectives were to publish a comprehensive, readable book that would give *practical* information on the entire realm of organic gardening, and to describe the relationship between soils and actual gardening and farming practices.

We realized that this was an ambitious undertaking; we hoped that a book of this nature would give new impetus to the already well-established organic gardening idea. To reach our goal, many gardening authorities were contacted; and much research was done. We received encouragement from everyone. Authors of articles in *Organic Gardening and Farming* gave us permission to use their material, and notified us they'd be willing to help in any way possible.

Special attention has been given to the subjects of major importance to organic gardeners. Composting, mulching, fertilizing, soils, vegetable gardening, flower gardening, orcharding and fruit trees, house plants, landscaping, nut trees, plant diseases and insect control, shrubs, borders—these topics are covered in detail.

Basic as well as more advanced information is given on growing plants in cold frames and greenhouses, for propagating plants by division, cuttings or layering. Growing details are given as well for thousands of plants in individual entries. In keeping with our desire to make the ENCYCLOPEDIA a practical book, most plants are listed under their well-known popular names instead of the Latin name. Cross-references will lead you from one related subject to another. For example, if you want information on liming your soil, the entry under LIME tells you which form is best, how much to apply, and why LIME is useful to plants. A reference to ACIDITY-ALKALINITY will take you to a further discussion telling you, among other things, which plants need lime, which ones do not.

Every gardening topic that we've considered of interest has been described thoroughly. For example, the subject of layering—an important one to many— was discussed in such a way that accurate coverage is given to *all* of the different methods. The same was true of LAWNS, PRUNING, HOUSE PLANTS, BERRIES, HUMUS, PROTECTING PLANTS, HERBS and ROSES.

And now the book is done. It is with a feeling of accomplishment that we realize that the last entry has been made. And we're sure this feeling is shared by the many others whose efforts went into the ENCYCLOPEDIA. People like Thomas Powell and Dorothy Franz, and the many other authors whose names are listed following their articles.

J. I. RODALE
ROBERT RODALE
JEROME OLDS

ENCYCLOPEDIA OF ORGANIC GARDENING

A

A HORIZON: All soils have a profile—a succession of layers in a vertical section down into loose, weathered rock. The individual layers are called horizons. The upper layers of the soil profile, known as the A horizon, generally contain the most organic matter, bacteria, fungi, and are darkened as a result. This upper layer is the surface soil with which we are most familiar.

The surface of this horizon, because of the humus, is generally dark brown to black. In the soils of the prairie and of the plains, this color extends to a considerable depth. In the soils of the forest regions, the color tends to change with depth to gray, brown, yellow, or red, depending on the geographic location. The A horizon is impregnated with humus and honeycombed with dead and living roots, the quantity varying with the geographic position. The structure too is characteristic for each soil, depending upon its distribution on the earth's surface. In some geographic regions the structure is granular; in others, it may be laminated, nutty, crumbly, prismatic, or lumpy. The depth of the A horizon fluctuates widely; from six to eight inches in the semidesert region to more than two feet in the semiarid great plains region, and to 15 to 16 inches in the humid temperate region. In the northerly section of the humid temperate zone, the lower portion of this horizon is sometimes ash-gray and is generally lighter in color than the upper portion. *See also* B HORIZON; C HORIZON.

ABELIA: Small to medium-sized shrubs of the honeysuckle family. The small, numerous and attractive flowers vary from white to pink or purple. Some varieties are hardy as far north as Pennsylvania.

Abelias do best in a sunny, fairly protected place. They prefer a well-drained soil, enriched with compost, leaf mold or peat moss. Propagation can be done with cuttings of green wood in summer, which should be rooted under glass, with cuttings of ripened wood in autumn, or with layers in springtime. They attain a height

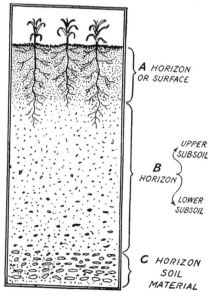

A HORIZON OR SURFACE

B HORIZON
UPPER SUBSOIL
LOWER SUBSOIL

C HORIZON SOIL MATERIAL

of three to five feet and bloom June through October.

The floribunda type can be grown in a cool greenhouse and prefers a sandy-compost potting mixture rich with leaf mold and peat moss.

ABIES: *see* FIR

ABSINTHE: (*Artemisia absinthium*) Often considered a weed, this perennial herb generally grows best in poor, sandy soils—prefers open sunshine and blooms during summer. Also known as wormwood, absinthe is used in the distillation of the liquor of the same name. *See also* ARTEMISIA.

ACACIA: Quick-growing trees and shrubs grown mostly in the warmer parts of the country, some kinds of acacias have been reported to grow as much as ten to 12 feet in one season. However, acacias are usually short-lived, reaching their full maturity when about 30 years old and then starting to die.

The Australian species is native to such states as Arizona, California, Florida, Oklahoma and Texas. Although hardier varieties are being developed, most current acacias cannot endure too much frost. Winter temperatures below 20° F. will be damaging.

In suitable climates, they are easily grown outdoors. Once established, acacias generally are drought-resistant, but for quick growth, they need good soil and sufficient water.

Propagating can be done with seeds, soaking them first in hot water and then cold, then planting while the seeds are still wet. Acacias can also be propagated by cuttings of half-ripened wood, from which a delicate taproot develops.

These attractive, free-flowering shrubs produce dense clusters of very small flowers, usually yellow.

ACCENT PLANT: Generally a shrub or tree (sometimes a group) that is used to accentuate some special feature in the garden design. A sense of form and arrangement requires careful use of an accent plant in just the right place, curtailing overuse and over-accenting. *See also* LANDSCAPING.

ACEROLA: (*Malpighia glabra*) Also called Barbados Cherry, acerola is a bushy tree native to the tropical and semi-tropical regions of the western hemisphere. When the Spaniards came to Puerto Rico in the late 15th century, they found these "acerola" trees growing wild in various sections of the island. There are no records to show that any serious attempts to domesticate these trees were undertaken at this time. However this tree may be the basis for a new industry for the island of Puerto Rico.

Often attaining a height of ten to 15 feet, the tree has fairly deep, penetrating roots; adapts itself easily to poor soil conditions; and requires comparatively little care. Its trunk is short and slender—about two feet in length and four inches in diameter. Abundant rainfall is a necessity.

The fruits look like cherries, produce a reddish-orange juice with a pleasant tart flavor. Their vitamin C content is highest just before the cherries ripen.

The buds are small, arranged singly and in clusters on slender, short stems. Flowers are also very small, about three-quarters of an inch in diameter when fully open. They range in color from white, through varying shades of light pink to deep pink, depending on the variety.

Tests have shown that juice from the acerola contains more than 85 times as much vitamin C as fresh orange juice. A six-ounce glass of acerola juice yields as much as 50 pounds of fresh raw cabbage.

ACHILLEA: These hardy perennial herbs include many species which are useful as border plants. The lower growing species are often used in the rock garden.

Able to thrive in ordinary garden soil, most achilleas prefer open sunlight and well-drained locations. The dwarf kinds are sometimes used as lawn material in areas too dry for regular lawn grasses. Care should be taken when growing achilleas, since some species may crowd out more delicate plantings in the garden. Summer-blooming, they produce attractive white, pink and yellow flowers.

Propagation is best done in spring by division, but other methods such as cuttings and seeds are also used. Some species of Achillea are called yarrow. *See also* YARROW.

ACHIMENES: (*Gesneriaceae*) Achimenes grow from small rhizomes, often called tubers, which vary in size and shape among the varieties; some are like small pine cones, others like pipe cleaners.

They can be grown like African violets. The rhizomes are planted as soon as they are received in late winter or early spring, about one-half inch deep in a light porous compost made of leaf mold, or of any combination of leaf mold, peat moss, vermiculite and loam.

Water the containers lightly and set them in the basement or under a greenhouse bench away from frost and where they will not get too wet, dry or hot. A temperature of 50° during storage is satisfactory. Don't let them dry out.

As soon as the sprouts show above the soil in the spring move them to a lighted window and topdress with well-rotted manure. They need considerable light, but resent full sunlight except in the early morning and evening. Repot in March or April and put in a greenhouse with a 60° temperature.

In fall as the number of flowers decreases, cut down on the water and allow the plants to dry off. When entirely dry, cut the stems above the soil and set the pot, with soil and tubers undisturbed, in the basement or under the greenhouse bench. Do not disturb them until the tubers sprout again in the spring, except to sprinkle the soil with water from time to time if needed.

The plants will make a fine show if left in the same soil and container for two seasons. If three to five tubers were planted in a 5- or 6-inch pot the first spring, the second season should find the pot full of blooming plants. Repot before the third season, however, using fresh compost.

Summer-blooming, the flowers have short tubes but with a wide lip, and the color range is broad . . . creamy white, blue, pink, deeper shades of red and purple. The hybrid varieties have flowers that measure several inches across.

Achimenes grow from seeds, corms, the scales from the corms and cuttings. It takes about three weeks for the bulbs to begin to sprout. They do well grown as a hanging plant or, if you want them to grow straight up, aid them by means of small canes or sticks.—*John Tobe.*

ACIDANTHERA: An African herb of the Iris Family. The stem is wiry, 2½ to 3½ feet tall and bears five to eight buds which open in water just as well as on the plant. The corms should be planted at the end of March or early June when the ground is warming up. The plants do best in full sunshine. Soak the corms in warm water for 24 hours before planting for a quick start because acidanthera needs about four months to bloom outdoors. Start them indoors in March like tuberous begonias for blooms in early August.

After the first frost the corms should be harvested with the stems intact, tied in a bundle and slipped into a paper bag which is hung from the ceiling of a warm cellar or room. The stalks should be removed in March. Acidanthera flowers in a long, loose, leafy spike; its fruit is an oblong capsule.

ACIDITY - ALKALINITY: Acidity and alkalinity of soils are the result of (1) the chemical nature of the rock from which the soil is derived, and (2) the partial or complete decomposition of vegetation. Alkalinity, so far as the growth of plants is concerned, is confined to the rather limited areas of limestone, the salt marshes, and the alkali deserts of the West.

The term pH means hydrogen-ion activity. This activity is nearly as important as temperature in many biological and industrial processes. It is of such great importance in the vital processes of soil organisms and of higher plants that every gardener and farmer should have a clear understanding of pH.

Correct soil pH can mean a bountiful harvest of fruits, vegetables, and flowers. The wrong soil pH can mean stunted, runty plants that can scarcely keep alive, let alone bear.

Yet soil pH is so easy to find out that no gardener or farmer should be without a general knowledge of pH and how to turn it to his advantage.

In old times, a gardener or farmer tasted his soil. If it tasted sour, he knew that it wasn't good for raising crops. The same thing went for a bitter taste. But if it tasted sweet, he knew that he could expect high yields. He didn't know it, but the soil that tasted sour was too acid to raise good general crops, and the soil that tasted bitter was too alkaline for the high yields that he wanted.

Rather than tasting soil, the modern gardener and farmer have an exact method for determining the amount of acidity or alkalinity in their soil. This method is called testing the soil pH.

Soil pH is the chemists' shorthand method of expressing the amount of acidity or alkalinity. Like secretarial shorthand, it cuts out a lot of unnecessary writing. It is very confusing to have someone tell you that their soil is sour or bitter. It doesn't tell you how much sour or how much bitter.

But with numbers standing for amounts of acidity or alkalinity, there is no such confusion. Hence, we use the chemists' pH scale just like we would a yard stick. The difference is that with the yard stick we measure inches or feet, whereas with the pH scale we measure amounts of acidity or alkalinity.

The pH scale runs from zero to 14. The zero end of the scale is the acid end, while the 14 end of the scale is the alkaline end. Logically then, halfway between 0 and 14 should be the exact neutral point where there is just as much acid as alkali. This is true, and 7.0 is the neutral point. A soil testing a pH of 7.0 will be exactly neutral. A soil testing any number greater than 7.0, for example, 8.5, will be an alkaline soil. Likewise, a soil testing less than 7.0, for example, 6.0, will be an acid soil.

In general, most common vegetables, field crops, and fruits, and flowers do best on soils that have a pH of 6.5 to 7.0, in other words, on a soil that is slightly acid to neutral. But if plenty of organic matter is present in the soil, this range of tolerance is increased, permitting plants to do fairly well on soils with a lower or higher pH. A few plants, such as azaleas, camellias, and gardenias do best on a quite acid soil. Others such as clematis, scillas, and campanulas do best on a quite alkaline soil.

The effect of soil pH on the yield of field crops has been clearly demonstrated. Corn which will yield 100 bushels to the acre at a soil pH of 6.8, will yield only 83 bushels to the acre at a soil pH of 5.7, and only 85 bushels to the acre at a soil pH of 7.5. Alfalfa which will yield 100 bales to the acre at a pH of 6.8 or 7.5 will yield only 42 bales to the acre at a pH of 5.7. The same thing is true for other field crops and fruit trees, flowers, and garden vegetables.

Obviously, for high yields, the gardener or farmer should know the pH

of his soil. Then he can either grow the kinds of plants that do best on soil of this particular pH, or he can take steps to change the soil pH to within the desirable range for the plants he wishes to grow.

For general use, and for being best suited to raising the majority of common plants, a soil having a pH of 6.5 to 7.0 is needed. A soil of this pH range offers the most favorable environment for the microorganisms that convert the nitrogen of the air to a form available to plants. It also offers the best environment for the bacteria that decompose plant tissue and form humus. In this pH range, all of the essential mineral nutrients are available to plants in sufficient quantities, and generally in a much greater amount than at any other pH. Also, soil having a pH within this range has better tilth, because a good crumb structure is more easily maintained.

Too acid a soil means that the bacteria which decompose organic matter cannot live. Manganese and aluminum are so soluble in very acid soil that they may be present in amounts toxic to plants. Yet strong acidity decreases total nutrient availability, and plants may literally starve to death for one essential mineral nutrient, while having so much of another that it poisons them.

On the other hand, too alkaline a soil is not desirable. Strong alkalinity decreases total nutrient availability. It causes loss of soil structure and development of "puddling." Strong alkalinity dissolves and disperses humus. "Black alkali" is caused by the accumulation of alkali and humus at the surface of the soil. Strong alkalinity causes a concentration of some salts in such quantities that they are toxic to plants and may completely inhibit their growth. In some of the desert regions the soils are so strongly alkaline that no plants of any kind will grow.

Soils developed from acid minerals are generally acid. Those developed from high-lime deposits are generally alkaline. Soils high in calcium generally have pH values up to 7.5. Large amounts of calcium carbonate in the soil, however, may run the pH up to 8.5. Soils high in sodium usually have very high pH values.

The effect of neutralizing a strongly acid soil is to increase and maintain a good supply of available nitrates and other essential plant nutrients. This is accomplished by furnishing microorganisms with a more favorable environment so that they are more active in converting ammonia or nitrogen into nitrates and in decomposing organic matter. Thus, the benefit of adding organic matter to the soil is utilized. A steady release of nutrients to the growing plants is maintained. However, in very acid soils, this is slowed down greatly. The best pH range for utilizing organic matter is between 6.0 and 8.0.

CORRECTING ACID SOIL: If soil is too acid, it may be brought back to a favorable pH by the addition of crushed limestone or Dolomite limestone. Dolomite has some magnesium present which is essential for plant nutrition and which is often deficient in many soils. Next to crushed limestone, wood ashes, marl, and ground oyster shells are best. All of these may be added in compost.

Slaked lime or quick lime must never be used, since they are so strongly alkaline that they very easily injure a soil. Too much lime causes oats to lodge, especially in wet years. It causes corn to show signs of potassium starvation, and causes chlorosis in soybeans. This is the reason why it is best to use crushed natural limestone. Natural limestone doesn't furnish an excess of lime all at one time. It gradually weathers or is dissolved by the excess acids in the soil to furnish alkalinity as needed but not an excess at any one time.

Gardeners and farmers have often been found adding lime or limestone to soils that were already naturally too alkaline. This happened because they did not know the pH of their soils and did not know what measures to take, if any were needed, to correct soil pH. Naturally, what they did was a waste of money, since the lime or limestone did not help the soil. In many actual cases, such unwarranted additions of alkali have been found to substantially decrease the yields of many crops.

In liming, it is best not to add all of the required limestone at one time. Just like adding salt to the soup, it is easier to add a little more later, than to try and take out any excess. Limestone of about 60 mesh is the grade generally considered best. This lasts for about three years on average soil before it has been completely used up. About a ton per acre is required to raise a clay loam soil containing a medium amount of organic matter up one unit on the pH scale, say from a pH of 5.5 to a pH of 6.5.

Overliming is easiest on a light sandy soil, whereas soils with plenty of organic matter tend to resist injurious overliming. Liming should be done when it is required to correct too acid a soil. For gardens, limestone is best applied in compost or just before spading so that it can be worked into the soil. Limestone may be applied to shrubs and trees and worked into the soil as needed.

One little considered aspect resulting in a tendency towards excess soil alkalinity is that introduced by watering during the hot, dry months. Test the water to see whether it gives an alkaline reaction. If it does, some extra organic matter should be added to the soil to correct for this extra addition of alkali, that is, provided the soil is sufficiently alkaline already.

Soils which are too alkaline may be brought back to a favorable pH range by the addition of organic matter. Organic matter contains natural acid-forming material and produces acids directly on decomposition. These acids combine with any excess alkali thus neutralizing it.

The nice thing about using organic matter is that a lot of it can be used. And it doesn't hurt the soil. It acts in a manner to control either excess alkalinity or excess acidity. Whichever way the soil is bad, either too acid or too alkaline, organic matter will tend to correct it. This is one of the reasons why gardeners get such good results by following the organic method. Regardless of what is wrong plenty of organic matter will tend to correct it.

The incorporation of abundant amounts of good compost helps correct an adverse soil pH to the range wherein most common plants thrive. Even though the pH of the soil is not the optimum for the plants being raised, many plants will do well in a soil having plenty of good compost thoroughly incorporated into it.

Before doing anything to his soil, however, other than adding compost, the gardener or farmer should check the pH and find out what it is. This is done by the use of soil test kits. Or, samples of soil may be sent to a laboratory for analysis. Most of the state universities have a laboratory set up just for this purpose. They do general soil analyses, including pH, for a nominal sum. Usually they have a special way in which they want samples of soil taken, so it is best to write to them first for this information. Write to: Director, Agricultural Experiment Station, your State University. This is the way to get the exact pH of your soil.

A simple test, which anyone can do, is with litmus paper. Neutral litmus paper works fine and will tell you whether your soil is acid, neutral, or alkaline. You can obtain this test paper at the local drug store for a few cents.

To use neutral litmus test paper, simply take a piece and press it with the thumb down into the moist soil after a rain. If the test paper doesn't

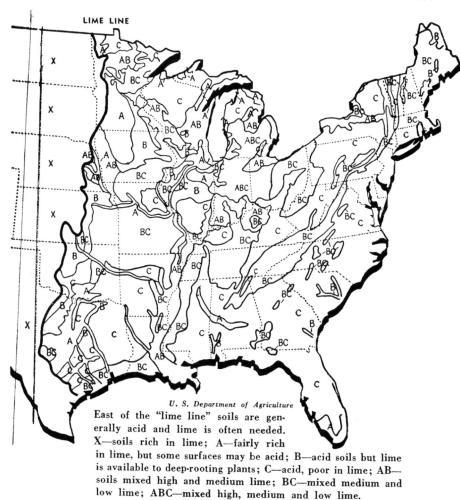

LIME LINE

U. S. Department of Agriculture

East of the "lime line" soils are generally acid and lime is often needed.
X—soils rich in lime; A—fairly rich in lime, but some surfaces may be acid; B—acid soils but lime is available to deep-rooting plants; C—acid, poor in lime; AB—soils mixed high and medium lime; BC—mixed medium and low lime; ABC—mixed high, medium and low lime.

change color, other than getting wet, your soil's pH is approximately 7.0. If the test paper turns blue, your soil is alkaline, if it turns pink, it is acid. Also test the water that you use for watering or irrigation.

The time to correct any excess acidity or alkalinity is after the soil has been tested and the pH found. This is easily done. Fresh organic matter corrects excess alkalinity. Natural limestone, preferably Dolomite, wood ashes, marl, or ground oyster shells, correct excess acidity. Plenty of good compost will tend to correct either excess acidity or excess alkalinity.

Following the scientific method of finding out first what the pH of your soil is, the taking of appropriate steps to correct any excesses will give surprising results in healthier plants and better yields.

The principal grain crops are mostly alkaline tolerant. This includes most wheat varieties, barley, maize, sugar cane, and some varieties of oats. Most varieties of oat are acid-tolerant, while rye tolerates both acid and alkaline.

ACID SOIL PLANTS: The following plants thrive best at pH 4 to 6:

Azalea	Marigold
Bayberry	Mountain laurel
Blackberry	Oak
Blueberry	Peanut
Butterfly weed	Pecan
Cardinal Flower	Pink potato
Chrysanthemum	Radish
Cranberry	Raspberry
Flax	Rhododendron
Heath	Spruce
Heather	Sweet potato
Huckleberry	Trailing arbutus
Lupine	Watermelon
Lily	Yew
Lily-of-the-Valley	

The following plants require a somewhat acid soil but can tolerate a neutral soil:

Apple	Gypsophila
Balloon Flower	Gold-banded Lily
Blazing Star	Lupine
Butterfly weed	Nicotiana
Cornflower	Pansy
Gardenia	Pumpkin
Gloxinia	Rice
Redtop Grass	Turnip

ALKALINE SOIL PLANTS: Moderately alkaline soil favors the growth and productiveness of many garden plants. The use of lime, wood ashes, and some of the natural rock powders create or increase the alkalinity of the soil. Certain alkaline-soil plants as peas, clovers, and alfalfa may become stunted or even sickly in acid soil. The more common alkaline-soil plants in the garden are listed below:

Alyssum	Lettuce
Asparagus	Mignonette
Bean	Nasturtium
Beet	Onion
Cabbage	Parsnip
Carnation	Pea
Cantaloupe	Phlox
Cauliflower	Rhubarb
Celery	Salsify
Cucumber	Squash
Geum	Sweet Pea
Iris	

Plants requiring a neutral soil: All plants not specifically mentioned in the lists given above require a neutral soil for best growth.—*Charles Coleman.* *See also* LIME.

ACID SOILS: *see* ACIDITY-ALKALINITY

ACONITE: Aconite (*Aconitum napellus*) Monkshood. A hardy, herbaceous perennial of the buttercup family, is native to the mountainous regions of central Europe. The value of the root, the part most used in medicine, depends on the presence of the alkaloid aconitine. The leaves also are used, but to a minor extent. This species is grown more or less as an ornamental in this country.

The plant appears to thrive best in a cool climate in a well-drained, gravelly loam in elevated situations, but it can be grown in any rich garden soil. Seed can be sown in the open late in the fall or early in spring, or plants can be started in a seedbed and the seedlings later transplanted and set about one foot apart in rows spaced two feet apart. Propagation by division of the roots after the stems have died down in fall is a better method because it is difficult to obtain seed that produces plants true to type. In the northern and central sections of the country, the plant requires some protection in winter.

Aconite ranges in height from three to six feet and are fine plants for late summer and early autumn gardens. Flowers, depending on variety, are pale yellow, white, lilac, blue and purple. The juice of plant is poisonous and children should be warned accordingly.

ACORN: The acorn is the fruit, or nut of the oak tree. Although today the acorn is regarded as a nut fit only for squirrels, it actually has been used as a standard food for ages and rates high in food value for human consumption. Some acorns are good to eat in the natural state, and most can be made palatable by removing the tannin (a useful product, easily removed), which makes some acorns taste bitter.

ACTINIDIA: (*Dilleniaceae*) A climbing shrub with handsome foliage, Actinidia also produces edible fruit which makes it doubly attractive to the organic gardener. They are an excellent choice for covering trellises and arbors. Two species, *arguta* and *chinensis,* produce many-seeded fruits up to two inches long with a gooseberry flavor.

Actinidias do best in a somewhat moist location with rich soil, and will climb well in either full sun or part shade. You can propagate them by seeds sown in spring, by cuttings of half-ripened wood in summer, or by layering.

ACTINOMYCETES: A group of soil microorganisms which produces an extensive threadlike network throughout the soil. They look like the soil molds but resemble bacteria in size. Actinomycetes are important in the decomposing and humus formation of organic matter. Some species produce the soil's valuable antibiotic substance.

They are found in some 90 species, and forming about 20 per cent of all the microorganisms in the average soil. Soils very high in organic matter may contain 40 per cent actinomycetes. Like most bacteria, they can stand little acidity. Although the largest proportion of them will be found in the top foot or so of soil, actinomycetes often extend to greater depths than the other soil organisms; they frequently work many feet below the surface at their job of breaking down dead plant matter, making food for the deeper-reaching roots of new plants.

Actinomycetes in most soils are only $\frac{1}{10}$ to $\frac{1}{5}$ as numerous as the bacteria. However, because they are much larger, their total weight in an acre-foot of soil roughly equals the weight of the bacteria, according to Francis Clark, principal microbiologist at the Agriculture Research Service in Beltsville, Maryland.

Wherever found, they are important soil-makers. One researcher discovered that actinomycetes reduce the gray, fibrous mud in lake bottoms to rich black mud, a process accompanied by the movement of iron and calcium to the upper mud layer.

Their activities are much the same in soil. They attack the roots, stems, straws and leaves of dead plants sheet-composted or plowed into the soil, converting them rapidly and efficiently into a dark brown mass very much like peat (their work is the first step in the formation of peat or brown coal). They secrete digestive enzymes that decompose the three most complex and abundant organic compounds in vegetable matter: protein, starch and cellulose. The cellulose, and the "woody" lignin material, too, is said to be "lignified." This is a humidification process resulting in the formation of black coloring substances and the synthesis, or building up, of cell matter into soil organic matter.

When large numbers of actinomycetes are at work, a musty, earthy odor rises like a rotting log in the woods or a damp haycock out in the field.

The actinomycetes do not fix nitrogen from the air, but instead liberate ammonia from complex proteins, and reduce nitrates to nitrites. They steal very little nitrogen from soil reserves, needing only one part of nitrogen for every 50 parts of cellulose they break down. And the humic material they produce, being very fine, has the ability to absorb nitrogenous materials and chemical compounds, residues of soil fertility which plants can then draw upon from the humus as needed.

The more fertile the soil, the higher its organic matter content and the more actinomycetes it will contain. *See also* MICROORGANISMS.

ACTIVATORS: A compost activator is any substance which will stimulate biological decomposition in a compost pile. There are organic activators and artificial activators. Organic activators are materials containing a high amount of nitrogen in various forms, such as proteins, amino acids and urea, among others. Some examples of natural activators are manure, garbage, dried blood, compost, humus-rich soil, etc.

Artificial activators are generally chemically-synthesized compounds such as ammonium sulfate or phosphate, urea, ammonia, or any of the common commercial nitrogen fertilizers. These materials are not recommended in the organic method.

There are two areas in which an activator can possibly influence a compost heap:

1. Introduction of strains of microorganisms that are effective in breaking down organic matter; and

2. Increasing the nitrogen content of the heap, thereby providing extra food for microorganisms.

Claims have sometimes been made that special cultures of bacteria will hasten the breakdown of material in a compost heap, and will also produce a better quality of finished compost. Products are manufactured which are reported to be effective in improving the action of a compost heap.

Experiments conducted at the University of California, Michigan State University, and Kyoto and Tokyo Universities in Japan have indicated that there is no benefit to be gained from the use of an activator which relies only on the introduction of new microorganisms to a heap. In addition, experiments with activators at the Organic Experimental Farm showed that activators were not effective in improving the action of the heap; that is, none of the trials indicated that a bacterial activator will increase the speed or degree of composting.

NITROGEN ACTIVATORS: It is generally agreed that the most common cause of compost heap "failures" is a lack of nitrogen. A heap that doesn't heat up or decay quickly is usually made from material which is low in nitrogen, since nitrogen is essential as a source of energy for the bacteria and fungi that do the composting work. Thus it is advisable to add nitrogen supplements or activators, such as bone meal, cottonseed meal, tankage, manure, or blood meal. How much to add depends on the nature of the material to be composted. Low-nitrogen materials like straw, sawdust, corn cobs and old weeds should have at least two or three pounds of nitrogen supplements added per hundred pounds of raw material. If plenty of manure, grass clippings, fresh weeds and other relatively high-nitrogen materials are available to be mixed with the compost, little if any nitrogen supplement will be necessary.

Some of the commercial compost activators that are sold are high in nitrogen, and it is probably this nitrogen value which accounts for their effectiveness.

The general conclusion is that commercial activators are not essential to efficient composting, since microorganisms are already present in the organic materials to be decomposed, and these are quite capable of doing the job if the proper environmental conditions are met. While certain commercial activators and supplements may improve the over-all nutrient value of the compost, it appears false to credit them with accelerating the decomposition process. *See also* COMPOSTING.

ADOBE SOILS: Adobe is the Spanish word for sun-dried mud brick; earth from which such bricks can be made is called adobe soil. Usually red or yellowish in color, adobe occurs in many parts of the American Southwest where, in conjunction with a dry climate and "hard" water, it confronts the gardener with numerous special problems.

Adobe soil is heavy clay, sometimes with an admixture of silt. It is likely to be rich in minerals, almost entirely deficient in humus. Of all soil types it is one of two (sand is the other) that will benefit most conspicuously from organic gardening methods.

Being heavy, it requires aeration. In its natural state it will contain no earthworms (ants and tunnelling gophers aerate it for the native vegetation). It will be alkaline, with a pH of at least 7.5 and probably higher. Because of this, some essential nutrients, phosphorus and iron among them, will be unavailable.

The first step will be to add humus. By doing this every one of the problems named above will be minimized, some entirely eliminated. The soil will become easier to till. Moisture will seep down and be held instead of running off. In this converted 'dobe, earthworms may be planted and will flourish. Since humus is a neutralizer, the alkalinity will be brought down to a point suitable for many garden plants. (Cottonseed meal, applied five pounds per 100 square feet, is said to be excellent for lowering the pH). Even the vital iron which has been there all the time (the red in adobe is iron oxide) and the locked-up phosphates may be freed to some extent. They should be supplemented, however, by using ground phosphate rock, and, if iron-deficiency symptoms appear, by the application of acid organic materials such as peat moss, sawdust and oak leaves.

There are many plants that can be happy in a properly conditioned, mildly alkaline soil. Those that can be grown in organically treated adobe include: acorn squash, asparagus, beets, broccoli, cantaloupe, chard, corn (sweet and Indian), cucumbers, several varieties of lettuce, peas, scallions, tomatoes, yellow squash and zucchini, alyssum (both annual and perennial), daffodils, dianthus, perennial gaillardia, iris, myrtle, shasta daisies, snapdragons, sunflowers, tithonia, tritoma, verbena and zinnias, apricots, figs,

peaches and pears. Even chrysanthemums, marigolds, pansies and corn flowers, apples, pumpkins and watermelons, all of which appear on the acid—or mildly acid-loving lists, do notably well, and roses will thrive even in heavy soil once it has been given a good dose of drainage-promoting organic material. *See also* ALKALI SOILS.

ADONIS: These hardy herbs of the buttercup family produce very attractive flowers. Growing them is easy, as adonis prefer any light, moist, fairly rich soil and will do well in either full sun or part shade. The perennial species are recommended for borders.

The annuals of the adonis group are propagated by seeds, sowing in autumn or very early spring. With perennials, dividing in the first part of spring is best.

The adonis attains a height of nine to 18 inches. Depending on variety, it produces blooms of yellow, white and red flowers.

AERATION: The exchange of air in soil with air from the atmosphere.

The average soil includes about 25 per cent air in its make-up—an obviously significant proportion while fertility and optimum root functioning depend directly on the extent of soil ventilation.

Air is needed in the soil for the proper workings of bacteria and fungi. It aids in the breakdown of organic matter. This is important in considering the decomposition of the roots of the previous crop. With sufficient air, these roots will turn to humus in time to feed the next crop. Air aids in the oxidation of mineral matter. In an air-poor soil not much of the minerals would be available for plant sustenance. The presence of sufficient air acts as a regulator of the supply of carbon dioxide, too much of which is detrimental to plants. In the process of soil respiration, oxygen is fed to the roots. Better aeration provides a bigger root system and higher yields.

In the process of plant growth, the leaves absorb carbon dioxide from the atmosphere and give off oxygen. The reverse takes place in the roots, which take in oxygen and give off carbon dioxide. In the decay of organic matter, carbon dioxide is given off.

The composition of the soil air differs somewhat from that of the atmosphere above ground. In the soil much of the air is dissolved in the soil water, but as such it is available to the needs of plants. The humidity is greater in the soil, which is a condition necessary for the optimum wellbeing of the soil organisms. The carbon dioxide content is much higher in the soil air and therefore the percentage of oxygen and nitrogen is less. In the soil there may be hundreds of times more carbon dioxide than in the air above it. While too much of this gas is detrimental, enough is needed to provide the needs for biochemical activities, the processes similar to human digestion, which in plant functioning begin to take place before the nutrients enter the roots.

DEVICES FOR BETTER AERATION: Among the methods used for increasing the air supply in soils are the addition of organic matter, the application of rock powders, soil drainage, sub-soiling, cultivation, mixed cropping, etc. By far the most important of all is to see that the soil is supplied with sufficient organic matter. It is axiomatic in agricultural literature that the more humus present in the soil, the better the aeration, the more pore spaces it will contain. There seems to be a direct relation between the amount of humus and the volume of pore space. The more of the former —the more of the latter.

CHEMICAL FERTILIZERS: It is often overlooked that some chemical fertilizers harden the soil and reduce the pore spaces. Nitrate of soda is a typical offender. In the yearly application of this fertilizer, the plant uses up much of the nitrate, but little of the soda, which keeps piling up in the soil. This soda combines with carbon which is always present in the soil, forming the compound carbonate of soda, which is washing soda. Where large amounts of nitrate of soda are used, the soil can become so hard that it can be cultivated only after a rain.

ROCK POWDERS: Part of the organic method of farming is the liberal use of rock powders rather than artificial fertilizers. In his book, *An Agricultural Testament,* Sir Albert Howard describes how the continued use of basic slag, which has a rock powder-like make-up, produced humus in a soil by its ability to aerate it. The application of rock powder to a heavy soil is bound to improve its aeration. Each tiny particle of rock will be completely surrounded by air, creating billions of new pore spaces where none existed before.

Rock powders may be roughly divided into two classes. One group consists of limestone, phosphate and the potash rocks. There is coming into use another class of rock which has been neglected—the basalts, traprocks, sandstones, etc.—what has been termed the bland rocks. These are well supplied with minerals but do not contain enough potash, phosphate or calcium to give trouble if overused. They are cheaper, and can be used much more liberally, thus greatly improving the aeration of a soil.

SOIL NUTRIENTS: The presence of sufficient air in the soil is necessary for the transformation of minerals to forms usable by plants. In an experiment it was found that forced aeration increased the amount of potassium taken in by plants. Nitrate formation in soils can take place only in the presence of a liberal supply of oxygen, and many of the processes in the soil are oxidatious—sulfur transformed to sulfur dioxide, carbon to carbon dioxide, ammonia to nitrate. Oxygen is essential to these processes.

THE EARTHWORM: Here we find one of the greatest aids to soil areation. The earthworm will burrow down six feet and more, leaving his passageways as means for the entry of air. Russell in his book *Soil Condition and Plant Growth,* suggests planting earthworm eggs in farm soils to increase aeration where it is poor. But applications of organic matter would be better because humus itself brings about better aeration, while the presence of organic matter automatically multiplies the earthworm population.

The hardpan that forms from lack of organic matter impedes the aeration of the soil below it, but the earthworm, if present in sufficient numbers can destroy it. In well-run organic farms and gardens there should be millions of earthworms per acre.

In helping to increase the soil's aeration, the earthworm serves a valuable purpose in one respect. There are many disease-producing bacteria that can thrive only under anaerobic conditions, that is, where there is a lack of oxygen. With a teeming earthworm population the conditions are kept aerobic.

Burrowing insects also help in maintaining soil aeration. For example, termites make tunnels which roots have been known to use.

SUBSOILING: The subsoiling tool, made by many tractor manufacturers, is pulled through the soil at depths of ten to 20 inches, shattering hardpans, and improving aeration. The soil must not be wet when subsoiling is going on or the hardpan will not be broken.

A legume crop is a good natural subsoiler. Alfalfa roots have been known to go down 15 feet or more. The decaying roots of this crop, after the plants are harvested, provide air passageways to very low depths. Tremendous increases in crop yields have been obtained by subsoiling. *See* SUBSOILING.

CULTIVATION AND TILLING: Plowing is an excellent means of improving soil aeration and reducing the carbon dioxide content of the soil. The increased air produces more nitrate nitrogen. Thus when one plows for corn and then cultivates three times, as the crop grows, much air is mixed with the soil, and crop yields increase. In the recent "no plowing" vogue many failures occurred and one of the reasons was the lack of aeration in heavy clay soils.

Drainage by means of soil tiles is an effective means of restoring aeration.

SOIL ORGANISMS: Air is an urgent need of many beneficial soil organisms that aid in transforming soil nutrients for plant use and that take part in the various oxidation processes, including the oxidation of humus. Oxygen gives the bacteria part of their energy. If it were not for the aerobic bacteria, no organic matter would decompose in the soil. These valuable organisms manufacture protein from these organic residues.

Aeration aids the formation of mycorrhiza on the roots of many plants. The mycorrhiza is a fungus organism that acts in partnership with the roots of plants to feed it valuable nutrients.

CARBON DIOXIDE: If the soil air contains too much carbon dioxide, given off by the roots, there will be a drop in crop yields. There are various methods of ridding the soil of an over supply of this gas such as changes in soil temperature, and rain water, the latter bringing oxygen into the soil. Soil that is more porous because of its organic matter content will absorb more rain water.

In the decay of manure much carbon dioxide is produced, but the effect of the application of manure is to increase the pore spaces in the soil which increases the rate of diffusion of this gas into the atmosphere. Sir E. John Russell has shown that green manuring, particularly if the crop is fairly succulent, will also raise the carbon dioxide content of the soil air. If seeds are sown too soon afterwards, the carbon dioxide may inhibit germination or harm the very young root system of the seedling.

WATER: Rain carries oxygen and brings it into the soil, soaking down to subsoil levels. In regions where there is plenty of rainfall there is much better soil aeration than in arid regions where the soil becomes silt, lacking porosity and forming crusts. Some soils that are low in organic matter may lose their permeability during heavy rains, and become water-logged. Percolation stops, asphyxiation sets in, and the root growth of crops are seriously affected.

In review, good aeration is required for the activities of the soil microorganisms, for the development of roots, for the break-down of organic matter, and for oxidation of minerals and other soil nutrients. For furthering aeration we have the earthworm and other insects, rock powder, soil drainage, subsoiling, plowing and other types of cultivation, and mixed cropping. *See also* CARBON DIOXIDE; COVER CROPS; GREEN MANURE; ORGANIC MATTER; COMPOST.

AEROBIC COMPOSTING: Most of the composting that is done by gardeners and farmers today is aerobic, that is, little attempt is made to eliminate air from the heap. *See* ANAEROBIC COMPOSTING; COMPOST.

AFRICAN DAISY: (*Arctotis stoechadifolia*) Gerbera jamesoni hybrids, also known as the Transvaal Daisies, are choice perennials flowering from May till November; coming from South Africa, they like heat.

SOIL REQUIREMENTS: Plant them in a sunny position in well-drained soil. The soil should not be heavy. A sandy loam suits them very well, so that in a season of excessive rains the water will not stand around the crowns and roots, causing them to rot.

If the soil is heavy, add sand and well-decayed compost, leaf mold or old manure, well worked into the ground. This will lighten it and put humus into the soil.

The Gerbera hybrids like heat since they come from South Africa. They appear to the greatest advantage when planted in a bed by themselves.

COLORS AND SHAPES OF FLOWER HEADS: The daisy-shaped flowers of the new hybrid strains are graceful and may be had in the following colors: white, yellow, orange, terra cotta, pink, salmon and red.

There are single and double flowers. The flower stems of well-established plants grow from eighteen to twenty inches high. They make a very satisfactory cut flower, with long-lasting qualities, and group well with other flowers.

CULTURE: Some gardeners consider these plants hard to grow. The culture is not difficult if a few essentials are observed. The plants may be grown from seed or by taking cuttings from side shoots, and rooting them in sand like any other cutting. In August seeds may be sown in flats, in light, sandy soil, and the seeds should be sown in rows or broadcast over the soil and lightly covered. When the seedlings are large enough to handle, transplant to flats filled with rich, sandy loam in which a little old manure is mixed. They are spaced two inches apart in the rows and the rows two inches apart. They are grown until they are large enough to set out in the ground, where they are to grow and flower.

How to Plant: In planting, make the holes deep enough so the roots will go straight down. They must never be doubled up. Always firm the soil around the plants in planting. The crown of the plant is kept a little above ground level, not below it. Too frequent watering or sprinkling is not desirable. Irrigate deeply so it will last for a week or ten days, depending on how hot the weather is. One must use judgment in watering.

After several years in the ground the clumps should be lifted and divided. The long roots can usually be pulled apart; each division should have two buds. Trim old leaves away before resetting the plants.

Gerberas appear to greatest advantage when planted in a bed by themselves. When grouped in a border of mixed perennials they generally get too much water.

They look well in a narrow bed along a garden walk in a sunny position, and shades of yellow and orange may be used, or terra cotta and reds.

The plants are long-lived if their growing conditions are congenial, and considering their long season of bloom, Gerberas are well worth growing. —*E. Hamilton Fairley.*

AFRICAN LILY: (*Agapanthus umbellatus*) A tuberous, rooted herb of the lily family, it has many long, narrow, dark leaves, from among which rises a stem two or three feet high, bearing a large umbel of very handsome blue flowers. Unlike the amaryllis, it flowers with its leaves, which adds to its beauty. The easiest way to grow it is in pots or tubs which are stored in a light cellar or other dry place during the winter. During the resting period give the plant just enough water to prevent the leaves from falling. In the spring, when danger of frost is past, the plants are put outdoors to flower and make their growth.

The agapanthus is easily forced into bloom at other seasons of the year, for the flowering season is controlled by the resting period. The earlier you wish it to flower, the earlier you dry it off; and then it does not have to rest all winter if the growth was made outdoors the previous summer, for it can be brought into the window after the turn of the year, and started into growth. When once established, the plants need not be repotted for several years if they are fed with manure water during the period of growth. Also known as Lily-of-the-Valley, its thick leaves are often almost two feet long.

AFRICAN VIOLETS: (*Saintpaulia ionantha*) No house plant has grown in popularity with the same speed as the African violet. Varieties have multiplied and their collection has become an obsession with some people. But it is only in recent years that it has really started to come into its own.

The African violet has a quiet charm and is one of the most generous of plants with its blossom. Many plants flower without ceasing for well over a year. Frequently a well-grown plant will carry 30 or more flowers open at the same time, almost hiding the foliage under its crown of beauty.

In their natural home, African violets grow in the woods near streams and waterfalls. The section is a limestone region and the plants grow close to rocks and boulders where they get constant shade and where the rock acts to keep the temperature of the soil at a uniform level.

Anyone can grow good, robust African violets by observing a few basic rules regarding proper lighting, temperature, watering, humidity and fertilizing.

Proper lighting is very important— too much light may cause burning; too little will check growth and flowering. Light from an east window from September to March, and from a north window from March to September, should give excellent results.

During the months when artificial heat is necessary, house temperatures should be about 70-72° during the day, falling to 65° at night.

WATERING: Proper humidity and watering can't be stressed too much. Many troubles will be avoided if greater care is given these two essentials. Water should always be tepid or at room temperature.

Three inch pots in saucers should be watered from the bottom. Pour enough water into saucer and permit plant to "drink" for a half hour, then pour off excess water. Larger potted plants should be watered from the top; do not overwater as this cuts off the air from the plants, and air is of the utmost importance.

Vases or pans of water set near radiators will increase humidity in rooms in which your flowering plants are growing, benefiting not only the plants but yourself too.

Plants should not be watered on cloudy or rainy days, unless, of course, they are very dry. It is well to check daily, since allowing soil to get too dry affects the tiny root hairs that absorb the food for the plant. These tiny hairs become incapable of absorbing water when dried out, causing a setback to the plant until new root hairs are grown.

If the water in your area is chlorinated, draw some off for watering, allow it to stand for 24 hours and then heat slightly. Try to use rain or spring water when available.

To feed the plant, choose a clear bright day, water the plant, wait several hours to prevent burning of root hairs and apply a liquefied organic plant food according to directions of the container. It is well to make a V-shaped hole against the side of the pot and apply fertilizer slowly at this point. Fertilizer should always be applied to the surface of the soil, and the watering following fertilizing

The African violet presents a challenge to gardeners everywhere. However, with proper care, it will flourish, its beauty a fitting reward.

should be surface watering; then return to usual method.

A three-inch pot will accomodate a plant for a long period of time. When there is a network of root hairs and a nine to 12-inch spread to the plant, then it is time to repot.

REPOTTING: For repotting, the soil should be a loose, friable one consisting of one-third good garden soil, one-third sand, and one-third peat or leaf mold. To this mixture add one teaspoonful of bonemeal for each quart of mix. The soil should be slightly acid, about pH 6.5. For the beginner and the inexperienced gardener, it is advisable to use one of the well-prepared organic soil mixes on the market. These mixes are complete and especially prepared for violets by experts.

When potting, remember that the roots are delicate and the fine root hairs absorb the nourishment, so care must be taken to pot loosely, gently firming the soil about the roots. The potting mixture should be moist, not wet.

Place a piece of broken flower pot over the drainage hole of a large pot, then one-quarter-inch layer of chicken grit (or crushed oyster shells or flower pot chips), followed by a wad of sphagnum moss and the potting soil. Just enough potting soil is placed in the pot so that when the root ball is set on it, the crown of the plant is one-quarter to one-half inch below the rim of the pot. Now fill in the sides of the pot, tapping gently to settle the soil and prevent air pockets.

Omit the drainage material and just cover the drainage hole with broken pot chips, if pots are to be watered from below.

The newly potted plants are ready for a bath to cleanse the leaves of dust and soil. Place them in the bathtub and sprinkle lightly with tepid water from a watering can equipped with a fine nozzle until leaves are clean and soil settled in the pot. Leave the pots in the tub out of drafts and keep them shaded until the leaves are dry. If leaves become wet and room temperature too cool, the leaves will spot.

The early spring months through the summer is the time for propagating leaves. Cut a few leaves from the center of a plant for best results. Trim the leaf stalk to about one and one-half inches in length and insert in a glass of water or vermiculite. By using a large pot, a number of leaves can be rooted at the same time.

When leaves have been set in position in vermiculite, add water gently until granular mixture is damp. The plantlets now need to be potted and fed. Have ready a mixture of one-half soil and one-half vermiculite. Place a piece of flower pot over the drainage hole, add some of the soil mixture, set one crown to a pot (one and one-quarter-inch size), and finish potting. Add water meagerly. Remove suckers as they appear. Feed once a week with liquid organic fertilizer.

When plantlets have outgrown the small pot, repot to a slightly larger one using a rich mixture, described above. Try to keep plants root bound to force blooms. If plants must develop roots, they will not develop buds at the same time.

VARIETIES: Choosing African violets for the home is most difficult, but here are a few that are worthy of space in your collection.

Strike Me Pink is everything the name implies with its diminutive rose-like blossom to the cupped leaves, dark, glossy green with white throat. The fluted edge of the leaves add extra enhancement.

Double Pink Cheer is a slightly darker pink rosette; flower rises above its pinked margin oval leaves supported by longer petioles than Strike Me Pink.

The lighter green foliage of the Fringed Snow Prince is most alluring topped with tall stems of big, fringed, dainty white blossoms. This one, coupled with contrasting varieties of deeper colors, adds more pleasure and interest to any collection. Blue Pom, with its lovely double bloom of deep blue, and fragile pale green foliage is appealing.

Leaves setting in a compound of half soil, half vermiculite should be root bound in order to develop blooms. Should the plants grow roots, they will not bloom. They should be fertilized weekly.

African violets are, indeed, the queen of house plants, a satisfying hobby to those unable to work in the garden, a source of joy to shut-ins, and to many, an enigma, utter despair to others. Knowledge of this plant's needs and understanding of its enemies will enable anyone to grow this favorite, and grow it best Nature's way!

One of the African violet's biggest enemies is the nematode—microscopic and eel-shaped that infests the roots of plants and the soil around them. Writing of the African violet and the nematode, Mrs. Harold Danne-miller, of Barberton, Ohio, has this to say: "An infested plant lacks luster; leaves and blooms, if any, are small and the plant is limp... so you see why I am after them."

Her potting formula which she has used successfully includes no chemicals but only organic ingredients. It follows:

1 pint natural ground phosphate rock
1 pint natural ground potash rock
½ pint natural ground limestone rock
½ pint bonemeal
1 pint dehydrated cow manure
1 pint fine charcoal
5 pints fine builder's sand
15 pints coarse baled peat moss, soaked, excess water squeezed out
2 tbsp. bacterial activator

Mrs. Dannemiller further advises us to "mix the ingredients thoroughly, keep moist and do not use for at least two weeks; the longer it works, the better."—*Esther Latting, Eva Wolf.*

AFTERMATH: The late summer and fall growth of grasses which have been cut earlier in the same season. Sometimes called Rowen.

AGARICUS: *see* MUSHROOM

AGASKARIZING: *see* ELECTROCULTURE

AGAVE: (*Amaryllidaceae*) The best known of this semi-desert American family is the century plant (*A. americana*), but many other agaves make fine succulents for outdoors in dry, frost-free climates. They also are recommended for the greenhouse or as house plants where there is plenty of sun, where they are best grown in large pots.

Aside from being decorative plants, agaves are also very useful. In their native Mexico, many species furnish fiber and soap. Other agave species produce *pulque* and *mescal,* two popular Mexican drinks.

Agaves are easy to grow, doing best in a sandy loam soil with good drainage. To grow small plants of the large-leaved kind into taller ones fast, put the plants in a sunny spot in the spring. Be sure the pot is large enough so that transplanting by fall is not necessary.

Flowers of the century plant are about two inches long and very numerous. Their large leaves are often up to five feet long and six inches wide.

AGERATUM: Sometimes called floss-flower, ageratum is a profuse-blooming, tender annual with fluffy flowers borne in dense heads. The dwarf varieties are high on the list of garden flowers used for borders, edgings, rock gardens, window boxes, and small beds. The tall varieties are good for cut flowers and may also be dried for winter arrangements. Ageratum is a constant bloomer and the popular blue-violet color combines with practically any other garden color.

CULTURE: Seeds can be started indoors and seedlings transplanted outside as soon as they are big enough to handle and all danger of frost has passed. Seed can also be planted directly in the open ground where they are to remain, and can be planted until early July and still make a showing. Care must be taken to water them while the weather remains dry. Ageratum will do well in sun or in semi-shade.

A finely pulverized seedbed is essential. The soil should be spaded to a depth of six to eight inches. Incorporating compost, woods soil, or other humus is ideal. This will provide a rich soil which will hold moisture well. Ageratum is not desirable for dry places because the plants are shallow-rooted and will wilt easily.

The seed of Ageratum is very fine, so cover only with a light layer of fine soil. This may be easily accomplished by sifting through a box or pan with a fine wire mesh on the bottom. After covering the seed, use a flat board or block to tamp the soil into close seed-soil contact. Do this lightly so as not to pack the soil.

After the plants are a couple of inches high, thin to six to eight inches for the dwarf varieties and ten to 12 inches apart for the tall-growing varieties. When the plants begin to bloom, keep the shabby seed heads picked. This not only improves the appearance but will also encourage profuse blooming throughout the entire season. In the fall, just before frost, you can pot plants of the dwarf varieties and take them indoors for several more weeks of blooming.

VARIETIES: The dwarf and compact forms are generally preferred to the tall varieties. Of the dwarf varieties the blue-violet color is the most popular. Among this group Blue Cap, Midget Blue, Blue Ball, Blue Perfection and Tetra Blue are good varieties. Imperial Dwarf White is a good white variety. Tall Blue and Tall White are good varieties in the taller-growing group. These make wonderful cut flowers for bouquets all summer and may also be dried and kept for winter arrangements. Cut the flowers just as they open, bunch about a dozen stalks together and hang from the ceiling of your basement. They require a dark, moisture-free place to dry satisfactorily. If dried in the light, the blue-violet color will fade considerably more than in the dark.

AGGREGATE, SOIL: Referring to soil structure, an aggregate consists of many fine soil particles held in a single cluster, such as a clod or crumb. The ideal soil structure is granular, where the rounded aggregates of soil lie loosely and readily shake apart. When the granules are especially porous, the term crumb is applied.

AGGRESSIVE: Of a plant, a vigorous

grower able to compete successfully with other types of plants.

AGRICULTURAL EXPERIMENT STATIONS: see GOVERNMENT SERVICES; EXPERIMENT STATIONS

AGRICULTURAL LIME: see LIME

AGRICULTURAL MARKETING SERVICE: see GOVERNMENT SERVICES

AGRICULTURE, A NEW APPROACH: By P. H. HAINSWORTH. See BOOKS FOR ORGANIC GARDENERS AND FARMERS

AGROSTEMMA: see LYCHNIS

AGROSTIS: An annual or sometimes perennial bent grass, often included in lawn mixtures. Agrostis species include Redtop, cloud grass, brown bent and Rhode Island bent. See also GRASSES, ORNAMENTAL.

AILANTHUS: These large trees, though sparingly branched, often give a tropical effect because of the large foliage. Planted widely in city streets because they resist smoke and are insect-resistant, Ailanthus trees (especially the Chinese species) are hardy in the Northern states. The foliage of the male plant gives off an unpleasant odor, and the pollen has been said to cause catarrhal troubles.

The trees grow best in a light, moist soil and are propagated by seeds or root cuttings.

AIR-PLANT: see BRYOPHYLLUM

AJUGA: Known as bugleweed, these are hardy herbs of the mint family. Ajuga grows in any garden soil, and is often used in rock gardens or as border plants. It can be propagated by division or seeds. The flowers are irregular and two-lipped; appear in a profusion of white, blue and occasionally reddish bloom.

ALBINO FLOWERS: True albinos are white sports or breaks from a normally colored species. These can be differentiated from non-albinos, the stems and foliage of which are pure green, whereas the typical form usually shows some pigment in the stem or foliage. The pure white Delphinium supposedly is a true albino, as is the white larkspur, *D. ajacis.* A recent American albino is *Dicentra spectabilis alba.* Another albino is the snowball, *Mertensia virginica.* In all, there are only about 100 recognized true albinos.

ALBIZZIA LEBBEK: *see* LEBBEK TREE

ALBRECHT, DR. WILLIAM A.: Dr. Albrecht, eminent agricultural scientist whose studies in the fields of soil microbiology, nitrogen fixation, inoculation of legumes, amino acids in soil fertility, animal husbandry and nutrition have gained world-wide recognition.

For the last 20 years he has been Chairman of the Department of Soils at the University of Missouri, where he has taught since 1916. During World War II, he served as an instructor of soils at the U. S. Army University in Biarritz, France. He is a consulting editor for several magazines and journals, including *Soil Science, Scientific Monthly and Plant and Soil* (Holland). Among the many scientific organizations in which he is an active member are the Soil Science Society of America (former president), the American Society of Agronomy, the International Society of Soil Science, the Society of American Bacteriologists, the American Naturalists and the American Academy of Applied Nutrition.

His perhaps outstanding attribute and contribution is his ecological insight into the fundamental relation between sound, natural soil care and the health and welfare of humanity.

ALCHEMILLA: These somewhat weedy herbs of the rose family make hardy rock garden and low border plants. Easy to grow, they produce small green or yellow flowers, small dry fruit, and attractive silver-grey leaves.

ALEPPO GRASS: *see* JOHNSON GRASS

ALFALFA: (*Medicago sativa*) A perennial plant with roots penetrating the soil for several feet, alfalfa was one of the first legume plants used. Besides having a deep root system and being highly drought resistant, alfalfa develops a crown at or near the surface of the soil from which goes up 15 to 30 leafy branches. The crop grows from one and one-half to four feet high.

It is suitable for general feeding purposes, pasturage, and, of special importance to organic growers—is an excellent permanent cover crop, increasing the yield of following crops. Alfalfa is grown in just about every state with best yields reported from the Southwest. It thrives best on a deep loam with an open subsoil, but does well on a wide variety of soils.

For information about specific varieties which will do best in your area, write to your state experiment station.

Alfalfa is a very heavy feeder, and each stand needs a good supply of plant food. Manure has been found to be very satisfactory, because it supplies the crop with the needed elements as well as humus. Rock phosphate is also recommended.

Alfalfa, like all leguminous plants, is a nitrogen-fixer. Certain bacteria attach themselves to its roots and form nodules which are rich in nitrogen. This nitrogen is largely derived from the air. Leguminous crops are therefore adding additional fertility to the soil because they encourage bacteria which make atmospheric nitrogen available for plant growth in the ground. Nitrogen is one of the main constituents of protein, and alfalfa, rich in nitrogen, is therefore an excellent growth food for animals. Animals fed on a high-nitrogen or high-protein diet produce manure richer in nitrogen than animals fed on poor grass low in nitrogen.

When green matter or even dried plant matter, like alfalfa hay, is available for composting, excellent results are secured, because the nitrogen in

The deep root system of the alfalfa does well on a variety of soils. The plant is a heavy feeder preferring manure as a good supply of food.

Nitrogen 2 per cent. Before bloom 3 per cent
Calcium 2 per cent
Potash 2-3 per cent
Magnesium 0.2-0.5 per cent
Phosphorus 0.2-0.4 per cent
Sulfur 0.2-0.4 per cent

Lahonton, a new variety of alfalfa, is reported to be practically immune to the stem nematode and resistant to the bacterial wilt disease. For growers in the Antelope Valley of California and Nevada's irrigated valleys, Lahontan fills a long-felt need for a persistent-growing, dependable-producing alfalfa variety.

Lahontan is the result of a 15-year intensive-search for disease-resistant stocks of alfalfa started at Reno, Nevada, by USDA plant breeder O. F. Smith, in cooperation with the Nevada and California Experiment Stations.

the plant matter produces quick breaking-down of the compost. An alfalfa compost heats quickly even during winter months when straw and hay composts are slow to get bacterial growth going. One reason for this is, however, that alfalfa hay can be more readily soaked than straw; another reason is that it packs better on account of its small leaves and thereby gets warm through pressure, when the large air spaces of a straw heap of ordinary compost size keep a heap dry and permit cold air to enter.

The fertilizer value of alfalfa is threefold: 1—Nitrogen fixation, 2—root residues which add much organic matter to the soil because the roots are among the most deep-reaching of all crops, and third, more valuable manure. The composition of alfalfa hay is dependent on the stage during which it was cut and on the quickness of drying. Young leafy growth is richest in nitrogen, and quickly dried hay is richer than slow-cured material.

An average composition of alfalfa hay is:

ALGAE: Most algae are microscopic green plants that live as single cells or as large colonies of one-celled individuals. Seaweeds are giant relatives of soil and fresh water algae. Diatoms are algae which live in glass houses; make outer skeletons or shells of silica, the main constituent in glass.

Most algae are green, but some are blue, blue-green, yellow, orange, red brown, black or colorless. A few change color. In the light they are typical green plants which make their own food material by photosynthesis as all green plants do. In the dark they have to eat bacteria, plant tissue, and other organic matter in order to live just as animals do.

Algae exist in fish bowls and large aquaria. They make the water cloudy and cover the glass with green slime unless eaten by snails which keep their numbers down. They are the green scum in ponds, drainage ditches, mud puddles, stagnant water, on greenhouse beds, and field soils.

Some algae grow on tree bark; others live in protozoa (one-celled animals) or together with fungi in the form of lichens. Even hot sulfur springs, coral reefs, the Dead Sea (which is not at all dead but teems with microbial life), glaciers in the polar regions, all have algae.

Algae are very active in connection with limestone. In the tropics and sub-tropics, certain marine algae coat themselves thickly with lime and contribute to the formation of coral reefs which eventually become calcareous soils. Layers of the mineral travertine are formed by algae in hot springs containing large amounts of calcium and magnesium in solution. Marl deposits on shallow lake bottoms and calcareous pebbles result from algal action. It is thought that the siliceous sinter deposits around hot springs may also be produced by algae.

In the economy of the soil, algae may play a surprising role. Under favorable weather conditions providing warmth and moisture, the growth of algae in the upper three inches of a soil may add as much as six tons of organic matter per acre.

To do this, algae must take about a quarter of a million (250,000) cubic feet of carbon dioxide out of the air. They use the energy in sunlight to produce the organic matter in their cells from this enormous amount of carbon dioxide gas.

The role of algae in connection with soil organic matter is even more interesting. Their growth results in a net production of organic matter, since they convert carbon dioxide gas into cell material.

Although other microbes, such as the bacteria and fungi, are important in transforming organic matter generally and in changing it into humus, their activities always result in a net decrease of organic matter. They oxidize some of the original material to carbon dioxide which passes into the atmosphere. It is the algae which helps turn this carbon dioxide back to organic matter and plow it into the soil, so to speak.

Other aspects of soil algae are equally interesting and important. Certain of the so-called blue-green algae are nitrogen-fixers. At the same times that they produce soil organic matter from carbon dioxide, these legume-like microbes enrich the soil with nitrogen since they make their cell protein from nitrogen in the air.

The important soil-forming activities of lichens probably depend on the nitrogen-fixing ability of the algal partners in these fungus-alga associations. Lichens on bare rock surface far above timberline can get their required nitrogen only from the atmosphere. It seems that by fixing nitrogen both for themselves and for the fungi with which they are intimately combined they make life possible for the resulting lichen.

It is also significant that blue-green algae are among the first living creatures to become established on volcanic ash and lava, after it has cooled, and there initiate the slow but inevitable process of soil formation. Primitive algae thus create conditions which permit more advanced plants to develop. In rice fields algae are believed to benefit the rice plants by taking up some of the carbon dioxide and providing oxygen which the submerged roots require for "breathing."

Algae are among the most important microbes in the soil. They are not responsible for serious crop losses as are certain disease-producing fungi and bacteria. They work quietly, unobtrusively, but constructively.—*Dr. Albert Schatz.*

See also MICROORGANISM; LICHEN.

ALKALI SOILS: Alkali means either one or both of the following conditions: 1—an accumulation of soluble salts, usually the chlorides and sulfates of sodium, calcium and magnesium, and sometimes potassium; 2—large amounts of absorbed sodium that either are directly toxic to plants, or harm them by making the soil impermeable by water. The former is called white alkali or saline soil, the latter black or true alkali soil. White alkali is the commonest type, found in almost all arid and semiarid regions.

White alkali soil is easily recognized—it frequently has a white crust on its surface, and streaks of salt within the soil. White alkali soils generally have good structure, and like the black, their pH range is from 8.5 to 11.

Both types may be caused either by a high water table which brings the soluble salts to the surface by capillary movement, or by the depositing of these salts in the soil by irrigation water. Digging into the rock substrata under the subsoil in many of these areas, will reveal large amounts of sodium there. If excessive irrigation or other factors raise the ground water level, this sodium will rise with it and be left in the surface soil when the water evaporates. This causes black alkali soil, the most damaging to crops because it has poor structure and puddles and packs easily. White alkali soils are formed in the same way, but they contain less sodium and thus do not pack.

What happens to plants in an alkali environment? The strong soil solution has a corrosive effect on the roots and stems, causing an actual shrinkage of the tissues that makes them less able to take up water. The large amounts of salts in the soil displace needed nutrients, causing nutritional deficiencies, especially of phosphorus, iron, and manganese.

Sodium causes a breakdown of the soil humus and clay. This results in the loss of good soil structure and the beginning of puddling and erosion. Water infiltration and root penetration are hindered, and aeration is reduced. The anaerobic conditions thus produced make toxic compounds of many of the elements present. Microbial life ceases, and the soil is dead.

Alkali soils, from the very nature of their development, are usually deficient in organic matter and nitrogen.

Here is a sound, safe program for rebuilding alkali soils:

Drainage is very important for reclaiming alkali soils, especially where the water table is high. The soil should be permeable to a depth well below the root zone. The ground water level should never come nearer the surface than at least ten feet. In the case of hardpans, subsoiling is a must to insure good drainage. Tile drains are sometimes necessary.

Once adequate drainage is established, leaching will help remove the salts. Here is an important point: whenever possible, irrigation water should be applied well in excess of the amount needed by the crop. And if the irrigation water itself contains harmful salts to any degree, apply extra-large quantities to make sure these salts, too, wash down. Don't conserve water at the expense of soil conservation! Each field should be carefully levelled, of course, so the water will enter the soil uniformly.

There are a number of other ways to restore the soil's organic content. Acid peats can be purchased in carload lots. Or you can collect waste organic materials and apply them as a mulch or partially disked in. An acre could use 40 to 50 tons, in conjunction with frequent irrigations to promote leaching of the salts.

In India, cheap organic materials like manure, oilcake and such by-products of the sugar industry as molasses and press-mud effected excellent reclamation. Gypsum was almost totally ineffective. Ten tons to the acre of molasses or press-mud on the fields produced 115 pounds of barley per acre.

Besides building up the soil's structure, organic matter exerts a "buffer" action, lessening the toxicity of the strong salts to plants. It also lowers the pH and improves the soil's capacity to supply available nitrogen.

Manure or sludge (20 tons or more to the acre) is also excellent, as is growing crops like sweet clover.

Plowing in a green manure crop increases the carbon dioxide content of the soil air, causing displacement of the harmful sodium by calcium. Other good alkali-resistant crops are sugar beets, cotton, rye, sorghum and barley. Alfalfa is very good because it requires a flooding type of irrigation that aids leaching, and its tough roots help break up the packed soil. Always prepare a good seedbed, have the soil moist to insure germination, and use more seed than usual.

In California, the Bermuda grass that often infests alfalfa fields has been found to be a fine alkali soil reclaimer. It provides valuable pasturage while at the same time preparing the soil for less alkali-resistant crops.

Keep a mulch on soil wherever possible to retard evaporation. The soil should always be moist enough to keep any salts in it dilute. Irrigate often, and lightly. Soils that show a tendency toward becoming alkali easily should have organic matter added to them as often as practical. *See also* ACIDITY-ALKALINITY.

ALKALINITY: *see* ACIDITY-ALKALINITY.

ALLAMANDA: These tropical climbing shrubs make excellent plants for the greenhouse, and are often grown outdoors in the south.

Allamandas are simple to grow; a favorite potting mixture is about one part sand, two parts loam and one part leaf mold. To aid drainage, add charcoal.

The vines bloom abundantly and rapidly climb trellises and fences, but should be tied. The flowers are bell-shaped, often yellow with a streak of white.

Plants should be watered frequently and every few weeks, fertilize with liquid manure. It's recommended that from late autumn to early spring, watering be almost eliminated.

Yellow bell (*A. nerifolia*) is one of the lower growing varieties, reaching about five feet.

ALLIGATOR PEAR: *see* AVOCADO

ALLIUM: These onion-scented herbs make up the vegetable family of onions, chives, garlic, leeks and shallots, but also include species popular for ornamental use. Most of these are hardy plants that bloom in spring; these can be grown similar to other hardy border bulbs. The bulbs can be planted in fall or spring; flowers are generally a ball-like cluster in a wide range of colors. *See specific plant listings.*

ALLUVIUM: The fine material, as mud or clay, carried by streams and redeposited is called alluvium. It is spread out by the streams in great alluvial valleys and deltas as along the Nile, the Mississippi, the Amazon, and other large rivers. Early civilizations grew up largely on these alluvial lands and probably today over a third of the people of the world get their food from soils developed from alluvium. Many of these soils are very fertile because a thin covering or film of fresh alluvium from eroding rocks is added to the surface every year or so during periods of high water in the river.

The largest uniform body of alluvium is located in the southern Mississippi Valley. Alluvial material ranges in texture from fine clay to large rocks and even to boulders. The fine sediments are washed into the drainage valley from the watershed surface. When the current is swift, the carrying capacity of the stream is high, but as the rate of flow decreases first the coarse and then the fine materials settle out. A common characteristic of all alluvial material is stratification, layers of different-sized particles overlying each other.

Most alluvium is carried and deposited during floods because it is at this period that erosion is most active and the carrying capacity of streams is at a maximum. When a flooding stream overflows its banks, its carrying power is suddenly reduced as the flow area increases and velocity decreases.

This causes the coarse sands and gravels to settle along the bank where they sometimes form conspicuous ridges called natural levees. As the water reaches the flood plains of the valley, the rate of flow is slow enough to permit the silt to settle. Finally the water is left in quiet pools, from which it seeps away or evaporates leaving the fine clay. Levees are characterized by good internal drainage during periods of low water, whereas flood plains exhibit poor internal drainage.

Large mature valleys like the Mississippi are characterized by rivers with many meanders which develop in a well-recognized cycle. As a stream swings back and forth across its flood plain, cutting new channels in flood periods, sections of the old bed, known as ox-bows, are left as lakes and swamps which fill with sediments during subsequent overflows.

Terraces are developed from flood plains as streams cut deeper channels because of lowered outlets. Several terraces may be found along a stream or a lake which has undergone repeated changes in level. Extensive terraces were formed as the glaciers receded and their outwash plains were no longer covered with water. Terraces usually are quite well drained and may be droughty. They exhibit stratification.

Streams flowing from hills or mountains into dry valleys or basins drop their sediments in a fan-like deposit as the water spreads out. These alluvial fans are usually coarse-textured, being composed of sands and gravels, and are well or excessively drained.

Flood plains as well as deltas are in general rich in plant nutrients and comparatively high in organic matter content. Terraces and alluvial fans, on the other hand, are more likely to be less fertile. Special crops such as vegetables and fruits frequently are grown on the latter formations because the soil warms up quickly and their good drainage and course texture permit free root development.

Along much of the Atlantic Coast and extending around the Gulf is a large area of land known as the Coastal Plains. This material was derived from sediments carried by streams and deposited in the ocean and gulf through decreased current velocity and chemical coagulation. Much of the area is sandy but is interspersed with beds of silt and clay which were deposited in estuaries or other sheltered bodies of water or farther out in the ocean. When raised above water level these deposits were subjected to soil-forming processes.

The solvent power of ocean water, coupled with the ceaseless grinding by wave action, pulverized soft minerals and extracted soluble salts. As a result large areas are quite sandy, composed mainly of particles of hard minerals, and are low in plant-nutrient content. Nevertheless a large acreage is used for the production of vegetables, fruits, and other special crops through the use of liberal quantities of fertilizer. There are also extensive areas of forest. Considerable acreages of loam, silt loam, and clay loam, especially in the coastal plains of Texas and Louisiana, are used for general farming and production of special crops. *See also* AZONAL SOILS.

ALLYCE CLOVER: *see* CLOVER

ALMOND: (*Amydalus communis*) The almond tree is as hardy as the peach but its production is more limited because it blossoms one month earlier, putting forth a mass of pink, five petaled flowers. The nuts ripen from peach-like, fuzzy fruits into the ripe almond and are ready for gathering in late August through September.

Propagation is by budding named varieties onto peach or almond seedlings. The wild, bitter variety is used in the latter instance because it is less expensive than the sweet.

Budding takes place in the early autumn. In the following spring the stock is cut back to the bud which is permitted to grow for a season. At the end of this period, the one-year tree is ready for planting in the orchard.

The almond requires a sandy, well-drained soil, neutral or tending slightly to the alkaline. Since good drainage is essential, plenty of humus should be present to hold moisture while permitting excess water to drain away.

Topsoil should be deep because the roots of the tree run deep. It is advisable to break up the topsoil thoroughly and to as great a depth as possible before planting and then fertilizing with plenty of organic matter.

Many commercial growers plant cover crops which are turned under for green manure, thus protecting the ground and enriching the soil. This practice should not be necessary for the small homestead where only a few trees are planted. At least two trees must be planted to ensure pollination.

Compost should be worked in late in the autumn and straw mulch placed under the tree but not next to its trunk because of nesting rodents.

Almond trees begin to bear in three or four years and should be in full production in 12 years. Nuts should be harvested when those in the center of the tree are ripe. Nuts which fall before the regular harvest time should be picked up daily to insure clean cultivation and prevent disease. *See also* Nut Trees.

ALOCASIAS: Foliage plants native to the tropics. Their foliage is truly beautiful; some varieties are silvery with green veins.

Alocasias do well in a mixture of one-half peat moss, one-fourth leaf mold and one-fourth garden loam or coarse sand. This mixture will give the plants food and drainage.

Water freely, especially when rapid growth is taking place; give them partial shade. Temperatures should be above 72° in winter. Alocasias can

be readily propagated by suckers or root cuttings.

ALOE: These perennial succulents, with large leaves and tubular red or yellow flowers, make very decorative plants. Their stiff appearance gives a "desert" effect.

Aloe plants often stay healthy for years in the same pot and flower abundantly. Potting mixture recommended is three parts sandy loam, one part broken brick (for drainage), and an addition of some lime, compost or manure. Pot firmly and be sure surplus water can easily leave the soil. Water very little, except when plant is growing rapidly.

Aloe thrives best when humidity in the house is low, and can stand full sunshine.

ALPINE: A term applied to very high altitude plants — strictly speaking, those above the timber line of a mountain. Many alpine plants are very delightful and have been adapted to Northern rock gardens.

In their native homes most choice rock garden plants are snow-covered from early fall to late spring. In our climate they must be well mulched to prevent their roots being heaved out of the ground by alternate freezing and thawing. Salt hay, peat moss, oak leaves, and evergreen boughs are all light mulching material and will protect the plants while not smothering them with weight. Peat moss and oak leaves should be used in large quantities only on plants that like an acid soil. *See also* Rock Garden.

ALPINE FIR: *see* Fir

ALSIKE CLOVER: *see* Clover

ALSTROEMERIAS: Brought from South America, these plants produce large flowers and are usually grown in a greenhouse or outdoors in Southern gardens.

One variety has deep yellow flowers known as the Peruvian Lily, can be planted outdoors in the spring, blooms throughout the summer, and then stored in a cool, dry place for the winter.

They should have some shade (a low ground temperature) and a soil well supplied with sand, leaf mold or other humus, and a good amount of bone meal.

ALTHEA: (*Althaea officinalis*) A perennial herb introduced from Europe, now grows wild in marshy places near the sea in Massachusetts and Connecticut and along tidal rivers in New York and Pennsylvania. The roots, leaves and flowers are sometimes used medicinally.

The plant grows well in almost any loose garden soil of moderate fertility but tends to winterkill under cultivation in situations where the ground freezes to a considerable depth and no mulch or other protection is provided. The plants can be propagated from seed or from divisions of the old roots made early in spring. The seed is sown in shallow drills at least three feet apart, and the seedlings thinned to stand 12 inches apart in the row. Under good conditions the plants attain a height of three or four feet.

The flowering Hibiscus shrubs, often grown in the garden, are forms of Althea.

ALUMINUM SULPHATE: *see* FERTILIZER, ARTIFICIAL

ALYSSUM: A spring-blooming perennial, the alyssum was known as madwort because it was supposed to help in treating sickness brought about by the bite of a mad dog. Fine for rock gardens and also in front of borders, low-growing alyssums have a decorative, "soft foliage," grow well in well-drained soils and should have prolonged sun. Propagation can be done by division, cuttings or seed. *See also* BORDERS; SWEET ALYSSUM; PERENNIALS.

AMARANTH: (*Amaranthaceae*) Member of a family of annual herbs, mostly coarse and weedy in nature. They are widely distributed, vigorous growers demanding full sunshine. The flowers are very small, without petals, but congesting in brightly colored clusters. The fruit is small, dry and single-seeded.

Sow the seeds in the garden after all danger of frost is past, allowing 18 inches on either side of the row so that the plants will not be crowded. After the seedlings are up, thin them to stand not less than a foot apart in the row.

The plants require well-drained soil which has been spaded deeply and enriched with plant food. They should have good air circulation. Under proper conditions the plants begin to branch freely while still quite small. When in full bloom they stand two feet or more in height with every one of the branches ending in a globular flower which has the general appearance of red clover. Where they are grown in a soil richly supplied with humus, they may be expected to add another foot to their normal height and under such circumstances light supports may be needed to protect them against wind damage.

All of them have an extensive flowering season, starting in June and lasting well into August. They are among the easiest of all annuals the gardener could choose for his garden, showing a high endurance to summer heat and drought. For best results, however, they never should suffer from lack of water, to which they are accustomed from their tropical homeland.

Although sowing outdoors is recommended as the easiest way to success, they are not difficult to start indoors if kept moderately moist and warm. If given plenty of light, they will develop rapidly requiring transplanting two or three times before the outdoor temperature permits their removal to the open. They may go from the seedpan to a flat or box, where they should stand two inches apart each way. The next transplanting should be to small pots, which will permit spacing them more adequately as they grow bushy.

AMARYLLIS: The garden amaryllis, *A. vittatum* (*Hippeastrum vittatum*), *A. belladonna,* and *A. reginae* and their

The amaryllis offers beauty, as a cut-flower or a potted plant. Their wide range of color, shape and bloom permit leeway in experimentation.

hybrids, are members of the *Amaryllidaceae* family. Native to South America and South Africa, many amaryllis grown today are hybrids of native varieties and are highly prized for their large flowers. The lily-like or bell-shaped flowers are red, pink, white and combinations of these colors.

Amaryllis are grown in the open field or in beds and borders around the home. They are excellent landscape subjects for use as individual specimens, in mass plantings, in beds or as part of the border planting around home grounds, and in park plantings.

It is common occurrence with many to fail with Amaryllis after the first or second year; to have no blooms or see the bulb gradually die. But the Amaryllis is one of the simplest of plants to grow for indoor beauty.

The reason for failure lies in the care given the bulbs, not so much in the potting as in the watering in the beginning, and subsequent care after blooming. Blooming the first season

was proof that the bulb was of mature blooming size and had formed bloom buds previously in its growth.

To water a bulb too much after the growth starts (thinking it needs it then) may cause it to rot, because there will be no assimilation of the moisture. A newly-potted, dormant Amaryllis should be kept fairly dry after an initial watering to settle the soil around the bottom of the bulb, until signs of life show. It should be watered sparingly; a syringing of the bulb itself helps, until you are sure there are roots growing. Once the leaf tip grows up from the center of the neck of the bulb, after the bloom stem has cleared the scales and is reaching up, it is definite that roots are feeding the bulb and it is time to apply more water to the soil regularly, keeping it moist but not soggy wet.

However, to start the foliage into full growth before the bloom and bud appear may cause the bud to rot or abort and there can be a healthy set of leaves growing up with no evidence of a bloom coming. It is wise not to water the bulb until the bloom bud shows, regardless of how promising the foliage looks.

Grow bulbs in a mixture of three parts rich loam, one part well-rotted leaf mold, with some sand and bone meal and another part of thoroughly rotted cow manure. Set the bulb one-third in the soil. Water carefully, individually and, as the bloom bud clears the neck of the bulb, use liquid manure once a week or every ten days, depending upon the growing conditions, until the color begins to show in the blossom buds through the sheath. Full sunlight is best for sturdiness, and a temperature between 55° and 60° grows them well. It is best to tie the bloom stem loosely to a stake to prevent its being broken.

After blooming, in February, March or April—the blooms can be cut and used for cut flowers—the plant is given less water and kept some cooler for a while. As weather becomes warmer the feeding of liquid manure is started again. As space and light permit, the pots can be placed in April or May in a cold frame or somewhat sheltered place, to prepare them gradually for planting outside in the garden to be kept growing.

In the fall, as the foliage matures, water should be gradually withheld and the bulbs lifted in cool weather before frost and placed in boxes of soil to "ripen" until around the first of the year. (In the method mentioned previously, the pots were lifted and stored without disturbing the roots.) A temperature of 40° is cool enough. Around Christmas, the bulbs should be checked for bloom buds showing, or possible injury, and all old foliage and loose dried scales cleaned off. As each is removed from the soil, the base and the roots should be checked to make sure they are dried and crumpled in the soil. These must be cleaned away, care being taken to protect the growing tips of new roots starting out from the base of the scales.

Amaryllis can be easily grown from seed and will bloom at 18 months old, if grown correctly. Fertilization is easily done, the pollen from one bloom being placed upon the pistil of another when it is ready to receive it. At that time the pistil is somewhat separated into three segments and becomes quite moist and sticky.

Cut the bloom petals back nearly to the neck of the flower after pollinizing it, to show definitely that it has been fertilized. There is no further use for the bloom as it would still take some of the energy from the bulb that should now help form healthy seed.

The seed is gathered when the pod has turned brown and the three sections about to open, and sown in a mixture of leaf mold and sand, and covered very lightly. They should be kept moist and warm. After two small leaves have formed, the tiny plants and bulblets are potted into small containers and kept growing in a healthy state, gradually increasing the richness of the soil to that used for mature bulbs, usually needing no larger size pot than a four inch, before blooming. There are differences, however, individualistic traits sometimes showing up in a bulb larger than usual, as well as others being long delayed both in size and bloom.

Amaryllis can be grown successfully and are worth the simple care they require. They offer a beauty a little different, either as a cut-flower or potted plant, and an opportunity for initiative in the art of breeding your own seedlings. Their color range, size, shape and bloom substance all offer mixed variation for experimentation. —*Louis Dodge.*

AMAZON LILY: (*Eucharis grandiflora*) This native of the Andes is a fine plant for the window garden. It has long stemmed basal leaves and clusters of dazzling white, trumpet-like blossoms with a perfume subtle yet potent enough to permeate the house. It can be potted in a coarse, fibrous soil with charcoal and sand, placed in an east window with other amaryllids and watered whenever dry.

During spring and fall, feed it once a month with liquid manure.

AMELANCHIERS: Commonly known as service berry, juneberry, and shadblow, the amelanchiers flourish in the woodlands of eastern United States. They are shrubs or trees of the rose family, some varieties of which are grown for ornament.

Amelanchiers bloom in the spring producing attractive white flowers in drooping racemes at about the same time the dogwood blossoms. The fruit has the appearance of a miniature apple, and is used for jellies. The plant is easily propagated from ripe seeds, sometimes by suckers. The trees attain a height of 30 to 45 feet, the shrubs extend from three to six feet.

AMERICAN ELM: *see* ELM

AMERICAN LOTUS: Member of the *Nymphaeaceae* family. One of the most picturesque aquatic plants in America is the American Lotus. Its stately flowers, exotic leaves, and salt-shaker-like, angular pods distinguish the species as one of the unique and most attractive plants of our native flora. It differs from the true Nymphaea or Water-lily by the distinct carpels or seed-bearers which are embedded in a receptacle, each carpel having a single seed. The leaves are round and attached in the center of the leaf to a long petiole or leaf stem, not on the end of the blade as leaves are usually attached. This form of umbrella-like attachment is described technically as peltate. The leaves, usually one to two feet across, stand two to six feet out of the water, are sunken a bit in the middle and have so characteristic a shape that they are often the theme of art studies.

Younger leaves may first be floating on the surface of the water before emerging to their mature height. The leaves arise from a strong and thick, usually tuber-bearing rhizome which creeps in earth or mud on the bottom of the pond or slow-moving stream. This rootstock system may spread over 50 feet if it has the room to expand. The tubers are like swollen bulges or spindles of the subterranean stem, firm and fleshy, and about one-half as thick as one's arm.

These bulges are from five to ten inches long and when severed form the rhizome, weigh from two to eight ounces. In the middle of the tuber there is a large cavity extending throughout its length with five or six smaller cavities within, all serving as air passages. The tuber is filled with starch in the fall, thereby acting as a storage tissue for the plant.

AMINO ACIDS: These consist of nitrogen-containing organic compounds, large numbers of which join together in the formation of a protein molecule.

AMMONIA: Colorless gas composed of one atom of nitrogen and three atoms of hydrogen. Liquefied under pressure, ammonia is used as a fertilizer. *See also* FERTILIZER, ARTIFICIAL.

AMMONIUM CHLORIDE: *see* FERTILIZER, ARTIFICIAL

AMMONIUM NITRATE: *see* FERTILIZER, ARTIFICIAL

AMMONIUM SULPHATE: *see* FERTILIZER, ARTIFICIAL

AMORPHA: Grown for their foliage and flowers, these shrubs are low to medium-sized with small blue or purple flowers on upright spikes. Most Amorpha are hardy as far north as Massachusetts.

They generally do well in average garden soil, in sunny and somewhat dry conditions. Also known as False Indigo, these shrubs are well suited for borders of shrubs.

AMYGDALUS COMMUNIS: *see* ALMOND

AMYGDALUS PERSICA: *see* PEACH

AMYLASE: *see* ENZYME

ANACARDIUM: This tropical species of trees and shrubs, which includes the Cashew, is only adapted to southern Florida in this country. The cashew is a large, spreading tree with leathery leaves and small flowers and grows to about 20 to 40 feet.

ANACHARIS: *see* AQUARIUMS

ANAEROBIC COMPOSTING: (Composting without air) The anaerobic method of composting was devised to improve upon the aerated composting of organic materials. There are two definite disadvantages in the latter method which permits air to come freely into the heap. First, it brings about an oxidation which must destroy much of the organic nitrogen and carbon dioxide, the vapors of which waste upward. Secondly, some of the valuable liquids, the essences, the juices of the materials, leach downward and out of the mass into the ground underneath where they are wasted. This can be seen by the gigantic weeds which grow in an empty compost pit with an earth bottom.

The purpose of keeping out the air is to prevent or reduce oxidation (combustion). Combustion of nitrogenous substances is always accompanied by the production of a great quantity of free nitrogen compounds. Manure kept in efficient conditions in an open pit loses 40% of the nitrogen originally contained. This loss is relatively small in comparison with the 80% or 90% we would have as a result of improper ways of keeping, but it is also relatively large in contrast to the 10%, 5%, or even 2% obtainable with the use of closed pits. In them the fermentation takes place out of contact with air, and the reduction in weight, when matured, is only one-quarter that of the original weight. If we were able to have perfect anaerobic fermentation, no nitrogen losses whatsoever would occur.

One big difficulty has been finding an efficient and simple way to practice anaerobic composting. The latest technique is to enclose the compost in a polyethylene wrapping.

There has been research that tends to prove that an anaerobic fermentation preserves more of the nutrients. Professor Selman R. Waksman and Florence G. Tenny of the New Jersey Agricultural Experiment Station did research comparing the aerobic and anaerobic decomposition of various types of organic matter. The authors reported: "In a study made on the decomposition of immature oak leaves under aerobic and anaerobic conditions, it was shown that when the leaf material was saturated with water, the celluloses and hemicelluloses were decomposed much more slowly than when the material was under aerobic conditions; the fats and waxes were much more resistant to decomposition and the lignins were preserved almost

quantitatively, whereas the protein content of anaerobic material was considerably greater than that of the aerobic compost because of the greater decompositions of the proteins and losses of the nitrogen in the form of ammonia in the aerobic compost."

The fact that the anaerobic storing of manure may be desirable is brought out in a recent book issued by the Food and Agriculture Organization of the United Nations entitled *The Efficient Use of Fertilizers,* which states: "In Norway, where cattle are stall-fed throughout the winter, the manure is dropped during the daily cleaning through a trap door into a basement extending the length of the cowshed. In this manner it is well protected until used in the spring." Further comments about this method stress that: "Under the efficient methods of storage described above, which are largely anaerobic (free of air) the rate of decomposition of organic matter is slow and the volatilization of ammonia reduced to a minimum. On the other hand, in dry, well-aerated manure piles there is much loss of organic matter and ammonia."

In the study of aerobic conditions against anaerobic it must be borne in mind that there is one place where conditions must be aerobic and that is in the soil itself.

Where land becomes water-logged due to standing water and the anaerobic organisms take over, crops will suffer. But good compost can be made by the anaerobic method and when it is applied to a well-aerated soil the aerobic organisms will prevail and begin to work on it to good advantage as far as crop yields and health of plants are concerned. *See also* COMPOST; MANURE.

ANCHUSA: A coarse-growing perennial which is of easy culture in any good garden soil. Among the best named forms, three to five feet high, is *A. azurea, Dropmore,* which from early June to September is covered with bright blue flowers resembling miniature forget-me-nots. An earlier bloomer, *A. barrelieri,* has blue flowers with a white tube and yellow throat. It opens its buds in early spring, at two feet, and can be set in the second border row, back of the edgings. The seeds germinate easily. It prefers sun, but tolerates some shade. If the stalks are cut back after the first flowering, and the plants fertilized with bone meal, you will get blossoms until frost.

ANDROMEDA: Low evergreen shrubs, with small, pink, bell-shaped flowers, andromedas are hardy in the north. They grow best in an acid humus-rich, moist sandy soil without full sun.

Andromedas germinate well from seeds, especially if sown in sphagnum, attaining a height of about one foot. It is also easily propagated by division or by layering. See also EVERGREENS; LYONIA.

ANEMONE: Popular garden plants comprising a large family of perennial herbs, most widespread in the north temperate zone. They are best described as hardy and attractive flower-garden and border plants. The stems are usually erect, varying in height from dwarf to tall, and, when tall, having graceful stems.

The anemone is widespread in the north temperate zone, thriving best in rich, well-drained loam. Propagation is by root division and seed.

The stem leaves are sometimes clustered together to form a crown near the flower. All the species are hardy perennials and generally cultivated for their showy flowers, and even for their delicate, finely cut leaves. The plants thrive best in fresh, rich, sandy loam that is well drained, although many will survive in any good garden soil. The tuberous species thrive best in a hardy border. Most of the other species fit in a rockery, and some are at home in partial shade.

Propagation, in general, is both by root division and by seed. The root method is best done in early spring before growth starts. Seeds are sown very shallow in a finely raked bed during the fall or in early spring. The good months for planting Anemones are September, October, November, December, February and March. The showy horticultural forms are divided into three sections: 1. The early spring Pulsatilla group. 2. The tuberous group of spring and early summer. 3. The tall Japanese forms of the late summer and fall.

THE EARLY SPRING PULSATILLA GROUP: The early species known as *Anemone* (Pulsatilla) *vernalis* is very shaggy and about six inches high or less. The leaves are finely divided, and all the flowers are purplish without and whitish within, blooming in April. They thrive best in a cool, moist location in a rock garden, and are always an attraction because they herald spring with the robins. *Anemone patens* of Europe is smaller than our American variety, known as "American Pasque Flower." The plant is four to nine inches high. The bluish-purple or white flowers poke out of the soil before the root-leaves develop. The flower blooms in April. *Anemone Pulsatilla,* the true Pasque flower of Eurasia, has very silky hairs three-fourths to one inch long, and the flowers are blue to reddish purple one and one-half to two and one-half inches across, also blooming in early April. Many varieties and variegated forms in color are known. This Pulsatilla group thrives best in well drained soil or stony places.

THE TUBEROUS GROUP OF SPRING AND EARLY SUMMER: The tuberous group of Anemones bloom almost whenever desired, depending on the culture and the time the tubers are planted. In sections, where it is too cold in winter, bulbs or tubers should be cured or ripened after the flowering period by being lifted from the ground to dry and store. If left in the ground to cure they must be protected against excess moisture; the bulbs cannot stand frost. The tubers are of unusual structure, some resembling a three-cornered horn. Florists use this group extensively indoors for late winter and early spring blooms, these being started in autumn in flats, and controlled like a bulb plant. The species is known as *Anemone coronaria* and in common terms as "Poppy-flowered Anemone." The flowers are deeply cut, one and one-half to two and one-half inches across, and poppy-like in appearance, being found in many colors and mixtures of colors from blue, white and red, with the anthers of the stamens blue. Many controlled varieties are listed, such as "Caen," "Scarlet" and "Victoria Giant"; these are single forms. Many double forms are also to be had in a variety of colors, although the scarlet colored are the most dominant. One variety known as *Anemone coronaria* var. *chrysanthemiflora* is a seedling produced in 1848, looking much like a full chrysanthemum.

THE TALL JAPANESE FORMS: The tall Anemones of late summer and fall are the Japanese forms called *Anemone japonica*. These are two to four feet tall with long slender flexible stems bearing white and rosy-purple to carmine flowers two to three inches across. These are excellent to use in a hardy border or colony. They bloom from September to late frost. Many beautiful varieties of the group are to be had, particularly in the white

color from the variety *alba*: such are "Coupe d'Argent" and "Whirlwind." —*G. L. Wittrock*.

See also FERTILIZERS.

ANGELICA: A European biennial plant sometimes grown in this country as a culinary herb and known commonly as garden angelica. It is a large, handsome plant which may reach six feet. The spreading leaves are divided into three-parted leaflets while the small greenish flowers are borne in rounded clusters (umbels) on the tops of the stems.

The fresh stems and leafstalks are used as a garnish and for making a candied confection. The seeds and the oil distilled from them are employed in flavoring, and the aromatic roots are sometimes used in medicine.

The plant thrives best in a moderately cool climate and may be grown in any good soil, but a deep and fairly rich moist but well-drained loam well prepared before planting will give the best results. The plant is most readily propagated from division of old roots, which can be set either in fall or in spring about 18 inches apart in rows. The seed germinates very poorly if more than one year old, and it is best to sow it as soon as it is ripe in a seedbed that is kept moist. Early the following spring the seedlings are transplanted and set in their permanent location about 18 inches apart in rows spaced three feet apart. Plants may also be obtained from seed sown in March in a spent hotbed or in a coldframe. In order to increase root development, the plants are often transplanted a second time, at the end of the first year's growth, and set three or four feet apart. For the same reason the tops are often cut back to prevent the formation of seed. During the growing season the soil should be kept mellow and free from weeds by frequent cultivation and mulching.

ANGLEWORM: *see* EARTHWORM

ANHYDROUS: Being dry, or without

water. For example, anhydrous ammonia is water-free as opposed to the water solution of ammonia known as household ammonia. Anhydrous ammonia is not recommended in an organic fertilizing program. *See also* FERTILIZER, ARTIFICIAL.

ANIMAL PESTS: *see specific animal listings*

ANISE: (*Pimpinella anisum*) An annual herb, which has been widely cultivated throughout the world. The dried fruits, which are usually called seeds, have been for centuries used for flavoring pastries, candies, and beverages.

The plant requires a light, fertile, sandy loam that is well drained and can be so pulverized that the small seed can be planted at a uniform depth and the very small young seedlings cultivated. A frost-free season of at least 120 days is required, and uniform rainfall throughout the growing season is essential because the plant is unfavorably affected by sudden changes from wet to dry periods. The temperature throughout the growing season should be fairly uniform without excessively hot periods, especially following rainfall. When the seed is near maturity alternate rainy and dry periods cause it to become brown, which greatly reduces its quality, and under such conditions the harvesting of the seed is difficult.

The seed is planted about one-half inch deep in the field in rows 18 to 30 inches apart at the rate of one to two seeds per inch. At this rate about five to ten pounds of seed are required to plant one acre. Growers in some European countries broadcast the seed, but as a rule weeds are a major difficulty and if these are present at harvest they are likely to affect the market value of both the seed and the oil. If it is necessary to broadcast the seed and cultivation is therefore impossible it is important that the land be fallowed and in clean culture the previous season. The harvesting of anise presents some difficulties in that the umbels ripen progressively and the seed ripens unevenly within each umbel.

In countries where the plants are grown commercially they are either pulled out of the ground or the tops are cut off by hand. The material thus obtained is tied in bundles and then stacked in a conical pile with the fruiting heads toward the center. This is usually done when all the seed of the umbel is still green. The seed then continues to ripen and when mature does not discolor and shatter from the plant. In foreign countries the seed is usually flailed out, but it can doubtless be threshed by machinery. After the threshed seed is cleaned it is bagged for the market. The oil is extracted from the seed by steam distillation. Under favorable conditions a seed yield of 400 to 600 pounds per acre can be expected.

Attractive in the herb garden, anise grows to two feet high. Its leaves are often used in salads.

ANISE HYSSOP: (*Agastache anethiodora*) Sometimes called Fragrant Giant Hyssop, this is a valuable honey plant that blooms from early summer until frost.

The anise hyssop blooms from early summer until frost. Growing well in ordinary soil, it attracts bees to its flowers much like sweet clover.

The seed of Anise Hyssop is quite small and grows slowly in the early stages. The small plants will not compete successfully with fast growing annual weeds which infest most cultivated land. Thus, under most conditions, there must be weeding or cultivation at least until the bed is established.

The abundant seed supply of Anise Hyssop furnishes summer and fall feed for some small song birds. It grows well in ordinary garden soil and attracts bees to its flowers as well as sweet clover does. *See also* HONEY PLANTS.

ANNONA: This family of tropical trees is most noted for the cherimoya. Grown to some extent in southern Florida and southwestern California, the cherimoya fruit matures in late summer.

Annonas do best in a heavy loam soil, and can stand temperatures in the middle 20's. Most begin bearing fruit when three or four years old. Generally, they suffer less from insect pests than most other fruit trees and require little pruning.

Fruits should be picked when mature; not permitted to fall to the ground and get bruised. The tree reaches a height of about 15 to 25 feet.

ANNUAL: To the botanist, an annual is any plant which grows from seed, produces its flowers, matures its seeds, and dies in one season. To the gardener, an annual is any plant of which seed sown in the spring will produce summer or fall blossoms and not live over the winter.

Many species of plants which in their native home are really perennial herbs (flowering plants that perpetuate their growth from year to year) or biennials (plants that live two years from seed, but bloom only or mostly the second year) are often classed as annuals. Since these plants are generally too tender to survive northern winters, it is better to treat them as annuals.

Most annuals are grown directly from seed, but some plants are grown from tubers or bulbs. For example, crocus and lilies are actually perennials that die back each year to the ground while the roots remain alive. This mixture earns them the name of false annuals.

CLASSES OF ANNUALS: There are a number of annuals which are easy to grow, and others which require pampering. These are easily separated into proper classifications by degrees of hardiness:

Hardy—may be sown outdoors before frosts have entirely ceased right where they are to grow. Generally sown from February to May, some hardy annuals such as sweet peas can be sown in autumn. Often the early seeding is done in a semi-protected area such as along a fence or wall and the seedlings are later transplanted to the desired location.

Half-hardy—usually sown before full warm weather; often these are planted inside in February or March, as half-hardy annuals need warmth to get a good start. Once established, they are quite hardy in the garden.

Tender—seed started in the house or greenhouse, as plants require more warmth than the half-hardy group; a temperature range of 60° to 70° is considered correct; be sure that seedlings get enough light and are not overcrowded; common practice is to transplant seedlings into small pots in which they later can be placed directly in ground.

ADVANTAGES OF ANNUALS: Every garden should include plantings of annuals. Most are easy to handle, inexpensive, ideal for temporary plantings, fine as fill-ins after perennials have stopped blooming; and offering a color range from pure white to a deep black.

As cut flowers, annuals are almost indispensable. Sweet peas, asters, calendulas, larkspurs, marigolds, snapdragons and zinnias are all easily grown decorative flowers. They are used for bedding plants, edgings, for rock garden subjects, as climbers for covering trellises and arbors. Included in the annual vines class are the morning glory and ornamental gourds, the common hop (*Humulus japonicus*), thunbergia, hyacinth bean (*Dolichos lablab*) and balloon vine (*Cardiospermum halicacabum*).

Annuals vary a great deal in form and size—ranging from prostrate, low-and-tall-growing, day-and-night blooming, and fragrant or scentless. The extremes of size can be indicated by the two-inch-high diamond flower or violet cress to the 12-foot castor oil plant (whose berries incidentally are poisonous).

Most annuals do best in an open, sunny location, that has added large amounts of manure, leaf mold, etc. worked into the soil.

CULTURE: The usual time to start a flower-bed is early spring, as most seeds germinate best during the moist spring weather, before it is sufficiently warm and settled for setting out plants. Early sowings give earlier and longer seasons of bloom, but with just a little more care anyone can have a fine display in the flower garden from plantings made as late as June.

How to Prepare the Bed: The preparation of the permanent bed should be given careful attention to make the best out of the planting. Before digging the flower-bed, mark out the dimensions, using the spade to get a clean-cut edge. Any good garden soil will usually produce a fine array of flowers if spaded to the proper depth and broken up to make a fine seed-bed. Heavy and moist soils can be made lighter by adding a good quantity of sharp sand. Usually it will help to spade well-rotted manure into the soil. The manure should be well rotted, since the heating effect of fresh manure can interfere with the growth of most seeds.

In manuring the ground a layer of well-rotted stable manure is spread evenly over the surface, two or three inches thick, and then spaded into the soil so that it is entirely covered. The depth to spade depends on the thickness of the good top soil. Usually six inches is deep enough. While spading the ground, break up the large clumps. After spading, use a steel rake to give a fine, smooth surface to the seed-bed. Stones and other coarse material must be raked out, as they interfere with the sowing.

The Seed-Bed: In many cases the seed-bed is used for raising seedlings which later are transplanted to their permanent place in the garden. The purpose of the seed-bed is to provide an ideal location for the germination and early growth of the seedling. A corner of the garden thoroughly spaded, with the top layer of soil enriched by compost, will make a suitable bed. A solid fence, wall, or a building on the north will hold off the cold winds from this direction.

The bed must be well drained and should be located where it receives the full warmth of the sunny spring days. Thorough preparation of the bed consists in raking the soil over and over until it is perfectly smooth and fine. Mark shallow drills (slight depression in soil) across the bed not more than one-half inch deep and about six inches apart. Sow the seed thinly in these drills and cover lightly with fine soil. Covering the seeds to a depth of two or three times their diameter is an excellent rule to follow. Each row should be labeled to show the variety of seed sown, as the seedlings must be identified when ready for setting out. Making the drills some little distance apart not only serves to keep the varieties well separated, but also permits frequent stirring of the soil between the rows. This is of great assistance in encouraging a quick growth of the seedlings and keeping down the weeds. The seed-bed is valuable for raising plants of almost all annuals except those which do not transplant well, as poppies, and the more tender kind, which should be started in the house or hot-bed.

Starting Plants in the House or Hot-Bed: Many of our choicest summer-flowering and foliage plants came originally from warmer climates, where the growing seasons are much longer than ours. These plants require considerable warmth and sunshine to start the seeds into growth, and the young plants should be kept at a uniform warm temperature. Plants cannot be set outdoors until the nights are quite warm and the trees are out in full leaf. They would receive a severe check in growth, or be entirely destroyed, by a touch of frost. Since they cannot be set out in the North until the latter part of May, it is a great advantage to have the young plants well grown before that time, so that they may quickly make an effective display. In nearly every home there is a bright, sunny window which will serve admirably as a nursery for these warmth-loving plants. If the window-sill is not deep enough for the seed-boxes, a shelf can easily be made with light brackets. When the days become warm and sunny in March, the seed-boxes should be prepared.

Seed-pans of about half the ordinary height of flower-pots are excellent for the purpose. Fill these two or three inch deep boxes nearly full with fine, rich soil or compost; if the soil is heavy or sticky, one-third sharp sand should be added and well mixed with the soil before filling the boxes. Settle the soil firmly in the boxes, and for very fine seeds, like begonias, coleus, etc., it should be well watered two hours before the seed is sown. Scatter the seeds evenly and thinly over the surface. If the box is of good size and several varieties with larger seeds are to be planted, the seeds may be sown in shallow drills three inches apart. Sprinkle the seed lightly with fine soil, barely covering it from view, and press the surface lightly with a small block so that the seeds will not wash out when watered. Now apply tepid water gently with a fine spray. Keep the soil slightly moist, being careful not to over-water nor to allow it to become dry while the seeds are sprouting. On very bright, warm days, when the soil dries out quickly, it may be shaded with a piece of newspaper during the heat of the day, but at all other times the box should be fully exposed.

When the young seedlings are well started, they should be carefully lifted and replanted in small flower-pots or set three or four inches apart each way in fresh boxes prepared in the same manner as for sowing the seeds. As they increase in size and strength they should be transplanted to larger pots, giving them more and more space and air as they grow larger, so that they may be strong and bushy in growth when the time comes for setting them in the flower-bed.

Sowing Outdoors: In the open, seed of the hardier annuals can be planted early in the spring, when the trees are starting into leaf. Usually the seed is sown directly into the bed where the plants are to bloom. Where a bed is to be planted solidly to poppies, petunias, or easily growing plants of like character, the seed may be sown thinly over the surface of the freshly prepared bed and lightly raked in. Where a border is desired, a drill, one-quarter or one-half inch deep, may be made around the edge of the bed with a small stick and the seed sown thinly in this drill, and lightly covered with fine surface soil. Sweet Alyssum, Bartonia, Mignonette, and others will do well for this purpose. Larger growing plants can be sown thinly in shallow drills in the border, or they may be started in the seed-bed, to be transplanted when three or four inches high. To save the time and trouble of transplanting, three or four seeds may be planted in a cluster where each plant is desired to stand, and, when well started, thinned out to the best plant in each place.

TRANSPLANTING: Choose a late afternoon after a good soaking rain, if possible, for transplanting the seedlings. If the soil has become dry, it would be well to water the seed-bed thoroughly a few hours before transplanting. Use a trowel or a stick to loosen the soil around the roots, carefully dig up each plant with all the roots possible, and set in a hole sufficiently large to allow the roots to be spread out in planting. Draw the soil over the roots and slightly up around the stem, and press it firmly into place. A good watering after transplanting will help the plants to become established in their new location. If the following day is warm and clear, shade with a newspaper during the hottest part of the day.

THE CARE AND CULTIVATION OF THE FLOWER-BED: When the young seedlings or transplanted plants are well established, the surface of the bed should be frequently loosened with a small hoe or cultivator. Mulching is even more effective for keeping weeds down and encouraging quick growth of the plants. In dry periods, plants may be kept growing by watering them, but such watering should be well done, wetting the soil thoroughly.

The neat and attractive appearance of the flower-bed will be much enhanced if all the blossoms are cut off and removed as soon as they fade. This will also prolong the flowering period. In the fall the blossoming period may be further prolonged by covering the flower-bed with sheets or newspapers on cold nights, as often there are several weeks of mild weather after the first light frost which injures the more tender plants.

WHAT TO PLANT INDOORS IN MARCH OR APRIL: Or in the hot-bed or cold-frame, to furnish plants for setting out in May:

Ageratum	Lemon Verbena
Asters	Begonias
Heliotrope	Browallia
Ipomoea	Cannas
Lantana	Celosia
Coboea	Cockscomb
Lobelias	Coleus
Marigold	Cypress Vine
Salvia (Flowering Sage)	Dahlias
	Geranium
Large-flowered and Double Petunias	Ricinus
	Torenia
	Verbena

WHAT TO PLANT IN APRIL: In the seed-bed or in the garden where they are to grow and bloom, making the planting when the trees are starting out in leaf:

Abronia	Poppies
Ageratum	Salpiglossis
Sweet Alyssum	Scabiosa
Anchusa	Snapdragons
Asters	Stocks
Balloon Vine	Calendula
Brachycome	Calliopsis
Browallia	Canary-bird Flower
Centaurea	Candytuft
Annual Chrysanthemums	Carnations
Cosmos	Godetia
Cypress Vine	Gypsophila
Datura	Larkspur
Dianthus	Lobelia
Eschscholtzia	Marigold
Forget-Me-Not	Ornamental Grasses
Gaillardia	
Mignonette	Sunflowers
Nasturtiums	Sweet Peas
Pansies	Verbena
Petunia	Zinnias
Phlox	Everlastings

WHAT TO PLANT IN MAY: Seeds of the following require considerable warmth to start them into growth, and the young plants are liable to injury from cool nights. Therefore it is best to defer planting the seeds in the open ground until the trees are in bloom, as the nights are then quite warm. If plantings of the varieties in the preceding list have been omitted, they can still be made at this time along with the following:

Abutilon	Cleome
Balsam	Coboea
Begonia	Cockscomb
Celosia	Coleus

Dahlia
Euphorbia
Four-o'clock
Ipomoea
Lemon Verbena
Momordica
Moonflower
Morning Glories

Nicotiana
Portulaca
Ricinus
Salvia
Sensitive Plant
Stocks
Torenia

See also FERTILIZER; FLOWER GARDENING.

ANNUAL BORDER: *see* BORDER, ANNUAL

ANTHURIUM: Widely grown as florists' plants, these tropical herbs need a warm moist greenhouse, about 60° both day and night. Also known as the tail-flower, Anthuriums offer a fine foliage and beautiful flowers.

A good potting mixture includes sphagnum moss, rotted manure or compost, and sand. Generally well-growing plants of Anthurium need repotting only once every two or three years, but they should have a top-dressing annually. The best time for this is before the end of January—that is, before active growth begins anew. They prefer a shaded place, without drafts.

ANTIBIOTIC: An antibiotic is a substance produced by certain microorganisms that inhibits the activity or life processes of other microorganisms. All antibiotics come from the soil.

The antibiotic age opened with the discovery of penicillin in 1941. Since then, over 3,000 antibiotics have been found, in soils from all over the United States, and from such widespread places as Malaya, Africa, India, Italy and the Philippines.

Antibiotics have practically wiped out human deaths from blood poisoning, mastoiditis, certain types of pneumonia, and typhoid, scarlet and childbirth fevers. They are effective aids against many other diseases, and often help cut the recovery period from still more illnesses. Used properly, they have saved the lives of numerous farm animals, too.

"Used properly" are the key words to the whole question of antibiotics.

For never in history has a substance with such potentialities for good been so misused and abused.

As one medical writer put it, "The 'wonder drugs' have become the 'blunder drugs.' " They have been incredibly overused: doctors have whipped out the needle or prescribed antibiotic pills—often at the patient's misguided insistence—for everything from colds to cancer.

The results have been disastrous. "It is conceivable," warns the New York County Medical Society in a report just issued, "that if the present trend of overdosing with antibiotics continues, soon physicians may have little or nothing with which to combat many infections." Some doctors believe that antibiotics will ultimately cease to be of any use at all—bacteria have already acquired resistance of varying degrees to every antibiotic used for human disease!

Medical societies also report increasing incidence of allergic reactions to antibiotics. Unexpected collapse with all sorts of symptoms, followed by rapid death, has occurred hundreds of times following the administering of penicillin, chloromycetin and other wonder drugs.

Worse yet, even if you have never been given antibiotics when ill, you get small amounts of these potent drugs every day in your food. Livestock feeds contain antibiotics, used as disease preventatives and growth stimulators. Bacteriologists point out that this is a very likely cause of the growing "mystery" disease rate. The antibiotics kill off beneficial organisms in the human body, allowing dangerous ones to become active. Highly troublesome fungus infections—one of them, *candida albicans,* is often fatal—are on the increase as antibiotics kill off the bacteria that normally hold them in check. Viruses, too, are becoming increasingly active.

And now we face the prospect of having all our food, not just our meat and milk products, loaded with these drugs.

A mere glance at the results of antibiotics on crops can make them seem highly attractive. Not only do they kill off disease bacteria, but they stimulate growth and yields (probably by destroying growth-retarding bacteria). Corn germination has been doubled and its growth rate accelerated by terramycin applied to the seed. Penicillin-treated soil, in one test, produced radishes three times as heavy as normal. An antibiotic dip for seed potatoes gave an increased yield of 72 bushels per acre, and tomatoes sprayed with an antibiotic solution gave a 42 per cent increase. Bigger yields and better market quality were reported for many crops.

But what of the other side of the picture?

It has already been proved that plant disease bacteria, just like those that cause human disease, can develop resistance to antibiotics—one company reports the appearance of a bean blight bacteria resistant to streptomycin concentration as high as 500 ppm. Often the wonder drug is as toxic to the plant as to the disease organism: actidione, an antibiotic that attacks fungi, damaged peach trees when applied as a preharvest spray for brown rot. When applied to the soil to prevent damping off of alfalfa seedlings, actidione destroyed the damping-off organisms, but greatly slowed the seedlings' growth.

Most antibiotics act as systemics. This means they enter the plant's tissues, moving through and thoroughly saturating them. Some antibiotics, scientists believe, are changed into more active toxicants in the plant— giving the consumer an even stronger poison to worry about.

Other wonder drugs, like thiolutin, now being tested for plant use, are highly toxic to man. Another, actinomycitin — highly beneficial when produced naturally in the soil by the actinomycetes—is the deadliest poison known to man.

There is a strong residue problem with a number of the antibiotics: streptomycin-terramycin residues have been found on apple surfaces a month after spraying with a 100 ppm solution. (When bacteria develop resistance to an antibiotic, synergism— combining with another antibiotic or chemical—may be resorted to, increasing the already dangerous amounts in the plant.) Some antibiotic residues last a whole season.

There is no doubt that antibiotics will save a crop that is being decimated by a disease epidemic. But how much better is proper soil treatment to prevent such an epidemic!

Organic soil, it has been proved time and again, has a very strong antibiotic reaction. A soil rich in humus has a huge microbial population, one of whose duties is the production of substances that protect plants from disease.

An unbalanced microbial population, many experts are beginning to realize, is one of the chief causes of many of today's crop troubles. Only one bacteria in 30,000 is harmful— but let chemicals or poor management destroy that one bacteria's enemies, and you have plant disease.

Selman Waksman, the world's foremost microbiologist, believes it is far more important to human life to feed the good microbes than to destroy the bad. By incorporating large amounts of organic wastes into our soils, he says, we keep the good bacteria busy producing materials to nourish and protect our plants—and without loading up our foods with foreign substances that may do us great harm.

Antibiotics are one of medicine's great tools. But if they are made a part of every food we eat, the day is near when we will find them worthless. As they stockpile in our bodies, those of us that don't die from allergic reactions to them will be in bad straits if we ever get seriously ill, for we will be immune to these wonder drugs and perhaps beyond help.

ANTS: Ants build nests or mounds in the garden, often spread aphids to plants, but few species actually eat vegetable plants. They can be kept off plants by banding. A suitable band to prevents ants from establishing aphids on the leaves of trees may be made as follows: first put a girdle of cotton around the trunk; over the cotton, place another band of roofing paper which can be secured by the use of small box nails; then, with a brush, apply tree tanglefoot over the band of roofing. This prevents crawling insects from going up the tree. Sprinkling steamed bone meal on lawns, flower beds and garden area has also been found to control ants. *See also* INSECT CONTROL.

APHIDS: Small, soft-bodied, pale green to black bodied insects; cluster on undersides of leaves and on stems; cause curling and cupping of leaves.

Humus-rich soil is the best means of prevention; for small gardens, they are easily removed by hand; aphid damage to fruit trees can be reduced by growing nasturtiums among the trees; rip out plantain weeds around trees, as aphids often harbor in these weeds; three per cent dormant oil spray in early spring and winter protects shrubs. In most cases, bad infestations of aphids can be prevented by watching the plants closely, removing infested leaves. Aphids can be washed off plants with a stream of water from an ordinary sprayer.

An extensive search by University of California entomologists and co-operating U. S. Department of Agriculture scientists has resulted in the discovery of two principal natural enemies of the destructive aphid: A tiny wasp-like parasite from Europe and the Middle East and a variety of ladybird beetle from Pakistan.

The rapid spread of the spotted alfalfa aphid has become a national agricultural problem. In order to propagate a sufficient quantity of the parasites to bring the situation under control, the University of California constructed five additional greenhouses at Riverside.

Cabbage aphids are green to gray or powdery blue; the potato aphid varies from flesh pink to green; the melon aphid is green to black; the pea aphid is pea green with black markings on its appendages; and the bean aphid is almost black. Aphids differ in size; some found on garden crops are about one-sixth inch long and the smallest are barely visible.

Aphids attack the leaves, stems, blossoms, pods, and practically all other parts of their host plants. All aphids are sucking insects, and their food consists of plant juices which they draw from the plants with their tiny needlelike beaks. Heavily infested plants become stunted, and their leaves curl around the colonies of aphids, thus affording the aphids both food and protection. Infested plants not prematurely killed will fail to grow normally or to produce normal crops. Migrating aphids transmit several important plant diseases.

Several natural enemies help to keep aphids under control. The lady beetle is a conspicuous example. Some others of equal importance are so small they can hardly be seen. Diseases also destroy many aphids, especially during warm, damp weather.

Aphids spend the winter either as eggs or as adults. The eggs are often found on the remains of cultivated crops, but they are found just as often on weeds or on plants not growing in the garden. The tiny aphids hatch in the spring. In a few weeks they are mature and give birth, without mating, to living young. Some of the mature aphids fly to cultivated crops during the spring and summer to start new colonies. Only females are produced during the summer; this fact, together with their rapid rate of reproduction, makes it possible for enormous numbers to develop in a short time.

As cool weather approaches in the fall, both males and females are produced. The females of this generation lay fertile eggs which go through the winter. *See also* INSECT CONTROL.

APIOS: These hardy herbs, which have a tendency to act like weeds, thrive in loose, rich soil. They can be used as a cover for trellises and are propagated from seed or by planting their tubers.

The pea-like, brownish, violet-scented flowers appear in clusters in the summer and are followed by long, flat, thickish, many-seeded pods. The tuberous roots were once an important source of food to the North American Indians.

APPLE: (*Malus pumila*) Native to southwestern Asia, apples have been growing since the beginning of recorded time.

They will grow in almost every type soil found in this country, although a clay loam is considered best. Authorities point out that the subsoil gives apple trees trouble more often than the topsoil. When the topsoil is shallow, the roots of trees go down into the subsoil in search of nutrients and water, where it is difficult to improve growing conditions. *See* SUBSOILS.

Vitamin C content of apples varies greatly with varieties. Two Winesaps or one Baldwin contain as much C-vitamin content as five Delicious apples.

There are two extremes to avoid in subsoils for apple trees as well as other fruits: (1) *hardpan*—usually clay layer which prevents penetration by tree roots as well as stopping drainage; and (2) *gravels* and *sands* that lose water quickly.

General advice is that apples thrive in soils on which the common cereals and potatoes grow well. Rolling or somewhat elevated lands are considered desirable, since they usually have better drainage of water and air.

North America is the leading apple growing region of the world, with an estimated annual production of 100 million barrels. All parts of the United States north of Florida and the Gulf borders, excluding the warmer parts of the Southwest, are adapted to apple growing. The area beginning with Nova Scotia and extending to the west and southwest to Lake Michigan is considered about the best.

Cultural information is listed under FRUIT TREES and ORCHARD.

OLD TREES: If the trunk or branches are badly rotted or about a quarter of the top is dead through disease or winter injury, it is not ordinarily worthwhile to attempt salvage. However, here's some general advice when trying to bring new life into old, neglected trees:

Cut out old wood and prune heavily to strong, new growth; remove all suckers that are not necessary to replace the top; prune out interlacing branches to open the trees to light and the circulation of air; break up the soil around the tree, working in a great deal of compost, manure and other organic materials; apply organic nitrogen such as dried blood, cottonseed meal or nitrogen-rich sludge—about 25 to 35 pounds per tree; mulch heavily. Do this regularly for several seasons.

GROWING PROGRAM: Even though commercial apple growing is usually carried on with the aid of 15 to 20 spray applications a season, it is possible to have fair to good results growing apples on a small scale if you follow these three steps:

1. Prepare your ground fully, to the highest degree of organic fertility.

2. Select varieties that are suited to your area, and that are less subject to insect and disease attack.

3. Take the time to apply a dormant oil spray during late winter, and take other preventive measures against insect and disease attack. The best time to plant your trees will be after their leaves have fallen, or from late October into early November. If freshly dug trees are planted early enough, planting can be done successfully in the spring. Nevertheless, land at this time dries up slowly and the growing season is generally well advanced by the time the soil becomes fit to work for the setting of the orchard. A more important reason for planting in the fall is that young apple trees withstand the shock of transplanting best when they are dormant, resting as it were from the growth which has gone on during the months before.

By planting your trees before heavy frost has penetrated the ground, new growth of the roots will take place at once and when spring comes, the trees will be well established and begin growing at the earliest possible period.

Set your trees forty feet apart both ways. This will leave room enough to avoid interference with each other as they grow older. Make the holes for them no larger than will accommodate the root development of each tree. As for how far down to dig, set the trees an inch lower in the ground than they stood in the nursery, and no more than that. A young apple tree will not root any deeper by deep planting and will suffer as truly from this as though it were planted in shallow earth.

If your soil is very acid, broadcast one pound of lime and one-half pound of phosphate rock per tree over your entire orchard before planting.

Once in place, the prime need of the trees will be nitrogen. Often a heavy mulch of alfalfa clippings, or other legumes will supply all the fertilizer required. Indeed cover crops stand high in the nourishment list for apple trees. If your ground is fairly good, sweet clover will be an excellent choice. Use as an annual seeding made late in July, and either leave it standing through the second summer or turn it under the following spring. If your surface soil is low in fertility, rye will be better for a cover crop than clover, as the latter is apt to take nourishment from the soil, thus depriving the orchard trees. Rye though, must definitely be turned under before it fully develops. Its tendency is to grow woody when mature, which is harmful for the young trees.

Apple trees will not thrive in simple sod. There will be too much competition between the grass and the trees. Mulching comes first and foremost in the early years of the home orchard. Alfalfa has been mentioned above. This will demand a good seed bed around the trees. After pulverizing the soil, sow the seed in July, and when the cover crop is clipped, pile the cuttings under the branch spread but keep them away from the tree trunks.

In the summer, when the grass in the orchard is cut, rake the hay and spread it in the form of a circle under the outer branches of the trees. Straw, as well as hay, may be used in this manner. Each one will provide the trees with an adequate mulch and rapidly build up the organic matter in the soil.

In laying these mulches, be sure to have them deep enough to smother the weeds beneath the branches of the trees. In fact it will be well to place them so that they reach somewhat beyond the spread of the branches. The depth or thickness of the mulches should be increased as the years pass. For an apple tree five years old, one hundred pounds of straw for each tree will be scarcely enough. Trees from two to four years old, will need a proportionately less amount.

Nitrogen may be applied in the fall after the foliage has dropped. Available from various organic sources, it may be used in the form of, say 2¼ pounds of dried blood or 4½ pounds of cottonseed meal to the tree, if the winter is not too severe. Otherwise it may be applied in the spring when the frost is well out of the ground, and a good three weeks before the time when the trees will be in blossom. The actual amount of nitrogen given in the form of dried blood or cottonseed meal, or any of the other basic materials from which nitrogen is released, will depend on the type of mulch which has been used on the young trees, as well as on the age of the trees, plus the nature of the soil.

One-half the amount recommended above may well be sufficient for young trees grown in a cover crop which is later used as a mulch around their base. For instance if apple trees are grown in sod and mulched with non-legume hay, obviously they will obtain little nitrogen under those circumstances and the dosage of dried blood or other material will have to be increased. Similarly, with each recurring season, the amount would have to be increased depending on the condition of the trees, reaching a maximum application of two pounds of nitrogen when the trees are seven or eight years old.

Irrespective of the amount of nitrogenous material, it should be applied in a circle about three feet wide under the outer extremities of the branch spread.

A deficiency of nitrogen will show up in the tree by the leaves being small and yellowish; the remedy has already been suggested. If the foliage rolls and scorches, though, that indicates a lack of potassium in the soil. A liberal mulch of manure, or a clover mulch to which lime has been added, mixed with from four to five hundred pounds of potash rock applied to the acre, will adjust the potassium deficiency.—*Milton Johnson.*

FALLING APPLES: The fall of apples, if not in excess, is a natural phenomenon. It is nature's way of removing fruit which is not properly pollinated. This occurrence also reduces excessive fruit which the tree could not normally bring to maturity without exhausting its nutrient supply. Two abscission periods are generally recognized among apple varieties; the "first drop" beginning shortly after petal fall and continuing for two or three weeks, and the so-called "June drop" which begins a few days after the completion of the first drop. The term "June Drop" is somewhat of a misnomer since its normal two- to four-week duration may begin anywhere from late May to early June.

APPLE SCAB: Apple scab spends the winter on dead fruits and dead leaves on or under the tree. It can be prevented largely by carefully removing all dead leaves and fruits to the compost heap and maintaining under the tree a mulch of compost and such mulching material as alfalfa hay or straw. It is also helpful to give the trees a dormant oil spray. This spray is in no way poisonous to soil organisms.

VITAMIN C QUALITIES: Apples are very important to health because they are one of the most readily available sources of vitamin C. Human beings, guinea pigs and monkeys are the only creatures on this earth that do not manufacture their own vitamin C in their bodies, and if we and our monkey friends are to stay healthy we must get our Minimum Daily Requirement of this important vitamin.

Although many people rely on apples to give them vitamin C, it is a fact that varieties of apples vary greatly in the amount of that vitamin they contain. You would have to eat five Delicious apples to get your minimum amount of vitamin C. But you could get the same amount by eating two Winesaps or one Baldwin.

Tomatoes and citrus fruits actually are richer sources of vitamin C than even the better varieties of apples, but vitamin C is so important to nutrition that it is important to have as many good sources in the diet as possible. Some people find the acid in citrus fruits objectionable, and tomatoes are available fresh for only a short time of the year. Canning and storage reduce vitamin C values in a fruit like the tomato.

The Minimum Daily Requirement for vitamin C is 30 milligrams per day. But that amount is just sufficient to prevent scurvy. You can easily see that if you are even *close* to getting scurvy you are in bad shape. So we should all count on getting much more than 30 milligrams of C per day. Some doctors recommend 200 or 300 milligrams per day.

The most comprehensive study of the vitamin C content of different apple varieties was made by the New York Experiment Station in 1946. They found that a French apple, the Calville Blanc, was several times richer in vitamin C than any American apple. But the joker is that the Calville Blanc doesn't grow well at all in this country, and even when grown in Europe it doesn't taste particularly good.

There are several good U.S. apples that are quite a bit higher in vitamin C than the general run of fruit. If you are planning on setting out some trees, you should give careful consideration to these high-vitamin varieties. Best of the American types are Northern Spy, Baldwin, Yellow Newton and Winesap. Apples that are low in vitamin C are McIntosh, Jonathan and York Imperial. Here is a list showing a selection of apple varieties rated according to their vitamin C content:

VARIETY	Ascorbic Acid (Vitamin C) Milligrams per hundred grams
Calville Blanc	35-40
Sturmer Pippin	29
Yellow Newton	16
Northern Spy	15-20
Baldwin	15-20
Winesap	10
York Imperial	8
McIntosh	4

You can see from that listing that there is a considerable difference in vitamin C values among different apples. However, when selecting varieties for a home planting it pays to consider whether the trees you want will grow well in your area. Yellow Newton, for example, is particularly adapted to the Shenandoah Valley region in Virginia, an important American apple area. It is not grown much commercially in other areas, but you might want to experiment with it in a home planting.

Baldwin is widely grown in the eastern U.S. It is sensitive to the climatic extremes existing west of Lake

This apple orchard is being sprayed, not with poisonous chemicals but instead with colloidal phosphate. This practice, combined with organic tree cultivation, keeps insect damage minimized.

Michigan, however. Northern Spy, another high-C apple, is also adaptable to the mid-continent and eastern region.

Northern Spy is an excellent dessert or eating apple, but is not too useful for cooking. Baldwin is just the reverse. It is good for making pies and apple sauce, but not too good for eating fresh. So by planting both of those trees you will get a good supply of both cooking and eating apples that are rich in vitamin C.

Tests have shown that most of the vitamin C in apples is right in or under the skin. The skin can contain five times as much of the vitamin as the flesh. It is also interesting that small apples are richer in vitamin C than large apples. Small apples have more area of skin per pound of fruit, and this greater percentage of skin is probably the cause of the higher vitamin C content.

One good thing about apples is that they lose very little of their vitamin C in storage. If stored at 36°, Baldwin apples will lose no vitamin C over a period of five or six months. However, if the storage temperature gets up to 45°, some of the vitamin will be lost. *See also* FRUIT TREES; ORCHARDING; INSECT CONTROL.

APPLE POMACE: The waste from apple processing plants, when available, is good material for composting.

Apple pomace decays readily if mixed with material that provides for proper aeration. Its value in the wet state is not high, since the nitrogen content is only one-fifth of one per cent. But when analysing the ash content of apple skins, it appeared that they had over three per cent phosphoric acid. Since apple pomace can be had in quantities, a goodly amount of phosphoric acid may be obtained from it at the cost of hauling. The potash content is, of course, much higher, amounting to about 12 per cent of the ash, which corresponds to three-quarters of one per cent of the pomace.

It would seem best to use apple pomace for mulching in the orchard whenever feasible, possibly mixed with straw to permit penetration of air.

In the compost heap, apple pomace should be used in thin layers because heavy layers tend to become compact and, as a result of this, fail to break down.

Apple pomace contains large amounts of seeds which are storage organs containing valuable nutritive substances, especially phosphorus and nitrogen. Hence the fertilizer value of the seed part must also be considered of value to organic gardening.

COMPOSITION	Protein %	Carbohydrate %	Minerals %
Wet	1.3	13.9	0.9
Dried	4.5	62.2	2.2
Silage	1.6	12.6	1.0

APRICOTS: (*Prunus armeniaca*) With an individual and superior flavor, ripening a week or two earlier than peaches, apricots deserve space in the garden. They are as easy to grow as peaches and, requiring the same temperature, frequently outlive them. But care must be exercised; a wet subsoil can kill the apricot tree.

The stocks on which apricots are budded affect their longer life: those whose host tree is a myrobalan plum stand heavy soils better; those on seedling peach and apricot stocks are best for hungry overporous land.

One drawback to apricot culture is that the flower buds, which open very early, risk being injured by late spring frosts. To overcome this, select a cool and not over-sunny spot, planting in a northern or western exposure to delay the opening of the buds, but avoid shade. An eastern aspect is objectionable, because the morning sun does not allow frost-bitten buds gradually to recover, as they may if sunlight does not get on them immediately.

Two-year-old six-foot whips are

good for planting. The average apricot tree covers a circle about 20 feet in diameter when fully grown; this means that apricots should be set at least this distance apart, and eventually they will need this space available to them on all sides. But shorter-lived brambles and bush fruits may be planted closer to them until they need their full room. The good varieties are:

Alexander. A cold-resistant Russian variety, with small freestone fruits.

Blenheim, Moorpark, and Scout. The last-named being non-self-pollinating.

Early Golden, which has large fruits, almost as big as peaches. An old-time reliable sort.

Some modern kinds, introduced from North China in the past 25 years, include such sorts as Chow, Manchu, Mandarin, and others, which are extra hardy, claimed to withstand temperatures down to 40° below in their native land.

Young fruits should be rigorously thinned; otherwise lean years may alternate with fruiting years. Important: when they are half-grown, snip out one of every two fruits that touch.

Multi-variety trees may be obtained: apricot, peach, and plum on one tree. They are recommended for the garden that is limited in area. *See also* FRUIT TREES; ORCHARD.

APRICOTS, HUNZA: American fruit growers, always seeking new and better varieties, may soon receive the benefit of a remarkable variety of apricot, developed over 16 centuries by a hitherto little-known people living high in the Himalayan mountains of northern Pakistan — the Hunzas.

These people have become famous since Western explorers discovered their valley and, subsequently, the remarkable vigor and stamina of its people. It is believed that the main reason for the robust health of the Hunzas lies in the food they eat; and one of the daily staples of the Hunza diet is the apricot. Americans who have been to Hunza report that their apricots are larger and more tasty than the fruit of varieties grown in this country. It is not unlikely that the food values in these superior fruits is one of the secrets of the Hunza people's strength and health.

To the Hunza, the apricot is a much more important part of the diet than it is to us. They cannot ship in fruits, so they must use what they can grow. There is seldom a surplus of staple foods in Hunza, so the apricots are nurtured carefully and dried to preserve them for winter use. Even the stones are cracked open and the inside kernels eaten.

For the last 1600 years the Hunzas have been propagating their apricot trees, and in that period of time they have developed several distinct varieties. Because Hunza is so isolated it is unlikely that any of these remarkable trees have been exported to other areas, and very little is known about them beyond the bounds of their little mountain valley.

The ruler of Hunza, the Mir, writes: "Regarding the apricots, there are several varieties of them in Hunza. Some of them are delicious for eating, some of them for drying and keeping them for dry fruit purposes and cooking. The custom is that when you will grow these seeds and when they are out and one-year-old, just cut the head of the small plant and graft it to the apricot tree so it will give you the real flavor and kind of fruit.

"We are growing good quality apricots between seven and nine thousand feet above sea level. Our temperature in winter sometimes falls to two or three below zero."

The editors of *Organic Gardening and Farming* magazine received some seeds from the Mir, and planted them at the Organic Experimental Farm in Emmaus, Pennsylvania. High hopes are held for this tree, if for no other reason than it is one of the prime food sources of a people who have been among the healthiest on earth. If the Hunza apricot thrives in this country, an attempt will be made to get some American nurseries to propagate it for sale to the public.

APRIL GARDEN OPERATIONS: see GARDEN CALENDAR

AQUARIUMS: There are no rules to follow in artistic aquarium planting except the general ones of proportion which apply to all garden compositions, indoors or outdoors. Mass the tall plants at the back and corners for background effects. Bushy plants should be placed at the side or in the corners and specimen plantings can be made of different varieties. In a large aquarium of more than five gallons capacity, nothing is better than Vallisneria, commonly called eel grass. It is a tall, thin plant with ribbon-like strands which swing to right and left below the surface of the water. Use it in clumps or as a solid mass across the back of the tank.

For the sides and corners Cabomba, Anacharis, and Ludwigia are extremely good. This last provides a spot of color for the planting, as the leaves are green in front and purple-red in back. Pinch back Anacharis, as it grows rapidly and will soon crowd the tank.

Sagittaria is a good specimen plant; so is spatterdock. Moneywort, a low green plant, very dainty in appearance and hair grass will carpet the aquarium with small grass-like needles which provide the fish, if any, with a good hiding-place. There are many other aquatic plants which may be used, if desired, such as water hyacinths or water lilies and the like.

Many fine vines, bulbs, and plants will live and thrive in water. English ivy, once established requires little care and will climb stucco walls or trail from a mantel with gorgeous effects. Nasturtiums, cut before heavy frosts, will bloom indoors all winter. Add a little fertilizer to the water each week. The Chinese evergreen (*Aglaonema simplex*), Roman hyacinths are all easily grown in water.

In starting his aquarium the beginner should keep in mind the following four basic functions that plant life performs.
1. Its ability, under the influence of light, to develop free oxygen and to absorb carbon dioxide. This function is absolutely vital to the animal life in the aquarium.
2. Absorbtion through its underwater roots and leaves of the fecal matter excreted by the animal life.
3. Helping keep the water clear by competing successfully for food with microscopic vegetal organisms. *Salvinia*, Duckweed and *Azolla* are excellent for this purpose.
4. Providing a breeding ground for the fish. Many fish deposit their eggs on the leaves of the plants and the younger fish subsequently seek refuge there from their cannibalistic elders. *Riccia* is especially recommended for this purpose.

AQUATIC GARDENING: see LILY POND; AQUARIUMS; WATER GARDENS

ARACEAE: This large family of herbs, sometimes called *Calla*, includes the Jack-in-the-Pulpit and skunk cabbage. While these are hardy, most araceae are tropical plants, containing a milky, bitter juice that is often poisonous.

ARALIA: Large herbs — sometimes shrubs or even small trees, aralias are almost hardy in the North. Preferring rich or heavy soil, their subtropical foliage makes attractive lawn plantings. Flowers are small and white, and are followed by black berry-like fruit. The perennial herbs are mostly woodland plants adaptable to the wild garden where they should be given rich humus and partial shade. Propagation may be through seeds sown in frames in the spring or by root cuttings over bottom-heat.

Ivy-leaf Aralia (*A. japonica*) makes a fine house plant. Its leaves may be four inches or more across, are dark green, and naturally glossy. They hold on the plant extremely well, showing no tendency to yellow or drop. For a bushy shape, Ivy-leaf Aralia should be cut back several times during its first two years; for a taller, more slender plant, allow it to branch normally as it matures.

Aralias need good drainage, fairly heavy watering, and a warm situation. They may be grown in a partially sunny exposure, but do best when given full bright light without direct sunlight. Pot them in good, humusy soil. One fine point about this plant is the ease and speed with which cuttings may be rooted in a glass of plain water. When roots on the cuttings are one-half to one inch long, pot these new little plants in small, clean clay pots.

Two other aralias are excellent indoor plants, and fairly fast growers, *A. balfouriana* and *A. balfouriana variegata*. These have fairly large, rounded, scalloped leaves, entire when the plant is young, but divided into three parts in mature plants. The all-green variety has not been seen much in the North, and until recently, the variegated sort was very rare. Cultivation and propagation of both the all-green and the cream-edged *A. balfourianas* is the same as for the Ivy-Leaved Aralias.—*Katherine Walker.*

ARAUCARIA EXCELSA: *see* PINE, NORFOLK ISLAND

ARBOR: All the material needed for this structure is a few cedar poles

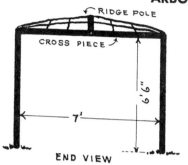

END VIEW

CROSS SECTION OF THE ARBOR shows simplicity of construction. The arbor should be adequate in size to permit freedom of movement within. The above dimensions, seven feet wide by six feet, six inches high, are recommended.

about nine feet long and four inches in average diameter, a coil of fence wire, a quantity of boards or two-by-fours, some nails and staples and a number of grape plants. Used lumber which is suitable will help cut costs.

Since it is to be used mainly in summer, its number one attraction will be coolness. The floor soon becomes bare of grass, and many experiments have proven that no plant life can long endure such heavy traffic. Re-sodding produces a lovely green carpet of about a one-month duration. A hardy growth of thyme will not last a full week. But down-to-earth flooring, bare, hardpacked Mother Earth has certain distinctive virtues.

SIDE ELEVATION OF THE ARBOR gives spaces between supporting wires and suggested length of 24 feet. The ends may be left open, permitting ready circulation of air for coolness or one end may be closed if privacy is desired. Building this arbor requires no special tools.

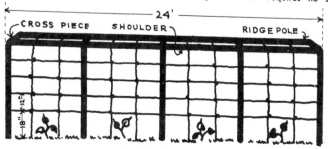

SIDE VIEW

It is comforting and relaxing—especially on a hot day—to rest the feet on the good earth. The floor is never fully exposed to the sun, its moistness always contributes to the general coolness. Once it becomes well packed, there is little tendency to muddiness.

The furniture must be of a flat-footed, non-gouging design, or can be made so by screwing a three-inch square of wood onto the bottom of each leg.

Above all things, the structure must be of adequate dimensions, allowing freedom of movement. This is the essential in which most arbors are lacking. They are usually constructed for the purpose of yielding much fruit and little human comfort. In a cramped-up arbor, to which no one is attracted, straying branches soon make the interior so impenetrable that most of the fruit cannot be reached.

An ideal size is seven feet wide by six and one-half feet high by 24 feet long. Such a structure will produce abundant fruit and allow complete freedom from a shut-in-cooped-up feeling. If coolness is the main object, both ends should be left open to the breeze. If greater privacy is desired, the ends may be closed, with one central entrance or a side opening at each end. Still more privacy is obtainable by making a "T," "U" or "L"-shaped arbor, and if the yard is of irregular contour, something like this may inspire an unusual or artistic design.

The most reliable vines to plant are Concord and Fredonia, but almost any variety will flourish magnificently on an arbor. A structure 24 feet long will support eight vines nicely, four spaced evenly on each side.

It will probably take two years for the arbor to become fully shaded by grape leaves, which are naturally shaped to give maximum shade while permitting free movement of air. No other leaves can equal the grape in this respect, but until the vines are sufficiently developed, ample shade can be had by planting climbing beans or morning glories. Tomatoes thrive excellently against the support of an arbor, the ripe fruit adding a delightful touch of brightness in the late summer.

Because of the extra shelter, these plants and vines retain their vitality well into the autumn. Some of the most enjoyable outdoor meals could be eaten in the protection of the arbor after the regular picnic season had ended. On every warm autumn day, the arbor invites you to prolong summer pleasures for a few more delightful hours. Such meals have a special zest—the added flavor of seasonal rejuvenation.

Actual building of the arbor requires no great ingenuity. Posts should be sunk about two and one-half feet into the ground, opposite each other in pairs, with a two-by-four or similar piece connecting their tops. These cross-pieces support a center ridge pole or board, which may be composed of several parts. The pairs of posts should be six feet apart, connected also with two-by-fours from top to top along each side.

Along the ridge pole, at two-foot intervals in each section, strands stapled in the middle reach to the ground on both sides. These wires are also stapled to the shoulder two-by-fours, then looped alternately around each of the horizontal wires. Along the top, strands run from end to end, one foot apart, looping the cross wires and stapled to the cross-pieces.

The use of wire in place of wood wherever possible will make your fruit easier to pick and your arbor less subject to rot. Life of the wood may be extended considerably by applying a coat of paint or preservative.

As a whole, the edifice need not be a masterpiece of carpentry. Odds and ends which can be made to fit will prove just as serviceable as new lumber.

Every five years or so, the accumulation of old wood makes an all-out pruning necessary. This should be done late in the fall. It can be accomplished by sawing all branches along the sides at a height of about three feet from the ground. The whole loose growth can then be raised on one side and rolled back over the top so that it comes clear in a complete mass to be carried away for compost or mulch use.

Now that the vines have strong roots, foliage will soon cover the arbor in spring with leaves larger and healthier as a result of pruning.

Considering the pleasant retreat they so readily provide, the scarcity of arbors is truly regrettable.

ARBORETUM: Defined as a place where trees and shrubs are cultivated for scientific and educational purposes, many of today's Arboretums are located on private estates, public parks and several experiment stations. Some of these include: the Arnold Arboretum of Harvard University; the Morton Arboretum at Lisle, Illinois; Myron Stratton, Colorado Springs; Childs Frick Arboretum, Roslyn, L.I.; Sanford Arboretum, Knoxville, Tenn.

ARBORVITAE: These evergreens, of the genus *Thuja*, are mostly low growers and come in a wide variety of shapes and are among the most popular of shrubs for foundation plantings. Usually found in moist, cool regions, arborvitae prefer areas free of smoke and dust, with sufficient rain and without too much summer sun. *See also* EVERGREENS.

ARCTOSTAPHYLOS: These evergreen shrubs produce red fruit and bell-shaped flowers. Native to the Pacific Coast, they make fine honey plants. One species, the bearberry, makes an attractive evergreen ground cover in the northern temperate regions.

ARCTOTIS STOECHADIFOLIA: *see* AFRICAN DAISY

ARECA: *see* PALMS

ARGEMONE: Preferring a light soil in a sunny location, these herbs have become popular annuals. Easily grown from seed, argemone produce a large yellow, white or purple poppy-like flower.

ARID CLIMATE: Refers to a very dry climate, such as in parts of the Southwest, where desert or semi-desert conditions exist. Generally there is only enough water for widely spaced desert plants. Annual rainfall varies from ten to 20 inches. The soil is generally low or deficient in nitrogen and organic matter. Shrubs and bunch grasses are the principal vegetation in areas where the rainfall is less than ten inches annually. The soils are light in color, alkaline in reaction, and often high in lime content and mineral nutrients. *See also* DESERT GARDENS.

ARMERIA: Often selected as border and rock garden plants, armerias prefer light, sandy soils. Thrift (*A. maritima*) grows about one foot high; has pink, purple or white flowers. Sometimes called *Statice*, these perennials belong to the *Plumbaginaceae* family.

ARNICA: (*Arnica montana*) A herbaceous perennial plant native to northern and central Europe, where it thrives in the cool climate of mountain meadows. The flowers, leaves, and roots are employed in medicine.

The plant requires a cool climate for best development. Seed in fall or spring. Seed may be sown in August in a seedbed and the seedlings transplanted the following spring. In the field the plants should stand about 18 inches apart in the row.

Arnica prefers a very acid soil; produces yellow flowers; is best propagated by root division.

ARROWWOOD: (*Viburnum dentatum*) A ten to 15 foot high shrub that does well in open areas. Its creamy flowers and bluish-black berries make it especially attractive. Hardy in practically every section of the United States, it has wine-colored foliage in fall. *See also* VIBURNUM.

ARTEMISIA: Known as the ghost plant, *A. albula* is a very interesting plant for the home grounds.

The foliage is densely hairy, making the plant appear white. In a mass in the evening, artemisia stands out in whiteness.

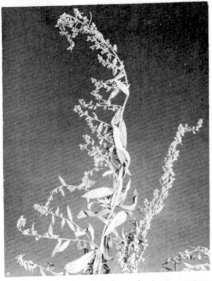

The artemisia is good for relieving monotony in the garden, because its whiteness makes it stand out against the general background. Propagation by division may be done in the spring.

Artemisia, which in general impression is white or gray (and some with purple stems), thrives in average soil; it blooms in August and September, or later, and retains its foliage in good condition long after blooming. The different species vary in size and height from six inches to 12 feet. These plants are fragrant and attractive even though somewhat elusive. Propagation is by cuttings or seed, but seedlings can be purchased of seed houses.

There are about a dozen species which may be briefly described. *A. albula* is one of the showiest wormwoods and has gray stems and embraces the Silver King, a form which is quite spectacular. Its leaves are white and finely hairy. It grows three feet tall and is often used in bouquets. It needs constant moisture. White mugwort (*A. lactifolia*), grows from three to four feet tall and has smooth green foliage with masses of fragrant white flower heads in September and October. The Common Mugwort (*A. vulgaris*), supposedly is tall with divided leaves and purplish stems and has yellow flowers in spikes. The leaves are white beneath.

"Old man"—Southernwood (*A. abrotanum*)—is shrubby and fragrant, also interesting. "Old woman" or Dusty Miller (*A. Stellerianam*), is well suited for rock gardens. It has densely woolly and deeply cut leaves which are aromatic when crushed. It is a slender plant, about two feet tall, and ghost-like in appearance. The Mountain Fringe, Fringed Wormwood (*A. frigida*), is 15 inches tall and has delicate foliage. The Summer Fir, also known as Russian Wormwood (*A. sacrorum*), has white leaves, is drought-resistant, and grows three to five feet high. It is good for borders and as lawn specimens. It has ornamental foliage, is pyramidal in shape and is white. *A. gnaphalodes* is tall and silvery, excellent for borders. Roman Wormwood (*A. pontica*), seldom blossoms, is finely cut, whitish and effective. It is useful for rock gardens. Tarragon (*A. dracunculus*), has masses of smooth, narrow, green leaves which are used for seasoning. *A. pedemontana* and *absinthium,* the source of absinthe and used for flavoring, are of minor importance.

The species of Artemisia will grow in ordinary garden soil, but do much better where there is plenty of organic matter. Composting the earth gives more luxuriant foliage and more abundant flowers. The fragrance is also more manifest when there is plenty of humus in the soil.

Clumps of artemisia are effective in the garden, since separate plants seldom spread more than two feet. The flowers continue in good condition for about six weeks, and the plants may be used at the rear of borders where large gaps are left by delphiniums when gone; so artemisia can be planted close to the delphiniums, and in due time will fill in the open places. Artemisia will relieve the monotony of many plants such as phlox.

In home propagation, one can best use division. When an old clump is 12 or more inches around, it may be divided into three or more sections in late September or in early spring. Use a sharp spade to cut the stool into sections. Then dig a hole large enough for each section and fill it with water. After the water has drained away, set the divisions in place, level with the rest of the soil, packing them well with earth. Then water again. The plants need full sun and will blossom well if fertilized. Use compost or mulches.—*M. B. Cummings.*

ARTICHOKE, AMERICAN: (*Helianthus tuberosus*) The American Artichoke, was originally called the Improved Mammoth French White Jerusalem Artichoke. Its large, potato-shaped tuber is characterized by a sweet nutlike flavor. Contrary to popular notion, it neither tastes nor looks like the green or globe artichoke, is not even related to it botanically.

Jerusalem is actually a corruption of the Italian *girasole,* meaning "turning to the sun," and this artichoke is really a prolific member of the sunflower family.

Over three hundred years ago, French explorers found the American Indians cultivating and eating what looked like a large, reddish peanut. They took it back to France whence it spread to England. Constant propagation and cross breeding have improved it ever since and in many European countries it has long served farmers as a practical, easy-to-grow stock and poultry feed.

The artichoke is 100 per cent *starchless.* It stores its carbohydrates in the form of inulin rather than starch, and its sugar as levulose the way most healthful fruits and honey do. It has practically no caloric value. Because of these facts, medical authorities strongly recommend it as a substitute for other carbohydrates on the diabetic's menu, and in the diet of all who should or must restrict their starch and calorie intake.

On the nutritional side, in addition to its non-starch feature, the Jerusalem artichoke offers a good source of some minerals and vitamins (particularly potassium and thiamine)—a result of its being a plant-world union of tuber

Many gardeners do not realize the difference between the common globe artichoke at left and the Jerusalem artichoke at right. The newer American variety is much less knobby and very nutritious.

roots and luxuriant sunflower growth.

They'll grow in almost any type of soil that gets a little sunshine. They are free from disease, highly productive and completely frost-hardy. In fact, it's important to remember that they spread very rapidly, and unless cultivated with a modicum of care, will become troublesome as weeds.

For this reason, it's best to give them an out-of-the-way planting, kept at a reasonable distance from other vegetables or flowers. If a check is needed against their spreading, roots should be dug in late fall or early spring and thoroughly removed.

Planting artichoke tubers is very much like planting potatoes, and is made from cut pieces each having a seed or "eye." Unlike potatoes, this frost-proof vegetable can be set out in the fall as well as early spring. A good location may be along the garden edge where the six-to-eight foot tall artichokes won't overshadow other plants. They're also useful where their screening effect and large, colorful blooms will improve the landscaping. (Some grow to heights of a modest 12 feet or so.)

In a row system, plant one medium piece per hill, a foot apart, in two to three-foot rows. In beds, set tubers four by four feet. As indicated, plants multiply quickly and soon choke out any venturesome weeds. Mulching is a good idea in row plantings, and compost applications maintain desirable fertility—although soil and climate extremes won't stop this persistant plant.

The sturdy artichoke's bright blossoms, upper stalk and leaf growth don't go to waste, either. Where they're not used for livestock or poultry feeding, the tops can be cut and fed to the compost or mulch-material piles.

Since freezing doesn't injure the tubers, they may be left in the ground indefinitely after fall frosts, a fresh supply being dug as needed throughout the off season. In fact, leaving them in the ground is a practical storage method for this vegetable whose tender skin doesn't make it a particularly good indoor keeper. Those that are brought in should be kept quite moist—if necessary given a daily soaking in water prior to use.

With the arrival of spring, tubers left in the ground should be dug, either for eating or replanting in rows. If an increased supply *is* wanted, some may simply be left to multiply.

Twenty-five-foot row will provide the average family adequately. And on a larger scale, it should be noted that *the Jerusalem artichoke will produce as much as 15 tons to the acre*—compared to about *three* tons for potatoes.

Of all the varieties of Jerusalem artichoke grown in the U.S., many of them wild, the American offers the greatest advantages. Contrasted to the knobby tuber shape of the others, this improved type is smooth-surfaced, resembling the Idaho potato, and about the size of a man's fist. In taste and in diversity of uses, it surpasses any previously developed.

ARTIFICIAL FERTILIZERS: *see* FERTILIZERS, ARTIFICIAL

ASEXUAL: Referring to propagation, asexual implies any method of reproducing plants except by seeds. Concerning flowers, asexual means that they have no stamens, pollen, pistils—therefore are sterile.

ASH: Belonging to the genus *Fraxinus,* the ash tree is primarily important as timber, although the flowering ash makes a showy tree for home landscaping with its large clusters of white flowers. Main growing requirement for ash trees is sufficient moisture. *See also* TREES.

ASPARAGUS: In the early spring the home garden offers few pleasures greater than the cutting of the luscious early spears of an established planting of asparagus. It was because of its

Asparagus in the field. This delicious vegetable will yield for many years if soundly established.

habit of producing early shoots that the ancient Persians named the plant "asparag" meaning sprout.

Until modern times asparagus was a medicinal plant. The great dietary value of the early and abundant supply of green spears restored men who must have struggled through the long winter upon a poorly balanced diet. But like many other medicinal plants asparagus later became a garden favorite. Its popularity is still increasing.

It is possible to grow fine asparagus plants from seed if care is taken to see that the seed bed is properly drained and well pulverized and that the seedlings are transplanted without too much injury to the root systems. But an established planting reaches the cutting stage much sooner if one year old roots of the best disease resistant varieties are used.

To establish a planting of asparagus it is best to select a site to one side of the garden. This site should be free from shade, the soil should be rich, deep, and well drained. The location should be so arranged that the permanence of the planting will not interfere with the cultivation of the rest of the garden.

In the spring as early as the ground can be worked, a trench 12 inches deep and about ten inches wide should be dug along the line where the first row is to stand. In the bottom of this trench place a three inch layer of mature compost humus. If well rotted manure is plentiful this may be added. This layer should then be well dug into the bottom of the trench. The second row should be made not closer than four feet from the first.

One year old crowns should then be placed in position about 18 inches apart and ten inches below the level of the garden. The crowns should be covered with a two inch layer of sifted compost humus and well watered. During the summer the trench should be slowly filled with a mixture of fine topsoil and composted material. Cultivation will tend to fill the trench, but it is advisable not to do the filling too rapidly or the growing plants are likely to be stifled.

Whatever care you take in the setting out will be well repaid to you later. The care you use in the selection of the site is an important item. The very careful, deep preparation of the area is of great value because the powerful fleshy roots of the asparagus plant often thrust their way five to six feet downward and spread out almost an equal distance in their search for the heavy supply of plant nutrients needed for the production of the large spears. Because of this, the plants require more garden space than their feathery brush would seem to indicate, and because of the great depth to which the roots develop, you will find it wise to see that an ample supply of rich organic matter is deeply placed before setting out the crowns.

After the planting is established it will thrive with little care for many years. But as with all vegetables, asparagus should be kept free from the damaging influence of trees, it should be kept free from weeds, and each season it should receive a liberal supply of added organic material. This supply can be arranged in two ways.

In the spring the rows should be

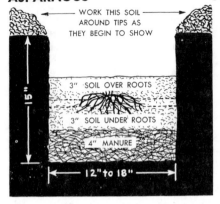

ASPARAGUS PLANTING TRENCH diagram shows overall depth, also materials for each layer.

ridged. Ordinarily this is done by drawing up to the row a good quantity of the topsoil between the rows by using a hoe. If you use compost instead of topsoil to form these ridges, this will serve two purposes; it will bleach the shoots by excluding the sunlight, and it will add much valuable plant nutrients to the soil.

After the cutting season, it is good practice to sow a cover crop of cowpeas, soybeans, etc. These should be planted between the rows of asparagus. A cover crop of this type discourages the growth of weeds and when dug under adds greatly to the organic content of the soil.

But the organic material added during ridging is the most important. This ridge should be several inches high because if it is shallow the shoots will tend to open before assuming sufficient length. Even if you decide to grow "green asparagus" that is, unbleached asparagus, you will find it necessary to form shallow ridges to overcome the tendency of the crown to get too close to the surface. This slow upward movement is caused by the formation each year of new storage roots on the uppermost side of the crown.

If a good growth is made the first year, it is possible to cut the shoots lightly the following spring, but it is generally better to encourage plant growth and to delay cutting for another season. Spears should be cut when about six inches high. Some gardeners cut them two inches below the ground level, others at the surface.

In cutting, place the knife blade close to the spear, run it downward the desired depth, then turn it enough to cut cleanly through the spear but no more. Careless jabbing during cutting time can cause very serious injury to a planting of asparagus.

As winter approaches the rows of asparagus should be lightly mulched with straw or similar material to prevent frost from penetrating too severely into the crowns. The brush should not be removed or burned but should remain as a part of the mulch. This mulch should be removed in the spring and the ground lightly cultivated.

The asparagus beetle is considered a serious menace, is very difficult to get rid of and does much damage. But most of the serious damage done by this beetle occurs when the beetle is allowed to overwinter in the adult stage by finding concealment in fallen sticks, trash, leaves and the like. In this case it emerges in the early spring to feed upon the young asparagus shoots. Garden cleanliness and fall cultivation will prevent the insects from overwintering. Also, a very old method for controlling asparagus beetles was to turn chickens, ducks, guinea hens, etc., loose in the asparagus planting. These birds invariably do an efficient job of wiping out the beetles and their larvae.

Asparagus rust is a plant disease affecting asparagus. Small reddish pustules appear first on the main stalks. These pustules, when they burst, release a fine rust-colored cloud of spores. Sometimes an entire planting is rapidly infected and dies. But the degree with which asparagus rust does damage is very largely dependent upon local conditions. The spores require dampness for germination. Areas subject to heavy dews and damp mists are poor locations for asparagus.

Mary Washington, an old reliable rust-resistant variety, is a safe bet for any gardener. It is the most popular variety grown today.

ASPEN: *see* POPLAR

ASPIDISTRA: One of the hardiest of foliage plants that can be grown indoors, the aspidistra (*A. lurida*) is extremely tenacious of life. It does not seem to mind the dust and dry air, or the spasmodic watering and insufficient light which seem to be the common lot of most house plants. It has been wintered outdoors at Philadelphia by giving it a heavy mulch of forest leaves. If given a fairly rich soil and plenty of moisture, the aspidistra will make a fairly rapid growth, but it never gets very tall; instead it broadens out. The simplest way to get new plants is by dividing the old one in the early spring (February), before any growth takes place so that the young leaves will not be injured, or in August.

The aspidistra has no stem, the leaves coming directly from the rootstock or rhizome. The leaves are from 15 inches to two feet long. The leaf stem is about one-eighth to one-quarter of an inch in diameter and wiry, and about one-quarter the length of the whole leaf. The blade is from three to five inches wide and very dark green in color. There is a variegated form of this having white stripes in the leaves. These are, however, almost lost if the plant makes a rapid growth, and in no two leaves on the same plant are they exactly the same.

ASTER: The name aster refers to two distinct genera of plants, both members of the Composite or Daisy family. It is the botanic name of the hardy asters which are perennials, and it is also the popular name of the tender China Asters which are annuals. The China Aster has been developed until it is now one of our most popular garden annuals.

CULTURE: For early bloom, the seeds should be sown in March in flats or pots. Use a soil mixture of one-third sand, one-third garden soil and one-third compost. Sow the seed in shallow drills about three inches apart and cover with a light layer of soil. Keep evenly moist, but not soaked, until the seedlings are up and growing well. When they have their first true leaves or are crowding, transplant them into paper cups or flats with at least four inches between plants. Do not delay the transplanting so long that the plants become spindly.

As the weather becomes warmer, gradually harden off the plants by setting them outside during the pleasant part of the day. When all danger of frost is over, the seedlings are ready to be transplanted to their permanent location. Set the plants about ten to 12 inches apart in rows about one and one-half to two feet apart or in groups, as you prefer. Add some wood ashes to the soil in early spring or at least two weeks before planting the seedlings; otherwise add well-rotted manure or compost. A light sprinkling of lime on an acid or neutral soil surface a few weeks before planting is beneficial, as they like a sweet or alkaline soil. Aster seeds can also be planted directly in the garden after the soil has warmed up if you are unable to start seedlings indoors.

Cultivate regularly throughout the growing season to keep down weeds. A good mulch can, of course, help control these and lighten the chore considerably. The roots of the aster are fine and close to the surface of the soil, so shallow cultivation is essential. During dry weather, water thoroughly about once a week.

USES: There are several features which make the China Aster one of the most desirable of the annual flowers. They are excellent cut flowers. They have good lasting quality, have long stems, are not easily damaged, and they have a wide color range. Bloom may be had from July until frost in October. They also make a wonderful display in the garden, as you may use them as a border plant, mass in groups in an informal fashion, or intermix them with your chrysanthemums.

VARIETIES: There have been so many types and varieties developed that it is difficult to discuss them all. Each variety has its own list of colors, some having many shades and tones. The Queen of the Market is usually considered to be the earliest bloomer. The Giant Branching type has very long stems. The California Giant type are quite tall and have very large flowers. There are also many other types of Pompon Asters, Fluffy Asters, and wilt-resistant strains. *See also* FERTILIZER; MICHAELMAS DAISY.

ASTILBE: *A. japonica* is commonly but incorrectly sold by many florists as spirea. It is a Japanese herb which grows from one to three feet high, and is an excellent plant to grow indoors. The flowers are a 'beautiful, creamy-white borne in long spire-like clusters. They require no special care. Pot the roots in the fall and keep in the cold frame or other cool place until the middle of November. Bring the plant into the house, give plenty of water and a little liquid plant food. It will bloom in about three months' time, or slightly less.

Astilbes also make fine perennial border plants, growing well in ordinary garden soil. The small flowers bloom mostly in late spring and sometimes through July and August. Some astilbe shrubs grow as high as six feet.

AUBRIETIA: A purple rock cress, growing to six inches, and an excellent mat-forming plant for the rock garden, wall garden, or sloping bank. Seeds may be sown in the open ground or in flats and transplanted. There are many forms of *A. deltoides,* some dwarf and others with larger leaves and pink, purple, crimson, and lilac

flowers instead of the common lavender. May be carried over the winter in frames or given winter protection.

AUGUST GARDEN OPERATIONS: *see* GARDEN CALENDAR

AUSTRALIAN PINE: Sometimes called Casuarinas, these native trees of Australia and the South Seas encircle the tropics of the globe. For binding shifting sand on the shores of the sea in windy locations, they have few equals. They may be trimmed into a windbreak hedge of a height sufficient to protect homes in its lee during severe storms.

Some trees bend with the wind permitting it to slide over and trickle through. Some, like the willows and gumbo-limbos, let their limbs snap off sprouting out fresh from the old stump after the storm is over. Casuarinas have adapted themselves to such conditions since they have no leaves. The green parts are pliant branchlets; stems are sturdy and give with the wind. They've adjusted themselves to the stormy seashore.

Casuarinas grow on salt marsh, seashore sand, and rock and muck at the rate of ten feet or more a year under favorable conditions and naturally grow straight into the air. They are long-lived, sometimes reaching a height of 150 feet. They have a very extensive and sturdy root system, fruit abundantly while very young and, although easily injured by fire and cold, are remarkably free from disease.

AUSTRIAN WINTER PEAS: Many southern growers have found this crop excellent for soil improvement. It is often used in rotation with winter wheat to increase organic matter and nitrogen content of soil. For good growth, it is important to be sure soil is well stocked with nutrients and is not acid.

AVAILABILITY: Referring to soil nutrients, this is the portion of the content of a plant food that can be taken up by plants for growth. *See also* FERTILIZERS.

AVENA SATIVA: *see* OATS

AVOCADOS: (*Persea americana*) One of the most practical fruit trees for the home grounds is the avocado tree.

It is one of the finest shade trees, thrives either in or out of the lawn area and may be planted from November through May.

In planting avocados, dig a hole twice as large as the ball of roots or larger. A hole three feet deep and as wide is worth the extra trouble of digging it, for it will give the new tender roots a soft run for some time to come.

In the bottom of the hole place two shovelfuls of well-rotted compost mixed with the same quantity of good topsoil, which may be a rich sandy loam. If the hole is three feet deep these amounts could be increased. Add enough topsoil to bring the top of the ball of roots level with the ground. Place the tree on this in the center of the hole and fill in with good soil in which some compost is mixed. This will put humus in the soil. Firm the mixture around the ball of roots as the filling in proceeds. When the hole is almost filled in, have a gentle stream of water from the hose run in to settle the soil, so there will be no air pockets. Let the water run long enough so it will reach down below the ball of roots, then fill in with more soil to bring it up to ground level. Make a basin around the tree to hold water. Give a thorough watering once or twice a week until the newly planted tree is established. When it has put out eight or nine inches of new growth, once in two weeks should be enough to water, unless the soil has very free drainage and the weather is very hot. Keep the water running from 45 to 60 minutes. Temperatures and soil conditions vary in different districts. No set of rules can be given that will cover all sections. A little experience will show what is the right amount. If there is good drainage any excess water will drain away.

As the trees grow, additional feeding may be given by applying a trowelful of blood meal and two of bone meal once in six weeks during spring and summer. Do not apply after August, for the new growth may be nipped in sections where there is danger of frost. Always give deep watering after applying fertilizer.

Do not cut off lower branches. They protect the tree from sunburn. There are preparations on the market with which to paint the trunk for sun protection.

No pruning is required except to keep the tree in shape, well balanced and symmetrical in growth. In old trees keep all dead wood cut out. At no time expose large bare branches to the sun, as they are easily sunburned.

Cultivation should not be done near the roots, as they resent being disturbed. Keep a mulch of compost, leaves or old steer manure on the ground around the trees throughout the year. There will have to be several fresh applications of compost, etc., as it gets washed into the soil. The mulch should be three to four inches deep. Keep it several inches away from the trunk of the tree. Water the trees well before putting on the mulch.

The following are some good varieties for the home garden:

Duke is a good hardy variety for the interior valleys, and is excellent in the colder districts. It is a green, oval fruit of pleasant flavor. The tree is large, well branched, and is one of the fastest growing avocados with the fruit ripening in September and October.

Fuerte is a fruit of fine quality and the leading commercial variety. The tree is large and spreading and it grows well in the Coastal belt. It ripens in various localities anywhere from November to May.

The fruit of the Edranal variety has a rich, nutty flavor, and does not discolor when fully ripe. The tree is of upright growth; excellent for the home garden, for it does not take up too much room. It has large fruit with small seed and ripens from May to August.

Anaheim is a large green oval fruit that bears heavily. The tree is of upright growth. Ripens May to August.

Hass has one of the longest ripening seasons and produces a heavy crop each year. This purplish black avocado is of fine flavor, and is perhaps the leading summer ripening avocado grown commercially. It is excellent in the Coastal and foothill areas, ripening from May through October.

Ryan has fruit of finest quality and ripens after Fuerte, bearing a heavy crop each year. The fruit, pear-shaped and green, ripens from May to October.

Nabal is particularly good in Coastal areas. The fruit is round with seed and smooth skin. The flesh is rich and of exceptionally fine flavor, ripening from June to September.

Pueblo avocado is a very fine home variety which is hardy to frost. The small trees bear heavy crops of large dark pear-shaped fruit, with superior flavor from November to January.

There are also other fine varieties from which to make a selection. Find out which ones grow best in your neighborhood. New varieties are constantly being introduced.—*E. Hamilton Fairley.*

AXIL: This is the point at which a branch, stalk or leaf diverges from the stem to which it is attached.

AZALEA: Azaleas can be grown successfully only by catering to their taste for a humusy soil.

This plant is an evergreen shrub all year, but with the advent of spring it comes into its glory. Suddenly the tip of each branch bursts into bloom; for sheer beauty few other plants are its equal.

Actually the azalea is the lazy gardener's dream plant if he will only cooperate with nature. Rarely, if ever, will an insect or disease do serious damage to a vigorous azalea. Most of the plant's ailments are caused by poor nutrition or an unsuitable location.

Its requirements are simple but rigid: acid soil organically formed, a heavy mulch, constant moisture with good drainage, filtered sunlight, and absolutely no cultivation.

The acid soil required may be achieved by organic means. Decayed pine needles have an extremely high acidity. Oak leaf mold and the decayed sawdust from oak, cypress or hemlock are also acid. If the soil where the azalea is to be set is alkaline, it should be dug out and replaced by acid soil. This may seem like a lot of trouble, but it will make the care of the plant simpler in later years.

Acid soil may be obtained from pine or other coniferous forests or from the woods where acid-loving plants such as mountain laurel and blueberry are growing. Coarse sand and leaf mold mixed in will make a loose, crumbly soil that retains moisture yet gives good drainage. The azalea will thrive in such soil, and after planting, the acidity can be maintained by proper mulching.

The importance of mulching azaleas cannot be over-emphasized. The roots are extremely shallow—most of them lie within three or four inches of the surface—and they must be kept moist at all times. They must also be protected from the heat of summer, the cold of winter, and must never be disturbed by cultivation. Thus, a mulch of at least four inches is necessary. The mulch will keep down weeds and is the natural home of frogs and lizards which eat any insect enemies of the plant.

Pine needles, oak leaves, and sawdust from oak, cypress, or hemlock make excellent mulches. A mixture of the materials is preferable since the mulch in decaying continually adds food to the soil.

Many growers find that a combination of pine needles and oak leaves is especially good. The needles keep the leaves from blowing and are high in acidity but slow in decaying. The oak leaves decay more rapidly and, while lower in acidity, are higher in food value. Seaweed added to the mulch from time to time adds trace minerals. Manure is not recommended for azaleas because of its alkaline reaction.

The most common symptom of an ailing azalea plant is chlorosis or a yellowing of the leaves. This usually means that the soil is not sufficiently acid. It may be prevented by proper planting and mulching. If the condition appears in spite of these precautions, check the water supply. Sometimes the water used contains lime which counteracts the acidity of the mulches.

Other than the food from the decaying mulch, azaleas require only a feeding of cottonseed meal once a year to keep them in good condition. This feeding is given immediately after the blooming season and is applied at the rate of about two and a half pounds per hundred square feet. It should be sprinkled over the mulch and watered in. Because of the shallow roots it should not be dug into the soil.

If the plant seems lacking in vigor, a second feeding of cottonseed meal may be applied three weeks later, but never after the last of June. Later feedings will encourage new growth that will not be hardened before the heat of summer begins.

Azaleas need some sun to bloom satisfactorily, but the direct rays of the summer sun are usually harmful. The buds for the coming spring form during the summer and fall, and the plants need plenty of moisture during that time. Any baking by the sun will result in a shortage of blossoms. The plants wilt quickly if not kept moist and are slow in recovering vigor after even a single drying out. For this reason azaleas thrive in the edge of woods where they get filtered sunlight, or in sheltered locations where they receive only partial sun.

They also need some protection

The Ghent Hybrid is highly individualistic; no two are exactly alike but are a blend of colors and shades from white to orange, yellow, and red.

from the wind. Wind does not harm the plants, but will damage the blossoms during the blooming season.

Winter hardiness of the azalea varies with the different varieties and with the condition of the individual plant. In general, the Indica varieties are perfectly hardy only in the South, while the Kurumes are grown successfully as far north as Long Island.

Plants grown in dense shade or those which are overfed or fed late do not withstand cold well. All growth should be matured before winter. The plant will survive severe cold if the roots are protected, but the flower crop may be injured by unseasonable cold, especially after the buds are showing color.

Azaleas are pruned to keep them at the desired size and to make them produce more flowers. Ideally, the plant should be thick headed and well branched since a flower forms at the tip of each branch. Pruning should be done immediately after blooming so that the blossoms can form during the summer.

The azalea is equally well suited for small gardens and large estates. It may be used as an accent plant, around pools, in hedges, or as a foundation plant. It is an excellent foundation plant in that it may be pruned to the desired size, is ever-green, and has low-growing branches which tie the house to the ground. Care should be taken that the color of the blossoms does not clash with that of the building, however.

The colors range from white through pink, lavender, salmon, orange and red. In small gardens a single color is most effective, especially when combined with plants of the same color which are in bloom at the same time. For instance, try white azaleas under dogwood or pink azaleas near redbud.

The azalea is exacting in its requirements, but once those are met no other plant is more rewarding. Other than its uses as an outdoor plant, it is a long-lasting cut flower. Furthermore, because of the compact, shallow roots it is easily transplanted. During blooming season the entire plant may be lifted, potted and moved into the house. Then it can be replanted without damage.—*Marilyn McAdams Sibley.*

See also SHRUBS, FLOWERING; EVERGREENS.

AZOFICATION: The process by which the azotobacter organisms add nitrogen to the soil. *See also* AZOTOBACTER.

AZONAL SOIL: These are soils without well-developed soil profiles because of extreme youth, steep relief, or very sandy parent material. They are found within any of the zonal soil regions. Azonal soils are of three types:

ALLUVIAL SOILS: Comprises recently deposited materials on which the soil-forming forces have acted for only a comparatively short time. Alluvial soils are widely distributed throughout the world.

SAND: Like Alluvial soils, loose, dry sands, commonly wind blown, occur widely.

LITHOSOL: *Lith,* from Greek, means stone; hence lithosols are skeletal soils, which are more or less weathered materials and rock fragments. There are stony parent materials and, commonly, stony ground surface, as on steep slopes and in rough, rocky, mountain areas.

AZOTOBACTER: A bacteria group in the soil that continually derives nitrogen from the air. These organisms—bacteria, algae, fungi—are free-acting, that is, not working in connection with the roots of any plants (as do those nitrogen-forming organisms living in roots of leguminous plants, such as peas or soybeans). These are said to be dependent upon the supply of organic matter in the soil for their energy. The nitrogen extracted from the air is incorporated into their bodies and given to the soil upon their death. *See also* MICROORGANISM.

B

B HORIZON: Every soil has a succession of layers in a vertical section known as horizons. The B horizon lies immediately under the A horizon and can be easily recognized by a distinct change in color, texture and structure. Usually the texture is heavier and the material is compacted. The B horizon contains very little organic matter, while its depth can often be greater than the A horizon. In the semidesert, arid and semiarid regions of the country, the B horizon is lighter in color and is only slightly more compacted than the overlying A horizon.

In the humid tropics and subtropics, little soluble organic matter reaches the B horizon. Sometimes a stone-like formation occurs at some point in the B horizon and this is known as hardpan. There is a wide variation in the depth of the B horizon: from eight to 20 inches in the humid temperature climate; somewhat deeper in the tropics; and deepest in the grass country of the arid, semiarid and subhumid climates, up to 30 inches. *See also* A HORIZON; C HORIZON.

BABY-BLUE-EYES: *see* NEMOPHILA

BABY'S BREATH: (*Gypsophila elegans*) The white, rose or carmine flowers of the three varieties of annual baby's breath are fine for filling in bare spots. This quick-growing annual with tiny flowers on wiry stems adds daintiness to any arrangement. Baby's breath blooms quickly from the time of sowing, but passes quickly into seed production; therefore several plantings at monthly intervals are recommended if the blossoms are wanted over a long period. Baby's Breath needs full sunlight and open, not-too-rich soils. Period of bloom extends through June 15 to October; height attained is ten to 18 inches.

BACHELOR'S BUTTON: (*Centaurea cyanus*) Often called Cornflower or Blue Bonnet, this garden annual normally produces blue flowers, also white, pink and purple. It grows to about two or three feet high. Seed in fall or early spring; thin plants to about one foot apart. Bachelor's Button seeds itself readily and often comes up as volunteers for several years without replanting. Many gardeners cut them six inches from the top after first blooming period to encourage second flowering. Fertilizing with liquid manure is effective. Plants will stand some crowding. Blooms make fine cut flowers. The plant is hardy and blooms until frost. *See also* ANNUALS.

BACTERIA: *see* MICROORGANISM; ACTINOMYCETES; FUNGI; SOIL

BALFOUR, LADY EVE: Author of *The Living Soil,* and a dynamic leader in the field of organiculture in Great Britain. In 1946, she became the first president of England's Soil Association—a group that has added much prestige and important research to the organic method.

This is the only body in Britain— and one of the first in the world—to be devoted to the furtherance of research into the biological aspects of soil fertility, and to the dissemination of knowledge on the subject.

BALLOON FLOWER: (*Platycodon grandiflorum*) A perennial herb of the bellflower family. The balloon flower is a most attractive plant, with large, showy, star-shaped flowers. Blossoms are pure white, blue, or white with blue veinings. Occasionally there are double-petaled blooms.

Balloon flowers may be propagated either by rootstock or from seed. The seeds germinate readily and should provide at least some blossoms the first year. Seeds should be started in frames in March. When about two inches high, transplant to permanent location, in a well-drained soil. Stems reach a height of about 18 inches.

BALM: (*Melissa officinalis*) A somewhat weedy perennial growing to about two feet in height. The entire plant has a strong lemon scent.

The leaves are sometimes used for tea, and sprigs are put into cool drinks to impart a lemony taste. Oil from the leaves is used in perfumes.

Balm is best planted where it is not too conspicuous because of its weedy habit. It has a tendency to spread and must be kept within bounds.

It thrives in poor soil in a warm, sunny spot. Can be propagated from seed sown in spring, or by dividing.

BALSAM FIR: *see* CHRISTMAS TREE FARMING; FIR

BAMBOO: An easy-to-grow and highly useful crop, which organic techniques have enabled to grow even in the North. True, we usually think of bamboo as a tropical crop. We know it's one of the staples of Oriental agriculture, serving dozens of human needs. The Chinese and other Asian peoples use it for food, clothing, weapons and all sorts of containers. They even construct their houses of it, build bridges, and lay bamboo water pipes to carry drinking and irrigation supplies.

But research is proving that bamboo can be grown in most parts of the United States, and that it is a potential raw material for dozens of things the Chinese never thought of.

At the Barbour Lathrop Plant Introduction Garden of the Department of Agriculture in Savannah, Ga., and at the Georgia Institute of Technology in Atlanta, hundreds of species of bamboo are being studied—*and the experts predict that bamboo may some-*

day become one of the nation's most important crops.

The edible bamboos under study are of special interest to health-conscious people. The delectable and healthful shoots or sprouts of certain varieties have long been recognized

Handsome groves of bamboo may soon be a common sight. Some 70 varieties, suitable for food and protection, are grown successfully here.

as a delicacy, but we've had to depend on canned imports from Japan and China for our entire supply. Today, however, edible bamboo promises to become a new easily-grown vegetable for American gardens and farms.

One of the most prized for its delicately flavored shoots is Moso (*Phyllostachys edulis*). It is a giant bamboo, growing as tall as 80 feet, with canes up to eight inches in diameter. Its wide-spreading branches and feathery foliage make Moso one of the handsomest and most impressive-looking bamboos.

A new Moso plantation should be established with the plants set 15 feet apart each way. They take about five to eight years to reach full size.

Thereafter, in early spring the tasty shoots appear (actually they are the sprouting buds, which if not cut will develop into full-sized canes or culms). They often grow at the fantastic rate of two inches an hour and attain full height in six to eight weeks.

Another fine edible variety is sweet-shoot (*P. dulcis*), known in China by the exotic name of "pak-koh-poo-chi." It grows to a maximum of about 30 feet, with stems up to three inches in diameter, and very sweet, tender shoots.

First of all, the list of varieties that produce edible shoots is bigger than was first realized. *Phyllostachys bambusoides,* the giant timber or Madake bamboo that grows well in the South and East, produces tasty shoots. So does the interesting green sulphur bamboo, *P. sulfurea viridis;* its shoots give off a lovely delicate aroma when cooked. Beechey bamboo, *Sinocalamus beecheyanus,* and *P. vivax,* another medium-tall grower, are other edible shoot producers.

The shoots of at least two other varieties, *Dendrocalamus asper* and *Bambusa multiplex,* are reported to be dug up before they emerge from the ground and used for food in the Dutch East Indies.

Incidentally, you have probably noticed from the foregoing that bamboos have more than one generic name. Every botany book and catalog seems to list them differently. Until this situation is cleared up by scientists —which will be soon, as interest in the plant grows—we can only suggest that you carefully study the catalog descriptions of any variety you plan to buy.

How do you cook bamboo? Gourmets recommend cutting them into one-eighth-inch thick slices, after peeling off the outer covering. Virtually all varieties, with the exception of sweetshoot, have a more or less bitter taste, so it is best to parboil them for six to eight minutes, then change the water. Further cooking for about 20 minutes will bring out their delicate flavor while retaining the firm, crispy texture.

Cooked this way, bamboo shoots taste very much like young field corn. You can serve them as a vegetable hot with butter, cold as a salad or in mixed salads, or use them in meat stews. They go well in numerous other American dishes, and of course, in dozens of Oriental ones, too.

BAMBOO HOUSE PLANTS: A particularly impressive one for a window with full sun is the Chinese goddess bamboo. Also good is *Sasa disticha,* a dainty fern-leaved bamboo that grows four or five feet tall outdoors, but will stay small for several years in a pot.

The same is true of the fascinating "Buddha's belly" bamboo, *Bambusa ventricosa,* so called because the portions between the nodes swell out oddly. This variety grows 40 feet tall outdoors, but will stay in miniature *for years* when potted.

Many of these bamboos, says the Department of Agriculture, may be grown from Virginia south along the Gulf Coast, and in the milder areas of the West Coast.

But—and here is the tip to organic gardeners—"success has been reported in colder parts of the country with edible bamboo when it was given a two- to three-inch mulch such as hay."

Another tip: contrary to what many people believe, bamboo does not prefer constantly flooded land. It needs a fertile soil with abundant moisture, but will not stand poorly drained soils that stay saturated for long periods. Ridges close to wet soil are suitable, provided its roots are not in the wet portion.

BANANA: (*Musa sapientum*) This is one of the most popular and important tropical fruits. Long-keeping and easily shipped, it is tasty, very digestible and rich in several major minerals and some vitamins.

The banana is a tree-like, herbaceous plant, and all of the numerous varieties belong to the *Musa* genus. Native of tropical Africa, Asia and Australia, its total height ranges from four to 30 feet, depending on species. From a crown formed by two to 20-foot-long feather-shaped leaves, hang branches of the fruit, each weighing up to 50 pounds or more and containing many bananas. After fruiting, the plant sends out suckers from the

The Dwarf banana, being hardier than the Common variety, stands a better chance in this country. Some gardeners are growing them.

base, then withers and dies. The new growth bears fruit the succeeding year.

Requirements for a banana plantation include rich soil, ample moisture and good drainage, plus a location receiving full sun and protected from strong winds. Commercially, most of the world's banana crop is grown in Central America and the West Indies. In this country, cultivation is limited to a few frost-free regions, principally along the southern coast.

The two main varieties are the Common Banana, which is the imported type widely eaten as raw fruit, huge quantities being picked and shipped green and ripening to yellow only as it reaches the consumer; and the Chinese or Dwarf Banana (*M. cavendishi*), which grows only four to six feet high, bearing many small, very tasty fruits. Since it is hardier than

most varieties, this dwarf banana is better suited to culture in this country, and many are grown as fruiting ornamentals in gardens as well as potted indoor plants.

BANANA RESIDUES: Analyses have shown that banana skins and stalks are extremely rich in both phosphoric acid and potash, rating from 2.3-3.3 in phosphoric acid and from 41 to 50 per cent in potash, on an ash basis. The nitrogen content is considered relatively high. When available in quantity, it would be thoroughly practical to utilize banana residues for gardening purposes. Table cuttings and kitchen refuse containing banana skins are valuable also for the reason that these materials contain large amounts of bacteria which effect quick break-down and act as activators for the rest of the compost material.

BANEBERRY: (*Actaea*) Perennial shrubs of the crowfoot family, baneberries are often seen in rich soils of northeastern woods. They grow best in the garden in a shady spot, in rich, fairly moist soil. The white form (*A. alba*) does better in a neutral to slightly acid soil; the red baneberry (*A. rubra*) prefers a more acid soil. Both can be transplanted in spring or fall.

BANTAMS: Small fowl capable of producing large amounts of eggs and meat. A small space is all you need for a bantam flock. They need but a small house six feet square and three feet deep, with a pen six by ten feet and three feet deep.

A pen of one bantam cock and 12 hens will supply all the eggs an average family can eat. There will also be plenty of dressed friers for broiling, baking or frying.

Bantams have been bred down through many years from large fowl, by crossing with other varieties, by inbreeding and line breeding for smaller size, and for particular qualities.

Bantams, like the large fowls, come in egg breeds and in a general-purpose egg and meat breed. The best family bird is the general purpose varieties, such as the Rhode Island Reds, the solid, blocky Cornish, the stocky little white, buff and the barred Plymouth Rocks, and the various Wyandotte varieties. The Leghorns, though smaller, lay well.

A good strain of Reds will lay 175-190 eggs per year. The Cornish Rocks, Wyandottes and Leghorns will lay from 135 to 160 eggs a year. They lay best during the pullet year, but often lay well on past their fifth year.

Three bantam eggs of above breeds will equal two large fowl eggs of the large grade, averaging around 18 to 19 ounces per dozen. Bantam egg yolks are larger in proportion than those of standard fowl, with correspondingly less white.

FEEDING: Table scraps, some all-purpose egg mash, some grain, and green trimmings from the kitchen and yard will about take care of a bantam laying flock. They don't fly much, so may be turned into the garden, flower beds, or onto the lawn every day or so for a while to pick up bugs, etc.

Bantams eat about one-fourth as much as large fowls and produce about two-thirds as much in eggs.

Almost any small house will do for bantams. It should have good light, no drafts, be dry. You should have sawdust or other clean litter on the floor. Give the hens box nests, tops covered to keep any from roosting on the edges and dirtying the grass or straw nests. The roosts should be inch thick rods suspended six inches above a wire-mesh grating so the droppings will fall through to a tray below. This keeps the house clean, and will let you remove the manure for use in the gardens and around flowers.

Fresh water is a must at all times, as is a box of small chicken grit and one of fine oystershell.

The eggs take 21 days to hatch. Keep the newly hatched chicks warm and dry. Give them tepid water and chick size grit for the first 24 to 48 hours. Then start them on baby chick scratch feed (ground grain). Give them what they will clean up of this feed for a period of five days. Then place them on starter mash. This will be their diet for the next two months.

You may start giving the youngsters greens at three weeks of age. A grassed pen or a time on the lawn or in the garden every day or two will help. You may raise them in a roomy house and pen, or you may bring them up in a brooder on wire. Many of the pullets of these breeds will start laying at five months of age.

Usual practice is to feed bantams twice daily, the heavier feed in the morning at any set hour, but with regularity. Feed an all-purpose mash. Just before dark throw the birds some scratch feed (oats, wheat, corn, milo). —*Gordon L'Allemand.*

BAPTISIA: Blue, Wild, or False Indigo. A native plant, bearing somewhat the appearance of the lupine; the pea-shaped blossoms are borne in long spikes of pale blue flowers in late May and early June. The foliage blackens and is unsightly in late summer; place late flowering plants in front of them to cover up the untidy appearance. Seed may be sown in the permanent location.

They do best in full sun and an open, well-drained sandy soil; can be propagated by division. *B. australis,* Blue False Indigo, grows to about three to five feet high, while *B. tinctoria,* often known as clover broom and shoofly, grows to 18 to 30 inches. *See also* PERENNIALS.

BARBERRY: (*Berberis*) The barberries are handsome shrubs much grown for hedges. Probably the one most generally planted for this purpose is Japanese barberry, (*B. thunbergi*), which makes a fine five-foot round-headed plant. The red berries and its fall tones of foliage colors—orange, scarlet, and crimson—are very attractive. It grows quickly and is easily propagated from seeds or cuttings. The dwarf form, commonly called the box-barberry, (*minor*), rarely reaches a height of more than 15 inches, if trimmed; if untrimmed, it can grow as high as three feet.

Best results with barberries will be obtained if they are planted in moist, well-drained, light loamy soils, although the more deciduous ones can stand drier conditions. Some deciduous species are *B. aggregata*—four to seven feet high, hardy in the southern half of the country, densely branched; *B. diaphana*—about five feet high, scarlet foliage in fall, hardy in south; *B. thunbergi*—described above, the Japanese barberry is hardy throughout most of the United States; *B. vulgaris,* common barberry—five to nine feet, though hardy, it's susceptible to rust infection.

Evergreen species of barberry shrubs include: *B. buxifolia* or Magellan barberry—one of the best of the upright evergreens, it grows up to eight feet, has a dark purple fruit, is hardy in the south; *B. darwini*—five to eight feet high, hardy with yellow flowers and purple fruit; *B. julianae* —wintergreen barberry, four to six feet; hardiest of the evergreen barberries and very popular.

Barberries germinate easily from seeds, which should be sown in flats or broadcast in beds in fall; in most cases, they will germinate by following spring. Barberries can also be propagated from green cuttings of young wood taken in June, placed in sand in shady bed.

BARK: Bark is the normal waste material of the lumber, pulp and paper industries, but research shows that it can be utilized as an inexpensive and unusually effective soil builder. Bark can (1) loosen the soil and improve its moisture holding capacity, (2) serve as a base for fertilizer, (3) control the rate at which the plants obtain their food from the soil, and (4) be used as a mulch.

BARK GRAFTING: *see* GRAFTING

BARLEY: (*Hordeum vulgare*) Barley was one of the first cereals to be cultivated by man and has been cultivated over a larger extent of the world than any other cereal with the possible exception of wheat.

Cultivated barley probably originated from the wild form (*H. spontaneum*) which is very similar in appearance to the present two-row forms of barley. The barley plant belongs to the same family as wheat and rye, but barley has three spikelets per joint of the rachis (segment of the head) while wheat and rye have only one spikelet per joint of the rachis.

The leading states in barley production are Minnesota, California, North Dakota, South Dakota, Wisconsin, Nebraska, and Iowa. Barley may be used for hay, pasture, or for grain as a stock food or for malt. Because of the generally short, lightly leaved straw, the crop has a value as a nurse crop. The crop is generally grown for the grain it produces. As a feed for livestock, barley compares favorably with corn. Barley contains about 1/3 more protein, about 40 per cent as much fat, 2-1/2 times as much fiber, and about 5 per cent less carbohydrates. In regions where corn is unadapted barley is successfully used in fattening cattle and swine.

Barley is more like wheat and oats in its soil adaptability. The root system is less vigorous than that of oats, hence barley needs a more fertile soil and a fairly well drained soil too. If fertilized, however, it can be grown on any loose open soil that is not too wet.

Barley thrives best in a moderately cool and moist climate.

BARREL ROOT CELLAR: Some garden produce can be stored for all or most of the winter in a state of freshness.

Onions, sweet potatoes, pumpkins, and squashes may be stored in a cool, dry place. A basement is ideal for this. Kale and collards may be left in the ground all winter since they readily stand quite cold weather. Parsnips and salsify are best left in the ground until used. Their flavor actually improves after freezing, however, they should be kept covered with about one inch of the stem left on to prevent "bleeding."

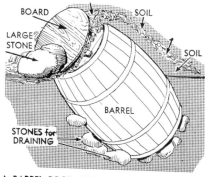

A BARREL ROOT CELLAR can store all or most garden produce in a fresh state over the winter. A strong, well-made barrel should be used and cleaned carefully before being set in trench.

A root cellar which is very satisfactory for the home garden is easily made from a large barrel. A barrel may be obtained for approximately one dollar from a grocery, hardware store, or a lumber yard. A strong, well-made one will last many years. Dig a trench a little larger than the barrel so that it can be set into the ground at an angle of about 45 degrees. Before placing the barrel in the trench, drop in a few large stones or bricks to facilitate drainage. Cover the barrel all around with about six inches of dirt, then six inches of straw or leaves, and finally with about two inches of dirt to hold the organic matter in place. After the vegetables are packed in the barrel, place the cover over the top and then pile about

a foot of straw, leaves or hay on the cover with a board and a rock to keep the covering in place. This covering is easily removed when it is desired to get into the root cellar.

BASALT: Basalt rock is widely distributed in the United States, the New England coast being especially seamed with deposits.

Dr. W. D. Keller, Professor of Geology at the University of Missouri, has stated: "Basalt rock is about the best-balanced rock I know of for supplying plant nutrients. Therefore, I believe that powdered basalt with an illite rock clay mixed with organic matter should provide the best average all-purpose plant food possible unless one would want to sweeten it up with a little extra phosphate rock." This agrees with the statement by Dr. Hans Heinz, of the Institute of Biodynamic Research, to the effect that the most fertile soils in Germany are those that have formed from an underlayer of basalt rock. In my opinion a mixture of phosphate, potash, and basalt rock powder would make the ideal mineral fertilizer, being well balanced in phosphate, potash, and the other needed mineral elements. The nitrogen would come from organic matter.

Basalt can be applied directly to the soil, as one would do with phosphate or potash rock. They have found at Griesheim, Germany that the basalt, if left on the surface, increases the temperature of the soil, but if worked in, it temporarily reduces it. Their practice is to leave the basalt powder on the surface of the soil one year and plow it in the next season. They claim that the basalt soon forms into clay, thus indicating that its nutrients are quickly available to growing crops.

The following chemical analyses of several basalts from Oregon show the relative abundance of the elements phosphorous, potassium, calcium, magnesium, and iron.

	Average of 6 Analyses
Silica	49.98%
Titanium Oxide	2.87%
Iron Oxide	13.97%
Alumina	13.74%
Magnesium Oxide	4.73%
Calcium Oxide	8.21%
Sodium Oxide	2.92%
Potassium Oxide	1.29%
Phosphorus	0.78%
Water	1.22%
Manganese Oxide	0.24%

In addition to the above constituents Oregon basalts contain the following trace elements.

0.1% to 1 % Strontium	0.1% to 0.01% Chromium Vanadium Barium
0.01% to 0.001% Cobalt	Below 0.001% Zirconium Copper Nickel Molybdenum

From the analyses, it is very obvious that basalt is an excellent fertilizing medium. Basalts from other sections of the United States may vary somewhat in their analyses, but generally speaking, basalt would be a worthwhile addition to the fertilizer program.

BASIC SLAG: An industrial by-product, resulting when iron ore is smelted to form pig iron. The ore contains, in addition to iron, small amounts of such elements as silicon, aluminum, sulphur, manganese, chromium, titanium, and traces of many other elements. In smelting the iron ore, large amounts of limestone and dolomite are used. The impurities unite with the limestone to form a sludge which rises to the surface of the molten mass and is poured off. In its cold, hard form this sludge is called slag.

The chemical composition of slag varies according to the ore that is used and with variations in the mixtures. The average ranges in the major constituents expressed in terms of the compounds indicated, are shown in the table below for a wide distribution of sources.

Material	Compound	Per Cent
Lime	CaO	38 to 45
Magnesia	MgO	4 to 9
Silica	SiO_2	33 to 39
Alumina	Al_2O_5	10 to 14
Manganese oxide	MnO	0.2 to 1.5
Iron oxide	FeO	0.2 to 0.7
Sulphur	S	1.0 to 2.0

Spectographic studies of slag indicate that it also contains traces of boron, sodium, molybdenum, tin, vanadium, copper, zinc, titanium, potassium, strontium, chromium and zirconium. It is because of the presence of so many kinds of essential nutrient elements that slag may be used as a soil builder.

For agricultural purposes, slag must be very finely pulverized. When slag is used in the soil, its efficiency varies directly with its degree of fineness. It is best known as a liming agent. It provides crop plants with calcium and magnesium. In comparative studies it has been found to be better than lime. This is doubtless due to the fact that it contains some of the trace elements which are so important in plant nutrition.

Slag is alkaline in action. It does best on moist clays and loams, and on peaty soils deficient in lime, but can be used in some light soils if a potash mineral is used with it.

It should be applied to the soil in autumn and winter. Slag is especially adapted to the needs of such leguminous crops as beans, peas, clovers, vetches, and alfalfa.

Ordinary iron and steel slags contain practically no phosphates but do contain other fertilizer constituents. Before using a slag for agricultural purposes, make sure that it contains soil-building constituents and especially the trace elements. Avoid slags which contain excessive amounts of sulphur.

Since slag is made up of finely pulverized but insoluble particles, it can be applied at any time and at any rate without injuring the plants. An average application is from one to several tons per acre.

BASIL, SWEET: (*Ocimum basilicum*) A pretty annual, about 18 inches tall, with light green rather broad leaves. The flowers are small and white, in spikes. There are several species of basil in cultivation, at least one having attractive purple leaves.

The spicily scented leaves are one of the most popular of all herbs used in cooking. They are considered especially good with tomato dishes, and are used fresh or dried.

The light green leaves are attractive, especially while the plants are young, and the purple-leaved kind gives an interesting color in the herb garden.

Grows easily from seed planted when danger of frost is over.

Green leaves can be picked about six weeks after planting. For drying, it is best to cut them just before the flowers open. *See also* HERBS.

BASSWOOD: *see* LINDEN

BAT GUANO: *see* GUANO

BEAN RUST: *see* DISEASE

BEANS, BUSH: Beans are one of the most valuable plants grown because they not only produce food for human consumption, but improve the fertility and physical condition of the soil. Nitrogen, a most valuable plant food, is added to the soil by the beneficial bacteria in the nodules which grow on the roots. These bacteria are capable of absorbing the free nitrogen from the air, which, after the plants are harvested, is left in the soil.

Bush Beans (also referred to as Snap Beans) are an excellent source of vitamins A and G and a good source of B_1 and C. They also provide calcium and iron.

CULTURE: Bush beans should be included in every garden because of the ease in growing and the wealth in harvesting them. Although beans are essentially warm-season plants, they can be grown successfully in all sections of the country.

Stringless bush beans like this are an excellent source of vitamins A and G and a good source of B_1 and C. They also provide calcium and iron.

The bush beans, while responding to rich soil and thorough cultivation, will succeed well in almost any garden soil. They thrive in a variety of soils, from heavy clay to light sandy soils. The soil should not be too acid and should receive a generous amount of rotted manure or compost.

The seed is sown directly in the garden after the last spring frost. Sow the seed thinly in rows 18 to 30 inches apart for hand cultivation. Plant the seed about one to two inches apart. When the plants are two or three inches high they may be thinned to four to six inches apart.

A continuous supply of beans throughout the growing season may be assured by successive plantings. Make additional sowings when the other crop is up and growing. Plant until midsummer, or until about 60 days before danger of the first killing frosts in the fall.

The cultivation of the crop consists of stirring the soil frequently during the entire season of growth. Scrape the weeds away and don't hoe deeply. The roots are close enough to the surface so that any deep or extensive cultivation will result in undesirable root pruning. It is essential that all weeds be kept down and that during times of drought a mulch is used to preserve moisture. *See also* FERTILIZER.

VARIETIES: There are two types of bush beans, the green-podded and the yellow-podded or wax beans. The variety or the color makes little difference except in individual prefernce. The quality is practically the same in all, provided they are pulled from the vine and eaten at the proper stage of maturity.

Of the green bush varieties, Bountiful, and Plentiful are both flat-podded and will develop beans from six to seven inches long. Stringless Green Pod, Wade, Stringless Valentine and Improved Tendergreen will grow round pods from five to six inches long. Of the yellow bush varieties, Pencil Pod Wax, Rustproof Golden Wax, Yellow Bountiful and Surecrop Stringless Wax are good varieties.

HARVESTING: Snap beans should be picked while the pods are immature. The seeds should still be small, the tips soft, and the bean should snap readily. The plants should be watered carefully as the proper time of harvesting lasts only a few days. If the pods are allowed to ripen fully, the plants stop producing and will die. Bush beans usually have several pickings, a few days apart or every day if the weather is warm.

Beans are one of the vegetables that are better when harvested young and eaten just after they are picked—an important reason for growing your own.—*Barbara Hardy.*

See also LIMA BEAN.

BEANS, DRYING: If, at harvest time, you find you have too many beans to use in the near future, think about drying them for future use. Drying beans is not difficult, and will reward the family during the winter.

There are several ways of going about drying the beans. One woman, who has "dried 'em all my life," does it the easiest way there is. She simply lets the bean plants alone until they're partially dried. She then pulls them up, shakes the earth off the roots, ties them up in bunches of three or four and hangs them up in a dry place. She forgets all about them until winter time when she wants beans.

Another lady picks the beans when they are so ripe that the pods show signs of drying up. The pods are then spread on papers or cooky tins and placed in the sun to dry. This is a slow process but not a time consuming one. The important thing to remember is that the drying beans must be placed indoors before sundown and not put out until the sun is up and shining brightly. Besides turning them each day so they dry evenly, there is nothing else to do until they have thoroughly dried. By this time, the pods are so brittle that they crumble when you handle them.

If the weather is against your drying program (not enough sunny days), then the beans may be hulled and canned before they are thoroughly dry. If, however they have thoroughly dried, then storing them in a dry place is imperative, for the beans may be wormy if dampness is allowed to get at them. Many people have had success by storing in jars in a dry place.

According to the "Home Canning Guide," by Anne Pierce, beans are blanched for eight to twelve minutes in boiling water, 212° F. Spread on trays $1/2$ to $3/4$ of an inch deep and dried in an oven at 160 to 175°. The only drawback here would be the greater loss of nutritive value and the beans could not be used for seed.—*Anne P. Didente.*

BEANS, SPROUTING: Bean sprouts can be used in a variety of tasty ways —as a vegetable, as a salad, in stews, or as a replacement for onions or mushrooms in fried or roasted dishes. Many people who use the fresh sprouts in salad prefer them to any other ingredient used.

1. Select clean, bright, new-crop beans. Yellow soybeans are less conspicuous than black, but black may be preferred.

2. Discard all except clean, whole beans.

3. Wash beans and place in one or two-quart fruit jar. Remember that sprouts increase about six times original volume.

4. Cover seed with four times volume of lukewarm water and let stand over night, until swollen, (no longer).

5. Pour off water and rinse thoroughly, pouring off last wash water.

6. Cover jar top with cheesecloth or quarter-inch mesh screening. Tie securely.

7. Invert jar in a pan and place in cupboard or dark place, in a slightly tilted position, so that excess water can drain away.

8. At least three times a day or every four hours, place jar under water tap or pour on plenty of cool water, to wash away molds or bacteria which may have developed. The better the washing, the better the sprouts. Return jar to inverted position.

9. In from three to four days, at room temperature, the sprouts will be from one to two inches long and ready for use. Pour sprouts into clean cold water and shuck off skins if desired, but this is not necessary.

A flower pot can be used for sprouting, but must have a piece of cloth over bottom drain and also a moist cloth over surface of beans to prevent drying. Otherwise the sprouts will be tough.

It is not wise to attempt sprout production in summer unless temperature can be kept about 70° F.

Refrigerated sprouts should be kept moist in covered container to prevent wilting. Bean sprouts freeze admirably. They should be blanched for two minutes, cooled in ice water and frozen in moisture-vapor-proof containers.

Cook with beans attached. Soybeans have chewy texture; crisp and waxy as a peanut. Cook only long enough to remove "raw bean" flavor—10 to 20 minutes. Use as little water as possible. As some of the vitamin C will be in the cooking water, it also should be used. The Chinese method of "panning" or sautéing saves Vitamin C. Sprouts can be fried without water —with or without onions.

Here is an anaylsis of the vitamin and mineral content of about one cup of soybeans and Mung bean sprouts:

	Soybeans	Mung beans
Calcium	48 mg.	29 mg.
Phosphorus ..	67 mg.	59 mg.
Iron	1 mg.	.8 mg.
Vitamin A ..	180 Int'l Units	10 Int'l Units
Vitamin B		
Thiamin ...	.23 mg.	.07 mg.
Riboflavin .	.20 mg.	.09 mg.
Niacin	.8 mg.	.5 mg.
Vitamin C ..	13 mg.	15 mg.

BEAUTY-BUSH: see KOLKWITZIA

BEDDING: Literally, this term applies to all plants suitable for garden beds, especially decorative beds. In practice, bedding plants have come to designate certain types which are set into the garden in a somewhat formal design. Frequently, these are perennials or sub-shrubs which can be closely sheared or pinched. Usually, they are propagated by cutting, rather than seeds, and bought each spring from nurseries or florists who have established them in greenhouses over the winter.

The purpose of bedding plants, although partly restricted, are also varied and give indication of those best suited. During the Victorian period, intricate and very formal carpet-bedding designs were the garden rule. Except in large public gardens and a scattering of strictly formal beds, however, this has now passed out of style.

Today many hardy annuals, some true perennials and a number of tender sub-shrubs are used as bedding to lend both cover and distinct, lasting color to the garden, and particularly to extend the blossoming and help to fill in those sections where early-flowering plants have lost their blooms and foliage. In addition, bedding plants are used to create complimentary borders and edgings, to improve banked areas, and to add often-lacking fragrance.

The list of suitable bedding plants is a long one. Among those best-known and popularly adapted are the following:

Calendula, Baby's-Breath, Sweet Alyssum, Poppy, Portulaca, Marigold, Nasturtium, Zinnia, Verbena, Garden Pinks, Carnation, Ageratum, Snapdragon, African Daisy, China Aster, Moonflower, Canterbury Bells, Cockscomb, Coleus, Cosmos, Dahlia, Chrysanthemum, Larkspur, Candytuft, Chamomile, Forget-Me-Not, Petunia, Annual Phlox, Salvia, Periwinkle.

BEE-BALM: (*Monarda didyma*) Also known as Horse-mint, Bergamot and Oswego-tea (because of the tea which is made from its leaves), it is a strong-growing perennial requiring moist soil. Plants spread quickly and should be divided about every three years, at which time the hard woody center portions should be discarded. Flowers of the Bee-Balm are red or lavender in the wild state, but new varieties offer the blooms in white, rose, maroon and salmon. The Bee-Balm is easy to grow and is remarkably resistant to disease and insect attack. Many gardeners use the tall, bushy plant for background plantings.

Bee-Balm will grow in sun or light shade, and is propagated by division or seed.

BEECH: (*Fagus*) A family of hardy deciduous trees, attractive in shape, foliage and color, and very useful as a shade and ornamental choice. Characterized by rounded tops and smooth gray bark, the beeches are a spreading type which attain heights of 80 to 90 feet. While they prefer an alkaline soil, they will also grow in moderately acid locales, and do especially well when protected with a mulch of their own leaves. Not only is this a long-lived tree (its beauty develops with age), but it is appreciably free from insects and disease. Upright types are adaptable for hedges if given frequent pruning. Propagation is by seeds stratified in winter and sown in the spring. Transplanting should be done in the spring and roots pruned by a nurseryman.

American Beech (*F. grandiflora*) holds its bluish-green leaves in the winter, has a light-gray smooth bark, and usually grows to about 60 feet.

European Beech (*F. sylvatica*) has darker foliage and bark than the American species, and is hardier in cultivation. Growing as high as 90 feet, it displays bright leaves which turn a deep red-brown in autumn and retains these through most of the winter.

BEEKEEPING: Thousands of gardeners are turning to beekeeping, as a rewarding hobby, and for the honey, and pollination which the bees perform.

You can find room for a few hives on a small lot, or for many on a country place. Even in some cities, beekeepers have bees on roofs. If you are situated where bees are an impossibility, you can be partners with a friend out of town, or in the suburbs, or you can have an out-apiary in the surrounding country, as do many city people. Bees don't mind being left alone.

Over the nation the methods of working with bees are similar. Thus, with variations, the honey season is made up of the May and June flowers; some clover through the summer; and fall wild flowers through September and October for winter stores for the bees. In other sections you will need to work up this information from local beekeepers.

The beginner in beekeeping can learn much from reading in the bee magazines and the catalogs of bee

Examining a frame of the comb to check on progress. Basic hive usually comprises a bottom brood box with a storage box and roof above it.

supply houses and maybe a book for beekeepers. He can take a course if he is close to a state university or a correspondence course in beekeeping; and he can attend local and state bee meetings to learn a lot from old-timers before spring arrives. The mail order catalogs carry a lot of bee equipment and supply-house catalogs are really mines of information on bee-keeping. All of them list what is known as a "beginner's outfit," complete from gloves to wax and your attention is directed to a study of what it consists and the use for each item.

There is a suitable time in spring in your area to start out with package bees which come in a three, four, five,

or six pound package; a screened box full of hungry bees, that will, in a short time, grow into a bursting, energetic 85,000 bee colony. Packages arrive with a queen inside in her own apartment, and since you must transfer them at once you need to have ready your larger empty hives in advance. Sometimes you can buy two hives of bees from a local beekeeper, which saves you all the trouble of the build-up period. If so, don't move your new hired hands until after fruit bloom as the present owner will know best how to build them up for the main honey flows.

You must decide on whether you want to make section (comb) honey, or extracted honey. If the latter, you will need an extractor and some few additional items of equipment to make the extracted kind. It has many advantages over comb honey. It is easier to store; easier to use in cooking; there is no wax when you eat it; you use the combs (supers) in which the bees make honey, over and over again, as you only cut the caps off and the extractor throws out the honey by centrifugal force. You can put the boxes full of frames holding these empty combs right back on the hives and have them filled up again and again.

Hives of bees should be disease free. As a beginner select Italian bees as they are relatively easy to work with; they make a lot of honey; and they glue up the inside of the hive only moderately. Some day in the future you may want to try Carniolan or Caucasian bees.

Whenever you find that No. 1 hive has lost its queen it must either raise one or you must supply one. The bees then make some queen cells, and rear a new queen, who in about three weeks or so will probably be laying 1500 eggs per day. As you increase your hives from two to four, from four to six, and so on, you decide to raise your own queens. You can raise them in little queen hives every summer and so always have a supply on hand if needed. Sometimes, too, you get a swarm and establish it in a new hive only to find that in a short time the queen loses egglaying capacity. This swarm needs a new queen and it must be supplied, otherwise the morale of the colony breaks down.—*Dr. Sterling Edwards.*

BEEKEEPING, A SIMPLIFIED METHOD: Here is a method of beekeeping that is especially suitable for the small diversified enterprise that may well include gardening, fruit growing, poultry or any other line of endeavor now practiced by millions of home owners on relatively small holdings.

The secret is to make two standard, full-depth hive bodies the home of the bees the year around. If package bees are bought to get started (a simple and convenient method), they are first hived in a single full-depth body; then as soon as they fill that in good shape, the second is added. The reason for using two full-depth bodies is simple. It gives the bees abundant room, allows them to store honey enough for their own use so that feeding should never be necessary, and it helps to prevent swarming. All the complicated manipulation described in some methods is done away with. The beginner may open his hives and study his bees if he wishes, or if he does not have the time or the inclination, they will do very well with no more attention than that advised in the description of seasonal operation.

The procedure of seasonal operation, beginning in the spring of the year, for established colonies in two full-depth bodies, is as follows:

When settled warm weather arrives the hives are opened to be sure that each colony has a laying queen, plenty of honey to use, and is otherwise in normal condition. If an occasional colony seems short of stores, honey is borrowed; that is, combs exchanged with one that has an abundance. If a colony has died, as one will once in a while, the dead bees are brushed

from the combs and the whole hive scraped and cleaned. These combs are then given to an extra strong colony, not only to protect the combs from wax moths, but to give the strong colony more room.

Normal colonies in two full-depth hive bodies will need more room at about the second month of settled warm weather or at the start of some major bloom. Over much of the United States this will be at the outset of clover bloom. For the purpose of easier handling we use shallow supers for this extra room, although more full-depth bodies may be used if one is capable of heavy lifting. When filled with honey the shallow super weighs about 45 to 50 pounds, the full-depth body about 80 pounds. The rule followed in giving extra room is to add one or more supers at any time that the colony shows signs of being crowded. The term "boiling over with bees" aptly describes a crowded colony, and extra room should be given before this stage becomes acute. If there is any question of when extra room is needed, it is better to give it a week early than a week late.

The bugbear of swarming or of having to watch for swarms which throws many beginners for a loss is considerably reduced by this method if one remembers the basic rule of giving extra room as soon as—or before—it is needed. At least one of the major causes of swarming is a crowded condition within the hive, and by giving abundant room swarming is reduced to a minimum. The occasional swarm that does issue may be hived if convenient, but if it does get away it is no killing matter.

As fall approaches, the honey gathered (that in the supers only) should be removed and the hives gradually reduced to two full-depth bodies. It is important to remember that in this method honey is never removed from the two lower bodies. The success of the whole thing revolves around having a strong colony of bees in a large self-sustaining hive.

In all sections hives should be in locations out of prevailing winds, and in the North will need some extra protection for winter. Being located in a section having severe winters, we first determine that the hive has abundant stores; secondly, we reduce the entrance both to prevent mice from entering and to help keep out the cold; and third we give added protection by first wrapping the hive in a mineral wool blanket and then capping that with tarred building paper.

The proper use of the two story hive, and removing only the honey produced above those two stories, can make beekeeping a thing of utmost simplicity.—*Robert Mead.*

BEES: Both in terms of direct cash in your pocket, and of indirect benefits like erosion protection, these buzzing creatures play an important role in Nature's scheme of things.

There are some 5,000 species of bees in North America. Most of them are important only to wild plants, but several hundred pollinate cultivated crops (over 100, for instance, visit alfalfa).

The value of those who pollinate only wild plants, of course, should not be minimized: they help to keep vital cover on millions of acres not used for farming.

Once, thanks to wild bees, we took pollination of our crops for granted —it happened as surely as the sun rose every day. But it's a different story today.

In the past 50 years, under the pressures of a growing population, more and more land was put under cultivation. But here's the paradox of progress: *the more crops we planted, the faster we destroyed the basic means for a full crop return.*

Forests were cut down, fields were made larger. Controlled burning of woods and wasteland destroyed the homes and food supply of the wild

pollinators. Implements ripped up the burrows of the beneficial earth-dwelling bees; and others who nested in reeds lost their homes and food plants as wire fences and close, clean cultivation replaced the old-time wide, overgrown fence rows.

Concentrated plantings of one crop over large acreages left the bees no wild plants to live on when the crop was not blooming; with nothing to fill in the gap in their food supply, they starved and disappeared practically overnight. Heavy grazing and trampling by sheep in woodlands and field further contributed to their progressive decline. And when indiscriminate spraying with powerful insecticides came along, the wild bees per acre could almost be counted on the fingers of one hand.

But, you ask, is this such a calamity? Don't we have ample numbers of domesticated honeybees to pollinate our crops?

No, we do not have enough honeybees. Farmers in every state, reports the Department of Agriculture, could benefit by having more hives on or near their farms. Some areas need two or three times the number of hives they now have, to insure adequate pollination of the crops grown there.

Here's where an increase in wild bees would be of immense help. Brought about by the farmers themselves, such an increase would bolster the efforts of the hard-working honeybees and show up in a direct rise in crop yields.

Too, wild bees have certain characteristics that make them more valuable than their domesticated cousins. They are hardier, going out to work in cold, rainy or windy weather, when honeybees will not venture from their cozy hives. Thus they will provide good sets of seed and fruit even in bad weather. In parts of New England and eastern Canada, this is especially important to apple growers, for the weather is usually bad there during apple-blooming time.

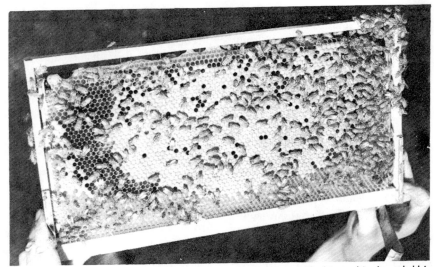

This close-up of a brood frame shows a large area of the sealed brood. The hive tool is always held in the hand while manipulating colonies. Department of Agriculture reports a shortage of bees; farmers could benefit by having more hives on or near their farms to insure more adequate pollination of crops.

Some species of native bees are more efficient pollinators than honeybees. Red clover blooms, having little nectar and the pollen at the bottom of a deep corolla tube, are often passed up by the honeybee; but the long-tongued bumblebee does an excellent job on them. Honeybees can steal the nectar from alfalfa blooms without "tripping" them to release the pollen. But alkali, leaf cutter and bumblebees are pollen collectors, thus trip every blossom they visit.

On rangelands, where it is impractical to supply honeybees for pollination, wild bees have a big responsibility to keep the range plants reproducing year after year. Every range reseeding program should include adapted legumes and other honey-producing plants to increase the wild bees, and thus improve the fodder and fertility of the range.

Practically all wild bees form no colonies, in the sense that the honeybee does. The exception to this is the bumblebee, who lives in a colony of some 50 to 500 individuals, with a queen and worker castes. Many new drones and queens are produced each year, but only the fertilized queens live through the winter, each one forming a new colony in the spring.

The other wild bees are solitary livers. Each female functions both as queen and worker. She builds her own nest, sealing her eggs in cells with honey-moistened pollen balls for the young to feed on. Once this is done, she has no further contact with her offspring.

Wild bees will nest almost anywhere. Sweat bees and mining bees construct underground burrows. Carpenter bees and leaf cutters chisel their nests in timber, or use old beetle holes. Some wild bees nest in the natural channels of hollow- or pithy-stemmed plants, others even make their homes in abandoned snail shells or cavities in porous rocks.

The majority, however, are soil-nesting. Almost any type of soil, moist or dry, loose or packed, flat or vertical, can be their homes. Alkali bees, in some areas the major pollinators of alfalfa, nest in fairly sandy soil, often in "communities" of several thousand nests less than an inch apart. Seed growers, knowing that communities like these will insure pollination of their alfalfa for two miles around, protect them from disturbance. Too, if small pieces of land are left unfarmed near the alfalfa fields, the alkali bees will spread to them and establish new communities there in one season.

Most wild bees, incidentally, rarely nest in rich organic soil, so you can leave small areas of your poorest soil for their nesting sites and thus not lose good land from production.

What are the best ways to increase your wild bees?

Tests by various experiment stations showed that on a cultivated plot situated next to overgrown land, wild bees were four times as numerous as on tilled plots surrounded by other tilled land. You can preserve some uncultivated or eroded land specifically for bees, and sometimes bee broods found on land that is to be tilled can be moved into these areas. Plant them to trees, shrubs, grasses and legumes, and keep your livestock out. On cropland, avoid working, flooding or trampling the burrows of ground-nesting bees whenever possible.

Field borders, fence rows, ditch banks and the sides of roadways should be planted to nectar-producing plants. Kudzu and bicolor or sericea lespedeza make excellent bee pasturage, or use whatever is suitable for your region. Pithy-stemmed plants like elderberry, sumac and tree-of-heaven make fine nesting sites. They will provide erosion protection and food and cover for other wildlife, too. Multiflora rose fences are very good, and bunch-type perennial grasses along the tops of banks are soil stabilizers as well as nesting sites.

Trees for windbreaks and streambank protection that also provide bee food and homes include the Russian olive, American elm, catalpa, honey locust, basswood, sycamore, wild plum and many others. In managing your woodlot, make sure the sawmill men do not cut down bee trees when they are selective-cutting.

Bee plants are often synonomous with soil-saving plants. The legumes used for green manures, orchard cover crops and in rotations provide bee food in plenty. Often a small planting of clover may be all that is necessary, with regular crop plants, to sustain a goodly population of wild bees all year. Improved pastures and grassed waterways should have some clover in their planting mixtures.

Bumblebees will nest in cans containing a handful of mattress stuffing or similar material, hung up in sheltered places in your outbuildings. Certain other species can be induced to set up housekeeping in cans with lids and entrance spouts, partially buried in well-drained soil. Some farmers break open bee trees in the woods, carrying the bees home in any handy container to be set up in suitable places around their farms. And when walking through your fields, you can break over the stalks of hollow-stemmed plants like canebrake, teasel, milkthistle and wild parsnip, to provide nesting and hibernating places.

BEES, DRAWN BY FLOWERS: Bees don't seem to be attracted to many flowering shrubs, but there are two perennials that attract honeybees and which are in bloom all summer. The first of these is Lythrum or Loosetrife, which comes in five colors including white. The other is a ground cover called Dropmore purple. The gray-green foliage has a pleasant, pungent odor. Bees are especially attracted to the latter and are there as long as it is in bloom—which is quite late. Here is a list of herbs which draw bees:

Balm, lemon	Chicory
Basil	Daphne
Bergamont, red	Dropwort
Borage	Fennel
Buglass, Italian	Germander
Butterfly weed	Ground ivy
Catnip	Hyssop
Chamomile	Lavender

Marjoram	Sage
Melilot	Savory, winter
Nettle, dead	Teasel
Queen-of-the-	Thyme
meadow	Fox glove
Rosemary	

See also Honey; Honey Plants.

BEET: (*Beta vulgaris*) Beets are one of the most important home-grown vegetables. They are a relatively easy crop to grow, quite resistant to insects and diseases, use little garden space, are reasonably easy to store, and are a good source of vitamins. Beets and beet greens can provide a valuable part of your diet. The beet roots are a good source of vitamin B_1 and C, and the greens are even richer, providing an excellent source of vitamin A and C and iron.

Beets can be grown all over the country, but seem to be particularly adapted to northern sections. They may be grown in the South during the cooler months of late winter and early spring. Since beets are hardy and can stand a light frost, you do not have to wait until all danger of frost is over to make your first planting. Sowing at intervals of three weeks insures a supply of tender young beets throughout most of the season. The last planting should take place 2½ months before the first fall frost date.

Good quality in beets depends largely on rapid plant development. Beets may flourish on any type soil, but they prefer a deep, well-enriched, sandy loam. The soil should be friable enough to permit proper development of the roots. Soil that packs or forms a crust after a rain is undesirable. A good application of well-rotted manure or compost will help condition the soil and promote the desired rapid plant development. Never plant beets in a soil full of fresh manure; well-rotted manure is the only kind they will tolerate.

Plant the seeds in rows 14 to 22 inches apart for hand cultivation, and approximately one or two inches apart in the row. Cover the seed with one-half inch fine soil. One package of seeds will sow approximately 25 feet of row. Later, when the plants are four-five inches tall, thin the seedlings to about three-four inches between each. Thinning is usually necessary with beets, because the "seed" is really a fruit consisting of two to six seeds, each of which may produce a plant. The thinnings with the tiny beets attached are highly palatable so you actually don't waste them.

Beets do not require intensive cultivation. Weeds must be removed before they interfere with the development of the beets. Otherwise, just an occasional shallow cultivation is sufficient. If the season is dry, a good thorough soaking of the ground is necessary occasionally.

There are two types of garden beets, the early type and the late or main-crop type. The early are planted in the spring and seem to grow best when the weather is cool. They have a sweet flavor and are used for canning and pickling. Crosby's Egyptian and Early Wonder are very popular early varieties.

The late or main-crop beets are planted in late spring or early summer in the North. They grow better when the weather is warm, and are the best varieties to use for winter storage. Detroit Dark Red, Winter Keeper and Lutz Green Leaf are good varieties of this type.

"Baby" beets are harvested when one to one and one-half inches in diameter. Simply pull the beets out of the ground, but, when removing the tops, leave an inch or two attached to the roots so that it will not bleed.

Beets to be stored for winter are reasonably mature when harvested. The late beets for storage are often allowed to stay in the ground until just before heavy frosts. The soil should be dry when the beets are harvested, and the tops cut off about one inch above the crown.

An even temperature and humidity

give the best results when storing beets. The maximum storage period is four to five months. Ideal temperature is slightly above freezing (33-40° F), but do not allow them to freeze. The humidity should be high enough to prevent shriveling. They may have to be kept in crates of moist sand to accomplish this.—*Barbara Hardy*.

BEET WASTES: In the sugar beet growing regions, beet wastes are easily available. Much of that material can be used for ensiling or feeding, but plenty could be composted. Numerous analyses of beet roots showed that their potash content varied from .7 to 4.1 per cent; the variation in nitrogen is less pronounced, and an average might be .4 per cent, while phosphorus ranges from .1 to .6 per cent. The leaves are not very different in their make-up, although their content in calcium and magnesium far exceeds that of the roots.

BEGGAR'S TICKS: (*Bidens frondosa*) One among a wide group of wild "pest plants" (those that cause skin irritation or infection, have poisonous berries or leaves, or injurious thorns). This vigorous-growing weed, from a few inches to five feet or more in height has a pair of down-pointed barbed spines at one end of the seed, which makes them cling stubbornly to clothing. The plant grows in damp, open areas, especially along lake shores, and sometimes even in relatively dry waste places. Control of beggar's ticks, also called Spanish needle, devil's pitchfork and bur marigold, can be aided by improving drainage on moist land and mowing before weed formation to prevent re-infestation.

BEGONIAS: A great group of tropical foliage and flowering ornamental plants. For gardening purposes, they can be divided into two groups: tuberous-rooted and fibrous-rooted (common bedding varieties).

Begonias thrive in a warm, humid atmosphere. East, south or west windows give correct exposures for most varieties in the winter, and the Rex types seem to like north windows, or shaded east windows.

If your begonias do not have enough humidity, the edges of the leaves are likely to be brown, and they will yellow and fall from the plant prematurely. Set the pots in larger containers, packing peat or spaghnum moss between the two and keeping this

Begonias do best in light, porous soil, pressed gently but firmly about the roots. They are very free of pests and diseases but fussy about water.

moist at all times. The air rising around your plants will then have a mist of humidity in it that will make them grow like mad.

You can also set the plants in trays filled with moist sand or peatmoss. A tinner will construct one of these at small cost. Have him make it at least two-inches deep.

Begonias are not especially fussy about potting soils, but they like a light, porous soil which should be pressed gently but firmly about the roots, not packed hard as for geraniums and ivies. Here is an ideal soil mixture for them: two parts sandy loam; one part clean, sharp sand; one-half part well-rotted cow manure; one-half part well-rotted leafmold, with crushed charcoal added to keep the soil "sweet," and for good drainage which is essential for begonias.

Begonias detest being over-potted, and they do not grow in pots without drainage holes in the bottom, so think about this when potting them. Water from the top of the pot with lukewarm water until it runs from the bottom of the pot and do not water again until the top of the soil feels dry. If you are new at window gardening, pinch some of the soil between your fingers, and if it sticks, they are wet enough; if it powders and falls from your fingers, they need water.

Begonias are very free of pest and diseases. Overwatering, or poor drainage may cause black rot in the roots which spreads up through the plant. If you want to save it, take cuttings from growth not yet infected by the rot and root in water, or in a mixture of equal parts peatmoss and sand.

They love conditions in a terrarium, and if you do not have a regular container for this, a discarded aquarium is ideal. Place one-half-inch pebbles and crushed charcoal in the bottom. Then place at least three inches of regular potting soil in the terrarium, but add another part of the sand to insure good drainage.

These terrariums which grow best in an eastern or northern exposure may become "catch-all's" for your houseplant cuttings, but they'll produce some nice surprises. Cover the top with a piece of window glass, keeping it slightly raised by placing a match under the edge to give ventilation.

You must go easy with the watering can with a terrarium. Keep the soil just moist at all times. You'll not have to water many times. If you want to grow varieties of Rex begonias, they'll grow lush, beautiful foliage in a terrarium.

Other kinds of begonias include the popular, easy to grow, Semper-florens or Wax Begonias. They come in single or double-flowered varieties. The Cane types are among the most popular for our Grandmothers grew and loved Angel Wing Begonias. The hirsute and rhizomatous groups offer more variety. The Beefsteak Begonia is found in the rhizomatous varieties, along with dozens of new varieties sporting beautiful foliage, not to mention the beautiful trusses of flowers in pink and white. Tuberous-rooted begonias for growing in the summer seem to fall into an entirely different category to the winter-window-garden begonias.

TUBEROUS BEGONIAS: These are excellent choices for shady spots. The tuberous begonia originally came from Central and South America, where it can be found mostly in cool, moist, shady places where the soil is rich and well-supplied with humus.

Plant in spring when soil is moist, but not wet; remove about top few inches of topsoil and cultivate remaining soil—removing stones and working in compost. If soil is heavy, work in additional organic materials, sand or peat moss. The goal is to have a spongy, loose humus-rich soil.

Plant tubers directly in bed—level with the soil surface and with the hollow side up. Water lightly at first until plants grow strongly; then keep beds moist. Mulch with about two inches of hulls, moss, etc.

Tuberous begonias generally begin to flower in July and continue until frost. Some gardeners produce earlier blooms—often in June—by starting tubers inside the house or greenhouse in March. Start them in shallow trays filled with peat moss, placing tubers close together. Trays should be in shady place; temperature about 60 degrees. Transplant in May.

BEGONIAS FROM SEED: Seed sowing is a form of propagation which is a favorite with many people. It provides many plants at a minimum of expense and the plants are more vigorous than those raised from cuttings. On the other hand, seedlings are not always true to name, even from species, if they have been grown where insects can cross-pollinate them. Seeds from hybrids usually revert to some of their ancestral characteristics and the resulting plant may be handsome. Unfortunately, many of these seedlings have been distributed, and are either nameless or falsely named, which merely adds to the existing confusion in the begonia world.

Seed sowing calls for scrupulous attention to details and for unremitting care for many weeks, but the reward is heart-warming. Not only will the plant lover have all the plants she wants for herself, but plenty to give to friends and neighbors, or to sell.

There are many methods for sowing seeds, and most growers have worked out their own plan. Various materials may be used—gravel, cinders, sand, leaf mold, peat, sphagnum or mixtures of these. Whatever medium is used, it must be clean, moist—not wet—and well-firmed in the container. A simple way is to use a clay flowerpot saucer, filled with one-half leaf mold and one-half sand, both finely sifted. Since begonia seed is very fine, mix a little—as much as will stick to your fingertip is enough for a four inch saucer—with one-half teaspoonful of sand, and scatter lightly over the prepared soil. Press down, but do not cover the seed. Set the clay saucer in water until it is dark and moist, then cover with cellophane or thin white paper, held secure by a rubber band. Make several pin holes in this to admit air. Set the saucer in a warm, shady place until the seeds germinate. As soon as the seedlings are plainly visible, remove the paper and sift a little fine sand over them, repeating once in two weeks.

Once a week, set the saucer in water for a short time to moisten the soil. If the tiny seedlings begin to "damp off" or rot at the soil surface, fill a salt shaker with sterilized, sifted sand and shake over seedlings. Sterilize sand by a thorough heating in an oven. While the organic method generally shuns the process of soil sterilization as damaging—particularly in large scale operations—there are indications that it is sometimes conducive to the subsequent development of beneficial soil organisms.

While the seedlings are still small, thin them with a pair of tweezers, and continue this as they grow. Do not let them become crowded, since this weakens and causes transplanting to be much more difficult. Better to have a dozen strong seedlings than twice as many weaklings.

Transplanting may begin after the seedlings have made the second pair of leaves. The new pots should be prepared in advance, filled with a mixture of equal parts of sand, leaf mold and sifted soil. Choose the largest, strongest seedlings, and lift carefully between two matches. Make a small hole and set the little plant in it, being careful to keep the thread-like root straight, without cramping. Then firm the soil gently around the seedling, just to the previous soil-line. If you use a four inch pot, do not set more than eight or ten seedlings in it. If a flat is used, set them in rows, well separated. Pots are easier to handle, especially in watering, which must always be with rain water. Set the pot in water until the soil is moist, then remove and cover with a pane of glass. A match under the edge of the glass will admit a little air. Bottom heat is almost a necessity, but difficult to supply in the house. A high shelf in a sunny window is good, but a thin muslin curtain should be used to temper the sun's heat.

One way to start begonia seed is to use an old-fashioned "brick grandmother" in pan of water.

When the seedlings begin to look crowded, transplant again, this time into two and a half inch pots. These small pots must be watched, because they dry out quickly. Set them in a pan of moist sand for safety. Seeds sown in May will grow to good size by fall, ready to give you early bloom in your plant windows when the world is cold and gray outside.

Another method of starting seed by using wide-mouthed bottle partially filled with soil mixture.

Since there are many ingenious ways to start begonia seeds, perhaps it would be of interest to describe a few. One of the oldest ways is to use "a brick grandmother." The old-fashioned red clay brick is good, because it is porous. Sterilize the soil and pack a thick layer on the brick, then set in a pan and add water until the brick is half submerged. When brick and soil are moist, scatter the seeds on the moist soil, pressing down firmly. Keep enough water in the pan to keep the soil moist at all times.

Some growers like to use a flat-sided, wide-mouthed bottle, partially filled with the soil mixture. Lay the bottle on the side and scatter the seeds with a long handled implement. Cover the bottle neck loosely, to admit some air. When the seedlings are ready to transplant, slip a wide-bladed knife under them and draw carefully out the wide bottle neck.

Seedlings sometimes show spotted leaves, which may be puzzling if they were not from spotted leaf varieties. As they get larger, the spots disappear, and the leaf takes on the appearance of the parent. The fresher the seed,

the better the germination, although there are always some sterile seeds. Begonia seeds bruise easily and this destroys fertility. They should always be packed in cotton wool to prevent bruising. Usually seeds germinate in from nine to fifteen days, but some times weeks or even months will elapse before the seedlings appear. The *semperflorens* begonias will bloom in six months from seed, the tuberous kinds in about the same time, but most of the fibrous kinds will not bloom until a year or more old.—*Elvin McDonald, Bessie Buxton.*

See also FERTILIZER.

BELLADONNA: (*Atropa belladonna*) Is a perennial herb with important medicinal properties, which are due to the poisonous alkaloids present in all parts of the plant. The dried herb (leaves, flowers, and small stems) and the roots are used in the preparation of a number of important medicines.

The plant thrives best in a deep and moist but well-drained loam such as will produce a good crop of vegetables. It will not survive long in situations where subsoil drainage is poor. Cultivation has been successful in the Northeastern and North Central States and under irrigation in the Los Angeles and Bay regions of California and in eastern Washington, which indicates that these are favorable regions for this crop.

Commercially belladonna is usually propagated from seed, although new fields can be planted with divisions of the fleshy rootstocks of old plants. Individual seeds vary greatly in the time required for germination. It therefore sometimes takes four to five weeks to obtain a good stand of seedlings from a given lot of seed. About one ounce of seed will provide enough plants for one acre.

The seed is sown thickly in pots or well-drained boxes in late winter in a cool greenhouse, a coldframe, or outdoor seedbed early in spring, as in the case of tobacco. When the seedlings grown indoors are large enough to handle they should be transplanted to light rich soil in small individual pots or seed flats in the same way as tomato or other vegetable plants intended for field planting. As soon as danger of frost is over they should be transplanted to a deeply plowed and well-prepared field by hand or with transplanting machines and set about 20 inches apart in rows 30 inches or more apart.

BELMOREANA: *see* PALMS

BEN FRANKLIN TREE: *see* FRANKLINIA

BENT GRASS: *see* LAWN

BERBERIS: *see* BARBERRY

BERGAMOT: *see* BEE-BALM

BERMUDA GRASS: (*Cynodon dactylon*) An important pasture grass in the South, where it prefers clayey soils, but also does well on sandy soils. It is commonly known as wire grass. Recommended seeding rate is five pounds per acre.

In the home garden, Bermuda grass is considered a weed, and it's a mighty tough one to eradicate. Many organic gardeners have found that deep mulching with over eight inches of hay, leaves, pine needles, etc., will smother out the Bermuda grass and still allow crops to grow in the garden.

Another method is where ground freezes, plow or fork shallowly in fall so roots are exposed to air through the winter months. Still another way is to try smothering the Bermuda grass with a crop of fall-sown rye followed by a crop of cowpeas or velvet beans.

Sometimes referred to as Devil grass, Bermuda has been found to be *an excellent base grass for permanent pastures*—besides being highly useful in stabilizing waterways, terrace outlet channels, steep slopes and embankments. These last uses are directly due to Bermuda's almost fantastic erosion-controlling ability.

Bermuda is an extremely tenacious, long-lasting perennial grass, first found in the tough growing conditions of the Bengal region of India and introduced into the United States about 1790. It produces above-ground runners (stolons) that root by themselves and form the crowns of new plants at the nodes, and fleshy underground runners (rhizomes) that also develop into new plants.

It makes excellent permanent pastures on land which cannot profitably be cultivated, and permanent meadows on formerly abandoned acres. Cattle find it highly palatable, and it is high in protein, calcium and phosphoric acid.

BERRIES: So many are the advantages of berries and other small fruits that it is difficult to see how any gardener can resist growing them. Here are just a few of their good points:

1. Flavor is unsurpassed. Many people feel that the greatest taste thrills in the garden are fresh-from-the-vine strawberries, grapes, blueberries and other small fruits.

2. Insects and disease cause less trouble. Strawberries, for example, aren't sprayed by many commercial growers. Fewer troubles with pests is one reason organic gardeners should concentrate on small fruit growing.

3. Quicker bearing. Almost all bush fruits start bearing the second year after planting, and some start bearing the first season.

4. Plenty of fruit in a small space. There is room for berries and vines in even the tiniest garden.

5. Food values are high. Fresh, organically grown small fruits are rich, natural sources of many vitamins.

The cultivation of most berries is very uniform, but there are some differences; therefore, cultural information will be given under the individual varieties.

NUTRITIVE VALUE OF BERRIES AND GRAPES PER CUP

FRUIT (1 cup, fresh, edible portion) (125 to 150 grams)	Calories (Food Energy)	Fat Gm.	Protein Gm.	Calcium Mg.	Phosphorus Mg.	Iron Mg.	Vit. A I.U.	Vit. B₁ Mg.	Vit. B₂ Mg.	Vit. C Mg.
BLACKBERRIES	82	1.4	1.7	46	46	1.3	280	.05	.06	30
BLUEBERRIES	85	.8	.8	22	18	1.1	400	.04	.03	23
CURRANTS	60	.2	1.3	40	36	1.0	130	.04	—	40
GOOSEBERRIES	59	.3	1.2	33	42	.8	440	—	—	49
GRAPES (American type)	84	1.7	1.7	20	25	.7	90	.07	.05	5
GRAPES (European type)	102	.6	1.2	26	33	.9	120	.09	.06	6
LOGANBERRIES	90	.9	1.4	50	27	1.7	280	.04	.10	34
RASPBERRIES (Black)	100	2.1	2.0	54	50	1.2	—	.03	.09	32
RASPBERRIES (Red)	70	.5	1.5	49	46	1.1	160	.03	.08	29
STRAWBERRIES	54	.7	1.2	42	40	1.2	90	.04	.10	89

See RASPBERRY; BLACKBERRY; DEWBERRY; LOGANBERRY; YOUNGBERRY; BOYSENBERRY; STRAWBERRY; CURRANT; GOOSEBERRY; BLUEBERRY; BRAMBLE FRUITS.

BETA VULGARIS: *see* BEET

BETULA: *see* BIRCH

BIENNIALS: The group of plants which normally requires two years to complete their life cycle (blooming the second season after seed is sown) before they produce seed and die. One group, known as the true biennials, includes Canterbury Bells, Sweet William, foxglove, hollyhocks, and Rose Campion. These are best sown in mid-June to mid-July to obtain healthy vigorous plants the following year.

The second group of biennials is comprised of pansies, forget-me-nots, English daisies and English Wallflower. Generally it is best to sow this group in August to avoid danger of winter-killing. Since biennials in this group are not very hardy, it's a good practice to protect them with a coldframe in regions where winter temperatures drop below 20°F. In any case, all biennials should be protected with a heavy mulch after the ground has frozen from weather extremes and heaving during warm spells.

When starting biennials, prepare the soil as for any good seed bed, making the soil fine, moistening it, adding leaf mold, peat moss or other humus material. A good practice is to mix the tiny seeds with dry sand in order to get even distribution in the rows.

Be careful when watering the seeds: if they get too little water, they'll dry out; if too much, damping off may result.

Once the seedlings have about four to six leaves and can be easily handled, it's time to transplant. Water sufficiently until they are well established. Mulch to conserve moisture. *See also* FLOWER GARDENING.

BINDWEED: (*Convolvulus*) The bindweed, or field bindweed is one of the most stubborn of all weeds to eradicate. Best control is continuous cultivation—which kills by starvation of the roots through the continual removal of the top growth. Cultivation every two weeks is necessary and the best time to start is immediately after harvest in the summer or about two weeks after the plant starts growth in the spring. Continue at intervals of 14 days as long as growth continues, about ten to 12 cultivations a season. If no plants are to be seen at the time a cultivation is due, that cultivation may be skipped. The depth of cultivation is not too important but make it deep enough to do a good job. Plows, duck-foot field cultivators and rotary rod-weeders all do a satisfactory job. *All* plants must be cut off at the time of cultivation. Extend the treatment to about ten feet beyond the patch. Unfortunately, it takes from two to three seasons for complete eradication. Soil erosion may result from this cultivation so be sure to use all plant residues. Winter rye planted in late September and plowed or disked the following spring and the cultivation started again helps. Do not allow the rye to pass the boot stage.

Other members of the bindweed family include the California rose (*C. japonicus*)—a perennial climber of about 20 feet; and Dwarf morning-glory (*C. tricolor*)—an annual often recommended where blue flowers are desired in the garden color scheme.

BIO-DYNAMIC METHOD: The bio-dynamic method of gardening and farming is closely aligned with the goals of the organic method in that both strive to improve the humus content of the soil. Whereas most organic gardeners don't differentiate between compost of varying materials, the bio-dynamic gardener mixes carefully portioned amounts of certain raw materials to form compost according to specified formuli. The bio-dynamicist is intent on producing compost in such a way as to lose as few nutritional elements as possible. Much research has been done at bio-dynamic experimental farms to show the effect of bacterial action on the decomposition of manure and compost. According to bio-dynamic adherents, this research has revealed what proper fermentation conditions should be and one of their major aims is to reproduce these favorable conditions so that compost and manure does not lose valuable elements.

Bio-dynamic preparations have been introduced to aid in the humus-forming process. Much of the original work in producing these preparations was done by the noted Austrian philosopher-scientist, Dr. Rudolf Steiner. Today the leader in this country is Dr. Ehrenfried Pfeiffer, once a student of Dr. Steiner. Studies are now being conducted at the Bio-chemical Research Laboratory, Three-fold Farm, Spring Valley, New York, under the auspices of the Biodynamic Farming and Gardening Association.

Following is one of the typical, recommended bio-dynamic preparations:

Preparation No. 502: This preparation is made from the yarrow blossoms (*Achillea millefolium*), fermented together with deer bladders over a period of six months in earth during the winter. The analysis of the available minerals shows a decrease of potassium from 1.05 per cent to 0.13 per cent, an increase of calcium from 0.05 per cent to 0.375 per cent, i.e. of 75 times; a slight decrease of magnesium from 0.01 per cent to 0.005 per cent. Phosphate remains stable at about 0.06 per cent. The major increase is again observed in nitrate nitrogen from 0.07 per cent to 2.5 per cent or 35.8 times the original. Nitrogen fixing bacteria have migrated into the preparation and lived and worked there. According to Dr. Rudolf Steiner, the originator of these preparations, No. 502 has a stimulating effect on the use of sulphur and potassium by plants in their growth. This in turn effects the building up of protein and carbohydrates and their balance. This preparation, as well as the others, acts as a biocatalyst.

Here in the words of Dr. Pfeiffer, is a brief explanation of the principles of bio-dynamics:

Bio-dynamic farming and gardening looks upon the soil as upon a living organism and regards the maintenance and furtherance of soil life as fundamentally essential in order to preserve the soil's fertility for generations instead of obtaining a certain number of cash crops and then giving up work on the land because of its exhaustion. The maintenance of soil life is vital also in order to protect the soil from erosion and to create, improve and augment the humus content. This will result in a fine, crumbly structure and provide the necessary organic colloids.

In addition it will grow a superior quality of products, which will mean better feeding for livestock and better food for human beings.

The nearer a soil is to the neutral state the better possibility it has for humus production. Increasing acidity deteriorates the humus.

The better a soil is protected against the bleaching and drying effects of the sun's rays, the better the humus is preserved.

The better a soil is aerated, the more soil life is developed and the more humus produced.

The more a soil is protected against dry and water-consuming winds, the better the humus production is maintained and hard-crust formation as well as loss of water avoided.

Each kind of plant develops its own type of humus through its roots and leaves which fall and decompose around it. Crops either consume, maintain or produce humus.

Mixed cultures are apt to preserve the fertility of the ground on account of certain beneficial effects from plant to plant, through mutual protection, through plant hormones and the kind of humus developed. The old-fashioned gardener obtains a black earth in his garden which a farmer never could produce in his fields.

The loss of humus must be replaced by humus. Soil life must be stimulated by means of organic decomposed material in the striving towards the state of neutral colloidal humus.

Soil improvement is obtained by proper humus management, e.g., by the application of sufficient organic manure and compost in the best possible state of fermentation, also by proper crop rotation, by proper working of the soil, by protective measures such as wind protection, cover crops, green manure, diversified crops rather than mono-cultures, etc., and mixed cultures so that plants aid and support each other.

Proper humus management is based on farm manure and compost as the most valuable fertilizers. They contain organic matter on which the soil bacteria and earthworms can feed and then revitalize the soil. They contain colloids which absorb moisture and mineral solutions in the ground, form a crumbly structure and eliminate the danger of erosion.

Farmyard manure usually loses 50 per cent of its nitrogen content from the day it is produced until it is plowed under. The careful storage of manure in heaps covered with earth, as taught by the bio-dynamic method, avoids this loss almost entirely. Organic matter has not yet reached the state of neutral colloidal humus. Complicated fermentation processes must first take place in the manure heap. The final result is either badly smelling decay with loss of nitrogen and break down to ammonia and carbonic acid or a transformation into neutral colloidal humus. The bio-dynamic method produces the right fermentation. Certain bio-dynamic preparations are inserted into the manure heaps in order to speed and direct fermentation and preserve the original manure values. This fermentation is usually completed in from two to five months.

The same principles apply to compost materials. When collecting and piling up such materials one obtains an additional source of organic fertilizer. Everything which is apt to decompose can be used, as leaves, grass cuttings, weeds, old rotten hay, corn stalks, garbage, pond cleanings, road scrapings, slaughterhouse refuse, bone, hoof and horn meal, wool, etc. These materials are piled up in alternate layers, interlayered with earth and a thin coating of quick lime and treated with the bio-dynamic preparations. The bio-dynamic literature describes this process clearly. The fermented compost material is especially good for the improvement of lawns, pastures, flower beds, vegetable gardens, shrubbery, alfalfa, clover, etc. If properly done the fermentation of compost material into humus takes place in about four to 12 months, according to climatic conditions.

Experience has shown that on a 100-acre farm with an annual manure production of 150-200 tons of manure about 100-120 tons of waste material in addition could be collected and composted.

Proper crop rotation is essential in order to preserve the fertility of the soil. The general rule is that soil-exhausting crops such as corn, potatoes and mangels in the fields and cabbage, cauliflower, etc., in the garden alternate with soil-restoring crops such as all plants of the leguminous family—peas, beans, clover, alfalfa, etc. Furthermore, deep rooting crops have to alternate with shallow rooting ones, crops which require manure with those that do without it. A carefully thought out crop rotation is the opposite of monoculture which in the long run completely exhausts the soil. The crop rotation plan must be made in accordance with soil, climatic, and market conditions and has, therefore, to be worked out individually for each case including farms, flower and vegetable gardens.

Proper working of the soil consists mainly of knowledge of the right time and right depth of plowing, of harrowing, disking, cultipacking, rolling, etc. Much skill and experience are needed. A cultipacker applied at the right time, at the beginning of dry weather, can preserve the moisture for a long period. Deep plowing of too wet a soil can ruin a field for many years. Only thoughtful experience combined with investigations, such as the taking of soil profiles, enable maximum efficiency in soil treatment.—*Dr. Ehrenfried Pfeiffer.*

BIOLOGICAL INSECT CONTROL: *see* Insect Control, Biological

BIOLOGICAL SOIL LIFE: *see* Microorganism; Actinomycetes; Fungi

BIRCH: (*Betula*) Deciduous and hardy, this striking family of tall-growing trees is best known for its distinctive bark, which in varying species ranges from a sharp, handsome white to shades of orange, red, brown and black. Added to this is its delicate, graceful foliage.

Most birches thrive in moist, sandy loam, and are hardy in cold climates, generally short-lived in warm areas. Propagation is by seed, sometimes by cuttings and by budding or grafting.

Among several species are the Canoe Birch (*B. papyrifera*), which grows from 60 to 80 feet high, has an extremely white bark that peels; the River or Red Birch (*B. nigra*), a hardy grower from Massachusetts to Florida and west to Kansas, it reaches heights up to 90 feet, has a reddish-brown bark which sheds in thin flakes; and the Cherry or Sweet Birch (*B. lenta*), found from Maine to Alabama and westward to Ohio. It is characteried by a smooth, dark bark like that of the cherry tree, and has aromatic twigs from which oil of wintergreen is distilled. For planting and culture, see also Trees.

BIRD-OF-PARADISE (*Strelizia reginae*) A member of the banana family. This plant should not be confused with bird-of-paradise bush, *Poincianna gilliesi,* or with the member of the pineapple family, *Billbergia,* which is sometimes given the same popular name.

Bird-of-Paradise, though it is the official flower of the City of Los Angeles and grows in Southern California like a native, is found wild only in South Africa. But it thrives beautifully wherever temperatures seldom go below freezing, and shoots up blossoms of orange and blue most of the winter and spring. In colder climates it can be raised in large pots and kept in a sunny indoor spot in winter.

Sometimes called crane flower, from a distance it does look like the head of a setting crane. The rose and green sheath that holds the blossoms juts out at an obtuse angle from its thick stalk resembling a huge bird's beak. Vivid orange petals and sapphire sepals stand up like plumes and could be mistaken for a crane's crest. Yet at closer view the flower looks more like a small bird perching.

The regions in South Africa that the wild crane flower chooses for itself are along rivers and in full sun. The only reason for shading at all would be to reduce heat in intensely hot climates where arid conditions prevail. More important than shade is additional water to compensate for the drying effect of sun.

What bird-of-paradise doesn't tolerate is freezing temperatures. Even a few degrees below 32° has been known to completely destroy the plant. In cold climates it would be best to treat bird-of-paradise flower as an indoor plant and raise it in pots on the patio in summer and in a sunny window in winter.

In climates where there are only occasional cold spells wrapping plants in burlap bags will insulate against light frosts. Another safeguard, where winters are on the border line between subtropical and temperate climates, is to force the plant into dormancy well in advance of the cold season, by holding back food and water at the end of the summer.

Watering, therefore, should be done thoroughly but not too often. Give the plant a chance to use up part of its reserve.

Humidity is highly desirable for most plants, and bird-of-paradise is no exception. It prefers the damp air of coastal regions but grows in more arid climes if it receives abundant water and is planted in soil that contains considerable humus. If the leaves begin to brown at the edges and become brittle, the plant is probably not getting enough water.

Under cultivation bird-of-paradise sometimes reaches six feet, while the wild plant seldom attains over four feet. One of the reasons for this is frequent fertilizer applications. Bird-of-paradise is a heavy feeder, and should be given a good application of a complete organic fertilizer in the spring followed by a second application three months later.

Where rains are scarce, add generous amounts of leaf mold or other humus. Where rains are heavy, add sand and gravel to improve drainage. Cultivation is not necessary except to remove weeds and incorporate fertilizer or compost.

Give bird-of-paradise ample room to spread lest it take the food right out from under the roots of its less hardy neighbors. Three feet between plants is the minimum; five feet is better. The exception is in planting very young plants which you intend to give more space later on.

Blossoms seldom appear unless at least ten leaves have developed, so do not be discouraged if a small plant you have had for a year or two has not flowered. It will, as soon as it is large enough, if it has had adequate care.

The bird-of-paradise flower is seldom bothered by serious pests. The occasional invaders include aphids, scale and mealy bugs.

To have new plants the fastest possible way, divide established ones. Each fan of leaves is a potential plant. The larger the clump taken, the sooner flowers will appear. Cut the fan from the parent plant carefully, taking as much of the root system as possible.

Spring is the best time of the year to divide plants. The weather is mild and humid and new growth has not begun, and the newly divided plant will have an opportunity to become established before the dormant season arrives. It is possible to divide well-established plants as late as August if you take ample roots, but those divisions made in the spring do best.

In climates with below freezing temperatures, bird-of-paradise can be raised indoors in sunny locations.

Plants will grow to three feet in seven inch pots. Watering should be done thoroughly but not too often. Plants should be fed an organic base liquid fertilizer about once a month during spring and summer and not at all during the winter.

Few cut flowers have better keeping qualities than bird-of-paradise. Several flowers come forth, one at a time, from each sheath. If you change the water every day and cut the base of the stem every other day, floral arrangements should last two weeks.— *Maggie Butanier.*

BIRDS: Many gardeners consider birds to be worth as much as $100 annually in their gardens. Their reason—harmful insects have never been able to build up an immunity to birds, as so many of them have developed against insecticides. For example, a yellow-throat warbler often eats 10,000 tree lice in a day. A single chickadee has been known to destroy 100,000 canker-worm eggs in a couple of weeks, plus thousands of tent caterpillar moth eggs. A nighthawk can gobble down 340 grasshoppers and 58 other assorted bugs in one meal; a killdeer can eat 300 mosquito larvae.

Many birds we consider pests do much more good than harm. Bluejays may rob some nests, but over 80 per cent of their food is weed seeds, grasshoppers, beetles and other bugs. Farmers hate crop-stealing crows—except in bug plagues, when they prove good friends to have. The bald eagle is accused of stealing poultry, but he's actually a scavenger who prevents water pollution by eating dead fish.

ENCOURAGING BIRDS: One of the best ways to encourage birds to make a garden their home is to provide plants that furnish cover and food. A great variety of these plants means a great variety of birds.

Choose plants that would provide food through most of the year: raspberry, cherry, currant, gooseberry and mulberry through the summer; bitter-sweet, dogwood, alder, pokeberry, honeysuckle and Virginia creeper in the fall; and barberry, bayberry, hawthorne and mountain ash in winter.

Many wintering birds like rose hips, and sumac supplies food that is eaten in the spring after being ignored all winter. Other good food-producers for various reasons are elderberry, shadblow, viburnums, sassafras, spice bush and the cornus shrubs. Many non-food plants like evergreens make excellent nesting sites, and some birds will nest high up in such trees as birches, oaks and elms. All sorts of hedges, too, make thick, well-protected sites for nests.

REAL BIRD SANCTUARY: If you have room you can make a section of your garden into a real bird sanctuary. Many of the shrubs listed above can be planted quite close together, with their branches allowed to intermingle as they do in woodlands. Quite a few will thrive in semi-shade, so you can group them around and under any high-branched shade tree. The birds will flock to such an ideal corner.

Even with such a multitude of fine nesting sites, birds will appreciate a few houses, too. You can build your own—the Fish and Wildlife Service, Audubon Society and Department of Agriculture supply designs—or buy some of the ones sold in garden supply houses.

They may be simple box-like affairs, or fancy 10- or 20-room apartment houses (for purple martins). Natural, weathered wood is best, or you can paint them a dull green or brown. You can locate them in low shrubs, in evergreens, under the eaves of your house, or on poles or attached to trees at varying heights. Always situate them with the entrance hole away from prevailing winds, and give them a sloping roof, a few ventilation holes under the eaves, and a drainage hole in the floor.

A good idea is to hang up short pieces of yarn, twine, horsehair and feathers for nest construction. Bits of cotton and lint from the dryer make fine soft "down" to line nests. Don't, however, put out brightly colored materials. They destroy the natural camouflage of the nests.

BIRD BATH: A drawing card for many species is a bird bath. Almost any large container with a rough interior surface and a maximum depth of two inches is good. You can put it on a pedestal or on the ground, but never close to shrubbery, flower beds or overhanging branches from which cats may leap upon the bathers. During warm weather, a popular bath may need cleaning and refilling daily, and a good scrubbing with a stiff brush weekly to remove algae.

Foods for birds include sunflower seeds, all kinds of cereals, and pumpkin, squash and melon seeds. Peanut butter mixed with crumbs and cooking fat is easier for the birds to swallow than plain peanut butter. Also good is "suet pudding," made by melting suet and mixing in crumbs, peanut butter, raisins and wild bird seed. Even steak or roast bones are relished by many species, as are apple parings and greens. And to attract hummingbirds, put out dishes of raw-sugar-and-water syrup as soon as the weather warms up.

Pans of warm water are a necessity in freezing weather. So is grit, in the form of sand or canary gravel, when snow covers the ground, and crushed eggshells for female birds prior to and during the nesting season.

The hopper-type "demand" feeders that hold large amounts of food are a must in case you have to go away or otherwise stop the feeding temporarily. Another good trick is to fill your feeders only once a day and let the birds forage for themselves the rest of the day, so they won't become too dependent.

BIRDS VS. INSECTS: Here is a brief description of what birds are most effective against what insects, according to Jane Green:

As you sit in the cool of your garden some evening, note the *air sweepers* such as bull bats, swallows, martins, night hawks and whippoorwills as they swoop through the air, gulping myriads of gnats, midges, mosquitoes and other such prey.

Another class of air experts take care of larger flying insects such as grasshoppers, horseflies, rose chafers and countless more flying pests. Among this force may be found kingbirds, pewees, mocking birds, catbirds and others.

Then, there are the *foliage cleaners.* Their job is to pick off caterpillars, plant lice, ants, cankerworms and their kind from the tender twigs and leaves where such pests are usually found doing the most damage. Warblers, vireos and humming birds are some of these careful workers, but other and stronger birds are needed also for this tremendous job. So we find cuckoos, both black and yellow-billed, and the Baltimore orioles taking over when it comes to tent caterpillars, wire worms, wasps, locusts and whatnots. The oriole, fastidious in habits and exquisite in appearance, gorges hungrily on click beetles, crane flies, grasshoppers, spiders and many other ugly destructive foliage despoilers.

The woodpeckers, sprightly and dependable, make up a wonderful *timber patrol,* capably aided by smaller helpers that climb trees and snatch any unwary bug, beetle, worm or ant *outside* the bark. Of course, the woodpeckers being outfitted by nature with chisels can go right *under* the bark and dig out tree borers, timber ants, and larvae of different tree enemies—and what a blessing for us that they can!

The *woodpecker helpers* are wrens, chickadees, brown creepers and other industrious small birds.

Wrens also work along with the *ground crews* of cleaner-uppers among which are bobwhites or quails, crows, sparrows, field larks, robins, wheat birds, blackbirds and a host of others that can clean up the grass roots, young grain and other valuable growth of such things as the dreaded chinch bugs, cutworms, crane fly maggots and innumerable other enemies that human ingenuity often finds overwhelming. *See also* WINDBREAKS.

BIRD'S-FOOT TREFOIL: *see* LOTUS

BITTERSWEET: (*Celastrus scandens*)
Ornamental vines or climbing shrubs with attractive foliage and brightly-colored fall fruit, bittersweet is excellent for walls, trellises or arbors. Bittersweet grows well in either shady or sunny locations, and in ordinary garden soil. It often reaches a height of 20 feet. Hardy throughout practically all of the United States, it can be propagated by root cuttings, layers or seed.

Another plant that is called bittersweet is *Solanum dulcamara*. This is a vine-like herb, growing up to eight feet, with scarlet fruit. Sometimes known as climbing nightshade, its berries are poisonous. *See also* SHRUBS, FLOWERING.

BLACKBERRY: (*Rubus*)
A very valuable member of the berry family, blackberries grow in just about every region of the United States. In addition to its hardiness, the plant will usually do well in ordinary soil, thriving best in a clay loam that is moist yet well-drained.

Roots of the blackberry plant need plenty of room. When set in hills, space them six to seven feet apart; in rows, allow four feet between plants and eight between rows.

Don't pick blackberry fruit until it is full ripe. (It is not ready for picking when it first turns black.) Keep berries cool and dry.

Barley, oats and buckwheat make excellent cover crops for blackberries, as they do not live over winter. These crops should be worked into the soil in autumn; in addition to adding humus, these crops also help in giving winter protection to berry canes. It is generally agreed that chemical ferti-

lizers, as the nitrates, only serve to increase cane growth, but not the formation of more fruit.

Many varieties of blackberry are self-sterile and need a pollenizer; at least two varieties should be in the garden that blossom at the same time so that the blossoms may be crossed and good fruit results.

Some variety of the blackberry family is found in every region of our country, excepting those which are extreme in climate, either hot or cold.

With all varieties, so far as possible, choose with reference to high quality, winter tolerance, and immunity to disease.

In other matters such as pruning, supporting and mulching, it is well to follow the suggestions given under raspberries. One will notice that blackberries need a moist soil during the fruiting season, for in comparison, the poor berries found on a dry soil show clearly the ill effects of the lack of moisture. This moist condition of the soil can be assured by using compost freely.

Blackberries increase their growth by means of suckers. Like the other brambles, they should be planted in early spring. They should be placed in furrows at a depth of from three to four inches.

During the summer strong roots will form on the bushes. In the fall take these up from the most vigorous of the bushes and cut them in pieces, two to four inches long. Store these in sand which is moist but not wet, or in sawdust if the location will keep a temperature above freezing during the winter. Set in the ground as soon as it can be worked in the spring.

There is no definite duration of berry plantings. Much depends upon the fertility of the soil and its humus content. Liberal applications each year of compost and free mulching will add much to the life and yield of plants. General good care, also in pruning, is needed, especially with regards to stubs, which should be very short. If the stubs stand up too high they can be recut and shortened, and the rows can be slightly mounded to cover the short stubs. This mounding will also protect buds of the new canes and the roots near to them. The duration of any plant depends upon the annual formation of buds for new canes. Compost, mulches and short close cuts of stems add materially to the potential life of berry plantings.

A healthy patch of black or purple raspberries produces on the average of six to eight good crops; and poorer ones afterward. The chief causes of running out are the virus diseases such as mosaic, blue stem, etc., winter-killing in severe weather, sometimes drought, and finally, lack of proper cultural conditions in growing the plants. Most of these shortening factors can be averted or diminished by giving full attention to the plant. Blackberries and red raspberries may produce well for twenty years, but the average over the country seems to be ten to 12 years. Loganberries are shorter-lived than blackberries. Dewberry plantings often last for 15 years and are productive all the while. In general, blackberries and purple raspberries are the most productive over a term of years, followed by black raspberries and red raspberries. But in all cases, good care is the most essential thing; and among them are the free use of compost and mulches to main-

tain the organic content of the soil. *See also* FRUITS; BRAMBLE FRUITS.

BLACK BINDWEED: *see* BUCKWHEAT

BLACK LOCUST: *see* HONEY PLANTS

BLACK MANGROVE: *see* MANGROVE, BLACK

BLACK NIGHTSHADE: (*Solanum nigrum*) An annual herb that belongs to the potato family, black or deadly nightshade is one of the more villainous "pest plants." In July and August it produces green berries which are poisonous when eaten, causing paralysis and narcosis. If such poisoning is suspected and a physician not immediately available, an emetic (anything which causes vomiting) should be given. These plants have wavy-toothed leaf edges, clustered small white flowers, and green berries that turn a dull, purplish-black as they ripen. They are found in waste areas, fields, yards, camp grounds or open woods. The USDA notes that the herbicide chemical 2, 4-D *will* NOT *kill* these plants, but that they are easily eradicated by pulling out the roots or hoeing.

BLACK RASPBERRY: *see* BRAMBLE FRUITS

BLACK ROT: *see* DISEASE

BLACK SPOT: A fungus disease which grows into the leaf and forms black spots by its dark threads just under the cuticle. It appears mostly on roses and related plants. Fungus fruiting bodies develop, ready to discharge their spores which are carried by rain, wind, beetles or even garden tools to healthy leaves. There they start another cycle if given six hours of continued moisture for germination. Black spots finally cause leaves to turn yellow and ultimately fall off.

There is no easy way to control black spots—even with chemical sprays. Be sure to pick off and destroy all infected leaves as soon as the spots appear, as well as removing infected leaves from the ground around the plant.

Then remineralize the soil by adding a pound of phosphate rock and a pound of finely pulverized potash rock to each plant. Also give each plant at least five pounds of compost worked into the soil lightly. Next mulch the rose bed with a four to six inch layer of pulverized corn cobs or similar material. These will absorb the rain and prevent splashing. The organism which carries black spot often is transferred from the soil to the plant by splashing caused by rain.

Much progress has also been made in developing roses with greater resistance to black spot.

BLACK WALNUT: (*Juglans nigra*) see WALNUT

BLACK WIDOW: The female of a common American spider (*Latrodectus mactans*), so called because of its shining black body and its habit of devouring its mate. Her bite (the males are harmless) is rarely fatal but causes terrific pain and violent illness. Like other animals, her populations rise and fall in cycles. In peak years, town dumps, stone fences, woodpiles and cluttered yards, garages and cellars may be crowded with them. Watch for a spider with a half-inch-long, shiny black body and a red mark on the underside of her abdomen.

The Widow, however, is more fearing than to be feared. She is extremely timid and will only bite if irritated, as when pinched or pressed in a fold of clothing. Black Widows are nocturnal in habit, but don't move around much, so there is no danger of being bitten in bed. The best way to get rid of them is to seek them out at night with a flashlight and a fly swatter. Better yet, keep the premises neat and free of all rubbish and clutter.

BLANCHING: This is a whitening or bleaching of various green vegetables, such as celery, cauliflower and endive. It is achieved by excluding light from the plants for a period just before ripening, and is usually done by piling up earth around them, setting up boards, or tying certain parts closely together.

With most of these vegetables, the blanching process serves only to alter the appearance; actually the food value is usually lowered, inasmuch as the plants' chlorophyll content is what gives it the green coloring. *See also* FREEZING VEGETABLES; ENDIVE.

BLANKET FLOWER: (*Gaillardia pulchella*) An annual, the red and yellow daisy-like blossoms are desirable for cutting on account of their cheerful colors, long stiff stems and excellent keeping quality. The blanket flower is cosmopolitan, volunteering annually and producing abundant flowers persistently, even on the light sands of the seashore.

It grows 12 to 20 inches high and has no special soil requirements. Grow many plants close together, but be sure they are placed near plants with which they will harmonize.

G. aristata, also called blanket flower, is a hardy perennial, growing two to three feet high. All Gaillardia prefer light, friable soils and full sun. Primarily summer bloomers, they can be propagated by division in spring or fall.

BLASTING SOIL: *see* DYNAMITE

BLAZING STAR: *see* LIATRIS

BLEEDING: When tree limbs are pruned or wounded, the exudation of sap is known as bleeding. Ordinarily, this has no harmful effect on the tree, except in very severe cases. *See also* TREES.

BLEEDING HEART: (*Dicentra spectabilis*) This perennial does well in average soil under part shady or sunny conditions. Fringed Bleeding-Heart, *D. eximia,* a fine rock garden plant, blooms from May to September, requiring no particular care other than watering during dry period. *D. spec-*

tabilis is known for its lovely, but, brief blooms in the spring, but does not bloom all summer. It grows from one to two feet.

Propagation can be done by seed or division by clumps. Transplanting can be done even when plants are in full flower.

Most *Dicentra* species do well in open borders or in the rock garden, can be propagated by division in spring.

BLIGHT: The term used to refer to any of a number of plant diseases. Usually, the term blight refers to a number of plants affected in one area, rather than isolated cases. Most blights are caused by pathogenic organisms, and are manifested by browning of foliage, generally undermining of the health of the plant, and often eventual death of the plant. *See also* DISEASE.

BLISTER BEETLE: A large, elongated beetle, gray or striped; eats foliage or blossoms. For control, handpick beetles; wear gloves while doing so, as the beetles discharge a caustic fluid that may blister the skin. *See also* INSECT CONTROL.

BLOOD, DRIED: Dried blood is the blood collected in the slaughterhouses, afterward dried and ground, which has a nitrogen content of 12 per cent or over. There are poorer grades and higher grades, all of which are nowadays mainly used for feeding purposes. The dried blood that finds its way to the fertilizer dealer or mixer is a small quantity. There is often a considerable amount of phosphorus in dried blood, ranging from one to five per cent; this is often not indicated on the bag, but may increase the value of the material considerably.

Dried blood can be used directly in the ground or composted. On account of its high nitrogen content, a sprinkling of it suffices to stimulate bacterial growth, and it is advisable either to soak the plant matter thoroughly before applying such a sprink-

ling or to apply the dried blood in moist form after a soaking or even to combine both methods.

Sources of dried blood and similar bagged fertilizers are the mail order houses, seed dealers, fertilizer plants and dealers, and the feed supply houses. *See also* FERTILIZERS.

BLUEBERRIES (*Vaccinium*) These insect-resistant shrubs, growing six to ten feet high, bear plenty of fine-tasting fruit and add beauty to the home.

When used as an informal hedge, they serve the double purpose of affording beauty as well as fruit.

Blueberry plants can be grown easily without spraying, because they have few insect pests.

The cultivated blueberry is still close enough to its wild ancestors to be appreciative only of natural, organic fertilizers. They like humus and soft, woodsy soil so much that it is almost a question of growing them organically or not growing them at all.

In nature the blueberry plant displays its blossoms and tasty fruit in the seldom-frequented spots of forest and wilderness whose soil is covered with a rich blanket of decaying vege-

Blueberries require a rather acid soil with a pH rating of 5 to 5.6. When planting, pack the soil firmly about the roots, using soil that is moist.

tation. It grows wild among the redwoods of California, on forest hillsides of the State of Maine and on the broad crests of the Appalachian ridges.

Blueberries are not self-pollinating, so more than one variety should be planted. Since each of the common varieties has slightly different characteristics, it is good home-garden practice to plant a selection of different types. They ripen at different times and vary slightly in flavor.

Here is a list of the improved blueberry varieties that are most widely used:

Atlantic	June
Burlington	Pemberton
Cabot	Rancocas
Concord	Rubel
Dixi	Stanley
Jersey	Weymouth

The Department of Agriculture has released five more varieties recently that are crosses of some of the varieties listed above. They are:

Berkeley	Earliblue
Bluecrop	Herbert
Coville	

SOIL: Soil should be from 5. to 5.6, which is quite acid. A liberal amount of peaty material is needed; a mulch of peat is fine. If additional acid is needed, use peat or compost made without lime to give the right acidity. The peat should be dug into the earth, and well intermixed with it. (*See* ACIDITY-ALKALINITY.)

Drainage must be ample for blueberry plants, despite the need for moisture. Water should not stand on the surface; and should not be held permanently nearer than 18 inches from the surface. If needed to keep the water condition right, dig an open ditch or install tile drains. Cool, moist, acid conditions are needed in the soil for the best growth of roots to support the plants.

CARE OF THE PLANTS: There are several items in the care of plants, each of which needs attention.

Pruning. In the wild, blueberry plants are pruned by the "burning over" process on the managed areas; the old stems are burned out. But in the garden the pruning shears need to be used after four or five years from set. Varieties vary much in growing habit; the somewhat open and flat-topped ones like Cabot, Harding, Dunfee, and Pioneer, should not be opened more; in contrast to upright and close growing varieties like Adams, Grover, Rubel and Pancocas, which need much opening to prevent them from becoming too thick and bushy. A little attention to the natural degree of openness will suggest what thinning-out there is to do—if any is needed. It is well to compare and contrast different modes of growth before starting the pruning.

There are two types of growth to cut out in pruning—the very slender stems which may not bear much; and the oldest and largest that have borne several years and may not bear much more, except at the tips. It is well to keep the clumps fairly open to avoid crowding and shading. More than one foot asunder for all stems is too open; less than four inches is too close.

Weeding. It is important to suppress all weeds. This is best done by the application of liberal mulches each year. Mulches are preferred and they should include some acid material as peat, oak leaves, etc. This material to maintain normal blueberry soil is better than sawdust or pine needles. Compost is helpful. Woodland soil is often suitable for the plants.

GENERAL DIRECTIONS FOR PLANTING: Upon arrival of plants (rooted shrubs) for setting out, it is urgent that the roots be protected from drying. Cover them at once with soil or burlap—if unpacked. Do not expose the roots to the drying effects of sun or wind. Put the plants in a cool moist cellar or in the shade till set. Dig the hole large enough to receive roots without bending or cramping them. When the subsoil is very hard break it up at the bottom of the hole. Use a pick or crowbar if necessary. Set the plants slightly deeper than they stood in the nursery. Spread all roots out naturally. Place good surface soil next to the roots and work it in with the hands. When the hole is half filled, tamp the soil firmly. Fill the hole and tamp the soil harder. Leave loose soil on top or cover with mulch. Leave a saucer-like depression at the top to catch water. If manure is used it should be well rotted and worked into and mixed with the soil. Manure can be used on top for a mulch. Never put fresh or unrotted manure next to the roots. It may heat or dry out and hurt the roots. The soil should remain moist—not wet and no long standing water should be left in the saucer-like depression. Add compost.

Planting is important work and should never be hastily or carelessly done. Careful operations pay well. In all cases pack the soil firmly about the roots and use moist soil for the purpose. Young plants, usually eight to 15 inches high, should be planted in early spring or late fall. Space them about five feet apart, and have rows about seven feet apart. Ten to 15-year-old bushes are estimated to yield about 14 quarts of berries.

The most troublesome blueberry disease is the mummy berry which causes berries to rot and fall off. Control by destroying old mummies by collecting off ground or turning under when cultivating.

BLUE BONNETS: *see* BACHELOR'S BUTTON

BLUEGRASS: *see* LAWN

BLUE GUM TREE: *see* EUCALYPTUS

BLUETS: *see* QUAKER LADIES

BOLTONIA: Also known as false camomile, false starwort or thousand-flowered aster, they are attractive perennials of the Composite family. Often grown in borders or in groups, two native varieties—*asteroides* and *latisquama*—are both tall (five to eight feet), with small flower heads ranging from white to the blue-violet-purple grouping. Boltonia are very easy to raise, are not particular about soil, and are easily propagated by spring or fall division. They generally prefer a sunny location; should be planted toward the rear of the border; bloom in late summer and early fall.

BONE MEAL: *see* PHOSPHORUS; FERTILIZER

BONESET: (*Eupatorium perfoliatum*) is a rather long-lived hardy perennial plant commonly found in low grounds throughout the eastern half of the United States. The dried leaves and flowering tops are used in medicine.

Divisions of clumps of wild plants collected early in fall will serve best for propagation. These are set about one foot apart in rows in well-prepared soil. During the first winter the newly set divisions are protected with a light mulch of straw or manure. Plants can also be grown from seed, collected as soon as ripe, and sown in shallow drills about eight inches apart in a moist, rich seedbed, preferably in partial shade. When of sufficient size the seedlings are set in the field spaced about the same as the divided clumps.

The plants are cut when in full bloom late in summer, and the leaves and flowering tops are stripped from the stems by hand and carefully dried without exposure to the sun. Yields of 2,000 pounds or more per acre of the leaves and tops of cultivated boneset can be obtained under favorable conditions.

BONSAI: This is a centuries-old method of tree dwarfing developed by the Chinese, that is fast becoming a popular hobby in the Western world. In short, it permits you to grow a tree in a flower bowl.

Bonsai isn't a difficult art. What it requires more than skill is patience since a fully mature specimen may take ten years or longer to produce.

Some plants are especially well adapted to bonsai dwarfing. Among these they list juniper, Japanese maple, cypress, Mugho pine and cryptomeria. In general, evergreens need less feeding, pruning and training, but deciduous varieties are sturdier and take shape faster. Deciduous kinds also show the change of seasons; their leaves turn color in the fall and, artistically trained, their bare winter form is as lovely as when they are full-leaved in the summer. (One caution: use small-leaved types because the foliage is not reduced in proportion to the trunk.)

In any case, whether you choose to grow a Biblical Cedar of Lebanon, a colorful firethorn shrub, or anything from an elm or pomegranate to a yew or even a giant Sequoia (scale: one inch to 25 feet), the method is the same:

You can start with cuttings or by layering, but experienced growers usually recommend seeds. You may be able to get very tiny seedlings from some nurseries, or dig them up while on a tramp through the woods. A flat of sandy loam is best for starting seeds. Keep them outdoors if possible, sheltered from hot sun and wind.

All seedlings should be transplanted when one year old. Use an organic soil mixture of 40 per cent loam and 50 per cent sand for evergreens, 70 per cent loam and 20 per cent sand for deciduous plants. All mixtures should contain ten per cent leaf mold. Use two-inch pots, with a bit of moss at the bottom to prevent clogging of the drainage hole.

Before potting, gently peel the dirt from the roots—the Chinese use chopsticks for this—and cut back the taproot about one-third with sharp scissors or pruning shears. Remove all old, dead parts of roots.

Do this operation quickly, in a cool room; a damp basement is excellent.

After transplanting, keep the plants indoors for several days, then gradually expose them to outdoor conditions. Thereafter, any roots that push through the bottom of the pot should always be cut away. You can also start pruning the tops lightly at this time, to develop a pleasing shape.

Ordinary pruning shears are best for cutting the roots back, a vital operation which must be done at each transplanting. Prune away all dead roots.

After this, your evergreens will require transplanting every three to five years, broadleaf trees every two, and flowering and fruiting plants yearly. Spring is the best time for each successive transplanting. Use only a slightly larger pot each time; any container with drainage holes is suitable.

Always make up a fresh soil mixture, and prune the roots fairly vigorously. Cut back the side roots irregularly and thin out the smaller roots to encourage the forming of a dense system.

Evergreens need little branch pruning, but deciduous trees, shrubs and vines should be pinched back to two or three buds on the previous year's growth. Always transplant and prune *spring-flowering* plants immediately *after* bloom has faded.

All bonsai experts use strictly organic fertilizers. You will probably have to work out your own fertilizing program to fit the needs of your specific plants. Most Chinese and Japanese growers advise very dilute applications of liquid fish fertilizer monthly or perhaps oftener, except when the plant is dormant. But others say feed.ing only three or four times a year is plenty. Excessive feeding will result in too vigorous growth, and you'll have a pot-splitting giant instead of an elegant dwarf.

If a tree looks weak, a sprinkling of one-eighth teaspoonful of high-nitrogen bloodmeal will perk it up. For regular feedings, very weak manure tea is as good as fish fertilizer. Occasional light sprinklings of manure compost are also excellent. Just enough fertilizer to keep the tree looking healthy is all that is necessary.

Water only when the soil feels dry to the touch, and don't overwater. The soil should never be either bone-dry or waterlogged. In dry, hot weather, you may have to water two or more times a day. (Some Oriental growers, incidentally, use extremely porous soil and water five or six times daily, on the theory that starving the plant by leaching out fertility elements makes for slower, more compact growth.) Syringe the foliage now and then to remove dust and soot.

Bonsai do best outdoors, although many people have had fine success raising them entirely on sunny window sills. They need abundant light, with some protection from the hot afternoon sun. Exposure to the elements makes the strongest trees, so let them spend as much time outdoors as possible—they provide a beautiful focus of interest for a patio, balcony or walled garden. You can, however, bring them indoors for a few days at a time if you put them in a cool spot away from heat sources.

Semi-hardy plants should be wintered in a greenhouse, coldframe or basement. An unheated garage or lath shelters covered with burlap or tarpaulins are also satisfactory except in the coldest weather. Hardy varieties can be kept outdoors all year.

When your trees are about four years old, you will want to start shaping them. Some look best knarled and twisted, others stately and dignified—pattern your dwarfs' shapes after those of their prototypes in the wild. Bend the trunks and branches in natural curves, winding copper wire around them to hold the new shape. This wire must be removed in a year or so, before it can scar or strangle the tree. This is a good time, too, to thin out excessive growth, cutting on a point just above the joint.

For added interest, when your trees are growing older, you can make a complete little garden in their bowls by mulching with smooth pebbles or granite chips, and decorating with moss, small rocks or shells and figurines.

BOOKS FOR ORGANIC GARDENERS AND FARMERS: The books listed here offer much information on what the organic movement can mean to all of us, individually and collectively.

AGRICULTURE: A NEW APPROACH: By P. H. Hainsworth. A closely reasoned appraisal of organic methods of farming and gardening. Mr. Hainsworth bases his study both on the scientific evidence provided by national research bodies, and also on practical information furnished by farmers and by his own extensive experience as a market gardener.

SIR ALBERT HOWARD IN INDIA: By Louise E. Howard. In this book Lady Howard describes the career and work of her late husband, during his residence in India, where he carried out 26 years of intensive research into the agricultural problems of the East.

THE LIVING SOIL: By E. B. Balfour. Lady Balfour's *The Living Soil,* first published in 1943, is now established as a scientific classic in soil biology and fertility relationships.

"My subject," writes the author, "is food, which concerns everyone; it is health, which concerns everyone; it is the soil which concerns everyone—even if he does not realize it—and it is the history of recent scientific research linking these three vital subjects. . . ."

SOIL BLOCK GARDENING: By J. L. H. Chase and A. J. Pouncy. Soil blocks are now replacing clay pots for a wide range of plants. They are used by amateurs and by commercial growers. The special techniques required for each group of plants are fully described in this book. The most important factor for success is making and using the correct compost. The authors give detailed instructions on this. Mr. Pouncy, an engineer turned nurseryman, was a pioneer of soil blocks, and uses them more widely than anyone else. J. L. H. Chase is the well-known market gardener and writer on gardening subjects.

COMMERCIAL CLOCHE GARDENING: By J. L. H. Chase. The principles and economics of commercial cloche gardening with chapters on strip-cropping, soil management, cloche management, irrigation, packing and marketing.

FOOD, FARMING AND THE FUTURE: By Friend Sykes. Sir Albert Howard once said that Friend Sykes was making the greatest contribution to agriculture since "Coke of Norfolk." Anyone who has seen the transformation wrought at Chantry will endorse this statement. Here one may see each summer the largest grain crops growing on land which looks not at all productive; magnificent dairy cattle, beef cattle, sheep, and poultry, grazing contentedly on luxuriant pastures, feeding the soil and being fed by it. This is accomplished without an ounce of imported feeding stuff or artificial fertilizers.

THE EARTH'S GREEN CARPET: By Louise E. Howard. The earth's green carpet can be kept flourishing only when we realize the importance of returning to the soil all plant and animal residues to serve as foods for the soil organisms, the author stresses.

THE WORKS OF SIR ROBERT MCCARRISON: Edited by H. M. Sinclair. Maj.-Gen. Sir Robert McCarrison worked for over thirty years on nutritional problems. The present book gives details of his classical work on the differences in health resulting from good and poor diets, as well as much other information about his work.

COMPOST: By F. H. Billington and Ben Easey. Compost is the cornerstone of successful organic cultivation and its production and utilization, whether for gardens or for farms, are covered in detail in this practical little book. It is one of the best books for the beginner-composter, who wishes to produce the best of all organic manures from miscellaneous materials which would otherwise be wasted.

CLOCHE GARDENING: By J. L. H. Chase. This book demonstrates the uses of cloches for the early production of all varieties of vegetables, fruits and flowers.

FERTILITY FROM TOWN WASTES: J. C. Wylie examines the conventional methods of refuse and sewage disposal and contrasts the treatment of the organic wastes of sewage and refuse together to produce composts. From rapidly accumulating evidence, the prospect is for better food and improved health from this new method.

STONE MULCHING IN THE GARDEN: By J. I. Rodale. Forgotten for two thousand years, mulching with stones is again coming into its own. Recent studies have shown that stone mulches preserve soil moisture, protect the surface roots of vines and trees, protect the roots and the soil organisms against light which is often injurious to them, prevent the growth of weeds and other plants in competition with food plants, act as a temperature regulator, and undergo slow decomposition to provide plants with important nutrient elements. The amazing effects of stone mulch tests on plants in the organic experimental farm are described.

CLIMATES IN MINIATURE: By T. Bedford Franklin. With simple and inexpensive apparatus, fully described the author has carried out experiments showing how some animals keep warm in the winter, the role of different soils and their temperatures, the way to forecast frost and achieve protection against frost damage, the effects of humidity, windbreaks and light and shade on plants, and why spring arrives first in hedgerow and wood.

RUSSIAN COMFREY: By Lawrence D. Hills. This book deals thoroughly with every aspect of this high-producing stock feed and compost material plant, which can produce more than 100 tons an acre in six to eight cuttings a year.

FARMERS OF 40 CENTURIES: By F. H. King. China can teach us many lessons on the arts of gardening and farming. Compost is the key to the continued fertility of the lands of the East. In this richly rewarding book, Dr. King reveals the East's secrets of keeping the soil healthy.

PRACTICAL ORGANIC GARDENING: By Ben Easey. Here is a standard textbook on organic methods. The English author describes how the change to organic methods is effected without disruption of labor or economics; how to conserve organic manures of all sorts and use green crops to increase fertility; how to improve the quality of vegetables, fruits and flowers, and how to manage gardens, greenhouses, orchards, and lawns so that pests, diseases and weeds are not an ever-recurring anxiety.

HUMUS AND THE FARMER: By Friend Sykes. Many years ago the author sold his property in the fertile Thames valley (England) and invested in some inexpensive land so utterly barren and neglected that it was described by one critic as "just so much space out-of-doors." This land is now eagerly visited by agriculturists as one of the most interesting farms in the country, and Mr. Sykes describes the exact methods of cultivation which brought about its high degree of fertility.

THE SOIL AND HEALTH: By Sir Albert Howard. The author spent his life studying the various crops of England, Europe, the West Indies, Asia and Africa. As a trained soil scientist, he specialized in investigating the diseases of crops and animals. From his findings, the modern organic agriculture movement began. In this book he shows why "one of the great tasks before the world . . . is to found our civilization on a fresh basis—on the full utilization of the earth's green carpet." His ideas were tested for many years in actual, practical farming, before he put them into this historic book.

THE HEALTHY HUNZAS: By J. I. Rodale. In the Hunzas, Mr. Rodale has found a living people who practice what he preaches, and in this book he brings us an interesting account of this remarkably healthy race. The Hunzas have long been known to explorers and scientists. Expeditions have visited them and marveled. *The Healthy Hunzas* tells about a culture we ought to know more about—one we could afford to emulate.

HOW TO HAVE A GREEN THUMB WITHOUT AN ACHING BACK: By Ruth Stout. Miss Stout combines a delightful writing style with the low-down on her now-famous year 'round mulching system, to give all gardeners a fine book for their libraries.

GARDENING WITH NATURE: By Leonard Wickenden. This is a thoroughly reliable, how-to-do-it guide to all phases of growing things for home consumption. A step-by-step exposition, by one of America's most successful all-around gardeners, of the way to raise the finest-quality food that nature can provide; food that by actual test contains the highest vitamin and mineral count—all without resort to chemical fertilizers or poison sprays.

ORGANIC GARDENING: By J. I. Rodale. Lists of diseases, insects, methods of making compost at different rates of decay and quality of product, and other suggestions make it a practical hand-book as well as a plea for a better understanding of how valuable organic matter is to the soil.

ORGANIC FARMING: By Hugh Corley. Perhaps this book's greatest value lies in its detailed description of the actual methods of organic farming, and in the author's observation of nature at work on his own farm. It will interest both the beginner at organic gardening and the non-gardening reader, while established farmers and gardeners will want to try some of Mr. Corley's organic methods including his practical ideas for making compost on farms. A variety of livestock is dealt with, and there is a stimulating discussion of pastures.

CHEMICALS, HUMUS, AND THE SOIL: By Donald P. Hopkins. This is an extensively revised edition of a book which has already proved its worth. It contains much fresh information about fertilizers and their use. "A big contribution to our literature on the feeding of crops, and no matter to which school of thought we may happen to belong, he has presented the other side so clearly that no one can fail to understand it."

BORAGE: (*Borago officinalis*) An annual with blue flowers, borage is a fine honey plant in most regions because of its continuous flowering season.

A close relative is the well-known Forget-me-not. In this family there are many herbs, for example alkanet (*Anchusa*), navelwort (*Omphalodes*), comfrey (*Symphytum*), lungwort (*Pulmonaria*), and others, besides the garden flowers, Mertensia and Heliotrope.

If the leaves were not covered with white hairs, they would perhaps be more welcome in the kitchen than they are. Roughly, they taste something like cucumbers, and some people like to add them chopped finely to lettuce and mixed salads. They can also be cooked as greens and added to stews. They are said to have laxative effects and it may be due to them that borage is effective also in cases of bad complexion.

This decorative annual, growing two to three feet tall, does best in dry sunny places. It blooms all summer; sow seed directly in garden.

B. laxiflora is a perennial rock garden plant, that should be mulched with straw as winter protection.

BORDER: This term generally refers to a long and narrow strip in the garden, sometimes between properties, often along front walks. The actual form that the border may take depends on the general contour of the land, the architecture of the house and its proximity to the garden, walk, and drives, and innumerable other details, such as can only be judged by personal preferences. Borders may be of straight or curving lines, following the boundaries of the property, or enclosures of lawns and open spaces. The planting of a general border may consist of shrubs only or a combination of shrubs and hardy flowers; or it may combine, as is the common practice, annuals and perennials. Shaded borders are more difficult to plant if flowers are desired. As a general rule the border should be located as to receive several hours of sunlight a day.

The preparation of the soil for the herbaceous border should be most thorough. It should be prepared on the assumption that the majority of the plants, except such as need dividing, are to remain there for a number of years without removal. In choosing plants consider carefully their cultural requirements, and then place them according to their likes and dislikes. All of these points must be given consideration in preparing the soil. After the soil is in good general condition, bury a liberal supply of well-decayed manure to a depth of at least 18 inches.

This encourages the roots to penetrate deeply, so that in times of drought they are out of harm's way. Prepare the soil in the fall and let it settle over the winter. Spring planting is to be preferred to fall planting, in most cases. Heaving of new plants often results when they are set out in autumn, as they have no time to make new roots to anchor themselves in the ground securely before frost. This is the strongest argument for applying a mulch to the surface of the perennial border in the fall. For plants that have special soil preferences, arrange a pocket in which to place the plant. This allows plants of different soil requirements to be grown as companion plants.

The size of the border depends mainly upon the size of the area available. Be careful of the curves, so that they are graceful and free-flowing. In a broad border such as this there are numerous opportunities for providing an element of variety and surprise which do much to make a garden desirable. Three or four heights of plants—very tall, tall, medium, and low—can be accommodated, and a background of shrubbery, a vine-clad wall, or trellis add to the effect. Irregular silhouettes, rather than straight ones, are always preferable. Some of the medium-sized plants may be brought toward the front of the border to form little coves in which smaller plants may be grouped. For instance, iris and peonies may be planted in drifts toward the back and then smaller drifts placed near the front in an uneven line, so that pansies, creeping phlox, and other low-growing flowers may blossom there. This irregularity applies to height as well as to the border line; a more artistic effect is obtained if plants of different heights are placed near each other. This provides variety in the skyline and avoids monotony, as a regular slope from back to front is apt to provide.

The distance at which plants are placed apart is dependent upon their habit of growth. Some of the stronger ones need as much as three or four feet—dahlias, for example. Mat plants, such as dwarf phlox and pinks, are placed only a few inches distant from each other. Crowded plants defeat their own ends, as they can neither be cultivated properly nor produce good flowers. The border may look skimpy the first year, but this is easily remedied by placing annuals between. After they reach maturity, many of the plants will need staking, to prevent their being toppled over by heavy winds. Provide supports that are as inconspicuous as possible and place them in such a manner that one scarcely realizes that the plants are dependent on artificial means of support. Hoops placed around them before they reach their growth will be hidden almost entirely by the subsequent growth. Peonies and delphiniums can always be cared for in this manner. Division of the clumps will help to keep strong plants from encroaching upon their less vigorous neighbors. Some kinds will need replanting. If the shoots in the center of the plant become weak and spindling with yellowish leaves, this means that they have used up the available plant food in the soil. When you reset such plants, place manure or a balanced fertilizer in the soil, to provide extra nourishment.

After it is once established the work required to care properly for the perennial garden is to keep down weeds, maintain a surface mulch to conserve moisture, thin out plants and young seedlings, provide support for topheavy plants, watch and destroy insects or diseases, and fertilize and replant such of the rampant growers as need it each year.

Winter protection, after decaying stems and leaves are removed from the perennials, will prevent heavy losses. Partly decayed manure, two or three inches thick, will not only protect the plants from loss of moisture, but provides a source of nutriment as well. Hay or cornstalks are also excellent. Inasmuch as you are covering the plants, not to keep them warm, but to maintain even conditions about them in periods of freezes and thaws, do not cover them too early. Wait until winter has set in in earnest.

Plan your border on paper first. In this way you can get a good general idea of what it will look like. Rough out approximately the amount of space given to each plant group and fill in its color or colors with water colors. Large plants should be figured as about three or four—no more—to a group, and of the small ones not less than a dozen. Try to get the border at least six feet wide, and if it is very small keep one or two dominating colors.

Perennials which require several years to bloom from seed: Monkshood, wild indigo, Christmas rose, peonies, and globe flower.

Perennials which bloom the first year from seed: Annual strains of hollyhocks, camomile, Chinese larkspur, pinks and sweet Williams and forget-me-nots.

Perennials to grow in the shade: Monkshood, lily-of-the-valley, bleeding-heart, plantain lily, trilliums, anemones (Japanese) and wild-flowers, bee balm, bugloss, foxgloves, pansies and bluebells.

Perennials with evergreen leaves: Candytuft, coral bells, flax, thyme, sedums of many kinds, and yucca.

Perennials for dry soils: Butterfly weed, columbine, blanket flower, cranesbill, and stonecrop.

DWARF BORDERS: In this group are edgings for perennial borders and some of them are little gems. The plants may be perennials or annuals that are used for this purpose.

For a sunny warm border, Dianthus or Garden Pinks has long been a favorite in gardens. Most of them have fragrant flowers and the tufty green foliage is attractive when the plants are not in flower. In recent years many new introductions have been added to the list. There are single and double-flowered species. Dianthus Allwoodii alpenus grows from four to six inches high and makes a compact plant. It thrives in good garden soil that has free drainage and flowers the first year from seed if sown in a greenhouse bench in late winter or early spring.

Dianthus Bristol Purity has large double white flowers; Bristol Maid, double pink, and both have a fragrance that is most refreshing. They bloom continuously.

Trim these plants after the flowering season is over for the year. This will encourage new growth to start and will keep the plants compact. Garden Pinks are easily raised from seed. Fill a flat or seed pan with light sandy soil and water thoroughly. This will settle the soil, which should come up to an inch from the rim of the flat; broadcast the seeds and cover lightly with soil.

When seeds do not germinate well, it is usually because they have been covered too deep. Put the flat in a shady place for a few days; at the end of the first week the seeds will be coming up, when they require more light and air to prevent them from being drawn up and becoming weak.

There are places in the garden where the Candy-tufts are good plants for finishing off a border of mixed perennials or a group of low-growing shrubs. Iberis sempervirens are covered with white flowers in spring, completely hiding the dark evergreen foliage. I. Little Gem begins to flower in May or June, depending on the climate. Its uniform neat habit of growth makes it valuable as an edging plant. I. Snowflake has flowers three times as large as sempervirens.

These Candytufts do best with a few hours of morning sun and a moderate amount of water. Cultivate the ground around them frequently.

Edgings give beds and borders a

neat trim appearance and make a nice finish to the planting.

Some edging plants of spreading habit lose favor with gardeners because they will not remain within their allotted space, but start off on a rambling career. A little trimming back of shoots will help matters and make the plants more compact.

A fine plant of neat habit and rich green foliage is *Arenaria montana*. The plants are covered with pure white flowers that are always admired. This plant should be more generally used. A sunny place in the garden and rather gritty soil that offers free drainage suits it very well.

When soil packs, mix it with coarse sand and well-decayed compost from the compost heap. This will open it up and make a soft root run for the roots to penetrate deep down and make a good root system, as well as giving the plant good development above ground.

The various fragrant Thymes make a nice informal edging to a border that has a flagstone path along the planting. Encourage the plants to encroach on the flagstones in a natural, irregular way, which gives an artistic effect and is a change from the well-trimmed edging.

From the Azores comes Thyme Azorious, growing four inches high and covered with purple flowers in early summer. The Lemon Thyme Citroidorus makes a small plant of bushy habit. T. serpyllum album forms a neat green mat only four inches high; during summer the plants are covered with white flowers, and there are other varieties.

For borders that are in light shade during the hottest hours of the day, use the dwarf Campanulas. They like a rich, well-drained sandy soil. Space them eight to ten inches apart. C. Carpatica, the Carpathian Harebell, is a neat plant, growing six to eight inches high. The flowers are a clear blue and are carried well above the foliage. There is also a white form

of this plant. Cullinmore is a hybrid form of Carpatica. Its blue flowers are produced during the summer, and there are many more species.

Violas and Pansies are popular as edging plants. They thrive in deeply dug rich loam with plenty of compost worked into the soil. They flower for a long time when used where the winter climate is mild. If they are planted in the early part of October, when buds have formed they will flower during winter and spring till May. Top dress the ground with old manure twice during that time, in January and March to have the flowers large.

The Hybrid Gazanias make a strong edging for a border of plants or shrubs in a sunny warm position as at the side of garden steps, or for shrubs in a warm place. These plants flower the first year from seed if it is sown in a greenhouse bench in winter. The color of the flowers may be white, yellow, amber, pink and various reds. These plants are good drought resisters, requiring very little water.

If it is only for the summer months that the edging is needed, annuals may be the best material to use. Buy young plants in flats at nurseries or sow seeds in the ground where the plants are to grow and bloom. Ageratum Blue Ball flowers over a long season. A. Midget Blue, four inches high, has azure blue flowers; and A. Blue Perfection, dark violet. In annual Alyssums, Carpet of Snow and Little Gem are excellent.

Lobelias do well in light shade and the light or dark blue flowers decorate the plants for most of the year in a mild climate.

Phlox Drummondi is a useful annual and is easily grown from seed, sown in the ground where the plants are to grow and flower. It does not make vigorous plants when seeds are sown in a flat and the seedlings transplanted to the border. Sow the seeds where plants are to grow and flower. They require a sunny position in good rich soil. The flowers may be had in a variety of colors.

Portulaca, another annual, has single or double flowers and does well in full sun. Seeds are sown in the ground where it is to grow and flower. If the seedlings come up too thick thin them out.

When any one of these plants need feeding use liquid cow manure once every two weeks during the growing season. This will build up the plants, produce larger flowers and more of them.—*E. Hamilton Fairley.*

See also ANNUALS; BEDDING; FLOWER GARDENING

BORECOLE: *see* KALE

BORERS: Generally, the group of insects termed borers include the small grubs of various insects. Their presence is detected by the sight of a small hole eaten in trees or plant stems. Many borers attack plants that are not growing vigorously, thus organic methods which build a healthy soil and healthy plants will go far to prevent attack.

Pruning and burning any weakened branches that may be infested with borers will keep new plantings in better condition and less susceptible to borer injury. The maintenance of clean, thrifty plants is one of the basic principles of borer control. *See also* INSECT CONTROL; BRAMBLE FRUITS.

BORON: Boron is required by living organisms in very small amounts. Elements which are used in such small amounts are called *trace elements.*

A deficiency of boron in the soil causes such degenerative diseases as internal cork in apples, yellow of alfalfa, top rot of tobacco, cracked stem of celery, and heart rot and girdle of beets.

The amount of boron to be added depends upon its degree of deficiency in the soil. *See also* TRACE ELEMENTS; DEFICIENCIES, SOIL; FRUIT TREES, DEFICIENCY.

BOSTON FERN: *see* FERN

BOSTON IVY: *see* PARTHENOCISSUS

BOUGAINVILLEAS: Among the most colorful and long-flowering of semitropical vines. There are about a dozen species and varieties: in addition, new ones are being introduced from time to time. If possible it is desirable to buy this vine when in flower in order to have the color that is wanted, for different plants of the same variety sometimes vary in the color of the bracts (colored leaves directly below the petals). Those listed as Crimson Lake (*B. spectabilis*) may show lighter or darker coloring.

Bougainvillea need a warm, sunny place to grow plus a good supply of well-rotted manure or leaf mold. Good drainage is also of great importance.

PLANTING: In planting Bougainvilleas make the hole twice as deep and wide as the container. In the bottom of the hole put fully a foot or more of well-decayed compost and mix some good soil with it. These vines are difficult to transplant; they have top growth out of all proportion to the small root system. The best method is to slit down the four sides of the five-gallon container and leave the plant in it; the slit sides will allow for plenty of drainage and the roots will not be disturbed. Cut away the rim of the container so it will not show above ground and place the can with the plant in it in the middle of the hole. Then fill in with good rich soil. When the hole is almost filled in, have water from the hose run in gently until it settles the soil thoroughly. Add more soil and finish planting by making a well around the plant to hold water. After it is established and growing well, it will need only a moderate amount of water. Good drainage is very important so eight or nine inches of gravel or cut stone should be placed in the bottom of the hole, if there is any doubt about the drainage being good.

Bougainvilleas are easily grown from cuttings which root in a few weeks. The cuttings may be six to eight inches long, and are placed in a flat of sand or a greenhouse bench in a temperature of 65 to 75°.

VARIETIES: *B. spectabilis braziliensis* is the hardiest of this family—a rapid and robust grower. During the flowering season the vine is a mass of reddish purple. As companion vines it should have those with light yellow or light blue flowers, for its color is so dominant that it does not blend well with many colors.

B. spectabilis praetorius has beautiful bronzy bracts with apricot shading. It grows best in frostless areas or near the seacoast.

There are a few vines that may be used to ideal advantage in covering a large wall space or a high wire fence. They may be trained up either side of windows to frame them in areas free from frost. They grow up and over tall trees and will cover the branches with warm rich color. A tree that has died and was needed in that particular position as a screen, may have one or more of these vines trained up through the branches to produce almost the same effect as the live tree. They make a fine covering for an arbor that is to be an outdoor living room during the summer months, and will climb to the roof of a garage, converting it into

a spectacular mass of color. *B. spectabilis* San Diego is excellent for this purpose. The large crimson bracts are particularly fine and the vine makes a vigorous growth. B. Sunset has beautiful rich golden yellow bracts with lilac shading—an unusual and beautiful combination of color.

These vines are natives of Brazil and South America, introduced by a French navigator, De Bougainvillea. The flowers are small and inconspicuous, but they are surrounded by large and showy bracts which constitute the decorative value of the plants.

Bougainvilleas are injured by heavy frosts, but after being cut back, come out again with renewed vigor. They need a sunny warm place in the garden. These plants should be given a mulch of well-rotted manure or leafmold.

Bougainvilleas can be grown successfully in greenhouses in the north. They grow well and bloom profusely during the winter months. They make an excellent wall cover in greenhouses which have one end abutted against a building.—*E. Hamilton Fairley.*

BOX: *see* BOXWOOD

BOX-BARBERRY: (*Berberis thunbergi minor*) *see* BARBERRY

BOXES AND BASKETS, FLOWER: In addition to window boxes, popular containers for flowers include hanging baskets, wheelbarrows and pushcarts—even old rowboats—that can be set out on the lawn in all its blooming glory. Drainage is important in all of these containers—either through holes in the bottom or with plenty of stones or broken pots in the box.

Generally, most gardeners prefer to transplant seedlings into the boxes, rather than planting seeds directly. In this way, a greater variety of plants with more pleasing color combinations can be obtained.

To make a good, full, professional appearance one should use enough plants in the box to just about fill up the space. If plants are put in sparsely in the box in the hope that they will "fill out," then the summer will be half gone before you have a really colorful box.

So whether you buy or grow your plants, be generous in using them in a window box. Later in summer you should remove those which are done blooming or which are not doing well, in order to make room for the others which have grown larger. But this "waste" is inevitable to gain a pretty window box for the summer.

It's best to choose plants that stand up well to the summer heat, as well as ones that bloom steadily throughout the summer. Cannas or geraniums are often used as "center pieces," since their bright color and sturdy nature make them ideal. When placing plants, put the high ones in back and lower ones in front for color, as marigolds, petunias and ageratum. The front edge might consist of vines to cover the front and sides of the box. Vinca is a favorite for this, since it is fast-growing.

After all your pots are in place fill in the space between with potting mixture and press it well into place to make a solid mass. Then water thoroughly and the job is completed except for nipping off flowers and straggling stems.

After a window box has been planted for a month it will begin to look rather wild. At this time it is best to take out one or two of the largest plants and a couple of the second row. Trim the others a little to make them bushy and fill up the space. At this time also dig out some of the upper layer of ground and add rich soil. This practice can be repeated again during the summer when the plants do not look well. Mulch with cocoa shells, buckwheat hulls or similar material.

INDOORS: In a sunroom or heated porch or conservatory, pot brackets and hanging plants always add to the appearance of the room. There are numerous varieties of wrought iron brackets to be had these days. The trick for the gardener is to find unusual plants to put in them rather than the usual ivy.

The strawberry begonia or geranium (*Saxifraga sarmentosa*) is an interesting addition to any room with its long trailers of baby plants. Other begonias lend themselves to this type of holder as well as trailing lantana.

Trellises add to the floral appearance of a room and aid the growth of vines. Occasionally one sees an ivy that has grown ten feet or more up the side of a window and over its top. Indoors it is always desirable to try for something like this which is a little unusual.

All of these indoor gardens should be given a vacation outdoors in summer for it is during the summer that they have their real opportunity to grow and gather strength. All plants are under a certain handicap indoors with a limited amount of sunlight, a dry atmosphere and sometimes gas fumes in the air. No matter how well your plant does inside during the winter it will do better outdoors in the summer.

BOX-THORN: *see* MATRIMONY VINE

BOXWOOD: (*Buxus*) Boxwood, or box, is a most valued evergreen for hedges and topiary work, just as it has been since the time of the Romans. The dwarf type, *B. sempervirens suffruticosa,* is the best for edgings. Box is expensive, but it can be grown easily at home from cuttings, taken from mature shoots in early fall.

CULTURE: Boxwood will grow well in most well-drained soils, and does best under partial shade. Some form of winter protection is necessary in the North. Boxwood is such a slow grower, and mature plantings are so valuable, that the pains of care are well worth the effort.

INSECTS AND DISEASES: The chief enemies of boxwood, other than severe winters, are boxwood canker (a fungus

[Nectria] disease), gray mottling of leaves caused by spider mites.

PREVENTION PROGRAM: In spring, go over the plantings very carefully, pruning out all dead wood and brushing out dead leaves and other debris with a whisk broom. Then apply a dormant oil spray. Check carefully through the season for signs of disease and prune out infected wood immediately.

B. japonica, which grows to about six feet, is considered the hardiest of the boxwoods, while *B. microphylla* in the dwarf class is of equal hardiness. It can be propagated by cuttings from mature wood in early autumn or by layers, while the dwarf forms can be increased by division.

When transplanting, always set them deeper than their previous ground level, making sure that the hole is deep and large. It is best to clip boxwood in late August or early fall. Give plants an annual dressing of organic fertilizer, such as compost or composted manure; boxwood will also benefit greatly from a mulch of similar materials.

BOYSENBERRY: The boysenberry is more like a blackberry than a rasp-

The boysenberry needs plenty of room for proper cultivation because of the height of its canes. Mulch heavily and protect well before the winter.

berry. Because of its woody, wandering stem it will need support. Set sturdy posts fully five feet tall, and string two wires between them, one at a three, the other at a five foot level. Canes which have borne fruit are cut down immediately after the harvest. Canes grow eight to ten feet high.

The root area of the boysenberry should be heavily mulched before winter sets in, and unlike our other brambles the canes should be laid on the ground and covered with a light layer of straw before there is any probability of snow flying. In spite of their apparent strength they are sensitive bushes. Culture is similar to that required by the loganberry.

Finally, a cardinal fact concerning the brambles. The canes of all these are biennial, but the roots live for several years and are perennial. So, unless *vigorous pruning* is practiced every year, the berry patch will soon bcome a wilderness of dead canes. *See also* BRAMBLE FRUITS.

BRAMBLE FRUITS: (*Rubus*) These fruits are of American origin from wild species, having stems that are more or less prickly. They are intermediate between an herb and a shrub, that is, the root is perennial but the stems die back nearly to the crown the second season of their life after maturing a single crop of fruit. There are, however, some exceptions to bearing, as in the case of the everbearing species, which bear terminally and continuously all summer. The cultivated brambles are prickly bushes bearing berries and include six species named below:

1. The American red raspberry—*Rubus strigosus.*

2. The European red raspberry—*R. idaeus.*

3. The blackberry—*R. nigrobaccus.*

4. The blackcap raspberry—*R. occidentalis.*

5. The northern dewberry—*R. villosus.*

6. The purple-cane—*R. neglectus.*

There are also the loganberries and the youngberries. The canes of the first three species listed above grow upright throughout the season; those of the second three grow more or less upright the first season but later droop down near the tip and may strike root.

The red raspberry is the most important species in this group, and is an especially desirable fruit for desserts, jams, drying, and deep freezing, which makes it available in apparently fresh condition as a garden berry. It has become commercialized in cultivation all over the United States and in southern Canada. With due care in selecting for hardiness, or with winter protection it can be grown as far north as any cultivated fruits.

PROPAGATION OF BRAMBLES: It is important to know how and when to propagate the bramble fruits. One can perpetuate his own plants if familiar with methods and devices that can be easily understood and practiced. Moreover, it is interesting to propagate and sometimes economically important to do it. Here are a few suggestions:

Tip layering. Several species are propagated by layering the tip of the plant in late summer. Among these plants are the black and purple raspberries, dewberries, loganberries, and trailing blackberries. A few of the red raspberries will tip layer. This work is usually done in the fall when growth for the season is nearly completed. The layering is done by hand. For best results the soil should be loose and moist. There are two important factors for good rooting. The land should be light, well drained but not dry; the plant nutrients, especially organic matter, should be fairly abundant. If the land is not fertile there will be poor rootage and inferior plants also. Layers from one-year-old plants are generally better than those from new ones. Under good conditions five or more layers may be obtained from each parent plant.

The time to layer is indicated by the tip becoming slightly thickened and snake-like or rat-tailed, and growing without leaves. Late August and early September are the best times to tip layer. On good friable soil the tip will root of itself but a little assistance will insure it, and more will set if slightly covered with soil or partially imbedded. Pegging down the tips or placing stones over them is unnecessary except on windy sites or where the surface soil may wash. Plants thus layered in early fall should have abundant roots and a strong bud before winter. A larger per cent of tip layers and better plants may be secured from cuttings of the roots one inch long and started under glass with mild bottom heat. Such root cuttings are made in autumn, packed in sand in shallow boxes and stored for callousing in a cool cellar until February or March when they are planted in the propagating bed from which they are set out in the garden in due time. Good plants can be secured by using a narrow spade or heavy trowel, better than by plowing a furrow for tip layering. In any case, if the soil is hard it should be loosened so that the tip may readily strike root. Three or four inches of earth make a good covering. A vertical rather than a horizontal placement is better for rooting. Inexperienced gardeners often use the horizontal placement and therefore do not obtain the best plants. One should use for planting the best specimens that he can get. Good roots are important. Healthy stock is also imperative.

In setting out the rooted plants one should be sure the soil is fitted for them. It should be open, deep, friable, enriched with manure or compost, and kept in good tilth. Set the plants three or four feet apart in rows six or seven feet apart. Some of the larger growing varieties should have an extra foot each way. Care should be taken in handling not to injure the bud at the crown as growth starts from this bud. One should also take care that the layered plants do not dry out in planting. Keep them moist.

In digging the tip—best done in spring after being attached to the parent plant all winter—one can use a four-pronged potato hook or fork. In separating the layer plants from the parent, one should leave six to eight inches on the tip; and these stubs may serve as handles in handling the plants but they may be shortened to four inches after being planted. It is well to discard any and all unhealthy or weak plants, using only the best that are well rooted. This results in more uniform plantings.

Suckering. Red raspberries are propagated by suckers that grow from underground stems or roots. These suckers appear in the spring and continue to form fairly well into the season and are the forerunners of new plants like the ones from which they came. One can get red raspberry plants by digging up the entire plant, or just the suckers. It is better to have separate plants for propagation and for production. The suckers may be set in permanent places or, what is better, grow them in a sort of nursery where they may build up strong root systems before being set as permanent plants. The small or so-called young plants can be pulled up, but it is better to dig them to save all good roots. When planting, it is well to follow the plant as to distance, etc., as given earlier for tip layered plants. Sucker plants generally do better if held over one year before permanent setting. There is less labor in handling sucker plants than tip layered ones. Blackberries can be propagated also by suckers as the red raspberries, but root cuttings are generally preferred.

Root cuttings. These are made of blackberry plants. They should be three to four inches long and the size of a lead pencil. These cuttings are best made in the fall and are then stratified in moist sand, or buried outdoors in a well drained location. When set out to grow in the spring they are placed horizontally in a trench covered with several inches of soil. Better growth is secured by setting the cuttings in a frame with bottom heat supplied with manure. After one year of growth in the frame they are set out in permanent places. Discard any weak plants at this time. It is urgent that the transplanting be done while the plants are dormant and before any growth starts. Good yields can only be secured when good foundation stock is used in the plantings. Look for good fibrous root systems.

INSECTS AND DISEASES OF BRAMBLES: Generally there are more losses and wastes the country over from insects and diseases than from any other cause, unless it be bad weather such as low temperatures or summer drought. This is due to lack of knowledge of pests and how to control them; consequently attention is drawn to the major enemies, so that control can be secured without the use of sprays.

Sawfly. Raspberry and blackberry leaves are often damaged by the worm stage of the sawfly. The injurious stage in its life cycle is the worm, which is a small green caterpillar one-half inch long and covered with numerous spines. These creatures strip the leaves by skeletonizing them into shreds, baring the ribs and veins. The adult is a fly about one-fourth inch long with a wing spread of one-half inch. The body and the wings are black, except some of the body segments which are rusty and yellowish on the under side. The male fly is smaller than the female. The sawflies appear about the middle of May in the Northeastern States and soon the female deposits her eggs under the skin of the leaf, forming white spots on the top surface. The young worms eat the tender foliage and later devour most of the leaf as indicated above. In the garden the egg clusters on the lower side of leaves can be collected and destroyed. Sticky fly paper or that smeared with molasses will catch and hold many flies till they perish. In some cases the small worms can be collected and destroyed before much harm has been done.

Mosaic. This is the most serious disease of raspberries and needs careful attention. It is characterized by a mottled condition of the leaves, with alternating green and light patches, a stunting of growth, and some curling of leaves. The plants are inclined to be somewhat dwarfed in protracted cases, with a lessened crop and poorer fruit. There are two forms of mosaic, red and yellow, both of which are transmitted by plant lice and leaf hoppers, which inoculate healthy plants with the disease virus. Latham, Chief, Viking, St. Regis and Dike are nearly immune to this trouble; Cuthbert, Queen and June are quite susceptible and need rogueing (cutting out affected plants) twice in June, once in July, and once in August each summer. Control consists in removing by pulling or digging or burning all affected plants and using only such land as is 200 feet away from wild or other cultivated raspberry plants. Watch all healthy plants adjacent to diseased ones, and eliminate them also if they appear infected.

Crown gall. This is recognized by the presence of galls or knots on the roots and sometimes on the canes and by symptoms on the foliage much like those of mosaic. Plants are weakened by the presence of this bacterium, which invades the tissues and causes the galls to form. As the gall decays, the germ lives for some time in rotted tissue in the soil and causes reinfection under favorable conditions, such as open wounds. Control measures are confined to the planting of gall-free stock in gall-free land (not recently used for Latham); together with absolute destruction of affected plants. Latham is quite subject to gall, and all new stock needs inspection. Do not replant Latham on the same area. Take a new plot.

Rust. The rust disease of raspberry plants, also known as anthracnose, cane spot, gray bark, and scab, occurs in larger or smaller quantities wherever raspberries are grown. It may be found in all small gardens. The amount of damage or the losses incurred depend much on the weather, general sanitary conditions, and the location of the planting. Rust is recognized by small spots unevenly distributed on the stems which at first are reddish brown and which are less than one-fourth in diameter.

Later these spots have white, slightly shrunken centers surrounded by a red ring. On the leaves may be seen small yellowish spots one-sixteenth inch in diameter which turn red as they grow and elongate and possess a light colored center still surrounded by a red ring. Prolonged rains, crowded plants, and dense shade favor the disease. The scars on the stems are scattered over the cane and seem more abundant on the young and succulent ones. Infection occurs after rains and the disease may spread rapidly. Sometime in June small whitish spots one-sixteenth of an inch across appear on the leaves. These leaf spots later turn red as they enlarge. The leaf lesions are somewhat similar to those on the canes. While leaf infections do not usually cause serious damage, under certain conditions the leaf spurs may be defoliated. Anthracnose spots on the leaves may easily be confused with septoria leaf spot; but anthracnose spot is angular and light in color, whereas septoria spot is always circular and somewhat darker.

While heavy infection on young canes can stunt them seriously, ordinarily the cane infections are not harmful but are noticeable. If the lesions develop sufficiently, the affected canes may crack open during the winter and subsequently dry out and break off during their fruiting year. It is interesting and important to be able to detect rust and deal with it.

All the brambles are subject to anthracnose, and any or all of the above-ground parts of the plants may be attacked. The severity of the disease varies with different kinds of brambles. The black raspberry and trailing blackberry plants such as dewberry, boysenberry, and youngberry are especially susceptible to injury, so much so that thorough control of anthracnose is a practical necessity for their successful production. Purple and red varieties of raspberry are more resistant to the disease than the black sorts. Protection against anthracnose is desirable. Plant only healthy stock that is certified so as not to introduce it into new plantings.

Rust or anthracnose is caused by a fungus, *Elsinae veneta,* which lives in infected canes. In the spring small spores, formed on the lesion of the previous year's canes, are blown about and spread the disease to young canes in wet weather. These infections produce thousands of spores which are spread by summer rains to still other uninfested plants nearby. During the winter the anthracnose fungus lives under the bark of infested canes and results in further spread the following spring. Rust lesions similar to those on young canes may also appear on the fruiting branches, leaf stems, fruit stalks, and small leaves around the unopened flowers. On these the lesions first appear as small purple spots which later become one-eighth to one-quarter of an inch long. The center of the lesion soon turns white and is surrounded by a purple border. In a healthy cluster of raspberries all of the berries ripen and remain attached until they have reached maturity. But a fruiting cane infested with anthracnose will have lesions on the main stem, fruiting laterals, and fruit pedicels. Lesions of the fruiting laterals of the fruit stem cut off the food material for the young berries. Small green, extremely hard berries which never increase in size or ripen to any degree are found. When the fruit is diseased the entire berry or such parts as are infected may remain

small and dry or they may develop without much flavor and turn a dull dark brown color. Affected canes should be destroyed.

The application of sanitary methods is the most practical way of controlling most of the diseases and insects of brambles; and in many cases is the only means. Eradicate all wild plants and stray bushes in the vicinity of cultivated patches and destroy heavily diseased plants before establishing new ones nearby. All prunings should be removed from the field and destroyed. By each treatment most of the less common troubles can be kept from developing to serious proportions. A careful check of the patch should be kept for such serious troubles as crown gall and virus diseases of raspberries and orange rust of blackberries. At their first appearance in the field all affected plants should be removed in their entirety—including all roots; and burned. Once such diseases as these have made much headway there is little that can be done to check them and new plantings should be started. In brief, plant only certified stock; destroy all old canes which may harbor the disease; thin out the canes to let in air and sun.

Borers. Wilting tips of raspberry stalks are symptoms of this insect trouble. The creatures are slender, cylindrical, long-horned beetles two-thirds of an inch in length which lay eggs in canes and cut two rings around the cane one or two inches apart in the twig about eight inches back from the tip. The part above the girdled ring soon wilts, and later dies. The work is done by a white grub which hatches from an inlaid egg, works down the stem sometimes boring the second year even to the crown of the plant. Control is by cutting off the cane below the lower ring, allowing the cut off ends to wilt on the ground, resulting in the death of the grub. It is important to repeat the tip pruning as long as wilting tips can be found. Begin inspecting in early July and continue each week with it until late summer. It will help much if attention is also paid to the neighboring plants, including the wild ones along the borders of fences and roadside and woodside; and to those in adjacent gardens. Insects and diseases often move rapidy from garden to garden so that constant vigilance is the price of healthy, productive plants.

Leaf hoppers. These creatures that, when disturbed, hop from plant to plant with the aid of strong hind legs, are properly named. They jump and hop, sometimes in groups, and there is no mistaking their identity. The leaf hoppers of the rose, feed on the older and lower leaves, causing discoloration in spots that are nearly white, but very small; sometimes there are curlings of leaves and defoliation. The species of hopper on the rose hibernates in the egg stage in little slits in the bark. There are only two broods in a season. Sticky fly paper will catch many of them.

Mildew. This makes a fine cobweb-like growth of a white fungus which is common and widespread. The fuzzy growth occurs most abundantly on the top surfaces of leaves and is quite abundant in wet seasons. Berry leaves are conspicuous sufferers from powdery mildew. The fungus is white but the winter spores are black as seen late in the season, and show as mere black dots over the surface of the foliage. Practically the whole fungus is on the exterior, the entire body of it being superficial. Control is by the collection and destruction of affected parts—or sometimes a whole plant is efficacious. Thin out the plants to let in sun and air. Keep the plants dry.

Red Spiders. The minute creatures known as red spiders affect many herbaceous plants as well as some woody ones. Phlox illustrates the first group and raspberry plants the second class. Spiders seem to be small red dots, usually enmeshed in fine webby growth which is their nest. They assemble on the underside of leaves, rarely on top, and occur in large numbers. They are so small they can hardly be seen without a magnifying glass but their bright red color distinguishes them. They eat the skin of leaves and some of the inside tissues, and in the aggregate do much damage. They are not true insects as they have eight instead of six legs and are a species of spider.

Red spiders eat ravenously on leaves of phlox, raspberries, carnations, and many other plants. They are rarely suspected until much harm has been done. Leaves of affected plants look pale, unthrifty or undersized and are of little value to the plant because of injury. Red spiders may spread disease, hence there is need of control.

The destruction of affected parts when generally infested, will suppress and control these creatures. Wetting down the plants with a forceful stream of water will wash off many of them, and they may perish before they can return to the plant. All applications of water from the hose should be made toward the under surface of the leaves and it is a hard task to get this thoroughly done. Use an angular nozzle or a curved one to get the right delivery to dislodge the creatures.

PLANTING BRAMBLES: There is a number of important points about starting a planting of brambles. Some relate to purchasing of plants, others to handling and planting, and still others to early care. Here is a little information about each point.

Buying Plants. In ordering plants from a nursery, it is urgent to insist on stock that is certified or true to name and free of disease. Most states have a certification system but not all nurserymen take advantage of it. Certification as clear of mosaic is the most important thing, as it can be done only in June and July, and the disease is not detectable in the winter season. Rust or anthracnose is easily carried on transplants, and is a rather serious disease, therefore it is important to avoid getting it. It is well to order plants far in advance of delivery to insure good specimens and ample time to ship them in advance of a rush season. They can be stored in a moist cool place or partly covered with soil till planted.

Setting Plants. Spring planting is generally preferred if not done too late. Often there is delay in shipments. The plants should be dormant and shoots should not be started. If prompt shipments are insisted upon, there will be less reason for delay and belated plantings.

The next most important thing after trueness to name and freedom from disease is a good root system. There should be many fibrous roots and few if any large ones. Good roots are the foundation of all plants. They should be packed so they will not dry out, for drying is fatal to the life of the plant. Waterproof paper outside the moss will give good protection, if crates are not used. *Tight boxes should never be used.*

In northern regions the best time to set tip plants is in early spring as soon as the soil can be prepared. In southern regions fall planting is preferred. Red raspberries and blackberries are carefully set in early spring, a season much preferred to late autumn planting. Fall planting is well enough, if not done too late. Six weeks is not too much time to get established before freezing weather. This is important. Red raspberry plants should have completed a year's growth from the sucker before being planted. Blackberry root cuttings also should have a year's growth before being sold or set.

Good surface earth should be placed about the roots of all transplants. Subsoil is less desirable and may result in a poor or tardy start of plants. Fall planting is open to the objection that it may be done too late, and if done early the leaves have to be stripped to prevent drying out. Moreover, if cold weather comes prematurely, the plants will not get estab-lished before cold comes to stay, and the plants do not survive the winter. Early fall planting is imperative if the plants are to do well. However, many nurserymen prefer to make sales and shipments in the fall to reduce their spring rush, and this is human nature. Fall planting often necessitates the removal of leaves from the plants which means extra labor and expense. So under all considerations spring planting is better for Northeastern states.

Care of Soil. In years gone by clean cultivation has been the rule. In addition, commercial fertilizer has been added, without due regard for the need of manures; and perhaps without full consideration of the value of mulches as an alternative to clean cul-ture. In many soils the need for or-ganic matter has far exceeded the need for ready made fertilizers. Hith-erto mulches have been viewed as chiefly valuable in winter to hinder deep freezing. These objectives are commendable and should be continued for their special seasonal values. But the building up of the organic content of the soil is also of tremendous impor-tance. As an alternative to continuous clean cultivation as some practice it and recommend to others, there is need for greater use of mulches. In the home garden mulching with straw or a loose covering of leaves or other material is a distinct advantage and should come into more general use. Some of the special advantages are to conserve moisture, avoid the expense of tillage; and to prevent the ground from becoming hard through tramping of pickers; and to lessen the amount of dirt on the fruit. The mulch also hinders the excessive development of unneeded new suckers. Then, too, in some cases where there is a slope it prevents erosion and wasting of rich surface soil. All these are important and the last is not the least important. Compost is recommended.

One can easily add a few more points in favor of organic matter. It has value in furnishing a medium for soil microorganisms, including those that fix atmospheric nitrogen. It contains major and minor mineral elements left behind in plant residues to be used in new crops. Mulches together with manure improve the physical properties of both light and heavy soils. It is therefore seen that organic matter is the key to many soil problems relating to soil fertility.

Winter Protection. The canes of some varieties need some winter protection, especially the first year ones, This relates to attention in addition to mulches for roots and low down buds. One plan is to bend the first year canes down and cover them with soil. This is done as late as possible before the ground freezes and when the canes are dormant, and the wood well hardened. Two men may work together; one bends down the tips and holds them in place while the other throws soil over them to hold them down. The pressure of the foot against the base of the cane helps to prevent breakage. Enough soil and mulch—three to four inches, is placed over the stems to keep them dormant and prevent freezing and thawing in variable weather. In the spring the canes should be uncovered while still dormant and before the buds begin to swell; otherwise, many buds may be broken off. This work is done as soon as the frost is out of the ground. *This type of winter protection is very special* for new varieties or somewhat tender ones, and particularly for the first year and for first year canes. It entails too much work as an annual practice. It may be pointed out that dewberries, loganberries, youngberries, and certainly boysenberries in the Northeast—if undertaken, will need covering especially the first winter till the plants get well established and the roots go down well into the soil. Coverings should be made before freezing weather in the fall and removed in the spring after all danger of freezing weather is past.

It is important that raspberry plants pass the winter in good condition. To insure a good crop next year and the maintenance of the plants for the years ahead, it is well to give the plants the necessary and suitable fall care. This embraces detopping when needed, the usual careful fall pruning, staking or wiring, and mulching in most places to reduce premature or over freezing of the roots. A few suggestions may be offered on each of these topics.

Some plants grow too tall and spindling. Slender canes may droop or break when weighed down with snow or ice; and they may be whipped in the wind beyond useful endurance and the buds may be brushed off. Consequently the slender canes should be cut back part way on the stalk. Canes that are more than six feet tall need detopping. An exception may be made with everbearing varieties such as Indian Summer, Raniere (St. Regis), etc., for these bear mostly at the tip where much of the fruiting wood grows. Some varieties like Herbert, when grown in rich moist soil, may send up canes to eight or ten feet, and in such cases nearly half of the growth should be removed. Detopping is especially imperative if the leaves do not drop at the normal time for they catch the snow and ice and are much damaged in case of early storms. Do not detop in summer; it has a bad effect: wait till fall.

Pruning Brambles. A few small tools for pruning and thinning bush fruits and other brambles are a convenience but one can get along with a strong sharp pocket knife. Much better work can be done and much time saved with suitable tools. In earlier years and to some extent in present times, the raspberry hook is handy. It is used for cutting off dead canes that have fruited and do not bear again. The cutting part is made of a rod of good steel, five-sixteenth inch in diameter, flattened and curved at the distil end with a thin edge on the concave side of the curve. The handle should be three feet long and the cutting edge placed at the base of a cane when a quick pull severs the stem. It is important to cut close to the ground with no tall stubs to be in the way, or to look bad.

The pruning knife is useful for small woody shoots and is all that some people use. The blade should be of good steel and the point should be curved forward a little to prevent the edge from slipping off when the cut is made. The handle should be large to avert blistering the hand and the base of the blade should be thick to furnish support for the thumb, and the rivet should be strong to sustain hard pressure upon the handle. In using the knife, the shoot to be cut off should generally be pressed with one hand toward the member that supports it, and the blade should be inserted at the proximal side. One needs to be cautious and careful in the work. Pruning shears are commonly used but they cut less smoothly and less closely. They should be kept sharp and the blades should articulate well. Cut but do not pry with them. Lever shears with three-foot handles are excellent and enable one to work among the brambles in pruning without scratching the hands. In any case, whatever tool is used, one should wear long wristed gloves to protect the hands and wrists. All prunings should be gathered and burned, for clearance of debris, to dispose of diseased canes and insect infested portions of the plants.

All old canes should be cut out, if not already done. Branched canes that have borne are useless and are an incumbrance. It is well to cut as low as possible so there will be no old stubs that protrude and annoy in another year. With the old dead canes out, then there is the further job of thinning out. Most clumps send up too many canes and they are too close together. Some are better than others. Choose to keep the sturdy ones. The stout thick ones are the most pro-

ductive; the slender ones are of little value as they do not bear very much. Take them out. Furthermore, some spacing should usually be done. Keep the canes from four to six inches apart if one can and still have enough left for good crops. Six or eight sturdy canes are enough for a clump. The yield depends more on the number of stocky canes well distributed than upon mere number of stems.

If the raspberries have not been pruned in the fall, it would do well to do the work at an early date in spring. To understand the principles of pruning one must recognize the fruiting habits. With the exception of a few new varieties, the raspberry cane fruits but once and then in the second year. The fruit is borne on lateral branches from one-year-old canes. The tops are biennial; the roots perennial. Shortly after fruiting, the branched cane dies and should be removed at once or before winter. In making the cut, be sure to make the incision as close to the ground as possible, leaving no stubs to bother another year. With the old canes once out, the only other pruning which is imperative is that which reduces the main canes of a plant to a number varying from four to six spaced about six inches apart. In cutting out surplus canes, eliminate first the slender ones; and thin out those which are too close together to permit full development. Cut out all diseased canes whenever found and burn them. The strong stocky canes which bear most of the fruit should be at least four or five inches apart. Although set in hills, the plants in spreading soon make a hedge row. Black raspberries sometimes need heading back to four feet of growth.

Cutting back the tips is necessary and desirable only in case of very rampant varieties or perhaps in the case of the Black Caps or Herberts which spread freely and extensively, or grow very tall in rich soil.

Winter Support. If it is likely that

winds and snows will break down the plants, they should be supported in some inexpensive way. A simple system of support may be made by a single small fence wire with posts 10 or 15 feet apart and one wire strung either side of the posts with the canes between the two wires held apart by a short cross bar. If substantial wire is used it should last for many years and be useful all the while by supporting the plants summer and winter.

Another simple way is to drive stakes in the middle of the clump and gather the canes loosely with a wire or strong string so that they may swing a little but not break down with snow and ice on them.

Mulching. Mulching in early winter before or after the ground is frozen to some extent before the snows come is often worth while. An application of eight to ten inches which will press down to four or five will not be too much material. Use leaves, straw, stover, or even small evergreen boughs which tend to hold the snow for a blanket, reduce danger from sudden deep freezing and winter injury resulting from drying out due to continuous cold dry winds. It will be well to mulch between the rows both fall and spring unless one prefers to practice clean cultivation. Build up also the organic content of the soil to enable it to retain the moisture better and to supply as well as to make available the necessary plant food materials in the land. Mulching is always advisable in localities subject to drought and in summer and autumn. Berry plants need plenty of water in developing the fruit so that the fruits may be large and luscious. A dry spell is likely to result in small berries that are rather dry and seedy.

Practical Hints. 1. *Soil.* No factor contributes more to the profitable production of raspberries than the location of the plot. The grower can afford the best land available. A fine deep sandy loam that holds moisture, contains much humus and retains moisture is ideal. Poor drainage is responsible for much winter injury. Mildew is serious on low land. Air drainage is important. Air pockets or low spots surrounded by higher ground are danger spots. Plant early varieties on a southern slope; late ones on a northern slope. In the latter case the soil dries out less and is cooler and better for for hot dry weather.

2. *Prepare land in advance.* Prepare land well before planting. Cultivate the soil six inches deep until it is mellow.

3. *Planting.* Do not let plants dry out at the roots before planting. Firm the soil about the roots. Plant four inches deep and practice shallow cultivation. Use lots of compost. Apply it late in the fall or early in spring, even in addition to the mulch. Let it take the place of commercial fertilizer. This helps the plants and holds up the soil.

BRASSICA: *see* MUSTARD

BRASSICA CAULORAPA: *see* KOHL-RABI

BRASSICA OLERACEA ACEPHALA: *see* KALE, COLLARD

BRASSICA OLERACEA BOTRYTIS: *see* CAULIFLOWER

BRASSICA OLERACEA CAPITATA: *see* CABBAGE

BRASSICA OLERACEA GEMMIFERA: *see* BRUSSELS SPROUT

BRASSICA OLERACEA ITALICA: *see* BROCCOLI

BRASSICA PEKINENSIS: *see* CHINESE CABBAGE

BRASSICA RAPA: *see* TURNIP

BREWERY WASTE: *see* HOPS

BRIDGE GRAFT: *see* GRAFTING

BROCCOLI: (*Brassica oleracea italica*) Broccoli is a hardy, fairly quick-maturing crop which belongs to the cabbage family. Nutritionists tell us that this vegetable should be a staple part of every diet. Producing both calcium and iron, it is also an excellent source of Vitamins A, B, and C.

Broccoli prefers coolness and moisture. In the regions of the country where summer arrives early, it will be most successful if planted as a fall crop. However, certain gardeners contend that it thrives best as a two-season crop for both spring and fall.

The Green Sprouting broccoli is a very promising vegetable and to be recommended to the seed buyer who desires to include it in his garden.

In the latter case, the seed is sown directly in the garden. When the stalks are three or four inches high, thin the plants, or better still, transplant them, so that they stand from eighteen to twenty-four inches apart in the row.

Seeds for indoor planting in the spring, are sown in a flat and covered with one-half inch of soil, and treated in the same manner as above when placed in the garden.

Broccoli seed may also be sown in the open garden at the end of May so that the plants mature their heads during cool autumn weather. Thus

you will readily see the wisdom of making two plantings: one by transplants set out about the end of March; the other, by seeds planted late in May.

Some watchfulness is necessary to see that the greenish heads are harvested before the flower buds expand and the curds dry out. After the main head has been cut the side shoots will continue to form smaller heads and provide a steady and heavy harvest over a considerable period. All heads should be cut off in such a manner that a fairly long stub of stem remains on the plant.

Broccoli is not a greedy feeder. It will do best in a moderately rich soil, provided that soil is well drained and easy to work. As to type of soil it is wonderfully obliging, thriving as it does in all kinds of lands from sand and clay to peat. It is a thirsty vegetable though and requires plenty of moisture.

The plant form of broccoli consists of a main thickened stalk, at the end of which develops a central cluster of tiny, dark green flower buds. Both stem and buds are edible, but care should be taken to pick them in time, for if not picked promptly the buds will open and their freshness will be dispersed. The leaves are edible too, but are not as tender as the stem and buds.

After the central head of broccoli has been cut for food, a number of small lateral roots will develop in the axils of the remaining leaves. These shoots, in their turn produce flower buds which are edible. So the welcome harvest of this important vegetable, even though taking eighty to ninety days to mature, will last for several weeks. Broccoli is a generous grower too. From four to six cuttings of stems and buds may be expected from every stalk.

There are two kinds of Broccoli; the heading type, which looks so much like a Cauliflower that it is sometimes marketed for such. This takes a long period to develop however. The Sprouting Broccoli, the kind which we have been dealing with here, is an exceptionally promising vegetable. One record of its growth tells of plants grown in the house during the very early spring, set in the garden the first of April, beginning to yield the middle of June. One of its most advantageous characteristics is its continuous harvest, which may be obtained from a single stem and one planting. The Italian Green Sprouting variety is one of the best known of its strains, and may well be the choice of the seed buyer.—*Leondra Sill Ashton.*

BROMFIELD, LOUIS: The late Louis Bromfield, well-known for his many fine novels, also contributed a great deal to the advancement of soil conservation methods. On his Malabar Farm in Lucas, Ohio, he demonstrated why organic matter was the founda-

Louis Bromfield combined in his lifetime the careers of author, soil researcher, organic farmer.

tion of any sound agricultural and gardening program. He also was one of the founders of Friends of the Land, an active conservation society. His books about his farming ideas include *Pleasant Valley, Out of the Earth* and *From My Experience.*

BROWALLIA: Tropical American herbs that are useful as hardy annuals. They can be grown from seeds or cuttings and will blossom into attractive blue flowers. Also grown as pot plants, browallias should be kept stocky by pinching and staking when necessary. Volunteers often occur. For indoor starting, plant in early spring, transplant outdoors in May.

Recommended for bedding plants, they do well in relatively poor soil, will bloom until frost. *B. americana* grows to about 15 to 20 inches high, while *B. speciosa* reaches a top growth of 14 inches.

BROWN ROT: Brown rot of stone fruits is caused by a parasitic fungus which spends the winter on dead fruits and leaves on the trees, or on the ground beneath the trees. You can stop brown rot before it starts. Remove all last year's fruits and leaves to the compost heap. Put a girdle of tanglefoot or other sticky substance around the tree trunk to prevent crawling insects from carrying the disease-producing fungus from the ground to the tree. Shake the trees frequently to displace any curculios which puncture the young fruits and enable the fungus to penetrate the fruit and cause the brown rot. *See also* DISEASE.

BROWSE: The tender portion (leaves, buds, twigs, and shoots) of woody plants consumed by animals.

BRUCE, MAYE: Miss Maye Bruce of Gloucestershire, Sapperton, England, is the acknowledged inventor of the so-called "quick return method" of composting, in which bacterial activators are used to speed up the composting process. Her main idea was to get organic methods applied to all our soil and to help gardeners in making compost. Her method is said to make possible the quicker return of living organisms to the soil, by means of an activator which accelerates decomposition of organic matter.

BRUSH CHIPS: Brush chippings and chipped tree branches, often available through local power company crews, are useful as a mulch around garden plants and trees. Since they are usually well-shredded, they can also be added to the compost pile where they will break down quickly. *See also* MULCH.

BRUSSELS SPROUT: (*Brassica oleracea gemmifera*) Brussels sprouts are readily distinguished from all other varieties of the cabbage tribe by the sprouts or buds, about the size of walnuts, which grow thickly around the stem; these sprouts are the parts used, and are equal in tenderness and flavor to cauliflower and broccoli. This vegetable has never come into general use in this country, probably because it is too tender to stand the winters of some of the northern states. Still, by sowing in April or May, and planting out in July or August, it may be had in fine condition until December; and in the Southern states may be harvested from November to March.

CULTURE: In early season, Brussels sprouts are treated exactly like any late cabbage. Till ample amounts of compost into the soil about two weeks before planting. When setting out plants, pinch off a few leaves and set plants 16-20 inches apart in rows of the same distance. Break off most of the lower leaves early in October, to concentrate the plant's energy on the immature buds. Begin harvesting the lower buds first. Shortly before the ground freezes, plants can be spaded up with some soil and transplanted in a moist greenhouse, coldframe or basement. If the soil is kept damp, sprouts will continue to mature. Brussels sprouts are a late season crop and are improved by a few fall frosts.

BRYOPHYLLUM: A fascinating indoor or outdoor plant that is characterized by its habit of sprouting new plants quite readily from leaves laid upon moist sand. Bryophyllum is a fleshy perennial of the Figwort family. Its small, hanging lantern-like flowers are pale green, shaded with red or purple coloring.

CULTURE: Bryophyllum will grow very quickly outdoors, but must be brought in during winter, since it is a tropical native. Bryophyllum is not particular about soil, but must have ample moisture and heat to thrive. Also known as life-plant, air-plant, floppers and lantern-plant, the *pinnatus* variety grows to a height of six inches.. Another variety, *crenatum,* grows to three feet, but has smaller flowers.

BUCKWHEAT: A very good cover crop, used for centuries in European and Asiatic countries. Buckwheat is grown mostly in the Northeast, particularly in Pennsylvania and New York. It can be grown on poorer soils than most crops, does well on acid soils. Buckwheat is very sensitive to cold and is easily killed by freezing, thus should be planted in the latter part of June or early July. On rich soils, seed 35 pounds per acre. On poor soils, as much as 60 pounds per acre may be applied.

Buckwheat itself is the tame brother of a group of weeds which is characteristic of sandy, light soils, as well as of acid soils. If soils are acid, with standing moisture, then their weedy brothers will also invade clay soils.

Buckwheat is a very old crop, much planted in the Old World. It grows well on acid soils and is of great value in rebuilding poor farmland.

Often the high, knotted, but erect stems, the red or reddish achenes and scaly lobes of the Dock and Sorrel varieties indicate that the soil is sour, has weed patches and insufficient drainage as well as a hard pan. The spreading of these groups can be used to measure the increase of soil acidity. Patience Dock (English Spinach) has been grown in England and on the continent in gardens, as a vegetable, for its slightly acid but refreshing taste. It prefers richer soils and grows near farm yards, manure heaps and roadsides. The Narrow-leaved, yellow, or curled Dock thrives in pastures, farmyards and moist places. The sorrels are frequently found in small quantities on pastures and meadows. They do not spoil the hay, although it is believed that the Field Sorrel is poisonous to horses. The young plants have been used in the past for savory soup and as a vegetable.

All are spread by seed, but the deep roots of the Docks, and the rootstocks of the Sorrels survive. The means of combatting them is therefore frequent cutting, in order to avoid seed formation and to starve the roots. Deep cultivation, in order to cut the roots is less successful. In small areas, pulling by hand, or prying deep with a spade may be helpful. The Narrow-leaved Dock has a widespread root system and is very damaging to grain crops through moisture competition. Fields with insufficient tillage and neglected pastures as well as roadsides, barnyards and edges of farm buildings and walls are most apt to spread the seeds. Commercial seed, especially alsike clover seed may contain sorrel seed. Where there are Docks and Sorrels on a farm, try to improve the soil by reducing the acidity and breaking the hard pan, through frequent and deep cultivation and proper aeration of the soil with a subsoiler or a spring tooth harrow. Once the field drains properly, half the battle is won. Frequent cultivation will do the rest. Some experts recommend much lime, which in itself is correct against acidity, but if drainage and aeration of the soil are not taken care of the lime is just "sunk" in the soil and rendered worthless after a few years.

On a pasture, mowing after pasturing is essential. Where there is an increase of acidity on a pasture, cattle will not graze and Sorrels and Docks will grow to seed unless frequently cut.

Most of the Docks like deep and good soil. They have deep-growing tap-roots, some two to three feet long and grow up to six feet tall. As the Sorrels indicate more or less acid soils, their size is almost an indication of the degree of acidity.

Another group of the Buckwheat Family is the Knotweed, (*Polygonum*), mostly on acid soils. The Prostrate Knotweed (*aviculare*) is very common all over the world, frequent on garden borders, along paths. The more trampled on, the better it grows. It is very rich in silica. All Knotweeds are characterized by "knots" on the stem from which branches come out. Some have white pinkish blossoms. Others are the erect and the bushy Knotweed.

The Swamp Smartweed indicates standing water or moist pockets, though it grows anywhere, spreading out from low fields. It is nasty because of its creeping roots, which are easily broken through cultivation and thus spread out. A typical inhabitant of wet meadows and damp places is the Mild Water Pepper (name from the bitter taste). Drainage will eliminate it as well as frequent cutting in order to starve the perennial roots. The Common Smartweed or Water Pepper has a very sharp juice that raises blisters on the skin. Lady's Thumb (*persicaria*) also called Spotted Knotweed is a very troublesome wide-spread fellow, growing in almost all crops and on meadows. It indicates a slight acidity, caused by insufficient surface drainage of the soil and lack of air.

Frequent and thorough cultivation is therefore the best preventative. Its seeds are one of the more frequent impurities in red clover, that is, it may be spread out where red clover is sown. The spotted Knotweed is easy to recognize by its reddish stem, the lance-shaped leaves, pointed at both ends with a dark brown to black spot in the center. The flower spikes are pink to purple.

The Wild Buckwheat or Black Bindweed is a moisture competitor in grain fields, climbing up and pulling down the grain by its weight. The seeds may be collected with the grain harvest and spread out with chaff and manure. They resemble the buckwheat seeds. The best way of combatting them is by early cultivation with a weeder. After the harvest cultivation, follow with a root crop. The Hedge Bindweed grows mainly along hedges, is bird planted or creeps along the ground. It prefers moist soil. *See also* COVER CROP; DEFICIENCIES, SOIL.

BUCKWHEAT HULLS: Buckwheat hulls make an easy-to-handle mulch. The hulls are disc-shaped, very light in weight, and after a rain they have the appearance of rich loam. When applied about one and one half inches deep, they will not blow away, but slither into place. After they have served as a mulch, buckwheat hulls can be worked into the soil to provide organic material for sandy soils and to help break up soils of clayey texture. *See also* HULLS; MULCH.

BUD-BLAST: *see* GLOXINIA

BUDDING: Budding is the method of plant propagation most commonly used by nurserymen throughout the world and is in truth a form of grafting. But there is one principal difference between budding and grafting. In grafting, a scion is used which usually consists of a piece of branch containing three or more buds. In budding, but one single bud is used and it is affixed to the other plant in the desired position or location.

When cutting your bud try to avoid getting too much wood, but get a nice section of bark with the eye intact. The length and width of the bud varies. It should be oval or shield-shaped, about one inch long and under one-half inch in width at the broadest point.

This method is the Shield or T Bud which is the one found most satisfactory in general practice.

When budding seedlings, always insert the bud as low as possible or as near the ground as practical on the seedling stock. Select a smooth location. Make a cut about one inch long along the length of the bark. Then make a cut across the top, at right angles to it, to form a perfect T.

Deftly open the slit. Then cut your bud from your scion and slip it down into position. Trim off the edge of your bud where the T-cut is made and then tie the bud in position firmly —leaving only the eye exposed.

Do not cut into the wood at any time—just into the bark.

Some budders say to leave a bit of wood in the bud when cutting it from the scion, since it gives firmness and rigidity.

In the South they practice what is known as June-budding, but generally the practice followed in the nursery trade is dormant budding which usually starts in July and extends into September, depending upon the stock to be budded.

Time for budding:

Roses—July 1st to July 15th.
Pears—July 10th to the latter part of July.
Apples—July 15th to early August.
Plum (Mirobolan)—August 15th to 1st week of September.
Cherry (Mazard stock)—Middle of July until early August.
Cherry (Mahaleb stock)—August 15 to September 1st.

Quince—July 15th to middle of August.

Peach—August 15th to the 15th of September.

Start budding roses as early in July as possible and continue . . . winding up the latter part of September with peach.

If you're doing budding on a fairly large scale, it would pay you to have someone go down ahead of the budder and clear off the lower limbs or branches to make it easier for the budder to work. The budder usually shuffles down the rows on his knees and is followed by an assistant who ties the bud firmly in its place. Raffia can be used although the elastic budding strips have been coming into prominence and general use during the past few years. They have one advantage over the Raffia inasmuch as they don't have to be cut off. The raffia has to be cut and removed. Otherwise it will strangle the tree.— *John Tobe.*

See also GRAFTING; PROPAGATION.

BUDDLEIA: Butterfly-Bush. These are lovely late-blooming shrubs, from July until frost in some varieties, especially *B. davidi magnifica.* The flowers are fragrant, a deep-rose purple in color, and much loved by butterflies. It is not very hardy and may winterkill north of Washington. Many persons cut them to the grounds each year, as they grow with extreme rapidity and flowering specimens are obtained without the loss of a season. Usually reaching a height of four to five feet, the plant must be cut back strongly. *See also* SHRUBS, FLOWERING.

Buddleias prefer a well-balanced, rich soil, also a mulch of manure.

The orange butterfly-bush, *B. davidi,* up to ten feet, is the hardiest of the Buddleias.

BUFFALO BUR: (*Solanum rostratum*) A noxious annual weed that frequently occurs first in field lots, then spreads to cultivated areas. A member of the potato family, it has poisonous, prickly stems and berries. Native to western areas, the plant generally reaches a height of one to two feet. Its yellow flowers are similar to those of tomato. These pesky plants can be controlled by clean cultivation; waste places where they grow should be mowed to prevent them from producing seed.

BUFFALO GRASS: *see* LAWN

BULB: Because of the remarkable beautiful flowers they produce, bulbs have become tremendously popular. They're versatile in the wide range of color, form and size of their flowers; they grow indoors as well as out; and in addition, they're relatively easy to grow.

Size alone does not constitute the value or quality of a bulb, but—firmness, weight and condition do.

If it is a true bulb (daffodil, lily or tulip) the layers or scales should be firmly adpressed, so that there is little or no feeling of looseness or squashiness when it is compressed in your hand. If it is a rhizome, corm or tuber (such as calla, crocus or dahlia) the flesh should be plump and fairly hard.

Good bulbs also present a distinct effect of being fairly heavy. It is not unusual to find bulbs of the same size and variety varying considerably in weight, those of inferior quality will tend toward lightness.

The condition of the skin or coating (as in hyacinths, tulips and others) should be smooth, bright, and innocent of deep cuts and bruises, noting in particular the disk at the base. Should this show signs of extreme injury or disease, the bulb will more than likely rot after planting.

It is best to plant them soon after purchasing; however, if this is impossible, keep the bags containing them in a cool, well-ventilated place where the air is not dried out by artificial heat. Remember, any condition causing the bulbs to shrivel will injure them.

In storing, also keep in mind (with the exception of daffodils)—squirrels,

To increase supply of glads, cut each bulb exactly in half, allowing one sprout per section. Store in warm, dark room for one month before planting. Work ground on planting site to obtain best results.

rats and mice regard them as delectable dishes.

BULB GARDEN: Millions of amateur gardeners have found that with a little effort in the fall and just a handful of Dutch bulbs they can add a maximum of color and beauty to their homes—and a genuine touch of Holland's bright charm next spring.

Moreover, they've learned that a bit of planning, careful selection and soil care bring this treat at a surprisingly low cost.

No matter where you live, you can turn local soil and climate to your advantage and get good results. Here are a few pointers that help:

Soil. Soil must have good drainage to help bulbs develop a strong root system. Where the soil tends to be heavy clay, loosen it up by using peat moss or sand.

Fertilizing. Compost or well-rotted manure are valuable for providing nutrients and improving soil structure. Place below bulbs when planting and cover with a layer of soil. Avoid fresh manure.

Other slow-acting fertilizers are excellent for bulbs. Bone meal, applied at five or six pounds per hundred square feet, is one of the most beneficial. Others include cottonseed meal, dried blood, tankage and wood ashes.

Mulches. Where winters are severe, bulb plantings should be mulched after the first heavy frost, or when the top two inches of soil are frozen. The purpose of this is not to keep the bulbs warm, but to reduce the danger of alternate freezing and thawing which often lifts and exposes bulbs or breaks roots. A winter mulch may be of straw, grass clippings, leaves, evergreen branches, buckwheat hulls, salt hay or pine needles, and should be removed when bulb growth starts in the spring. Summer mulching can help to hold moisture, keep the ground cool and discourage weeds. Clippings, peatmoss, hulls, and decayed sawdust are all good for this.

Make sure plantings have plenty of water in early spring. Lack of moisture may stunt bulb growth.

After Flowering. If flowers are not cut for indoor decoration, be sure to cut them as soon as they fade. Do not let petals lie on the ground. When leaves have dried, cut them off. Then you may leave the bulbs in the ground or lift them. If you lift them, place in a cool, dark spot to dry. When dry, clean off dirt, remove roots and old loose skin. Store in dry, airy place.

For planting, follow these simplified rules:

1. Plan where your bulbs will give you the most attractive results. Pattern your garden after those of the Dutch for a real Holland effect.

2. Consult the planting chart to determine how deep to plant the bulbs and the proper distance between them.

BULB PLANTING CHART

FLOWERS in order of appearance in garden	PLANTING TIME	FLOWERING TIME	HEIGHT IN INCHES	HOW TO PLANT	WHERE TO PLANT
CROCUS	Sept. 1-Dec. 15	March 15-30	5"	3" Deep 3" Apart	Rock Garden, Border, Lawn
GRAPE HYACINTHS	Sept. 1-Dec. 15	March 25-April 10	5"	3" Deep 3" Apart	Rock Garden or Border
TULIP Species For Rock Gardens	Sept. 15-Dec. 15	April 1-30	5"-15"	4" Deep 5" Apart	In Rock Gardens
DAFFODILS- Large Trumpet	Sept. 1-Dec. 1	April 10-25	18"-20"	6" Deep 6" Apart	In Beds, Groups or Borders
DAFFODILS- Medium Trumpet	Sept. 1-Dec. 1	April 10-25	16"	6" Deep 6" Apart	In Beds or Groups
DAFFODILS- Short Cups	Sept. 1-Dec. 1	April 10-25	14"	6" Deep 5" Apart	In Beds or Groups
TULIPS-Fosteriana	Sept. 15-Dec. 15	April 15-30	20"	4"-5" Deep 6" Apart	In Groups
TULIPS-Early	Sept. 15-Dec. 15	April 15-30	14"	4"-5" Deep 5" Apart	In Beds or Groups
HYACINTHS	Sept. 15-Dec. 15	April 15-30	10"	6" Deep 6" Apart	In Borders or Groups
TULIPS-Triumph	Sept. 15-Dec. 15	April 25-May 5	20"-24"	5"-6" Deep 6" Apart	In Beds, Groups or Borders
TULIPS-Darwin	Sept. 15-Dec. 15	May 5-20	26"-32"	5"-6" Deep 6" Apart	In Beds, Groups or Borders
SCILLA Campanulata	Sept. 15-Dec. 15	May 5-20	10"-14"	4" Deep 3" Apart	Rock Garden or Border
TULIPS- Mayflowering (Cottage)	Sept. 15-Dec. 15	May 5-20	28"	5"-6" Deep 5" Apart	In Beds, Groups or Borders
TULIPS-Parrot	Sept. 15-Dec. 15	May 10-25	22"-28"	5"-6" Deep 6" Apart	In Beds, Groups or Borders

SOUTHERN CLIMATE—If you live in a warm region store bulbs in a cool spot till planting time. Plant deep: add 4 inches to recommended depth for daffodils, hyacinths and all tulips except species. Plant in partial shade. Water frequently. You can plant from early fall through January.

3. Remove topsoil to required depth.

4. Loosen soil below, add fertilizer, cover and level it. Soil should be moist when bulbs are planted.

5. Place bulb nose (pointed end) up.

6. Replace original topsoil and smooth over the bed.

7. Plant before the first heavy frost in the fall.

By using various types of bulbs, your garden will have flowers in bloom from early March until June.

PLANTING: There are two popular ways of putting bulbs into the ground: the evacuation method and surface planting.

The former is done by removing all of the soil to the desired depth, setting the bulbs on the exposed ground and then replacing the earth.

The latter merely entails making a hole in the ground with a trowel or dibber, plopping in each individual bulb and then covering with soil.

In either method, it is advisable to lay out each group of bulbs before the actual planting begins.

In preparing a formal bed, a planting stick can be helpful, as it has notches to depict distances for accu-

As shown here, it is advisable to lay out each group of bulbs before the actual planting begins. Water thoroughly immediately after the planting.

rate spacing. Another useful tool for surface planting is a gadget which removes a circular piece of sod and a core of soil beneath it. When the bulb is planted, soil and sod can be returned.

The depth to which bulbs are covered varies with species and varieties, also with soils and exposures. Here are a few general rules to follow:

To delay flowering, place them in a northern exposure. Contrary to belief, extra-deep planting delays flowering very little.

A thorough watering is a must when planting is finished. This brings about rapid root developments which anchor the bulb firmly, thus decreasing the danger of injury by heaving.

Crocuses, daffodils, tulips and the usual early spring-blooming bulbs are considered extremely hardy and once they are established, do not need protection from freezing. But if they are planted very late, mulching can be beneficial in two ways:

First to extend the period during which root growth can develop in the soil, and second to prevent heaving by keeping the surface frozen.

On the other hand, narcissus, galtonia, montbretias, bulbous irises, anemones and ranunculus are not reliably hardy, but thanks to mulching can be grown outdoors in many sections where it would be otherwise impossible.

Another use of mulching is to *keep from freezing* ground which has been set aside for bulbs, such as the hardy lilies, which are unobtainable until late in the season. A mulch will keep this soil workable when there are early frosts. It is removed to plant the late bulbs; then, after the planting is completed and the soil frozen two or more inches, replace the mulch.

Since mulching is rarely required until late December or January, Christmas tree boughs are considered excellent mulching material. They are not only easily applied, but lie flat and catch and retain light snow falls. Also they present a pleasant appearance for the greater part of the winter, and in the spring their removal takes only a matter of minutes.— *Doris W. Weinsheimer. See also* Flower Gardening.

BULBS, FORCING: Bulbs are easy to grow indoors. They can be forced successfully in the window of an apartment, the home, the cold frame or in the greenhouse. No special skill is needed and if light, sufficient moisture and a temperature high enough to enable growth is provided, bulbs will flourish. The flower bud is preformed in the bulb before it reaches you. Containers can be pots, bulbs or azalea pans, or flats according to the number of bulbs or the desire of the grower.

Tulips: Some varieties of tulips will force more rapidly than others and for that reason it is important to consult your bulb dealer about selection. Plant them as soon as possible after purchase and preferably by the end of October. Early planting is important for the establishment of good root growth which takes from six to eight weeks.

Choose containers that have ample holes in the bottom for drainage. Roots cannot grow in a moist soil that can easily stagnate. The soil should be moderately rich garden loam, slightly alkaline. Some shredded manure or thoroughly decayed farmyard manure can be added with advantage at the rate of two parts loam to one of manure. In the case of clay soil, leafmold is helpful in equal parts.

The prepared soil is then put in the containers to within three-quarters-of-an-inch from the top and leveled off. The bulbs should be set about half-an-inch apart in pots or pans. When planting tulips in pots it should be remembered that the flat side of the bulb should be toward the rim of the pot. Pack the soil lightly around the bulbs, water liberally and store in a cool, dark place.

The best method of storing tulips, however, is to dig a shallow trench in the garden about six to eight inches deep, place the containers on a level surface and thoroughly water before covering with eight or ten inches of soil. A covering of straw or leaves should also be added to keep out frost.

On February 1, the earliest varieties can be brought into a temperature ranging from 60 to 65 degrees F. Keep in slight shade for one week and then set containers in as light a place as possible, giving them water in the morning as needed. Flowers will appear in from 26-36 days according to the variety. Remove all pots from the trenches by February 15 and store in a cool place until time for forcing. If bulbs are brought in at carefully timed intervals, it will be possible to have a succession of flowers up to Easter.

Daffodils: In many ways the procedure for forcing daffodils is similar to tulips, but there are several important differences. Daffodil bulbs benefit by being soaked in water for several hours before planting. They also prefer a slightly acid soil enriched with compost or decayed farmyard manure.

Hyacinths: These hardy bulbs are undoubtedly more colorful and worthy of use as potted plants than almost any others. Their culture is simple and the fragrance delightful. Hyacinths are also the ideal gifts at Eastertime.

As with the other bulbs, it is most important that a good root growth is established before the forcing process begins. The earlier you begin, the earlier the flowering period. "Prepared" bulbs (those stored by commercial growers at 80 degrees F. after digging) can be potted up in September and kept indoors at 50 degrees F. for Christmas blooms; ordinary bulbs can be started as late as December for Spring flowering. Results will be good as long as conditions are cool enough during the rooting period.

Either the largest or second-size bulbs can be selected for planting in the same type of soil as recommended for tulips. Pot singly in four- or five-inch size bulb pan for the living room. There are white, yellow, red, pink and blue shades for home decoration.

If pots are used, it is better to set the bulbs deeper in the soil with the "nose" of each slightly above the surface. Place bulbs close to one another, packing some soil around them to keep in position.

Storage outdoors after planting is recommended the same as for tulips except that daffodils require copious watering before covering with six or eight inches of soil. Sand or screened cinders would even be preferable as they would provide an even cool temperature for good root growth. Allow at least eight weeks outdoors before bringing in to a temperature of 50 degrees F.

However, as the flower buds advance they can stand a temperature as high as 65 degrees F. Early varieties can be brought in around January 15 and flowers will bloom four to five weeks later. During this time daffodils respond to ample supplies of water.

When the potting has been completed, the tips or up to one-quarter of the upper part of the bulbs should be showing above the surface. Then there must be liberal watering before the pots are buried eight or ten inches deep in a convenient location, preferably shaded. Hyacinths need about eight weeks for full root growth and then they can be brought indoors. If you allow two weeks between starting dates, hyacinth pots can be brought in at different times to make possible a succession of bloom.

At the time that the pots are removed from the ground, the tops will be blanched and therefore the pots should not be placed in direct sunlight. At that point the young growth will be at least one and one-half inches long. When this growth is green, a week or ten days later, the pots can be placed in direct sunlight at a temperature of 55 to 60 degrees F. They can tolerate a temperature as high as 70 degrees F., in which case the mature flowering stage would be reached in 25 to 30 days. However, the cooler they are grown, the better the flowering results. During the growing period liberal supplies of water are helpful.

Hyacinths can also be grown in the home or apartment without soil. Your dealer will guide you in selection of varieties to use on hyacinth glasses. These are filled with water and a little charcoal. The bulbs must be set so the base just meets the water. Place the glasses for about two months in a dark and cool closet or cellar, until root formation is well advanced. At that time the young growth should be at least one-and-a-half inches long. Add fresh water to keep the level of the original volume. Allow filtered light for ten days and then strongest light in an airy window.

MINOR BULBS: It is also possible to have these dainty bulb specimens in the indoor garden but care should be taken to keep them in cool temperatures. They appear outdoors early in the season at about 50 degrees F. and similar conditions should be provided indoors.

Select a sun porch, cold frame or greenhouse as ideal places for snow-crops, crocuses, chionodoxas and early varieties of scillas. Allow about a half an inch between the bulbs in the container. Use a loamy soil and be sure of good drainage. During the growing period care should be taken to see to it that the soil is neither soggy nor very dry. Place the pots where they get the greatest amount of light possible. The minor bulbs flower naturally and easily in this way.—*Margaret Herbst.*

BULL THISTLE: (*Cirsium vulgare*) Also known as common and spear thistle, this biennial pesty weed produces a prickly rosette of leaves the first year and a spiny-winged, flowering stem in the second. Unlike Canadian thistle, the heads are solitary or only a few, at the tips of short, prickly-winged branches. The purple flowers produce seed one-eighth of an inch or more long which are straw-colored with black stripes. Bull thistle can be best eliminated through cultivation and regular mowing.

BULRUSHES: (*Scirpus*) Widely distributed in ponds, lakes, and marshes, its floating vegetation sometimes produces odors on decay. River bulrush (*S. fluviatus*) is common in pond borders and bays; Great Bulrush (*S. validus*) grows in shallow ponds. Either annuals or perennials, bulrushes vary in height from several inches to several feet.

BURBANK, LUTHER: Luther Burbank produced more new varieties of useful plants than any one person before or since, although only a relatively few have withstood the test of time. One of his chief desires was to make it possible to produce more food and flowers and forage crops. In order to accomplish this ambition, he developed new varieties of fruits, vegetables, nuts, forage plants, flowers and grains to a total of about 1,000 new varieties.

BURDOCK: (*Arctium*) Two species of burdock (*A. lappa* and *A. minus*) are large biennial plants well known as common and troublesome weeds in the Eastern, Central, and some Western States. The dried root from these plants of the first year's growth and the seed are used medicinally.

Burdock will grow in almost any soil, but the best root development is favored by a light well-drained soil rich in humus. The seed germinates readily and can be sown with a small seed drill directly in the field in rows 18 inches to three feet apart either late in fall or early in spring. When well up in spring the seedlings are thinned to stand about six inches apart in the row. Cultivation is continued until the plants get too large.

The roots are harvested at the end of the first year's growth, in order to obtain the most acceptable drug and to prevent the plants from bearing seed and spreading as a weed. The tops of the plants can be cut with a mower and raked off, after which the roots can usually be turned out with a deep-running plow or with a beet lifter. In a dry and very sandy soil the roots frequently extend to such depth that it is necessary to dig them by hand.

Burdock is considered a pesty weed when occurring in neglected farmyards, fence rows, or rich soils of uncultivated areas. Plants can be eliminated by cultivation, especially during the first year.

BURNET: (*Sanguisorba minor*) A pretty perennial with very small white or rosy flowers, Burnet grows to about one foot high.

The leaves are somewhat like that of cucumbers, and are used in salads and in cool drinks.

The graceful appearance and pleasant green of burnet leaves make it a useful plant near the front of a border, especially if the rather untidy flower heads are cut off.

It grows in any garden soil and is easily raised from seed or propagated by division.

BURNING FIELDS: The burning of weeds, grass or trash is a destructive practice and should always be avoided. Earthworms, bacteria, fungi, protozoa, algae and other soil organisms are killed. Soil organic matter in the upper few inches is consumed. Moisture is dried out of the soil and the water table is lowered. The tilth of the soil is harmed because soil particles are broken down. There is always the danger of the fire spreading to nearby buildings, fields or forests.

BUSH BEAN: *see* BEAN

BUSH CHERRY: *see* CHERRY, BUSH

BUSH FRUITS FOR LANDSCAPING: Today more and more home owners with limited space are finding ways to combine small fruit growing with attractive landscaping. In these days of suburban living, home owners can be found using bush cherries as foundation plantings . . . dwarf trees as hedgerows . . . blueberries as property dividers . . . even strawberries as flower borders. In addition, many small fruits are being used in spots where ornamental shrubs were used before. Every day, gardeners are finding that they can "have their hedges and eat them, too."

BUSH CHERRY—A TAME HEDGE: The bush cherry is perhaps the most likely fruit to replace many small hedges and foundation plantings. This variety can be planted in close rows, and can be trimmed to almost any height desired. Blossoms are beautiful in spring, and the silvery-green foliage is always attractive, but the real payoff comes when quarts of succulent cherries are picked in late summer for canning, pies and preserves. Bush cherries are also adaptable for singular plantings. Use this just as you would any ornamental of comparable size. (Up to five feet.)

WILD HEDGES: The "wild" hedges, those which should not be trimmed, include the blueberry, raspberry and Rosa Rugosa. They may best be used for spots where larger, rambling hedges would ordinarily be used, such as along property lines, farm pastures, and along roadways. These plants generally grow with amazing speed, and are perfect for shutting out undesirable views, or for secluding a patio from a roadway or other houses. Raspberries generally grow about six feet high, and should be planted about three feet apart. A trellis can be used to help train canes, prevent wind damage, and keep fruit off the ground. Blueberries grow six to ten feet high, and for commercial purposes are planted five feet apart. You may, however, wish to sacrifice some of the fruit surface to gain a more dense hedge, planting three to four feet apart.

THE REMARKABLE ROSA RUGOSA: The Rosa Rugosa is famous for its "hips," or fruits that form on its branches after the blossoms fall. Rose hips are nature's most compact source of Vitamin C. A quarter pound of rose hips contains as much C as 120 oranges. The plant itself will grow to a height of five or six feet and, when planted about two feet apart, will grow into an attractive, thick hedge, with beautiful blossoms appearing all summer long.

DWARF TREES: Another family of plants which are both attractive and fruit bearing are the dwarf trees. Full-sized apples, pears, cherries, and other fruits can be enjoyed all summer in the space which otherwise might have been devoted to ornamental shrubs. Most of these trees are very attractive, especially at spring blossom time, and the fruit they bear is equal in all respects to full-sized trees. Dwarfs usually range from six to 15 feet in height. In Europe, dwarf apples are commonly seen used as hedgerows.

STRAWBERRIES: Useful as a border for the flower bed. The plants are very attractive, and provide another example of how you can combine landscaping with fruit growing. One expert says of the strawberry plant, "it does make an extremely attractive low hedge or border, and when a vigorous upright growing variety such as Empire is used it forms a very attractive picture, both in bloom and in fruiting."

With care and planning, strawberries can be used for a border, yielding a double bonus of a most attractive border plus a supply of delicious fruit.

The examples mentioned should give you some idea of the almost endless possibilities of the fruit-landscaping idea. *See also* Bramble Fruits; Shrubs.

BUTTER-AND-EGGS: *see* Linaria

BUTTERCUP: (*Ranunculus*) Also called crowfoot, these plants have yellow flowers usually; often give weedy appearance. Over 300 species are accredited to the genus, which is considered almost cosmopolitan in range over the earth, particularly in the North Temperate Zone. The name *Ranunculus* was derived from the Latin: "*rana,*" a frog, in allusion to the fact that most of the species inhabit humid, swampy marshes and banks of streams in woods where frogs are at home.

The herbs contain an acid, caustic juice or sap, that with some people, when applied to the skin will raise blisters. This rubefacient property is most notable with three local species of our woods, *R. septentrionalis* being the worst. They are usually the guilty culprits that cause a skin rash for which the poison ivy is accused. The sap of most of the species taken internally is considered poisonous; producing violent effects; one should drink much water as an antidote, if the plant is eaten raw by mistake. In spite of this poisonous property *R. arvensis* and *R. sceleratus* are eaten by sheep and goats, and they are actually used as fodder in some European countries, since drying the plant tends to remove the poisonous properties.

Many interesting traditions are associated with the Buttercups, originating in legends and stories handed down through the ancient history of man. One of these stories to survive time is that of *"Ranunculus,"* a mythical figure of many thousands of years ago. *"Ranunculus"* was pictured as a young man possessing uncommon accomplishments, particularly in qualities that made him attractive to young ladies. He was fond of music and

gifted with a beautiful voice. His sweet melodies, when heard by the nymphs, would attract them. Though charmed and delighted by his voice, the nymphs failed to show their appreciation sufficiently to be wooed and submit to marriage, with the result that the poor fellow died broken-hearted. The Gods, in pity for this unfortunate youth, turned him into a pretty yellow flower of the woods near streams. This flower still bears his name, the *Ranunculus*. One must not forget the popular belief also about the Buttercup, that it is supposed to indicate whether an individual is fond of butter; the test is to hold a flower under the chin; if the chin reflects yellow, the subject is guilty.

The native Buttercups are described as both perennial and annual herbs with alternate, simple or compound and finely dissected leaves, and with flowers that are yellow, white or red with five separate petals and sepals, and many stamens or pollen bearers. When the flower matures the head consists of many hard fruit called *achenes*. Honey is secreted at the base of the petals, serving as a lure to insects. The flowers are terminal, solitary or panicled and rarely stemless. Most of the native species are propagated either by seeds or root divisions. One of the common European species, much used here in the States in Rock Gardens, is *Ranunculus acris*. This species has a rich, glossy, yellow tone in the flower, and the doubled variety, known as "florepleno," is called in the trade "Yellow Bachelor Button." Many of the species are grown in flower gardens, borders and in Rock and Aquatic gardens since they are naturally at home as alpines, boreals, and aquatics, thus well adapted in formal landscape. The *Batrachium* section of the Buttercups embraces the true aquatic species; these species are natural pond plants, living in shallow water and are used extensively in horticulture for colonizing in ponds along their margins.

The truly beautiful Buttercups species most popular in Europe and with florists in America is a species of Asia known as *R. asiaticus* and its many varieties. This species is known as the "Asiatic Crowfoot," "Common Garden Crowfoot" and "Turkey Crowfoot." It supersedes all other European and American species of the genus in beauty of form and color. The group is also classed into two major sections: the *Persian Ranunculi* and the "Turbans." The species, with its many varieties, has since been greatly improved not only in form and size, but into a variety of bizarre colors. The flowers are usually double, more than two inches across, globular in outline, and they are found in almost every tone of possible color-shade except in blues. Some are variegated and striped in different colors. They suggest Pompon Dahlias in texture and beauty. A mass planting of mixed or controlled colors is a sight not soon forgotten. Unfortunately, the group is not as popular in the States as it is in Europe. This may be due to the culture that is required. They bloom in this country in late May to early June. They should be planted in an herbaceous border where some shade is present during the warmer parts of the day. The roots suggest miniature dahlia tubers and like them, are not hardy, particularly in the northern States. The tubers should be lifted after the foliage has signs of withering or "ripening off" which usually is in late August. The tubers are then dug up, cleaned, and stored in a cool root cellar until the following spring. They should be divided and planted in the spring as soon as the danger of frost is past. Planting is about two inches deep and six inches apart, dressing the top soil with a layer of sand so that the leaves can push through easily without injury and strain. The plants like much moisture, a characteristic of all the species of the genus. Propagation is by seed, but the bulb, as the tuber is called, is the

easiest method to propagate and is naturally more selective since the colors can be controlled.

BUTTERFLY-BUSH: *see* BUDDLEIA

BUTTERFLY FLOWER: (*Schizanthus pinnatus*) This delicate, graceful plant, when properly grown, is covered with tiny orchid-like blooms and always attracts a great deal of attention. It does require constant care and rather exacting conditions. The butterfly flower is usually grown as a house plant, or in greenhouses. For winter flowering, seeds should be sown one-eighth inch deep in August. During growing period, temperature should remain between 45 and 55 degrees. Sometimes called "poor man's orchid."

BUTTERNUT (*Juglans cinerea*) The butternut, or white walnut, was once a very familiar and pleasant sight along the country lanes and in woodlands, but in recent years it is little to be seen.

The old butternut trees would probably still be here, were it not for the blight, and oyster-shell scale. A great deal toward preventing these has been accomplished through organic fertilizers and mulching. Its main fertilizers are organic nitrogen and finely-ground phosphate rock. It is the phosphate that makes and fills the nuts.

To those who know nut tees, it is common knowledge that the butternut growing on its own roots is usually a weak tree because the root system is not too sturdy. Nurserymen have grafted the butternut on the strong and vigorous black walnut rootstock, and behold, you have an entirely different type of butternut tree to plant now. The new butternut trees come in varieties of proven cracking and extraction quality, just like the apple and peach trees you buy. There is one drawback with butternut tree production in the nursery. Trees are usually in limited supply because of the difficulty in getting the grafts to grow.

Use a leaf mulch around them for a couple of years and water newly set trees weekly near the trunks, where you should leave a vacant place in the leaves.

Hardy throughout most of the United States, butternuts reach a height of 90 feet. *See also* NUT TREES.

BUTTON BUSH: (*Cephalanthus occidentalis*) Fragrant ornamental shrub. The nature lover will do well to explore the marshy ground and banks of quiet streams in August. Even before he sees the plants he will become aware of an unusual, delicate fragrance which permeates the atmosphere. More than likely this fragrance will be found to be emanating from hundreds of small creamy-white flower-balls that dangle in clusters on long stems from the gracefully drooping branches of low, rounded bushes. These shrubs are button bushes with their small flowers arranged in globose heads. The fragrance of these flowers seems to be one of the greatest delights of bees and butterflies, which hover over them to partake of the natural sweetness found so abundantly supplied deep in their nectar wells.

Although this plant is at home in swamps, it is perfectly capable of living in ordinary garden soils and is hardy over most of the United States, blooming from August to late Septem-

Although it grows naturally in swamps, the button bush can be cultivated in almost any garden and is hardy over most of the country.

ber. This beautiful, fragrant shrub deserves a place in your garden. In many respects it is more ornamental than many of the cultivated shrubs. It is especially desirable in that it blooms in late summer when relatively few other shrubs are in bloom. It will do well in almost any location in your garden but if you have a pool or stream, button bush will more than repay you for remembering that it is by nature a water-loving plant.

BUTTON SNAKEWOOD: *see* LIATRIS

BUTTONWOOD TREE: *see* PLANE TREE

C

C HORIZON: Below the B horizon of the soil profile begins a layer of material known as the C horizon. As a rule, it is lighter in color than the overlying A and B horizons. Its texture is not as heavy as that of the B horizon, if the soil has formed from a column of weathered material of homogeneous texture. The texture of the C horizon can be heavier or lighter than that of the B horizon, if the soil has formed from alluvial or other sedimentary deposits which may vary in texture from point to point in the column. In these deposits one may find a clay layer where the A horizon is formed, a sandy layer where the B horizon is formed and a clay layer below it or vice versa. Under such circumstances, the C horizon will be heavier or lighter in texture than B, depending on the texture of the material when deposited.

The C horizon varies in depth, according to the geologic history of the deposits. If, for instance, the C horizon is of sedimentary origin it may be either fairly shallow, as in the soils formed on outcropping red shale, or very deep, as in the soils of the Coastal Plain. If the C horizon is of residual rock deposits, its depth depends on the depth of the weathered material. From the standpoint of pedology, the soil body terminates a few inches below the surface of the C horizon. Below that lies the subsoil. *See also* A Horizon; B Horizon.

CABBAGE: (*Brassica oleracea capitata*) A common vegetable in gardens with temperate climates. It grows well only where there is a good supply of moisture and the weather is cool. It won't stand extremely dry spells or intense heat.

Midsummer crops are grown in some parts of the country, but such crops are considered secondary and seldom are very successful except in limited areas.

Cabbage can thrive in almost any kind of soil. Soil moisture is a bit more important than soil texture in the growing of cabbage. Since cabbage does not favor periods of intense heat and dryness, heavy mulches on the soil will compensate for these hot dry spells.

As a fertilizer, well-rotted animal manure can be used to great advantage with cabbage. It will make the sandy soils produce a good crop and it tends to hold water well.

Decayed leaves are excellent provided they are buried deeply enough in the garden.

In using well-rotted manure with cabbage plants, it is best to cover the entire part of the garden which is to be used for the cabbage. It can be spread at least three inches thick and then thoroughly plowed under. This job should be undertaken about two weeks before the cabbage plants are ready to be set out in the garden.

Many gardeners prefer to grow their own cabbage plants from seed. The early varieties grown from seed should of course get an early start in the greenhouse. They can be successfully grown in the house in a cool room or in the cellar. In such cases, the seed is sown in fine soil in flats or in pots. In the northern states, this can be done in February or March. Much depends upon the climate in the various states when figuring the time to sow seed. The soil in which the seeds are planted should not want to be too rich. When the soil becomes too rich, the seedlings will grow too fast and become "leggy."

The later varieties of cabbage are handled in the same way except that the flats or boxes are kept outside instead of under glass. When the seedlings reach a height of three or four inches, they should be picked out and replanted in flats or boxes some distance farther apart. This action will assure the grower of good stocky plants. The seed-sowing should be timed six weeks or at least a month ahead of the time at which the plants are to be set out in the garden.

In setting the plants out in the garden, a good deal depends upon the variety chosen. The early varieties are best set 14 inches apart in rows 28 inches apart. Midseason varieties should be planted 16 inches apart in rows 28 inches apart; and the late varieties, 24 inches apart in rows 36 inches apart.

Set out the early varieties as soon as danger from frost is over and check the date with local facilities. The late varieties should be planted not later than the first of August in the northern states. Depending on the variety, it takes up to 67 plants of the early types to fill a 100-foot row. For the later types, 40 plants are enough. A 100-foot row will produce enough cabbage for a family of five.

Beware of the cabbage maggot. This is the larva of a small black fly. It lays small white eggs about the size of a grain of rice on the surface of the ground near the stem of the plant. Look for these eggs and remove them by hand. But the midseason and late cabbage varieties are not apt to be attacked by this pest.

The green cabbage worm is well known. It is the larva of the white butterfly and feeds on the leaves. The eggs are laid at the base of the leaves and are hardly noticeable. A sharp look-out will do much in preventing damage from this insect. The cabbage looper, like the former pest, eats small holes in the leaves. If they are not removed promptly, they will prove disastrous to the crop. In the south, the Harlequin cabbage bug attacks the plants by sucking the juice from them. Removal by hand is the only practical method of destroying them.

Cabbage aphids can usually be discouraged when they appear in cool weather by using a fine forceful spray from the garden hose.

Of the many cabbage diseases to be found in different parts of the country, club root and blackleg are probably the most common. Club root occurs in acid soil. It can be held in check by working plentiful amounts of limestone into the soil. Blackleg can be detected when the plants are set in the garden after being removed from the flats or pots. This disease works in the stem of the plants and once it gets a start, the plants are doomed. Mulching and compost will keep down these diseases to a minimum.

Winter Supply of Cabbage: Late varieties of cabbage can be salvaged way into the winter. Pull the entire plant and stack each one upside-down in a protected corner of the yard. Cover the cabbage pile with a foot layer of leaves or straw. Perfectly good cabbage heads will then be easily available for consumption anytime during the following winter or early spring.—*Charles Booth.*

See also Fertilizer; Deficiencies, Soil.

CABBAGE APHIDS: *see* Cabbage; Aphids

CABBAGE MAGGOT: To control the cabbage maggot, pull the dirt away from the plant where the maggots can be seen working on the stem. Place a heaping tablespoon of wood ashes around each stem, mix some soil around with the ashes, firm the plants in and water. When setting out winter cabbage in early August, mix wood ashes, lime and rock phosphate and bonemeal (4 parts wood ashes to 1 part each of the other ingredients) and stir two cups of this mixture in a 2-foot radius for every plant. *See also* Cabbage.

CABBAGE WORM: These pale green or striped worms eat leaves and holes in heads of cabbage. Yellow jacket hornets thrive on cabbage worms. For control, during early morning when dew is heavy on cabbage plants, sprinkle with rye flour; (one pint will cover large patch) later in the day, you'll find cabbage moths with dough sticking to their wings, feet and bodies. Acts the same way with worms; they crawl around and then sun bakes dough hard and worms die. *See also* Cabbage; Insect Control.

CABOMBA: *see* Aquariums

CACTUS: (*Cactaceae*) These oddities of the plant world come in sizes from an inch tall to 63 feet high. You can grow them in cups, trays, pots and pans, window boxes, and outside gardens as well as in the ground.

The flowers of many cacti are exotically beautiful. There are the huge ten-inch flowers of the night-blooming *cereus* cactus with its overwhelming perfume; and the range of flowers of the world of the orchid cacti that equal and often surpass the loveliest of conventional orchids. Nature seems indeed bent upon making up in the forms and color of cacti flowers what she has saddled their world in drabness of plant shapes and coloring.

Anybody can raise a cactus garden. Anywhere citrus grows you can grow cacti outside the year around. Elsewhere where there are snows and frosts and freezing you can grow your cacti plants in pots, trays, boxes inside in sunny windows during cold weather. When the last freezes are past, you can place your "gardens" outside in semi-shade on benches, plant them in the ground—and for the long months until the frosts return.

Window gardeners plant their cactus specimens in tiny pots, large ones, all shapes and trays; even make miniature gardens in flat bowls. Some are placed in the sun on window

A cactus hybridizer in California semi-desert country inspecting some of the many hundreds of varieties of plants now available. Such cultivated species combine beauty and hardiness; need little water.

ledges or on tables; others have glass greenhouses. But through it all cactus plants will thrive happily and blossom and grow in sunny south windows just about anywhere in the world. You can safely expect to grow them outside within the limitations of most flowers. But—they won't stand frosts.

Nevertheless, they are tough plants. Millions of years of desert life made them that way. Go away on a trip and forget to water them for a week, a month—throw them on a cement walk for two, three months—then replant them and water them and they are gaily off on a growing spree, happy and healthy, as jaunty as ever.

You will learn mighty soon not to take liberties with the protective array of spines, spikes, thorns and needles with which cacti are adorned. They are meant to keep animals and men from destroying the plant. In the ever-hungry desert, animals and birds would soon devour all the cactus world were it not for this protection devised by Nature.

There are literally thousands of varieties of cacti and succulents from such far places as the Andes, South Africa, South America, the Central American jungles, the West Indies, Mexico, and the American Southwest to stir the collector's urge in you. Specimens of most of these can be bought for from 50 cents up to as high as you want to go. And you have a galaxy of sources: the popular five-and-ten cent store, plant nurseries, farms that specialize in producing cacti and that ship them anywhere via parcel post. So, there is no reason why the flower-lover can't have a cactus "garden" outside or in his sunny south window.

You can buy varieties of cacti so that you will have them flowering practically the whole year. Some bloom with the fall rains, some with the spring rains. Your nursery or the cactus nursery farm can tell you what months every variety blossoms.

Those of you who can't have cacti planted outside in gardens due to freezing weather, or living in apartments, can have window gardens—grow all varieties in pots and miniature gardens—and enjoy their blooming as much as if they were outdoors. Use a fine, simple growing mixture for potting and for the little gardens—equal parts sifted leaf mold, sand, fine loam, a little peat moss. Water your plants only when their soil is bone dry. *Don't* over-water. That is the surest way to rot out and kill plants. Water once a week or ten days should be enough.

How hybridizing is done. Onto the top of every plant another cactus is grafted. Vari-colored and unique flowers result from this procedure.

Roughly speaking, we can divide the cacti world into three sections: cacti generally, orchid cacti, succulents. But there are many thousands of varieties of cacti, and growers are creating more by hybridizing.

Succulents: Colorful and charming desert plants from Africa, Mexico, South America, Madagascar, etc. Rare, curiously shaped, beautiful flowers. They are fine for window gardens. Thrive in a sandy, porous soil of one part easily crumbled loam, two parts coarse river sand, one part sifted leaf mold. Keep pots small. The succulents love lots of sunshine.

Among the members of this group you will find such odd-named characters as White Jewel plant, Cockscomb, Hairy Starfish, Painted Lady, Arab's Turban, the Inch Worm, Tricolored Jade, and many others. Flowers quaint and pretty. You'll love the Mexican Firecracker, the Scarlet Paintbrush, and the Split Rock with its eruptions of lovely little blossoms.

The *orchid cacti* or Epiphyllums are among the easiest grown of all cacti. Their blossoms surpass many orchids in size and brilliance of coloring. Found wild from the Isthmus of Tehuantepec to Guatemala. Hybridists are having a field day producing more lovely crosses in this great classification.

Grow the orchid cacti in a mixture of equal parts light loam, gritty sand, leaf mold. Keep near windows, but out of direct sun. When frost is past put them outdoors in shade of trees. The flowers are on last year's stems, and from April to July.

The amazing world of the *Opuntias* —the pincushion cactus, the gorgeous, showy, night-blooming cereus, the jolly clan of the barrel cacti or *Echinocactus* will leave you simply overwhelmed with their myriad shapes, their diverse personalities, the colors of their flowers. Imagine having in bloom in your window such fabulous little plant folk from the Upper Cretaceous Age of 40 million years ago, and with such names as: the Bishop's Cap, Pink Pearl Chin cactus, Strawberry cactus, Old Man of the Andes, Violet Sea Urchin, and Fire Crown. They may be two inches tall, they may even tower to the 63 feet of the Giant Mexican Cereus cacti. *See also* DESERT GARDEN.

CACTUS DAHLIA: *see* DAHLIA

CACTUS, ORCHID: *see* EPIPHYLLUM

CAJEPUT: (*Melaleuca leucadendron*) This tropical tree is sometimes known as the broad-leaved tea-tree. The volatile oil yielded by its leaves and twigs is a valuable solvent and of use in medicine.

Originally from Australia, the bark of this tree is white and papery on the outside and corky and spongy to a depth of ½ inch or more, even on small trees. The aromatic leaves and twigs are fine for decorative garlands. They remain green a long while and emit a pleasant fragrance. It belongs to the same order, and is closely related to the genus Eucalyptus.

The seeds of this tree are very minute and therefore difficult to sprout, in the usual way. (Scattering of these seeds over shallow water is all that is necessary. The minuteness of its seed is therefore not a disadvantage since it can be started by the "flotation" method by shaking the seeds from a saltcellar from an aeroplane on the surface of any swampland covered with shallow water). These seeds are, in fact, as fine as finely-ground red pepper.

It produces seed while very young, sometimes when a year old. The seed spreads on shallow water and when the water disappears germinates and grows quickly in the mud. The tree grows straight up and rarely assumes a bushy or shrubby form. Owing to the corky nature of its bark it is rarely killed by fire.

From its botanical name, *Melas* is *black*, *leukos* is *white*, and *dendron* means *tree*. It is called "black-white tree" because in its native land, owing to bush fires, the lower part of the tree is black.

The tree is most excellent for decorative purposes for homes close to the seashore. Its tall straight white trunks are effectively used close to houses of certain types of architecture.

The capeput-tree blooms in fall and winter in southern Florida, can be propagated by cuttings.

CALADIUM: A striking, large-leaved foliage plant of the *Arum* family. Caladium is a popular house plant, loved for the beautifully delicate veining of its leaves. The coloring of the caladium is varied. Some have pink leaves, others have green leaves streaked with white, dark green streaked with black, white leaves with pink and green coloring, and many other combinations. Caladium is often moved to the outdoors in summer, but remember that it is native to the tropics and can't stand temperatures lower than 70°.

CULTURE. Caladium likes an acid soil, similar to that of azaleas. A good mixture consists of equal parts of good garden loam and peat moss, with a little sand. During the growing period, caladium likes plenty of water, and in very late summer and early fall, when foliage color begins to fade and lose lustre, it's time to prepare the plant for its natural dormant period.

For planting outdoors, dormant tubers should be set out about two inches deep, several weeks after the average last frost. Indoor and green-house plants are grown from bulbs, which are set in four-inch pots. As growth continues, it will be necessary to repot.

Caladium is often erroneously called elephant's ear, a plant which actually belongs to the *Colocasia* family.

See also HOUSE PLANTS; FOLIAGE PLANTS.

CALCEOLARIA: Showy-flowered herbs and shrubs, widely grown in the green-house and outdoors. The herbaceous kinds are treated as annuals and grown from seeds usually. Grown mostly for their slipper-like flowers, the shrubby forms generally do not do too well in the summer heat.

Seed is planted from the beginning of April through August in shallow pans in a mixture of sand and peat, finely sieved. Tamp down seeds lightly and water by dipping the pan in water. After transplanting to larger pots and the plants are well rooted, fertilize with manure water. When plants are ready to flower, be sure to give them plenty of room to properly develop.

The most popular specie, *Crenati-flora*, has yellow flowers, grows about two feet high.

CALCITE: A calcium carbonate occurring in many crystalline forms, such as chalk or marble.

CALCIUM: One of the mineral elements, calcium ranks as the fifth most abundant constituent in the earth's crust. However, it does not occur alone in nature, but is always found combined in varying concentrations with other elements.

Known also as one of the "alkaline earths," calcium is important agriculturally because it is the principal element concerned in the reaction of soils, especially in humid regions, and has a primary role in determining soil pH, availability of several nutrients and the general fertility level. Commonly called lime (CaO), it forms a major part of limestones, marbles, corals, natural chalks and shells.

Like potassium, calcium is present in plants mainly in the leaves. One of its important functions is to neutralize certain toxic acids which form in many plants as a by-product of their metabolism. It also serves in the building of plant proteins, in preventing magnesium toxicity, and in aiding healthy cell structure.

Best gardening and farming sources for calcium fertilization are natural ground limestone, dolomite, wood ashes, bone meal, oyster shells and marl.

See also LIME; ACIDITY-ALKALIN-ITY; DEFICIENCIES, SOIL; FRUIT TREES, DEFICIENCIES; OYSTER SHELLS.

CALCIUM CYANIDE: *see* FUMIGATION, SOIL

CALCIUM HYDROXIDE: *see* LIME

CALCIUM NITRATE: *see* FERTILIZERS, ARTIFICIAL

CALCIUM SULPHATE: *see* GYPSUM

CALENDAR OF GARDEN OPERA-TIONS: *see* Garden Calendar

CALENDULA: Also known as pot marigold (*C. officinalis*) an annual plant native to southern Europe, is frequently grown in flower gardens in the United States. The dried flower heads are sometimes used in soups and stews, and the so-called petals (ligulate florets) constitute the drug used in medicine.

Calendula grows well on a variety of soils, but a moderately rich garden loam will give best results. The seed, which germinates rapidly, is sown in open ground early in spring in drills 18 inches apart. As soon as the seedlings are established they are thinned to stand about one foot apart in the row. Plant does best in full sun.

The plants blossom early and continue to bloom throughout the summer.

Fine for cutting, flowers of the pot marigold varieties vary from white to orange; the plant grows one to two feet high.

CALICO-BUSH: (*Kalmia latifolia*) *see* Mountain Laurel

CALIFORNIA POPPY: (*Eschscholzia californica*) Especially effective when grown in large groups in a sunny garden. Varieties are offered in creams, white and reds that are striking deviations from the typical yellows. The California Poppy is very hardy, is easily grown from broadcast seeds, and volunteers readily. The blooms are excellent as cut flowers when arranged in low containers with their own foliage. Flowers close in the evening. Plant grows one to two feet high, blooms from July to early fall.

CALLA LILY: Popular florists' flowers, calla lilies belong to the tropical herb genus *Zantedeschia* and are mainly grown for their beautifully-colored leaf-like bracts. In the greenhouse, they need a good supply of light, food and water. The soil mixture should be rich in manure, leaf mold with some bone meal added. It should have some shade, and winter temperatures should range between 55 and 65°. After blooming, dry the tubers before repotting for the following season.

In central California, calla lilies are grown outdoors in moist lowland areas. *Z. Aethiopica* grows to two and one-half feet.

CALLIOPSIS: *see* Coreopsis

CALOCHORTUS: Many fine species of this native of our Western states have been slow in receiving recognition in the East. The butterfly or Mariposa type are forms of *C. venustus*.

The plants should have perfect drainage, and fresh manure should never be used where they are to be planted. Full sun is important. Space the tiny bulbs two inches apart and cover with two inches of fine soil. Plant any time before the ground freezes. There is no need for winter protection, except in exposed locations, where a thin layer of dry leaves or a few evergreen branches should be used to shade the soil surface. If heavier layer of leaves is used it must be removed before the sprouts break through the soil. They usually bloom during the latter part of June.

CALYCANTHUS: These fragrant deciduous shrubs, most of them hardy in the North, prefer well-drained, rich soils, and do well in both sunny and shady locations. They bear a fruit similar to rose hips. *C. floridus* grows three to six feet, has dark green leaves, and is hardiest of all calycanthus. They can be propagated by division, layers set down in summer, or division of older plants. *See also* Shrubs.

CALYX: *see* Flower

CAMASSIA: Entirely hardy, camassias produce showy blue, bluish-white or rich purple blooms that make them a fine attraction for the border or large rock garden. They will thrive anywhere in the United States. Some varieties send up their lovely spikes of lacy florets, 18 to 36 inches high, at the same time as the daffodils. Others bloom up to three weeks later.

These members of the lily family do equally well in sun or semi-shade. Plant them four inches deep in a rich, sandy loam in the fall and don't disturb them. The recommended planting distance is usually three to five inches, but their basal foliage spreads so widely it's better to space them eight or nine inches apart. Camassias will thrive for many years, and may even increase from self-sown seeds.

The Indians used to eat the bulbs, which they called quamash. Camassias are not to be confused with death camass, a variety of zigadenus and a plant which poisons stock in the West.

CAMBIUM: The soft formative tissue which gives rise to new tissues (wood, bark, etc.) in the stems and roots of most shrubs and trees.

The green inner bark of trees, this cambium layer carries the foods produced in the leaves to the roots. Therefore, when the complex ring of a tree's cambium layer is cut, the tree eventually dies.

CAMELLIA: The showy flowers of camellias make a handsome contrast on these woody evergreen shrubs or trees. They thrive best in well-drained soil to which manure or other humus material has been added. If not mulched and fertilized regularly, camellias tend to be slow growers, but the lasting quality of the beautiful flowers makes the extra care worth while.

Colors of the flowers include white, pink, red and violet; varieties are single, semi-double and double. Planting is usually done in early autumn, making the hole about five times larger than the balled shrub. Mulch heavily as the plant can suffer from drought. Many growers have found that white camellias generally

do better in part shade and sometimes even in full shade. Most varieties of camellias have the same climate requirements as azaleas.

It is generally agreed that a camellia planted in fall will be able to tolerate more heat and sun than one that is planted in spring or summer. Don't place camellias near walls or sidewalks or else the reflected heat may damage the plant. As mentioned above, camellias do best in light shade, such as under trees where they are protected from the hot noon sun. Try to protect them also from strong drying winds.

Drainage is particularly important in selecting a location for camellias, as soggy soils around roots are damaging. Be sure to make planting hole extra deep—about one foot—to insure proper drainage; fill in with some gravel and topsoil. But do not plant camellias too deep as this is a most common cause of camellia trouble. The camellia is shallow-rooted, and its surface roots suffer from deep planting. Generally the top roots should be no more than one inch from the soil. Camellias have two most active growth periods—late spring and late summer. Do not transplant during or between these two periods.

CAMOMILE: German, or Hungarian, camomile (*Matricaria chamomilla*) is a European annual herb cultivated in this country in gardens, from which it has escaped in some localities. The dried flower heads are used in medicine.

This species does well on moderately heavy, rather moist, soil rich in humus. Since the plants bloom about eight weeks after the seed is sown, a crop can be grown from seed sown either early in spring or late in summer, following early vegetable crops. Seed sown early in fall will give a good stand of plants that will produce a crop of flowers the next spring. The seed can be sown in drills and barely covered or broadcast, since the plants will soon occupy the ground and exclude the weeds.

When the plants are in full bloom the flower heads are gathered and spread thinly on canvas sheets and dried in the sun. As hand picking is extremely tedious the use of some kind of box stripper is recommended.

Roman camomile (*Anthemis nobilis*), also called English camomile, is a European perennial herb frequently cultivated in gardens in this country and sometimes found growing wild.

Camomile is one of those plants that, like the mints or marjorams, do not have a very clear description botanically. Two genera are distinguished, *Matricaria* and *Anthemis*, but they are by no means so easily separated and, as a result, species in both have the common name camomile. It is a daisy-like flower, the inside of the heads consisting of yellow tubes, the outside rays being white. It is related to the chrysanthemums and similar composite flowers. With the chrysanthemum it has a certain relation in the smell of the leaves.

There are two varieties that are suitable for brewing teas, the so-called rayless and the genuine German camomile. The rayless is not without ray flowers, but only has them subdued, while the German species is distinguished by its cone-shaped, hollow, yellow baskets. The older flowers in this variety or species lend the best distinguishing mark, because all the white petals turn downward. Unfortunately, you cannot fully trust your nose in picking, because all these chrysanthemums or daisies have, at least in the open, some odors which are not easily kept apart. In fact, the real fragrance and the fine flavor of the true camomile does not appear until after it is dried and used in a tea.

CAMPANULA: Often known as the bellflower, campanula makes up a large group of flowering herbs. Its several hundred species include fine plants for borders, perennials, annuals as well as rock garden specimens.

C. medium, for example, the popular Canterbury Bells, is a biennial that grows two to four feet high. *C. pyramidalis,* the Chimney bellflower, makes a busy perennial from three to five feet high, often used for a border. *C. rotundifolia*, often called blue-bells-of-Scotland, is a slender perennial with bright blue flowers, and *C. trachelium* or Coventry Bells makes a vigorous border perennial about three feet high.

Blue is the usual color of campanulas, though white and yellow flowers are sometimes seen. They can be raised from seed, by division or cuttings. Seeds are started under glass, with a shallow covering. The area where transplanted should be a light, well-composted soil, while some of the varieties used in rock garden plantings do best in sandy humus. In the North, open sites are preferred; for the South, partial shade is recommended. Mulch with several inches of organic material to provide winter protection.

See also PERENNIALS.

CAMPION: *see* LYCHNIS

CANADIAN THISTLE: (*Cirsium arvense*) A deep-rooted troublesome weed with purple flowers. The most economical means of eradicating these in fields is to plant alfalfa. The alfalfa shades the rosettes of thistles and cutting the crop twice a year so reduces the storage reserves of the roots that they die in the second or third season. Black fallow, using a duckfoot cultivator to cut off the shoots as soon as they appear in spring and continuing until time to plant alfalfa, helps to deplete the underground storage reserves and will eradicate most of the plants.

CANDYTUFT: The common name for *Iberis*, an attractive, low-growing half-hardy annual, available in white and many pastel tints. Candytuft is very easy to grow, requiring no particular care or special soil. It's perfect for rock gardens and edgings, and some varieties are even grown as house plants. An annual shearing should be made, after blooms have begun to fade.

Annual seeds can be sown outdoors in mid-spring, and should begin to bloom in about eight weeks.

There is a perennial candytuft, much like the annual, which can be propagated by division, or by sowing seeds in fall. *I. sempervirens* has evergreen foliage, white flowers.

See also BORDERS.

CANKER WORMS: The female canker worms, which cause so much trouble, fortunately do not have wings. This makes it necessary for this sex to crawl up the trunks to reach a satisfactory place in which to lay eggs. There are two types, the fall and spring canker worm. By placing a sticky band around the tree trunk in the fall and spring, many of these insects can be eliminated. However, care should be taken that the bands are fresh and that there are no gaps or bridges over which the insects can cross.

See also INSECT CONTROL.

CANNA: A genus of the Banana family, growing from thick, fleshy, tuber-like roots.

In the flower border they can be used in groups of several roots for a bright splash of color from midsummer until frost. Cannas may be used as a bright background in a flower bed along a wall, or in the center of a bed in the lawn with annuals planted around them. They even look nice in rows in the garden with dahlias for cutting. In fact cannas are good anywhere you want color. Their tall, torch-like beauty can set off other flowers to a good advantage.

Cannas can be purchased in two or three eye divisions from most bulb dealers. The roots should be planted as soon as the soil has thoroughly warmed up in the spring. Set them

Canna do not bloom in shade, must have sun for at least half the day. The soil should be moist and never allowed to harden or become very dry.

about two inches deep and 12 to 24 inches apart. A good shovelful of compost should be mixed in the soil around each root. If you want earlier flowers, the roots may be started in four inch pots, inside, early in April. Use good soil with some compost mixed in. After warm weather comes, transplant them to the garden. Cannas need as much sunlight as they can get. They do not bloom in shade. They may be shaded for a short time, but should have sun at least half of the day. Also, the soil must be moist at all times, and should not be allowed to become very dry. By mid-summer they will make good growth and will be ready for another feeding of compost. With correct culture, each root division will have grown into a large clump by fall. Let them grow until the leaves are frosted. On the morning you find them frosted, cut off the stalks just above the soil line. Cut them off *before* the sun shines on them and turns them black. This improves the keeping quality of the roots. Lift each clump carefully and let some soil adhere to it. One of the best methods of storing is to put the clumps with soil adhering in boxes and cover with dry sand. Cannas should not have a very low temperature in storage or they will rot. If it is too high they will dry. A temperature of about 60° is best. The roots should be examined several times during the winter and spoiled ones removed, or the temperature changed if necessary. When planting time comes again, remove all dirt from the roots and divide them into sections with two or three points, or "eyes." Each of these will grow into a stalk.

The new light colored cannas are difficult to keep successfully. If you have trouble keeping them, here is a method which may be helpful. Cover the cannas when frost is expected. After a frost, when the others are lifted, lift these that have not been frosted with a large ball of earth on them. Cut the stems back half way, and pack the plants in boxes or buckets with moist soil around them. Set them in the basement near the window so they can get as much light as possible. Keep the soil just moist enough through the winter to keep the leaves green. They should be rather cool so they will not make too much growth. A temperature about the same as for completely dormant roots is correct. In the spring these plants can be divided and started in pots or in the open ground in the usual way.

CANNING: Canning is, by far, the most widely used method of home food preservation. Government and Gallup surveys indicate that approximately 20,000,000, or 42 per cent, of all home-makers can every year. In rural areas the proportion of home canners jumps to 80 per cent!

An obvious advantage of canning is that there is practically no storage problem. You may can until your basement bulges, whereas your freezer space is definitely limited. Thus it would be wise to freeze those foods which are not suitable for canning before freezing foods which may be either frozen *or* canned. Otherwise,

you may find your freezer filled with foods which could have been canned just as well, and your berries, which are better frozen, will be out of luck.

It would seem that the recent rise of freezing popularity would cut into home canning. However, the reverse is true, according to sales reports of Ball Brothers Co., makers of Mason Jars and Closures for home canning. The reasons for this parodox are: (a) Space in home freezers' and lockers is limited, and many prefer to use it for such things as strawberries, raspberries, cauliflower, etc., which are more satisfactory frozen than canned. (b) Tomatoes, pickles, and most relishes are not suitable for freezing. (c) Many persons prefer peaches, the most universally liked fruit, canned.

SUGGESTIONS FOR CANNING

There are a few cardinal points for proper canning procedure. Can only fresh food, in tiptop condition. Use the boiling-water bath method for fruits and tomatoes. Use the steam-pressure canner for other vegetables. Make sure your equipment is in good working order. Keep your equipment clean. Follow up-to-date directions backed by research. A good booklet on canning is available from the Superintendent of Documents, U.S. Government Printing Office, Washington 25, D.C. Send a dime and ask for *Home Canning of Fruits and Vegetables,* Catalog No. A 1.77:8.

GENERAL RECOMMENDATIONS

The following listings can serve as a general guide in your choice of foods for canning and freezing. If you have gotten results contrary to these recommendations, by all means follow the wisdom of your own experience.

Best Foods for Canning

Tomatoes, Pickles, Relishes, Cabbage, Cucumbers, Snap Beans, Peaches, Apples, Pears.

Best Foods for Freezing

Strawberries, Red Raspberries, Cauliflower, Broccoli, Peas, Carrots, Turnip Greens, Spinach, Brussels Sprouts, Kohlrabi, Cherries.

Foods Suited to Either Method

Asparagus, Lima Beans, Beets, Rhubarb, Squash, Sweet Corn, Green and Wax Beans, Green Snap Beans, Apricots, Vegetable Greens.

See also FREEZING.

CANTALOUPE: (*Cucumis melo cantalupensis*) Actually a hard-rind variety of muskmelon, the cantaloupe is closely similar in requirements and culture to this and all vine-melon-type crops.

Cantaloupe seeds may be started indoors in pots or plant bands and then transplanted to the garden where they should provide an earlier crop.

Named for an Italian castle where it was first grown, the cantaloupe, like all the melon family, does best in somewhat sandy soil. It should not be grown in heavy clay, as melons thrive best in humus-rich, well-drained soil. Another essential is frost-free, warm and sunny weather. Cool temperatures and prolonged cloudiness, even where no freezing occurs, are hard on these sensitive plants. For this reason, melons should not be planted until the soil has thoroughly warmed in the spring—which for the northeastern states usually means June.

Before planting, an application of well-rotted manure to the soil is advisable. Seed should be sown in hills four feet apart each way. To prepare a hill, dig out two shovelfuls of soil, insert one shovelful of rotted manure, and cover with six inches of well-firmed soil. Plant about six to eight seeds per hill and cover with one-half inch of soil. Keep seeds two inches apart and each hill at least 12 inches in diameter. One ounce of seed will plant 20 hills. In about two weeks, the seed should germinate and plants appear. When these are three to four inches high, thin out to three strongest plants per hill.

Seed, incidentally, may also be started indoors in pots or plant bands, then transplanted to the garden to provide an earlier crop. This method allows one serious insect pest, the striped cucumber beetle, less opportunity to damage young plants.

The soil should be cultivated lightly between the rows, but not close to the plants. A constant moisture supply is very necessary to vine development and production, and is particularly important while the fruit is forming. Melons are ripe and ready for picking when the stem begins to part from the vine and comes off with a very slight pull. Yields average ten to 15 melons per hill and vines continue producing from three to four weeks.

Two of the more popular older varieties are Hearts of Gold (80 to 90 days, deep orange flesh) and Rocky Ford (100 days, light green flesh).

CANTALOUPE RINDS: These are quite valuable in the compost heap; their ash contains almost ten per cent phosphoric acid and over 12 per cent potash; they decay most readily and, owing to their moisture, may help in activating decomposition in a heap composed of different plant residues.

CANTERBURY BELLS: *see* CAMPANULA; BIENNIALS

CAPE-MARIGOLD (*Dimorphotheca aurantiaca*) Daisy-like flowers, about two inches across, in shades of yellow, buff, orange and salmon, are produced in abundance by the dwarf spreading plants of *Dimorphotheca*. The flowers of this annual close in the evening. Sometimes blooming from seed the first year, it is sometimes referred to as African Daisy. Grows to about one foot high. *See also* AFRICAN DAISY.

CAPILLARY ACTION: Capillary water is water which surrounds soil particles and which moves in the soil from a moist to a less moist portion of the ground, in opposition to gravitation. Capillarity moves water from the water-table level toward the surface. The distance it can move depends upon the air spaces between the soil particles. The roots of plants derive all of their water supply from this capillary water. *See also* SOIL.

CAPSICUM: *See* PEPPER; CAYENNE

CARAWAY: (*Carum carvi*) An annual or a biennial herb that has been cultivated in many parts of the world for flavoring purposes. The dried fruits, which are known commercially as seed, are used in bakery products and also to flavor cheese and confections. The oil distilled from the seed is used for certain medicinal purposes and in the manufacture of liqueurs.

The plant grows in a wide range of soil conditions, but probably does best on an upland fertile clay. As cultivated in Europe it is usually a hardy biennial that withstands a rather severe continental climate and matures seed early in the second season. The plant is best adapted to the cool climate of temperate regions. When selecting suitable locations for this crop consideration should be given to possible damage from heavy rains and severe winds at harvest time.

When grown as a biennial the seeds are usually drilled early in spring about ½ inch deep in rows 16 inches apart at the rate of six to eight pounds to the acre. In foreign countries when the biennial variety is grown it is common practice to plant some early annual vegetable crop between the rows of the slow-growing caraway. By this means some return is obtained from the land the first season. The biennial caraway crop is harvested in June of the second year.

In California, where the annual variety has been grown, the seed is sown early in spring and the crop matures late in summer. When the first seeds are mature caraway should be cut with some mowing machine that will deposit the cut material in windrows in which it is allowed to cure to some extent. Several methods of handling are used, depending on the size of the crop, the weather conditions, and the implements available at the time.

After partial drying in the windrow the herb may be moved indoors to complete drying or it may be placed in shocks or piled on large pieces of canvas in the field. As the seed comes to final maturity in the curing process, shattering is likely to be excessive unless the crop is handled carefully. For this reason curing on canvas or in barns or open sheds where the shattered seed can be collected has a definite advantage. Seed that does not shatter from the plant after the drying process can easily be removed by flailing or with a grain thresher. In some sections of the Pacific Coast States and adjoining Mountain States where dry clear weather prevails when the caraway matures, the crop has been allowed to ripen thoroughly in windrows and it is then harvested with a combine with a special attachment for elevating the material into it with a minimum loss of seed. Grows about 30 inches high. *See also* HERBS.

CARBON: This makes up from 40 to 50 per cent of organic matter. Carbon is the element at the base of carbohydrates. We eat it, but depending upon what other elements it is combined with, and in what form, hinges the fact whether it is a poison or not. Carbon rarely stands alone as it does in a diamond, which is pure carbon. In coal, in charcoal, in graphite, in a plant, it is in compound form. In limestone it is in the form of calcium carbonate; in washing soda it is sodium carbonate.

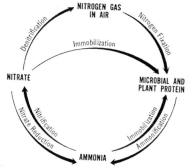

The soil carbon-nitrogen cycle. All plants and soil bacteria must have carbon dioxide. Its presence is denoted in the soil by healthy foliage.

In the air and in the soil carbon is found in the form of carbon dioxide —CO_2—a gas consisting of one atom of carbon and two of oxygen. It is a colorless and odorless gas which is used in making carbonated soft drinks. When one atom combines with only one atom of oxygen we have CO, carbon monoxide, a violent poison which comes from the exhaust of automobiles.

Carbon dioxide is present in the air to the extent of only .03 per cent which means three parts out of 10,000, but its presence in the atmosphere is absolutely necessary for the existence of man, plant and animal. Without it life would come to an end. It is the source from which the plant gets its carbon for the energy it needs to grow. Carbon forms carbohydrate which is an energy food, and it is one of the most important foods for man, plant and microbe. In addition to furnishing energy, part of this carbon is converted into living protoplasm.

Carbon dioxide is a very heavy gas and therefore in a silo, where the fermenting matter is giving it off constantly, there is danger of suffocation

if a person enters without first leaving the doors wide open so that the gas can escape. Being heavy, it accumulates at the bottom of the silo.

THE CARBON CYCLE: When organic matter decays, carbon dioxide is given off. This process is the basis of life itself for this gas goes into the soil atmosphere and is used again by growing plants through their leaves. This is known as the carbon cycle. In this cycle not only does carbon dioxide come from decaying organic matter, but also in the respiration of plant roots. Some of it is also brought down in rain water. For many years it was believed that plants secured their carbon only from the atmosphere, but Lundegardh in 1924 discovered that decaying organic matter in the soil was a more important source. Modern farming, however, with its accent on chemical fertilizers and the neglect of the maintenance of adequate supplies of organic matter, reduces the quantity of carbon dioxide in the soil. This may seriously reduce crop yields.

It is known that plants can use much more carbon dioxide than is normally present in air. In Germany recently experiments have been conducted to add carbon dioxide to the air of greenhouses in order to make plants grow better.

Photosynthesis refers to the manufacturing process which goes on in a plant's leaves, which is made possible through the action of sunlight, and which takes in the manufacture of plant food out of carbon dioxide, water and other nutrients. Sunlight is the basis of photosynthesis.

ORGANIC MATTER: Scientific workers have found that the amount of carbon dioxide in a soil is directly dependent on the amount of organic matter present. It rises and falls with it. In fact the amount of carbon dioxide escaping from soil has been used as a measure of the amount of organic matter present in the soil. The factors that aid in decomposition of organic matter are the same factors that are good for the production of carbon dioxide—namely, high temperature, sufficient moisture and adequate aeration. In one experiment it was shown that four times as much carbon dioxide was given off from a manured as compared to an unmanured soil.

COMPOSTING: The question is, with regard to the production of carbon dioxide in a soil, which is the better method—composting of organic materials, or applying them raw to the soil. Here is a comment by Edward Faulkner, author of *Plowman's Folly,* a few years ago:

"Composting, unless done with such perfection that none of the gaseous carbon dioxide escapes, must necessarily be less efficient in producing carbonates from the soil—per ton of original organic matter. When raw organic matter is intimately mixed with soil (so intimately that there are no bunches) each fragment is surrounded by soil; and the carbon dioxide it releases immediately finds the minerals upon which it can work; and abundance of plant food carbonates necessarily results. I believe that in this way the maximum effect from a given amount of organic matter is obtained. It is conceivable that equal success might be had by compost methods, but for large areas I feel sure that composting can be no better; besides being laborious as compared with the mere mixing in by machinery of a green manure crop."

Research shows that in composting, large amounts of carbon dioxide dissipate into the atmosphere because of the heat generated. For this reason an anaerobic form of composting, where as much air as possible is kept from the fermenting matter, is sometimes considered the better means of conserving more of the carbon.

The soil benefits if raw material is placed there to decompose. In the same way that there is a continuous stream of nitrogen coming from such material, there is also a faster going off of carbon dioxide. In finished com-

post the carbon-nitrogen ratio is much lower than in raw organic material. The rate of going out of nitrogen as well as carbon is therefore less in the former. The compost holds these nutrients for a more gradual release. As far as carbon is concerned a material like sawdust can be an excellent source of carbon, if an excess of carbon is required.

The use of chemical fertilizers retards the formation of carbon dioxide for many reasons. Its use results in lower moisture, aeration, and even temperature. Tests have shown that a soil high in organic matter will have somewhat higher temperatures. Certain fertilizers, like nitrate of soda, cause a severe hardening of soils, reducing their aeration, and good aeration is important so that a sufficient supply of carbon dioxide might be given off. It is a known fact that many farmers who use chemical fertilizers forsake the manure pile and overlook the use and importance of organic matter. Organic farmers and gardeners can have a feeling of security that there is sufficient organic matter in their soils to supply a steady and adequate stream of carbon dioxide gas.

Just as the plant must have carbon dioxide so must the microorganisms of the soil. It furnishes their energy. In fact, the formation of carbon dioxide from organic matter is almost entirely due to the action of bacteria. They make it and use it. The soil bacteria and other microorganisms also produce carbon dioxide as a waste product of their own metabolism. This is what makes the heat in composting.

A sufficient supply of carbon dioxide in the soil will create a healthy, dark green foliage in plants. The abundance of carbon dioxide in soil varies at different seasons. In certain experiments it was found highest in May and in August. This may be a combination of seasons when organic matter decays most readily, plus the time when organic matter is plowed under —added organic matter put in the soil by the farmer, plus crop residues plowed under.

CARBON DIOXIDE: In decomposing organic matter, bacteria release this gas. Combining itself with water, carbon dioxide forms a weak acid which helps to release minerals and other plant food elements from their "holding companies" of colloidal clay and humus.

Some carbon dioxide is also loosed into the air, and an abundance of this rising from the soil insures a healthy dark green foliage color in your crop plants—not the "poison green" caused by nitrate fertilizers. But trap this carbon dioxide in a compacted soil, and it will kill your plants, whose roots need oxygen to live.

The same three essentials, then, that are absolutely necessary for the proper utilization of all other vital soil components, are needed for the formation and proper use of carbon dioxide: an open, friable soil structure, ample organic matter, and the presence of every other element in sufficient quantities so that none may have a limiting or unbalancing effect on any of the others. *See also* AERATION; CARBON.

CARBON DISULPHIDE: *See* FUMIGATION, SOIL.

CARBON-NITROGEN RATIO: There are two chemical elements in organic matter which are extremely important —especially their relation or proportion to each other. They are carbon and nitrogen. This relationship or proportion is called the *carbon-nitrogen ratio.* To understand what this relationship is, suppose a certain batch of organic matter is made up of 40 per cent carbon and two per cent nitrogen. Dividing 40 by two one gets 20. The carbon-nitrogen ratio of this material is then 20 to one, which means, 20 times as much carbon as nitrogen. Suppose another specimen has 35 per cent carbon and five per cent nitrogen. The carbon-nitrogen ratio of this material then would be

seven to one. Anyone who handles organic matter, who mulches or who composts—regardless of which method is used—should have some idea about the significance of the term carbon-nitrogen ratio.

EXAMPLES OF RATIOS: Before we go further and study the significance of the carbon-nitrogen ratio, let us look at some figures—examples of typical materials and their specific carbon-nitrogen ratios. Here is a list as obtained from several sources:

Young sweet clover	12 to 1
Alfalfa hay	13 to 1
Rotted manure	20 to 1
Clover residues	23 to 1
Green rye	36 to 1
Sugar cane trash	50 to 1
Corn stalks	60 to 1
Oat straw	74 to 1
Straw	80 to 1
Timothy	80 to 1
Sawdust	400 to 1

Note the high carbon-nitrogen ratio of sawdust. Such a material would be called highly carbonaceous, and has a very low nitrogen content. If much of it is put into the soil, there would not be enough nitrogen, which is the food of bacteria and fungi which have the function of decomposing it. They would thus have to consume soil nitrogen and create a deficiency of it, thus depressing the crop yield. It would do well for the farmer and gardener who applies organic matter to be conversant with the carbon-nitrogen ratio of the different materials he handles Generally speaking, the legumes are highest in nitrogen and have a low carbon-nitrogen ratio which is a highly desirable condition. The above figures are not standard, but vary greatly, depending on particular conditions under which the plants grew. Straw, for example, could go to as high as a 160 to one ratio, whereas the above gives it as 80 to one.

There is a difference between the carbon-nitrogen ratio of raw organic matter and that of humus. The nitrogen in a leaf may be only one per cent, but by the time it turns to humus, the percentage of nitrogen of that more or less refined substance would be about five per cent. The average of nitrogen of practically all humus is about five per cent, but that of organic matter fluctuates considerably. However, with regard to carbon, a different condition exists. While organic matter in decomposing does lose large amounts of carbon as it turns to humus, the percentage of it to the total mass does not seem to go up or down too much. Thus, if you start with some rotted manure that has a 40 per cent carbon and two per cent nitrogen content which gives a carbon-nitrogen ratio of 20:1, you may wind up with a 10:1 ratio when it turns to humus: that is, a 50 per cent carbon and a five per cent nitrogen content. There is always a narrowing down of the carbon-nitrogen ratio when organic matter decomposes. The content of carbon in humus does not vary too much. It averages about 50 to 52 per cent.

THE SOILS' CARBON-NITROGEN RATIO: The carbon-nitrogen ratio of the soil is on the average much less than that of organic matter. By the time green matter is decomposed in the soil the C:N ratio has dropped to much lower figures. Selman Waksman in his book *Humus* gives typical figures. Some brown silt loam soils of Illinois were about 12:1 in the topsoil, 11½:1 in the subsurface layer and 9:1 in the subsoil. The ratio always declines as one goes downward. In the Broadbalk plots (England) the C:N starts at about 9:1 and declines to about 6:1 seven feet down. Waksman cites a black clay loam at 12:1 in the topsoil and 9:1 in the subsoil. As the age of the humus increases, says Waksman, the C:N ratio of the soil in which it is, becomes lower. In eight soils in Northwestern United States the C:N average was 12½:1 in the top six inches and 9:1 about 3½ feet down.

THE BACTERIA AND CARBON-NITROGEN RATIO: The C:N ratio of the microorganisms of the soil is usually much lower than that of organic matter, humus, or soil. The average C:N ratio of the bodies of bacteria and fungi falls between 4:1 to 10:1. Why is their C:N ratio always less than that of the humus in which they work? The answer is that they require more protein than carbohydrates. Protein is needed for tissue building mainly, while carbon of carbohydrates is for energy. Humus is made up to a great extent of lignins and other high-carbon material. In other words humus has more carbohydrates than the bodies of microbes, which are extremely high in protein, and since about 16 per cent of protein is nitrogen, we can see that the microbes' bodies will have a very high percentage of nitrogen to carbon. Usually the tissues of bacteria are richer in protein than that of fungi.

When much raw organic matter is applied to a soil, the microorganisms will multiply rapidly, but in this process of working they have to consume nitrogen. That is an absolute necessity to their existence. Now, if the material that is plowed under has a low C:N ratio, that is, it is low in nitrogen, the soil organisms in decomposing it will have to look for their nitrogen in places other than in the decomposing substances. They will draw on the soil's store of nitrogen, thus depleting it, with a depressing effect on the crop yield. But their bodies are now gorged with nitrogen and when they die, future crops will benefit. This shows that when plowing under highly carbonaceous organic matter, a sufficient period of time should elapse before the crop is planted. It will give the soil organisms time to die, so to speak, to give their bodies to their country. Or, one should try to use organic materials with a low C:N ratio, which means a high nitrogen content.

One investigator (Broadbalk) discovered that where the C:N ratio of added organic matter plowed under, was 33:1 or more, a withdrawal of nitrogen occurred. Between 17 and 33 nothing was added or withdrawn; in other words, nitrification ceased. But if it was under 17, the nitrogen store of the soil was increased. This shows the value of adding compost to the soil, because its C:N ratio is usually quite low.

The practice is, when plowing under organic matter with a high C:N, to apply with it a high nitrogen fertilizer. The organic gardener can use for such purposes dried blood, bone meal, hen manure, cotton seed meal, fish scraps and dried ground fish, peanut shells, silk and wool wastes, castor pomace, cotton gin wastes, cowpea and soybean hay, felt wastes, feathers, hoof or horn meal, a number of other organic materials having a high nitrogen content.

Russel in his book *Soil Conditions and Plant Growth* (Longmans) gives an interesting illustration of a comparison between the earthworm and microorganisms in reducing the C:N ratio of rye-straw. He says, "Thus, L. Meyer found that earthworms feeding on rye-straw composted with basalt meal reduced its C:N ratio from 23 to 11 during a period of two years while the soil microorganisms alone reduced it to about 18 during the same period." This means that the earthworm is a better conserver of nitrogen than microorganisms.

THE SIGNIFICANCE OF THE C:N RATIO: We have already seen that the C:N ratio of plowed under organic matter is important to the conservation of the soil's store of nitrogen. It is also of great significance to the general operation of soils. Mainly, it is a matter of having enough nitrogen available. There is a difference in the way a low C:N ratio works, depending on whether it is in raw organic matter or in humus. Organic matter, applied to the soil, represents nitrogen on the move. In a finished compost it is in a more static condition. Less is given off. In terms of C:N ratio we can express it in the following manner. In the application of raw organic matter, the extent of nitrogen movement depends on its C:N ratio. If it is high, like in sawdust (400:1) there will be no nitrogen movement, but if it is a material like young sweet clover (12:1), there will be a very satisfactory rate of nitrification.

In humus, however, although the C:N is low, let us say 10:1, there is a resistance to rapid decomposition. The movement is slower, and will take place over a longer period of time. This is of some value as it means the nitrogen is stored for future use. In the case of fresh organic matter with a low C:N, not only is there a fast nitrogen movement, but much carbon is given off in the form of carbon dioxide. It is thought by some that this may kill off some of the larvae of destructive insects.

AGE OF ORGANIC MATTER: The younger the plant material is, the lower the C:N ratio, which means that it will not only decompose more quickly, but will release more nitrogen and increase the yield. Louis M. Thompson in his book, *Soils and Soil Fertility*, gives the figures of an experiment with wheat that is typical:

Stage of Growth	C:N Ratio
Very young	16
Well headed	27
Almost ripe	41

This experiment showed that the lower the C:N the more nitrates were added to the soil and more growth of wheat occurred.

RAINFALL AND TEMPERATURE: As rainfall goes down, the C:N ratio also declines. The higher the rainfall, the lower the nitrogen. The C:N ratio of arid soils is always lower than those in regions of higher precipitation. In a soil which had a rainfall of 15 inches per annum the C:N was 13:1. Where it was 10 inches or less of rain the C:N was about 11:1. It has also been found that the higher the temperature the lower the C:N. To review: Higher rain—higher C:N.

Higher temperature—lower C:N. Also: Higher acidity—higher C:N. *See also* COMPOSTING; CARBON.

CARDINAL CLIMBER: *see* STAR GLORY

CARDINAL-FLOWER: (*Lobelia cardinalis*) The bright scarlet spikes of the cardinal flower can be found in July along a brook or a sluggish stream, usually in semi-shade. If you wait until the seeds are ripe, you can gather them, plant them in a flat and raise excellent little plants easily. When they develop into rosettes of dark green leaves with sturdy roots, they are ready to be placed in their permanent setting. Although they prefer a damp soil, they have been known to grow in an ordinary flower garden.

A sister of the cardinal flower is the blue cardinal flower, *syphilitica*. The flowers are bright blue touched with white, fading to pale blue. Its requirements are much the same as its cardinal sister. It likes moist soil beside a stream or pond.

There are other lobelias. The brook lobelia is a graceful little plant with racemes of light blue flowers on thread-like stems, found in companies among the long grass along a brook. The cardinal flower grows three to five feet tall. *See also* MOISTURE-LOVING PLANTS.

CARDOON: (*Cynara cardunculus*) An old vegetable, known to the ancient Romans, cardoon has been largely overlooked by American gardeners. Small quantities have been imported from France, and it is a minor market vegetable in a few places in California. A close relative of the artichoke, cardoon grows rapidly in any good rich organic soil, in well-drained soils with plenty of moisture. Plants should be raised in hotbed, transplanted after last frost about three feet apart. In plant and leaf structure it suggests a cross of burdock and celery. The plant grows about three feet high when it should have straw, burlap, or paper wrapped around it to blanch or whiten the main leaf stalks, which are the edible portion. The blanched plant looks something like an oversize celery bunch, but the stalks are used as a cooked vegetable, boiled or like French fried potatoes.

CARNATION: (*Dyanthus caryophyllus*) In its sweetness of perfume, beauty of color, and symmetry of form, the carnation is unexcelled. These attributes, combined with the ease of culture and the certainty of flowering,

Carnations such as this Dorothy Gordon variety are not hard to grow. New stock plants may be grown from cuttings; rooting takes three weeks.

give the carnation preeminence among our flowering plants. As a cut flower the carnation is more durable than is the bloom of most plants, for it has lasting quality in a vase.

These half-hardy perennials grow to two feet high; it is a nice plant for the garden where it can be used for borders as well as in beds or in simple mixed plantings. Furthermore, its adaptability to pot-culture makes it possible to grow it in the house, where it may blossom much of the year. Separate pots of it may be made to bloom successively to prolong the peak of flowering, if preferred, or all may be grown at one time for greater abundance of flowers on special occasions. In the greenhouse plants are set into permanent beds, worked into strong sandy loam that is porous in structure and possessed with a liberal organic content. Tankage, as steamed refuse from slaughter houses, at the rate of three pounds to 100 square feet of soil gives good results. In greenhouses or garden culture, applications may be made every two months. In pot-culture, one teaspoonful of tankage to one quart of soil can well be given at the start and at eight-week intervals. House plants should not be allowed to become "pot-bound" by being beset with roots, giving a crowded condition. It is urgent to repot the plants every six months.

Tankage is an excellent organic fertilizer, having 5-10 per cent nitrogen and 8-30 per cent of phosphoric acid. Leaf mold and compost in the soil are also good, may be used as a part of the surface mulch.

CULTURE: Carnations are not hard to grow; in fact, the culture is simple. New stock plants are grown from cuttings which are easy to root. Side shoots which develop along the main stem are used. Rooting takes place in about three weeks. Bottom temperature of 60-65 degrees F. and room temperature of 55 degrees F. is conducive to rapid rooting. The species of carnation are cool-temperature plants but need sunshine to do well. It is better not to try to grow them in diffused light or in shade. The new stock is potted or put into flats to "grow up." See also FERTILIZER.

CARNIVOROUS PLANTS: There are a few plants which are capable of capturing and devouring small insects. For example, the sundew (Drosera rotundifolia), has a foliage that is covered with sticky hairs. Insects are attracted to the plant and cannot escape once caught in the "trap." The more they struggle, the more sticky hairs their bodies come into contact with. Eventually the sundew secretes sufficient juices so that the insect is completely digested. Butterworts (Pinguicula) work similarly, with the additional feature of having the sticky-haired leaves roll up—thus starting the digestive process.

The Venus Fly-Trap (Dionaea muscipula) is a wild, semiaquatic herb, that has leaves ending in two plates. These snap together to trap and devour insects. Once the trap is shut, the victim is digested, after which the trap again opens.

Another group of carnivorous or insectivorous plants is the pitcher plant. These are any one of a number of plants whose leaves are formed in the shape of a pitcher. Insects which enter the pitcher are trapped by a sticky fluid in the hollow base, where they are eventually dissolved. In this category are the common pitcher plant (Sarracenia) and the Darlingtonia. There is an additional plant, the bladderwort (Utricularia), which are found in pools and trap many water insects with a form of trap door. See also DARLINGTONIA.

CAROB: (Ceratonia siliqua) For thousands of years, the carob tree has flourished in countries bordering the Mediterranean Sea. It bears large, brown pods containing 40 per cent sugar and six per cent protein.

The tree belongs to the legume or bean family and is a handsome evergreen, medium-sized tree with glossy leaves.

While carob has a wide range as a handsome shade tree, commercial production of pods is limited to areas not far from the sea, where the summers are dry and warm and fall rains do not come before harvest.

In the Mediterranean countries where water for irrigation is scarce, carobs are grown dry farmed. No fertilizer is used and the trees are never sprayed as these trees are practically free of diseases and insect pests. Therefore the cost of production is low.

The carob made its United States debut in 1854, when the U. S. Patent Office distributed 8,000 plants throughout the southern states. Since that time, the development of the carob has been limited mainly to parts of southern California. Many California communities sport very large carob trees today—the result of the work of the California Experiment Station over 75 years ago.

Carob flour, made from the flesh of the pod, is now made in this country from imported pods. This flour has a flavor resembling chocolate and is used, when mixed with wheat flour in making bread, hot cakes, waffles, etc. Mixed with hot milk, it is an excellent drink. The coarsely ground flesh is a superior breakfast food.

Carob syrup is made by reducing the pods to coarse powder, dissolving the sugars in water and boiling down to the thickness of honey.

Carob thrives on a rather warm climate, free from severe frosts and requires at least 12 to 14 inches of rain per year. An average of 23 inches is ideal.

On the other hand, carob suffers from too much water, as is shown by the sickly condition of trees planted in wet places, or in lawns which are frequently sprinkled.

The carob requires a near rainless autumn when the pods are reaching maturity. Ripening occurs in September and October according to variety. Harvest is in October-November. Early fall rains of short duration do little or no harm, especially if followed by dry East winds. A long wet spell after the pods have reached high sugar content is likely to cause loss of quality by moulds and fermentation. Near the coast in Southern California, in the fog belt, carobs often mould at maturity and are quickly infested with worms. While carobs are quite popular as street trees in coast towns, commercial carob culture is not recommended for a narrow belt immediately adjacent to the ocean.

Many types of soil, from adobe to sand, are suitable for the carob. Recommended, however, is a rather deep heavy loam with good subdrainage. The root system is very extensive with relatively few fibrous feeder roots.

Carob seeds, when collected fresh from recently ripened pods, germinate readily. They may be planted in beds or flats, and when the second set of leaves is well formed, they are planted in small pots or paper containers. At 12 inches high, the plants are set in boxes four by 12 inches deep, or planted in nursery rows in open ground where there is little danger of frost. When the seedlings have developed a stem three-eighths of an inch or more in diameter, they are budded after the fashion of citrus trees.

For soil conservation and improvement, carob trees should be planted on contours of one per cent gradient. They are spaced about 30 by 30 feet or about 50 to the acre and, if desired, may be rowed in one direction. Trees should be set at the same depth. The best time to plant is at the end of the rainy season, while the soil is still moist. All weeds must be kept hoed from around the trees.

Rabbits and gophers must be controlled until the trees grow beyond their reach. It's a good idea to protect them the first year by surrounding each tree with poultry netting. Other than that, pests are negligible.

Carob pods are easily shaken down; the few remaining ones can be knocked off with a light pole. They are then spread in the sun for a few days until completely dry. When the market is further developed and volume production is common, no doubt some type of evaporator will be developed for drying more quickly. After drying and fumigating, the pods may be stored indefinitely if protected from mice.

The budded carob tree, under favorable dry farm conditions should begin to bear the sixth year and produce an average of five pounds per tree. The size of the crops will increase gradually, reaching an average of 100 pounds the twelfth year.—*Dr. J. E. Coit.*

CAROTENE: *see* CARROTS, NUTRITIONAL VALUE

CARPET GRASS: *see* LAWN

CARPETWEED: (*Aizoaceae*) A low-growing weed, forming mats in gardens, on paths, and thriving well on lighter, sandy soils. It will not resist hoeing and cultivation.

CARRANZA, ERWIN K.: Erwin Knohr Carranza was born in Costa Rica, where he farmed organically for many years. During the Second World War, he lost his farm and, at the end of the war, he went to Germany. Here he studied more about the organic method on a farm operated by bio-dynamic experts. After four years, he took his knowledge back to Central America and constructed a composting plant in Heredia, Costa Rica. Several years ago, Carranza took over a larger plant in San Salvador, which processes up to eight tons of garbage an hour.

CARROTS: (*Daucus carota sativa*) Increasingly important because of their high Vitamin A content, carrots should occupy a prominent place in every home garden.

Carrots were well known by the ancient Greeks. In the middle ages they were greatly esteemed because of the beauty of their delicate foliage. No stylish corsage was considered complete without a few carrot leaves.

Carrot seeds are very small, but there are several ways of overcoming the difficulty of handling the tiny, slow-germinating seeds.

They can be mixed with clean, dry sand using about a teacupful of sand for a quarter ounce of seed. This mixture, thoroughly stirred, can then be planted easily enough in the drill or

No vegetable garden is complete without the carrot. A fine source of Vitamin A, it is hardy and easy to grow and stores well during the winter.

trench. A quarter ounce of seed is plenty for a fifty foot row.

Or you might prefer to sprout the seed before planting them. Seeds can be sprouted between sheets of wet paper for four days. They are then allowed to dry out just enough to make handling feasible.

The soil in which they are to grow must be well prepared. It should be deep, mellow, and well pulverized. Although the carrot gets along well in almost any type of soil, the soil should be free from lumps and stones because these force the roots into deformities and cause them to split.

A good supply of humus from a well made compost heap will do much to put the soil into condition.

Carrots are hardy. That is, they may be planted just as soon as the garden can be worked. In most of the northeastern states this is some time in April.

If the soil is light, the seeds should

be covered with half an inch of earth. Less covering is necessary with heavier soils.

You will find that this is most easily done by stretching a tight guide line across the garden close to the surface. Following the guide line a small trench should be opened using the corner of the hoe.

After the seeds have been placed in this trench, they may be most readily covered by using a rake to draw the removed earth back into the trench. The seed should be carefully firmed after planting to secure good contact between seed and soil and to remove air pockets.

Because of their slow germination, you will find it a good idea to mark the rows while planting by dropping an occasional radish seed, as well as using stakes to mark the ends of the rows.

For hand cultivation, the rows should be about 14 inches apart.

Carrots should be thinned to stand about two inches apart in the row. Conscientious thinning often makes the difference between a good crop and a poor one. Some gardeners wait until the young carrots are a bit less than half an inch in diameter. Creamed young carrots, fresh pulled; or raw young carrots, grated for salads, are a delicacy.

To secure a steady supply, successive plantings of carrots should be made. The last planting may be made as late as July 15th to August 1st.

Nantes has high quality and is suitable for sandy soils. Chantenay is very reliable for heavy soils and is an excellent storage variety.

Of all vegetables, you will probably find the carrot the least affected by disease and insect pests. In suitable soils they are usually thrifty. But if you know from experience that wireworms are common in your locality, you can greatly reduce their activities by sprinkling wood ashes along the rows.

If the soil in your garden is by nature excessively acid or lacking in natural calcium (and most soils in the northeastern states have through cultivation and the leaching action of rainfall become deficient in lime) you might return this material to the garden by the application of finely ground limestone.

During their growing period carrots should be weeded carefully. Mulching will eliminate the tedious hand weeding job.

Except for those grown for immediate use, carrots are customarily left in the ground in the fall until after the first frosts. They are then dug and stored.

The proper storage of home-grown food is very essential. It is both practical and necessary to conserve foods. Carrots can be stored in many ways depending upon the quantity and the limitations placed upon the gardener.

Properly stored carrots keep well, retain their flavor, and have a higher food value, than canned ones.

Carrots in storage require for best results cool, moist surroundings, with the temperature ranging from 32 to 42° and a humidity of between 90 and 95 per cent.

For the home gardener the storage barrel is perhaps the most handy.

After the temperature at night has dropped to freezing, enough carrots should be dug and topped to fill a barrel. If a barrel is not available, a packing box can be used provided it is closed on all sides except one. After the barrel has been filled, its mouth should be plugged with straw or grass and it should be placed in a trench, deep enough to take it lying on its side.

A layer of straw should then be placed under and around the barrel so that the whole thing appears as a mound of straw. A thin covering of earth is then applied.

It is best to wait then until the temperature is down almost to freezing before applying another layer of straw and a foot thick layer of earth as a complete cover.

This method is convenient because the stored material is started and held at about the right temperature and humidity and is easy to get at by removing the straw plug.

A couple of storage barrels of carrots should be ample for most families over winter. If you have a larger quantity it will probably be necessary for you to store them by mounding them in a straw-lined trench about a foot deep and five feet wide and as long as may be necessary. Alternate layers of straw and earth are then applied as with the barrel pit.

Whichever method you use, select for storage only sound, uninjured and mature roots.

CARROTS, NUTRITIONAL VALUE: The orange-yellow pigment abundant in carrots is scientifically known as carotene, a substance that becomes Vitamin A when used up by the cells of the intestine.

Carotene is absent in such root vegetables as parsnips and turnips so carrots have become important in our bill of fare. Although green vegetables are a greater source of Vitamin A, carrots can be made available by the home gardener throughout the year and can be used in the diet in various ways.

Scientists tell us too, that when we have consumed more carotene or Vitamin A than is required for immediate needs, it is stored in the liver in quantity sufficient for three months. When we have learned that a deficiency of carotene in our bodies may cause night blindness and may make one susceptible to infections of the epithelial tissues of the eyes, the digestive glands, the kidneys, the respiratory system and the alimentary canal, we can understand not only its great importance but will prize more highly the successful results of our efforts in the culture of our carrot crop.

The highest content of carotene is found in varieties with bright golden orange flesh. Red Cored Chantenay is still one of the best. Pale sorts are not recommended. While we find all carrot seedling roots to be colorless, the thinnings that are usually removed in late Spring and enjoyed as a delicacy are claimed to possess substantial amounts of carotene.

CARTHAMUS TINCTORIOUS: *see* SAFFLOWER

CARUM: *see* CARAWAY

CASSAVA: *see* MANIHOT

CASTOR BEAN: (*Ricinus communis*) Fruit of the castor oil plant which is a robust perennial in tropical countries, but in regions subject to frost it is grown as an annual. The seeds of this plant, called castor beans, yield castor oil.

The crop is adapted to corn or cotton land, which should be prepared as for these crops. Corn planters with certain modifications can be used in seeding. The spacing of rows and of plants within the rows may be such as to permit the use of available planting and cultivating equipment. The seed should be planted 1½ to three inches deep, depending on the moisture in the soil. From seven to ten pounds of seed are required to plant an acre, depending on the variety. Weeds must be kept under control by frequent shallow cultivation early in the season.

Besides the actual cash value of castor beans, it is the rich fertility of the castor bean pomace or residue left after the beans are hulled that is of prime interest and importance to organic-minded farmers and gardeners. Analysis charts show the hulls to be richer in appreciable amounts of nitrogen, phosphates, potash and a number of other minor plant food elements than either fresh barnyard manure or cottonburs.

In addition to the value of the hulls, the stalks are high in cellulose content and easily decomposed, and when they and the leaves are chopped and turned under the soil can assimilate them readily. It is estimated that from 35 to 50 per cent of the gross weight of the castor beans and capsules can be returned to the soil for its improvement.

As a periodic rotation crop, as a side crop grown for the rich organic soil-building benefits of its pomace, hulls, roots, etc., or as an actual cash crop, castor beans are proving remarkably helpful in boosting fertility. They more than repay the effort and space given their cultivation.

In harvesting, the beans are either hauled to the hulling plant, or a portable huller goes to the grower's field. In either case, the hulls are saved and the farmer takes his home in most instances to spread on his field, orchard or garden.

Many farmers find in rotating other crops with castor beans that their succeeding crops are more vigorous and productive. Potatoes especially are found to be greener and healthier from the organic contribution of castor bean humus. City gardeners are seeking the hulls for mulches on rose gardens and other flowers, strawberries and asparagus and are also spreading it over lawns. Admirably serving further, the bean plant wastes provide a valuable contribution in building and enriching any gardener's compost pile.

Ricin is the poisonous agent in castor pomace, and scientists have not yet been able to remove it; consequently the rich protein pomace cannot be fed to livestock. They are also trying to produce paper from the stalks, but it may well be that the present organic use of the castor pomace and stalks is of more value to more people than the industrial use could be.

The soil for beans requires plenty of organic matter if they are to give good yields. This organic food can usually be supplied by crop rotation and by plowing green manure under awhile before planting.

Poisonous Bean: Growers of cas-

tor beans should realize that the ricin from the seeds or beans must be regarded as a blood poison. The beans are contained in three one-sided parts which form spiny capsules. If eaten by humans or animals, they can cause nausea, pain, extreme thirst or dullness of vision.

Castor Pomace: After the oil has been extracted from the castor bean, a residue is left that is widely used as an organic fertilizer in place of cotton seed meal, because the latter is valuable also as feed. The nitrogen analysis of castor bean pomace is the decisive factor. It varies from four to 6.6 per cent, while phosphoric acid and potash analyze from one to two per cent, with greater variation occurring in the phosphorus content.

Where animal matter is unavailable and where plant matter alone is present, compost could be easily made with castor pomace, especially if it were first moistened and spread over the green matter in semi-liquid form. The finer the plant matter to be broken down, the more intimate the contact between the plants and the pomace, and consequently the quicker the bacterial action.

Castor pomace is handled by fertilizer dealers in various parts of the country. Recent studies have indicated that castor pomace is fully comparable to cottonseed meal, if used on an *"efficiency"* basis. This means that 160 pounds of nitrogen in castor pomace will have the same crop-producing effect as 200 pounds of nitrogen in cottonseed meal. For farm practices, castor pomace may be substituted, pound for pound, for cottonseed meal.

CASUARINA: *see* Australian Pine

CATALOGS: For many people, the peak of the year's garden enthusiasm comes not with the first blooms of spring, but in the first week in January when the new seed and nursery catalogs arrive.

There is good reason for this excitement over the garden catalogs, because they serve an important function. Only the very largest of seed stores and local nurseries carry the variety of plant materials that are available to gardeners everywhere through the catalogs. And since some of the finest gardening pleasures come with growing things that are unusual —plants that will make friends and neighbors thrill with admiration and envy—the coming of the spring catalogs has become one of the most important garden events of the year.

Some common plant materials— fruit and nut trees for example—are available almost exclusively by mail because many local nurseries don't sell enough to warrant propagating them. And mail order nurseries are just about the only source for "lining out stock," seedlings and small plants for stocking home nurseries.

Seed and nursery catalogs have performed an important service by educating gardeners. After many hours of studying illustrated catalogs you are bound to improve your ability to identify plants and trees. And they give an idea of the current market value of seed and nursery stock and offer cultural information about many plants.

CATALPA: Handsome flowering trees often used for front lawns and streets. Chief disadvantage is their relatively short life, so they are not recommended for permanent tree plantings. Fast-growing, they can be planted in ordinary garden soil, propagated by cuttings or layering. Also known as bean tree, *C. bignonioides* grows up to 40 feet, produces white flowers in summer.—*See also* TREES.

CATCH CROPS: In intercropping, a quick-maturing crop that is grown along with a major crop, but is matured and removed by the time the major crop expands to occupy its adult dimensions.

Improving the organic matter content of soils by growing and plowing under catch crops has proven to be

worth over $33.00 an acre in some Illinois field tests. Obtaining these catch crops required very little extra labor, only a small outlay of actual cash, and as a rule they did not occupy the land long enough to prevent growing the usual grain crops in the rotation.

A rotation of corn, oats, and wheat allows a grain crop each year and a catch crop in the wheat plowed under for corn. There is scarcely time after oat harvest and the preparation of the seed-bed for wheat to make it worth while to attempt a catch crop in the oats.

With the wide corn row coming into use there is now a possibility of seeding various legumes successfully between the corn rows and have a desirable catch crop immediately following the corn. The legume seeding or legume-grass mixture does not always have to be used as a plow-under catch crop in order to obtain the highest value. It is evident that if a legume crop is allowed to stand over a year there is the possibility of hay and pasture which will add to its farm value. In fact there were some experimental field results which indicate that the stand over legume-grasses gave a larger increase in crop yields than did the in-between catch crop.

Of the many legumes that might be used, sweet clover is probably the best for catch crop purposes. The sweet clover weevil has in recent years become so destructive as to about rule out this valuable legume. Next in line is alfalfa which has proven its ability to survive adverse weather especially drouth conditions. One soil requirement which is a must for alfalfa is that the land be well limed. Alfalfa has the extra advantage of supplying large amounts of hay and good pasturage if the catch crop is allowed to stand over.

It is advisable to use a mixture of legumes and grasses in a catch crop seeding. A good mixture almost insures a survival of one or more of the varieties seeded. This is also likely to give a more uniform coverage of a field. There may be areas or spots in a field where one legume will fail and the other succeed, or the grasses will succeed where the legumes thin down or fail completely. Alfalfa and red clover make a good legume mixture and such grasses as timothy, brome grass, orchard grass or fescue go well in legume-grass mixtures. Grasses are very desirable in a catch crop or a stand over crop because the fine grass roots in the topsoil are very desirable and almost necessary if highest corn yields are to be obtained.

The wide corn row seeding as a means of obtaining a catch crop, hay crop or pasture is gradually developing in the Midwest. In this plan the conventional 40 inch corn row is too narrow for successful growing of legumes or legume-grass mixtures between the corn rows. The 80 inch row is more desirable for the legume-grass but it generally gives a 20 per cent lower corn yield. Not many corn growers wish to take such a loss in order to get a stand of legumes on the land. The 60 inch corn row has proven to be good for the legume seeding and also allows a corn yield which will generally equal and sometimes exceeds that in the 40 inch row. This is on the basis of 16,000 plants an acre for each row width.

The best legume to use in the corn field seeding depends on the season. Since we cannot determine the weather in advance, it is necessary to use a legume which has been found to survive consistently in adverse seasons. In seasons of an abundance of rainfall the following legumes and grasses have been successfully grown between corn rows: alfalfa, red clover, alsike, ladino, vetch and the grasses, ryegrass, orchard grass, brome grass, fescue and timothy. Grasses in this type of seeding have not been as successful

as have the legumes with the exception of Balbo rye.

In seasons of drouth and extreme heat, alfalfa has proven to be the most successful for corn field seeding. This corn field seeding has many possibilities of obtaining catch crops, hay crops, pasture and in addition has considerable potential in soil conservation.

Catch crops should generally be plowed under in the spring after the growth has started. Fall plowing is advisable only on heavy clay soils or gumbo soils which may be difficult to handle when spring plowed. Fall plowing should be done as late as possible in order to prevent the legumes from coming on in the spring, through the plowed land. Fall plowing on rolling land is subject to serious erosion.

The value of the catch crop varies with type of soil and also with the crop rotation in which it is used. In all cases it would seem that the legume catch crops are highly profitable. This profit is derived from the increase in crop yields brought about by adding active organic matter to the soil.—H. J. Snider.

CATENA: Refers to the association between soils on the basis of drainage or of differences in relief. Soil surveyors make use of this relationship when classifying soils in a given region.

CATERPILLAR HUNTER BEETLE: One of the most valuable of ground beetles is the caterpillar-hunter, or searcher. It is about an inch and a half in length, and is strikingly pretty. Its wing covers are violet-green with a red margin, and the under parts of its body are violet, green and gold. Another true ally of the gardener, it is particularly fond of the tent caterpillar, which it destroys in untold numbers. The larvae, living just below the surface of the ground, live on other insects; especially the leaf-eating varieties that pupate in the ground.

This useful insect is a boon to city gardeners, as it is usually found in greater numbers within the city limits than it is in the country. Protection should be offered to such a valuable asset. *See also* INSECT CONTROL.

CATNIP: (*Nepeta cataria*) A European perennial plant that frequently occurs in this country as a weed in gardens and about dwellings. It has long had a popular use as a domestic remedy. Both leaves and flowering tops are in some demand in the crude-drug trade.

Catnip does well on almost any good soil, but thrives best on a well-drained and moderately rich garden loam. It will be more fragrant, however, if grown in sandy situations rather than in heavy soils. The plant may be propagated from seed or by root division. The seed is sown in rows either late in fall or early in spring and covered lightly. Fall-sown seed usually gives a more even stand and a heavier growth. When the plants have reached a height of four to five inches they are thinned to stand 12 to 16 inches apart in the rows. In some localities field sowing does not give good results, in which case plants may be started in a coldframe and later transplanted to the field. Shallow cultivation will favor vigorous growth. Does well in sun or shade; grows to four feet.

The flowering tops, harvested when the plants are in full bloom, are dried in the shade to preserve their green color. When larger quantities are grown the herb may be cut with a mowing machine with the cutter bar set high. The plants should lie in the swath until partly dry, and the curing may then be finished either in small cocks in the field or in the barn, care being taken to preserve the natural green color as far as possible.

CATTAIL: (*Typha*) Sometimes referred to as a reed, tule, flag, rush or reed mace, cattails are tall spiked plants that grow on swamp or marsh land. In the north, plants begin to emerge from the water around April first, and in the first few weeks may grow as much as three inches a day. By the last of July, they range from eight to 15 feet in height.

Cattails are a neglected crop whose potentialities appear almost unlimited. The roots are edible like potatoes and the flour good for baking.

Cattails are a perennial plant that spread rapidly. There can be as many as 35 offsets from a single plant in one growing season, and as many as three acres of cattails have been judged to be all one plant. A good cattail stand will average around 86,000 stems per acre.

Once cattails are established successfully in an area, they crowd out all competition, so there is no weeding problem. Unlike other plants, no insects or molds are known to interfere with their growth to any practical extent.

One kind of cattail which grows in Egypt thrives in salt water, and the Egyptians have discovered that when they plant it on the delta where the Nile meets the Mediterranean, the cattail will make the soil less salty, and it can then be used for other crops.

Researchers speculate that if this cattail were planted in the coastal areas of Texas, and Louisiana, which are periodically overrun by salt water, the cattails would purify the land so that it could bear other crops. This would give the country thousands of additional acres of valuable farm land.

Experimental studies show that you can get a larger crop by cultivating the cattail, and that it can be grown on lands unsuitable for other crops, providing the land can be irrigated. Cattails need ample water, but they don't require swamp conditions.

The potential uses of cattail products seem almost unlimited. The root can be eaten like potatoes. The flour has a potato-like flavor and makes truly good cookies, taste testers say. The flour is so high in starch that it can substitute for cornstarch in making puddings. It can also be fermented to form alcohol, or used as a media for penicillin production.

Cattail harvesting is almost a year-round business. The leaves can be harvested from July until the first frost, and the stalks and spikes from the first of September until the 15th of May. Two crops can be harvested each year in the South.

A survey made by the Federal Government during the last war showed that the United States has approximately 140 thousand square miles of swamp land with cattail stands of varying densities. If these cattails were processed, approximately 34,000,000 pounds of oil could be extracted from the seeds, leaving 166,000,000 pounds of meal for cattle or chicken feed.

CATTAIL REEDS: Such material, often easily obtainable when ponds are cleared, should be used in fresh form in the compost pile since the straw is very hard to break down, partly because the nutrients have receded into the roots, partly because stalky material cannot be properly moistened and brought into intimate contact with nitrogenous material, such as manure,

dried blood, etc. Where dry material is available, it had best be used for mulching. The nutrients in reeds are not negligible, especially not when water lily stems and similar material are included to balance it. The contents are estimated at 2.0 per cent nitrogen, 0.8 phosphoric acid, and 3.4 potassium.

CATTLE MANURE: *see* MANURE

CATTLEYA: Perhaps the most popular of the orchids, cattleyas are extremely showy and very valuable commercially. Native to Central and South America and epiphytic in habit, cattleyas have been of great importance in popularizing the idea of growing orchids at home.

Here are general instructions for growing cattleyas: from May through October, inside house temperatures are generally satisfactory; during winter, a temperature range of 50 to 55° at night is recommended; best potting material is osmunda fiber and it is vital that the plant be firmly set or else the roots will be injured when the plant is handled; also loosely-packed material will hold too much water for the proper growth of the plants.

Growing plants should be repotted about every two years. During hot dry weather, spray the plants with water in the evening. *See also* ORCHIDS.

CAULIFLOWER: (*Brassica oleracea botrytis*) To produce the circular head of pure white curds, which give this vegetable the deserved name of "flower," plenty of attention is needed. First of all comes the soil in which the cauliflower is to grow. This should be deeply dug, pulverized, rich in organic fertilizer, and above all, contain a high per cent of nitrogen.

Nitrogen is the element most needed for the full development of the cauliflowers. Too little will cause leaves to droop and die, the head to be stunted, and turn yellow.

There are almost 40 varieties of cauliflower but only six of a definite species. Do not buy plants with small leaves which separate curds.

In preparing space for the cauliflower, do not forget that a rapid, vigorous growth is necessary for its development. So, in addition to maintaining organic matter in the earth by plowing under green manure crops, feed the ground generously with compost. If your soil is very acid, give it a medium application of lime well in advance of planting time.

Set cauliflowers in rows of furrows dug two feet apart. Place the large, late varieties two feet apart, and early, smaller ones, fifteen inches from each other. Make a shallow furrow between the rows, and use this for watering when the weather is dry. Some successful gardeners run a stream of water through the planting rows, and allow it to soak in before setting the plants. Others plant them in dry soil and water them generously, immediately after setting in the ground. Either method gives the added advantage of settling the soil firmly around the roots.

In most of the home gardens in the East, cauliflower is grown either in the spring or the late fall. The last few days in May will be the spring planting date; the tenth of July, the approximate one for fall. The spring seeding is started in flats in the house. Sow the seeds sparsely here, so as to give the small plants plenty of room to develop. When these have four leaves apiece, thin them, leaving a full two inches between them. If the spring weather is mild enough to allow planting the seeds directly in the ground, put three or four of these in the place where one is to be left standing. In this case you will have to thin the plants as soon as possible to avoid their crowding each other.

Only when mild weather has come to stay, plant the early crop directly in the ground. A late frost will stunt the plants, and cause a premature growth of the head bereft of leaves, which should be avoided at all cost.

When the head first pushes itself above the level of the ground, small incurving leaves close around it, and protect it from the sun. As the head enlarges however, these leaves are forced apart and away from it, and human hands are needed for further care. The gardener must then shield the head from the sun by bringing the largest leaves up over it, and tying them in an upright position with soft tape, raffia or string.

Even after the leaves are tied, watchfulness should still be the order of the day, for you must make sure that the heads do not overdevelop. It will be better to cut cauliflower a little too early than too late. The weather will help you decide when to harvest. If it is warm, a cauliflower will be ready to cut in from three to five days after its leaves have been tied. On the contrary, if the weather is cool, as much as two weeks may pass, before it reaches the accepted size for cutting.

The general rules for cutting are: when the head is six inches in diameter, and while its curds are compact, not after they begin to separate and resemble grains of rice. When the times comes for harvesting, cut the plant with a sharp knife, leaving one or more whorls of leaves around the head to keep it from breaking.

There are nearly forty varieties of cauliflower known by different names, but only six of a definite species. The various strains are known by different characteristics of their leaves, and of the manner in which these enclose the head. In buying seeds, avoid any type which has very small leaves, for these will push their way through the head and separate the curds.

CAYENNE: Cayenne and other pungent red peppers used as condiments are obtained as dried fruits from an annual herbaceous plant, *Capsicum frutescens*, widely cultivated in many parts of the world and variable in the character of its fruit. They are closely related to the so-called sweet, or mild-flavored, varieties commonly grown in home gardens. The pungent varieties used in the dried form are designated in the trade as dry peppers to distinguish them from the others used in the fresh condition and classed as vegetables. Included among the dry peppers is the paprika, a mild type.

The pungent red peppers as they appear in the trade vary in size, shape, and degree of color and pungency. The pungency is greatest in the tissues near the seed, and the extent to which these tissues are removed determines to some degree the pungency of the finished product. The varieties of pungent peppers are known under various names, such as chili, cayenne, and tabasco.

The pungent peppers require a warm climate and light warm soil. The plants bear fruit throughout the late summer and fall and to produce a full crop must have a long growing season. The plants are propagated from seed planted under glass or in outdoor seedbeds, and the seedlings are set in the field later and cultivated like other truck crops.

CEDAR APPLE GALLS: *see* FUNGUS

CELASTRUS SCANDENS: *see* BITTER-SWEET

CELERY: (*Apium*) The growing of celery is often believed difficult. This is not especially so if a few simple precautions are taken.

Celery needs good air and water drainage. With a good supply of composted humus, it is resistant to fungus diseases; producing good stalks.

Before you start, it is advisable to get some idea of the conditions under which the ancestors of modern cultivated celery thrived. Wild celery still flourishes in the marshes of Western Europe and Northern Africa. These marshes are usually brackish and underlain with limestone or calcareous soil. Some drainage is generally supplied by the close association of the marsh with a river or the action of tidal waters.

Wild celery is a rather bitter flavored, aromatic herb. The cultivated plant has retained much of the aroma but has to some extent been bred away from the marshes. In this connection it is interesting to note that the ancient Greeks named celery "selinon" and considered it a lowland plant. They associated it with "petroselinon," rock celery, known to us as parsley.

Tests have shown that ordinary celery grows better if excessive soil acidity is corrected by the use of lime, and that it will tolerate a certain amount of alkalinity. It has also been demonstrated that celery plants will tolerate salt to such an extent that the growing stalks may be caused to absorb enough salt to give them a pleasant and definitely salty flavor without apparent damage to the plant.

You will find it best to grow your own plants. One packet of good seed should produce as many plants as you can use and probably leave some surplus.

About the end of February or the beginning of March, celery seed should be sown in a flat or small wooden tray indoors. This flat should be about three-quarters filled with a finely sifted mixture consisting of two-thirds mature compost humus and one-third clean washed sand, and have good drainage. Upon the surface of this mixture the seed should be placed one-half inch apart in evenly spaced rows also one-half inch apart. The seed should then be evenly covered with a careful sprinkling of washed sand and firmed. The sprinkling of sand is very important as you will later discover.

The flat should be bottom watered by being placed in a bathtub or similar container in which has already been placed enough water to reach half way up the sides of the tray. It should remain there until the layer of surface sand becomes damp.

Before two weeks are up the seedlings should appear and during that time the surface of the flat should not be allowed to dry out. During this period also, as you have guessed, the problem consists of keeping the sanded surface of the flat moist without causing "damping off" and the loss of the seedlings. However, if you use clean surface sand, good drainage, keep the flat in an airy sunny place, and do not allow it to become soggy from excess water, the seedlings should thrive.

Additional flats should be prepared so that when the young plants are a month old they may be moved to roomier quarters where they may stand two inches apart in each direction. Four weeks later they should be ready to move to the garden but they should not be set out until all danger of long, cold spells of rainy weather is over.

At least a week before the setting out of the young plants, the ground should be properly prepared to permit the settling of the soil. Add nitrogen, phosphate and potash fertilizers, plus lime, if necessary.

This mixture should then be deeply dug in and the soil worked to a depth of 14 inches. If you prepare the soil during very dry weather, it is advisable to follow the digging by a thorough drenching. In any event the soil should be supplied with sufficient water to penetrate several inches a couple of days before the setting out of the plants.

Moisture is essential, for you will remember that celery is a gross feeder. For best results its steady and quick growth is necessary. But if the supply of compost material is low, poultry, stable, or sheep manure comes in handy provided it is well incorporated in the soil before the setting out of the plants.

The plants should be set out in the garden six inches apart in rows over two feet apart. Care should be taken to see that they are not set deeper than that which they stood in the flat in which they grew. They should be well watered during and immediately following transplanting.

When you come to the matter of the cultivation of celery you will again find yourself faced with the problem of seeing that sufficient moisture is supplied at all times to prevent the drying out of the soil. Anything which approaches the condition which causes the wilting of the plants should be avoided. On the other hand, the moisture should not be so excessive as to encourage mildew and plant disease. Of course, weeds must be kept down. Mulching will do both. And if you add to this mulch a generous supply of unleached hardwood ashes, healthy plant growth will be greatly encouraged.

Hardwood ashes have value because they supply much needed potash without adding nitrogen. Two very destructive diseases of celery, Blackheart and Pinkrot, are probably traceable to the use of excessive quantities of inorganic nitrogen. Many disastrous failures of celery crops have been found upon investigation to have been brought about by the use of excessive quantities of water saturated with chemical fertilizers and applied shortly before the plants matured. Celery plants are easily damaged by excess nitrogen but demand much potash, hence the unleached wood ashes. Ten pounds of unleached hardwood ashes contains the same amount of potash as ten pounds of commercial inorganic fertilizer without the other very undesirable elements.

Many diseases of celery, notably the blights, are no doubt largely due to poor environment. If your garden site has been chosen with decent regard to air and water drainage, these should bother you little; and if you use properly composted humus, your plants should be immune to plant-fungus diseases. These do their greatest damage in damp, undrained, poorly ventilated areas.

Bleaching. Some very good gardeners believe that green-stalked celery has finer flavor and greater nutritive value than the crisp, bleached type. Just the same, when the plants are about two-thirds mature you may want to bleach a number of them.

This is easily done by using boards. These boards, about ten or twelve inches wide, should be placed on edge alongside the rows and held in place by short stakes driven into the ground. Care should be taken to permit the tufts of the leaves to protrude so as not to suffocate the plants. Lacking boards, you will find that a handy scheme is to tie each plant loosely and then wrap it with several layers of old newspapers, securing these wrappings with pins or string and permitting the leaves to protrude.

After ten or 12 days the boards, or other bleaching materials, should be removed and the plants harvested.

The arrival of cool fall weather will cause you to think about storage, for you will want to store a number of fine plants for use later on. A very easy way to do this is to dig a trench 14 inches wide and of sufficient depth so that the plants, when placed in it, will have only their tops exposed a couple of inches above garden level. In this trench the plants, which have been dug and cut with a sizeable portion of their roots left on, should be stood close together. Any unused portion of the trench should be filled in and firmed.

With the advent of colder weather the boards which were used for bleaching the stalks may be placed over the trench to form an inverted V-shaped roof. This covering may still later be augmented by straw, dry weeds, topsoil, etc.—*Roger Smith.*

CELL-SAP: *see* FLAVOR

CELLULOSE: Although we do not eat cellulose, it is none-the-less a most important item in our lives. Wood, paper, cotton, and linen are some of the more common forms. A large percentage of all plant tissue is cellulose. Fruits, vegetables, grains, and nuts, as well as hay, ensilage, and other livestock feeds contain a lot of cellulose. Coal was formed from plant material that was originally mostly cellulose.

But it is also important to microbes. Like most sugars and starches, cellulose is a carbohydrate manufactured by plants. And like all other plant substances, it decays. That is why cellulose is important to plants. Those that cause it to rot do so because they use it as food. The rotting that we observe is the way in which microbes "eat" this food material.

Some mushrooms and toadstools which you may have seen on living trees, dead stumps, and fallen logs and branches were able to grow there just because they could "eat" the cellulose in the woody plant material. In the presence of moisture, these fungi even grow on and destroy stored lumber, the wooden foundations of buildings, fence posts and poles, the hulls of fresh water boats (fungi are not significantly active in the ocean), and the automobile bodies of wooden station wagons. Their growth produces a soft, pulpy, rotted wood that has no strength and gives no support. In such places as composts, barnyard and stable manure piles, and in the soil, many microbes grow on the cellulose they find in plant materials.

CELOSIA: The red or yellow plumes of the annual celosias or cockscombs, borne on robust, quickly growing plants, are often seen in summer gardens and occasionally as dried bouquets. Tender, but of easiest culture, the celosias succeed during the summer months. However, the root-knot nematode is a serious pest and sometimes will take a heavy toll of the seedlings growing in infested soil.

Most varieties grow about one to two feet, but *C. Floribunda* makes a shrubby plant about ten feet tall. *See also* COCKSCOMB.

CENTAUREA: A large group of herbs, that includes Bachelor's Button (*C. cyanus*) and other popular annuals as well as perennials. Many of the annuals in this family prefer crowding, are readily grown from seed. The perennial species make fine border plants, as the dusty millers, which bloom in summer, do well in ordinary garden soil. Genus also includes Basket Flower (*C. Americana*)—a four to six foot annual; Dusty Miller (*C. cineraria*)—one to two foot perennial; Sweet Sultan (*C. moschata*)—one to two foot annual. *See also* BACHELOR'S BUTTON.

CENTIPEDE - GRASS: (*Eremochloa ophiuroides*) *see* LAWN

CENTRANTHUS: Handsome perennial, Jupiter's Beard or Red Valerian (*C. Ruber*) grows one to three feet high, with red flowers, bushy appearance. *See also* PERENNIALS.

CENTURY PLANT: *see* AGAVE

CEPHALANTHUS OCCIDENTALIS: *see* BUTTON-BUSH

CEPHALARIA: A tall perennial with white or yellow flowers, *cephalaria* often appear in the back of border plantings. They often reach six feet high. *See also* PERENNIALS.

CEREALS: Agricultural grains of the grass family, such as barley, rye, wheat, oats, corn, rice and sorghum. Rye is commonly used as a cover crop on sandy, rocky and poor soils. Barley is also recommended for cover cropping, since it makes a heavy, quick growth. It is often used in preparation for crops that must be planted early in spring.

CEREUS: This night-blooming flower likes a light, porous soil with good drainage. Like other true cacti, it likes a reasonable amount of water—almost as much as ordinary house plants—during the growing season, but while not active give it only enough water to keep it from shriveling. Feeding should be light and chemical fertilizers avoided. Some *Cereus* varieties, as *C. peruviana*, native to South America, grow 40 feet high. *See also* CACTUS.

CHAMOMILE: *see* CAMOMILE

CHARCOAL: A black, porous form of carbon, prepared from vegetable or animal substances, usually made by charring wood in a kiln from which air is excluded.

Pieces of charcoal are often recommended as additions to potting soils, as they improve drainage.

CHARD: *see* SWISS CHARD

CHELATORS: Research proves that the grabbing action of organic compounds makes elements more available to growing plants. This grabbing or claw-like action gives these organic compounds their name—"chelating compounds," which actually mean claw-like.

By definition, a chelator is a compound which literally clamps onto metals. An iron chelate is a kind of iron compound in which the molecules of the chelator have locked onto the atoms of the metal in a vice-like grip.

The iron is held much more strongly in a chelate than in ordinary salts, such as iron chloride, where the iron separates easily from the chloride part of the molecules. Chelators grab and hold iron so strongly that they can literally pull it out of soil minerals and rocks. And they may do this more effectively than certain strong acids which are not chelators.

Humus itself functions as a chelator. Most organic matter has some chelating ability which may at times attain considerable importance in the mineral economy of the soil.

Many soil fungi normally produce a variety of compounds that behave as chelators. This may well be a major function of the mycorrhiza fungi which act in the role of root hairs for certain trees and other plants. Without their fungus partners, these plants either grow poorly or are unable to develop at all.

Many chemical compounds produced by lichens are powerful chelators. This is how these creatures are able to live luxuriantly in barren places where other forms of life cannot even survive. They have their own "built-in" chelators. These dissolve rocks and in this way provide them with vital trace metals. This is one of the best examples of biological weathering or the chemical breakdown of rocks and minerals by living organisms.

Research shows that this chelating action of manures is one explanation for the greater availability of phosphate fertilizers when they are applied with farm manures.

CHEMICAL FERTILIZERS: *see* FERTILIZERS, ARTIFICIAL

CHEMICALS, HUMUS, AND THE SOIL, *by Donald P. Hopkins. See* BOOKS FOR ORGANIC GARDENERS AND FARMERS

CHEMURGY: The science that deals with the industrial utilization of farm crops.

Chemurgists have three major aims: 1—the improvement of present crops and methods of processing them; 2—the development of new crops and uses for them; and 3—research to find new, non-food uses for farm crops, their residues and by-products.

CHERIMOYA: *see* ANNONA

CHERNOZEMS: The word *chernozem* means black earth in Russian, but chernozem soils vary from dark brown to black. Chernozem signifies more than merely color; it is a process of soil formation. Mere blackness does not signify chernozem, since there are other types of soils which are black in color, such as peats and mucks which are not chernozem. Some poorly drained soils are well supplied with organic matter and are very dark in color as a result, but are not chernozem.

In chernozems, the color is usually black in the North and as it goes southward it changes to brown, because there is less organic matter in southern soils. The heat is a factor in burning out organic matter. Due to the lesser amounts of rainfall of chernozem soils, and the hot, dry summers, the organic matter does not decay as fast as under podzol conditions. It thus accumulates in larger quantities, which causes the darker color. Another element in the black color is the fact that in chernozem soils there are large amounts of lime which is conducive to a type of decay that brings about a very black humus. The cold winters and dry hot summers may also be a factor in producing the very dark color, as well as the fact that the rainfall, as little as it is, comes mostly in the spring.

In the subsoils of chernozems the color is a grayish or yellowish brown with spots of calcium carbonate or lime, but the subsoils of the southern chernozems are reddish or yellowish.

GEOGRAPHY OF THE CHERNOZEMS —In the United States the chernozems take up a wide north-south belt in the eastern part of the Great Plains, the tall grass regions which are located in the central part of the country. In North Dakota about three-fourths of the soil is chernozem; in South Dakota and Nebraska, one-half; Kansas and Oklahoma, one-half each. It takes in a large part of Texas, small section of the eastern parts of Washington and Oregon, and some of west Idaho, as well as some other areas on a small scale. In all, there are about 280,000 square miles of chernozem soil in the U. S. compared to 614,000 of podzol.

CLIMATE—Chernozems occur in sub-humid regions, with a cool climate, sometimes being very harsh. There are cold winters, hot summers, high winds, and the rainfall which is only between 16 to 28 inches, can bunch itself in the spring in sharp showers. Water is usually scarce in such regions and there is always a threat of drought.

ACID - ALKALINE CONDITIONS — While podzols are usually on the acid side, chernozems are usually neutral or somewhat on the alkaline side. This is because there is not suf-

ficient rain to leach the lime out of the soil, and at two to five feet below ground there is a definite layer of lime. In fact the process of chernozem soil formation is usually considered a calcification process. Because of the neutrality of the soil, much of the aluminum and iron remain in the topsoil. *See also* PODZOL; SOILS.

CHERRY: (*Prunus*) Valuable fruit producing trees for centuries, cherries include the sweet, sour and hybrids. Sour cherries are among the hardiest of fruit trees, standing up well to heat, cold, neglect, and even insects. On the other hand, sweet cherries are more sensitive, doing best on light sandy loams.

Young cherry trees are sensitive to cold, so remember to keep them away from regions which are subject to spring frosts. On clear frosty nights the cold air will naturally drain down to low levels. For this reason, slopes or places which are somewhat higher than surrounding areas will be the best location for them. And, if you have a lake or pond on your grounds, plant the trees near that if possible. Water always reduces the danger from frost. Besides, the cool air blowing from it prevents, what frequently proves a peril to young fruit trees—an early flowering in the spring.

As for soil for the cherries, be sure that this is well drained. Given this prime requisite, both sweet and sour cherries will thrive on many different types of soil. It should be added, however, that a sandy loam will always be the best. This will not only provide good drainage, but will also help the trees to a deeper rooting than will lighter soils.

The roots of most cherry trees do not go much below two feet in the ground. While with this shallow rooting the trees may appear thrifty and even produce satisfactorily for a time, a long severe winter or a period of abnormal rainfall will work havoc with them if left in this condition. If set in a sandy loam the roots will easily reach a depth of four feet.

To aid this accomplishment, at the time of planting mix some peat moss and compost with the soil which you work in around the root.

Cherry trees need plenty of room. There is good reason for this. The development and ripening of their fruit depends upon sunlight. If the trees are so close together that the branches overlap, they will shade each other and the cherries on them will fail to mature.

If you are cramped for space in your garden, you will likely choose some of the dwarf varieties of cherries. If this is the case, set the trees 18 feet apart. If you have ground available for larger specimens leave a space of 25 feet between; and if you aspire to the large growing sweet cherry trees and have room for them, plant these 30 feet apart.

The old tradition was always to plant cherry trees in the spring. Now, it has been proved that both spring and fall are equally appropriate; but if you do plant in the spring, be sure the place where they are to grow is plowed in the fall.

As for the actual planting, as soon as your trees—presumably at the age of two years—arrive from the nursery, water the roots without delay, and if possible plant them at once. If this is not feasible, prepare a trench in a sandy, well-drained spot, place the trees in it at an angle which slants to one side, fill the trench with soil, and as you do so, work it into the roots. Be sure never to let the roots become dry.

Before you set the trees in the ground, trim off any roots which have been broken or injured in moving, and shorten any straggling ones. Plant the trees where they are to stand and a little deeper in the ground than they were at the nursery. A good way to settle the earth around the roots will be, as you throw the first few

shovelfuls in place, to move the tree gently up and down.

Provided the soil of your site is deep and plentifully supplied with nitrogen, you may well grow your cherry trees in sod. Always remember, though, not to allow the sod to compete with the growth of the trees in using up its needed moisture and nourishment.

If you do decide upon sod, also remember that a mulch will be a necessary accompaniment to it. Use straw, hay or cut up corn cobs for this and do not fail to cut the grass two or three times during May and June.

If your cherry trees are not grown in sod, then a cover crop for the orchard is worth while. Before this is sown, give the young trees a generous amount of manure or compost, digging it in over the roots but not allowing it to touch the trunks of the trees.

A spring cover crop is sown as early in this season as possible. The best choice for this is rye. Sow this at the rate of one and one-half bushels of seed to the acre, and do not fail to turn it under before the crop matures. Otherwise, it will compete with the young trees.

A late summer cover crop will be of even more value to the cherry orchard than the spring one. For this, use buckwheat, oats or millet. Not one of these will survive the winter, and lying withered on the ground, will add nitrogen to the soil.

The late cover crop will be best sown when the fruit is ready to pick. According to the weather, this will be sometime during the first two weeks of July. As the season advances, you will find this late crop of value in improving the soil, especially if it tends to be heavy; while in helping to prevent erosion and loss of nutrients, it will improve the wood of the tree during the late summer and fall.

At the time of planting, have the main stem higher than any of the branches. Thin the others from about four to six inches apart, leaving the lowest ones about 16 inches from the ground. After that, cut only to keep the center of the tree free from sprouts and from inward growing branches and those which cross each other.

Although sweet cherry trees produce good pollen, none of them are self-fruiting. Generally speaking, pollination will take place when any of these are planted together, but there are exceptions to remember; namely, the group of sweet cherries composed of Bing, Emperor Francis, Lambert and Napoleon.

The Duke cherries, grown primarily for home gardens because they are noted for their hardiness, are hybrids of the sweet and sour ones. These will pollinate both the sweet and sour varieties.—*Leonora Sill Ashton.*

See also FRUIT TREES; ORCHARD.

CHERRY, BUSH: The bush cherry makes an attractive hedge, or foundation planting, and in late summer produces tart, black-purple cherries suitable for pies and preserves.

One of the easiest fruits to grow, it is bothered little by insects or diseases. Clean cultivation, good soil, and proper care of the bush cherry will help to keep plants strong and healthy for years to come.

The hardy bush cherry will grow to a height of four or five feet in as many years, delighting owners with fruit the second year, along with two weeks of small, white blossoms early in May. The silvery-green foliage is also attractive, as it turns red in autumn.

New plants are usually obtained from softwood cuttings. The bush cherry was originally called the "sand cherry," probably because it was developed on a sandy soil. Tests, however, have proved the plant to thrive on a wide variety of soils, including clay loam. Almost any soil can be altered to meet its few requirements. Annual applications of compost will usually do the trick.

Most authorities recommend early spring as the best planting time, but many owners have successfully started plants in fall. If they are started in fall, a heavy winter mulch is a requisite. When planted as a continuous hedge, plants should be spaced 12 to 15 inches apart. Of course, individual plants may be staggered into the general landscape scheme, as you wish. The bush cherry takes well to pruning, which should be done before August. Flowers are borne on both new and old wood in late summer, and late pruning would remove many flower buds.

The old standard is the Hanson Bush Cherry, named for the developer of the plant. Over the years, this variety has been improved, and others have been added to the family. Such varieties as Hansen Improved, Brooks, Black Beauty, and Sioux are making their appearance on many home grounds.

CHERRY, DWARF: *see* FRUIT TREE, DWARF

CHERRY, FLOWERING: These wonderful ornamental shrubs and trees include *Prunus yedoensis, P. serrulata* and *P. lannesiana,* all Japanese flowering cherries. These trees generally grow between 30 and 40 feet high; their culture is similar to fruit trees, as cherries, plums and peaches. All of them grow well in open sunlight and well-drained soils. Mulch them during winter with compost or well-decomposed manure, as this encourages early spring blooms. Plant about 25 feet apart. These flowering cherries are hardy throughout most of the United States. *See also* CHERRY.

CHERRY, SOUR: The sour cherry is one of the most resistant of all fruit trees to insect damage and disease.

This might well be termed "the universal fruit tree," for no other fruit tree will thrive in so many different zones as the sour cherry. You'll find it growing from southern gardens all the way up to Canada, in regions where winter temperatures of as much as *30 degrees below zero* have no harmful effect on some varieties. The sour cherry is also known to grow and bear in dry and drought-affected areas, where other fruit trees wither and fail to produce. Add to these the advantage of having dead-ripe fruit in early summer, and it's easy to see why the sour cherry is one of the most popular fruit trees in America today. Paradoxically, sour cherries are not always sour. Many prospective planters have been led away from the sour cherry, not knowing that there are varieties which are only slightly tart, and are good for tangy eating, as well as for cooking. This is an important point, because sour cherries are generally easier to grow than sweet cherries.

The three most popular varieties of the sour cherry are Early Rich-mond, Montmorency, and English Morello. Early Richmond is an early producer of small fruits, used almost exclusively for cooking. Trees are hardy, vigorous, very large, and productive. Montmorency produces large, tart, red cherries. It is the most popular of all varieties, thriving from Virginia all the way up into Quebec. The trees are large, very hardy, vigorous, and productive. English Morello gives a medium-sized reddish-black fruit, produces rather late, and is excellent for cooking. The tree is small, vigorous, and hardy.

Sour cherries are not exceptionally difficult to care for, and they will encounter fewer difficulties than most fruits, including the sweet cherry. The most important operation to be considered is the actual planting. Trees often suffer greatly in the period between nursery and permanent loca-

The sour cherry is beautiful in springtime and an early and bountiful yielder as well. Given proper care, it will produce many quarts of delicious and nutritious fruits, good for eating and preserving.

tion, so take pains in preparing soil.

The few pests which *do* bother sour cherries are not likely to present serious problems. They can be controlled largely by clean cultivation methods, such as removing fallen fruit regularly, destroying harboring places, and regular cultivation. Scale insects, a serious threat to other fruit trees, are seldom a problem of sour cherries. Brown-rot, black-knot, and yellow leaf are three diseases to watch for. At the first sign of any of these symptoms, removal of dead or injured wood, cankers, and knots should prevent further infestation. *See also* CHERRY.

CHERVIL: (*Anthriscus cerefolium*) This annual kitchen herb is easily germinated from seed, but often stunts if transplanted.

Chervil grows to less than two feet high, has lacy green leaves resembling parsley. It does best in shady area; seed should be planted in early spring. *See also* HERBS; PARSLEY.

CHESTNUT: (*Castanea*) Tall group of nut trees. The American chestnut (*C. dentata*) grows 100 feet high in forests, its green leaves changing to bright yellow in fall. The nuts are brown and sweet-tasting. Japanese chestnuts (*C. crenata*) grow to about 50 feet, produce large nuts that are tastier when cooked. Blight has drastically reduced the number of native chestnuts in New England and North Atlantic states. Researchers are trying to develop blight-resistant chestnut varieties. *See also* CHESTNUT, CHINESE.

CHESTNUT, CHINESE: (*Castanea mollissima*) A tree which is grown easily in almost any soil and climate; grows quickly, beginning to bear after four years; can produce heavily; is practically blight-free; and best of all, the Chinese chestnut offers a nut which is comparable in taste, and is larger than the old American chestnut.

The Chinese chestnut will thrive under a greater variety of soils than most nut trees. It requires a well-drained soil and does best on a slightly acid soil. These trees will thrive from the southern temperate zone to the Great Lakes region, although they do better in southern states. Roughly, they will thrive anywhere a peach tree will thrive. Another gauge is the maple tree, which has somewhat the same climatic requirements.

Organic matter content of the soil is vital to the Chinese chestnut, to provide proper nutrients for young seedlings and to hold moisture in the soil. This tree is comparatively shallow-rooted, thus not requiring as deep a soil as most nut trees. This characteristic has both advantages and disadvantages: It is not necessary to work the soil as deeply when planting seedlings, and shallow roots will absorb water more quickly than deep-rooted trees. On the other side of the ledger, roots will tend to dry out quickly in surface soil, and will be subject to surface soil temperature changes, especially in some areas.

Because roots are shallow, mulching is a necessity for the Chinese chestnut. The homesteader or suburban gardener who wants only a few trees for beauty, shade, and food, can do very well with a straw mulch of four to six inches, placed around each tree to the outer extent of its branches. To discourage field mice, keep mulch two feet away from the trunk, and lay a six-inch layer of coarse stones in this mulchless area.

The mulch should never be removed and, in fact, there is no reason to remove it. Cultivation is unnecessary and impractical, since roots may be injured by this practice. A good mulch will break down slowly, year after year, feeding the soil and retaining a good tilth in the surface soil.

Some commercial growers use a permanent sod mulch system. A grass sod is cut and allowed to act as a growing mulch around each tree. This system is easier than straw mulching, but may cause a nitrogen deficiency. This can be easily corrected, however, by feeding applications of manure or cottonseed meal in late winter or early spring, before new growth starts. A word of caution here—some growers have had very unfortunate experiences with fertilizers, killing trees with heavy applications. Because of this, some growers advocate a fertilizing policy of non-interference.

In the limited experience of American growers, newly-transplanted trees have begun to bear in as few as three years, with crops increasing annually until, at maturity, trees produce well over 100 pounds of nuts per season. The best characteristic of this tree is that it bears comparatively heavily in its early years. You won't have to wait forever to enjoy the fruits of your labor.

The nut itself is somewhat larger than the American chestnut, but smaller than the Japanese variety. Its meat is sweet and, although it is slightly inferior in quality to the American, it is the best chestnut available today.

Trees should be planted 25-30 feet apart. Frost pockets are sure death and should be avoided. Air drainage must be good. After 10 to 15 years, every other tree should be cut out, so that the planting distance is enlarged to 50 x 50 feet. This may seem like a great distance, but it is essential. *Yields will not be increased by crowding trees.* The Chinese chestnut is formed on the order of an apple tree, low and rounded.

It is wise to plant several varieties in close proximity. Trees will not bear nuts without being cross-fertilized. Plenty of moisture for young trees is vitally important for good spring growth and for the very life of the tree. A good idea is to form a shallow basin around the tree to catch and hold water. The mulch around trees will protect the topsoil from drying and caking, while plenty of humus will hold water which is absorbed into the soil. It would be a good idea to buy a moisture meter to keep constant check on young trees until they are well-established.

At the same time, trees cannot stand soggy soil, but good drainage should prevent this condition.

Grafting and layering the Chinese chestnut, although successfully attempted by some growers, are rather difficult for the home gardener. Therefore, most propagation is accomplished by the planting of seedlings. Since the career of this tree in America is still in infancy, experimenters are constantly working to improve the variety. Some experts maintain that in due time the Chinese chestnut will surpass the American variety in quality and yield.

Thus far, the trees in this country have suffered little from blight. Those trees which are affected should be treated immediately, and will probably recover within two seasons.

Chestnut weevils can become a major problem, but they may be controlled by gathering nuts from the ground daily. This practice prevents the worms from entering the soil. Chickens running under the trees can do this cleaning up for you.

Growers who have used DDT sprayings to control the weevil have found that red mites often follow spraying, because of the destruction of their natural predators. We suggest avoidance of any spraying. A healthy soil will nourish a healthy tree, resistant to diseases and insects.

Commercial aspects of the Chinese chestnut are very favorable. There seems to be a definite market for the nuts, as they surpass imported Italian and Spanish varieties and can, of course, be sold profitably at a lower retail price. Considering the comparatively heavy yields in early years, the tree surpasses other nut trees in cutting the period of deficit operation. *See also* NUT TREES; NUTS, FOOD VALUE OF.

CHICKEN: *see* POULTRY; BANTAMS

CHICKEN MANURE: *see* MANURE

CHICORY: (*Cichorium intybus*) Also called coffee weed and blue dandelion, chicory has been used as an additive to or substitute for coffee for around two centuries. A four to six foot perennial, the chicory plant is a botanic relative of the endive, and several varieties of chicory are likewise used. Chicory root is also sometimes cooked as a vegetable like turnips and carrots.

The roasted root of the large rooted variety is the "coffee chicory" of commerce. While coffee with chicory is more preferred in our southern states, particularly in the New Orleans region, chicory growing is largely centered in the east-central or Saginaw Bay territory of Michigan. Chicory is also a commercial crop in many places in Europe and in South Africa.

For some years most of the "coffee" served in Europe has been little more than a mixture of roasted cereals and chicory with possibly a little real coffee added. Some of the South African coffee mixtures are more than half chicory.

In some places chicory has escaped from cultivation and has become a roadside weed, the blue flowers being a familiar sight. However, there is no danger of its becoming a serious weed nuisance and possibly it has some use as a bee pasture or honey producing plant.

Chicory is a hardy plant not especially sensitive to heat or cold. Like other root crops it demands a deep, rich, loamy soil, well pulverized for the satisfactory formation of its penetrating roots.

Any well-dug, properly drained, garden soil is suitable but in most gardens it is best to incorporate quite deeply a moderate amount of mature compost humus so as to ensure normal fertility of the soil. Raw manure should be avoided for this, somewhat like stones, encourages malformed, pronged, useless roots.

Witloof Chicory (French Endive) requires about ten days from the sowing of the seed to the maturing of the root. If seed is sown too early the plants are likely to "bolt"—go to seed —and form useless roots. It is better to sow a little too late than too early.

Seed should be sown thinly in drills 18 inches apart and covered with about 1/4 inch of sifted compost humus. The plants will develop their best roots if they stand about three feet apart.

Chicory requires about the same cultivation as carrots, shallow but sufficient to keep down weeds. It is a husky plant, rather free from insect pests and plant disease, even so it will strikingly reflect any extra care you manage to give it. A little consideration such as a thorough soaking with water at the beginning of a prolonged dry spell followed by a light mulching of rough, partially composted materials will keep the plants thriving.

There is also an early spring type of chicory, Asparagus or Celery Chicory. This very pleasing form of leaf chicory has much to recommend it and it may be that it will eventually displace endive in popular favor when it becomes better known.

Asparagus chicory is sown, much like lettuce, in early spring. It is grown for the value of its young leaves. The head may be blanched or the leaves used green. Young leaves and shoots are very tender, celery-flavored, and make excellent salad-bowl material. The older leaves may be boiled much as spinach.

CHILEAN NITRATE: *see* FERTILIZERS, ARTIFICIAL

CHINCH BUG: Very small black and white sucking insects, red when young, which cause large brown patches in lawns. For control, seed lawn in soil made up of one-third crushed rock, one-third sharp builder's sand and one-third compost. Soybeans grown as a companion crop with corn shade the bases of the corn plants so that they will be avoided by the chinch bug.

Experiments conducted by Professor Leonard Haseman of the University of Missouri have shown that when this insect is fed on plants grown in nitrogen-poor soil, it not only lives longer but lays more eggs. Haseman feels that well-fed soil and crops will give better insect control. *See also* INSECT CONTROL.

CHINESE CABBAGE: (*Brassica pekinensis*) Chinese cabbage is sometimes called celery cabbage, although it does not taste too much like cabbage. It is perhaps best described as a sweetly flavored, lettuce-like vegetable with large crisp leaves. It is used fresh for salads or boiled as greens.

Chinese cabbage is an annual requiring cool weather during the greater part of the growing season in order to develop to perfection. A continued period of heat tends to force the plant into flower before the leaves have reached any size or formed heads, at the same time giving them an undesirable cabbage taste.

Where the summers are cool you may plant early in the spring, at the time lettuce is sown. In sections of the country where the summers are hot, a fall sowing is advisable. Plant the seed in the early part of August, and keep the seed bed well cultivated from the time the rows can be recognized.

The best growth is made in a rich, light loam. Apply a generous amount of compost or well-rotted manure to the soil before planting. If the soil is reasonably rich, a three-inch layer of compost can be lightly dug in along the line where the rows are to stand. An application of dried cow manure during the growing period will also be beneficial. It is important to encourage a quick and fleshy growth. In soils known to be acid, lime should be raked into the soil to correct this condition.

Sow the seed in the open ground, as the plant is somewhat checked in its growth by transplanting. Plant one-half inch deep in rows about 12 to 16 inches apart. When the plants are three to four inches high, thin out to stand about ten inches apart in the row. You may use the thinnings for greens or salad. This crop requires a good amount of moisture. Cultivate frequently to keep down weeds and save moisture. Water during dry spells, if possible, with a thorough drenching every evening.

Most varieties reach maturity in approximately 70-80 days after planting. When the heads reach maturity they may be cut for use as you need them. The heads can be harvested after the first light frost and stored for a couple of months in a cool cellar or outdoor storage pit. In gathering, pull the plants with the roots, remove the outer leaves and store in layers protected by dry straw and cover with soil.

Most seedmen recommend Michihli as the best variety, and have dropped Chihli, which used to be the most popular variety grown. Michihli is more uniform and dependable than the Chihli. Pe-Tsai grows more like Swiss chard and usually does not form solid heads.

CHINESE FAN PALM: (*Livistona chinensis*) see PALMS

CHINESE FORGET-ME-NOT: (*Cynoglossum amabile*) This annual offers blue flowers in the late spring garden. Although injured by frost, it is easy to grow, volunteers readily and blooms in a relatively short time. As the flower spikes wilt rather quickly, it is best used for blue masses in the spring border. Grows 1½ to two feet high.

CHINESE LANTERN: see PHYSALIS

CHINESE SACRED LILY: (*Narcissus tazetta orientalis*) see NARCISSUS

CHINESE WOOLFLOWER: see COCKSCOMB

CHINKERICHEE: see ORNITHOGALUM

CHIONANTHUS VIRGINICA: see FRINGE-TREE

CHIONODOXAS: These beautiful spring-flowering bulbs are especially suited for planting in clumps about such shrubs as forsythias and the early magnolias, in sunny spots in the rock garden, and in the herbaceous border. Do not disturb them, but let them reseed themselves from year to year. They will soon form a dense carpet of blue and white in early spring. The best varieties are *C. luciliae* and *C. sardensis*—both about three inches high. Plant them in October about three inches deep and three inches apart. *See also* BULBS, FORCING.

CHIVES: (*Allium schoenoprasum*) This useful herb makes neat clumps of grass-like leaves and is not out of

Chives are hardy and grow well in all temperate and warm climates. They require a rich, coarse soil and like the sun but not too much moisture.

place in the perennial border. The flowers are rose-purple, and quite attractive.

There are so many uses for chives in the culinary field. The fresh leaves are chopped up and used as seasoning in appetizers, cheeses, butter, omelets, sauces, soups, and they add a zest to any fresh vegetable salad.

CULTURE: Chives may be grown from seed planted in a rich pebbly soil. Germination is slow however, and the usual and easiest method of propagation is to plant a clump of three or four tiny bulbs to each pot. The bulbs multiply very fast so it won't take long for them to fill the pot. Plant the bulbs about one inch deep.

Chives require a rich, coarse soil, so make a mixture of gravel, compost, and a little garden soil. Use proportions of approximately ½ compost to ¼ gravel or small pebbles, and ¼ garden soil. Chives like plenty of sun so they will appreciate wintering in your sunniest window. Keep the soil moist by watering regularly, but do not overwater. That's about all the care they require, and shortly you will be enjoying the "harvest."

Chives are a hardy perennial and will grow well in all temperate and warm climates. In the spring you may wish to start a bed outside. Select a sunny location and plant small clumps of two or three tiny bulbs about six to ten inches apart. The bulbs will multiply so quickly that it is advisable to dig them up every two or three years and separate them. Keep the beds well cultivated and free from weeds. Clean culture is especially important during the early stages of growth.

LOCATION: The slender, dark green, tubular leaves of chives grow in clumps, and the flowers are tiny lavender-colored pompons. Some gardeners like to raise chives for the flower. The plant and flower could make a charming and decorative border or edging to beds of other plants, or perhaps add color and interest to a rock garden. The faded flowers should be cut promptly before the seed matures; otherwise self-sown seedlings may prove to be troublesome weeds. Grows about one foot high.

HARVESTING: It is simply a matter of cutting the slender, tubular leaves as you need them. These are usually chopped up fine and added to whatever foods you wish to season.

The leaves are cut at the ground level. New shoots will soon appear. Usually the more they are cut the more vigorously they grow. *See also* HERBS.

CHOKEBERRY: (*Aronia*) Adapted to a wide range of soils, these early-blooming shrubs range in height from four to eight feet. Black Chokeberry (*A. melanocarpa*) is a summer-blooming shrub and is one of the most showy with its clusters of white blooms. The black berries hang on until well into winter. The fall foliage is red; shrub grows to about five feet. The red chokeberry (*A. arbutifolia*) grows to about eight feet and shows foliage in autumn.

CHRISTMAS CHERRY: (*Solanum pseudocapsicum*) The names Christmas Cherry, Jerusalem Cherry, Winter Cherry, and Cleveland Cherry are all used interchangeably by amateurs, though most of the plants seen around Christmas time are selections from the Cleveland Cherry. The plant is not really a cherry, but is a decorative pot plant, loved by many amateurs for its attractive red to yellow fruits.

As the Cleveland Cherry is quite variable, several types are to be found on the market, some with small round fruits, others with larger elongated ones.

Keep the plants in a sunny window of a fairly cool room with an even temperature of from 40 to 45° F. Keep the soil moderately moist at all times, using water of room temperature. Make sure that no water is standing in the saucer for any length of time, and protect against cold drafts. Sooner or later, according to conditions, the berries will shrivel and the leaves drop off. When the plants have lost their attractiveness, prune them back severely, retaining only two or three eyes on each branch. A cool place (40°) must now be provided and water must be restricted to keep the soil barely moist. To encourage

development of new shoots, syringe the tops daily with temperate water.

In May, when all danger of frost has passed, the pots may be sunk outdoors up to the rim in a sunny place in the garden. Some gardeners prefer to remove the pots and set the plants into moderately rich soil. Do not delay too long in setting out the plants, or the crop of berries to follow will be scarce. If the plants have been hardened thoroughly before planting out, a light frost will not do much harm. Firm planting is essential, and plenty of water is needed during dry weather. By the end of June weak liquid manure may be given once a week. By fall the plants will have made strong, rounded bushes of good appearance.

Early in September is a good time to take up the plants and carefully repot them. Soak the ground thoroughly a few hours before potting to prevent the soil from dropping from the roots. A five-inch pot will be found large enough to hold all but extra-large plants, which may need six-inch pots. Place a piece of crock over the drainage hole and use a mixture composed of one part rich garden loam and one part leaf mold to which has been added a little dried sheep manure and fine sand, to fill the space between the walls of the pot and the root ball. Pot firmly, but allow enough space at the top to make thorough watering possible. Keep the plants, after they have been thoroughly watered, in a coldframe, with the sash in place, or in a cool room without much ventilation. Wind and drafts, which dry out the leaves and soil, must be avoided until the plants have recuperated from the ordeal of transplanting. Plants which were sunk outdoors in pots may remain in the garden a little longer than those that need potting. Before frost appears, all plants must be placed indoors in a greenhouse or a sunny window, where they should be kept from 45 to 55°. They need plenty of light, fresh air, and regular watering. Weak liquid manure may be used again when the plants show signs of having taken hold of the soil in the pots.

The growing of new plants can be accomplished either by sowing seed saved from fully ripened berries or by cuttings. Sow the seed thinly and barely cover with fine soil. Place a pane of glass over the receptacle after watering and keep moderately warm (55 to 65°). Soon after sowing, the seedlings will break through the soil, and the glass must then be removed. From then on keep moderately moist at all times and give as much light to the plants as possible. When the seedlings are large enough to be handled, pot them up in individual small pots. To encourage a well-branched, bushy growth, nip out the tips of the shoots. Additional branches may be forced into growth later by removing the tips of the side branches. As the plants increase in size they require repotting once or twice into one-size-larger pots. After repotting keep the plants well protected against wind and drafts, and water cautiously but regularly. Spray the top daily with lukewarm water. The remainder of the culture is the same as for larger plants.

If cuttings are to be made, wait for the young shoots to appear after the plants have been cut back. Take these with a heel, which means that each new sprout is to have part of the old stem attached, and insert them in small pots filled with sandy soil. To prevent excessive evaporation of moisture, place the pot in a box covered with a tight-fitting pane of glass. Keep watered and spray the tops daily. Rotting will take place quite quickly, and a somewhat warmer temperature than that required by the old plants will be needed until the plants make an active growth. Gradually accustom them to the cooler temperature of the old plants, and from then on handle in the same manner.

CHRISTMAS PLANTS: Plants that are received as holiday gifts may be kept for a long time if carefully tended and given three to five hours of sun. Some will even bloom the following year. Cyclamen is a very popular florists' plant which is prized for its long keeping qualities. Remove the flowers as fast as they fade, and take off any leaves that turn yellow. It requires an abundance of water throughout the flowering season. After flowering, decrease the amount of water given it and repot in April or May with new soil. Set it outdoors in early summer, watering it well during the entire season. Next winter it will have smaller blossoms, but many of them.

Poinsettias are beautiful plants and can be cut off, dried, and forced to flower again the next year. If they drop their leaves when in the living-room, they are either getting too much or too little water, or the roots have become chilled. Set the pot in a pail of warm water, almost as hot as the hand can endure. This will warm the earth and roots.

Tiny so-called orange trees are very attractive and hold the fruits for a long time. These dwarf orange trees will sometimes blossom, if given plenty of water and not too much heat. The blossoms and ripe fruits may be on the little trees at the same time. These little trees are commonly known as Otaheite or Tahiti orange. *See also* HOUSE PLANTS (CARE OF GIFT PLANTS); CYCLAMEN; POINSETTIAS.

CHRISTMAS ROSE: (*Helleborus niger*) Belongs to the Buttercup Family (*Ranunculaceae*) which includes such diverse plants as buttercups, meadow rue, hepatica, anemone, clematis, columbine, delphinium, globeflower, baneberry, and hellebore. This cosmopolitan family of plants offers many beautiful flowers for our enjoyment, some blooming in early spring, some during the summer months, some in autumn when the days are growing shorter and cooler, and some in midwinter.

Helleborus niger grows natively in

the shade of trees and shrubs in northern Italy, and other parts of southern Europe. It is commonly called the Christmas rose because its blooming season usually begins before the holidays and extends through and beyond them, and also because the flower resembles a single rose. It grows best in a shaded place where the soil is stony and contains much humus and moisture. But it can endure the summer sun better than the bright light reflected by snow and the biting winds of winter. Against these the Christmas rose should be protected. This can be accomplished most simply by planting it on the off-wind side of evergreen shrubs and trees, and by covering the plant lightly with evergreen boughs during the months of December to March or until the snow disappears.

TIME TO PLANT: The best times to plant Christmas rose is from August until winter and in early spring before much growth has been made. A common mistake with Christmas rose as with the peony is to plant it too late in the spring. Unless planted early, the plants will not build up enough reserve energy to enable them to bloom the following winter so that flowers will not be formed until a year later.

HOW TO PLANT: Like peonies, Christmas roses must not be planted too deep and special care must be taken that the roots are not damaged. The soil should be well prepared with humus and pulverized rocks because a planting lasts for decades. Leaf mold and peat moss are also good materials for further enriching the soil humus.

TIME OF FLOWERING: Christmas roses are unique in that they bloom in midwinter when practically all other plants are out of bloom. Not only do these plants provide beautiful winter flowers, but because of their beautiful evergreen leaves they are unexcelled for ground cover. For this purpose, they should be planted in groups of from ten to hundreds of plants. The leaves are palmately divided. There usually is only one long-petioled leaf,

but the flower stem may bear one or more sessile (unstalked) leaves or aborted leaves called bracts. The leaves are leathery and evergreen. The plants have creeping rootstocks. The white flowers are borne on either simple or once-branched stems about 12 inches high so that the flowers are elevated a few inches above the leaves. Common horticultural varieties of *H. niger* include *H. altifolius* or *maximum* which has taller flower stalks and larger flowers, *H. praecox* which blooms as early as October and continues until after the New Year, and *H. niger angustifolius* which has narrower leaves and smaller flowers than the typical Christmas rose.

INDOOR BLOOMS: To be absolutely sure of having plants in bloom at Christmas, one moves strong plants into the greenhouse. Or before freezing weather, entire beds can be brought into bloom for cut flowers by covering them, or plants about to bloom may be balled and placed under a protective covering. If one wishes to sell blooming plants, they should be potted in six-inch pots (or larger pots for the larger plants) in early spring, and the potted plants should then be sunk in the soil to a depth of about five inches in the shade of a high tree and provided with water during the summer. At the proper time in late autumn, the pots must be taken up and put under conditions which will bring them into bloom at the desired time.

Christmas roses do not require high temperatures for forcing. In warm weather, they should be aerated and eventually shaded. After the buds appear, the plants should be kept in the dark for a time. This will insure longer flower stems. Later, however, the plants must be given full light again but not bright sunlight. The forcing of the broad petaled variety must be started somewhat earlier than that of *H. niger* and the early-flowering varieties. An experienced gardener will know how to hasten or retard the flowering of the plants, by controlling the temperature. If plants seem to be coming into flower too early, they are exposed to the air during the day or during both day and night. If the plants are developing too slowly, the plants are kept covered and the temperature somewhat higher. If greenhouses are available, the plants can be moved from a warm house to a cold house or vice versa. At temperatures just above zero, the flowers of all forms of *H. niger* remain fresh for many weeks. In some of the forms the flowers assume a yellowish or pinkish tinge as they get older. —*Dr. William Eyster.*

See also PERENNIALS.

CHRISTMAS TREE FARMING: It is feasible to grow Christmas trees from seed, but most farmers prefer either two-year or four-year plants. Two-year seedlings come about eight inches tall, and should be planted in a replant bed until they are four years old and able to stand the rigors of open plantings.

A replant bed should have rich, well-drained soil. Plant the seedlings about six inches apart in rows about 15 inches apart. Plant them with their roots slightly deeper than they were in their original bed, and pack the soil very firmly around the roots, trampling it down with your feet—air pockets mean death to the young seedlings. Keep weeds out of the bed, and supply a three-inch mulch of straw, old hay or leaves after the first frost to protect the roots from cold.

The field in which the four-year-old trees are to be planted should be cleared of all briars and brush, so they won't compete with your crop for light and nourishment. It's not necessary to plow, but get rid of all briars, the Christmas tree man's worst enemy.

Spring is the best time to plant your seedlings. Fall is equally good—provided the soil has plenty of moisture in it. You can plant your trees haphazard, or check-row them (if you plan to cultivate) in rows about four feet apart. The latter method will give you approximately 2,700 trees per acre. Norway spruce, which has bigger branches, should be spaced five feet apart, giving you about 1,700 per acre. Contour planting will help hold the soil on slopes.

Dig a hole with a spade or mattock, a little larger than the clump of roots. Set the tree in straight, firming the earth around it and stamping it down to eliminate air pockets. Firs and pines should be set slightly deeper than they were in the original bed, but set spruces at the same depth they were before.

Keep the roots moist while handling and planting. Most farmers carry the seedlings to be planted in a bucket of mud or water. How many can you plant a day? One man alone should be able to manage 600 to 1,000.

Once established, the trees need only a few days care a year. You'll have to grub out all hardwood seedlings once a year, to give your young trees a chance to live to go to market. And weeds and brush should be kept down to a minimum, for in dry weather they can feed a brush fire that will wipe out your plantation in minutes. Keep your stock fenced out from your evergreens, too—they can eat a tree to death pretty fast.

Once-yearly pruning every June or July, cutting back half that year's new growth, will insure the full, conical shape consumers like to see in their living rooms. Equipped with a shears, you can prune about 50 trees an hour. A light dressing of manure the year before harvest year will give the trees a better color.

Early December is the time to check your Christmas tree planting to pick out the best trees for harvesting.

You can get a higher price by digging up the trees and wrapping the ball of roots, complete with soil, in heavy burlap. Tell the buyer to keep it well watered and replant it as soon as he can after Christmas.

Norway spruce and Douglas pine are the most popular throughout the Midwest Christmas tree belt. Both are well-formed with short, dark needles.

Balsam fir is a slower grower, taking about 10 years to grow to a six-foot height, but its pleasant odor makes it a fast seller. Blue spruce and white spruce are fairly expensive as seedlings and grow slowly, but their beautiful shape and foliage color attract many Christmas buyers. Both of these, as well as the Douglas fir (a very slow grower) are often sold live to home owners who want to re-plant them in their lawns.

CHRYSANTHEMUM: Long after many flowers have said farewell, and long after we have put summer activities behind us and started our heaters, chrysanthemums challenge winter with late and lavish blooms. In some favorable seasons these perennials defy frost and carry on even into December with fresh, crisp and beautiful blooms. These last blooms terminate a procession which begins late in August and reaches its height in October.

PROPAGATION: Hardy chrysanthemums may be propagated by division, cuttings, or seed. Most named varieties will not come true from seed and, therefore, must be propagated by one of the two vegetative means. Cuttings are taken in March or April and rooted in sand. Divisions are done as early in the spring as possible. Garden plants should be divided once every year or once every two years. Young chrysanthemum plants bloom better than huge clumps. Divide the root into as many small rooted divisions as the outside of each crown will supply. Discard the hard woody centers. Set the divisions out 12-18 inches apart. After the spring resetting, when the plants have six leaves, pinch the tops out to induce side branching. As each new branch devel-

The Bobolink variety of the quilled spoon type, is a coral burnt orange in the bud, later flowers as a sharp pastel orange-gold, brightly gay.

ops six leaves, pinch these also. Discontinue this practice about mid-July and let growth go on, otherwise flower formation may be greatly delayed. Plants purchased from nurseries are set out in the spring when the ground can be worked.

CULTURE: Chrysanthemums grow well in any normally-cultivated garden soil, but will profit greatly in a soil enriched with rotted manure, compost, or humus. Chrysanthemum beds need to be prepared about ten inches deep unless natural drainage is poor. An extra five-six inches is then dug, and a layer of coarse gravel laid in the bottom. Good drainage is essential for safe wintering. Plants which are alternately frozen and thawed rarely survive an average winter. A light mulch may be placed over the roots in the late fall and the plants can be protected with burlap screens. Do not cover the plants heavily as they are easily suffocated. If the season is dry, regular and deep waterings are necessary to prevent the stems becoming woody.

LOCATION: Location is an important factor. It is best to plant chrysanthemums in a spot that is protected from winter winds. They should also be protected from a cooking sun which may destroy plant tissues. A southwestern exposure is best with house wall, fence, or shrubbery behind for a windbreak.

Varieties include: Aster daisy (*arcticum*)—one to one and one-half foot high, hardy perennial with white or lilac flowers; Pyrethrum (*coccineum*)—summer-blooming perennial that grows to two feet, fine border plant, also known as Painted Lady; Costmary (*balsamita*)—hardy, two to three foot high perennial; Crown daisy (*coronarium*)—hardy, three to four foot high annual; Corn marigold (*segetum*)—one to two foot annual with white or yellow flowers; and Giant daisy (*uliginosum*)—four to seven foot high hardy perennial. *See also* FERTILIZER; PERENNIALS.

CHUFA: (*Cyperus esculentus*) Listed in some seed catalogs under the name "earth almond," it is sometimes grown in northern gardens as a curiosity.

The plant is a botanic relative of the papyrus plant of which the ancient Egyptians made paper. It looks much like a coarse, heavy bunch marsh grass, but should properly be called a sedge, the edible portion being the small tubers attached to the roots. These vary much in size and shape but average the size of medium sized beans, from a fourth to three-fourths of an inch. They have a sweet taste, very much like that of coconut, but are not much used for human food, as when matured and dried they become hard and woody.

Chufa tubers are grown in a bunch at the base of the plant, and as the roots do not spread or run through the ground, can be easily dug or harvested.

This plant can well be a valuable adjunct in the reclamation of much sandy land now of low fertility and classed as sub-marginal.

The chufa grows well and can be easily harvested in any loose, friable soil and relatively high yields are reported, sometimes 200 bushels or more an acre.—*Archer Whallon.*

CIDER: Most recommended apple varieties for cider include Winesap, McIntosh, Jonathan and Baldwin.

A bushel of apples gives two gallons of cider when made with a hand grinder and press. After grinding and pressing, allow juice to stand in deep containers overnight.

Then, siphon off the juice from the sediment. Pasteurize the juice for ten minutes at temperature of 170°F. and store in a cool place.

CIMICIFUGA: Also known as bugbane, these hardy ornamental perennials are satisfactory for partially-shaded locations at the far end of the garden. They grow best, becoming taller and with showier blooms, if the soil is rich in humus. Varieties range in height from two to four feet; often give off a foul odor. *See also* PERENNIALS.

CINERARIA: Cinerarias are popular florists' flowers which may be grown from seed each year. They are not difficult to grow, but plants may be bought from the nurserymen if you do not care to go to the trouble of raising your own. The seed is very fine and may be mixed with sand to secure even distribution. Do not cover it with earth; just press down firmly with some flat surface. After transplanting, keep shifting the plants until they are in a six-inch pot, which will give you large specimens. They require a great deal of water and sun, but not enough sun so that the leaves wilt and are burned. After the flower spikes appear, fertilize with liquid fertilizer about every two weeks. Keep all the old blossoms picked off to prolong bloom and be sure they get plenty of fresh air, but avoid cold drafts. Stakes may be needed to support the flowers. They are sometimes afflicted with red spider. Remove all leaves which show any signs of disease. *C. maritima* is highly recommended; though not hardy in the North, its low growing foliage is attractive as a summer bedding plant. *See also* CENTAUREA.

CINNAMON FERN: *see* OSMUNDA

CINQUEFOIL: *see* POTENTILLA

CITRUS FRUITS: The first requirement of any citrus tree is a warm climate, so most of the fruits are grown in Southern California, along the Gulf of Mexico, and in Southern and Central Florida. A great many gardeners in those areas use groupings of orange and grapefruit trees as shade trees around their homes.

Citrus trees are broad-leaved evergreens. The trees vary in height from ten to 15 feet (lime), ten to 20 feet (lemon), 15 to 40 feet (orange) and 30 to 50 feet (grapefruit). There's little difference in their growth pattern. When young, the trees are upright and spreading. As they become older, they become somewhat pyramidal in shape. Generally, citrus trees are long-lived and begin bearing at four to six years.

Unlike the peach and apple, citrus trees are non-hardy, able to withstand temperatures only a few degrees below 32°F. For example, the critical temperature of the sweet orange is about 24°F, while the lemon is about 26°F. In the subtropical zone of the citrus growing districts, temperatures below these critical points frequently occur; that's why the unique practice of orchard or grove heating has been developed. Oil or gas heaters, burning small piles of wood, wind machines that mix warm and cold air, protecting trunks of young trees by mounding them with soil high enough to shield the bud union—these are some methods used by growers to save trees from cold.

Experts estimate that about 35 inches of water is necessary for the annual production of most citrus fruits. That's why horticulturist J. C. Johnston of the University of California calls irrigation the most important single factor in caring for a mature orchard. Florida is more fortunate in this respect, however, since most of their vital water is supplied by rain.

Similar to other fruit trees, citrus trees require well-drained, well-aerated, and fairly fertile soils. Excellent drainage is particularly important. Therefore cover cropping and the addition of organic fertilizers are vital to the success of every citrus grower, if soil structure is to be improved.

The time cover crops are grown usually coincides with the period of heaviest rainfall. In California practically all of the rain occurs during the winter, and so cover crops that grow in cool weather are started in the fall just before the rains stop. In Florida, most of the rain takes place in the summer; cover crops are started in the spring and worked into the soil in fall—usually just before the harvest season.

To get an idea of how to fertilize your citrus trees, let's take a look at how Will Kinney of Vista, California, handles his 24-acre orange grove. When he was first building up the soil, Kinney used 20 tons each of natural limestone and gypsum, plus 30 tons of a rock phosphate mixture that included many trace elements such as cobalt, zinc, boron, molybdenum, iron and magnesium. Comments orange grower Kinney: "Seventy tons of this material on 24 acres is a very heavy application. However, this program will be continued, with some changes, for several more years to bring the grove into maximum production of maximum food value fruit.

"Each month throughout the year, the permanent cover crop is chopped at the rate 6,000 pounds per acre. These chopped plants return a high-nutrient green manure residue to the soil. I have been using grasses and clovers for cover crops, and they pro-

This transplanted orange tree bore fruit the following season. When it was nine years old it was cut back and moved and treated with greensand and colloidal phosphate compost on its new location.

duce an abundance of organic matter for our soils. In addition, I've been able to add hundreds of tons of cow manure, which is an excellent organic nitrogen carrier."

Recently more and more reports have been issued about the decline in citrus production, especially in Florida. To a great extent, the cause seems to be excessive use of concentrated chemical fertilizers. In general, California growers have been making better use of organic nitrogen fertilizers, such as manure, alfalfa hay and straw, than orchardists in Florida, where only a small percentage of the nitrogen is derived from organic sources. Other troubles have been cropping up as shown by the increased use of artificial preservatives and color additives so common to citrus sold in supermarkets.

PLANTING: Citrus trees grow best in direct sunlight; when planted in partial shade, they tend to be weak.

Most varieties are fast-growing, averaging about one foot per year growth in over-all height and spread. Therefore, when choosing a location for trees, remember that distance between trees is most important. Usual spacing for most orange trees is 25 x 25 feet; grapefruit 25 x 30 feet or 30 x 30 feet; mandarins and hybrids (as Temple) 20 x 20 feet; kumquat, lime and lemon 15 x 15 feet.

If you have to plant in poorly-drained soils, it's essential to prepare the soil deeply and add as much organic materials as possible. Trees are usually obtained from nurseries (1) bare-rooted; (2) bare-rooted but placed in sphagnum; (3) balled—burlap placed around the small root system that was lifted with soil still around roots and (4) potted trees. The last two are preferred, since roots are more protected. Never let the rootlets be exposed for any length of time, or else they will become dry and permanently damaged.

Healthy nursery stock will have large leaves and bright, clean bark. Bud union should be smooth and about three inches from the ground. Don't buy trees with a hard, stunted look; bark on these trees is generally dark grey, trunk crooked, with joints reflecting stunted growth.

When roots are bagged, remove the bag and set the tree so that it is growing a little higher than it was in the nursery. Do not bend roots.

Recommended planting time is when trees are dormant, about late January or February. Area where tree is to be planted should be spaded deeply, all rocks, sticks, etc., removed. The hole should be large enough to accommodate root system without bending roots. If roots are bagged, remove bag and set the tree so that it is growing a little higher than it had been in the nursery. If the tree was bare-rooted, inspect for damaged or broken roots and prune these off with sloping cut.

When mulching citrus trees, it's a good practice not to let the mulch come into direct contact with the tree trunk; allow a space of about eight inches in diameter around the trunk exposed to sunlight and air to reduce possibility of fungus attack.

To protect young trees from cold weather and freezing temperatures, bank them with soil to well above the bud union—around one to one and one-half feet high. Remove bank of soil when freezing danger is over. This protection is especially important until tree is two or three years old.

In reference to pruning, keep in mind that removal of leaves retards growth and delays bearing. The general rule is avoid pruning unnecessarily. Sprouts can be removed when tree is young in order to develop a better fruiting structure; leave the tops unpruned until the tree is bearing; trim only to remove dead wood.

BENEFICIAL INSECTS AND FUNGI: Many beneficial parasites and predators exist that prey on the various pests of citrus trees. Here is a list of the three most common ones according to Citriculturist Fred P. Lawrence of the Florida Agricultural Extension Service:

Ladybugs (for detailed description, see listing); *Red Aschersonia*, commonly found on citrus trees, is a beneficial fungus that kills immature whiteflies. It forms pink and reddish pustules one-eighth inch or less in diameter, on the underside of leaves. It is so colorful that many growers are quite concerned when it appears and sometimes mistakenly think that it is harmful. Brown whitefly fungus also aids in control of whiteflies. It appears as cinnamon or brownish-colored pustules about one-eighth inch in diameter on underside of leaves. This fungus is often confused with Florida red scale. However, it can be quickly distinguished from red scale because it does not have the raised reddish-brown center peculiar to red scale.

Oil sprays during the summer months have been found to control scale and also remove sooty mold from foliage as well as other pests.

HARVESTING: While all varieties of citrus have peak ripeness times, fruit can be left on tree for quite some time after maturity without serious deterioration. One thing to be very careful about—overly mature citrus fruit will start to have its juice absorbed by the tree, so do not let it hang too long after ripening.

Here is a brief listing of the better known citrus varieties:

Orange: sweet orange (*sinensis*)—growing 15 to 25 feet with fragrant, white flowers; king orange (*nobilis*)—small white flowers, large-size juicy fruit; mandarin or tangerine (*deliciosa*)—small, attractive tree whose fruits have become so popular; Seville or sour orange (*aurantium*)—medium-sized tree whose stock is extensively used for budding other citrus fruits since it is especially adapted for growing in wide range of soils, even low wet areas; Tahiti orange (*taitensis*)—attractive miniature orange tree, growing about two to three feet high.

Lemon (*limonia*)—small sensitive tree with rather large, reddish-tinted flowers.

Grapefruit (*paradisi* and *grandis*)—large tree, round-topped with large, white flowers.

Lime (*aurantifolia*)—small tree with small white flowers, considered the most sensitive to cold of any of the citrus trees.

COVER CROPS FOR CITRUS ORCHARDS: "Cover crops have always played an enormous role in the maintenance of fertility in our sandy soil, and they are just as important today as ever—if not more so. . . . The need for leguminous cover crops on all of our sandy soils has been recognized for many years, because they not only furnish organic matter in our soils, they also furnish a readily available form of nitrogen to other plants when they decompose." This analysis of the value of cover crops is made by R. E. Norris and Fred P. Lawrence, Florida citrus experts.

Although Beggarweed, Cowpeas, and Velvet Beans were the earliest legumes used in citrus groves, Norris and Lawrence highly recommend hairy indigo. Here's why:

"Hairy indigo looks quite promising as a leguminous cover crop for citrus in Florida. It grows well on our light sandy soils. It is highly resistant to rootknot. It is not an acceptable food plant for the pumpkin or stink bug and it gives a comparatively high tonnage of green manure per acre. Yields have been checked up to slightly over twenty-two tons (green weight) per acre; however, it appears that under average conditions the yield should be between five and seven and one-half tons green weight per acre. The plant reseeds itself and apparently requires no inoculation or special fertilizers. Its chief drawback as a cover crop in citrus is that it does not produce seed until late in the year. Usually it is mid-October before mature seed spikes are produced.

When to Plant:
   March to June when good moisture is present.

Rate to Seed:
   Four to eight pounds per acre (on solid acre basis) depending on method of seeding.

How to Seed:
   Sow on well prepared middle or seed-bed. Cover not more than one-half inch. It is not imperative but it helps to pack the soil with a cultipacker, roller, or drag.

Green Manure Crops:
   Chop, disc, or plow after seed matures in the fall, before the first killing frost, to assure reseeding for the following year."

OTHER CROPS

Here are descriptions of several other crops to consider:

Cowpeas
   Locale: Southern States
   Soil: Does well on almost all

types of soil. Like buckwheat, is good for returning poor soils to fertility.

Planting Time: Seeding should not be done until the ground is thoroughly warmed. All varieties are susceptible to cold.

Growth Rate: Yield is comparatively high.

Seed: When planted in rows 3 feet apart, about 20 pounds of seed per acre are needed. When sown broadcast, 80 to 100 pounds per acre are needed.

Disease and Pests: Subject to attack by nematodes, bacterial canker and fusarium wilt, all of which often do considerable damage.

Red Clover

Locale: Thrives in practically all areas.

Planting Time: Often planted in early spring to allow time for two stands.

Growth Rate: Has upright growth and heavy yields, making it one of the best crops for soil improvement.

Seed: 15 to 20 pounds per acre are recommended.

Sudan Grass

Locale: Adapted to almost all parts of the United States.

Growth Rate: Rapid growth makes it a suitable plant for green manure when the period in which such a crop can be used is very short.

Seed: Should be sown in close drills or broadcast, 20 to 25 pounds per acre.

Disease and Pests: In the humid region of the Central and Southeastern states, Sudan grass is subject to serious damage by foliage diseases. Much of this can be overcome by using a recently developed

variety known as Tift Sudan. This variety is especially valuable in the Southeastern states.

Vetch, Austrian winter peas, rye and rye grass, are all used to a certain extent as winter cover crops. Vetch is well adapted to sandy soils, along with rye and rye grass. *See also* ORANGE; LEMON; GRAPEFRUIT; LIME; TREES, PLANTING; FRUIT TREES.

CITRUS WASTES: Citrus wastes are most easily composted, nor is there any danger to the soil in their oils and resins, because these disintegrate in the composting process. The fact that some citrus peels may have spray residues on them need not be overestimated, since such residues are small and will not likely harm the soil after the material is broken down into compost. Orange skins and citrus skins of all kinds are richer in nitrogen if the skins are thick; their phosphoric acid content is extremely high, and an ash analysis shows about 3.0 per cent of the valuable element in orange skins, while the potash content of the ash only surpassed by banana skins; the former analyzing about 27 per cent, the latter almost 50 per cent in potash. Lemons, as a rule, have a lower potash, but a higher phosphorus content than oranges; grapefruits seem to hold the middle between the extremes: 3.6 per cent phosphoric acid and 30 per cent potash. Whole fruits, so-called culls, are also useful, though their fertilizer value is necessarily lower than that of the skins, because they contain great amounts of water.

CLARKIA: This annual is native to the western United States, is hardy and comparatively easy to grow during the cool weather of winter and early spring. The plants attain a height of about two feet, produce spikes of single or double flowers in shades of white, pink, salmon or red. Seed should be sown before the earth freezes in November or when the snow is leaving the ground in late

February. Broadcast the seed on a mild day where it is wanted; they do best in light soil in a spot where there is full sun or part shade. An early start will insure quick growth and bloom before summer. Flower from July to October.

CLAY SOIL: A typical "clay" soil may be composed of approximately 60 per cent actual clay, 20 per cent silt, and 20 per cent sand. The particles in a clay soil are so fine that it tends to compact, which makes cultivation difficult and interferes with the oxygen supply for plant roots. Water can do little to enter the impervious clay soil, and runoff is very common during rainfalls. *See also* ORGANIC MATTER; SOILS; MOISTURE-LOVING PLANTS; AERATION.

CLEARING LAND: *see* LAND, CLEARING

CLEFT GRAFT: *see* GRAFTING

CLEMATIS: During the past several decades there has been a greatly increasing interest in the ornamental vines known as Clematis. In England, there are a great many varieties, colors and shapes of these plants which seem to thrive in their special type of climate. In this family of vines there are over 400 small and large-flowered

Clematis are prolific bloomers with many uses and arrangements. They combine well, make good borders, and may be grown alone for an accent.

varieties, although many of them are not practical for the home gardener.

There are now about 90 different colors and shades available to those who are enthusiastic about growing Clematis. Most of these are own-root plants, which are generally considered to be much better than grafted stock because of their ability to start from the collar in cases where the stem has been injured, still maintaining their own original variety. These own-root plants also produce a better root system and are more resistant to temperature changes of our various seasons.

The Clematis family of vines is mainly divided into two general groups. The first group comprises the small-flowered varieties which range in shape from flat blooms to a variety of urn, bell, lantern and star-like flowers. The second is the larger-flowered hybrids which are available in a number of different sizes and colors and are usually platter shaped. These larger-flowered Clematis blossoms will often produce blossoms up to eight or ten inches across.

By careful selection of the varieties planted, a gardener can have continuous blooms from early spring until frost. In our New York region, the hybrids usually start to bloom in July and continue for six or eight weeks, with an interruption in September for new growth. After this, they will often resume blooming just before frost. Depending upon the variety, a growth in one year may be from six feet to 30 feet.

In general, Clematis are prolific bloomers, with this condition: the larger the size of a flower, the less profuse in bloom it is apt to be. A compensating factor is that those which do not bloom so profusely generally make up in quality of bloom for what they lack in quantity.

There are a great many uses and arrangements in which the Clematis excels. You can combine them with other flowers on your favorite garden arch, trellis or fence; you can grow them alone on a pillar, post, stone wall or terrace, or to completely cover and hide an old stump. When used as a perennial border, they will make a very fine arrangement and will cover a surprisingly large area completely. A good method is to use some old branches over the bed area so that the vines can grow up on them away from the ground. It is sometimes helpful to arrange the branches so that they are lower in the front and higher at the back. In one season, the vines will completely cover the area giving a mass of green foliage with bright accents of colored blossoms scattered about.

WHAT THEY NEED: Some people who are not too familiar with Clematis consider them difficult to grow. This may be due to the fact that they are unaware of the needs of this plant, or do not take their needs into consideration. Clematis need nothing that the average gardener cannot provide with a little work. Naturally, they do not do their best unless given the conditions they like, and if too badly abused, may give up and die completely after a few disappointing years. Don't let this discourage you— the conditions are not difficult.

The first thing is to buy own-root plants, two years old. These two-year-old plants are the right age for a rapid top growth and will give you good blossoms without having to wait too long.

WHEN TO PLANT: Planting can be done in the fall or in the spring. Fall-planted stock should be mulched well in order to prevent damage from frost action on the soil. Clematis start their growth early in the spring, so they should be planted as early as possible, and especially before the weather becomes hot and dry. Plants from pots can even be set out throughout the summer if kept well watered at reasonable intervals so that they do not dry out too much.

WHERE TO PLANT: The location for planting Clematis should be selected with these factors in mind: good drainage, but no standing water; four or five hours of sunlight a day; soil at the base of the plant should be cool and damp; a good rich loam soil, well loosened and with a little well-rotted manure mixed in if available. Because the roots of the Clematis like to be cool and damp, it is often well to select the shady side of a wall or fence where the vines can climb into the sunlight. A good summer mulch of straw, grass clippings, peat moss, buckwheat hulls or some other type will help to retain the moisture during the hot summer days and prevent the soil from becoming baked and hard. This mulch will also have the advantage of keeping the weeds under control better.

HOW TO PLANT: In planting the Clematis, you should dig a hole about 18 inches across by about 18 inches deep, and fill it with good loose soil, with some well-rotted manure mixed in if you can get it. If your soil is too heavy, you might add a little peat moss to loosen it up. About two months after planting, you can add a good fertilizer once or twice but do not work it in too deeply so as to disturb the roots. Clematis also like lime and if your soil is not on the alkaline side, you can add a little lime and work it in to help the plants.

Plant the Clematis with the collar (the point where the roots branch from the stem) two to three inches below the soil level. Firm the soil well around the roots and water thoroughly after planting. However, be careful not to overwater so as to cause mud. Do not fertilize for at least two months after planting.

USE SUPPORTS: A support for the vines to start climbing should be provided right from the start. This will prevent the wind from whipping the vine around and will also help to keep the leaves off the ground. Clematis does best when its stems and leaves are able to grow up into the air and have light and air circulation around them.

LITTLE PRUNING NEEDED: For the first two years after planting, it is generally not necessary to do any pruning, as you want to give the plants plenty of time to get established When the roots have become large, you can thin them out in early spring by removing the old and dead wood. If you are trying to cover a special spot, you may prefer simply to cut out the dead wood only. Trim summer and fall-blooming varieties early in March, but the spring-flowering varieties should get their pruning in late January by simply taking out the old wood. These spring-flowering varieties bloom on last year's growth and you, therefore, must leave the old wood in order to avoid cutting off the new flowers.

Summer-flowering varieties may be cut back to two or three feet above the ground in early spring. You need have no fear in doing this as their rapid early growth will still make the tops as large as ever by blooming time, with better foliage and larger blooms.

MULCH IS IMPORTANT: North of Washington, D.C., it is very good and inexpensive insurance to provide a good winter mulch in November, before heavy frost time. This mulch prevents any sudden changes in temperature from causing heating of the ground which would cause serious winter damage to the plants. A good mulch will more than pay for the extra work in the protection of your plants and the better early start they will get in the spring.

WIDE CHOICE OF VARIETIES: Here are a few of the good varieties that you might select in starting out.

COMTESSE DE BOUCHARD (range in color from satiny rose to rich pink; strong grower, profuse bloomer from June to September; reaches eight to ten feet height.)

DUCHESS OF ALBANY (gorgeous pink, trumpet shape flowers, bloom July to September, often called Scarlet Clematis of Texas.)

DUCHESS OF EDINBURGH (pure white, similar to a gardenia, ideal for use on a pillar or post.)

JACKMANI SUPERBA (dark violet purple, large flowered.)

JACKMANI RUBRA (bright red variety of Jackmani, vigorous growth and free flowering.)

LAWSONIANA (beautiful blue flushed with mauve, large flowers, long blooming, soil rich growth.)

HENRYI (hybrid of rare beauty, large white flowers often eight inches across, vigorous growth, climbs as high as eight feet.)

NEVILLE (rich textured petals, like plum colored velvet; average height, long blooming.)

MRS. CHOLMONDELEY (wisteria-blue, a color of rare delicacy with large open flowers in profusion. An extraordinary summer flowering variety.)

MONTANA UNDULATA (soft mauve pink flowers, ideal for growing on a wall or terrace, makes a mass of bright flowers in spring.)

See also FERTILIZER.

CLEOME: This annual is one of the most prolific seed bearers, and seeds have a remarkably high rate of germination. It is extremely resistant to insects, making it one of the easiest annuals to grow. Plants start to bloom when about six inches high, early in July, and keep blooming and growing until frost kills it in mid-fall. In this way, some plants grow to a height of six feet. The most common variety grown as an ornamental is *spinosa,* sometimes known as "spider-flower," or "spider plant." Another variety, *serrulata,* is grown as a bee plant in the western part of the country. *Serrulata* is also known in some locals as Rocky Mountain bee plant, or stinking clover. They do best in sandy soils and in a sunny location.

CLETHRA: Sweet Pepper Bush. A four or five foot shrub blooming from July to September. *C. alnifolia* will flourish in a damp spot or in any ordinary garden soil. The flowers are very fragrant (pure white spikes about five inches long). These combine excellently with many uncultivated plants such as wild roses and grapes, and also with the butterfly bush—the white of the pepper bush setting off the rich purple tones of the buddleia. It can be propagated by seeds sown indoors in spring, division, or by layers and cuttings. There is a delicate pale pink variety. All are said to grow best in slightly acid, peaty soils.

CLEVELAND CHERRY: *see* CHRISTMAS CHERRY

CLIMATES IN MINIATURE: *By T. Bedford Franklin. See* BOOKS FOR ORGANIC GARDENERS AND FARMERS

CLIVIA: Clivias belong to the amaryllis family. Their rich orange glory sheds a luminous glow over their spot in the garden. Because they thrive in the dense shade, they are often used in out-of-door plantings under the shade of massive oaks. Although it is somewhat tender, only the leaves are injured by frost. The strong succulent roots and heavy strap-like leaves are long lived and the heavy umbels of richly colored flowers make them one of the most decorative plants you can select for your garden. They need shade, plenty of water and very crowded roots, if you are growing them in pots. In the garden they should be grown in rich heavy soil and never be allowed to dry out. Even the common *C. miniata* is a very desirable plant. It is much hardier and has long narrow dark green foliage. It is free flowering and you find wonderful clumps of it in many of the old-time gardens. The flower umbels and individual flowers are smaller. The sal-mony orange flowers fade to light yellow in the center. However, the fine Belgian hybrids are the superfine strains which have been developed in Europe over many decades. Even out of bloom the plants are very decorative with their three-inch dark evergreen leaves.—*Charlotte Hoak.*

CLOCHE GARDENING: The underlying principle of "continuous cloches" is to take glass protection to a growing crop instead of growing the crop inside a fixed greenhouse or frame.

The continuous cloche, designed by L. H. Chase, of England, over 40 years ago, is intended to protect rows of growing crops at their normal field or garden spacing. Each cloche is a rigid entity, weighing about five pounds and consisting of two or four sheets of glass held together by a galvanized wire framework. The continuous cloches fit together end to end to form long glass tunnels not more than 24 inches wide and of any required length. The ends of these tunnels are closed with sheets of glass to prevent excessive draft.

The maximum width of the cloche is important, as the method by which water reaches cloche-protected crops is unique, although similar in principle to the methods of irrigation used

A bottomless gallon-sized glass jug will serve as a home-made cloche but the top cover must be removed periodically for adequate ventilation.

in tropical countries. The surface of the soil in which the crops are growing under the cloches is never wetted, as it is in the case of open-air crops, or in greenhouses or frames. According to J. L. H. Chase, son of the designer, the rain falls on the glass roofs of the cloches, runs down the sides and seeps into the soil and so laterally to the roots of the plants.

The result is that the soil never cakes under the cloches, and the original tilth is preserved. "This means that hoeing to keep the surface soil aerated is unnecessary, and it also means that 'the soil temperature is considerably raised, for the fine surface tilth prevents frost from penetrating, even at very low temperatures," states Mr. Chase.

Cloches offer good protection against frost, as well as against wind. Although relatively small and light, the individual cloches are not shifted by heavy gales unless the ends of the rows are not kept closed or they are put down unevenly on the soil.

Since they are constructed almost completely from glass with just a small amount of framework, cloches offer practically no obstruction to the sun's rays. In addition, light reaches the plants from the sides, signifying that growth will not be distorted vertically and there will be no "drawing" of the plants, as is effected when light is obtained only from above.

Cloches also give protection from impurities in the air, which prevent crops from growing properly, although it is necessary to clean the glass from time to time as it quickly becomes dirty in industrial areas. This advantage becomes increasingly important, when one considers the extensive damage to crops caused by smog last year.

Some crops are grown throughout under cloches from sowing until harvesting, but the majority of crops are merely started under the glass and then allowed to finish in the open. Half-hardy crops, for example, can be sown or planted five weeks before the danger of killing frosts has passed. At the end of that period the cloches can be removed and the plants can grow on in the open in the normal way. Strawberries, on the other hand, have been cloched for three months, from March until picking is finished approximately at the end of May.

Cloches are not used to cover just a single crop in the year, but a succession of crops. In England, during the winter and early spring, the choice lies between lettuces, carrots, asparagus, peas and radishes. During April or May, the first crop is followed by a half-hardy crop, such as one of the following: tomatoes, French beans, runner beans, marrows or sweet corn. The third crop is a summer crop, covering the plants from June onwards, and consisting of a late crop of tomatoes or melons, cucumbers, capsicums or onion sets.

There are also a number of profitable flower crops which are grown with cloche protection. Most important are: sweet peas, larkspur, pyrethrum, scabiosa, dahlias, zinnias, anemones, violets, daffodils, tulips, iris and gladioli. Some need more height than is afforded by the continuous cloche in its normal position, and this is provided by using what are called elevators, which effectively raise the height of the cloches by about 12 inches.

Early in the 1940's, when the shortage of labor became an acute problem in England, a work-saving technique—"strip-cropping"—was evolved for the use of cloches commercially. Instead of using the drift of cloches in a solid block over one crop and then, when that crop reached maturity, shifting all the cloches to another part of the field to cover a second crop, "strip-cropping" was introduced. In this method crops were grown in alternate strips of the same width, and when one crop no longer needed protection, the cloches were merely moved six feet sideways on to the adjoining strip in order to cover the succeeding crop.

Cloche cultivation is most widespread in England. It has been estimated that there are about 15 million cloches in use in the United Kingdom, with about two-thirds used commercially and one-third by amateur gardeners.

In Canada, the greatest interest has been shown in British Columbia, for in eastern Canada the spring is so short that cloches only have a limited value in the production of early crops.

In the United States, continuous cloches were first marketed in 1950 and are known as "P. M. G.'s"—portable miniature greenhouses. Here experimentation has been primarily done by amateurs who like the chance to grow a greater variety of crops. *See also* HARDENING-OFF; GREENHOUSE; BOOKS FOR ORGANIC GARDENERS AND FARMERS (CLOCHE GARDENING).

CLOVE PINK: (*Dianthus caryophyllus*) Perennial, with jointed stems and blue-green, grass-like leaves and small carnation-like flowers. The fragrance of the flowers is penetrating and spicy, resembling cloves. Clove pink is a useful plant for a low border and can be propagated from seeds, cuttings, or by layering. It is hardy, but needs protection in cold climates; should have good drainage.

CLOVER: (*Trifolium*) For many centuries, clover has been grown for soil improvement purposes. A valuable green manure crop, species of clover have absorbed free nitrogen from the air and added it to the soil. In addition, all clovers are excellent bee plants.

The small leaves of some of the clovers, especially when cut young, decay readily and make excellent compost, while stalky material does not pack well enough to keep moisture uniformly. Where old clover is used, care must be taken in aerating the heap well, so that the stalky material can break down.

RED CLOVER: (*T. pratense*) Red clover used to be the leading forage plant in the United States. It is still widely grown and is an important hay plant and component of grass mixtures. Recently alfalfa, ladino clover and birdsfoot trefoil have become more widely used.

While red clover is actually a perennial, it acts as a biennial. It has a comparatively deep and much branched tap-root system. The plant will range from one to two feet in height. It produces its greatest growth the season after planting. If allowed to produce seed during the first year of establishment it usually dies, hence, clipping or grazing in the early fall are recommended to prevent it from setting seed the year it is sown.

The diseases to which it is susceptible are mainly: fusarium, anthracnose and mildew. The grown borer also causes serious injury to this plant.

The soil fertility requirements of red clover are lower than for alfalfa. It is adapted to a wide range of soil conditions. It will not thrive on thin, open, gravelly soils which suffer from drought. It requires soil high in organic matter and a pH of 6.0 or above. It is also a heavy user of phosphorus. Good corn land is considered good clover land.

It is not as tolerant of drought as such deep-rooted legumes as alfalfa, white clover, or birdsfoot trefoil. It does best in regions with abundant rainfall and without extremes of either winter or summer temperatures; so it is confined to the humid, temperate regions of the United States.

Its most common use is for hay purposes. It is one of the most nutritional of forage crops.

ALSIKE CLOVER: (*T. hybridum*) Alsike clover is similar to red clover with which it is frequently confused. This legume is limited in acreage to conditions unsuited for red clover, particularly wet soils. Like red clover it is a perennial but acts as a biennial. The plant is smooth rather than hairy and its flower heads are partially pink and white. This plant will vary in height from ½ to three feet. It has a branch tap-root, but the stems are rather weak and hence the crop lodges easily.

Soil and climatic adaptation. Alsike clover is adapted to soils with poor drainage and of less fertility than required for red clover. It is not as sensitive to acidity, hence, it can be grown successfully on wet, cool and sour soils on which red clover fails. It prefers heavy silt or clay soils with plenty of moisture for best growth.

It thrives best in a cool climate but it does stand severe winters better than does red clover.

Uses. Alsike clover is used for hay primarily and makes a better quality hay than red clover but doesn't yield as well. The nutritive value of alsike and red clover hay is as follows:

Kind of Hay	Dry Matter %	Protein %	Carbohydrates %	Fat %	Fuel Value Calories
Red Clover	84.7	7.38	38.15	1.81	92.32
Alsike Clover	90.3	8.15	41.70	1.36	98.46

—*J. B. Washko, Penna. State University.*

See FORAGE CROPS.

LADINO CLOVER: (*T. gigantrum*) Another great legume becoming ever more popular in the northeastern states is ladino clover. Typical of current opinion in New England is the statement that "ladino clover has done more for Vermont dairymen than any other legume. It can be grown under such a wide range of soil conditions that there is a place for ladino on nearly every farm in the state." And, it might be added, in every state in the northeast.

Ladino is of such great value because it lasts long under proper management, produces a heavy amount of fodder with its great size, gathers nitrogen and creeps so that only a small amount of seed is needed. Usually a pound or two is sufficient per acre in mixture with other grasses; there are three-quarters of a million seeds per pound, so it goes a long way. The fertilizing recommendations for

alfalfa apply to ladino, too, for both are heavy feeders and the latter is especially fond of potash, supplied by greensand or granite dust. In mixture with alfalfa it would, of course, get the same food. It is unwise to use ladino alone, particularly for pasture, for it will cause severe bloat in cattle unless dry hay is fed first. Grown with brome grass, timothy or orchard grass, this danger is averted. It should not be grazed shorter than four inches and, as with alfalfa, should be allowed free growth for six weeks at the end of the season to build up a food supply in the crowns and roots.

Many farmers in the northeast have wet fields they don't quite know what to do with and ladino furnishes an answer as long as the field is not swampy. Together with reed canary grass, another moisture lover, ladino provides good hay and pasture on moist fields. In fact, it is not recommended for dry hillsides or droughty conditions.

The small leaves of some of the clovers, especially when cut young, decay readily and make excellent compost, while stalky materials do not pack well enough to keep moisture uniformly.

SWEETCLOVER: Biennial legume; all parts of U. S. Just about any soil, if reasonably well supplied with lime. Will pierce tough subsoils. Especially adept at utilizing rock fertilizers, and a fine bee plant. Sow 175 pounds of scarified or 25 pounds of unscarified seed, fall to early spring. Fast-growing Hubam, annual white sweetclover, can be turned under in the fall; other varieties have their biggest roots in the spring of the second year, so turn them under then.

CLOVER, ALLYCE: This is a summer

legume that makes a fast, lush growth, recommended for soil-building, grazing and hay. It has been grown successfully primarily in central Florida, and other southern states are testing it now.

Sweetclovers have strong roots that penetrate compacted subsoils. They use rock fertilizers efficiently, making their nutrients available.

CRIMSON CLOVER: (*T. incarnatum*) An annual that grows two to three feet high, crimson clover has been widely used for soil building as well as a forage crop. Farmers have found it excellent as a winter legume capable of stopping erosion, enriching soil and providing good pasture. About 15 years ago, reseeding crimson clover was developed and is highly recommended. It resists severe cold, requires less than 35 inches of rainfall. While their seeds look like common crimson, they don't crack open but begin germination around fall, so they are not killed during summer.

As a result, farmers get five to seven months winter grazing, a spring seed crop, and plow the crimson under or mow it for hay—all without affecting the next year's crop.

Reseeding crimson is a good neighbor to other crops, too. It grows well in combination with sericea, kudzu, oats, ryegrass, vetch, Bermuda grass and other permanent grazing crops. With some, like Johnson grass and sweet sudan, it furnishes nearly year-round grazing.

After making good winter and spring pasture, crimson dies as the summer crops, of which corn, grain sorghum, cotton and soybeans are widely used, begin their growth. And the nitrogen it has stored up stimulates the following crop like a shot of vitamins. When used for green manure, it should be turned under a few weeks before planting the next crop to allow time to decompose. Or, it will yield two tons of hay per acre, cut near the end of April. It also provides cover and organic matter when grown in combination with late fall and winter truck crops.

Livestock can start grazing crimson when it is about six inches high. Rotation grazing—allowing them to graze one clover field for a week or so, then shifting to another—will keep both pastures thick and prevent overgrazing.

It should be planted one month to six weeks before the average date of the first frost. Lightly harrow and disc the land and allow it to settle a few weeks before seeding. The best method is to plant during or after a light rain on a firm seedbed and cover the seeds lightly. Use 20 pounds per acre when broadcasting the seed, 15 if drilling (½ inch deep).

CLOVER DODDER: *see* CONVOLVULUS

COAL ASHES: Although coal ashes will lighten heavy soils, there is serious danger of adding toxic quantities of sulphur and iron from this material. Some ashes do not contain these chemicals in toxic quantities, but the coals from various sources are so different that no general recommendations can be made. The safest procedure is to regard all coal ashes as injurious to the soil.

An analysis of 32 samples of soft coal ashes showed from 4 to 40 per cent iron oxide and from 0.3 to 10 per cent sulphur trioxide. When water is added to sulphur trioxide, sulphuric acid is formed in such amounts as to destroy all vegetation. Hard coal ashes have lesser amounts of iron and sulphur, but it is best to play safe and not use them to lighten heavy soils. It is much better to lighten the soil by adding compost or plain sand.

COBALT: One of the trace mineral elements occurring in both soils and plants, cobalt has been the center of considerable research and dispute over the past several years. Originally, it was contended that cobalt had no function in the nutrition of plants, animals or man. Research has since shown, however, that it makes up four per cent of the dried weight of crystalline vitamin B_{12}, an important part of the essential B-complex.

Evidence has been established that a common wasting disease of sheep and cattle (which has a number of names in various areas throughout the world) is the result of cobalt deficiency in these animals, and can be treated successfully by overcoming this shortage in their feed. In addition, treatment of humans suffering pernicious anemia with the cobalt-containing vitamin B_{12} has brought similar success.

While agricultural science is as yet uncertain of the precise role cobalt plays in plant nutrition, it is apparent that this is a vital one—as it is with others of the trace element group—and that this in turn is significant in both animal and human health. The organic method's principle of incorporating natural, thoroughly balanced materials into the soil to maintain fertility assures the crops grown on that

soil, and the animals and people fed by these, an ample share of all the trace elements, including cobalt. *See also* Trace Elements; Compost; Rock Fertilizers.

COBRA ORCHID: *See* Darlingtonia

COCCINELLIDAE: *see* Ladybug

COCKLEBUR: (*Xanthum chinense*) The rough, hooked burs of this coarse annual weed often get tangled in clothing and the wool of sheep, can injure the hides of farm animals. First seed leaves are reported poisonous to some · animals. Cocklebur frequently grows on lowlands, lake beaches and waste lands. It should be mowed to prevent seed formation.

COCKSCOMB: (*Celosia*) A member of the *Amaranth* family and a tender annual. Chinese Woolflower is another common name given it. In form and color it closely resembles the comb of a rooster, but is considerably larger. Other forms are plumed or feathery, some spiked or pyramid-shaped.

Cockscombs are easily grown and make exceptional plants for the garden border. Sow seed indoors eight to ten weeks before spring frost-free date. Transplant to a light, rich soil. Keep leaves and soil reasonably moist. Syringe plants if red spiders appear. Seed can also be sown outside a short time before last spring frost, flowers forming where there is a long season.

C. cristata, the variety known as cockscomb, grows one to two feet high. *See also* Celosia.

COCOA BEAN SHELLS: Coarse cocoa shells are excellent as a mulch and soil builder when applied to garden and flower beds. The fine shells are used for lawns, and can be applied with a spreader.

Cocoa shell dust analyzes rather high in nitrogen for a product of this woody kind, namely one per cent. The phosphorus content is about 1.5 per cent, the potash content approximately 1.7 per cent. Usually theobromine and caffeine are first extracted from the shells, and the residues analyze 2.7 nitrogen, .7 phosphoric acid, and 2.6 potash. The raw, untreated shells are slightly higher, but must of course be finely ground to be useful as fertilizer material. Cocoa pressed cake has also been sold for fertilizing purposes, but the analyses vary according to treatment. As a rule, this cake is rather high in nitrogen, but lower than the shells in potash, while the phosphorus content is close to .9 per cent.

The chocolate factories have begun to market cocoa shell wastes which have been freed of the oil and the theobromin. In the extraction process, lime is used. The finished product is without odor, weed seeds and acids, and therefore useful for mulching soils in acid regions, because the lime content will balance the acidity of the soils while the organic matter of the residue acts as a fine water-storage medium.

When the shells are spread on the ground about one inch in depth, they furnish fine protection against drought. At the same time, rain will remove a great deal of the soluble plant food contained in the shells. During the winter months, they afford excellent protection against the damages caused by alternate freezing and thawing of seed beds and roots.

Cocoa bean shells can also be applied on lawns and when used in landscaping, they provide a very colorful, light even-brown color around shrubberies and evergreens as well as flower beds. *See also* HULLS; MULCH.

COCONUT: (*Cocos nucifera*) A tropical palm tree growing over 80 feet high, the coconut grows best in areas where the annual temperature is above 70°, and is therefore limited to southern Florida in this country. Produced only by seed, the shallow planted nuts usually germinate in about six months and can be transplanted when six to ten inches high.

It requires some 20 years before coconut trees reach full bearing, and annual yields are from 20 to as many as 100 nuts. Fertilizing with organic materials has been found of great importance, and cover crops that will add nitrogen to the soil are also recommended.

COCOS WEDDELLIANA: *see* PALMS

CODLING MOTH: The larva is ¾ inch long; pinkish white and brown heads. Larvae winter in cocoons in the crotches and under the bark of trees. Moths emerge to lay their eggs in warm dry weather about a week after petals have fallen. For control, traps using sassafras oil have been found effective; a solid bait for codling moth may be made by filling a small ice cream cup two-thirds full of sawdust, stirring into the sawdust a teaspoonful of sassafras oil and another of glacial acetic acid. Then add enough liquid glue to saturate completely the sawdust mixture. When the cup is dry, after a day or two, suspend it in a mason jar partly filled with water. A dormant oil spray is also effective in protecting trees. In addition to the use of a dormant oil spray, an application of tanglefoot around the upper part of the tree trunk to trap the larvae may help. Scraping the bark on the trunk up to ten feet during the winter will be very helpful in reducing codling-moth infestation.

Feeding the trees, if it hasn't been done for some years, will help to correct many of their ills.

Apply the fertilizer in February. To determine the amount of complete plant food required by the tree, measure the diameter of the tree about four feet from the ground. To each inch of diameter allow three pounds of complete plant food. With a crowbar or ground auger make a series of holes 18 inches deep and about two inches wide under the drip line of the branches. Fill the holes half full of the plant food and complete filling with soil.

Cleaning up all drop fruit from under the trees at least once a week is good practice. Mulch with compost if available or straw, keeping the materials at least 18 inches from the trunk of trees. *See also* INSECT CONTROL.

COFFEE WASTES: The average gardener has usually access only to coffee grounds. As a seed, the coffee bean has some nitrogen. Coffee grounds have up to two per cent nitrogen in them, a third of one per cent phosphoric acid, and varying amounts of potash. Drip coffee grounds are richer than grounds that have been boiled, but the potash content is still below one per cent. Coffee grounds sour easily because they preserve moisture well and seem to encourage acetic-acid-forming bacteria. If mixed with lime and applied to the compost heap or fed to earthworm cultures they are by no means negligible additions to the fertilizer resources of the average family. Being acid, they are good for blueberries, evergreens, and all acid-loving plants. When using on plants that like lime, mix some ground limestone with the grounds before using as a mulch. They seem to have a remarkable effect on stimulating the growth and health of certain plants. Chemical analyses show that the grounds contain all sorts of minerals including trace elements, carbohydrates, sugars, and even some vitamins. They also have some caffeine present.

A waste product from coffee manufacturing, coffee chaff seems to be an excellent material for use in home gardens as well as farms. Over two per cent in both nitrogen and potash, chaff also appears very suitable for use as a mulch material, where its dark color is an asset.

COLCHICUM: (*Autumnale*) Commonly called autumn crocus or meadow saffron, it is a bulbous plant native to the temperate parts of Europe and northern Africa, where it is found in moist pastures and meadows. The corm (usually called bulb) and the seed contain colchicine, a poisonous alkaloid, used in medicine. In the last ten years, colchicine has also been used in increasing quantities by breeders in developing new varieties and types of plants. Colchicum is grown as an ornamental in this country. The corm and seed used as a source of colchicine have been obtained mainly from abroad.

Colchicum is best adapted to rather moist, rich, light sandy loam. It will grow in partial shade but can be successfully cultivated in sunny situations. The seed is sown just after it ripens in June or July. The seedlings will not emerge until the following spring and they do not bloom for several years. The plant is also propagated from the corms, which are planted two or three inches deep late in summer or early in fall. In cold regions some protection in winter is necessary. The new corms are formed from the old ones in much the same way as in tulip bulbs.

The plant blooms in fall, sending short flower stalks directly out of the ground, hence the name autumn crocus. The seed capsule develops underground in the corm and emerges with the leaves in spring. The corms develop their maximum growth during July. *The corms and seed must be handled with much caution, because of their very poisonous nature.*

Recommended as a rock garden plant, there is a wild pink variety of *autumnale* that is becoming quite popular.

COLD FRAME: If you have even a fairly large vegetable garden and flower beds, you should learn to grow most of your own plants. You will save money, raise superior plants, get plants that are directly acclimatized to your locality, and you can produce a far greater variety of plants.

A great advantage in growing your

own plants in hotbeds and cold frames is that you can send off for seeds from any part of the world, and thus raise and experiment with varieties and with new plants unobtainable from local seedmen. Nurseries usually limit themselves to a few good selling varieties of plants. If you want to experiment with some new hybrids, or with new varieties developed abroad or elsewhere in the U.S., you should by all means learn to grow your own plants.

What is the difference between a hotbed and a cold frame? If you want to grow peppers, tomatoes, egg plants, or any of the other heat-loving plants, a hotbed is best to grow them in. A cold frame has the same construction as a hotbed, except that there is no heat used inside it. In a cold frame you can propagate such cold-loving plants as cabbage, the broccoli family, cauliflower. Or you can use your cold frames to taper off and harden plants that have been moved into them from the hot beds, to get them hardened between the hotbed and setting out into open garden or field.

There are two types of hotbeds. One is heated by a great deal of fermenting straw or fresh manures (preferably horse or chicken) which has been placed in a pit two and one-half feet deep. The manure is packed down to a depth of 18 inches, well watered to soak. Then you shovel into the pit five to six inches of composted soil or good rich top soil. This soil—which will make the seedbed—must be sieved fine.

Hotbed type 2: This kind of growing bed is made by arranging electric heating cables, five inches below the surface of the topsoil seedbed. No manure is needed for heating this type bed. The coils produce a steady heat day and night, while the manure is effective for a few weeks.

The electrically-heated hotbed is much more expensive than the old-fashioned manure-heated hotbed. For the small to average gardener the manure-heated hotbed is best.

Both types of hotbeds and cold frames are made the same way as concerns construction of frame and top. A heavy frame of two-inch thick planking a foot wide should be made to cover the bed, and to act as base for the hinged or removable lid or top. You can use the inexpensive glass-like Sun Ray cloth. It won't break, lasts a long time. For permanent frame tops you may use glass windows.

Planting the seeds: In the germinating hotbeds or cold frames you plant seeds plentifully, cover them lightly, and keep the rows one inch apart. You may later thin out to suit. In planting lots of seeds remember this: while most seeds will produce sturdy plantlets, others will be thin or weaklings. With plentiful planting you may pluck out all but the finest, sturdiest plants.

A *must* to remember: The grower must constantly watch moisture and heat with an eagle eye. You must not allow the heat to rise too high, or above 75-80 degrees while the plants are small. If the growing beds get too hot—and there is no ventilation—the hundreds of plants may easily damp off and die. To ventilate you simply raise the lids a bit. Leave lids closed at night.

How and *where* to build your hotbeds and cold frames:

Use two inch thick rough lumber for all frames. Have these planks from 12 to 14 inches wide, ten inches above the surface of the ground. Always locate the beds in the warmest spot possible, your best southwestern exposure. No matter how cold or windy the day is—if the sun is shining —the beds will gather a wonderful warmth through their transparent lids.

Be sure to make one long side of the beds two inches lower than the other so water will run off. Hinge the lids on the high side. It's best to lay out the beds with their lower, longitudinal sides facing south. Just sink

Cold frames and hotbeds are identical in construction but no heat is used or added to the interior of the cold frame. Make heavy frames of two-inch-thick planking to act as a base for the hinged top.

the southern edge of the heavy board frame two inches or so into the soil. Drive stakes around outside the frame and nail to frame walls for solidity.

Water the beds daily after planting. Use a fine can sprinkler and *tepid* water. Don't muddy the seed bed; just water it enough to be nicely damp. Once the plants have sprouted and are several weeks old—and there is the delightful feeling of their crowding one another—lift the lids more and more. As the growing season progresses, and the bedding plants grow faster, there will be nice days when you should take the lids off and get the full benefit of the sun.

First transplanting: When your plants have grown to a size large enough to be handled, they are ready to transplant over into the cold frame beds. There they will grow rapidly and harden off so that the shock of final planting into the open garden won't hurt them.

Wet down the bed well before transplanting. Next take out the little plants in clumps; place them in a tray or flat. Transplant these into flats or cold frames with enough space for growing larger. Allow these plants to grow several weeks at this second planting, or until all danger of frost in open garden or fields is past. Plant the seedlings one inch apart.

Final setting out of seedlings into garden or field: When you are ready to transplant the seedlings to their final places in the garden, again wet down beds or flats well. When you dig up the plants be careful to preserve the root systems with earth well packed, undisturbed around them.

When you have your rows or beds ready in the garden, set out the new plants from the hotbeds or cold frames. Firm them in well in fertilized rows. Then give them a good soaking, and they are on their way.

About the only thing that can harm growing plants in the hotbeds or cold frames is overheating, drying out for lack of water, or being attacked by the fungus disease known as *damping off*. This damping off or "black root" or "wire stem" in the seedbed is caused by about a half dozen or more fungus parasites. They usually grow near the surface, and enter the tiny plants at the point where they emerge from the ground. All of these fungus parasites require a high moisture content of soil and air for quick growth.

To prevent trouble from *damping off* the best defense is to keep the air and surface of the seedbed as dry as is consistent with good growth of the plants. Getting the beds heated without proper ventilation, and not allowing the moisture to escape, is what causes damping off.

PROPER SOIL FOR PLANTS: Make a mixture of two parts good garden loam, one part fine, but sharp sand, and one part leaf mold or old, decayed compost. Mix well and put eight inches of it into the bed. You might loosen the bottom soil first to insure good drainage.

There is enough plant food in this mixture without adding manure or organic fertilizers high in nitrogen. Used too soon, these often cause the young plants to grow too rapidly, unbalancing their natural growth.

After the soil has been evenly distributed throughout the two sections of the bed, pour several pails of boiling water over it. This will sterilize the soil and prevent the damping off disease common in cold frames. Allow the ground to cool, then cover with window sashes. When the sun reheats the soil to 70°, it is ready for planting.

WHEN TO PLANT: Two separate compartments are helpful in the cold frame. All vegetables do not require the same temperature for germination. Where some will sprout in the heat, others will rot. To get the maximum number of plants from the seed, the plants must be divided into two groups. Celery, cabbage, lettuce, cauliflower, and broccoli require low temperatures for germination. Plant these together in one section of the cold frame, dropping the seeds evenly in rows two inches apart. Plant about the first week in April or eight weeks before transplanting time. An inch of fine mulch may be spread evenly over the seeded area to keep the ground moist and to discourage early weeds. The growing plants will push their way through as they grow. Water lightly, then close the frame.

About the middle of April, when the sun is warmer, plant tomatoes, peppers, eggplants, muskmelons, summer squash, and cucumbers. Plant these in the other half of the bed. The plants in the first half of the bed should have sprouted by now and need ventilation. Close the cover on the tomato bed until the plants sprout, then ventilate along with the other half.

Cucumbers, muskmelons, and summer squash are grown in parts of milk cartons, and set out in the open after danger of frost. This is not absolutely necessary. It merely helps produce an earlier yield.

VENTILATION: No matter what the germination temperatures had been, all growing plants do best around 70°. Regulate temperature each day by slightly lifting the two sashes. On cold days, allow the beds to remain closed. Never lift covers into the wind. A cold wind can damage the tender shoots. Open away from the draft, and secure the windows so they will not be broken.

WATERING: A sprinkling can is best for watering a cold frame. The bed will require more water on hot days than cloudy ones. One gallon sprinkling can to a six-foot section is fine. But water only when needed, and with water at a temperature of about 70°.

For an added boost to growth, you might open the bed to a warm, quiet rain.

HARDENING OFF: Your garden yield depends entirely upon how carefully you execute this step. Do it slowly. Remember, the plants are delicate. Start about one and one-half weeks before transplanting time. Cut down on the water supply, and begin to expose the plants to the direct sunlight and wind. Remove the covering entirely for a half-hour the first day. Increase the exposure each day. Take care not to under-water as this condition may cause the plant stems to turn woody. After the seventh day, the plants should be hardened enough to withstand a full day of sun. You may now remove the windows, and allow the plants to remain uncovered until transplanting time. Water well every night.

TRANSPLANTING: An hour before you take up the plants, water the beds well. When taking out plants, never yank. The tiny feeder roots are delicate, little hairs. If the plant is yanked out, these roots are torn off and the plant suffers. A ball of earth should be taken with every plant to insure an unharmed root system.

Transplant on cloudy days, or during a light drizzle. This will help to prevent shock. Should a plant refuse to take, replace with one from the bed.

Once you have grown your own plants and found what satisfaction it brings, you will never be without a cold frame again. Build it of simple, second-hand materials, plant the seeds according to directions and germination temperatures, ventilate, water wisely, harden off with caution, and always transplant with a ball of earth clinging to each root system. After plants have caught, mulch heavily.

USING THE COLD FRAME FOR WINTER VEGETABLES: A cold frame is really a protected seedbed and can be used in the first frosty days of autumn just as advantageously as in early spring. Tender lettuce and crisp endive can be enjoyed until after Thanksgiving by properly utilizing the cold frame.

Plant seeds in early autumn. For lettuce, endive and parsley, plant seeds in one compartment in rows three inches apart and about one-quarter inch deep, covering the seed with vermiculite to prevent damping off.

Then water the rows with a fine spray, and adjust the sash and place a covering of light boards over it. As soon as the seeds sprout, remove this cover and raise the sash several inches to allow good circulation of air.

Seedlings will grow rapidly, and when they begin to crowd each other, they are ready to transplant. Set the little plants in another compartment, about three inches apart each way. Mulch again with vermiculite and keep them shaded for a few days. As plants grow, they can be thinned and the thinnings used in salads. The remaining plants will then begin to form heads.

When nights grow frosty, close the frame tightly before sundown to hold the day's heat within, opening it again each morning. If nights are very cold, cover the frame with a blanket and bank leaves around the sides. If the day remains cold, remove the blanket to allow light to enter, but keep the frame closed.

You'll be amazed at how much cold the plants could stand under glass. As the season grows late, plants may be frozen occasionally, but by sprinkling with cold water and keeping in the dark for a while, they will revive and come back in good condition. It is possible to have fresh salads until winter.

You can also use the cold frame in winter for storing vegetables. Before the ground freezes, remove about 18 inches of soil and place in vegetables like turnips, rutabagas, beets, carrots and celery on a layer of straw. Over the vegetables cover another layer of straw with sash boards. Vegetables should keep crisp and unfrozen all winter. *See also* HOTBED.

COLEUS: Coleus is an old plant, but it is still high on the list of popularity as a bedding or decorative plant. Coleus can be used in window boxes, borders along walks, foundation plantings, and one of the cleverest uses is to plant coleus as a filler between small, newly planted shrubbery. Advantage is then taken of its fast growth and easy culture.

Another big advantage of the coleus is that you can grow it all year. If you have sunny windows, you can grow several colorful pots full of coleus, and not only add beauty to your home during the summer months, but you will have plants ready to set out in the spring.

CULTURE: Usual way of propagation is by cuttings. These cuttings are taken about September before frost. Coleus is very tender and will be hit by the first frost.

When making a cutting, cut at the node or the slightly enlarged portion of the stem where leaves and buds arise. Root formation is more rapid at these points. Clean sand is the best rooting medium. Place the cuttings firmly in the sand and keep quite moist. Keep the cuttings out of direct sunlight for the first few days to prevent wilting. In approximately three weeks, root formation should be well underway. You may then begin to pot the cuttings in individual pots. Make a mixture of one-quarter sand, one-quarter compost and one-half garden soil.

Coleus require plenty of sun to keep their brilliant color, so the more sun the better. Keep soil slightly moist; be sure not to overwater. Coleus must be pinched back to make well-formed bushy plants. The night temperature shouldn't go below 60°F.

When transplanting coleus in the spring, be sure all danger of frost is passed. They require little care in the summer other than an occasional pinching back and an ample water supply.

VARIETIES: For hanging baskets and window boxes the pink and yellow Trailing Queen and Verschaffeltii are the best when you want yellow and red effects for bedding. Good varieties for both bedding and pot culture are: Butterfly, Beckwith's Gem, Firebrand, Pink Verschaffeltii,

and Defiance. These are only a few of the many varieties available.

COLLARD: (*Brassica oleracea acephala*) As a vegetable, it is of major importance in the South, where, by its hardy constitution, it can stand summer heat and winter cold. It is easily cultivated, and is highly esteemed for its flavor. The collard is a member of the cabbage family. It has been described as a non-heading cabbage, resembling the tall kales in growth. Since it will stand more heat than cabbage, it is substituted for that crop in warm regions of the country. In the North where heading cabbage is successfully grown, collards have not become popular.

CULTURE: In general, the culture of collard and that of cabbage is similar. In the South, sowing is usually done in both the spring and the fall. In the North, collard may be planted in the summer for late greens. Some believe it to be improved by the first frosts. Plants may be started early in the spring and set out later in the same way as cabbage, or they may be sown in the garden row and later thinned to sand about two feet apart, with three feet between the rows. Seedlings may be thinned to stand six inches apart if the crop is to be used while plants are still small.

A good fertile soil will produce a more desirable growth. High quality relies on quick growth, and generous applications of rotted manure or compost are important. The soil should be worked into good tilth before planting.

Collards require full sun, and although they can withstand more drought than the cabbage, ample moisture should be supplied. No weeds should be allowed to establish themselves, so cultivation is necessary. Shallow cultivation is best to prevent cutting roots close to the surface. The hoe should be put into action about once a week until the plants are half grown, after which the shade of the plants will help to keep down the weeds.

HARVESTING: Whole young plants may be cut or the tender leaves at the top stripped off. A cluster of leaves may be picked a few at a time as required and before they mature so as not to be tough. As the plants are gradually stripped of their lower leaves, they may need the assistance of a stake to support the top cluster.

VARIETIES: The standard variety is Georgia or Southern collard which endures adverse conditions, including poor soil. It grows 30 or more inches in height and bears a loose cluster of large cabbage-like leaves. Louisiana Sweet has compact centers and short-stemmed leaves. Cabbage collard is more resistant to warm weather and forms small cabbage-like heads.

Collards are rich in vitamins, particularly B and C, and in minerals, so they will add a measure of health to your diet.—*Barbara Hardy.*

See also CABBAGE.

COLLOID: The soil colloids are of great importance to the soil. "Colloid" is derived from the Greek word for glue, and refers to the very finely divided, jelly-like residue plant material in the soil. Colloidal clay is made up of those particles less than .0002 mm. in diameter. Some clays are much more active than others. Organic colloidal matter, or humus, has the same properties as does colloidal clay, and is much more effective, pound for pound, than any mineral colloid.

The properties of soil colloids include water-holding capacity, formation of good granulation through their swelling and shrinking upon wetting and drying, and their peculiar ability to "adsorb" or hold on their surface, in a form available to plant roots, most of the mineral nutrients of the soil.

It is this adsorptive power of the colloidal fraction of a soil that furnished the key to its natural productivity. Laboratory tests measure the amounts of the significant nutrient elements adsorbed by a given soil, their sum being expressed as the "total exchange capacity" of the soil.

These nutrient elements are present on the colloids as "ions," or electrically charged elemental units of matter. While precisely speaking there may be many different elements present, for all practical purpose only four are in significant amounts. Three of these—namely calcium, potassium and magnesium—are classed as bases, being alkaline in their effect. All are essential to plant growth. The fourth—hydrogen—is acid-forming and being in fact, a by-product of plant root activity, is therefore of negative nutritional significance.

When the colloidal complex of a soil has its entire capacity occupied with hydrogen ions, it is said to be "unsaturated." When the other ions satisfy a part of the total exchange capacity, the degree of saturation is expressed as the percentage of the total capacity occupied by such ions. This is called the "total base saturation" of the soil being tested.

To protect the colloid against an excess of hydrogen ions, it is necessary to provide a supply of basic ions to replace the acid-forming ones. Calcium, or in some cases calcium and magnesium, are the elements best suited to do this. These two are found in satisfactory proportions, for most cases, in limestone, which is about 13 per cent magnesium and 22 per cent calcium. *See also* SOIL.

COLLOIDAL PROPERTY OF HUMUS: *see* HUMUS

COLLOIDAL ROCK PHOSPHATE: Like raw rock phosphate, colloidal phosphate is an excellent natural source of phosphoric acid. Colloidal phosphate is found in a very fine or colloidal state, contains somewhat less phosphoric acid. The main source of this product is Florida, where it is found in natural sedimentary deposits of soft phosphate with colloidal clay.

Either raw rock phosphate or colloidal phosphate is a natural soil nutrient. Superphosphate is not. *See also* ROCK PHOSPHATE.

COLORADO FIR: *see* FIR

COLOR IN THE GARDEN: *see* LANDSCAPING; FLOWER GARDENING

COLOR OF HUMUS: *see* HUMUS

COLUMBINE: (*Aquilegia*) Attractive perennials of the buttercup family, their showy flowers have made them popular in rock garden and border plantings. Plants do best in open, sandy loam; can be increased by division of the clumps in spring. The common columbine (*A. canadensis*) grows one to two feet high, has yellow flowers and grows well in shady spots. *A. longissima* is recommended for the southwestern United States, where its golden flowers on plants two to three feet high make it a fine perennial choice. A fine rock garden plant of this family is *A. alpina* which grows no more than one foot, has blue flowers.

COMFREY: (*Symphytum*) Sometimes called Quaker comfrey, Russian comfrey, or prickly comfrey, the *asperum* variety is a farm crop of relatively recent importance.

A perennial fodder crop, comfrey does best on clays, loams and sandy loams, with a *p*H no lower than six. It has a deep, powerful root system that helps it tap the subsoil for water and nutrients, and making good growth possible on very poor soils. Spring and fall are equally good for planting.

Ten to 15 tons per acre of manure are recommended, with lime as needed. Comfrey is propagated by root-stocks, in rows three feet apart and plants three feet apart in the row. This makes 4,840 plants to the acre. Row-crop cultivation is necessary only rarely after the first two cuttings, as comfrey's fast, heavy growth chokes out most weeds.

Comfrey should be cut a minimum of five times a season, six times the first. The initial cut on a new plot is usually made when the plants are one to two feet high. All cuts should be at about two inches above the ground.

COMMERCIAL CLOCHE GARDENING: *by J. L. H. Chase. See* BOOKS FOR ORGANIC GARDENERS AND FARMERS

COMMODITY CREDIT CORPORATION: *see* GOVERNMENT SERVICES

COMMON SMARTWEED: *see* BUCKWHEAT

COMPACTION, SOIL: Referring to the hardening of soil into a hard mass after continuous passage of heavy

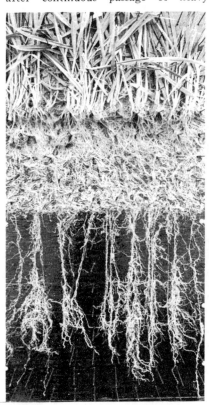

A hard subsoil makes for root scantiness past the ten-inch mark. The use of heavy equipment is held responsible for this unhealthy state.

weights over it. Plants growing on soil compacted by heavy machinery travel or by general bad cultural practices cannot develop healthy roots. Loosening the lower soil levels with a subsoiler and the working in of green manure crops helps plants to send roots much deeper in soil.

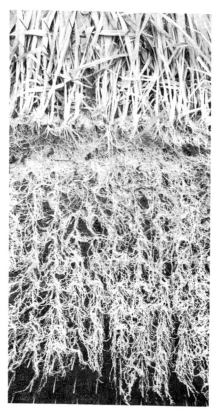

With loosened subsoil, the 11-week-old oats in this comparison plot sent its roots down to the two-foot mark in sound and vigorous profusion.

Here are four rules for healthy root growth:

1. Tractors and implements should travel on plowed land as little as possible to minimize compaction of the soil just below the surface.
2. Lighter weight tractors should be used for cultivating where possible.
3. The incorporation of consider-

able amounts of organic matter should also help prevent the development of compaction zones.

4. Annual cover crops should be planted whenever possible to provide green manure and to provide a cushion which will resist the compactive effect of implements.

COMPANION CROPS: Wherever plants grow without cultivation there is a colorful mixture of plants, which, in accordance with the soil type and local climatic conditions, are able to live together and mutually complement each other. Such a mixed culture of plants in nature is called a "natural plant association." The plants in an association are such that they utilize to the fullest extent such environmental factors as light, moisture, and soil. Plants that require less light live in the shade of those which must have full light. Also the roots of some plants live close to the surface, while those of others penetrate to greater depths.

The plants in an association do not all grow and fruit at the same time in the growing season. Some plants hurry into growth and flowering early in the season before those, which might cut off their source of light, produce leaves at all. The different kinds of plants in an association produce an endless succession of green leaves, flowers, and fruits from early spring to killing autumnal frosts.

In planting our vegetable garden, we may well imitate so far as possible nature's mixed plantings, using such plants as are mutually compatible and make demands on the environment at different times. Horticultural plants may be divided into *heavy feeders, light feeders,* and *soil conserving* and *soil improving* crops. The heavy feeders should preferably be planted in the soil that has been newly fertilized. Among the heavy feeding vegetables are cabbage, cauliflower, all leaf vegetables as chard, head lettuce, endive, spinach, and celery, celeriac, leeks, cucumbers, squash and sweet corn.

Other heavy feeders which, however, are perennials and are not included in a crop rotation include rhubarb, raspberries, blackberries, and strawberries. Tomatoes also are heavy feeders.

The heavy feeding vegetables should be followed by such light feeders as pole and bush beans, and other legumes. The roots of legumes tend to reach down into the deeper soil layers and absorb essential elements which are brought to the surface where they again become available to the roots of other plants. Also, as is well known, the roots of legumes are inhabited by nitrogen-fixing bacteria which can take large amounts of nitrogen out of the air and make it available to the roots of other plants. The fact is that light feeding vegetables are really compost lovers. Also they can, better than other kinds of plants, utilize the finely pulverized raw rocks and make phosphorus, potassium, and many trace elements available to other plants.

Other light feeders are such root crops as carrots, beets, radishes, turnips, and rutabagas. Other compost lovers are the herbs which help conserve the soil and enliven the vegetable garden.

Some plants, which have a beneficial effect upon the garden by virtue of the peculiar character of their growth, their scent, and their root formation and soil demands, have a beneficial effect upon the garden. Among these plants are sunflower, hemp, blossoming hyssop, thyme, savory, borage and other good bee-pasture plants. Odoriferous plants, including those with aromatic oils, play an important part in determining just which insects visit the garden. Hemp, for instance, is said to repel the cabbage butterfly.

COMPANION PLANTING: It is not a matter of indifference in what associations plants are grown. Good plant neighbors are those whose roots occupy

different levels in the soil or find in each other's company the light requirements which best suit them. Pole beans planted with sunflowers grow most unsatisfactorily as a result of root and light interference. Sunflowers and potatoes are equally incompatible and we run the risk of getting stunted vines and small potatoes. Other incompatible combinations are tomatoes and fennel, tomatoes and kohlrabi, pole beans and beets, pole beans and kohlrabi, and red and black raspberries.

Compatible combinations of vegetables are cabbage and beans, beets and onions, celeriac and leeks, cucumbers and sweet corn, leeks and beans, carrots and peas, cucumbers and beans, kohlrabi and beets, onions and beets, early potatoes and corn, early potatoes and beans, early potatoes and horse radish, tomatoes and parsley, bush beans and celery, and cucumbers and bush beans.

Compatible plants are those which supplement each other in the soil as well as above the ground. The compatibility of celery and leek, for instance consists in the upright nature of the leek thus finding room near the bushy celery plant, and both are potash-lovers. Lettuce and kohlrabi, for instance, are compatible for intercropping, as the lettuce will be harvested by the time the larger kohlrabi plants need all the space in the row. Mixed cultures, as in intercropping, provide a more complete ground cover, thus preventing the ground from crusting and drying out, and holds the weeds in check.

Here are some of the important likes and dislikes of plants mentioned in the book *Bio-dynamic Farming and Gardening* by Dr. Ehrenfried Pfeiffer:

Asparagus—The asparagus beetle is repelled by tomatoes growing close to the asparagus plants.

Cabbage—To repel the cabbage maggot, plant mint, hemp, tomatoes, rosemary or sage in the next row.

Carrots—Peas are good for them when growing nearby.

Celery—Plant bush beans in next row.

Cucumber—Plant beans or corn next to them. Also peas and bush beans.

Herbs—Aromatic herbs as border plants are helpful.

Kohlrabi—Beets are a good companion.

Leeks—Do well with celery next to them.

Onions—Do well with beans. In poor soil, camomile sown thinly between will help.

Potatoes—Corn is a natural and beneficial neighbor. Early potatoes like beans to grow nearby.

Radish—Will do extra well and become tender if there is a row of lettuce growing on each side of them.

Tomatoes—Plant parsley in next bed.

Turnips—Peas are excellent neighbors.

NEGATIVE EFFECTS

Fennel—Do not plant them near tomatoes or bush beans.

Tomatoes—Do not plant next to kohlrabi.—*Dr. William Eyster.*

COMPOST: In the soft, warm bosom of a decaying compost heap, a transformation from life to death and back again is taking place. Life is leaving the living plants of yesterday, but in their death these leaves and stalks pass on their vitality to the coming generations of future seasons. Here in a dank and mouldy pile the wheel of life is turning.

Compost is more than a fertilizer or a healing agent for the soil's wounds. It is a symbol of continuing life. Nature herself made compost before man first walked the earth and before the first dinosaur reared its head above a primeval swamp. Leaves falling to the forest floor and slowly mouldering are composting. The dead grass of the meadow seared by winter's frost is being composted by the damp-

ness of the earth beneath. The birds, the insects and the animals contribute their bodies to this vast and continuing soil rebuilding program of nature.

The compost heap in your garden is an intensified version of this process of death and rebuilding which is going on almost everywhere in nature. In the course of running a garden there is always an accumulation of organic wastes of different sorts—leaves, grass clippings, weeds, twigs—and since time immemorial gardeners have been accumulating this material in piles, eventually to spread it back on the soil as rich, dark humus.

Because the compost heap is symbolic of nature's best effort to build soil and because compost is the most efficient and practical fertilizer, it has become the heart of the organic method. The compost heap is to the organic gardener what the typewriter is to the writer, what the shovel is to the laborer and what the truck is to the truckdriver. It is the basic tool to do the job that is to be done. In the case of the organic gardener the job is the creation of the finest garden soil he knows how to create, and compost has proven itself through thousands of years of use to be the best tool for the job.

In many parts of the world today, composting is practiced just as it was hundreds or even thousands of years ago. Farmers and householders in backward countries of Asia, Africa and even Europe often have no source of commercial fertilizer, and consequently make rough compost piles of cattle manure, garbage, human wastes, straw and weeds. These piles decay into humus, which is then used as a soil conditioner for the kitchen garden and farm fields. Such compost is not very rich in plant nutrients, but it is a manageable form of humus which maintains the tilth and general condition of soil that has been used for many years.

More often than not, though, farmers in primitive countries have

Bacteria in compost heaps multiply rapidly producing temperatures up to 160°. The tractor-powered loader stirs the heap to give the bacteria plenty of air. Airless composting is also practiced now.

been and still are wasteful of material that could be used for composting. Where trees are scarce, cow dung is dried and used for fuel. Human wastes that might be saved safely in a properly made compost heap are scattered dangerously in streams and village alleys. Agricultural scientists who have observed this waste of compostable material have formulated simple methods of making heaps that can be used by people in backward countries. These methods have been designed to make fullest use of the microbiological activity that goes on in compost heaps. Sir Albert Howard, an agricultural scientist who worked about 40 years ago in the Indian state of Indore, was one of the first men to create a sophisticated method of composting, and out of his efforts has flowered the entire organic idea.

Within the last twenty years, a great amount of progress has been made in adapting composting methods to solve various waste disposal and agricultural problems. In 1949, the Sanitary Engineering Department of the University of California started a compost research project that culminated in the first detailed scientific analysis of the phenomena of composting. The California project concentrated mainly on compost made in heaps. Several years later, a project in digester composting was started at Michigan State University, under the leadership of Prof. John R. Snell. A vertical silo digester on the Earp-Thomas pattern was constructed at East Lansing.

An important result of the California project was the outlining of a method that home gardeners could use to make compost in as short a time as 14 days. The method will be described in detail later in this section.

The composting of garbage is a problem that has intrigued many entrepreneurs. Dr. G. H. Earp-Thomas is the originator of a silo digester that is the basis of a plant at Paris, France. The DANO firm of Denmark builds a "bio-stabilizer" that is possibly the most successful commercial composting method. A plant on the DANO system was set up at Sacramento, California, in 1957. The path of commercial composting in the U.S., however, has been marked by a number of failures and disappointments. Probably, the two major reasons for this slow progress are:

1. Unsatisfactory equipment. Very large grinders and digesters are necessary to compost garbage economically. Engineering of such equipment is extremely costly.

2. The mixed character of American garbage. Many cities collect trash and garbage together. Consequently, most "garbage" consists of up to half paper, cans, bottles and other scrap materials. Pure food wastes would be much easier to compost.

The best review of the whole subject of commercial composting is the book *Composting, Sanitary Disposal and Reclamation of Organic Wastes* by Harold B. Gotaas. It is published by the World Health Organization, United Nations, New York.

THE PURPOSE OF COMPOSTING: Composting in heaps is an extension of a process that is going on almost everywhere in nature. When a lawn is mowed and the clippings are left on the ground, they compost. The straw that is left on fields by the combine decays into humus. Leaves that fall turn the forest floor into a compost area. The fertility of all the soils of the earth has been achieved and maintained principally by the decay of vegetable matter.

Gardening and farming disrupt the natural pattern of the return of plant matter to the earth. Compost is the link between modern agriculture and nature's own method of building soil fertility.

In addition to returning rotting vegetable material to the soil, there are two major reasons for making compost:

1. To render certain materials such as manure and garbage pleasant to handle.

2. To increase the nitrogen content of low-nitrogen materials such as sawdust, straw and corn cobs.

The high heat of composting rapidly "cooks" the smell out of manure and garbage. This is a significant gain because gardeners are often reluctant to use those materials fresh.

The composting process also increases the nitrogen content of the pile. Microorganisms "burn off" much of the carbon, reducing the cubic bulk of the heap but correspondingly increasing its nitrogen portion.

Organic matter is valuable to the soil only while it is decaying. Even "finished" compost is actually only partly decayed. It continues to break down in the soil, providing food for increasing populations of microorganisms. When building tilth on a farm, it is frequently practical to spread fresh manure which will do more for the soil than the same amount of composted manure, because a greater part of its decay will take place in the soil—where it will do the most good.

Even though it may not be necessary to compost some materials, most organic gardeners prefer to compost almost all the organic matter they get. The compost heap is a convenient place to store leaves, weeds and grass clippings until they are needed. Pound for pound, compost is the finest soil conditioner to be had.

BACTERIAL ACTION IN COMPOST: The microbiological processes that occur during composting are a form of rotting or decay, but without the unpleasant smell that often accompanies such decomposition. A well-made compost heap creates an environment in which decay-causing bacteria can live and reproduce at the highest rate of activity. As a result of this activity of microorganisms, fresh manure, garbage, leaves, weeds and other compost materials are converted into dark humus.

There are two types of bacterial activity taking place in compost heaps: anaerobic breakdown (without air) and aerobic breakdown (with air). Some bacteria that cause decay function in a lack of air or oxygen. Others need plenty of air. Aerobic composting is more common and practical than anaerobic because it is faster.

During aerobic composting, the microorganisms convert the carbon in the heap materials into energy, creating heat. The temperature in an active heap can rise to 160°. Nitrogen, phosphorus and potassium are required in the nutrition of the microorganisms. Phosphorus and potassium are usually plentiful in all compost material, but there is quite often a lack of nitrogen. The relationship between the amount of nitrogen in compost material and the amount of carbon is called the carbon/nitrogen ratio, often stated as the C/N ratio. Raw garbage, for example, has 25 times as much carbon as it has nitrogen. Its carbon/nitrogen ratio is therefore expressed as simply the number 25. Sawdust has a C/N ratio of 511. Farmyard manure, which is much higher in nitrogen, has a C/N ratio of 14. The higher the number, the more carbon is present. It is generally stated that a carbon/nitrogen ratio of 30 is required for compost activity to take place at an optimum rate. By determining the C/N ratio of all materials placed in the heap a good balance of carbon to nitrogen can be obtained. Such care is required for commercial composting operations, but for home or farm composting, only rough estimates of the C/N ratio need be made.

A heap that does not have sufficient nitrogen will compost very slowly. It may not heat up at all. A pile of ordinary sawdust will take several years to break down into dark humus. But if an organic nitrogen supplement is added in the form of dried blood, tank-

age or poultry manure, the composting of the sawdust will be much more rapid. A lack of nitrogen (represented as a high C/N ratio) is probably the chief cause of composting failures—heaps that fail to heat and decay quickly.

Actually, there are many factors other than the C/N ratio which influence composting. Here is a list of some of the other factors:

a) moisture

b) air temperature

c) pH (Acidity-Alkalinity)

d) absorbency of the material

e) mineral content of the material

It is readily seen that since all those factors are variable, no two compost heaps will be exactly alike unless they are made in the same place at the same time of the same materials. The chief effect of this variability is to vary the type of microorganisms that multiply in the pile and effect its breakdown. If the heap is made of acid materials, types of microorganisms that can live under acid conditions will multiply. This variability in compost heaps is one factor that makes it highly unlikely that a bacterial activator preparation would be useful. A bacterial activator or "starter" is supposed to introduce into the heap particular strains of microorganisms that are efficient composters. Controlled experiments with activators conducted at the Sanitary Engineering Project of the University of California and at Michigan State University have shown that activators did not influence composting results. (*See the entry under* ACTIVATORS.)

Moisture can have an important influence on microorganisms. A heap that is soggy can smother air-loving organisms—the type that work the fastest. The ideal heap is moist, but not waterlogged. Some composters cover their heaps with a plastic sheet to help keep the moisture content constant. This can be a useful technique in very dry areas, also in times of heavy rainfall.

Because air-loving microorganisms are the most efficient composters, compost heaps are turned primarily to assure a continual supply of air. Even so, parts of a heap can become sealed from the air in a short time after being turned, and anaerobic decomposition sets in. Shredding or grinding of material being put in compost heaps creates a fluffier mass and enables aerobic decomposition to take place for longer periods. Aerobic microorganisms convert the carbon in the heap into carbon dioxide, which is passed off into the air.

Anaerobic (air-less) decomposition is generally carried on in tanks, bins or silos. The chief advantages of this type of composting are that no turning of the mass is required and that the compost can produce methane gas for heating and lighting purposes.

TYPES OF COMPOST: Compost can be made in a number of different ways. The method used is determined by the following circumstances:

1. Amount of material available.
2. Type of material available.
3. Machinery that is available.
4. Time limit for completion of composting.
5. Climate.
6. Cost or availability of labor.

On large farms, it is usually most practical to use the sheet composting system, whereby compost material is not piled in heaps at all but just spread on the fields in "sheets." Where compost must be made quickly, the 14 day system is used. (See subsequently.) Some cities use the digester system to make compost out of garbage. A review of the most common composting methods follows:

SIR ALBERT HOWARD'S INDORE METHOD: Compost can be made by the Indore method either in open piles or in bins. Piles are more satisfactory when machinery is going to be used to turn the heaps. Bins are sometimes used by gardeners who dislike the unkempt appearance of an open pile. Bins also have the advantage of affording better control of moisture and temperature.

The average Indore pile is made six feet wide, three to five feet high and ten to thirty feet long. First, a six inch layer of plant wastes is spread over the area to be covered by the pile. Materials for this layer can include spoiled hay, straw, sawdust, leaves, garbage, wood chips, etc. Then a two inch layer of manure and bedding is added. This is followed by a layer of topsoil approximately one-eighth inch thick. Sir Albert recommended urine-impregnated topsoil as being particularly valuable. On top of this layer of earth, a sprinkling of lime, phosphate rock, granite dust or wood ashes can be spread. These materials increase the mineral content of the heap. Of course, lime is not added if an acid compost is wanted.

This "sandwich" is then watered and the process of layering is continued in the same manner until the desired height of the heap is reached. Care is taken not to trample on the heap. If the heap is matted down, aeration will be impeded. Vertical ventilator pipes are placed along the center of the heap approximately 3½ feet apart. The pipes are made of tubes of wire netting.

Within a few days, the heap begins to heat up and starts shrinking in size. The heap is turned with a pitchfork two or three weeks after being made, and again about five weeks after being made. Care is taken during turning to place the outer parts of the heap on the inside, so they can decay fully. The heap heats up to almost 150° at the outset. After the first turn the temperature will again rise, but it will then settle to a steady temperature of about 130°. The compost is finished after three months.

A tremendous advantage, especially in backward countries, of the Indore method is the fact that only hand tools are needed. The purpose of making the heaps in layers is to make sure that ingredients are used in the correct proportion—and that they are mixed evenly throughout the heap.

THE 14-DAY METHOD: When the Sanitary Engineering Department of the University of California set out in 1949 to design a good method for composting municipal refuse, they found a maze of conflicting claims in the semi-technical literature, but very few proven facts. The 18 scientists on their staff set out to clear the air with a broad and basic scientific study of the mechanism of composting. Out of their work evolved the "14-day method." This technique is suitable for garden, farm and municipal use.

The keystone of the 14-day method is the grinding or shredding of all material going into the compost pile. Grinding has these effects on compost:

1. The surface area of material on which microorganisms can multiply is greatly increased.
2. Aeration of the mass is improved, because shredded material has less tendency to mat or pack down.
3. Moisture control is improved.
4. Turning of the heap is much easier.

No layering of material is used in the 14-day method. Material is mixed either before or after shredding, then piled in heaps no more than five feet in height. After only three days, the heap is turned. Turning is continued at two- or three-day intervals. After 12 to 14 days, the heat of the pile has dropped, and the compost is sufficiently decayed to use on the soil.

If compost is being made for garden use, turning can be done by hand. Turning a shredded heap is not laborious, because the material is light and fluffy. For larger applications, turning is usually done by a manure loader, or a machine specially designed for turning large compost piles. Several such machines are manufactured.

Shredding the material prior to composting presents more of a mechanical problem than turning, especially for large composting projects. A number of good machines are available for garden use, however. Horticultural shredders made primarily for potting soil preparation can be used as compost material grinders. Small rotary lawn mowers also shred compost material efficiently and easily. Weeds, leaves, straw or stable manure to be cut up are piled on the ground and the lawn mower is run over them. It is helpful to do this near a wall which can prevent the cuttings from spreading out too much. Eventually, large grinders may be designed that will shred municipal garbage at high speed.

Compost made by the 14-day method is often superior to compost that has been allowed to stand out in the weather for many months. Less nutrients are leached out when compost is made quickly.

SHEET COMPOSTING: In farm practice, it is often unnecessary to make compost in heaps. Raw organic materials can be spread on fields during fallow periods. The initial stages of decay will then take place before the next crop is planted.

An excellent method of "sheet composting" is to grow a green manure crop on the fields to be treated. Soy beans, clover, cow peas, and many other forage plants make good green manure crops. When the green manure plants are still immature (and rich in nitrogen) the compost materials are spread over the fields with a manure spreader. Low nitrogen materials like sawdust, corn cobs and wood chips can be spread over a young green manure crop without fear of causing later nitrogen shortages. After spreading, the whole mass is worked into the soil, preferably with a farm-size rotary tiller. A rotary tiller is superior to a plow or a disk for this purpose because it works the organic material evenly into the top few inches of the soil, enabling plenty of air to reach the decaying material. Very often, the field is first run over with a rotary cutter to shred any long grass that might wind up on the tiller tines.

Sheet composting is not satisfactory for most garden purposes, because a gardener is seldom willing to take a section of land out of production for several months. Bacteria which break down the cellulose in sheet compost consume nitrogen which ordinarily would be contributed toward plant growth. In a few months this nitrogen is returned for plant use through the bodies of the microorganisms, but for the initial period of sheet composting a nitrogen shortage does exist. In a very rich soil this temporary nitrogen shortage is often not noticed. Also, if low-nitrogen materials are just spread on the surface as a mulch they will break down very slowly and no nitrogen shortage will result.

It is a good idea to add limestone, phosphate rock, granite dust or other natural mineral fertilizers along with the other sheet compost ingredients, because the decay of the organic matter will facilitate the release of the nutrients locked up in those relatively insoluble fertilizers.

DIGESTER COMPOSTING: Compost digesters can be divided into two classes: 1. Small machines intended for garden and farm use. 2. Large machines for composting of municipal garbage.

The Bard-Matic Garbage Eliminator is a small anaerobic cabinet, into which the usual household vegetable wastes and meat scraps are placed each day. It consists of a steel tank about four feet high which is buried partly in the ground. The hatch on the top of the tank has a rubber gasket which keeps out all air.

Organic Gardening and Farming magazine tested the Bard-Matic unit and found that it would accept three or four pounds of garbage daily for a period of about six months without filling up. The accumulated garbage does turn into humus, which can be removed periodically and used on the garden.

Various wooden compost digesters for garden use have also been manufactured. Most are approximately three feet square and about six feet high. They are raised a few feet off the ground by stout legs. Wooden digesters are primarily aerobic in action, and are ventilated on the sides. They are intended to receive daily amounts of garbage. Frequently earthworms are introduced to help break down the garbage.

Farm-sized anaerobic manure digesters which produce methane gas for household use have been in use in India, France, Germany, Algeria, England and the U. S. since about 1945. These installations consist of one or more air-tight pits with a capacity of four to five cubic yards, and a tank for collecting gas with a capacity of two or more cubic yards. The slow reduction of the carbon in manure and litter produces sufficient gas to make practical an investment of about $1,500 in such a unit. They are most economical in areas which do not have gas or electric service, and which have a mild climate. Prolonged freezing weather requires extra attention to prevent freezing of the digester and its contents.

The gas tank is similar in construction to the large gas tanks used to hold gas for city use. It rises and falls as the supply of gas increases or decreases. Gas digesters are becoming especially popular in areas in which manure is used for fuel, as they enable both fuel and humus to be obtained from the manure. After several months, the manure in the digester tank is expended and it can be removed and used on the soil. Pathogenic organisms have been killed by the prolonged anaerobic digestion, making it practical to use human wastes if desired.

Gasoline engines, gas furnaces and stoves can be run on methane gas.

Large garbage digesters for municipal use are primarily of the aerobic type, although Verdier and Beccari anaerobic digesters have been used for garbage composting in Europe. The anaerobic digesters are large concrete tanks which are filled and emptied at intervals.

The goal of designers of aerobic digesters is to make a machine that will convert garbage into compost in a period of hours instead of days. Compost has been made in pilot plants in as short a time as 48 hours. Basically, there are two reasons for the use of digesters instead of open heaps in the design of municipal compost plants:

1. Digesters enclose the raw wastes, cutting down odors and reducing fly and rodent problems. They also enable decomposition to take place under any weather conditions, an important consideration in northern areas.

2. Digesters can make compost more quickly than any method using heaps. A fast composting process requires less space for storage of garbage and compost, a very important point when the high cost of real estate near cities is considered.

The basic function of digesters is to create those ideal conditions which make for fast growth of aerobic micro-organisms. For ideal composting an ample supply of warm, moist air must be able to penetrate all parts of the compost mass at all times. Digesters either provide compressors to blow warm, moist air into the compost, or they accomplish the same means through continuous agitation or mixing.

The Earp-Thomas digester is about the size and shape of a large silo. Inside, the silo is divided into a series of stages or "floors" several feet apart. A large shaft runs down the center of the silo, and to this shaft are attached mixing arms which continuously agitate the material on the various floors. Raw garbage or compost material is introduced into the digester at the top by means of a conveyor. As it decomposes it passes down from one stage to

another. Finished compost is removed from the bottom of the machine. Garbage must be ground before being fed into the digester.

The DANO process is apparently the most successful of the digester systems. Its main feature is a long, rotating drum, called a "Bio-Stabilizer," set at an angle of five degrees from the horizontal. Garbage is fed into the upper end of the drum. Two rows of air jets on the inside of the drum provide aeration. The garbage moves so slowly through the drum that it can be retained for three to five days. No grinding of the raw material is required, as the abrasive action of the sides of the drum reduces the particle size of the garbage. There is a DANO plant at Sacramento, California, but all the other DANO installations are in other countries. *See also* ACTIVATORS; DEFICIENCIES, SOIL; SOIL.

COMPOST BINS AND BOXES: Gardeners who are not satisfied with composts in heap fashion have come up with a great variety of bins, boxes, pits, and other containers. These structures make composting easier and can improve the appearance of the compost. They also protect the compost from washing rains and baking sun. The type of container you select for your home grounds depends on your personal taste, the amount of labor you wish to expend, and the materials

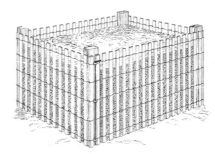

The picket-fence compost box is inexpensive and easily constructed. Snow-fencing may be used if it is securely attached to rigid, strong stakes.

you have on hand. Here are a few of the more popular types which have evolved throughout the years:

Block or brick bin is easily constructed with concrete blocks or bricks, laid without mortar. Blocks are laid to permit plenty of aeration spaces. This bin is sturdy, long-lasting, easily accessible with its open end, can be built to match a brick house.

The picket fence bin can be made by fastening prefab picket fence in a square. Four posts are sunk into the ground at corners.

Another compost or leaf mold maker consists of several fence posts in the form of a circle, surrounded by chicken wire fencing.

A rough stone or log enclosure also makes a nice, informal appearance.

COMPOST, MATERIALS FOR: Here are brief descriptions of some materials that can be used in making compost. (For complete descriptions, *see* specific listings.)

LEAVES: Leaves are valuable fertilizer material, since they are rich in minerals. For fast composting, never use leaves as the exclusive green material. They should be mixed with weeds, lawn clippings, plant residues, etc., so as not to pack and impede aeration.

HAY: Hay such as alfalfa or clover will during its first year's growth, break down fast in the compost heap. However, it's worth while using all hay available—young or old; shredding with a mower or shredder to hasten decomposition.

SAWDUST AND WOOD WASTES: Sawdust has excellent properties for building soil, and can be added to the compost heap. Sawdust probably can be obtained free at the local lumber mill.

GARDEN RESIDUES: Tomato and squash vines, corn stalks, flower stems —all plant remains make a rich harvest for the compost heap.

WEEDS: Weeds are a very valuable addition to the compost heap because they belong to different plant families and therefore extract different elements from the soil.

GRASS CLIPPINGS: Cut grass is usually sufficiently wilted by the time it is added to the compost heap so that it will soon start heating. Grass cut before blooming is richer in nutrients.

SEWAGE SLUDGE: As a rule, sludge is classified as a source of nitrogen and will act as a bacteria stimulator in the compost heap, even though the nitrogen content may not be above one or two per cent.

GARBAGE: In using garbage, it is best used as a part of the green matter of the compost heap. Its relatively high nitrogen content produces quicker decay.

BREWERY WASTES: Spent hops are the residue after hops have been extracted with water in the brewery. In their wet state, they have about 75 per cent water, 0.6 per cent nitrogen, 0.2 per cent phosphoric acid.

LEATHER DUST: Leather dust makes an excellent fertilizer material, high in nitrogen. The nitrogen content varies from 5.5 to 12 per cent, and it also contains considerable amounts of phosphorus. Available from leather tanneries.

NUT SHELLS: The composition of nut shells varies according to the nuts. Almond shells and pecans decay readily, black walnut shells which contain greater amounts of lignin, take longer; filberts and English walnuts decompose without trouble; while Brazil nuts and coconuts could be used only in ground-up form, in the same manner in which cocoa shell meal is utilized.

PEANUT HULLS: Peanut hulls are rich in nitrogen.

	Nitro-gen	Phos-phoric Acid	Potash
Peanut shells ..	3.6	.70	.45
Peanut shell ashes	.8	.15	.50

TOBACCO STEMS: The nutrients contained in 100 pounds of tobacco stems are 2.5 to 3.7 pounds of nitrogen, almost a pound of phosphoric acid and from 4.5 to 7.0 pounds of potassium.

COFFEE WASTES: Coffee chaff appears an excellent material for use in home gardens as well as farms. Over two per cent in both nitrogen and potash, chaff also appears very suitable for use as a mulch material. Coffee grounds can also be added to compost heap.

DRIED BLOOD: Dried blood collected in the slaughter houses, afterwards dried and ground. The nitrogen content of dried blood is 12 per cent or over, while the phosphorus content ranges from one to five per cent. It can be used on the ground but in sound gardening practice is composted.

COMPOST, WHEN AND HOW TO APPLY: The principal factor in determining when to apply compost is its condition. If half finished, or noticeably fibrous, it can be applied in October or November. By spring it will have completed its decomposition in the soil itself and be ready to supply growth nutrients to the earliest plantings made. For general soil enrichment, the ideal time of application is a month or so before planting. The closer to planting time it is applied, the more it should be ground up or worked over thoroughly with a hoe to shred it fine. A number of garden cultivating tools and machines are excellent time-and-labor-savers. Several will help spread it evenly and mix it thoroughly with the soil.

If compost is ready in the fall but not intended for use until spring, it should be kept covered and stored in a protected place. If it is kept for a long period during the summer, the finished compost should be watered from time to time.

HOW TO APPLY: For general application, the soil should be stirred or turned thoroughly. Then the compost is added to the top four inches of soil.

For flower and vegetable gardening, it is best to pan the compost through a half inch sieve. Coarse material remaining may then be put into another compost heap.

SIDE DRESSING: Where compost is to aid a growing crop, it is absolutely necessary to avoid injuring plant roots growing near the surface. To avoid disturbing roots of established plants, compost should be mixed with topsoil and applied together as a mulch. This is the best means of adding what is often termed side dressing. It serves a double purpose: providing plant food which will gradually work itself down to the growing crop, and it also affords an effective mulch for the soil, giving protection from extremes of temperature, hard rains, and growth of weeds.

HOW MUCH TO APPLY: For best results, compost should be applied liberally, from one to three inches per year. There is no danger of burning due to overuse, such as is always the case with artificial chemical fertilizers. Apply compost either once or twice a year. The amount will depend, of course, on the original soil fertility and on what and how much has been grown. The average weight for one cubic yard of compost (27 cubic feet) is 1,000 pounds.

FOR ORCHARDING AND TREES: Compost should be applied under each tree, starting about two to three feet away from the trunk, and extending about a foot beyond the drip-line at the end of the branches. An annual application should be between $\frac{1}{2}$ and one inch thick. The grass mat under the tree should be first worked into the soil and the compost added, keeping it in the upper two inches. It is a good practice then to apply a mulch of old hay or other green matter. A layer of compost about three or four inches thick would be sufficient for three or four years.

Where there are poisons in the soil from many years of spraying, a three or four-inch layer of compost worked into the soil will tend to counteract somewhat their harmful effects.

THE RING METHOD: To save time, the compost can be made right under the tree. Thus it acts as a mulch also. The reason it is called the *ring method* is that starting from about three feet away from the trunk, the material looks like a ring. Apply the raw materials under the tree as if for making compost, but make the heap two feet high instead of five. To hasten the formation of compost, a large quantity of earthworms can be placed in the material.

FOR FLOWERS: Flowers, like other growing plants, respond to the organic method and to applications of compost. Compost may be safely applied even to acid-loving flowers such as the rhododendron. If a gardener has a considerable number of acid soil plantings, which include several of the berries as well as many flowers, it would be advisable that he prepare an acid compost. This is done by making the compost without lime or wood ashes, just as it is for those soils that are quite alkaline.

For potted flowers, compost should not be used alone, but should be mixed with soil. Try screening and applying friction to it before using in a flower pot. Then mix about one-third compost and two-thirds rich soil. *See also* FERTILIZERS.

COMPOST SHREDDER: *see* SHREDDER

COMPOST WATER: Often, some of the valuable nutrients in compost are dissolved in water quite readily, and in solution these nutrients can be quickly distributed to needy plant roots.

Since plants drink their food rather than eat it, the use of compost water makes quite a bit of sense, particularly during dry periods when plants are starved both for food and water.

Many problem plants and trees can be nursed back to health by treating them with compost water. You can use it on bare spots on your lawn, on

trees that have just been transplanted and on indoor plants. You can even use it on vegetables in the spring to try to make them mature earlier. Compost water is also good in greenhouses, where finest soil conditions are needed for best results.

It is really no trouble to make compost water on a small scale. For treating house plants or small outdoor areas, all you have to do is fill a sprinkling can half with finished compost and half with water, stir gently ten or 12 times, and pour. The compost can be used several times, as one watering will not wash out all its soluble nutrients. The remaining compost is actually almost as good as new, and should be dug into the soil or used as mulch. It takes the action of soil bacteria and plant roots to extract the major value from compost.

COMPOSTING, VERTICAL: *see* MULCH

COMPOSTING WITH EARTHWORMS: For the small gardener, this method of compost making is recommended. While earthworms breed, they work with the raw materials of their boxes and turn it into a rich fine compost in only 60 days. This does not have the disadvantages of compost made outdoors which has the objection of resting on an earth bottom and which is open to the air.

Use wooden cases about two or three feet square and a little more than two feet high. In the boxes, put a mixture of raw materials. A typical mixture would be about 70 per cent weeds, leaves, grass clippings, etc., about 15 per cent manure and 15 per cent top-soil. This can be greatly varied. If no manure is available parts of your table wastes can be substituted. You can try almost any formula.

First, however, it is advisable to start with the purchased earthworms as they thrive best under domestic conditions. Secondly, before placing them in the boxes, mix all the ingredients thoroughly. This will prevent the high heating which takes place in the regular compost heaps. (Don't let the heaps get too hot, or else the earthworms will either leave or perish.)

The earthworm compost is also rich in the castings or manure of the earthworm which is superior to animal manures.

The material in the boxes should be piled to a height of two feet and kept sufficiently watered, but do not put too much water in, or it will create an anaerobic condition. It is the combined action of the earthworms, bacteria, fungi, etc., which produces the best kind of compost.

The process takes about 60 days. Then you take out half a box of material and fill it up with the raw materials again and in 60 days the new stuff will be completely composted. It is advisable to feed the earthworms with something equivalent to chicken mash, but you can make your own feed, using ground leaves, ground grain seeds such as wheat, barley, corn, etc. *See also* EARTHWORMS.

CONEFLOWER: (*Rudbeckia*) These attractive native American members of the daisy family, also called Blackeyed Susans, will grow on fertile soils in full sun. The plants can stand about two feet apart. They make useful border plants, can be increased by division or seeds. Orange coneflower (*R. fulgida*) is a perennial that grows two feet high; Blackeyed Susan (*R. hirta*) is an annual, sometimes biennial, that grows one to three feet, has golden flowers with purplish-brown disks. The hedgehog coneflower (*Echinacea purpurea*), sometimes called Black Sampson, is a hardy perennial, useful in open borders; blooms in summer; grows two to three feet high. *See also* LEPACHYS.

CONIFERS: Evergreen family of cone-bearing trees and shrubs, including pines, spruces, and firs.

CONSERVATION: The word *conservation* means many things to many people. Generally, it includes the process of preserving forest, wildlife and soil. Of these, the organic method is most intent on preserving the virgin soil of the nation. Each day, the soil of America is being depleted in various forms. The once virgin soil is being reduced in organic matter, the life of the soil. The nutritive elements of the soil are transformed into feeds for livestock or food for human consumption. Some of the manure is returned to the soil, but too little to stem the disastrous trend.

The second way in which precious topsoil is lost is by erosion. Each day, untold tons of topsoil are being washed down streams and rivers, just because farmers and public officials lack the foresight to take precautionary measures against erosion. In Wisconsin, for example, it has been estimated that 25 to 50 per cent of the original topsoil on nearly all the rolling fields of that state has *washed away*. In 100 years of farming, Wisconsin has lost over one-fourth of the topsoil formed by nature in thousands of years.

There are four kinds of erosion—sheet, gully, wind, and streambank. Wind erosion takes place when high winds sweep over dry, bare soil; it is most common on the larger areas of level sand. The wind generally carries away the finer soil particles and organic matter, leaving behind coarse sand particles to pile up into choking drifts. On the farm, wind erosion can hit a field of very young plants. Shelterbelts of pine trees, special techniques of stripcropping can cut down soil losses from wind.

Streambank erosion is the carrying away of topsoil by streams and rivers. When fields are baked dry and hard, hard rains will not be absorbed by the soil, but will run off into streams, thus creating floods which carry off soil by streambank erosion. Thus one type of erosion fosters another in a vicious spiral to infertility.

Sheet erosion is the result of improper farming methods, taking place on sloping fields that have not been plowed properly. It is a most serious kind of erosion, because it attacks precious farm land, and often the erosion pattern is set before the farmer realizes what is happening.

Gully erosion is so obvious, anyone can recognize it. Gullies develop in warped and wrinkled places in fields where water concentrates as it flows into streams. As water collects in these natural drainageways, it develops great cutting power, forming large gullies. Many farms have been greatly reduced in value because gullies have destroyed parts of fields.

WHAT TO DO ABOUT EROSION. Steep lands should be covered at all times, by trees and cover crops. Croplands should always be covered when not in use. A wise rotation program will further reduce erosion losses, as will proper contour cultivation.

Strip cropping protects soil against sheet erosion. Fields are divided into strips or belts about 100 feet wide. These are laid across the slope on the contour to keep them level across the entire length. The same rotation is followed on all the strips in the field, but the order of rotation is staggered so that each corn or grain strip is protected on either side with a thick-growing cover crop.

Meadow belts save soil. When soil runs off cropland, it can be caught and held by belts of alfalfa or clover. Gullies that start in the corn strips end at the "meadow" belt, which again saves soil. And a field that is strip-cropped holds rainfall better than one which is cropped up-and-down.

A series of earth terraces will hold excess rainfall. Water flows slowly in the terrace channels and is discharged into a safe grass-covered outlet. Because of the slow rate of flow, much of the rain is absorbed by the soil.

In the draws or "wrinkles" of a field, permanent grass waterways should be maintained. Grass belts placed in danger areas such as these will prevent the formation of gullies. Each farmer should contact his county agent and work out a sound conservation program to follow. Not only will it increase profits for the farmer, but will help to save the soil of the nation for future generations. *See also* WILDLIFE; ROTATION; STRIP CROPPING; TERRACING; MULCHING; COVER CROP; COMPOST; EROSION; WINDBREAKS.

CONSERVATION SERVICE: *see* GOVERNMENT SERVICES

CONTAINER STOCK: A term for nursery plants that have been grown in tin cans or other impervious containers.

CONTOUR: A sound soil conservation practice, farming on the contour refers to the plowing, planting, cultivating and harvesting of sloping fields on the level. Thus instead of making straight up-and-down-hill furrows on hillsides, the object is to have curving furrows to fit the slope of the land, thereby saving both soil and water. The curved furrows hold rainfall and reduce the amount of soil that is washed away.

Another conservation practice, terracing, means ridging land on the contour. Ridges or embankments of soil are built to retain rainfall on sloping fields.

If the garden slopes, this is recommended practice. The curving furrows save water and soil, preventing erosion. Terracing is also recommended.

CONTROLLING INSECTS: *see* INSECT CONTROL

CONVOLVULUS: In gardens and fields, field bindweed or morning glory (*C. arvensis*) with long creeping brittle roots spread over plants wherever they can. This and the Hedge Bindweed (*C. sepium*) can be real pests in fields. Much cultivation, particularly with the duck-foot-type of weeder and spring tooth harrow will help as well as thick growing crops like soy beans, vetch, field peas, *i.e.*, crops which, by means of their roots, maintain humus and produce a crumbly soil. In persistent cases temporary pasture may solve the problem, instead of tillage.

In the garden, dig out wild morning glory as much as possible, keeping the soil surface cultivated. Try to prevent new shoots from growing more than two inches high.

To the Convolvulus Family belong some surprisingly beautiful garden flowers, the Sweet Potato (*Ipomoea batata*) and the Rosewood, a native shrub of the Canary Islands, used for perfume and fine cabinet work.

The Wild Sweet Potato Vine (*I. pandurata*) has a large edible root, deep under the ground and grows as far north as Eastern Canada, contrary to the Southern Sweet Potato.

COOKING FOR NUTRITION: *see* NUTRITION; CANNING; FREEZING.

COPPER: A trace element, copper has recently been recognized as one of the many minor elements essential to plant growth. The peat and muck soils of some states have been reported deficient in copper, as have the acid sands of Florida. Copper is present in most plants up to 100 parts per million—in certain soils up to 50 ppm. Mushrooms have a high copper concentration. Readily absorbed by soil colloids, copper content in soils varies from five to over 100 pounds per acre. Some researchers believe copper is important in the synthesis of chlorophyll. Copper-

deficient tomatoes appear bluish-green; dieback occurs in copper-deficient citrus trees. Such fertilizers as copper sulfate and other copper salts are not recommended because of the danger of toxic effects on plant growth. Agricultural frit, supplying copper as well as other trace elements to the soil, is the safest way to make up for any minor element deficiency in soils. *See also* TRACE ELEMENTS; DEFICIENCIES, SOIL; FRIT.

CORAL-BELLS: (*Heuchera sanguinea*) A tall, but diffuse, perennial, popular mostly in rock gardens and wild gardens. Propagated by division, coral-bells are not particular about soil, but prefer a humusy, rich one. They like sun, but do well with at least some shade. Annual application of compost is recommended. Grows from one to two feet high, blooms throughout summer. *See also* PERENNIALS.

COREOPSIS: Deep golden flowers, long wiry stems, and very hardy and abundant. Excellent for cutting and a good border plant, sometimes requiring staking. Keep withered flowers picked off, to extend the period of bloom and water in dry weather. Not particular as to soil, coreopsis blooms in summer. Golden-wave (*C. drummondi*) is a tender annual, grows one to two feet high. The sea dahlia (*C. maritima*) is considered a perennial, reaching a height of three feet. Golden coreopsis (*C. tinctoria*) is the most popular of the annuals, growing from two to three feet; it does best when crowded, blooms from July to fall. Also known as Calliopsis.

CORIANDER: (*C. sativum*) An annual herb, has long been cultivated in many parts of the world. The dried fruits, known commercially as seed, are used for flavoring candies, sauces, soup, beverages, and tobacco products. The oil distilled from the seed also has a variety of uses as a flavor.

The plant is indigenous to southern Europe, Asia Minor, and the southern

Coriander thrives best in sunny locations on a rich garden loam of limestone origin, well-drained. Plant seed when all danger of frost is past.

part of the Union of Soviet Socialist Republics and has been planted in most parts of the world where the climate is suitable. Although small acreages have been grown in various States from time to time, there has been no sustained commercial production.

Coriander will grow in a wide range of conditions but thrives best in sunny locations on rich garden loam of limestone origin with good drainage. Excessive nitrogen may delay the ripening of the seed and reduce the yield unless the growing season is long. Well-distributed moisture and fairly even temperatures throughout a growing season of 90 to 100 days are favorable for the crop. Rain or wind during the harvest period will discolor the seed and cause loss through shattering. The seed is planted as soon as the soil is warm enough for germination but after danger of frost has passed. It is planted at the rate of (ten to 15 pounds per acre, about one inch deep in rows 15 to 30 inches apart. Frequent and light cultivation to keep the weeds under control is recommended, but some hand weeding is usually

necessary. Broadcasting the seed is not practical, because coriander does not compete successfully with weeds. Plantings made early in May will usually bloom in about nine to ten weeks and mature seed early in August. When grown in the Southwest as a winter crop the seed is sown in November and the crop matures in May.

See also HERBS.

CORK: Natural cork occasionally is used as a mulch. Because of the tannic acid in cork, it is of value where increased acidity is required in the soil. Cork has been used as a mulch for azaleas, laurel, and other acid-loving plants.

CORK ELM: *see* ELM

CORK TREE: *see* PHELLODENDRON

CORM: A corm looks very much like a true bulb, as it is a solid, underground stem. It has no scales, but nourishes the plant and bears roots at the base. It ultimately produces young cormels, which are a source of propagating material, as they in time become corms. The gladiolus is a good example of a plant growing from a corm. *See also* BULBS.

CORN: Corn is usually divided into five or more types: (1) dent corn (*indentata*), (2) flint corn (*indurata*), (3) pop corn (*everta*), (4) soft corn, and (5) sweet corn (*rugosa*). A sixth type known as pod corn is sometimes grown as a curiosity. The dent and flint types are the ones grown for general farm use. There are a number of varieties of each type. In the great corn growing regions of the United States almost the entire crop is dent corn. Flint corn requires fewer days to ripen than dent and is therefore grown at a higher latitude and altitude. Nearly all New England field corn is flint.

Sweet corn is the only type raised for table use, and is one of the few native American vegetables. Sweet corn can be grown in all 48 states, and generally is. All that is required is a growing season of 70 to 80 days and plenty of summer heat. Any average garden soil will suffice, but for best results, dig in well-rotted compost about two weeks before planting.

A sunny, well-drained corn-patch means little or no trouble with insect pests. Mulching of corn is recommended practice; ends between-row hoeing.

Many seaside gardeners take a tip from the Indians and put a dead fish in each hill.

Early varieties are usually planted in shallow trenches, or drills, as are most garden vegetables, while late varieties (which grow taller) are planted in hills.

ORGANIC CULTURE: The organic raising of corn under a heavy layer of mulch has the advantage of ending between-row cultivation in the hottest time of the year. Early objections that corn needs direct sunshine and will not thrive in mulch have not been borne out by results.

Commercial corn growers in various parts of the country have been experimenting growing corn under black polyethylene strips—reportedly with success. The strips are laid the length of the row and the corn is planted by a tractor drill attachment which punches holes in the plastic and plants seeds at set intervals. The strips reportedly serve two or three seasons

before being replaced. Time, labor and money saved by ending between-row cultivation more than justify the extra expense of the plastic while results have reportedly been highly satisfactory.

Mulching and composting corn will appeal to the organic gardener on the basis of obtaining produce of superior nutritional value. There is the added benefit of eliminating unnecessary between-row cultivation. Finally, building up the soil structure by the gradual addition of slowly decomposing organic matter as the mulch breaks down is essential organic practice.

Because corn takes relatively large amounts of nitrogen out of the soil, it is advisable to fertilize heavily. Using weathered animal manures plus a concentrated nitrogen source such as cottonseed or soya meal while planting is gaining acceptance. There is no possibility of burning the tender shoots because the organic fertilizers are slow-acting.

The organic fertilizer goes directly into the planting site. A mixture of one part aged animal manures plus one part cottonseed or soya meal is recommended. If the ground is somewhat heavy a third part of ground rock powder may be added.

Mulching with straw or hay between the rows immediately after planting will keep the weeds down from the start. Mulching between the young stalks of corn along the row should be done when they are six to eight inches high.

Side-dressing corn during the growing season is practiced on many organic homesteads. The two-part mixture of weathered animal manure plus the cottonseed or soya meal is again recommended.

Results appear to justify the mulching and composting technique. The corn is remarkably insect-resistant, ears are full while the kernels are tender and flavorful.

The mulch should be left on the ground at the end of the season. If necessary, it should be reinforced with an extra supply of straw, hay or other vegetable matter to act as a ground cover during the winter. If plowing or rotary tillage is practiced, a winter cover crop of vetch or clover should be sown. In this case, the partly decomposed mulch can be turned under and the cover crop sown.

Sweet corn can be planted one row each week starting with the last week in April and continuing until mid-July. The rows will come into bearing just as the older rows are harvested, ensuring an evenly spaced yield.

If the garden is sunny and well drained, there will be little trouble with fungi and insect pests. These troubles usually indicate a wrong location, a damp unsunny, undrained location.

But if the crows are numerous it is advisable to plant seed corn a little deeper than recommended for the type used.

Do not leave any excess seed corn around and firm kernels planted so that they will not float to the surface during the first rain.

At harvest time it is advisable to pick all ears just as soon as they reach the milk stage. When the tassels turn brown, watch the ears. If you do not gather them promptly the crows, if they are numerous, will make a meal of them. *See also* DEFICIENCIES, SOIL; FERTILIZER; HOMESTEAD (*Farm Crops*).

CORNCOB: Like almost all plant residues, corncobs can find a welcome place in the garden scheme. Ground into a spongy material, corncobs have been found to be an excellent mulch. First tried on greenhouse roses, with near phenomenal results, a corncob mulch is now considered to be one of the best, because of its moisture-holding properties. As a mulch, corncobs should be applied to a depth of three or four inches. Corncobs may sometimes use up much soil nitrogen when decomposing, so a nitrogenous organic fertilizer should be applied before the mulch is laid. The best organic materials for supplying nitrogen are dried blood (15 per cent), cottonseed meal (seven per cent), tankage (six per cent), bonemeal (four per cent), compost or manure.

COMPOSTING COBS: Corn cobs are an excellent material for making compost, but they should be first cut up with an ensilage cutter, shredder, or grinder that will break it down, otherwise it will take years for the material to compost.

The cobs mixed with leaves prevent the latter from caking and impeding aeration. Corn cobs can be left to weather in the open for a few months. They will then break down much finer in the shredder.

Corn cobs are a valuable ingredient for the compost heap and should be carefully preserved, rather than burned up as many farmers do. Tests show that the cob, in nutrient value is equivalent to two-thirds that of the corn kernel. This is amazing when one considers how sinfully the cobs are gotten rid of.

If gardeners or farmers will contact the mills in their community that shell corn they will find that they can get mountains of cobs merely for the hauling. *See also* MULCH.

CORN COCKLE: (*Lychnis githago*) The Purple Cockle or Corn Cockle is a troublesome weed in the grainfield, particularly in winter grain. It is an annual and is propagated by seed. It mixes with the grain in harvesting and threshing. Due to its poisoning effect, it spoils the grain for feeding and flour. The seeds are black, somewhat similar to the caraway seed and are particularly poisonous to sheep, pigs, rabbits, geese, ducks and poultry. The chaff from threshing should be checked for its presence before being fed to animals. The rather large flowers have five reddish-purplish petals, slightly mottled on the edge with dark spots inside. If grainfields become infested with the Purple Cockle, hand pulling may be necessary. Do not grow grain crops on such fields for several years but plant crops requiring much cultivation, such as—corn, potatoes, soy beans, vetch or peas, to choke out the weeds.

CORNELIAN CHERRY: *see* CORNUS; MOISTURE-LOVING PLANTS; DOGWOOD

CORN FLOWER: (*Centaurea cyanus*) *see* BACHELOR'S BUTTON

CORN SMUT: *see* FUNGUS

CORN STALK: Like most plant residues, corn stalks are good composting material. They are very difficult to break down in the pile, however, unless they are shredded or ground first. For the garden, any commercial compost grinder is sufficient. On the farm scale, an ensilage cutter can handle the job. *See also* MULCH.

CORNUS: Dogwood and Cornel. The Cornelian cherry (*C. mas*) is a hardy shrub with yellow blossoms in late March or April. It stands smoky conditions extremely well and is valuable for city planting. The red osier (*C. stolonifera*) to six feet, the gray dogwood (*C. racemosa*) to ten feet, the silky cornel (*C. amomum*) to eight feet, and the Tartarian dogwood (*C. alba*) are shrubs with brilliant red bark and gray or purplish twigs; the flowers are white and the fruits, according to the variety, red, blue, and white. Hardy everywhere and easy of culture in ordinary garden soil. Propagation by cuttings of old wood or layering.

Two Cornelian-cherry Dogwoods (*C. mas* and *C. officinalis*) rate high on the list of edible-berried shrubs. Attractively colored jelly of fine flavor can be made from the tart fruit of either. *See also* DOGWOOD.

COROLLA: Petals of a flower. *See also* FLOWER.

CORSICAN MINT: *see* MINT

CORYLOPSIS: This shrub has varying shades of yellow which differ considerably from the forsythias and are not so brilliant in color. The shrubs are related to the witch-hazels, and require no special care, provided they are grown in sandy soil which is not too heavy. Propagated preferably by layers, although they may be grown from seed or cuttings under glass. *C. spicata* has fragrant blossoms in clusters of seven to ten, which in protected spots open late in February or early March; six to seven feet. *C. pauciflora* resembles the above species, except that it has smaller leaves.

COSMOS: Annual members of the *Compositae* family, often used as background plants. It develops as a loose bush, usually reaching a height of three to five feet. The old type has single flowers, and the cosmos foliage is delicate and fern-like. Cosmos does not demand a rich soil; in fact, too rich a soil will produce leggy plants with few blooms. Seeds germinate in eight days and blooms are usually about four inches in diameter. *See also* ANNUALS.

COSTMARY: (*Chrysanthemum balsamita*) Perennial that may grow to as much as five to six feet, and flowers like small daisies.

Leaves are used for tea, and for their fragrance. They are also supposed to be useful as a moth preventive.

Best kept in the background as it grows large and is somewhat coarse.

Costmary is hardy and easily cultivated by division. Does well in average soil, in dry sunny place. *See also* CHRYSANTHEMUM.

COTONEASTERS: These decorative shrubs, many having decorative fruits remaining throughout winter, supply the garden with some choice specimens, both tall and low-growing. For example, rock spray (*C. microphylla*,

C. adpressa, C. dammeri and *C. horizontalis*) are low shrubs, useful in the rock garden, under windows or as an edging to a border of shrubs.

Tall upright shrubs in the cotoneaster family include:

C. acuminata—eight to 12 feet high with pink flowers and red fruit; *C. acutifolia*—same height as above with pink white flowers and black fruits; *C. foveolata*—four to eight feet high, pink flowers and black fruit; *C. hupehensis*—four to six feet high, white flowers and deep red fruit; and *C. salicfolia*—eight to 12 feet high, white flowers and red fruit.

The cotoneaster shrubs thrive in well-drained slightly alkaline soils, in a sunny spot. Usually planting in spring is advised, and bad results are had generally if shrubs are transplanted.

Doing best in southern areas, the evergreen forms make attractive plantings with their arching branches that in winter are covered with large quantities of red berries. During spring clusters of white flowers decorate many varieties.

COTTON GUM: *see* NYSSA

COTTONSEED HULLS: *see* COTTON WASTES; HULLS

COTTONSEED MEAL: An excellent by-product organic fertilizer, cottonseed meal is made from the cotton seed which has been freed from lints and hulls and deprived of its oil. Since cottonseed cake is one of the richest protein foods for animal feeding, relatively little finds its way for use as fertilizer. The special value of cottonseed meal lies in its acid reaction which makes it a valuable fertilizer for acid-loving specialty crops. The meal is used mainly as a source of nitrogen, of which it contains varying amounts, usually around seven per cent. Phosphoric acid content is between two and three per cent, while potash is usually 1.5 per cent. *See also* FERTILIZERS.

COTTON WASTES: Often called cotton gin trash. Cottonseed burrs are a source of potash, but need considerable moisture before breaking down into compost. The fine waste and the more voluminous amounts of wastes containing cotton fiber are, as a rule, rich in nitrogen because seed parts and lint are contained in them. When piled up in the open, this material will decay in a few months under southern conditions into a rich and valuable compost without further additions. These materials can also be used to activate compost heaps by covering other plant material, including cotton burrs, with them.

One of the major fertilizers nowadays are cottonseed hulls and cottonseed hull ashes, especially the latter, which are used as a source of quickly available potash, of which there is from 15 per cent to 23 per cent in the commercial product. Phosphoric acid content is also considerable and usually above that of other plant products, namely seven to nine and a half per cent.

COTTONY-CUSHION SCALE: *see* INSECT CONTROL, BIOLOGICAL

COUNTY AGENT: *see* GOVERNMENT SERVICES

COVER CROP: One of the most important cultural practices is that of the cover crop. Cover crops increase soil organic matter which in turn will increase absorptive activity and stimulate biochemical processes.

In addition, cover crops prevent soil erosion. They bring leached nutrients back to the surface where these will be available for the new planting. In fact, cover crops get their name because the seed is planted in late summer or the fall, and enough growth comes up so that the soil surface is covered during winter.

Choices among cover crops are many. A good cover crop should make as large an amount of growth as possible in the shortest possible time. To assure good growth, the crop must be adapted to climate and soil.

To facilitate soil preparation it is advisable to choose a crop that is easy to incorporate into the soil.

In making a decision in the choice of a cover crop, the considerations will dwell with the use of legume or non-legume. Here it should be noted that the legume has an added advantage in supplying extra nitrogen as well as organic matter. Among the individual crops which have cool temperature requirements the legumes include crimson clover and vetches. The non-legumes encompass rye, oats, wheat, buckwheat and rape. Those with warm temperature requirements in the legume group are cowpeas and soybeans. The non-legumes are millet and Sudan grass.

Soybeans are an excellent green manure crop for the heavier soils of the North. Rye, although difficult to turn under, is one of the best recommended since it can be planted from August first to October 15.

The actual planting of these crops can be accomplished at vegetable harvest time or somewhat earlier by planting between the vegetable rows. Planting should not be done so early that it may compete with the main crop.

In putting under these materials, whether they be cover crop or soil improving crop, it is best to work them under while they are still succulent.

WINTER COVER CROPS: The best winter cover crops are rye, wheat, and rye-grass. Any of these may be sown from mid-August to mid-September. These crops will become well established before cold weather begins. During the winter they serve to hold the soil in place, and thus prevent erosion. All of them have large fibrous root systems which add extra organic matter to the soil when they are plowed or spaded under. They should be plowed under in the spring before they make much growth, usually by

May 1. Winter vetch is sometimes used with rye, but the mixture must be left growing longer in the spring, to give full benefit. Rye-grass provides an excellent cover for the soil during the winter and an abundance of organic matter when plowed or spaded under; it has a particularly large root

One winter's growth of vetch like this produced 99 bushels of corn the following year on "worthless" sand soil with the help of phosphate rock.

system. It is not so coarse as rye or wheat, and has a darker green color. It is especially useful when it is sown in the vegetable or cutting garden in late August or September. Seed can be scattered between the rows, and the rye-grass will not interfere with the maturing of the plants already there.

SUMMER COVER CROPS: Summer cover crops are particularly suitable for areas to be made into lawn. Soybeans, oats, millet, and Sudan-grass are useful for this purpose, and may be sown in the spring and plowed under in the late summer or fall. These plants are ready to be turned under by mid-August or early September, in time for fall lawn-making.

Buckwheat is another crop sometimes used to provide organic matter.

It may be sown any time from June to late summer, and is usually plowed under while it is in bloom. It is killed by cold weather; but it may be left on the ground all winter and plowed under in the spring. It returns to the soil the least amount of organic matter of all the crops mentioned here; but it has the advantage of being able to grow on rather poor soil. It shades out weeds fully as successfully as any of the pre-lawn crops, and is easily spaded under.

In large areas being prepared for planting, fertilizer should be applied to the soil before green manure crops are sown. The cover crop will be stimulated in growth by such fertilization, and will eventually add more organic matter to the soil as a result of it.—*Conrad Link.*

CROPS FOR GREEN MANURES: Suggestions for northern United States:

to work the material into the soil. Some rotary tillers that have a cutting action as well as digging are especially effective for this job.

The time to work in a cover crop is usually determined by the time a crop in that section is to be grown. Since so much of the value of cover crops depends upon the quantity of organic matter produced, many growers postpone working them in for as long as planting schedules permit, allowing them to get increased growth from early spring warmth.

PLANT FOOD IN COVER CROPS: The amount of plant food in a well-grown cover crop is equivalent per acre to a ton of high-grade fertilizer. The availability of plant food from such a cover crop depends upon the type of cover crop grown, the fertility level or fertilizer applied, and the time it is plowed under. Properly grown cover and green manure crops

Crop	Date of Seeding	Rate per 1000 Sq. ft.	Time of Plowing Under
Summer Crops			
Buckwheat	June to Sept. 1	2-2½ lb.	Aug.-Oct.
Millet	May 20 to June 10	6 oz.	Aug. 15-Sept. 15
Oats	March 15 to May 1	2 lb.	May 15-June
Soybeans	May 15 to June 15	2 lb.	Aug. 15-Sept. 1
Sudan-grass	May 20 to June 20	8 to 10 oz.	August
Winter Crops			
Rye	Aug. 15 to Sept. 15	2½ lb.	April
Rye-grass	Aug. 15 to Sept. 15	½ to 1 lb.	April
Wheat	Aug. 15 to Sept. 15	2½ lb.	April

WORKING IN COVER CROP: If the crop is heavy, it's best to chop up the growth before working it into the soil. Farmers can do this with a heavy cover crop disk. Often two or three diskings are needed to work in a heavy crop; as a result, it decomposes quickly enough so that a crop can be planted in only a few weeks. In orchards, the usual method is to disk only to kill the growing plants.

For the gardener, often a rotary mower is used to cut up the growth into smaller pieces; then several passes are made with a rotary tiller

will contain approximately two per cent nitrogen, 0.5 to 0.8 per cent phosphorus, and from three to six per cent potassium of the dry matter. The amounts vary greatly with the state of maturity and the fertility levels or fertilizer application.

Much of this plant food can be obtained from the residues left from the cash crop. For legumes, the nitrogen is obtained from symbiotic action. Tilth and porosity are greatly influenced by the type of root system for the cover crop selected. For soil aeration, this is quite important.

COVERCROP CHARACTERISTICS

Compiled by B. A. MADSON, Agronomist, California Extension Service

Crop	Density of growth	Soil	Type of growth	Cost of seed	Rate of seeding (pounds per acre)
Legumes					
Common vetch	Moderate	Loam	Succulent	Moderate	60-75
Purple vetch	Moderate to heavy	Loam	Succulent	Moderate to low	50-65
Hairy vetch	Moderate to heavy	Sand loam	Succulent	High	40-50
Calcarata vetch	Moderate	Loam to heavy	Succulent	High	30-50
Monantha vetch	Moderate	Loam to heavy	Succulent	Moderate to low	50-60
Hungarian vetch	Moderate	Loam to heavy	Succulent	Moderate to low	60-75
Bitter vetch	Moderate	Loam to heavy	Stemmy	High	35-50
Horse beans	Moderate to heavy	Loam to heavy	Stemmy	High	125-175
Tangier peas	Heavy	Loam to heavy	Succulent	High	80-110
Wedge peas	Light	Loam to heavy	Succulent	High	80-110
Field peas (Canada)	Moderate	Loam to heavy	Succulent	Moderate	75-100
Field peas (Aus. winter)	Moderate	Loam to heavy	Succulent	Moderate	70-90
Fenugreek	Light	Loam to heavy	Stemmy	Moderate	35-45
Bur clover	Light	Loam	Succulent	Moderate	20-30
Nonlegumes					
Mustards	Heavy	Loam to heavy	Stemmy	Moderate	15-20
Wheat	Moderate	Loam to heavy	Succulent	Moderate	60-90
Barley	Moderate to heavy	Loam to heavy	Succulent	Moderate	60-90
Oats	Moderate to heavy	Loam to heavy	Succulent	Moderate	60-90
Rye	Moderate to heavy	Sandy to heavy	Succulent	Moderate	60-90

The availability of the plant food for the cover and green manure crops is influenced by the fertility condition under which it is grown, the state of maturity when plowed under, together with the temperature and moisture conditions in the soil. *See also* CONSERVATION; CITRUS (COVER CROPS); GREEN MANURE; CLOVER.

COW: A milk cow can save many families on their milk bill. If five people in a family drink the usual amount of milk, they pay out about $300 a year for milk. Since it costs only around $140 a year to feed a family cow producing two and one-half gallons of milk per day, this family would save about $150.

Proper housing is of key importance, but generally an existing outbuilding can be converted to a suitable cow barn. Following are some suggestions made by Milton Wend in his booklet, *The Family Cow*, published by the Country Bookstore of Noroton, Conn.

Unless the cow is to be kept in a stanchion, the minimum floor area for a stable is 200 or more square feet. In northern areas, the cow stable should be windtight; all winter ventilation should be under control. An economical job can be done, when necessary, by nailing unslated roofing paper over the sides. A cow can stand more cold than generally realized. If a stable has but one window, cross-ventilation must be obtained by means of a transom over the door provided with a sliding panel or controlled through openings into other parts of the barn.

The cow may be confined by some sort of stanchion or allowed the freedom of a box stall. The box stall is recommended, since the cows can keep warmer by moving around occasionally on very cold nights. Milk production has been found to increase about five per cent when cows are kept in a stall as opposed to a stanchion.

A calf pen is required. This should preferably be a duplicate of the cow stall since the calf may be raised through the heifer stage to a second cow or for beef. If there is visibility between the two stalls, both cow and young calf will be more content after the calf is weaned.

A family milk cow will generally yield about 12 quarts daily for from eight to 12 months, consuming about 18 pounds of hay daily. A Jersey heifer is best bred at from 15 to 17 months; Guernseys at from 17 to 18 months; and the heavier breeds on up to 25 months. After freshening, a cow will reach maximum production during the second month. She will then decline in production at the rate of six to seven per cent a month. A cow that freshens in the fall or early winter will usually yield an average of ten per cent more milk and fat than one that freshens in spring or summer.

COW MANURE: *see* MANURE

COWPEA: (*Vigna sinensis*) The cowpea is a multi-rooted legume popularly grown today for food, hay, grazing and soil building. A native of central Africa, the cowpea spread to practically all warm, tillable areas of the earth.

With sufficient warm weather cowpeas grow wherever corn grows, and may be found in some parts of Michigan. But the cowpea area is really south of a line running westerly through Pennsylvania to southern Kansas, then southwesterly across the Panhandle to the Gulf. In this zone cowpeas are grown as a secondary crop with corn, as a main crop and as a soil builder, the latter in places where cotton and tobacco have depleted soil fertility.

With suitable climate cowpeas grow on practically any type of well drained soil, withstand drought well and make forage at time of year when most needed. As soil conditioners they make sandy ground more compact and heavy clays more friable through added humus. And the legume reactivates dead soil with countless bacteria from nodules supplying nitrogen, the important growth factor.

For food cowpeas are served like snap beans, shelled green or cooked like dried beans. This is the recommended method of cooking dried cowpeas:

Soak peas in lukewarm water several hours, then let simmer at low heat until tender. *Do Not Add Soda.* Season with pork fat, onion, cheese, green pepper or celery, or a combination of all, and you have a tempting, sustaining dish. Fried cowpeas have 19.4 protein, 54.5 carbohydrates and 1.1 per cent fat, being higher in protein and carbohydrates than oats but lower in fat.

Their vitamin content is high, especially B-1, and the green sprouts, ready to cook 24 hours after germination, are high in Vitamin C and carry a fair amount of B vitamins.

Cowpea straw is popular as litter, mulch and feed, some growers even preferring it to cowpea hay for the latter. In protein the straw runs 3.4 per cent, higher than soybean, oat, wheat, rice or barley straw. And as litter and mulch it is very satisfactory.

CRABAPPLE: (*Malus*) The white to pink flowers of the flowering crab or crabapple trees can be favorably compared to the beauty of the Japanese flowering cherries. In addition to their beautiful blooms, these ornamental crabapples also produce edible fruit. The showy crab (*M. floribunda*) makes a large bush-type tree with its spreading branches reaching about 20 to 30 feet high. The American crab (*M. coronaria*) also known as sweet crab grows to about 30 feet, has rose to white flowers. The Oregon crabapple (*M. fusca*) has white flowers, grows to 30 feet, is hardy throughout most of the United States. *See also* APPLE; TREES; FLOWERING.

CRABGRASS: (*Digitaria sanguinalis*) Sending its tentacles spreading out over good lawn grasses, crabgrass gains

a foothold in a lawn that often can't be dislodged by ordinary means. Soon, the proud lawn-builder finds that his rich green sward has turned into a blotchy mass of brown weeds, and the more he pulls them out the faster they grow.

A dense lawn, fed by plenty of compost and growing in topsoil rich in humus, will defy crabgrass. Cutting grass under three inches is not advisable after arrival of the midsummer season.

Lawn weeds weren't always such a problem, because before the days of power mowers and suburban developments the average man confined his grass-producing efforts to a small patch in front of his house which he dosed liberally with manure donated by the family cow. An occasional cutting with a scythe or sickle allowed the grass to grow at a reasonable height. The good lawn grasses grew well on this plot because a good, fertile soil gave them the strength they needed to crowd out weeds.

Today, the new homeowner usually sets out to make a lawn on clay or sand that the contractor has hauled to the house site as fill, with perhaps two inches of topsoil spread over the surface like icing on a cake. The whole mass is packed down solid by the steel tracks of the bulldozer. A few bags of chemical fertilizer are brought in to give the grass a start, and from there on it is pretty much on its own.

To make matters worse, when the owner sees the weeds getting ahead he usually confines his efforts to killing them, rather than to giving the valuable lawn grass the help it needs to get ahead.

The real secret of crabgrass control is contained in this simple formula:

Crabgrass and good lawn grasses thrive on a different set of growing conditions. You can encourage the weed or discourage it by altering its environment.

Here is what good lawn grasses need to grow:

1. A fertile topsoil, preferably no less than six inches deep and rich in humus.

2. Cutting at a reasonable height. Perennial ryegrass, one of the most common good grasses, grows six feet high in its normal habitat. When it is kept trimmed to an inch or an inch and a half it finds the going difficult. So during the hot summer months when weeds take hold it helps to trim your grass as high as three or four inches.

3. An occasional drenching watering.

Crabgrass has a slightly different set of likes:

1. It doesn't grow as strongly on good soil as do good lawn grasses. It can't stand the competition of ryegrass and bluegrass when those plants have a good soil to back them up.

2. Crabgrass likes to grow low to the ground, so it is not stunted by low mowing. Quite the contrary, low mowing gives it the room it needs to spread out and grow strongly.

Here is a program which will show results:

1. First, if you have a lawn sweeper, use it after several midsummer mowings to pick up crabgrass seeds that will sprout the following year. Put the clippings in your compost heap.

2. Aerate your soil as much as possible, using either a hand aerator or an aerating attachment for a tiller or garden tractor. Don't be afraid to really shake up your soil, because air and moisture are needed below the surface to give encouragement to good grass roots.

3. Spread on your soil liberal amounts of phosphate rock, potash rock and lime, if needed. For an average soil, apply these amounts:

Phosphate and potash rock—ten pounds per 100 square feet.

Lime—5 to 10 pounds per 100 square feet, depending on soil pH. (Larger amount for acid soils, less for those nearer neutral pH.) If soil is alkaline, do not apply lime.

Bone meal is also an excellent mineral supplement for lawn soils. Apply in the same proportions as the ground rock fertilizers.

These natural mineral fertilizers will make sure that the good grass you want to grow has ample mineral food.

4. Now comes the most important step—the creation of a good soil structure. It is hard to get across how much can be accomplished in producing a good lawn by improving soil tilth and structure. And the only practical way to do this is to pack plenty of compost, humus, leaf mold, peat or other organic material into your lawn soil.

You should not be concerned about nutrients in the materials you use, because in promoting good growth of grass, nutrient value is secondary to tilth. You have to be a little cautious about spreading sawdust or chopped straw on your lawn (they are low in nitrogen content), but small amounts of those things can be spread without harm.

Spread your "structure builders" in installments that will give the grass a chance to grow a little between spreadings. Basically, what you are doing is *mulching* your lawn, but you still want to encourage the grass to grow through the mulch. Peat moss is one of the best materials for this type of work. Compost is excellent, but it should be ground or shredded before application.

Other organic fertilizing materials that will go a long way in boosting lawn growth include dried blood, cottonseed meal and soybean meal. These three are especially rich in growth-promoting nitrogen, and should be applied as liberally as needed and available.

The result of this program will be a vigorous lawn with a minimum of crabgrass and other weeds. *See also* LAWNS.

CRANBERRY: (*Vaccinium macrocarpon*) Cranberries were found growing in wild abundance when the Pilgrims first set foot on American soil. Originally cultivated in Cape Cod, most commercial growers are now located in Massachusetts, New Jersey and Wisconsin.

An experienced cranberry picker averages as many as 100 pounds of berries in an hour. Cultivation is specialized, requiring well-drained soil.

Cranberry cultivation is a special kind of farming. It requires an acid soil containing peat, sand, plenty of water and good drainage. Despite its name a cranberry bog is usually dry except when flooded for protection against frost.

The building of a bog on Cape Cod begins in the latter part of the season. When swamp lands freeze, trees are cut down just above the ice. In the spring, when the ice thaws, the stumps are pulled up. Ditches are dug around the edge of the bogs, with a network of ditches through the interior for drainage. The exposed peat is leveled and smoothed out. A layer of sand about three or four inches is sometimes spread over the peat to make a soft dry bed.

By early April the bog is ready for planting. Cuttings taken from a producing bog are set out by machine in the newly prepared ground, in rows about eight inches apart. As the cuttings grow, roots extend down into the peat and vines send out runners, much as do strawberry plants. Constant care is necessary in cranberry cultivation. In the spring and fall there is danger of sudden frost which can kill an entire crop overnight. When the Weather Bureau issues a frost warning growers flood their fields. The water, flowing through the ditches and in among the vines, produces a vapor which rises above the bog. This serves as a protecting blanket between the vines and frost. Strangely enough, the vines may remain under water all winter with no harm done. If thick ice remains on the bog too long, the water level must be dropped and the ice shattered to save the plants from smothering from want of oxygen.

Cranberries are native to acid marshlands in the cooler sections of the country. Its slender stems and evergreen leaves—with the well-known red berries that ripen in early fall—can be seen in those muck regions.

CRANBERRY TREE: (*Viburnum opulus*) Also called High Bush Cranberry and Pimba. This beautiful native shrub occurs in woods and along streams in northeastern United States and as far west as Wisconsin and Iowa. Because of a margin of sterile florets around the flower clusters, this viburnum is highly ornamental. The well-known snowball tree is a cultivated variety of viburnum in which all the flowers are sterile and showy. The leaves have the shape and general appearance of maple leaves. The dense and vigorous growth of the shrub makes it suitable for border or hedge. The showy red fruits are excellent for foods for birds in winter, and may be used as a substitute for cranberries.

A dwarf form may be used in rock gardens or low hedges.

All viburnums can easily be identified by their flat, disk-like seeds. *See also* SHRUBS, FLOWERING; VIBURNUM.

CRANE FLOWER: *see* BIRD-OF-PARADISE

CRAPE JASMINE: *see* TABERNAEMONTANA

CRAPE MYRTLE: *see* LAGERSTROEMIA

CREEPING CHARLIE: *see* LYSIMACHIA

CREEPING LILYTURF: (*Liriope spicata*) *see* GROUNDCOVERS

CREOSOTE: Not recommended to preserve wood in seedling flats or wood for compost bins. It is highly poisonous. Linseed oil is satisfactory substitute.

CRESS: (*Lepidium sativum*) Sometimes called pepper grass, it is an early spring vegetable, used as a salad, and of easy culture. It is sown thickly in early spring in rows one foot apart; as it runs quickly to seed, succession sowings should be made every eight or ten days. There are several varieties, but the kind in general use is the Curled which answers the purpose of garnishing as well as for salads. *See also* WATERCRESS.

CRESTED WHEATGRASS: *see* LAWN

CRINUM: The word is derived from the Greek which means lily. Botanically it was put in the Lily family for many years, but it is now rightfully classed with the Amaryllis family.

Especially fine for Southern gardens, the crinum is a very ancient plant, mentioned in Biblical literature. There is no part of the sub-tropical world without a representative. Some of the crinums, if sufficiently mulched,

are able to withstand the winters as far north as Philadelphia and Kentucky with occasional reports of a few farther north, though these are very rare. Many species and hybrids grow well in Texas where they are frozen to the ground each year. Greenhouses all over the country grow many crinums.

There are two main types of crinums. In the first the flowers are salverform (the petals set flat on the tube as in the phlox). The long, narrow, erect tubes in different species have petals (limbs) long and narrow; some are lance-shaped; some are white, pure white; some are faintly lined with rose down the center; some purple or wine down the outside of the entire flower and white inside. The number of flowers varies from five to 35 in number on the umbel. All are variously and deliciously fragrant.

In the other group the flower has what is called the lily shape. A short or long tube broadens out in the "cup" in varying shapes. In two species the "cup" is quite open or tulip shaped. The lily shaped crinums are far more numerous than the salverform type because it is from the "lily-shaped" *C. moorei* that the wealth of crinums has descended. It is really the "Mother of Crinums."

Crinums grow best in the mild climate of the South, usually requiring much space. They require a rich soil, therefore thrive in high-humus soil, mulched with compost or manure.— *Margaret H. Walmsley.*

CROCUS: With the first warm rays of the spring sun the crocus pops its colorful head out of the ground to announce the coming of spring. Sometimes this little flower seems almost too impatient to wait for spring and, defying late winter snows, is seen pushing its way through snow covered lawns.

FALL PLANTING: These spring, flowering bulbs are easy to grow even for the new gardener. Good growing conditions contribute to the best display of flowers and the continued year-after-year performance of the bulbs. The bulbs are planted in the fall any time before the ground freezes. Rich soil is not necessary but it must be well-drained. A bone meal or a thin coating of well-rotted manure, or compost spaded in the soil will prove beneficial. Crocuses should, for showy effect, be planted in masses about two inches deep and three to four inches apart. The depth refers to the distance from the soil surface to the neck of the bulb.

The crocus lends itself well to many garden locations such as the rock garden, borders, the base of trees, or informal scattering in the lawn. The best position is where they will get sun for part of the day. If planted in the lawn, select a southern exposure to encourage early blooms so that the foliage has matured before the grass needs to be cut. This is essential if flowers are wanted in future years.

To avoid formal arrangements scatter the bulbs on the lawn and plant them where they fall. Lift the sod with a trowel, stir soil underneath and plant the bulb, right side up, and press sod back. In the lawn, plantings must be free and natural.

WINTER CARE: In localities with severe winters, after the ground has frozen hard, a mulch of hay, straw, or evergreen boughs may be used. This prevents the alternate freezing and thawing of the soil, and disastrous heaving of the bulbs. This covering should be removed early in the spring.

SPRING CARE: In the spring allow the foliage to ripen. After blooming, the foliage continues to grow until it turns yellow and withers of its own accord (four to six weeks). Crocus may remain in the same planting and make a splendid show for years. Do not disturb plantings unless replanting becomes necessary due to overcrowding.

Every garden, large or small, can partake of the beauty of the crocus. The bulbs are inexpensive and with a little care will not only persist for many years but will increase considerably. The bright showy colors of their blooms are a joy to the eyes very early in the spring when few other flowers are to be had in the garden.

Varieties include Scotch crocus (*biflorus*)—purple spring-blooming choice for rock gardens; Cloth of Gold —(*Susianus*)—orange-yellow, spring-blooming; *Longiflorus*—autumn-blooming, delicate purple flowers; Saffron Crocus (*Sativus*)—autumn-blooming, sometimes white flowers; common crocus (*Vernus*)—spring-blooming.

(When making Saffron for cooking, the flowers of the Saffron Crocus should be picked as soon as open and orange stigmas removed and dried.) *See also* BULBS, FORCING; BULB GARDEN.

CROP, CATCH: A short-season crop occupying the land for a short period between the main crops in the rotation. Catch crops are frequently sown following a seeding failure. *See also* CATCH CROPS.

CROP, FORAGE: A plant grown primarily for livestock feed and of which all, or nearly all, the plant parts are harvested by man. Forage crops include all grasses and legumes cut for hay or silage and also harvested root crops such as turnips, rutabagas, sugar beets, and mangels when they are fed to livestock.

CROP RESIDUES: Working crop residues into the soil helps maintain soil productivity and is an integral part of the organic method. Research has shown that these residues increase crop yields under the right management.

Most of the nutrients which plants obtain from the soil remain in the unharvested portion of crops. These nutrients become available to succeeding crops as the residues decompose in the soil. Burning these materials results in an almost complete loss of the nitrogen and carbon which they contain. The carbon portion of residues adds to the organic matter content of the soil. Better soil structure could be obtained if farmers and gardeners returned all crop residues to the land. Residues also have considerable value when mulched on the surface of the soil for the control of erosion and increased infiltration of rainfall.

Decomposition of these residues is caused by microorganisms which live in the soil. Like all living things, these microscopic bacteria and fungi require carbon, nitrogen and additional inorganic elements which are largely obtained from the organic matter of the soil. According to researchers at the Ohio Experiment Station, for every ten parts of carbon used by the soil microorganisms, one part of nitrogen is required. If such a carbon:nitrogen (C/N) ratio is not present in the crop residue, the microorganisms will then use and "immobilize" the inorganic forms of nitrogen in the soil. This process makes such nitrogen temporarily unavailable to higher plants and is the cause of the characteristic yellowing (nitrogen deficiency) of crop plants grown on soils to which residues having high C/N ratios have been applied. An example of residues with high C/N ratios is wheat straw or corn stalks.

This difficulty can be overcome in three ways: (1) use the residues for bedding and return the strawy manure (manure contains considerable nitrogen) to the land, (2) seed a leguminous green manure crop in corn at the last cultivation or seed legumes with small grain crops, (3) add enough nitrogen fertilizer to reduce the C/N ratio of the residues. *See also* Cover Crops; Green Manure; Organic Matter; Carbon-Nitrogen; Compost.

CROP, SOILING: A crop fed to animals immediately after cutting and while it is in a green and succulent condition. No curing process or storage is undertaken prior to feeding.

Green corn, sorghums, and kale are frequently used as soiling crops.

CROSS-BREED: *see* Crossing

CROSSING: In plant propagation, this term designates the intentional combining of two varieties of the same species. Frequently, it is called cross-breeding or cross pollinating, although strictly speaking there are several methods of crossing plants. The interbred or cross-bred result is known as a hybrid, and the process is also referred to as hybridizing.

Variety breeding has many important purposes. Because the crossed offspring of two plant varieties will generally retain the dominant characteristics of each parent used to produce it, improved traits can be sought and achieved through this method.

In all types of plants, such things as frost and drought hardiness, disease and insect resistance, high productivity, earlier maturing, desirable harvesting, shipping and marketing qualities are often brought about by selective cross-breeding. In food crops, higher nutritional value, improved flavor, size, appearance, etc., have been accomplished. With flowers and other ornamentals, efforts have similarly been directed to vigorous growth, increased blossom size, lengthier blooming, soil and climate adaptability, and various other helpful characteristics.

CROSS POLLINATION: *see* Plant Breeding; Pollen

CROTALARIA: Yellow-flowering pea. Mostly grown in California and Florida, crotalaria is considered a valuable green manure crop in warmer sections of the country. *See also* Green Manure.

CROWFOOT: *see* Buttercup

CROWN GRAFT: *see* Grafting

CROWN IMPERIAL: (*Fritillaria imperialis*) Blooms in early spring. Often growing to three feet, its bell-shaped blooms are yellow, orange or red. After the foliage ripens, the plant goes dormant.

Soil should be rich and friable, neither too moist or dry. Use compost or well-rotted manure. Plant the large bulbs, ones that are three to four inches in diameter, about 12 inches deep. These large-size bulbs should be spaced about six to 12 inches apart, depending on when you want to dig them for transplanting. Deep, far-apart planting permits you to leave them alone for as much as ten years.

Tiny bulbs, one-half inch or less in diameter, need not be planted more than an inch deep, but make sure they are well mulched.

Transplant when the bulbs are dormant. Don't wait too long after the foliage has died down to dig the bulbs. Plant them where they do not get the hot afternoon sun. They should not be crowded by other plants, shrubs or trees, either above or below the soil. Mulch when the plants die down. Bulbs can be multiplied rapidly if transplanted every year or two.

CROWN VETCH: (*Coronilla varia*) A creeping legume perennial which may be the answer to problems of roadside slope and gully erosion for highway and conservation departments.

This hardy legume maintains a solid green foliage during a long growing season on raw steep roadside banks. During the summer, it blooms into a mass of pink, rose, and white flowers. The foliage provides a thick soil-protecting mat which holds the rainfall and retards runoff. The soil conditioning action of the roots renders the soil exceedingly receptive to moisture; an important factor to good slope development.

Plants seed from mid-June to September, and spread by strong fleshy underground stems. These grow to lengths of ten feet or more and produce new plants at each node.

Among the many advantages crown vetch seems to possess are exceptional vigor under extreme drought and cold conditions, disease resistance, and a remarkable ability to grow well even on subsoils. Crown vetch is quite competitive and chokes out undesirable plants. *See also* VETCH.

CUCKOO FLOWER: (*Cardamine pratensis*) An attractive member of the weed family, Cuckoo Flower, Lady's-smock or Meadow Pink prefers moist, shady areas. Introduced from Asia Minor and Siberia, its blossoms are bright red; the well-known garden varieties are pink, white or blue, known as phlox. Some believe it derived its name, Cuckoo Flower, from the fact that it blossoms when the Cuckoo calls or, perhaps, because of the foam pockets of the Foam Cikade, which in the old world are called Cuckoo's saliva. *See also* LYCHNIS.

CUCUMBER: (*Cucumis sativus*) Thanks to research and the development of new strains, cucumber-growing has become increasingly popular with the commercial grower and home-gardener alike. The new strains are both drought and disease resistant which takes the risk out of their cultivation.

Cucumbers are heavy users of organic materials, demanding a balanced diet of the basic elements. Soil should be medium, level and well-drained.

When choosing a field for planting cucumbers, a flat, well-drained one is preferred to a slope. A level field will retain moisture longer during the hot, dry spells. If possible, it should be a clover or bean field that had been plowed under last fall or early spring.

The soil should be medium—not too light and sandy. A sandy soil will grow the plants too rapidly, and dry them up the moment drought hits. A heavy, wet soil, on the other hand, interferes with proper growth.

Cucumbers are heavy users of organic materials and produce better and more heavily when organically fed. They also require an equal balance of such elements as phosphate, nitrogen, potash, lime, copper and iron.

A balanced rock fertilizer should be used if the soil is deficient in the necessary elements. This should include a minimum of five per cent nitrogen, and about 20 per cent of such organic materials as ground up cottonseed, dried blood, dehydrated manures, bone and fish meal.

Cucumbers may be planted any time in May after danger of frost is past. About the middle of the month is best. Before plowing the field, scatter plenty of seasoned manure over the area. It must have aged at least four months so as not to burn the tender plants. This manure will serve two purposes in the soil: one, feeding the plants; two, helping retain moisture during the hot spells, and keeping the soil porous. Adequate moisture in the soil at all times spells the difference between weak, unproductive plants, and green, robust ones.

Plant the seed just one inch below the surface to prevent damp rot in case of heavy rains.

Most cucumber rows are planted six to seven feet apart running from east to west for maximum sun. If space permits, eight feet is better. This gives the vines more room to grow without getting matted, and will make picking easier.

Space hills six feet apart in all directions. This allows for cross cultivation which eliminates hand hoeing to keep down weeds. Plant six seeds to a mound. When four inches high, thin out to three because there is not enough plant food in the small area to feed all.

Start cultivating as soon as the plants are three inches high. One cultivation a week is necessary until the vines begin to creep. Since the cucumber plants grow so vigorously, the soil must be kept as loose as possible so as not to hamper the rapid growth.

When the vines have attained the length of about 18 inches, stop cultivating, and apply a moderate amount of organic fertilizer along both sides of each row. A rock fertilizer, high in nitrogen, is excellent. If possible, apply during a light rain or drizzle so the water will immediately carry it down to the roots where it is needed. As the weather clears, hill the plants to protect their somewhat shallow roots from the hot sun.

Six to seven weeks after planting, small cucumbers begin to form on the vines. They bear watching because they grow into full-sized cucumbers over night. Start picking as soon as two or three are found in a clump of vines. The first picking is usually small. But it is necessary in order to encourage the plants to produce more.

CUCUMBER BEETLE: The adult is colored from yellow to black; black stripes down back; the larva is white, slender, and brownish at the ends. Adults feed on leaves and spread bacterial wilt. Larvae bore into roots and also feed on stems. For control, mix a handful of wood ashes and an equal amount of hydrated lime in two gallons of water; then spray both the upper and lower sides of the plant leaves; cucumber beetles are also known to be repelled by marigolds. *See also* INSECT CONTROL.

CULINARY HERB: *see* HERBS

CULTIVATION: To the gardener, cultivation refers to the entire job of taking care of the soil surface and in some cases, the subsoil. When referring to soil, cultivating means the operations that are done prior to planting the crop.

For small areas, most gardeners use a spading fork, since it's lighter to use than a spade and breaks up clods with less effort. For loose, sandy soils, regular garden spades do a satisfactory job.

An important thing to remember when cultivating with either spade or fork is that your object is never to pulverize the soil. You do want to loosen and aerate it, but this does not mean that when you're through, the soil has to pass through a sieve.

Use a rake to make the top two or three inches fine and smooth enough for planting and sowing.

When loosening the topsoil, you may be tempted to go all the way, and put the subsoil on top. This is a dangerous practice, especially since—as in the case of so many new homeowners—the topsoil layer is no more than several inches deep. Remember, your object is to loosen, not invert. This again is another reason why a fork is a better tool than a spade, since there is less tendency to invert the soil when using a fork.

Cultivation should never be done when the soil is wet, unless your soil is extremely well drained. It's not only a lot more work to cultivate a wet soil, but it's also a harmful practice. Wet soils tend to bake, puddle, and form brick-like clods after drying that defeat the entire purpose of cultivation.

Your soil is ready for digging when a handful, firmly compressed, crumbles when the pressure is released. If it remains in a wet sticky mass, with moisture on the surface, it's still too wet to work.

Soil cultivation, after the crop is planted, is done to keep weeds down and save moisture in the soil. Mulching has become the recommended method for accomplishing these objectives, and has saved much time and labor on the gardener's part. *See also* MULCHING; WEEDING; NO-DIGGING; AERATION.

CUMIN: (*Cuminum cyminum*) A small slender herbaceous annual widely cultivated in India and the Mediterranean region of Europe. The aromatic fruit (known as seed) is used as a condiment. Large quantities are used in the preparation of curry and in combination with other aromatic seeds in flavoring sausages, cheese, and numerous other food products. The seed has not been produced commercially in the United States.

The plant thrives best on a well-drained rich sandy loam in regions where temperatures are mild and even during a growing season of about three or four months. It is grown from seed. In the Mediterranean region the seed is frequently broadcast after winter crops of cereals, potatoes, or cabbage. Complete control of weeds is necessary because the plant is small and tender. For this reason planting the seed in rows spaced to permit maximum use of cultivators would be preferable in regions where hand labor is costly.

The crop is ready for harvest when the plants wither and the seed loses its dark-green color.

CUPFLOWER: (*Nierembergia caerulea*) The small plants of this annual bear showy pale lavender cup-shaped flowers that have purple centers. The small leaves, wiry stems and closely-packed blossoms combine to make this an annual of fine texture that is good as an edging plant, pot plant or window box subject. Seeds should be planted in flats in the autumn, but plants can be propagated by tip cuttings. The most popular variety is Purple Robe.

CURCULIO: A name given to any snout beetle, especially one which attacks fruit. Curculio can be controlled by cleaning up all the areas near the orchard that provide places where the beetle might winter. This should then be followed by disking under the trees to break up and kill the pupae in the ground. During early morning, trees may be jarred so that the beetle will drop on to sheets spread underneath. From here they may be gathered and destroyed. Finally, it is suggested that drops found beneath the trees be collected and gotten rid of while the larvae are in them. *See also* INSECT CONTROL.

CURLY PALM: (*Howea belmoreana*) *see* PALMS

CURRANT: (*Ribes*) The fruits of the currant are rich sources of Vitamin C, so that there is a nutritive reason for growing these species in the home garden. The currant plants are relatively easy to grow and are dependable— more so than fruit trees, if given good care.

New currant plants may be obtained by cutting. Short canes should be taken from eight to ten inch stems of one year's growth in the autumn.

The growing of bush fruits such as currants is not difficult, but there are practices that are important for good results. The plants will live most anywhere, doing best in a relatively cool moist climate and well-drained soil. Plant growth and fruitfulness are most satisfactory on soils well supplied with organic matter. Stable manure or its equivalent in humus-making medium is important. Mulches of leaves and litter can be worked into the soil after being used on the surface.

Pruning is necessary. It is well to do a little each year. The practice should be based on the fruiting habit. The best fruit is borne on canes from two to four years old. The old canes should be cut to stimulate new ones to bear for three or more years. It is well to space the canes six to eight inches apart, so far as possible, always removing the oldest, saving the larger stocky ones for fruiting. Cut out all slender canes as they are nearly useless; diseased or injured canes as short as possible. The season of pruning is immaterial but preference should be given to the fall season. Do some pruning each season. Spasmodic and severe cutting has a bad effect on yields.

New plants. Small plants for setting out can be secured by propagating from old ones. The usual way is by making cuttings. These are short canes taken from one year's growth of stems eight to ten inches long. They are cut in the fall from medium sized canes after growth has ceased and when the wood is mature. They are called hardwood cuttings. The cuttings are tied in bundles of a dozen or more and stored in cool sand or sawdust and kept moist enough so they will not dry out, and cool enough so the buds will not swell. In the spring the cuttings which have now calloused at the cut ends are set in a garden row with severed end down to root and grow for one year. Soil should be packed about the cuttings which are set four to six inches deep and three to twelve inches apart. When they are well rooted they may be set out in permanent places in the fall or the following spring. Fall planting is often practiced. It requires from two to three years to get plants built up to bearing age. It is well to space the permanent plants four feet apart in rows six feet apart. As currant and gooseberry plants have many shallow roots, the soil should not be worked deeply enough to injure the roots. Special care is needed the first year after setting in order not to harm the roots. Suppress weeds by mulches; add manure generously each year.

New plants can also be secured by a process known as mound layering at the base of a clump of plants. The first step is to cut back the stems severely—two-thirds to three-quarters their length—to stimulate numerous new side shoots. In midsummer, about July or soon after, earth is mounded half way up the cut off shoots. By fall or the next spring many shoots will have rooted and these can be dug away with stems and roots attached and set out for new plants. If any variety has not rooted well by fall, leave it undisturbed for another year. Mound layering is more work than cuttage but also more certain of good results. Some varieties do not set well by cuttings but only a few are eccentric in that way.

INSECT AND DISEASE PROBLEMS: Insect and disease problems are real and recurring ones unless one is familiar with the means of control. There are five troublesome insects and three harmful diseases that need attention.

Currant aphis. This damaging creature often called the leaf louse, stands at the head of the list of injurious insects because it is likely to occur anywhere and everywhere, but indirectly the creature harms the whole plant by dwarfing and starving it, and diminishing fruit production. The foliage of the currant is commonly distorted and discolored, being pale or yellowish, rolled and wrinkled by yellow-green plant lice on the undersides of the leaves. Later in the season the seriously injured leaves drop, and defoliation hinders the full development of the fruit. The eggs of this insect are shiny black, cucumber shaped, and are attached to the bark of the new growth—near the nodes. The eggs hatch soon after the leaves open in spring. The young lice crawl to the leaves and feed on the under surfaces by sucking the juice of the foliage. This causes curling. Toward the end of summer true males and females

develop, copulate, and winter eggs are deposited on the twigs in October. The eggs can be washed off with water sprayed on the canes.

The currant plant louse is not easy to control, which is the reason why this creature is a major insect. The eggs may be transported on nursery stock, if infested and uncertified, so that new plants may be the source and origin of the louse on newly planted stock. The sprocket-like cavities of curled leaves give some protection to the lice and hinder control. Plucking of affected foliage where too much curling of leaves has occurred is important. Sharp eyes will detect the shiny black eggs on the canes and they can be rubbed off and destroyed before hatching in the spring.

Currant worms. The green as well as the imported currant worms are often destructive to foliage. They can be shaken off the bushes and stepped on.

Berry worm. A small, white worm, a sort of maggot, sometimes infests the fruit of currant and gooseberry. It is believed that the eggs are laid in the fruit and the worms from them feed inside the immature berry and damage it, leaving it unfit for use. For control pick and destroy all affected fruit, leaving no berries on the bushes or on the ground.

San Jose scale. This pernicious and inconspicuous scale insect often damages many plants. It forms an ashen gray coating in mass on the canes and sucks the juice and life out of them. It is a common garden insect on ornamental shrubs. Set out only clean healthy plants, and use clean cuttings as helpful preventive measures.

COMMON DISEASE: Among diseases there are several of economic importance such as rust, mildew, and anthracnose. Each needs attention when present, and search should be made for them to protect all cases at the start, forestalling much later trouble and loss.

Rust. The red rust on currant leaves is often the most evasive disease of currants. It is intimately associated with blister rust of white pine as an alternating host for the disease. The red blister rust of pine and leaf spot of currant are one and the same disease with different manifestations on each. Both alternate from one species of plant to the other with the change of seasons. Black varieties of currant and the species of white pines are the most susceptible, and these should not be planted nearer than a half-mile apart. It is unwise to plant currant where white pines grow in the near vicinity.

The symptoms of rust on each host species are easy to recognize. On the trunks of affected pines there are in midsummer red rusty eruptions of yellow dust which are the spores. On the under leaf surfaces of the currant there are spots with small curved pointed projections, manifesting the growth of the fungus. If only an occasional pine is affected, it can be cut and the spread of the disease forestalled.

Mildew. This very common disease of cultivated plants often occurs on currants and gooseberries. The symptoms on these plants are fine, tender, white cobwebby growths on the top surfaces of the leaves. It often occurs in patches not far away and is most prevalent in wet seasons or in moist areas. It is urgent to give the plants full exposure to sun and provide good air circulation to keep the plants dry. One should remove all incipient cases of mildew as soon as detected to prevent its spread. These preventive practices are of much importance.

Cane blight. A wilting of the cane due to a fungus invasion is of occurrence in the garden. The canes die suddenly while loaded with fruit; and non-bearing canes contract the disease. Small black cushions on the canes reveal the disease. It is best to examine all plants during the summer and remove all affected stalks and burn them. General sanitation is important, as refuse is often a menace to healthy plants.

In the home garden currants are often grown in partial shade of trees, buildings or fences, an unwise practice which makes them more liable to disease if not to insect damage, than if grown in full sun and in free ventilation, hence the need for more frequent attention to keep them healthy. Flowering and ornamental species of these plants are subject to the same enemies as are those grown for edible fruits. *See also* BRAMBLE FRUITS.

CUT FLOWERS: Giving cut flowers the proper care prolongs the length of time you'll enjoy them.

One suggestion is to cut the stems at a long slant. They'll absorb more water and stay fresh longer. Another authority recommends adding a lump of sugar to the water to keep cut flowers fresh. Flower stems should never be cut with scissors, which crush the stem tissues. A sharp knife should be used to make a long slanting cut. The stems should also be cut every day. Never let any of the foliage come below the water level. Also, never let flowers lie around out of the water, as the stems seal themselves thus interfering with their water absorption.

Always keep your vases and flower containers immaculately clean. A dirty bacteria-laden container will shorten the lives of the flowers. Another rule to follow is not to crowd too many flowers into a container. It bruises the flowers and also makes an unattractive arrangement.

Poinsettias when used as a cut flower are sealed before delivery, so if it becomes necessary to cut the stems again the flowers can be resealed by placing the stems in boiling water for five or ten minutes or singeing them over a flame. This is done because poinsettias are full of a white milky fluid, and would bleed to death unless the ends are quickly sealed.

Roses need careful handling. Cut at least an inch from the stem with a sharp knife, making sure that the cut is slant-wise to avoid crushing. Roses have a porous stem which takes up water to nourish the bloom. If the pores become clogged the flowers wither, no matter how nice the buds are.

Whatever you do, don't jam too many in a small-necked vase or suffocation will result. Be sure to use a vase that will allow your flowers to take water right up the stem. And keep in mind not to put them over a fireplace with a cozy fire burning. If you do, the only place for your roses will be in the ash can.

If, in spite of proper care, your roses droop without opening, cut two or three inches off the stem to clear the shaft, and place them in water deep enough to reach to the bottom of the bud. Then put in a cool place, not out of doors, until they revive. A good point to remember is that all flowers kept in a cool place will last longer.

A long-lasting flower which can stand a great deal of handling is the carnation. That is one reason these flowers have become the standby of sick rooms and hospital wards. All one needs to do to keep them looking their best is to cut an inch off the stem each day and place them in fresh water.

In caring for chrysanthemums, you'll find that it's much like caring for roses—although "Mums" last longer. Care should always be taken to support the head of a large "Mum" because this flower is allergic to bumps. Bumping causes the numerous petals to shed.

Never lift a "Mum" by its head and make sure one hand is supporting the flower from underneath as you lift it to gently place it in water. Instead of cutting the stem each day, the method is to break a little off the stems, about an inch or so, and then pound them a bit so they'll take up water.

In the feeding of many varieties what is one flower's meat is another's poison, you'll find in dealing with plants. Cyclamen plants come in a wide range of colors and are very popular around Christmas time. This plant thrives best in a cool place and should be watered every other day at the rim of the pot. Pouring water directly on the foliage or bloom spots them, making dark patches on the plant.

There are also plants that love sunshine. A favorite is begonia. Allow your begonia to become thoroughly dry before watering; then water well. Keep the plant out of drafts and when begonia blossoms fall, pinch off the stem ends. New shoots will appear, which means more blossoms to take the place of those that fade.

The following families, such as hydrangeas, rose bushes and azaleas, must be thoroughly watered each day with care taken so that they do not become waterlogged.

Here is an example: forgetting to water your hydrangeas, then leaving them in a tub of water over night. The safe way to do it is to immerse them in a bucket of water to reach the rim of the pot. Leave them in the pail of water for an hour and when you remove them they will be all right.

Ferns are governed by the amount of water they receive and shouldn't be watered more than two or three times a week. The best way to water them is to place the plant in a pail of water for enough time to let the soil become moist, drawing up water from the bottom of the pot. Ferns should not be allowed to stand in water longer than this, as the soil becomes soggy and dries out so hard that roots are damaged and finally die.

Keep your fern in a light airy place out of hot or cold drafts. You may put it in a jardiniere, but before you do, place pebbles or a saucer in the bottom of the jar to allow for drainage.

CUTTINGS: One of the easiest and most effective methods of propagating plants is by cuttings. Cuttings are parts of plants cut from a parent plant and inserted in water, sand, soil, peat moss, or some other medium where they form roots and become new plants. By this method of propagation, plants which are identical with the parent are reproduced. This is especially helpful to increase stock of new varieties created by hybridization or discovered as variations through mutations. Seeds from such new forms, if produced (sometimes such plants are sterile), are likely to revert to a previous type, but cuttings will reproduce in kind the plant from which they are taken. Hence cuttings are referred to as an asexual method of reproduction, and they provide a simple, convenient, and inexpensive method for increasing stock of a particular plant.

Cuttings may be classified in two ways: either according to the plant part used—as roots, tubers, rhizomes, stems, or leaves—or according to the stage of development of the parts—as dormant, ripe or hardwood cuttings; active, green, immature or softwood cuttings.

SOFTWOOD CUTTINGS: Green or softwood cuttings are generally rooted in greenhouses or cold frames or, on a small scale, in boxes or pots in a warm room in the house. The cuttings should be taken from vigorous plants at a stage when it breaks with a snap when bent. If it merely crushes between the fingers, it is too young to use; if it bends without breaking, it is too old and tough. After a little practice, the favorable stage can be recognized without difficulty.

Most softwood plants may be increased by greenwood cuttings. Bedding plants are universally propagated this way. Tender growing tips of ornamental shrubbery and other hardwood plants may also be used for propagation, provided that cuttings are taken in early summer when growth is most rapid.

Convenient lengths for greenwood cuttings are two to four inches. The base should be cut straight across just below a node or joint. In most cases with any type of cutting it is best to cut at a node or "cut to a bud" (to have a bud at the base of the cutting), as roots seem to form more readily near the nodes. The top should be cut slanting with a bud (or a node from which a bud will sprout) just below the tip. There should be two or three nodes on each cutting. Lower leaves are usually cut off, both to facilitate handling and to reduce transpiration. If the remaining leaves are large, as on a begonia, from a third to a half of each is cut away to prevent too much water from being evaporated from their surface. But some leaf surface should be left to carry on the life processes while the cutting is forming roots.

Sand or fine gravel is an excellent medium to start these cuttings, because it provides good drainage. To prepare a propagating bed for cuttings, level the sand perfectly, water it, and pack it firmly by pressing it with a level board. Then take a straight-edged board and at regular intervals with a blunt-tipped dibber make holes for the insertion of the cuttings. Press each cutting gently but firmly against the flat bottom of the hole, and bring the loose sand around it so that it can stand alone. Softwood cuttings should be transferred as rapidly as possible from parent plant into the propagating bed. They should be kept cool and shaded while the work is being done.

When they are placed in the bed of sand, drench them with water from a fine sprinkler and cover them lightly with newspaper or else keep in a shaded place until roots begin to form. When the root system develops, they can take in from the soil all the water they need, and can then be given more sunshine to aid their growth. During the first two weeks, at least, they need protection from strong light, as well as good ventilation and constant moisture.

When roots are one-fourth to one-half inch long, the cuttings may be transferred to two-inch flower pots, one to a pot and again given plenty of water to encourage their growth.

Greenwood or softwood cuttings are widely used because they root easily, and the great majority of plants, whether soft or hardwooded, can be propagated in this manner.

LEAF-CUTTINGS: Cuttings may often be made from leaves of certain plants that are succulent or fleshy. A mature leaf of the Rex Begonia can be cut from a plant, slashed at each point where two large veins unite, placed flat on wet sand and weighted down with pebbles or pegs. If handled from this stage like a softwood cutting, such a leaf will develop tiny new plants at many if not all of the points where cuts were made. Some leaves should be pulled from the parent plant with a bit of the main stem adhering to the base. This stump should be buried, and the leaf itself held flat on the sand. This will increase the leaf's intake of moisture, and prevent excessive loss through transpiration.

Gloxinia leaves, when inserted in sand, form tubers at the base of the stem. When dried and rested for a while, they can be planted like ordinary tubers. Hyacinth leaves placed in wet sand often develop bulblets at their base.

HARDWOOD CUTTINGS: Nearly all soft and loose wooded plants grow readily from hardwood cuttings. These cuttings are generally used in propagating such soft-wooded trees as willows and poplars, and bushes such as gooseberries and currants.

Hardwood stem cuttings are made from the ripe wood of the past season's growth or older wood. The leaves may or may not be retained. If retained, they should be reduced in number and the cuttings handled in the same way as softwood cuttings. Many hardwood cuttings are made in the spring for spring planting, but many more are made in the fall and stored over winter. In late fall, after the leaves have fallen, the stems are cut to the desired length (usually three and one-half to eight inches), tied in bundles and buried, butt-ends upward, below the frost line in the soil. Or, they may be taken in winter and buried in sand or peat moss and kept moist and cool in a cellar. These fall and winter-made cuttings form good calluses (protective coverings of new cells on the cut surfaces), and therefore root more freely than hardwood cuttings made in spring.

When spring comes, the calloused hardwood cuttings are unearthed and planted, usually four to eight inches apart, in the rooting medium. Both root and stem development will be facilitated if the lower buds on the cutting are removed. Plants grown outdoors from such ripe or hardwood cuttings may be transplanted to nursery rows or to a permanent location after the first season.

Broad-leaf evergreen cuttings are not stored but planted directly after being prepared. All leaves except the one or two at the top of each cutting are removed and these leaves are reduced a half more by cutting with a knife or shears. The cuttings are then planted in the usual manner in the rooting medium.

Many narrow-leaf evergreen varieties are propagated by cuttings since they do not come true from seed. The cuttings, three to five inches long, are made in October (or later) of well-ripened wood and are not stored, but planted directly in flats of sand and kept in a cool, moist place. Most species root slowly, often remaining in the original flats a year or more. The usual practice is to trim off the needles with a sharp knife for two to three inches, none of the needles being buried in planting. Most hardwood cuttings take a longer time to root than do softwood cuttings.—*Barbara Hardy.*

See also LAYERING; DIVISION; PROPAGATION.

CUTWORMS: Dull gray, brown or

black larvae of various genera of noctuid (especially *Agrotis*) moths. They may be striped or spotted. They are stout, softbodied and smooth, up to one and one-fourth inches long, and curl up tightly when disturbed. Cutworms can be disastrous to plants, usually attacking young plants at ground level. For control, place a stiff three-inch cardboard collar around the stems, allowing it to extend about one inch into the soil; clear the stem by about a half inch. Another suggestion is to put a ring of wood ashes around the plants and soak the ashes. Keep down weeds and grasses on which the cutworm moth lays its eggs. Toads consume cutworms. *See also* INSECT CONTROL.

CYCLAMEN: Perennials that are popular as potted plants. Cyclamens can be kept in full bloom for many weeks if they are given proper care. Place them in an airy room where they will receive plenty of light without being subjected to the rays of the mid-day sun. The temperature should be as even as possible—anywhere from 42 to 55°F. The cooler, the longer will be the flowering season. The utmost care must be taken in watering the plants. Do not splash the foliage and flowers, but carefully pour the water on the soil and make sure that the center of the corm, where the new flower spikes are forming, is kept dry to prevent decay. Have the water at room temperature and apply enough each time to moisten the soil through and through. Never let the soil dry out completely. However, a continually soggy condition is as harmful as excessive dryness. Examine the saucer an hour after each watering and pour out any water that may have settled in it. Weak liquid plant food or organic fertilizer may be given once a week.

Flowers which have lost their attractiveness should be removed when

The cyclamen is almost equally at home indoors as in the garden outside. But great care must be exercised in moving them from one environment to the other. They need moderate moisture and some shade.

they begin to wilt—by pulling them loose at the corm, as any stumps left by cutting them off are likely to cause decay. Though you have been warned against watering foliage, a fine, dew-like spray applied to the tops once a week in the late forenoon of a bright day is decidedly beneficial. The spray should be so light that it will evaporate completely within an hour or so. While the plants must be kept free from drafts, they must be doubly guarded against cold air currents while the foliage is moist. An occasional careful sponging of the leaves may be needed where dust is likely to clog the pores of the leaves.

After a prolonged flowering season the plants will show by the yellowing of their leaves that they are ready for a resting period. When they show this sign, gradually withhold water until the soil is quite dry. In another week or two, the wilted leaves will pull off at the base without leaving any fleshy wound. Lightly dust the top of the corm with a little finely pulverized charcoal as an extra guard against decay. Lay the pots on their sides on the north side of the house or a solid fence where occasional rains will prevent complete drying out of the soil. The placing outdoors must not be attempted until all danger of frost has passed and the nights have become balmy. If the plants have been kept flowering indoors under proper conditions, they will have reached their dormant stage at the proper season. Four to eight weeks after having been placed outdoors, signs of new growth will be noticed in the center of the corm, and the pots should then be set up straight. Place a layer of cinders or coal ashes beneath the pots to prevent worms and insects from entering through the drainage hole in the bottom. Drying out of the soil must be carefully prevented through regular watering. As the plants increase in size, replanting to a size-larger pot is necessary. For potting use a special soil mixture composed of one-quarter garden soil, one-quarter rich compost soil, one-quarter moistened peat moss, and one-quarter fine sand. Add a cupful each of coarse bone meal, dried sheep manure, and finely pulverized lime to each bushel of soil. Mix well and have the material in a slightly moist condition for use. Place a crock over the drainage hole of each pot and fill with a little of the new soil. Transfer the plant from the old pot into the new one without disturbing the ball of earth, adhering to the roots. Carefully work some more soil around the old root ball. When all is finished, the top of the corm should be level with the rim of the pot, but the soil level must be about three-quarters of an inch below the rim to make watering easy. Keep moderately moist and shaded all during the summer and fall. When colder weather arrives in the fall, bring indoors again to a cool, airy room kept at from 42 to 55°.

A second method of storage may be followed by apartment dwellers not having a garden. Treat the plant in the same manner as outlined until the foliage has withered and shriveled so that it will come off at the base with just a touch. The pots must then be placed on their sides in a cool, dark room where the soil will not become bone dry. In July, August, or early September, the corms are taken up with care and freed carefully from the longest old roots. Each corm is then replanted into another pot large enough to permit an inch of space between the outside of the corm and the flower pot. Water and place in a light airy room with a temperature of from 45 to 55°. Keep moderately moist at all times. Transplant to a size-larger pot when the plant has reached a fair size, and otherwise treat it the same as already described. *See also* CHRISTMAS PLANTS; CUT FLOWERS; HOUSE PLANTS.

CYMBIDIUM: Among the most decorative of epiphytic orchids, cymbidiums produce flowers that last many weeks and with spikes often two to three feet long. They may be grown in a minimum temperature of about 50° during winter; the roots should never be dry, and the plants themselves should not receive strong sunlight after early spring. *See also* ORCHIDS.

CYNARA SCOLYMUS: *see* ARTICHOKE

CYNODON DACTYLON: *see* BERMUDA GRASS

CYPRESS VINE: *see* STAR GLORY

D

DAFFODIL: (*Narcissus*) Daffodils, as well as all of the hardy bulbs, require an interval of low temperature during their dormant period before they will flower properly. That is why they must be planted in the fall. Late September or the month of October is the best planting time for daffodils.

Types and forms of the daffodil are varied and many. They range through the double-flowered varieties and also include bicolor specimens.

Daffodils are hungry plants and thus fast growers. Before planting, spade the soil to about 12-18 inches and incorporate generous amounts of compost and well-rotted manure. Peat moss or leaf mold may be used generously in sandy soil, and heavy clay soils should be loosened by working in sand and humus material, such as compost. These bulbs are very intolerant of raw manure, so be sure it is well composted.

Set the bulbs about six inches deep and six to eight inches apart. Shallow planting results in dwarfed plants. It is better to plant a little deep than too shallow. Be sure to press the flattened base of the bulb firmly into contact with the soil beneath it. Air spaces will delay the formation of roots or may allow rotting of the bulb to take place. The roots must be well established before hard frost.

Most bulb plantings do not require a winter cover, but in areas where winters are severe it is wise to mulch with straw, leaves, grass clippings, or pine boughs. Remove the cover early in the spring so you'll let the small plants poking through have a breath of spring air. As with all the spring bulbs, let the foliage ripen naturally. They need to store energy for next year's array of bloom.

LOCATION: Scatter the bulbs at random and plant them where they fall. Of course they look lovely in more formal beds, too, but keep them in clumps or groups, not in rows. Once planted, daffodils may remain several years before you need to replant them. Be sure they get a top dressing of compost each year to insure a good display of flowers. When the plantings become too crowded and blooms are small, it is time to dig up the bulbs, separate them, enrich the soil, and replant.

VARIETIES: The type and forms available are varied and numerous. If you are interested in the double-flowered varieties, try planting Mary Copeland or Twink. Some of the single-flowered varieties are King Alfred, Golden Harvest and Carlton. There are also bicolor varieties which are very attractive, such as Spring Glóry, Lovenest, and Dick Wellhand. —*Barbara Hardy*.

See also BULB GARDEN; NARCISSUS; BULBS, FORCING; FERTILIZER.

DAHLIA: A tuberous genus of the *Compositae* family. Dahlias have become as popular an annual as they are a perennial. They can be grown from seed as an annual or can be grown from tubers as perennials.

Modern dahlias offer a vast range of colors and forms which can give a striking yet harmonious picture in any garden.

Small dahlias can be grown as annuals and can, in a single season, produce masses of vividly colored single and double flowers from seeds.

CULTURE: Dahlias do well in different soils, but seem to do best in one that is light with enough loam to retain moisture and fertility and plenty of sand for good drainage. Select a location sheltered from the wind and where the plants will receive the sun's direct rays at least four to six hours each day.

Plant tubers outdoors in the spring after the soil has become quite warm. In most sections of the country May and early June are preferred planting dates. Allow four feet of space each way between the large flowering varieties and about three feet between the pompons. If soil is sandy, dig a hole six inches deep, for heavier soil four inches is enough. Make the hole wide enough so that the tuber can be placed in it in a horizontal position. Never place the root on end. If the soil is dry at planting time, it must be well watered after which the roots should be covered with two inches of fine soil, filling in the remainder of the soil as the plant grows.

Many people do not realize the small dahlias can be grown as annuals and that in one season from seed, they can easily produce masses of brilliantly-colored single and double flowers of many forms in a wide range of colors. These small dahlias make excellent cut flowers. Plant seed within a week or two of the last frost. The seed will not germinate well if the weather is cool, but do not delay planting too long or you will also delay flowering. Sow seed in the garden by putting three or four seeds in spaces 12 inches apart. When the seeds germinate, thin leaving just one plant in each position. Seed may be started indoors and plants transplanted when there is no danger of frost. Choice plants from these seeds can be dug in the fall and tubers saved for next year.

PINCHING AND DISBUDDING: Dahlias should grow and branch naturally. However one main stem is likely to branch and provide enough of the best quality flowers. When additional sprouts come from the root they should be eliminated. Pinching and disbudding are correlated and controversial problems. One method is to pinch out the top to two pairs of leaves as soon as four pairs are formed and allow three or four stalks to develop. The first tie to the stake will be necessary when the stems are ten to 12 inches high. Use a soft but strong string—binder twine is good—tying tightly to the stake and loosely around the plant. Further support should be given to every 18 inches of growth.

Disbudding should be begun July 10-20. Best flowers result when side branches and flower buds are removed, leaving only the strongest terminal bud and perhaps a branch at the lower end of the stem. Never disbud every branch of a plant at one time, but stagger the operation by stretching it over two or three weeks.

MULCHING: Dahlias enjoy an even temperature at the roots. Baking of the top soil by the sun is detrimental to good growth. Weeds will be kept in check by maintaining a mulch to a depth of three inches. Water will only be necessary in extended dry spells. A thorough soaking, down as far as roots reach, is important. As soon as terminal buds are set, give each plant about three gallons of diluted cow manure, applied when the soil is wet.

FALL CARE: After the tops are killed by the first heavy frost, the clumps should be dug. Cut the tops off an inch or two above the ground level. Loosen the soil all around and under the clumps so that it may be lifted without breaking off any of the tubers. A tuber with a broken neck is useless for planting again and should be discarded.

Cut the stalk about two inches from the crown; let the clump dry in the sun and air for a few days. Place under cover for continued drying. There is no need to remove any adhering soil as this will help to keep the roots plump. Spread a two inch layer of dry sand in the bottom of a box. Place the roots on top; then fill in around clumps and over them with the same material until there is at least a three inch covering over all. Store boxes in a cool but frost-proof cellar. Examine roots from time to time and if there is any indication of shriveling, place clumps in moist peat moss or between layers of wet newspapers for a few days to restore moisture. Repack as before.

Two or three weeks before your outdoor planting time, put the roots on damp paper, moss, sand or soil in a light position. If no shoots appear, sprinkle every day with water to encourage the eyes to swell. Separate the clumps so that a piece of the crown has an eye on each one. A root without an eye will not grow.

VARIETIES: There are several types of dahlia roots to choose from. There are the formal and informal decorative dahlias, the Cactus Dahlias and Pompon Dahlias, and they come in a wide range of colors.

The popular varieties planted from seed are *Unwin Dwarf Hybrid, Coltness Hybrid, Zulu,* and *Mignon Mixed.*

FERTILIZERS: Bone meal is valuable for its phosphorus compounds and can be recommended as safe and effective. While most soils are rated as well supplied with potash, it has been found that applications of unleached wood ashes bring a healthier, more vigorous growth. Five pounds of raw bone meal mixed with ten of wood ashes may be raked deeply into the surface after spring spading or plowing.

Dahlias thrive best when surface-fed, after making a sound start. The middle of August is a good time to start top-dressing with two pounds of raw bone meal mixed with five pounds of wood ashes. *See also* FERTILIZER; PERENNIALS.

DAISY: Common term for members of the *Compositae* family of flowers. Originally, the only daisy was the *Bellis perennis*—the English daisy of literature and poetry fame. Today, the term has come to be applied to many other plants, including the chrysanthemum, arctotis, aster, rudbeckia, and townsendia.

Some daisies are favorites in the garden, while others are perennial weeds, such as the whiteweed (*Chrysanthemum leucanthemum*).

Long-time favorites as border and edging plants, daisies do best in cool, moist location. The true English daisy—with its yellow center—is a low perennial, often grown as an annual. Plant in rich soil about six inches apart; mulch in winter lightly. Grows three to six inches high.

DALEA: Relatively little-known perennials with white flowers that change to purple. They are mostly grown on the dry soils of prairie lands—sometimes being used as border plants.

DAMPING-OFF: Damping-off is a name given by gardeners to the wilting and early death of young seedlings usually soon after they emerge from the soil. The fungus attacks the seedlings at the ground line and causes them to break over at that point.

Damping-off may be caused by different organisms which live in or near the surface of the soil. Conditions which favor damping-off are: (1) crowding of seedlings due to sowing the seeds too freely, (2) high humidity, and (3) lack of sufficient aeration. Remedial measures consist in proper ventilation, drying off the soil in which the seedlings are growing and sprinkling on the soil powdered charcoal or finely pulverized clay which has been heated in an oven.

Damping-off can be prevented by providing seed flat with proper drainage, sowing the seeds in a mixture of compost and sand (equal parts), covering the seeds with pulverized, heated clay, keeping the young seedlings in a well-ventilated, well-lighted, cool place so that the tissues of the stem become well differentiated.

DANDELION: (*Taraxacum officinale*) A well-known and troublesome perennial weed, occurring abundantly al-

While the dandelion is frequently rated a nuisance, it is actually quite valuable because of the medicinal and vitamin value of its roots.

most everywhere in this country except in the Southern States. The root is used in medicine. Valued for salads, dandelions grow well in any good soil. The seed is planted in spring in rows 18 inches apart and covered ½ inch deep. The seedlings are thinned to stand one foot apart in the row, and the crop is well cultivated, and kept free from weeds. The roots are dug in the fall of the second season. They are washed and dried whole, or cut into pieces three to six inches long and the larger portions sliced. A serious objection to growing this crop is the danger of seeding adjacent land with an undesirable weed. Best control is digging out and cultivating regularly. *See also* LAWN; WEEDS.

DAPHNE: Flowering shrub "sometimes evergreen" of the *Thymelaeaceae* family. This genus offers some beautiful, outstanding early-flowering and fragrant shrubs. Most varieties grow no taller than four feet; the Daphne is very popular in landscaping schemes, perhaps even more so because it is resistant to diseases and insects, though less resistant to hot, dry, sunny conditions. Hard winters pose no problem for the hardy shrub, and in spring little sunshine and nourishment is needed. The red berries, ripening in July, attract birds and other wildlife. Berries of the white-flowering variety are yellow.

SOIL: Daphne often grows wild, nearly always near water and in low places. From this observation, it can be seen that Daphne should be planted in a partial, if not wholly shady place, in a gravelly and well-drained soil which retains moisture because of a mixture of clay and humus. A high water table in summer will also help to keep the leaves green and fresh appearing. Seeds collected in summer and sown then, will germinate without trouble the following spring.

ROSE DAPHNE: The rose daphne (*D. cneorum*), sometimes known as the garland flower, is one of the best known varieties. It is a low, bushy, evergreen shrub which produces masses of rosy colored flowers in May. Propagation is easily accomplished through cuttings taken in mid-autumn, or simply by layering trailing branches or by mound-layering the ascending stems.

DARLINGTONIA: Often referred to as the Cobra Orchid ("the plant that catches insects"), and as the *Chrysamphora,* darlingtonias normally reach a height of between one and three feet. The plant can be described as a group of slender, erect, tubular leaves starting narrow at the base but wind-

The darlingtonia is an insect catcher unknown to many gardeners. With care they can be propagated from seed or plants started by division.

ing up with a broad, rounded, hooded, membranous, spotted top which, to all intents and purposes, does look like the head of a cobra.

Underneath this hooded head is a rounded opening or small mouth about three-quarters of an inch in diameter, and hanging from this mouth is a pair of tentacles similar to a moustache

of vivid, streaked, spotted reddish color. Each tentacle is about three inches long. They sit at the entrance to the mouth and move with the slightest breeze.

When the plant is more or less mature, this appendage has a bright reddish color and gets redder with age. It seems to attract insects by its shimmering, iridescent glow and perhaps by some odor.

Insects in large numbers do enter the opening and once they are in, the inner part of the smooth globe-like head affords no foothold whatsoever on which the insects can walk or climb —and thus only descent is possible. The walls of the tube of the plant contain very fine hairs, all running one way. It is very easy to go in and to descend via these hairs but it is absolutely impossible to get out by the same means.

The diameter of the tube or leaf varies from approximately ½ inch at the base where it comes up out of the root to as much as four inches where the curve of the head or hood takes place. The plant forms these pitchers newly every year. The base or the root is perennial.

The average plant will run from five to nine leaves or pitchers. Some are small, some medium-sized and some are quite large. (*C. californica,* known as the California pitcher-plant, grows in an acid moss with a pH of five or lower and needs a great deal of water.)

When growing Darlingtonias, sow seeds on fresh sphagnum moss that has been carefully prepared and levelled. Beneath should be a mixture of sharp sand and peat. This seed-starting medium should be set where it will be partly in water all the time. It is important that this be maintained at a cool, moist, even temperature—at 50 to 60° for best results. If you added a bit of finely ground charcoal to your medium, you might prevent souring of the soil.

Starting Darlingtonias is not easy.

The safest means in under a belljar or glass. The seed is not hard-coated but soft and fluffy, and germination should take place in 14 to 21 days.

Keep them away from the direct sun and simulate their native habitat as much as possible. The optimum time for starting seed is the months of April and May.

Plants can also be started from divisions or side-shoots inserted in small pots at almost any time of the year. For plants growing or even an older plant that's established, daily syringing is practically a must from March till September because it does want lots of moisture.—*John Tobe.* See also CARNIVOROUS PLANTS.

DATE: (*Phoenix dactylifera*) Dates have furnished mankind with a delicious food from the dawn of the world, but it is only just recently that their full nutritional value has been determined.

Of 15 different varieties grown in Arizona, all were found to contain measurable quantities of Vitamin A, B_1 and B_2. For years, people have perhaps thought of this fruit merely as a dessert item—a desirable sweet— and have given little thought to its high nutritive qualities: 80 per cent sugar, three per cent fat, three per cent protein, together with mineral salts and vitamins, all of which add to its delectability and its food value.

CULTURE: The date palm can be grown anywhere in these United States where there is a hot, long-growing, frost-free season, moderate winter temperatures and a low atmospheric humidity during the blossoming and ripening period. California leads in date production, with Arizona and Texas next so, obviously, certain sections of the Southwest are particularly adaptable for the growing of this fruit. While the date probably originated in the Mediterranean countries, we can grow an equally good product here.

In America, we make a practice of planting date palms usually 30 feet apart, as their beautiful fronds take up much space while their feeder roots grow until they are interlaced to a considerable depth all through the soil.

In California, Arizona and Texas, it is the custom to bury the dead fronds and fruit stems from the previous season's growth in deep furrows between each row where they soon become part of the soil. Fertilizer can be spread over the surface of the date garden and then disced under. A heavy crop of clover, cow peas, or some similar green fertilizer plant can follow. The cover crops are then normally turned under during May or June.

The date enjoys a high nutritional rating, the equal of wheat or corn flour. The tree requires a hot, long-growing, frost-free growing season.

Since the date palm must have its "head in the sun and its feet in the water," date gardens are irrigated regularly about every two weeks during the spring and from every ten to twelve days during the summer. During the ripening season the irrigation program is slowed down to about once a month. The heavy application of water during the growing season helps to make plant food available more quickly and develops a very high quality date.

The date palm, of which there are many varieties, is propagated by removing the young offshoots from the base of the palm and transplanting in orchard form after they have established a root system of their own. If a single date seed is planted, it may germinate, but the resulting plant may originate a new variety; seldom reproducing its kind. Of every stray seed so planted, the chances are 100,000 to 1 that it will produce a bearing date palm. Therefore, commercial growers can only obtain uniform plantings of a specific variety by planting offshoots.

The date palm is technically known as a dioecious tree, which means one tree bears male flowers, which supply the pollen, and another bears the female flowers, which develop into fruit. It is necessary to have both male and female trees in order to mature dates. The blooms are protected in a spathe appearing behind a leaf axis in the crown of the palm. As the bloom develops the spathe bursts open. Pollination must take place within the next four to six days. Bees, unfortunately, are not attracted to the fruit blossoms so workers must take care of this operation by hand as each fruit spathe bursts into bloom. One of the improvements made by American growers is that they can now regulate ripening, due to their improved methods in artificial pollination. Palms bloom over a period of about ten weeks.

The fruit develops through the long, hot summer months. When the dates reach the size of olives, they are thinned out. Each cluster is then covered with paper protectors to safeguard the fruit against rain or moisture; one drop of rain actually can ruin a 50 pound cluster of dates so, while the added work and expense of placing protective coverings lessens profits, it pays off in a full crop. In the fall when the dates ripen, they are really nuggets of concentrated sunshine. In full production, a mature date palm will yield an average of 200 pounds of dates a year, though exceptional trees may yield as much as 500 pounds.

Some varieties such as the Khadrawi are the earliest, ripening even in mid-August. The Deglet Noor dates begin to mature in early September and harvesting continues until January.

You can grow dates organically in your own back yard if you live where temperatures do not go below 20° for prolonged periods. The date is a sub-tropical tree and while it will grow in a very damp climate, it will not produce commercially under such climate conditions.—*Ruth Anderson.*

DATE PALM: *see* PALMS

DAYLILY: (*Hemerocallis*) Daylily is the term applied to lily-like plants whose flowers remain open but a day. The term, however, is applied most commonly to plants belonging to the genus *Hemerocallis,* which comprises about a half-dozen wild species of lily-like herbs occurring from Central Europe, through Asia to Japan; and some recently developed hybrids. The roots are somewhat fleshy and often occur in clusters or fascicles. Nearly all the leaves are basal, narrow, sword-shaped, and keeled, so that the leafless flower stems extend some distance above the leaves. It is interesting to recall at this point that the word *Hemerocallis* is a Greek word which means "beautiful for a day."

Daylilies are among the most valuable herbaceous perennials. They will adapt themselves to a greater variety of soil and climatic conditions than almost any other perennial. They are hardy, easy to grow, and free from disease. Their leaves are attractive, and they give us a long period of bloom by the daily succession of the flowers. By selecting suitable varieties, daylilies may be kept in bloom from spring to late summer. Daylilies have been made even more valuable and decorative by the many new hybrids that have been developed, particularly by Dr. A. B. Stout of the New York Botanical Garden.

Few perennials can equal daylilies for giving brilliant and abundant colors to the garden in the midsummer months of July and August. It is at this season that many gardens are sadly lacking in colors. Daylilies get along with almost no care regardless of wind or weather, but repay the gardener manyfold for any garden courtesies extended to them. They will succeed where many other flowers fail, and will give you a great profusion of flowers as large and as beautiful as the finest true lilies. It is not unusual for a plant to bear as many as 50 flowers. These beautiful flowers seem to be at their best when the heat and drought of July and August have parched the lawn and the spring-flowering perennials have long since disappeared from the scene.

Daylilies are special favorites of week-end gardeners because they thrive with a minimum amount of care. They definitely dislike heavy applications of fertilizers, preferring conditions as they find them in the ordinary garden. Even after the flowering season is ended and the flower stalks have been removed, the daylilies are decorative as the grassy green foliage makes attractive mounds of green. Although most of them lose their leaves in the fall, some tend to be evergreen and give promise through the winter of another summer made colorful with their blossoms.

SPECIES: A number of the species of daylilies deserve a high rank among garden plants. *H. flava*, commonly known as lemon daylily, is early flowering and the lemon-yellow flowers are odorous. Other yellow-flowered daylilies are *H. minor* which is small and has grass-like leaves, and *H. thunbergi*, which does not bloom until early July, thus extending the blooming period of the yellow varieties well into the summer.

The common roadside daylily with tawny-red flowers is *H. fulva,* which includes the well-known types such as Kwanso, Flore-Pleno, and Variegata. For the rock garden, the low-growing and dwarf types of *H. dumortieri* and *H. minor* are recommended.

HYBRIDS: With few exceptions the species of *Hemerocallis* briefly described above are surpassed by the new hybrids. Hundreds of seedlings of hybrid origin are being grown and selected. These provide the gardener with a wide diversity in types in respect to habits of growth, season of bloom, range in color of flowers, and in size of the flowers. It is possible to have daylilies in bloom in the garden from spring to fall. Most important of all is the wide range of flower colors from light yellow through golden, copper, bronze, salmon, red, maroon, to purple. Many flower colors are light-proof and storm-proof. The flowers of some of the new hybrids remain open evenings. Daylilies can be grown in practically all parts of the garden except in wet or swampy places and in dense shade. They are especially valuable for keeping the garden colorful in midsummer when so many gardens show a lack of color. In making selections of the new daylilies, the gardener should first visit a nursery and see the plants in bloom. This is especially advisable for the fulvous and red-colored daylilies which are now being introduced in large numbers.

CULTURE: Daylilies thrive in almost any soil, and may be grown in all climates from Panama to Alaska. They may be established in naturalistic plantings as on dry rocky slopes, banks of streams or ponds, or anywhere except in swampy land which is constantly saturated with water and in dense shade. They may be planted at almost anytime the ground is in condition for planting. An old plant may be divided into sections of convenient size having at least one bud of the crown and some roots. In the garden a planting of daylilies may be left undisturbed for several years. When the plants become crowded to such an extent that the central part of the crown is pushed up, it is time to take them up, divide them, and reset the divisions to grow into new plants. The separation of old plants pay big dividends, as the rejuvenated plants will be much more vigorous and beautiful. With reasonable care, daylilies may be transplanted at any time, but the best time for this is in early spring before the season's growth begins. Be sure that the ground level is not more than one inch above the crown.

Daylilies are excellent for creating garden pictures. Select those which will blend in with the other plants in any particular part of the garden. Also in grouping the daylilies, care must be taken to select varieties that will have harmonizing colors. *See also* FERTILIZER; LILY; PERENNIALS.

DECEMBER GARDEN OPERATIONS: *see* GARDEN CALENDAR

DEFICIENCIES, SOIL: Sick plants exhibit to the trained eye of the plant doctor certain symptoms which are characteristics of specific nutritional deficiencies. In fact, micronutrient deficiencies are best noted by observing "hunger signs" in plants. It takes time to learn the many hunger signs, but experienced growers and other experts can often pinpoint the deficiency at first glance . . . by an off-shading of a leaf, or the peculiar shape of the fruit. Plants have ways of "calling out for food," and with careful diagnosis many hunger symptoms can be corrected with the proper organic fertilizer.

NITROGEN DEFICIENCY: Nitrogen is especially important for vegetables of good quality since it is essential for the synthesis of natural proteins. Plenty of nitrogen gives a good normal deep-green color to foliage and stems. In general, a nitrogen deficiency is characterized by slow growth, slender fibrous stems, and foliage and stems that fade to yellow in color.

Tomatoes: Tomatoes deficient in nitrogen exhibit very slow growth at first. This is followed by the green of the leaves becoming lighter. This starts at the tip of the leaves at the top of the plant. The leaves remain small and thin, and the veins may become purple. The stems are stunted, brown, and die. Flower buds turn yellow and shed, and the yield is reduced.

Cucumbers: When deficient in nitrogen, cucumbers exhibit stunted growth. The green of the plant turns to a yellow color. Roots turn brown and die. Nitrogen deficiency is also what causes cucumbers to point at the blossom end. These market as low-grade produce.

Radishes: Radishes deficient in nitrogen are retarded in growth. The leaves are small, narrow, thin, and yellow in color. The stems are slender and weak. And the edible roots are small and imperfectly developed. They have a faded reddish color.

Corn: The most prominent symptom for corn that is deficient in nitrogen is the yellowish-green of the plants rather than the normal deep-green color.

While these are specific examples they indicate the general symptoms exhibited by most vegetables for deficiencies in nitrogen.

TREATMENT FOR NITROGEN DEFICIENCY: Use compost or any organic fertilizer high in nitrogen. Some of the best products available commercially are bloodmeal (15% nitrogen), hoofmeal and horndust (12.5% nitrogen), and cottonseed meal (7% nitrogen). These products could be mixed with compost in ample quantities and applied to the soil in fall, or in very early spring.

PHOSPHORUS DEFICIENCY: In general, plants which are deficient in phosphorus are slowed in growth. The underside of leaves assumes a reddish-

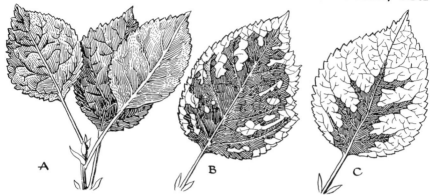

A: Yellow-green apple leaves show a nitrogen deficiency. B: Scorched leaves near twigs mean a severe potassium deficiency. C: A great lack of magnesium is manifested by heavy blotching near vein.

purple color, and the plants are slow to set fruit and mature.

Tomatoes: A phosphorus deficiency causes a reddish-purple color to develop on the underside of leaves, and the whole foliage eventually assumes a purplish tinge. The leaves are small, and the stems are slender and fibrous. The plants are late in setting fruit.

Radishes: The leaves of radishes deficient in phosphorus may be a reddish-purple on the underside.

Celery: Celery deficient in phosphorus exhibits poor root development and slender stalks.

Corn: Corn deficient in phosphorus has a yellowing of leaves similar to nitrogen starvation. After the ears set with kernels, check them to see if all the rows are filled, and if the stalk becomes brown, the inner portion grayish-green, and finally bronzed.

POTASSIUM DEFICIENCY: *Cucumber*: Leaves of cucumbers deficient in potassium exhibit a bronzing and dying of the leaf margin. The fruit has an enlarged tip. This is just the opposite symptom of nitrogen starvation where the fruit has a pointed tip.

Radishes: Radishes which are deficient in potassium have leaves which are dark-green in the center while the edges curl and become pale yellow to brown. Extreme deficiency is indicated by deep yellow color of leaves and stems. The leaves may become thick and leathery. The roots are more bulbous than normal.

Beets: Beets deficient in potassium develop long tapered roots rather than the preferred bulbous type.

TREATMENT FOR POTASSIUM DEFICIENCY: By placing six inches of green matter to every two inches of stable manure in your compost heap, you supply adequate amounts of potassium for gardening purposes. Once the moisture of green plants is eliminated and the material is broken down, a great percentage of the solids consists of potassium. If your soil is particularly low in potassium, add potash rock, granite dust, wood ash, or some other potassium-rich organic material to the compost—or apply these materials directly to the soil.

Heavy mulching also seems to help maintain the potassium supply. At Purdue University, Clarence E. Baker found that mulching with manure, straw, and soybean hay eliminated symptoms of potassium deficiency in a peach orchard. Check trees, which received no mulch, did not recover.

CALCIUM DEFICIENCY: In general, plants exhibiting calcium deficiency are retarded in growth and develop thick woody stems.

Tomatoes: The upper leaves appear yellow in color. This distinguishes the deficiency from that of nitrogen, phosphorus, or potassium where the

A: Peach leaves with a potassium deficiency show it by curling and spotting. B: A phosporus-potassium deficiency gives added curling and spotting. C: A lack of calcium kills tissues of mature leaf.

lower portion of the plant has discolored leaves while the upper leaves and stem remain more or less normal. The plants are weak and flabby and lacking in firmness. The terminal buds die and the nearby stem becomes spotted with dead areas. The roots are short and brown in color.

Peas: Red patches appear on the leaves near the center and spread out. The healthy green of the leaves changes to a pale green, then white. Growth is slow and the plants are dwarfed.

Corn: Corn deficient in calcium exhibits the most startling symptom of all plants. The tip ends of the leaves are stuck together as if they had been glued.

TREATMENT FOR CALCIUM DEFICIENCY: Use any good grade of ground natural limestone. About 60-mesh is a good grind.

MAGNESIUM DEFICIENCY: Magnesium deficiency is widespread. Plants deficient in magnesium are, in general, late to mature, and do not mature uniformly. They have poor market quality. They exhibit a characteristic lack of green color with the lower leaves being affected first. The areas between the leaf veins turn yellow, then brown, while the veins remain green.

Tomatoes: Tomatoes deficient in magnesium have brittle leaves which

curl up. A yellow color develops in the leaves. This is deepest further from the vein. The older leaves of mature plants are the ones which most commonly show the symptoms. There is little effect to be observed on stems or fruit.

Cabbage: Mottled light-colored spots appear on the leaves of cabbage deficient in magnesium. The lower leaves pucker. The edge of the leaves may turn white or very pale yellow. These may turn brown and die. If only magnesium is deficient, the entire leaf becomes mottled with dead areas. If nitrogen is also deficient the entire leaf turns a light-green color, then yellow, and finally develops a mottling of dead areas. Potassium deficiency, which is sometimes confused with lack of magnesium, can be distinguished by the bronzing which occurs before the dead areas appear.

Turnips: The leaves of turnips deficient in magnesium develop brown areas around the rim. These dry up and drop out. The inner areas are mottled with light-colored spots.

Carrots, cucumbers, squash and *lima beans*: These show the typical characteristics of mottling and then browning of foliage.

Corn: Magnesium deficiency is very easy to tell in corn plants since they develop a yellow striping or white streaks only on the older leaves.

TREATMENT FOR MAGNESIUM DEFICIENCY: If obtainable, add a quart of sea water to each 100 pounds of compost. Or, use dolomite limestone since this contains quite a bit of magnesium.

BORON DEFICIENCY: A deficiency of boron in plants causes plants to grow more slowly. Severe deficiency causes crop failures since plants die. Unlike the other nutrient elements which produce general changes in most truck crops, boron deficiency produces more specific changes in different vegetables. Beets and turnips develop cork-like areas in the edible root, and a hollow stem develops in cauliflower, while celery cracks. The leaves may be stunted and twisted with dark spots on the tips of young leaves which grow larger as the leaves mature.

Celery: Celery deficient in boron develops a brownish mottling of the leaf. The stems become brittle and have brown stripes. Crosswise cracks appear in the stem, and the tissue curls back and turns brown. Roots turn brown and die.

Beets, turnips, and other *root crops*: These, when affected by boron deficiency, develop what is commonly known as brown-heart disease. Dark-brown water-soaked areas appear in the center of the roots. Sometimes a hollow, discolored center results. The roots do not grow to full size and may have a rough, unhealthy, grayish appearance. The surface may be wrinkled or cracked. The plants are stunted, the leaves smaller, twisted and less numerous than normal. Leaves sometimes develop yellow and purplish-red blotches, and the stalks may show splitting.

Tomatoes: Blackened areas appear at the growing point of the stem, and stems are stunted, and terminal shoots curl, then turn yellow and die. The plants have a bushy appearance, and the fruit may have darkened or dried areas.

Lettuce: Lettuce deficient in boron exhibits malformation of the more rapidly growing leaves, and spotting and burning of leaves.

Cauliflower: Deficiencies of boron cause discolored, water-soaked areas in the stem of the cauliflower. These may spread. The leaves around the curd may be stunted and deformed.

IRON DEFICIENCY: Iron deficiency in plants is characterized by spotted, colorless areas developing on young leaves. Yellow leaves appear on the upper parts of the plants. The growth of new shoots is affected and plant tissues may die if the deficiency is severe. Too much lime causes iron deficiency to develop.

TREATMENT FOR IRON DEFICIENCY: Plenty of manure and crop residues, dried blood and tankage are the best methods for correcting iron deficiency.

COPPER DEFICIENCY: Copper deficiency is usually confined to peat or muck soils. Plants deficient in copper exhibit slow growth or complete cessation of growth. Leaves become bleached-looking, and leaves and stems are flabby. Normal bright color is lacking.

Tomatoes: Tomatoes deficient in copper have stunted shoot growth, and very poor root development. The foliage may be a bluish-green, and the leaves curled. There is an absence of flower formation, and leaves and stems are flabby.

Lettuce: Leaves become bleached-looking. The stems and the rim of the leaf are affected first.

Onions: Onions which are deficient in copper have an abnormally thin scale which is pale yellow in color rather than the usual brilliant brown. Growth may be stunted or fail entirely.

ZINC DEFICIENCY: Zinc deficiency occurs often in peat soils. It is particularly characterized in plants by leaves which are abnormally long and narrow. The leaves may also turn yellow and be mottled with many dead areas.

Squash, mustard, tomatoes, beans:

These plants usually are the first to exhibit the typical symptoms of zinc deficiency as described above.

Corn: Corn deficient in zinc, exhibits older leaves which are dead, while yellow striping appears between the veins on the newer leaves.

TREATMENT FOR ZINC DEFICIENCY: Use plenty of manure.

MANGANESE DEFICIENCY: Plants deficient in manganese are slow to grow, and mature late and unevenly. The areas between the veins of leaves become yellow, then brown, while the veins remain green.

Tomatoes: Leaves have a typical lightening of green color which gradually turns to yellow farthest from the major veins. Dead areas appear in the center of the yellow areas and spread. Growth is stunted, and there are few blossoms and no fruit.

Spinach: Spinach deficient in manganese exhibits a loss of color at the growing tips. This spreads in towards the center of the plant. The normal green color gradually changes to a golden yellow. White, dead areas eventually appear.

Beets: The leaf takes on a deep red to purple color which gradually becomes yellow. Dead areas finally appear between the veins. The growth of roots and tips is stunted.

Snap beans: Whole leaves turn a golden yellow and small brown spots appear between the veins.

Cucumbers, cabbage, peppers: These plants when deficient in manganese have small, slender and weak stems. The leaves turn yellowish white while the veins and midribs remain green. The blossom bud may turn yellow.

Although, at first glance it may appear somewhat difficult to diagnose the problem in a garden where the plants are sick, it is easy if you pick out one vegetable and concentrate on that. For example, if cucumbers are pointed at the end, then the soil is deficient in nitrogen. If cucumbers are narrow at the stem and bulging at the flower end, then the soil is deficient in potassium.

In general, it can be stated that plenty of manure, or good quality compost made with kitchen scraps and a wide variety of plant materials such as weeds, grass clippings, etc., will correct all soil deficiencies. Whenever there is doubt concerning the cause of sick-looking plants, it is recommended that heavy applications of manure or compost or both, be used. —*Charles Coleman.*

See also names of individual crops and elements; FERTILIZER; TRACE ELEMENTS; DISEASE.

DELPHINIUM: Delphinium is a genus of over 250 species of annual and perennial herbs of the buttercup family. This family is sometimes referred to as the crowfoot family, because the leaves of most species are three-lobed and thus have the general form of a crow's foot. The flowers are unusually showy and are generally borne on a long terminal cluster or spike which may be several feet in length. The annual species of this genus are commonly called *larkspur,* while the perennial species are referred to as delphiniums.

Delphiniums are widely distributed over the northern hemisphere, occurring from California, the Swiss Alps, Kashmir, Sikkim, Tibet and on to China. Although there are many species, only a few have played a part in the development of the modern garden delphinium, which is a hybrid. The exact parentage of this hybrid is not known, but *D. elatum* which has tall and stately stems bearing long spikes is believed to have played a leading role. The pioneer work in the development of the garden delphinium was done in England during the first quarter of this century.

Growing delphiniums from seed, an extremely fascinating garden chore, requires no special equipment. The seeds can be sown when gathered in early fall. Early sown seeds germinate better than those which have been stored for a time, as the seeds do not long retain their ability to germinate. For best results, sow the seeds in a mixture of two parts of garden loam and one part of sand, avoiding materials used for enriching the soil. Sow the seeds thickly in rows, and cover them with a fine soil, not deeper than twice the shortest dimension of the seeds. Then spread a damp cloth on

This Larkspur Giant Imperial variety of delphinium may be grown from seed and does not require any special garden equipment or technique.

the surface of the seed-bed or flat, and water thoroughly with a fine sprinkler, using only rain, spring, or well water. Good drainage is important. To insure this, coarse sphagnum moss should be placed in the bottom of the flats. Sphagnum moss may also be used, if finely screened, as a top dressing in the flat. When sphagnum is used, the seed-flats remain moist for a long time so that watering need not be done often. If for any reason seeds cannot be planted immediately after they are gathered, they should be sealed in an air-tight enclosure and kept at a temperature of about 50° F.

To prevent slugs and snails from feeding on the delphinium seedlings, place the flat on inverted flower pots which are surrounded with ashes. The seedlings will lose most, if not all, their leaves and the small crown will remain dormant until the arrival of warm weather in spring. When growth is resumed, the seedlings should be transplanted into other boxes with three-inch spaces between adjacent plants. They will be ready to be planted out in the border or into the nursery beds for subsequent removal to the herbaceous border. Many seedlings transplanted in spring will bloom during the late summer and early autumn, but it is not until the second year that they will attain their full stature and their real quality will become apparent.

GROWING FROM CUTTINGS: Since all garden delphiniums are highly hybrid, particular varieties can be kept true to type only by asexual propagation by cuttings. The best cuttings consist of young shoots severed from the crown of the plant in the spring. These cuttings should be taken when about three inches long, taking care to get the heel of the cutting by making the incision close to the rootstock. As a rooting medium, use clean sand or vermiculite. Try to maintain an even temperature, but a very high temperature must be avoided. Rooting requires from four to eight weeks. Rooted cuttings should be transplanted in much the same way as seedlings.

Plants may also be propagated asexually by division. This is best done in spring when the growths are from three to four inches high. Lift the old plant from the ground, remove all old and decayed parts, and divide the plant into a number of parts, each having one or two strong crowns and an ample supply of healthy roots. In replanting, it is advisable to prepare the soil well with compost and pulverized phosphate and potash rocks.

TRANSPLANTING AND PLANTING: Seedlings from spring-sown seeds should be transplanted after they get their first true leaves. Within from one to two weeks, the seedlings will be up. Remove the cloth or other material that was placed on the soil when the seeds were sown. Remove the seedling-flat to a cool, sunny place. Transplant the seedlings to deeper flats or in the cold frame. One purpose of transplanting is to encourage root development. In dry weather, a mulch of leafmold or peat moss around newly transplanted seedlings will insure a sufficient supply of moisture.

The time to plant will be determined largely by suitable conditions, but plantings should be completed by the end of October so that the plants will be well established before winter. Plants can be set in soils rich in humus at almost any time. It is well to prepare the soil carefully, as delphiniums are voracious feeders. Delphiniums are definitely partial to well-fermented composts, and abhor chemical fertilizers. A liberal application of phosphate rock and potash rock is a good investment and will pay large dividends in healthy plants and superior flower spikes.

In setting the plants in the garden, the crown should be just above the level of the ground, which should be mounded so that water will not collect around the crown. The distances between plants will be determined somewhat by the purpose for which they are grown. In the herbaceous border, plants should be set from 18 to 24 inches apart. If planted for exhibition purposes, they should be set from two to three feet apart.

Delphiniums are most effective in the border when planted in groups of three or more plants, the number varying with the width of the border. In very narrow borders, they may have to be planted singly. For the first year after planting it will be well to limit the number of spikes to not more than three. When a foot or so high, the thinnest spikes should be cut out so that the three strongest ones remain to develop further. At this time the growing spikes should be supported by suitable stakes. Supporting the plants is an important operation, and it is best done by placing three stakes per plant and tying around them, thus leaving the plant free to move within the stakes and tie. At this period a good application of compost will benefit the plants considerably, sprinkling it on the ground and then covering it with a mulch of shredded plant materials. The mulch should be thin on heavy soils and correspondingly thicker on lighter soils.

If the first spikes are cut out as soon as they have finished blooming, secondary spikes will develop which will bloom for two or three weeks after the main spike.

WINTER CARE OF DELPHINIUMS: It is well to give delphiniums some winter protection, but be sure to use some loose material like straw, excelsior, or similar material. Before winter mulching, all dead foliage and the supporting stakes should be removed and the flowering spikes cut down to within a foot of the ground. From now on, the plants will develop their crown buds (eyes) for the following year's growth. Do not apply the winter mulch until the ground is hard-frozen, and remove it in early Spring before growth begins.

About every three years it is necessary to divide roots. This is an early spring job, just when the shoots are breaking through the ground. Dig plants carefully, wash dirt away, cut clumps into sections, each with plenty of fibrous roots and one strong stem. Plant immediately in well-prepared soil, setting plants so the crowns will be two inches below the surface. In most sections winter protection of older plants is not needed. In colder areas, a two-inch porous mulch over the crown provides excellent protection. *See also* FERTILIZER; PERENNIALS.

DEPARTMENT OF AGRICULTURE: see GOVERNMENT SERVICES

DEPTH OF PLANTING: see GERMINATION

DERRIS DUST: see ROTENONE

DESERT GARDEN: Great deserts cover one-third of the world's surface. But not all of them are barren wastes of heat and sand. The American Desert of the Southwest, stretching from California to Texas and north to Utah, boasts a multitude of plants of unsurpassed beauty.

The trend toward using these native plants for desert gardens is growing. Many nurserymen now carry stocks of them because gardeners are finding that, given their own environment, they need almost no care and make the loveliest gardens imaginable.

Even trees are not rare in the desert landscape. Few of them, however, look like the tree gardeners of more verdant climes are used to seeing. Some of them are cacti, like the giant saguaro that rises in towering pillars of primitive majesty. But the Joshua tree, growing 40 to 50 feet is the "tall timber" of the desert. Growing slowly, it lives for 200 years, brightening the desert with its panicles of rich white blossoms.

The smaller trees include the ironwood, with its fragrant purple blooms that bring the June bees from far and wide, and the desert willow that boasts a profusion of crimson flower trumpets. The Jerusalem thorn or the brilliant yellow palo verde are other favorites, especially in the higher altitudes. A lesser-known tree is the coral, which has cylindrical scarlet flowers which appear before the leaves, making it look like they are blooming on dead branches.

Flowering plants of all sizes, shapes and colors abound in the desert. Yucca of a dozen different varieties sends up its white blooms surrounded by the "bayonets" of its green, needle-pointed leaves. Sometimes 500 buds can be found on one stem.

Golden yellow flowers tip the 15- to 20-feet high stalks of century plants that bloom once in 22 years. Orange-yellow poppies, desert marigolds, Jimson weeds, evening primroses make the desert floor a brilliant carpet of blossoming wild flowers every spring.

There is a shrub for every use, too. Senna has lovely gold flowers whose sweet scent is heightened by the sharp desert air. The silvery desert holly is now popular, and the dense-growing, broad goatnut with its leathery leaves and little pale tan pods is found increasingly around desert homes. The white blooms of the ragged rock flower and the cream and blue "Chinese Lantern" calyces of the paper-bag bush vie with the feathery pink-gray tails of the Apache plumes. Many gardeners prefer the creosote bush, called the "spirit of the wastelands" because it seems to shun the slightest trace of moisture. Five feet tall, it is sweet-scented and has pale gray seed puffs, black-banded bark and curved branches that can be pruned into arches or other garden shapes.

But it is the cacti on which Nature has lavished her fondest care. The grotesque shapes and ferocious spines of the tall organ pipe or the lowly hedgehog, the vicious cholla or the silken-haired Old Man, take on thrilling beauty when the plants burst into a riot of color after a rare desert shower. The gardener has over 2,000 varieties to choose from, and the study of cacti can become an all-absorbing hobby, as attested to by the more than 10,000 collectors in the United States.

Common names include the lobster claw, owl's eyes, Cuban baby, beaver tail, popcorn, boxing glove and rattlesnake. They can stand the toughest conditions.

One picturesque and very pointed example of the seemingly limitless variety offered by cacti is the Prickly Pear cactus. When the armored pad of this cactus, sometimes called "elephant ears," puts out its beautiful and fragile red flowers, friends of the desert know that it is spring. Belying the unapproachableness of the pad, the blossom is delicate and lovely.

Good drainage is essential, and planting—to be done any time from September to February in most areas —should include some humus mixed with gravel and the desert soil. Water well at the roots, then let the ground dry out completely. A loose, porous soil is best. A little bone meal, dried manure and compost once a year is all the feeding native desert plants require to be at their best. *See also* CACTUS; ARID SOIL.

DESIGN, GARDEN: *see* PLANNING GARDEN PLANTINGS; LANDSCAPING

DEUTZIA: These are graceful, spring-blooming shrubs with single or double flowers in white or pink. They are not very hardy and should not be planted north of Boston, in the East, unless protected. The loveliest is *D. gracilis,* also the smallest. The flowers are white, blooming in May, and the bark is a soft grayish-green. The bushes can be clipped and formed into round, compact balls, three feet wide, which are lovely as accent plants in either the herbaceous or shrubbery border. If potted and brought indoors in late fall, it can be forced into bloom without difficulty. Grows readily from soft wood cuttings in spring and attains a height of five to seven feet.

DEWBERRY: A form of blackberry. *See* BRAMBLE FRUITS

DIABASE: Diabase rock is equivalent to basalt and can be used in the same manner. Diabase and basalt vary from one deposit to the next and contain a relatively small amount of potash, but have usable quantities of iron, calcium, magnesium and trace elements. The average application for diabase dust should be around two tons to the acre every three or four years. *See also* BASALT.

DIANTHUS: Commonly known as pinks. Many of the plants of this group are important garden flowers. They are easily raised from seed and can be further increased by division, layerings, or cuttings. Keep a supply of young

Dianthus may be raised in the average garden, is tolerant of most soils and moderate in needs. It is best to increase the perennials by cuttings.

plants coming along, as many of the pinks die out if let alone over a period of two or three years. The grass pinks (*D. plumarius*) have delicate white and pink flowers with fragrant tufted foliage; Maiden pinks (*D. deltoides*) form dense mats of foliage with tiny blossoms in white, pink, and red; Sweet William (*D. barbatus*) is a biennial with many named forms— two of the best are Newport Pink and Sutton's Scarlet. Grows one to two feet; usually blooms in spring. Dianthus also includes the carnation(*D. caryophyllus*). *See also* BORDERS; CARNATION.

DICENTRA SPECTABILIS: *see* BLEED-ING HEART

DICHONDRA: *see* GROUNDCOVERS; LAWN

DICTAMNUS ALBUS: *see* FRAXINELLA

DIEFFENBACHIA: Low, shrubby perennials, Dieffenbachia are popular greenhouse plants because of their attractive foliage. Members of the Araceae family, they grow best in a light potting mixture, prefer a temperature between 70° and 80°, much moisture, and a partially shaded location. Except for the extra-large leaved plants as *D. triumphans* and *D. nobilis,* usually three or four plants can be placed in a single large pot. Fertilizing with liquid manure has been found effective. Propagating can be done by placing cut sections in moist sand.

DIGESTER: *see* COMPOST; EARP, THOMAS, DR. G. H.

DIGGING, NECESSITY OF: *see* CULTIVATION; NO-DIGGING METHOD; MULCH

DIGITALIS: (*Digitalis purpurea*) Digitalis, also known as foxglove, a fairly hardy European biennial or perennial, has long been grown as an ornamental in flower gardens in this country. In addition to being an important medicinal plant, digitalis is one of the handsomest garden herbs. Digitalis leaves and their products are heart-ailment medicines, and no satisfactory substitute for them has been introduced. The numerous horticultural forms developed differ principally in the size and color of the flowers. All are known to be medicinally potent, and their leaves are therefore acceptable for drug purposes. The species also grows wild in the general region of the coast ranges of mountains in the northern Pacific Coast States.

The plant thrives in ordinary well-drained soils of open texture and reasonable fertility. Propagation is by seed. Direct field sowing is not usually successful, because the seed is exceedingly small and does not germinate well except under favorable conditions. To facilitate even distribution it may be mixed with sand and sown early in February in flats in a greenhouse or in a hotbed. When danger of frost is over, the plants are hardened off and transplanted to the field about one foot apart in rows conveniently spaced for cultivation. They do not bloom until the second season. Mulching for winter protection is advisable where very low temperatures prevail. The plant is usually cultivated as an annual or biennial crop although it also grows sometimes as a perennial.

The digitalis flowers in long, racemic, one-sided clusters of showy purples, yellows or white.

DILL (*Anethum graveolens*) An annual or biennial plant often grown in gardens for the herb and seeds (fruits), which are used for flavoring foods and pickles. It is grown as a commercial crop in the North Central States, where it is used by pickle manufacturers. The volatile oil, which may be distilled from the same material, is now to some extent replacing the dill herb, and limited acreages of dill are being grown for oil production. Some years ago the oil was produced mainly in Indiana, but at present Oregon is the principal source.

Although a native of southern Europe, dill will grow well in a much cooler climate. On fertile loam soil it will grow to a height of three or four feet and makes a good seed crop in the Northern and North Pacific Coast States. If planted early in spring, dill will produce seed the same season, but, if conditions do not permit prompt germination and rapid early growth, the plants may not reach full development and will produce only a small seed crop. Good results have been obtained by late fall sowing so the seed can germinate as soon in spring as conditions become favorable. The

Dill has long been a favorite herb with house-wives and gardeners. A late fall sowing permits early spring germination and a good fall harvest.

seed is drilled in rows usually one to three feet apart, depending on the method of cultivation to be followed for weed control. The plants must be thinned when about three inches high, and the distance between plants in the row may vary from six to 15 inches. A better seed crop will be obtained if the plants are not too crowded.

The progressive ripening of the seed and the tendency of fully ripe seed to shatter present the same difficulties in harvesting as in other aromatic seed crops. The best practice seems to be to mow the plants when the earliest seed is ripe. In very dry weather this is preferably done early in the morning when the plants are damp with dew. In the garden, it grows to about three feet high, has yellow flowers; sow in spring after last frost. *See also* HERBS.

DISBUD: In the cultivation of several flowers, especially roses, peonies and dahlias, disbudding means cutting or pinching off the side buds when these first appear, in order to allow all the strength to go to the terminal or main bud so that a larger flower is produced.

DISEASE: A plant disease may be defined as any abnormality in a plant produced by some causative agent. The causative agent may be a bacterium, a fungus, or other parasitic organism; or it may be some unfavorable environmental condition as, for instance, a deficiency of one or more of the elements which are necessary for the normal growth and development of plants.

A living organism which causes a disease in plants is usually referred to as a *pathogene*. Pathogenes belong to the groups of bacteria, fungi, viruses, slime molds, and some animals, such as nematodes. Some of these, like the powdery mildews, are external parasites but send absorbing organs into the tissues of the plant on which they live. The plant from which a parasite takes its food is known as its *host*. Some parasites live on a single host, like grape mildew, while others live on two or more different kinds of host plants, like the wheat-rust fungus which lives alternately on wheat and the American barberry.

The successful establishment of a parasite on its host is called *infection*. The infection of plants of a garden or field from an outside source is known as *primary infection*. The spreading of the disease from one plant to another in the same garden is known as *secondary infection*. Many diseases can be controlled by preventing secondary infection. This can be done by eliminating all diseased plants as a result of primary infection.

Most plant diseases are caused by parasitic fungi. Effective control involves the creation of conditions in plants which will be unfavorable to the growth of these parasitic fungi. Plants which are nutritionally well balanced are, as a rule, healthy and relatively free from the common plant diseases. To have such plants in the garden consideration must be given to (1) well-adapted varieties, (2) a well-prepared soil rich in humus and the essential elements, and (3) cultural practices.

Plants are covered with an effective, often disease-resistant epidermis. It is only after the epidermis has been broken that disease-producing fungi and bacteria can gain an entrance into the plant. Even slight damage is sufficient to make a plant vulnerable to these fungi, as brushing against and breaking off a few epidermis hairs of a squash leaf. Who knows how many diseased plants are the result of slight injuries to plants in the cultivating and hoeing processes? Such injuries not only provide an entrance for disease-producing organisms but lower the vitality of the plant to the point where it cannot resist the parasite.

Signs and Symptoms of Diseases Produced by Pathogenes: Every part of a plant—root, stem, leaf, flower, bark, wood, seed—is subject to disease, and the same disease may manifest itself in many or all parts of the plant body. Those marks or evidences which indicate a diseased condition in a plant are known as the *signs* and *symptoms* of the disease. The most common signs of disease are (1) a dying of the tissue (necrosis), resulting in such conditions as rot, canker, blight, wilt, damping-off, spot, streak, burn, and shot hole; (2) an overgrowth of tissues (hyperplasia), resulting in such abnormal growths as witches'-broom, galls, hairy root, curl, and scab; and (3) an undergrowth of tissues to produce such conditions as dwarfing and chlorosis (incomplete development of the leaf pigments).

How to Recognize Diseases:

1. *Seedlings fail to come up; seedlings wilt, fall over and die soon after coming up.* This is "damping off," a disease caused by fungi in the soil that attack the seed and seedlings.

2. *Plants wilt or turn yellow and die before maturity.*

A. *Roots distorted with many small to large swellings or "knots."* This is "root knot" caused by microscopic worms called "nematodes." It is present in many soils and is one of the main reasons for the premature

Severe boron deficiency, as in the plant on the left, causes heart and dry rot of beets, and can completely ruin the crop.

dying of tomatoes, cowpeas, okra, root crops and melons in midsummer.

B. *Roots appear sound but the tissue just under the bark of stems and roots is discolored brown and abnormally wet.* This is one of the "wilt diseases," caused by fungi or bacteria in the soil. Wilt diseases occasionally become very destructive, especially on tomatoes, potatoes, cabbage, beans, cucumbers, cantaloupes, peas, watermelons, and sweet potatoes. Wilt-producing parasites live in the soil for years; but each parasite is restricted to one crop so that, as a rule, land that contains one type is safe for growing other vegetables. For example, the tomato wilt fungus attacks only tomatoes.

C. *Roots are dead and decayed.* This is a root rot disease, and affected roots have brown, hairy, fungus, threads on the surface.

In another type of root rot, the roots are usually blackened, with a foul-smelling decay. This is the result of excessive water in the soil, which kills the roots by excluding the air.

3. *Leaves, stems and fruits show numerous roundish, angular or irregularly shaped dead spots.* There are many of these "spot diseases," affecting various vegetable crops, caused by fungi or bacteria.

4. *A grayish-white mold or mildew covers the leaves.* This is "powdery mildew," a fungus disease particularly common on peas, cowpeas, and cucumbers. Severely affected leaves may turn yellow, dry up, and fall off; as a result, plants are usually stunted and yield poorly.

5. *Leaves are mottled with light and dark areas, curled or twisted, but not dying; plants are stunted and yield poorly.* This is "virus disease," a common type of what is called "mosaic." It especially affects beans, potatoes, tomatoes, cucumbers, and cowpeas.

ORGANIC PREVENTION OF PLANT DISEASES: In plant diseases, as in so many other matters, an ounce of prevention is worth a pound of cure.

Sanitation is of the utmost importance in the prevention of plant diseases. Diseased plant parts, including stems, leaves, and fruits, should be put in the compost heap to be converted into compost.

Crop rotation has been advised for the prevention and control of many plant diseases. If the same kinds of plants are grown in the same soil year after year, parasites are likely to accumulate to the point which makes growing this kind of plant unprofitable.

Rotation of crops and change of location are helpful in all cases and indispensable where root knot and root rots are concerned. Tomatoes, melons, okra and other summer growing crops should not be grown on the same land oftener than once in three years. The land should be devoted to other crops like corn, grains, and early vegetables that are harvested by June. After harvesting, the land should be kept free of weeds.

The small garden can be divided into thirds with summer vegetables susceptible to root diseases grown on a different plot each year.

A living soil, one rich in soil organisms, is usually one having a high organic-matter content and all the nutrient elements in good balance. Such a soil is the best kind of insurance against plant diseases. Tillage of the soil also is an important factor in the control of plant diseases, as it provides conditions favorable to a vigorous growth. Waksman and others have recently shown that in artificial media different bacteria and fungi manufacture substances of varying degrees of antibiotic activity to other bacteria and fungi. It is possible that antibiotics are produced in living soils which keep crop plants free from disease. It is a common observation in pot experiments that a great variety of diseases, such as the root rots of cereals, are more destructive in sterilized soil than in comparable non-sterilized soil, both being equally inoculated with the pathogenes. In such experiments, if bits of the original soil are introduced into the sterilized soil, the microflora is quickly re-established, the pathogene checked, and the disease controlled.

The physical condition of the soil has an important bearing on the prevention and control of diseases. Important are such factors as temperature, aeration, moisture, and soil reaction. Some disease-producing organisms attack their host plants in soils of certain temperatures, but not when soils have a different and, apparently for the pathogene, unfavorable temperature. For instance, yellows in crucifers caused by *Fusarium conglutinans* occurs in soils with a higher temperature but does not show up when the crucifers are grown in cooler soils. An entire tomato crop may be destroyed by wilt caused by Verticillium in wet soil, while the plants will be entirely immune when grown in a well-drained soil. It has long been recognized that potato scab is less prevalent in soils that have a reaction below 5.2 than in soils with a higher pH value. The pH value becomes less important as the humus content of the soil increases; the humus acts as an effective buffer in the soil. The physical factors of the soil and air are so interrelated when it comes to their possible effects on pathogenes that it is not easy to say just what effect each has separately.

Some Common-sense Measures: Use healthy plants. Many diseases start in young seedlings in greenhouses or plant beds and later cause heavy losses in gardens. One can rarely detect disease at transplanting time. If possible, grow your own plants, or at least purchase plants from a thoroughly reputable grower in whom you have complete confidence.

Eliminate weeds that carry vegetable diseases. Many vegetable diseases spread from weeds to nearby gardens. Cucumber and muskmelon mosaic may spread from milkweed, pokeweed, ground cherry, and catnip. Tomato mosaic may come from ground cherries, horse nettle, Jimson weed, nightshade, bitter sweet and matrimony vine. Many cabbage diseases come from any wild members of the cabbage family, such as wild mustard and shepherd's purse. Weed destruction in the garden, around the garden, and along the fences destroys sources of disease-causing organisms.

Make the environment unfavorable to disease occurrence, and, cultivate, weed and harvest vegetables when foliage is dry. Most disease-causing fungi and bacteria require moisture and some other agent for their spread from plant to plant. Bean blight and anthracnose are easily spread by picking beans when the vines are wet. Any movement of animal or man through wet plants, if disease is present, is certain to spread the causal organisms to healthy plants. Do not take chances.

Practice fall clean-up. Disease-causing organisms in most cases can live through the winter and until the next spring in the old diseased refuse. When plowed under, they rarely cause disease unless brought to the surface through cultivation. If plowing under is not feasible, the raking together of old plant parts and hauling to a refuse heap or to some part of the yard not used for vegetables may save the humus for future use.

Control of Some Common Plant Diseases: The actual occurrence of a plant disease is a sure sign that one or more requirements of the plant for normal health and growth has not been met completely. The trouble, as a rule, is in the soil and can be corrected. Sometimes the difficulty is in the atmosphere, such as a prolonged period of inclement weather.

Asparagus Rust. Remove all badly infested plants to the compost heap.

Bean Rust. Include all diseased plants in the compost heap to be used later in fertilizing the bean rows. Be careful to plant varieties of beans resistant to the rust.

Powdery Mildew. Remove infected plants as soon as they can be recognized and remove them to the compost heap. Mildews can be largely prevented by properly enriching the soil in humus.

Potato Scab. This is a common disease of the potato and can be inhibited to a large extent by keeping the soil reaction low, say at pH of 5.2.

Early Blight of Potato. Vigorous plants are said to withstand the attack, so that a soil that will insure rapid, healthy growth is the key to this disease.

Late Blight of Potato. This blight, like so many other blights, can be largely prevented by keeping the soil in good heart. The most important factor is a high humus content.

Tomato Blight. Same as late blight of potato.

Downy Mildew. Downy mildews occur on many food plants as a result of unfavorable growth conditions. If any plant shows downy mildew, it should be removed immediately to the compost heap.

Black Rot of Cabbage. Remove infected leaves as detected, and practice sanitation in every way possible.

Brown Rot of Stone Fruits. Remove all fruit mummies from the tree and ground and all dead leaves from beneath the trees. Band the trees to prevent crawling insects from climbing them.

A sufficient number of examples have been given to indicate the use of natural methods for preventing or controlling plant diseases. The occurrence of a disease should be regarded as an indication of a mistake in cultural practices rather than as a sign that poisonous sprays should be used. By studying the situation carefully, an intelligent gardener can usually learn the cause of the disease, not in terms of a pathogene but rather in terms of cultural practice.

PLANTING RESISTANT VARIETIES: Some varieties of plants seem to be much more resistant to pathogenes than others. Seeds taken from plants grown in your own garden are apt to be better adapted to your conditions than seeds grown elsewhere, especially if they have been grown and selected over a number of years.

Since many garden plants are natives of other countries, it is important to become familiar with the environmental conditions of their native lands. Plants of the desert and open meadow require lots of light, while plants of the woodland prefer some shade.

For each kind of plant, learn whether it prefers an acid or slightly alkaline soil, a northern or southern exposure, a heavy or light soil, a well-drained or wet soil, a long or short day, a dry or humid atmosphere.

A garden planted to one kind of vegetable and a field planted to one kind of crop represent monoculture, a practice which usually is avoided by Nature. Out of cultivation, plants grow in mixed cultures—that is, they grow together to form a more or less complex plant society. Our grandmothers' gardens contained vegetables, flowers, herbs, and small fruits, and for this reason, perhaps, were damaged less by pests than present-day vegetable gardens in which are grown only a few kinds of plants and no flowers and herbs.

DISEASE-RESISTANT VARIETIES: The need for multiple resistance is becoming more and more important. It is no longer enough to have varieties resistant to only the disease present in the areas where the crop is grown for market or processing. They must also be resistant to the diseases in the seed-producing areas.

Some of the accomplishments in developing resistant vegetable varieties, together with some hint of things to come, are presented below.

Asparagus. Rust (caused by *Puccinia asparagi*) was first noticed in the United States in 1896. By 1902 it had become serious throughout our commercial asparagus-growing sections. In 1906 an intensive breeding program was initiated, and by 1919 the two resistant varieties, *Mary Washington* and *Martha Washington*, had practically replaced the other varieties. Their resistance was obtained from a male plant of unknown parentage and two female plants selected from the Reading Giant variety from England. *Mary Washington* is still the most widely grown variety of asparagus.

Bean and Lima Bean. Anthracnose (caused by *Colletotrichum lindemuthianum*) before 1920 was possibly the most important disease of beans. The wide use now of western-grown seed has reduced it to a minor position. In 1915 *Wells Red Kidney*, was used as a parent in developing a resistant strain of *White Marrow*. Because of the relative unimportance of the disease at present, little emphasis is directed toward developing anthracnose-resistant varieties in the United States.

Powdery mildew (caused by *Erysiphe polygoni*) often attacks the fall crops of beans in the Southern States and also is serious in bean crops along the Pacific coast. Differences in varietal resistance have been observed. Some of the recent varieties listed as being resistant to certain races of powdery mildew are *Contender, Florida Belle, Logan, Wade, Fullgreen, Ranger, Tenderlong* 15, and *Flight.*

Rust (caused by *Uromyces phaseoli typica*) attacks pole beans particularly. Most of the efforts to obtain resistance have been with them. The existence of more than 30 races of rust makes it difficult if not impracticable to breed varieties resistant to all of them. Some of the pole snap beans resistant to certain races of rust are *Coaster, Kentucky Wonder Rust Resistant Brown Seeded, Kentucky Wonder Wax, Morse Pole No. 191, Potomac, Rialto, Stringless Blue Lakes Nos. 228 and 231,* and *U. S. No. 4 Kentucky Wonder.*

Halo blight (caused by *Pseudomonas phaseolicola*) is often serious on beans when the environment is favorable for its development. Many of our important field bean varieties have acceptable field resistance to halo blight. One, *Great Northern,* has been used as a source of resistance by several workers in developing resistant snap beans. It was one of the parents of *Fullgreen,* a bush snap bean with good field resistance to halo blight. *Tenderlong* 15 has also been reported to have some tolerance to halo blight.

Virus Diseases. The most important virus disease of beans is common mosaic, but with the rapid development of resistant varieties it may soon be of minor importance. The first-developed resistant varieties were *U. S. No. 5, Wisconsin,* and *Idaho Refugees.* All of the new *Refugee* varieties are resistant. Some of the new resistant bush snap beans are *Topcrop, Wade, Tenderlong* 15, *Improved New Stringless, Ranger, Contender, Idagreen, Improved Brittle Wax,* and *Pure Gold Wax.* Many of the pole varieties such as *Kentucky Wonder,* most of the *Blue Lake* strains, and *Ideal Market* are resistant to common bean mosaic.

Curly top frequently occurs on beans grown in Utah, Idaho, Washington, Oregon, and California. From a cross made in 1936 between the *Burtner* variety, a white pea bean type, and *Blue Lake,* the resistant snap bean *Pioneer* was released in 1943.

Southern bean mosaic and pod mottle viruses have been reported as causing serious damage on fall-grown crops of snap beans in southern Illinois. Most pole bean varieties are resistant to southern bean mosaic virus. *Low's Champion, Ranger, Corbett Refugee,* strains of *Idaho Refugee,* and *Tennessee Green Pod* are the only bush snap bean varieties known to be resistant to this virus.

Downy mildew (caused by *Phytophthora phaseoli*) has seriously damaged lima beans in the North Atlantic States since 1945. Resistance was found in some selections from

India, Guatemala, southeastern United States, and California. None was acceptable commercially, but crosses were made between them and several small- and large-seeded market and processing types. It will be several years before resistant commercial types are available.

Root knot, to which beans are very susceptible. is caused by certain nematodes (*Meloidogyne* species). The disease is prevalent in the Southern States on light, sandy soils. Two resistant selections of pole beans have been released as *Alabama Pole No. 1* and *Alabama Pole No. 2. Spartan* and *State* are resistant half-runner types.

Lettuce. Downy mildew (caused by *Bremia lactucae*) is serious in the coastal lettuce-growing areas of California. Factors for immunity were found in *Lactuca seriola* and were incorporated in *Imperial* 410, which was released in 1945. New strains of mildew to which none of the varieties mentioned are resistant have appeared since then.

Bronze Beauty variety is highly tolerant to mosaic in that it stands up under field and greenhouse tests better than any of the varieties tested. A strain of lettuce tolerant to mosaic was obtained from progeny of a cross between *Paris White* and another European cross type. This was released to the trade in 1951 as *Parris Island.*

Tipburn, physiological disease, occurs during warm weather and causes necrosis in the marginal and submarginal parts of head leaves of lettuce. *Great Lakes,* "456," and *Progress,* of the present commercial varieties, are somewhat resistant.

Muskmelon. Alternaria leaf blight is caused by *Alternaria cucumerina.* Resistance to this fungus, which defoliates the plants and sometimes causes sunken spots on the fruit, was found in a selection of New Seed Breeders, a variety of the *Hale Best* type. It was released in 1944 as *Purdue 44.*

Downy mildew (caused by *Pseudo-*

peronospora cubensis), a destructive disease of muskmelons in the Atlantic and Gulf Coast States, defoliates the plants. Resistance to it was found in several foreign varieties and in a wild type growing in Texas. *Texas Resistant No. 1*, a shipping type released in 1945, was the first resistant variety developed. It was a selection out of a cross between the resistant West Indian melon *Rocky Dew Green Flesh* and *New Seed Breeders* variety, a variety of *Hale Best* type. It also is highly resistant to aphids. *Riosweet* is another downy mildew resistant variety, which is moderately resistant to aphids. The new *Georgia 47* is resistant to powdery mildew, downy mildew, and aphids. *Granite State* is a resistant cantaloup developed primarily for the short growing season in the North. Another resistant variety is *Smith's Perfect,* which was originated in the West Indies.

Fusarium Wilt (caused by *Fusarium oxysporum* f. *melonis,* a soil-borne fungus) is important in some sections of the Central and Eastern States. *The Persian, Honey Dew, Honeyball,* and *Casaba* varieties are relatively resistant but are not adapted to culture in those states. Other resistant varieties are *Iroquois* and *Delicious 51. Burrell Gem, Paul Rose,* and *Pollock 10-25* have fair tolerance.

Mosaic virus causes dwarfed plants and small mottled fruits. In the Central and Eastern States the most common form of mosaic is caused by the ordinary cucumber mosaic virus. Resistance to it has been found in the *Freeman Cucumber, White Melon,* and *Gin-Makuwa (Kin-Makuwa)* varieties of the oriental pickling melon (*Cucumis melo* var. *conomon*).

Onion and Shallot. Downy mildew (caused by *Peronospora destructor*) has been reported in most states, but in the North the damage is chiefly to the bulb crop. Losses in the seed crop in winter and spring in California are often heavy. *Italian Red 13-53* was observed in 1934 to be resistant to downy mildew. It was crossed with *Lord Howe Island,* and a resistant selection named *Calred* was released in 1947. The seed stalks of *Calred* show a higher degree of resistance to downy mildew than do the leaves. The resistance in *Calred* is being incorporated in a Creole type.

Pink root (caused by *Pyrenochaeta terrestris*) is an important soil-inhabiting disease in the onion-growing districts of California, Texas, New York, Ohio, Indiana, Michigan, and shallot-growing districts of Louisiana. *Yellow Bermuda* is one of the most resistant of the commercial varieties. The green bunching onion *Nebuka* (*Allium fistulosum*), leek (*A. porrum*), and chives (*A. schoenoprasum*) are highly resistant. The green onion variety *Beltsville Bunching,* released in 1945, is resistant.

Smut (caused by *Urocystis cepulae*) attacks the bulbing onions, in none of which has resistance been found. The green bunching varieties *Nebuka* and *Beltsville Bunching* are resistant.

Yellow dwarf is a virus disease. Selections immune to certain strains of it have been made in some of the commercial varieties of the Spanish type, such as *White Sweet Spanish* and *Yellow Sweet Spanish,* and also in *Yellow Bermuda, Lord Howe Island,* and *Crystal Grano.* Resistance to the yellow dwarf virus to three other viruses known to attack onions is found in *Nebuka and Beltsville Bunching.*

Pea. Wilt is caused by *Fusarium oxysporum* f. *pisi* race 1. Most of the varieties listed in seed catalogs are wilt-resistant.

Near-wilt (caused by *F. oxysporum* f. *pisi* race 2) is another race of *Fusarium* that attacks most of the varieties resistant to race 1 of the fungus. *Delwiche Commando* is resistant to both races.

One strain of *Perfection* is tolerant to septoria leaf spot (caused by *Septoria pisi*). Other strains of the variety are resistant to several viruses, including yellow bean mosaic and common pea mosaic.

Pepper. Mosaic is due to several viruses, which cause mottling of the leaves and distortion of the fruit of garden pepper. Resistance to one of these, tobacco mosaic virus, has been found in several pungent varieties including *Tabasco, Rutgers World Beater No.* 13, a new mosaic-resistant variety, was selected out of *World Beater.* Several lines of *California Wonder* type resistant to a pepper mosaic occurring in Puerto Rico have been selected out of a cross between the susceptible *California Wonder* and the Mexican hot pepper known as *Cuaresmeno.*

Several pepper varieties—*Santanka, Anaheim, Chile,* and *Italian Pickling* —have high degrees of natural resistance to nematode galling. *Santanka* has also been reported as resistant to bacterial spot. *Tabasco* was observed by workers in the South to be more resistant to southern blight (caused by *Sclerotium rolfsii*) than other varieties when infection occurred about the time of the first blossom formation.

Potato. Late blight, caused by *Phytophthora infestans,* is severe in cool, humid regions. From crosses between susceptible lines the mildly resistant varieties *Sebago* and *Sequoia* have been selected. The latter has resistance to vine infection but not to tuber infection. A resistant German variety, *Ackersegen,* was used in developing the moderately resistant *Calrose.* Immunity from field infection occurs in *Solanum demissum,* which is related to our cultivated potato. Workers at Cornell University have used *S. demissum* as a source of resistance in developing *Empire, Placid, Virgil, Chenango, Ashworth,* and *Essex.* The so-called "W" lines from Germany are believed to have derived their resistance to late blight from *S. demissum.* They have been used in this country as a source of resistance in developing the resistant varieties *Kennebec, Pungo,* and *Cherokee.*

Verticillium wilt (caused by *Verticillium albo-atrum*) is increasing in importance throughout the potato-growing areas of the United States. It has been present in Maine, in the South, in sections of California, and in rather large areas in Idaho and Washington. Field tests have shown that several varieties are resistant; *Menominee, Saranac,* and *Sequoia.*

Ring rot is caused by *Corynebacterium sepedonicum.* The varieties *Friso* and *President* from the Netherlands and a number of seedling varieties developed in the United States resist this bacterial disease. One of these seedlings, released as *Teton,* has shown a high degree of resistance in Maine and Wyoming. *Saranac* is also highly resistant.

Scab (caused by *Streptomyces scabies*) is the result of a soil-borne organism that infects the tubers and causes losses wherever potatoes are grown. Three resistant but poor-quality European varieties, *Hindenburg, Jubel,* and *Ostragis,* have been used in this country for hybridization. Some of the resistant varieties that have been released in this country are Menominee, Ontario, Cayuga, Seneca, Yampa, and Cherokee.

Extensive breeding work by several cooperating agencies is under way to develop resistance to the common virus diseases such as mild mosaic, latent mosaic, rugose mosaic, leaf roll, and net necrosis. *Chippewa, Earlaine,* and *Katahdin* are immune to virus A. *Katahdin* is also resistant to virus X, virus Y, and the virus causing leaf roll. *Warba, Sebago, Red Warba, Mohawk, Kennebec, Menominee,* and *Houma* are resistant to virus A. *Houma* is also resistant to the leaf roll virus.

Spinach. Downy mildew is caused by *Peronospora effusa.* In a collection of spinach varieties made in Iran in 1940 two lines contained a mixture of plants resistant and susceptible to downy mildew. The resistant plants had small, thin leaves, which had a high content of oxalic acid, and the plants were early bolters. By crossing the resistant plants with the different popular commercial varieties, good progress is being made in developing resistant shipping, canning, and freezing types.

Mosaic, or blight, on spinach is due to several viruses, but the chief cause of spinach blight in this country is the cucumber virus. A wild spinach from Manchuria was found to be highly resistant. It was crossed with several commercial varieties, and a Savoy type was selected and introduced about 1921 as *Virginia Savoy.* From a selection of a cross between *Virginia Savoy* and *King of Denmark,* mosaic-resistant *Old Dominion* was developed. It was released in 1930. Since then *Domino* and a strain of *Virginia Savoy,* resistant to fusarium wilt, have been released.

Squash and Pumpkin. Curly top is a serious virus disease of many vegetables in some sections of the Pacific Northwest and the Mountain States. *Marblehead, Long White Bush,* and some strains of *Vegetable Marrow* squash have been found resistant.

Resistant varieties of pumpkins are *Big Tom, Cushaw, Large Cheese,* and *Tennessee Sweet Potato.*

Sweet Potato. Fusarium wilt (caused by *Fusarium oxysporum* f. *batatas*) attacks almost all of the present market varieties of sweet potato. *Goldrush,* a new, resistant, orange-fleshed, moist type, was released in 1951. Its resistance was obtained from a seedling of a Cuban variety, *Americano.*

Tomato. Early blight (caused by *Alternaria solani*), a fungus disease, is often serious on tomato stems, foliage, and fruit. When infection occurs at the soil line, the lesion is known as collar rot. The variety Southland possesses high resistance to collar rot and some resistance to early blight. The *Manahill* variety is somewhat resistant to foliage infection.

Fusarium wilt (caused by *Fusarium*

oxysporum f. *lycopersici*) is a soil-borne disease that is particularly serious in the Southern States.

In 1910 selections were made by workers at the Tennessee Agricultural Experiment Station, and in 1912 *Tennessee Red* was released. In the same year *Louisiana Wilt Resistant* was distributed by the Louisiana Agricultural Experiment Station. Then followed many moderately resistant varieties. Two of them *Marglobe* (1925) and *Rutgers* (1934), are still widely grown. The *Red Currant* tomato from Peru was a real advance in the development of truly wilt-resistant tomatoes. Since 1935 it has been crossed with a number of commercial types. *Pan America*, introduced in 1940, was the first variety to possess the new type of resistance. Since then other varieties with this resistance have been developed; among them are *Cal 255*, *Sunray, Southland, Jefferson, Golden Sphere, Fortune, Ohio W. R. Globe, Boone, Tipton, Kokomo, Homestead, Tucker, Manahill,* and *Manasota.*

Leaf mold (caused by *Cladosporium fulvum*), a leaf-spotting disease, is serious on tomatoes grown in greenhouses. Resistance to it was observed in Ohio in an off-type plant of the *Globe* variety. This plant was probably the result of a natural cross with *Red Currant* tomato, which was the only known resistant type. By using that species as a source of resistance, several varieties (*Globelle, Bay State,* and *Vetomold*) have been developed.

Verticillium wilt is caused by *Verticillium albo-atrum*. The *Riverside* variety, released in 1937, had tolerance to both verticillium wilt and fusarium wilt. It was a cross between *Cal 2*, moderately resistant to fusarium and verticillium wilts, and *Marvana*, resistant to only fusarium wilt. This variety and *Essar*, released in 1939, are adapted to areas in California. A high degree of resistance was found in a small-fruited strain of tomato called *Peru Wild*. Crosses between this and commercial types have yielded promising lines, two of which, *Loran Blood* and *VR Moscow*, are now available.

Curly top is a virus disease, to which none of the domestic tomatoes are resistant. It is serious in some sections of the West. Three wild species, *Lycopersicon glandulosum, L. peruvianum* var. *dentatum,* and *L. peruvianum* var. *humifusum,* have an appreciable degree of resistance.

Mosaic. A line of *Lycopersicon hirsutum* with high resistance to ordinary tobacco mosaic virus, which causes a mosaic disease of tomato, has been crossed with several of the commercial tomato varieties. Some of the progeny have shown tolerance to the virus when artificially inoculated. Mostly, however, the resistance is expressed as a delay of the symptom development.

Spotted wilt, a virus disease spread by thrips, is serious in parts of the *Red Currant* tomato, of *Lycopersicon hirsutum,* of *L. peruvianum,* and of the variety *German Sugar* are resistant. *Pearl Harbor,* a resistant variety, was released in 1945.

Immunity to the gray leaf spot fungus (*Stemphylium solani*) was found in the currant tomato. The Hawaii Agricultural Experiment Station has released seven varieties immune to the disease. They are named after the islands: *Hawaii, Kauai, Lanai, Oahu, Maui, Molokai,* and *Niihau.* Another resistant variety, developed in Florida, is *Manahill.*

Watermelon. Anthracnose, caused by *Colletotrichum lagenarium,* is perhaps the most destructive disease of watermelons. *Congo,* released in 1949, is somewhat resistant. *Fairfax,* introduced in 1952, is the first shipping variety available to southern growers which offers combined resistance to anthracnose and to fusarium wilt. The resistance to anthracnose came from the same source as Congo and the resistance to fusarium wilt from *Leesburg* and *Hawkesbury.*

Downy mildew is caused by *Pseudoperonospora cubensis.* A source of resistance to it was found in native watermelons of poor quality from the Dominican Republic. They were crossed to varieties resistant to fusarium wilt and anthracnose.

Fusarium wilt is caused by *Fusarium oxysporum* f. *niveum*. Since the release of *Conqueror* in 1911 there have been developed many resistant varieties that are adapted to the principal watermelon-growing areas. Among them are *Improved Kleckley No. 6* and *Stone Mountain No. 5* for the Midwest; *Leesburg, Hawkesbury, Blacklee, Georgia Wilt-Resistant, Miles, Missouri, Queen,* and *Ironsides* for the South; and *Klondike R-7, Baby Klondike,* and *Blue Ribbon* for the West.

Many serious diseases remain for which resistance is needed: Common blight of bean, bean and pea root rots, ascochyta blight of pea, aster yellows and mosaic of lettuce, and curly top and late blight of tomato, to mention only a few.

New diseases and strains of old diseases will appear as cropping becomes more intensive and as vegetables are grown in new areas. New sources of resistance will be needed.

To meet the future problems, continuous research by plant breeders, pathologists, and other biologists is needed.—*H. Rex Thomas; W. J. Zaumeyer.*

DISH GARDENS: One of the most popular forms of exotic indoor planting is the dish garden, an outgrowth of the Japanese miniature garden.

Dish gardens may be arranged in various containers that are several inches deep. Pottery, bronze, brass or wooden bowls that have received several coats of spar varnish may be used.

Drainage is essential if the plants are to survive. Bits of broken pots and pebbles covered with sand should serve as a foundation for the potting mixture with a few pieces of charcoal added.

Plant arrangement depends largely on location. Small dish gardens are generally viewed from one side only. Tall plants are arranged in one grouping while an unusual plant takes the center with other plants serving as a frame.

Dish gardens are best watered with a small bulb spray. The watering must be done carefully because if the plants become too wet they soon die. This is particularly true of arrangements of cactus. Little water and plenty of drainage are their requirements. They are ideal plants for hot, dry homes since they thrive on heat if they have sunlight with it.

Petunias, dwarf marigolds, ageratum, geraniums, and vinca vines are among the standard fillers. All of these grow with little attention and will withstand a wide range of heat and cold, wetness and drought. They also bloom prolifically.

These arrangements need sunlight and thrive best if given a little fresh air outdoors on a sunny day. As soon as frosty weather is gone they make pretty additions to the porch.

DISH WATER: The organic gardener is inclined to utilize every waste in some form and frequently would like to dispose of dish water by adding it to the compost heap. This is not advisable for the following reasons: Dish water invariably contains some fat and soap, and since soap is highly alkaline, an excess amount of soda would gradually be added to the compost if dish water were regularly poured on the heap. In addition, the chemicals in modern detergents are very detrimental to soil bacteria.

DIVISION: Division is a form of plant propagation in which new plants are not grown from seeds or bulbs but separated from the parent plants.

This includes plants that have (1) bulbs, tubers, corms, or rootstocks, (2) runners or suckers, or (3) breaking up of large clumps of old plants or the separation of plants with crowns.

Certain perennials, such as phlox, form "crowns" or groups of new shoots which must be divided at intervals to avoid crowding and secure plants which come true to type. Parts already naturally rooted, as strawberry runners and blackberry suckers, may be severed from the original specimen and transplanted. Or there may be simple separation of parts not already rooted, as tulip bulblets, but which root readily after being removed from the parent, especially at the close of the growing season.

Practically all perennials can be divided—but annuals and biennials are best grown from seed. The division of perennials not only increases the number of plants, but stimulates more vigorous growth and profusion of bloom.

Methods of division vary widely. Rough division consists of using a sharp spade to cut across large clumps of such plants as phlox and rhubarb. The pieces are then dug and replanted. Finer practices include digging and breaking the clumps apart with the hand or fingers, or cutting them apart with a sharp knife. Suckers which develop from plants such as red raspberry and snowberry are dug individually. Crowns or rooted buds, which form (usually at the tips of rhizomes) toward the close of the growing season and push forward in the soil, are often severed and planted. The best example of this type is lily-of-the-valley, millions of whose "pips" are forced annually by florists. Tubers (short thickened parts of subterraneous branches such as dahlia) are broken apart from the main stem and clumps and then planted separately.

Division and separation are two of the easiest methods of propagation which amateur gardeners can utilize in increasing plants suited to these types of multiplication.

The best time for division depends largely upon the variety. Most spring and summer-blooming perennials may be separated in the autumn, while fall-blooming species should be left until spring. Replant the divisions at once and water them thoroughly until (in the case of fall planting) the winter mulch is put in place or new growth starts. *See also* PROPAGATION; CUTTINGS; LAYERING.

DOG MANURE: Dog manure as well as cat manure is, owing to the diets of these animals, rich in phosphoric acid. The nitrogen content is about two per cent, while the phosphoric acid content may be about ten per cent. When the dogs eat bones, their manure is higher in phosphorus and calcium than when they are fed canned foods. *See also* MANURE.

DOGWOOD: A large family (*Cornus*) of hardy, ornamental small trees or woody shrubs. Desirable for many decorative purposes, and especially effective in winter because of their colored twigs, dogwoods are considered among our loveliest and most popular plants. A spring blaze of highly attractive flowers plus colorful autumn

Dogwood may be adapted for many garden purposes, grouping well in ordinary soil. Few shrubs do better in the shade or, with care, in the open.

leaves and fruit makes the native Flowering Dogwood a beautiful landscaping feature along the Atlantic coast and mid-Eastern states, and an understandable garden favorite.

General recommendations for soil preparation, planting, transplanting and after-care of trees and shrubs (which see) pertain to the dogwoods. They thrive in ordinary soil, different types preferring wet or dry areas, some favoring acid soil.

For most species, propagation is by fresh seed, sown in a coldframe in the fall, and usually germinating the following spring. Others are increased by cuttings, suckers, grafting or budding. Generally, home gardeners seek established nursery stock to start their own plantings.

Popular among the many varieties are:

Flowering Dogwood (*florida*), the prized native, which ranges from central New England south to Florida and west to Texas and Ontario is also the state flower of Virginia. Growing from ten to 30 feet high, it is characterized by a low, spreading head of horizontal-tiered branches, and small greenish-yellow blossoms surrounded by blunt-ended white bracts, which team to make the species one of spring's most beautiful small trees. Then, in autumn, this dogwood displays bright red leaves and showy red fruits in dense clusters.

Pacific Dogwood (*nuttalli*) is the 75-foot giant of the family common in western North America, but not hardy in colder regions. With white or pinkish bracts spreading six inches across and bright red-orange fruits, it is a striking species which in Oregon frequently blooms twice during the fall.

Gray Dogwood (*racemosa*) is a dense, spreading shrub, native from Maine to Georgia, which grows in heights ranging from three to 15 feet. Highlighted by handsome gray branches, long sharp-pointed leaves, varying from autumn red to purple,

white spring flowers and white fall fruits on red stems, this variety is well-suited to banks and roadsides.

Blood-Twig Dogwood (*sanguinea*) is a low-growing (ten feet or more) upright shrub noted for its dark red branches, which retain their attractive color through the winter, deep red fall leaves, greenish-white flowers and black fruit.

The berries of the dogwood are not the least of this shrub's many attractions. The *nuttalli* is especially beautiful; bears red or orange fruit.

Cornelian-Cherry (*mas*) has large cornelian-red edible fruits. An attractive, good-sized shrub, it is one of the prettiest dogwoods in early spring with clusters of greenish-yellow blooms, showy yellow leaves that last until late fall. A native of Europe, this species grows slowly, but is long-lived and hardy.

Others include the Pagoda Dogwood (*alternifolia*), a 20-foot native shrub or small tree noted for its whorled, spreading green branches, white May flowers and deep blue fruit; the Red-Osier Dogwood (*stolonifera*), a liberally spreading shrub with dark green foliage, large clusters of white blossoms with a red center and white fruit. This species tolerates shade, grows well in wet soil. Bunch-Berry (*canadensis*) is a spreading, herbaceous shrub which grows just a few inches high, requires cool, shaded, woodland soil; and an evergreen dogwood, (*capitata*), which is one of the best for use in the far south.

DOLOMITE: A rock similar to limestone, and is interchangeable with limestone for uses in which physical properties are the determining factor.

Limestone is composed of the mineral calcite, calcium carbonate, whereas dolomite rock is composed of the mineral having the same name which chemically is a double carbonate of calcium and magnesium. Theoretically pure dolomite contains 45.73 per cent magnesium carbonate, and 54.27 per cent calcium carbonate. *See also* LIME.

DORMANT OIL SPRAY: Dormant oil sprays are recommended for insect control in the orchard. They are effective against practically all the common chewing and sucking insects such as aphids, red bug, red spider, thrips and many others. The orchard can be sprayed early in the spring before any of the buds open, with a three per cent oil spray. *See also* SPRAYS, OIL.

DOWSING: The ancient art of water-divining—practiced since the 15th Century—has long been an object of controversy.

What makes a forked twig bend toward water in one person's hands and not another's? Science can't explain it. Not even the "water-witches" themselves seem to know.

Estimates of the number of people with dowsing ability range from seven out of ten to one in 12. This wide variation may be due to the great differences in sensitivity between dowsers.

The dowser grasps a forked twig firmly at the outer ends of the fork, thumbs out. If he possesses true divining power, it will bend down sharply as he passes over a water vein—sometimes strongly enough to tear off the bark where he is holding it. Some dowsers can even figure the depth and rate of flow of the underground water by the rod's movements.

Dowsers use willow, hazel, peach, apple, horse-chestnut and beech twigs. Some prefer only twigs with bitter bark, others say any green wood will do. Modern dowsers are proficient with brass or steel rods, and Henry Gross, a famous Maine dowser who once accurately located water sources in Bermuda while in his home 800 miles away, finds he can use anything from grass to wire.

Scoffers say there is underground water practically everywhere, so finding water where a dowser's rod points is not at all remarkable.

DRAINAGE: Adequate drainage and aeration are vital to the health of soil and directly affect its fertility index.

Inadequate or defective drainage can take either of two extreme forms. One—the land drains too rapidly and does not hold moisture for its plant-life. Two—the land drains slowly or practically not at all and has degenerated into a bog or swamp. (*See* AERATION.)

Really severe bog-like conditions can best be relieved by a thorough drainage system, including the laying of pipes or drains and the digging of drainage ditches. The average farmer or gardener is advised to consult local experts, including the state or country farm agent, on how to proceed. *See also* DRY WEATHER GARDENING.

DRAINAGE, HOUSE PLANTS: Drainage is very important in the successful growing of house plants. A small hole is usually found in the bottom of each pot, to allow excess water to escape. A piece of arched crock or broken pot may be laid over the hole of small pots. Large pots, say ten-inch size, require two or three inches of drainage material. This may be broken crock in the bottom layer, with gravel, cinders, or pebbles placed over it. Sphagnum moss may be laid over the drainage material, if desired, to keep the soil from washing through it, but it is not essential. *See also* HOUSE PLANTS.

DRIED BLOOD: *see* BLOOD, DRIED

DRIED FRUITS AND VEGETABLES: Sundrying is one of the best ways of preserving food for winter use, with proper equipment. The Indians used this method centuries ago.

Many fruits can be sun-dried. The method is not only easy but also preserves vital nutrients and adds foods to the menu that require little space.

In the drying process, most of the water content is, of course, removed. On a pound-for-pound basis the dried food then has a substantially increased concentration of many nutrients, especially minerals. Two exceptions are vitamins A and C. These are usually lowered in drying, and that fact should be kept in mind.

FOODS FOR DRYING: Some of the many foods which can be sundried include: pumpkin, squash, raspberries and strawberries, dandelion and other greens, apples, peaches, apricots, prune-plums, cherries, beans, peas, rhubarb, and many others. Next to quick-freezing fresh produce, which isn't practical with all foods, sundrying does the best job of keeping part of the garden's surplus and retaining its nutritive values.

When storing indoors in unwaxed deep-freeze containers, open containers at least every two weeks and examine for mold in wet weather.

Shallow cake pans, covered with screening are frequently used in sundrying. These have the advantage of stacking easily, also of ease in carrying from the kitchen to the outdoors and back.

DROUGHT-RESISTANT PLANTS: Not all plant growth is equally able to withstand varying and often adverse environment. Some by nature have been provided the capacity and characteristics to thrive in harsh climate and poor soil. And while diligent soil-improvement measures—application of compost, natural ground rock, cover-cropping, mulching, irrigation, etc.—can accomplish much to help overcome or lessen the effects of these conditions, the thoughtful gardener (especially in selecting ornamental plants) will choose from those most suited to his locality.

One of the more common and difficult problems is that of drought or near-drought—very inadequate rainfall, lack of humid air, parched and sandy soil. The following lists are of plants recognized as drought-resistant, those best adapted to dry soil and hot weather areas:

Annuals:

    Calliopsis (*Coreopsis tinctoria*)

    Cape-marigold, Winter (*Dimor-photheca aurantiaca*)

    Convolvulus, Dwarf (*Convolvulus tricolor*)

    Cornflower (*Centaurea cyanus*)

    Drummond's Phlox (*Phlox Drummondii*)

    Four-o'clock (*Mirabilis jalapa*)

    Ice Plant (*Mesembryanthemum crystallinum*)

    Larkspur, Rocket (*Delphinium ajacis*)

    Morning-glory (*Ipomcea purpurea*)

    Perilla, Green (*Perilla frutescens*)

Rose Moss (*Portulaca grandiflora*)

Sanvitalia (*Sanvitalis procumbens*)

Scarlet Sage (*Salvia splendens*)

Showy Pricklepoppy (*Argemone grandiflora*)

Snow-on-the-Mountain (*Euphorbia marginata*)

Summer-cypress (*Kochia tricophylla*)

Sunflower (*Helianthus annuus*)

Zinnia (*Zinnia elegans*)

Shrubs:

Barberry (*Berberis vulgaris*)

Bayberry (*Myrica pensyvanica*)

Beach Plum (*Prunus maritima*)

Blackhaw (*Viburnum prunifolium*)

Burnet Rose (*Rosa spinosissima*)

Bush Clover (*Lespedeza formosa*)

Dogwood (*Cornus racemosa*)

Fragrant Sumach (*Rhus canadensis*)

Indian Currant (*Symphoricarpos vulgaris*)

Juniper (*Juniperus Sabina*)

Pentaphyllum (*Acanthopanax Sieboldianum*)

Prairie Rose (*Rosa setigera*)

Rose Acacia (*Robina hispida*)

Rose Rugosa (*Rosa rugosa*)

Savin Juniper (*Juniperus Sabina*)

St. Johnswort (*Hypericum aureum*)

Staghorn Sumac (*Rhus styphina*)

Wayfaring-tree (*Viburnum Lantana*)

Trees—Deciduous:

Amur Maple (*Acer Ginnala*)

Black Cherry (*Prunus serotina*)

Black Locust (*Robina Pseudoacacia*)

Box Elder (*Acer Negundo*)

European White Birch (*Betula alba*)

Gray Birch (*Betula populifolia*)

Hedge Maple (*Acer campestre*)

Largetooth Aspen (*Populus grandidentata*)

Monarch Birch (*Betula Maximowicziana*)

Pignut (*Carya glabra*)

Quaking Aspen (*Populus tremuloides*)

Scarlet Oak (*Quercus coccinea*)

Sour Cherry (*Prunus cerasus*)

Tartarian Maple (*Acer tartaricum*)

Tree of Heaven (*Ailanthus grandulosa*)

Wafer Ash (*Ptelea trifoleata*)

White Poplar (*Populus alba*)

Trees-Evergreen:

Canadian Spruce (*Picea alba*)

Chinese Juniper (*Juniperus chinensis*)

Norway Spruce (*Picea excelsa*)

Pitch Pine (*Pinus rigida*)

Red Cedar (*Juniperus virginiana*)

Scotch Pine (*Pinus sylvestris*)

Swiss Mountain Pine (*Pinus montana*)

White Pine (*Pinus strobus*)

DRY WEATHER GARDENING: While the gardener cannot control the amount of rain that falls on his land, he can control and increase the ability of his soil to retain the water it receives. In doing so, he must realize that the type of soil determines how often and how much it needs water.

Department of Agriculture experts Victor Boswell and Marlowe Thorne state that "the coarser the particles that make up a soil, the less water it will hold under most field conditions. Sandy soils hold only about one-fourth inch equivalent rainfall or irrigation water per foot of depth. Sandy loams commonly hold about three-fourths inch of water per foot; fine sandy loams, about 1.25 inches; silt loams, clay loams, and clays, about 2.5 to 3 inches."

There is a wide variation in water-holding capacity of soils—enough to make the difference between one-fourth of an inch per foot of soil to three inches ... the difference between garden success or failure during a drought.

To improve soil, large amounts of

organic matter to increase the water-holding capacity of sandy soils and sandy loams, as well as make it easier for water to soak into heavier-type soils such as loams, silt loams and clays.

Sheet composting, green manuring and applying organic fertilizers are the best and fastest ways to increase the garden's humus content.

Subsoil conditions influence the plant-water relationship. Some soils that look all right on the surface are actually covering up a hard, tight layer only a few inches below. It may be practically impossible for roots or water to enter this layer at all. The result is a shallow zone, which prevents normal root development.

"The limited amount of water that can be held by such a shallow layer is soon exhausted in dry weather," observe Boswell and Thorne, "and the plants suffer for water relatively soon after a rain or irrigation. Rock near the surface of the soil is even more unfavorable in this respect. Under such conditions water must be supplied in moderate to small amounts frequently. Heavy watering may virtually drown the plants by overfilling the soil pores and preventing proper aeration of the root zone."

On a farm, the best and most universally used method of breaking up a hardpan is by subsoiling, using a heavy-duty rotary tillage tool. After several passes with the tiller, the tines dig down to about a ten-inch depth.

However, a hardpan that is located more than ten inches below the surface requires more power to eliminate it than any present gardening machine has. One suggestion is to loosen the soil structure by using small, slow-detonating explosive charges.

A rather slow, but sure, way of loosening a hardpan is through sheet composting and green manuring. Many organic gardeners have successfully used this method, but it will take at least several years to do the job.

At the other extreme to the hardpan, there are some surface soils that are underlain by very open, deep deposits of sand or gravel. Roots can pass readily into these coarse layers but may obtain little water. Crops on soils having such open subsoils suffer quickly for the lack of water just as do those above a tight layer near the surface. Heavy watering of subsoil not only wastes water but leaches some plant nutrients down to levels where the roots fail to reach them. Here again, the best solution is to incorporate large amounts of organic matter into the soil.

To protect plants from the hot, dry summer weather, the following steps are recommended:

1. Make a list of materials available locally which can be used for mulching. This can include: weeds, native grasses, leaves, leaf mold, compost, stones, grass clippings, packing materials, peat moss, buckwheat hulls, rakings from under trees and shrubs, straw, hay, sawdust, woodshavings, corncobs, coffee grounds, cocoa bean shells, seaweed and vegetable garbage.

2. Jot down *next to each of the above items* the name of the place where it can be obtained.

3. Don't delay contacting these sources of possible supply until the hot July sun is baking the land. Get in touch with the sources and find out if the material is available for the taking or if a charge is involved.

4. Renting a small pick-up truck and collecting the needed mulching materials will take a few hours and should not cost more than $15.

Here's some advice from expert mulcher Ruth Stout on the best ways to use these materials around vegetables:

For spinach, lettuce and peas: place six to eight inches of mulch around them. Shade the lettuce if possible.

For beets, carrots, parsnips and kohlrabi: first thin plants; then water thoroughly and put mulch all around them at once, six inches deep and be-

Mulching the year-'round provides the best means of gardening successfully in all kinds of weather, dry or wet. The thick cover of organic materials keeps evaporation to minimum and improves soil structure.

tween rows. If the mulch is wet, so much the better.

For bush beans: if already planted, thin, water and mulch. Make a drill four inches deep; plant the beans sparsely; cover with two inches of soil; water; cover with a board or cardboard and mulch. Remove board as soon as beans sprout.

For corn: if planted already, thin to two plants in a hill instead of customary three. Water and give it six inches of mulch. (If mulch is short, use as many layers of wet cardboard as you can collect. The cardboard is only an emergency measure; it is not, of course, as satisfactory as hay or leaves, because the latter provide valuable nutrients to the soil as they decompose.) Each time you plant corn, advises Miss Stout, soak the seed overnight, make four inch drills and cover the seed with two

inches of soil. Water thoroughly, put a board over the seed and mulch immediately.

For late cabbage, broccoli, cauliflower, peppers, and tomatoes: if not planted yet, put very deep and four feet apart instead of three and mulch heavily. If peppers and tomatoes aren't in, put them very deep and farther apart than customary. If already planted, water and mulch heavily (six to eight inches).

For flowers: "All flower beds should be under a constant mulch, drought or no drought." Miss Stout points out that this can be done without making them look ugly. Peonies can be mulched with dead leaves and their own tops. Well-rotted hay, mixed with crushed leaves, makes an excellent cover for roses. Put it on six inches deep and then scatter soil on top. It all looks like soil then, but the mulch is so deep that weeds can't sprout. The same method works well for large annuals, such as zinnias.

For small, low-growing annuals, Miss Stout used a fine mulch. "Since I keep my whole vegetable garden mulched constantly, there is always material there, not quite rotted enough to be rich soil, but rotted enough to look like it. I put this around my small annuals. If you don't have such material, you can use crushed leaves mixed with a little soil and wood ashes. This may sound like quite a job, but it is done just once a season. And it greatly enriches the soil and keeps the moisture in the ground and carries you through a drought."

GARDEN IRRIGATION: Many gardeners may also be interested in setting up a small irrigation system. However, in terms of ordinary household usage, irrigating a large backyard garden may require amounts that appear enormous. Before going ahead with any irrigation set-up, the home gardener should first check whether an ample water supply will be available at reasonable cost. (Remember also that many communities place restrictions on the use of water during dry spells.)

To get an idea of how much water is required, the following estimate appeared in the USDA's Yearbook of Agriculture for 1955:

"Consider a garden 60 by 70 feet, approximately one-tenth of an acre. Suppose this garden is in a district that normally depends on rainfall but still needs additional water from time to time during the summer and early fall—a good watering during a half dozen short dry spells. Under average conditions the equivalent of an inch of rain may be considered an adequate single application. That amounts to about 2,700 gallons for one application."

If a large supply of water is available for irrigation, then your next question is *how much* water is needed. Briefly stated, the amount of irrigation

water a plant requires during any season is the difference between the use of water by the plant and the effective rainfalls received. However, this is complicated by the variations in *intensity* of rainfall. For example, five inches of water received in a month may be far less effective when it falls as one five-inch rain than when it falls in five one-inch rains.

Average amounts of water used by vegetable crops vary from 0.10 to 0.20 inches a day, and peak rates as high as 0.32 inches a day have been reported to the Department of Agriculture. Thus the moisture requirement of vegetables can vary from a low of about three inches to a high of nine inches a month, depending on the crop and the conditions under which it is grown. Potatoes, tomatoes, beans and sweet corn are reported to have higher water requirements than many other vegetables.

In the home vegetable garden, where many different vegetables are grown close together, it is obviously impractical to attempt irrigating with different and specific amounts of water for each kind of crop.

The difficulties in setting up an irrigation system for the home garden clearly emphasize that the most practical and efficient ways of conserving or even *adding* water is via a mulch.

FERTILITY AND WATER: Regardless of the extra water supply, bear in mind that plants need plenty of fertility to be able to use water. While irrigation does supply water it will not make up for deficiencies in organic matter, mineral nutrients or other essential features of a good garden. This brings up two points:

1. Compost irrigation.

Although irrigating an entire garden area is not practical in most cases, try this two-in-one fertilizing method on a limited basis. Very often, some of the valuable nutrients in compost dissolve quite readily, and in solution these nutrients can be quickly distributed to needy plant roots.

Since plants "drink" their food rather than eat it, the use of compost water makes good sense, particularly during dry periods when plants are starved both for food and water. It is no trouble making compost water on a small scale. For treating small outdoor areas, fill a sprinkling can half with finished compost and half with water, stir gently ten or 12 times, and pour. The compost can be used several times, as one watering will not wash out all its soluble nutrients. The remaining compost should be dug into the soil or used as a mulch.

2. Deep fertilizing.

When drought strikes, it is always the top layer of soil that dries out first. A week of dry weather will probably dry out the top two inches of soil. It takes a severe and prolonged drought to dry things up to a depth of a foot to 18 inches.

Therefore a key way to protect the garden from drought damage is to build fertility deep down in the soil, where plant food will stay moist longer. This can be done by drilling in granular organic fertilizers with a fertilizer drill attached to a garden tractor. Or, spread fertilizer on the surface—and then work it in as deeply as possible with the plow or tiller.

DUCK: Ducks are very easy to handle, taking less time and work than any other fowl. Also, their housing needs no insulation and less heat than for chickens.

One of the big dividends of duck raising is the manure. It is twice as rich in nitrogen, and contains approximately six times the phosphorus and the same amount of potash as average farm manure.

Ducks relish green feed—especially grass clippings and weeds—and do particularly well on deep litter. Adding new straw, shavings or ground cobs as needed to keep it clean and dry will build up a deep litter (as beneficial to ducks as to chickens) and provide a goodly amount of high-humus material when cleaned out and used on the garden.

An accumulation of manure, incidentally, in ducks' houses or yards, will burn their breasts. While ducks are subject to few diseases: sanitation, which includes clean quarters, feeders and waterers, is always important. Flies and moldy, off-quality feed are other causes of losses.

The most popular breeds are Pekin and Rouen. Pekin makes up about 80 per cent of all ducks sold. It is a hardy, fast grower, and its white feathers are a valuable by-product. On commercial farms, the sale of feathers pays the cost of picking and cleaning. Rouen is a slow-maturing breed—six to seven months. It is a descendant of the wild mallard, and like the old-time favorite, the Muscovy, has dark feathers but a most delicious, high-flavored meat.

A ten by 12 brooder house will accommodate 200 to 300 ducklings, or a pen may be used in a laying house. Quarters should be cleaned and aired thoroughly before the ducks arrive.

Put the day-old ducklings, immediately under the brooder at a temperature of 90 degrees. Reduce it ten degrees each week for three weeks.

After the first few days, ventilation is vital: pure fresh air is the cheapest "feed" available. Ventilate enough to keep dampness down, but avoid drafts. The temperature of the brooder house should be 70 degrees the first week, and thereafter reduced five degrees each week.

Fast-growing Pekins need a high-flock raisers feed a crumbly, wet chick-growing mash, keeping it before them at all times in self-feeders. At eight weeks, they switch to a fattening ration, or feed pellets, if these are available. They go further and are easier to handle (they require no wetting). The first two weeks the ducks get starter pellets, then growing pellets, and finally fattening pellets at eight weeks.

Ample fresh, clean water is essential. Running water in shallow narrow troughs will let the baby ducks submerge their bills and eyes without getting their bodies wet. Ducklings seem to need grit even more than chickens.

If ducks are to be raised entirely in confinement, they will need three square feet per bird by the time they are six weeks old. If ranged in cool weather they can be let out after the first three weeks. In the spring, they can go outdoors at two weeks. Cool temperatures make them feather out faster and eat better for smooth, plump flesh. It's a good idea in cool weather to harden them off first by admitting increasing amounts of outdoor air for a week previous to ranging. Trees and tall weeds, or frames covered with boards or building paper, are sufficient protection from sun and rain on the range until their breasts are completely feathered. Move the mash hoppers and water fountains around frequently to avoid bare spots.

On places where there is only room for small yards, try to locate them on gently sloping land with light sandy soil. Manure must be scraped up regularly, or a couple of inches of gravel to make the yards self-cleaning with each rain can be put down. It's possible to raise 100 ducklings in a yard 50 by 75.

A pond or brook will considerably reduce the amount of water hauled or piped to your flock. They don't need a particularly large or deep stream, just one big enough to clean themselves in without getting excessive exercise. It should be shallow and flowing. Many farmers put a dam with a floodgate across the stream, so it can be flushed out to remove manure. A settling basin is an excellent way to catch the sludge after flushing, for use on the soil. A pond should be continually charged by a spring or brook, and handled the same way.

Does it pay to keep a breeding flock? Not for a hundred or so ducklings in the summer for local trade.

But for a steady supply during a large part of the year, a breeding flock is the answer. Select breeders carefully: keep a sharp watch for healthy recruits during the summer. Separate them from the rest of the flock and check them again at ten weeks for general health and vitality. They need about five square feet of housing space per bird, outdoor exercise in all but the worst winter weather, and swimming water to keep in top condition.

Duck eggs are incubated four weeks before they hatch. They require a lot more moisture than hens' eggs, and must be turned twice a day. Whisk the babies to the brooder as soon as they are dry and fluffy, and see that there is ample feed and water available in the brooder.

Properly grown Pekins weigh between five and six pounds at nine to eleven weeks. After 12 weeks or so, they won't grow any bigger without considerable extra feeding, and the meat is apt to get tough and stringy.

Dry picking is generally rated best— the birds keep in finer condition and hold their flavor better than if dressed by scalding.

Another good market is for duck eggs: the old-time prejudice against them is disappearing as people discover their food value.

DUTCH ELM DISEASE: Transmitted by bark beetles, this blight is extremely hard to control. Symptoms include wilting followed by yellowing, curling and dropping of leaves. No adequate remedy for checking the disease has as yet been found. Blight diseases imported into this country from abroad, work havoc on indigenous vegetation which apparently requires exposure to the disease for many centuries before developing resistance.

Destruction of all affected trees is advocated as a drastic control measure. Short of this extremity, it is advisable to follow good basic orchard practice.

Keep trees healthy by proper feeding and watering as well as pruning reduces infestation of the bark beetle carriers which lay eggs only in weakened or diseased tissue. *See also* ORCHARDING; ELM.

DWARF FRUIT TREES: *see* FRUIT TREES, DWARF

DWARFING TREES: *see* BONSAI

DWARF PLANTS: *see* BORDERS

DYNAMITE: This explosive can be used, safely and effectively, where extremely difficult soil conditions such as hardpan exist. But a permit for its use is necessary and local authorities, on the county, township or village level, should be contacted before proceeding further.

The use of dynamite is advisable in those cases where it is obvious that half-measures will not properly loosen the soil to permit adequate aeration and drainage. These are some of the farm chores it does best:

1. Cracks hardpan and loosens soil structure.

2. Loosens soil for tree planting holes—enabling root structure to expand quickly.

3. Digs drainage ditches.

4. Excavates for ponds.

5. Removes stumps and cracks boulders.

6. Digs post holes.

7. Splits logs.

The first chore is the most important. Hardpan and general soil compaction are among the gardener's worst problems. Very often the upper 12 inches of a garden's soil will be in fine and loose condition—but below that depth may exist a hard and impervious layer that is hindering proper root development. Roots of most garden plants *try* to penetrate as deep as six to ten feet in search of water during dry weather. But they can't if the soil down below is hard.

It is true that building up the surface health of the soil by mulching and using compost will gradually loosen a hardpan below. But waiting for that to happen will occupy several years at least.

Blasting will kill many of the earthworms in the soil, but ultimately the looser conditions that result should actually increase the earthworm population. Where a serious hardpan exists, only a few earthworms will be found.

Dynamite is dangerous but it can be used and if simple precautions are followed, dynamite becomes a safe and reliable tool.

Many people don't realize that there are different kinds of dynamite. Some blasting powder is so sensitive that a simple shock will set it off. Others are relatively mild and slow acting, and require a strong detonation to explode. For soil blasting purposes the slowest grades are used, and can be used without fear.

To improve the soil structure of a large garden area, set off only 30 or 40 charges, spaced from 12 to 30 feet apart. For work on that scale there is no need to buy an electric detonator. An ordinary match fuse will work. The blasting procedure is quite simple. Make a hole with a soil coring tool, attach the fuse to the detonating cap and the cap to the dynamite, place the charge in the hole with the fuse extending; and tamp in the fill or "stemming."

To improve soil structure by using explosives, the following procedures are recommended:

1. Make a map or paper plan of the desired results. Blasting near buildings can only be done with great caution and is probably out of the question on suburban holdings. Dynamiting can be done safely on homesteads situated outside or bordering on town limits.

2. Locate the position—depth and extent—of the hardpan. It is important to place the charge *in* the hardpan, not above or below it. In this way, the strength of the charge will

be directed where it is most needed. Do the actual blasting when the soil is dry. Wet soil may be compacted by a blast, rather than loosened.

3. Bore holes straight down, using a driving bar or soil auger. The charge used is usually one-half to one cartridge. Be sure to fill in or "stem" the hole in which the charge is placed. Sand makes a good stemming.

4. Make one test shot to start with, then excavate the blasted earth to determine just what effect you are achieving.

5. If unsure of your "do-it-your-self" abilities, hire someone with experience to do the job. The cost of even a custom job will be less than the benefits gained.

Large, tractor-powered subsoilers have generally taken the place of dynamite in correcting farm hardpan problems. In a large area, there is no doubt that a chisel blade penetrating 18 inches to four feet is faster and cheaper than blasting. But it is doubtful whether mechanical subsoilers can do as shattering a job as dynamite. Furthermore, most gardeners don't have access to mechanical subsoilers.

E

EARP-THOMAS, DR. G. H.: A pioneer of municipal composting in the United States. Many years ago, he developed his principle of the "continuous-flow digester," a vertical cylinder divided into eight sections or floors and fitted internally with rotating booms. The organic waste, after having been ground to a pulp-like consistency, is introduced to the top section of the digestor where it is inoculated with bacteria.

The waste "works" its way down, floor by floor, heating up as it descends. After 24 hours, it has reached the bottom layer and the composting process is considered complete.

EARTH ALMOND: *see* CHUFA

EARTH'S GREEN CARPET, THE: *by Louise E. Howard see* BOOKS FOR ORGANIC GARDENERS AND FARMERS

EARTHWORM: The earthworm is a valuable adjunct in the soil's expression of fertility. He digests the soil—eats it and conditions it. To an important extent, our topsoils have practically been made by earthworms. That is why Aristotle called them the intestines of the soil. Their castings are far richer minerally than the soil which they ingest. It is said that an average earthworm will produce its weight in castings every twenty-four hours. They burrow into the ground, as far as six feet down, aerating the soil, making holes for rain to pene-

There are more than 2000 species of earthworms, extending in size from the microscopic to several feet. They are rated invaluable aids to the farmer because they both aerate and enrich the soil.

trate. They break up hardpans. Each year their dead bodies furnish a considerable amount of valuable nitrogenous fertilizer, which may amount to more than a thousand pounds per acre in a highly "organic soil."

The division of invertebrate animals, of which the earthworm is a member, is composed of five families or classes. These, in turn, are divided into two orders. The *phylum annelida*, that is to say, the entire division of earthworms contains upwards of two thousand species.

Some earthworms come to the surface of the soil and travel many miles especially in rainy weather, when their burrows or tunnels are flooded. All throw their bodily excrements, technically known as castings, behind them. Some species throw their castings above the surface of the soil, forming small hillocks or mounds.

Earthworms range in size from microscopic to several feet. Some common names are orchard worm, rain worm, angle worm, brandling, night crawler and fish worm—descriptive names familiar to certain areas of the United States. Hybrids have been developed by cross breeding. All are "headless," eyeless and toothless. There are no external antennae or feelers. From tip to tail the body is composed of ring-like segments. A short distance from the head, there's a band, lighter in color than the balance of the body, which is usually a deep red.

Noted earthworm researcher Charles Darwin found that the amount of soil these creatures pass through their bodies annually can be as much as 15 tons of dry earth an acre. In so doing, the digestive juices of the earthworm make the soil's organic matter and mineral content more valuable to plants. Their manure makes excellent fertilizer. Aerating, drainage, mixing—these are a few other reasons why earthworms are rated so highly.

Usual methods for earthworm breeding are: culture box, ground-top bed, pit and compost heap. For beginners the box method is considered simplest.

Earthworm manure is known as castings; capsules are the gelantinous egg sacs containing wormlets, each capsule about half the size of a grain of rice. Culture is the mixture in which earthworms breed; the basic mixture generally consists of manure, earth and pulverized vegetable matter as grasses and grains.

Earthworms are bi-sexual, with both male and female reproductive organs; each earthworm is capable of producing egg capsules, but must first have contact with another worm to be fertilized. Under favorable conditions, an earthworm will produce an egg capsule every week to ten days. Two to three weeks after the capsule has been deposited (usually near the soil surface), the wormlets emerge as minute white threads about one-sixteenth of an inch in length and are self-sufficient from that time on, with an average life span of two years.

Earthworm eggs hatch in about 21 days. The new-born appear as short bits of whitish thread about one-quarter of an inch in length. In from 12 to 48 hours they become darker, but are visible to the untrained eye only after a painstaking search for them.

Worms begin to mate from 80 to 100 days after birth, depending upon the richness or poorness of the soil in which they live or in which they are cultured.

Mating follows at periods of from six to eight days. Thus, if we are to follow the average fertility of each capsule laid, that is, three worms, one mature worm will beget over 150 worms each year of its life.

Certain species of earthworms, particularly those that come to the surface and crawl about during wet or rainy weather, seemingly are chiefly active during the nocturnal hours. Other species are, apparently, active throughout most of the day and night. This specie seldom, if ever, comes to the surface, remaining throughout its life from six to 30 inches beneath the surface, depending on the porosity of the soil.

Every morsel of soil and decayed vegetable and animal matter taken in by the earthworm passes through its digestive system. This is equipped with a gizzard-like organ. Here the food value in the swallowed matter is extracted for use by the worm. The balance is carried by muscular action down through, and out of, the alimentary canal.

Earthworms abound in practically every geological section of this planet. The exceptions to this rule are the extreme northern and southern latitudes where extended cold periods preclude the existence of this branch of invertebrate animals. But in torrid and temperate zones more than 1000 species of earthworms live, prosper and procreate.

The dense, humid jungles of equatorial climes give us the largest specimens of the earthworm. These are the direct antecedents of all terrestrial worms that have spread from one end of the earth to the other. *See also* AERATION.

EARTHWORMS, BREEDING: The "culture box" is the simplest method for beginning earthworm breeders.

Any good-sized wooden box will work well. Fruit or vegetable lug boxes, approximately 17 by 14 by six inches, are fine and can usually be obtained from any food market. Place the boxes in a corner of the basement, garage or shed, under the house or outside in a sheltered place.

This size box accommodates 500 full-grown breeders, or half a pound of pit-run (mixed sizes), which ordinarily amounts to 800 or so worms from babies to breeders. Since the usual earthworm order is for either 1,000 breeders or one pound of pit-

run, you'll need two made-over boxes to start off with.

CULTURE BOX MIXTURE: This mixture will make enough for just one box.

Spread a 12-quart pail of finely-screened topsoil out on a flat surface (floor or work-table) until it is leveled out to a layer three inches high; similarly spread over this a 12-quart pail of finely-ground peat moss that has been thoroughly soaked beforehand in water, for 24 hours, and then drained or squeezed free of dripping water; spread over this a 12-quart pail of crumbled horse, cow, sheep or rabbit manure; sprinkle whole surface of this layered pile with a mixture of food made by thoroughly mixing a cupful of dry cornmeal with one (or two, if you have it) pound canful of coffee grounds.

Now with a small trowel, start at one end of the pile and systematically toss, turn, mix and aerate this compost, until you get to the other end of the pile; then go back and forth again—tossing, mixing, fluffing—taking only a little at a time.

The ideal moisture-content is reached when you can squeeze a handful of compost in your fist and have it hold together in a wet but not dripping mould. Test your compost now. It it needs more moisture, sprinkle some water over it gently and evenly and let it penetrate through the loose pile. Repeat this whole tossing, mixing and moistening operation once a day for five days.

On the fifth day, before you toss it put your hand down into the heart of the pile to test it for heat. If it is cool to the touch, your work is done; if there is the slightest warmth, keep mixing and moistening once a day until it is thoroughly cooled. Earthworms will crawl out en masse if your compost is warm; if they can't escape, they burn up—actually melt and die.

FILLING AND STOCKING THE CULTURE BOX: It usually takes the average earthworm hatchery from one to three weeks to fill and ship your order. Find out when you place your order and get your boxes and compost ready ahead of time. We are now going to assume that your worms have arrived and are setting in their containers waiting to be planted in your culture boxes.

1. Toss and fluff up your compost again, just in case it got lumpy or packed while waiting for the worms to arrive. Also test it for moisture and re-moisten, if necessary.

2. Lay a piece of burlap, corrugated cardboard, or a few folded sheets of newspaper over the loose-lath false bottom of box.

3. Evenly spread about a half-inch layer of dried lawn clippings, withered small weeds, or crushed dried leaves. (Note: Use no grass that has had weed-killer or chemical fertilizer applied to it. Earthworms are very sensitive to chemicals and won't work in compost that is not to their taste, but will pile up in bunches along the walls of the box and eventually crawl out.)

4. Fill with compost to within three inches from the top of box.

5. Dump half of your breeders into each box (don't tire them out by trying to count out exactly half—just guess it). Or, if you've purchased pit-run, put half of those (by guess) in each box. If you are stocking your box indoors, turn on a 100-watt light about a foot above the box to make the worms go down into the compost quickly.

If you're working outdoors, the sunlight will accomplish it. Worms don't like being exposed to strong light. If the weather is raw or dark, go inside with this operation. Cold worms scarcely move. Under right conditions they'll burrow down in five to 30 minutes.

6. Now fill your box with compost up to within an inch from the top. This gives your worms a depth of six inches of compost to work in, which is their *minimum* requirement.

7. Mix a handful of very dry cornmeal with three handfuls of coffee grounds. (This will be enough to do two boxes.) Sprinkle two handfuls of this in two ridges on top of compost (in each box), keeping two inches away from both the sides and the ends of the box. These open spaces will give the worms a chance to escape from this feed in case it heats up temporarily.

8. Fill box to rim with dried lawn clippings or similar material. Press these into a mat by using a light board, being careful to tuck all the grass inside the walls of the box. Lay a piece of well-soaked burlap over the grass, or any kind of cloth the size of the box, being sure to tuck it in so none of it hangs over the rim. The burlap should be about half an inch from upper rim when pressed into place. Worms will crawl along overhanging burlap or grass and get out.

9. Improvise a sprinkler by punching small nail holes in the bottom of a two-pound coffee can. Pour a quart of water into the can and sprinkle your box evenly through the burlap, covering the whole surface. Avoid wetting the outside surface of your box.

After your culture boxes multiply and you begin stacking them four or five high, make yourself a pipe and right-angle nozzle sprinkler, thus eliminating the need to lift your boxes around when all the attention they require is weekly watering. The reason to water through the burlap and grass from now on is to distribute the water evenly and gently, thus causing a minimum of flooding of the channels that the worms have made for themselves down below.

STORING AND STACKING: Except for watering your boxes once a week, and keeping an eye on those two ridges of cornmeal-coffee mix after about the third week, your first two culture boxes will need no more attention until it comes to subdivide them into four.

The *temperature* of your storage place should get no lower than 50°, nor higher than 75°, for best results. Worms work best and breed best at 60 to 75°. Below 60 they begin to get sluggish, and at 32° and lower they are completely dormant—merely balling up somewhere to await better conditions.

While it is all right to keep your stack outdoors during the milder weather, where it is protected from excessive heat, wind and rain, you must bring it in for the winter if you live in a cold climate.

DIVIDING BOXES: Here's a time-table for subdividing culture boxes:

boxes stocked with breeders—divide after 30 days;

boxes stocked with pit-run—divide after 40 days;

boxes stocked with eggs and spawn (babies)—divide after 90 days.

The week you are planning to divide, don't water the box. The mealier the material, the easier it is to handle the worms. The last operation after dividing will be the usual watering. A good tip when handling worms is to keep a can of dry soil at hand and keep rubbing your palms and fingers in it to keep them from getting gummy.

Dividing a culture box is about a 15-minute job. It should be done in strong sunlight or under a 100-watt light hung about a foot above the box. This encourages the worms to go down quickly into the compost, as they don't like being exposed to strong light.

HARVESTING THE CASTINGS: Beginning about the fourth month after starting your original boxes, you will notice that the bottom four inches of material (the breeders' home) is getting blacker and blacker, and finely granulated. It will look as different from the original coarse compost as day is from night. These are the castings.

Don't water the culture box during the week you are planning to do this job. Turn the breeders' box upside down onto a cardboard under a strong light. Pile the castings up in a tall, tight cone, and give the worms time to get clear down to the bottom-center of the cone in a solid mass. This should not take more than 20 minutes. Then go back and start lopping off the top of the cone in double handfuls — collecting same in a pail.

Then start cutting in around the base of the cone. Keep these two maneuvers up until you see the boiling mass of worms at the bottom. Lift them up in both hands and immediately plant them in a newly-prepared culture box as you did in the beginning, when they first were shipped to you.

In the castings there may still be eggs and white spawn. The eggs you can lift out with a spoon, as mentioned. The spawn will go down and roll up in balls and masses under the light, if given plenty of time, and may be planted in another box.

BRANCHING INTO OUTDOOR PITS: After you've racked up ten or 15 culture boxes full of worms, you are ready to introduce as many as you want to spare into outdoor pits. Remember that the worm works best in the upper six to ten inches. It's folly to throw a pile three to five feet high at him. Rather, make your pit long and shallow.

Plan to plant 500 breeders or 1000 mixed sizes per cubic foot of compost and they will do their job quickly and well. Be sure to have a solid, or a one-half-inch wire netting bottom on your pit to keep the moles from ravaging it. Planking, shiplap, or a thin layer (one inch) of concrete will do. The sides can be similar wood, four-inch concrete walls, or concrete blocks. An over-all height of two feet provides room for ten to 12 inches of compost on the bottom and protective layers of dry leaves, wilted grass, weeds, green garbage, or hay, to shield the worms from the elements.—*Dorothy Hewett.*

EARWIG: Both adult and nymph are reddish-brown, prominent forceps at tail end, growing up to three-quarters inch long. The earwig hides during day and forages at night. It discharges a foul odor, seldom causes severe damage to vegetables, but is chiefly a health hazard. For control, use of traps has been found very effective; here is one trap used: take four pieces of bamboo a foot in length—each piece open at both ends and tie with nylon yarn into a bundle at both ends. Lightly paint them with a green paint and when dry, put under bushes, against fences and any place where earwigs are likely to gather; leave them there for a few days; early one morning, shake earwigs out of holes into bucket of hot water or kerosene; bantam hens have also been reported as an effective control against earwigs. *See also* INSECT CONTROL.

ECHINACEA: (*Brauneria angustifolia*) A native perennial plant found on the prairies of the Middle West, most abundantly in Nebraska and Kansas. The roots are used medicinally.

This plant has been found to do well under cultivation in moderately rich and well-drained loam. It grows fairly well from seed, which is planted thinly in a well-prepared seedbed in drills about eight inches apart. The plants develop slowly and may be left in the seedbed for two years and then transplanted to the field in spring and set about 18 inches apart in rows. Thorough cultivation is essential for best results.

Blooming in summer, these plants are fine in the open border, as they can stand wind and sun well. The purple daisy (*E. angustifolia*) grows two feet high, while the Hedgehog

coneflower (*E. purpurea*) often reaches three feet high.

ECOLOGY: The science (actually a branch of biology) which deals with the mutual relations between organisms and their environment. In agriculture, it is the important study of the relationship between plant communities or groups of plants and their environment, including soil types, composition and development, climate, rainfall, temperature, light, etc. *See also* SOIL.

EDELWEISS: (*Leontopodium*) A lovely alpine perennial herb (and an emblem of purity), edelweiss grows four to 12 inches high, and is covered with a whitish wool with small yellow flowers. It has become a recommended rock garden plant, preferring light, well-drained soil and full sun. Seeds are sown in early February indoors and transplanted to regular location in May.

During the winter, edelweiss often appears to have died away completely, but as soon as the soil is warmed by the first spring sunshine, its silvery leaves begin to peep through once more.

EDGING: Low-growing plants or materials such as bricks, rocks or metal, used to mark the outline of a flower bed, lawn or roadway.

Many commercial edging materials are available, most of them made from metal, but for a more rustic appearance, rough bricks or rocks are more effective. Low-growing plants such as candytuft, box barberry and violas, can make effective edgings. The width and type of the border depend for the most part on the edging plants used. *See also* BORDERS; FLOWER GARDENING.

EELWORM: *see* NEMATODE

EGGPLANT: (*Solanum melongena*) This tropical vegetable, often substituted for meat, has a mild flavor similar to that of fried oysters. It can be grown successfully in any good garden soil but is very sensitive to weather conditions.

Eggplant is a member of the *Solanaceae* family of which the potato, pepper and tomato are other members. Not only are these crops related botan-

Eggplant is sensitive to the cold and should be started in a hotbed or greenhouse, allowing six to eight weeks from seeding to transplanting.

ically but their culture is quite similar. Eggplant is grown as an annual, and if not killed by disease, will bear until frost is past. They are not hardy and should not be set out until danger of frost is past. Eggplant is primarily a warm season crop which produces best in sunny weather.

CULTURE: Start the seed indoors in pots or flats and cover with a one-quarter-inch of soil. One packet of seed will provide more than enough plants for the average family. It takes about two months to produce eggplants large enough to set out. Most home gardeners prefer to buy plants which can be set outdoors after all danger of frost has passed.

If your average, free frost date is April tenth, eggplant seedlings would be due in the ground early in May. If that date is later, around the twentieth or thirtieth of April, wait until the first two weeks in June to plant them in the open. Count back eight weeks from either of these dates, and you will have the one for sowing your seeds.

It will be well to soak these seeds in water first; then sow them in flats, covering them with one-half inch of mellow well-pulverized soil, remembering to keep them always in a warm room. Where the seedlings are about two weeks old, or about three inches high, transplant them singly in small clay pots.

The soil for this first transplanting should be particularly rich. A good combination for it will be: two parts of rotted sod and one part of compost in which a small amount of sand has been mixed. Later on in the garden, eggplant will flourish in almost any type of soil, provided it is well fed. Someone has expressed it, "the best soil for eggplant is that which is very fertile as the result of long-continued good treatment."

This "good treatment" consists first of all, in not using fresh manure, but in nourishing the bed with well-rotted manure or compost. Apply these at the rate of about two pounds of either to each plant.

Because of their sensitiveness to the weather conditions, protection of some sort is a necessity for the young plants when first set in the open. Paper cones or wooden boxes covered with a piece of glass, will both be useful for this purpose. There are those who fashion a box with four panes of glass set edgewise, with a piece of cheesecloth placed over the top. Or, the plastic containers in which many household supplies come today, will, if their size permits, make excellent miniature greenhouses for the tender plants.

Given good drainage and a very fertile soil, the eggplant tract will require moisture equal to about one inch of rain a week. In very dry weather this must be given with watering by hand. Do not forget at such times when this is necessary, that it is always better in the vegetable garden to give the ground a good soaking once a week, than to sprinkle it every day.

When the ground is thoroughly warmed in the spring, and the young plants are putting forth new growth, one may know the time has come to give the necessary adjunct—a mulch. Use hay or straw for this, laying it about two inches thick.

All mulches are valuable, but one is especially so for the eggplant with its necessarily unhampered development. Besides smothering the weeds, it will help to conserve a uniform supply of moisture which in turn will enable the roots to feed on the top, moist two inches of soil with which they are surrounded.

By the middle of July, your eggplants will be in need of extra food. This is best given as a side dressing of compost or other natural fertilizer.

It is generally conceded that warm, sandy soils are best adapted to eggplants. This crop is seldom grown in clay soils, except under the most favorable climatic conditions. It is important that the soil be deep, rich and well drained. A liberal amount of compost is essential to the largest yields.

Manure may be applied heavily for an early crop, like lettuce or radishes, to be followed by eggplants.

Allow two and one-half feet between plants and about three feet between rows. Water thoroughly after transplanting.

VARIETIES: Black Beauty is the most generally grown. It is a sturdy grower, and produces very large fruits. New York Improved Spineless is a little later, with more elongated, lighter purple-colored fruits. Early Long Purple is more dwarf, earlier maturing and therefore may prove better for cool sections of the country.

HARVESTING: The fruits are at their best edible stage when the skin has attained a high gloss. Fully matured fruits are not as desirable as those somewhat immature. When young, the seeds will be small and

hardly noticeable. Keep fruits picked off as they become ready and plants should bear until frost.

Eggplant is very easy to cook and does not need the salting process so often described. Simply peel and cut the eggplant into slices about one-quarter-inch thick. Either dip in an egg batter or cover with flour and saute in olive oil.

EGGSHELLS: A good source of eggshells is a chicken hatchery, which usually will be glad to have them hauled away. The analysis of eggshells is over one per cent of nitrogen and about 0.4 per cent of phosphoric acid; the main substance is, of course, calcium. Where eggshells are regularly added to the compost heap, they will supply a considerable amount of lime to the soil over a period of years.

ELDERBERRY: (*Sambucus*) Often called elder, the plant is a widely found member of the Honeysuckle family. There are five or more prin-

American or Sweet Elder is also known as the elderberry. It does well in the informal garden, and is easily raised, preferring a moist soil.

cipal species, but the American or Sweet Elder (*S. canadensis*) is most recommended, since it produces abundant purplish-black berries richer in vitamin C than any other garden fruit except rose hips and black currants.

Frequently found wild, this shrub is one of the easiest to grow. It is hardy in the North, a rapid grower that does best in rich, moist soil and partial shade. Propagation is by cuttings, seeds or occasionally by suckers. Relatively free of insect and disease trouble, its chief pest is generally the currant borer which can be checked by cutting out affected canes. At maturity, it reaches a height of six to ten feet.

As a food, the berries are considered a superior jam and pie-fruit; the berries and flowers both serve as a source for wine. In landscaping, the elderberry—properly used—is a highly practical ornamental shrub, attractive in hedgerows, roadsides, back borders and especially adapted to moist soil areas near water.

In addition, the berries are used in dye-making as a source of deep red and purple colors. The hollowed stems are employed in various crafts, including blow-gun toys and boyhood whistles. Medicinally, the elder's usefulness dates back many centuries. As an herbal remedy, it was and still is regarded beneficial in treating all sorts of common ailments in man and animal. A favorite of the Greek doctor, Hippocrates, and a sacred plant to the gypsies, the elderberry was used in a wide variety of ointments, powders and potions to alleviate internal and external disorders.

Flies are said to have an aversion to the elder's highly scented leaves. Dried and powdered, these are used as an insect-repellent by the Arabs. A concentrated brew of the green stalks and branches is used as an external application against gadfly for cattle and horses. *See also* FRUITS; BRAMBLE FRUITS.

ELECAMPANE: (*Inula helenium*) A European perennial plant now growing wild along roadsides and in fields throughout the northeastern part of the United States. The root is used in medicine. Elecampane will grow in almost any soil but thrives best in deep clay loam well supplied with moisture. The plant is best propagated by divisions of old roots, which are set in the field in fall about 18 inches apart in rows three feet apart. Plants can also be grown by sowing seed in spring in seedbeds and setting the seedlings in the field in the same manner as the root divisions. Those grown from seed do not flower the first year. Cultivation should be sufficient to keep the soil in good condition and free from weeds.

Doing best in a sunny location, elecampane grows as high as six feet.

ELECTROCULTURE: Electroculture is a method of setting up an electrical field to influence the growth of plants. The word *electrical* in this sense does not mean a conventional electric current, but an atmospheric, magnetic electricity. According to research, this electricity has been found to have very beneficial properties for plant growth and germination.

Tests at the Massachusetts Experiment Station many years ago have indicated that plants benefit from electricity.

ELECTROCULTURE TECHNIQUE: The following methods have been used by experimenters in electroculture:

1. *Radiomagnetic.* The seed is sown in a bed provided with a sheet of iron-wire netting, one-half inch. For plant or tree a *jacket* or *apron* is formed, one inch to one foot wide, depending on the girth. For individual branches of a tree a *collar* of the same wire netting is formed.

2. Preliminary treatment of seed before sowing, either in *dry* way, by spreading it out in a thin layer on an insulated metal plate and then giving the plate a high-tension spark of say

2,000 volts for one minute and then sowing the seed *without touching;* or in the *wet* way, by soaking the seed in *electrified water* in an insulated vessel for one or two hours and then sowing the seed without touching it as before.

3. *Agaskarising* the plant or giving it electrified water. Whenever a growing part is given such a mantle of electrified water, its growth is increased. This is much more than irrigation, which is watering the roots. Water is electrified by taking it in an earthenware container, placing it on a rubber mat, dipping one end of a high-tension cable into the water while the other is hooked on to the ignition plug of a motor car and the engine run for a minute. A complete set of such pitchers, containing as many as 100 gallons, can be electrified at once by dipping one end of a wire into each, collecting and connecting the other ends together and then using a cable in the same way and running the engine as above.

4. *Interculture* of the growing plant with other suitable plants such as are rich in M-Rays or Gurwitch Rays or Ultraviolet Rays like onions and other root crops.

5. Combination of the above methods. Other radiations are also effective, such as X-Rays, Ultraviolet Rays, Violet Rays, etc., but the exposure should not exceed one minute as a rule.

The *Basic Principle* is that wherever there is cellular activity there is electrical energy developed, and conversely, wherever electrical energy is applied, cellular activity is increased and better growth obtained. *Electroculture* is the science of securing this growth through the application of electricity by using suitable technique.

ELECTROCULTURE, HOME EXPERIMENTS IN:

Experiment One: With any low-growing garden vegetable, such as broccoli, etc., set rows of metal cans (ordinary tin cans), with the tops and bottoms removed, beside each seed-

ling plant in the row. The metal cylinders should be placed firmly—about an inch or so—into the soil. At a distance from these, raise another

row or more of the same vegetable in the same way, omitting only the cans.

Experiment Two: In the soil next to a number of potted plants such as

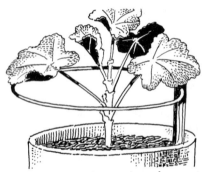

radishes—or in the garden plot next to these or carrots, etc.,—insert a piece of wood through which a circle of copper wire is suspended. Allow enough circumference so that the suspended wire does not touch the plant. Again, provide several check plants, treated equally, without the wire arrangement.

Experiment Three: Directly over a row of vegetables, stretch a wire fastened to poles at the ends of the row. Keep this just high enough so that here, too, no plant is touched. Grow one or more rows of the same vegetables as a test comparison. A variation on this idea is a metal grid, or iron-netting, placed in the soil around

each of the plants—but not in contact —in the row.

Experiment Four: On the stalk and branches of tomatoes, beans or any vine-type plant, hang metal balls (as

Christmas tree balls). Attach these carefully, being sure that they are not tied too tightly and are not heavy enough to hamper the plant's development.

ELM: (*Ulmus*). These tall ornamental trees are widely planted as shade and street trees. They are the most commonly planted ornamental tree in the northeastern states.

Most are hardy in the North, especially *U. americana* which is favored for street and park plantings. It grows up to 120 feet high. Its wide-spreading head on a straight trunk has become a standard sight in American towns.

Elms are easily transplanted, best in rich, rather moist soil, and are not sensitive to severe pruning. Generally

little pruning is needed. Many insects and fungi attack the elm, especially the American elm. The elm leaf beetle is destructive of the foliage, and the canker worm is also troublesome. To keep it from doing damage, band the trunks a few feet above the ground

This American or White Elm is native to Durham, N. H. This species attains a height of 120 feet, is hardy and abounds east of the Rocky Mountains.

with cloth covered with a sticky substance. This prevents the wingless female from climbing.

All elm leaves, no matter what variety, are lopsided at the stem end. The more advanced botanist will notice strong ribs or veins branching out from the main rib that runs down the middle of the leaf. Elm leaves, also, on the whole are rather hairy and rough.

The English Elm (*U. campestris*) is a more compact tree than the American Elm, growing to 100-150 feet. It is just as hardy and can be grown in the same types of soil. The leaves will stay green longer in the fall than the American Elm.

The Wahoo or winged Elm, one of the smallest of the elms, can be grown only in the South. It does very well south of Virginia and west to Arkansas and Texas, "Petite" can be used to describe its oblong-headed growth. Use on upland soil near streams and lakes.

The red-barked Slippery Elm (*U. fulva*) is suited to most eastern regions, rarely growing over 60 feet.

The Cork or Rock Elm (*U. racemosa*) has not the elegance of the American Elm, being a large, stiff-looking tree, but it can be planted as far north as Quebec. Watch for corky ridges on most of its branches. Growing up to 90 feet, its foliage turns yellow in fall.

Charming in spring is the Scotch or Wych Elm (*U. glabra*). It produces large rosettes of flowers that can almost be mistaken for leaves. The variety of Camperdown Elm will form a natural arbor when mature.

CULTURE: Mulching with leaves or sawdust is helpful if grass under the tree is not important. If soil is acid, correct *p*H to about neutral. Insert ground rock fertilizers into mulch.

The dread Dutch Elm Disease, a product of neglected care of the elms, is caused by a fungus imported from Holland, causing a wilting or yellowing of the leaves. In severe cases trees suddenly wilt and die without excessive yellowing of leaves. The fungus mycelium gets into the water passages so that supply from the roots is cut off.

The organic method is a strong point in fighting the Dutch Elm Disease. A healthy tree can usually resist attacks from all kinds of parasites. Since it is carried by the Elm Bark beetle, it is best to look to him first. Prune away all sick branches which might be breeding places for the beetles. Be careful of all wounds, because the Dutch Elm fungus enters mainly where the bark has already been broken. See also TREES; DUTCH ELM DISEASE.

EMMAUS (ee-may'-us): A borough (pop. 10,000) in central-eastern Pennsylvania, five miles south of Allentown. Emmaus was settled in 1741 by Moravians, and was named after the Biblical city located near Jerusalem, mentioned in St. Luke 24:13. Emmaus is the home of the organic method in America, and holds the offices of Rodale Press, Inc., publishers of *Organic Gardening and Farming* magazine and *Prevention* magazine. The Organic Experimental Farm, scene of much of the practical experimentation of the organic method, is located near Emmaus. *See also* ORGANIC METHOD, HISTORY OF.

ENCLOSED GARDEN: If you own a year-round place you will doubtless secure privacy for your outdoor living-room by permanent plantings—perennials, shrubs, and evergreens. If you occupy a country home only for a few months during the summer or rent property, a row of tall-growing annuals may be needed. Annual vines, such as morning glories, trained on arbors or trellises also make a quick and effective screen. *See also* SCREENS, PLANTS FOR.

Only very tall-growing annuals are suitable for a temporary hedge. The tallest of all is the castor-oil plant (*Ricinus*), which probably originated in Africa. It grows readily in almost any garden soil with good drainage, and reaches a height of about 12 feet in the North. It becomes a tall tree in the tropics. Its foliage creates something of a tropical atmosphere, as the plants look coarse and heavy. Next in height comes the annual sunflower which in good soil grows to a height of ten feet or more. Cosmos are very attractive, but the late-blooming kinds are often cut down by hard frosts before flowering. The early ones are preferable for planting in the North.

Trellises, fences, either wire or wooden, or walls covered with vines make the most satisfactory screening. The moonflower (*Calonyction*) blooms only at night, except on cloudy days, but will make a growth of 30 to 40 feet in a season. Other climbers of more delicate growth are the cardinal vine (*Quamoclit*) and the scarlet-runner bean, the latter a perennial usually grown as an annual. The clock-vine (*Thunbergia*) is a dainty trailer to clamber along a wall. The leaves are very decorative and the creamy, purple-throated flowers are excellent for cutting. *See also* ARBOR.

ENDIVE: (*Cichorium endivia*) This salad plant will succeed in any ordinary garden soil not deficient in humus and normal moisture. Like lettuce, its succulent growth must be rather rapid to enable it to form tender leaves. On poor, dry, exposed soil its growth will be slowed up so that its leaves, if they

Full Heart Batavian Endive like this measures a full 15 inches across. In addition, it is highly valued for its A, B₁ and C vitamin content.

form in quantity, will be hard and unnecessarily pungent.

An excellent plan for success in endive growing is to use the same area where lettuce succeeded early in the spring. A thin layer of compost lightly dug in along the lines where the rows of endive are to grow will insure success.

Seed should be thinly sown, covered with not more than 1/3 inch of finely sifted, mature compost humus, clean sand, or a mixture of the two. To make easier the job of sowing, seed, sand, and humus may be well-mixed first in a suitable container and the mixture spread in a narrow ribbon along the bottom of a shallow trench formed by drawing the corner of the hoe along a line indicated by a tight string stretched across the garden. The rows should be placed about one foot apart and the plants early thinned to stand one foot apart in the row.

For a fall crop, seed must be sown in late summer. Growing the tiny seedlings during a time when the garden surface is hot and dry, has its difficulties. You may find it best to raise the plants in a flat or similar container set in a partly shaded spot, or by using a shaded seedbed. Flats and seedbeds may be protected from excess summer heat by stretching cheesecloth over them in some manner. This covering may be in the form of a small tent or an awning, either is easily built upon stakes driven into the ground around the seedbed. A removable slat roof, a frame a bit larger than the seedbed is a handy garden accessory. Such a slat roof is easily made. Across a reasonable firm rectangular frame of the desired size, laths are nailed with spaces equal to the width of the laths between them.

The flat should be built of boards thick enough to prevent the undue escape of moisture and have adequate drainage. It should be deep enough to hold three inches of a fifty-fifty mixture of clean sand and mature compost, plus a bottom layer of small stones or broken flower pots. Later prick out the little plants and transfer them to flower pots or small containers as their demand for space increases. Seedlings of endive are usually ready for transplanting to the open garden when they are three weeks old.

Young plants should be set slightly deeper than they grew in the flat, be well firmed and protected against excessive heat if necessary for a day or two by inverted baskets. Usually such protection is not necessary. A little work with the hoe to keep down weeds, or a light mulching of straw or rough compost, is about all the cultivation the plants need.

BLANCHING: Endive differs from lettuce in many ways. One of its striking differences is the slightly bitter, appetizing flavor of its leaves. This bitter flavor can be reduced sufficiently to make it a really pleasant and refreshing quality by blanching.

When the plant is about half grown and the head fairly well formed, the long outer leaves should be drawn up around it and tied together with soft string or a strip of muslin so as to cause them to exclude sunlight from the heart.

Some three weeks later you will be able to cut and examine the first blanched head.

Blanching, the exclusion of light, may be accomplished in a number of ways: by inverted flower pots over the plants; by placing planks about a foot wide on edge so that they cover the row with a light-tight miniature roof. Unless you grow a very large number of plants it will probably be easier for you to tie up the heads.

Although blanching reduces the bitterness natural to the leaf, it also reduces its food value. The green, unblanched outer leaves so casually placed upon the compost heap are highly recommended by dieticians because they are rich in Vitamins A, B₁, and C, and recommended as protective foods to ward off colds and maintain normal eyesight. The bitterness of these outer leaves can become a savory asset when cooked in soups with a "flat" flavor and with ordinary "greens." This quality can also be used to add distinction to the ordinary salad-bowl.

Plants which reach maturity in late fall are commonly dug up with a good ball of earth around their roots and with as little disturbance as possible, and set in a dark corner of a cool, unheated cellar. Here the heads will

soon blanch without the necessity of tying.

There are many fine types of endive from which you may choose. Cos type Batavian (100 days to maturity) has broad, flat leaves much like Broad-Leaved Batavian (90 days to maturity). Giant Fringed Oyster endive (65 days to maturity) has finely cut, lacinated leaves. Before tying up for blanching most of these plants form a rosette some 15 inches in diameter.

Lettuce and endive belong to the same family as the dandelion. But endive, *C. endivia,* is much more closely related to chicory, *C. intybus.—Roger Smith.*

ENGLISH DAISY: (*Bellis perennis*) Also known as bachelor's button, this biennial bedding plant blooms early, grows to six inches high. *See also* DAISY.

ENGLISH ELM: *see* ELM

ENGLISH IVY: (*Hedera helix*) Capable of climbing as high as 100 feet and covering walls and trellises, this evergreen vine does best in a shady location. Also useful for outdoor boxes and baskets, as well as a ground cover under shade trees, it can be propagated by cuttings. *See also* IVY.

ENTOMOLOGY: Branch of zoology that deals with insects. Research experts in the field have stated that it is essential that insect biology and *ecology* be included in their studies. The most economical and desirable way to control insects is through the use of plant varieties that resist insect attack. According to Dr. E. F. Knipling of the Entomology Research Branch, U. S. Department of Agriculture, "This means of reducing insect losses, when incorporated in varieties having other desired qualities, is accomplished without cost to the grower, without creating a residue or other toxicological hazard, without damage to pollinating insects, and without upsetting nature's balance between host insects and their natural enemies." It is hoped that government researchers will be able to devote more time than is currently being spent to this important aspect of controlling insects, as well as the field of biological control. *See also* INSECT CONTROL.

ENZYME: Any of a class of complex organic substances, such as amylase, pepsin, etc., that accelerate, or catalyze, specific chemical transformations, as in the digestion of foods, in plants and animals.

Without enzymes, plants would not grow, seeds would not germinate, organic matter would remain unchanged on a compost pile, microbes would not function, and there would be no soil. Enzymes are therefore among the most important things in our world.

EPIPHYLLUM: The orchid of the cactus family. While there are only 16 wild species of Epiphyllum—there are probably better than 3000 varieties recognized, including both the American and European hybrids. The flower size varies from two inches to some as large as ten inches across for a single flower and have a complete color range, with the exception of a real blue. The flower grows directly off the leaf-like stems which in turn are of many shapes and sizes, some long and slender and some wide and meaty.

The original orchid cactus was found in the jungles of Central America and the northern parts of South America and in Mexico.

A good potting mixture for the orchid cactus is one which contains a moister and richer soil than required by desert types of cacti. A suggested ideal composition consists of two parts loam, two parts leaf mold, one part sharp sand, and half part dried rotted manure, plus a pint of bone meal to each bushel. This soil should be kept rich in humus but porous. Shade well from all strong sunlight.

The California climate is especially favorable to growing orchid cactus under lath or in the open. However, they are easily grown anywhere outdoors in the summer and kept indoors in the winter months. During this latter period they should be given an eight to ten week rest, being kept as dry as possible without allowing the

The Ackermanni Epiphyllum is day-blooming with flowers four to six inches wide, scarlet exterior and carmine inside. Origin of species is unknown.

leaf-like stems to shrivel. This winter rest is necessary to assure satisfactory summer blooming.

Growing these lovely flowers from seeds is a long process and they do not always come true to the parent plant. Asexual propagation is the sure way to get the same plant. This is done by taking a cutting from the main branch at the joint where the small branch starts off. A 10-16 inch cutting gives quick bloom.

When taking cuttings, allow them to cure for from five to ten days before replanting. Then they should be set in a dry soil mixed with equal parts leaf mold or good compost material and building sand. When transplanting the rooted cuttings, plant them in perfectly dry soil and withhold water for at least three days. Water the plant sparingly until it is re-established. Plants which are damp or watered at once after transplanting may rot off at the base. A dry plant cannot rot. Be sure the containers have good drainage. The more crowded the plant, the better the blooms. It takes about two years for a plant to bloom from cuttings.

After the first year some feeding is necessary. Diluted cow manure and bone meal several times a year are recommended. If a dry fertilizer, such as well-rotted steer or rabbit manure is used, it is not necessary to feed so often. Just before and after the bloom season will do for the balance of the year. Blooming time is from the last of April to the middle of June.

Plants should be kept well moist all through the growing and blooming season. While the name cactus would imply the characteristics of the desert cactus, these plants like partial shade, moisture and good drainage. *See also* CACTUS; ORCHID.

EPIPHYTE: The name given plants that grow on other plants, commonly known as "tree-perchers." Epiphytes are not parasites, but receive nourishment from the atmosphere. This is evidenced by the fact that in tropic zones epiphytes are often found growing on telephone wires and other man-made structures.

In their natural tropical climate, for example, epiphytic orchids grow on tree branches, high off the ground. Their roots firmly grip the coarse bark of the tree for support. Epiphytic plants never steal food from the tree, but use the tree as a place to perch in the light, rather than dying out in the dense forest. *See also* ORCHIDS.

EROSION: Each year millions of tons of topsoil are lost through erosion. Both good as well as poor lands suffer from this loss. Here are some of the forms that erosion takes:

Gully erosion in this Santa Fe vineyard resulted from mountain runoff. Earth fill dams are advised as a remedy in this case. Control of such runoff calls for careful, expert, on-the-site observation.

Sheet erosion: Worst damage occurs on bare cultivated soil; rain puddles the soil and seals it so that runoff results; best protection from sheet erosion is by keeping continuous cover on soil by way of green manure and cover crops, also working in organic matter to improve soil structure.

Gully erosion: A further development of sheet erosion, gullies tend to lengthen, completely divide farm fields until they must be developed. One vital step is to seed gullied areas with soil-binding crops such as Reed canarygrass.

Wind erosion: Dust bowls are the end result, but wind erosion is a too-common happening on soils that have been continuously cultivated. Experience has shown that any cultivated soil where strong winds occur regularly is a potential dust bowl.

It has been said that most of the soils in this country are practically ruined when they have lost six inches of topsoil, and they are generally abandoned before they lose ten inches of the surface layer. In fact, our entire farm economy is dependent upon that six to nine inches. It is obvious then why the organic method stresses sound practices that will hold down as well as build up the soil. *See also* CONSERVATION; GREEN MANURE CROPS; COVER CROPS; MULCHING.

ERYNGIUM: Also known as sea holly, these perennials with their blue flowers are often recommended for the rock garden and border. Summer-blooming and requiring sufficient space, they do best in a moist, fairly rich soil. Varieties include button snakeroot (*E. aquaticum*)—four to six feet; *E. bourgati*—1½ feet or less; and *E. giganteum*—over six feet.

ESCAROLE: *see* ENDIVE

ESPALIER: A method for training fruit trees to grow in a shape best suited to the grower. More specifically, the objective is to train the trees in a manner similar to vines or grapes, so that the branches grow flat along a wall or trellis. Therefore an espalier tree becomes a two-dimensional growth; it grows up and across the wall but not out from it.

The espaliered fruit tree, such as the pear, offers top-quality produce on a comparatively limited growing area. Trees should be of dwarf stock.

Coming from the French word, epaulet, which refers to a shoulder strap, espalier got its name because of the way the branches go out from the trunk almost at right angles or shoulder-like. It's based on the principle of sap flow control. In practice, this means that you may have to prune or kill off stronger branches in order to help along weaker ones, so that the tree has a more even shape.

All trees grown espalier fashion should be dwarf stock, which bears fruit within three years or less after planting. Apples, pears, peaches, plums, nectarines, and cherries are dwarf fruits suitable for espalier.

Espalier *trained* fruit trees are available from several nurseries. With trained trees, your main job is only upkeep rather than the more involved original training. However, since it takes six years or more to train espalier trees, they are fairly expensive to purchase.

WHERE AND HOW TO PLANT: Plant espaliers against sides of buildings, walls, or fences; below or in between windows; or even along driveways or between properties as a hedge.

These trees can be trained to grow horizontally to cover low or medium high walls; upright as a screen or for high walls; or fan-shaped to stretch out over broad wall areas.

When planting espaliers, use the same methods described for dwarf fruit trees. The soil should be moderately open and well-drained; the hole should be big enough to take the tree roots without bending them. Cultivate the soil deeply, making certain to loosen the soil at the bottom of the hole.

Espaliered trees do best planted against a wall or building. Planting technique is the same as for dwarf trees; the graft union is above ground.

If you plant trees close to the foundation of your house, you may run up against a heavy, hard-pan subsoil—probably full of bricks, stones and maybe a few pipes left by the builders. Clean them out and work in compost, peat or other humus material, so that the roots of your tree won't be cut off from water, air and nutrients.

Both tree roots and top should be pruned at time of planting. Use good quality top soil in filling hole to a few inches of the top. By leaving a slight depression around the tree, rain water can collect there., Tamp the earth gently but firmly around the roots leaving no air pockets; next water and mulch two to three feet

around the tree and several inches deep.

Keep in mind that dwarf fruit trees should always be planted with the graft-union above ground. The graft-union is an onion-shaped knob at the base of the trunk and can be recognized by a change in the color of the bark. This graft serves as a guide for how deep to plant the tree and generally should be about an inch above the soil surface.

TRAINING TREES: The final shape of the tree depends on the equal flow of sap throughout the branches. You may have to hold back certain portions that are naturally stronger and faster-growing and encourage the slower and weaker branches. There are several ways to do this:

1. Prune the strong branches short but allow the weaker to grow long;
2. Kill off the useless buds on the strong parts as soon as possible. Do this as late as possible with the weaker parts;
3. Tie up the stronger branches very early and close to the wall but delay doing this to the weaker branches;
4. Pick off some of the leaves on the stronger side;
5. Leave as much fruit as possible on the stronger branches but pick all fruit off the weaker one;
6. Keep the strong side close to the wall and keep the weak part away;
7. If necessary, even place a covering over the strong side to deprive it of light.

Here are a few general principles to keep in mind:

1. Branches cut short develop more vigorously than those left long;
2. Sap has a tendency to flow to the end of the branch, making the terminal bud develop more than the lateral buds;
3. You'll get more buds and less

wood if you slow up the circulation of the tree's sap;

4. The side shoots—not the leaders — need constant summer pruning. Pinching back these shoots induces the formation of fruit spurs, fruit buds and, finally, fruit;

5. Leaders, the principal branches coming from the main trunk, are headed back in the dormant or late winter season, if and when necessary.

EUCALYPTUS: The common name for this fragrant and picturesque broad-leaved evergreen tree is the Gum Tree. Handsome foliage and flowers in addition to varied, interesting bark, make them popular as ornamental trees for streets and lawns. Many of them are especially valuable as windbreaks. They are native to Australia and grow in warm or semitropical areas. Rapid growers, they reach heights up to 300 feet. Among the numerous varieties there are also several attractive dwarf forms, particularly suitable for gardens.

The Blue Gum (*E. globulus*) species is widely used in California and the Southwest. It is quite sensitive to abrupt weather changes and freezing temperatures, but adapts very well to the dry soils of this region. Red Gum (*E. rostrata*) resists both drought and flooding, withstands extreme heat, and thrives in alkaline soil. Red Ironbark (*E. sideroxylon*) has blue or gray-green leaves, dark-hued bark, and a profusion of rose-colored blossoms. Red mahogany (*E. resinifera*) has small flowers, grows to 100 feet.

Since it is adapted to warm temperate climates, most eucalyptus trees in this country are grown in California. They grow well in a variety of soil types, considered to grow best in a rich loam.

EUCHARIS GRANDIFLORA: *see* AMAZON LILY

EUONYMUS: These include a wide number of deciduous and evergreen shrubs or small trees that are popular for many garden and landscaping uses.

The Euonymus is tolerant of most soils and climates, but not all are hardy. They may be grown from cuttings of old wood or by stratified seeds.

Several have colorful fruits; shrubby evergreen types are good for hedges; creeping forms serve as ground cover. Propagated by seeds, layers or cuttings, they do well in any soil and in sun or partial shade. Generally found in the warmer sections, although most deciduous and a few of the evergreen types are hardy in the North, where they thrive under city and seashore environment.

Some of the popular-named species in the Euonymus family include: Running Strawberry Bush (*obovatus*), Spindle-Tree (*Europaeus*), Burning-Bush (*Americanus*), growing respectively 1½, 15 and eight feet high.

All are spring-flowering, sometime in May or June, while the fruit is set from July to frost. *See also* SHRUBS; EVERGREENS.

EUPHORBIA: Also known as spurge, these cactus-like succulents are often grown in the greenhouse. The plants secrete a milky juice, which in many varieties, is poisonous. They grow well in winter in a dry house with a temperature of about 50°, preferring sufficient light but little water. They can be placed outside in summer in a hot dry spot that has good drainage. There are a few hardy species that do well in rock gardens, as Cushion spurge (*E. epithymoides*). This is a hardy perennial with attractive foliage that grows about one foot high. Milk purslane or flowering spurge (*E. corollata*) is a fine plant for bedding, adapted to sandy soils; it grows 1½ to two feet. Snow-of-the-mountain (*E. marginata*) is a popular annual, growing about a foot high. Crown-of-thorns (*E. splendens*) is recommended as a vine in greenhouses, blooming most of the year, and spreading about three feet.

EVENING PRIMROSE: (*Oenothera*) These night-blooming showy plants are easily grown in an open, sandy soil. Blooming in summer, they offer the gardener a wonderful array of colors. The sundrops, the day-blooming counterparts of the evening primrose, include: *O. fruticosa*—two to three foot high perennial with yellow flowers that does best in dry areas; *O. perennis*—one to two foot high perennial. Missouri primrose (*O. missouriensis*) is a day-blooming perennial, about one foot high, as is the showy primose (*O. speciosa*).

EVERFLOWERING LOCUST: see HONEY PLANTS

EVERGREEN: Evergreen shrubs and trees lend enchantment, dignity, and an air of permanence to the home grounds and gardens. While garden enjoyment in winter may be somewhat limited, there are countless ways in which evergreens, etched against a cold gray sky, can form a beautiful picture to be seen from windows. For the year-round home they are necessary as a setting for the house. In spring they form ideal backgrounds for the vivid coloring of early bulbs and flowering shrubs. Nor does this

Evergreen trees and shrubs may, with careful planning, make a formal setting for the homegrounds. Appreciated for their beauty, they may be used to form a windbreak, protecting the house and land.

value abate as the color pageant progresses through summer until late fall.

Used with restraint, the practice of planting evergreens around the base of the house is both artistic and sensible. But the malpractice of planting them so closely together that no room is allowed for growth, or of planting trees where shrubs ought to be, has brought them into disrepute. Tall-growing specimens are often useful and necessary to emphasize a corner or to break the lines of a long, low house.

BROAD-LEAVED EVERGREENS: The Heath family is an important one horticulturally. It includes the heath, mountain laurel, rhododendron, azalea,

The rhododendron is a member of the Heath family of broad-leaved evergreens. These plants require acid soil which should be tested before planting and the results carefully checked.

trailing arbutus, cranberry, blueberry, and many other shrubs. Nearly all have showy flowers and many are broad-leaved evergreens of great garden value. Practically all the plants of this family demand acid soil. This can be determined by the use of litmus paper or a soil-testing kit. The hardiness of the individual plants varies greatly. (See acidity-alkalinity.)

Rhododendrons and azaleas are kept as two separate genera by most gardeners, but included as one genus— Rhododendron—by most botanists.

WINTER GARDENS: Evergreens, both broad and narrow-leaved, are the most important from the viewpoint of contrast with the snow and as shelter from cold winds. Deciduous trees outlined against a winter sky are often more interesting than in summer. Deciduous vines form delicate covers over house walls.

Choose your location carefully; it should face south and have a windbreak of high wall to shut out the prevailing winter winds. The wall of a house may be used as one side, or an angle may form two sides. Use evergreens, planted close together and kept clipped so they will grow thick and interlock, for the other side or sides of the enclosure. Keep your winter garden small. Too large a one is not practical, either for the plants or the individual who makes use of it.

Practical evergreens for the northern states are pines, spruces, cedar, hemlock, yews, and juniper. The bright, shiny foliage of many of the broad-leaved kinds contrasts well with the dense growth of the conifers. Rhododendron, laurel, *Andromeda polifolia*—which is very hardy in the North—and Fetter-bush (*Leucothoe catesbaei*) and many hollies are hardy in the North. Nandinas, cherry laurel, crape-myrtle and the evergreen privets may be used for winter gardens in the South.

Shrubs and trees with lovely bark and colorful twigs are beech, birch, willows, bush honeysuckles, Kerria japonica and various members of the dogwood family. The dogwoods have especially bright-colored twigs in varying shades of red, yellow, and purplish-brown. Prune these heavily, for the young branches bear most of the fruits and are the most colorful.

Berried-shrubs which hold their fruits well into the winter are extremely desirable, as many of them have brilliant autumn foliage. They are ideal plantings for bird covers and food. The common coralberry (*Symphoricarpos orbiculatus*) sometimes called the Indian currant, is literally covered in the fall with brilliant crimson berries which last a long time, usually from early in October until late in March. The flowers are not particularly attractive, but the foliage is good, and it is an excellent shade-tolerant plant. Prune heavily. Wild roses have lovely red twigs and red fruits in autumn and early winter. Cut these down to the ground every two or three years and let them come up again from the roots. This will keep plenty of young shoots coming on for color effects.

The hawthorns (*Crataegus*), especially the native species, are particularly attractive when they flower in May and June and when they fruit in September and October. Birds are not so fond of the berries of the hawthorns as of those of the dogwoods, which are stripped of their red berries early in the fall. Consequently, the brilliant orange and red berries of the hawthorns last well into December and in a few cases even longer. The bush honeysuckles have attractive red and yellow fruits, but unfortunately they do not last long. The European privet has shiny black berries, while its close relative, the Siberian privet, has blue berries borne in long, ornamental clusters. Both the common barberry and the Japanese barberry have red and orange fruits. The Viburnums have splendid fruits in reds and blues, but *V. opulus* must not be planted close to the dwelling-house, as the fruit has a vile odor. The cotoneasters hold their berries late—if the birds do not get them. Both the tall shrubs and the dwarf types are interesting in form and color, the berries being red or black.

The deciduous holly, or black alder, *Ilex verticillata,* has more bright red fruits than any other species of holly. It is a large shrub, wide-spreading, reaching a height of at least eight feet. The Japanese variety has black fruit, but is a better holly to grow on a small place.

Among the plants which may be grown for their ornamental flowers during the winter and very early spring are the witch-hazels, the yellow jasmine (*Jasminum nudiflorum*), the daphnes (*D. odora* and *D. mezereum*), the fragrant honeysuckle, *Magnolia stellata, Erica carnea, Pieris floribunda.*

This Crus-Galli variety of Hawthorn flourishes from Quebec to Michigan and North Carolina. It may be grown as a sizeable shrub or small tree.

and *P. japonica,* the early primroses, the wall cress, the Christmas rose, the winter heliotrope (*Petasites fragrans*), and pussy willows for their catkins. Winter aconite, snowdrops, crocus, early tulips, and other bulbs may be planted in sheltered locations to produce extra early blooms. To have and enjoy these plants at unseasonable times, give them shelter and protection.

MASS PLANTINGS AND ACCENTS: Dividing evergreens into two categories, "mass plantings" and "accent plantings," makes it easier to secure beautiful and tasteful arrangements. Small trees used in a limited area, such as the vast spaces below windows or to hide a high foundation, are mass plantings, and consist of the low, spreading-type evergreen. Yews and dwarf junipers, and such shrubs as rhododendron, privet or boxwood fall into this category.

Accent plants are the important trees on a large lawn, or placed near the entrance or corners of a house. They serve to blend the house into the surrounding landscape, providing an interesting frame. The accent plants are tall, pointed, large-limbed and have generous foliage. Arborvitae, upright junipers and cedars are good choices. Remember you want a pleasing frame, not a screen for your home.

INFORMAL PLANTING: If you keep in mind that the shrubbery and house should have equal prominence, you'll find it simple to work out the best informal planting for your home. You won't grow many types of evergreens clustered in tight little bunches. Neither do you want to obscure your second-story windows with an overgrown forest. Consider the future growth of the plants you choose.

Color is important, too. Select plants of a uniform tone. Brightly colored, exotic specimens might be fine in a large garden or estate, but stand out like sore thumbs by the average sized home.

Perhaps you will use flowering shrubs like rhododendron. Because most of them have blooms of short duration, it's smart to plant for successive bloom—unless, of course, you prefer a colorful spring showing.

Always buy stock that is fully guaranteed. Be especially careful to get plants at least three years old, as they will have vigorous root systems and top growth. They can be expected to survive the shock of transplanting and adapt to new conditions rapidly.

PLANTING EVERGREENS: The shock of moving either conifers or broad-leaved evergreens is greater than with other woody plants. Evergreens are never entirely dormant. All of these plants should be dug with a large ball of soil, and then tied up at once in burlap or canvas. Burlap is generally used on small plants and not removed when they are planted. Just slit it in a few places. Canvas is used for large, heavy trees and must be removed before planting, as it rots very slowly.

Drainage is particularly important. Excessive moisture can kill the tree, especially if the soil is naturally heavy. Even if there is good soil as deep as two feet, check to see that there is no layer of hard gravel or rock below. Dig the planting holes deeper and wider than the roots require. A hole two to three feet wide is right for a small tree if the soil is of good quality —wider if the soil is poor. Pile the topsoil to one side, and dig out and discard the poorer subsoil to a depth of about two feet.

Always handle the tree by the burlap-covered root ball. Branches can be tied to prevent breakage. Above all, avoid deep planting, the cause of ill health and early death of many trees: place the tree at the ground level it had originally. Don't cut back the roots of an evergreen at planting time, and never cut off the tops of any trees; both will stunt its growth. If it is necessary to remove any of the lower branches, cut them off individually. Remember to turn the best side towards the direction from which it will be seen.

If you are unable to plant the specimens immediately, place them in the shade with the ball and burlap left on and water them thoroughly. The wrappings keep the roots from wind and dry air. Plant early in the spring or in late August or early September. If you set them out too late in the fall, the roots do not have an opportunity to get a fresh start. Keep them well watered.

FEEDING AND TRIMMING: These plants thrive best in an acid soil. The soil should be rich in humus and provided with good drainage.

An occasional top-dressing of well-rotted manure can be given, but if the soil is well supplied with humus and if a plentiful leaf mulch is maintained, any special feeding is best done with fertilizers of an acid-forming nature.

After the plants have become established, the soil surrounding them should be disturbed as little as possible, for the roots are very near the surface. It is known that there is a definite mycorrhizal association between the feeder roots of most of the evergreen plants and shrubs and certain fungi.

Sometimes a balanced organic food or one rich in nitrogen is given to stimulate growth. This should be dug into the soil, and the area well watered; or it may be applied in solution or in crow-bar holes driven at two-foot intervals down to the feeding roots, starting the holes at least 18 inches from the trunk.

Evergreen shrubs can be trimmed any time during the growing season— July and August being the best.

Trim each shrub as close as you would a formal hedge. For each branch you snip off, you will get four or five in the spring growth, giving the shrub that solid, compact appearance so necessary to its beauty. This close trimming will also prevent that leggy appearance found so often in uncared-for shrubs.

LOSS OF MOISTURE: Evergreens can't protect themselves during the winter by dropping their leaves, so they continue to lose water by evaporation through them. Too much wind and winter sun may cause an extra loss of moisture, and this drying injury is winter burn.

Two excellent means of protection are either a covering of burlap, stretched on a wire frame over the entire plant, or a screen (made from laths, straw mats or burlap) set up on the east and south sides of the plant. Both are recommended for the smaller conifers, especially if they are in an exposed position. Well-ventilated boxes can be used, too, but remember—all protectors should be kept beyond reach of the branches.

MULCHING EVERGREENS: Excellent materials for mulching are evergreen boughs, threshed rye straw, salt hay, oak leaves, peat moss, grass cuttings, and coconut fiber. They should be applied in a layer not in excess of three inches and extending a little beyond the natural spread of the roots.

SEVERE WINTER WINDS: Slender evergreens with long, erect branches, such as the Irish Junipers, are often the whipping posts for winter gales. The dwarf evergreens, used in foundation plantings, also suffer—but windbreakers made from slatted fencing and held in place by steel posts will protect them. Breakers made of lath and wire, like highway snow fences, will also guard them sufficiently from severe sweeps of cold wind.

Where evergreens are being grown in extremely exposed areas, if necessary, wrap your foundation conifers in burlap. This is easy to do if you start at the bottom and tie a stout cord to one of the branches, then walk around the specimen, lifting each branch and holding it in place with the cord until the top is reached. Now, tie the end of the cord to the next lower strand.

Next, apply three-inch strips of cloth (burlap preferred) starting at the bottom. Fasten the end to the first round of cord with wire nails used like pins, and walk around the specimen as before, winding the burlap spirally upward and fastening each lap in several places with the nails. If desired, the top may be covered with a square of burlap pinned in place, or with any other cap that will shed the snow.

When staking, arrange three stakes in a triangle with the tree trunk held centrally by means of wires or stout non-stretching cords which pass between the stakes and around the trunk.

Protect the bark from being cut by applying pieces of rubber hose, automobile shoe, or even a thick wrapping of several layers of burlap.

HEAVY SNOW AND SLEET ON THE BRANCHES: As soon as a storm stops and while the snow is soft and fluffy, the excessive loads should be jarred from the branches. This should never be done by striking them from above, because such blows only increase the strain and often break the branches. Instead, lift each bough, give it a slight shake from side to side, then a stronger one, and so on until at least half the snow falls off.

Keep the snow and ice off of your foundation shrubs, such as the Yew. This conifer, unlike most evergreens, has several main stems which are generally hidden by the outer mass of foliage. This is so dense that a heavy blanket of snow could split apart or otherwise injure some of the boughs. The remedy is either to shake the snow off or else tie the entire plant together.

Props placed under heavy branches of old conifers will prevent breakage under heavy snow and ice loads, but be careful to avoid tearing the bark. If you nail boards on the prop, it will give support on both sides of the branch, as well as from below. In some cases, you may find it more practical to eliminate props and use cables. —*Doris Weinsheimer.*

See also names of individual evergreens.

EXHIBITS, VEGETABLE:

To select a prize-winning plate of vegetables for exhibition purposes, a grower or exhibitor must place himself in the role of a judge. The judging of vegetables consists in selecting the best specimens of any particular vegetable by eliminating the undesirable exhibits and scoring the remainder on merit and varietal characteristics. The judge should have a knowledge of vegetables, and be familiar with different types and varietal characteristics.

There are definite points to look for in selecting prize specimens of each vegetable, and the judge must be ready at all times to give his reasons for awarding premiums to certain plates or specimens. The exhibitor must also follow the same course in selecting his exhibit.

In all vegetables, choose those specimens that are regular and typical of the variety.

ASPARAGUS: Shoots should be thick, of standard length (nine inches) and uniform in thickness, tender, and free from rust and insect injury. Should show no signs of branching, and no more than $1\frac{1}{2}$ inches of white at bottom. Bunches from $2\frac{1}{2}$ to three pounds in weight.

BEANS: *Size:* The specimens should be large but not overgrown or coarse.

Uniformity: Specimens should be uniform in size, form, color, and maturity.

Condition: The specimens should be sound and without blemish.

Color: The color should be typical for the variety shown.

Broad Beans: Straight, broad, well-formed pods filled with large tender beans. Free from disease.

Snap Beans: Pods should be long, well formed, typical of variety, fresh, brittle, uniform and free from disease. Seeds well developed but tender. Color according to variety.

BEETS: *Long:* Not more than $2\frac{1}{2}$ inches in diameter, smooth and free from side roots, firm, free from cracking or signs of disease. Top small and compact. Roots uniform; showing little of scaling or sunburn, color judged by outer indication and by slight abrasion on side.

Turnip: Not over three inches in diameter, firm, with smooth round shape and fine terminal root; no side roots. Roots uniform, typical of variety and showing as little scaling or sunburn as possible. Free from cracks or signs of disease.

BRUSSELS SPROUTS: Stems straight;

densely covered with medium-sized, firm sprouts.

CABBAGE: *Early:* Generally round or pointed, typical of variety if named, should be of medium size, four to six pounds in weight, fresh, hard and free from insect injury or disease.

Late: Heads round or flat with two layers of green outer leaves. Specimens should be fresh, uniform, hard but not excessive in size. Free from disease or insect injury.

Red: Slightly conical or round in shape. Dark red color, solid, heavy.

Savoy: Round or flattened, firm and heavy. Dark green color with close curl in leaf.

CARROTS: *Roots:* Medium in length and size, straight, free from side roots and without green top or split roots, gradually tapering or with blunt tip according to variety. Skin smooth, color clear and bright with a small core and larger outer ring. Roots uniform in size, shape, and color. Free from disease.

CAULIFLOWER: *Head:* Large in size, of a well-formed curve, with a dense formation of flower, showing no tendency to open; pure white in color and without small leaves in the head. Free from all blemishes. A few of the lower leaves attached. Specimens uniform.

CELERY: Stalks large, stems long, well-blanched except in winter varieties, firm, medium thickness, none hollow, free from rust and rot, showing no flower stems. Roots trimmed short or to pyramid shape. Heart large and carried well up. Ribs not prominent. Uniform in shape, true to type of variety.

CITRON: Large, well-rounded, heavy specimens, finely mottled and well-colored throughout. Must be firm and of good weight.

CORN, GREEN: An exhibit of green corn shall consist of ten ears.

Size: The ears should be large but not overgrown.

Uniformity: The ears should be

uniform in size, form, color, and maturity.

Condition: The ideal condition is just between the milk and the dough stages. The kernels should be tender and sweet.

Color: The color should be typical for the variety.

CUCUMBERS: *Outdoor:* Specimens should be smooth in form, uniform, straight, not over eight inches long and $1\frac{3}{4}$ inches in diameter which is well-carried out towards the ends; of dark green color.

Pickling Cucumbers must not be over $4\frac{1}{2}$ inches in length and $1\frac{1}{4}$ inches in diameter, smooth, of even diameter from end to end. Gherkins not over $2\frac{1}{2}$ inches long and $\frac{3}{4}$ inch in diameter.

EGGPLANT: Color should be dark purple all over, specimens even in size, large, smooth, and solid. Free from any signs of decay or injury.

KALE: Specimens in pots generally, should have a close, even curl on all leaves. Size according to particular variety.

LETTUCE: *Cabbage:* Heads should be large, well-rounded, firm, free from any blemishes. Fresh, no flower stems.

Cos: Conical in shape with straight, upright growing leaves, well-bleached and crisp, and with a firm heart. No flower stems.

Leaf: Heads of crisp, well-crinkled leaves, showing medium green, without any blemish. No flower stems. Leaves forming dense mass.

MELONS AND CUSHAWS: *Size:* Size shall be medium to large.

Uniformity: All specimens should be uniform in size, color, form, and maturity.

Condition: Specimens should be mature, free from blemishes, thick meated and sweet.

Color: Color should be uniform and typical of the variety.

Muskmelons: Medium to large according to variety, firm evenly ribbed and closely netted. When fit for use melon pulls easily from stem and flower end is somewhat soft and yielding to the finger. Readiness for eating is the first requirement. This is indicated largely by the smell. Closeness of the netting denotes the quality.

Watermelons: Medium to large according to variety, firm, smooth. Melon must be tapped to get quality.

ONIONS: *Large:* Shape, globe or flat and of color of variety. Clean but not peeled, uniform, of good weight and have a small well-ripened neck, firm, especially at the base of the neck. Showing no section. Thorough ripening essential. Should be separate classes for seed. Transplanted, and sets.

Pickling: Should range from 1/2 inch to 3/4 inch in diameter, uniform in size and shape, clean, firm and white in color. Thoroughly dried.

PARSLEY: Head, large and filled with numerous, finely curled, dark green leaves. Crisp and free from any discoloration.

PARSNIP: Roots straight, of good length, broadly shouldered, not less than three inches crown well hollowed, free from side roots, gradually tapering from crown to tip, clean, smooth and free from discoloration or disease, firm with a small core.

PEAS: Pods long and straight, dark green in color and well-filled with medium, sweet-flavored, tender peas. Pods uniform in size and color with no signs of ripening.

PEPPERS: Either red or green. Should be smooth, firm and typical of variety. Free from disease and injury. Should be of even color.

POTATOES, IRISH: *Size:* The most desirable size is medium.

Uniformity: All specimens should be uniform as to form, size, frequency, depth of eyes, and maturity.

Skin, etc.: The skin should present a uniform surface, should be clear, smooth, or uniformly netted. An undue amount of dirt will be scored against. The eyes should be of medium depth and normal in number for the variety. The market prefers shallow-eyed varieties, but this characteristic usually denotes weakness; hence, showings of seed potatoes should have eyes rather deep than shallow. Showings of fall grown crops may be immature; others must be mature.

Condition: The flesh should be solid, fine grained, and of uniform color. It should be free from discoloration and hollow heart. The presence of disease would be heavily scored against. Specimens with any mechanical injury, such as broken skins, bruises, cuts, scratches, or holes, and insect injuries should be excluded.

POTATOES, SWEET: *Size:* The size should not exceed three inches in diameter and seven inches in length, nor be less than two inches in diameter and four inches in length. Potatoes 2 1/2 inches in diameter and five inches in length are preferable.

Uniformity: All specimens should be uniform in size, form, and color.

Condition: All specimens should be bright in color, smooth, and the skin dry. The soil should be wiped off, not washed.

Freedom from Blemishes: All specimens should be free from cuts, bruises, and defects of whatever nature.

PUMPKINS: Round or oblong in shape, symmetrical, medium size, thin-skinned, closely ribbed, firm, heavy; deep yellow or creamy yellow color all over.

RADISH: *Summer and Winter:* Medium size, according to variety; clean, smooth, and even form; free from insect or disease injury, cracking and side roots; crisp, firm, not spongy, uniform in size, no stem, leaves close to fleshy root.

RHUBARB: Stalks medium in diameter, long, straight, fresh and tender. Well-colored over all the stem.

ROOT VEGETABLES: *Size:* The size should be medium to large, very large or small specimens will be rated down.

Uniformity: All specimens should be uniform in size, color, form, and maturity.

Condition: Specimens should be clean, bright, free from root hairs, and blemishes. They should be free from pith and hollow hearts, and should be crisp and firm.

Color: The color should be typical for the variety.

SALSIFY: From 1½ to two inches at top, smooth and straight, gradually tapering to tip, free from side roots, firm, fresh and clean, skin white in color. Core small.

SPINACH: Specimens should be large with close heavy foliage, fresh and free from all coarse, outer leaves; broad, dark green, tender leaves, typical of the variety, free from diseases and insect injury.

SQUASH: *Summer:* Medium size and weight, color and shape of variety, firm but with rind soft enough to admit thumb nail readily.

Winter: Should be large, heavy and firm, of color and shape according to variety. Hubbard should be heavily warted.

TOMATOES: *Size:* Specimens should be large but not overgrown.

Uniformity: All specimens should be uniform in size, form, color, and maturity.

Condition: Specimens should be mature but not over-ripe. They should have small seed cavities and thick fleshy walls, and should be firm and solid.

Color: The color should be bright, clear, intense, and characteristic of the variety. The color should also extend right down to the stem.

TURNIPS: Medium size with smooth, symmetrical form, small tap root and free from side roots, firm and heavy. Small core, as free as possible from splitting or sunburn, showing no insect or disease injury. Color varies from white to light yellow, according to variety.

VEGETABLE MARROW: Medium size, oblong in form, smooth and even, with uniform thickness and good weight. Fresh, firm but with a rind soft enough to readily admit thumb nail. Color varies from a cream yellow to a mottled green.—*C. H. Nissley.*

EXOCHORDA: Pearl Bush. A well-shaped shrub attaining a height at maturity of ten feet, with a graceful, slender habit of growth. It is an excellent shrub for forcing blooms in water indoors, and receives its name from the unopened flower buds, which resemble pearls. Blooms in late April or May. Very easy of culture in any ordinary soil and is propagated by seeds, softwood cuttings, or layers. Usually catalogued as *E. grandiflora,* but known to botanists as *E. racemosa.*

EXPERIMENTAL FARM: *see* ORGANIC METHOD, HISTORY OF

EXPERIMENT STATIONS (AGRICULTURAL): Each state has an experiment station which does research and publishes reports of particular interest to the gardeners and farmers in the state. For example, you can find out which plant varieties are best suited for your particular climate and soil by writing to the experiment station. Experiment stations also make soil tests either free or at a nominal charge. Here are the addresses of state colleges and experiment stations:

Alabama Agricultural Experiment Station, Auburn, Ala.

Alaska Agricultural Experiment Station, College, Alaska

Arizona Agricultural Experiment Station, Tucson, Ariz.

Arkansas Agricultural Experiment Station, Fayetteville, Ark.

California Agricultural Experiment Station, Berkeley 4, Calif.

California Agricultural Experiment Station, Davis, Calif.

Colorado Agricultural Experiment Station, Fort Collins, Colo.

Connecticut Agricultural Experiment Station, New Haven 4, Conn.

Connecticut Agricultural Experiment Station, Storrs, Conn.

Delaware Agricultural Experiment Station, Newark, Del.

Florida Agricultural Experiment Station, Gainesville, Fla.

Georgia Agricultural Experiment Station, Experiment, Ga.

Hawaii Agricultural Experiment Station, Honolulu 14, Hawaii

Idaho Agricultural Experiment Station, Moscow, Idaho

Illinois Agricultural Experiment Station, Urbana, Ill.

Indiana Agricultural Experiment Station, Lafayette, Ind.

Iowa Agricultural Experiment Station, Ames, Iowa

Kansas Agricultural Experiment Station, Manhattan, Kans.

Kentucky Agricultural Experiment Station, Lexington 29, Ky.

Louisiana Agricultural Experiment Station, University Station, Baton Rouge 3, La.

Maine Agricultural Experiment Station, Orono, Maine

Maryland Agricultural Experiment Station, College Park, Md.

Massachusetts Agricultural Experiment Station, Amherst, Mass.

Michigan Agricultural Experiment Station, East Lansing, Mich.

Minnesota Agricultural Experiment Station, University Farm, St. Paul 1, Minn.

Mississippi Agricultural Experiment Station, State College, Miss.

Missouri Agricultural Experiment Station, Columbia, Mo.

Montana Agricultural Experiment Station, Bozeman, Mont.

Nebraska Agricultural Experiment Station, Lincoln 3, Nebr.

Nevada Agricultural Experiment Station, Reno, Nev.

New Hampshire Agricultural Station, Durham, N. H.

New Jersey Agricultural Experiment Station, New Brunswick, N. J.

New Mexico Agricultural Experiment Station, State College, N. Mex.

New York (Cornell) Agricultural Experiment Station, Ithaca, N. Y.

These are test cylinders at the New Jersey Agricultural Experiment Station at Rutgers University, New Brunswick. They are three feet deep, containing soil and subsoil brought in from the field and set in place just as each was in the field. Such stations are sources of information for the home gardener.

New York State Agricultural Experiment Station, Geneva, N. Y.

North Carolina Agricultural Experiment Station, State College Station, Raleigh, N. C.

North Dakota Agricultural Experiment Station, State College Station, Fargo, N. D.

Ohio Agricultural Experiment Station, Wooster, Ohio

Ohio Agricultural Experiment Station, Columbus, Ohio

Oklahoma Agricultural Experiment Station, Stillwater, Okla.

Oregon Agricultural Experiment Station, Corvallis, Ore.

Pennsylvania Agricultural Experiment Station, University Park, Pa.

Puerto Rico Agricultural Experiment Station, Rio Piedras, Puerto Rico

Rhode Island Agricultural Experiment Station, Kingston, R. I.

South Carolina Agricultural Experiment Station, Clemson, S. C.

South Dakota Agricultural Experiment Station, State College Station, S. D.

Tennessee Agricultural Experiment Station, Knoxville 16, Tenn.

Texas Agricultural Experiment Station, College Station, Tex.

Utah Agricultural Experiment Station, Logan, Utah

Vermont Agricultural Experiment Station, Burlington, Vt.

Virginia Agricultural Experiment Station, Blacksburg, Va.

Virginia Truck Experiment Station, Norfolk 1, Va.

Washington Agricultural Experiment Station, Pullman, Wash.

Washington Agricultural Experiment Station, Puyallup, Wash.

West Virginia Agricultural Experiment Station, Morgantown, W. Va.

Wisconsin Agricultural Experiment Station, Madison 6, Wis.

Wyoming Agricultural Experiment Station, Laramie, Wyo.

See also GOVERNMENT SERVICES.

F

FALLOW: In a rotation schedule, this refers to "letting the land rest." However, this does *not* mean that nothing should be grown on the land. Growing nothing on a soil is the opposite of sound conservation practice. Very soon a wild vegetation will take over in a bare fallowed field, as weeds and bushes grow fast. Insects such as wireworms, larvae of grubs, etc., may multiply undisturbed. When it comes time to put the field back in production, the grower may have a very difficult struggle. Besides, the crop of weed seeds and troublesome insects may spread to adjoining fields. Therefore the practice of untreated fallow is not recommended.

What is advised is a fallow under a green manure crop. This kind of fallow in the rotation is especially good for soils with a low humus content. By growing the leguminous plants, such as vetch, soybeans, sweet clover, etc., on a fallow field and then plowing it under as green manure, the soil will be greatly improved. Sweet clover is recommended for a green manure fallow since it turns a considerable amount of organic matter into the soil, and does an excellent job of making the phosphorus in rock phosphate available to crops following in the rotation.

FALSE CAMOMILE: *see* BOLTONIA

FALSE DRAGONHEAD: *see* PHYSOSTEGIA

FALSE INDIGO: *see* AMORPHA

FALSE STARWORT: *see* BOLTONIA

FAREWELL-TO-SPRING: *see* GODETIA

FARMERS HOME ADMINISTRATION: *see* GOVERNMENT SERVICES

FARMING ORGANICALLY: *see* ORGANIC METHOD, HISTORY OF

FAULKNER, EDWARD H.: A noted agricultural writer, Mr. Faulkner is best known for his unorthodox book, *Plowman's Folly,* published in 1943. Faulkner advanced the concept that plowing is not only unnecessary, but actually harmful to the soil. He stressed the importance of returning humus to the soil and using rock fertilizers. In 1947, *A Second Look,* a sequel to *Plowman's Folly,* was published. Faulkner's earlier background includes work as a county agent, agricultural teacher, field tester of soil management theories, and farm editor for a Cleveland radio station. *See also* NO-DIGGING METHOD.

FAUNA: The fauna of the living soil is one of the most valuable assets that the gardener has.

As soon as the leaves fall to the ground, decay sets in by way of moulds, fungi, bacteria, other minute soil fauna, such as springtails, mites, various grubs of small flies, worms, etc. These in turn are devoured by other soil fauna, beetle grubs, centipedes, and others. Woody material is chewed up and eaten by woodlice, the grubs of various species of flies, beetles, moths, etc.

One feeds upon another, and they or their dead bodies are in turn attacked. The waste products of each is again consumed, first as before by the bacteria, moulds, etc., then again by the organisms that feed on these. And the leaf that fell in the autumn is passed through the body of many living things, one consuming another, forming a continuous living chain, reducing the leaf, link by link, until, still a living thing, it is in such a state that the new plant can absorb it and become a real living thing in its turn.

The living soil fauna are instrumental in conditioning our soil by their biting, chewing, tunnelling, and crawling through the mass of material. They loosen the soil, thoroughly mix the mineral with the organic matter, and by the very nature of the physical structure of their excrement, create that valuable crumb structure so desirable.

Where there is an abundance of organic matter there is also a proportionate number of soil fauna.—*J. H. Burman.*

See also MICROORGANISM.

FEATHERED COCKSCOMB: *see* COCKSCOMB

FEATHERS: Feathers are similar to silk and wool in that they contain considerable amounts of nitrogen. That is their main value, which is about equal to that of good hoof and horn meal or horn dust. An analysis of feathers revealed that they contained 15.30 per cent nitrogen. Feathers decay very rapidly in a compost heap, but must be kept unusually moist to do so.

Poultry raisers who sell their manure commercially have not infrequently byproducts of lesser value, they think, namely those wastes of feathers, matted with droppings; they are frequently to be had for the hauling and should by all means be used for composting. Feathers in large amounts, estimated to be about 40,000 tons annually, are available at poultry dressing plants. This figure represents approximately 25 per cent of all the feathers from poultry processed on farms, in homes, and by dressing plants.

Experiments in which fresh waste feathers were treated by steam-pressure cooking and drying have yielded a friable, easily handled, animal feed and fertilizer.

Feather meal, made from poultry feathers, has also been developed into a valuable fertilizer.

A process, developed by the USDA Western Regional Research Laboratory, makes these feathers into a high-nitrogen fertilizer. The feathers are pressure-cooked with steam for 30 to 60 minutes, then dried to an eight to 12 per cent moisture content, and ground. This yields a dry, friable

meal or powder. There is no appreciable loss of nutrients during the steam treatment.

The finished product weighs about 50 to 60 pounds per cubic foot. Its total nitrogen content averages between 12 and 13.5 per cent, of which 10 to 13 per cent is water insoluble.

The slow release of nitrogen makes feathers and feather meal valuable for all crops requiring a steady, long-lasting supply of that element. Put on the cover or green manure crop late in the fall, it will release nitrogen slowly all winter and spring, and prevent a nitrogen shortage caused by bacteria attacking the green matter of the crop when plowed under.

FEBRUARY GARDEN OPERATIONS: *see* GARDEN CALENDAR

FEIJOA: *see* GUAVA

FELDSPAR: A closely related group of minerals, all silicates of aluminum, with either potassium, sodium or calcium. *See also* MINERAL ROCKS.

FELT WASTES: Hatteries have a certain amount of hair and wool wastes, which may analyse as high as 14 per cent nitrogen. The same that is true of hair and wool applies to felt wastes. If included in a compost that is teeming with bacteria, hair and feathers as well as felt wastes break down rather easily, provided the heap is kept moist enough. It is always wise to mix some manure or other high-protein material in with dry refuse, such as felt wastes, in order to supply bacterial life from the outset and to hasten the compost process.

FENNEL: (*Foeniculum vulgare*) A herbaceous perennial occasionally cultivated as a garden herb in the United States. The dried aromatic fruits, commonly referred to as seed, are used for flavoring bread, pastry, candies, and liqueurs and in medicine. A volatile oil is present in the seed and may be obtained from it by steam distillation. It possesses the characteristic flavor of the seed and is used for flavoring and medicinal purposes. The several varieties of fennel are quite different in growth habit. The Indian fennel matures at about three and one-half to four feet in height when grown

Sweet fennel, also called finocchio, has an enlarged leaf base and is used as a food when it is blanched. It is grown extensively in California.

under favorable conditions. The Moroccan variety requires about three weeks longer to mature and grows about six feet tall.

Fennel grows well in a fairly mild climate and on almost any good soil but thrives best on nonacid, well-drained loams. It is readily grown from seed but can also be propagated by root and crown division. The seed is sown thickly directly in the field late in fall or early in spring, in rows three or four feet apart and covered lightly. When well established the plants are thinned to stand eight to 12 inches apart in the row. The plants can also be started in a seedbed and transplanted to the field when three or four inches high. The cultivation required is the same as for ordinary garden crops. If the plants are grown as a winter crop in the warmer valleys of

the Southwestern States the tops are injured by winter freezing, but they will make a good growth under favorable conditions early in spring.

Fennel is believed to be adapted to the Central and Northern States and probably to some sections of California, where it has escaped from cultivation in some places and grows to large size. *See also* NIGELLA.

FENUGREEK: (*Trigonella foenum-graecum*). A stemmy annual legume closely related to sweet clover. The plant is erect, more or less branched, attaining a height of 12 to 24 inches. It has three leaflets, very similar to those of sweet clover. The small flowers, white with dark markings, are borne in the axis of the leaves. The pods are long, slender, and needlelike, and bear several seeds. The seeds are yellow to brown, roughly rectangular in shape, and about as large as a small grain of wheat. The whole plant has a pronounced odor and taste, and is not relished by livestock, although sheep will eat it fairly well.

It is sometimes made into a tea.

FERN: Perennial, flowerless plants. Ferns are the "old men" of the plant kingdom. Long before the appearance of man, great forests of giant ferns covered the earth. Today all that remains of these dense jungles are vast beds of coal, formed by the decay of the plants when they were submerged by flood waters.

However, quite a few of the descendants of these prehistoric ferns—over 7,000 varieties, in fact—still exist.

Ferns are ideal for damp, low spots by fences; shady areas under trees, and on north side of houses. There are ferns to suit almost any conditions. Some, of course, are strictly tropical and not for temperate climates, except perhaps in the greenhouse or terrariums. But many of them will thrive in cool, moist, shady spots, even swampy areas. And some even like hot, dry conditions, like the resurrection

Ferns make excellent backgrounds for the garden and are invaluable for rock gardens, walk borders, bog gardens and banks. Autumn plantings are recommended with a protective winter mulch of leaves.

fern that seems dead and sere until the first rain makes it spring into life.

Ferns make a fine background for many flowering plants. The deciduous types are especially valuable to fill the empty spaces after spring-flowering bulbs have bloomed. Their fronds hide the untidy browning bulb foliage and continue to look well even when the shrubs and trees leaf out and make dense shade.

The ferns that stay green all year, like the evergreen wood fern (*Dryopteris marginalis*) and the Christmas fern (*Polystichum acrostichoides*) can be a garden mainstay right up until snow blankets them. And the larger ferns are excellent for "fill-ins" around newly planted shrubs, to give needed height for good landscape design.

Too, they cool the ground and moisten the atmosphere, shading the plants beneath them like a lacy parasol —very helpful for young plants or for delicate flowering ones.

PLANTING: Spring or fall is the best time to plant or move ferns. Those with running rootstocks, however, will send up new fronds if transplanted in any season. One caution concerning these: use them only where you want a good-sized mass planting; running rootstock types like hay-scented, bracken and ostrich tend to overrun their sites.

If you are hesitant about moving ferns from the wild, you can purchase those you wish from a wildflower nursery. Planting directions vary: most ferns with spreading roots do best if the roots are barely covered, while some central-crown types like the crown exposed and others prefer the crown at the soil surface.

A woodsy location, with shade, moisture and an organic soil high in leaf mold is perfect for the majority of ferns. Dig a fairly deep hole and put in a mixture of leaf mold, sand and loam. Oak leaves and compost are good substitutes for the leaf mold. If the soil is acid, a little limestone is advisable, and a mulch of organic materials is always recommended.

Rock-growing ferns are hard to establish directly on the rocks. But plant them alongside and they will quickly spread over the rocks. For sunny rocks the best varieties are hay-scented, *Woodsia,* ebony spleenwort, bracken and cliff-brake. The fragrant hay-scented fern will thrive in the shade, too. You can use these ferns to blend in a big boulder that would be hard to remove, or to soften the outlines of a rock ledge.

Also good around rocks with some shade are hart's-tongue, royal, northern lady, New York, maidenhair and the evergreen and marginal woodferns. The smaller kinds among these, and the polypodies as well, look very pretty planted in soil placed in the crevices of fieldstone fences.

For massing in low shady spots, you'll like the handsome cinnamon or the interrupted fern. Like its cousin, the royal fern, cinnamon has colorful fruiting fronds that resemble flower heads. The leathery fronds of sword ferns are also eye-catching planted thickly under dense shade trees.

Some ferns, like hay-scented and lady fern, are indifferent to varieties of light and moisture. They will flourish almost anywhere. But for dry, shady places, Christmas fern is your best choice. And for boggy spots, try marsh fern, sensitive fern or the lovely chartreuse-plumed New York fern. Royal fern prefers full sunlight but will tolerate very wet conditions like lake borders, even growing in shallow water if its crowns are above the high water line. Crested woodfern is another that likes damp sites, but with much shade.

The popular maidenhair is easy to establish in any well-drained soil. The hardy climbing fern, however, likes acid soil and grows well among mountain laurel and blueberry bushes. A heavy mulch of oak leaves will keep it thriving. For limestone sites, walking fern (its thread-like frond tips "walk" to root and form new plants) spreads to a tangled mat over mossy rocks in the shade.

You may find that you have a place for a real fern garden. A brookside, a damp rocky slope, or even an old garage or barn foundation might be an ideal place to establish dozens of varieties in a natural setting. But even if you don't, you'll find room for at least a few ferns in your outdoor decorating scheme.

INDOOR PLANTING: How about indoors? Here, too, ferns are highly valuable. Given dim light—too strong illumination yellows the fronds; a north window with two hours or less sun a day is good—plus rich organic soil with good drainage, and a temperature range of 50 to 70°, a large number of ferns will thrive in the home.

A popular fern is the common sword fern (*Nephrolepis exaltata*). The type is rarely seen in the florists' shops, it having been superseded by the Boston fern (*N. exaltata,* var. *Bostoniensis*). This is the best of all the sword ferns. Even when young in small pots the plants are attractive, but as they make a fairly rapid growth one does not have to wait long to obtain a large plant. The fronds of the Boston fern are two to three feet long and two to three inches across, and of a rich green color. Unlike most of the ferns this will stand some abuse. With all the other ferns if the soil once becomes dry the plant is ruined for the season at least, if not absolutely killed; but should your sword fern be neglected for a day or two, becoming dry, it will recover if carefully looked after.

Another variety of the *exaltata* which has given satisfaction in many window gardens is known as *N. philip-*

pensis. The fronds are smaller, being only about 18 inches long and one and one-half to two inches wide and are very dark green. The variety *Scotti* is a miniature Boston fern, the fronds being shorter and narrower, thus making a dense, more compact plant.

There are several plumose forms in which the pinnæ are much divided. The fronds are usually a foot or so long and quite broad. They are known under such trade names as *Piersoni, Barrowsi, Whitmani,* etc. These do well in the house but with the exception of *Whitmani* the fronds are more or less liable to revert to the type. This is caused by the conditions in the room —a dry heat and insufficient light.

The sword ferns will grow in almost any soil but a well drained sandy loam is best.

The glossy, dark green foliage of the holly fern (*Cyrtomium falcatum*) always attracts attention. The upper side of the pinnæ is very dark green, the under side is somewhat lighter green and studded with brown spots —the spores. The pinnæ are large, four to six inches long and one to two inches broad, the fronds about two feet long and very stiff. Altogether it is very attractive.

MAIDENHAIR FERN: The graceful, feathery fronds of the maidenhair ferns always excite interest. The most beautiful one, *Adiantum Farleyense,* often seen in the florists' shops, cannot be grown in the window garden, but there is a good substitute for it in the so-called "hardy Farleyense" (*Adiantum Capillus-Veneris,* var. *imbricatum*). This will withstand the trying conditions of the house just as well as will the Boston fern.

The soil in which maidenhair ferns are growing must never be allowed to become dry—the fronds immediately wither and nothing can be done to recuperate them. Should such an accident happen, remove the injured fronds and keep the plant in as good a condition as possible until the fol-

lowing spring when new growth will be made.

SPIDER FERNS: The best small ferns for the home are found among the spider ferns (*Pteris*). The fronds are once divided, the divisions being long and narrow, and pointed.

One of the best of the spider ferns is *P. cretica.* It grows nearly a foot high. The stalks are straw colored and the foliage is dark green in the type but there are several varieties, some of which have white markings.

Another spider fern very commonly grown is *P. serrulata,* which differs from Cretica in not being such a strong grower, the stalks are brown and the edges of the pinnæ are sharply serrulate or saw edged. Like Cretica, this has many forms, mostly more or less distorted, and to which such descriptive Latin names as cristata, cristata variegata, densa, etc., have been given.

The best variegated fern for the window garden is *P. argyræa.* This is somewhat stronger growing than those already mentioned, but its chief feature is a broad, white band down the middle of each division of the frond.

All the spider ferns are used more for fern dishes than for specimen plants, to which they are, however, admirably suited.

One of the shield ferns (*Polystichum angulare*) somewhat resembles the sword ferns. The fronds are from one to two feet long and rather narrow. The pinnæ differ from those of the sword ferns in that they are triangular rather than oblong. This fern seems to withstand the unfavorable condition of the house well.

The hare's foot fern (*Polypodium*) is always interesting because of its rhizomes. These rest on the ground and are densely covered with long, coarse, yellow hairs. Sooner or later these hang over the edge of the pot and bear a strong resemblance to a rabbit's foot.

Another interesting fern is *Davallia*

bullata, usually seen in the form of "fern balls," but equally at home in a pot or on a sphagnum covered board. As a fern ball this fern is particularly

Pteris argyraea is well-suited to window-garden cultivation in the North. It belongs in the soil-tolerant group and does well with normal treatment.

interesting. The balls are composed of the rhizomes wrapped around sphagnum moss. The balls are received in this country in December and January and all that is needed to start them into growth is a thorough soaking in water. Have them in a light window, preferably a north one.

In the coldest weather the temperature in which ferns are growing ought never go below 55° at night. A raise of temperature during the day of 10 or 15 degrees is enough; no room should be above 70°. A north window or any window which has lots of light and but little or no direct sunlight will suit ferns; the sun injures the delicate fronds.

Ferns do not like a heavy soil, one composed of four parts of a sandy loam, one part sand, and one part manure, will give good results. For most of the ferns a little leaf mold may be added. Pack the soil fairly firm about the roots but do not make it hard. The soil in which ferns are growing must never become dry, neither must it become water-logged. It is a common assumption that, because ferns grow naturally in damp places, they cannot be over-watered, but while the soil in which ferns thrive outdoors may be very damp it is always well drained and aerated.

Keep the roots cool. This can be easily done by placing the pots in jardinieres or vases and packing damp sphagnum moss about them. If you want to use the plant for table or other decoration it can be removed from the receptacle, used in the decoration, and returned when the occasion is over.

Keep the leaves of the ferns clean. This is best done by syringing them with clear water on all bright days. If done on dull days, there is some danger of the fronds turning black.

Thrips and red spider are troublesome, especially in a dry atmosphere. The two can be kept in check by frequent syringings of water, being sure to hit the under side of the fronds.

Annual repotting is necessary only for young ferns, and monthly feedings of dilute manure tea will keep all of them healthy and vigorous for years. Never use chemical fertilizer— ferns are extremely sensitive to its unbalanced formulations. Give them plenty of water: only the leaf-losing kinds should be allowed to dry out, during their resting season.

Small ferns or young plants of the larger varieties that require lots of humidity are perfect for terrariums. For a lovely conversation piece, put some humusy soil in any good-sized glass container and plant polypodies, rattlesnake and grape ferns, oak and beech ferns, small spleenworts, baby maidenhair and walking ferns, along with other wild plants you pick up in the woods and fields. Be careful never to overwater. A glass cover over the top will conserve humidity.

You can propagate ferns by division of the crown or rootstock. But most fascinating is propagation by the spores, those tiny dust-like "seeds" clustering on the backs or edges of the leaves. Brush them off into a paper bag, let them dry for a week or two, then shake them onto a pot of moist leaf mold and sand. Set the pot in a saucer of water, cover it with glass to retain humidity.

FERTILITY: A fertile or productive soil, one which produces satisfactory yields of crops, has certain characteristics. In the first place, it contains an abundance of organic matter or humus; this is brought about by the incorporation of stable manure, green manures, crop residues, and other forms of organic matter into it. A fertile soil, also, has a favorable texture, not too loose and light, nor too heavy and stiff. A fertile soil is well drained. Further, a fertile soil is one which is not too acid, having had an occasional application of lime. And lastly, a fertile soil has an abundance of available plant-food.

How to Increase Soil Fertility: There are many ways to increase and maintain the valuable nutrients of your soil which contribute to its fertility. The best way is to set up and follow an organic program to fit your particular garden needs. Some plants need a rather acid soil, while others need a more alkaline soil. They need different nitrogen, phosphorus and potash ratios, too.

Each plant changes the soil and has different soil needs than other plants. You won't have to worry much about having *exactly* the right amounts of each element for each plant you grow, however. As long as your soil is generally fertile and rich in organic matter, your plants will not suffer. *See also* Fertilizer; Cover Crop; Compost; Organic Matter.

FERTILIZER: If plants are to have good growth, they must have:

1. space in the soil to get air (*see aeration*);
2. room to grow roots;
3. proper soil pH (*see acidity-alkalinity*);

4. adequate water, sunlight and mineral nutrients.

Air space, root room and availability of water to plants depend mostly upon soil structure, which is closely related to the organic matter content. It also depends on suitable distribution of mineral particles of different sizes to keep the soil open and porous, permits water to drain away, and air to enter. This dependence upon humus and minerals shows clearly why an organic fertilizing program must include organic fertilizers as well as the rock minerals, such as potash rock, rock phosphate, greensand, basalt, etc.

Storehouse of Soil's Nutrients: Organic matter has been called "the storehouse of the soil's nutrients." Briefly, the reasons it is so vital to soils are that it (1) improves tilth and structure, (2) improves water-holding capacity, (3) aids in nitrogen fixation and (4) makes nutrients available to plants.

Wesley Chaffin and Robert Woodward, agronomists at Oklahoma A. and M. College, have written: "Nearly all of the nitrogen and sulfur, and more than one-third of the phosphorus that become available for plant use are supplied by the organic matter.

"Smaller quantities of the other plant nutrients also come from this source: consequently, an increase in the rate of organic matter decomposition likewise increases the quantities of nitrogen, phosphorus, potassium, calcium, magnesium, and other plant nutrients in the soil solution."

All soils differ widely in their content of plant nutrients. This difference is caused not only by the fact that soils differ greatly in the original content of nutrients which they had but also because soils lose these nutrients through erosion, leaching, and the harvesting of crops. Some of these losses are made up by the weathering of minerals, rainfall, action of earthworms and bacteria in the soil, and

TWENTY KINDS OF ORGANIC FERTILIZERS

TOP ROW (l. to r.): wood ashes, basic slag, leaves, sawdust, blood meal. SECOND ROW: rock phosphate, greensand, bone meal, peat moss, cottonseed meal. THIRD ROW: seaweed, dried manure, tankage, peanut shells, leaf mold. FOURTH ROW: wood chips, manure, cocoa-bean shells, compost, grass clippings. Organic fertilizers build the soil structure in addition to feeding the plants.

other natural soil phenomena. But serious deficiencies must be corrected if the soil is to produce adequate and healthy crops. This is the reason why organic fertilizers and mineral nutri-ents should be added—to increase crop yields as well as to produce crops with the proper nutrients.

One of the best ways to gain an understanding of the major nutrient problems of soil is to have it tested—either with your own soil test kit or sent out to your state experiment station or commercial laboratory. Generally a test of this kind will answer whether or not your soil has a sufficient amount of the major nutrients—nitrogen (N), phosphorus (P), potassium (K). A test of this kind will also tell you whether your soil is acid or alkaline.

When fertilizing, always remember that the objective of the organic method is to feed the soil, not necessarily the plant. Therefore the major objective is to increase the over-all fertility of this soil and not just supply the minimum amount of nutrients to produce a single crop in one season.

The chemical fertilizer user has long made use of special proportions of fertilizers, such as 5-10-5, 4-8-4, etc. Such a fertilizer formula is merely a simple way to show the amount of nitrogen, phosphorus and potash in the mixture of fertilizer. For example in the combination 2-4-2, 2 per cent is nitrogen, 4 per cent is phosphorus and 2 per cent is potash.

THE IMPORTANCE OF NITROGEN: Nitrogen is a major element in plant nutrition. It is responsible for producing leaf growth and greener leaves; lengthening the growth period tends to increase set of fruits. Deficiency causes yellow leaves and stunted growths; excess delays flowering, causes too much elongation of stems, reduces quality of fruits, causes lodging of wheat, renders crops less resistant to disease.

If you believe your soil is deficient in nitrogen, you can correct it by adding compost, manure or other nitrogen-rich organic fertilizers such as dried blood, tankage, cottonseed meal, cocoa bean and peanut shells, bone meal or sewage sludge. Returning weeds, grass clippings and other garden wastes to the soil will add to its humus content and improve its nitrogen content at the same time.

ORGANIC VERSUS CHEMICAL

NITROGEN: Organic forms of nitrogen are more stable in the soil and become available for plant growth more gradually than nitrogen from chemical fertilizers. When concentrated chemical nitrogen is applied to the soil, it produces a shot-in-the-arm effect to plant growth. The plants are subjected to too much nitrogen at one time. Then, if a sudden heavy rain storm drenches the field, the chemical form of nitrogen is to a large extent washed out, and the plants can become starved for lack of the element. *See* NITROGEN

THE VALUE OF PHOSPHORUS: All growing plants need phosphorus. It is important for a strong root system, for brighter, more beautiful flowers and for good growth. If plants are unusually small and thin, with purplish foliage, it may be an indication of a phosphorus deficiency in the soil. Phosphorus is also said to hasten maturity, increase seed yield, increase fruit development, increase resistance to winter kill and diseases, increase vitamin content of plants, while a deficiency causes stunted growth and sterile seed.

SOURCES OF PHOSPHORUS: You can best add phosphorus to your soil with rock phosphate, which is a natural rock product containing from 30 to 50 per cent phosphorus. When the rock is finally ground, the phosphate is available to the plant as it needs it. Rock phosphate is especially effective in soils which have organic matter.

Besides rock phosphate, other phosphorus sources are basic slag, bone meal, dried blood, cottonseed meal and activated sludge.

HOW MUCH TO APPLY: Lawns—apply at rate of 100 lbs. to 1,000 sq. ft., raking it into first inch of top soil. Vegetable and flower gardens—apply liberally around plants and carefully mix with first inch of the top soil. In most areas, barring any great deficiencies or excesses, one lb. for ten sq. ft. is a good amount to use and would be sufficient for three to five years. *See* PHOSPHATE

THE VALUE OF POTASSIUM: Potassium is the third major nutrient and is very important to the strength of the plant. It carries carbohydrates through the plant system, helps form strong stems, and helps to fight diseases which may attack. If plants are slow-growing and stunted, with browning leaves and stunted fruits, there is probably a potassium deficiency. Potassium is said to accomplish the following: improves keeping quality of fruit; aids in the production of starches, sugar and oils; decreases water requirement of plant; makes plants more resistant to disease; reduces winter kill; promotes color of fruit; is essential for cell division and growth; aids plants to utilize nitrogen; balances effect of excess nitrogen or calcium; reduces boron requirements.

Deficiencies can cause firing of the edges of leaves which later turn brown and die. This affects lower leaves first, causing shrivelled, sterile seeds. Corn ears also can fail to fill out when there is a potassium deficiency.

POTASH SOURCES: Natural mineral fertilizers supply insoluble potash which the plant can only take up as it needs it. That's why rock potash and other rock powders rich in potash are recommended. It has been found that the more soluble potash there is in the soil, the more of it plants will take up. And this "potash feast" will actually prevent the plant from taking up other elements it needs. Since the natural mineral fertilizers are insoluble, there is no worry about this occurring.

There are three main sources of potassium used by organic gardeners and farmers:
1. plant residues
2. manures and compost
3. natural mineral sources, like granite dust, green sand and basalt rock

Included in these categories are wood ashes (six to ten per cent), hay (1.2 to 2.3 per cent), and leaves (0.4 to 0.7 per cent). The best plan is to use both organic and mineral potash fertilizer—organic for short term potash release and mineral for the longer period. *See* POTASH

Other plant foods needed by crops include calcium, magnesium, sulfur, iron, zinc, molybdenum, tin and iodine. These are called trace or minor elements and for details about how to supply these elements to your soil, *see* TRACE ELEMENTS AND DEFICIENCIES.

These trace elements are very important to proper growth of plants even though they are only needed in small amounts. Some in fact have been found to serve as partial substitutes for other nutrients and also have been found to increase plant resistance to diseases.

PLACE FERTILIZERS DEEP: An important idea recently developed is the concept of the deep placement of fertilizer. Particularly in regions where the soil is poor or there is scarcely enough rainfall during the growing season for proper growth, deep placement is most effective.

The whole concept of deep placement is based on the placing of fertilizers deep down at the very bottom of the root system of plants. If this is done, the roots of the plants work themselves deep down in the soil to reach the nutrients. This means that the plants will become especially well-rooted. When there is a shortage of rainfall, the plants thus well-rooted will be able to stand up under the drought conditions. Plants that are inadequately rooted in the shallow top soil will dry up and die when the top soil dries out.

Another important reason why deep-placement of organic fertilizer is better than chemical fertilizer is water retention. A good compost has billions of pores and absorptive plant cells per cubic yard. Chemical fertilizers have few and will retain no water except what little is held by the surface wetting of the chemicals. Good compost is like a sponge taking up water. It soaks it up when there is plenty of rainfall and releases it to the growing plants when there is insufficient rainfall.

How to Mix an Organic NPK Formula: In the chart are listed 51 different plants, both flowers and vegetables, along with fertilizer recommendations for each plant. Note that, in many cases, we recommend fertilizers in NPK formulas. You can mix your own formulas by consulting the *Organic Fertilizer Formulas* chart which follows the *Fertilizer Recommendations* chart.

To make up, for example, a 2-4-2 mixture, the proportions of one part bone meal, one part leather dust, and three parts granite dust are needed. If you want five pounds of it, weigh out and combine one pound of bone meal, one pound of leather dust, and three parts granite dust.

If a fertilizer formula contains raw organic matter, try to turn it under at least several weeks before planting. Even more time may be needed if the bacterial population of the soil is low from past use of chemical fertilizers. If you can grind up organic matter such as leaves, alfalfa, or straw, they will decay much quicker.

Don't worry about getting exactly the correct proportion when mixing organic fertilizers. Do not hesitate to substitute cottonseed meal for blood meal. One reason that the organic method of fertilizing has so many staunch supporters is that it is almost impossible to go wrong.

By no means have all possible organic fertilizers been used in the listing. Many others could be substituted if their exact chemical compositions are known. We have chosen these to give you a good idea of what you can do with organic fertilizers in the way of mixing to get desired analyses. There are commercial preparations of

rock fertilizers and **organic** matter that can also be used.

Fertilizing your soil organically is a simple procedure. For example, when manure is not available, don't worry. Your local hardware or garden supply store most likely has bone meal. If you mix dried blood with it, you'll have an effective balanced fertilizer.

Fertilizer Recommendations

Vegetables: (*per 100 sq. feet*)

Artichokes: three lbs. of 2-4-2.

Asparagus: 3.5 lbs. of 1-5-5 and 115 lbs. of rotted manure. For sandy soil, use seven lbs. of 2½-5-5.

Beans: three lbs. of 2-4-5.

Beets: five lbs. of 3-6-2½ or six lbs. of 2½-5-5.

Cabbage: eight lbs. of 2½-5½-2½.

Carrots: seven lbs. of 2½-6-6.

Cauliflower: seven lbs. of 3-4-3 and 70 lbs. of rotted manure. A soybean cover crop is excellent.

Celery: seven lbs. of 3-4-3, 100 lbs. of rotted manure, leaf mold and wood ashes (especially from hardwoods).

Corn: three lbs. of 2½-5-5. Also add 7½ lbs. of wood ashes.

Kale: seven lbs of 3-4-3.

Lettuce: five lbs. of 2½-6-6.

Onions: four lbs. of 3½-3½-3½, two lbs. of rotted manure, and a sprinkling of wood ashes.

Parsley: five lbs. of 2½-5½-2½.

Peas: three lbs. of 2-4-2.

Peppers: four lbs. of 0-6-6.

Potatoes: for sandy soils, use four lbs. of 2½-5-5. On heavier soils try five lbs. of 2½-5½-2½.

Radishes: six lbs. of 3-7-5 and 120 lbs. of rotted manure.

Spinach: 2½ lbs. of 3-7-5 and 120 lbs. of rotted manure.

Sweet Potatoes: three lbs. of 2-4-5.

Tomatoes: seven lbs. of 4-6-6 or nine lbs. of 2½-5-5.

Turnips: three lbs. of 2½-5½-2½.

Flowers: (*per 100 sq. feet*)

Anemone: Mulch with peat moss, leaf mold or hay.

Annuals: Add four bushels of manure

per 100 square feet: spread on four-six lbs. of 2½-5½-2½ per 100 square feet.

Asters: When planting, use six lbs. of 2-5-2 per 100 square feet and double the quantity for poor soil. Mulch with oak leaf mold, rotted pine needles or cottonseed meal.

Begonias: Dig in small amounts of cottonseed meal, fish meal, or bone meal, but avoid using too much nitrogen. Never cultivate. Mulch with leaf mold or peat moss.

Bulbs: Planting: dig in two bushels of peat per 100 square feet.

Camellias: Dig in small amounts of rotted manure, cottonseed meal or leaf compost. Don't use blood meal or fish meal. Mulch with bean or alfalfa hay.

Carnations: Planting: Use rotted cow manure, peat moss or acid compost. When they are beginning to bloom, add two lbs. pulverized sheep manure and 2½ lbs. wood ashes per square yard.

Chrysanthemums: Use rotted manure, compost, bone meal. Mulch with loose material such as salt hay, straw or rotted manure—or add four lbs. of 2-5-2 per 100 square feet.

Clematis: Dig in two lbs. of bone meal per 100 square feet and some well-rotted manure. Mulch with leaf mold or cocoa shell, preferably semi-decomposed.

Daffodils: Planting: three-eight inches of rotted manure, a liberal sprinkling of bone meal. Mulch with leaves or salt hay.

Dahlias: Planting: two-inch layer of rotted manure, a handful of bone meal and tobacco dust in each planting hole. If possible, grow a legume cover crop the previous year. Later, fertilize with five lbs. raw bone meal and ten lbs. glauconite marl (or five lbs. wood ashes) per 100 square feet. If the soil is deficient in nitrogen, use three lbs. dried blood.

Daylilies: Not much fertilizer is needed. Use a three-inch layer of rotted manure and add 1½ lbs. bone meal per 100 square feet. Mulch with peat moss or a light layer of leaves.

Delphiniums: Add plenty of compost, rotted manure and bone meal. Use leaf mold at the rate of eight-ten bushels per 100 square feet. Mulch with ground corn cobs, buckwheat hulls, or grass clippings.

Fuchsias: Mulch with leaf mold.

Gardenias: Use rotted manure on quite acid soil, peat moss or leaf mold on slightly acid soils.

Geraniums: Wash in a sprinkling of wood ashes. Manure water can be used, but avoid peat (too acid).

Gladiolus: Grow a cover crop of rye or vetch, fertilized with four lbs. phosphate rock and one lb. wood ashes per 100 square feet. Then at least four or five weeks before planting gladiolus, turn under the cover crop and add ten lbs. 2½-5½-2½ per 100 square feet. Mulch with leaf mold.

Irises: Very little fertilizer needed. If soil is especially poor, use small amounts of phosphate rock, bone meal, or wood ashes. Avoid nitrogen and manures.

Lilies: On highly alkaline soil use peat moss or leaf mold. Treat ground with six lbs. glauconite marl per 100 square feet.

Narcissus: Planting: three inches of rotted manure and eight-ten lbs. of 2½-5½-2½ per 100 square feet in trench. Use liquid cow manure during the growing season.

Pansies: A cover crop of clover or peas is excellent before pansies. Also use five lbs. phosphate rock, two lbs. oyster shell dust, and a sprinkling of blood meal per 100 square feet. Mulch with a thin layer of dry leaves, lawn clippings, partly rotted straw or evergreen branches.

Peonies: Planting: Put three inches of rotted manure and a sprinkling of bone meal in the planting holes. Manure should not touch the crowns of peonies. In fall, add well-rotted manure and eight lbs. of $2\frac{1}{2}$-$5\frac{1}{2}$-$2\frac{1}{2}$ per 100 square feet. Mulch with ground corn cobs or a light layer of pulverized leaves.

Phlox: Turn under a three-inch layer of manure several weeks before planting.

Primroses: Fairly rich soil is needed. Planting: use a three to one mixture of peat moss and dried cow manure. Mulch, especially in dry climates, with straw, salt hay, or hardwood sawdust (oak is very good).

Roses: Planting: Use four lbs of 6-8-3. In early spring or late fall apply five bushels of cow manure or one bushel of hen manure per 100 square feet. Bone meal is good on acid soils.

Snapdragons: Dig in plenty of rotted manure or leaf mold. When coming into flower, use liquid manure.

Sweet Peas: Apply three-four inches of rotted manure. Bone meal can be used at the rate of five lbs. per 100 square feet.

Tulips: Planting: Mix in five lbs. bone meal and five lbs. dried manure per 100 bulbs used. Keep the nitrogen fertilizers low. Use only weak solutions of liquid manure. In fall, double the amount of fertilizers used at planting.

Violets: Use small amounts of wood ashes.

ORGANIC FERTILIZER FORMULAS: Below are listed more than 20 NPK formulas which you may have cause to mix for your garden. Under each formula is listed the organic and natural ingredients needed for their construction. Of course, you may experiment and mix your own formula if the materials we recommend are not available. The easiest way of doing this is to approximate NPK values based on two or three types of organic material, and then to proceed as suggested before.

0—6—6
1 part phosphate rock
3 parts greensand
2 parts wood ashes

1—4—3
1 part basic slag
1 part tankage
4 parts greensand

1—5—5
1 part tankage
3 parts wood ashes
2 parts basic slag

2—$3\frac{1}{2}$—$2\frac{1}{2}$
1 part bone meal
3 parts alfalfa hay
2 parts greensand

2—4—2
4 parts coffee grounds
1 part bone meal
1 part wood ashes

2—4—2 (alternate construction)
1 part bone meal
1 part leather dust
3 parts granite dust

2—4—5
1 part tankage
1 part wood ashes
1 part granite dust

2—5—2
2 parts coffee grounds
1 part tankage
1 part bone meal

2—5—2 (alternate construction)
5 parts basic slag
2 parts wood ashes
2 parts leather dust

2—5—3
3 parts greensand
2 parts seaweed
1 part dried blood
2 parts phosphate rock

2—12—2
1 part cottonseed meal
2 parts phosphate rock
2 parts seaweed

$2\frac{1}{2}$—$5\frac{1}{2}$—$2\frac{1}{2}$
2 parts cottonseed meal
1 part colloidal phosphate
2 parts granite dust

$2\frac{1}{2}$—6—6
1 part dried blood
1 part phosphate rock
4 parts wood ashes

PERCENTAGE COMPOSITION OF VARIOUS MATERIALS

For use in calculating your own formulas, we present a listing of many common organic materials, along with their NPK percentages:

	Nitrogen	Phosphorus	Potash
Activated Sludge	5.00	3.00	. . .
Animal Tankage	8.00	20.00	. . .
Alfalfa Hay	2.45	.50	2.10
Apple Leaves	1.00	.15	.35
Bloodmeal	15.00	1.30	.70
Bone Meal	4.00	21.00	.20
Brewers' Grains (wet)	.90	.50	.05
Cattle Manure (fresh)	.29	.17	.35
Castor Pomace	5.50	1.50	1.25
Cocoa Shell Dust	1.04	1.49	2.71
Coffee Grounds (dried)	1.99	.36	.67
Corn Stalks	.75	.40	.90
Cottonseed	3.15	1.25	1.15
Cottonseed Meal	7.00	2.50	1.50
Dried Blood	12.00–15.00	3.00	. . .
Fish Scrap (red snapper)	7.76	13.00	3.80
Greensand	. . .	1.50	5.00
Hen Manure (fresh)	1.63	1.54	.85
Hoofmeal and Horn Dust	12.50	1.75	. . .
Horse Manure (fresh)	.44	.17	.35
Incinerator Ash	.24	5.15	2.33
Oak Leaves	.80	.35	.15
Peach Leaves	.90	.15	.60
Red Clover	.55	.13	.50
Seaweed	1.68	.75	5.00
Sheep Manure (fresh)	.55	.31	.15
Swine Manure (fresh)	.60	.41	.13
Tankage	6.00	8.00	. . .
Tobacco Stems	2.00	. . .	7.00
Wood Ashes	. . .	1.50	7.00

3—4—3
  3 parts basic slag
  2 parts wood ashes
  2 parts leather dust

3—4—3 (alternate construction)
  3 parts wood ashes
  5 parts basic slag
  2 parts dried blood

3—6—2½
  2 parts tankage
  1 part colloidal phosphate
  3 parts seaweed

3—6—2½ (alternate construction)
  1 part leather dust
  1 part phosphate rock
  3 parts seaweed

3—7—5
  1 part dried blood
  1 part phosphate rock
  3 parts wood ashes

3—8—5
  1 part leather dust
  1 part phosphate rock
  1 part fish scrap
  3 parts wood ashes

3½—3½—3½
3 parts granite dust
1 part dried blood
1 part bone meal
5 parts seaweed

4—6—6
2 parts dried blood
1 part phosphate rock
4 parts wood ashes

6—8—3
2 parts fish scrap
2 parts dried blood
1 part cottonseed meal
1 part wood ashes
1 part phosphate rock
1 part granite dust

ORGANIC FERTILIZERS ARE DIFFERENT: To prove that organic fertilizers are different and superior to chemical fertilizers, W. D. Keller, Professor of Geology at the University of Missouri writes:

Scientific proof has been discovered in another way that organic compounds will feed plants where otherwise similar inorganic compounds will not. This new, important discovery has been announced in a recent issue of the technical magazine *Science* under the title "Influence of Humic Acids on Plant Growth" by P. C. de Kock, at the Macaulay Institute for Soil Research, Aberdeen, Scotland.

Opponents of the organic method have said many times that it makes no difference to a non-intelligent plant whether a nutrient element is presented to the plant in an organic or an inorganic compound, and thereby condone the practice of deluging a soil with concentrated, highly soluble chemicals. Organic supporters have not always had a scientific answer with which to refute, or to come back at such a statement. They could always say, "We see the difference in our plants, and in the flavor of our foods," but although that answer is truthful, it is not a quick squelch to the fast talker who was selling inorganics. The report by Mr. de Kock and accessory references give

proof now that a plant may starve on an inorganic source of iron but that it responds healthily if humic material is added. Because the experiments were conducted so as to meet strict scientific requirements, organic farmers will find comfort and assurance in the report.

First, Mr. de Kock referred to an experiment on a sunflower plant, which was described by other authors in 1954. The roots from a sunflower plant were divided, part of them being placed in a compartment which contained iron and phosphate nutrients, and the other part of the roots in a second, separate compartment whose contents could be changed. When an organic compound which is a chelator, in this case ethylene diamine tetracetic acid (also called EDTA), was placed in the second compartment, the plant could utilize the iron and phosphate in the first compartment, and the plant grew healthily. If the organic compound, EDTA, was withheld, the sunflower plant became chlorotic (meaning malnourished and leaves discolored).

Second, Mr. de Kock found from one of his experiments that the humic substances from lignite (a coaly, organic material) likewise made iron available to the plant even in the presence of a high concentration of phosphate. If the organic humic substance was not present, as in the second compartment, iron was immobilized in the roots, and the upper part of the plant was starved of iron. This is a remarkable experiment in several ways.

It shows that a plant thrives if some roots are picking up one set of nutrients and other roots are picking up entirely different nutrients. Plants can therefore provide themselves with a favorable mixed "diet" from different sources. It shows that a plant can combine, redistribute, transfer, or translocate, widely different chemical compounds within the plant. It shows that part of the plant's "diet" may be extracted from inorganic rock fragments and part from organic matter and solutions elsewhere in the root system. It shows that organic substances act as transmitters, or translocators for other nutrients, as well as providing them.

To go a step further, it is possible that a large proportion of the transfer of nutrient elements in plants may be carried on solely as mobile chelated organic compounds, even though they start out inorganically. It is entirely logical that organic nutrients are more easily absorbed, more completely absorbed, and spread through the plant more quickly, more efficiently, and more thoroughly than as isolated inorganic ions. Inorganic nutrition may be far more widely dependent upon organic assistance than the most rabid organic farmer has previously imagined.

Whether all or only part of these effects are obtained beneficially from organic substances, the facts remain that organic matter contains quickly available and quickly assimilable nutrients for plants, that it imparts most desirable physical properties to the soil, and that it is an effective weathering agent of rock and mineral particles which hold the reserves of fertility for long lasting soil. Therefore, in any case, one cannot go wrong when he goes organic. *See also* DEFICIENCIES, SOIL; COMPOST; ORGANIC GARDENING; MANURE; TRACE ELEMENTS; NITROGEN; PHOSPHORUS; POTASH.

FERTILIZER, ARTIFICIAL: It was in reaction to the increased use of artificial fertilizers that the school of organic gardening and farming grew. With the inception of the motor age, manure became scarcer for many farmers, necessitating a new method of fertilization. Thus, shortly after the turn of the century, scientists developed a series of artificial fertilizers, most of which combined natural rock bases with additions of soluble chemicals.

The organic school does not accept the use of artificial fertilizers for many reasons. Chemical fertilizers are quick-acting, short-term plant "boosters," and are responsible for: (1) deterioration of soil friability, creating hardpan soil, (2) destruction of beneficial soil life, including earthworms, (3) altering vitamin and protein contents of certain crops, (4) making certain crops more vulnerable to diseases, and (5) preventing plants from absorbing some needed minerals.

The soil must be regarded as a living organism. An acid fertilizer, because of its acids, dissolves the cementing material, made from the dead bodies of soil organisms, which holds the rock particles together to form soil crumbs. It spoils the friability of the soil. On the surface of the soil such cement-free particles settle to form a compact, more or less water-impervious layer. This compact surface layer of rock particles encourages rain water to run off rather than to enter the soil.

For example: A highly soluble fertilizer, such as 5-10-5, goes into solution in the soil water rapidly so that much of it may be leached away without benefiting the plants at all. But the sodium in the fertilizer like sodium nitrate tends to accumulate in the soil where it combines with carbonic acid to form washing soda, sodium carbonate. This chemical causes the soil to assume a cement-like hardness. Other minerals, when present in large concentrations, percolate into the subsoil where they interact with the clay to form impervious layers of precipitates called hardpans.

Hardpans seal the topsoil off from the subsoil. Water cannot pass downward into the subsoil, and water from the water table cannot rise to the topsoil in which the plants are growing. Many plants cannot live when their roots are kept too wet. Then too, the subsoil below the hardpans is anaerobic and rapidly becomes acid. In such anaerobic acid soils, the soil organism population changes radically and in ways which are unfavorable to crop plants.

Such highly soluble chemicals as chlorides and sulphates are poisonous to the beneficial soil organisms, but in small amounts act as stimulants. These chemicals stimulate the beneficial soil bacteria to such increased growth and reproduction that they use up the organic matter in the soil as food faster than it can be returned by present agricultural practices. When chemical residues accumulate in the soil, the microorganisms may be killed off by hydrolysis (water-removing). The high salt concentration in the soil water will pull water from the bacterial or fungal cells, causing them to collapse and die.

ARTIFICIAL FERTILIZERS CHANGE THE SOIL ORGANISM POPULATION: Many artificial fertilizers contain acids, as sulphuric acid and hydrochloric acid, which will increase the acidity of the soil. Changes in the soil acidity (pH) are accompanied by changes in the kinds of organisms which can live in the soil. Such changes often are sufficient to interfere greatly with the profitable growth of crop plants. For this reason, the artificial fertilizer people tell their customers to increase the organic matter content of the soil, thus offsetting the deleterious effects of these acids; also to use lime.

NITROGEN - CONTAINING FERTILIZERS, LIKE SODIUM NITRATE AND CYANAMID, AFFECT THE NITROGEN-FIXING SOIL BACTERIA: About 78 per cent of the atmosphere is made up of gaseous nitrogen. Living soil contains enough nitrogen-fixing bacteria to fix enough atmospheric nitrogen to supply abundantly the needs of crop plants. In the presence of soluble nitrates, these bacteria use the nitrogen which man has provided in his artificial fertilizers and fix absolutely none from the atmosphere.

ARTIFICIAL FERTILIZERS ARE RESPONSIBLE FOR POOR AERATION OF THE SOIL: There are several ways by which artificial fertilizers will reduce aeration of soils. Earthworms, whose numerous burrowings make the soil more porous, are killed. The acid fertilizers will also destroy the cementing materials which bind rock particles together to form crumbs. Lastly, hardpans result which seal off the lower soil levels, keeping them more or less completely anaerobic.

THE TYPE OF FERTILIZER USED INFLUENCES THE AMOUNT OF VITAMINS PRODUCED BY THE PLANTS: Several Experiment Stations have found that supplying citrus fruits with a large amount of highly soluble nitrogen will lower the vitamin C content of oranges.

THE USE OF ARTIFICIAL FERTILIZERS CAN MAKE CROPS MORE SUSCEPTIBLE TO DISEASE: Chemical fertilizers rob plants of some natural immunity by killing off the policemen microorganisms in the soil. Many plant diseases have already been considerably checked when antibiotic-producing bacteria or fungi thrived around the roots.

When plants are supplied with much nitrogen and only a medium amount of phosphate, plants will most easily contract mosaic infections also. Most resistance is obtained if there is a small supply of nitrogen and plenty of phosphate. Fungus and bacterial diseases have then been related to high nitrogen fertilization, as well as to a lack of trace elements.

ARTIFICIAL FERTILIZERS DO NOT PRODUCE THE SAME AMOUNT OF PROTEIN IN CROPS THAT ORGANIC FERTILIZERS WILL: It has been found that fertilizers that provide quickly soluble nitrogen will lower the capacity of hybrid corn, in particular, to produce seeds with high protein content.

WHY CROPS GROWN ON LAND CONTINUALLY DOPED WITH ARTIFICIAL FERTILIZERS OFTEN ARE DEFICIENT IN TRACE ELEMENTS: To explain this principle will mean delving into a little physics and chemistry, but you will then easily see the unbalanced nutrition created in artificially-fertilized plants. The colloidal humus particles are the convoys that transfer most of the minerals from the soil solution to the root hairs. Each humus particle is negatively charged and will of course attract the positive elements such as potassium, sodium, calcium, magnesium, manganese, aluminum, boron, iron, copper, and other metals. When sodium nitrate, for instance, is dumped into the soil year after year in large doses, a radical change takes place on the humus particles. The very numerous sodium ions (atomic particles) will eventually crowd out the other ions, making them practically unavailable for plant use. The humus becomes coated with sodium, glutting the root hairs with the excess. Finally the plant is unable to pick up some of the minerals that it really needs.

Beware of fast-acting fertilizers. Repeated tests by organic gardeners have shown that they are short-term feeders and that they can't build up soil to virgin goodness. Only ten to 15 per cent of their nutrients are used by plants. The rest is washed out or locked up chemically in the soil.

Extremely few fertilizers are complete plant foods—despite what you read in advertisements for chemicals. No man yet knows all the nutrients that a plant needs. The only way to be sure of putting into your soil a complete plant food is to duplicate the way soil was built originally. Add the natural rocks and silt that supply minerals plus compost, manure or other organic matter to supply, in a shotgun manner, the humus that is the key to soil balance.

LISTING OF CHEMICAL FERTILIZERS

The following fertilizers are classified by organic farmers and gardeners as not acceptable in an organic fertilizing program. These are the types of common chemical fertilizers.

Aluminum Sulphate. 15 per cent aluminum, 28 per cent sulphur. Highly acid, aluminum sulphate may release toxic amounts of the trace element aluminum.

Ammonium Chloride. 26 per cent nitrogen, 66 per cent chlorine. Seed germination is reduced when chlorine is built up in the soil.

Ammonium Nitrate. 32½ per cent nitrogen. It is manufactured by passing ammonia gas through nitric acid.

Ammonium Sulphate. 21 per cent nitrogen, 24 per cent sulphur. Ammonium sulphate is strongly acid in the soil and is death to certain beneficial bacteria.

Ammo-Phos. Grade A, 11 per cent nitrogen, 15 per cent available phosphorus; grade B, 16 per cent nitrogen, 6½ per cent available phosphorus.

Anhydrous Ammonia. 82 per cent nitrogen, containing more nitrogen than any other fertilizer. Farmers force it into the ground as a gas.

Calcium Nitrate. 15 per cent nitrogen, 24 per cent calcium.

Coal Ashes. Bituminous or soft coal ashes show from 0.3—10 per cent sulphur trioxide, which forms sulphuric acid when water is added. Some of the ashes also have as much as 30 per cent aluminum. Anthracite or hard coal ashes are less toxic but should be avoided.

Iron Sulphate. 37 per cent iron, 21 per cent sulphur. Iron and sulphur residues are toxic especially if the drainage is poor.

Magnesium Sulphate. 20 per cent magnesium, 26½ per cent sulphur.

Manganese Sulphate. 27 per cent manganese, 24 per cent sulphur.

Muriate of Potash. 53 per cent potash, 47 per cent chlorine. Continued use lowers the protein content of certain food crops, particularly potatoes and damages their quality.

Nitrate of Soda. 26 per cent sodium, 16 per cent nitrogen (similar to Chilean nitrate). Natural fixation of nitrogen by legumes will be practically stopped. Crops forced with nitrate of soda may accumulate extremely high amounts of nitrogen, which can cause poisoning in human beings.

Potassium Nitrate or Saltpeter. 39 per cent potash, 13 per cent nitrogen. Long application ruins soil structure by separating clay particles. Then the land is no longer granulated and porous.

Potassium Sulphate. 45 per cent potash, 18 per cent sulphur.

Sodium Nitrate. Same as nitrate of soda.

Soot. High ammonia and sulphur content.

Superphosphate. Raw ground phosphate rock treated with sulphuric acid. A ton of the acid is generally used to treat each ton of phosphate rock.

Urea. 42 per cent nitrogen.

Many gardeners use too much chemical fertilizer because of a lack of knowledge of the make-up of these strong chemicals. Because commercial fertilizers are so highly concentrated, they must not be allowed to come in contact with the plant, so a trench is dug from two to four inches away from the stems. Also, care must be taken to remove immediately any that may be spilled on the leaves, for if allowed to remain, burning may result. Many gardeners do not realize the potency of commercial fertilizers and use far too much. This is both dangerous and wasteful; dangerous because roots can be burned by large amounts not properly blended with the soil, and wasteful because plants can only take up so much food at a time, and when too heavy an application of fertilizer is made, a large portion leaches away before the plants can use it. *See also* FERTILIZERS; ORGANIC GARDENING.

FESCUE: *see* LAWN

FIELD BINDWEED: *see* BINDWEED

FIELD DODDER: *see* CONVOLVULUS

FIG: (*Ficus carica*) This tree (it actually looks more like a bush) is seldom found in commercial orchards, and when it is, the fruits are almost always either preserved or dried. The reason is that the fig does not continue to ripen after being picked, and by the time it reaches its peak, it is too perishable to ship without expensive precautions. Therefore, to enjoy delicious fresh figs, your own "dooryard" tree is a requisite.

The Trojano or Black Kadota fig is a very heavy bearer, frequently yielding a crop after the first year. Trees are started from cuttings or layering.

REQUIREMENTS OF THE FIG: Different varieties thrive in different localities, according to their resistance to cold weather. The fig requires warm summers, mild winters, ample moisture, and excellent drainage. It thrives well when planted next to a house, for the building offers some winter protection. If the trees are protected by heavy mulch, or by about 15 inches of soil over the roots during winter, they will come out from the root and produce fruit that year, although the top may be killed back by severe cold. Older trees are usually more resistant to cold. Young trees are sometimes pulled over and are covered with soil during the winter.

INSECT AND DISEASE PROBLEMS: The fig meets with little trouble from insects or diseases. It is an ancient tree, having been popular for thousands of years, and has survived the test of time. In the Gulf Coast area, the most common insect pests are nematodes and tree borers. To discourage nematodes, the tree should be planted in deeply cultivated heavy soil and encouraged to root deeply. Shallow-rooted trees in sandy soil are more susceptible to nematodes. Planting near a building also discourages nematodes, which do not infest the roots under the structure.

Tree borers are discouraged by good housekeeping in the garden. Any dead or broken limbs should be pruned immediately, and the scars and any other breaks in the bark should be promptly painted with tar or some other healing preventative.

Rust and cotton root rot are the most common diseases in the South. The rust, like the tree borer, is prevented by careful housekeeping. Strong, healthy trees are seldom attacked. Cotton root rot can be prevented only by not planting the tree in land where cotton has been grown.

FIG PROPAGATION: New trees are usually started from cuttings, or by layering. The cuttings should be about 3/8-inch in diameter, ten to 12 inches long, and from one or two-year-old wood. It may be rooted where the tree is desired, set deep with only one bud left above ground.

Like all fast-growing semi-tropical plants, the fig responds quickly to fertilizer. There is danger in overfeeding, however, as lush tender growth is easily damaged by cold. A slow, mature growth is preferred to a fast one. A heavy mulch in the summer to retain moisture, and in the winter to protect against the weather, plus a spring application of good compost, will usually guarantee even growth. A tree treated like this needs no cultivation.

This Trojano fig is sometimes called the Black Kadota. It is a very heavy bearer; frequently starts after the first year; needs no pruning except to keep the tree shaped.

With a choice location and proper winter protection, the average tree will produce fruit in three years, and the gardener can fulfill the prophesy of Micah in the Old Testament: "They shall sit every man under his fig tree."—*Marilyn Sibley.*

VARIETIES OF PLANT: Other members of the *Ficus* are also well-known. The rubber plant (*F. elastica*) is one of the most popular ornamental foliage plants for indoor growing. The creeping fig (*F. pumila*) is a very common and well recommended climber. Almost as dark in color as English Ivy, it clings close to walls, makes a dense growth and is sometimes used for hanging baskets. There is also the banyan tree (*F. benghalensis*), some varieties of which ripen their fruit underground. This tropical tree sometimes outgrows all others in its native habitat.

CAPRIFICATION: This refers to the fertilization of Smyrna figs done by the fig-wasp, the Blastophaga. Its history in this country is a fascinating one—how the first Smyrna fig growers in California blamed the inability of their trees to bear fruit on local weather conditions; scoffed at the silly ideas of Greek farmers who claimed that the fig harvest depended on an insect. Then as the situation grew more and more serious, government and California state researchers tried desperately to propagate the Blastophagas. Finally in 1869 the fig-wasps became accidentally established on a farm near Modesto, California, and that was the real start of the fig industry in this country. Research has now discovered much of the procedure for keeping the insects abundant. Only about 30 Capri figs are needed to fertilize a large fig tree, as the insects and pollen are so numerous; in fact, just one tree of the wild fig is enough for over 100 Smyrna trees. The pollen-coated insect forces itself into the tiny openings of the undeveloped figs, fertilizing the female flowers inside.

Commercial fig-growing is mostly

restricted to California, but it is spreading also into Arizona, New Mexico and Texas. As stated above, fig trees are often grown as bushes in the central as well as some northern areas, where they are protected in winter by covering the branches with a heavy mulch or several inches of soil. *See also* FRUIT TREES, RESISTANT VARIETIES; RUBBER PLANT.

FIG MARIGOLD: *see* MESEMBRYANTHEMUM

FILAMENT: *see* FLOWER

FILBERTS: (*Corylus maxima*) A filbert tree, with a single trunk, is about the size of a thrifty plum tree. Set out in orchard form, the trees should not be closer than 25 feet. If you grow the filbert for nuts, you will prefer it as a single-stemmed plant, and will find it bears more prolifically that way. If you have an orchard of filberts, the single-stemmed trees will probably be a trifle easier to handle.

In the West, however, where the commercial crop of filberts is grown, many orchardists let their filberts have three or four main stems. The plant will send up innumerable shoots, so that the grower can train it with as many heavy branches as he desires. A filbert with several stems grows like a clump of white birches, with the several stems arching outward from one another in a most artistic manner. Such a growth is highly ornamental.

If the gardener elects, he can grow the plant as a bushy shrub. He allows several stems to come up and then prunes them to outside buds to spread out the growth and keep the plants at any desired height. Thus he can make a very beautiful hedge of filberts. Preferably the plants should be set not closer than six feet. Such a hedge can be anywhere from a few feet high to 12 or 15 feet. It is all a matter of deciding what you want, and training the plants accordingly.

The leaves of the filbert are large and are very lovely. Although the female blossom is so inconspicuous that one can hardly find it, the catkins stretch out at the first touch of warmth in the spring, the pollen turns a beautiful yellow.

BLOOMING PERIOD: But here is one of the weak points of the filbert. It blooms *too* soon. Forced out by a prematurely warm day, the catkins may be frozen stiff by the frosty night that follows. That won't hurt the tree, but it may ruin the nut crop. However, the same thing is often true of other nut trees and also of the apple and the peach. The difference is that the filbert comes out much earlier in the year and so is more likely to suffer. Don't plant in a southern exposure as the warmth would be apt to force the flowers; the cooler the site the better.

Another beautiful feature of the filbert is the husk or involucre that encases the nut. "Encases" is exactly the right word, for the involucre grows out around the nut much like a pillow case about a pillow. The difference in length of involucres is a matter of interest. Some of these vegetable pillow slips are not as long as the nut to be enclosed. Some fit the nut very nicely. Others extend well beyond the nut, the outer ends of the husks being more or less wrapped together, like the slightly-twisted end of a long pillow case. All these husks are beautifully fringed or pinked at the ends.

Furthermore, filberts are borne singly, in pairs, as triplets, or in groups of four or five, depending probably upon how well pollination was effected. As the nut ripens, the husk fades in color from a vivid green to a yellow and then a brown. Now the nuts are ripe. They will rattle out of their little cases, although some varieties retain the nuts within the husks.

Filberts will grow almost anywhere in the country. They are easy to grow. Being propagated almost exclusively by layering, they come to the purchaser with a generous growth of roots and begin to grow promptly and vigorously. They will not stand wet feet, so make sure drainage is good.

A most striking characteristic is their tendency to "sucker up." The nurseryman will send you a plant with a single stem, but in no time you will have many more shooting up from the roots. So you must decide promptly what sort of filbert you want to grow. If you want a bush, let the suckers come. If you want a tree with three main branches, cut out all but two of the suckers. If you want a tree with a single trunk, remove *all* volunteers. Then be watchful, for the plant will continue from year to year to send up suckers.

This, however, is not an undesirable trait. If your main stem is injured or diseased, you can remove it and soon you will have a good substitute. You can't do that with a peach or apple tree. They are grafted, and shoots from the roots would probably be from inferior and undesirable stock.

The filbert is a close relative of the hazelnut, both belonging to the genus *Corylus*. The one ailment that affects the hazelnut is a blight, but it rarely seems to infect the filbert. The hazels are resistant to it and suffer little damage, having acquired a large degree of resistance, just as the Chinese chestnut is resistant to the chestnut blight. But with regard to blight the filbert is like the American chestnut. It has no age-long experience with the disease to help it develop immunity, so it has little resistance. Therefore, do not grow hazels and filberts together. If your plants do become blighted, cut away all blighted stems and in no time you will have fresh, healthy substitutes.

The filbert is one of those plants that simply *must* have cross-pollination. If you want nuts, you will be wasting time by planting a single filbert plant. Buy two or three varieties. Local nut nurserymen will tell you what to use in your locality. Many varieties of filberts have now been developed. Some are excellent polli-

nators. Some are not so good. All are practically self-sterile. So be sure to secure at least two varieties that work well together.

FILBERTWORM: The filbertworm cannot enter nuts until after the husks have begun to crack, so the nut crop should be harvested at the earliest possible date. Further, the filbertworm is unable to complete its development on dried nut meats. Therefore, the crop should be dried thoroughly as soon as it is harvested.

FIR: A handsome tree that thrives in cooler climate areas, this hardy conifer, a member of the pine family, is one of the most beautiful evergreens. Tall and stately, firs form pyramids of stiff branches with upright cones and bristly, blunt-tipped leaves arranged in flat, spiralled sprays. The new cones appear in a variety of bright colors—everything from blue to red, green, purple and brown, depending on the particular species.

In the northern latitudes, firs are deservingly popular for the home grounds, serving attractively in landscaping designs and providing desirable winter color and windbreaking protection.

Botanically named *Abies,* firs prefer a moist soil, shade and cool, humid air free of dirt and city smoke. Although some types may become spindly when mature, most will keep their fine form under favorable conditions and care. As with many evergreens, they require little pruning, although removing the terminal buds will develop side branches and add to the tree's foliage and compactness.

Young firs are especially suitable and pleasing in the home garden. Careful placement is important when first planting if the trees are not to be moved later. However, their fibrous root system allows even large trees to be transplanted.

As for difficulties and precautions, the root and wood diseases which generally afflict conifers in a forest setting are seldom noted or serious in ornamental plantings. Several rust diseases, though, are often troublesome, including witches' broom. This dwarfs young twig growth and causes a broom-like effect on upright branches. Any infested branches should be carefully cut out, and weeds which host the disease should be destroyed. Most fir species are relatively free from insect pests.

Among the best-known fir varieties is the Colorado or White Fir (*Abies concolor*), most adaptable and widely used species. It is a fast grower, reaching 120 feet at a rate of about 18 inches a year. A native of the area from Colorado to California, this tree is hardy north to Massachusetts, Nebraska and Iowa. It tolerates heat and dry weather, prefers a rich, well-mulched and moderately moist soil, which helps it keep its lower branches well into maturity. A smooth light-gray trunk and branches, gray-green cones from three to five inches long, and bluish needles are features which make this fir attractive and popular.

Other species include the Balsam Fir (*A. balsamea*) which attains 75 feet, is common in wet soils and hardy in the Northeastern states; the Nikko Fir (*A. homolepsis*), a very hardy, popular native of Japan which is found throughout the eastern U. S., Minnesota, Montana and North Dakota, and grows to a 90-foot symmetrical pyramid with dark green foliage and purple cones; the Alpine or Rocky Mountain Fir (*A. lasiocarpa*) thrives in Canada and the Northwest, has a silver-gray bark and serves well in group plantings; the Silver Fir (*A. alba*) is a graceful native of China and southern Europe, reaches heights up to 150 feet, features bright, dark-green leaves with whitish undersides, and is not hardy in colder sections, requires protected location; and the Himalayan Fir (*A. spectabilis*), which displays large purple cones and is a good species for the south-central states. *See also* CHRISTMAS TREE FARMING.

FIRE ANT: The imported fire ant is an annoying and destructive pest in many Southeastern states. It kills vegetation by sucking the plant juices. It attacks young animals and destroys eggs. It has a vicious sting. It builds hard-crusted mounds as high as three feet that wreck farm machinery. All indications are that insecticides do far less harm to the ants than to other forms of life.

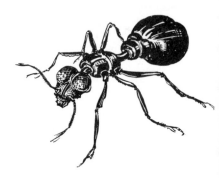

The Fire Ant is presumed to have been first introduced into this country in 1930 by boat from South America. Place of origin was Mobile, Ala.

The fire ant was presumably brought to Mobile, Alabama, by a ship from Argentina. It was first identified near there about 1930, but until a few years ago it remained a minor nuisance and confined itself to lower Alabama.

Then suddenly the fire ant population "exploded." It spread rapidly over the South and has now reached North Carolina and Central Texas without signs of stopping. The deep underground habits of the ants make it unlikely that they will be stopped by severe cold. It is the opinion of the U. S. Department of Agriculture, however, that the imported fire ant cannot survive north of Tennessee and North Carolina.

During 1956 and 1957 thousands of acres in lower Alabama were treated by poison broadcast according to government specifications. Cattle have grazed on that land and crops have been grown. Untold damage has been done wildlife and human life. According to the USDA bulletin the land will be toxic for three years.

Yet this area is *still* heavily infested with ants. Apparently the insecticide does not kill the ants in great numbers. It merely forces them to move to a new location. This they do by tunneling underground to an untreated area, moving their eggs and queens with them.

Obviously the insecticides have not controlled the ants. It is plausible that the poisons have actually triggered the increase of the ants by destroying their natural enemies. Quite possibly the poisons have served to scatter the ants further afield.

Only the natural enemies and diseases of a pest can offer a safe control.

In Argentina where the ant is native, it has never been a menace. It is the natural enemy of other worse insects, and in turn has been controlled by enemies of its own.

The native Southern fire ant is a close relative of the imported fire ant. Yet it has never presented a major problem.

FIRE BLIGHT: Kills back branches and blights blossoms on fruit trees so they appear burned by fire. It also produces cankers on twigs or the main trunk. Cutting out infection well below the visibly blighted area is most important, and so is breaking out blighted fruit spurs. A dormant oil spray has also been found effective.

FIREFLY: One of nature's most fascinating wonders is the light of the firefly. It is light without heat, made by a mysterious substance called luciferin contained within the firefly's abdomen. By opening a special tube, he exposes the luciferin to oxygen, which makes it glow. When temperature, moisture and light conditions are just right, the male flashes his light every six seconds, to be answered two seconds later by the female. Thus they seek each other out in the soft summer dusk.

In the tropics, fireflies grow considerably larger, and their light rivals the stars. Some varieties truly deserve the name of lightning bug, for when a number of them flash simultaneously, the whole landscape is brilliantly illuminated.

Actually a beetle, the firefly is a friend to the gardener. He feeds on snails and slugs, and his larvae eat small insects and cutworms underground and in rotting wood.

FIRETHORN: *see* PYRACANTHA

FISH, DRIED: Mainly used for feed mixtures, but also available for fertilizer needs, dried fish analyzes around eight per cent nitrogen and seven per cent phosphoric acid; these analyses are so high that such material can be handled like dried blood when used for composting. Since fish meal or dried ground fish is very malodorous, care must be taken not only to comply with health department regulations but also to protect escape of the nitrogen into the air. The best method is to use heavier layers of earth with the compost and to pay particular attention that heaps are kept evenly moist so that bacterial action is not interrupted. To get the proper balance of bacterial energy food or plant matter to the growth food, supplied as ground fish, is absolutely essential. One bag of dried ground fish of a hundred pounds should be composted with several hundred pounds of plant matter or a heap the size of a kitchen table. If sawdust is added, the amount of wilted plant matter can be somewhat reduced, because sawdust is highly absorbent and requires more nitrogen for complete composting.

FISH, ORNAMENTAL: *see* LILY POND

FISH WASTES: Fish scrap is often available locally; its nitrogen and phosphorus value is high, frequently about seven per cent for each and over, computed on a dry basis. While dried ground fish is free from fats, fish scrap contains much fish oil and may thereby attract fat-eating ants, besides being slower to break down. In tropical regions where citrus or banana wastes are easily available or near canneries where refuse is obtainable, composting of fish refuse with plant refuse can be easily undertaken on a large scale, because those plant residues supply good amounts of potash while the fish scrap contains the other two major plant nutrients besides such minor elements as iodine. In warm regions the outside temperature hastens furthermore the breakdown of the material. But care must be taken to have the heaps well covered with earth and in a good state of moisture to secure quick action and absence of odors. The pit method is recommended. By sinking trenches about three feet deep, the composter will still supply enough air surface to stimulate aerobic bacterial growth, especially if the plant material is bulky. In the small garden, fish scrap can hardly be used successfully; but on a farm scale, the inclusion of wastes from fish markets or canneries in the compost is by no means impossible, and in the Northeast as well as Northwest cannery wastes of fish material could profitably be used for making sheet compost.

Where much fish material has to be disposed of, it may be advisable to use the drastic method of sprinkling the fish with quick lime. After some period has elapsed, the resulting substance should be ready for inclusion in a compost heap. We do not otherwise recommend the use of quick lime, but suggest for all other purposes agricultural lime or ground limestone.

FLAG: see CATTAIL

FLAMBOYANT TREE: (*Delonix regia*) Also known as the royal poinciana or peacock-flower, this summer-blooming tree grows to about 40 feet, has lovely flowers. Generally restricted to the warmer climate of California and Florida, the tree produces clusters of bright scarlet blooms. *See also* POINCIANA.

FLAME-FLOWER: see POINCIANA

FLATS: see SEEDS; COLD FRAME; GERMINATION

FLAVOR: Flavor is one characteristic that food scientists have found impossible, chemically speaking to define. They know it is a result of concentration of "cell-sap"—a blend of sugar, acid, tannins, volatile oils, organic compounds and probably other substances. They also know that enzymes play a role in flavor development, and that processing can easily destroy or alter flavor. Not surprisingly, efforts to make synthetic flavors out of the identified components of cell-sap have never been successful.

There are three things the grower can do to insure good flavor in his fruits and vegetables: grow them on a balanced, naturally fertilized soil; pick them as nearly full ripe as possible; and if irrigating, reduce the amount of water as the produce approaches maturity. *See also* NUTRITION.

FLAX: (*Linum usitatissimum*) Its history in the United States goes back to the 17th century. Thrifty New Englanders grew small plots of fiber flax to provide linens for family clothing. The invention of the cotton gin in 1792 reduced the demand for the fiber flax. It was not until the middle of the 19th century that seed flax assumed commercial importance.

Almost all of the flax grown in this country today is for the production of linseed. The seed flax varieties have shorter stems than the fiber varieties. Linseed cake, a by-product left after extraction of the oil from the seed, is a valuable concentrated protein feed for animals. Some of the flax straw is used in industry, particularly for making high-grade papers, while linseed oil is used a great deal in manufacturing paint, varnish and lacquer.

Flax is an excellent companion crop for legume and grass seedings.

Flax does best in a fertile soil, but

fertilizer applications are rarely made directly for the crop. In much of the flax-growing area of the North Central States, it is preferable to apply most of the fertilizer to some other crop in the rotation. Older soils are capable of producing good crops provided they have been well managed so that fertility and organic matter have not been seriously depleted and they have not become too weedy.

Flax occupies a place in a rotation similar to small grains. It does well following oats, wheat, barley, soybeans and corn. Small grain stubble may be plowed immediately after harvest, and soybean stubble that has been kept clean is excellent for the sowing of flax. A seedbed is prepared by shallow working in the spring.

About 95 per cent of the flax production is concentrated in the Dakotas, Minnesota, Montana, Iowa and Wisconsin. A considerable acreage is grown in Texas as a fall-sown crop. Flax is also grown in California and Arizona as a fall-sown crop under irrigation.

Mr. Culbertson lists the following as improved flax varieties in the North Central States: Redwood, B-5128, Marine and Sheyenne. All of these are immune to races of rust found in North America and have a good resistance to wilt, but none is resistant to pasmo. Generally, Marine is damaged less by pasmo than most other commercial varieties.

FLAX DODDER: *see* CONVOLVULUS

FLEA BEETLES: There are many species; black, brown or striped; jumping beetles; about 1/16 inch long; attack potatoes, tomatoes, peppers, beets and related crops. Leaves look like they have been shot full of holes.

For control, practice frequent cultivation; they are driven away by shade, so interplant susceptible crops near shade-giving ones; do not keep piles of materials around the garden during the winter, as the flea beetles

will nest there. *See also* INSECT CONTROL; INSECTS.

FLOODS: Suppose it were possible to trace the whereabouts of a soil particle for about ten years. This piece of soil starts out on a sloping bit of land that is being farmed up and down hill, rather than on the contour.

Then when the rains come, the water turns the steep rows into a little canal taking the soil particle along. Its temporary destination is a roadside ditch.

Again the rains begin. This time our particle reaches a mud bar on a small stream. After resting there for several years, more rain forces the particle to leave the mud bank and carries it downstream to a large river.

Dikes of earth along the river could not hold back the water—and the particle plus others like it leave a muddy trail on highways, in factories and homes. Floods hit the headlines again, and the soil particle never again has a chance to feel crops rising above it.

This is not a false dramatization of how floods can arise. Millions of particles just like the one described are being taken off our fields—leaving behind a bare, hard surface that has little capacity to absorb water. Rains and melting snow, that should have supplied needed moisture to growing plants, instead mass up as they rush downhill and never slow down until they have inundated everything in their path.

The destruction done by floods makes it urgent to correct mismanagement of the land. Erosion is not only a force that can wipe out our source of food in the far-off future; it is a very real immediate danger that can—and does—allow waters to charge down upon us each year.

SOIL DESTRUCTION: More than 300 million acres out of the 400 million acres of farm fields are now eroding faster than soil is being formed. That means destruction of the land if erosion is not controlled, according to

Soil Conservation Service experts. SCS erosion experiment stations, set up across the nation, have come up with accurate information on this problem.

Figures over a five-year period at the Statesville, North Carolina, station show that, on an eight per cent slope, land lying fallow without cropping lost an average of 29 per cent of rainfall in immediate rainfall and 64 tons of soil per acre in wash-off *each year*. This means that in only 18 years, seven inches of soil (the average depth of topsoil) would be washed away.

Under continuous cropping to cotton, as was once the general practice in the North Carolina region, each year the land lost an average of ten per cent of rainfall and 22 tons of soil per acre. At this rate, it would take only 44 years before the soil would be lost.

Rotations were found to reduce, but not stop, erosion for the land lost nine per cent of the rain and enough soil so that it would take 109 years to erode away seven inches of soil.

There is no reason for erosion to be a master of agriculture. Under the natural cover of woods, where fire was kept out of the woods and litter accumulated on the forest floor, the land lost less than one-third of one per cent of the rainfall. And, according to the SCS calculations, it would require more than 500,000 years to wash away seven inches of soil. This rate of erosion is far below the rate of soil formation.

Farmers who have learned the wisdom of keeping some of their acres in grass will find that less than one per cent of rain is lost. So little soil is washed away when land is under grass, that it would take 96,000 years to lose all of the topsoil. This rate is also no faster than soil is formed.

"Grass farming" and continuous cover are not just good ideas; they are *musts*. The greatest part of our lands is sloping. By clearing and cultivating these sloping areas, we expose soils to accelerated erosion by water and wind —and we expose our cities to floods.

An analysis by SCS researchers shows that there are only about 100 million acres of flat alluvial land where the erosion hazard is slight. On the remaining portion of suitable crop lands—over 350 million acres—the hazard of soil erosion is always present.

The job is to eliminate self-destructive agriculture. If we can accomplish that, we shall not only defeat erosion, but we shall also discover that floods are *not* inevitable. *See also* CONSERVATION; EROSION.

FLOPPER: *see* BRYOPHYLLUM

FLOSS FLOWER: (*Ageratum*) For blue flowers during the summer, a fine choice is the floss flower or ageratum. Equally desirable as garden material or for cutting, the soft, lacy flowers lend themselves very well to color combinations and special effects. There are dwarf sorts as well as tall varieties in white, pink or shades of blue. The plants are of easiest culture, seedlings usually volunteering in abundance about old plants. Ageratum is injured by frost, so bedding out should not be done until danger of frost has passed. Tip cuttings root readily in early summer. *See also* AGERATUM.

FLOWER: The flower is an essential part of every plant, as it contains the reproductive organs without which the species could not continue. Many gardeners forget that the flower is primarily a reproductive organ, and tend to assume that flowers were placed on earth to tickle man's esthetic sense. Such is not the case; the flower gardener should always remember the true function of the blooms of which he is so proud.

In a complete flower, there are many separate components, each of which has been given a name by botanists. The outermost covering of a flower bud is composed of leaf-like parts called sepals; collectively they are called the calyx. Inside the calyx are the petals, the showy part of the organism which provide color and beauty for the gardener, and protection for the vital organs within them. Inside the petals (which collectively are known as the corolla) are the male and female reproduction organs.

Usually, the female organs are located in the center of the male organs. Among the female organs are the ovary (containing the ovules), the style, and the stigma. Around the style and stigma are the male organs, the stamens, shank, filament, anther (containing the pollen—the male fertilizing material). The union of the pollen and the female ovules produces seed for future generations.

FLOWER ARRANGEMENT: Experts in the art of placing plant material in vases and containers have developed certain rules and formulae to help novices in the craft. These rules are based on recognized principles of color harmony and design, skill in preserving cut plant material, with latitude for individual taste and ingenuity.

Recognition of all these points is made in the scale used to judge flower arrangements in shows and exhibitions. Points awarded for arrangements in a general class are usually apportioned as follows: color combination, 25; relation to container, 10; design, 25; distinction and originality, 20; suitability of combination of material, 10; condition, 10.

CUTTING: Cut plant material will stay fresh and crisp only as long as it is able to take up water. This it can do only at the cut end of the stem, not through additional leaves and stems, which may decay under water.

Cutting is done either in early morning or in the evening, never during the hot hours when material may be wilted. Side leaves are immediately stripped from cut material, and stems are plunged to the flower head in a pail of water. Foliage material may be completely submerged. Arrangements are not made until the plant material has taken up enough water to make it crisp and firm to the touch.

Plant stems are cut with a sharp knife on a slant to permit the extra surface to absorb more water. Stems are all cut longer than will be required, and are shortened when the arrangement is made. Curves which will be desired in the finished arrangement may be made in the stems before they become firm in the case of evergreens, which may need to be slightly wilted for the purpose. Most other material may be shaped after crisping.

Flowers with woody stems such as stock, marigolds, snapdragons, and chrysanthemums may be crisped more completely if the ends of the stems are split back about half an inch with a sharp knife. Delicate specimens such as tulips, dahlias, poppies, poinsettia, and heliotrope will keep best if their stems are flamed immediately after cutting. This may be done by holding a match to the end of the stem. If shortening is necessary later the flaming must be repeated.

EQUIPMENT: Container may be any receptacle which will hold the plant material and is appropriate to the material. The proposed design will dictate the shape of the container, whether it is to be tall, as a vase, or low, as a bowl. The character of the plant material and its use will determine the size and texture of the container. General rule for size is that the tallest sprig or leaf should rise above the container $1\frac{1}{2}$ times the height of a tall vase or the diameter of a low bowl.

Delicate material may be best displayed in a container which is delicate in character and shape, if it is intended for a sheltered position in the house. If the arrangement is to sit on the floor or in an exposed part of the house such as a porch or patio, the container should be appropriately rugged.

In color and shape the container must be considered a part of the completed arrangement. Its color must harmonize with colors of the materials placed in it, and with the room decoration in the position it will adorn.

Support for the material in the arrangement may be supplied by pin- or needle-point holders, by wire mesh crumpled in the bottom of the container, or by sheet-lead cut into strips and bent over the back rim of the container. Whatever the support used, it is completely masked by plant material at any angle from which the arrangement may be viewed.

Floral clay, a type of plasticene developed for this purpose, may be used to stick the flower holder to the bottom of the container, to prevent tipping. The base of the holder is spread with a thin layer of clay, which is then squeezed to the bottom of the dry container. Only after the clay is tightly bonded is water added. Cellophane tape is sometimes used to hold material in place, as are strips of sheet lead. In tall vases a T-shaped piece of sheet lead may be used to hold the whole prepared arrangement. Arms of the T are wrapped around the stems of the material, and the base of the T bent over the back edge of the container. If more than one cluster of stems must be held, the arms of the T are split in two, each side holding one cluster.

DESIGN: A number of conventions of good design have been adopted by flower arrangers, and some have become standard practice. Arrangements are made in the shape of an L, a triangle, an oval or circle, or an inverted T. Whatever design is chosen, its weight is centered over the center of the container.

Most popular design is based upon a triangle. It is put together as follows: 1. The longest shoot is curved and placed left of center, with its tip over the center of the container. 2. A second shoot shorter by about one-third than the first and curved similarly is placed left of the first one. 3. A still shorter shoot is placed right of the first. 4. A fairly long piece, approximately the length of that in

2, is placed horizontally at right, extending out over the rim of the container. 5. A small shoot is placed horizontally at left, extending over the rim of the container. 6. A block

Whatever its design, the weight of the ideal flower arrangement is centered above the center of the container. It may be an "L," a triangle or an oval, as long as it remains in balance.

of material, roughly round or triangular in form, is placed at junction of all shoots, covering holder and overlapping front edge of container.

In general, a center of interest is established in each arrangement—in this case the mass at the base—and the other material grouped around it. Heaviest color and mass accent is placed near the bottom of the arrangement for balance. Light, slender material is usually used in the silhouette. The container is tied in with the arrangement by material allowed to over-lap its edges, and by carrying the heaviest mass of the design down over an edge.

Materials which may be used include not only flowers and leaves, but fruits, seed pods, vegetables, dried material, moss, woody branches and drift wood, even rocks, shells, and bits of statuary.

Perhaps the best criterion of a good flower arrangement is its avoidance of the following faults: *overcrowding*—too much material which clutters the design; *crosscutting* — stems or branches cross each other where they can be seen; *flower-stepping*—regular spacing of flowers of same size one above another; *sandwiching*—too regular alternation of materials; *equal ranging*—placing of spikes, flowers, or branches on the same horizontal level; *spottiness*—too many scattered flower or leaf accents, or not enough massing of detail; *lack of strength*—use of insignificant material which scatters the accent; *fillers-in*—use of insignificant material such as baby's breath or asparagus fern to hide stems, holders; *hole next to container*—arrangement does not meet container so

that they appear to be two units; *poor graduation*—too abrupt a change from light to dark colors or from thin to heavy material; *poor transition*—too abrupt changes in line, color, or form. *See also* HOUSE PLANTS; ANNUALS; CUT FLOWERS; BOXES AND BASKETS, FLOWER; FLOWER GARDENING.

FLOWER BOX: *see* BOXES AND BASKETS, FLOWER

FLOWER GARDENING: Cultivated flowers fall into two groups based upon soil preference. One group will grow only in acid soil with a pH below 6.5, while the others prefer or will tolerate only alkaline soil, pH 6.5 or above.

Acid-lovers are plants that thrive on raw humus, such as their ancestors found in the woods where leaves drop from the taller trees. Leaves, leaf-mold, peat moss, or other humus should be incorporated in soil where

The garden reflects the personality and tastes of the home-maker. It may be small and informal or extended and estate-like. No hard-and-fast rules can be made; the gardener will make his own.

they are to be planted. Especially recommended are oak leaves, which produce an acid humus. A special potting mixture for house plants contains leaves grated through a half-inch wire mesh mixed with equal quantities of coarse sand and garden loam, with a handful of bone meal and one of cottonseed or blood meal mixed with each bushel. Bone meal supplies phosphorus; cottonseed or blood meal supplies nitrogen. These materials may be obtained from the larger seed houses. Dry chicken manure, sheep manure, or compost can be added to leaf mulches and to potting mixtures as one-fourth of the total.

Soil for seedlings which are to be started in a sunny window or greenhouse needs special handling. A mixture of equal proportions of sand, compost, garden soil, and grated leaves is placed in cypress flats in the fall, before the ground freezes. It should then be stored in a well ventilated dry cellar or garage until needed.

Seeds may be started in sand and sphagnum moss and transferred to flats as soon as their first true leaves appear, or they may be sown directly in the flats.

Before being used, the seedling flats are sometimes sterilized to prevent damping-off. Boiling water is poured over each flat, drained, and saved for later use in the open garden. It will contain some of the soil nutrients dissolved in the soil. The water bath destroys dangerous bacteria and fungi that cannot easily be controlled under artificial indoor conditions.

HARDY BULBS AND ROOTS FOR SPRING FLOWERING AND SUMMER BLOOM: Hardy bulbs are those which not only survive, but actually demand a cold season—tulips, crocus, daffodils, hyacinths, grape hyacinths or muscari, scilla, sometimes named Spanish hyacinth, snowdrops, and a group of others. Most lilies also like a period of cold weather.

Lilies are planted as soon as received, whether it is August or December. If the ground is frozen on top it must be thawed enough to permit digging the lilies in at about ordinary spading depth. Lilies will arrange their growing level themselves. They should not be grown in bare spots but in front of shrubs, in places where a

Lilies, with their stately stalks, may be planted between other perennials. The speciosum variety is easy to grow and produces white flowers.

tree throws shade during the hot hours of day, and where the ground is covered with some growing plant. Whether petunias or vincas, mignonette or nasturtiums are grown above does not matter much, as long as the ground is shaded and kept from drying out. Lilies, with their stately stalks, can be placed between other perennials. *Lilium candidum,* the Madonna lily, fidgety, but fragrant and fine if successful; *L. speciosum*, white with beautiful long lasting flowers, also in other shades, is easy to grow. *L. tenuifolium,* a small kind of the Turk's cap, but delightfully fragrant, *L. superbum,* the American Turk's cap, a safe bet. *L. Henryi, Davidi, dauricum* are found in most lists and worth having, but *L. regale, L. formosanum,* and *L. auratum* are the big show plants. None of them is really difficult, though all like a well-drained ground, rich in humus, but not too moist.

Crocus, winter aconite or *eranthis*, grape hyacinth, hyacinth, snowdrops, the host of daffodils and jonquils in various shades and colors and many forms and fragrances, and the innumerable varieties of garden tulips as well as the earlier-flowered species tulips, *Scilla campanulata* in colors of white, rose, and blue are planted as soon as obtained, about as deep as the trowel reaches. Their only need is that they should not stand in water and that the rodents can not get at them. Some gardeners place a trowel full of sand under them, to insure drainage. Usually, this is not necessary. For the ground is either well-drained and does not need this addition, or the ground gets soggy and a handful of sand will not make any difference.

The Crocus speciosus blooms in the late fall and keeps the garden colorful for extra months. Hardy bulbs not only survive the cold but require it.

Mertensia virginica or Virginia bluebell is a native plant sold in the bulb trade. It blooms at the same time as yellow daffodils and narcissus, and makes a splendid contrast to them with its blueish hues. The fall-flowering crocus, *Colchicum autumnale*, is usually sold in late summer for fall blooming. It too is hardy and will bloom again each succeeding fall.

Iris varieties are so numerous that no general rule can be given for their performance. Iris, daylilies, funkias, and peonies are the most easily grown and showiest plants from rhizomes or rootstocks. Some iris bloom twice, once they are well established. Some, like the *Iris reticulata* or netted iris, are delightfully scented.

Most bulbs are best planted in groups. Iris must be planted close to the surface, and never in wet ground. All the bulbs except some lilies are buried at two to three times their diameter.

Daffodils fall mainly into two groups, scented and unscented. Fragrant ones are usually those with white petals and small trumpets. Tulips are similarly offered in many classes. Many dealers have abandoned the division into breeder, Darwin, and cottage tulips which have lost their old significance. Double tulips, parrot tulips, and the smaller but striking and highly recommended species tulips are listed separately. Others are now listed only according to height and blooming period.

There are many hybrid forms of the daffodil or trumpet narcissus. Because of their great number, they fall into two groups, scented and unscented.

CHARACTERISTICS OF MAJOR BULBS

Names	Blooms in	Color	Heights
Camassia	May, June	blue	20 in.
Chionodoxa	March-May	various	6 in.
Colchicum	Sept., Oct.	lavender, blueish	7 in.
Spring Crocus	March, April	blue, white yellow	6 in.
Fall Crocus	Sept., Oct.	various	4 in.
Crocus Sieberi	Feb., March	blue	3 in.
Winter Aconite	Feb., March	yellow	3- 6 in.
Snowdrops	Feb., March	white	5- 6 in.
Hyacinths	April, May	various	7-15 in.
Muscari (Grape Hyacinths)	April	blue, white	9 in.
Dutch, Spanish, English Iris	May-July	various	16 in.
Iris reticulata	March-April	purple	6 in.
Bearded Iris	Spring or Spring and Fall	various	2- 4 ft.
Leucojum (Snowflake)	May, June	white	12-15 in.
Auratum Lily	July-Sept.	white and gold	3- 5 ft.
Lilium canadense	June, July	yellow, red	2- 4 ft.
Lilium candidum (Madonna Lily)	May, June	white	2- 4 ft.
Lilium formosanum	July	white	3- 4 ft.
Lilium martagon	June, July	purple, red	3- 6 ft.
Lilium pardalinum	June, July	gold and crimson	5- 6 ft.
Lilium regale	June	white	3- 5 ft.
Lilium speciosum	Aug., Sept.	white, red	2- 4 ft.
Lilium tenuifolium	May, June	orange	1 ft.
Lilium testaceum	June, July	apricot	5 ft.
Lilium tigrinum	Aug., Sept.	orange red	4 ft.
Lilium washingtonianum	June	lilac purple	4 ft.
Lilium wilmottiae	July, August	orange red	3- 6 ft.
Mertensia	April, May	amethyst	10-30 in.
Narcissus (Daffodils)	April, May	yellow, white, rose	6-13 in.
Scilla sibirica	March, April	blue, white	4- 6 in.
Scilla campanulata	April, May	blue, white, rose	14-18 in.
Sternbergia lutea	October	yellow	3 in.
Triteleia	May	light blue	3 in.
Tulips	April, May	various	10-30 in.
Tulipa Eichleri	April	crimson	12 in.
Tulipa Kaufmanniana	March, April	cream, red	10 in.
Tulipa Marjoletti	May	red	10 in.

THE TENDER BULBS: The *Anemone coronaria*, not the hardy Japanese anemone, and the large-flowered hybrid *Ranunculus* appear in fall bulb lists. It is best to buy them then, keep them in their bags in a not-too-warm spot, and to set them out at the planting time for sweet peas, larkspur, poppies, and other hardy annuals.

Oxalis can go out then, too, but callas, cannas, tuberoses, tritonias or montbretias, gladiolus, dahlias, and amaryllis must wait until the frost is entirely out of the ground. Amaryllis in pots that have flowered in the window are set out in their pots. The others go into the ground when the sun has warmed it. The growth of some, especially tuberoses, will be hastened if they are potted early inside to start root growth.

Tender bulbs are dug in the fall when the leaves have died down, washed and dried in the shade, and stored for next year's planting. Dahlias should be stored in sand, sawdust, or peat moss to prevent drying out. Others may be kept rather dry and warm. None must be exposed to freezing.

Some relations of the amaryllis, the now more and more popular *All-*

stroemerias are hardy in the temperate regions and can stay out as most plants can in the South. The *Zephiranthes* lily, the summer hyacinth or *galtonia*, and the *eremurus* or desert candle, also called foxtail lily, are more sensitive to cold weather. Eremurus grows best if planted in fall and heavily mulched, but it is best to grow it where it would naturally succeed, regions of hot and long summer and mild winters, down south. *Callas* can be treated as pot plants, like amaryllis, but *cannas* are southern plants which, up north, must be treated like dahlias and tuberoses. The *freesia*, a most beautiful and fragrant flower for the window box, is best treated like paper-white narcissus (tazetta). It is worth some effort and will reward the patient gardener with unusual beauty of coloring and scent. The inexpensive companion of the gladiolus, the *tritonia* or *montbretia*, is one of the best cut flowers and bedding plants and easy to grow. But it, like the glads, does not want a ground cover. It does best when the soil is rich in phosphorus, which can be supplied in form of bone meal, and it does so well in some southern regions, like Florida and Hawaii, that it becomes wild and spreads like Jerusalem artichokes. In the more temperate regions, it is handled like the gladiolus.

SUMMER ANNUALS: Summer and fall-blooming annuals like petunia, clarkia or zinnia are, as a rule, sown when the soil gets warm. However, many of them may be sown late in fall, before snow covers the ground, and will then make an earlier growth. Or they may be sown as soon as the earth thaws in spring. This applies, for instance, to poppies, both shirley and somniferum (or opium) poppy, to larkspur, mignonette, and petunia. Plants which reseed themselves, and survive the cold season will make the sturdiest plants. Unfortunately, home-grown seeds and self-sown plants are not always the best in appearance.

Flax remains the same, portulaca may even become more widely varied in colors, but petunias tend to become more and more faded and must be replaced sooner or later. Prize petunias of the varicolored or ruffled kind will hardly ever continue sound from home-grown seed, because they become hybridized with less attractive varieties. The same is true of zinnias; the reddish and speckled lavender colors seem to survive, while the white and yellow heads disappear, and the lavender or purplish ones fade out.

The cornflower does best treated as a hardy annual, sown on the growing site. It seems to flower better when crowded and needs little thinning.

Relatively hardy and therefore suitable for earlier sowing are the following: ageratum, alyssum, amaranthus, anchusa, calendula, california poppy, Canterbury bell, candytuft, celosia, cornflower, centaurea (sweet sultan), cosmos, chrysanthemum, clarkia, delphinium and larkspur, euphorbia, cynoglossum (Chinese forget-me-not), hollyhock, linaria, linum (flax), lupinus, matthiola (nightscented stock), mignonette, nicotiana, periwinkle, pansy, shirley poppy, salvia, scabiosa, snapdragon, sunflower, sweet pea, verbena, wallflower. Also a plant of profuse flowering and useful for bees, listed usually under herbs, the borage.

Relatively tender and therefore to be sown when the soil is warm are:

balloon vine, balsam, cobaea, four-o'clock, geranium, godetia, heliotrope, lantana, lobelia, morning glory, moon-flower, nasturtium, nemesia, nolana, portulaca, ricinus (castor oil bean), salpiglossis, schizanthus.

Other flowers of the garden are usually raised in flats before planting out in order to make an early growth. Some of these are: asters, stock, marigold, though most of the tender ones already mentioned can also be sown inside.

Those garden plants not mentioned are usually sown outside as soon as the soil becomes warm and danger from frost is past, though they are not as warmth-loving as the second group. Zinnias, for example, can be put out in the early spring; their seed will not rot readily, but they will not make a growth until air and soil get warm. If sown later, they make a quicker initial growth and catch up with those put out earlier. Thus, there really is no advantage in sowing them early and risking loss from excessive rains or washing of soil. It usually pays to wait a week longer when in doubt as to the proper sowing time. A good rule-of-thumb for planting annuals is: hardy annuals should be planted when maple trees are in bloom; tender annuals should be planted when the maples are in full leaf.

Many perennials may be sown early if space is available. They will make a growth and become sturdy plants by the end of summer, much more able to weather the cold season, and ready for transplanting in September. After all, they seed themselves usually in spring when growing in the wild, because most perennials flower earlier than annuals. Of the earliest flowering annuals, the clarkia is the most reliable when sown into the open, as soon as the soil can be worked.

Some annuals grown from seed need not necessarily be treated as annuals. Clove pinks and snapdragons are easily propagated by cuttings after flowering, when hardy ripened offsets have formed. Early weak cutting or slips should not be used. Most annual cuttings will root in ordinary garden soil if the spot is not too moist, but if the air is moist. A flat placed on the north side of a building is a satisfactory place for rooting such cuttings. In dry regions a glass or bell over the flat will keep the air moist around the cuttings. The rooted cuttings are then taken indoors for the winter, where they are kept in a cool, light room, and can be planted out to produce flowers early in spring. If they are well fed they will produce good plants and prolong their growing period but delay flowering, so that they may be set out in spring to flower in late May or early June.

Below is a list of selected annuals, arranged according to height:

VERY TALL: *Amaranthus* (red), *celosia* or cockscomb (red or yellow), *ricinus* or castor oil plant (showy

The chrysanthemum-like marigold produces a golden yellow flower, three or more inches across. It blooms until frost and is excellent for cutting.

foliage), *helianthus* (sunflower of many varieties, some blooming orange), *tithonia* or Mexican sunflower (orange red) and the *dahlias*. Also some of the balsams (*impatiens*).

MEDIUM TALL: Tall *ageratum* (blue), tall *antirrhinum* or snapdragon (varied), *arctotis* (white), *argemone* (yellow), *borago* (blue), the kitchen herb, but an excellent flowering plant, *browallia* (violet), tall *calliopsis* (orange-red), annual Canterbury bells or *campanula* (blue, lavender, pink), annual *chrysanthemum* or daisy (colored bands and white), *cleome* or spider flower (pink and red rose), *cosmos* (sulphur yellow, orange, white, pink, red), dwarf *dahlias*, grown from seed, *delphinium* or larkspur (white, pink, blue, purple), *euphorbia* or snow-on-the-mountain (green and white); *gaillardia* (gold and brown) *gilia* or bird's eyes (light blue, lavender, purple), tall *godetia* (purple and red), *hunnemannia* or tulip poppy (yellow), *impatiens* or balsam (red, pink, white), *kochia* or summer cypress (red coloring, often a weed), *lavatera* (pink and white), *leptosyne* (yellow), *mirabilis* or four-o'clock (white, yellow, rose, red, purple, speckled), *nicotiana* or flowering tobacco (white and fragrant; deep crimson), *poppies* (shades and mixtures of red and white and lavender purple), *salpiglossis,* the most gorgeously colored annual (red, purple, blue, yellow and gold), *salvia* or flowering sage (blue and scarlet), *scabiosa* (white to dark brown, blue, rose), *tagetes* or marigold (gold and mahogany), *matthiola* or stock, tall varieties non-branching (white, pink, lavender, fragrant), *zinnia* in tall varieties (yellow, purple, red, pink, white).

MEDIUM LOW: *Ageratum* varieties (lavender blue), *anchusa* (blue), *antirrhinum* varieties or snapdragons in many colors, early asters, *calendula* (yellow and orange), *calliopsis* (yellow and brown), *clarkia* (pink, white, and purple), *cynoglossum* (blue),

delphinium or larkspurs (white, pink, blue, purple), *diascia* (rose), a much too much neglected charming flower, *dimorphotheca,* a daisy-like plant of great flowering capacity (orange and buff shades), *eschscholtzia,* the well-known california poppy (yellow, orange, even red), *gomphrena,* a straw flower (purplish), *gypsophila* or baby's breath (white), *lavatera,* a mallow kind (white and rose), *lupinus* (white, red, blue, purple), sometimes getting very big later in the year, *lychnis* (rose and scarlet), apt to become a weed, *matthiola* or stock (purple, rose, cream, white) and *night-flowering stock,* a much more easy-flowered and scented kind than the ordinary garden stock, *mimulus,* the monkey flower, red and yellow (loves shade and moisture), *myosotis,* the common forget-me-not (blue), which loves moisture, *nemesia* in all colors from white and red to blue, *nigella* or love-in-the-mist (blue), *petunia,* often balanced by the contrasting colors of nasturtium or *tropaeolum,* as it is properly called, *phacelia* (blue), another shade lover, the Shirley poppies, *schizanthus,* one of the easily grown and very beautiful flowers with mixed colors, and called butterfly flower, dwarf marigold (*tagetes*) in golden shades, *verbena,* tall or small varieties, all tending to sprawl (red, purple, white), and wallflower or *cheiranthus,* one of the best-scented of flowers, in colors of rich gold and purple.

LOW: Sweet *alyssum* (lavender and white), *anagallis* (red and blue), candytuft or *iberis* (white), *dwarf asters* and *snapdragons, brachycome* or swan river daisy (blue, rose, white), forget-me-not or *myosotis* (blue), *lobelia* (dark and light blue), *malcolmia* or virginian stock (lilac, white, red), *nemophila* (blue), *nierembergia,* a quick grower and mat-former (violet), *mignonette* (yellow-ish-green), a moisture-lover that cannot be easily transplanted, *portulaca,* which thrives in blazing sun and flowers in all shades of white, red, yellow, purple, and mixed, *sanvitalia*, the creeping zinnia, a sun lover, too (golden), *pansy* (all shades), *thunbergia* (white or yellow with dark eye), a tender climber, that in the North grows like a low annual, and dwarf varieties of *verbena*.

TRANSPLANTING: Most annuals are easily transplanted, with the exception of poppies, mignonette, and Eschscholzia. Transplanting sets a flower back, and postpones its flowering. But many plants become more safely established and make bigger growth because of transplanting. Period of bloom may be extended in some cases if part of a planting is transplanted. The flowers which were moved will bloom later, while those left where they sprang up will have finished before the others open. This is true of *schizanthus*, and to a certain extent of *salpiglossis*, two flowers highly recommended for warm spots.

Many plants can be held over a second year if they have made good growth during the first year, and if the weather is not too cold. This is especially true of pansies and snapdragons. In their case, transplanting will increase the root systems and make stronger plants. A winter mulch will help them survive the heaving of the soil that occurs where the sun strikes the bare frozen ground.

When spring transplanting is indicated, the job should be done when the soil is damp but not puddled. Best time is late afternoon or evening of a warm spring day after a gentle rain. The ground then is rich and moist and ready to envelop young plants without stifling their fine rootlets. Planting should be followed by gentle watering.

Watering in the summer must be heavier. Then it is best to let the water soak in. Canvas hoses which can be attached to the rubber hose are good for the purpose. Overhead sprinkling is dangerous because it packs the soil. Watering should be done in the evening, except on roses, because plants are given the whole night to absorb the moisture before it is dried by the sun. If days are very hot, irrigation in the morning is also good, provided water can run into the beds plentifully and slowly.

FAILURES: Failure of annuals may be due to the following factors: premature sowing, ants that carry off fine seed, crowding, drying of seed bed or germinating seeds, or seed planted too deep.

Plenty of compost will keep the moisture level of the flower bed too high for ants, and will discourage them.

Seed should be sown thinly enough to avoid crowding seedlings. When the second set of leaves has developed, any excess of plants may be moved to a new position, and rows thinned.

Seed should generally be planted to a depth equal to three times its diameter. Since this will be very close to the surface in most cases, it may be necessary to cover the seed bed with burlap to prevent drying. Cover must be removed as soon as germination has taken place.

Some flowers will make a good growth and then not send up the flowering spike expected. Stocks and tall cosmos are sometimes disappointing in this respect. The reason is that those plants bloom only during the weeks when the days get shorter. Stocks can easily be potted and brought to bloom inside, a method that is also recommended for the deliciously scented wallflowers (*cheiranthus*), but the tall stocks must be grown in a greenhouse in the North.

PERENNIALS: Perennials form the most essential part of the flower garden. Biennials are included in this group, because they do not bloom the first year, but will perpetuate themselves by their own seedlings after the second season. Perennials do not require constant attention and cut down on the work and time required for gardening.

Perennials will remain many years

where they are sown or planted. The soil must therefore be well prepared before sowing. This can be accomplished best by the inclusion of liberal amounts of compost—a bushel per square yard—and the additional application of leaves from deciduous trees, which may be dug into the ground in fall along with some rotted manure.

The perennial garden is usually in front of hedges or along walls. If empty spots develop, there will always be enough seedlings to fill out vacant places; but annuals may be sown between the perennials. Bulbs make a good foreground or may be set in groups and clusters between leafy perennials. Some will do well in the half shade of the shrubs or sheltered by low-growing perennials. Excellent color contrasts can be achieved if before planting or sowing, time is taken to plan groupings of those plants which bloom at the same time and have colors that do not clash. It is important in planning to consider the relative heights of flowering plants. While *lilies* and other beautiful specimen plants may stand up amid a cover of low-growing annuals or perennials, the ordinary small-flowered perennials must be employed in groups and masses. The same holds true of mixed perennials and annuals. The general rule is to let large-flowered beautiful specimens stand out for individual admiration, but to mass those plants that have many flowers.

PROPAGATION: Most perennial seed may be sown early in spring while the ground is wet. All but the relatively difficult columbines, or *aquilegia*, can be sown thickly and will make a growth by August or September. They may be transplanted then to their permanent positions, after fall rains have moistened the soil. Or they may be set out in spring when other beds are cleared. Columbines are best sown separately, because they are comparatively slow growers, and trans-

planted in spring with plenty of earth around their roots.

Some perennial seeds will not germinate without a cold-storage period, equivalent to a freezing winter. These are best planted in the fall or early winter in the north. In the south they must be artificially refrigerated before germination can be induced. For refrigeration treatment, seed may be placed in damp sand or peat moss in a tight glass jar in the food compartment of a household refrigerator for eight-12 weeks. Seed given refrigeration treatment is best sown during the cool season. Some perennials which demand a cold winter for germination are *Colchicum lutem,* Lenten rose or *Helleborus orientalis*, and some primroses. Some other perennials must have a long cool period for germination, though not necessarily freezing. Those which prefer fall planting are aconite, *allium*, anemone, armeria, asphodel, perennial asters, callirhoe, clematis, Shasta daisy, *dicentra*, edelweiss, *euphorbia*, fritillaria, gentians, coral bells, hardy gloxinia, lythrum, mertensia, perennial phlox, penstemon, primroses, sempervivum, scabiosa, and thalictrum.

Many perennials are propagated by root division. Iris, chrysanthemum, peonies, and dahlias are propagated most easily in this way. Iris which have become crowded in their beds are dug and divided as soon as their blooming period is over. Chrysanthemums may be dug and divided in spring, when growth is about to start. Peonies may be divided and replanted either in the fall, when the leaves begin to yellow, or in the spring when the first red sprouts push through the ground.

Cuttings of some perennials may be rooted in the garden to provide additional plants. Chrysanthemums are easily propagated in this way. The cuttings are made in spring when the new shoots are eight to 12 inches high. A six-inch piece is cut off the shoot, all leaves removed except the tip

MOST POPULAR PERENNIALS

VERY TALL PERENNIALS OR BIENNIALS

	Color	Flowering Time
Aconitum (Monkshood)	Blue	July and August
Althaea (Hollyhock)	Various	June to October
Anchusa azurea	Blue	June, July
Aster novae-angliae	Purple	September, October
novi-belgi	Varied	September, October
cordifolius	Lilac	September, October
Astilbe davidii	Mauve	June
Baptisia	Blue	June
Boltonia	White	September
Campanula lactiflora	Blue	June to August
Cephalaria	Yellow	June, July
Chrysanthemum	Maroon, Purple, White	July to October
Cimicifuga	White	August
Dahlia (tender roots)	Varied	Summer and Fall
Delphinium hybrids	Blue, White, Varied	June till Fall
Dictamnus	White, Purple	June
Digitalis (Foxglove)	Rose, Purple, Yellow	June, July
Euphorbia	White	August, September
Helenium	Yellow, Brown	August, September
Helianthus (perennial sunflower)	Yellow	July till September
Heliopsis	Yellow	July till September
Hemerocallis (Daylily)	Golden, Yellow, Maroon	May to August
Hibiscus	Rose, White	July to September
Kniphofia pfitzeri (Tritoma) tender	Orange	August, September
Lilies of many kinds, blooming from late spring till autumn		
Lythrum salicaria	Purple-Red	July, August
Papaver orientale (Oriental Poppy)	Red, White	May, June
Pentstemon	Reddish shades	July, August
Phlox paniculata (some varieties)	Red, Purple, White	July till September
Physostegia	Purple	July till September
Rudbeckia	Golden	July till September
Verbascum (Mullein)	Yellow spikes	July

MEDIUM TALL

	Color	Flowering Time
Achillea	White, Purplish	June to September
Anchusa	Blue	June
Anemone Japonica	Cerise, White, etc.	August, September
Hupehensis		
Aquilegia (Columbine)	All colors and blends	April till August
Asclepias (Butterfly weed)	Orange	July
Aster, varieties	Purplish	Fall
Astilbe (Spiraea)	Pink	June, July
Campanula persicifolia	Blue	June, July
Centranthus	Red	June, July
Chrysanthemum varieties	Varied	July to October
Coreopsis	Gold	June till November
Dicentra (Bleeding Heart)	Reddish and White	May, June
Doronicum	Yellow	June, July
Eryngium	Blue	June, July
Eupatorium (Hardy Ageratum)	Blue, White	August, September
Gaillardia	Yellow, Brown	May till November
Geum	Yellow, Red	July till September
Hemerocallis (Daylily)	Yellow, Red	May to August
Many varieties		
Hosta varieties	White, Blue	June to August
Iris varieties	All shades	June, and some spring and fall
Lupinus	Red, Blue, White	June to October
Lychnis	Red	June, July

MOST POPULAR PERENNIALS
(Continued)

	Color	Flowering Time
Malva	White, Rose	July, August
Mertensia	Blue, Reddish	May
Oenothera (Evening Primrose)	Yellow, White, Red	June to September
(Annual, but roots can be saved like Dahlia tubers) There are perennial species, too.		
Papaver orientale (Oriental Poppy)	White to	May, June
Papaver nudicaule (Iceland Poppy)	Red	May-October
Paeonia (Peony) numerous varieties, many varieties	White, Red	May, June
Phlox paniculata	White, Red,	July to September
Phlox divaricata	Mauve,	June
Phlox arendsii	etc.	May till Fall
Scabiosa	White to Maroon, Blue	June to September
Thalictrum	Yellow	June, July
Veronica many varieties	Blue	July to September

Low (Not Over 18 Inches)

	Color	Flowering Time
Alyssum	Yellow	April, May
Anemone	Reddish Purple	April to June
Aster alpinus	Lilac	September, October
Begonia Evansia	Pink	September
(Mulching necessary)		
Campanula varieties	Blue	June to October
Chrysanthemum dwarf		
Azaleamum		
Shasta Daisy	Varied	June to October
Delphinium varieties	Blue, Red	June, July
Dianthus (Pinks) numerous varieties	All colors, but Blue	Spring till fall
Erigeron	Lavender	June, July
Geranium	Purple	June
Helleborus niger (Christmas Rose)	White	Winter
Heuchera (Coral Bells)	Red	June, July
Lavandula (Lavender)	Lavender	June till August
Linum (Perennial Flax)	Blue	June till August
Lobelia	Blue	August, September
Phlox, dwarf varieties	Varied	May till October
Platycodon, a very beautiful bell-flower	Blue, White	July to October
Primula species	Varied	April to June
often difficult to start from seed		
Ranunculus	Varied	May till August
Rosemary	White-lavender	Summer
Verbena	Red, White, Purple	Summer to late fall

Very Low (Not Over Ten Inches)

	Color	Flowering Time
Arabis (Rock Cress)	White	April, May
Armeria (Statice armeria)	White, Pink	May, June
Aster alpinus	Purplish	Fall
Aubrietia	Purplish	April, May
Campanula carpathica	Blue	July till September
Convallaria majalis (Lily of the Valley)	White	May
Gypsophila	White	May, June
Hepatica	White, Blue	April, May
Iris, miniature varieties	Purple	
	White, Yellow, Blue	April, May
Myosotis (Forget-me-not)	Blue	June till September
Papaver alpinus	Yellow	June till September
Phlox subulata	Reddish and Purplish	May
Phlox drummondi	Varied	
Sedum	Cerise	August to October
Thyme (Thymus)	Lavender, White	July to September
Vinca (Evergreen)	Blue	June
Viola (Violets, Pansies)	Varied	June to October

leaves, and the stem plunged into a moist bed, where it is kept shaded. After the cuttings are rooted, they may be moved to permanent beds.

Some plants disappear during summer. Some Iceland poppies as well as the oriental poppies have leaves in spring and fall, but not in summer. Positions of such plants should be marked, to avoid cutting them with the hoe or digging them up. Some of the lilies wander underground for some distance and may spring up at a different place. This too must be watched, though lilies are as a rule too deeply rooted to be hurt by summer attention.

Other plants are straggly and need staking. Unless much taste and great care is used, staked flowers look like an artificial enterprise. It is always best to plant straggly plants, including the clove pinks, in groups so that they can naturally sway and support each other. An alternative is the sowing of a low ground cover, let us say, *arabis, phlox subulata,* or even better, *sedum* and similar rock garden plants, between straggly flowers, so that they do not dip to the ground but can hang over lower plants.

ROTATION: If long-lived perennials such as iris or chrysanthemums are grown in one spot for a long time they will deplete the soil. They will continue to grow, but their health will suffer. They may be top-dressed or side-dressed with compost, but some perennials do not want too much cover. It may be impossible to give them enough food to prevent rust and other infestations. The only way to treat them is to move them to new and more fertile positions.

A heavy dressing of manure, compost, and possibly leaf-mold may be given the spot from which an old perennial has been moved, and it may be given a rest during the winter. In the spring, after an application of wood ashes, phosphate rock, or bone meal the spot will be ready to receive a different kind of perennial.

Often the gardener fails to observe that the rains of several seasons tend to lower the soil level considerably, washing earth off into the paths or down into the deeper spots of the garden. This means that the volume of earth from which growing plants in the higher spot could draw nourishment is somewhat reduced, if not largely depleted. To counteract this, especially with peonies and other plants that stay put for many years, nothing is better than to make a top-dressing of plain garden soil, possibly enriched a little with compost. New earth is thus added and the nutrients in it are washed down to feed the plants and give more profuse bloom the following season.

How do different flowering plants stand in regard to compatibility? There are for example acid-loving evergreens that need very little nitrogen, no rich compost, just leaf mulches and occasionally some bone meal. Likewise there are lilies that like humus and a deep mellow shaded soil; these two can go together. But will a lime-loving plant, like the campanulas grow next to them? Theoretically this looks like a real puzzler. The inexperienced gardener thinks that he should prepare different subsoil and make for himself a great deal of extra work. Practically, the matter is not serious at all. Many hundreds of thousands of gardens grow both azaleas and columbines; both campanulas, foxgloves, coreopsis, carnations and rhododendrons. It seems, indeed, as if the question of acidity were overemphasized. Organic matter in the ground will act as a buffer against extremes and enable the plants to seek with their roots what they need, lime as well as acid humus. But since the acid-loving shrubby plants will usually be in the background, more leaves may be left there, while in the foreground, where carnations and tulips may be planted a slight sprinkling of lime is made in fall.

See also Individual Varieties, AN-

NUALS; PERENNIALS; BIENNIALS; BORDER; BULBS; MULCH; PROPAGATION; HOUSE PLANTS; and related subject entries.

FLOWERING CHERRY: *see* CHERRY, FLOWERING

FLOWERING CRAB: *see* CRABAPPLE; TREES, FLOWERING; APPLE

FLOWERING MAPLE: (*Abutilon*) Also known as Chinese bellflower, this tropical shrub makes a fine indoor plant. Its blossoms are papery bells, resembling somewhat those of the hollyhock. Colors range through shades of pink and rose to red; there is a yellow-flowered variety. Leaves are maple-shaped, large, and slightly fuzzy; plants are usually large and bushy. Established plants should be cut back sharply once a year in order to promote best flowering; young plants normally tend to flower well without cutting back. Flowering maple requires plenty of moisture, bright exposure with some sun, and rich, humusy loam.

FLOWERING QUINCE: *see* QUINCE

FLOWERING TOBACCO: *see* NICOTIANA

FLUORESCENT LIGHT: In growing house plants, light, along with temperature and humidity, can be controlled and they become tools in our hands for producing luxuriant healthy growth. With fluorescent light you can give plants the same amount of illumination all the time.

Here are the figures for fluorescent lighting. If you have a double light, 40 inches long with a reflector, bought or painted, you will get

1 inch from lights	1,000 footcandles
2 inches from lights	950 footcandles
3 inches from lights	750 footcandles
4 inches from lights	650 footcandles
5 inches from lights	560 footcandles
6 inches from lights	460 footcandles
7 inches from lights	430 footcandles
8 inches from lights	370 footcandles
9 inches from lights	360 footcandles
10 inches from lights	350 footcandles

There is the added consideration that the light is not the same all along the tube. The most light is right in the middle, the least at the ends. Therefore, a light-loving plant, like a geranium can be placed on a little block if necessary to make its tip just clear the light in the middle of the tube. Start cuttings, which are satisfied with little light, right in the peat moss at the ends of the tubes.

Fluorescent lights are considered better than the incandescent ones, which give out a light in which red rays predominate. These are good for making roots, but not for top growth. Fluorescent lights are predominately blue which helps produce flowers and deepens color. Also they are cool and can't overheat plants.

It's not hard to learn at which distance from the lights your plants do best. Just watch them. If the leaves turn brown or bleach out, and if the plant tends to hug the sides of the pot, too much light. If plants grow tall and willowy with little or no bloom, too little. Generally, plants that don't bloom need much less light than those that do.

PLANTS TO GROW: Many beautiful plants. African violets love fluorescence. Their flowers, drawn by the lights two inches above them, bloom profusely above rich glossy foliage. Gloxinias, just clearing the lights, are beautiful; begonias, at 750 footcandles, do well; caladiums and ferns flourish with not more than 400 footcandles and a minimum of care; fuschias do well in dimmer zone of the lights. Geraniums, orchids and miniature roses are right at home high under the lights; gardenias bloom well with 650 footcandles.

As an extra humidity control, put a plastic curtain around shelves; just a strip of clear plastic thumb-tacked to the top and bottom shelf give plants their own little greenhouse. Plants grown in this plastic enclosure seldom need watering, and they have that shining-with-health look that goes

African violets do best when kept about 12 inches from the lights. However, the individual grower is advised to work out his own set of factors which, with time, will give the most desirable results.

with plenty of humidity. Open the curtain every day to give them change of air.

Here is another way in which plants gain by controlled light. There are three kinds of plants growing in most of our homes; short-day plants, which start to form buds only when days become shorter, like poinsettias, gardenias and chrysanthemums; plants that respond to long days to flower, tuberous begonias and calceolaria; then a third group of which african violets and roses are members, which doesn't seem to care what the day length is. Florists use this knowledge to control the light their plants receive and produce flowers when they are most easily marketable.

Once in a fluorescent case must plants stay there or suffer from the change? Not at all. Plants can come and go without apparent bad effect. You can put them under the lights until they attain desired growth and luxurious foliage or bloom, then take them out and place them where they show to best advantage.

FEEDING: The more nearly perfect growing conditions are the faster plants will grow, the healthier they will be and the more food they will need. That is another way of saying that the plants close to the lights, which is the sun-substitute for turning plant food into carbohydrates into new tissue, need more food than plants farther away. Watch for new growth; it is lighter and thinner than the old. If they are growing fast, feed them well.—*Dorothy Schroeder.*

See also HOUSE PLANTS.

FODDER: Corn and sorghum forage (including leaves, stems, and grain) which is cut, dried, and fed to livestock whole.

FOLIAGE PLANTS: Those plants grown not for flowers, but for the beauty of their leaves. Foliage plants are easier to grow, as a rule, than flowering plants, and their beauties can be enjoyed at all times, unlike flowering plants which have periodic blooming periods.

Foliage plants require less care than flowering plants. They need less sunlight, will stand higher temperatures; many are not injured easily by drying —the main cause of failure with flowering plants. Furthermore, there are fewer insect and disease troubles with foliage plants.

A mixture of one part compost and one part good garden loam is a fine potting mixture for most foliage plants. Other than that, they should need no food at all, except for annual changing of potting soil.

Watering foliage plants is the same as for most house plants. Soak thoroughly, but let the soil dry out for a day or two before the next soaking. Keep a happy medium between a water-logged and a baked dry soil. Either extreme will be harmful.

Many foliage plants have been selected for breeding because they will stand quite a bit of neglect in the normal household. They do need *some* care, however, and of course the more, the better they will thrive.

Insects are rarely a major problem with foliage plants. Mealybugs, whiteflies, thrips and red spider mites can be controlled easily by washing plants weekly with a rather strong jet of water. Scale can be controlled by pruning off infested leaves.

Many foliage plants can be propagated by division. Plants with stems are suitable for propagation by cutting.

See also names of individual plants; DIVISION; CUTTING; PROPAGATION; VINES; IVY; HOUSE PLANTS; GREENHOUSE.

FOLIAR FEEDING: The process of spraying or otherwise applying fertilizer to the foliage of plants. This process was originally developed in 1950 (although limited use of foliar feeding had been used before) by two wheat-quality researchers at Kansas State College. In this original experiment, the researchers increased the protein content of wheat by foliar feeding with a quickly soluble formulation of urea, a highly concentrated nitrogenous food.

Feeding plants through the leaves is not recommended by the organic method. We believe that leaf feeding is too clearly a violation of nature's intended function of roots. Roots were made to pick up nutrients from the soil, and are the most effective entrance into the plant's bloodstream. Leaf feeding was originated in order to give plants a quick shot-in-the-arm. Such temporary stimulation is not necessary if your soil is built up naturally into a permanent state of good fertility.

FOOD PRESERVATION: *see* FREEZING VEGETABLES; CANNING

FOOD VALUE: *see* NUTRITION

FORAGE: Any plant or plant part (fresh, preserved, or processed) used as feed for livestock. Forage may include hay, silage and pasture.

Forage crops come from two great botanical families—the grasses (*Gramineae*) and the legumes (*Leguminosae*). Here are some of the factors which influence the choice of forage crop, according to Pennsylvania State University:

Long-lived meadows for hay. Good choices are alfalfa and birdsfoot trefoil.

Soil conservation and improvement. Deep-rooted legumes are generally selected for their ability to hold down the soil; also increase its nitrogen content.

Short-lived meadows for hay. A mixture of red clover and timothy is a good example of a short-lived

DISTRIBUTION OF FORAGE CROPS

Crop	Distribution in U. S.
Timothy	Northern grass, north of latitude 36°.
Kentucky Bluegrass	North of latitude 36°—cornerstones Maine, Virginia, Missouri, Minnesota.
Redtop	Over most of the U. S. except extreme South and dry regions.
Orchardgrass	Over most of U. S.—East of Mississippi and North of Alabama and Georgia.
Tall oatgrass	Over most of U. S.—East of Mississippi and North of Alabama and Georgia.
Bromegrass	Northern Great Plains and Mediterranean region.
Fescue grasses	Grown on limited scale over most of U. S.
Rye grasses	North Central and Northeastern U. S.
Reed Canarygrass	Northern U. S.
Bermuda	Southern U. S.—Pennsylvania to Kansas, to Gulf of Mexico, Arizona, New Mexico, California, South of Latitude 36°.
Alfalfa	Over most of U. S.
Red clover	Most extensive in North Central and Northeast U. S.
Alsike clover	North of Ohio River and Potomac. West to North Dakota.
White clover	Widely spread over U. S., especially Midwest, Northeast and Northwest.
Crimson clover	Atlantic coast plain from South Jersey to South Carolina and west to Mississippi.
Hop clover	Over most of U. S., especially in South.
Sweet clover	Over most of U. S.
Bur clover	South—from North Carolina to Arkansas and southward.
Black medic	From Ontario to Gulf of Mexico.
Common lespedeza	South—from South Jersey to Kentucky and south.
Kobe lespedeza	South to Gulf. South Jersey to Kentucky and south.
Korean lespedeza	South to Gulf. South Jersey to Kentucky and south.
Sericea lespedeza	South to Gulf. South Jersey to Kentucky and south.
Kudzu	Florida to Maryland. Best in middle and lower South.
Soybeans	Cornbelt, Eastern and Southern U. S.
Cowpeas	South.
Peanuts	South.
Vetch	South and Pacific Northwest.
Field Peas	North Central, Northeast and Pacific Northwest.
Sudangrass	Over most of U. S. except extreme North and Florida.
Sorghums	Over most of U. S., especially semi-arid west from South Dakota to Texas.
Millets	Great Plains and Eastern U. S.

meadow which is used for hay purposes.

Annual hays. Millets, sudan grass, and soybeans grown alone or in combination, falls in the category of annual hays.

Coarse grasses for silage or fodder. Examples of coarse grasses for silage or fodder are corn, sorghum, and pearl millet.

Permanent pastures. Species for permanent pastures are Kentucky bluegrass and white clover in various more or less complex mixtures.

Semi-permanent pastures. Species particularly adapted for semi-permanent pastures are orchard-ladino, brome-ladino, reed canary-ladino, orchardgrass-alfalfa, brome-alfalfa, timothy-birdsfoot trefoil as well as other tall growing grasses and legumes.

Supplementary pastures. Species adapted for supplementary pastures are the small grains, sudangrass, domestic ryegrass, and field brome.

Soiling crops. Soiling crops are cut

and fed to cattle green. Such crops are corn which has been thickly planted, sweet sorghum, soybeans and the like.

Adaptability to environment. Different forage crops are adapted to widely different climatic conditions, as climatic conditions frequently limit the area in which each species can profitably be grown. See listing below.

Yielding ability and feeding value. The yielding ability and feeding value of forage crops is very important. Unless high yields are obtained and the forage is highly valuable nutritionally, it doesn't pay to grow it. Tall meadow fescue is an example of such a species. This coarse grass grows very well in Pennsylvania. However, it is not recommended for pasture purposes because it lacks palatability and cattle have to be starved to eat it.

Length of life. Species are classified as annuals, biennials and perennials. In the long run, perennials are preferred because they yield more and last longer, making their production much cheaper.

Cost of seed is sometimes a factor. One of the limitations to the expansion of the birdsfoot trefoil acreage in the Northeast is its high seed cost.

Versatility of species. The more uses a species can be put to, the greater is its forage value. It is highly desirable that a species be used interchangeably for pasture, grass silage, hay or seed as needs dictate.

Ease of harvesting, curing, etc. In order for forage to have maximum value it should be comparatively easy to harvest and to cure for later feeding. Many species fail to satisfy this requirement, hence, lose much of their potential value. For example, sweet clover is sometimes so coarse as to make it difficult to handle and cure. Kudzu is another example of such a species. This plant has a very prostrate viney habit of growth which makes for difficult handling.

See also LEGUMES; COVER CROPS.

FORCING: Refers to the growing and blooming of plants outside their usual season. Flowering branches that are most commonly brought into the home for forcing include: forsythia, pussy willow, winter hazel, hardy jasmine, flowering quince, red maple tree, magnolias, flowering crabapple, native white and pink dogwoods, spring-blooming spireas, all kinds of cherries, lilac, fruit trees, rhododendron, mountain laurel, winter honeysuckle, wintersweet and andromeda.

Many of these will spread anything from a delicate perfume through a room to a heady fragrance throughout your whole house.

Some of them, like pussy willow, will force in ten days or less. Others, like apple and peach, which are woodier and also naturally later blooming, may take as long as three to four weeks. The gardener who wants a continuous supply of blooms cuts a fresh lot every week or so from early February to late March. Of course, the closer you cut them to their date of outdoor blooming, the quicker they will flower indoors.

For a fine display, select branches heavily laden with fat flower buds. (On fruit trees, you can distinguish between flower and leaf buds by the short gnarled spurs that hold the flower buds in position.) Try to cut the branches two to three feet long, although some shorter ones may be valuable for arrangements with other material. Don't cut too lavishly from any one bush or tree, or you'll have few blooms to enjoy on the plant at its normal flowering time, and be careful not to spoil the symmetry of the plant.

The middle of a mild day, when the temperature is above freezing, is the best time to cut. Use a sharp knife or shears and make a clean diagonal cut. If the branch is hard and woody, crush the end with a few strokes of a hammer or split it through the center for an inch or two up the stem. This will help it to absorb water.

To soften the hard outer covering of the buds and encourage movement of sap in the stems, the branches should be completely submerged in a tub of water for three or four hours. Then put them in deep containers of water and keep them in a cool, dim place until the buds begin to show color. Remember, the slower they are forced—the more gradually heat and light are increased—the longer the blooms will last. If the water in the containers is not changed daily, a piece of charcoal will keep it fresh.

Daily spraying or dipping under a stream of lukewarm water—like spring showers—will further soften the hard bracts which protected the flower buds during the winter. As soon as they start to open, bring the branches into your living room. The blooms should last a week or more. Pussy willows, incidentally, will remain handsome for several months if removed from water and kept in a dry vase after the "pussies" are fully developed.

For other interesting effects, you can try forcing the branches of almost any tree or shrub. The buds of birch and alder produce novel catkins, and oak and maple also provide unusual materials for arrangements. Commercially, the forcing of vegetables, flowers and potted plants has developed into a relatively large industry, in which forcing houses are much in use. *See also* BULBS (FORCING).

FOREST SERVICE: *see* GOVERNMENT SERVICES

FORGET-ME-NOT: (*Myosotis*) A large group of annual or perennial, low-growing herbs. Hardy in the north, flowers are often purple when plants are young, later turning blue. Generally forget-me-nots prefer moist, partial shady locations, but also grow satisfactorily in open sunny borders. Seed can be sown from spring through summer for bloom the following year. Perennials can be propagated by cuttings or division. Forget-me-nots make excellent bedding plants, especially

under bulbs as tulips. Mass together for best effect.

FORM IN LANDSCAPING: *see* LANDSCAPING

FORMAL GARDEN: Contrasted to the unconstrained design of the informal garden, which generally aims to duplicate a setting of nature, the formal garden is a carefully precise study in layout and arrangement. Everything is planned and kept in exact geometric balance and symmetry. Trees and shrubs are clipped uniformly. Color is kept restrained and in a single scheme. Ornaments and accessories are chosen in discreet scale to maintain the balance and style. Frequently, one major feature, such as a fountain, bird bath, figure or pool, is centered as a highlight.

The formal garden is not necessarily forbidding. It can often lend a feeling of spaciousness and charm where these characteristics are difficult to achieve, such as in a small urban garden. Both formal and informal garden styles have beauty and usefulness. *See also* LANDSCAPING.

FORMALDEHYDE: *see* FUNGICIDE

FORSYTHIA: Golden Bell. Of all the upright forms of this lovely spring-blooming shrub, *F. intermedia spectabilis,* to nine feet, is by far the best in cultivation. The flowers are a bright, brassy yellow. The variety, *primulina,* has pale yellow flowers more numerous at the tips of the branches. *F. suspensa* is the old weeping golden bell and if left untrimmed may be trained as a vine over a wall. All the forsythia are rapid growers, so you can save money by buying small plants a foot to 18 inches high. Give them plenty of space, at least six feet apart, and even then they will have to be thinned when they reach maturity. They grow readily in any good garden soil and are easily propagated from cuttings in midsummer or from the new shoots, which root as easily as privet. Early April and May—height six to eight feet, with a spread of approximately 10 feet at maturity. They are hardy; but in extreme winters they are sometimes partially winter-killed, especially the tips of the branches and the flower buds. *F. ovata,* a five-foot species from Korea, is extremely hardy and blooms earlier than any of the others, producing amber-yellow flowers occasionally even in late March. This is an excellent shrub for places with severe winters, such as Maine and the other northeastern states. Do not prune any early spring-blooming shrub until just after it has flowered, as the blossoms are borne on last year's wood. *See also* SHRUBS, FLOWERING.

FOSTERIANA: *see* PALMS

FOUNDATION PLANTING: A foundation planting is one which ties your home, garden, shrubbery, walk, and surrounding territory together and contributes to its general beauty. On the street side especially, it is important that your general planting scheme shall be in harmony with the architectural character of the adjoining houses, as well as with your own. To plant the front of your home with a showy assortment of specimen plants of riotous colors, or various odd foliage and form effects, can single it out as gaudy, even though the planting is costly and would be of immense value if used elsewhere.

Study the character of your architecture before you decide on the type of shrubs to use for your foundation planting. The primary purpose of such a planting is to soften the outlines of harsh man-made materials and blend them gradually into the natural lines of the home grounds. Plantings serve to act as anchors for the house.

Many plants that are valuable for the color and texture of their foliage are useless for the front of a planting because they are bare of leaves near the ground. If small, compact bushy types are used in front, they appear to fit pleasingly into the picture. These are the types that must be placed beneath

windows—shrubs that are less than three feet in height. The staghorn sumac, for example, is large and attractive during the summer, and might well be thought of as one of the plants to reach high up against the house and tie it down to the ground. But look at it in the autumn, when the large leaves have fallen, and nothing is left but the bare branches! High plantings are often needed to create balance, as tall-growing poplars against apartment houses or the customary use of trees for framing purposes. If the house is located close to the street, however, this type of planting may interfere with the street trees. Extremely large trees placed in front of any house tend to dwarf it, whereas any of the smaller trees, such as the flowering cherries or hawthorn, will make the house appear large. On the home grounds high plantings can be accomplished by the use of a lovely deciduous shrub such as the mock-orange or large rhododendrons or dwarf evergreens which are tall enough for this purpose. An occasional cedar or arborvitae may be used to accent a corner and a few other evergreens planted against large bare surfaces of a house, but trees in a foundation planting as a general rule are in poor taste. With the hundreds of shrubs to choose from, don't ruin beautiful trees by putting them in places where they are misfits.

The following suggestions for type plantings will assist you in determining the kinds best suited to your architectural style. Substitutions can be made for personal preferences of certain shrubs:

DUTCH COLONIAL: This style of architecture traces back to the houses of the early Dutch settlers in the Hudson Valley, western Long Island, and New Jersey. The building may be of brick, stone, and timber or of wood with shingled walls. This is a very modest type of house and requires a simple foundation treatment without any dominating color to detract from the architecture. For a planting close to the base, a globe-shaped boxwood may be placed on either side of the entrance, with a very low hedge along the face of the building. Yew or Regel's privet could be used instead. A mixed group or a single specimen shrub could be used at the corners to blend the house into the planting of the grounds. Use a tall plant, such as the Persian lilac, parallel to the corner, next a few of medium height—as the sweet pepper-bush—and in front some of the dwarf deutzias, as *D. gracilis.*

NEW ENGLAND COLONIAL: Throughout the New England States the preferred building material has been wood, usually painted white with green trimming. The doorway may be flanked by boxwood, Regel's privet, or any of the well-rounded forms of the dwarf evergreens. A few shrubs at the corners will usually suffice for this type of house, as there are often beautiful shade trees on the lawn. A tall, slim red cedar might be used with a few low-growing evergreens, such as Pfitzer's Juniper. Sunny corners or sides of the house, if bare-looking, could be planted with forsythias and bush honeysuckle; the shaded or north side might be planted with Japanese barberry or a mixed planting of rhododendrons and laurel. In sections where the cold is extreme, these plants may need protection during the winter.

A farmhouse is usually constructed of siding and shingles, but sometimes of field stone or brick. Broad-leaved evergreens should be used to hide any exposed foundations and accent plantings should be placed at the corners and entrance to tie the whole together. Flowering and berried shrubs are better for this simple type of house than the more formal evergreens, as a general rule.

Cottages at the seashore require very simple shrubbery planting. Small groups of low-growing plants may be spaced irregularly about the foundation of a house, broken here and there at intervals with groups of two or three medium-sized shrubs chosen for bloom and berried effects, if for all-year occupancy, or perhaps only for bloom if used a few months during the summer.

BUNGALOW: Base plantings must be very colorful and attractive and tie house and garden plot together, as the architecture is not distinctive enough to carry the house alone. Plant tall shrubs at the corners, and grade them down and out in full curves, to break the square outlines of the house. Broad-leaved evergreens are excellent for shaded spots, and colorful effects may be introduced by using tuberous-rooted begonias in front of them. Never, of course, must you plant solidly around the house. Pull some of the higher plants toward the front and keep the height of the plants varied, in order not to get an absolutely straight line except in very formal effects. The principles of border planting apply in large degree to foundation planting.

PLANT TYPES: The following so-called types of plants used in foundation planting are a general guide, so that you may decide into which category shrubs of your own choosing are to be put.

High bushy types. Common, French, and Persian lilacs, European privets and the Tartarian honeysuckle.

Low bushy types. Barberry, bush honeysuckles, deutzias, box, and deciduous cotoneasters.

Rounded, dense-headed types. Vanhouttei spirea (Bridal Wreath), snowball, mock-orange, barberry, Regel's privet, globe arborvitae, and Mugho pine.

Vertical accent types. Pyramidal varieties of juniper, white fir many of the arborvitaes, Irish yew and some of the cypresses.—*Cecile Matschat.*

See also BORDERS; LANDSCAPING.

FOUR-O'CLOCK: (*Mirabilis*) Popularly grown tender annuals. *M. longiflora* grows two to three feet high, the flowers opening after sunset. In the southern half of the country, it is often treated as a perennial; the plant is not hardy in the North. Four-o'clock (*M. jalapa*), also known as Marvel-of-Peru, grows one to 2½ feet high; its one-inch wide flowers in white, red or yellow open up toward sundown.

FOXGLOVE: *see* DIGITALIS; BIENNIALS

FRANGIPANI: *see* PLUMERIA

FRANKLINIA: In the autumn of 1765, John Bartram of Philadelphia was making an exploration of southern Georgia, following generally the course of the Alatamaha River. Few settlers had come inland as yet in the new colony, and the country was thoroughly wild. But the high point of interest on that trip was not Indians or strange animals. It was the discovery of a small shrubby tree that

Today the Franklinia is found only under cultivation. It was originally discovered growing wild by John Bartram while traveling through Georgia.

looked a little like a stewartia. Though its leaves blazed with autumn red and gold, the tree was still covered with large white flowers. A thrilling sight, for Bartram was a botanist.

When he got back to Philadelphia he checked it carefully against his herbarium specimens and all the books

he could find. It was unknown to botany and he named it Franklinia, after his friend Benjamin Franklin, the well-known printer of that day.

Nine years later, in 1774, Bartram's son William introduced this fall-blooming tree into England, where Franklin was also at the time—endeavoring to persuade the home government not to drive the colonists to open rebellion. There it was renamed Gordonia, the earlier naming of Franklinia being unknown. (Franklinia is now the recognized name, however.)

In 1778 Bartram went back to Georgia and collected carefully all the good plants he could find. These came back to his gardens in Philadelphia and were propagated and distributed (as soon as the War of Independence permitted) through America and England. Twelve years later a search along the Alatamaha River located just one living tree. Since that time the plant has never again been seen growing wild. Possibly within the enormous Okeefenokee Swamp some plants may still survive, hidden on some islet, but all the plants now in the world's gardens—and there are many highly prized specimens—are descended from those collected in the second expedition in 1778.

Franklinia likes moist soil; not wet, but not dry, either. It is hardy north to Boston, Rochester and Chicago; not a tender plant. A peaty soil suits it well, even a sandy soil, provided the moisture requirement can be met. Full sun is best.

It can be propagated by seeds, but is usually grown from hardwood cuttings, since this is quicker. They root in sand, with bottom heat, in a few weeks. If taken in late autumn, cuttings seldom succeed better than 50 per cent. But if not taken from the plant until after January first, they root much better, close to 90 per cent rooted being the usual crop.

In transplanting small plants, under five feet, no earth ball is needed in late fall or early spring. However, a certain amount of the top is likely to die back on transplanting, and it is important to prune this away, down to living wood. Once the new leaves start to come out late that spring, your new Franklinia can usually be depended on for many years of beauty. —*Lawrence Manning.*

FRAXINELLA: (*Dictamnus albus*) Also called burning bush and gasplant, since the strong odor of its foliage will sometimes ignite if a match is placed to it. Fraxinella prefers a deep rich soil and a sunny well-drained location. Because its foliage is as attractive as its blossom, the plant is often grown singly. Plant in the spring, at least 12 inches apart; once established, transplanting is not recommended.

FREESIA: Beautiful, South African herbs with yellow or white flowers that bloom in winter.

Since the introduction of hybrid varieties with large flowers in many lovely and delicate shades, Freesias have still further gained in popularity. These hybrids are the results of crosses made between the white *refracta* varieties and the colored *armstrongi.* Flowers bloom in salmon-orange, buff, lovely lavender-pink, golden yellow with orange blotch, rosy salmon with golden yellow throat, light purple, and many other fine shades. The old white Freesia, *refracta alba,* is also still most desirable. It bears its snow-white blooms on stems 15 inches long, whereas the colored hybrids grow a few inches taller. Under proper conditions the plants remain in bloom for about two weeks, and through succession plantings, made two weeks apart, a continuous supply of blooms may be obtained in the greenhouse or house.

Freesia corms, usually but incorrectly called bulbs, should be planted indoors in August. The large corms, measuring ¾ inch in diameter, are the first ones to bloom; smaller ones, ½ inch in diameter, require a longer time and are likely not to bloom until April.

CULTURE: The culture of Freesias is quite simple. The corms and plants are tender and must never be subjected to freezing temperatures. They are suited to house culture exclusively. Success depends primarily upon correct temperature. Prepare a special soil mixture composed of one-third each of leaf mold or shredded peat moss, good rich garden soil, and fine clean sand. Moisten the mixture moderately and place it in pots or deep bulb pans, first covering the drainage hole with a few pieces of broken flower pot. Five or six corms can be planted in a five-inch pot, from eight to ten in a six-inch pot. Some gardeners have found that Freesia corms are surer to bloom if they are dried thoroughly for about two weeks on a sunny windowsill. When planting, space the corms about two inches apart and press them into the loose soil mixture so that the tips are covered with from one half to one inch of soil. Next place the pots or pans, without watering them, in the shaded window of a cool room where the temperature remains between 45 and 50° F. Under such conditions root growth will commence promptly. When the sprouts break through, place in a south window. It seems that the colored varieties do better if the temperature is kept five degrees warmer.

WATERING: When the surface soil shows signs of drying out, give a light sprinkling of tepid water with a fine spray. Excessive watering is harmful and so is cold water. Repeated sprinkling with small quantities of water must be done so that the soil will at no time be water-soaked. Keep the temperature just above 50° during the night, if you are growing the colored varieties, until the flower buds begin to form, when it should be raised to 60-65° during the night. Place a thermometer near the plants to be sure of the temperature, as many may be spoiled if this is left to guessing.

Always keep the plants as close to the window as possible, but beware that they are not harmed by the frost during cold nights. The foliage must never be allowed to touch the glass of the window. A few thicknesses of paper placed between the plants and the glass during extra-cold nights will be an added protection. At all times water moderately only, but do it often and never let the soil dry out. When the buds begin to open, very weak liquid manure may be substituted for the water to encourage long flower spikes set with larger blooms. Support the flower stems with four or five short, thin stakes stuck around the edge of the pot and connected with thin twine. For cutting, remove each spray when the first two blooms have opened on it.

RIPENING CORMS: When the blooming season is over, gradually withhold water and dry off in a cool room. The process of ripening the corms requires about a month or so. When perfectly dry, shake the soil from the corms and store in a perfectly dry place until next fall or early winter, when they may be replanted. Corms which started into growth during storage are undesirable, as they fail to bloom in most cases. The new growth during storage consists of the formation of a new, small corm at the growing tip of the old corm hidden beneath the fibrous skin. Most gardeners will not be bothered saving the old corms, as they require quite exacting storage conditions in order to do well the following year. There is another point that will be a problem to the gardener saving his corms, and that is the fact that they remain dormant for a certain set period of time, after which they will commence growing no matter what the conditions are. —*Alfred Putz.*

FREESTONE: Refers to varieties of peaches and nectarines in which the flesh of the fruit easily separates from the stone. The fruit of other varieties, known as clingstone, sticks more to the stone.

FREEZING: *see* FROST

FREEZING VEGETABLES: An intelligent approach to the subject of vegetables for quick freezing is to determine which are the most nutritious and the tops in family popularity. Then, plan your garden accordingly, not only for serving produce directly from the garden but for quick freezing so that it will be available in off-seasons. This fore-planning will actually reduce the garden work as the selected vegetables may be grown in larger plots depending on your needs and there'll be a consequent minimum of maintenance and harvesting effort. Harvesting and freezing will be made easier, too, for a complete supply of one vegetable can be frozen in one session.

Vegetables for freezing should be tender, succulent, fully colored and free from wilting so that all their delicious freshness may be retained to add zest to the off-season dinner table. Try not to freeze old, tough vegetables. An important tip to remember is that the quicker you prepare and freeze vegetables after picking, the more delicious—and nutritious—they will be when served. Freezing of vegetables and other foods has brought a revolution in home health and happiness. Quick freezing is a modern time and temper-saving invention which makes food preservation simple.

Usually vegetables should be blanched (scalded) before freezing as it inactivates the enzymes which would otherwise produce unpalatable flavors and disagreeable odors. Blanching tends to prevent spoilage. Put the vegetables to be blanched in a wire-mesh basket and drop it into boiling or near-boiling water or, better yet, suspend it above steam for the best results. Over-blanching may cause a difference in flavor or texture, but it's better to over-blanch than not do it sufficiently. As soon as the process is completed, remove the wire basket from the boiling water or steam, and cool the contents as quickly as possible either by plunging the basket in ice water to which ice cubes may be added as necessary, or under very cold running water. Vegetables *must* be completely cooled before freezing or there would be a loss in color, texture, flavor and nutrients. Fortunately, properly frozen, thawed and served vegetables lose little of their basic nutrient value. It's only if they're allowed to thaw and the juices leak away that we cheat ourselves. Some of the vitamins are water-soluble, others are destroyed by the action of air—a process which is hastened by a combination of light, warm room temperature, and by oxidative enzymes acting within the plant tissue. Freezing actually aids in retaining vitamin value, retarding enzyme activity if vegetables are properly blanched.

Scalding, though essential, causes some loss, 10-30 per cent of vitamin C. Less loss takes place when the vegetables are subjected to blanching over steam. There is a 10-50 per cent loss of vitamin B_1, depending on the variety of vegetable, and the blanching time involved. There is a very slight loss of vitamin A. Actually the losses by quick freezing reported in scientific literature are comparatively insignificant for a high vitamin content is retained, and what is most important we actually consume more green vegetables than would be the case were it not for this revolution in the home preservation of foods.

FREEZER CONTAINERS: For the actual containers of vegetables preserved by quick freeze methods, any may be used that will prevent contamination and loss of moisture. Ice cream containers, waxed inside, are ideal. If tin cans with friction lids or glass jars are utilized, don't fill them to within more than an inch of the top as that space would allow room for the normal expansion of the food without accidents. Vegetables which are to be packaged loose, should be placed in moisture-proof cellophane bags, heat-sealed with a hot iron, at a point close to the vegetables as possible so that there's a minimum of air in the package, or waxed containers could be used. It's advisable to overwrap cellophane packages with stockinette to prevent the plastic material either breaking or tearing.

There's plenty of choice in home freezers, and the local appliance store will have a good variety of them, without doubt. The one selected should obviously be placed in the most convenient, coolest, dry and best ventilated place, whether that be in the cellar, kitchen or garage. It will require no attention, other than to be defrosted.

Recommended times for scalding vegetables:

Vegetable	Minutes
Asparagus	2 to 4
Whole green beans	3
Cut green beans	2
Lima beans	2 to 4
Beets	Until tender
Broccoli, split	4
Brussels sprouts	3 to 5
Small whole carrots	5
Diced or sliced carrots	2
Corn on the cob	4
Eggplant, peeled and sliced	4
Spinach greens, trimmed	2
Green peas, shelled	1½
Green peppers, seeded, cut in strips	2
Summer squash	3

FRIENDS OF THE LAND: This is a non-profit society whose purpose is to educate people to a wiser use of our natural resources. The Society sponsors many programs designed to stress the importance of conserving soil and water. Some of these programs include annual clinics and tours of model watersheds and conservation projects, such as in the Muskingum Valley and the late Louis Bromfield's Malabar Farm. Friends of the Land also sponsors an annual institute on soil, food and health, which points up the interrelationship of these three factors.

Mr. Bromfield helped found and

had been an ardent supporter of Friends of the Land. *Land and Water* is published quarterly by Friends of the Land; publication offices are 386 S. Fourth St., Columbus, Ohio. Editor and president is Dr. Jonathan Forman, also editor of the *Ohio State Medical Journal.* Other officers and board members include Dr. William A. Albrecht, head of the Department of Soils at the University of Missouri; Rep. Clifford R. Hope of Kansas; Miss Doris Duke of the Duke Foundation; Dr. Paul B. Sears, Chairman of the Department of Conservation at Yale University; Ollie E. Fink, manager of the Friends' Hidden Acres Farm in Zanesville, Ohio; and a score of additional devoted conservationists, educators, agricultural leaders and industrialists.

FRINGED GENTIAN: *see* GENTIAN

FRINGE-TREE: (*Chionanthus virginicus*) . The ornamental fringe-tree grows natively on river banks in the

This Fringe-Tree or Old-Man's Beard grows up to 25 feet high. It ranges from Pennsylvania to Florida and Texas; is hardy below the bluegrass line.

Eastern States and as far west as Missouri. Its fleecy white flowers are produced in the utmost profusion. The stamens and pistils are usually borne in separate flowers, the male flowers being larger than the female

flowers. Fringe-tree is closely related to the lilac, and should be given much the same care. It drops its leaves in the autumn and is one of the last shrubs to put out leaves in the spring. It has a coarse-textured habit that goes well with a modest country home, and blooms in May and June. It adds charm to an informal foundation planting.

FRIT: *see* TRACE ELEMENTS

FRITILLARIA: Mostly low-growing and spring-blooming hardy plants, fritillarias resemble lilies since they have drooping flowers. Most popular kinds are crown imperial (*F. imperialis*) and checkered lily (*F. meleagris*); these are hardy, easy to cultivate and have flowers about two inches long. Depending upon the species, fritillarias are grown in rock gardens, in pots or in borders. *See also* CROWN IMPERIAL.

FROG: The common name applied to any of a number of tailless, leaping amphibians (genus *Rana* and allied genera of the family *Ranidae*) of aquatic habits. Among the best-known American species are the bullfrog (generally applied to any large frog, especially *R. catesbeiana*, *R. grylio* and *R. aurora*), leopard frog (*R. pipiens*), and pickerel frog (*R. palustris*).

The frog is not an enemy of the gardener, and could even be classified as an unknowing friend. Like the toad, the frog will quickly devour anything moving close to it. However, since frogs generally inhabit ponds instead of gardens, their food consists mainly of pond life, including minnows, crayfish, water-bugs and smaller frogs. Frogs which live in marshes thrive on spiders, beetles, crickets, grasshoppers and other small ground creatures. The toad is more of a land lover, and thus is of more value to the gardener.

FROG FARMING: There is a limited amount of frog farming, especially in deep Southern states. Markets are found only in large urban areas, like New York, Chicago, St. Louis, Baltimore and New Orleans. Most of the so-called "frog farms," and those which are least expensive and which require the least labor, are simply natural marshy areas or ponds adapted as to food supply and environment to the needs of frogs. In such areas the frogs, left to themselves, will thrive and multiply. *See also* TOAD.

FROST: The term "frost" or "hoarfrost" is used to designate the deposit of feathery ice crystals on the ground or other exposed surfaces the temperature of which has fallen to 32° F., the freezing point of water, or lower. It is customary, however, when such a temperature occurs to say that there has been a "frost," even if it was not accompanied by a deposit of ice crystals.

In order to understand the underlying principles of frost protection, it is necessary to know something of the processes through which the ground surface and the air at lower levels cool during the night.

HOW FROST IS FORMED: Whenever two adjacent objects or different portions of the same object have unequal temperatures, the colder always gains heat at the expense of the warmer, unless insulated from each other or otherwise prevented from doing so, the tendency being to equalize the temperature between the bodies or throughout every portion of the same body. The interchange of heat may be accomplished by radiation, conduction, or convection, which will be discussed as far as they bear on the occurrence of frost.

WHEN TO EXPECT FROST: Frosts or freezes may follow almost any type of local weather, and predictions based on local indications alone are likely to prove disappointing. However, there ?re a few local indications that may prove to be of some value.

The weather of the United States is largely governed by the movement of, and interaction between, great moving masses of air which originate in different regions and have different characteristics of temperature, moisture and wind; these air masses may be divided broadly into two main types —polar, or cold, originating in the north, and tropical, or warm, originating in southerly latitudes. Each air mass carries with it its own particular type of weather. The most changeable weather, accompanied by cloudiness, wind, and often by rain or snow, normally is found near the boundaries between two air masses, of differing characteristics, called "fronts." A boundary at which warm, moist air is over-running relatively cold air is known as a "warm front"; while a front at which cold air is pushing under, and lifting a warm air mass is known as a "cold front." Speaking very generally, the passage of a warm front is accompanied by a blanket of heavy low clouds and more or less continuous precipitation, while a cold front passage is characterized by intermittent precipitation, followed by broken cloudiness and, later, clearing skies.

Practically all freezes and a large proportion of local frosts follow the passage of a cold front and the subsequent influx of polar air. Cold rain or sleet is followed by intermittent showers or thunderstorms, then clearing skies and falling humidity. At times, however, frost does not immediately follow the cold front passage because of wind conditions. Relatively cold polar air masses usually move southward in the westerly portion of a cyclone, or low-pressure area, and in the eastern portion of an anticyclone, or high-pressure area.

Although moisture in the ground after a rain tends to prevent warming of the ground during the day, it also tends to prevent a large fall in temperature during the night. When the dew point is reached the latent heat given up checks the rate of cooling, and when the abundant surface ground moisture freezes, the liberated heat also aids in checking the rate of fall in temperature.

By the second night after the rain the surface of the ground usually has dried out considerably, the dew point is likely to be lower, and there is more danger of a damaging frost. Before the third night the day temperature usually has risen high enough to make a heavy local frost unlikely, although there are exceptions to this rule. In California heavy frosts sometimes occur following a strong influx of polar air without any local indications of the passage of a cold front. Low night temperatures occur immediately following the cessation of strong dry north to east winds.

Large bodies of water exert a modifying influence on the climate of nearby localities to the leeward, and such localities are less liable to damage by frost. A light wind blowing from a large body of water is generally more or less laden with water vapor, which retards the rate of surface cooling; and as the temperature of the water is usually considerably above freezing, that of the air passing from it to the land is often high enough to prevent the formation of frost.

Rivers often give up a large amount of moisture to the surface air, so that when the temperature falls to the dew point a surface fog forms which covers a part or all of the lower land in the valley, absorbing and returning radiation and preventing a further fall in temperature. In valleys near the ocean, fog sometimes drifts in from the water toward morning and prevents a damaging frost. On nights with ground fog the hillsides are practically always colder than the lowlands unless the fog extends high enough to cover both hillsides and valley floor.

PROTECTING PLANTS AGAINST LATE FROST: Much damage may be wrought in the garden by the unexpected late spring frosts which not uncommonly follow a period of warm growing weather. Removal of the pro-

tecting evergreen boughs and leaves from the perennial beds will have been necessary in most sections, as an extended delay yellows the growth beneath the cove and causes it to be weak and lanky. Keep this material handy in an out-of-the-way place. Plants indigenous to the section where they are grown are less likely to be caught by late frosts than those that are natives of other zones.

It is remarkable to see the resistance the early-spring-flowering bulbs show to cold. Snowdrops will push through the soil while the ground is still covered with snow. Crocus, Scilla, and Chionodoxa are almost equally resistant to cold weather and need no emergency protection if they have not been coddled by a winter cover. Narcissus and Hyacinths also are endowed by nature to withstand a cold snap after they have made quite some top growth. But a light protection of evergreen boughs will be of aid. Particular care must be given to the more tender bulbs like Brodiaea, Camassia, and Calochortus, which are easily injured by late frost. Early-blooming bushes, like Cydonia japonica, are sometimes caught unawares, and large old sheets placed over them will usually save the display of flowers.

Seedlings coming along in the coldframe need particular watching. Close the sash upon the approach of freezing temperature, and if the drop is severe bank the outside of the frame with soil or litter and place burlap bags over the glass panes. These keep the cold out during the night, and the shade prevents an undue rise of temperature during the day. When the temperatures rise above 32°F., give air by raising the sash with a brick or block on the side of the frame opposite to the direction of the wind.

Young plants of hardy annual flowers sown outdoors early in the spring are sometimes affected by late frosts. Individual plants may be covered with berry boxes, held in place by stones or earth placed upon them. Where they are planted in rows the boxes may be placed a foot or two apart over the row to keep sheets of paper placed over them off the ground. Cover the sides of the paper with soil.

Cover perennials that have started into growth early with berry boxes, wooden boxes, flats, flower pots, pails, and even cardboard boxes. One of our finest Lilies, *Lilium hansoni*, needs particular attention, as it starts growth early, yet is quite easily injured by late frosts. Often the young shoots of this Lily are quite tall and require the tall five-eighth fruit basket to cover them. Line the inside of the basket with a couple of thicknesses of newspaper as a further protection and place a heavy stone on the top. Where dry leaves are still at hand, cover the perennial plants with them before using the inverted boxes.

The purpose of all covering is first to keep the severe cold off as much as possible and second to accomplish a gradual warming up afterwards. Use good judgment as to the length of time it is kept on, as the young plants or shoots beneath it need light as well as air to make a normal growth. Fortunately these late cold spells do not last long enough to necessitate protection for more than a few days. In most cases it will be just for a night or two that they cause harm, but that may be enough to do severe damage.

Planting close to the foundation of the house deserve special attention, as the proximity to a heated cellar or a chimney wall warms the soil in such positions and causes an advance in growth. As plants in such locations are usually well established, they can stand a cover of double-thickness mulch (even newspaper held in place by stones or soil). A light covering of leaves below the paper serves as an additional protection.

The work of protecting plants against frost injury extends also into the house. Though there may be little danger of the temperature in the con-servatory or the enclosed porch falling below the freezing point, one must be sure that none of the plants touch any of the window panes. Remove the plants a few inches from the windows, or if this is cumbersome, place three or four layers of newspaper between them and the glass pane. But with house plants freezing temperatures are not the only ones that may cause injury. Make sure the warmth-requiring specimens have a night temperature of not less than 60°F. In this class we have Amaryllis, Begonia, Bouvardia, Caladium, Geranium, Impatiens, Justicia, Lily-of-the-valley, Thunbergia, and Torenia. Those classed as cool greenhouse plants, which need at least 45° at this time, include Abutilon, Calceolaria, Cineraria, Cyclamen, Fuchsia, Gerbera, Gloxinia, Grevillea, Hydrangea, Primula, Solanum, and Streptocarpus.

Last but not least, make sure that the tender bulbs, corms, and roots in storage are not affected by the cold through an open window, etc. Gladiolus, Dahlias, Cannas, Oxalis, Zephyranthus, Tigridia, Begonia, Caladium, Calla—they all need checking for storage temperatures when late cold spells make their appearance.— *Alfred Putz.*

See also VEGETABLE GARDENING.

FRUIT, FOOD VALUE: Looking at them analytically, fruits contain considerable amounts of several vitamins; they are major contributors of most essential minerals; and their role in aiding digestion, body development and tone is particularly important. But beyond the ordinary nutritional statistics, fruits have some unique and delightful functions in the well-rounded diet that make them deserve far more consideration—and use—by those who do the family food planning *and* the family gardening.

More than any other food group, fruits introduce a fascinating variety of color, taste and texture to meals and snacks. Fruits have a very low caloric content and, with the exception of avocados and olives, a practically negligible amount of fat.

AID TO DIGESTION: Fresh fruits, because of the cellulose and organic acids they contain, have a natural laxative effect, constantly aiding the passage of food along the gastro-intestinal tract. What's more, they yield an alkaline residue or ash that neutralizes the acid residue formed by meat, eggs and other protein-rich foods. Because of this, fruits are exceptionally important in maintaining acid-base neutrality—that balance so essential to good health, nutrition and digestion.

Most of us know the citrus fruits are especially valuable for their ascorbic acid (vitamin C) content. Along with these go berries and melons as fairly good suppliers. All fresh fruits, in fact, make some contribution of this highly perishable vitamin that needs constant replenishing.

Another nutritive factor found in fruits is carotene, which our bodies convert to vitamin A. Such fruits as apricots, peaches, cantaloupes and bananas supply appreciable amounts. And although tree crops in general offer only small quantities of the B-complex vitamins, several of the dried fruits and citrus varieties contribute some thiamine (B_1) to the diet. Speaking of dried fruits, make sure those you select are *sun-dried*, not sulphured. There's an important difference in the over-all health value.

On the mineral side of the ledger, fruits shine even more brightly. Their potassium content is quite high and is usually combined with those vital organic acids. Large amounts of calcium are present in the dried fruits and somewhat more moderately in oranges, raspberries and strawberries. Iron makes an appearance in dates, figs, bananas, peaches, prunes, raisins, and apricots. In the last four, it is found in quite high amounts—and, what is another important consideration, mostly in an *available* form.

Since fruits have a high water content and low proportions of fat and protein, they represent especially good sources of food iron and other minerals because they can be added to the diet without replacing other foods or making the total calorie consumption too great.

While fresh fruits, as emphasized before, are to be preferred (any processing or other treatment lowers the nutritional value), they may of course be cooked and prepared in numerous ways to lend further variety to our eating, and to make them suitable for infant or invalid feeding. What the cooking—either stewing, steaming or baking—accomplishes is a softening of the cellulose so that they are more readily digested. It's also one way to add to their keeping quality and, second to freezing, it is the best solution to a sizable surplus.

FRUITS

Species	Ascorbic Acid (mg./100 g.)		
Rosa rugosa rose hip	1700 to 6977		
Barbados cherry (Acerola)	1000 to 4676		
Myrciaria glomerata	706 to 2417		
Phyllanthus emblica	625 to 1814		
Guava	23 to 486		
Cashew apple	147 to 348		
Green pepper	86 to 275		
Adansonia digitata	300		
Ceylon gooseberry	66 to 245		
Brysonima crassifolia	90 to 192		
Mango	7 to 147		
Crataegus pubescens	90 to 119		
Papaya	36 to 109		
Lychee	42 to 84		
Naranjilla	31 to 84		
Jujube	56 to 82		
Strawberry	41 to 81		
Muntingia	81		
Spondias purpurea	26 to 73		
Sour orange	43 to 103		
Lemon	50	(23 to 60)	
Orange	49	(37 to 80)	
Grapefruit	40	(23 to 50)	
Tangerine	31	(15 to 57)	
Lime	30	(25 to 49)	

FRUIT TREES: Growing fruit trees is one of the most important as well as the most challenging activities for the home gardener. There are the pome fruits (apples and pears), the drupe fruits (cherry, peach and plum) and the citrus fruits (grapefruit, orange, lemon and lime) ; selection of the fruit and the specific variety must be done carefully.

CHOOSING TREES: Before buying fruit trees, study the varieties offered. Compare them for growth characteristics and soil needs. Check these against your needs and the kind of soil and climate prevailing in your area.

When you choose—choose trees that should do well in your vicinity. Then, make up your lists with care and really work at making your selections.

Another factor to keep in mind—planting the single tree. When you order such, *make sure it is self-fertilizing.* Study your dealer's catalog; don't be afraid to ask questions. You should know in advance if a single tree is sterile, that it depends upon the presence of other trees for propagation.

Buy first-class trees, as a rule. Select those which are medium-size for their age, shapely in body and head, stocky with straight, clean trunks and abundant roots. They should not be stunted and they should be free of borers and injuries. In the case of budded trees, the union should be very near the ground.

Vigor, cleanness, stockiness and firm, hard growth are more important than mere bigness. The toughest and best trees are usually medium in size. In dollars and cents, the difference between first and second-class trees is small compared to the return you will get from each tree.

Age of the tree is also important. The proper planting age varies, depends on varieties and circumstances. But, in general, the younger trees stand the shock of transplanting better and you will suffer fewer losses.

Work with the younger tree as a rule and where you have a choice. There will be exceptions to this and you will find yourself experimenting with a recommended older planting because it has a good background.

WHERE TO PLANT YOUR TREES: Beauty and an anticipated landscaping plan are important but they cannot be the sole or even determining factors. This is common-sense reasoning and you should acknowledge it as such right now. The important factors in deciding tree sites are:

1. Soil
2. Soil Drainage
3. Exposure to sun
4. Exposure to prevailing winds

Whether you plant one tree or 100, plant them in fertile, well-drained soil. Plant them where they are accessible, where you can compost and mulch them readily and well. Don't plant them in low-lying, swampy spots where the frosts come early in the day and stay late. Give each tree a good home with plenty of humus and a good rich supply of organic nutrients.

Plant your trees where there is good circulation of air. Avoid spots where extremes in temperatures prevail. Plant on the north or northeast slope when possible. Don't plant on the sunny slope where the sun will blister your tender trees during the day and the winter frosts will chill them at night.

PLANTING DISTANCES: Never forget that trees are wide feeders. Their roots stretch out and out in a ceaseless search for the food necessary to their growth. Remember that the root system of the average tree just about equals the extent and volume of its system of branches.

PLANTING DISTANCES:

Apples	40 ft. each way
—Dwarf	10-15 ft. each way
Apricots	20 ft. each way
Cherries, Sour	20 ft. each way
—Sweet	30 ft. each way
Figs	20-25 ft. each way
Oranges, Lemons	25-30 ft. each way
Pears, Standard	20-25 ft. each way
—Dwarf	12-16 ft. each way
Quinces	16 ft. each way

The above distances are recommended as safe. Again, where the soil is particularly fertile and a good, thor-

THE ONE-ACRE ORCHARD

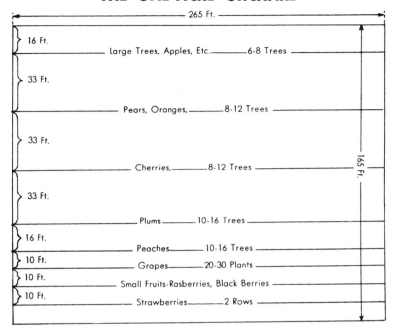

Your preferences as owner and those of the family can be given full rein here. Pick the trees and berry bushes whose fruit appeals to all. It's also a good idea to check with the neighbors; find out what varieties do best in your area.

The rows must run the length of the plot. Remember not to plant in a frost pocket where the cold likes to stay all winter. Also, a northern exposure is better for your trees than a southern; the sun won't scald your trees so badly there.

Be scrupulous in pacing off distances between rows. Don't plant the maximum number of trees in every row; give the young root and branch systems a chance to spread out and grow.

Last but not least—try to grow a cover crop a year before you plant. Turn it under in the spring and let it break down in the soil over the summer before you plant in the autumn. And when your trees are all planted—remember to give them plenty of mulching and composting as they grow.

ough organic groundwork has been established—they may be pared a trifle.

WHEN TO PLANT: Experts differ on the respective planting merits of the fall versus the spring. Fall planting is considered preferable, particularly for the hardy tree fruits. But the soil should be thoroughly drained. If the ground is in good condition, fruit trees can be set out as late as October with success, even in the northern states.

The advantages of fall planting are numerous. The trees take hold in their new sites during the benevolent Indian Summer weather. Then, later next spring, they are already making an early start in ground which is still too hard to permit spring planting.

This early start not only means a better growth during the vital first season but—and this is very important —*trees that get an early hold in the soil endure the midsummer dry weather much better than trees planted in the spring.*

Planting is almost invariably done better in the settled weather and workable soil of autumn than during the changeable days and hurry of the early spring. There is still another gain: the fall planter has plenty of time in the following spring to start cultivating his young trees instead of just starting out with them.

However, some tree planters consider fall planting too risky, especially in the North. The majority argue this point by stressing that there is small chance of excessive tree loss—as long as you prepare your ground and follow the rules.

COVER CROPS: In the days of our fathers plowing the land was considered a "must." Plowing filled a double purpose; it got the cover crops under and it loosened and aerated the soil, making it easier for the young trees to send out their roots.

Today the average homesteader is working in a smaller space and, unless he has commercial aspirations, is more modest in his ambitions as a tree-grower. But, it is axiomatic that an organic gardener will grow a cover crop to protect and enrich his soil, particularly when he is growing a tree crop.

The putting in of a cover crop on the larger plot will pay dividends far beyond the time and trouble invested. In addition the earnest and hard-working gardener of today has a whole host of power tools to ease his task for him.

Outstanding among these is the rotary tiller which can turn a cover crop under in addition to performing other chores.

The advantages conferred by the propagation and subsequent turning under of cover crops are many. The cover crop serves a double purpose; it protects the soil from the elements and it improves its nutritional qualities. Kinds of cover include the various clovers, vetches, and leguminous crops such as mixed beans. All of these will, when turned back into the soil, add valuable nutrients as they break down and will also promote better

soil structure through the addition of humus.

The function and benefits of the cover crop may be itemized as follows:

1. Directly improve the physical condition of the soil,
2. Prevents hard soils from puddling or cementing,
3. It holds the rain and snow until they have time to soak into the land,
4. Serves as an added protection against frost,
5. Catches and holds some of the leaching nitrates,
6. Renders plant-foods available.

A last word on the cover crop—plant it one full year before you put your trees into the soil. That's right; try to plan in this case a year ahead. This means putting in a winter cover of vetch or clover and then turning it under in the spring. Permit it to age in the soil until September or early October when you plant your trees.

The reasons for this are sound and if you follow this plan—it can save you a lot of trouble. First: don't put raw manure or any kind directly into the soil when you plant the trees. By plowing under in the spring and waiting three-four months you give the green manures time to age and weather. Second: you may stimulate late tree growth which means that your trees will carry tender, sensitive wood into the chilling frosts of winter. It is almost certain beyond all doubt that this wood will be killed and the young tree itself seriously weakened if not killed outright itself.

HOW TO PLANT: By knowing why you are planting, what varieties and stocks you are going to plant, where and when you will plant them, you have already gained some idea of how they should be planted.

You realize that your holes should be dug in advance, that the ground should be well prepared and on a favorable site where your trees will be neither blistered by the sun nor frozen by the winds. The ground is well-drained and the air-ventilation is satisfactory. Remember: do not plant in low-lying, swampy, frost-pockets.

The holes for your fruit trees must be dug broad and ample. In hard soils,

Do not leave any air around the roots when filling the hole. Good procedure is to water while placing soil and gently agitating the tree.

make the hole a little larger, break up the ground a bit more and give your roots a better chance to spread out. It is hard for the young tree to send its roots out into hard-packed soil and everything you do to make that job easier will pay dividends later.

While you are advised to plant your trees a little deeper than they stood in the nursery you are also warned *not to plant them too deep!* Trees which are properly planted develop a strong feeder root system which spreads out and takes firm hold of the ground *close to the surface.*

This means a series of spreading, tenacious roots which provide a sure, firm base for your tree when the season of high winds arrives.

At the same time you should provide a good, regular source of organic nutrients by compost-mulching around the tree. This will stimulate feeder

root growth and ensure its taking hold during the critical period.

Take great care to set your tree well and firmly into the hole. Make a small mound of topsoil and place the young tree on this gently. Keep the roots in their natural position as much as possible.

Fill with more topsoil around the roots with your hands. Work the soil around the roots gently with your fingers. Try, as much as possible, to avoid air pockets. When the hole is partly filled, tamp the earth down as firmly as possible. Repeat this operation often, working with extreme care.

You can get air-holes out from around your roots by filling the half-full hole with water and then gently rocking the tree on its mound while the water settles, carrying soil with it into the air pockets. Continue by filling the hole with more dirt and repeating the flooding. Then add more dirt firmly tamped into place.

It is good practice to leave a depression immediately around the tree. This is to encourage movement of

As soon as the tree is firmly in place, it should be pruned back to keep the branch and root systems in balance. Fill the basin for a thorough watering.

water toward each tree where it will be held in a natural basin. You will find in time that the depression will gradually fill in with soil.

Water your tree immediately after it is planted. Be sure to give it a thorough soaking—not a sprinkling. Fill the depression with water and allow it to soak into the ground slowly. When you water the tree thereafter, water it once a week only—but give it a thorough soaking. If you have a good, soaking rain that week—you can skip watering. But if you have a brief sprinkle or a shower—be sure to give your tree its full watering.

Use well-weathered compost or straw or hay as a first-season mulch. Cover the ground around the tree up to the drip-line but keep a few inches to one-foot clear space immediately around the tree. This will keep mice and rodents away from the tender bark of the tree.

You might also place a protective bank of wire mesh around the tree. Make it 18 inches high and no less than nine inches across. Make it sturdy and you can press it firmly and deeply into the ground so that rodents can't burrow under it. You will also find that the wire protects the tender bark of the trunk from sun-scald by deflecting the rays of the sun and also by absorbing their heat.

BEARING TIME FOR FRUIT TREES

	Years Start	Years Bear
Apple	3-10	50-100
Apricot	3-4	10-25
Blackberry	2-3	5-10
Cherry, Sour	3-4	15-25
Cherry, Sweet	4-5	25-75
Currant	2-3	5-10
Dwarf* (See note below)		
Gooseberry	2-3	5-10
Grape	1-3	10-50
Peach & Nectarine	2-3	5-15
Pear	3-5	25-75
Plum	3-4	10-20
Quince	3-4	10-20
Raspberry	1-2	5-10

* Dwarf fruit trees usually bear one to three years earlier than standard varieties, but are not normally as long-lived.

FAILURE TO BEAR FRUIT: There are many reasons why a fruit tree will not bear or why it stops bearing after being a regular producer or why it does not bear abundantly.

While these reasons may sometimes be obscure and not readily explainable, failure to bear is in the majority of cases due to one or several well recognized factors. The following is based on research made by the U.S. Dept. of Agriculture:

WEATHER CONDITIONS: If a frost occurs during the period when fruit trees are in bloom, injury frequently results, its seriousness depending on the severity of the frost and the attending conditions. The injury may range from the killing of a few abnormally weak or tender blossoms to the complete destruction of the entire crop prospects.

Frequently, when cold weather prevails at blossoming time, the fruit does not set well, even though the trees blossom abundantly and no killing frost occurs. The pollen does not germinate when the temperature approaches the freezing point. Probably there is little germination of the pollen if the temperature during the blossoming period falls much of the time below 40° or 42°F. Other essential parts of the blossom, including the pistil and ovules, may be adversely affected by low temperatures, so that should the pollen germinate, fertilization may not take place even though no actual freezing of the flower parts occurs. Sometimes the blossoms open during a warm period which is immediately followed by a cold spell that continues during the remainder of the blossoming period. Under such conditions a very poor set of fruit may be looked for. An exceedingly heavy June drop commonly follows a blossoming period such as has been described, continuing sometimes until practically the entire set of fruit is gone.

If a very heavy beating rain occurs immediately after the blossoms open, it may result in much of the pollen being washed away, especially in recently opened blossoms; this, at least, is a claim that is sometimes made.

Many fruit varieties are self-sterile or self-unfruitful, and the blossoms dependent upon the pollen from other varieties to fertilize them. The common honeybee is the principal agent in carrying the pollen from one tree to another and from blossom to blossom. Bees are inactive during very windy weather, also when the temperature drops to within 10° or so of freezing. If the blossoming period is so windy or temperature so low that the bees are inactive, self-sterile varieties are likely to pass through the blossoming period without cross-pollination.

Extremely cold winters can kill or injure peaches and some of the other more tender fruits. It rarely occurs in the case of apples, although it may happen under extreme conditions. But peach buds even in a perfectly dormant condition are killed or injured by extreme temperatures. The most tender parts of the blossom are the pistil, or the small embryo fruit, which occupies the center of the flower. The temperature may be low enough during the winter to destroy these central parts of the flower in many of the buds. Such buds may open normally, and unless the blossoms are carefully examined, injury may not be suspected until it is found that the trees are not setting any fruit, or perhaps only a very light crop, although there was a profuse bloom.

SELF-STERILITY: Reference was made above to self-sterility or self-unfruitfulness.

Self-sterility is very common. It occurs in many varieties of apples, most varieties of pears, probably in all varieties of sweet cherries, in most if not all varieties of the native and Japanese plums, and in some varieties of the European or domestic plums and prunes. Sour cherries are considered largely self-fertile, although there is some evidence of partial self-sterility.

Most peach varieties are self-fertile; the J. H. Hale and June Elberta (Mikado) are notable exceptions, as they require cross-pollination. Sterility in plums, cherries, and perhaps other fruits may sometimes be due to deformed or imperfect pistils. Some grape varieties must be cross-pollinated in order to be fruitful.

There is every conceivable degree of self-sterility, from one extreme where no fruit sets without cross-pollination to where it is not a serious factor in fruit production. Even varieties considered self-fertile to a high degree will set a better crop of fruit if cross-pollination occurs. With self-sterility prevailing to so large an extent in the common fruit varieties, the relation of weather conditions favorable to the greatest activity of honeybees is apparent, since the fruit grower largely depends on them for the cross-pollination of his fruits.

In planting orchards the grower must take into account the self-sterility problem in choosing varieties and in so planting them that cross-pollination will be insured. Every third tree in every third row is usually regarded as a safe proportion for a minimum number of pollinizer trees. Many other cases occur where a home owner has planted single trees of a number of different kinds of fruit in his yard or about his buildings. When self-sterile varieties are planted and there are no other trees of different varieties of the same kind growing near enough to insure the passing of bees from one to the other, it will be found that trees blossom but do not set fruit.

Where self-sterility occurs under such conditions as those described, the permanent remedy is to top work a certain number of trees or branches to a variety that blossoms at the same time as the trees themselves and is known to be effective as a cross-pollinizer of the variety. This remedy, however, requires several years. This temporary expedient frequently proves quite effective: when the tree to be cross-pollinated is in bloom, secure some blossoming branches from a tree of another variety of the same kind of fruit and place them in a pail or other water container in the top of the tree. The bees, visiting the trees, will also visit the blossoms on the branches and will thereby transfer the pollen as they revisit the blossoms on the tree.

NUTRITIONAL CONDITION: The nutritional feature of nonfruitfulness is somewhat complicated. In general, trees that are overvigorous and those that are seriously lacking in vigor are not in a favorable condition of growth for the formation of fruit buds. In general, trees low in vigor need fertilizing in order to be fruitful. Nitrogen is most commonly the limiting nutrient, but this deficiency can be corrected by the application of generous amounts of compost, cottonseed meal, soya meal, or dried blood. Fertilizer may be applied at any time, but preferably in the late summer or early fall.

The blossom buds of the common deciduous fruit trees form during the season preceding the spring when they open. Conditions in any season that affect the vitality or nutrition of a tree may affect correspondingly its next season's crop of fruit by influencing fruit-bud differentiation. Excessive shading by nearby buildings or large trees, uncontrolled diseases or insects which may destroy or greatly reduce the normal functioning of the foliage, or the production of an excessively heavy crop of fruit, with its effects on the storing up of plant foods within the tissues of the tree, may all be factors influencing the next season's crop.

PRUNING AND PRODUCTION: Pruning may havé a decided effect on productiveness. Excessive pruning of a young tree delays its bearing. This effect is especially marked with apple trees, but it is true also of other kinds. Instances are also known where apple trees 12 or 15 years old in reasonably satisfactory bearing condition have been very heavily pruned and the internal nutritional condition

so thrown out of balance thereby that the trees have borne little or no fruit for several years thereafter. On the other hand, old trees that aré somewhat lacking in vigor may be rejuvenated and stimulated into better fruit production by judicious pruning. Just what constitutes excessive pruning for a young tree or a judicious amount for an old tree of low vitality must be determined through experience under the local conditions. The tendency with young trees, however, is to over-prune rather than to prune too lightly. *See also* NAMES OF INDIVIDUAL FRUITS; ORCHARD; PRUNING; INSECT CONTROL; TREES; FERTILIZER.

FRUIT TREES, DEFICIENCIES: Deficiencies in fruit trees can cause new twig growth to die back, abnormally twisted leaves and blotchy fruit.

Possibly your trees have symptoms of mineral deficiency. Potash or phosphorus may be low or your soil may be too alkaline to allow certain minerals like iron and aluminum to become available. The following list can perhaps solve your problem. These symptoms apply for all deciduous fruit trees.

NITROGEN DEFICIENCY: Examine the leaves on the old branches. With a lack of nitrogen, these older leaves turn a yellowish-green, working toward the tips. You may also notice reddish or reddish-purple discolorations. If nothing is done to relieve the deficiency, leaves become very small, and the twigs slender and hard.

PHOSPHORUS DEFICIENCY: The young twigs develop a ghost-like hue; stems show purple coloring; leaves are abnormally small and dark green. Old leaves become mottled with light and dark green areas. Occasionally bronzed leaves will show up on mature branches.

POTASH DEFICIENCY: The key to potash deficiency is purplish discoloration and scorching of leaf edges. The dead spots will be found on mature leaves, but under continued deficiency, even very young leaves are affected. Peach foliage often becomes crinkled and twigs are unusually slender.

MAGNESIUM DEFICIENCY: The large, old leaves will display flesh-colored patches of dead tissue, not restricted to the leaf edges. Watch for dropping of leaves, first on old branches, then on twigs of the current season. Defoliation may be so severe that only tufts or "rosettes" of thin, small leaves are left.

ZINC DEFICIENCY: Both zinc and magnesium deficiencies are very much alike. Each of them can cause rosettes of leaves in the advanced stage. But without zinc, crinkled leaves are common, which are also chlorotic (rather washed-out yellow in color). In peach trees this is very true. With citrus fruit, very small, smooth fruit and pointed leaves are the symptoms. There may also be striking contrasts in leaf patterns—dark green veins and yellow tissue.

CALCIUM DEFICIENCY: Calcium and boron shortage will show up first on young twigs rather than the mature branches. Dead areas are noticeable on the young, tender leaves at the tips and margins without calcium. Later, the twigs will die back and roots are injured.

BORON DEFICIENCY: Immediately coming to mind should be internal cork of apples, which is the commonest boron deficiency problem. Early in the season, hard, brown spots with definite margins form inside the fruit. As the season progresses, the spots soften, become larger, and lose their definite outline. The leaves may be entirely unaffected. .

In other cases, the young leaves can become very thick and brittle, then cause dieback of twigs. Some trees may also form wrinkled, chlorotic leaves.

IRON AND ALUMINUM DEFICIENCY: With an overdose of lime comes an unavailability of certain minerals like iron and aluminum. These minerals may be right in the soil, but are held insoluble when the acidity is low. Look for yellow leaves with brown patches, and loss of flavor in the fruit.

CORRECTIONS

Nitrogen—apply cottonseed meal, dried blood, tankage, raw bone meal, fish wastes, legume hay, or one of the organic nitrogen commercial products now on the market.

Phosphorus—raw or colloidal phosphate rock, bone meal, fish wastes, guano, or raw sugar wastes.

Potash—granite dust, glauconite marl (greensand), wood ashes, seaweed, or orange rinds.

Magnesium—dolomitic limestone or raw phosphate rock.

Zinc—raw phosphate rock.

Calcium—raw pulverized limestone.

Boron—raw phosphate rock (avoid lime, add manure and acid organic matter like peat moss, sawdust, or ground oak leaves).

Iron and Aluminum—glauconite marl (avoid lime, use the acid organic matter recommended under boron).

See also DEFICIENCIES, SOIL; TRACE ELEMENTS; FERTILIZERS.

FRUIT TREES, DWARF: Dwarf trees, usually growing only from five to seven feet tall, are truly Tom Thumbs compared to the 35 feet or more their regular variety relatives reach. To the busy part-time gardener, this means a number of important things: They are considerably simpler to prepare soil for, plant, fertilize and mulch. In each of these operations, there's much less land area, material and tree itself to handle and give attention to.

Dwarf trees usually begin fruiting far sooner than standard varieties—most by their second year. Standard trees take up to ten years to start bearing, and usually a minimum of five. Dwarf apples, pears, peaches, plums, nectarines, apricots and sweet cherries begin yielding within a couple of years, producing well by the time they're three-year-olds.

The fruit from dwarf varieties is

equal in size to that of standard types. As a matter of fact, because these trees can be given individual care more readily, the fruit they bear is frequently *larger* than on the full-scale kind, and often is of better quality,

Dwarf Red McIntosh apples growing at a convenient picking height. True dwarf varieties produce fruit of fine quality; require little care.

color and taste. To top it off, they are obviously easier to harvest and there's less waste or spoilage from fallen fruit. All in all, dwarf trees produce more fruit faster in any-sized area than any other method.

The dwarfing idea isn't new. Europeans have successfully dwarfed apples and pears for hundreds of years, and the limited space of most of their homesteads has long made this a primary factor in planning fruit plantings.

A dwarf fruit tree, as one plant scientist very simply defines it, is made by grafting the bud of a standard fruit tree to the rootstock of a dwarfing variety that does not yield a desirable fruit. Since the rootstock controls the size of the tree and the grafted bud

determines the fruit it will produce, many dwarf varieties are possible and several highly satisfactory ones have been developed and made available.

Rootstocks for dwarf apples and pears have become generally fixed. For the apple, these stocks are known as Malling, a name derived from the East Malling Research Station in Kent, England, where much of the initial testing and investigation was done. Numbered consecutively according to their degree of controlling tree-size, hardiness, and other characteristics, Malling VIII and IX rootstocks have proved the most suitable and widely used. No true rootstock for pears has as yet been fully developed, and this fruit is usually dwarfed by grafting on quince stocks.

Various methods for dwarfing peaches, plums, apricots, nectarines and cherries have evolved and been made practical, although not to the extent of the apple and pear. Current research and testing holds strong promise of making these and other fruits as widely popular and successful in dwarf varieties.

At the same time, reliable, generous-bearing dwarf peaches, plums, and cherries (in addition to pears and apples) are available from a number of nationwide nurseries.

PLANTING: For best results, dwarfs should be planted in soil that is moderately open and well drained—not in fine-textured clay or soil so coarse that it does not retain moisture. If it's too light and porous to hold moisture, nutrients needed by the tree's roots in a soil-moisture solution just won't be there, and a starved tree is the outcome. On the other hand, a heavy clay soil keeps water from draining, holds rainfall up in close contact with the roots and literally suffocates them.

As for where to plant your dwarfs, two factors are important: wind and frost. While good air circulation through fruit trees is necessary, strong winds are deadly. Have your trees planted on a site that's open and

Dwarf trees like this Dwarf Lincoln Pear produce sooner but are shorter-lived than standard trees. Its fruit suffers no loss in flavor or sweetness. Trees should be protected against spring frosts.

sunny, but which has protection from north and east winds or from south-westerly gales. Buildings, hedges or fences can help. Remember—besides the danger of toppling young dwarf plantings, spring winds are capable of stripping the trees' blossoms—and these are essential for them to set fruit.

On the temperature side, spring frosts are the greatest damage-doers. A few degrees dip on the thermometer may be enough to kill all or most of the blossoms. Primary precaution is to avoid valleys or low-lying sections of land. Cold air moves downhill, fills up any hollow or pocket before overflowing into upper portions. Best location, then, for fruit trees is one that is not appreciably lower than the surrounding area.

One vital note regarding how to plant dwarf fruit trees: They will stay dwarf only if planted correctly.

Because the dwarf is produced by grafting, *it must be planted with the graft-union above ground.* This is a knob at the base of the trunk and can be seen by a change in the color of the bark. Be sure this union is kept above ground. If it is placed below, the upper part of the tree (standard variety) will form its own roots—and instead of growing six to eight feet, it will shoot up 35 or 40!

Plant dwarfs in early spring if you live where winters are severe; in late fall or early spring in more moderate climates. Place them ten to 12 feet apart each way, or six to eight feet apart in rows with 15 feet between them. Pack good topsoil firmly around the roots.

Not all varieties in either standard or dwarf trees are self-fertile. In order to set fruit, some must be cross-pollinated by another variety planted

Grading nursery apple trees to show the type of root system that will produce dwarf trees (left and right) compared with the root systems of normal trees. Plant dwarfs with graft-union above ground.

nearby. With apple or pear trees it's best to plant two dwarfs of different named varieties to assure cross-pollination and get more fruit. Peaches, nectarines and apricots are usually self-fertile, as are plums which set a better crop, however, when several varieties fertilize each other.

Sour cherries, by the way, have some special advantages that make them doubly attractive for dwarf fruit planting by home gardeners. They're hardier, more disease and insect-resistant than any of the others. They are self-fruitful, do not require cross-pollination. And they're early bearing, yield fruit in June or by mid-July, starting with the third year.

PRUNING, THINNING AND MULCHING: Not much pruning is needed with the dwarfs. When planting dwarf apples, the lowest branch should be about six to 12 inches above the ground. Prune back any on the trunk below that height. After that, simply watch for water sprouts or suckers, trim off broken ends, and let the tree take its natural shape.

Against a wall or trellis, the ornamental or "espalier" dwarf fruit tree is an attractive variation. Popular in Europe where they achieve a double purpose in providing food and decoration, the espaliers are trained by special pruning, bending and tying into flat, interesting designs.

Another recommendation is that excess fruits (anything more than one fruit along each six inches of a branch) be thinned by picking off the small fruits. If not thinned, say the experts, dwarfs may set more fruit than they can carry and develop to good size and quality, and may not bloom the following year.

As with all fruit trees, mulching is ideal for dwarfs. Mulch with straw, grass clippings or other organic material, and make it deep enough around each tree to smother grass and weeds. Keep mulch a few inches away from the trunk to avoid attracting bark and root-damaging mice or rabbits. Protect trees from rodents or other animal pests by applying a shield of fine wire mesh (hardware cloth) around the trunk base.

VARIETIES: There are several varieties of most dwarf fruits available in just about every part of the country. Weather extremes and soil conditions can, of course, make a difference. Your state agricultural experiment station or county agent can advise you on the adaptability of a specific dwarf type or variety to your locality. For the most part, those fruits that grow well as standard trees in the area may also be grown as dwarfs.

Here are just a few dwarf fruit tree varieties from which you can choose.

Apples: Baldwin, Cortland, McIntosh, Red Delicious, Northern Spy, Yellow Delicious, Rome Beauty, R. I. Greening, Jonathan, Stayman Winesap, Gravenstein, Redwin Spy, Spitzenberg, Wealthy, Yellow Transparent.

Pears: Bartlett, Seckel, Kieffer, Clapp's Favorite, Duchess, Anjou, Fame, Lincoln, Flemish Beauty, Red Bartlett, Gorham, Easter, Sheldon.

Peaches: Elberta, Golden Jubilee, Red Haven, Eclipse, Rochester, Valiant, Crawfordy, Red Bird, Hiley, J. H. Hale, Belle of Georgia.

Plums: Italian Prune, Burbank, Stanley, Damson, Abundance, German Prune, Reine Claude, Red June.

Sweet Cherries: Bing, North Star, Meteor, Black Tartarian, Royal Anne, Windsor, Emperor Francis, Schmidt's Bigarreau, Hansen's Bush, Korean, Golden Bay, Lambert.

Sour Cherries: Early Richmond, Montmorency, English Morello.

Apricots: Alexander, Early Golden, Moorpak, Perfection, Riland.

Nectarines: Boston, Hunter, Napier, Newton, Sure Crop, Red Roman.

See also ORCHARD; FRUIT TREES.

FRUIT TREES, RESISTANT VARIETIES: Insects and disease are the most troublesome problems facing fruit growers. Organic techniques of soil improvement can often reduce the intensity of insect and disease infestations, but it helps to start out with varieties that thrive well in your area and which have some natural ability to ward off attackers.

Here are recommendations from agricultural experiment stations of the more resistant fruits and nut trees in these states:

ALABAMA: Pecans, Black Walnuts, Hickory, Chinese Chestnut, Filberts, Pears, Cultivated Crabapples, Mulberries, May Haws, Black Haws, Jujube, Persimmons (both American and Oriental), Bronze Elaeagnus, Blueberry, Pomegranate, PawPaws, Strawberries, Sapa Plums, Compass Cherries, Oka Cherries, Figs, and Muscadine grapes.

Varieties of pears are Seckel, LeConte, Garber, Kieffer, Baldwin, and Oriental.

CALIFORNIA: Varieties of the following kinds of fruit will do reasonably well if given normal garden care without the use of sprays for disease and insect control: Blueberry, Carissa, Chestnuts, Feijoa, Fig, Jujube, Macadamia, Olive, Papaya, Pecan, Persimmon, Pistachio, Pomegranate, Quince, Strawberry Tree (*Arbutus unedo*), and Black Walnut.

Not all of these species are immune to insect or disease problems, but most of them will do quite well with minimum attention.

FLORIDA: A few fruit trees that will do reasonably well without chemical means of controlling insects and disease are: Banana, Pineapple, Pear, Stewart Pecan, Japanese Persimmon, Sapote, Sea Grape, Catlic Guava, Mulberry and Loquats.

NEW HAMPSHIRE: Pears as a whole are very much less subject to insects and disease than are apples. The varieties we recommend are

Clapp's Favorite for early, Gorham for mid-season, and Bosc for late.

NEW MEXICO: The Arkansas Black Apple is a vigorous, disease-tolerant tree which produces a firm, thick-skinned apple. The growing season requirements for the Arkansas Black, however, are long and only in southern New Mexico will it reach proper maturity.

TENNESSEE: Pears and strawberries (resistant varieties) come as near being free from insect and disease attack as any fruits. The Orient pear is practically immune to fire blight, a bacterial disease, and in addition is resistant to leaf spots. Ayres and Morgan are two new varieties that are very resistant to these diseases. Orient and Ayres have sterile pollen and must be cross pollinated by another variety that blossoms at the same time. Many growers in Tennessee have managed these new varieties for seven or eight years without a drop of spray chemicals.

Home plantings of strawberries, using resistant varieties, rarely if ever receive any spray chemicals. Tennessee Beauty, Blakemore and Tennessee Supreme are commonly planted in Tennessee.

UTAH: In this area the native American plum, *Prunus Munsoniana,* or Pottawattamie Plum and the Stanley and Italian prune are not bothered too much by insects. The apricot and sour and sweet cherry are grown commonly without spraying.

VIRGINIA: The York apple is more resistant to scab. In our home fruit planting recommendations we also recommend the planting of early season maturing varieties such as Lodi, Williams Early Red, Summer Champion and Rambo. It is our feeling that these early season maturing varieties will become ripe before the insect and disease problems are too serious.

WEST VIRGINIA: The Seckel pear is one of the most satisfactory varieties to plant for a supply of home fruit. As you know, it thrives relatively well under neglect and is reasonably resistant to fire blight. Codling moth will not attack pears as much as it will apples, and the pear is fairly resistant to scab and other foliage diseases. The principle problem with pears in this country happens to be spring frost because of their early blooming habits. Other fruits which we sometimes recommend for home planting are Lodi, Yellow Transparent, Wealthy, and Rome for the apple varieties. Kiefer and Winter Nellis are often recommended along with the Seckel of the better pear varieties. Among cherries we like the Montmorency and Windsor, which is a sweet cherry.

See also ORCHARD; FRUIT TREES; DISEASE; INSECT CONTROL.

FRUITS FOR DRYING: *see* DRIED FRUITS AND VEGETABLES

FRUITS, GROWING INDOOR: House plants which produce edible fruit have always been of great interest. Perhaps the most commonly-grown window fruit is the Ponderosa lemon. The Ponderosa bears fruit and flowers simultaneously, which makes the plant interesting as well as attractive. The fruits last extremely well on the plant, and may be allowed to remain on it for months without danger of deterioration.

In addition to the Ponderosa lemon, which is readily available from many nurseries, several growers are now offering other citrus fruits for the indoor garden. Otaheite orange (*Citrus taitensis*) is a dwarf plant of great beauty, although its small fruits are not as useful as those of the Ponderosa lemon. The leaves are glossy, and the fragrant blossoms are pink-tinted, waxy white. Plants in five-inch pots may carry as many as a dozen oranges.

The dwarf tangerine not only has glossy foliage and fragrant flowers but the brilliantly-colored fruit is very good to eat. Kumquats, limes and other small citrus fruits are equally attractive and useful.

Figs are no novelty in the indoor garden. The flavor is completely different from the dried figs. Fig plants begin to bear very early, although more fruit is obtained from larger plants, naturally. If you find it inconvenient to handle the large plants indoors, grow them in tubs, in the basement during the winter, and on the porch or patio during the summer.

If you want to grow an edible fig, but lack the space for the standard types, try Creeping-fig (*Ficus pumila*). This is naturally a climber, and support should be furnished to which its aerial rootlets can cling. While small, the Creeping-fig has tiny, heart-shaped leaves, but when the plant is fully mature and ready to bear fruit, it sends out very large leaves.

Dwarf pomegranates are beautiful plants, evergreen, glossy-leaved, and with fragrant flowers. These plants have edible fruits, as do the Strawberry-guavas. If you want to grow another "strawberry," try the Strawberry-tree (*Arbutus unedo*); a handsome shrub with red or white flowers and small, scarlet, warty fruits.

Lady-finger bananas are edible, and the plants are attractive. Many other varieties are equally decorative as foliage specimens, and some mature at only three feet.

Although tomatoes and peppers are classed as vegetables, by many people, they are in fact fruits. In their native tropical habitat, both are perennials. You can grow the ordinary "bell" peppers for years indoors, in eight-inch pots, and have them remain in good health, bearing flowers and fruit, for fresh salad garnish. Tomato plants intended for indoor growing should be potted in the spring in large pots, using plenty of rough compost in the soil. Fasten a three-foot trellis to the pot, and plunge the pot outdoors during the summer. Bring it indoors in late summer, treat it to your sunniest window and a daily shower-bath. If your winter is sunny, you may have ripe fruit for Christmas.

Growing fruit indoors can be a lot of fun, and more often than not, you harvest a reward for your gardening efforts. But to grow fruit, or anything else, indoors with the maximum success, you must apply the same gardening know-how that you use in your outdoor gardening.

CULTURE: First, remember that potted plants cannot send their roots very far in search of food; it must be brought to them. This is done by potting in compost-enriched soil. (Use acid-type soil for acid-loving plants, alkaline for the others.) Be sure to incorporate generous amounts of compost in the soil to be used for repotting; or, if repotting is not indicated but a "boost" is, wash out the top inch of soil and replace it with a humus-rich material.

Next to soil, the most important point in indoor gardening is exposure. All plants need good light for best growth; flowering plants need at least three hours sunlight a day; and fruiting plants need all the sun they can get. Some fruit can be expected in a partially sunny location, but heaviest bearing will result from full sun. Along with exposure, temperatures are important, and contrary to what you may have heard, all house plants do not need hot-house temperatures. Fifty-five to 60° at night, with 65 to 70 during the day, usually provide ideal growing climates. The night drop in temperature is important; it allows the plant to rest and mature the growth made during the day.

Watering can literally kill any plant, if done improperly. Too much is worse than not enough, although no plant should ever be allowed to suffer from lack of moisture. It is best to keep the air as humid as possible, then give water amply at the roots whenever the surface soil begins to dry. This is better than giving small amounts of water more frequently. Too, water-spray the top growth at regular intervals, to increase humidity, to keep the plants clean, and to discourage insect pests. *See also* HOUSE PLANTS.

FUCHSIA: (*Conagraceae*) Fuchsias are, to a great extent, shade-loving plants. A few varieties will stand full sun, but their roots must be shaded or well mulched.

Fuchsias are started by both seed and cuttings. The seed route is at times very disappointing. However, the hybridizers follow this system to obtain new varieties. For the average grower try the cutting method. In February cut or prune back, leaving two nodes or buds on each stem. Soon the sap starts up and the new green growth comes out. These are called cuttings. When they are about three inches long, take them from the parent plant, having prepared a box of ½ coarse sand and ½ peat moss. Insert the cuttings about one half their length in this mixture. Remove all leaves where they would be in the ground. They root in about fourteen days. Try to lift them out of the soil. If you feel a pull on them, they are rooted, if not, wait a few days. After they are fully rooted, lift them and plant them in three inch pots. The soil for growing fuchsias is composed of one part of leaf mold, one part compost or sand, one part well rotted cow manure, one part peat moss.

Keep plants moist at all times. A plant started in spring will be a beautiful blooming plant by August.

Fuchsias are fast growers and little pigs for eating, so twice a month, give them a feeding of *"cow tea."* Put five pounds of cow manure in two gallons of water. Keep well stirred for two or three days. Then take a quart of *cow tea* and add to two gallons of water and stir.

You will find most any variety you wish in both hanging baskets and up-rights. You can espalier fuchsias to form a beautiful effect. They can also be trained as a tree. The basic colors are red and purple; however, the newer varieties are red and white, pink and white, all white, all red, all pink, and some so deep a purple they look almost blue.—*Merriel Teaney.*

See also FERTILIZER; SHRUBS, FLOWERING.

FUMIGATION, SOIL: Fumigation is a standard commercial greenhouse practice used to combat insects and diseases. Chemicals usually used are carbon disulphide, hydrocyanic acid, calcium cyanide and paradichlorobenzene, along with nicotine preparations. Fumigation is not a recommended practice in the organic program because of its harmful effect on beneficial soil life.

A practice long used in Germany and more recently in this country is to "fumigate" the greenhouse with smoke from burning oak leaves. Growers find that this is an effective, safe way to control ants, aphids and small mites. Wet down the leaves first; place them on straw and newspaper which is set on fire. The greenhouse should be tightly closed to allow the smoke to accumulate. A half hour of this treatment has been found effective.

FUNGI: *see* FUNGUS

FUNGICIDE: Any of a number of chemical preparations employed to destroy fungi or inhibit the growth of the spores or hyphae. Among chemicals used in the preparation of fungicides are various forms of sulphur, copper, mercury, formaldehyde, and minor elements; none of which are recommended in the organic method. *See also* FUNGUS; SPRAYS; FERTILIZERS, ARTIFICIAL.

FUNGUS: Any of a group of thallophytic plants comprising the molds, mildews, rusts, smuts, mushrooms, toadstools, etc. These growths are destitute of chlorophyll and reproduce mainly by means of asexual spores. The world of the fungi includes the large woody bracket or shelf fungi seen on trees, mushrooms and toadstools, as well as the realm of molds, mildews and yeasts. Many plant diseases, such as wheat rust, corn smut and cedar apple galls are fungus infections. Technically, bacteria and viruses are also in the fungus group. However, most fungi are basically valuable and essential to the processes of life.

We are familiar with fungi which cause plant diseases, food spoilage, and human and animal infections such as athlete's foot and ring worm. We also know that fungi are responsible for rotting damage in moist wooden structures, mildew destruction of cotton cloth, and even death from poisonous mushrooms. But despite these undesirable attributes, most fungi are of considerable value, so much so that it is doubtful whether life on earth could continue as we know it if all fungi were suddenly to die.

To learn something about them, let us begin with their spores. These are the microscopic seeds of fungi.

Without knowing it, you have probably seen them by the millions as green or blue powdery blotches on rotted oranges or in Roquefort cheese.

Fungus spores are fascinating. For one thing they are produced in astronomical numbers. One giant puffball fungus about five feet by four feet in size was estimated to contain over seven trillion spores! A particular bracket fungus shed almost two and a half pounds of spores in twenty days! (Each of these spores, by the way, weighed about 5/1,000,000,000,-000 or five-trillionths of one ounce.)

One interesting fungus which grows on the dung of herbivorus animals actually aims its spore-bearing "branches" toward bright light and shoots its spores in that direction with a propelling force of approximately 82 pounds per square inch. Some fungi shoot their spores out at a rate of 20 feet per second to a vertical height of six feet and as far as eight feet horizontally.

In some cases, thousands of spores are ejected at the same instant as a "puff of smoke" and at the same time the fungus gives off a distinctly audible hissing noise, like the fizzing sound of a carbonated beverage. Still other fungi get rid of their spores by jack-in-the-box devices, or shoot them out in closed sacks which burst like rockets in the air to liberate the spores individually.

Fungi Reproduction: Some fungi have sex while others are completely sexless. Therefore, spores may be produced as a means of sexual reproduction or in a purely asexual (sex-free) manner. But either way, the spores behave as seeds which under suitable conditions develop into fungi. This may be even thirty years later, since spores have been known to develop after that long a time.

The different kinds of fungi are in themselves fascinating. Some so-called slime-molds actually crawl around as slimy masses on decaying vegetation, and literally feast on bacteria and other microbes. Certain fungi spend much of their lives in the water. Others grow as looped threads and use themselves as living lassos to capture protozoa (one-celled animals) and microscopic nematode and other worms which they then devour. Some fungi prefer an insect diet and specialize in growing on and killing the grub or larval forms of insects in the soil. Even arsenic compounds are handled by many molds which actually convert these materials into poisonous gases that have caused the death of people who inhale them.

Activity: Certain fungi can do such interesting things as move about, align themselves with the direction of light, produce noises, and capture microbes and worms. A few even produce light. On a dark night, some mushroom species can be seen glowing so brightly that it is possible to photograph them by their own light!

One group of mushrooms when mature dissolves their gills into a black inky fluid. The yellow or white inner flesh of other mushrooms quickly turns blue, red, or brown when broken open and exposed to the air. Some fungi live only on the manure of herbivorous animals. Others grow only on burnt-over ground.

So, these are the fungi and their remarkable attributes. These are the creatures which form the very important mycorrhizal associations with orchids, evergreens, and other plants. These are the organisms which help convert rock material into valuable agricultural soils and which contribute to the manufacture of humus.

Fungi are also active in decomposing dead vegetation and animal bodies. In this way they restore minerals to the soil for further use. (Just think, what would happen if organic matter didn't rot but piled up from year to year!)—*Dr. Albert Schatz.*

See also MICROORGANISM.

FUNKIA: *see* LILY

FUSARIUM ROT: Fusarium rot is a disease that produces very small, reddish-brown spots with water-soaked margins on the corms and lesions on the husks, causing them to become discolored and brittle. If the storage conditions are right—high humidity and high temperature—the rot progresses rapidly, producing irregular, circular spots from $\frac{1}{8}$ inch to one inch in diameter. By planting time the whole corm may become a black, worthless mummy.

Often there is no external evidence of fusarium rot on unbrushed corms, even though these may be completely mummied under the husk. The most important diagnostic character of fusarium rot is the existence of more or less concentric ridges or rings in the lesions. These rings are not an absolute proof of the presence of the disease because they are often absent, so that there is a possibility of confusing fusarium rot with dry rot and hard rot unless a microscopic examination is made. If corms attacked by this disease are planted, it might happen that there may be vacant spaces in a row of plant.

Corms that are even moderately infected may produce stunted growth, and rarely produce flowers, because they cannot develop a healthy root system. They are usually attacked by fungi that live on dead or dying material, and thus die prematurely. *See also* DISEASE.

G

GAILLARDIA: *see* BLANKET-FLOWER

GARBAGE FOR COMPOST: Garbage is a neglected source of compost which is particularly rich in nitrogen and other nutrients essential to soil building and plant growth.

The individual gardener should compost his kitchen wastes whether he lives in a rural area or a suburb. In either case, animal-proof bins should be used to avoid the committing of nuisances. If the gardener lives in a comparatively densely settled community, local statutes should be consulted.

Commercially-built anaerobic bins are available to the suburban gardener. These are moderate in cost and are designed to hold six month's garbage, producing a good quality compost.

If the local situation permits, the gardener can build his own compost bin. It need not be anaerobic but it should be animal-proof. To start his joint garbage disposal-composting program, he merely dumps his garbage in it daily. It is advisable to add a little soil, spoiled hay or straw to the garbage, covering each day's layer of kitchen waste.

Some gardeners bury their garbage on next year's planting sites, thus rotating their garden and leaving some land "resting" in anticipation of next year's crop. They take the precaution of burying the kitchen waste deep enough to escape detection by scavenging animals.

Still another course is open to the homesteader. He can build an enclosure of cement blocks, high and strong enough to be animal proof. Here he can dump his garbage, permitting it to break down partially. From time to time he removes some of this highly nitrogenous material, adding it to new compost heaps composed mostly of vegetable manures. In this way he is assured of a steady supply of activating material for his composting program. *See also* COMPOST; VEGETABLE GARDENING (TRENCHING).

GARDEN BOOKS: *see* BOOKS FOR ORGANIC GARDENERS AND FARMERS

GARDEN CALENDAR: It is manifestly difficult, if not impossible, to work out a planting schedule and program of activity with any degree of close accuracy. But the wise and observant gardener will read the seasonal signs and follow the monitions of the weather forecaster and old-timer alike. Despite all calculated precautions, he will make mistakes, will get caught by early and late frosts and his plantings will suffer accordingly.

To hold these down to a bare minimum, this GARDEN CALENDAR has been arranged according to region, as shown on the accompanying map. Separate monthly calendars appear under each geographic heading.

Any discussion of the weather and the havoc its vagaries can cause is incomplete without reference to the organic system of composting and mulching. While no system can be perfect, the organic method follows a pattern established aeons ago by Nature; that of replenishing and protecting the soil with organic matter.

Experimentation and observation show that the soil has a greater tolerance of all plant life when it contains plenty of humus. Plants thrive better in such a soil, disease is held to a minimum and insect pests are better resisted by sound healthy plants.

But, of prime importance here, the weather itself can cause less damage to plant life and the soil when these are guarded by mulch and compost. This protective layer of organic matter acts as a shield, moderating and conditioning the severity of the wind, the rain and the hot summer sun.

It will be advisable, then, for the

careful gardener (and reader) to keep this significant fact in mind when consulting the following GARDEN CALENDAR.

The North and East

JANUARY

At this low ebb in the gardener's year, there are still some things to be done, especially in preparation for next season. Tender evergreens should be protected now with burlap screens in time to defend against the extreme cold to come.

Orchard. Scions of fruit trees for

from drafts or chilling on loosely-insulated window sills. If plants are in the dormant season, water less often than in growing periods. If some house plants have spent the summer in the garden, they are used to a rather high degree of humidity . . . probably greater than that of the artificially heated home. Spray plants regularly with water, on both sides of leaves. A fine mist is best for this purpose. African violets can stand a limited amount of sunlight during the winter, when outside light is limited.

Other Activities. Start growing mushrooms this month. With spare

use in making grafts later may be cut now, tied in bundles, and stored in a cool place. Ornamental trees with branches infested with borers may have all dead and infested wood removed. Clean cuts should be made flush at the juncture of an infested limb and the main artery.

Flowers. Put up gloxinias late in the month. Allow buds of hyacinths to develop in the dark—otherwise, the flowers will be short-stemmed.

Vegetables. Rhubarbs can be forced quickly in the basement at this time of year, as may roots of French endive and several other vegetables.

House Plants. Keep house plants

room in a cellar, shed, barn, or under the greenhouse benches, this enjoyable venture can be profitable, too.

FEBRUARY

Flowers. Set potted bulbs in a sunny window for early spring forcing. To get a head start, sow in flats snapdragons, delphiniums, penstemons, asters, ever-blooming begonias, Shasta daisies, canterbury bells, and many other annuals. For seeds sown indoors, use prepared potting soil or bring in some mature compost, mix it with an equal part of leaf mold, and add plenty of sand. Some people use straight compost, and some use only leaf mold. Repot non-blooming house plants; don't let them get potbound. Bulbs in storage should be looked over for possible rotting. Place unusuable ones deep in the compost pile. If bulbs appear shrivelled, the storage place is too dry. Start cuttings of chrysanthemums, making sure that the soil mixture is low in nitrogen, to prevent too fast and resulting "leggy" growth.

Vegetables. During the month, in hotbeds, cold frames, greenhouses, and indoors, sow seeds of early cabbage, cauliflower, celery, tomatoes, radishes, peppers. This pleasant pre-spring chore will bring fine rewards in spring, and will save the expense of buying many nursery plants.

Orchard. Check the orchard mulch. If the weather is mild, apple and pear trees may be pruned now. To prevent disease, make sure no fruit is lying beneath trees. Collect and bury in the compost pile.

Other Activities. Garden tools need a thorough cleaning and mending before the hectic spring season starts. Do it now! Repair cold frames and hotbeds—they should be ready for heavy use next month.

MARCH

Flowers. Keep the spring flowering bulbs covered as long as possible. If not kept cold, they may flower too soon, and the blossoms may be harmed by frost. Uncover perennial beds if weather permits, and place the litter between the rows to serve as a mulch. In warmer regions, sow sweet peas, poppies, larkspur, mignonette and calendula, if soil can be worked.

Orchard. Many fruit trees can be planted this month, including dwarfs. These miniature trees which provide giant fruits can fill that empty spot in the landscape. Finish off pruning left over from last month. Also cut scions of fruit trees and bury them in sand. Next month is grafting time.

Vegetables. Sow asparagus seed or set out roots, and give the bed a good

application of pulverized phosphate and potash rock. Cabbage and cauliflower seed may be sown now in sheltered spot, if not already in hotbed. Also set out horseradish, onions and rhubarb. Dig any parsnips which have over-wintered in ground before the tops get too high. Early potatoes may also be planted, and in hotbeds, sow seed of garden sage and tomatoes.

Lawns. Top-dress lawns with compost. If there is moss on the lawn, there is a lack of nutriments; spread on a liberal application of screened compost over the affected areas or over the entire lawn.

APRIL

Flowers. It's time to set out lily-of-the-valley clumps, planting them so the tops of the pips are level with the soil surface. When the weather has settled, set out pansies, forget-me-nots, Canterbury bells, foxglove, Japanese lanterns. Gladiolus plantings can be made in the latter part of the month, and can be repeated at two week intervals until well into the summer. This is the month to put out many varieties of perennials and other ornamentals. Check planting details in catalogs, or on seed packets. Spread compost over the perennial borders to give them a good start. Rock fertilizers, including greensand, will add vital nutrients and trace elements to the compost, the benefits of which will be noticed for a long time to come.

Vegetables. Many vegetables may be planted now . . . which ones, of course, depend upon the specific varieties and the particular location. Among sure bets are the very hardies, such as asparagus, horseradish, parsnip, rhubarb, salsify, and winter onion. Varieties recommended for sowing or planting around April tenth include some varieties of asparagus, beets, cabbage, lettuce, mustard and parsley. Some peas may also be sown now. If tomatoes were sown last month, they may be transplanted into beds or boxes. Transplant cabbage plants for an early crop. Transplant onion plants from hot beds to open ground.

Other Activities. Top-dress all bush and cane fruits with compost, fortified with pulverized rock phosphate and, where easily accessible, granulated seaweed. Grafting may be done as soon as buds show signs of swelling. Drain and clean lily pools, and put in hardy water lilies now. Reseed bare spots in the lawn, and feed a lawn mixture of screened compost and rock powders. Also check climbing vine plants to be sure staples have not pulled away or rotted through. Fruit trees which have been badly girdled by the feeding of mice, should be bridge grafted now.

MAY

Flowers. There are many beautiful varieties helping to welcome warm May but there are some things to be done in the flower garden. Disbud the peonies for larger blooms. Since they are heavy feeders, give them a top dressing of bone meal or well-rotted manure mixed with compost. For pink hydrangeas add a handful of lime to the soil around the plant. A heavy dose of acid peat moss will provide blue flowers. Water hydrangeas with liquid manure while they are in bud to increase the size of the blossoms. Sweetpeas may be planted. Add bone meal at the rate of five pounds per 100 square feet. Before transplanting house plants to the garden, they should be exposed to outdoor conditions for hardening. Chrysanthemum cuttings made by mid-May will do well in six inch pots and make very satisfactory house plants for fall. Seeds of biennials and perennials for flowering next year may be planted the latter part of May. Work compost into the soil together with pulverized potash and phosphate rock. Empty places in the border may be filled with sowings of larkspur, candytuft, poppies, marigolds or nasturtiums.

Vegetables. Beans, corn, cucumbers, melons, potatoes and squash may be safely planted in open ground in mid-May, assuming the ground is not too cold. If the season is mild, early corn may be planted during the first week. Add plenty of compost and a pound each of pulverized phosphate rock and potash rock to every ten square feet of soil. Harden off tomato plants and plan to set them out the beginning of June. Work in phosphate and potash rock; tomatoes require little nitrogen.

Other Activities. Clean out and prepare the lily pool for the coming season. This year, try to add some unusual water plants in addition to the usual lilies.

JUNE

Flowers. Now is the time to sow seeds for next year's perennials and biennials—they'll get a much better start now for a better showing next season. Cultivate rose beds thoroughly, and water them with liquid manure or liquid compost. Dahlia roots may still be planted, and set stakes for the dahlias at the same time so that roots will not be injured by staking later. Perennial seeds may be sown either in the cold frame or in the open garden. Preparation of the beds should be quite thorough with a good mixture of compost, bone meal and, if necessary, lime. For shady places plant tuberous begonias, gloxinias and primroses. Potted palms and ferns may be put out, buried to the rims of the pots in such spots. Annuals are better planted in the garden than in flats. It is not too late to put in zinnias, marigolds, balsam, portulaca and other heat-resistant flowers. For transplanting, pick an overcast day and shade until plants are established.

Vegetables. Plant seed for late cabbage, cauliflower and broccoli first week in June at the latest, to be transplanted in mid-July. Sweet corn planted early this month will make rapid growth, and could be followed by a mid-month planting. Plant beans, beets, carrots, kohlrabi and turnips for a late crop, digging in one-half pound each of phosphate and potash rock for each ten square feet. Thin root crops planted earlier. They need ample room. Use the tops of beets and turnips for salads. Generally, they contain more vitamins than the more popular root parts, and they taste good, too. Peppers should be kept well watered, but not kept too moist. If the fruits have not set, overwatering may produce too much leaf growth.

Other Activities. After the spring-flowering shrubs have made their showing, prune moderately, removing some of the old wood, also the climbing roses and ramblers after their flowering. On ramblers, remove at the base the canes which produced flowers during the spring. Untie climbers, separate the canes, and cut down one or two of the older ones. Return the tropical fish to the pool and begin to plant tropical water lilies if the water temperature stays up around 75°. Canes of blackberries and black and purple raspberries should be "topped" when new growth reaches 26 to 30 inches in height. When shoots are permitted to grow unchecked during the entire growing season, they become tall, unproductive, spindly, and difficult to handle during the fruiting season the following year. Gather wooden stakes for the flower and vegetable gardens, getting suitable scraps at a lumber mill, or at an old house being torn down.

JULY

Flowers. Shear off dying blooms of lilac and rhododendron while conserving the plant's strength. Remove tips of chrysanthemums. Remove at ground level the canes of climbing roses which have finished blooming. Divide spring-flowering perennials, including iris and golden alyssum. Glads planted now will be appreciated in fall. Remove the seed pods of rock plants, and don't let weeds go to seed in beds. Water regularly sweet peas and cornflowers. Cut back delphini-

ums, bachelor's button and phlox for fall flowering. There's still time to plant many annuals, including lupines, balsam, portulaca, zinnias and mignonette, including pansies—they'll make a colorful fall.

Vegetables. Fill up empty spaces in the garden with second plantings. Beets, carrots, beans, chard, endive, kale, kohlrabi, lettuce, broccoli, Brussels sprouts, late cabbage, cauliflower, late beets, celery, turnips, radishes, spinach and others may be planted now. Check the number of frostless days left. Dig in plenty of compost for each planting. Mulch to preserve moisture, keep down weeds, and protect soil from temperature changes. A mulch will also keep ripened vegetables and fruits from rotting on the ground.

AUGUST

Vegetables. Make sure the mulch is in place, especially for plants like tomatoes, cucumbers and melons, whose fruits come into contact with the ground. There's still time for second plantings: turnips, spinach, lettuce, beets, radishes, chard, endive, kale, mustard, winter onions and late kohlrabi. Check the date of maturity on the seed packet against the average date of first frost.

Flowers. Remove any sucker growth on hybrid roses which might be springing up from the ground. Divide iris clumps; dig up and transplant the rhizomes a foot apart. Also disbud dahlias and chrysanthemums. The size of the blooms will justify the August work.

Other Activities. The biggest job this month is the summer pruning of the fruit trees. Cut out any water sprouts (suckers on upper branches), and prune away branches which have poor shape and poorly colored fruit. Make sure the mulch is about a foot away from the trunk, to discourage field mice, and keep a circle of crushed stone between the mulch and the trunk. Only the most strong-willed mice will bother to burrow through the stones. If rain has been sparse lately, be sure to keep the lawn grass up to two inches or higher. Now is a good time to set out strawberries. When planting runners, work plenty of organic matter deep into the soil. Plants should start bearing next spring, but the big yield should come the following season.

September

Flowers. Time to plant bulbs—narcissus, hyacinths, crocus. The narcissus family (including daffodil and jonquil) should be planted about four inches deep in well-spaded soil. A little manure placed about two inches below bulbs, and bone meal and wood ashes mixed in with topsoil, should give bulbs a good start in spring. Crocus should be planted in clumps, about two inches deep. These spunky little flowers will be welcomed early next spring, when they push aside winter's dull days and pioneer a new season. Chrysanthemums should be boosted with compost water, and buds should be pinched out for large blooms. Most perennials should be divided and transplanted . . . it gives them a chance to become established before winter.

Vegetables. There's still time to plant radishes, corn salad, mustard spinach (for overwintering), and turnips. Rootcrops can be left in the ground until serious freezes start. Parsnips must be exposed to a slight frost to become best tasting. Asparagus bed should be mulched. In the cold frame, you may sow parsley, lettuce, spinach and chives.

Other Activities. Parsley and other herbs for winter-growing indoors will do better if potted this month and left in a cold frame or cool cellar until December. Pick grapes before they get soft . . . allow them to ripen in a cool, dark place. The compost pile should be building up with waste materials from the garden. In case of a dry Indian summer, be sure to keep the heap moist. Put up some screened soil for potting mixtures for winter and spring flats, and for house plants.

October

Flowers. Dig up dahlias, glads, montbretias, cannas, tuberoses and tuberous begonias before the first frost. Leave a little soil clinging to each while they ripen. Store each variety in a separate container in a cool, dry place protected from mice. Be sure to label carefully to avoid mistakes next spring. Now is the time to re-make flower beds. Pull out annuals and divide perennials flowering in spring and early summer so good root growth can be made before the ground freezes. Mulching the soil after planting divided perennial plants or seedlings will hold soil warmth and allow a longer time for root growth. Set out most spring-flowering bulbs. Try camassias with tulips, and fritillarias for new combinations. Plant daffodils before October 15. Hill up soil around established roses. Mulch lily-of-the-valley with any good organic material. Stake mums, even though they are flowering, so that the stems will be straight and the blooms clean. Cut back canes of roses so they don't whip. Tie up vines and loose climbers against wind damage. It's time to sow hardy annuals such as larkspur and sweet peas.

Vegetables. Harvest all remaining vegetables before frost. Tomatoes, squashes, pumpkins, peppers, and ornamental gourds are damaged by the first frost. Give rhubarb a liberal application of manure, compost, or kelp.

Cleanup. Close the season with a thorough cleanup to destroy weeds and control pests and diseases. Compost weeds and discarded plants. Shred woody stalks before composting. Clean out coldframes, line with dry leaves, hay or straw. Close sash and cover with manure or earth. Bulbs for winter forcing can stay here until Christmas time.

Other Activities. Early this month, sow cover crops for the nut orchard. Many nuts are now ready for harvest. Those ready for picking can easily be shaken down with a long pole with a hook on the end. This is also the time to prune nut trees. Mow newly planted lawn when grass is about two inches high and reseed bare spots in old lawn.

NOVEMBER

Now is a good time to incorporate compost and green matter into the soil. It will blend in with the soil over winter. Rotary till the material into the garden soil and let it rough surfaced until spring.

Clean-up Time. Gather up and add leaves to compost pile . . . or shred up on location with one of the new rotary mowers. A few passes of the mower will shred leaves fine enough to sift in between the blades of grass. Turn under the last of the vegetable remains. Test soil. If acid, add a layer of lime. If lacking in nutrients, prepare to get some organic materials to add now or in spring. Remove a little of the water from the fish pond to allow for expansion when freezing. Hardy goldfish will take care of themselves over winter. Don't mulch strawberry bed until after first hard freeze. Remove nests of tent caterpillars and cocoons attached to branches with a stiff brush or broom. Save the egg masses of the praying mantis. Learn to distinguish between the cocoons of both. Get winter protective mulching materials together now. Hay, buckwheat hulls, peat, and leaves are good. Mix some potting soil now, before the ground freezes.

Vegetables. Heap manure on rhubarb when the weather gets cold to stay. Sow radish and cauliflower in frames.

Flowers. Standing puddles of water can kill perennials. After a November rain, check the run-off and if necessary, dig little drainage ditches. Don't cover the plants until late November, when they are safely dormant.

Orchard. Prop up any weak limbs on fruit and nut trees for protection against possible ice storms towards the end of the month. Cut out any black spots on stone fruit trees to prevent further infestation. Grapevines may be pruned now, but most growers wait until spring.

DECEMBER

Remove heavy, wet snow from hedges—but not if ice has formed—otherwise the weight of the snow may break the branches. Mulch shrubs and trees with shredded leaves. Hold them down with branches. Mulch acid-loving plants with pine needles or peat. Set evergreens and berried branches in window boxes. They can be watered when necessary and will last all winter.

Flowers. Remove, climbing roses from their supports, the canes laid carefully on the ground and covered lightly with earth. Bush roses, on the other hand, should be hilled up for about a foot over the crown, and a mulch should be added. Tea roses and hybrid teas may be successfully wintered in cold frames. Place them on their sides, cover with earth and, in severe weather, add blankets of leaves. This is the time to look at potted bulbs in the cellar. If full of roots, they are ready for forcing. Mulch pansies with straw or leaves, now that the weather has been cold for some time and the plants have hardened themselves to the rigors of winter.

Vegetables. Sow radish and cauliflower in frames. Mulch strawberry plants as soon as the ground freezes. Most people use straw, but at famous Malabar Farm, home of the late Louis Bromfield, they use sawdust with success.

Orchard. Grapevines may be pruned now, but many growers wait until early spring. A hint on discouraging field mice: tamp down the snow under the branch to crush burr.

The South

JANUARY

Flowers. Dogwood, redbud, rhododendron, camellias, and native azaleas may be planted this month. Most losses in plantings of these five large-growing beauties occur because it's so easy to plant them too deeply. The tap root must go down, but the feeder roots must grow just under the surface of the soil. For this reason, they require a heavy mulch at all times, and must never even be scratched around.

grow crops that withstand a spell of cold weather. Rhubarb does well only in the higher altitudes of the upper South. Plant now.

Other Activities. January is the month to get scions (before the sap rises) and graft pink dogwood, camellias, fruit trees, etc. In camellias it is most important to bank the soil up around the graft, invert a large painted jar over the graft, keep moist at all times. Remove jar when two-inch growth is obtained on scion. Four-o'clocks make good shading for tender

Check to be sure they don't settle and raise with the trunk in a depression. Last call for planting sprng flowering bulbs like hyacinths, tulips, ixias, and the Dutch bulbs. Many of the hardy bulbs can be planted: regale, speciosum, tiger, Philippine, shuksan, auratum, and others. With rocks below bulb for perfect drainage, sand around the bulb itself, plus compost and a sunny location, they will remain for years and increase in beauty with each season.

Vegetables. Plant Bermuda onion plants, onion sets, cabbage plants, rape, mustard, turnips, and carrots. Garden peas may be planted in mid-South, using only the smooth-seeded varieties for early planting. In lower South, many more vegetables may be planted. Gardens well-fortified with humus will

growth, though must not be planted too close and must be removed at the end of summer.

FEBRUARY

Flowers. For all-around satisfaction, one can hardly select a more desirable ornamental plant than the hibiscus. It is one of the easiest to grow in the South, and never tires of blooming. This beautiful plant can be started readily from cuttings, preferably taken from the lower branches. Many other flowers can be started this month, depending on the locality. Among these are alyssum, calendula, candytuft, godetia, lupine, nigella, poppies, and sweet peas, all for outdoor sowing. Transplant seedlings of foxgloves, Shasta daisies, and others previously started.

Vegetables. Many vegetables can be seeded now, including beets, broccoli, cabbage, carrot, cauliflower, chard, endive, kale, kholrabi, lettuce, leek, onion, parsley, peas, potatoes, radish, spinach, turnip. Start plants of asparagus, beets, cabbage, cauliflower, leek, lettuce, onion and rhubarb. Check the local frost date. Cucumbers respond to heavily composted soils, doing away with fusarium wilt and being free from insect pests. Make a hole the depth of a shovel, and a foot or more in diameter, and fill with compost. Mix fine soil and compost deep enough to cover the seed. Allow three plants to the hill.

Other Activities. This is a good month to trim and shape a prize boxwood. Set out peaches, pears, plums, persimmons, mulberry, fig, and pecan trees.

MARCH

This is the big planting month. Just about everything goes in, from cockscomb to mustard, from balsam to beans, all the annual flowers and kitchen garden.

Flowers. Look after the gardenias. Give them a dressing of compost to prepare them for the enormous quantity of blooms that begin opening up in May. Scarlet runner beans, classed among the flowers, can also be used as a food. Crape Myrtles may still be planted. The more they are cut back, the more profusely they will bloom. Try these for background plants: palms, elephant's ear, ricepaper plant, castor bean, globe artichoke and tall goldenrod. Bulbs need attention now. Divide and reset tuberoses from two to three inches deep. Put amaryllis bulbs in partial shade. Oxalis bulbs set in March will make a fine border for beds. Plant gladiolus bulbs every two weeks from now until July.

Vegetables. Set out tomatoes, eggplant and peppers along Gulf Coast and in Florida when danger of frost is past. In upper South the hardiest of vegetables may be planted: beets, kale, carrots, kohlrabi, mustard, smooth varieties of English peas, radishes, spinach and turnips. In Middle South, add collards, blackeye peas, lettuce, parsley, Swiss chard and Irish potatoes. In lower South, English peas, Irish potatoes and onion sets may still be planted. Also, all kinds of bush and pole beans, limas or butterbeans, squash, cucumbers, cantaloupe, pumpkin and watermelons.

Lawns. Evergreen lawn grass mixtures and Kentucky bluegrass may be planted now. Do not plant Burmuda grass until June. Centipede grass may be planted now. Sprigging centipede grass may be done now and continued through June provided it is kept watered during dry spells. Mow winter rye grass regularly.

Other Activities. Put up birdhouses, baths, and feeding stations to encourage flocks of feathered friends to live nearby. Get a hive of bees to help pollination.

APRIL

Flowers. This is the month to plant all flower seeds. Dahlias may be planted now. Tubers left in the ground all winter should be taken up, divided, and replanted immediately, before sprouts begin to show. Use a knife to divide, taking care to have a portion of the stem on each division, to be sure to have an eye or bud from which the sprout comes. Tubers that break off without an eye will not sprout. After preparing the hole with compost in the bottom, set stake firmly, for later support; lay tuber on side, four to six inches deep, with neck close to stake; cover two inches deep and fill hole as shoots develop. A generous helping of granite dust will give strength to stalks. Magnolias are best moved when in active growth. They like a deep, rich soil with lots of humus and plenty of water—through the second summer after planting. An acid soil with a pH of about 5.5 is best. Feed bulbs, roses, shrubs, and the lawn this month, using compost and natural pulverized rocks. Let the foliage on bulbs ripen and turn yellow before pulling it off and composting. The growing period after blooming is the time next year's blooms are set, and if cut down, the bulbs will "go blind." Foliage may be tied up for neatness, and to allow rain to get to bulbs if the season is dry; if wet, to keep it from rotting. Give pansies an application of compost and peat moss.

Vegetables. In sections where an Easter freeze is usual, plant tomatoes, peppers, eggplants, cauliflower, onions, celery, sweet potatoes, and cabbage plants immediately after the freeze. In frost-free sections, plant anytime during the month. Make sure soil is workable before planting.

Other Activities. Try mulching strawberries with pine needles during the harvest season. Work the needles up under the leaves to keep the berries off the soil, to avoid washing sand from them later. There's nothing like a good mulch to keep the weeds down, and to conserve moisture too.

MAY

Flowers. Time to plant cosmos, Shasta daisy, gaillardia, globe amaranth, petunia, zinnia. These old favorites require little care, but will respond gratefully to applications of compost or other organic fertilizers.

Vegetables. For better health, more tasty vegetables and economical living, grow ample garden produce for the family. Planting must be done immediately for summer crops. Be generous with compost, and when plants are four to five inches high, apply a mulch at least three inches deep. Use old sawdust, hay, leaves, pine needles or rocks to hold moisture, lessen weed growth, and cut down on labor. Practically all of the vegetable seeds may be planted in May, including heat-loving ones, such as okra, squash, watermelons, cucumbers, cantaloupes, summer spinach, and second plantings of corn. Set tomato plants four to six inches deep. Pinch out suckers that

develop between the main stalk and the branches while they are quite small. This will prevent them from utilizing plant food and making too much foliage. Cut okra pods before they mature, so the plants will continue to bear all season. Plant in wide rows with stalks every two or three feet. Use compost liberally. Cauliflower, celery, cucumbers, pumpkins, cowpeas, gourds, spinach and crowder peas may be planted now; also vegetable plants, such as sweet potato slips, tomatoes, eggplants, collards, peppers, and cabbage for fall crops.

JUNE

Soil should be tested now. With a sandy soil especially, watch out for potash and phosphorus deficiencies. Replenish the mulch around shrubs and perennials; apply to garden and flower beds around new plants. Water for the garden's sake, don't merely sprinkle down the dust. This shallow watering method encourages roots to force their way up to the top inch or two of soil—the depth to which the water soaked. To do an adequate job, place the hose so that it shoots a diffused spray over one area for about an hour; then change its position. Better yet, take time now to install an automatic sprinkler system; it need not be elaborate, they come in many price ranges. Don't water during early evening, before foliage can dry off for the night; early evening watering encourages rot and disease. Best of all is to lay a good mulch to preserve what rain may come.

Flowers. Feed roses, dahlias and mums now, and work into the upper inch of soil under the mulch. Also make use of locally available mulching material such as cotton wastes, cottonseed hulls and dehydrated sugar cane pulp. Bigger phlox heads will result when the number of stalks is reduced. Feed well with compost and supply plenty of water to roots. Water on the foliage will cause mildew. Azaleas, magnolias, jasmine, tea olive, camellias, climbing roses and many other plants may be layered now. Bend a branch down to earth and cut or crack it near a joint. Cover with thin layer of good soil and place a rock or limb over the joint to hold it down. By next spring sever the rooted plant from its parent and transplant. When iris has finished blooming, large clumps may be dug, separated and replanted anytime from now until fall. Inspect carefully for borers and cut out and remove from bed any damaged or rotted parts. Use compost, well-mixed, in iris bed and plant rhizomes just under the surface. Do not mulch iris, as they rot easily.

Vegetables. In harvested rows, plants of tomato, eggplant, sweet potato, and pepper can be set out in the middle and upper South. Sow seed of bush and pole lima beans, pole snap beans, crowder peas, blackeye peas, pumpkin, cantaloupe, watermelon and sweet corn. In the lower South, try planting collard, eggplant, mustard, okra, peanuts, peppers, rutabaga, New Zealand spinach, sunflowers, turnips, sweet potatoes, pole snap beans, and pole lima beans.

Other activities. Take care of the compost heap this month. Water if it has dried out, and keep adding material. Warm weather is breakdown time, but the bacteria cannot do their work in dry material. Make a four-inch soil dam around shrubs and trees planted last winter. Fill with water every week, and after watering replace mulch to keep the ground moist. Transplant palms, bamboo and yuccas in lower South. Settle each at its former level, water thoroughly and apply a three-inch mulch. Stake in windy areas.

JULY

The compost heap needs plenty of attention this month. For best results, grind all material with a shredder, or a rotary mower and keep the heap moist to let bacteria do their work faster.

Flowers. July is a good time to sit back and enjoy masses of blooming beauties, including oleanders, crepe myrtles, hydrangeas, altheas, magnolias and phlox. Many gardeners report success in mulching roses with ground corn cobs. In the lower South, roses should rest—hold back water and fertilizer until next month. Poinsettias should be cut back to encourage branching. Prune hydrangeas right after blooming, and keep watering regularly. Plant Madonna lilies now, and store spring-flowering bulbs, including narcissus and tulips. Pinch back chrysanthemums for better results later. Now is the time to divide iris and daylilies, after blooming.

Vegetables. Keep tomatoes well watered and staked. Use soft cloth cords to tie them—a strong wind will break stalks against hard cords. Lots of vegetables can replace those which are being harvested now. Think of tomatoes, turnips, beans, beets, cabbage, cauliflower, carrots, eggplant, lettuce, squash, spinach, radish, rutabaga, pepper, peas, onions and cucumbers.

AUGUST

Flowers. Biennials and perennials can be started now in frames. Think of sweet William, hollyhock, veronica, delphinium, hibiscus, Oriental poppy and many others. Water flowers deeply during the dry spell. Spray foliage of camellias every night during hot weather, being sure to reach the underside of leaves. A strong stream of hose water should wash off red spiders, especially from ageratum, phlox, delphinium. Lift and divide Siberian, Dutch and Louisiana iris. Feed, water and mulch dahlias and chrysanthemums this month to insure best results. Order bulbs now for spring blossoms. Give all flowers a mid-summer boost by applying liquid compost. A shovelful mixed in a pail of water should do for each plant.

Vegetables. By the middle or latter part of the month, start the winter vegetables in seedbeds for early September planting. The different cabbages and cauliflowers, Italian broccoli, Bermuda onions, Fordhook chard, parsley, and winter lettuce are all good bets. In many places the fall crop of Irish potatoes can be planted in thoroughly irrigated rows. Dig in plenty of compost before planting. It's also time to plant tomatoes, winter squash, drought-resistant Black-eye beans, radishes, rutabagas, Chinese cabbage, cabbage, broccoli, Brussels sprouts, chard, kale, leaf lettuce, fall peas, salsify, late spinach, turnips, bush and pole beans, sweet corn and pumpkins.

SEPTEMBER

Flowers. Apply compost around each rosebush, dahlia, and chrysanthemum plant. Keep them watered to encourage large fall blooms. Keep plants mulched. Don't water calla lillies, but divide and transplant as soon as they are dormant. Root-prune wisteria and bougainvillea that failed to bloom. Order trees, shrubs, vines, and evergreens for fall planting. Popular fall and early winter-blooming annuals for Gulf Coast and Florida planting are sweet alyssum, snapdragon, calendula, cornflower, cosmos, gypsophila, annual lupine, marigold, nasturtiums, pansies, petunias and sweet peas. In the upper South, plant columbine, hardy asters, Canterbury-bells, hollyhocks, perennial poppies, and candytuft.

Vegetables. Plant as many greens this month as needed. They like rich soil, so apply plenty of compost. September is usually a dry month, so keep mulching to preserve moisture. In the garden planting, it is a good idea to include a few rows of sweet potatoes for early spring use. They should be far enough along to stand a slight frost if it comes in early winter. If a hard frost is expected, cover the plants with hay or grass or, if available, burlap bags. Beets, Brussels sprouts, carrots, Swiss chard, cress, corn salad, kale, spinach, radishes, rape, turnips, leeks, mustard, and let-tuce may be planted now. In Florida and the warmer regions of the South, tomatoes and many frost-tender vegetables may be planted.

Other Activities. Start strawberries now. Select sturdy runners and prepare beds well with compost. Renew mulch in the flower and vegetable garden, and around trees and shrubs, particularly those set out in the last two years.

OCTOBER

Flowers. Plant madonna lilies and peonies now, remembering good drainage and shallow planting are musts with these wonderful bloomers. Place liberal helping of compost below plantings. Plant ranunculus, anemonies, hyacinths, tulips, pansies, crocus, freesias, muscari, and daffodils. For dramatic color, plant Oriental poppies now, being sure the crown of the plant is even with the top of the ground. Mulch with shredded leaves. Dig glad bulbs as stalks turn brown and store in cool place, packed in sand or vermiculite, for successive plantings next spring and summer. Dig and store fancy leaf caladiums.

Vegetables. A dozen or more vegetables may still be planted. They are beets, carrots, radish, cress, leaf lettuce, leek, turnips, mustard, Swiss chard, kale, kohlrabi, and onion sets. In the lower South, cabbage, Chinese cabbage, head lettuce, parsley, broccoli, and collards. Gather matured tomatoes just before frost. Wrap in paper and store in a cool dark place on shelves or in wire baskets. Bring them out into a warm room two days before using. Store rutabagas and turnips soon after cold weather. Cut off tops to half-inch of root. Place on well-drained ground and cover with soil to prevent freezing. Thin fall plantings of carrots, beets, and turnips when they are three to four inches tall. After frost, cut asparagus tops and put them on compost heap. Apply heavy feeding of well-rotted stable manure or compost, and a good mulch.

NOVEMBER

Flowers. Set out roses, many kinds of shrubbery, peony crowns, iris. Divide and replant daisies. Many lilies may be planted now. Check catalog for varieties which may be planted. Plant hollies, azaleas and camellias in acid soil during the latter part of November and on through the winter. Prune out all dead wood and mulch well. Dahlias may be dug, dried and stored this month. Sweet peas planted now will produce earlier, larger, and have more blooms than those planted in spring. Plant peonies in upper South. Be sure camellias, azaleas, and other shrubs have enough moisture to go into the cold weather. Water well if rain is lacking.

Vegetables. Put in an asparagus bed now. Place it on one side of the garden so it will be out of the way of annual vegetables. Asparagus crowns may be planted in rows or beds, 18 to 24 inches apart, in rich soil. If fed properly and not cut until the third year, they will produce for as many as 50 years to come. Plant head lettuce in cold frame and transplant (to another cold frame or hot bed) 12 inches apart when large enough. Other vegetables which may be planted now include cabbage, endive, kale, lettuce, radishes, onions, spinach, beets, Chinese cabbage, turnips, kohlrabi, mustard, and parsley. Check catalog for varieties suitable for your region.

Orchard. November is the best time to plant many kinds of fruit and nut trees, berries and grapes. Trees set in November and December will make root growth during winter and be in better condition for rapid growth in spring. Prune muscadine grapes soon after fall. Train on three wires instead of two, as is recommended for bunch grapes.

Other Activities. Set strawberry beds now and mulch well before freezing weather. Clean and store garden implements before putting away. Oil applied to wooden parts will prevent cracking and rotting. Collect and save

leaves. They can be used either on the compost pile, shred right on location with a rotary mower, or as leaf mold.

DECEMBER

Now is a good time to test soil. Transform findings into organic formulas, using raw ground phosphate rock and granite dust or greensand. After the powders have been broadcast, spade up the ground. Allow it to lie rough over the winter unless you plant a cover crop. Broken ground will warm up more quickly in spring.

Flowers and Shrubs. All summer and fall-blooming shrubs should be cut back now. Prune crepe myrtle severely for best bloom. Feed and mulch camellias and azaleas. Plant roses, California poppies, and sweet peas. Transplant snapdragons, calendulas, pansies, stock, alyssum, Sweet-William, and candytuft to blooming site.

Vegetables. For a long-term investment, start an asparagus bed now. Plant crowns two inches deep, 12 inches apart in rows five feet wide. Prepare the soil deeply. Remember, you are making a bed for a 50-year crop. In parts of the South, strawberries may still be planted. Don't overlook this opportunity for good eating. Many vegetables may be planted now, depending upon your particular location. Check into onion sets, carrots, English peas, beets, cabbage, lettuce, greens, and radishes.

Orchard. Many fruit and nut trees can be planted now, including scuppernongs and berries. In Florida add citrus trees. Established fruit trees may be pruned now.

The Southwest

JANUARY

Flowers. Sow seeds of double petunias, lobelia, verbena, and dwarf bedding dahlias in electric-heated cold frames. Plant bare root dormant roses in the holes prepared in December. Buy only number one stock. Set hybrid glads for early flowering. Row up in your cutting garden. They like vegetable soil. Amaryllis bulbs may still be potted to come on for the spring flower shows. Plant azaleas and camellias. The latter may be selected in bloom. Use leaf mold and compost instead of peat. Keep pods clipped off your winter sweet peas, so as to prolong their blooming period. Keep mulches, and shade occasionally from a too hot winter sun. Continue

turning of sheet-composted material preparatory to spading under for the February planting. Mulch winter vegetables and flowers with unsifted compost. It will keep down winter weeds, conserve heat, and provide nourishment. All hardy evergreens can go in now. Handle balled specimens carefully. Avoid root-bound canned material. Set bare root deciduous fruits. Be sure to avoid defoliation and insure continuous cropping. Trellis

to make plantings of ranunculus and anemones for later blooming. Plant lately arrived lily bulbs. Cannas can be dug and divided.

Vegetables. Plant perennial vegetables, artichokes, asparagus, rhubarb, and horseradish while the roots are dormant. In warm sandy soil, potatoes may be planted. Spread well-prepared compost over the area before planting. Also plant warm weather vegetables—tomatoes, egg plant, and peppers—if your area has a mild, frostless belt.

Other Activities. Make the last

and arbor grapes can be set. Buy the expensive old vines with large trunks for first-year grapes. See that your tree trunks are properly protected. Winter sunburn is bad.

FEBRUARY

Humus is lacking in the sun-baked soils so spread plenty of compost in rows before planting. Start new bins or fill old ones immediately. Add neither lime nor ashes to compost, for Southwest soils are generally high enough in pH. Make good use of the lush growth of winter weeds before they go to seed They may be spaded under along with other cover crops. The waste from winter crops, which are now waning, furnishes more good material. Save lawn clippings for mulch. Spade in cover crops and sheet composting materials early in the month.

Flowers. In electrically heated frames, sow seeds of begonias, lobelia, petunias, dahlias, and verbenas. In covered seed beds in the open, seed hardy perennials, such as anchusa, delphiniums, hardy pinks, pentstemons, gaillardias, rehmannia, stokesia, and merembergia. Sow in open seed beds rather than in flats.

Vegetables. By the middle of February, the time has arrived for planting the early spring garden. Plant the first crop of Irish potatoes in well-composted soil; the second crop to follow in July. Set out plants of cabbage, Italian sprouting broccoli, kale, chard, leaf lettuce, and onion seedlings and sets. Sow seeds of beets, carrots, mustard, kohlrabi, parsley, turnips, Swiss chard, and radishes.

MARCH

During the first week of March plant fruit trees, grapes, berries, roses and shrubs. Cover crops should be spaded or disced in so as to get the ground ready for warm weather crops. Sheet compost should be now worked in.

Flowers. For brilliant spots of color in the flower garden, try some Red Hot Poker, both dwarf and tall. Put out dormant clumps of hardy phlox, gerberas, and Pacific hybrid delphiniums. Mulch thoroughly and incorporate plenty of compost in the ground before planting. Continue planting summer bulbs, cannas, gladiolus, dahlias, ismene, montbretias, tigridias, Mexican tuberoses, etc.

Vegetables. Make a late planting of the hardy vegetables: onion sets and seedlings, beets, carrots, kohlrabi, chard, lettuce, broccoli, savoy cabbage. Watch heated cold frames carefully

and transfer peppers, eggplant, and tomatoes to plant bands or cartons made from milk containers. Discard all weaklings. With a warm location in a sheltered area, use hot caps on tomatoes, eggplant, and peppers — planting directly a few seeds in a place and selecting the strongest one. Plant the last week in March. By the end of March, plant bush beans and summer squash. Holes for squash return double the yield if they are carefully prepared beforehand.

Other Activities. Spade in cover crops if they are planted on contoured sections. Watch night temperatures. Do not rush to plant the heat-loving plants when the night temperatures drop below 50 degrees. Beware either a very hot spell in March or a sudden frost. Finish all the work of planting bare-root deciduous material, fruits, trees, grapes, berries, roses, and deciduous trees and shrubs. Prepare holes for citrus and semi-tropicals to be put in the last of the month. Establish dwarf citrus fruits in redwood containers. Prepare all holes for planting with organic activators several weeks before planting. Use plenty of compost. Basin carefully and mulch thoroughly. Whitewash trunks of all trees or use yucca protectors.

APRIL

April is a midseason planting month. Conserve every bit of moisture by spading in compost and mulching all plantings. Return all waste material to the soil, especially the abundant greens of the spring weeds and lawn clippings.

Flowers. Bulbs conserve moisture, are easy to grow, and are highly decorative. There are so many to choose from . . . yellow callas, the showy billbergias, dahlias, fragrant crinums, tuberoses, liriope, to mention only a few. Feed deciduous bulbs with compost and bone meal until the leaves have turned brown. Never cut off leaves while still green. These two precautions will insure blooms for the next year. Feed azaleas and camellias with compost and leaf mold, and do not let them dry out at any time. Camellias are slow growers in poor soil, but being such stunning plants, they are worth a little care.

Vegetables. Continue to plant vegetables this month. In the area with the last killing frost occurring between April first and April 20, the warm weather crops should be planted in April and May. These include New Zealand spinach, tomatoes, cantaloupes, etc. But root crops and other hardy vegetables may still be sown. The more hardy ones, including beets, broccoli, cabbage, leaf lettuce, radish, carrots, turnips, should be planted in April for the first time in regions where the last killing frost may occur between April 20 and May tenth. In the cooler parts, only asparagus, onions, spinach, radishes, parsley, and Chinese cabbage are sown out by the end of April, but the warm weather crops must be started early in the month inside, especially cucumbers, peppers, and tomatoes, so that they can be set out in late May or early June. If vegetable garden space is limited, plant chives and parsley as an edging to flower borders. Leaf garlic can be used in the bulb border, as well as the handsome rhubarb chard.

Other Activities. As weather permits, plant citrus fruits and other subtropicals. More attention should be given to dwarf types which are being used in the redwood containers. Bare root plantings should be rushed to completion rapidly.

MAY

Flowers. Have succession plants ready for the long dry season ahead. Some heat-resistant perennials include arctois, salvias, hardy asters, marigolds, zinnias, cosmos.

Vegetables. In carefully prepared rows plant okra, bush squash, bush and pole beans, lima beans and corn. Mulch heavily. For small home gardens use as many vertical growers as

possible. Chinese and Armenian cucumbers, pole beans, and tomatoes should be trained to stakes. Plant summer cover crops of the drought-resistant legumes. Tepary and Black Eye beans give a food crop, and can be plowed under later as a soil renewer. Plant the leaf lettuces which do not get bitter in summer in a little shade. The heat-loving vegetables— lima beans, summer squash, peppers, eggplant, tomatoes—should be planted in deeply composted holes. Watercress can be planted in a shallow tub or discarded sink.

Other Activities. The importance of compost and mulches cannot be overstressed for the season to come. Continue to add to the compost heap, and gather mulch materials because they hold soil moisture and improve soil tilth.

JUNE

Keep soil pH low, mulch and compost continually. Add minerals and humus to cultivation-weary soils. Cultivate little, keep weeds down, use flat culture and water economically.

Flowers. Plant the heat-loving annuals—cosmos, marigolds, annual gaillardias, dwarf Tithonia, annual phlox and petunias. Water spring bulbs until the leaves die down and feed with a mixture of bone meal and compost. Set hardy chrysanthemums in permanent rows in well-prepared soil. Mulch heavily and water lightly during the summer. Bird-of-Paradise, one of the most exotically beautiful of all ornamentals, is making its chief growth now; be sure to water and feed freely with compost.

Vegetables. Plant in deep, well-prepared holes well-established plants of tomatoes, eggplant and peppers. Put compost in the bottom of the holes and sink water down before planting. In deep, well-prepared soil, plant okra, lima beans, bush and pole beans and corn. Mulch heavily and water with soil soakers. Plant summer cover crops of drought-resistant legumes such as tepary and black-eye beans. Plowed under later as a green manure, they help renew the soil. Put lettuce for summer in partial shade. Sow such annual herbs as dill, summer savory and sweet basil in your herb beds. Keep parsley, evergreen garlic and sorrel growing for your salad bowl. Water sweet potatoes and melons, using a soil soaker and mulch heavily afterwards.

Citrus. Set citrus trees and semitropicals. Use dwarf citrus fruits for small areas. They are attractive, and can replace many ornamentals.

JULY

July is a crucial "mulch month" in the Southwest. Many gardeners have an aversion to sawdust as a mulch, but experiments have found it to be excellent for protecting soil and for breaking down slowly into humus. Keep the compost pile moist during the dry spell, and keep adding materials. Spend lots of time out in the garden and on the patio this month.

Flowers. It's time to divide and replant iris. Other spring-flowering bulbs, including narcissus, hyacinths and daffodils can be lifted and stored in a dry basement. If results with bulbous plants were not very satisfactory this year, they probably need division. Plant the heat-loving annuals now, including cosmos, marigolds, annual gaillardias, tithonia sunflowers and zinnias.

Vegetables. Continue setting out plants of eggplant, tomatoes and peppers. This is also the time to fill bare spots in the garden with a variety of vegetables, including okra, summer squash, string beans, hybrid sweet corn, spinach, kohlrabi, chard, beets, broccoli, carrots, cauliflower, endive, lettuce, radishes, turnips and potatoes. Conditions vary from area to area, so check seed packets for maturity dates against the number of frostless days left in your area.

Other Activities. Keep moisture high and keep mulching berries. After bearing, cut back berry bushes. Select four or five of the strongest brambles of new growth for next year.

AUGUST

It's time to start planting operations for the winter season. Bulbs and seeds of many flowers and vegetables can be sown in seedbeds. All new seedings must receive special care, especially in watering, and established plants must be protected from the baking sun by a mulch.

Vegetables. Start winter vegetables in seedbeds in the latter part of the month. The variety is endless; radishes, rutabagas, Black-eye beans, cabbage, broccoli, Brussels sprouts, chard, kale, leaf lettuce, fall peas, late potatoes, salsify, late spinach, tomatoes, turnips, bush and pole beans, sweet corn, pumpkins and winter squash. In many areas, the fall crop of Irish potatoes can be planted in thoroughly irrigated rows. When summer crops are harvested, pull out old plants and weeds and add them to the compost heap. The internal action of the heap should provide enough heat to kill weed seeds. For better results, shred materials before composting, and keep the heap moist.

Flowers. Many bulbs can be planted now, including Madonna lilies, iris, callas, freesia and watsonia. Winter-blooming annuals can be planted now, including tetra-snapdragons, candulas, pansies and violas. Pinch back dahlias, and give roses a summer boost with an application of compost water. Mix a shovelful of compost in a bucket of water for each plant. Have compost ready to apply to flower beds. When summer-blooming annuals have spent themselves, turn under the old plants (or add them to the compost pile) and prepare the beds for the winter-blooming varieties.

SEPTEMBER

This month marks the beginning of the "second spring" of the Southwest. Planting of winter vegetables and winter-blooming annuals should be rushed as soon as the soil is warm and night temperatures are favorable. Keep an eye on your thermometer and, when the night temperature drops down to forty and lower, the dormant period has set in. In September, when the soil is thoroughly warmed up and the night temperatures are favorable, rush plantings of winter vegetables and set in plants for winter-blooming annuals.

Flowers. Sow seeds of deep-rooted annuals like poppies, scarlet flax, candytuft, and larkspur in permanent locations, as they don't like to be transplanted. This is bulb planting time . . . including lilies, glads, leucojums, narcissus, iris, ixia, sparaxis, grape hyacinths, and other favorites. Check catalogs for varieties.

Vegetables. Sow seeds of beets, carrots, chard, early onions, winter radishes, Chinese cabbage, mustard, turnips, Canadian Wonder bush beans and Pencil pod wax beans will mature about the middle of November if planted the first week of September. In water-saturated and compost-enriched rows, set out stocky plants of cabbage, cauliflower, Italian sprouting broccoli.

Other Activities. Mulch every planting if possible. Use lawn clippings, leaf mold from the home grounds. Prepare orchards for winter cover croppings. *Mililotus indica* is one of the more dependable ones. Purple vetch and barley are also good. Encourage the natural growth of lupine and bur-clover. Always protect the soil from wind and water erosion.

OCTOBER

Make the most of favorable planting weather while the soil is warm. Watch the thermometer for night temperatures. When they drop to 50 degrees and lower, slow up on garden operations. "Shooting to seed" in early spring is easily prevented by this precaution.

Flowers. Set winter annuals by first week in October, if they are not already in. Calendulas, Iceland poppies, snapdragons, stock, pansies, and violas. Sweet peas already started in plant-bands may be set where they are to bloom. Sow deep rooting annuals such as centaureas, scarlet flax, field poppies, larkspur, and godetias. Broadcast daisies for a colorful winter carpet. Set hardy perennials of all sorts so that they make strong roots for the early spring blooming. Use coral bells, columbines, Scotch pinks, gaillardias, geums, Shasta daisies, rehmanias, and delphinium. Set such hardy biennials as Canterbury bells, foxgloves, hollyhocks and Sweet William for a long winter growth. Plant bulbs as soon as they are available, getting the natives and South Africans in first. Plant narcissus of all types, iris, blue bells, hyacinths, and anemones. Use compost and bone meal in preparing the soil.

Vegetables. Continue setting plants of such winter vegetables as cabbage, cauliflower, kale, kohlrabi, Italian sprouting broccoli, celery, seedling onions, Romaine, leaf and head lettuce. Chinese edible pod peas can be trellised like sweet peas. Telephone peas and Windsor beans are excellent winter crops.

Other Activities. Plan to sheet compost any unused areas of the garden this fall. Use waste raw materials; in our section "turkey poult" is good with dry grass, straw, spoiled hay, and vegetable refuse, which can be layered, watered first, soaked by the winter rain and spaded or disced in early in the spring. Plant hardy evergreens, both conifers and broad leaved ones. Use more natives. They are drought and frost resistant, fine for erosion control. Tropicals and subtropicals should not be set out unless in a "frostless belt." Hold water off of tender material so that it can harden up for winter frosts.

NOVEMBER

Sheet compost for early spring planting. Add manure for nitrogen insurance. Have the soil tested now for pH and analyzed to find out what minerals are lacking and add mineral rock and other soil amendments. Use pulverized seaweeds if obtainable locally. Make compost by the quick "dry method" to keep pH down so that the minerals which are in the soil can be absorbed.

Flowers. Plant bulbs of all sorts throughout the month . . . daffodils, hyacinths, bulbous iris, glads, scillas, hybrid amaryllis. Take your tulips out of cold storage and pot or set in borders the last of the month, planting from ten to 12 inches deep. Broadcast or sow in rows the deep-rooting annuals, such as poppies, clarkias, godetias, candytuft, linarias, and scarlet flax.

Vegetables. Sow telephone peas, Chinese edible pod peas, Windsor beans. In sunny and light soils, put in more onion sets and set plants of leaf lettuce.

Orchard. Survey and contour plow sloping sections of the orchard to prevent winter erosion. Prune, shape and stake trees before the rainy season.

DECEMBER

Cover crops may still be planted. Start your winter pruning as soon as the leaves have fallen. Delay rose pruning until the first week in February.

Flowers. Dig and prepare big generous holes for your dormant root roses to be planted in January. Use well prepared compost. Dig and transplant camellias. Select your plants while they are in bloom. Make sure you shallow plant, mulch, and provide good drainage. See that your Christmas and New Year's blooming chrysanthemums are securely staked and mulched. The first week in December, continue potting and planting bulbs. At this time many bargains are offered.

Vegetables. Asparagus, artichokes and rhubarb can be set as soon as available. Make new strawberry beds and renew old ones. Other vegetables which may still be planted in parts of the Southwest are beets, chard, cucumber, broccoli, Brussels sprouts, cantaloupes, carrots, leaf lettuce, muskmelon, green onions, parsley, peppers, potatoes, radishes, rutabaga, spinach, tomatoes, and turnips. Divide and reset garden herbs. Use chives as edgings, along with parsley. Divide your chives while they are dormant.

The Northwest

JANUARY

Take a tour of the garden this month. Make sure all mulches are in place. Replace plants which have heaved out of the ground. Eliminate

standing puddles with down-grade ditches. Plan to prune trees this month.

Flowers. Plant California poppy, mignonette, linaria, godetia. If Christmas poinsettias are looking sickly, they may be too hot and dry. Try them in the coolest corner of the kitchen, where humidity is higher. Follow instructions for house plants in a recent issue. Fuschias may be brought to light this month, if desired. Cut back severely. They love food and enjoy a rich soil. Remove all plant material from window and porch boxes. Fill the space temporarily with evergreen branches, such as holly, mahonia, skimmia, or acuba. Kept moist, they will stay green for a long time. Try forcing the blooms on some cut branches of flowering shrubs, such as flowering quince, forsythia, and such trees as apple, dogwood, pussywillow, and flowering cherries. Soak entire branch in luke-warm water overnight. Watch for the blooms in about ten days.

Other Activities. If the two-year old canes of the raspberry and other bramble fruits have not yet been removed, it can be done now. However, care should be taken not to injure the canes which will bear fruit this year, and, by all means, do not top them until all danger of freezing back is passed. In the greenhouse, make carnation cuttings to produce flowers for summer. First call for annual pruning of fruit trees in the area west of the Cascades. On one of the nicer days, turn the compost heap. Add a layer of soil on top, keep moist, and protect from rains.

FEBRUARY

Flowers. Start removing the mulch from snowdrop, crocus, primrose, daffodils, and tulips. Many others may be seeded in flats now. Use old cigar boxes with holes punched in the bottom.

Vegetables. Seed-onions, early potatoes, and carrots can be seeded this month if the soil is sandy. If soil does not crumble and fall apart when a handful is squeezed, it is too wet. Wait until a later month to make the garden planting. In colder parts of the Northwest, cold-frame or hotbed seedings should be made of many vegetables, including peppers, tomatoes, early cabbage, cauliflower, celery and radishes. Gardeners who seeded the ground to rye and vetch for green manure should turn it over now and prepare at least that strip which is to be seeded to early peas. Washington's Birthday is the date on which the peas are sowed in the Pacific Northwest.

Indoor. Clean up and repot any house plants which appear potbound. Prepare plenty of soil for flats. Remember not to include any nitrogenous material in seeding soil. Too much nitrogen produces too fast growth.

Other Activities. Turn the compost heap, and "feed it" with table scraps, to stimulate activity of the angleworms and bacteria. Pruning should not be put off any longer. Do it now, before the sap begins to rise. Saw off any weak limbs, and clean up the ground.

MARCH

Warm, sunny days near the coast may be tempting, but avoid planting until the latter part of the month, when seeds will be fairly safe from rotting in the wet ground.

Flowers. Now is the dormant season for Helleboros Niger. It may be transplanted this month. Fertilize bulb beds, violets, pansies and primroses. Liquid manure or fish emulsion may be used. Continue to feed primroses once a week during blooming season. Plant glad bulbs which show signs of sprouting. Save the others to plant later for succession of bloom. Pruning roses is a must for March. The 15th day of the month is accepted as the best average day west of the Cascades. Any earlier pruning might subject tender new growth to freezing.

Vegetables. Plant some lettuce as a border for flower beds. It fills the gaps in the spring and will be harvested before the space is needed. East of the Cascades, plant only cabbage, lettuce and onions in the vegetable garden this month. West of the Cascades, the following may also be planted: peas, carrots, spinach, turnips, celery, radishes, early potatoes, cauliflower, rhubarb and asparagus roots. Wait for the soil to ready itself for digging. If a spadeful breaks apart when hit with the spade, it is ready. If not, wait until later in the month. Near the middle of the month, put in another planting of peas. The first one should be made around Washington's Birthday. Place a two-by-four on the ground, and plant the first planting on one side of it, the second on the other, using the same strings for both plants.

Other Activities. Sawdust is plentiful in this region, so take advantage of it and use it to mulch berries. It will keep out the weeds, retain moisture in soil, and assure a hearty crop. There are also many fish canneries in some regions, and waste material is an excellent fertilizer. Bury one fish head to a hill of strawberries for splendid results.

APRIL

Never plant seeds in poorly prepared soil. See to it that compost is well worked in, the seed bed raked over, the surface pulverized. Lime may be needed, particularly if your soil is low-lying and wet. Don't, however, add lime without testing to see if it is needed.

Vegetables. In the West, approximate dates for seeding or setting out plants are: Asparagus and early potatoes until April 8; spinach, peas, onions, Swiss chard, beets, and lettuce, during the first half of the month. Strangely enough, parsnips and salsify, both among the hardiest crops, are recommended for April 25 only. Sometimes, not coolness but light conditions may require a late or early planting, since too early planting may produce

seed formation with some crops. In all cases, check catalogs and seed packets, as dates also vary with different varieties. In general, if the ground is friable and ready for use, these vegetables may go out in the open: Cabbage and broccoli plants, seeds of turnips, beets, lettuce, carrots, chard, potatoes, spinach, parsnips, radish and salsify. Partially fill the seed furrow with compost containing a small amount of ground steer manure to furnish a little warmth. Plant and cover as usual.

Other Activities. The winter compost pile should be ready to yield some returns now. Turn the top layer over into a new heap and sift the well-rotted compost out of the remainder. Place the residue on the new heap for further decomposition. Take advantage of the lush new growth of grass and use the clippings for mulching. Try saving them for flower beds if other mulching material is less neat looking. This is the last month recommended for setting out blueberry bushes. If a cherry tree doesn't produce any fruit it may need a pollenizer. It won't necessarily mean a new tree, as bee experts say that a bouquet of blossoms from a pollenizing variety placed in the sun under the tree will do the trick. Keep the bouquet fresh. Find the particular pollenizer by writing the state experiment station.

MAY

Flowers. Stake up perennials now, before a hard rain levels them. Plant glads and dahlias. Spade deeply and sink the bulbs to a good depth. Old clumps of chysanthemums can be dug up and divided. Choose outside roots, plant at least ten inches apart, and feed with compost. Mums need plenty of sun. Perennial candytuft makes a grand border to follow up the primrose. They will bloom throughout May. Delphiniums and pyrethrums will be stately if well staked.

Vegetables. Prepare the vegetable garden well with standard organic methods. The reward will come as the large humus content of the soil keeps the garden from drying out, the mulch keeps the weeds down and the compost, bone meal and manure furnish the food needed. All plants may be set out now—cabbage, cucumbers, cauliflower, tomatoes. East of the Cascades, be sure the frost date has passed. Stop cutting asparagus the latter part of May.

Other Activities. Bury table scraps under the raspberries for large size fruit. Clean up the patch and tie up the canes into summer position. Watch out for moonweed. Logan, boysen, and Olympicberries are perfect for Northwest gardens.

JUNE

Continue mulching to control weeds. A little effort now will be doubly rewarded next month. The warm weather is just right for bacterial action in the compost heap. Give the bacteria a chance by keeping the heap moist. Try to use rain water, if possible.

Flowers. Spring is in full glory in the Northwest, and summer planting is just around the corner. It's time to lift the spring-flowering bulbs, after the foliage has completely withered, or if bulbs are less than three years old, to simply remove the foliage. Don't give chrysanthemums too much water for best results in late summer and fall. They like it a little on the dry side. Cut delphiniums back to about 12 inches after blooming. A second blooming will probably come along later if the plants are fed and watered well. Dahlias and gladiolus may still be planted in the early part of June. They will grow well during the summer weather and will make color in the fall garden. Continue to pinch tips from chrysanthemums for bushier plants. Be sure to cut rose blooms properly. One accepted method advocates cutting just above an outward-pointing group of five leaves. Continue feeding roses with

liquid manure. Try planting gladiolus with iris, as the similar foliage helps relieve barrenness after iris have bloomed.

Vegetables. It is late, but several vegetables may still be planted, such as sweet corn, carrots, pole beans, and heat-resistant varieties of lettuce. Prepare a seed bed and plant seeds, for transplanting later, of winter crops such as cabbage, broccoli, chard and Brussels sprouts. Tomatoes should be set out when they flower. Set paper bags about them and stake down the bags to prevent blowing away. Put sawdust or grass cuttings around the plants. Drop root vegetables into a bucket of water after harvesting them. Ready them for the kitchen by washing and removing the tops. Contents of the bucket and the tops may then be put on the compost pile. Don't throw out the turnip and beet tops, though; they're loaded with vitamins.

Other Activities. Now is the time to grow next year's stock of rockery plants. Ideal soil for them is a mixture of sand, compost, peat, a handful of lime and some wood ashes containing burnt bone. Raise the mower blades to 2½ inches to prevent scorching lawn. Keep picking off blossoms of everbearing strawberries until the end of July.

JULY

Spring-applied mulch should be doing a good job in keeping down weeds this month. If it isn't, the material may be too loose. New straw, although it is a fairly effective mulch, isn't much good in smothering weeds. Better for this purpose are rotted or ground straw, ground corncobs, buckwheat hulls, sawdust, grass clippings, or any other fine-textured material. The mulch will also improve results tremendously during the present dry season, especially east of the Cascades.

Flowers. Time to dig up and store spring-flowering bulbs in a cool, dry place. If too crowded, divide and replant iris, violets and lily-of-the-valley. Glads and dahlias can still be planted early in the month in warmer areas. Now that the blooming season is here for many varieties, don't let the masses of blooms droop or break. Stake with soft cloth cords. Sow seeds of pansies and violets this month and next. Disbud mums and dahlias for better fall results.

Vegetables. In those empty spaces in the garden sow kale and kohlrabi. Also plant beets, carrots, rutabagas, bush beans and a fall crop of peas. Also think of radish, head lettuce, St. Valentine broccoli, cauliflower, beets, cabbage, endive and leaf lettuce. Check the number of frostless days left against maturity date and hardiness of individual varieties.

Other Activities. Renew peat mulch around broad-leafed evergreens. This month is also the beginning of the berry season. Keep them mulched and water if necessary.

AUGUST

Things are moving a little faster in the Northwest than in most parts of the country. August is the time to think of next season, and to start to prepare for it. Many flowers should be sowed, divided, or transplanted this month. August is also a dry time, making it absolutely necessary to keep the garden well mulched to preserve what moisture may come.

Vegetables. Make enough second plantings now to insure food until spring. Try fall and late varieties of artichokes, beets, cabbage, carrots, parsley, peas, radishes, spinach and turnips. Check maturing time of individual varieties against the date of the first fall frost.

Flowers. August is a busy time in the flower garden. Clip dead rose blooms to prevent mildew. Disbud chrysanthemums and mulch well to prevent drying out from now until September. Many perennials can still be planted, including hollyhocks, delphiniums, canterbury bells, coreopsis, forget-me-not, wallflowers and violas. Fall and winter bulbs, starting with

the crocus, can go in the ground in mid-August and on into the fall. Biennials, including pansies, campanulas and foxgloves, can also be seeded now. Start paper narcissus, Roman hyacinths and freesias for indoor plantings. All perennials which have finished blooming can be divided now. Early-planted glads might be ready to dig, if their foliage has died down. Keep feeding the glads which are just coming into bloom.

Other Activities. Be sure to have a mulch on evergreens, to insure ample moisture during the dry season. Peat moss is perfect for evergreens. Water the peat after applying it, to prevent its blowing away with strong winds. Keep the mower up to two inches or higher, as the grass needs all the strength it can maintain. Now is the time to add materials to the compost heap, keeping it watered. When strawberries are finished bearing, the patch can be cleaned up. Old plants can be thinned out if runners are taking hold. Feed the patch generously now with both compost and phosphate and potash rock to give plants a good start for next year.

SEPTEMBER

Flowers. Take tuberous begonias into the house before frost comes. Allow them to keep on blooming in a sunny window. Plant crocus, grape hyacinth, snow drop, glory of the snow, lady tulips, Spanish bluebells, early scilla, water lily tulips. All these will make a colorful spring around the house. Some work with chrysanthemums now, pays dividends. Feed lightly with fish emulsions or compost water while buds are forming. Disbud if large flowers are desired. Keeping the ground moist, but not soggy, is important, and a mulch will help. Support the plants before the rains come. It's time now to divide or transplant peonies. Planting too deep is a common cause of non-blooming, but starvation is another. They need very rich soil. Transplanting will often hold up blooms for one year. Put at least a bucketful of compost and a cup of bone meal in the bottom of each hole.

Vegetables. Keep carrots and beets in moist sand. Allow an inch or two of top to remain. Too much moisture will cause them to put out feeders, so be careful. Cucumbers, should now be producing. Keep them well watered and pick them every day. Cut ends of squash to within leaf of a fruit. Vines need moisture now. Keep mulching. Set out plants of late cabbage, cauliflower, Brussels sprouts and broccoli. Rhubarb clumps may be divided now. Set at ground level, leaving one or two eyes per root. Cover mulch of straw manure about five inches. Plant spinach in a sunny spot before the 15th. It should be ready in October or November. Plant radishes now in time for Thanksgiving garnishes.

Other Activities. Now is the time to add plenty of material to the compost heap . . . garden wastes, lawn clippings, weeds, any organic material. Prepare some potting soil for the winter. Sifted compost mixed with rich loam makes an excellent soil to use during winter months, when rains and snows make it difficult to secure. Sand or peat may be added according to the structure of your soil. Take in houseplants to accustom them to indoor temperature before starting the furnace.

OCTOBER

October is the harvest month. Canning, freezing, and storage activities are at a peak now. The less time lost in getting fruits and vegetables from garden to freezer, the less vitamins are lost. Vitamin C is particularly vulnerable to this danger period.

Flowers. Divide perennials now. Plant Epimedium, a fine ground cover, under camellias and rhododendrons. There is bloom in spring and bronzy effect in the fall. Prepare the ground now where lilies are to be planted in November. This does not include lilium candidum and its hybrids. Put plenty of bone meal and compost with the soil. Roses can be moved safely this month.

Vegetables. October is a good time to divide rhubarb. Even the smallest garden can find room for this coarse, yet beautiful plant. It is a heavy feeder and likes lots of manure.

Compost. Clean out all plant residues and throw them on the compost pile. Now is the time when the heap should be built up for next year's use. Grass clippings, leaves, and any other organic matter can help. The difference between a compost pile and a pile of green matter, is the presence of manure and layers of soil put between each application of green matter. Soil and manure will help the pile to decompose much more quickly. Another trick is to shred up all green matter with the rotary mower before applying to the heap. Add nutrients to the heap, with rock powders to each layer of soil. The result will be a beautiful combination soil conditioner and fertilizer.

Other Activities. Mulch rose beds, asparagus, rhubarb, and lily-of-the-valley with manure, mixed with straw or wood chips. A local lumber mill will probably supply chips and/or sawdust for the hauling. Sawdust is fine for a strawberry mulch. Get the paved sections of the garden free of weeds, especially west of the Cascades where the weeds grow all winter. Cut gourds before frost, but seeds should rattle when shaken. Handle them carefully, like ripe fruit. Dry thoroughly before decorating. Last call for planting new lawns. If planting is impossible before the middle of the month, postpone it until spring. Reseed bare spots. Now is a good time for an annual application of bone meal to the lawn. The fall rains will wash it down. Use 80 to 100 pounds for an average-sized lawn on a city lot.

NOVEMBER

Keep planting bulbs, seeds of hardy

annuals, roses, trees, and shrubs as the weather permits. Clean up generally all diseased and insect-infested foliage, leaves, fruits, and stalks, placing them deep in the compost heap so its heat will destroy all disease spores and insect eggs. Think of a mulch now as a winter garden blanket. It protects roots against temperature variations, conserves moisture (a necessary measure for evergreens). Whether in the perennial border, rock garden, among the shrubbery, or in the garden generally, a mulch of peat moss and cedar sawdust is popular, and in the spring, this may be worked into the soil. Transplant fruit and ornamental trees and shrubbery, being sure that holes are wide enough to take the root-spread without twisting. Compost, well-rotted manure, or other organic fertilizers should be worked into the bottom, as well as the soil which is to act as a fill. Set trees and shrubs one inch lower than in their former location. Phosphate rock and potash rock, bone meal, well-rotted manure, and compost may be worked into the ground around trees and shrubs. Spread manure and compost in any vacant beds and spade in later. Gather up all available leaves and use them for composting or for leaf mold.

Flowers. Keep planting lilies until ground freezes. Clean away all dead foliage from roses, hilling soil around tender varieties. Work in bone meal around old rose bushes before covering for winter. When hardy chrysanthemums finish flowering, cut stalks back to within a few inches of the ground. Last call for lifting tuberous begonias. Keep them from freezing over winter. Fuschias should be kept in a cool, frost-free place. They must have moist soil, even though resting, but darkness is not essential.

Vegetables. Earth up celery for the winter. Replant winter varieties in deep frames. Heap manure around rhubarb plants. Where possible, plant vegetable garden in fall to expose hibernating insects to freezing. Plant peas in well-drained soil. Leave a ridge of soil to the south of the row to shade the row of small plants from sudden temperature extremities. Onion sets put out now bring the earliest green onions. The size of harvest may be small, but none the less rewarding. Onion seeds can be sown now and will germinate at the first sign of spring.

DECEMBER

The garden should have been put to bed last month. Remember to keep the compost heap covered to protect it from the heavy Northwest rains. Devote a Saturday afternoon to a final pruning of all trees and shrubs. Watch for broken limbs. Inspect stored bulbs, fruits, and vegetables frequently to prevent spread of rot or infection. Don't disturb trees, shrubs, or hedges when ice-coated, or they may break. It's time to remove plant material from windows and porch boxes. Evergreen boughs or holly branches may be used to fill the space temporarily and make for all-winter beauty. Kept moist, they will stay green for a long time. Give gardening friends gift-wrapped plants for Christmas.

Flowers. Miniature roses can be grown in pots indoors, and require about the same treatment as African violets. Older, large-flowering camellias may be disbudded this month. One bud every three inches is recommended. This will permit the flowers to develop.

GARDEN CLUBS, ORGANIC: Over 150 Organic Gardening Clubs have been organized throughout the United States, the District of Columbia and Canada. These groups, varying in membership from a dozen or so to hundreds, are an active, meaningful part of the organic movement. As organized units, they provide an important community-level meeting ground for all who are interested in natural gardening and farming and better health. In some areas, state-wide federations have been formed and have expanded the scope and effectiveness of this work.

A full list of active Clubs is available without charge. Write for complete information on getting started if you'd like to help organize. Address: Club Director, Rodale Press, Emmaus, Pa.

GARDEN GERANIUM: *see* GERANIUM

GARDENIA: Named after Dr. Alexander Garden, who lived in Charleston, S. C. in the 18th century, gardenia belongs to the family, *Rubiaceae,* and is related to other tropical plants as coffee and chinchona. Genus gardenia includes about 60 evergreen trees and shrubs. Best known representatives are *G. florida,* or cape jasmine, and *G. veitchi,* the florist's gar-

Plenty of moisture is the most important factor in gardenia culture. Place containers in bowls of water whose depth equals gravel level in pot.

denia, with its waxy fragrant white flowers and glassy foliage.

G. florida is a summer-blooming variety, with flowers slightly smaller than those of *G. veitchi.* It is grown in pots or tubs as a house plant, being summered in the garden in a shady place, and wintered in the house in a

relatively cool room. During its blooming season, *G. florida* must be kept thoroughly wet, and not allowed to dry out. During the winter it is kept fairly dry.

G. veitchi is an everblooming gardenia, the most popular hot-house or house plant variety. It is also summered outside, in a shaded moist location, and kept wet summer and winter. It must be returned to its partly sunny window indoors before the nights become cool.

Gardenias demand a very acid soil, with a pH of 4.5 to 5. This may be supplied in well-composted sawdust or oak leaves. Leaves which fall from the plant, as well as its own faded flowers, may be placed on top of the soil to form a self-mulch. In addition, if the foliage shows a tendency to turn yellow, a handful of rotted manure or of cottonseed meal may be mixed with the top layer of soil.

An abundance of moisture is the most important factor in successful gardenia culture. Plant containers may be placed in trays or bowls in which water is allowed to stand to a depth equal to the depth of gravel or rubble in the bottom of the flower pot. If sufficient water is supplied, the plants will be free of bud-rot, which causes the buds to drop before flowering.

Insects which trouble gardenias are thrips, red spider, and mealy bug. Red spider may be combatted by a daily spraying of the foliage with clear water. Thrips and mealy bug may be hand-picked, but will trouble the plant little if it has been fed sufficiently for robust health.

GARDEN PLANNING: *see* LANDSCAPING; PLANNING, GARDEN

GARLAND FLOWER: *see* DAPHNE

GARLIC: (*Allium sativum*) This vegetable is of easiest culture, growing freely on any soil suitable for onions. It is propagated by divisions of the bulb, called "cloves," or "sets." These are planted in early spring, in rows, one foot apart, one to two inches deep, and from four to six inches between the plants in the rows. The crop matures in August, when it is harvested like the onion. It is always sold in the dry state. Garlic grows to two feet, has pinkish flowers in small heads.

The crop is harvested by pulling when the tops begin to turn yellow, which takes place from May to July, depending on the locality and the time of planting. The bulbs should be thoroughly dried and cleaned by removing the outer loose parts of the sheath and trimming the roots close to the base. They may be stored loose like onions, tied in bunches, or plaited into the strings such as are sometimes seen on the market.

To control meadow garlic when it becomes a weed problem, plow in autumn and follow with a clean cultivated crop for one or two years before reseeding. To control field garlic, disk to destroy the tops and plow in late autumn, followed by early spring plowing and planting to a clean cultivated crop. Repeat yearly as necessary. *See also* HERBS; ONION.

GAS-PLANT: *see* FRAXINELLA

GAZANIA: Members of the daisy family, their attractive flower heads— often with yellow rays—bloom in the daytime, close at night. *G. longiscapa,* often known as 'African daisy, makes an excellent summer-blooming annual, useful as a border plant. *G. rigens* and *G. splendens* are both perennials, the latter growing about 1½ feet high. *See also* AFRICAN DAISY; BORDER.

GEESE: Many rural families have found that it is worthwhile to include a flock of geese in their poultry operations, especially since they require so little attention and housing facilities. From the age of two weeks to maturity, it is possible to raise geese on good pasture without any other food. Geese graze closer than most other animals; ten to 20 birds are recom-

mended for an acre of pasture; if the pasture is excellent more birds can be kept safely.

The Toulouse breed lay from 15 to 35 eggs each year and usually start laying in February. The eggs require more humidity to hatch than other eggs.

The goose can cover 12 to 15 eggs, but the chicken hen has a nestful with four to six. If a hen is used, the eggs should be turned every day, as they are too large for the hen to handle. In a dry climate, a warm-water sprinkling every day after the first two weeks helps hatchability.

Goose eggs require from 30 to 35 days to hatch. If an incubator is used, the temperature should be the same as for chicken eggs, with higher humidity. After the goslings hatch, they should not be fed for the first 24 hours, but be allowed to dry off.

FEEDING: Stale bread soaked in warm milk—or wet mash—is a good starter for the goslings. Chopped green feed may be added to either of these and the goslings like it. Feed all the food the goslings will clean up in 15 minutes four times daily for the first two weeks, gradually adding more green feed and at the end of that time the goslings will be able to get their entire living from good quality pasture.

If the pasture is not too good, cut greens, grass clippings, alfalfa, turnip tops, beet tops or cabbage make a good supplement. During winter, mixed hay or silage with small amounts of grain are good for the breeders, though not an absolute necessity.

Geese need plenty of grit and a constant supply of drinking water, as do all fowl. If fattening geese for the market, feed twice daily on mash and a mixture of grain. Heavy grain feeding adds that nice color to the flesh. —*Nell W. Evans.*

GENTIAN: (*Gentiana lutea*) The common, or yellow, gentian is found in the mountainous regions of southern and central Europe. The root is used extensively in medicine, as indicated by the quantities imported.

The plant is poorly adapted to cultivation outside its natural range, and experimental plantings in this country have not been encouraging. It appears to require partial shade and would probably best be grown as a companion crop to ginseng and goldenseal in open woodland or under an artificial shade structure and with much the same cultural methods. It is a slow-growing plant and takes several years to produce a marketable root.

Gentian is probably best adapted to the milder mountain sections of the Eastern and North Pacific Coast States where ginseng and goldenseal are now grown. Also known as bitterwort.

Many of the Gentians make fine rock garden plants, well adapted to cool, moist areas. The bright blue flowers of Fringed Gentian (*G. crinita*), a biennial, are very attractive. *G. acaulis* grows to four inches high, is a perennial, and a good choice for the rock garden.

GENUS: A major classified group of plants, actually a category between family and species. Genus (the plural is genera) includes one or more species which have structural or floral characteristics in common. Species represent plant groups forming a subdivision of a genus which differ too slightly to be classed as separate genera. Subdivided types within species are termed varieties. In the scientific name of a plant (formal or Latin name), the first word (capitalized) is the genus, the second the species.

GEOLOGY: Science which treats of the history and life of the earth as indicated by rocks. *See also* MINERAL ROCKS.

GERANIUM: A large family of popular, cultivated flowering ornamentals. Geraniums are usually perennial or biennial, but there are a few annual varieties. The common garden geranium is not a true geranium at all, but is a member of the genus *Pelargonium*.

CULTURE: Geraniums are not difficult to raise. They need only a moderate amount of water, a fairly cool, well-drained, moderately rich (but not

Geraniums offer a rich and varied diversity of foliage and abundance of brilliant flowers. Many zonal geraniums are used successfully for hedges.

too rich) soil, and plenty of sunshine. In the northern regions of the country, they should be planted in full sun, but in the South and Southwest, half a day's exposure should be enough to make the plants bloom freely without burning. An annual top-dressing of decayed manure or rich compost should be ample stimulation for geraniums. The fact that geraniums are fairly drought-resistant makes them a popular cultivated plant of the Southwest.

POTTING: A recommended mixture for potting geraniums is two parts garden loam, one part leaf mold or compost, and one part sharp sand. Some gardeners recommend including one part well-rotted manure, and some add a teaspoonful of bone meal to a five-inch pot when planting. If the soil in your outdoor beds is heavy, it should be lightened with leaf mold and sand. And although geraniums may be planted directly in the earth, it is sometimes better to sink them in clay pots for easier removal.

CUTTINGS: Cuttings are best made in late summer or early fall from new tip growth taken from earlier flowering plants that have been cut back a month or so before. Select stems about three or four inches long with two or three leaf nodes, remove the lower leaves and any flower buds, then allow the cuttings to dry several hours before sinking them in damp, sharp sand. Some gardeners have success rooting geranium cuttings in water, and some merely plunge them into the soil near the mother plant.

The length of time required for the roots to form seems to vary, from as little as two weeks to as long as six or eight. The usual procedure is to plant the rooted cuttings first in $2\frac{1}{2}$-inch pots, later transferring them to progressively larger ones, although some commercial growers are said to start them directly in four-inchers. If you try this, be sure that your soil is light and well-drained. As the new cuttings grow, pinch the tips every once in awhile to keep the plants from getting leggy, and don't allow them to bloom until they are well grown. Wait until all danger of frost is over before taking the new plants outside.

If the leaves of your potted specimens begin to turn yellow, you can take your choice of two diagnoses—not enough sun or too much water.

Once in a while your indoor geraniums may develop leaf spot, particularly if you have been wetting the foliage when you water. If you find evidence of this disease, isolate the sick plants for the sake of the healthy ones, place them where they will get plenty of light and fresh air and where the humidity is low, and remove the affected leaves and flowers.

For mealy bugs, which seem to favor geraniums, particularly the scented varieties, the isolation ward is also recommended. Often mealy bugs can be eliminated by cleaning the infested parts with swabs of cotton dipped in alcohol. The same treatment may prove effective for onslaughts of aphis. Also try rinsing these pests off with water, but if you do this be sure to keep the plants away from the sun until foliage is dry.

PROPAGATING: The average home gardener is going to be most successful by propagating from cuttings taken in September. This is particularly so in reference to the *P. domesticums* or Lady Washington. As early as the first week in September, take three or four inch cuttings of leaf bud not flower bud material. Use a very sharp knife and make a cut straight across, just below the bud. Never use pruning shears for there is a danger of crushing the delicate tissue. Do not allow your cuttings to get dry, but set them in moist sharp sand immediately. Protect with a muslin shade, and do not allow them to dry out. Pot up, as soon as the roots are well started (about three to six weeks), using a potting soil that is not too highly fertilized.

RAISING GERANIUMS FROM SEED: Plant seed in December; geraniums started from seed bloom in about four to six months. Sow seeds, covering them with about $\frac{1}{8}$-inch of fine soil. Keep moist by watering with a fine spray or by setting containers in a pan of water until soil surface is moist. Some seeds may germinate in several days, but sprouting usually continues two to three weeks. When seedlings have first pair of true leaves, transplant to individual pots; when plants have several leaves, pinch out growing tips to encourage bushier growth. Keep them in a sunny, cool window (55 to 60°). Slightly pot-pound plants often give better results than those with a lot of room for roots.

LANDSCAPING BEAUTY: Geraniums present such a rich and varied diversity not only in the foliage, but in the abundance of brilliant flowers. Many of the zonal geraniums can be used for hedges, and when you want a brilliant splash of color, the vivid orange scarlet Maxine Kovaleski can be employed for it is seldom out of bloom.

The versatile ivy-leafed geraniums are more and more being employed for the planting of baskets and window boxes of lasting and colorful beauty. You can combine them with harmonizing colors of the zonals for upright: some of the fragrant mint geraniums, such as the plushy-leaved peppermint geraniums, and the queen of all of them, the lovely Clorinda. —*Elizabeth Rigby, Charlotte Hoak.*

GERBERA: *see* AFRICAN DAISY

GERMAN CAMOMILE: *see* CAMOMILE

GERMAN-CATCHFLY: *see* LYCHNIS

GERMINATION: The power to grow (viability) in seeds varies greatly with different varieties of plants. Some seeds keep this power for many years, while others will not germinate after one year's time. Seeds are said to have "germinated" when young plants first appear at the surface of the soil.

Usually it is not advisable for young gardeners to save their own seed. Many of the resulting seedlings would not resemble the parent plant either in appearance or coloring. It is best and cheapest in the end to buy good seed from reputable dealers. Seed purchased from a good seed-house is sure to be fresh, and you need not worry about its germinating quality.

If you should have any seeds of which you are doubtful, however, you can easily test them. Count out a few seeds and place them between moist, not wet, pieces of blotting-paper. This must be kept moist until germination takes place. Keep them at a temperature of 70 to 80°, and in a few days, depending upon the kind of seed sown, most of them will have sprouted, if the seed is fresh and healthy.

Darkness, moisture, air, and heat are all required for proper seed sprouting. Unless they have these in the soil in the proper proportion, the seed cannot germinate. The following general rules must always be observed: (1) the soil, whether in flats (shallow boxes) or seedbeds must be properly prepared; (2) flats and seedbeds must be carefully placed to secure the proper amount of sun and shade for the varieties being grown; (3) soil temperature should be governed according to whether the seeds need heat or cold to develop; and (4) moisture must be carefully watched so that the seeds are kept neither too wet nor too dry. Some seeds require "winter freezing," that is, living in the frozen ground over winter before germinating. Other seeds will sprout only when the soil is very hot and dry. You need not worry about this if you will follow carefully the directions usually printed on the seed packets. The following table gives the approximate time required for the germination of a few common flower seeds.

TABLE OF GERMINATION

PLANT	DAYS
Ageratum	5- 8
Alyssum	4- 5
Anchusa	18-20
Arctotis	12-15
Baby's-breath	18-20
Balsam	5- 8
Butterfly weed	10-12
Calendula	8-10
Candytuft	5- 8
Canterbury-bells	12-15
Clarkia	7-10
Cockscomb	5- 8
Columbine	15-18
Coreopsis	15-20
Cornflowers	5- 8
Cosmos	5- 8
Dahlia	8-10
Delphinium	10-15
Dianthus	8-10
English daisy	5- 8

Forget-me-not	12-15
Four-o'clock	5- 8
Gaillardia	15-20
Godetia	12-15
Heliotrope	15-18
Hollyhock	15-18
Larkspur (annual)	15-18
Lobelia	8-10
Love-in-a-mist	8-10
Marigold	5- 8
Mignonette	8-10
Morning-glory	8-10
Nasturtium	8-10
Nicotiana	18-20
Nigella	8-10
Pansy	10-12
Peas, sweet	15-18
Penstemon	18-20
Periwinkle	15-18
Petunia	10-18
Phlox (annual)	15-18
Poppies (Iceland)	18-20
Portulaca	15-18
Rose mallow	15-18
Sage, Blue	12-15
Shasta Daisy	18-21
Strawflowers	5- 8
Zinnias	5- 8

DEPTH TO PLANT: In sowing seeds the general rule is to cover them two or three times the diameter of the seed. Plants, such as sweet peas, which have a short season of bloom, often do better when the seeds are sown deeper. On the other hand, very tiny seeds, as petunia and begonia, should be pressed down with some flat object so that they are just below the surface of the soil. Very fine seeds may be mixed with sand before sowing to allow more even distribution. Hard-shelled seeds, such as moonflowers and castor-oil beans, may be scraped with a sharp knife until the outer shell is pierced. This will allow the entrance of moisture and hasten germination.

AFTER-CARE OF SEEDLINGS: Thin out the seedlings promptly if they come up too thickly, so that they will not crowd each other. Pull up enough of them, carefully, to give the other plants plenty of room. Never pinch them off at the surface. This allows the remaining roots to rot in the soil, which is bad for the health of the others.

When the little new plants are large enough to be handled (usually when they have their first true leaves), they should be pricked-out; that is, taken from the flat or seedbed in which they germinated and replanted in other flats, pots, or permanent beds, at a greater distance apart than previously. The first leaves which appear on seedlings are the "false" leaves, and do not resemble those of the parent plant.

Soak the flats or beds thoroughly a few hours before the seedlings are pricked-out. The earth then will stick to the roots and lift out in a small ball. A sharpened bit of shingle, or a lead pencil, will lift the plants out more easily than can be done with the fingers. Do not pull them out. If you do, you will tear apart and injure the tender roots.

You can be almost certain of good germination if you will sow the seeds in a mixture of equal parts of compost and sand. When the seedlings are large enough to be transplanted, transplant them into a seed flat filled with one part compost, one part sand, and two parts leaf mold.

It is important also to provide suitable conditions of moisture and temperature. Expose the young seedlings to full light to keep them from becoming leggy. *See also* PROPAGATION; SEEDS; COLD FRAME.

GESNERIA: *see* NAEGELIA

GEUM: Also known as avens, these perennials of the rose family are often recommended for use as border or rock garden plants. Prairie smoke (*G. triflorum*) grows to 1½ feet; the popular summer-blooming *G. chiloense* grows to two feet, is a fine choice for the perennial border. These plants do well in average garden soils, can be propagated by division. *See also* PERENNIALS.

GHENT AZALEA: *see* AZALEA

GHOST PLANT: *see* ARTEMISIA

GIANT REED: *see* GRASS, ORNAMENTAL

GIFT PLANTS: *see* HOUSE PLANTS (CARE OF GIFT PLANTS)

GILIA: Showy hardy annuals that do best in well-drained soils and an open, sunny location. The foliage, lacy and fern-like, is attractive; flowers are rough, globular heads, about one inch in diameter, and are produced abundantly over the plant. Prickly phlox (*G. californica*) is a sensitive perennial shrub, two to three feet, generally not able to withstand eastern winters. *G. rubra* makes an attractive three to five foot perennial in the South. Also known as Tree Cypress and Trailing Fire.

GINGER: (*Zingiber officinale*) A biennial or perennial herb native to the Tropics and cultivated in tropical countries in both hemispheres. The rhizome (the underground stem often referred to as the root), which has a characteristic, pungent taste, is used to some extent in medicine, but its principal commercial use is in flavoring foods, confections, and carbonated beverages.

Ginger is an exhaustive crop and requires fertile soil with good drainage. The rhizomes are likely to rot in poorly drained soil, and the plant will not thrive in gravelly or sandy soil. For maximum growth, much rain and high temperatures during the growing season are required, and it is therefore best grown in tropical and subtropical regions.

Since the rhizomes may be harvested early in winter, however, and the crop will not be replanted until early in spring, its culture need not be restricted to regions that are entirely frost-free. Ginger is readily propagated from small divisions of the rhizomes, each division containing at least one bud or so-called "eye." In Florida, these may be planted in February or early March about three inches deep and about 16 inches apart in rows two feet apart. Experiments there have shown that the plants come up slowly and in the early stage of growth are much benefited by some protection from the sun. Cultivation and hoeing sufficient to control weeds is necessary. As the season advances and the rhizomes enlarge, the plant develops numerous leafstalks, followed in fall by flower stalks.

In Florida the roots may be harvested early in December. This is readily accomplished with a garden fork. The soil is shaken off, the top cut off close to the rhizomes, and the fibrous roots removed. To facilitate removal of the soil, it is advisable to break the rhizomes into its several branches, or "hands."

Often grown in a greenhouse, it does best in about 75° temperature; needs much water, a large pot; responds well to applications of liquid compost or manure.

GINSENG: (*Panax quinquefolium*) A fleshy-rooted herbaceous plant native to this country and formerly of frequent occurrence in shady well-drained sites in hardwood forests from Maine to Minnesota and southward to the Carolinas and Georgia. The roots have long been believed by the Chinese to possess pronounced medicinal value.

Ginseng must be grown in partial shade in open woodland or under lath structures. The soil must be fairly light and well fertilized with woods earth, rotted leaves, or fine raw bone meal, the bone meal applied at the rate of one pound to each square yard. Seed is planted in spring as early as the soil can be worked to advantage. It is placed six inches apart each way in the permanent beds or two by six inches in seedbeds, and the seedlings are transplanted to stand six to eight inches apart when two years old. The roots of ginseng plants, especially in woodland, are sometimes damaged by mice. Protection from these rodents may be necessary. The beds should at all times be kept free from weeds and grass and the surface of the soil slightly stirred whenever it shows signs of caking. A winter mulch is needed, applied when freezing weather begins and removed early in spring.

GLADIOLUS: Gladiolus, with their stateliness, bring beauty and color to gardens and flower beds the summer through. And they may be found tossing their proud heads in the wind from Maine to California, and from North Dakota to Texas. Their brilliant florets, crisp and full, adorn spikes that sometimes attain the height of five feet.

Each individual bloom is a delicate blend of pastel shades. The few varieties of gladiolus that boast heavier and deeper tones of red, blue, and purple, have a texture of pure velvet. Each variety, regardless of height, color or size of bloom, produces beautiful, proud flowers that are a pleasure to behold.

The extreme beauty of this flower, its versatility in adapting to soil and climatic conditions, and the simplicity of its culture, are responsible for its nation-wide popularity.

Many years ago, this summer-blooming member of the iris family was first discovered growing among the tall grass along the river banks in the hot, steaming jungles of Africa. At that time the florets, although, extremely beautiful, were small compared to the hybrids of today. Through cross-pollination, a multitude of colors have been created to bring even greater beauty to the glads, and more buds and better height to the spikes.

Here are a few of the more beautiful gladiolus, which can be grown with reasonable success in all parts of the country. They are Bagdad—a smoky old rose with large florets; Peach Blossom, a beautiful peach-blossom pink; Purple Supreme—a nice deep purple; Blue Boy—a pure shade of blue; Green Light—a yellow-ish-green; Bouton d' Or—a deep yellow; Maria Goretti—an almost pure white; Picardy—an apricot-pink, and Palet—a lovely vermilion red.

All of these are of the hybrid type

There are many varieties of gladiolus ranging in size from miniature to five feet. It is advisable to buy different-colored bulbs for best effects.

with spikes measuring from three to four feet high. The florets are all large and very showy. There are many other varieties and colors on the market which range from the miniatures to the giants that reach five feet.

One more thing concerning the purchasing of gladiolus corms: You may be fond of only one color, and are interested in growing just that one. It is wiser to buy six bulbs of a different color. Variety in colors makes prettier bouquets. The bulblets, or cormels, can be saved from year to year, and, in time, you will have large numbers of each color at no additional cost.

INCREASING CORMS: If you are interested in growing giant spikes, you may do so with a twist of the wrist. In order that the corm be made to concentrate all of its energy into growing just one spike, all "eyes" must be removed from the corm except the main one located near the center. Cut deep enough, with the tip of a knife, to remove all "eye" cells. Allow wounds to heal for a few days before planting. This is the method flower-growers use to create Grand Champions.

A good way to increase your bulb supply is to cut each large bulb in half. Those corms that have sprouted are best to work on. Cut right down through the corm between two sprouts. Each half will then produce a large spike. This dividing will in no way affect the size of the flower, or dwarf the new bulb in fall. When divided, the corms often produce lovelier and more robust florets.

Saving bulblets, or cormels, of course, is another way to increase your bulb supply at no additional cost. Save all those over $\frac{1}{4}$-inch in diameter. In spring, break the hardshell, and peel each clean. Plant as you would peas. Within three years these tiny bulblets will reach blooming size.

WHEN TO PLANT: The best rule to follow here is to make the first planting just as the leaves are bursting on the trees in your area. For a succession of bloom, make plantings every ten days for about ten weeks.

These plantings may create problems, for, no sooner does the weather turn warm, than corms sprout and grow. What we usually do is pick out all of the sprouted ones, and plant them first. The others are equally divided into the number of intended plantings, and stored in paper bags where temperatures are around 45°.

HOW TO PLANT: All garden soil that has good drainage, and is rich in organic matter, is excellent for gladiolus culture. Plant the corms in small, circular beds among other flowers for summer color, or plant in rows in the garden for a steady supply of cut flowers.

When planting in flower beds, dig a round hole eight inches deep and 12 inches across. Loosen soil in the bottom, and add one quart of old manure, or a pint of dehydrated manure, two fistfuls of an organic fertilizer that is balanced, and a fistful of lime if the soil is acid. Work the fertilizer well into the soil, cover with an inch of dirt, then set in six large corms spaced two inches apart in all directions.

Refill the hole, leaving a slight depression to catch water. The earth should be firmed only enough to eliminate air pockets.

If planting in rows in the garden (which, by the way, produces the largest flowers), work the soil well to a depth of 12 inches. Turn in any organic matter you have on hand such as compost, aged manure, leaf mold or green manures. Rake area smooth, then make trenches eight inches deep about two feet apart.

Since gladiolus are such heavy feeders, some organic food should also be incorporated into the bottom of each trench for immediate use. We like to mix old manure equally with compost, and apply two inches deep in each trench. Then we give each furrow a good dusting of bone meal. All of this is then worked into the soil, and covered with an inch of dirt.

The larger corms are then set individually six inches apart. The smaller ones are planted alternately four inches apart. Gladiolus that are planted six inches or deeper will require no staking when spikes appear. If spikes should become quite large, however, staking would be wise to prevent breakage.

When choosing a planting location, select one that receives full sun all day. The shorter the photoperiod, the shorter the flowerheads. Under ordinary conditions, glads bloom within 70 to 90 days. In Southern California, they'll bloom twice if the first spike is cut off immediately after blooming.

SUMMER CARE: Unless rains are extremely heavy, water gladiolus at least once a week. Most failures are due to insufficient watering. These flowers require an inch or more of water a week. Even those glads that are not fed, do better when watered adequately. We solve this problem of watering by allowing an overhead sprinkler to run all night every seven days. The earth around the bulbs should be damp at all times, but no puddles should be allowed to remain as gladiolus dislike wet feet.

When plants are eight inches tall, loosen soil between rows, and apply an organic fertilizer high in phosphorus. This early feeding determines the bud count on each spike and its final length. Water in fertilizer with a fine spray. When ground has dried sufficiently, hill each row to a height of six inches for later support.

To cut down on weeds, and to keep the soil constantly moist, mulch heavily with at least eight inches of hay, straw or grass clippings.

CUT FLOWERS: There is a slight disagreement among professional gladiolus growers as to the best time to cut spikes. Some believe it is wise to gather them after sundown when the spikes are fortified with extra food. Others prefer to cut them in the early morning.

When gathering spikes, use a sharp knife, and cut on a long slant to expose as many cells as possible. More water will be absorbed if cut this way, resulting in crisper flowers. Do not take any leaves if possible, as they are needed to mature the corm properly. Cut when two lower buds show color.

Spikes cut in this early stage bloom more beautifully, and last much longer. However, if you prefer to gather your spikes after half of the florets have opened, do so in the middle of the day. Allow to wilt for an hour, then rearrange the florets into a more clustered group.

FALL CARE: Right after all blooms have faded, rake away the mulch and give the plants another feeding of organic fertilizer. This feeding produces massive corms, which, in turn, will bring forth larger and more beautiful glads each year. Any balanced organic fertilizer will do. Soak fertilizer in, then replace the mulch.

Allow bulbs to remain in the ground until a light frost, then take them up with a garden fork. If you have large numbers of bulbs, break them off immediately, and place in open trays in some outdoor building to dry. Smaller amounts may be tied together like onions and hung in a well-ventilated room until dry.

After three weeks, husk the corms by completely removing the paper-like covering. Gather all suitable cormels and place in a shoe box. Return the peeled corms to their trays and allow to cure for two or three weeks, or until nice and dry. When ready, place in a carton with peat moss, or into strong paper bags into which a few moth balls have been dropped to discourage mice and thrip. Store in a cool, dry place until spring.—*Betty Brinhart.*

GLAUCONITE: Glauconite is an iron-potassium-silicate that imparts a green color to the minerals in which it occurs. It is a rounded, soft but stable aggregate of finely divided clay. The most common and best known glauconite mineral is the greensand of New Jersey which was deposited near the "mud line" surrounding the continental shores many millions of years ago. As an oceanic deposit, glauconite is developed principally in the interior of shells, and organic matter is believed to play a part in its formation.

Sand-sized glauconite acts like a sponge, absorbing and storing moisture. Its unique rounded shape also prevents the interlocking of soil particles and retards soil compaction. According to Dr. J. C. F. Tedrew, Rutgers University soil specialist, glauconite may have considerable capacity for gradual release of certain plant food elements, particularly the so-called trace elements or micronutrients, which plants need, but only in minute quantities. Once glauconite is thoroughly impregnated with the micronutrients, they may later be released at a very slow rate, a condition highly desirable in soils. *See also* GREENSAND.

GLOBE-FLOWER: (*Trollius*) Globe-Flowers require a moist soil and thrive best when planted in swampy parts of a rock garden, in shady wet beds or on margins of ponds and streams. The species make most attractive spring-flowering clumps of yellow and orange. The plants are propagated either by seed or by division of the roots. Clumps should be lifted, divided and replanted every three to four years. This can be done from October to April. During dry weather the plants should be watered freely. Seeds should be sown outdoors in a loamy soil in a shady location in September or April.

The plants are low perennial herbs, erect or ascending from thickened, spreading fibrous rootstocks. The leaves are dark to bronzy green, basal and on the stem, and palmately lobed or cut, like those of the Buttercups. The flowers are most showy, whitish, yellow, orange or even purplish, and are usually borne solitary at the ends of the stems and branches. The fruit is a one-seeded follicle, a number being clustered in a colony.

The species most planted in rock gardens is *T. europaeus*, which has incurved sepals so that the flowers have a ball-like appearance. A large

number of hybrids between this species and *T. asiaticus* are also to be had.— *G. L. Wittrock*.

GLOXINIA: (*Sinningia*) These houseplants offer the grower a wonderful variety of colors that range from pink and dark purple to pure white. Gloxinias thrive best in a soil rich with compost and may be grown from mature tubers, young potted plants, leaf cuttings, or seed.

Buell hybrids, like other gloxinias, are splendid houseplants whose appearance is an asset to the arrangement or decor of any room in the home.

A good potting mixture is one-third part each of sand, peat moss or leaf mold and good garden loam soil. The main thing to remember is that gloxinias like the potting mixture to be rich and fibrous.

Charcoal in the bottom of the pot helps drainage. As a general guide, gloxinia tubers less than $1\frac{1}{2}$-inches can go into five-inch pots, while larger tubers require a larger size pot. A temperature range of 60° at night and no higher than 85° during the daytime is best. Extreme temperatures will shorten the blooming season.

During the winter time, give gloxinias as much light as possible; generally an eastern or southern exposure is best. In summer, give them some shade.

Water them at the soil surface until the water runs out the bottom of the pot. Don't water again until the surface shows signs of drying, as this prevents the soil from becoming water-logged.

Give gloxinias a short rest after they bloomed during the spring and summer. This should start in September or October. Then repot the tubers as soon as the plants die down and before storing them for the rest period. Potted tubers should be kept in the basement or in a dark closet until new growth starts and keep them only slightly moist. When you see signs of new growth, it's time to move the plants to warmth and sunlight.

LEAF CUTTINGS: You can start leaf cuttings in the spring or summer and they will usually produce tubers and flowers the following year. Cut the leaf as closely as possible to the stem of the plant, where the leaf stem is hard. Remember to take leaves while the plant is in active growth, preferably while in bud or bloom.

Root the cuttings in sand, vermiculite, peat moss, or a mixture of sand and peat moss. After dampening this mixture, put the leaf stem in the entire length of the stem. Cover the top of the container until the leaf is established, and a new tuber will form on the stem end of the leaf. Don't permit the rooting medium to dry out. When the leaf starts turning yellow, it's time to dig the new tuber that is formed and to pot it in the usual manner for mature tubers.

GROWING GLOXINIAS FROM SEED: It is not difficult to grow gloxinias from seed. Make sure the seed you use is as fresh as possible. If you sow in July, they will develop into lovely flowering plants within ten months.

Since the seeds are fine, it's best to sprinkle them thinly over a well-screened mixture of good soil, compost, peat moss and sand. Instead of covering them or pressing them into the soil, put a piece of glass over the container to conserve moisture; then set the pot in a shady, warm place and don't allow it to dry out.

The seeds should germinate in ten days to three weeks after sowing. The first transplanting can be done when the initial leaves measure about ⅜-inch. After germinating, plants should be moved to an east window and the glass removed from the container for several hours daily.

For this first transplanting, prepare four-inch pots with drainage and rich soil. Use a sharp lead pencil and a pair of tweezers to help you in transplanting. Plant 20 or 30 seedlings in one pot. The tiny gloxinias can be grown in these pots for four to six weeks and then potted individually into 2½-inch pots.

The gloxinias can remain in these pots for about eight weeks and at this time it's recommended to place them in five-inch pots where they can be grown through their first blooming season.

INSECTS AND DISEASES: One of the most common enemies of gloxinias are thrips. They cause a rusty appearance on the undersides of the leaves and stems; also buds often fail to mature and form into hard little balls. Most often gloxinias won't be bothered with thrips, if you give them the right humidity and a well-composted soil mixture.

Bud-blast, another enemy of gloxinias, is usually caused by insufficient humidity. If your plants are troubled with this, you can correct it by setting the plants on moist trays of sand.

Try not to get water on the leaves of plants especially when they are in the sunshine. This will cause holes to be burned in the leaf. If you do accidentally splash some water on the leaves, set the plant in a shady place until the water has evaporated.

If plants are "spindly," give them more light. Move them closer to the window or, if necessary, place them in a different window with more sunshine. If gloxinias are grown under fluorescent lights, and have this problem, apply boosters in the form of inverted pots or cans to get the plants closer to the lights.

GNEISS: *see* MINERAL ROCKS

GOAT: Goatkeeping is one of the simplest livestock operations; equipment for the "backyard dairy" can be just as simple—a homemade stanchion and manger for feeding is the basic requirement. You may wish to add a folding milking stand, attached to the wall, to ease the milking task a bit.

By their nature goats are affectionate and gentle. They are highly intelligent and can be taught almost any trick that can be taught a dog. This, together with their small size, makes them excellent projects for women and children. Dairy goats are growing in popularity as 4-H projects, providing excellent training for the youngsters as well as a profitable activity. Boys and girls secure a real satisfaction in productive activity working with animals that are highly responsive to their care and attention.

BREEDS: There are four principal breeds of dairy goats in America.

Nubians are of English, African and Oriental origin. They are characterized by large size; long drooping ears; arched nose; and any color or combination.

French Alpines range from white to black spotted. Ears are upright; face dished; eyes prominent.

Saanens are of Swiss origin. They are white; good size; short, erect ears; face dished or straight.

Toggenburgs are a Swiss breed, medium-large; brown in color with light markings down the face, on legs and under body; ears short and erect; face dished.

Many beginners start with grades of one of the recognized breeds. A grade is one with a registered, purebred sire, with the other parent of unknown or mixed breeding. Carefully selected grades carry many of the best characteristics of the purebred blood they contain, and are usually available at a lower cost than a purebred of comparable productive ability.

Goat milk is more easily digested than cow's milk because of, among other things, its smaller, finer and more easily assimilated fat globules. For the same reasons, it is also more nourishing, for people are nourished not by what they swallow but by what they digest. Tuberculosis does not exist among goats, so their milk needs no pasteurization because of it, and runs no danger of losing its vitamins or having its calcium salts altered by heat.

It is significant that many people have started to use goat milk to help them through an illness, and then have continued to use it—both as a preventive and because of the fine flavor and quality of carefully-produced goat milk.

Goat milk is sweet and pleasant to the taste. Goats are particularly discriminating in their feeding habits. The doe, or female goat, is absolutely odorless and of utmost cleanliness in her habits, and it is quite easy to produce high quality milk of the finest flavor.

A fairly good goat will give three to four quarts of milk a day—more than the usual amount purchased by an average family. To produce this amount of milk about four pounds of hay and two pounds of grain is required. You should purchase two or more goats, however, and by having them freshen at different times of the year a reasonably constant milk flow can be maintained throughout the entire year.

Young females may be bred to freshen at 14 or 15 months of age if they are well developed. The gestation period is five months, and the usual practice is to have the does freshen once a year. There are fine, purebred males available within driving distance of any community and it is seldom necessary or advisable for the small owner to maintain a male for breeding his does.

The average city lot can provide much of the maintenance for goats, and the leaves and trimmings from the family garden—if not damaged with sprays and poisons—will go far to meet the feed requirements. These feeds, otherwise waste except as converted into compost, are made into milk at a great saving in grocery bills and improvement of family health. Add alfalfa hay, or any good leguminous hay, with a light grain ration and the goats will thrive at nominal cost.

Keep in mind, too, that while producing milk the goat is also converting feed into high-grade manure. The goat's digestive system is such that few if any weed seeds pass through her undigested. The composition of goat manure is about the same as that of sheep manure, but of course varies depending upon the kind and quality of feed she receives. The goat is, by nature, a browser rather than a grazer; she utilizes leaves and twigs of deep-rooted plants to good advantage. Disregarding trace minerals and some other similiar ingredients, goat manure will contain about:

Water	64	per cent
Nitrogen	1.44	per cent
Phosphorus	.22	per cent
Potassium	1.00	per cent

The manure of the goat, being dry and in pellets, is clean and odorless. In fact, the modern dairy doe is perhaps the most nearly odorless and the cleanest of any animal, and your premises can be absolutely free of any odor, if reasonably sanitary conditions are maintained. Does are normally quiet if well cared for, but even the rare noisy doe can be "debleated" by a veterinarian. Your backyard goat dairy can be clean, sweet, odorless and quiet!

Goats do not need expensive or elaborate housing. Only a few essentials must be remembered: House them in a clean, dry place, free from draughts but well ventilated. If this is done, they will stand almost unlimited cold or heat in any climate.

Where animals are kept stanchioned, a minimum of about 2½ feet by five feet is required for each animal, plus whatever alleyways, feedways, and so on may be desired or required. This presupposes that the goats will receive some exercise in an outside pen or on a tether. If goats are shut in the barn during part of the day or night, but not confined to stanchions, a minimum floor space of three square yards should be provided for each goat.— *Corl A. Leach.*

GOAT MANURE: *see* Manure

GODETIA: The godetia or satin-flower, though not hardy, will succeed especially in a partially shaded location, and deserves consideration as a spring-flowering annual. The open, primrose-like flowers of white, rose or red are borne on spikes about 18 inches long. The seeds germinate well in autumn and the young seedlings, which closely resemble snapdragon plants, grow off quickly and the losses from transplanting are negligible.

Farewell-to-spring (*G. amoena*) grows one to two feet high, is fine for cutting, prefers being crowded together.

GOLDEN BELL: *see* Forsythia

GOLDENROD: (*Solidago*) These are any plants of a widespread genus (*Solidago*) of summer and fall-blooming perennials of the aster family. Descriptively, they have wandlike stems, variously shaped leaves, and heads of small yellow, or occasionally white, flowers. Species from this group have been adopted as state flowers by Alabama, Kentucky and Nebraska.

Most of these plants are striking in appearance—but have odors that are not pleasant. One, however, that appeals to both sight and smell is the Sweet or Anise-Scented Goldenrod (*S. odora*), named for the aroma of its crushed leaves.

Sweet Goldenrod ranges from Maine and Vermont south to Florida

The goldenrod responds well to cultivation, making handsome groupings with other fall-blooming wild flowers. They propagate readily by division.

and west to Missouri and Texas. It grows in fertile but sandy or dry soil along thicket borders, in open woods, or on sunny hillsides. Often reclining, it is a slender species that reaches only two to three feet high, and blooms from July to September. The leaves have many small, clear dots which secrets an anise-like scent; also a good honey plant.

These fragrant leaves, when dried and steeped in water, make a very pleasing drink. The plant is sometimes called Blue Mountain Tea, and the beverage is regarded as a tasty and wholesome tea substitute.

GOLDENSEAL: (*Hydrastis canadensis*) A native perennial formerly abundant in open woodlands having good natural drainage and an abundance of leaf mold. Its range is from southern New York and Ontario, west to Minnesota, and south to Kentucky and Georgia.

Like ginseng, goldenseal must be grown in open woodland or under lath shade. The soil should be well-fertilized, preferably by decaying vegetable matter, such as woods, soil and rotting forest leaves, well worked in to a depth of ten inches or more. Raw bone meal and cottonseed meal can also be used to advantage. Seed may be broadcast or planted in October half an inch apart in rows six inches apart in a well-prepared seedbed and covered with fine leaf mold to the depth of one inch. In winter the seedbed should be protected with burlap or fertilizer sacks. The seedlings when large enough, usually at the end of the second season, are transplanted to their permanent beds six to eight inches apart each way, the rootstocks covered to a depth of about two inches. The soil should be kept free from weeds and the plants liberally watered throughout the growing season. For satisfactory growth the plant requires about 75 per cent of shade during the summer.

Under favorable conditions goldenseal reaches its best development in about five years from seed, or in one

Belonging to two main species, American and European, the gooseberry has been neglected here although its fruit makes fine preserves.

or two years less when grown from root buds or by divisions of the rootstocks. The roots are dug in fall after the tops have withered. They are washed clean of all soil and dried on lath screens in an airy place in mild sunlight or partial shade, or indoors on a clean dry floor. When dried in the open they should be protected from rain and dew.

GOOSEBERRY: (*Ribes*) This bush fruit is fine for the home fruit garden. Wonderful for jellies and jams, as well as for fresh fruit, there are several ornamental varieties of gooseberries useful in front yards and border plantings. Growing gooseberries is not difficult. Its culture, insect and disease problems are very similar to that of currants. *See also* BRAMBLE FRUITS; CURRANTS.

GOPHER: Gophers are small rodents from six to ten inches long. They are really miniature bulldozers, digging new tunnels with their front feet and their two long projecting front teeth. Their numerous tunnels range aimlessly around, usually from a few inches to two feet beneath the surface. At intervals they throw out lateral tunnels to the surface, push freshly dug soil out into their telltale mounds, plug up the tunnel mouth, and go their nefarious way.

They eat nearly all sorts of plants, vegetables, flower bulbs, weeds, chew the bark from tree roots, often girdling and killing them. Masses of roots, plant crowns and grass are stored in underground pockets for future eating.

Gophers have from one to five litters of five to eight youngsters each a year. In California alfalfa fields they live by the tens of thousands. On the grounds of small homes and estates, wastelands, even in town and city lawns and gardens they appear as if by magic. Their tunneling and moundmaking propensities can ruin lawns, create havoc among flower gardens, and they can wipe out a young orchard in weeks.

CONTROL METHODS: First encourage the natural enemies of gophers: your pet cats, dogs, gopher and king snakes, skunks, and particularly barn owls. A pair of breeding barn owls—who do no harm to poultry and little to birds, will eat from three to six gophers a night.

Your cats will take care of many gophers, but cats and dogs cannot get at gophers that stay underground. So you must trap, flood out, or exclude gophers with inch mesh underground fencing.

You may stick a water hose in a gopher burrow and flood it, but the wily gopher often plugs off flood water, poison gas from "gopher bombs," and sometimes snake enemies.

One good way to get rid of gophers is to trap them with a wooden box trap. (Especially designed gopher traps are available commercially.) With this trap you cut a spot at the burrow entrance, set the trap and push it against the hole, put a bunch of grass or weeds on top of the trap, then stake down.—*Gordon L'Allemand.*

GOURDS: (*Cucurbitaceae*) More and more people today are discovering that gourds are one of the most fascinating crops they can grow. For one thing, they have a long and colorful history. Gourds 4,000 years old have been found in Egyptian tombs, and musical instruments made from them were used in Indian ceremonies. Back in pioneer times, they were the universal drinking cup, as well as being made into cooking utensils, dishes and toys. Historians believe gourds were cultivated even before that earliest of crops, maize.

Now, gourds are enjoying a new popularity. They're fun to grow. Too, gourd craft work is proving a most rewarding yet inexpensive hobby.

Yielding bountifully, the vines take up little space and require almost no attention while growing.

CULTURE: Seeds are planted as soon as all danger of frost is past.

The ideal location is one that provides plenty of sun, with some protection from the hot afternoon sun.

Gourds will thrive anywhere pumpkins and squash do well. A deep, well-drained soil of good fertility is best. Some growers add a handful or two of compost per plant. Too much fertilizer will produce a lot of foliage and not much fruit.

You can plant five seeds to the hill, about an inch deep, and later thin to three plants a foot apart. When the vines are to be allowed to ramble on the ground, some growers recommend a mulch of excelsior, straw or wood shavings to prevent spotting of the gourds. A concave spot dug around

are very hard to the touch, or at the first sign of frost. They are cut with a sharp knife, leaving on several inches of stem. Handle them very carefully to avoid bruising.

Wipe off any moisture, and never wash or disinfect gourds. Any mold that appears on the lagenarias while drying can be scraped off with a knife.

The hard-shelled gourds are put on a rack or indoor clothes dryer in a cool, dry place where air can circulate around them. The thin-shelled ornamentals are waxed, shellacked or varnished immediately. They will rot if cut or carved, and anyway only last several months, unlike the lagenarias which will last for many years if

The Luffa is a most versatile gourd whose cultivation is well worth the gardener's while. Its gourd and leaves are edible and it also has medicinal and industrial value. Up to 25 gourds grow on one vine.

trellised plants will help to retain water. Gourds are shallow-rooted plants, so should never be cultivated deeply. They are subject to only one disease, wilt, which may be avoided by planting in a different location every few years.

Some gourd gardeners like to shape their gourds while growing to make them even more interesting. Soft tape works well with the smaller varieties, while the long kinds can be bent gently and frequently with your hands. One fancier succeeded in actually tying a knot in the four-foot-long handle of a Knob Kerrie gourd! Growing gourds are sometimes encased in bottles or jugs, which are later broken off to let the gourd mature in its new shape. Gourds can be harvested when they

properly treated. One museum has a Japanese wine bottle over 200 years old.

The drying time of the lagenarias may vary from a month to six months or more. They are cured when the seeds rattle inside upon shaking. Scrubbing with steel wool will remove the thin outer skin, leaving a surface which will take a beautiful polish.

When the gourd is completely dry, it may be cut for whatever use you wish to make of it, and the seeds scooped out. The shells can be carved or designs burnt in with an electric needle—the name of a friend and a greeting is especially fine for a gift.

You can use feathers to paint the gourds with a quick-drying enamel. Lacquer or varnish are equally good.

Many craftsmen prefer several coats of high-grade wax to give a natural mellow glow—the Indians accomplished the same thing by rubbing the gourds for hours with the natural oils from their skins. Decals look well, too.

GOVERNMENT SERVICES: In 1862, the United States Department of Agriculture was established. Its purpose: "To acquire and diffuse useful information on agricultural subjects in the most general and comprehensive sense."

Thus today advice and aid in many forms is available to any farmer or gardener.

The Department of Agriculture carries on research at the experiment stations at the federal land grant colleges—one in each state—and at some 600 field stations. In addition, the states maintain over 450 research centers. Together they have nearly 13,000 scientists working individually and cooperatively on current and long-range farming problems. All of the findings of this huge amount of practical research is channeled through the Extension Service of the state colleges.

Over 3,500 extension county agents are available to help rural people with everything from planting to marketing, from rose growing to clothes making.

One vital word of caution: Make it known that you want recommendations in line with organic principles— no artificial fertilizers, poison sprays, or any other substitutes for what your soil, plants, trees and livestock should get.

To find out how to contact your county agent and other experts, it will pay you to get the "Directory of Organization and Field Activities of the USDA," available for 55 cents from the Superintendent of Documents, Washington 25, D. C. It tells the address of all national and local agricultural agencies and the people to contact at each.

Another valuable booklet from the same source is the "List of Available Publications of the USDA" for 45 cents. It lists thousands of bulletins and reports of all types you can get free or for a nominal charge.

The Office of Information, USDA, Washington 25, D. C., also distributes free publications to farmers, and the experiment station will send you their bulletins on request.

At Beltsville, Maryland, is the Agricultural Research Center, the biggest experiment station in the world. Thousands visit it every year to see its 11,000 acres of garden, field crop, livestock and greenhouse projects. It's well worth a trip, but write first for information on visiting regulations.

Several other agencies offer direct and indirect aid to the farmer:

The Agricultural Marketing Service conducts marketing research, makes crop and livestock estimates, and sets the standards for farm products. Most of its information is sent out through its press service to newspapers, farm magazines and radio stations.

The Forest Service conducts research in woodland and range management. In particular, it distributes planting stock for woodlots and shelterbelts, and aids in the conservation of water and other wildland natural resources.

The Farmers Home Administration makes or insures loans to buy or improve family-sized farms, to install conservation practices, and to purchase equipment, seed, fertilizer and the like. There are 1,500 local offices.

The Commodity Credit Corporation makes loans for the construction or expansion of farm storage facilities, and also administers price support programs. One of its chief duties is to assist the Commodity Stabilization Service to adjust the production, price and carry-over of farm products to prevent shortages or gluts.

The Rural Electrification Administration extends loans and technical assistance to local electric and telephone service for rural users.

Since it was formed in 1935, the Soil Conservation Service has grown until it is today one of the most valuable organizations working for and with the farmer. Its activities have demonstrated conclusively that the best use for land—based on the way that nature made it—is the most profitable use.

There are now some 2,700 locally organized, farmer-directed soil conservation districts. They take in over 90 per cent of the nation's farm- and ranch-land.

When you apply to the SCS for advice, or become a conservation district "cooperator," the Service's whole staff of technicians swings into action for you. They survey your farm, acre by acre, analyzing its soil, typography and other factors influencing its productivity and long-range usefulness.

Many conservation practices, by the way, will be paid for in part by the government, under the cost-sharing provisions of the Agricultural Conservation Program. And the new Watershed Protection and Flood Prevention Act also provides funds for establishing conservation measures on whole watersheds where flood damage and other upstream land and water problems may be proving costly to the farmer.

See also EXPERIMENT STATIONS, AGRICULTURAL.

GRADING LAWNS: *see* LAWNS

GRAFTING: A graft is a shoot or part of a tree or plant inserted into another tree or plant and fixed or protected so that it becomes attached and a living part of the new identity.

Probably the oldest purpose of grafting is for reparative purposes. But today the most important use of grafting is for propagation of new or desired varieties of fruits or flowers for their perpetuation and multiplication . . . and these are the chief rea-

sons that grafting is used universally today.

There is one other important reason that grafting is used and that is for making dwarf trees—for most dwarf trees are grafted trees.

But grafting is also used to make trees more fruitful or to improve the quality of the fruit and to adapt plants to adverse soils and varying climatic conditions. For example, in the southern states they bud plum on peach roots because the peach root is more adaptable to sandy soil. In the North they bud peach on plum roots to make them stand up better where the soil is damp. Then again, they'll put plum on peach roots because the peach tends to make the tree bear sooner.

In Russia and in the northern parts of Canada they bud or root-graft apples onto Siberian crab rootstocks because this is an exceptionally hardy variety and it is readily compatible to all varieties of apple.

There are approximately 125, more or less, different kinds and types and varieties of grafting. But the art of grafting revolves around six proven and tried methods and these are as follows: (1) Whip—or Tongue Graft; (2) Cleft Graft; (3) Bark, Crown or Rind Graft; (4) Bridge Graft; (5) Budding; (6) Double Top-working or Double Grafting.

Grafting is not confined solely to woody plants or trees because grafts take very readily on cactus . . . and, on tomatoes, melons, cabbage, asters, phlox and coleus. Sunflower has been grafted on melon, cabbage on tomato, aster on phlox, coleus on tomato, maple on ash.

However, it has never been recorded that a graft was successful of a monocotyledon on a dicotyledon or other plant divisions.

It was the Russian agriculturist T. Lysenko who really showed how simple grafting can be. He just sliced a tomato in half while it was still attached to the vine, put the top of one on the bottom of another and vice versa and kept them in position by means of an elastic band and seed was developed. This actually was a case where grafting was used to create a hybrid.

WHIP OR TONGUE GRAFT: This appears to be the best method where the stock and scion are close to the same thickness. When the stock that is to be grafted is greater than ¾-inch in diameter, it is best to use some other form of grafting because it would be very difficult to make the proper cuts with the grafting tools.

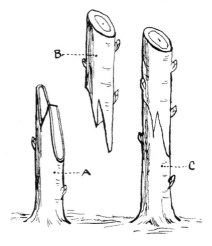

The top of the rootstock is cut off diagonally. If the stock is ½-inch in diameter, the diagonal cut should be 1¼-inches long. This diagonal cut should be greater or less, depending upon the size of the rootstock. The scions are usually prepared before and should be between four and six inches long and should contain at least three eyes. If the scion wood is scarce, as it sometimes is, especially with new varieties, two eyes or even one eye will be satisfactory but your chances are better of meeting with success if you use a three-eyed scion. (A scion is defined as the shoot of a woody plant containing two or more buds to be used in grafting.)

The cut on the rootstock should be made heavenward and that on the scion should be made earthward. Make sure the cut is smooth and clean because you don't want anything to stand in the way of perfect contact between the two cambium layers.

Now make your second cut to form a tongue. It should be about one-third distance in each case from the apex to the base and running towards the base. Then they are spliced together and the tongues interlocked. Make sure that the cambiums coincide on both sides. If you do that, you will get optimum results.

It is not necessary or required to apply grafting wax on whip grafts. You can use string, wool or raffia to hold them firmly in place. Back 25 years ago the method used when whip grafting our apples (root-graft) was to put the scions in pine sawdust and they were kept in the cellar until time came to plant. Of course many other types of insulating material can be used but we found the old pine very, very satisfactory. Nowadays with modern storage, they can be kept to the exact temperature desired with little or no chance of failure.

The scion is generally grafted directly onto the root but you can also use only a part of the root.

CLEFT GRAFT: The cleft graft means exactly what it says. It is just chopping down into the center of the limb and inserting the scion. The cleft is held open with a wedge and then the prepared wedge-shaped scions are put in. Make a cut in the bottom end of your scion between two and three inches long. Be careful not to split the wood when you're tapering your scion.

One scion should be placed at each end of the cleft so as to come in contact with the cambium layer. Actually only one of these growths is wanted but if you set two and both of them take, you can cut back the one that you don't want. But if you set one and it doesn't grow, failure is the result.

It's difficult to get the cleft made as deep as you want it without doing harm or splitting further than you intend. Cleft grafting is employed only where large stocks are used— preferably where the branch is more than an inch in diameter . . . generally in the larger or mature trees where a new variety is wanted. It is advisable to wax the entire surface to prevent drying out and other troubles.

The cleft graft should be made in the early spring. The best time is when the sap is beginning to run. The scion wood however should have been prepared long before while still dormant and the buds not opened. They can be kept in cold storage, in a refrigerator or buried in the earth— properly wrapped and protected. In this way you will get good results.

Cleft grafting is the method usually employed in, or is often in itself called, top-working.

Cut the limbs off squarely at the place where they are straight. Make a clean square cut at the point where you want the new limbs to grow. Never completely de-horn a tree. Always leave a few branches prior to grafting. They can be removed later.

BRIDGE GRAFT: The main reason for bridge grafting is when a large area of bark has been injured or removed by rodents or accident. Often complete girdling has happened in a specific area, spelling certain death to the tree because the bark cannot carry the sap for nourishment and life to all parts of the tree.

In such cases, trim both jagged edges of the bark where the injury occurred, leaving the part to be grafted clean. Then cut the scions in each case an inch or two longer than the area to be bridged. About four scions would be required to encircle a normal limb; even more is recommended. Both ends are tapered sort of wedge-shaped and then slits in the bark are made where they are to fit in.

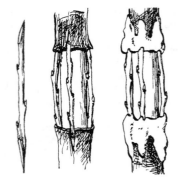

Tack them with a very fine tack, or use a pin—just the ordinary plain straight pin. And if tapped carefully, it will penetrate and do the job. Again, be careful not to split the scion wood.

Then cover the joint with grafting wax. The entire exposed area need not be covered . . . just the contact points.

In making the choice of scions, don't use wood that is too heavy nor scions that are too light. Get something of a medium size that looks good, sound, healthy and pliable.

BARK, CROWN OR RIND GRAFT: Cut back the branches just as you would in preparation for the cleft graft but instead of splitting the center, place the scions under the bark— thus causing little damage and resultant quick healing and rapid growth.

The right time is in the early spring when the sap is running and the scion wood must be prepared in advance and kept dormant.

Slit the bark with a sharp knife and insert your tapered scion. Where the individual branch is more than two inches in diameter, use two scions— one on each side. Make sure cambium is touching cambium. Then tie or tack tightly in position and cover the entire exposed surface with wax.

DOUBLE TOP-WORKING OR DOUBLE GRAFTING: There are some fruit varieties in apple and in pear where the variety or scion is positively not compatible with the rootstock. But if you want to have that variety, you must find some way or means of getting this thing to work.

The accepted method is to first graft onto the rootstock a variety that is compatible—usually by budding or whip grafting. Then after a season's growth, put a graft of the variety you want onto this graft. This means that you have three distinctly different plants on one tree. Two are scions and one is the root. But the resulting fruit is the fruit you wanted and the rootstock is also of your choice. However, you had to use an intermediary to achieve your goal. This system is practiced quite widely throughout the world.—*John Tobe.*

See also BUDDING; LAYERING.

GRAIN CROP: Term applied to cereal grains, including barley, buckwheat, corn, rye, sorghums and wheat. *See names of individual crops.*

GRAMAGRASS: *see* LAWN

GRANITE DUST: Granite dust or granite stone meal is a highly recommended natural source of potash. Its potash content varies between three and five per cent and sometimes more.

One of the first researches showing the value of granite dust to plants took place at the Connecticut Experimental Station. Tests there showed that the potash in granite rock is available to a growing crop of tobacco, a plant which needs a liberal quantity of potash for optimum growth. The opinion popularly held by most agriculturists is that only the chemical fertilizers, such as the sulfate or muriate compounds, contain potash in an economically available form.

This work in Connecticut definitely shatters that idea. The experiment was written up by the Connecticut Agricultural Station in a booklet entitled *Granite Stone Meal as a Source of Potash for Tobacco,* Bulletin 536— April 1950. The work was done by T. R. Swanback, of the Tobacco Laboratory, Windsor, Connecticut.

The value of using potash rock

over the chemical form is that it is cheaper and leaves no harmful chemical residues. It also contains valuable trace mineral elements. There are sources of granite and other rocks

Granite dust can be spread by hand or by adapted seed cart. Recommended application is two tons to the acre plus added nitrogen and phosphoric acid, according to soil test findings.

that contain potash all over the country and the agricultural experiment stations should make detailed surveys in each state in order to best serve the interests of the farmers within their states.

NATURAL POTASH: Here are some excerpts from the Connecticut report:

An "ideal" form of potash-bearing materials is the potash carried in the organics, which are widely used in fertilization of Connecticut tobacco. However, the organics (*cottonseed meal, castor pomace,* etc.) are mainly used as carriers of nitrogen and only a limited quantity of potash is derived from that source.

The common sources of commercially available potash, such as sulfate, nitrate, carbonate of potash and ashes, all have limitations in their usage.

Too much sulfate of potash should not be employed because of its sulfur content. This element is commonly known to affect adversely the burn of tobacco and also, in excess, may impair the grading (quality) of the finished product. Nitrate of potash is limited because of the restricted usage of nitrate nitrogen in tobacco fertilizer. The general use of carbonate of potash and ashes is unsatisfactory because of their alkaline effect on the soil.

Recently, experiments were started with a type of granite stone meal with an unusually high content of total potash, obtained from granite quarries in Massachusetts.

The potash-bearing minerals in granite are the potash feldspars and the micas, of which the latter contain the most easily released potash. . . . Granite stone meal used in the experiment carried a total potash content of at least eight per cent. In addition, the material contained small amounts of trace elements.

An application of two tons of stone meal per acre, combined with the usual amount of nitrogen and phosphoric acid, produced fully as good a yield and quality as a standard six-three-six formula.

RATE OF APPLICATION: Granite dust can be used as a top dressing, worked directly into the soil, or used when establishing a cover crop. In the garden, suggested rates of application are ten pounds to 100 square feet, 100 pounds to 1,000 square feet; on the farm two tons per acre.

Hybrotite, Soil-Con and Super Gran-its are some brands of granite dust now marketed. *See also* MINERAL ROCKS; POTASH; FERTILIZER.

GRAPE: Of all the fruits grown in America, grapes are the most widely adapted to varying soils and climates. Our first settlers found grapes growing from the coast of Maine to Florida and inland to the Rockies. Besides growing over a wide area, no fruit offers so many different flavors or is more delicious. Grapes are nature's oldest and most healthful fruit, and being easy to grow should be included in every home planting.

The fruit of the Golden Muscat is golden-yellow, and the cluster and individual fruit very large. The vine is not vigorous but the fruit is tasty.

LOCATION: Grapes are one of our easiest fruits to grow and much less subject to attacks of insects and diseases than most other fruits. Every garden can produce good grapes. Selection of a favorable site for planting is important. The best site is one that has a gentle slope to provide good air circulation. Low frosty pockets should be avoided because of the danger of injury from spring frosts. Plant where the vines will receive full sun and away from trees so that they will not have to compete for moisture and other elements necessary for growth. Where growing seasons are very short, ripening can be hastened by planting on the south side of a building and training the vine against it. Heat radiation from reflected sunlight will make the fruit ripen as much as a week earlier.

Grapes are not particular as to soils. As long as they are well drained and fairly deep, they grow well on both heavy and light soils. A soil of average fertility is best because too rich soils stimulate too much cane growth causing poorly formed clusters. A slightly acid soil is best but good growth and production is possible on neutral soils. Since grapes are productive for as long as 50-60 years it is important to maintain high organic content for increased yields and better quality fruit. Waste hay, straw, sawdust, wood chips and other organic materials should be applied every other year.

FERTILIZING: Potash is a very necessary element for healthy vines and for the production of high quality fruit. Many growers apply finely ground granite rock in the fall to bring the potash content up to requirements. This is reflected in healthier vines and increased yields of fruit. Potash deficiency can be recognized on growing vines by yellowing of the margins of the leaves, and on some varieties by purplish-black leaf areas, known as black leaf.

Grapes do not respond to phosphorus, but nitrogen is necessary to stimulate growth and increases yields.

A good fertilizer program for a home planting is to apply for each vine two to three pounds of finely ground granite rock in the fall and about $\frac{1}{2}$-pound of some good source of organic nitrogen in the spring. Spread evenly over an area of from six to eight feet in diameter from the base of the vine. Grape vines have long roots that extend as much as eight feet from the base of the vine. Most of the feeder roots are from three to six feet from the base so much of the benefit will be lost if the fertilizer is placed next to the trunk.

PLANTING: Planting can be done either in spring or fall. Late October and early November is the best time for fall planting. Spring planting can be done from March through May, but it is better to plant as early in spring as the ground can be worked.

Either two-year No. 1 or one-year No. 1 vines are best. Older vines and so-called bearing age types are not satisfactory since most of the roots are lost in digging. They do not transplant well and actually take longer to produce.

Usual spacing is eight by eight feet, but if space is limited a seven foot spacing will do. Holes should be dug 12-14 inches deep and 16 inches in diameter. Before planting, the top should be pruned back to a single cane and this cut back so two buds remain. When planting in the fall, delay pruning of the top until spring. Any broken roots are pruned off and those roots that are too long to fit in the hole without crowding are cut back.

If available, it is a good plan to place some bone meal, compost or ground granite rock in the hole. Set the vine so that the two buds left on the top are just above the soil level. Either mulch or cultivate the first year.

No trellis is necessary the first year as the vines can be trained on stakes placed next to the base of the plant. The second year a trellis is necessary. A trellis with posts spaced 24 feet apart and two wires strung between the posts is ample for home plantings. Posts can be either metal or wood, about eight feet long and driven two to $2\frac{1}{2}$ feet into the ground.

The top wire of the trellis should be about $5\frac{1}{2}$ feet from the ground and the second wire about two feet below this. Grapes on a $5\frac{1}{2}$ foot trellis will ripen a week before those on a $4\frac{1}{2}$ foot one. The reason is more leaf area is exposed to sunlight.

PRUNING: Pruning is one of the most important of all operations in growing good grapes. Grape vines must be pruned every year or so much fruit will set that it will not ripen, fruit will be of very poor quality and cane growth will be weak. The purpose of pruning is to limit the production of fruit so that cane growth and fruit yield is in balance.

Strong growing vines will support more fruiting canes than those making a weaker growth. A general rule to follow in pruning is leave two buds the year planting is done. Second year, prune off all growth except one strong cane and leave three to five buds. Tie this cane to the first wire of trellis. Third year, leave two fruiting canes of six to eight buds each. Fourth year, leave two longer fruiting canes of eight to 12 buds each. Fifth year, three fruiting canes of ten to 12 buds on each.

In selecting fruiting canes use those of the previous season's growth. Leave one spur for each fruiting cane. A spur is a cane cut back to two buds. The reason for leaving these is that the canes growing from the spur is used for a fruiting cane the following year. Thus the fruiting canes are kept near to the trunk of the vine. Late winter and early spring is the best time to prune.

CULTIVATING: Cultivation should begin as soon as the ground is in condition to work. Either a mulch or cultivation is necessary to maintain yields and vine vigor. Grape feeder roots develop near the surface of the soil and working the ground more than four inches deep will injure them.

For a small home planting a heavy mulch is just as good as cultivation. The mulching material should be applied early in spring before weed growth begins and spread thickly so that weeds will not grow through it.

Grapes should not be cultivated after August first as this will stimulate late growth and delay the ripening of the fruit. Three or four cultivations during the season at about two-week intervals will control weed growth and conserve moisture.

DISEASES: The most serious disease of grapes are black rot, which attacks the fruit causing it to turn black and drop, and downy and powdery mildew. Powdery mildew affects the fruit and downy mildew causes the leaves to russet and may cause defoliation.

These diseases occur when rainfall is heavy and the days are hot and humid. These conditions are more prevalent in the southern part of our country and it is best to plant only those varieties that are very disease resistant there. Ontario, Buffalo, Sheridan and Steuben are all very resistant. Good air circulation is very important and a site where there is constant and free movement of air reduces disease to a minimum.

VARIETIES: Through efforts of plant scientists, new varieties have been developed that further extend the grape growing area. Thanks to modern plant breeding we now have varieties like Van Buren that will stand 30° below zero and produce a full crop. Ontario, an amber-colored grape that ripens three weeks before Niagara, has been entirely free from disease in our planting.

California or European grapes are too tender to survive northern winters, so plant breeders at the New York State Experiment Station have crossed hardy native grapes with California types and have produced some fine varieties. Interlaken Seedless, a cross of Ontario and Thompson Seedless, is entirely seedless and has solid, crisp, meaty berries, sweet throughout and compares with the best California Seedless varieties.

In selecting varieties for planting there is a wide choice of new and time-tested kinds. A balanced planting should include varieties that ripen from early to late to provide grapes from mid-August to November.

It takes about two to three years from the time of planting before the vines start to bear and at maturity most vines will yield from ten to 15 pounds of fruit.

Interlaken Seedless is a new fine

seedless grape that ripens by August 15th. It is hardy to about 15° below zero. Van Buren, an early blue grape, will stand 30° below zero and still produce a full crop. It ripens in late August and is of excellent quality with well-formed clusters.

Ontario is also very hardy and very disease resistant. Mildew or rot rarely occurs even in the most unfavorable seasons and with no spraying. The cluster is long and loose, and when fully ripe the golden berries are very sweet and fine flavored. It ripens a few days before Van Buren.

Buffalo is another fine early grape that is hardy and free from disease. The large blue berries and clusters have a very delightful flavor and are fully ripe by the first week in September. It should do well in more southern locations where summers are hot and humid.

Delaware and Brighton are the two best red grapes ripening in midseason or about September 15-20th. Delaware is one of the finest of all grapes with small, sweet, highly flavored berries and compact, attractive clusters.

Brighton grows long loose clusters with medium-sized berries that have a deep lilac color. It is the only variety in this list that is self-sterile and needs another variety planted with it for cross pollination.

Alden is a new midseason grape that is entirely California in character. It has very large, blue oval berries that are crisp, meaty and sweet throughout. It is hardy to about 15° blow zero.

Steuben is one of the finest blue grapes of all. Clusters are very large and well formed, with medium to large berries that are very sweet and distinctive in flavor.

Concord is included in this list because it can be grown in so many different areas. It has no equal for making grape juice and jellies as no variety has such a pronounced grape flavor after it is processed.

Sheridan is a fine late blue grape

that has very large berries and attractive, compact clusters. It is hardy and disease resistant and will keep in good condition in storage until Christmas.—*J. E. Miller. See also* FRUITS; ARBOR.

GRAPE ARBOR: *see* ARBOR

GRAPEFRUIT: (*Citrus paradisi*) Largest of the citrus family both in tree and fruit size, the grapefruit is not especially suited to the small home garden—although it may be successfully grown in favorable climate and soil areas. Like the orange, lemon, lime, etc., the tree is an evergreen, has dark green glossy-topped leaves, large white flowers and fruit up to six inches or more in diameter. Also termed a Pomelo, this fruit is generally round, with a thick, smooth peel and juicy flesh divided into many segments.

Originating in the West Indies, the grapefruit was introduced here first in Florida. California, Texas and Arizona also produce a share of the nation's supply.

Grapefruit trees grow vigorously, and when mature are better able to withstand cold than other citrus types. Their care and culture is similar to that of the citrus fruits in general.

Varieties include the Marsh Seedless, which has a less acid pulp and juice than others, although its fruit size is smaller; Duncan, Walters, Innman, McCarty and Conner's Prolific, which are better-sized but contain many seeds; and Foster, Pink Marsh and Ruby, which are popular pink-fleshed varieties.

See also CITRUS.

GRAPEFRUIT WASTES: *see* CITRUS WASTES

GRAPE-HYACINTH: (*Muscari*) Spring-flowering perennial member of the lily family. Relatively simple to grow, they do best in a loose, deep rich soil and a sunny location. Bulbs should be planted in early fall about three inches deep and apart. Blue-bells or Starch hyacinth (*M. botry-oides*) grows to about ten inches, has white flowers and also a pink variety. *See also* BULBS; BULB GARDEN.

GRAPE POMACE: The left-overs from wineries, consisting of the pressed parts of the grape, containing beside a varied bacterial flora, especially yeasts, a certain amount of nitrogen, usually about one per cent, and smaller amounts of phosphorus and potassium. Such material should be treated like other green matter in the composting process. The seeds of grapes contain valuable stored elements that will break down without much trouble through the action of fungi.

GRASS: A member of the plant family *Gramineae*. *See also* LAWN.

GRASS CLIPPINGS: Almost everyone who has a garden also has a lawn and therefore a regular supply of grass clippings. If the grass is cut once a week it is sound practice to leave the clippings right on the lawn so that they may become natural humus as they would under field conditions; but sometimes, the growth is so heavy or rain prevents the regular cutting, and leaving a heavy crop of clippings would lead to wads of yellow hay covering parts of the lawn. In that case, the material had better be raked up and added to the compost heap as part of the green matter. By the time the lawn is cut and the grass is raked it is sufficiently wilted and will soon start heating.

Grass clippings are not different from hay except in the matter of curing; after all, hay is nothing but dried or cured grass clippings, possibly mixed with herbs and legumes. The quality of the soil and the maturity of the growth have much to do with the nutritive content of the residues. A fertile soil, rich in nitrogen and phosphorus, produces a grass richer in nitrogen than a poor light soil; and

grass cut before blooming is richer in nutrients than grass that has grown long stalks with flower heads or, worse still, that has set seeds and turned into straw.

Comparing dried green grass and hay, the main distinction is this: green grass has a higher phosphorus and potash content than hay if the latter has been weathered long; otherwise there is no difference. Kentucky Blue Grass hay analyzes, for example, 1.2 per cent nitrogen, .3 per cent phosphoric acid, and 2.0 per cent potash. Timothy is a bit lower, perennial rye-grass often noticeably higher. Redtop analyses show a relatively high percentage of phosphorus. A mixed lawn, composed of several grasses should therefore mean over a pound of nitrogen and two pounds of potash for every hundred pounds of clippings in the dry state.

USES FOR CLIPPINGS: Grass clippings can play an important role in soil-improving. First of all, a good lawn doesn't need as much enrichment, added organic matter or mulching as do the more heavily cropped plots. As such a rich source of nitrogen, these clippings can most often be better used elsewhere. They can be a valuable fertilizer in the vegetable garden, a helpful addition in all mulches, and a major aid in converting leaves and other low-nitrogen wastes into best-quality compost.

Then, too, collecting grass clippings is one way to curtail unwanted weed growth in the lawn, since doing this helps to remove the weed seeds. Also, periodic collection of the clippings promotes better appearance, aids in keeping a neater lawn.

Don't remove all grass clippings. Some can and should be left as occasional replenishment for the lawn itself.

Grass clippings, freshly cut, contain a very large percentage of nitrogen. That is why grass is such a good soil builder. Perhaps too few gardeners are aware of this fact. As proof of

A mulch of grass clippings, as shown above, helps produce topsoil of excellent tilth. It contains plenty of nitrogen when freshly cut, is easily applied and protects the soil. It is fine for early vegetables.

that statement, if cut grass is allowed to remain undisturbed on a pile for two days, extreme heat will build up within the very center of the heap. If not moved, the grass will soon turn into a slushy, brown muck. This heat and reaction are caused by the rapid release of nitrogen as the grass decays.

Because green grass clippings are such a wonderful source of nitrogen, they should be utilized to the utmost. There are three excellent ways in which they can be put to work in the garden and flower beds: They may be used as a mulch; they may be turned in as green manure; and they may be used in the compost heap to create the necessary heat for good decomposition.

MULCHING: As a mulch, lawn clippings surpass most others. They are easy to handle; will remain in place nicely; will fit in the smallest spaces with no trouble, and when dried, will give your rows and beds a very neat appearance. Of course you will not have enough mulch for your entire garden from the first cutting, but mulch as much as you can each week. In a short time, all of your rows will be mulched. It is a good idea to mulch first those vegetables that mature early, then work on the others.

Because it is so finely chopped, these clippings disappear completely into the soil by fall. The mulch may be replenished in late summer, but it is not necessary. For some reason, grass does not like to grow in areas covered with decayed clippings.

Green mulch, such as this, may temporarily rob the soil of available nitrogen, including both ammonia and nitrates. But this condition is so short-lived that it can, in no way, stunt the rapid growth of the plants.

GREEN MANURE: Later in the season, you may have a surplus of grass clippings on your hands. The garden has all been mulched. What to do with them now? Don't throw them away, by any means, or add to other mulch where it is not necessary. If you are not planting a second crop in your pea patch, or in the section where the lettuce or string beans have been, scatter a few inches of the green clippings over the entire area. Turn these in immediately as green manure along with the mulch previously applied. Work a small plot at a time, depending upon the amount of excess clippings on hand. Later, you may remulch the entire area and allow it to remain thus until the following spring.

When green vegetation is mixed with the soil under favorable conditions of temperature and moisture, decomposition immediately begins. This rapid decomposition is brought about by many species of bacteria and fungi found in the earth. These micro-organisms require a source of energy such as nitrogen, which green grass supplies in abundance. Because of this large amount of nitrogen in grass, these hungry bacteria and fungi will tend to draw from it, instead of robbing the soil of its necessary supply. In no time, the grass is digested into humus, and the soil made many times richer for plant growth. The nitrogen in the earth has, also, been stepped up, which will cause plants to become stronger and greener.

If you care to turn in green grass clippings as green manure before planting a second crop in a vacant plot, you may do so. Give the section a week or ten days to return to normal, then plant as before. Many times, if the plot has thus been treated, the second crop surpasses the first.

When used as green manure, grass

clippings greatly improve the physical condition of heavy-textured soils. But to all, they give the much-needed humus and nitrogen. If acidity is a factor, a small amount of limestone may be applied with the clippings.

The third use of grass clippings is incorporating them into the compost heap to create the necessary heat for proper decomposition. The best principle to follow here is to use two-thirds grass clippings and one-third stable manure or other high-nitrogen material.—*Betty Brinhart.*

See also MULCH.

GRASSHOPPERS: Most grasshoppers feed on any available vegetation. When abundant, they can destroy complete plantings. Here are some characteristics: brown, gray, black and yellow; strong hind legs; up to two inches long; most grasshoppers are strong flyers.

CONTROL: One control measure is to plow soil at least five inches deep; most species deposit their eggs in the ground in late summer and fall; the common injurious species spends six to eight months of the year as eggs in the top three inches or so of soil, the surface layer well compacted by later cultivation—prohibits the hoppers which are hatching, from emerging from the eggs. Working the soil also may bring the eggs to the surface where they are destroyed by the drying action of sun and wind. Fall tillage is preferable, but spring tillage is sometimes just as effective. *See also* INSECT CONTROL.

GRASSLAND FARMING: Grassland farming means giving grasses, legumes and other sod crops a more important place in the farming system. It means more and better pastures and ranges and more livestock. It means more grasses and legumes in the crop rotations and more and better hay crops and silage. It means more and better cover crops, grass waterways, strip crops of grasses and legumes, and the use of sod crops in other ways to help conserve land and water. It also means better balanced and more profitable farming. This vegetative program greatly helps wildlife.

Practically all grasses and legumes conserve and improve the structure of the soil. They are the principal agents for controlling erosion on sloping land. Nearly always they improve both soil tilth and fertility and increase the water-absorbing and water-holding capacity of the soil—while growing and after being turned

Crops for grassland farming include: alfalfa, timothy, red clover, sand lovegrass, tall fescue, wheatgrass, birdsfoot trefoil, adino clover, lespedeza, vetch, kudzu, smooth brome grass and orchard grass.

Professor William A. Albrecht of the University of Wisconsin adds a word of caution about grassland farming: "Crops don't make the soil. Only soils of high fertility will feed the crops to feed us.

"To believe that merely scattering

Harvesting alfalfa which is fed green on this Orange County farm in California. Grassland farming means a better balanced and, in the long run, more profitable operation due to improvement of land.

under as green manure or left on the ground surface as a mulch.

The advantages of grassland farming, moreover, often are not limited to beneficial effects on the land. Grassland farming often takes less labor than cultivated crops, as the labor is usually distributed more evenly over the year. It has increased the income of nearly all the farmers who have tried it. Furthermore, it is usually a more interesting and enjoyable way of farming. Many farmers enjoy work with livestock, and good grass is the main base for profitable livestock farming.

grass seed is grassland farming is false. It is bunk to believe that any kind of crop farming will succeed unless we feed the crop well by means of fertile soils suited or balanced so as to provide the crop's need for its own complete nutrition."

GUARDIAN OF WATER: One way that grass conserves water is by hastening the movement of rainwater into the soil. Experiments near Guthrie, Oklahoma, showed that 30 inches or 98 per cent of the annual precipitation went into the soil when the cover was native grass. This corresponds to 26 inches of precipitation that soaked into the soil under cultivated and terraced conditions. A grass cover thus permitted four additional inches of rainfall to soak into the soil.

Grasslands are very effective in increasing infiltration of water into the soil. Grasslands also permit runoff water to flow over watersheds without erosion of the soil. This protection results in clean water and prevents siltation of the reservoir. In contrast forests encourage more water to enter the soil and less to flow over the surface as runoff. Grasslands generally yield more surface runoff than do forests on comparable land. For this reason, grass usually is the better watershed cover for areas which drain into reservoirs.

Grass protects bare soil from the beating raindrops and shades the soil from excessive heating by the sun. Grass furnishes food for earthworms and insects whose burrows permit the soil to "breathe" and "drink" more freely. Holes made in the ground by worms, insects, and grass roots, increase the amount and rate of water entering the soil. Some of the water is stored in the soil for use by plants. This reserve supply of soil moisture enables plants to withstand dry weather. Another portion of the water which enters the soil percolates deeper and increases the supply of ground water. Some of the ground water emerges as springs and some raises the water level in wells.

Probably no crops grown in the United States have more conservation uses or more all-around value than do the grasses. Grasses protect land from wind and water erosion and maintain or improve soil quality. In addition the same grasses produce pasture and hay. Grasses are being seeded to restore badly eroded land to useful production, to heal gullies, to prevent damage by runoff water on steep slopes, and to line waterways so that excess water from cultivated fields can be disposed of without erosion.

Grasses commonly used include Brome, Sudan, Orchard, Timothy, Johnson, Reed Canary and Kentucky blue.—*Roy Donahue.*

See also FORAGE CROPS; GREEN MANURE.

GRASS-OF-PARNASSUS: *see* PARNASSIA

GRASS, ORNAMENTAL: Ornamental grasses range in height from the tiny tufted varieties to those of ten feet or more. These grasses are beautiful in form; their waving feathery plumes and soft pastel colors are ideal with the bolder colors grown in the garden. Many of them are suitable, when cut or dried, for winter decorations in the home.

Seeds of the perennial grasses are available and easily grown, and develop rapidly. Still others may be increased by division; one large clump can be cut into three or four pieces and these will soon grow to make nice-sized clumps. The latter may then be divided in early spring as soon as the soil can be worked. It is advisable to follow this method with the variegated sorts as most of them will not come true from seed.

Crowded plants cannot develop, so allow at least a foot between plants. Their rapid growth and how quickly they fill the space allotted to them is amazing. As the perennials keep growing year after year, they will require more space, or will have to be thinned out regularly. The annuals are easily raised from seed sown in early spring where plants are to stand. Thin to about ten inches apart when they are quite small; give them plenty of room to assure success. The common mistake of most gardeners in growing ornamental grasses is leaving them in a crowded condition and they fail to grow.

Some of these grasses do well in a dry location while others love the water. Planted in such spots, they cast beautiful reflections in pool or brook. They do well in any good soil with plenty of humus worked in

Blue Fescue Grass

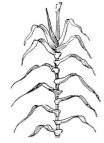

Giant Reed Grass

Spear or Feather Grass

Manna Grass

Marram Grass

Eulalia Grass

Ribbon Grass

Tropical Pennisetum

around the roots both spring and fall. Most of the grasses will adapt themselves to the soil condition and, given all the room they need, will grow into their full grace of height and form.

Hare's-tail Grass (*Lagurus ovatus*), also called Rabbit's-tail Grass, is an excellent edging plant preferring a sunny location and a well-drained soil. It grows to a height of one foot, with leaves four inches long and less than 1/2 inch wide. Spikelets two inches long are rather broad and have dense wooly heads. The plants look well in the garden and also make up into very attractive bouquets.

Cloud Grass (*Agrostis nebulosa*) is like a soft, fine hair. It grows to 18 inches tall and likes a dry situation. Quaking Grass (*Briza minor*), growing to one foot, has spikelets that are flat and tremble in the slightest breeze. Brome Grass (*Bromus brizaeforms*), with its drooping spikelets resembling those of the Quaking Grass, grows to two feet and the plant is often a biennial.

Blue Fescue (*Festuca ovina glauca*) produces fine blue-gray foliage about nine inches high and does well in a dry location. Sandy soil and moderate shade is all that is needed for this beautiful little edging plant.

Stipa, is often called Spear Needle or Feather Grass. It grows to three feet, having rolling leaves at the edges, while the spikelets are borne in clusters. *S. elegantissima* bears purple bearded spikelets in loose clusters half the height of the plant. These grasses are considered and treated as annuals.

Beach Grass (*Arenaria*), is a genus of tall-growing perennial grasses for the edge of pools or for growing along streams. Sow seed where plants are to stand. When the plants attain the height of four to five inches, thin to eight inches apart. It is a good sandbinder. *A. arenaria* (Marram Grass, Sea Sandreed or Psamma) grows to three feet and has panicled flowers to one foot, with long branching root-stocks. Prefers a sandy soil.

The Giant Reed (*Arundo donax*) is the largest of the grasses, except for the Bamboos. It is a perennial but will need some protection in the north. The plant grows from eight to 20 feet in a single season, according to clime and soil. It bears loose feathery flowers spikes one to three feet long which are very effective in the border.

Plume Grass (*Erianthus*) is hardy from New York, southward. This genus of the perennial grasses is tall growing and attains the height of ten to 12 feet in a single season. Ravenna Grass (*E. ravennae*) is the tallest with leaves three feet long and about ½ inch wide, and a plume-like flower which grows to about three feet long. *E. divaricatus* and *E. saccharoides* may grow to ten feet, have loose panicles one foot long and are very good used as accents in the border or garden. Planted in the formal garden they are most effective when used as accents in the center or for the corners.

Manna Grass (*Glyceria*) is a tall coarse perennial grass used in damp, poorly drained places—by the pool or pond. The elongated flower clusters are usually purple and are borne on branching racemes. Reed Meadow Grass or American Manna Grass (*G. grandis*) grows to five feet with leaves that are rough on the top side, growing to one foot long and ½ inch wide. May be grown from seed or the clumps may be divided.

Pampas Grass (*Cortaderia*) is a native of South America and one of the best and most popular of the ornamental grasses. It is tall-growing with silky blooms which are borne in late summer and are beautiful for many weeks. Cut when fully developed, the plumes may be dried and used to give an airy grace to winter bouquets. This very decorative grass is not hardy so must be grown as an annual. It thrives in sandy soil, in a sheltered location.

Eulatia (*Miscanthus sinensis*) is the best ornamental grass for the northern regions. Once established, it will remain for years. Good soil and enough moisture will develop this grass into attractive clumps for border or around the lawn. The leaves are three feet long and one inch wide, and have a large central vein which is a ridge-like extension of the petiole or main ridge on the leaf-like part. The panicles of silky plumes grow to two feet long. The leaves of *Var. variegatus* have white or yellow stripes. Those of *Var. zebunus* (Zebra Grass) are yellow branded.

The Ribbon Grass (*Phalaris arundinacea picta*) with green and white stripes, grows to about five feet tall and makes thick clumps in the border.

Pennisetum, grasses native to the tropics and sub-tropics, are grown for their ornamental foliage. There are both annual and perennial varieties and either makes a good garden subject. Seed started indoors or in the hotbed will get an earlier start than those planted out-of-doors. They prefer a sandy loam in a well-drained soil and a sheltered site. In the fall the plants may be lifted and placed in the cellar or under glass. *P. japonicum* has foxtail mahogany plumes tipped white. *P. ruppeli* grows to four feet and has narrow leaves two feet long. The flower spikes, a foot or more in length, are purple, coppery-red, and rose.

Supplying soft tones to the garden is the silvery Beard Grass (*Andropogon argenteus*) growing to about three feet. It bears silver plumes which are good for drying and then make an effective contrast in the winter bouquet.

Love Grass (*Eragrostis*), some annuals, some perennials, are valued for their ornamental sprays of delicate beauty. The small panicles are carried in open spikelets, growing four to 15 inches long. *E. elegans, E. interrupta* and *E. japonica* all grow to three feet and are very useful in dried bouquets.

Uniola, one of our native perennial grasses, known as the Spike Grass, includes several varieties. There are *U. latifolia* and *U. leptochloa fascicularis.* The former, a native of America, is a perennial grass, growing to five feet in height. Planted for landscape effects, it is ideal as a background for a border planting, and is hardy from Pennsylvania to Texas. The latter variety is used for the same purpose, but is a native of the warmer and more temperate parts of Eastern United States. It grows to 2½ feet, and has thread-like leaves eight inches long and flower panicles to one foot long. It thrives in a sandy loam and a good top dressing of humus.

Everyone knows the corn or maize of Mexican origin. It is grown for its handsome foliage. They are very good ornamentals for the garden where a bold effect is needed. Their large coarse leaves of all varieties are variegated, white, pink and cream. As we know, corn needs a rich soil with plenty of humus and a good supply of moisture in the growing season.—*L. Pillars.*

GRASS PINK: *see* DIANTHUS

GREEN CABBAGE WORM: *see* CABBAGE

GREENHOUSE: Any glass-roofed building or part of a house whose sole purpose is to contain plants may be considered a greenhouse. Conservatories and sun parlors which may still be in use in older houses were primarily part of the living quarters of the house, and secondarily plant rooms.

Modern home greenhouses fall into four types: free-standing buildings heated with their own heating systems, or by underground pipes from the house, or merely by heat from the sun; glassed buildings attached at one end to the house, from which they may be heated; lean-tos, that is, glassed areas which slant in to the house walls on one or more sides, and vary in size from enlarged cold frames to room-size; or plant windows, consisting of glassed enclosures extending

A prefabricated greenhouse of the English type with the sides slanting to the sun to absorb the maximum amount of sunlight. Note the hinged windows on the roof and sides to facilitate ventilation.

out from a normal house window from which the glass has been removed to provide heat.

Time was, and not so long ago, when a greenhouse was an expensive luxury that only the wealthy could afford. This is no longer so. New designs, modern materials and equipment have brought the greenhouse costs down to a fraction of what they formerly were. Now for no more than the price of a second-hand automobile, prefabricated parts may be purchased to put up a good-looking, practical glass house, or anyone adept at carpentry, can get the indivdual glazing bars and fittings and build one for even less.

Prefabricated greenhouses are usually about nine, ten and 13 feet wide. Lengths are in sash sections or about $2\frac{1}{2}$ feet, so the greenhouses can be built in any length. They come with slanted or straight sides. These greenhouses are made in sash panels that any handyman can put together with a screw driver, wrench and hammer. All the parts are furnished cut to fit in place. The glass is cut to size and is not putty glazed. It goes into glass grooves in the sash and is held weather-tight with a special caulking rope.

While the prices for the materials for a prefabricated greenhouse are higher than purchasing parts such as glazing bars, sills, eaves, ridge and fittings of a conventional type greenhouse, the time they save in labor greatly offsets the difference. The building of such a greenhouse should never be attempted by an amateur for it takes skill in carpentry and glazing to do a good job.

Greenhouses with plastic instead of glass are becoming popular for economy reasons. They are light, so require less rigid supports. Plastic is strong, and withstands wind, rain, hail, and cold. Its principal drawback is that it generally must be removed before the hot summer sun strikes it, or it will be damaged and will need

replacement before the following winter.

A greenhouse constructed entirely of inexpensive screenglass has been reported by an organic gardener living in Michigan, where temperatures drop very low. It was used only for starting seeds for a truck garden, so was probably not in use in winter months. Flats were heated from below by electric heating units running through soil in the tables on which they stand.

FOUNDATIONS: The walls below the sills are the hardest part of building any greenhouse. Masonry walls are best because they are more permanent than those of wood. Poured concrete, brick, cut stone, or cinder blocks are used. Cinder blocks provide the easiest means of building a wall. But since they leave an unsightly finish, the outside should always be coated with stucco and painted. The attractiveness of a greenhouse depends a great deal upon its walls, for this is the largest solid area.

The walls of a prefabricated greenhouse should extend below the frost line. This would be about $2\frac{1}{2}$ feet in most areas but may be less in the southern states and more in the north. The footings below the ground can be of poured concrete and gravel. A conventional type greenhouse is built with steel posts set on footings and encased in piers that extend below grade. The side walls need only go down to solid ground, a few inches below the grade.

LOCATION: It is important to locate the greenhouse where it will receive a maximum amount of sunlight particularly during the days of December and January when every bit of sunshine is important, especially that of the morning sun. In the North, above the Mason-Dixon Line, the recommended direction to run the greenhouse is on a line ten degrees N.E. and S.W. of east and west on the compass. Farther south, this is not important, in fact, many greenhouses that are built in other directions are giving excellent results.

SIZE: Never build a greenhouse too small, even to start with. In a small area, it is impossible to maintain an even temperature and a healthy atmospheric condition. On sunny days, even in the winter, the temperature in a four by six foot greenhouse would run over 100° in a matter of a few minutes. Then at night when the sun goes down, it would cool off just as rapidly. Plants will not grow under such conditions. The smallest of greenhouses should never be less than five by ten feet, but it would be better to build them larger, for a large house contains a greater volume of air. An even temperature is more easily maintained and ventilation is more simple to regulate.

LEAN-TO GREENHOUSE: This greenhouse may fit on the side of a home to make an extra sunny room, or it might be located along the side of the garage or tool shed. A south wall should be chosen for the location of the lean-to type because more sunshine will be caught during the winter months. With only one side, ceiling, and one or two ends glassed in, the adjacent building can be staged with tiers for extra plant space.

Heating costs for this type of house can be kept to a minimum by having a basement or porch window open into the greenhouse. It is possible to circulate the warm air with an electric fan. The glass house also will hold a lot of the sun's warmth through the day, and padded mats rolled down across the sash at night will help keep in the warmth.

Though the space is cut by the upright building wall in the lean-to greenhouse, every inch can be put to work by the use of plant benches, ground beds, eave shelves, ledges and hanging baskets. But the straight sided lean-to makes it possible to grow tall plants close to the glass. Straight sides accommodate eave shelves better too, and they provide better ventilation

and temperature control. The straight sided houses are somewhat more expensive, however, because there is more glass area. On the other hand, slanting sides capture more sunshine.

ATTACHED GREENHOUSE: This type is also constructed for economy since it saves the cost of one glass end. Heat is supplied by pipes from the home furnace, or by circulating warm air from the home by fan. Due to greater glass area, this house will absorb more warmth from the sun. There is usually room for two or three plant benches.

FREE-STANDING GREENHOUSE: This type may be built if space permits and a sunny location is available. Its advantages are more plant space, light may be caught from every direction, and it is more adaptable for ground beds. Free-standing houses may be heated by pipes from the home heating system, but usually need additional heating units of their own.

A free-standing greenhouse which is unheated except by the sun is the pit-type house. An old root cellar can be used for the pit of the house. If this is not available, a four foot excavation can be made and lined with concrete or cinder blocks. In heavy, poorly drained soils, drainage tiles around the foundation are recommended.

The pit-type house, except for severe sub-zero weather, is sun heated. The only additional heat needed under conditions of extreme cold is a 200-watt electric light bulb or a small electric heater. Temperatures in the pit-type house make daily watering unnecessary. Usually only the south side is glassed in, and this is set at a 45 degree angle to admit the most sunshine. Ordinary hotbed sashes can be used.

To add warmth to the pit house, the ends and unglassed side should be double walled with about three and a half inches of insulating material between. Doors and ventilators should also be insulated. After sunset, the glassed areas should be covered with padding, the thickness of which is determined by climatic conditions. When pads are used to cover the sashes, tarpaulins are rolled down over them to keep them dry. Wet padding makes poor insulation.

The Dutch door is best for the pit house because the upper half can be opened for ventilation during the winter. The door should be at the east end of the house to be better protected from prevailing cold westerly winds. A ventilating window can be placed at the west end. This is most important in the pit-greenhouse. It should be open during the warmest hours of every day. Some pit houses use skylight openings on the top of the unglassed side for ventilation.

BASEMENT GREENHOUSE: From the outside a basement greenhouse looks like a sloping coldframe backed against the foundation. Inside, it is an alcove in the cellar wall, with a concrete floor raised above the basement floor. Like the foundation, it is built of concrete blocks.

The floor should be at least 3½ feet above the basement floor because of the high angle of the midwinter sun. The foundation wall in front of it should be about two inches higher than the greenhouse floor to prevent water from running out on the cellar floor. This front wall should be finished with a neat concrete cap that makes an attractive shelf or parapet for placing plants in the foreground where they display to advantage.

A shelf placed high up beneath the glass at one end is used for sun-loving plants and can be duplicated at the other end. The greenhouse should face south, southeast or southwest. A wide crack left open just behind the parapet gives invisible drainage, though there is little to drain. With only one hot air vent in the basement, the temperature will stay between 55 and 60°.

In any type greenhouse ventilation is of the utmost importance. Ventilators, comprising about ten per cent of the roof area, should be placed on both sides of the ridge, or at the top of the lean-to. Automatic regulators are very useful for greenhouse operators who are not always on hand to open and close vents themselves. No provision need be made for air intakes, since enough air may be expected to enter through cracks. The purpose of ventilators is to reduce temperature and humidity, rather than to supply fresh air.

GREENHOUSE MANAGEMENT: Details of greenhouse management may be divided into two heads, control of the house, and handling the plants. Under the first head is included:

1. Regulation of temperature to imitate natural outdoor rise and fall, from cool at night to warm or hot in the middle of the day. Sturdier plants will be obtained if the temperature is kept slightly on the cool side. Under a too-high temperature plants become quickly overgrown, are tender, and susceptible to mildew greenfly, and other pests.

2. Space being at a premium, greenhouse plants should be kept only so long as they are healthy and productive, then immediately discarded.

3. Roots of greenhouse plants are confined in flats, pots, or benches, and

BASEMENT GREENHOUSE

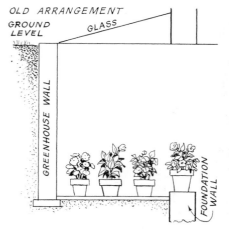

OLD ARRANGEMENT
GROUND LEVEL
GLASS
GREENHOUSE WALL
FOUNDATION WALL

cannot spread freely to seek food and moisture. Soil must therefore be prepared to the liking of each plant. Texture of the soil should be looser than that in the garden to assure good drainage and retain moisture. It should be screened to eliminate stones and unnecessary debris.

Always keep a plentiful supply of screened compost on hand as well as peat moss, clean sharp sand, sphagnum moss and vermiculite for rooting purposes and special mixtures. For seed flats, many greenhouse growers use a light, porous soil, low in fertility, since small seedlings are not able to assimilate the elements in a rich mixture. A mixture of ⅓ soil, ⅓ finely shredded peat moss, and ⅓ sharp sand is often used.

4. Greenhouse watering should be done in the mornings of sunny days, if possible. Water should be supplied sparingly, rather than too freely, to minimize the hazards of fungus disease. When watering is done it should be thorough, but plants should be permitted to show signs of thirst before it is repeated. Water should also be withheld, if possible, in cloudy weather when evaporation is slow and fungus spores will not be destroyed by hot sun rays.

5. The greenhouse should be kept clean at all times, and free of diseased plants or those infested with insects. Care should be taken to inspect each plant that is brought in from outside, and leaves or stems found to be diseased on existing plants should be immediately removed and destroyed before the disease can spread. It is far easier to maintain healthy conditions than to reestablish them after infection has taken place.

6. Shade must be provided during the summer months to protect plants which cannot be removed to the outdoors. Bamboo or slatted matting may be spread over the top lights, or the roof may be whitewashed. By autumn most of the whitewash will have flaked off, and the balance must be removed with a brush.

CARE OF PLANTS: Plant handling principles most important in the greenhouse include:

1. Conditions favorable to each plant's growth when it is grown in the garden should be duplicated as far as possible in the greenhouse. If it demands a period of rest in the garden, such a period should be allowed in the greenhouse. Sun, shade, and soil requirements outdoors should be duplicated as far as possible.

2. Flowering periods may be forced by potting and handling conditions. If a flower has crowded roots, its flowers will form early If it is repotted and fed, its flowering period may be delayed. Bloom may be obtained throughout the winter months by regulation of the flowering period of greenhouse plants.

3. Most important use of the greenhouse is for plant propagation. Cuttings, seedlings, even grafts for the garden may be prepared during winter month in the greenhouse. Winter greenhouse gardening falls into three classes: cool, moderate and warm. The cool house, with a night temperature of 50°, is usually best for the person who wants to grow the largest variety of plants. Too, fuel

IMPROVED ARRANGEMENT

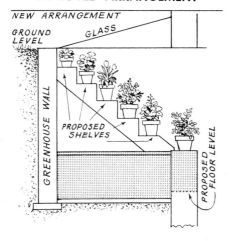

NEW ARRANGEMENT

GROUND LEVEL

GLASS

GREENHOUSE WALL

PROPOSED SHELVES

PROPOSED FLOOR LEVEL

cost practically doubles for every five degrees rise in temperature. Plants needing higher temperatures can be grown in the cool greenhouse if they are placed high on shelves where it is several degrees warmer.

COOL GREENHOUSE: Practically all the popular annuals and perennials do well in the cool greenhouse: asters, pansies, stock, carnations, sweet peas, marguerites, chrysanthemums, winter-flowering marigolds, calendulas, alyssum, candytuft, schizanthus, snapdragons, Goston yellow daisies—the list is endless.

Potted roses do fine as do some of the hanging basket plants like oxalis, miniature ivy, browallia, strawberry begonia, trailing fuchsias and periwinkle.

In cool temperature and organic soil, bulbs such as tulips, Dutch iris, lilies, daffodils, hyacinths, ranunculus and anemones are very easy to grow and give amazingly fine blooms.

The biggest advantage of a greenhouse lies in its ability to produce fresh vegetables for the organic gardener's winter table. The poor flavor and low food value of commercially-raised winter vegetables has long been a source of despair to people who know the value of fresh, organically-grown produce.

PLANTING PLAN FOR YEAR-ROUND GREENHOUSE BLOOM

WHAT TO PLANT (Seed unless otherwise specified)	WHEN TO PLANT	BLOOMING PERIOD	SPECIAL TREATMENT
African violets	March (seed & division)	Sept.-March	Plenty of humus Screen sunlight
Arctosis grandis	April	July-Oct.	Grow cool. Full sun
Balsam, camellia flowered	Jan. and Feb.	Apr. and May	Water freely
Begonia brightness (fibrous rooted)	Feb.	Jan.-March	Part shade
Begonias (tuberous rooted)	Jan. and Feb.	Aug.-Oct.	Mix seed with flour to germinate.
Browallia speciosa major	Seed in Feb., cuttings in March	Oct.-May	Pinch back often
Calceolaria hybrids	May	May and June	Cold frame in summer
Calendula	August	Feb.-April	Sow in pots and thin
Campanula isophylla	July, Aug. (cuttings)	July-Sept.	Plenty of lime
Canterbury bells	May	Feb.-April	Outdoors to Oct.
Carnations, perpetual flowering	Dec.-March (cuttings)	Oct.-Mar.	Take cuttings from center of plant
Celosia plumosa	March	Aug.-Oct.	Avoid stem injury
Chrysanthemums	Dec.-March (cuttings)	Nov.-Jan.	Grow cool. Sun
Cineraria, large flowered and stellata	June or July	March-May	Grow cool
Clarkia	August	March-May	Water carefully to prevent collar rot
Cyclamen, triumph hybrids	Aug. or Feb.	Nov.-March	Summer in cold frame
Didiscus coerulea	Feb.	May and June	Screen sun
Francoa ramosa	March-May (seed & division)	April-July	Divide regularly

Vitamins A, B₂, and C are especially lacking in vegetables on the market in the cold months. Long storage and transportation, plus the fact that the plants are grown with chemicals and poison sprays, make them of dubious value.

Lettuce, radishes, Swiss chard, kale and scallions do very well in the cool greenhouse. So do carrots, cauliflower, peas, red and green cabbage and beets, if you have the extra space they require. Tomatoes and cucumbers need more room, too, and a night temperature of 60 degrees or higher. Many growers prefer to start their tomatoes from seed in January, and thus have tomatoes two months before their outdoor plants begin to bear.

Slips may be taken from garden-grown tomato plants in mid-August, and rooted in tubs for the greenhouse. These plants may be staked and pruned to one main stalk to save space. They will begin to bear at about the time when frost nips garden plants, and will sometimes continue to bear until next year's garden plants begin to ripen their fruit. Italian plum tomatoes are especially good for this purpose.

Herbs are another good crop. A few pots or boxes of rue, sage, mint, marjoram, parsley, chives and the like

PLANTING PLAN FOR YEAR-ROUND GREENHOUSE BLOOM

(Continued)

WHAT TO PLANT (Seed unless otherwise specified)	WHEN TO PLANT	BLOOMING PERIOD	SPECIAL TREATMENT
Gardenia	Cuttings—March	Nov.-Feb.	Part shade — keep moist
Geraniums, winter flowering	Cuttings—March	Nov.-March	Full sun
Gesnera hybrids	Seed and division —Feb.	Sept. and Oct.	Part shade — grow warm Plenty of humus
Gloxinia	Feb.	June-Aug.	Grow warm Plenty of humus
Helipterum (rhodanthe) manglesi	Jan.	Apr. and May	Sow in pots and thin
Poinsettia	Cuttings—March and April	Dec. and Jan.	Avoid bruising
Primula kewensis	Feb.	Dec.-March	Grow very cool
Primula malacoides	Aug.	Feb.-April	Plenty of leaf mold
Primula obconica hybrids	Feb.-May	March-July	Dryish in winter
Primula sinensis and p. stellata	Feb.-May	Nov.-March	Water carefully to prevent damping-off
Salpiglossis	Oct.	May and June	Pinch back twice
Salvia splendens	Seed—Feb. Cuttings—Jan.	Oct.-Jan.	Summer outside
Schizanthus hybrids	April Aug.	Aug. and Sept. March-May	Pinch back at 4 inches
Streptocarpus hybrids	April or May	April-July	Grow cool. Plenty of humus
Stocks—winter flowering	June	Nov.-April	Grow cool all the time
Sweet pea	Oct.	April and May	Full sun. Prune to single stem
Torenia fournieri	March	June-Aug.	Plenty of leaf mold
Trachelium	Seed—Feb. Cuttings—Aug.	June-Aug.	Plenty of lime

will provide garnishes for winter meals.

Cucumbers and melons are only practical as a summer crop in the small house for they need space and higher temperatures. It is grand to have the large, juicy melons that can be grown to perfection under glass in the summer and cucumber with seeds so soft there hardly seem to be any at all.

One of the most profitable things done in a greenhouse is to raise plants for setting out in your summer garden. They can be grown by the thousands in a home greenhouse. Husky plants for tomatoes, cabbage, cauliflower, lettuce, melons, broccoli, celery and peppers, as well as all of the bedding plants for the flower garden. Seed is inexpensive and the plants are much finer than those offered for sale, and may be raised in strains not available on the market.

WARM GREENHOUSE: While it costs almost twice as much to bring the home greenhouse up to moderate or warm temperatures in comparison with a cool house, many exciting plants can be grown that make it well worth while for those who like the unusual. Orchids are among them. With a collection of 50 to 75 plants of different varieties, it is possible to have something in bloom every day of the year. Some of them last a very long time. Cymbidiums will keep for as long as three months. Any orchidist will tell you the plants are not difficult to grow. In fact, they will stand more abuse than most of the annuals previously mentioned. Insects are not a serious problem. Orchids can be grown in any greenhouse where it is possible to maintain an even temperature and keep the atmosphere fresh and healthy. High humidity is essential and this is usually provided by placing a tray of coke underneath slat plant benches. This coke holds tremendous quantities of moisture and gives it off slowly.

Other flowers and plants that do well in the moderate to warm greenhouse include: amaryllis, azaleas, begonias, ferns and tropical foliage plants, bougainvillea, cactus, gardenias, gloxinias, poinsettias, potted roses, Saintpaulia, and lantana. Those who enjoy growing unusual things will include such plants as *Tacca chantrieri,* the devil plant whose curious blooms have long drooping whiskers and which is seldom out of flower; *Columnea gloriosa* with its fleshy leaves on long trailing stems that make it excellent for hanging baskets; and *Rondeletia odorata* that blooms more or less continually with bright coral red flowers.

Perhaps the most satisfying thing about greenhouse gardening is the great therapeutical value and contentment it gives to so many people, young and old. Almost suddenly, taut nerves loosen and you capture the exhilaration that goes with living close to nature.

GREEN MANURE: The recent development of power equipment has opened the door to one of the most helpful practices for the organic gardener—utilizing green-manure crops. Until the innovation of rotary tillers and garden tractors, green-manuring was an awesome, if not impossible task. But now that many gardeners classify power equipment as "indispensible," the practice is becoming more widespread—and for good reason.

Green manure plants are one of the best soil conditioners ever discovered. They cost little, take little time to use and provide the answer to good soil tilth. Aside from the fact that it is sometimes impossible to compost enough material for some larger gardens, green-manuring saves hours of hard work and retains soil fertility economically.

Especially in a large garden it is worth while to devote a part to build a green-manure crop. It's no secret that farmers have been doing it for years and now consider it a very necessary part of the normal farming rotation. The dividends received in the form of soil building are worth far more than the original investment calls for.

Green manuring fertilizes soils deeply, which is something which cannot be accomplished by composting without undertaking an almost impossible task. By far, the most important source of organic matter is plant roots. These roots, penetrating often to considerable depths and decaying year

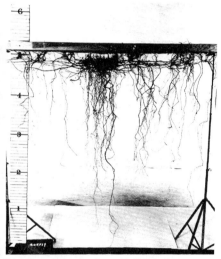

This Canadian creeping alfalfa is three years old and has 48 crowns in a five feet square area. Gauge is marked in feet; shows plant root depth.

after year, have in the course of time left great stores of organic matter to be broken down into humus. This type of deep fertilization cannot be duplicated in any other form so cheaply and easily.

Another advantage of green manuring is that, when these green manure crops are rotated season after season, plant diseases and insects are discouraged. They are not willing to attack a healthy soil and will turn to more susceptible fields.

Green manuring has a certain advantage over usual composting methods in

that it supplies the soil with succulent organic matter at the peak of its nutritional benefit. Compost, no matter how carefully tended will lose some of its nutrients due to leaching and other actions of the elements. But, by careful treatment of green manure, the soil will hold its nutrients (especially the minerals found only deep in the subsoil) until they may be assimilated by the following stands.

Green manure crops decay in the soil fairly quickly. To get the greatest benefit from your crop, take advantage of the new soil fertility soon after decay is completed. In warm weather with moisture present, almost complete decomposition takes places in less than six weeks. Young, succulent material decomposes more readily than older plants. The fertility liberated in the process of decomposition should be utilized immediately by growing plants, or some will be lost by leaching or escaping into the air in the form of gas.

GREEN MANURE CROPS: Here are some of the more common green manure crops:

Alfalfa—deep-rooted perennial legume; grown throughout U. S. Does well in all but very sandy, very clayey, acid, or poorly-drained soils. Inoculate when growing it for the first time, apply lime if pH is six or below, and add phosphate rock. Sow in spring in the North and East, late summer elsewhere, 18 to 20 pounds of seed per acre on a well-prepared seedbed.

Alsike Clover—biennial legume; grown mostly in the northern states. Prefers fairly heavy, fertile loams, but does better on wet, sour soil than most clovers. Sow six to ten pounds per acre in spring, or may be sown in early fall in the South.

Alyceclover—annual legume; lower South. Prefers sandy or clay loams with good drainage. Sow in late spring, 15 to 20 pounds of scarified seed per acre.

Austrian Winter Pea—winter legume in the South, also grown in early spring in the Northwest. Winter-hardy north to Washington, D. C. For culture, see *field pea*.

Barley—annual non-legume; grown in the North. Loams, not good on acid or sandy soil. In colder climates, sow winter varieties, elsewhere spring varieties, two to 2½ bushels per acre.

Beggarweed—annual legume; South, but grows fairly well north to the Great Lakes. Thrives on rich sandy soil, but is not exacting; will grow on moderately acid soils. Inoculate when not grown before. Sow 15 pounds of hulled and scarified seed or 30 pounds of unhulled seed when all danger of frost is past. Volunteers in the South if seed is allowed to mature.

Berseem (*Egyptian clover*)—legume for dry and alkali regions of the Southwest. Usually grown under irrigation. Will not stand severe cold.

Black Medic—legume; throughout U. S. A vigorous grower on reasonably fertile soils. Sow seven to 15 pounds of scarified, inoculated seed in the spring in the North, fall in the South. Needs ample lime.

Buckwheat—non-legume; grown mostly in the Northeast. Tops for rebuilding poor or acid soils; has an enormous, vigorous root system, and is a fine bee plant. Sow about two bushels to the acre, anytime after frost. Can grow three crops, 40 tons of green matter per acre, in a season. Uses rock fertilizers very efficiently.

Bur Clover—a fine winter legume as far north as Washington, D. C., and on the Pacific Coast. Prefers heavy loams, but will grow on soils too poor for red or crimson clover, if phosphate is supplied. Sow in September, 15 pounds of hulled seed or three to six bushels of unhulled seed per acre. Volunteers if allowed to set seed.

Cow-Horn Turnip—non-legume; widely adapted. Its value lies in its enormous long roots that die in cold weather and add much organic mat-ter in the spring. Plant in late summer, two pounds per acre.

Cowpea—very fast-growing annual legume. Thrives practically anywhere in the U. S. on a wide range of soils. A fine soil builder, its powerful roots crack hardpans. Inoculate when planting it the first time. Sow any time after the soil is well warmed, broadcasting 80 to 100 pounds or sowing 20 pounds in three foot rows.

Crimson Clover—winter-annual legume; from New Jersey southward. Does well on almost any fairly good soil; on poor soil, grow cowpeas first for a preliminary build-up. Sow 30 to 40 pounds of unhulled seed or 15 to 20 of hulled, about 60 days before the first killing frost. Inoculate if not previously grown. Dixie hard-seeded strain volunteers from year to year in the South.

Crotolaria—annual legume. For very poor soil in the South and as far north as Maryland. Sow scarified seed in the spring, ten to 30 pounds, depending on the variety. Makes sandy soil like loam.

Dalea (*Wood's clover*)—legume; northern half of U. S. Still being tested, but shows promise for strongly acid, sandy soils. Volunteers for many years.

Domestic Ryegrass and Italian Ryegrass—non-legumes; many areas. Wide range of soils. Sow 20 to 25 pounds in the spring in the North, fall in the South.

Fenugreek—winter legume; Southwest. Loam soils. Sow 35 to 40 pounds in the fall.

Field Brome Grass—non-legume; northern half of U. S. Widely adapted as to soils. Good winter cover, hardier than rye. Sow in early spring or late summer, ten to 15 pounds per acre.

Field Peas—annual legume; wide climatic range. Well-drained sandy to heavy loams. Sow 1½ to three bushels, depending on the variety, in early spring in the North, late fall in the South. Inoculate first time grown.

Hairy Indigo—summer legume;

deep South. Moderately poor sandy soil. Makes very tall, thick stand. Sow in early spring six to ten pounds broadcast, three to five drilled.

Kudzu—perennial legume; South to Central states. All but the poorest soils. Commonly allowed to grow for several years before plowing under. Seedlings planted in early spring.

Lespedeza—legume; South and as far north as Michigan (Korean and sericea varieties in the North). All types of soil, but sericea is particularly good for poor, sour soils—for these,

Many soils. Winter oats suitable for mild winters only. Sow two bushels in the spring.

Pearl Millet—non-legume; as far north as Maryland. Fair to rich soils. Commonly planted in four foot rows, four pounds per acre.

Persian Clover—winter-annual legume; South and Pacific states. Heavy, moist soils. Sow in the fall, five to eight pounds. Inoculate. Volunteers well.

Quaker Comfrey—a relatively new crop currently being tested. Prefers

This rye green-manure crop was grown in Bristol County, Mass., and turned under to restore plant nutrients which had been taken out of the soil. Green manure crops decompose rapidly in warm weather.

it's one of the best fertility builders available. Sow in spring 30 to 40 pounds. Benefits from phosphate rock. Inoculate first time grown. Will volunteer if seed is allowed to set.

Lupine—legume; Southeast to North. Sour, sandy soils. Blue lupine is a fine winter legume in the South; white and yellow are most often grown in the North. Sow in spring in the North, late fall in the South, 50 to 150 pounds, depending on the variety. Always inoculate.

Oats—non-legume; widely grown.

clays, loams and sandy loams. Its huge leaves are generally chopped up for green manure. Rootstocks planted in spring or fall.

Rape—biennial non-legume; many areas. A rapid grower in cool, moist weather. Sow five to six pounds per acre.

Red Clover—biennial legume; practically all areas, but does not like high temperatures, so is most useful in the North. Any well-drained fair to rich soil; needs phosphorus. Its decay is of exceptional benefit to following crops. Sow early in the spring to allow time for two stands, 15 pounds of seed per acre. Inoculate the first time grown.

Roughpea (caley pea, singletary pea)—winter annual legume; southern half of U. S., and the Northwest. Many soils but best on fertile loams. Sow 30 pounds of inoculated, scarified seed in the fall. Needs phosphorus. Will volunteer.

Rye—non-legume; grown mostly in the Northeast and South. Many soil types. Sow 80 pounds in the fall. Tetra Petkus is an excellent new giant variety.

Sesbania—legume, as far north as Washington, D. C. Prefers rich loam, but will grow on wet or droughty land, very poor or saline soils. Very rapid grower in hot weather. Broadcast or drill 25 pounds in the spring.

Sourclover—winter legume; South and West. Many soils. Sow in early fall, 15 to 20 pounds of scarified inoculated seed.

Soybeans—summer legume; deep South to Canada. Nearly all kinds of soil, including sour soils where other legumes fail. Will stand considerable drought. Use late-manuring varieties for best green manure results. Sow 60 to 100 pounds, spring to midsummer. Inoculate first time grown.

Sudan Grass—non-legume; all parts of U. S. Any except wet soils. Very rapid grower, so good for quick organic matter production. Use Tift Sudan in Central and Southeastern states to prevent foliage disease damage. Sow 20 to 25 pounds broadcast, four to five drilled, in late spring.

Sweetclover—biennial legume; all parts of U. S. Just about any soil, if reasonably well supplied with lime. Will pierce tough subsoils. Especially adept at utilizing rock fertilizers, and a fine bee plant. Sow 175 pounds of scarified or 25 pounds of unscarified seed, fall to early spring. Fast-growing Hubam, annual white sweet clover,

can be turned under in the fall; other varieties have their biggest roots in the spring of the second year, so turn them under then.

Velvetbeans—annual legume; South. One of the best crops for sandy, poor soils. Produces roots 30 feet long, vines up to 50 feet long. Sow when the soil is well warmed, 100 pounds, or 25 to 30 pounds in wide rows.

Vetches—annual and biennial legumes; varieties for all areas. Any reasonably fertile soil with ample moisture. Hairy vetch does well on sandy or sour soils and is the most winter-hardy variety. Hungarian is good for wet soils in areas having mild winters. Sown in the North in spring, elsewhere in the fall, 30 to 60 pounds, depending on the variety.

Weeds—whenever weeds will not be stealing needed plant food and moisture, they can be used as green manures. Some produce creditable amounts of humus, as well as helping make minerals available and conserving nitrogen.

Soil Conditioners: Recent experiments reveal that after the addition of green manures and other crop residues, the soil bacteria produce materials called polysaccharides. These are the glue-like materials which stick the soil particles into aggregates so essential for a good structure.

The amount of these valuable polysaccharides, produced by decomposing green manures, can be tremendous. For example, agronomists at the University of Delaware report that decaying alfalfa and oat straw produced as much as 5,500 and 4,000 pounds per acre, respectively, of these glue-like materials only one week after they had been added to the soil. *See also* Cover Crop; Compost.

GREEN MATTER: Under this classification is included all substances derived from plants.

The main sources for obtaining green matter around the modern home include left-overs from the kitchen, the weeds and culls from vegetable and flower garden, weeds and grass clippings from lawns, meadows, roadsides, etc., and special plant material gathered for composting (including cannery refuse, spoiled silage, cotton gin refuse, hay, straw and leaves). These materials contain various minerals, but also large amounts of carbohydrates; they supply nutrients for the growing bacteria and are, in the process of being digested, broken down into compost, if animal matter is also included.

Green matter is usually used in the compost heap, but it can also be used quite profitably as a mulch, in sheet composting, and in green manuring.

Even diseased green material of any kind can be used for making compost. By placing diseased material in the center of the heap where the temperature is highest, the disease-producing organisms are killed. Many cases have been reported where the compost, made from diseased tomato vines, has produced heavy crops of clean, healthy fruit on disease-free plants. If there is so much diseased material that it might not be completely composted in one operation of the heap, it might be better to burn it and use the ashes as a fertilizer.

See also COMPOST; GREEN MANURING; MULCHING; ORGANIC MATTER.

GREEN PEPPERS: *see* PEPPERS

GREENSAND: Glauconite greensand or greensand marl is an iron-potassium-silicate that imparts a green color to the minerals in which it occurs. Being an undersea deposit, greensand contains traces of many if not all the elements which occur in sea water. Greensand has been used successfully for soilbuilding for more than a hundred years. It is a fine source of potash.

Greensand is commonly called a glauconite potash mineral, because it contains from six to seven per cent of plant-available potash. The best

deposits contain, in addition to the potash, 50 per cent of silica, 18 to 23 per cent of iron oxides, three to 7.5 per cent of magnesia, small amounts of lime and phosphoric acid, and traces of 30 or more other elements, most of which are important in the nutrition of the higher plants.

ADVANTAGES: The factors underlying the immediate response of grasses to greensands seem to be the following: (1) absorb and hold large amounts of water in the surface layer of the soil where the plant roots feed; (2) round up and feed to the grass roots the nutrient elements which are already in the soil; (3) provide an abundant source of plant-available potash which stimulates photosynthesis and rapid growth of grasses; and (4) contain the trace elements which may be deficient in the soil or in the surface layer of the soil in which the grass roots feed.

Greensands are so fine that they may be used in their natural form with no processing except drying if the material is to pass through a fertilizer drill. An application consists of about $\frac{1}{4}$ pound of greensands per square foot of soil. It may be applied at any time without danger of injuring plants. In gardens and fields it may be applied when the soil is prepared for planting or to growing vegetables and crop plants. It may be applied on the surface with the organic materials in sheet composting, or used in the compost heap to stimulate bacterial action and to enrich the compost. *See also* GLAUCONITE.

GRINDER: *see* SHREDDER, COMPOST

GROUND CHERRY: *see* PHYSALIS

GROUND COVERS: These practical plants should be considered as an important asset to your landscaping scheme, especially if you've had trouble growing other plants under shady trees or on banks.

Almost all the common ground cover plants are as vigorous as weeds.

Of course, you wouldn't expect grass to grow on a windswept or rain-washed slope; neither will most ground covers. You could plant really tough specimens as crown vetch or gout weed in such spots, but they grow with such abandon you'd have a hard time holding them in check. Preparing the soil for a suitable ground cover is wiser than planting potential pests.

Soil rich in organic matter holds moisture and prevents leaching on slopes, besides aiding a quick, dense thus using a smaller number of plants, and battle weeds in the longer interval the plants take to cover. Others buy seed, seedlings, or rooted cuttings from nurseries in order to produce the ground cover more cheaply at home. But if these are planted directly outdoors, many will die, giving a ragged effect to the bed. It's better to start them in your "home nursery" or pots, carefully shading and watering before setting them out. Some economy-minded gardeners transplant-

Cerastium tomentosum is a plucky ground cover which will grow in pure sand if necessary. It stays close to the ground, forming large patches of cover while its white flowers and leaves give a pleasing effect.

plant growth that refuses to give weeds a chance.

Dig to a depth of at least eight inches, removing all weeds and foreign material. Mix in a two to three-inch layer of organic material such as compost, peat moss, rotted manure or aged sawdust. Soak well a few hours before planting.

Since ground covers are higher in initial cost than seeding a lawn, there are many schools of thought on how to economize. Some gardeners prefer to set plants a good distance apart, ed wild plants from nearby fields and woods.

PLANTING: The ideal method is to set small plants close together. The proper distance apart depends on the rate of growth and size of the plants at planting time. Three to eight inches apart is correct for most ground covers, while some vines can be up to three feet apart.

What height should your ground cover be? Tall vines and some shrubs up to two feet tall are suitable for large open areas and some slopes, while small areas like the flower garden borders or odd angle corners where the lawn mower can't reach, call for something low with delicate foliage.

Partridge berry (*Mitchella repens*) adapts itself readily to a woodland garden. The trailing vines with their oval evergreen leaves bear small flowers of a creamy-white to pink color. This plant takes root along its stem as it creeps over the ground; it blossoms in April, May or June, and later develops red berries. It is one of the finest ground covers for densely shaded spots. It does well in acid soil, but needs humus and moisture. Partridge berry has been grown with success in both northern and southern sections of the country. Birds love the red berries, so planting partridge berry is an ideal way to attract them.

Dichondra (*D. carolinensis*) is a round-leaved herb that grows to a height of two inches. Because of its very low growth, it is widely used as a lawn substitute. Dichondra prefers moist soil, full sun to deep shade. Native to California and the South, it thrives in warm climates. Used extensively in Palm Beach as a covering material, it can be walked upon or mowed without harm.

Periwinkle or myrtle (*Vinca minor*) is a very successful glossy-leaved evergreen ground cover that develops cheerful violet-blue blossoms from early spring until late in the season. It grows to a height of four to six inches in sun or shade and in ordinary soil, if not too dry. Periwinkle holds banks well.

Creeping lilyturf (*Liriope spicata*) is unsurpassed for planting under trees or shrubs. Very hardy, it withstands extreme heat, drought and poor soil, in full sun to deep shade. It is often preferred to grass as it has a coarse, dark green foliage that blossoms with attractive lilac-colored blooms in summer. Growing to a height of 15 inches, it also tolerates salt spray. Dwarf lily-turf (*Ophio-*

pogon japonicus) grows to a maximum of 12 inches.

Japanese spurge (*Pachysandra terminalis*) has turned many an eyesore into something pleasant to look at. This hardy evergreen grows six inches high, endures shade and drought, but grows equally well in sunshine. It needs slightly moist soil. The cuttings root easily if planted in rich soil; it spreads easily if the tops are cut back occasionally. The lovely dark green foliage has a neat appearance which makes it excellent for use as a border for walks. A really vigorous plant, try it where everything else fails.

Other evergreen ground covers to consider are *ajuga* and *iberis,* both of which grow to a height of eight inches or less. *Ajuga* will grow in sun or shade but the others require some sun for good growth.

Ajuga reptans or common blue bugleweed is easily grown in ordinary garden soil, ranges from four to ten inches. Flowers are purple or blue.

The evergreen variety of ground covers are quite popular in the North, but with evergreens there is little or no blossom color. Brighten up green beds by underplanting spring flowering bulbs. Crocuses, hyacinths or daffodils peeking up through the leaves add to a colorful accent. Strengthen the bulbs that are in competition with the ground cover's roots by applications of a good organic fertilizer.

A SELECTED LIST OF GROUND COVER PLANTS

Scientific Name	Common Name	Ever-greens	How it spreads	Rate of spread
PERENNIALS				
† Ajuga reptans	Bugle		R	Fast
† Arabis procurrens	Rockcress	Yes	T	Fast
† Arenaria verna	Sandwort			Slow
* Asperula odorata	Sweet Woodruff		U	Fast
* Asarum canadense	Wild Ginger		R	Slow
† Campanula poschsharskyana	Serbian Bellflower	No	R	Medium
† Convalaria majalis	Lily-of-the-Valley		U	Fast
s Coronilla varia	Crown Vetch		T	Medium
† Dianthus deltoides	Maiden Pink	Yes	T	Fast
† Euphorbia cyparissias	Cypress Spurge		U	Medium
† Iberis sempervirens	Candytuft	Yes	T	Slow
† Myosotis palustris semperflorens	Forget-Me-Not		T	Medium
* Pachysandra terminalis	Japanese Spurge	Yes	UT	Slow
s Phlox subulata lilacina	Moss Pink	Yes	T	Fast
† Ranunculus repens and R. acris	Buttercup		T	Fast
s Sedum album	Stonecrop	Yes	T	Fast
s Sedum reflexum	Stonecrop	Yes	T	Fast
s Sedum sexangulare	Stonecrop	Yes	T	Fast
s Sedum spurium	Stonecrop		T	Fast
* Sedum ternatum	Stonecrop		T	Fast
s Thymus serpyllum coccinea	Thyme	Yes	T	Fast
s Thymus album	Thyme	Yes	T	Fast
† Teucrium chamaedrys	Germander	Yes	U	Medium
s Verbena canadense	Hardy Verbena		T	Fast
* Veronica filiformis	Speedwell		T	Fast
† Veronica rupestre	Speedwell		T	Fast
† Vinca minor	Periwinkle (Myrtle)	Yes	TU	Fast
† Violet papilionacea	Common Violet		Seed	Fast
† Viola canadensis	Canada Violet		Seed	Fast
ANNUALS				
Ipomoea purpurea	Heavenly-blue Morning Glory		T	Fast
Sanvitalia procumbens	Common Sanvitalia		T	Fast
Verbena erinoides	Moss Vervain		T	Fast
WOODY PLANTS				
† Akebia quinata	Akebia	Yes	T	Medium
† Ampelopsis quinquefolia	Five-leaf Ivy		T	Fast
† Euonymus fortunei (radicans)	Wintercreeper	Yes	T	Medium
† Euonymus fortunei colorata	Wintercreeper	Yes	T	Fast
† Euonymus obovatus	Running Strawberry-bush		T	Medium
* Hedera helix	English Ivy	Yes	T	Fast
* Hedera helix baltica	Baltic English Ivy	Yes	T	Fast
† Lonicera japonica halliana	Japanese Honeysuckle		T	Fast
s Rose wichuraiana	Memorial Rose		T	Fast
† Zanthoriza apiifolia	Yellow-root		U	Slow

* Shade only   † Sun or shade   R Runners; roots
s Sun only   T Trailing   U Underground stems

VICTOR H. RIES, The Ohio State University

Vines make attractive and inexpensive ground covers. Best for large open areas where there are no shrubs or small trees for them to climb, they make a thick, well-interlaced cover. Most vines tend to cluster together and lump up after a while, but you can cut them back severely without harm.

English ivy (*Hedera helix*) makes beautiful rapidly spreading cover for shade or sun and moist soil. In many parts of the North where this plant doesn't do well trained upright, it will thrive when grown on the ground. Its creeping foliage thrives under maples and beeches, where few other plants survive. The leaves remain green in winter, though they usually develop a purplish tinge.

Ground ivy (*Nepeta*) bears small blue flowers throughout the summer. Adaptable to any type soil, it thrives in sun or shade. Ground ivy is so sturdy you can run a lawn mower over it without doing any damage.

A trek in the woods can pay off with wild strawberry plants. This plant, with its white flowers and delicious berries, thrives in any soil, but does need some sun. Another woodland plant, moneywort (*Lysimachia*), so named because of its bright "gold piece" flowers, requires light shade and dry or moist soil. Since these are wild-growing plants, they are apt to be just as wild in the garden. Keep them in check by cutting.

CULTURE: Give plants on banks or slopes a chance. Cut toeholds into the bank at different heights along its length, and wedge stones deeply into these holes. Then cover with a good rich soil and plant the ground cover. *Pachysandra terminalis* and *Hedera helix* are good evergreens for shaded banks and slopes. The flowering *Vinca minor* or *Ajuga reptans* will thrive if there is some sun available.

Narrow areas around walks or house foundations which are too small for tall, elaborate plantings are fine for ground covers. Choose those that suit the location, be it sun or shade.

English ivy, *pachysandra* and *ajuga* serve excellently in areas along sidewalks and streets where continuous traffic makes growing a lawn difficult. These borders of plants give a neat, landscaped appearance that will deter habitual trespassers who love to cut corners on lawns.

Thymes are dense masses of tiny leaves that fairly hug brick walls or stepping stones; they prefer a lime soil. Sedums, widely used in gardens, are pretty but squash easily under traffic.

Ground covers can also be planted under and around permanent garden furniture where it's difficult to cut grass.

Once established, ground covers need no coddling, but while they are getting started they do deserve some care. Water occasionally during the first season. Top dressing with compost, humus or well-rotted manure will supply the nitrogen needed for dense growth, to cover the ground without any "holes." As the plants grow, they will strangle any crabgrass or plantain.—*Audrey Stephan.*

GROUND IVY: *see* GROUND COVERS; NEPETA

GROUND RATTAN: *see* PALMS

GUANO: The droppings, dead bodies, and other residues from bird and bat colonies in regions without rain or in caves are a rich source of nitrogen. Rain would leach this important plant food out, but the dry air keeps it in a good state of preservation. Some of the guano is imported from the coastal islands of the Southern Pacific west of the Andes; some is mined in caves of the Southwest. The nitrogen varies from one to ten per cent and the phosphoric acid content may go as high as 25 per cent. When available, guano can be substituted for manure, dried blood, hoof and horn dust, and similar sources of nitrogen. In the earlier history of bagged fertilizers, guano was most popular with gardeners and even farmers, but in our day the supply is limited. *See also* MANURE.

GUAR: (*Cyamopsis tetragonoloba*) This summer legume is adapted to a wide range of soil types, but grows best on loamy to sandy soils, free of excess alkali. It requires a warm seed bed for germination, and so seed should not be planted until the soil is warm and all danger of frost is past.

In the Southwest, planting is usually done between June 15 and July 15.

Besides being a nitrogen-fixing plant, guar grows a heavy tonnage of residue for return to the soil. These factors result in substantial increased yields on other cash crops following on the guar land for a period of three to four years when guar should again be included in rotation for its soil conditioning benefits and subsequent increased yields.

There are many varieties, varying in physical appearance and size, but generally they are vertical stalk plants, three to six feet high, having large leaves and clusters of bean-like pods. Each of these pods contains from six to nine pebble-shaped seeds. As maturity approaches, the leaves fall off leaving only the stalk and clusters of pods.

A sizable percentage of farmers, who have been using guar in rotation, have been growing it strictly for a green manure crop or a cover crop for soil protection and improvement. Guar is used in rotation with lettuce, spinach and other vegetable crops because it does such a fine conditioning job. Another prime use for guar is where it is planted on marginal or submarginal land and plowed down prior to converting these lands to grasses.

GUAVA: (*Psidium guajava*) A small, tropical tree which grows about 15 feet in height and is considered of value in landscaping as well as for its fruit. The tree has a smooth bark, greenish-brown in color, smooth, oval light-green leaves, and white flowers. Its round or pear-shaped fruit, up to four inches long when mature, is usually yellow, has a number of hard, small seeds, and a sweet, musk-like taste and aroma. In addition to being eaten raw, it is often used in preserves and jams.

The guava is grown principally in Florida and southern California. It is easily propagated from seed and increased by budding or cuttings, and has no special soil preferences as long as good drainage is provided. Left to itself, the plant spreads rapidly and may become a nuisance.

Other varieties include the strawberry guava (*P. cattleianum*) which is hardier, has a darker, maroon fruit with a more delicate flavor; and the lemon guava which is extremely tender, must be grown with particular protection, and is not regarded suitable for home gardens.

Pineapple guava (*Feijoa sellowiana*) is actually the *Feijoa*. The "pineapple guava" term is simply a popular name—the plant and fruit are completely distinct from the common guava. It is a member of the myrtle family; grows wild in Brazil and other South American countries; was introduced to France in 1890 and about ten years later was brought to California.

Guava fruit has a penetrating aroma and tastes like a blend of pineapples and strawberries. Fully ripened, it contains about ten per cent sugar and is high in vitamin C.

CULTURE: Guavas can be grown wherever the temperature does not go much below 15°; although they can take ten degrees for short spells. Most nurseries carry them in one and five-gallon cans all year around and they may be planted at any time. They are partial to heavy loam if the drainage is good. All varieties do best in full sun. Allow 12 to 15 feet between plants.

To get them off to a real good start, dig a hole about two feet in diameter and depth; replace the soil with a mixture of loam, compost and well-rotted manure. It will help to mix in a cupful of bone meal or ground rock phosphate.

Set the plant about an inch or so higher than it was in the can to allow for settling and pack the earth firmly for good root contact. Make an irrigation basin about 18 to 24 inches in diameter and four to six inches deep. Fill two or three times and then mulch it well, keeping the trunk clear. Water about once a week until it shows new green growth; then increase time between waterings to two weeks or when the soil is dry four to six inches below the surface. If you live where it rains in the summer, treat it as you would any of your other shrubs. As it grows, increase the size of the basin out to the tips of the branches. Keep soil heavily mulched.

No pruning is needed except to keep it in bounds. Home garden plantings are seldom bothered by insects; an occasional attack by white flies or scale can be easily controlled by weak dormant oil sprays.

Guavas bear fruit when quite young, often the second season after planting. Best varieties are Andre, Coolidge, Superba, Choiceana. Coolidge will fruit when planted alone; the rest need another variety planted close by for pollination.—*Warner Tilsher.*

GULLY: Severely eroded conditions of gullies can sometimes be noted on neglected farm areas. If neglected or ignored, such conditions result in rapidly increasing loss of soil. For correction, gullied areas can be sloped with a bulldozer, planted to soil-binding crops. Soil Conservation Service reports many cases where destructive gullies have been transformed into rejuvenated pastures or useful farm ponds. *See also* CONSERVATION; COVER CROPS.

GUMBO: (*Hibiscus esculentus*) *see* OKRA

GUMMOSIS: Gummosis is a symptom of disease in trees that causes cracks in the bark and oozing of a pale-colored liquid gum. It is most often found on the trunks of plum, cherry and citrus trees. A recommended practice is to loosen the soil around the tree and work in about 20 pounds of compost.

GUM TREE: *see* EUCALYPTUS

GYMNOGRAMMA: *see* PITYROGRAMMA

GYPSOPHILA: Baby's-breath. A fine mist-like flower with small pink or white flowers, especially useful as cut flowers. *G. paniculata,* single or double, has gray-green foliage and white cloud-like blooms which are very attractive in the border. Put it behind other plants, however, as the blossoms turn brown in about a fortnight, and then it is unsightly. No special soil requirements, but the plant prefers full sun and does not like to be disturbed. The creeping variety, *G. repens,* is excellent for rock gardens and walks. *See also* BABY'S BREATH.

GYPSUM: The use of gypsum for agricultural purposes has been closely questioned by organic gardeners. A hydrated calcium sulfate, gypsum is often used to reclaim alkali beds. For this purpose, it is finely ground and is generally applied with a lime spreader. It is claimed that gypsum replaces the sodium of alkali soils with calcium and improves drainage and aeration.

New Jersey Experiment Station Bulletin 772 reports as follows: Gypsum is a highly effective ammonia-conserving agent when applied to manures or other types of rapidly decomposing organic matter. As a result of its use, the escaping ammonia is changed to ammonium sulfate, in which form the ammonia is stable. When used in the gutters in dairy barns, gypsum not only saves ammonia but virtually eliminates objectionable odors. Since it is white, it gives the stable a cleaner appearance.

Before going ahead with any large scale application of gypsum to increase soil acidity or improve drainage, we suggest your trying it on a test basis first. See also FERTILIZERS, ARTIFICIAL.

GYPSY MOTH: In recent years large areas of New York, New Jersey and Pennsylvania were completely covered with an aerial spray of one pound per acre of DDT in an effort to stop the spread of the gypsy moth. The job was paid for and planned by the Federal government.

Both private and public lands were sprayed, and in the case of private lands, owners were not consulted. Many organic farmers had the horrifying experience of seeing converted World War II twin-engine bombers roar across their fields dropping acrid clouds of DDT that killed insects, birds and fish alike. Fields that had been cared for and nursed organically for years were covered without warning with a dose of poison that even the U. S. Department of Agriculture warns should be used carefully and should not be allowed to get into livestock feed and human food.

Out of the gypsy moth tragedy, perhaps one small benefit can result: The public has become so aroused at this forced poisoning of millions of acres of farms that in future years more people can be counted on to fight any similar spray programs that may be planned.

The plan to spray 3,000,000 acres with DDT in 1957 was a desperation effort to curb a pest the mere mention of whose name sends shudders up and down the spine of entomologists and people who have seen the damage it does. Whole forest groves

and orchards have been stripped of leaves by the hungry gypsy, which up to now has not spread beyond a relatively small area of the Northeast.

For thousands of years the gypsy moth has existed all over the European continent, but it has natural enemies there to keep it in check. In 1868 the moth was brought to Massachusetts by the French astronomer, Leopold Trouvelot, who thought that crossbreeding them with the silkworm would produce a master race of silk-producing moths.

He fully realized the damage that would result if the moths got loose, so he confined them to one bush that was completely covered with cloth to prevent their escape. But one windy night the cover blew off. Trouvelot realized how dangerous the moths were and he tried to get help in stamping out the few that were loose. No one was interested, however, and the matter was soon forgotten.

The few gypsy moths, adrift in a strange country, took the next 20 years to get acclimated to New England weather and food. By 1889 they began stripping whole trees of their leaves, and in 1890 the first public action was taken to organize an eradication campaign. About $50,000 was appropriated by the Massachusetts legislature and progress was being made in wiping out the gypsy when an economy drive cut short the program. After that the moths started multiplying again, and this time there was no stopping them.

Some entomologists feel that the only hope for permanent control of the gypsy moth is to establish here the natural enemies it has in France and other European countries. Already some of these predators have been brought over, and they are preventing the gypsy from doing the severe damage it did in the early days of the infestation. One of the gypsy's enemies that has been brought over is *Calosoma sycophanta L.,* a large, green

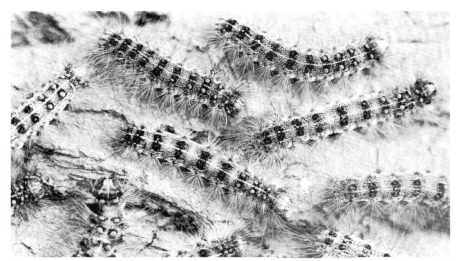

The adult gypsy moth lays her eggs in July and August in clusters on a tree trunk or twig or bark. In May of the following year the caterpillars emerge to feed destructively on foliage of preferred trees.

metallic beetle ¼ inch long. A pair of these beetles and their children destroy more than 6,000 gypsy caterpillars and pupae in a single year.

Unfortunately, the gypsy moth is such a vicious pest that not one predator can keep it in check. Entomologists are using the "sequence theory" to try to curb it. They are building up a whole series of predators that will attack the gypsy at each sequence of its development.

Spray Dangers: Admittedly, the gypsy moth is one of the most serious insect pests now confronting farmers, gardeners and homeowners. But the spraying of whole geographic regions with DDT is a cure that could be worse than the disease. There is a great deal of similarity between poison spray and the H-Bomb. Both are powerful weapons, but their use in an all-out struggle with an enemy—be it man or insect—causes secondary damages which are all out of proportion to the benefits they can accomplish.

The DDT "fallout" from the gypsy campaign will not only poison people and food as well as insects— it will destroy the natural predators of the gypsy which have been so carefully sought out and brought here over so many years. The spraying will render useless the biological control of the gypsy which is our major hope in the long run. *See also* INSECT CONTROL.

H

HACKBERRY: (*Celtis*) Related to the elms, the common hackberry tree (*C. occidentalis*) grows as high as 100 feet, is hardy throughout almost all the United States. It is also known as the nettle tree. The sugarberry (*C. laevigata*) grows mostly in the southern states, has red fruit changing to dark purple, grows to 60 to 80 feet high. The trees generally do well in ordinary garden soil.

Nettle trees are considered valuable as shade trees; their wide spreading head and light green foliage are very attractive in lawn plantings. Rarely susceptible to insect or disease damage, the nettles even do well in dry areas.

HAIR: Hair, in common with wool and silk, has a high nitrogen content. If the sweepings from a barber shop were regularly applied to a compost heap, an enormous amount of nitrogen could be saved, since six to seven pounds of hair contain a pound of nitrogen or as much as 100 to 200 pounds of manure. If kept in a well moistened heap, hair will disintegrate as easily as feathers.

Experiments with 32 varieties of roses by William Stafford, of Austin, Texas, indicate that human hair used around the roots of bushes produce longer stems, larger buds and deeper color tones.

The chemical constituents of human hair are nitrogen, hydrogen, oxygen, carbon and sulphur, approximately the same as bone meal which is a popular rose food.

Stafford experimented with hair at the base of plants, found it accelerated growth—but slowly—since it took a long time for the hair to decay. It seemed to work best on roses, also.

He wanted the hair to decay faster and worked out a recipe for a compost material which chemically decays the hair more rapidly.

His recipe—enough for 50 rose bushes):

10 pounds of hair clippings (should be clipped to ¾ inch lengths to prevent matting)
20 pounds of cottonseed meal to help hold moisture and encourage rotting
1½ yards of leaf mold

Mix the dry ingredients together; then wet down well. Keep in a compost pit 30 to 60 days, turning it until it is all rotted, then put about three quarts around each bush. Water frequently the first ten days and keep watering until results show.

Hair used alone will get the same results, but takes longer. Spread the hair around the surface as a mulch and water until it decays. Keep the hair on the surface. It is good insulator for the roots of all tender plants in severe cold and Stafford has a blue ribbon as proof it helps roses bloom longer in winter.

HAIRY INDIGO: *see* GREEN MANURE

HALF-HARDY: *see* HARDINESS

HANGING BASKET: *see* BOXES AND BASKETS, FLOWER

HANSEN BUSH CHERRY: (*Prunus besseyi*) *see* CHERRY, BUSH

HARDENING OFF: Refers to the process of preparing young plants to meet outside weather conditions. Young plants, especially non-hardy ones, are very vulnerable to sudden temperature changes. To put them outside, after their propagation in the protection of a greenhouse or other warm place, may easily be fatal. Therefore, young plants have to be introduced to the elements by degrees—the hardening off process.

There are many ways of hardening

off plants. If they were propagated in a greenhouse or indoors, they can be transferred to a cold frame and exposed gradually. If grown in a cold frame, they can be put outside with a burlap covering and can be taken indoors on cool nights. Another way of hardening off is to put plants beneath *cloches,* an English innovation. Cloches are miniature greenhouses, designed for a single or a few plants. During the hardening off process, less water is generally given to plants. *See also* PROPAGATION; GREENHOUSE; COLD FRAME; HARDINESS; CLOCHES.

HARDINESS: That quality in plants which enables them to survive the climatic conditions of the particular area where they are to be placed. When gardeners speak of a "hardy" plant, they usually mean one which will survive the winter. But the term can also be applied to plants of a northern climate which will survive the heat of a more temperate climate. *All* plants are hardy in their natural climates, but when transported by man to foreign environments, many cannot survive.

HALF-HARDY PLANTS: A plant which will survive under the normal conditions of a climate, but may be injured by abnormalities, such as an unusual cold snap, an excessive fall of rain, or lack of rain, or a prolonged period of high temperatures. Half-hardy plants are also those which are taken indoors during parts of the year, or those which must receive special treatment of some kind.

A mulch applied in fall is the best protection for half-hardy plants. The mulch will protect the plants against extreme temperature changes. It is also best not to induce growth of half-hardy plants in late summer and fall. Cut down on water and do not apply nitrogenous fertilizers. New growth is usually unable to meet the rigors of winter. *See also* PROPAGATION; GREENHOUSE; COLD FRAME;

MULCH; FERTILIZING; HARDENING-OFF.

HARDPAN: Hardpans are impervious horizontal layers in the soil that may exist anywhere from six inches to about two feet below the surface. A true hardpan is formed by the cementing together of the soil grains into a hard stone-like mass which is impervious to water. A more common condition is an impervious layer in the subsoil caused by the pore spaces becoming filled with fine clay particles. Such "tight clay" subsoils, called claypans, are generally associated with an extremely acid condition, so that from both the physical and chemical standpoint they are objectionable.

When hard or claypans exist, the surface soil is cut off from the subsoil; no new minerals are added to the lower part of the soil; plant roots often are unable to penetrate these layers. Plant roots usually grow down to this hard layer and then extend horizontally over the top of it. This results in shallow-rooted plants which may suffer from lack of nutrient elements otherwise available in the subsoil and from water during the dry summer months. Often such shallow-rooted plants die out completely from lack of water during dry periods, while plants nearby where there is no hardpan flourish and grow vigorously.

If land is characterized by poor drainage and large water run-off after a rain or if water stands in ponds after a rain, there is good reason to suspect the presence of hardpans in your soil. Hardpans are horizontal layers sometimes one-sixteenth to one-half inch in thickness. These structures are usually detected by experiment station agents by passing a blunt-pointed steel rod, attached to a handle, down through the soil profile. If resistance to the downward descent of the rod is observed at a certain depth, the depth of the obstruction is then observed. The procedure is repeated many times in the general area of the first test. If resistance to the downward thrust of the rod is observed at about the same depth on all tests, a hardpan is undoubtedly present.

Further surety may be obtained by digging several small holes in scattered places to a depth greater than that at which the hardpan was detected and by observing the soil profile. The hardpan area may be detected by testing the friability of the soil at that depth with a penknife. Gently scratch along the area with the knife; if it crumbles easily and falls away loosely the layer is not an impervious one. If the layer is hard and compact a hardpan is present.

The best and most universally used method of breaking up hardpans is by subsoiling. Subsoiling consists of cutting into the soil with a subsoil chisel or "killifer," usually from 16 to 30 inches deep. In exceptional cases, the chisel may go to a total depth of over five feet. The power requirements for these heavy deep-working tools are obviously high. Sometimes the combined power of three of the biggest track-layer tractors is needed. For the lighter tools, with a single chisel, penetrating up to 30 inches deep, the power of the ordinary wheeled two- to three-plow farm tractor is usually sufficient. *See also* DROUGHT; DYNAMITE; SUBSOILING; AERATION.

HARDWOOD CUTTINGS: *see* CUTTINGS

HARDY: Refers to plants that will endure the cold within a zone or area designated. Trees and shrubs are considered hardy when the entire woody structure remains alive through the winter and plant withstands cold. Perennials may sometimes die back to the ground, but the root system will remain alive to produce new growth and increased beauty each spring. *See also* HARDINESS.

HARE'S FOOT FERN: *see* FERN

HARE'S-TAIL GRASS: *see* GRASS, ORNAMENTAL

HARLEQUIN CABBAGE BUG: *see* CABBAGE

HARROWING: The farming operation that usually follows plowing; its objective is to break up soil clods, similar to the job done by raking in the home garden. Harrowing is done prior to seeding a crop.

HARTFORD FERN: *see* LYGODIUM

HARVESTING: The primary aim of many organic gardeners is the harvest of high quality foods. The continuous supply of vegetables depends greatly on a careful planting schedule. Harvesting details are given under the specific food crops. *See also* PLANTING; PLANNING; STORING FOOD.

HAUGHLEY EXPERIMENT: A closely-supervised, long-term agricultural experiment conducted by The Soil Association in England.

The Haughley Experiment comprises *three full-sized farms*, each operated completely independent under different methods of soil treatment, as follows:

1. A 32-acre farm operated without any livestock but with the use of chemical fertilizers and green manures.

2. A 75-acre farm operated by organic methods. Livestock is kept on the farm, all manure is composted, deep-rooted soil-building plants are used in the pastures and *no fertilizers or compost-making materials are brought onto the farm from outside.*

3. A 75-acre farm operated by chemical methods. The same type and numbers of livestock are kept as on the organic farm, but only regular pasture plants are used, not the deep-rooted kind. Artificial fertilizers are brought in from outside and all manure and crop wastes pro-

duced on the farm are returned to the soil, but are not composted.

The three farms that make up the Haughley experiment have been operated under those conditions for almost 20 years—even through World War II—and the point has now been reached where the data being collected have meaning and importance.

EXPERIMENT RESULTS: The stockless chemical farm has lost humus in its soil and the organic farm has gained humus. The chemical farm with livestock has maintained its humus content approximately the same. Most important, here is a demonstration that organic farming can increase humus content of the soil without bringing in fertilizers or organic materials from off the farm.

Crop yields on the organic farm have been equal to or greater than yields on the chemical-livestock farm. And soil tests show that even though the yields on the organic farm are greater, the fertility of the soil is actually increasing, while on the chemical-livestock farm it is decreasing.

Also, ash determinations of silage and hay crops show that most often the organic samples have the greatest ash analysis, which indicates that a superior fodder is being produced on the organic farm.

Vitamin analyses made of the various crops produced have not shown significant variations, but it does appear that the animals on the organic farm are reacting better to their diet than are the animals on the chemical-livestock farm. Not only are the organic cows producing more milk, but their milk has a higher protein content. Protein production per year of the organic cows average 254 pounds, while that of the chemical cows is only 228 pounds.

SEASONAL VARIATIONS IN SOIL ANALYSES: One of the most arresting discoveries made at Haughley concerns the seasonal variation in the plant food content of the soil. Dr. Reginald F. Milton, the consultant biochemist who supervises the analytical work at Haughley, has observed that great fluctuations in plant food take place on the organic farm, and lesser variations occur on the mixed chemical-organic farm. On the exclusively chemical farm the variations are not great.

During the winter the nutrient level of the soil on all three farms is about the same. But when the warm weather comes and plants need more nutrients, the plant food level on the organic section increases greatly. In the case of one series of tests, it was found that the phosphorus content of the organic soil doubled between January and July on the organic farm, while it stayed the same on the chemical farm.

Undoubtedly, the cause of these welcome nutrient increases in the organic soil is the natural and bacterial life that exists there. Warm weather stimulates the microorganism into increased activity just at the time when growing plants need the most food.

The staff of the Haughley Farms has made 25,000 separate soil analyses over the last five years. Every month of the year accurate tests are made of many different locations in all fields.

In future years The Soil Association, sponsor of the experiment, hopes to be able to finance additional work in animal feeding, so that observations can be made of the effect of chemical and organic diets on laboratory animals. Such work is necessary, because frequently the chemical tests of food quality that are so commonly used do not indicate the real worth of that food in supporting animal and human life.

SIGNIFICANCE OF THE HAUGHLEY EXPERIMENT: The Haughley Experiment is a complex of three farms, each operated independently, offering scientists the chance to experiment and observe on a truly meaningful scale. The soil can be tilled and planted in the usual manner and live-stock can be managed just as it is on the average farm.

Because Haughley is such a large and long-continuing experiment, the scientists and farmers of the world will no doubt look at its results with more than the usual amount of interest.

HAWKWEED: (*Hieracium aurantiacum*) A low-growing weed with attractive flowers that is especially abundant in northeastern wasteland areas. Although they are troublesome weeds, bees work the flowers readily producing an amber honey.

HAWTHORN: (*Crataegus*) The hawthorn is a medium-sized tree, desirable on the lawn for its form, bloom, autumnal leaf colors, and showy fruit. The flowers are white, pink, or red. The hawthorns comprise a large genus of thorny shrubs and trees belonging to the rose family, and are hardy and native throughout the eastern United States. Some of the hawthorns seem to enjoy the wind-beaten atmosphere along the seashore.

The native hawthorns are exceedingly attractive in flower in spring, in leaf coloration in autumn, and in fruit in early winter. The flowers and fruits occur in showy clusters. The fruits are really small pomes and thus resemble miniature apples.

Because of their thorns, impenetrable barriers can be made of them, although they may suffer when pruned back for hedges. Hawthorns can be recognized by their long, sharply pointed thorns which really are modified branches, small spherical buds, showy flowers borne in corymbs, and clusters of brightly colored fruits.

The American hawthorns come true from seed. Before sowing, it is advisable to soak the fruit in water until the flesh has decayed and the seeds may be rubbed free of the pulp. Sow the seeds in flats and keep in a cool cellar, basement or shade house for two years, watering them occasionally. Germina-tion will not occur until the second spring, possibly the third.

Transplant the seedlings in the first year to encourage the formation of a fibrous root system. Rare varieties are obtained by grafting on seedling stock of the English Hawthorn (*C. oxyacantha*).

VARIETIES: The English Hawthorn grows to 15 feet, forming a small tree or bush. The white flowers are followed by bright red fruit. The *pauli* puts out bright scarlet, double flowers and is the most popular variety in this country.

Mollis is native to the Midwest and the state flower of Missouri. It is an attractive species with glossy leaves, short thorns, and small, scarlet, pear-shaped fruit which drop shortly after ripening.

Cockspur-thorn (*Crus-galli*) has widespread, often drooping branches, frequently covered with long thorns. The small, dry, round fruits often remain on the tree all winter while the glossy leaves assume vivid autumn hues. This variety frequently attains a height of 40 feet but can be kept dense and short by careful pruning.

The Washington thorn grows to 30 feet, is a native of the South and makes an excellent hedge with pruning. It puts forth flowers in dense clusters which are followed by lustrous fruit which remain until midwinter.

HAY: The dried top growth of certain fine-stemmed grasses, legumes and some other plants used for feeding livestock. It is considered the best and cheapest feed for forage-consuming livestock.

Cows and the other ruminants were designed by Nature to efficiently consume large quantities of roughage. A cow's four stomachs and big intestinal tract have a capacity of 80 gallons of feed. Hay thus plays a vital role in the diet of cows, as well as of sheep, and to some degree poultry and pigs.

But the hay must be of the best quality to do its job well. A cow that eats a ton of poor hay will need 500 pounds of additional grain to maintain her maximum production.

HIGH-QUALITY HAY: A definition by the New Jersey Experiment Station states: "Quality hay is any legume or grass of economic value to livestock, grown on well-limed, fertile soils, cut in the early bloom stage and cured rapidly with a minimum loss of nutrients and minerals. This hay is green in color, the leaves are intact upon the stems, has a pleasant aroma and is free from dust."

he cures it into very good hay, that acre will yield 1,440 pounds of protein. The same acre of alfalfa, if the soil is infertile and the farmer's curing methods poor, will yield only about 800 pounds of protein of poor digestibility. To make up the difference of 640 pounds would take *118 bushels of corn or 28 bushels of soybeans.*

Total digestible nutrients, or energy values, follow the same pattern. Poor hay will have about 175 pounds per ton less total digestible nutrients— 700 pounds less for that acre of alfalfa

Hay is an invaluable product of the farm. Once grown mainly as a food for cattle, it has since come into its own as a cover crop, soil conditioner and material for composting and mulches.

Such hay will produce most or all the protein needed for high milk production, without concentrates. Very good alfalfa hay contains 18 per cent protein, while a poor alfalfa hay may have only ten per cent. Even more important, the protein in fine hay is more digestible than that in poor hay. A brown, leafless timothy hay will have less than half as much digestible protein as a rich green timothy hay.

What does this mean to the farmer who feeds this hay? If one acre of his farm produces four tons of alfalfa, and

—than very good hay. You have to feed 16 bushels of corn to get back that much T.D.N. (Total Digestible Nutrients). Put another way, four tons of good alfalfa or clover and timothy hay will yield as much T.D.N. as 80 bushels of corn or 12 tons of corn silage.

POOR QUALITY CAUSES DISEASE: Poor quality hay is one of the main reasons for sickness, breeding troubles and lack of thrift in livestock. An animal's health is tied up with the food it eats. Hay that is low in vitamins, minerals and trace elements, say authorities, is very often responsible for everything from digestive disturbances, rickets, pneumonia and death in calves and lambs, to a dozen baffling ailments in older animals.

These deficiency diseases are directly traceable to the soil on which the hay was grown. Which brings us to the three factors causing poor quality in hay: poor soil, cutting at the wrong time, and improper curing.

Low soil fertility is the worst culprit. Says the New Jersey Station, "The plant reflects the nutrition of the soil." Soil low in nutrients and having little organic matter and poor structure, will not produce plants of good food value.

Acid soils or those low in calcium will grow calcium-deficient plants (such soils are extremely widespread today). The animal eating these plants will not have strong bones or teeth, and will suffer from generally poor health. Lime your soil, and lime it deeply and plentifully, to grow high yields of good quality leguminous hays.

A lack of phosphorus causes a craving for unnatural foods and other eating troubles. Rock phosphate, in the amount dictated by your soil's needs, is a must for good hay and healthy animals.

Organic matter content of the soil is definitely related to the carotene and protein content of the hay. Little carotene (pro-vitamin A) is found in plants grown on soil low in nitrogen. Build up the organic matter and bacterial activity in soil by plowing down a crop of grasses and legumes every few years, instead of continually taking them for hay.

Trace minerals are equally vital. Copper, cobalt, manganese, iron, magnesium and iodine have all been proven important to the health of livestock. An imbalance of micronutrients (mainly an excess of molybdenum and a deficiency of manganese and cobalt) is believed to be the cause of the mysterious "X-Disease" of cattle. A good diet of rock fertilizers, with plenty of organic matter, will supply all the necessary trace elements in goodly amounts.

Use every bit of manure properly to build up the soil. Make good seedbeds and use high quality seeds to insure thick stands that crowd out weeds, let hay plants develop good-textured stems.

Improving soil to grow highly nutritious hay plants is not all there is to the job. Numerous experiment station researches show it is possible to increase the value of a hay crop *one-third* by earlier cutting and better curing, handling and storage methods.

STAGE OF MATURITY: The stage of maturity at harvest is all too often ignored. Carotene reaches its maximum before or at the early bloom stage in nearly all hay plants. Digestible matter is also greatest at the pre-bloom stage. Practically all the valuable constituents of a hay plant—carotene, sugars, ascorbic acid, vitamins B-1 and B-2—decrease as the plants mature, while crude fiber increases. The latter makes the hay less palatable, too.

The late date which gives the greatest number of tons per acre generally gives the least digestible protein and feed values. Says the Tennessee Experiment Station, "The protein in a ton of alfalfa hay cut just before the plants start to bloom is worth about $28, in terms of cottonseed meal. Cut after the seeds are formed, it's worth $16."

Good hay has plenty of leaves—they contain two-thirds of the digestible protein and most of the minerals. Natural green color indicates good curing, palatability and plenty of the vitamin A necessary for normal reproduction and growth.

Average methods of haying fall miserably short of accomplishing their purpose. Poor curing and storing can make a hay worthless. Excessive handling causes shattering of the leaves.

Over-curing in the swath and window causes bleaching (sunlight, not wet weather, destroys carotene), leaching of nutrients by rain and dew, heating and other fermentation changes due to the action of enzymes and bacteria. *These can destroy from 20 to 50 per cent of the nutritional value of a hay.*

CURE AND STORE PROMPTLY: Nutrient losses start piling up the minute hay is cut. The sooner it is cured and stored, the better.

To consistently produce top quality hay by field curing is almost impossible since weather cannot be controlled. Field curing lets much protein and carotene vanish into the air.

Even if there is perfect curing weather, the sun will destroy some carotene. And to rush wet green hay into the barn can mean overheating and fire. Even if the barn doesn't catch fire, poorly cured hay stands to lose up to 25 per cent of its feeding value from mow heating.

Field curing can make for a frantic, and often profitless, haying season. Some experts go so far as to say that crushing may be the only thing that will keep field curing in the picture in the future—nothing else yet invented can make it consistently produce the high quality hay farmers want today.

The USDA Station at Beltsville, Maryland, has conducted experiments over several years on the relative merits of various haymaking methods. Here are some significant results:

In good-weather years, cows gave eight per cent more milk from an acre of mow dried hay than from an acre of field cured; from an acre of wilted silage, 12 per cent more. In a rainy year, when field cured took a beating, mow dried gave 48 per cent more milk, silage 40 per cent, and dehydrated hay 60 per cent.

In average years, dairymen in the Beltsville area could count on about 20 per cent more milk from hay barn dried without heat than from field cured; barn drying with heat gave them 30 per cent more.

Both nutrients and actual tonnage yield are saved by mow drying and dehydrating. Quick, thorough curing saves most of the leaves, which contain over two-thirds of the digestible protein and most of the minerals and vitamin A. Losing only one leaf in five means enough protein lost from ten acres of hay to cost $75 to $100 in concentrates.

The biggest advantage of barn drying is that most of the handling is done while the leaves are still too moist to shatter. Also, the total time for the operation is less than for field curing, permitting more of the crop cut at the proper stage of maturity. There's no waiting for clear weather, and practically no weather risk after cutting. Barn-dried hay may have 20 per cent more leaves and 50 per cent more green color.

The county agent or extension service engineer will look over present facilities and usually help install one. Here's how one works:

Turning hay once in the windrow lets it dry to the necessary 40 to 50 per cent moisture content in four to eight hours. Forced air in the drying space then keeps it cool while more water evaporates, until the hay has about 20 per cent moisture. Supplemental heat naturally speeds up this operation. Barn drying with heat, if done properly, generally costs from eight to 15 cents a bale. Farmers find this is absorbed by the reduced amounts of grain and protein they need to feed when they have fine artificially dried hay.

The layout for your system will depend on the size and shape of your mow, rate of filling, kind of hay, etc. These are essentials: an airtight floor, strong enough to support the heavier load of high-moisture hay to be dried. Windows or other ventilators are needed to let the moisture-laden air escape. Air ducts for channeling and directing the air can be made in all shapes and sizes to fit individual requirements.

A system employing heat usually costs twice as much as an unheated-air system. Some farmers build special sheds through which heated air from a portable crop drier can be forced. Another recent development is hay curing on the wagon—less than an hour is required to reduce hay with 35 per cent moisture to 20 per cent. A wire or slatted tunnel for an air duct is run up the center of the wagon. Other farmers with no barn drying facilities or sheds stack baled hay on a slatted platform, put a tarpaulin securely over it, and cure it rapidly with a portable drier—in pouring rain.

Dehydrated hay—sort of a "baked silage"—is made by cutting, chopping, then immediately putting the green material through a huge oven or kiln to bake out the moisture. This method makes far and away the best hay, but it takes more time and work, and needs expensive equipment.

USDA tests showed dehydrating saves 96 per cent of the dry matter, 85 per cent of the protein and 23 per cent of the carotene. Efficient mow drying with heat saves about 75 per cent of the protein, 12 per cent of the carotene. Dehydrating plants which buy crops from the farmer and sell him back the finished feed, are found in increasing numbers in the South and Central states.

The consensus on forage harvesters, generally regarded by agricultural engineers as the most worth-while equipment for hay and silage harvesting reveals:

A forage harvester saves one-third the time required to put up hay with a loader and hay fork. Too, chopped hay needs less than half the storage space of loose hay; it's also easier to feed and because coarse stems and fine leaves are thoroughly mixed, cows leave none of the rougher material in the manger. Less labor and time make a forage harvester the cheapest method of harvesting the crop—on a large tonnage basis. The University of Wisconsin estimates that 160 tons

of hay and about 20 acres of row crops for silage are the lowest figures for profitable operation of a harvester.

However, efficiency — the farmer himself, in other words—is the most important factor in how well a machine pays off. A recent survey showed the difference in haymaking labor and time is greater between farmers using the same machinery than between farmers using different types.

How often should cows be fed hay? This has long been a controversial point among farmers. The answer seems to hinge, once again, on the quality of the hay. Good leafy green hay, organically grown, has plenty of "appetite appeal." Dairymen with good hay toss their cows some forkfuls every time they go into the barn, usually six or eight times a day. The cows clean it up, and their production records show slight but definite rises. *See also* MULCH; COW.

HAYFEVER PLANTS: *see* RAGWEED

HAZELNUT: (*Corylus*) Hazel or Hazelnut includes many forms of the birch family, some producing the tasty filbert and hazelnuts. The shrub types, American hazel (*C. americana*) and Beaked hazel (*C. cornuta*) grow to eight feet high and are hardy throughout most of the United States. They grow well in ordinary garden soil.

The filberts (*C. maxima*) range in height from ten to 30 feet, are grown commercially mostly in the Northwest, but varieties are being developed for the eastern parts of the country. General requirements for filberts are fairly rich, well-drained soils, and a climate without mild periods during winter and late spring frosts. Trees should be planted about 20 feet apart in autumn or spring. Gather nuts when ripe, indicated by the browning of husk edges. *See also* FILBERT; NUT TREES.

HEALTH AND SOIL: The idea that health can possibly be related to the soil was—and in many cases, unfortunately, still is—considered an extremely radical one. The fact that there is a direct strong relationship between health and soil is an integral concept of the organic method. In short, better soils produce better quality crops, which in turn produce better-fed and healthier people. More and more researchers — both agricultural and medical—are coming to agree with this concept.

The late Sir Albert Howard, over a period of 30 years in India, discovered that the use of chemical fertilizers was devitalizing the soil and the food that was grown in it.

As a mycologist in the West Indies, Sir Albert had an opportunity to study the diseases of sugar cane. He came to the conclusion that the existing methods of scientific research would never solve the problem of plant disease. In 1905, he was appointed to Imperial Economic Botanist to the Government of India.

Around his farm Sir Albert kept a close watch on the methods of the natives and saw how careful they were that all animal and plant residues were returned to the soil. Every blade of grass that could be salvaged, all leaves that fell, all weeds that were cut down found their way back into the soil, there to decompose and take their proper place in the natural cycle. The crops in the region surrounding Sir Albert's experimental farm were practically immune from disease.

Sir Albert also observed a gradual lessening of animal disease. When his oxen rubbed noses with other cattle that had the dreaded hoof-and-mouth disease they did not contract it, in spite of the fact that they had not been inoculated. Their bodies had become strengthened and could fight off dangerous disease organisms because their food came from a soil rich in living humus matter, that had not been defiled with dead chemicals. Sir Albert sums up his work with the classic statement, "Artificial fertilizers lead to artificial nutrition, artificial animals and finally to artificial men and women." Another author put it in a different way. He said: "The only crop that can be raised on poor land is poor people."

LIVING SOIL: The soil is not a dead, inert substance. It is very much alive and teems with such microorganisms as bacteria, fungi, molds, yeasts, protozoa and algae. As a group, these lower plants and animals are referred to as the biologic life of the soil.

These tiny living organisms are part of the digestive processes of the soil. They are the wrecking crews that turn anything with which they come into contact into soil, even rocks. Without the aid of this microorganic world man would cease to exist.

Sir E. John Russell, in his book *Soil Conditions and Plant Growth,* describes a study which was made in a field treated with farmyard manure. It had a bacterial count of 28,860,000 per gram of soil. Where chemical fertilizers were used only 15,100,000 bacteria were present. Practically all investigators agree that the application of organic manures stimulates and increases the biologic life of the soil.

Professor Selman A. Waksman of Rutgers University who isolated antibiotic streptomycin says, "Plant deficiency diseases are usually less severe in soil well supplied with organic matter, not only because of the increased vigor of the plants but also because of antagonistic effects of the various soil microorganisms which become more active in the presence of an abundance of organic matter." *See also* NUTRITION.

HEALTHY HUNZAS, THE, by J. I. *Rodale. See* BOOKS FOR ORGANIC GARDENERS AND FARMERS

HEARTNUT: (*Juglans sieboldiana*) Introduced into this country from Japan almost 100 years ago, the heartnut is now recognized as one of the best ornamentals of the nut tree species. With its luxurious, almost tropical foliage, the heartnut provides a dense shade, yet grass grows well under it.

Heartnut trees seldom grow larger than apple trees, as they have a tendency to grow rather low and very spreading. Because of this tendency, it's necessary to "fight" it for the first few years to get the tree headed high enough. Do this by cutting off one or two of the lower limbs each year and cutting back some of the longer laterals. Any of the new growth that threatens to compete with the leader should also be cut back. Sometimes growers find it necessary to place a high post beside the tree, to which they can tie one of the most vigorous branches in an upright position to form a leader.

In a survey of the entire Northern Nut Growers' Association made by nut tree expert John Davidson, ratings of heartnuts were as follows:

Hardiest — *Walters, Fodermaier, Gellatly, Faust* and *Bates.*

Best yields—*Walters* and *Bates.*

Best filled (with best husking and cracking quality)—*Gellatly, Walters* and *Bates.*

The heartnut—along with other members of the Japanese walnut species—thrives in both clay and sandy soils. J. Russell Smith, nut tree expert, describes it as "a veritable goat in its feeding habits," making it a very rapid grower, "and in rich soils a single leaf is sometimes a yard long."

In form, the nut is distinctly heart-shaped with a short, flat base and sharply pointed tip. Produced in clusters—sometimes of ten or more, their flavor is mild, except with the choicest varieties, which taste much like the butternut. Generally the tree tends to bear annually, though not as heavily as the black or Persian walnut.

Because of its many good features, the heartnut and other Japanese walnut trees should receive a lot more attention from plant breeders in the future. In its native home, the trees grow throughout the climatic range of Japan, which includes climates similar to Nova Scotia all the way down to Georgia.

At the present time, the heartnut's average life span in America seldom exceeds 30 years. *See also* NUT TREES.

HEATH: (*Erica*) A large group that includes low-growing shrubs as well as tree-like ones. The tree heath (*E. arborea*) grows ten to 20 feet, has white flowers. Scotch heath (*E. cinerea*) makes a dense low-growing shrub to one and one-half feet with rosy-colored flowers. Corsican heath (*E. stricta*) reaches about ten feet, has blooms similar to Scotch heath, is hardy only in the deep southern states. One prostrate form, excellent for rock gardens, is winter or spring heath (*E. carnea*), growing less than one foot high. Culture is similar to heather, which see.

HEATHER: (*Calluna*) Belonging to the *Ericaceae* family, the common heather (*C. vulgaris*) is most often grown in dense clusters, reaches one and one-half feet high; it is recommended for sandy banks along northeastern seacoasts. Many varieties offer the gardener a wide choice of flower colors—from white and crimson to pink and golden yellow. Blooming from mid-summer to fall, heather grows best in a light, sandy, but humus-rich, soil and in an open or part shady location. They need much care to grow well. After the plants have bloomed, they should be cut down in order to keep them bushy and attractively shaped.

HEAVING: A type of winter injury in which plants are loosened and frequently lifted from the soil as a result of successive freezing and thawing. It occurs in soils containing a considerable amount of clay or silt which alternately freeze and thaw in the spring.

Protecting the plants and soil with mulch should eliminate the condition. A long-range remedy is to compost heavily, adding large amounts of humus to the soil and proportionately reducing its clay content.

HEAVY SOIL: Soil which contains a high percentage of clay and/or silt. Heavy soils generally hold too much moisture and have poor drainage. *See also* SOIL; CLAY; AERATION.

HEDERA: *see* IVY; ENGLISH IVY; HOUSE PLANTS

HEDGE: A hedge is a row of plants, generally woody, used as a border, fence, screen, or windbreak. It is usually trimmed to a more or less formal shape. Plants used for hedging are chosen for their capacity to hold a shape, and to form a thick intertangled growth from the ground up. Hedges, though sometimes used as borders around formal gardens, are to be distinguished from edgings, which are mostly temporary borders along walks, or enclosing flower beds.

Hedges along property lines where it is desirable to screen in the property or provide a windbreak may be as high as a line of poplars or a row of evergreen trees. Where a lower wall or fence would be used, the hedge may be equally low. In formal European gardens dating back to the seventeenth and eighteenth centuries, six to 12 inch hedges of box or similar material were used to outline flower beds of fancy shapes. Hedges are often used abroad, especially in England in place of fences around fields and pastures.

Evergreen or deciduous plants may be used for hedging. Evergreen hedges are usually slower-growing, and are preferred for that reason. But any shrub which makes a dense growth may be trimmed to perform the function of a fence.

PLANTING AND MAINTENANCE: To obtain a good hedge, it is necessary to prepare the soil deeply, set the plants close, and shear them at least twice each year. Distance between plants will be determined by the plant, and by the proposed height of the hedge. Privet, planted for quick effects, is spaced about nine inches apart. Most evergreens are best planted at least 18 inches, and some 24 inches apart. Arborvitae may even be set three feet apart.

To insure a dense growth, deciduous plants are usually cut back almost to the ground when planted. Plants especially grown for hedges may not need such drastic pruning, but it is advisable to cut back tip growth by at least 30 per cent.

Shaping should begin the year after the hedge is planted, though the first few years pruning should be light until the desired height and general shape is attained. Deciduous hedges should be pruned after the first strong growth of the spring has slowed down, in May or June, and again in midsum-

A formal hedge of Colorado spruce not only confers privacy but also acts as a windbreak and natural snow fence. For healthiest growth, hedges should be denser at the bottom than at the top.

mer when the secondary growth may need to be shaped. Evergreens grow more slowly, and should never be severely pruned. Shaping once each year in midsummer should be sufficient.

For densest growth to the ground, hedges should be kept narrower at the top than they are at the bottom, shaped in cross-section like a truncated pyramid. This shape will permit the lower branches to get enough light to keep them healthy and thickly foliated. When permitted to broaden at the top, a hedge will lose its lower leaves and become leggy. This effect is also sometimes the result of pruning neglect. When a hedge has not been pruned for several years, it becomes thin at the bottom. The only remedy is frequent and careful pruning for a year or two.

To maintain its health, a hedge should be kept clean at its base, particularly in wet seasons when fungus diseases may attack. Because the foliage protects the soil under it from the rays of the sun mulching is usually unnecessary, and leaves that blow under the hedge from neighboring trees should be removed.

Plants recommended for low hedges under 18 inches are: deciduous—dwarf cranberrybush, *viburnum opulus nanum; spirea* Anthony Waterer, *spirea bumalda*; box barberry, *berberis thunbergi;* privet, *ligustrum* various; evergreen—box, *buxus sempervirens* var. *suffruticosa, nana;* pygmy Hinoki cypress, *chamaecyparis obtusa pygmaea,* formerly called *retinospora obtusa nana*; common thyme, *thymus vulgaris.* Evergreens which will not grow to a height of more than two feet are: globe arborvitae, *thuja occidentalis,* var. *globosa*; Hinoki cypress, *chamaecyparis* obtusa nana; Japanese yew, *taxus cuspidata brevifolia*; Japanese holly, *ilex crenata microphylla*; inkberry, *ilex glabra.*

Deciduous shrubs which can be grown for medium height hedges are: California privet, *ligustrum ovalifolium*; Ibota privet, *ligustrum ibota*;

Amur privet, *ligustrum amurense*; Japanese barberry, berberis thunbergi; flowering or Japanese quince, *cydonia japonica*; rugosa rose, *rosa rugosa*; Vanhoutte spirea, *spirea vanhouttei*; arrow-wood, *viburnum dentatum*; Peking cotoneaster, *cotoneaster* acutifolia.

Evergreen trees which make a close growth for good hedges are: American arborvitae, *thuja occidentalis*; hemlock, *tsuga canadensis*; Irish juniper, *juniperus communis hibernica*; Norway spruce, *picea excelsa*. Deciduous trees that make good hedges are: European beech, *fagus sylvatica*; English hawthorn, *crataegus oxyacantha*; cockspur thorn, *crataegus crusgalli;* and hornbeam, *carpinus betulus,*

FORMAL OR INFORMAL: There are two types of hedges—formal and informal. The formal hedge has definite lines and clean-cut surfaces. The informal hedge is allowed to grow freely, and is not clipped close. The only trimming which is done is an occasional pruning to keep it within bounds. Trimmed hedges are often used in landscape design as horizontal lines and seemingly to tie buildings and formal gardens together.

Plants for formal hedges include the privets, boxwoods, yews, and arborvitae. Some plants for informal hedges are the barberries, mock orange, lilac, spirea, viburnum, and dwarf deutzia. *See also* EVERGREENS; SHRUBS.

HEEL-IN: The practice of covering plants temporarily with soil before planting them permanently.

Plants set out in the spring require little attention before planting, except to unpack them in a cool, shady place and examine for any signs of damage. If they are to be planted at once, cut off any broken or ragged roots with a sharp knife or shears so as to make a clean cut. Should the stock be received in the fall too late for planting, or for some reason cannot be cared for at once, heel-in as follows: Dig a shallow trench in a well-drained spot with one side vertical and the other sloping. Lay the plants close together in the trench with the roots against the vertical side and the stems resting on the slope. Cover the roots completely and water them thoroughly. If the plants are to stay heeled-in all winter, tamp the earth firmly around the roots and cover the trunks and lower branches as well. Heeled-in material can be pulled out and permanently planted at a later date.

HELENIUM: Known as sneeze-weed, these are mostly hardy yellow-flowering perennials, that bloom from summer to fall. Yellow star (*H. autumnale*) grows about five feet, is usually placed toward the rear of flower borders. They do best in a moist, rich soil, preferring a sunny location.

HELIANTHEMUM: Belonging to the *Cistaceae* family, these are low-growing woody plants often used in the rock garden. Known as rock roses and sun roses, helianthemums are native to North and South America. *H. nummularium* is the commonest sun-rose, generally growing less than one foot; *H. halimifolium* grows to about two feet. Both have yellow flowers. They are especially adapted to the California climate, where they are well suited to dry, sunny rock gardens.

HELIANTHUS: see SUNFLOWER

HELIOPSIS: Summer-blooming perennials that in many ways resemble the sunflower. Sometimes known as false sunflower, *H. helianthoides* grows to five feet high, has yellow flower heads. Orange sunflower (*H. scabra*) is similar to the other variety except for bloom color. They grow well in a variety of soils, often give a weedy appearance. They are propagated by division.

HELIOTROPE: (*Heliotropium*) Popular tropical plants for their large fragrant flower heads, heliotropes range in height from one to four feet. The common heliotrope (*H. arc cens*) is

generally grown as an annual, growing two to four feet. They require a rich soil and much warmth, therefore are planted late in spring. They are recommended for grouping in a mixed flower border, the dwarf kinds for edging in the rose garden. The name "heliotrope" means "turning to the sun" and refers to the plant's desire for a warm, sunny location. They should be given sufficient water.

HELIOTROPISM: The power of sunlight to retard growth on the side of the plant facing it. During the day the side of the plant that is in the shade grows faster than the side facing the sun. At night the unshaded side grows faster than the shaded side to catch up. Some plants therefore seem to move along with the sun.

Sunflower heads, for example, seem to follow the sun's movements across the sky, and then—during the evening —they slowly return to the east again.

HELLEBORUS: see CHRISTMAS ROSE

HEMLOCK: (*Tsuga*) The very popular evergreen tree of the pine family so often seen in the garden landscape. This graceful tree, with its fan-like sprays of greenish-blue foliage, bears quantities of small cones which add to its beauty. Although usually small, the cones are somewhat woody but not stiff, and are generally borne on the twig ends.

The small, flat needles, one-fourth to one-half inch long, are arranged in rows on each side of the twig, and drop off quickly when dry.

The two most common species are the Canada (*T. canadensis*) and Carolina (*T. caroliniana*) hemlocks. Canada hemlock, often called hemlock spruce, is the common one so popular in the northeastern section of the country. It is conical, tapering evenly from a broad base to a long, straight head. Capable of reaching almost 100 feet, it usually grows much shorter. It is commonly used as a hedge.

The Carolina hemlock is often called

spruce pine, has dark dense foliage with sweeping branches.

Actually very hardy trees, hemlocks do best in a rich, moist soil, and a somewhat wind-sheltered location. They do not stand up well to intense summer heat or drought periods.

Other varieties include Japanese hemlock (*T. diversifolia*)—pyramid-shaped; western hemlock (*T. heterophylla*)—adapted mostly to the West Coast; and mountain hemlock (*T. mertensiana*)—also restricted mostly to the western part of the country. *See also* EVERGREEN.

HEN MANURE: *see* MANURE

HENBANE: (*Hyoscyamus niger*) A poisonous annual or biennial herb of the potato family introduced into this country from Europe and occasionally found as a weed in some of the Northern and Great Plains States. The herb (leaves, flowers, and small stems) contains several poisonous alkaloids used in the preparation of important medicines.

The soil and climatic requirements of henbane are very similar to those of belladonna, but the plant is less subject to root decay under poor drainage conditions. The seed germinates uniformly in about two weeks.

If the annual type is grown, the crop is harvested when the plants are in full bloom. The biennial type makes a large rosette-like growth the first year and blooms early in the second season.

HENSEL, JULIUS: Julius Hensel's concept of mineral nutrition is very different from that of the famous Liebig School in Germany. The German chemist Liebig was the founder of Agricultural Chemistry. As a result of his findings the major mineral nutriments in soil have been discovered, such as potassium, nitrates, phosphates, calcium. Even now, a hundred years later, these elements are considered basic for plant nutrition. The entire modern fertilizer industry bases its existence on this discovery of Liebig's.

Hensel felt, however, that the use of potassium, nitrates and phosphates alone does not replenish the soil. A soil analysis reveals the truth of this position as well as the existence of calcium, magnesium, manganese, silicium oxide, aluminum oxide, and many other substances, including all the trace elements.

Hensel observed that, in mountain valleys, on virgin soil, plants were always healthy, vigorous, and almost without disease. He thought that the origin of life must be here, where the water, coming down the hills, deposits all the substance of the mountains which has been dissolved in it, and thus builds the fertile, valley bottom land. In the plains, where no new alluvial soil is added, the land gradually becomes exhausted. This simple observation was the basis of his plan to powder mountain rock and apply it where nature herself could no longer do it. Then he analyzed plants and found that different plants vary widely in their mineral constituents.

With the addition of finely ground stone-meal, Hensel obtained very good results. He particularly observed that plants not only grew in quantity but were also very healthy and free of parasites. Another important observation was that roots grew particularly well in soils thus treated. We quote from Hensel's book, *Bread From Stones*: "If we desire normal and healthy crops, and that man and animals living on them should find in them all that is necessary for their bodily sustenance, phosphate and fluorite of lime and magnesia for the formation of the bones and teeth, potassium and iron and manganese for the muscles, chloride of sodium for the serum of the blood, sulphur for the albumin of the blood, hydrocarbons for the nerve fat, it will not suffice to merely restore the potassium, phosphoric acid and nitrogen. Other things are imperatively demanded . . ."

Today the replacing of trace minerals in the soil through the application of rock powders or dust is gaining acceptance. This practice, when combined with a composting and mulching program will more than fulfill the vision of this pioneer organiculturist.

HEPATICA: Also known as the Mayflower and liver-leaf, hepatica is a low-growing perennial that blooms in early spring. They do best in partial shade, but also grow well in open areas, as long as the soil is rich and well-drained. Root division is the usual means of propagation; plant seeds in moist soil under shade. Common hepatica (*H. americana*) is also known as blue anemone; grows to six inches high, has mostly blue, sometimes white or pink flowers.

HERB: Botanically speaking, an herb is a plant without a permanent, woody stem. This definition is broad enough to include most plants of the world, the major exceptions being trees and shrubs. Most herbs are herbaceous, *i.e.,* they have fleshy stems and die down during winter.

When the average gardener speaks of herbs, though, he generally refers to a very special group of herbaceous plants that are used for delicate flavoring, scenting, and occasional medicinal purposes.

Herb Culture

Following is some detailed information on growing herbs in the home garden, as described by F. H. Scott and L. B. Wilkins, Extension horticulturists from Virginia:

Culinary herbs are garden plants grown for seasoning food and for preparing beverages.

Herbs may be grown any place near the house where there is reasonably good, well-drained, garden soil. Some gardeners prefer to plant herbs in the vegetable or flower garden. Others maintain a little herb garden which, if planted with care and well tended, can be quite attractive.

ANISE: (*Pimpinella anisum*)—An annual herb, growing about 18 inches

high. Seeds are the part of the plant mainly used, but occasionally fresh leaves are used as garnish and in salads.

Seed should be sown in the garden in early spring at a depth of one-half inch. Use eight or ten seed per foot of row and later thin to eight inches apart. Six to eight feet of row should be enough; but for large plantings space rows two feet apart. Keep weeds under control. Hilling, which is pulling soil around the lower part of the plant, keeps the heavy heads from bending over onto the soil.

In about 75 days, when the seeds turn grayish-brown, clip the flower clusters, called "umbels," from the plant. Thoroughly dry by spreading in a warm, dry, shaded place. Then clean the seed by rubbing the umbels between the hands and blowing away the chaff. Store in a cloth bag.

SWEET BASIL: (*Ocimum basilicum*)—The usually planted variety of this annual herb will grow about 18 inches tall with a taller flower stem. The tender fresh leaves or dry leaves are the parts used and have a clove flavor.

Sow seed in the garden in the early spring about one-half inch deep. Space the seed about one inch apart

one seed to the inch and later thin to about four to six plants per foot. The plants will grow to a height of about 18 to 24 inches. You need only a few plants; but if you want a larger planting, space the rows about 24 inches apart. Germination is slow and so is the growth of the plants in the early part of the season; therefore, considerable care is necessary to keep down weeds. The biennial caraway will flower early in the second season after planting and mature their seed by midsummer.

When the seeds turn brown, they should be cut from the plant before shattering begins. Thoroughly dry the seed by spreading them in a warm, dry, shaded place. Then clean them by rubbing the umbels between the hands and blowing away the chaff. Store seed in a paper bag or closed container.

CHIVES: (*Allium schoenoprasum*) —A perennial herb that grows to about eight or ten inches high and has an attractive violet-colored flower.

Bulbs are usually planted in the early spring, about five inches apart. Usually they are set about one-half to one inch deep. The bulbs multiply so rapidly that it is necessary to take up clumps either in the fall or spring and subdivide them every two or three years to prevent crowding. A few clumps of bulbs may be potted late in the fall and kept indoors or under glass in a cold frame during the winter, so that the fresh leaves can be used as needed.

Fresh tender leaves are always used, as the bulbs or dried leaves lose their flavor. The tender leaves or the entire plant can be harvested any time during the season and used fresh. Sometimes it helps to cut back the seed heads after flowering to stimulate new leaf growth. The leaves should be chopped and used soon after harvesting.

CORIANDER: (*Coriandrum sativum*) —An annual herb growing to a height of 24 to 30 inches with finely cut foliage and white flowers.

The seed are sown in the early

and, if the tops are not pinched out, it will not be necessary to thin the plants. Some gardeners prefer to pinch out the tops which will make the plants grow into little bushes that should be thinned to ten inches apart. Only a few plants will be needed; but for a larger planting, space the rows 24 inches apart.

Just as the plants begin to flower, in about 85 days, harvest the tender leaves by cutting the stems, usually six to eight inches above the ground. The green tender leaves may be used fresh at any time. Several cuttings may be made during the season. The leaves and stems can be tied in small bundles and hung in a well-ventilated dark room or spread thinly on a screen to dry. After thorough drying, the leaves may be stripped from the stems and packed in closed containers.

CARAWAY: (*Carum carvi*)—This is the biennial variety of caraway that will not produce a crop the first season. The seed generally matures about midsummer of the second year. This herb has a carrot-like foliage and white flowers.

The seed of the biennial varieties may be sown in late summer or early spring at a depth of about one-half inch. Sow the seed at a rate of about

The herb garden has been more or less neglected in this country. Herbs are propagated like other plants; from seeds, bulbs or roots and are neither more nor less difficult to cultivate successfully.

spring about one-half inch deep. Usually the seed are spaced about one inch apart. Some gardeners suggest thinning the plants to six inches apart while others suggest no thinning at all. Either way will usually produce satisfactory results. A row several feet long should supply enough coriander seed for the family; but for larger plantings space the rows three feet apart. No special care is necessary except to keep weeds under control.

The plants should be cut for seed in about 90 days when the fruits have turned brown and before much shattering has occurred. The pleasing flavor of the coriander fruit is not thoroughly developed until it is completely dried. The whole plant may be tied in bundles or spread on screens to dry. As soon as dry, the fruits should be separated by threshing and blowing the chaff away. The clean seed should be stored in bags or closed containers for sometime before using.

DILL: (*Anethum graveolens*)—A good variety of this annual herb is Long Island Mammoth. The plant which has yellow flowers will grow to a height of two to three feet, so it is advisable to plant it on the north side of the garden in order not to shade other crops.

Sow the seed in the spring about one-quarter inch deep using 15 to 20 seed per foot. Germination takes place in ten to 15 days. Thin the plants to about four to eight inches apart in the row. Several feet of row would be enough for the family; but for larger plantings space the rows 36 inches apart.

The fruiting umbels are ready to harvest for seasoning in about 70 days when the fruit is fully developed but not yet brown. They may be used fresh or dried. The umbels may be dried on screens in the shade and stored in closed containers for winter use. The leaves are used fresh as they lose their pleasing flavor when dried.

GARLIC: (*Allium sativum*)—This herb is a perennial that is frequently treated as an annual. Its culture is very much like that of the onion. The cloves are obtained by separating the bulbs.

Cloves of garlic must be planted in the early spring in order to avoid hot weather. The cloves are pressed into the soil, base downward, one to two inches deep and four inches apart. The amount of cloves to buy depends on their size but usually three-quarters of a pound would be ample for a 25 foot row. If you should want to plant more than one row of garlic, space the rows 15 inches apart.

The crop is harvested by pulling up the bulbs in about 90 days when the tops begin to turn yellow. The bulbs should be fairly well dried and then cleaned by removing the outer loose parts of the sheaths and trimming the roots close to the base. They may be stored loose like onions, tied in bunches, or plaited into strings. Store the garlic in a cool well-ventilated place.

SWEET MARJORAM: (*Majorana hortensis*)—This herb is a tender perennial which must be grown as an annual where freezing temperatures

are frequent. There are also the pot and wild varieties of marjoram but we are concerned with the sweet marjoram which is sometimes called "knotted."

The seed should be sown in a cold frame or window box and covered with a thin layer of sand. Keep the sand moist but not soggy. As early in the spring as possible when the plants are two or three inches high, transplant them to their permanent outdoor location. Space the plants six to eight inches apart in the row. They usually reach a height of 12 to 24 inches. Sweet marjoram also can be propagated by crown division and cuttings. Stems from the latest growth make the best cuttings and usually can be rooted in late summer or early fall. Cut the stems into four-inch sections, each having a set of leaves or leaf buds near its upper end. The leaf area should be reduced about two-thirds by removing the larger leaves and allowing only the buds or young leaves to remain on the upper third of the section. Place the cuttings in water as soon as they are removed from the plant. Fill a flat, which is a shallow box, with about four inches of clean sand. Insert the cuttings about two-thirds their length in the moist sand. Pack firmly and water thoroughly. Cover the flat with glass so that a one-inch opening remains along one side for ventilation. Place the box in a protected, sunny place and keep moist, but not wet, at all times. The cuttings should be protected from the direct sunlight by paper for about ten days. On hot sunny days, the ventilation should be increased by raising the glass cover higher on one side. Roots should develop in about two weeks. In about five weeks, the cuttings should be ready to set in pots or coldframes or in other places where they can be protected during the winter. Early in the spring, the plants can be transplanted to a permanent location.

When the plants begin to bloom, they can be cut back several inches, and a second or third cutting can be made before the frost. The leaves and flowering tops should be dried rapidly, the stems removed, and the clean dry leaves stored for winter. The fresh leaves can be used as needed during the season.

PARSLEY: (*Petroselinum crispum*) —This is a biennial but the leaves may be used the first season as well as the early part of the second season before the flower stalks appear. An excellent variety of parsley is Moss Curled. This has very dark, finely cut, and curled leaves.

Seed should be sown early in the spring and covered to a depth of one-quarter inch. About 15 to 20 seeds are used per foot of row and later the plants are spaced six inches apart in the row. The plants grow to a height of seven to ten inches. Usually a small bed of parsley is all that the family requires; but if you want more, space the rows 15 inches apart. You need give parsley little other attention except to keep weeds under control.

Green leaves may be harvested at any time during the season when sufficient growth has been made, usually in about 70 days. The plants remain green until early winter. During the second season, the leaves may be harvested until the flower stalks appear. The leaves are nearly always used fresh, but they will retain their flavor if dried and stored.

ROSEMARY: (*Rosmarinus officinalis*)—This herb will develop into a dense perennial shrub with glossy green foliage and tiny light blue flowers. By the end of the second season, the plant may be two feet in diameter and three feet high and later may reach a height of four feet or more.

This herb rarely produces seed except under the most favorable conditions so that it will be necessary to obtain plants or rooted cuttings to start. If you wish to develop rooted stem cuttings, you should follow the procedure as outlined under sweet marjoram. The plants should be spaced 36 inches apart. One or two plants

are all that a family would ordinarily require. For large plantings, space the rows 36 inches apart. The plants or rooted stem cuttings should be set out in the spring.

The growth can be pruned back several inches once or twice each season after the plants become large enough which is usually in the second season. The leaves and stems from the pruning should be dried on a screen and the leaves stripped from the stems and stored in a closed container. The leaves may be used fresh.

SAGE: (*Salvia officinalis*)—This perennial herb is grown for its leaves, which are used for seasoning. There are other sages such as scarlet and clary sages. The sage used for seasoning is a perennial, although it will probably be necessary to renew it every three or four years as the plant becomes woody.

The plants may be grown from seed, crown divisions, or stem cuttings. Sage should be planted in a cold frame or window box and the young plants transplanted when two to three inches high. Because plants grown from seed are generally of mixed types, propagation by cuttings made from desirable plants is preferred. Cuttings may be developed as described under the heading sweet marjoram. Plants which may reach a height of 24 inches should be set 18 inches apart in the row. A family seldom needs more than a few plants, but if you want a large planting, space the rows 18 inches apart. After the plants have become well established in the garden, they need little attention except weed control.

Six to eight inches of the top growth can be cut from the plant about twice during the season. The leaves should be harvested before the plant blooms. The tops may be tied in small bundles or spread on screens and dried in a well-ventilated room away from direct sunlight. If the leaves are dusty or gritty, they should be washed in cold water before drying. When they are thoroughly dry, remove the stems and place the clean dry leaves in paper bags or some other closed container.

SAVORY: (*Satureia hortensis*)—This annual herb may reach a height of 12 to 18 inches. The tender leaves and stems are used fresh or dried.

Savory should be planted in the early spring about one-half inch deep. Sow about ten seed per foot and later thin to five inches apart in the row. Only a few feet would be required for a family; but if a larger planting is desired the rows should be spaced 36 inches apart. Pull soil around the lower parts of slim plants when the leaf tips are first cut to keep the plant from bending over onto the soil. Little other care is necessary except to control weeds.

The tender leaves and stems may be used any time during the season, but for drying, six inches of top growth should be cut when blooming begins. Sometimes two or more crops can be harvested in one season. The top growth as cut from the plants may be tied in small bunches or spread on screens or paper to dry. When thoroughly dry, the leaves should be stripped from the stems and stored in closed containers. Remove all small pieces of woody stems, as they interfere with the use of the leaves in flavoring foods.

SPEARMINT: (*Mentha spicata*)— This perennial herb grows to a height of 12 to 24 inches and spreads by means of surface or underground runners that may grow several feet from the parent plant.

Spearmint is always propagated from surface or underground runners, as plants produced from seed are not uniform. The herb will do well in partial shade. Early in the spring, runners should be set in moist but not soggy soil, either in beds or rows. The runners should be covered to a depth of about two inches. New plants spring up at the nodes of the runners during the season. In spring or early summer, these plants with the roots attached can be transplanted to another bed. Unless confined by boards or metal strips set several inches in the ground, the underground runners will spread in a few seasons to cover several times the area of the original set. After planting spearmint, it needs little attention except to control weeds.

As the plants grow rapidly, fresh green sprigs are available for use as needed from early in the spring until late in the fall. The leaves and flowering tops should be cut for drying when the plants begin to flower. The upper part of the plant may be tied in small bundles and hung up or the leaves and flowering tops spread on screens and dried in the shade. Spearmint must be dried rapidly away from light if it is to retain its green color. Use a well-ventilated darkened room such as an attic. As soon as the leaves and stems are brittle, remove any excess stems and pack the clean dry leaves and flowering tops in a closed container.

THYME: (*Thymus vulgaris*)—This perennial herb is the common garden thyme which grows to a height of 12 to 18 inches.

Seed may be sown one-quarter inch deep in hotbeds or window boxes and when two to three inches high transplanted to their permanent location. The plants should be set about 15 inches apart in the row. The family would require only a few plants; but if you want a large planting, the rows should be 36 inches apart. In three or four years when the plants should be renewed, you can do this easily by layering. This is accomplished by covering some of the side branches of the old planting with soil, leaving much of the top exposed. When the covered parts of the stems have rooted, they can be cut from the parent and set as individual plants.

When the plants are in bloom, six inches of the flowering tops should be cut with clippers or a sharp knife. Sometimes two or more crops can be harvested the same season. The flowering tops should be spread on a fine screen of newspaper in a well-ventilated room to dry. After thorough drying, the leaves and flowering tops should be stripped from the stems and stored in a closed container.

STORING HERBS: The old admonition to "cut the herbs just before they start to bloom" can be taken seriously or ignored according to conditions at harvest time. The essential oils are a bit stronger then and there are more leaves in proportion to the amount of stem. However, home-dried herbs are so much more flavorful and pungent than any which can be purchased that it doesn't matter if you do your harvesting after they have flowered.

After sage has gone to seed, shear them back to within six or eight inches of the ground and use the new foliage which breaks out then for drying in August. Because sage gets so woody in a few years, try to start some new plants from seed each season just for the purpose of drying First year sage offers the tenderest leaves for drying.

With basil and savory try to catch them before the flower buds open. It may mean a second crop of tender shoots will be available before frost takes the basil and flowering savory turns from green to almost purple in color.

Lavender and tansy to be dried for winter bouquets should be cut before the blossoms are fully open because the color is more intense.

The sooner the clipped greens can be washed and started drying the better. If they lie in the sun too long, decomposition begins with a consequent loss of flavor.

After cutting and washing the herb, take as large a bunch as can be held in one hand easily, and holding the tops down tie the stems loosely with string. Thick, fat bunches wouldn't dry as quickly or thoroughly.

The following section appears through the courtesy of THE HERB GROWER MAGAZINE.

DRYING HERBS: "Hands" of herbs may be hung outdoors after washing to drip dry. They will wilt slightly but they can afford to lose as much moisture as possible. The reason for not leaving them hung in bunches on the clothesline all day is that the sun would turn the leaves somewhat yellow and evaporate the volatile oils which provide the flavor in the herb.

When dried off, put the bunches of herbs in brown paper bags, one kind to a bag, and tie the neck of the bag around the stems. Hang the bags on a line in the attic or any dry place. If the bunches were not drained first before placing in the bag, the dripping water would ruin the bottom of the bag. Label the side of the bag with the name of the herb.

Drying herbs in brown paper bags in this excellent way is not at all the same as storing an herb in a cardboard or paper container. None of the oils are absorbed by the bag while the bunch is drying in it. The leaves do not touch the side or bottom of the bag until ready to be removed—when they are crispy dry.

In a week or two, depending on the amount of humidity in the air, the herbs will be dry enough to remove from the stems while still in the bag. By rolling the bag in the palms of the hands and squeezing, the really dry leaves will fall to the bottom of the bag leaving the stems still in the bunch. Open the top of the bag to see how this process is coming. When no more leaves will separate by this simple method, take out the bunch and pick off the rest of the leaves from the individual stems. Save the stems to tie in bundles again with a bit of ribbon. They make fragrant kindlings for a fire.

If the weather should be consistently damp when drying savory, thyme, mint or basil, it may be necessary to spread the stemmed herb on a cookie sheet for further crisping in a cool oven (not over 100° F.). Do not put dried materials into air-tight containers until they are dry enough to powder easily when rubbed.

Lavender and other flowers desired for use in dried bouquets may be treated the same way; by hanging upside down in brown paper bags. However, the blossoms will be left on the stems, unless it is necessary to use the lavender in sachets. The petals of roses and other flowers to be used in potpourri are spread on screens to dry after all the stems and solid parts of the flowers have been completely removed from them.

HERBS IN COOKING

The most simple, everyday cookery becomes exciting and tastier when a subtle flavoring of herbs is added. A palette of herbs adds variety, color, and flavor to almost any type of food.

The Orientals have used saffron for centuries—to add color and flavor to chicken and rice dishes. Our own garden marigolds, dried and crushed, add the same delicate yellow coloring, and an enjoyable, delicate flavor.

One of the most delicious ways in which to cook peas is in a watertight nest of outside lettuce leaves—with a pat of butter and a few mint leaves added.

Certainly a leg of lamb rubbed with a cut garlic clove, and sprinkled with finely chopped rosemary is a culinary treat—and so simple to do.

If herb cookery is a new adventure for you—go slowly—and use them sparingly, but try them.

Angelica—Angelica is a most pleasant and aromatic tasting herb, the candied roots and stems of which can be helpful in cooky and cake baking and in decorating bonbons. The fresh leaves lend themselves to use in tossed salad, fruit cup, and are a pleasant addition to jam and jelly.

Anise—The sweet pleasing odor of anise is faintly reminiscent of licorice. The taste is quite agreeable. Use the fresh leaves in salad, and add to cooked vegetables. It has a special affinity for shellfish such as lobster, crab and shrimp. The dried seed may be applied in cooky and cake baking and in liquors.

Basil—Basil has a clovelike, mildly peppery taste which adds zest to almost any food, especially tomato dishes. Use it with fish, egg dishes, poultry, game, meat or fish casseroles, soup, stew and salad, or sprinkle it over cooked vegetables.

Bay Leaf—Bay leaf (laurel) is a wonderful, aromatic, seashore-smelling herb. Use it with fish, game, poultry, shell fish, salad, in aspic, and in sauce, soup, stew, ragout, and with almost any cooked vegetable. It is one of the most versatile and widely used of herbs.

Bee Balm or Bergamot—The fresh fragrant leaves are delicious in iced tea, fruit cup or salad, and in herb tea. The dried leaves add savor to roast meats, may be sprinkled over creme soup, and used in poultry seasoning. The flavor is pleasantly lemon-like. Sprigs of the herb are a fine addition to wine punch, lemonade or fruit drinks.

Borage—Borage has a subtle flavor that makes it a good substitute for the more commonly used parsley. Use wherever you would use parsley, such as in a tossed salad, as a garnish for meat, fish, or poultry. It is a pepper-up for cooked vegetables. The candied leaves and stems are for use in baking and in decorating cookies and cakes. The fresh sprigs and flowers improve iced tea and fruit punch.

Camomile—The dried flower heads of camomile make a delightful herb tea. In many European countries it is used in place of tea or coffee.

Celery—There are few new suggested uses for celery. Make the most of it in cheese dishes, with fish of all varieties, meat, poultry, game, and in

Borage may be used as a substitute for parsley.

salad. It is suitable as a garnish, and stuffed with cream cheese preparations as an appetizer. Celery root is tasty in stew, soup, or ragout. Chop fine and combine with chopped meat, shellfish or cream cheese; it serves excellently for sandwiches or canapes. The dried seeds flavor soup, stew, and ragout.

Caraway—The fresh young leaves of this herb have a very different, spicy taste. They flavor salad, cooked vegetables, soup, and mashed potatoes. The fresh leaves season roast pork well. The roots, boiled, serve as a vegetable. In taste they resemble parsnips. Add fresh chopped leaves to cream cheese, as an appetizer. Use the dried seeds to flavor Christmas cookies and cakes.

Chives—Tasting like mild onions, the minced fresh leaves of chives flavor all foods where onion is indicated. Use in salad, egg dishes, in salad dressing, in cream or brown sauce, add to cooked vegetables, or to cream cheese as an appetizer, and as a garnish.

Dill—Dill is a pungent, aromatic herb, having a pleasing taste and flavor. Use the fresh leaves and stems, chopped fine, with salad, meat of any sort, stew, soup, or ragout. The seeds are valuable in pickling, and in making herb vinegar. Sprinkle chopped dill on potato salad, or almost any cooked vegetable.

Garlic—Garlic, when used sparingly, is the most versatile of all seasonings. For salads, rub your wooden salad bowl with a cut clove of garlic. Use it in pot roast, with meat, poultry and game, and in sauces, gravy, soup, ragout and stew, but be miserly with it. Crushed garlic added to vinegar makes a wonderful ingredient for salad dressing.

Horehound—A delightful, fragrant, old-fashioned herb, adaptable to making herb tea, and flavor honey. The crushed leaves and juices go into making a hard, brittle candy which soothes the throat.

Horseradish—Freshly ground horseradish root is a peppery, hot herb that makes a wonderful condiment. It is a necessary addition to cocktail sauce. Use it with shellfish, and with cold meats, game, and poultry, in a cream sauce with boiled meat and fish, and in salad dressing.

Hyssop—Hyssop has a slightly bitter, aromatic flavor. Use the fresh minced leaves in cooking game, fish, meat, soup, stew and ragout. The crushed leaves add piquancy to vegetable juices and are excellent in cranberry juice. A few leaves make an unusual addition to fruit pies. Add to tossed salad sparingly.

Lavender—Lavender has a lovely, haunting fragrance that is distinctly its own. Use the fresh petals in wine cup, fruit drinks, jelly, gelatin dessert and custard. The dried flowers make nice sachets or potpourri to scent linen closets and lingerie drawers and chests.

Leek—Its mild delicate onion flavor makes a splendid flavoring in any food where onion taste is desired. Use as a cooked vegetable, boiled, creamed or braised. They are the prime factor in that famous cold soup, Vichyssoise. Put them in stew, soup or ragout, with meat, game and poultry.

Lovage—Used sparingly in soup, stew, ragout, fish chowder, and cooked vegetables, or rubbed in the salad bowl, as one uses garlic, lovage adds a delightful, celery-flavored zest. Use fresh lovage leaves, boiled or steamed, as spinach is used.

Marigold—Marigold has a sweet, mildly spicy taste, and a lovely golden color. Use the fresh petals in salad, as a garnish, and to flavor cup custard or pudding. It may also be incorporated in fish stew and chowder, or with beef, game or poultry, and in cooking rice. It may also be used in any cookery which calls for saffron.

Mint—There are many varieties of mint. The basic flavor is one familiar to everyone. Crushed mint leaves enliven fruit drinks, herb or mint tea, iced tea, fruit cup, and ice cream, or to flavor icings and candy. It may be used in cooking lamb or mutton, in sauce, for jelly, or made into a syrup. The spice lends itself to use in salads, cooked with vegetables, and as a garnish.

Marjoram—A sweet, spicy herb, quite commonly used in chowders, with fish, meat, roasted or boiled, game and poultry, or in salad, as well as in cream or brown sauces. It is employed in the manufacture of sausage products. Remove the marjoram from cooked vegetables before serving.

Mustard Plant—Mustard plant is a favorite "green" in the Southern states. It has a tangy, slightly peppery taste—and is believed to have a tonic effect. Use it in mixed tossed salad, or cooked as spinach.

Nasturtium—The Orientals use nasturtium leaves and flowers in salad and in making delicious tea. The young, tender leaves may be minced and added to cream cheese for canapes, and in tossed salad. The flower petals add piquancy to fruit salad. Use the seeds, pickled, as capers.

Onions—They are the most widely used seasoning in the world. Add them chopped fine to any sort of appetizer, or caviar, sea food, meat and game spreads and poultry appetizers. Use in omelets, souffles, with fish, game, poultry, stew, soup, ragout, roast, broiled or boiled meat, salad, or in sauces, and in combination with other vegetables. They may also be eaten by themselves, raw, boiled, creamed, baked, braised—and as a garnish.

Oregano—Oregano has the pleasant, aromatic flavor of sweet marjoram, but is somewhat stronger, so is used more sparingly. It is excellent with guinea hen, pheasant, grouse, hare or venison —and is used in tomato sauce, and in Italian cookery.

Parsley—Parsley is a widely-known and much used herb. Use it as an enjoyable garnish. Minced, it can be added to almost any egg dishes, soup, ragout, stew, and in the preparation and serving of meat, poultry, game, fish and with potatoes, salads, and cooked vegetables.

Rose—The petals, dried or fresh, add an exotic taste and odor to many foods. Use fresh rose petals to flavor fruit cup, custard, desserts, ice cream, jellies and honey. Add them to brewed tea, fruit drinks and lemonade.

Rose Geranium—Rose geranium tastes and smells like aromatic rose, adding savor to potpourri. A leaf in the bottom of jelly and jam jars imparts a subtle flavor to the sweets. Sprinkle in iced drinks, teas and

punch. Use as a garnish in fruit cup. Place a leaf under apple, pear, peach or quince, when baking them and in the bottom of a cup custard.

Rosemary—This lovely herb with a lovely name and odor is one of the best-liked of all herbs. The fresh tops may be used in fruit drinks, the chopped leaves in stew, soup, ragout, sauces, roasts, in game, partridge, venison and rabbit. Chopped, it is a delicious addition to biscuits. Use it with duck, pheasant, grouse, or quail, and sparingly, with cooked vegetables.

Rue—Rue is a slightly bitter, aromatic herb and must be used sparingly. Add it to vegetable cocktail, tomato juice, beef or lamb, in salads, stew and ragout.

Sage—Sage is a wonderfully aromatic and fragrant herb which has an affinity for pork and sausage. Use it to flavor cheese, in poultry fillings, with turkey, chicken, duck and goose, fish and game. It is wonderful with meat loaf, in sauces, or used sparingly with cooked vegetables.

Savory or Summer Savory—Savory has a piquant, slightly tart flavor which improves the appeal of tomato or vegetable juices, eggs, omelet, fish, game, meat of all sorts, and poultry. Use it in salads, sauce, soup, stuffings, and chopped into cooked vegetables. It may also be served as a garnish.

Shallot—This herb has a very delicate, onion-like flavor. Use it with fish, game, meat of all sorts, poultry; in sauces, stuffings, and cooked vegetables.

Sorrel—Sorrel leaves have a sharp, pleasantly acid taste. It spices tossed salad, omelet, souffle, or scrambled eggs quite well. Use it in soup, stew and ragout, and with cooked vegetables.

Tansy—Tansy makes a faintly bitter herb tea, and is useful in garnishing meat, in salads, omelets, fish, and meat pie if sparingly mixed.

Tarragon—This herb has a delightful, slightly acid, faintly anise-like flavor. Use in herb vinegar, vegetable cocktail, omelet, and scrambled eggs;

24 Favorite Garden Herbs

Name	Type Height Flowers	Distance Apart	Propagation	Cultural Directions	Uses in Cooking
ANISE *Pimpinella anisum*	annual 18" white	6"	seed (self-sows)	Full sun, fairly dry and medium rich soil.	Leaves for salad; seeds for garnish, cakes and cookies. In Holland, seeds are steeped in hot milk to induce sleep.
BASIL *Ocimum basilicum*	annual 24" white	10"	seed	Full sun, rich soil; needs some protection from wind. Several shearings of top three to four inches can be made in a season.	Superb for tomatoes and tomato dishes. In soups, and with meat, fish and vegetables. Place in water when boiling shellfish. Use in salads and in egg, cheese, rice and spaghetti dishes.
BORAGE *Borago officinalis*	annual 36" white, blue	15"	seed (self-sows)	Full sun, medium soil. Matures in six weeks, so make two sowings.	Adds piquant cucumber flavor to salads and drinks. Blossoms used as garnish for drinks.
BURNET *Sanguisorba minor*	perennial 12"-18" white, rosy	12"	seed (sow yearly for tenderest leaves) divisions	Full sun, poor dry soil. Sow early spring, fall. Is almost evergreen.	Cucumber flavor for salads. Good for tea and vinegar.
CARAWAY *Carum carvi*	biennial (treat as annual) 24"-36" white	6"	seed (self-sows)	Full sun, medium soil.	Seeds with bread, cookies, baked apples, ragouts, cheese.

Name	Type Height Flowers	Dis- tance Apart	Propa- gation	Cultural Directions	Uses in Cooking
CHERVIL *Anthriscus cerefolium*	annual 18" white	6"	seed (self-sows)	Semi-shade, rich, moist soil. Likes humus (best plants often come from old seed heads thrown on compost pile). Sow early spring and late summer.	Fish, soups, salads, omelets. Combine with butter sauce when basting chicken for broiling. Flavor is best preserved by freezing herb rather than drying.
CHIVES *Allium schoenoprasum*	perennial 18" lavender	6"	seed divisions	Full sun, richer soil than most herbs. Sow thickly to make clumps. Dress with compost or manure. Divide every year. Only herb that is best dried in oven.	Gives zip and color cut fine into cream soups, salads, omelets, scrambled eggs, cheese dishes, potato soup.
COSTMARY *Chrysanthemum balsamita*	perennial 60" yellow	12"	divisions	Good soil, sun or semi-shade. Great under-ground spreader.	Strong anise flavor. Use sparingly in green salads, poultry dishes, some jellies. Used for tea.
DILL *Anethum graveolens*	annual 36" yellow	sow in clumps	seed (self-sows)	Full sun, good soil. Sow seed in clumps so plants can lean against each other.	Seeds for vinegar and pickling, in seed cakes and bread. Leaves to flavor soups, sauces, fish, lamb. Cook with beans, sauerkraut, cabbage, cauliflower. Mix into potato salad, macaroni, coleslaw.
FENNEL *Foeniculum vulgare*	perennial (treat as annual) 60" yellow	18"	seed	Full sun, good soil. Sow early spring and fall. Has heavy flower heads and should be supported against a fence.	Stems used like celery. Seeds and leaves impart licorice tang to fish sauces, chowders, soups, pickles. Seeds for bread, tea.
HYSSOP *Hyssopus offiainalis*	perennial 12"-18" blue, pink, white varieties	10"	seed (self-sows) cuttings divisions	Full sun, limey soil.	Very strong. A few leaves give an interesting flavor to green salads and beef soups. Dried flowers sometimes used in soups. Leaves, shoots and tops for tea.

Name	Type Height Flowers	Distance Apart	Propagation	Cultural Directions	Uses in Cooking
LEMON BALM *Melissa officinalis*	perennial 24" white	18"	seed (self-sows) divisions	Part shade, moist soil.	With fish, lamb, beef, and in salads. Used like mint in beverages. Dried leaves for tea.
MARJORAM *Marjorana hortensis*	perennial (treat as annual) 12" white	6"	seed	Full sun, dry soil.	In stews, meat loaf, green salads, poultry stuffing. Cook with beans, peas, carrots. Rub on meats before roasting.
MINT *Mentha viridis*	perennial 12" purple	12"	cuttings divisions of stolons	Part shade, moist soil, pH 5.2 to 6.7. Avoid manure—causes fungus disease. In late fall, cut to ground, mulch with compost.	Sprinkle on fresh fruits, peas or squash. Use in salads, drinks, make tea. Combine with lemon balm for delightful lemint vinegar. Mint sauce.
OREGANO *Origanum vulgare*	perennial 20" pink	12"	seed layering divisions	Full sun, fairly dry soil.	In Spanish, Mexican and Italian dishes. Rub on veal and lamb before roasting. In goulash, stew, sauces, soups.
PARSLEY *Petroselinum hortense*	biennial (treat as annual) 10'-15" yellow	6"	seed	Part shade, medium soil. Slow to germinate, soak seeds overnight.	With all vegetables, salads, soups, stews, omelets, etc. One tablespoon equals adult daily requirements of vitamins A and C.
ROSEMARY *Rosemarinus officinalis*	tender perennial 36" blue	18"	seed cuttings layering	Poor light soil with ample lime, full sun. Bring indoors in winter, or store dormant in cool cellar.	In chicken dishes, soups, stews, gravies, muffin batter. Add to water when cooking peas, potatoes, turnips. Sprinkle on meats before roasting or broiling.

Name	Type Height Flowers	Dis- tance Apart	Propa- gation	Cultural Directions	Uses in Cooking
SAGE *Salvia officinalis*	perennial 24" blue	15"	seed cuttings layering divisions	Full sun, sandy soil. Soak seeds a few hours to aid germination.	With meats and fish. In dressing, stuffing, egg and cheese dishes. Leaves for tea to relieve colds, sore throats.
SAVORY *Satureia hortensis*	annual 12"-18" pink	5"	seed	Full sun, medium rich and fairly dry soil. Does not transplant well.	In meat loaf, hamburger, beef stew, bis- cuit and dumpling batters, egg dishes, pea and bean soup. On fish and pork, and in cooking beans, peas, cabbage, sauerkraut.
SESAME *Sesamum indicum*	annual 18" lavender	6"	seed	Full sun, medium soil.	Seeds in bread and cake. Grind and mix with nuts, figs, poppy seed or honey to make a healthful candy.
SHALLOTS *Allium ascalonicum*	perennial 24"	4"	cloves	Full sun, medium soil. Bulb breaks up into many cloves.	Good with any dish calling for onions. Wonderful with steaks, roast beef, game. Take four or five cloves when recipe calls for one shallot.
SWEET CICELY *Myrrhis odorata*	perennial 24"-36" white	18"	seed (self-sows) divisions	Part shade, acid, moist soil. Usually sown in July, comes up next spring.	Leaves add anise flavor to green salads. Seeds good with cabbage and many other foods.
TARRAGON *Artemisia dranunculus*	perennial 24" yellow	12"	cuttings divisions	Full sun, medium soil, some protection from wind.	Poultry, steak, fish and egg and cheese dishes. In green salad and salad dressing, and tartar and lemon butter sauces. Rub roasting bird inside and outside for taste treat.
THYME *Thymus vulgaris*	perennial 12" lavender	8"	seed cuttings divisions	Full sun, sweet, sandy soil. Likes a stone mulch. Will layer if mulched with earth in fall.	A universal herb—use with meat, fish, vege- tables, egg dishes, soups, stuffing, chow- ders. Tops with tomatoes, cheese canapes.

as a marinade with vinegar for lamb, mutton, pork and veal, in salads, and with porterhouse and sirloin steaks and filét mignon; in sauces—Hollandaise, mayonnaise, and tartar; also in soup, stew, and ragout.

Thyme — Thyme is a seasoning standby. Its aromatic flavor adds zest to appetizers, vegetable and fruit cocktails, and vegetable juices. It is minced and mixed with various types of cheese. Use it in chowder, soup, all egg dishes, rabbit, hare and venison cookery, add it to sauces, stew and ragout. Is widely used in chicken, turkey and veal stuffing as well as with cooked vegetables.

Verbena—A delicate, lemon-flavored herb. Use it in fruit cup and as a base for a delicious herb tea. The leaves serve as flavoring and garnish for salad, meat and poultry.

Watercress—The leaves and stems are pungent and tangy. Use it by itself, and chopped, in appetizers, canapes, and garnishes. Minced, it is a pleasant addition to biscuits. It is tasty chopped in combination with cottage or cream cheese, and with softened butter. Use chopped and added to pie crust dough for meat pie.

Woodruff—The sweetest smelling of all herbs used in the famous German "Maytrink" or May wine. Add it to lemonade and fruit drink, and wine cup, and fruit cup.—*Murii Manahan.*

HERBIVOROUS ANIMALS: Those animals which habitually rely upon plants and plant products for their food, as contrasted with carnivorous animals which live primarily on meat.

HEREDITY: Heredity is what a plant possesses, its characteristics, from its beginning, when the egg and sperm unite. It may be contrasted to environment which is the sum total of all phenomena surrounding each living organism from its conception until its death.

Not all of a plant's inheritance manifests itself or appears superficially. Characteristics which are the results of ancestral genes may or may not

appear or function under a given set of environmental circumstances.

The third factor in this organic trilogy is variation. Variations are contrasts or differences. They may be either hereditary or environmental. In order clearly to understand plant breeding, a knowledge of all three factors, heredity, environment and variation, is necessary. *See also* ENVIRONMENT; VARIATION.

HIBISCUS: A genus of more than 200 species of trees, shrubs and herbs of the mallow family. The *Hibiscus* is of great horticultural interest because of its great variety of garden annuals, perfume and food plants, decorative perennials, beautifully colored tropical trees and shrubs.

The leaves alternate, sometimes lobed or parted while the veins are invariably arranged finger-wise. Its flowers are generally large, usually bell-shaped, with five petals and sepals; sometimes the sepals unite to form a five-tooth calyx. The stamens are united in the tubular structure which surrounds the stylex while the fruit is a dry five-valved capsule.

The plants are most popularly known as mallow or rose mallow. (*See* MALVACEAE.) As in other genera of this family, there is often a series of bracts appearing beneath the calyx. The diversity of Hibiscus is extremely great; those annuals mentioned below may be treated as hardy plants and the seeds sown directly into the planting site.

ABELMOSCHUS: The *Abelmosk* or *musk mallow* is a tropical Asiatic annual or biennial hairy herb two to six feet high. A native of India, it is grown mostly for its seeds which give a musky perfume. It needs more summer heat than is found in most parts of this country but it will flower even in the Northern sections.

ESCULENTUS: Known as *Okra* or *Gumbo* this plant is a favorite in the South where it is grown for its mucilaginous pods which are used in cooking. It reaches from two to six feet while the ribbed and beaked pods are four to 12 inches long. *See also* OKRA.

GRANDIFLORUS: Use for seaside planting along the Gulf Coast and in Florida.

MOSCHEUTOS: Variously called *rose mallow, swamp mallow* and *sea holly-hock.* It grows three to seven feet high with generally oval leaves, three to seven inches long, sometimes angled or lobed. Its flowers, useless for picking because they wilt almost immediately, are four to seven inches wide.

The rose mallow is a typically salt-marsh plant and can be dug out of its wild habitat and transplanted into the garden with complete success. But this is rarely done today because of the domestic varieties available which are the result of selection and cross-breeding. These improved mallows are at home in any rich garden soil but need plenty of room.

MUTABILIS: A native of China, a shrub or sometimes tree-like, called *cotton rose* or *Confederate rose.* The leaves are broad and oval, four inches wide, three to five lobed. The flowers are three to four inches wide, opens white or pink, changing to deep red, and hairy on the outside. The fruit is globe-shaped.

OCULIROSEUS: *White rose mallow* indigenous to the marshes of eastern New York and New Jersey and the District of Columbia.

ROSA-SINENSIS: *China-rose* or *rose of China,* also called *shoeblack plant* because its flowers are used in the trop-ics to polish shoes. This beautiful Asiatic shrub frequently attains 20-30 feet in the tropics. It can endure no frost but is a familiar plant through-out the tropics and is grown in this country chiefly in Florida and Califor-nia. The leaves are broadly oval, three to four inches long and tapering. The flowers are mostly solitary in upper-leaf axils, four to six inches long, rose-red and spectacularly showy because of the petals and long column of stamens. Can be grown in warm, moist green-houses where it requires rich feeding

with liquid manures and potting mix-ture.

SABDARIFFA: *Roselle* is a tropical annual whose culture here is confined to the warmest parts of this country. It is also known as *red sorrel* or *Ja-maica sorrel,* attains four to seven feet, much-branched from the base and with reddish stems. The flowers are stalk-less, solitary with yellow petals longer than the thick, red calyx and its bracts for which the plant is grown. These contain an acid which may be used as a substitute for the cranberry in the making of drinks and jelly. Harvest-ing however must occur while the calyx is immature. The plant may be grown very much like eggplant.

SYRIACUS: The *rose-of-sharon* is highly valued because of its late bloom and the only hardy shrub in this genus. It grows five to 15 feet high with unlobed, oval leaves two to five inches long, sharply toothed. The flowers are solitary, short-stalked, three to five inches long, red, purple, violet or white in color, broadly bell-shaped and most showy on dark days. Hardy generally south of the Bluegrass Line and offered there in many forms.

TRIONUM: A flower garden annual, 18-24 inches high, whose seed should be sown on the planting site. The flowers are pale yellow or yellow-white with a dark eye. *See also* OKRA: MALVACEAE.

HICKORY: The Hickories (*genus Carya*) are tall trees, valuable as timber and for their nut crops. Leaves are alternate and compound while both male and female flowers appear on the same tree, in different clusters.

The fruit is a flesh drupe, hardens with age and separates into four woody sections within which is the edible nut. The three most popular species are the Shelbark (*Carya laciniosa*), the Shagbark (*Carya ovata*) and the pecan (*Carya pecan*).

Many other wild species occur but are not cultivated because their crop is largely inedible. Those listed below bear well in most temperate regions and may be planted with good prospect of success by the average homesteading gardener.

Hales: Shell thin and easily cracked. Kernel plump and sweet. Originated in New Jersey.

Kentucky: Medium-sized, fairly easy to crack; flesh plump, rich and sweet. Originated in Kentucky.

Kirtland: Rather large with thin shell, easily cracked. Kernel plump and rich.

Vest: Medium or small in size, quadrangular in shape, with very thin shell. Originated in Virginia.

Weiper: Shell rather thick but easily cracked. Kernel plump and good flavored. Originated in Pennsylvania.

Since the species is being improved steadily, it is advisable to check the latest catalog before ordering. On the whole, it is best to favor varieties recommended for the particular region where they will be planted.

Hickories have deep tap roots and much care must be taken not to injure them when planting or setting the young tree. The hole should be adequate as usual and filled only with topsoil. *Put no manure in the hole.* Do not allow the roots to become dry for even a few moments. Heel-in all young trees waiting to be planted.

After planting cut back the growth one-third and stake carefully. Water thoroughly if there is a dry spell at the beginning. After the trees are established this should be no longer necessary. In general, cultivate and mulch the trees the same as most fruit trees, giving them the same seasonal care. *See also* NUT TREES.

HIMALAYAN FIR: *see* FIR

HIP: *see* ROSE HIP

HISTORY OF ORGANIC METHOD: *see* ORGANIC METHOD, HISTORY OF

HOARFROST: *see* FROST

HOARHOUND: *see* HOREHOUND

HOG MANURE: *see* MANURE

HOGS: *see* PIGS

HOLCUS HALEPENSIS: *see* JOHNSON GRASS

HOLLY: Two genus of the *Aquifoliaceae, Ilex* and *Nemopanthus,* are commonly known as hollies. Varieties number more than 275, mostly evergreen shrubs and trees.

Ilex opaca or American Holly ranges from Massachusetts to Texas, grows naturally in acid soil. A spreading tree, it attains a height of 40 feet.

Most popular garden varieties are *I. aquifolium,* English holly; *I. opaca,* American holly; *I. crenata,* Japanese holly, with black berries; and *I. verticillata,* black-alder or winterberry.

Christmas hollies are usually the English or American holly. Hanging holly at Christmas time is an old custom, not necessarily related to Christmas. Originally it was considered a charm against witches and evil spirits. Farmers believed that holly hung in the barn would insure fertility of their stock.

English holly, though considered more beautiful than American, is not much grown here because it is more delicate, and responds to American climate only along the North Pacific coast. American holly may be delicate in more northerly locations unless it is given large quantities of acid humus, such as oak leaf mold. They do best in rich, well-drained soil; the evergreen holly types prefer a partly shady location. Of all the leaf molds, oak seems the best in character and richness. Most any woods leaf mold is good, other than maple, which tends to be sweetish and not much to the liking of hollies.

The top surface of the woods consists of fresh leaves and the leaf mold itself is permeated by the rootlets of trees and shrubs. Men must go out and gather it by hand, scraping off the top fresh leaves, spading out the layer of leaf mold and roots, avoiding the poor subsoil beneath. By dint of shaking out the roots, the rich brown oak leaf mold remains. Composting can yield the same product from home-gathered leaves, and the use of a shredder will hasten the process.

PLANTING: Holly should be planted either early in spring or early fall after the season's growth has commenced to ripen. At either time the foliage should be stripped from them to avoid loss of moisture. Or they may be moved without stripping if dug with a large ball of earth and severely pruned. In either case they should be sprayed daily with the hose for several weeks.

In planting hollies, a hole is dug at least twice as big as the ball of the holly to be planted. This hole is filled with oak leaf mold, placing the holly so that the top of the root ball is level with the surface of the surrounding earth. A thick mulch of leaf mold, two or more inches deep, is placed over the top of the roots and surrounding area. Hollies should be soaked thoroughly with water when planting to compact and settle the leaf mold around the roots so that no air spaces remain. Potted hollies should have the pot removed when planting. Basketed hollies may be planted in the wire basket, for the basket will rust out long before

the roots constrict. Burlapped hollies should be planted in the burlap, for the burlap does no harm and holds the root mass together until the tree has "settled in."

It seems to matter little what kind of soil they are planted in as long as there is plenty of oak leaf mold around the roots of the holly. Like most broad-leaved evergreens, hollies like water but need a well-drained location. American hollies will tolerate cold climates and temperatures of as low as 20 below zero. In the colder climates hollies should be planted as much out of the winter winds as possible. The thorny leaves batter each other in the wind when frozen hard.

Holly plants are either male or female. Only the female bears berries but the male is necessary and must be planted nearby if the female is to have berries. One male is sufficient for up to at least ten females. By the same token, a small male holly will be ample to plant near a single large female.

Most any named variety of American holly is good, though some are famous for certain qualities. It is usually best to buy potted or basketed hollies, especially if they are to be shipped any distance.

Few hollies are grown from seed, for they do not come true and have many faults. For the same reason very few hollies are collected from the wild, for they too have come from seed. It often takes two to three years for a holly seed to sprout.

Most hollies grown from rooted cuttings will berry at any age, no matter how small, although they do not berry every year. Little hollies (from rooted cuttings) berry often enough to please most everyone.

Grafted hollies often sprout from the understock and for this reason are not usually as desirable as rooted cuttings. The advantage of rooted cutting named varieties is that they are reproductions of the parent tree from which they are cut.

It does not take many years to grow

a beautiful specimen holly from a baby. When pruned back each year for Christmas, a dense, bushy, four-foot specimen may be eight years of age; a lovely eight-foot tree perhaps 16 years of age. Left to grow without much pruning, hollies will become larger in that length of time, but will be less dense and broad. Hollies may be pruned freely without harm. No matter where a holly is pruned, new branches will start, either out of the bark or from leaf buds or twig ends. Unlike Christmas trees, which are destroyed by the cutting, hollies are improved by the annual Christmas shearing.

HOLLY CARE: The yearly care of hollies is both easy and simple. They love water and should be thoroughly soaked once every week or two during the growing season, for summer rains are rarely heavy enough to please a holly. Waterings by hose or bucket are well repaid by more beautiful growth. Aside from the yearly surface mulch of well-rotted oak leaf compost or woods leaf mold, hollies are benefited by a blanket of tobacco stem mulch placed over the root area underneath the entire branch spread of the tree. Tobacco stems are rich in nutrients and perhaps are also detrimental to insects. Hollies respond with darker green leaves and more berries when fed with a yearly mulch of tobacco stems.

Pruning is a delightful Christmas time prospect and thought should be given to shaping the tree at pruning time. Unusually long twigs or leaders should be cut back to the general pattern or shape of tree desired.

The following varieties are most esteemed for hardihood and beauty.

ENGLISH HOLLY: (*Ilex aquifolium*) Attains up to 40 feet but none too hardy north of the Bluegrass Line and susceptible to hot, dry summers. Does best in Oregon and Washington.

DAHOON OR YAUPON: (*Ilex cassine*) A shrub or small tree attaining up to 25 feet. Strictly for the South, from North Carolina to Florida.

JAPANESE HOLLY: (*Ilex crenata*) Extremely handsome evergreen shrub, hardy south of the Bluegrass Line, occasionally just north with protection. Dark green, oblong leaves, with black fruit.

INKBERRY: (*Ilex glabra*) Also called WINTERBERRY and BEARBUSH. Evergreen to the South but only half evergreen to the North, turning a rusty green in the autumn. Generally not more than six feet high with oblong wedge-shaped leaves and black fruit. A bog shrub, native to Eastern part of the country but growing well in any good, sandy garden loam. Does very well when mulched with leaves.

SMOOTH WINTERBERRY OR HOOP WOOD: (*Ilex laevigata*) Not an evergreen, growing from five to eight feet planted mostly for its orange-reddish fruits. Hardy below the Bluegrass Line, but also cultivated from Maine to Pennsylvania and Virginia.

AMERICAN HOLLY OR WHITE HOLLY: (*Ilex opaca*) A spreading tree attaining up to 40 feet. Evergreen leaves are yellowish-green beneath, dull green on top. Hardy in the South, it also ranges from Massachusetts to Florida, west to Missouri and Texas. Grow naturally in acid soils with a pH of five to six. It is hardier than the *English Holly* but is difficult to transplant.

BLACK ALDER, WINTERBERRY, DOGBERRY: (*Ilex verticillata*) Not an evergreen, grows up to eight feet, is noted for its profuse showy growths of bright red fruits. Hardy in the South, ranges through the East.

HOLLY FERN: *see* FERN, POLYSTICHUM

HOLLYHOCK: These garden favorites are members of the genus *Althaea* of the mallow (*Malvaceae*) family. Included, in addition to the garden hollyhock, are the true marshmallow and the Antwerp hollyhock. This genus comprises about 15 species of tall, leafy annual, biennial and perennial herbs.

They are noted for hairy alternate leaves and terminal raceme-like clusters of attractive flowers whose five petals are usually notched, and originally red or white.

Hollyhocks will do well in any suitable garden soil but the varieties, due to constant hybridization are unstable, particularly the annuals.

The hollyhock was grown originally in China and was imported into England about 400 years ago. It attained an early popularity in early American colonial gardens, being suited then as now, for cultivation under windows and along fences, bringing a fresh, bright note of color to these places.

CULTURE: Almost any suitable garden soil will do. If grown for biennials, sow the seed in frames or flats outdoors in July or August for next year blooming. Grow the seedlings until the first frost when they should be mulched lightly and left in the frame or flat but without any added heat.

Move them to their final site in the spring. Take care to keep the roots pointing down because they are susceptible to frost-heaving; also plant a little deeper than before. This safe-guard protects the roots and permits the plant to secure a firm hold.

VARIETIES: Due to constant hybridization, the varieties are quite unstable. This pertains particularly to annuals which will run not much better than 50 per cent true from seed. Biennials are somewhat more reliable, although instability will be noted. The following colors can be relied on: crimson, pink, rose, salmon-pink, scarlet, yellow, white. Forms are single-flower, double and semi-double. The first is still most popular, possible because simplicity constitutes the essential appeal of this flower.

The following varieties enjoy considerable popularity and may be grown with common-sense precautions in almost any garden.

ANTWERP HOLLYHOCK: (*Althaea ficifolia*) A biennial herb not much grown here with showy lemon-yellow or orange flowers in terminal spikes. It is related to the common hollyhock with the leaves divided into seven irregularly-toothed, narrow segments.

MARSHMALLOW, OR SWEATWEED: (*Althaea officinalis*) A perennial herb, grows three to four feet high. Its leaves may be unlobed but are generally three-lobed, ovalish, with the mid-lobe largest. Grows here in a wild state in the salt marshes of the eastern seaboard.

COMMON GARDEN HOLLYHOCK: (*Althaea rosea*) Originally a tall, perennial Chinese herb; grown today mostly as a biennial or annual. Erect, five to nine feet high, with a leafy, spire-like stem. Flowers are stalkless in terminal clusters, single, and red or white. *See also* MALLOW.

HOME NURSERY: *see* NURSERY, HOME

HOMESTEAD, ORGANIC: In recent years, the sharp dividing line between farm and urban life has been breaking down. More and more people have moved from city and suburban areas to several or more acres in the country. To organic gardeners, this move is particularly important since it gives them a chance to raise better food and more of it.

THE HOUSE: There need be nothing luxurious or expensive about the homestead. Here are some of the characteristics that a good homestead house might possess:

1. A full basement for storage and expansion room. A basic necessity is a root cellar which is cool in winter and summer, for storing fruits and vegetables.

2. The basement should have an exit directly to the outside with a large door, so supplies and equipment can be taken in and out easily.

3. A very desirable feature is an attached greenhouse. New models are not as expensive as generally thought.

4. The kitchen of the homestead is more than a place to prepare meals. It should be large enough to provide ample room for canning, freezing and other harvest chores.

5. A large back porch provides room for relaxation and work during bad weather.

TREES AND SHRUBS: One of the major advantages in having an organic homestead is the supply of natural food it provides. To get maximum food production from an acre plot, don't overlook the *food* that trees and shrubs can grow.

The fruits of Rosa Rugosa (small red "apples" that form after the petals fall) are a fine rich source of vitamin C. It is truly a plant made to order for the organic garden.

When it comes to planting shade trees, use the many fine nut trees that will provide all the growth and shade of maples and elms, with a bonus harvest of nuts thrown in. A nut tree can do the job that any ordinary shade tree will do.

Chestnut. Chinese blight-resistant variety now produces chestnuts as fine

as those from native American varieties used to be.

Shagbark. Grows tall and stately and the full grown tree produces three or four bushels of nuts.

Mulberry. A small tree that grows a big harvest of fine-tasting berries.

English Walnut. New varieties are arousing new interest in this tree that has been popular for thousands of years.

Black Walnut. A beautiful tree that adds character and open shade to the lawn and ground. Pleasant winter evenings can be spent opening the nuts.

Don't fail to investigate these other nut trees: persimmon, pappaw, hickory, honey locust, northern and southern pecan, grafted hiccans and even the oaks whose acorns can be used for fodder.

THE VEGETABLE GARDEN: Here is the heart of the homestead. The major benefit from the homestead is the supply of natural food available. Most of it will come from the vegetable garden.

The vegetable garden in the ideal organic homestead is something special. The plants grown in it are only those varieties that have special merits adapting them to use by organic gardeners.

Tomato—Doublerich. Highest production of vitamin C along with large fruit size characterizes this variety perfected by the University of New Hampshire. *Sunray:* Unusual golden orange color combined with high content of vitamin A and C and resistance to fusarium wilt.

Carrots. Grow plenty so you can store some for winter in your cold cellar. *Imperator:* Best variety for vitamin A. *Yellow Belgian:* Highest in vitamin C.

Kale. Special Dwarf Green Scotch variety is rated best nutrient producer of this vegetable well known for value in healthy salads. Other varieties are good too.

Lima Beans. Burpee's Best, Cangreen and *Carpenteria* all merit special attention for the ideal homestead gar-

The organic homestead represents an integrated way of life in which the functional parts contribute to the whole naturally and without forcing. The gardens and house thus become a unit or planned entity.

den because of superior vitamin content.

Okra. Louisiana White Velvet I variety is recommended.

Peas. Pedigree Extra Early and *Alaska* showed high vitamin C content in government tests.

Sweet Peppers. Sweet peppers produce more vitamin C than any other garden vegetable. *Neapolitan, Perfection Pimento* and *Florida Giant* are good varieties.

Pumpkin and Squash. Delicious Banquet and *Buttercut* rate high in vitamins.

Snap Beans. Improved Tendergreen is resistant to mosaic. *French Horticultural* rates high for nutrients.

Soybeans. This useful plant should have an honored place in the ideal organic garden. It is very high in protein content, easy to grow and adds an unusual flavor to healthful meals. It also is needed as a protein supplement in animal rations. *Bansei* variety is suitable. *Jogun 2* and *Wolverine* have high ratings.

Sweet Potatoes. Source of many healthful menus and needed food values, should be included in the organic garden. *Allgold* is highly recommended.

Cabbage. Golden Acre, Early Jersey Wakefield and *Marion Market* are resistant varieties.

Space doesn't permit mention of all the fine vegetable varieties available. Many of the old favorites not mentioned above—broccoli, beets, chard, cauliflower, cabbage, celery, sweet corn, lettuce, onions, parsley, radishes, spinach, turnips and others should be grown. Remember, one of the prime objectives of the ideal organic homestead is to supply as much family's food as possible. So give a lot of thought to vegetables that store easily and can be used during the winter.

The real payoff of the homestead garden will come when the winter snows fly and you can live off your own larder.

Livestock. One of the basic differences between a homestead and merely a house on a large country plot is live-stock. A few sheep or goats and a small flock of chickens will get far greater benefits from land.

THE ORCHARD: For homestead orchard on a 175' x 250' plot, you could include four apple trees and six pear trees. These are full-sized trees, not dwarf varieties. In selecting trees for an orchard, try to keep insect problems to a minimum by picking varieties of trees that are less prone to damage and make use of the unpoisonous dormant oil sprays and tanglefoot.

Pears are quite easy to grow without insecticides. The following varieties are good: *Clapp Favorite* (very early ripening); *Bartlett; Seckel; Kieffer, LeConte,* and *Garber.*

Apple varieties recommended are: *Early McIntosh; Milton* (also early); *McIntosh* (best for North); *Macoun* (good flavor); *Rome Beauty* (very productive); *Stayman* and *Winesap* (these two good for South and West).

Add a few dwarf trees for some variety and earlier bearing.

THE GREENHOUSE: So many things can be accomplished with a greenhouse that it would be difficult if not impossible to plan an Ideal Organic Homestead without one. Even an unheated greenhouse augments the gardening program, especially if it is attached to the house so some warmth can be passed into it.

A "cool" hothouse will grow lettuce and other hardy greens all winter.

Adding a little heat permits a wide range of vegetable crops that will add taste appeal and needed vitamins to the family winter diet. Vegetable and flower plants for spring use are easily grown in the greenhouse.

THE FLOWER GARDEN: Flowers give so much pleasure to mankind that it is unthinkable to plan an ideal homestead without giving ample space and thought to them. Organic gardeners especially can get the maximum pleasure from flowers because they have conquered the major limiting factor to success—poor soil, humus, it has

been demonstrated, will make even the desert bloom.

Roses, flowering shrubs, tulips, iris, petunias, lilies, mums—the list is endless to choose from. Plan a garden of blooms that will grace the homestead.

MAKING COMPOST: A good place for compost heaps on the homestead is near the vegetable garden. This location will reduce handling.

While grass clippings, straw and weeds are needed for mulching, compost heaps are needed too as a source of humus ready to use and as a means of "converting" materials like manure and garbage. You will need compost for your flower beds, for the lawn, for planting trees and shrubs, for the vegetable garden, for the greenhouse and the orchard.

Remember, the true strength and value of a homestead is the land. Make that soil as fertile as it can be made, within the budget. Make it a project to collect as much organic material as available. Use your car or station wagon to pick up things like corn cobs, gin waste, wood shavings, leaves, spoiled hay, straw.

POWER MACHINES: The homestead plan described here is made practicable by the small internal combustion engine. Without a small gasoline engine and tools like a rotary tiller that it propels, homesteading would be the backbreaking job it was during the last century, when all members of the household had to pitch in and work from dawn to dusk.

The rotary tiller is the most important and useful implement for the organic homestead. It not only builds soil fertility by working organic material into the soil, but it makes it possible for one person to work a large vegetable garden as a spare time project. Attachments to the tiller enable it to mow the lawn, haul hay and other materials, plant, cultivate, pump water, saw wood and cut weeds.

To work a plot of one acre, you should have a tiller of three to five horsepower.

A compost shredder is a most invaluable machine. By running manure and other organic material through it prior to composting you will cut the amount of labor needed and turn out a finer product in less time, too.

Extra Income

A homestead can do more than save $1,000 or more on food. If the whole family pitches in on the food-raising job—it can realize extra cash income ranging from several hundred dollars up.

The opportunities for making extra money on an organic homestead are practically limitless.

The following is only a partial list of proven part-time money makers:

Specialty Crops: Quality asparagus can bring you $800 per acre. Hint: use surface planting and mulch for less work and better plants. Or asparagus plants grown from seed and sold to gardeners will net $25 to $35 per 100-foot row.

Sweet corn and winter squash are worth $300 an acre. Pop corn can bring $300. An acre of green peas can net $500 if planted and matured as early as possible; three plantings (in rich, humusy soil) will give a four- to six-week selling season.

Cucumbers are always a good bet—one organic homesteader makes top profits selling them with dill to people who like to make their own dill pickles. A half acre is enough for cucumbers, or for beets, another good seller if grown to luscious perfection organically. You can make a sizeable profit, too, from less than half an acre planted to endive, radishes, broccoli, parsley or string beans. Don't ignore the possibilities of succession cropping: a New Jersey homesteader does very well by growing dandelions which are cut as greens early in the spring, following with spinach for forcing and cutting by May, and finally planting leeks for harvest in October.

Horseradish is a top seller ground, bottled and sold by mail or to restaurants, hotels and stores. Herbs take little acreage and make a fine job for the country wife. For sale on the roadside stand, she'll want to grow a few rows of gourds and Indian corn—they're a big attraction. And a dark cellar or shed, plus some boxes, manure and compost, and a bottle of spawn, will give plenty of mushrooms for daily harvest and sale.

Fruit: Here's what you can *net* per acre from fruits using organic methods and getting high top-quality yields: strawberries, blueberries, red raspberries, $1,000 or more; peaches (in areas where the buds won't be winter-killed), $500, sold in small basket lots; melons, $300; grapes, $400. Hint: grow everbearing varieties of strawberries, or late-bearing raspberries like Durham, to get the top profits from out-of-season sales.

If you have some favorite recipes, you may find the biggest money lies in selling jams, jellies, fruit butter and candies. (The same, of course, goes for relishes, bread, cakes and pies, mincemeat, gingerbread and the like, if you raise most of the ingredients.)

Growing Under Glass: Gardening work is light in the winter, and profits are nil outdoors. But in a greenhouse you can grow holiday plants, common or rare house plants of all kinds, seedlings for sale in the spring, or organic vegetables. Simple cold frames and hotbeds serve equally well for many purposes: for a good profit with tomatoes, lettuce or carrots, for instance, get plants started as early as possible from seed sown under glass.

Livestock: Goats are easy to care for. They need only simple sheds, and eight goats can be maintained for the cost of one cow, on six tons of hay from two acres plus ten cents a day per goat for grain. Goats provide excellent meat, cheese and milk which sells for almost twice the price of cow's milk.

Rabbits are cheaper to raise and take less time and work than chickens.

A combination hotbed or cold frame in a sunny and sheltered corner of the house. Heat from basement window can be used to maintain the desired temperature and windows removed on sunny spring days.

A 50 by 100 foot area will hold 200 rabbits and their litters. Self-cleaning hutches require less than five minutes work a day. Rabbit meat is becoming increasingly popular, and the skins and furs bring a good price.

POULTRY: Squabs are easy to handle; each pair will produce about 15 marketable squabs a year at a profit of $5 to $8. Broilers are equally profitable and take little room raised in

Prices change with the times but a steady income can be made from eggs if the chores are done promptly and a retail business is built.

batteries. But to make a sizeable profit with laying hens, someone must be on hand to do all the chores called for several times a day, every day of the year. You'll have to keep at least 300 layers, and sell eggs at retail. Turkeys raised on wire can pay well—if you grow and feed green crops to build top health.

Keep in mind that the manure from all animals and poultry is a valuable soil-building dividend.

BEES: For a $25 investment and few hours of work, a hive will produce 50 to 75 pounds of luscious honey—and a lot of fun. Bees serve double duty by pollinating crops, too.

EARTHWORMS: Many a homesteader has made a tidy profit selling worms for soil enrichment. Boxes or a simple pit 20 by 40 inches will raise 50,000 worms a year, worth a cent apiece.

FLOWERS: Specialize in growing favorite plants. A 50 by 50-foot bed will raise $1,000 worth of pansies, for instance. Or set up a weekly flower service to shops and offices. Seasonable bouquets (don't forget dried flowers, grasses, pods and leaves in the fall) are good sellers, too.

HOME NURSERY: Grow trees and shrubs from seed and cuttings on a small plot. It takes very little work, and landscaping plants double in value.

WOODLOT: Fireplace logs are worth $2.50 a dozen, white birch logs for decoration $1.50 each. Make wreaths and sprays from evergreens, or sell holly, bayberry and mistletoe. Successive plantings of Christmas trees on waste land can bring $200 an acre per year; get inexpensive seedlings from the state Forest Service.

CRAFTS: These offer golden opportunities: weaving, furniture building or refinishing, pottery, hooked or braided rugs, quilts, gourd craft, embroidery, fancy candles, fence building, jewelry making, toys. Or collect and sell anything from old iron kettles and horseshoes to butter molds. Hint: specialize, and make your product unique.

OTHER IDEAS: Buy cull apples, and with a cheap hand press turn out 100 gallons of cider a day, at a profit of 40 cents a gallon; board plants for people on vacation; breed, board and train dogs; lecture on gardening; be a taxidermist; raise giant bullfrogs in a tiny pond (very prolific and marvelous insect controllers); if you have a larger pond, let tourists catch all the fish they want, at a flat rate per pound; keep ponies and sell rides to youngsters; or raise game birds—an acre or two and modern methods will raise an astonishing number of pheasant, mallards or quail.

Hints for success:

Sell at retail. A roadside stand will bring double the price you'd get for your crops at wholesale. Small stands can be run on the honor system, left unattended with a box for change. Many homesteaders pool their products and time to run a big cooperative stand.

A "must": grow or make the best, and package it attractively. Study the market, and advertise with signs and ads in the local papers. And above all, don't try to take on more than you can handle in your available time and space.

GROWING FARM CROPS

To get the full benefit from the organic homestead, grow farm crops as well as fruits, nuts and vegetables. Hay and straw are needed for small stock and chickens, also corn and possibly wheat and barley for feed. Even for your own family's use you will want to raise wheat for breadmaking.

You can grow these crops efficiently without the resources for plowing, planting, cultivating and harvesting that a farmer has, by making full use of the power gardening equipment available—plus ingenuity in adapting them to special needs and chores.

The major jobs necessary to growing farm crops on about a quarter of an acre can be done adequately by a rotary tiller or garden tractor of three to five horsepower. The ten horsepower small tractors are more efficient for several acres. Preparing a seedbed is done the same as for a vegetable plot. There is no problem to that. But when it comes to planting various crops, some original work is necessary.

Wheat and other small grains can be sown by hand just by broadcasting the seed. This should not be done on a windy day, and there is a knack to it. Some prefer to invest a few dollars in a seed broadcaster, a small crank-operated machine that hangs around the neck and distributes even quantities of seed as they walk down the field. They also use it for seeding the pasture area and for planting winter cover crops and green manure crops.

Corn has to be planted in rows. Make a row marker out of scrap boards in a short time, to do the job by hand, or, get a planting attachment for the tractor or tiller, which makes the job much easier. Corn rows should be planted about 40 inches apart, with the plants 40 inches apart in the row In each hill plant four or five seeds. Plant closer together in the row if the soil is very fertile. Sunflowers are planted with the same spacing, but only one seed to the hill.

Cultivating corn can be done efficiently with the tiller set at a shallow depth—or with a garden tractor. However, you still may have to get out the hoe to chop weeds growing between the plants in the row. Of course, it is better to mulch cultivated crops to help preserve moisture and keep down weeds (in addition to feeding the plants).

Harvesting corn is easily done by hand. Get a small husking tool which fits in the palm of your hand, to make it easier to husk the ears as you pick them off the plants. It is not possible to shell corn efficiently by hand. Try to find a neighbor willing to rent his sheller or do the job for a small fee.

SMALL GRAINS: Small grains are more difficult to harvest than field corn, because you've got to do it at the right time and the weather must be on your side. Get a custom harvester to come in with his combine and the job is done in no time at small cost, but the field may not be large enough to make that worth while. In this case invest in a scythe with a cradle to cut the wheat when the heads are filled out, but before they become so dry that the grain falls out readily.

Tie the stalks into bundles about ten inches in diameter, using binder twine, then stack the bundles into shocks and let them cure for a couple of days or until they are thoroughly dry. The next step will be either to thresh the grain (remove the grain from the stalk and the chaff). Much of the grain produced in the world is still threshed by hand.

A clear floor, preferably indoors is needed for threshing. The stalks are first beaten with a flail, a wooden rod with a flexible joint about in the center. This loosens the grain from the stalks. Fan the grain to blow the chaff away or do the work outside on a windy day.

Be sure to grow sunflowers—the Mammoth Russian variety. They are very good to eat because they are high in protein and valuable oil and they are a fine chicken feed. Removing the seeds from the heads is done easily by rubbing the heads back and forth over a screen of quarter inch muskrat wire. This screen can be placed over a barrel to catch the seeds that pass through.

Shelling the seeds is a little more difficult. It is not necessary if they are used for chicken feed, as chickens can do that for themselves.

Growing farm crops on the homestead is an important part of the plan for producing food for the family. With a little ingenuity you can produce good yields of crops of the highest nutritive value—crops that are organically raised and free of spray residues.

See also NUT TREES; FRUIT TREES; ORCHARD; GREENHOUSE; FLOWER GARDENING; VEGETABLE GARDENING; MULCH; COMPOST; GOATS; RABBITS; POULTRY; BANTAMS; BEES; EARTHWORMS; NURSERY; HAY.

HONESTY: (*Lunaria*) Also known as silver dollars and the money plant, because the seed pods are round and flat. The showy purple flowers are most attractive in June, and the seed pods add much to winter bouquets of dried flowers. Lunarias are easy to grow in most garden soils. *L. annua*, known also as satin-flower is an annual, often grown as a biennial, that reaches one and one-half to two and one-half feet. Perennial honesty (*L. rediviva*) is not as showy as *annua*, can be increased by division.

HONEY: Honey is nature's most perfect food. According to chemical analysis it is the saccharine exudation of flowering plants, and is composed of

Lunaria annua or Honesty plant, also known as satin-flower, is an annual often grown as a biennial and a showy plant reaching over two feet.

33 to 40 per cent fruit sugar, 32 to 39 per cent grape sugar, one to four per cent saccharose, minute amounts of iron, calcium, manganese, potassium, sulphur, phosphorus, and *water*. The requirement for sound honey, in the United States, is that the water content is not more than 25 per cent.

For every pound of honey, it is said that a bee makes from 40,000 to 80,000 trips, collecting from many times this number of flowers. From one to one and one-half miles is covered in each trip.

With the ligula, the worker bee extracts from flowers the nectar, which after being held in the mouth for a while, passes into the honey sac, or honey stomach. Upon filling her honey sac, the bee returns to the hive and regurgitates the juices into a cell of the honeycomb. She departs at once for more nectar, while other bees add invertase which converts the nectar into honey. The cells are then hermetically sealed and the ripening process continues until the substance reaches the stage of "ripened honey," and is ready for consumption.

One pound of honey contains 1,600 calories, and since an important part of the digestive process took place in the honey sac, honey is easily digestible. Often it is given as supplementary food to small children and elderly people.

Among primitive races honey is widely used as food. In Central Africa it is said the sole food of the Anyanha tribe consists of a mixture of maize flour, bananas and honey.

A germ-free product, honey has long been successfully used for dressing stubborn old sores, or fresh wounds. In as much as it is water-absorbing, honey acts as a disinfectant on infected mucous membranes, especially recommended in the case of a cough.

Honey is also important in the preparation of various medicines. Prescriptions, of which honey was the main ingredient, have been found in ancient papyri in Egypt.

Honey derived from flowering plants and leaf trees is considered better than that gained from coniferous trees though the latter has its special friends. Honey produced in May and June seems richest in aroma and flavor. The bees visit the flowers for nectar, and this the bee turns into honey—just as the cow turns grass into milk. Nectar contains up to 60 per cent of water in which sucrose is dissolved.

It is becoming important to blend the various qualities of honey in order to produce a good general standard of the product. This is particularly so in England where much honey is imported. Most consumers of honey always like the same accustomed taste in the honey they buy at any time. This can be obtained more easily by blending different kinds of honey.

Honey should be stored where it is dry and warm. If it is kept for a long time, particularly in cold weather or under cold conditions, it will change from its original liquid form to a semi-granular condition which does not mean spoilage but which is not liked by the consumer. The most important thing to remember about honey is that it should be *used*. In almost any cookbook, the woman of the house can find innumerable recipes for dishes which can be made more tasteful by using honey rather than sugar or other sweetener.—*Jewell Casey and Dr. W. Schweisheimer.*

See also BEES; BEEKEEPING; HONEY PLANTS.

HONEY PLANTS: Not even the hardest working bee can produce an appreciable amount of honey or do a good job of pollination without a plentiful supply of rich blossoms to forage on.

For more bees and better bees, one must improve their range. All during the growing season a succession of honey rich plants should mature—one this month and a different one the next. Do not deprive a bee of her blossom even for a day. The greater the succession of nectar plants present throughout the season—the more bees will be present to perform the pollination chores of the field and garden.

A good succession of maturing honey plants will make for stronger colonies, more bees per hive, will foster the development of new apiaries and may possibly restore the now almost defunct population of wild pollinating insects.

In view of the pressing need for more and better honey and pollen plants, a honey plant testing ground—known as Pellett Gardens—has been established at Atlantic, Iowa. It is run in cooperation with *The American Bee Journal.*

Here hundreds of plants have been tested for their value as honey plants and for possible other uses. Native plants, foreign plants, trees, shrubs, mints, oil plants, common plants and uncommon plants all have been tested. Of the hundreds tried, a number appear promising. If used with careful planning by conscientious farmers, these plants may reverse the present trend toward the decimation of bee populations.

The following are some of the more unusual plants:

Trifolium ambiguum, or Pellett Clover is a perennial clover which spreads rapidly underground and has attracted a wide interest. It spreads and thickens up by the root system until the soil is very heavily bound with coarse roots. It is apparently entirely winter hardy and looks good for erosion control. It blooms in June and July and the nectar is readily accessible to honeybees.

Pellett Clover shows up early in the spring. At first only basil leaves appear which may be considerably larger than those of most clovers. In late May the flowering stems appear and the growth is heavy where it does well. Animals like it.

Everflowering Locust (Robinia pseudoacacia semperflorens) is a very unusual tree because it blooms in varying amounts all summer long. Apparently this variety originated in eastern Europe and is little known in this country. They bloom all summer from the time of the first heavy bloom almost constantly until near the first of September. This is a quick-growing tree and expected to be similar in requirements to the black locust which is noted for adaptability to a wide range of soil and climatic conditions.

Mountain Mint (Pycnanthemum pilosum) is a native plant which holds promise as a source of essential oils. Tests indicate that it is capable of yielding much heavier amount of oils than most mints now in cultivation. Apparently having commercial possibilities, it is yet in the experimental stage. It blooms very heavily over a long period in late summer and fall and seldom fails to find the bees working it. Mountain Mist is suited to garden cultivation and an attractive plant with very pronounced minty flavor.

Anise Hyssop (Agastache anethiodora) reportedly attracts the bees most consistently over the longest blooming period of any honey plant. It begins blooming in June, blooms heavily through most of the summer and usually continues with some bloom until frost. The bees consistently work the flowers from daylight until dark. It was a native plant of pioneer times which has since almost entirely disappeared. It was estimated in the old days that an acre of Anise Hyssop might be sufficient pasture for 100 hives of bees. Thus it is sometimes termed "Wonder Honey Plant."

As is the case with a good many honey plants, reports indicate it to vary in bee attractiveness in different localities. Where suited, it is very good for bees and an attractive herb.

For honey plants to be of any great value they must be sufficiently hardy to withstand competition, to take care of themselves; or else to have some other use to encourage their cultivation. Naturally the most important honey plants are those which are forage crops or others which are grown extensively in large acreage. But also important are the smaller areas of some plants which bloom at the off season. In so many cases plants can be used which will serve the original purpose and at the same time be good honey plants. This factor may well be considered when making selections for conservation programs as erosion control and wildlife conservation. Plantings of trees and shrubs can usually be those which also will furnish some bee pasture.

Some very good honey plants may be growing wild in waste places and fence rows. In many localities wild asters and goldenrod give a good fall honeyflow. Catnip and motherwort, often thought of as weeds are among the best of honey plants. When the "weeds" are good honey plants and are doing no harm it is well to leave them. More honey plants make for a better beekeeping location—more bees and better pollination.—*Melvin Pellett.*

MAJOR HONEY PLANTS BY STATE

Beekeepers rank honey plants according to their value as nectar pro-

ducers. It should be emphasized that the ratings given are for each state as a whole; they may not represent certain areas within the state. The plants included are those that were given a rating the greatest number of times, and they are listed below in the order of their ratings. For a few plants the ratings were equal; these plants are joined by braces.

The terms "major" and "minor" honey plants are frequently used in beekeeping literature, but usually without any definite explanation. It is doubtful whether a definition satisfactory to the entire country can be applied, owing chiefly to the variations in the size of honey crops in different states. Probably beekeepers in any area think of a major honey plant as one that usually yields nectar in sufficient amounts above the needs of the bee. A minor honey plant is one that yields some nectar but usually does not supply a surplus of removable honey. Listings of honey plant preferences by state follow. The report was prepared by Everett Oertel of the Department of Agriculture's Bee Culture Division.

ALABAMA:
  Sweetclover
  Tuliptree
  Rattan
  Cotton
  Blackberry
  White clover

ARIZONA:
  Mesquite
  { Arrowweed
  { Catclaw
  Alfalfa
  Tamarisk
  Sweetclover

ARKANSAS:
  White clover
  Persimmon
  Spanish-needles

CALIFORNIA:
  Sage
  Alfalfa
  Orange
  Wild buckwheat
  Star thistle
  Mustard

  Lima bean
  Manzanita

COLORADO:
  Sweetclover
  Alfalfa
  Cleome
  White clover
  Rosinweed
  { Alsike clover
  { Sunflower

CONNECTICUT:
  { Sweetclover
  { White clover
  Sumac
  Alsike clover
  Goldenrod
  Aster

DELAWARE:
  Tulip poplar
  Crimson clover
  Tupelo
  Gallberry
  Persimmon

FLORIDA:
  Tupelo

Mangrove
Thistle
Orange
Palmetto
{ Sunflower
{ Titi

GEORGIA:
Tulip poplar
Gallberry
White and black tupelo
{ Mexican-clover
{ Sourwood
Sumac
Titi

IDAHO:
Alfalfa
Sweetclover
White clover
Alsike clover

ILLINOIS:
Sweetclover
White clover
Heartsease
Alsike clover
Spanish-needles
Aster
Basswood

INDIANA:
{ Alsike clover
{ White clover
Sweetclover
Aster
Tulip poplar
Basswood
Goldenrod

IOWA:
Sweetclover
White clover
{ Alfalfa
{ Alsike clover
{ Basswood
{ Heartsease
Goldenrod

KANSAS:
White sweetclover
Alfalfa
White clover
Heartsease

LOUISIANA:
White clover
Willow
Peppervine
Goldenrod
Palmetto
Vervain

MAINE:
Alsike clover
Wild raspberry
White clover

Goldenrod
Milkweed

MARYLAND:
Alsike clover
{ Tulip poplar
{ White clover
Locust
Goldenrod

MASSACHUSETTS:
Alsike clover
{ Goldenrod
{ White clover
Blackberry and raspberry
Fruit bloom

MICHIGAN:
Sweetclover
White clover
Alsike clover
Basswood
Buckwheat
Goldenrod
Alfalfa

MINNESOTA:
Sweetclover
White clover
Alsike clover
Basswood
Goldenrod
Heartsease
Alfalfa

MISSOURI:
White clover
Heartsease
Sweetclover
Spanish-needles
{ Alsike clover
{ Goldenrod
Basswood

MONTANA:
Sweetclover
Alfalfa
Alsike clover

NEBRASKA:
Sweetclover
Alfalfa
White clover
Heartsease
Goldenrod

NEVADA:
Alfalfa
Sweetclover
Sunflower
Rabbitbrush

NEW JERSEY:
White clover
{ Aster
{ Sweetclover

{ Alsike clover
{ Goldenrod
Sumac

NEW YORK:
Alsike clover
White clover
Sweetclover
{ Aster
{ Goldenrod
{ Buckwheat
{ Sumac
Alfalfa
Basswood

NORTH CAROLINA:
{ Sourwood
{ Tulip poplar
{ Basswood
{ Locust
Sweetclover
{ Black gum
{ Tupelo

NORTH DAKOTA:
Sweetclover

OHIO:
Alsike clover
White clover
Sweetclover
Basswood
{ Alfalfa
{ Aster
{ Goldenrod
Buckwheat

OKLAHOMA:
Sweetclover
Alfalfa
Horsemint
Cotton
{ Goldenrod
{ Heartsease

OREGON:
Alfalfa
Sweetclover
Fireweed
Alsike and white clover
Vetch

PENNSYLVANIA:
Alsike clover
White clover
{ Aster
{ Locust
Buckwheat
Sweetclover
Goldenrod
Basswood

SOUTH CAROLINA:
{ Sourwood
{ Tuliptree
{ Basswood
{ Locust

{ Goldenrod
{ Sumac
Persimmon
Aster

SOUTH DAKOTA:
Sweetclover
Alfalfa
White clover

TENNESSEE:
White clover
{ Sourwood
{ Tulip poplar
{ Locust
{ Persimmon
{ Sweetclover
Thoroughwort
Goldenrod

TEXAS:
Cotton
Horsemint
Mesquite
Huajillo
Catclaw
Marigold

UTAH:
Alfalfa
Sweetclover
Alsike clover
White clover

VERMONT:
White clover
Basswood
Alsike clover
Raspberry
Goldenrod
Alfalfa

VIRGINIA:
White clover
Tulip poplar
Sourwood
Persimmon
Blueweed
Aster

WASHINGTON:
Fireweed
White clover
Alsike clover
Sweetclover
Alfalfa

WEST VIRGINIA:
White clover
Sumac
Blue thistle
Tulip poplar
{ Basswood
{ Sourwood
Locust

WISCONSIN:
White clover
Sweetclover

Alsike clover
Basswood
Alfalfa
{ Aster
{ Goldenrod

WYOMING:
Sweetclover
Alfalfa
Dandelion
Alsike clover

The most widely distributed major honey plants—alfalfa, alsike clover, sweetclover, and white clover—with the states in which the reporters gave them first or second place as honey producers, are as follows:

Plant and rank — States

ALFALFA

First: Idaho, Nevada, Oregon, Utah.

Second: California, Colorado, Kansas, Montana, Nebraska, Oklahoma, South Dakota, Wyoming.

ALSIKE CLOVER

First: Indiana, Maine, Maryland, Massachusetts, New York, Ohio, Pennsylvania.

SWEETCLOVER

First: Alabama, Colorado, Connecticut, Illinois, Iowa, Kansas, Michigan, Minnesota, Montana, Nebraska, North Dakota, Oklahoma, South Dakota, Wyoming.

Second: Idaho, Indiana, Nevada, New Jersey, Oregon, Utah, Wisconsin.

WHITE CLOVER

First: Arkansas, Connecticut, Indiana, Louisiana, Missouri, New Jersey, Tennessee, Vermont, Virginia, W. Virginia, Wisconsin.

Second: Illinois, Iowa, Maryland, Massachusetts, Michigan, Minnesota, New York, Ohio, Pennsylvania, Washington.

See also BEES; BEEKEEPING.

HONEYSUCKLE: (*Lonicera*) A large group of shrubs and woody vines, all of which make fine garden plants. The taller shrubs are used in hedges, borders and single specimens, while many of the lower-growing forms appear in rock gardens. The showy fruits range in color from white to black, are popular with birds. They prefer a moist, loam soil, and usually thrive in almost any location, whether shady or open.

Varieties include common or Italian honeysuckle (*L. caprifolium*), a climbing type often reaching 20 feet with yellow-white flowers and orange fruit; like many other varieties, it's hardy in the central and southern states. Yellow honeysuckle (*L. flava*) is more of a spreading vine, considered by many as the most attractive of the honeysuckle family.

Japanese honeysuckle (*L. japonica*) is a strong-growing climbing vine, reaching as high as 30 feet with white flowers and black fruit. Woodbine (*L. periclymenum*) is another woody climber that grows to 20 feet, has red fruit. Trumpet honeysuckle (*L. sempervirens*), also known as coral honeysuckle, is an evergreen climbing vine, has showy orange flowers. European or bush honeysuckle (*L. xylosteum*) is a bushy type shrub that reaches about ten feet high, has yellow flowers and red fruit.

Most honeysuckles are spring and summer bloomers, produce a great quantity of the showy fragrant flowers.

HOOF AND HORN MEAL: There are many grades of hoof and horn meal; the granular material breaks down with some difficulty unless kept moist and well covered; it also tends to encourage the growth of maggots because it attracts flies. The finely ground horn dust, which gardeners use for potting mixtures, is on the other hand quite easily dissolved. In fact, it can be smelled clearly which shows that small particles break off all along. The nitrogen content is from ten to 16 pounds per hundred pound bag or as much as a ton of manure or more, while the phosphoric acid value is usually around two per cent. If available, this is a very handy source of nitrogen for flower growers and gardeners with small compost heaps, because it can be easily stored, is pleasant to handle, and relatively less costly than other forms of bagged organic nitrogen.

HOPS: Spent hops is a by-product, the residue after hops have been extracted with water in the brewery. In their wet state, they are 75 per cent water, 0.6 per cent nitrogen, 0.2 per cent phosphorus. Moisture content varies considerably, and the analysis expressed on the dry matter is the most satisfactory figure. On this basis the nitrogen ranges from 2.5 to 3.5 per cent and the phosphoric acid about one per cent. Spent hops in their natural condition are to be regarded mainly as a source of nitrogen. In many areas, gardeners and farmers have been successfully using the hops in their natural condition, spreading it in the same way as farmyard manure. Many other growers have been composting the hops before applying to the soil.

Another brewery waste available is the material left over from the mashing process, composed of grain parts. This wet brewer's grain, which decays readily, has been found to contain almost one per cent of nitrogen.

Spent hops have been used as a mulch with excellent success. For the owner of the small garden, however, they have their disadvantages because of the very strong odor, but this disappears in a short time.

Used in larger areas, where the odor is not seriously objectionable, spent hops prove to be a very effective mulch.

Like other mulches, it conserves the soil moisture, raises the soil temperature in the late fall and early spring, and aids bacteria in their work in the soil. Spent hops, direct from the brewery, are very wet and have a pH of about 4.5. One six-inch application about a plant will last at least three years and sometimes longer. Stirring the material once or twice during the growing season aids in keeping down any of the weeds that may have grown up through it.

In the Arnold Arboretum two of the most important characteristics of this material are that it does not blow away when dry and does not burn if a lighted match or cigarette butt is thrown into it. Many other mulch materials burn easily.

Because of the tremendous amount of water in them, fresh spent hops heat very readily when freshly applied in the summer months. Keeping them at least six inches away from any young stems will overcome this difficulty.

HORDEUM VULGARE: *see* BARLEY

HOREHOUND: (*Marrubium vulgare*) A hardy perennial herb that occurs as a common weed in many places in the United States, especially on the Pacific coast. The leaves and flowering tops are in some demand as a crude drug. Their greatest use is in the manufacture of horehound candy, although they are sometimes employed for seasoning.

Horehound grows well in almost any soil and can be started in cold frames, either from cuttings or seed and later transplanted to the outdoors.

The plant grows well in almost any soil and thrives in those that are light, dry, and rather poor. It grows readily from seed, which is usually sown in drills early in spring and covered with about one inch of soil. Plants can be started in cold frames, from either seed or cuttings, and later transplanted to the field, or divisions of old plants can be used. Plants may stand six, 12, or 18 inches apart in the row; those standing close together have small stems and hence yield a crop of finer quality.

HORMONE: Synthetic hormones are being used a great deal in today's livestock programs. The object is to speed up the rate at which cattle put on weight. One such synthetic hormone, stilbestrol, is being used by almost 50 per cent of the cattle growers, even though actually little is known about how the hormone works.

Synthetic hormones are manufactured from a variety of chemicals by a complex process. A dictionary definition states that a hormone is "any of various chemical substances formed in the endocrine organs (that is, ductless glands that secrete internally) which activate specifically receptive organs when transported to them by the body fluids." Named from the Greek verb *hormanein,* meaning "to arouse or excite," the principal hormones are the internal secretions of the glands that manufacture pituitrin, thyroxin, insulin, adrenalin and the hormones of sex.

Natural hormones in humans function in the control, coordination and stimulation of all vital body activities, including secretion, metabolism, growth and reproduction. Needless to say, it is impossible to have good health if the body's hormones are not working properly.

Stilbestrol, for example, has all the properties of an estrogen, a type of female sex hormone. For some years, this synthetic female hormone—estrogen—has been used by doctors for the treatment of disturbances in women during their change-of-life. However, the *Journal of the American Medical Association* has frequently warned that estrogen should only be administered when symptoms are very severe and even then not over an extended period of time.

These warnings about estrogen have been issued, because it is so powerful a drug. Medical reports state that a dose as small as 1/56,000th of an ounce will cause response to some illnesses.

A look at stilbestrol's history offers further insight to its potential dangers. Some years ago, stilbestrol made its first appearance in poultry houses. The general idea was to inject a pellet of stilbestrol under the skin near the top of the chicken's head.

The purpose of using stilbestrol was to produce a bird which was essentially a capon. Here is what happened to the bird: externally it showed up in the shrinking and paling of comb and wattles; the bird became sluggish and tame and had no desire to fight; internally the sex organs shrank; the final result—and most important to commercial growers—the bird took on flesh and fat at a rapid rate.

The hormonized bird was ready for market in 20 weeks from hatching and possessed a size and quality comparable to that of an eight-month-old true capon. Stilbestrol also cut the poultryman's costs.

During the last few years, however, poultrymen have been warned about using stilbestrol pellets. Main reason: residual pellets of stilbestrol have been found in the birds. In one case, an official of the Food and Drug Administration bought a drawn chicken which had four pellets in its neck, one of them three inches down from the skull. A Congressional committee has been alerted about the possible dangers of stilbestrol to humans.

It is readily apparent that stilbestrol pellets were not regarded as "safe" for use. This again leads to the belief that farmers are committing a major blunder by accepting stilbestrol as a feed supplement for cattle so wholeheartedly.

Another word of caution comes from *Farm Journal,* in excerpts from a report which appeared in that publication of August, 1955:

"If you feed stilbestrol to your cattle, better not say anything about it when you send them to market. You might end up getting less money.

" . . . For some reason, the whole trade is wary of stilbestrol-fed cattle. But there's no good reason for it, as far as anyone can tell.

" 'The plain facts are,' says one old-time commission man at Chicago, 'that stilbestrol won't *help sell* any cattle—and it *might* cut the price if the buyer knows about it. We just don't talk about stilbestrol any more.'"

One packer has this to say: "Stilbestrol cattle just don't cut out a carcass that's as good as they look on the hoof. But it's not only stilbestrol that's responsible—it's the short-cut, cheaper fattening methods promoted by every agricultural college around.

"The beef we're seeing today doesn't measure up to the old cornfed beef. It looks plump and good on the outside, but when you cut it open the quality isn't there.

"The way things are going, cornfed beef will be a thing of the past in four or five years.

"One yards veteran admits, 'I've probably seen 100,000 stilbestrol-fed cattle come through here, and have been able to tell that less than 5,000 of them have had it. They're the ones with the high tail heads, and the steers that look like a heifer "making bag."

"So while it's hard to nail down anything concrete at these markets," concludes *Farm Journal*, "one fact stands out: If you feed stilbestrol, better keep mum about it."

Farmers have also been warned against giving stilbestrol feeds to dairy cattle, beef bulls, suckling calves or female beef to be kept for breeding purposes or to steers being fed for shows. This is because the hormone tends to cause such animals to develop unwanted sexual characteristics.

Dairy cattle would go off milk production, beef bulls can become too female and not sire calves, female beef breeders might not conceive, or would abort, or in different ways not produce a good calf crop.

It has been stated by research agencies that stilbestrol fed to cattle never lodges in the meat, and that it is only in the blood and passes through the animal very quickly. The Food and Drug Administration has made a ruling that cattle should be taken off stilbestrol feeding 48 hours before slaughter as an extra precautionary measure.

HORNBEAM: (*Carpinus*) Belonging to the birch family, these slow-growing trees or shrubs are fairly hardy. The American hornbeam (*C. caroliniana*), also known as blue beech, prefers a shady, wind-protected location; grows to about 30 feet. The European hornbeam (*C. betulus*) grows about 50 feet high, but usually much lower when cultivated in the garden. The variety *columnaris* is often used as a hedge, growing straight and slender.

HORNBLENDE: A common dark mineral, generally black, composed of a light to dark green silicate of iron, magnesium and calcium with aluminum.

HORNWORM: *see* INSECT CONTROL

HORSE-CHESTNUT: (*Aesculus*) Often used as a street tree because of its dense shade, the horse-chestnut is a very attractive tree, especially when in flower. Ohio buckeye (*A. glabra*) grows to 30 feet, is hardy in central to southern states. The common horse-

A handsome Horse chestnut in a public park in Washington, D. C. Species such as the *hippocastanum* above reach 100 feet, bear white flowers.

chestnut (*A. hippocastanum*) reaches as high as 100 feet, has white showy flowers in spring. Red buckeye (*A. pavia*) is mostly a shrub growing ten to 30 feet, producing egg-shaped fruit. Sweet buckeye (*A. octandra*) and Japanese horse-chestnut (*A. turbinata*) grow around 60 feet high, produce yellow flowers. *See also* TREES.

HORSE MANURE: *see* MANURE

HORSE NETTLE (*Solanum carolinense*) A close relative of the buffalo bur, this plant is not only a pest as a weed in spring, but is also poisonous when leaves or berries are eaten. In addition, it is susceptible to tomato mosaic which makes it objectionable near tomato fields. Horse nettle is not poisonous in all stages of growth, but because the presence or absence of the poison cannot be known at all times, it should never be eaten.

Resembling the buffalo bur in appearance and size, this perennial weed spreads by creeping rootstocks up to three feet long, its vertical taproots penetrating to depths of eight feet. It is troublesome both in meadows and in crops, especially on loose, sandy soils. It can be controlled in fields by clean cultivation, and can be choked out on camp grounds or in resort areas by establishing a good sod of bluegrass. Patches of this weed should be mowed in uncultivated areas to prevent seed formation.

HORSE-RADISH: Horse-radish is a perennial with a very thick, fleshy taproot system. The taproot gives rise to many fleshy laterals in the surface foot of soil, where also frequently the main root divides into several rather equally prominent branches.

The great extent and rapid development of the horse-radish roots explain why the plants grow best in a very deep, moist, fertile loam soil; why deep cultivation is beneficial; and why a good soil structure is an important environmental factor for growth.

In planting, the roots are placed with the upper end of the cutting two to five inches below the soil surface. The soil should be packed firmly about them to insure good contact and resultant prompt growth. Weeds should be kept out so that sufficient water and nutrients will be available late in the season when the plants make their best growth. On hard, dry, or shallow soil the roots are very likely to be crooked, unshapely, and scarcely fit for use. The growth of long, straight roots of more uniform size is promoted by preparing and maintaining a deep, mellow soil. The usual distance is ten to 18 inches in rows three to four feet apart.

Belonging to the mustard family, horse-radish is often found growing wild along streams, in meadows and other moist locations. It makes an excellent condiment for meats and many fish courses.

Horse-radish grows best in the cool months of autumn, steadily improving after September. Many gardeners dig a few roots at a time, allowing the remainder to lay in the soil, since the root is hardy.

HOSTA: Often known as plantain-lily, *Funkia* and *Niobe,* these are perennials of the lily family native to China and Japan. Hostas are hardy and relatively easy to grow, attractive because of their masses of root-leaves and blue and white flowers. They are often used along walks. The soil should be deep and rich; large-leaved types prefer moist, shady locations. The plants bloom in summer. Tallest growing of the Hostas is *H. undulata*, reaching three feet. *H. caerulea* grows to 1½ to two feet high, as does *H. japonica*. *See also* LILY.

HOTBED: The location of either hotbeds or cold frames should provide full exposure to the sun and good protection from cold winds. A southern exposure is best, providing that water from the eaves of the protecting structure does not drip onto the beds.

The excavation or pit for a hotbed is usually dug from ten inches to three

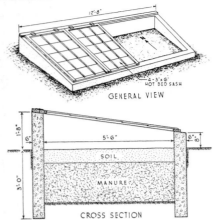

GENERAL VIEW

CROSS SECTION

Sturdy construction is required for outdoor hot-beds or cold frames. As a rule, use wood at least two inches thick, weatherproofed against decay.

feet in depth. The length is always made some multiple of three feet, which is the width of standard hotbed sash. The width of the bed should also be made to accommodate standard sash. On smaller beds, used storm or window sash may of course be utilized, in which cases the exact size of the bed will be dictated by these dimensions.

For a four-sash frame, the excavation should be laid out $6\frac{1}{2}$ feet wide by $12\frac{2}{3}$ feet long. The latter dimension allows for necessary sash supports or bars which run across the bed. Walls should be made about six inches thick.

The bed is usually made so that the top of the south wall is about six to eight inches and the north wall from 12 to 20 inches above the ground. This gives a slope of from six to 12 inches. As it is difficult to dig a six-inch trench for concrete walls, it is customary to make the excavation for the bed first and to utilize the earth for the outer forms up to ground level. One-inch-wide boards are used above-grade and for the inner forms. If desired, recesses may be cast in the top surfaces of the wall to receive sash.

The recommended concrete mixture for hotbeds and cold frames is $1:2\frac{1}{4}:3$ —that is, one part portland cement by volume to $2\frac{1}{4}$ parts clean sand and three parts gravel or crushed stone. The coarse aggregate (gravel or crushed stone) should not be more than $1\frac{1}{2}$ inches in diameter. These ingredients are mixed to a stiff, fairly dry consistency, and then tamped into place in the forms. Not more than five gallons of water per bag of cement should be used for this mix when the sand is in average moist condition. Good concrete is not difficult to make, but always measure your ingredients carefully.

The newly placed walls should be protected from drying out too quickly. Hang moist canvas or burlap over them and wet down the covered walls with a garden hose. Do this frequently for a week or ten days after pouring. In cold weather the work should be protected, but does not have to be kept moist.

When the curing is completed and the concrete has hardened, the hotbeds are banked with earth and the embankment sometimes covered with straw in order to prevent heat loss.

Good drainage, both surface and underground, is essential. The ground should therefore slope away from the site of the bed. Without ample drainage, water may possibly collect in the pit, delay the growth of the plants and seriously check the fermenting of the manure. Lengths of four-inch drain tile are often placed around the perimeter of the bed and connected to a suitable outlet so that the bed will be drained in case water happens to collect. However, in well-drained soil, this is probably not necessary. *See also* COLD FRAME.

HOUSELEEK: (*Sempevivum*) Often used in the rock garden, these foliage plants prefer a rather dry, somewhat poor soil. Mostly summer bloomers, houseleeks frequently appear in the open border. Common houseleek (*S. tectorum*), also known as roof house-leek and hen-and-chickens, grows about one foot high. Cobweb houseleek (*S. arachnoideum*) produces many cobwebby leaves, red flowers.

HOUSE PLANTS: Any plant which will grow under the adverse conditions of aridity, temperature, and light encountered in an ordinary house may be a house plant. If special conditions not normal to the ordinary household must be supplied to a potted plant to ensure its survival indoors, the plant may be considered a hot-house subject, but not properly a house plant.

Special equipment which supplies atmospheric moisture, additional sunlight, or temperature control has been designed to enlarge the range of plants which may be brought inside. This equipment may be as simple as a tray for holding water under plant containers or as elaborate as a special plant window which verges on becoming a greenhouse.

Some plants may be grown indoors with no special provision for light or moisture, and with little sunlight. These are mostly foliage plants whose native habitat was tropical or desert. Generally speaking, any flowering plant will need plenty of sunlight, and almost any foliage plant may be grown with little or no sun. Some desert plants, as the many varieties of cactus, need sun but little atmospheric moisture. On the other hand, many deep-woods plants, like many varieties of fern, need almost no direct sun but must be surrounded by moist air.

MOISTURE CONTROL: Except cacti, all house plants need more atmospheric moisture than is available to them in an artificially heated house. Water constantly evaporates from all foliage, though the rate of evaporation differs according to leaf structure. Usually plants with smooth, leathery foliage will lose less water through their leaves than those with hairy or spongy textured leaves. The former are easier to accommodate in the house, and the latter will need special handling.

Because of water expired by each plant, a group of plants in a small area will be surrounded by a more moist atmosphere than one plant by itself. Any plant stand designed to hold a number of plants, or a window with shelf-room for more than one plant will improve the atmospheric conditions for all the plants.

A bulb spray syringe may be used to spray water over house plants daily, if their surroundings will not be damaged by the moisture. Or they may be moved to sink or tub weekly for a spray bath of all foliage. Flowers are sometimes damaged by strong streams of water, so care should be exercised. Most house plants benefit from a weekly soaking in a tub with water up to the pot rim. After it has absorbed enough water to make the surface moist, the plant should be thoroughly drained before being returned to its window. The amount of water given between soakings will differ according to the plant, the size pot, and the accidental clogging or opening of the drainage hole in the bottom of each pot that takes place after it is filled.

Most plants should not be allowed to stand in saucers filled with the water that has drained after their daily watering. However, if their need for moisture is greater than can be supplied in any other way, the plant saucer may be filled with pebbles which are kept moist, and the plant will stand on the pebbles above the water-line. This treatment may be given to individual plants, or a tray large enough to hold many plants may be constructed of wood or metal and waterproofed. If the planter is deep enough, the pots may be set into it, and the space between them filled with damp sphagnum moss. Or a shallower tray may be filled with water and covered with heavy wire screening on which the plants may be set. If the plant window is over a radiator, a humidifier may be made tank-shape to cover the top of the radiator, and the plants set on shelves above it.

For special moisture-lovers, like orchids, it may be necessary to build a special glass case to contain their own atmosphere. A glass cabinet like an old china cupboard with its wooden back replaced by glass makes an ideal miniature hot-house for these prima donnas. Or a case may be specially constructed of plexiglass using the window itself for one wall. Supplemental daily spraying with a bulb syringe will keep the humidity high enough in such a case for the most demanding plants. Thermometers with humidity gages are available, and should show a humidity of 60 to 80 per cent for orchids.

TERRARIUM: A Lilliputian garden with its own moisture control may be built in a glass container such as a bottle, bowl, or even a light bulb or discarded coffee-maker. Such a terrarium should be supplied with miniature plants which may be purchased, or may be dug in the woods. It will need to be watered only once in two or three weeks. Unless the opening of the glass vessel is small, it should be covered by a piece of window glass which should be raised once or twice daily to permit fresh air to enter.

Plants suitable to a terrarium are tiny ferns, like ebony spleenwort, baby maidenhair, and rock fern; rattlesnake plantain, partridge berry, wintergreen, or pipsissewa for bright berries; sedums and mosses in large varieties; ground pine, or seedlings of evergreen trees, such as white pine.

TEMPERATURE: Conditions ideal for house plants are almost the same as those best for human beings. Temperatures of 65 to 70° in the daytime, and 50 to 55° at night are optimum.

Temperatures in a plant window may fluctuate much more than this, especially if curtains or dividers behind the plants prevent circulation of air from the room. During the day the sun will quickly heat a small enclosed space to shoot the mercury up ten to 25 degrees. Unless glass is double between plants and the winter cold, temperatures in a deep window may drop to freezing near the glass on a very cold night.

Circulation of air near the plants is not necessary to provide them with oxygen, which they manufacture themselves during the day, but to moderate the temperature. Changes in temperature are achieved more slowly in a large than in a small space. If the air circulating through an entire room flows around the plants, or around the case or glass jar containing them, they will suffer less from abrupt temperature changes than if they are isolated in too small a space.

Specially constructed plant windows, described below, must be built with air vents in the roof to allow the escape of hot air on sunny days. A small electric fan kept running during hours when temperatures in the window may be expected to reach extremes can also help to circulate air from the room into the window embrasure.

When plants grow in too hot an atmosphere, even though they are given plenty of moisture and food, the growth is too soft, is easily injured, and is easy prey for insects.

LIGHT: Light is important to almost all plant life—light, but not necessarily sun. Just as some plants thrive outdoors in the shade or half-shade, so house plants may not want more than a small amount of sun, filtered through a thin curtain or screen.

Ideally, house plants should be supplied light on all sides. A bow window, or specially constructed plant window, may permit almost as much all-round light as if the plant were outside. If such conditions are not possible, the plants must be turned often to prevent their reaching toward the light supply and becoming lopsided.

African violets, gloxinias, and gardenias are among the flowers which prosper with something less than direct sun, but all three need bright situations, possibly in north or northeast windows. Ferns usually like the same light conditions—the more delicate ones are dried up by direct sun. Other plants that will flourish with no sun are ivy, philodendron, rubber plant, sanseviera, strawberry geranium, caladium, and dracaena.

In windows that can catch only one to three hours sun each day, African violets will also grow, provided the sunny hours are in the morning. Some of the others that need only a small amount of sun for bloom are shrimp plant, azalea, begonia, the bromeliads, cyclamen, spring flowering bulbs, ivy geranium and scented geranium.

Although many flowers can be brought to bloom in windows with a few hours' sun, most will be improved if they get all the sun short winter days provide. For these a glass case with three glass sides and a glass roof may be built outside an ordinary window frame to form a miniature greenhouse. Several of these, prefabricated, are offered on the market. They are equipped with vents at the top to let out hot air, and may be made with double glass to protect against cold.

SOIL: The window box and flower pot must be regarded as miniature, portable gardens. In addition to holding the soil, these containers must be of such nature and construction as to provide adequate drainage and aeration so that the soil will be a favorable environment for the plant roots and the microorganisms which live in the soil and play important roles in the plant's nutrition.

Some house plants, such as Bromeliads and Cacti, thrive in a soil that would prove to be inadequate for most other plants; others, like the Chinese Evergreen, can get along very well for long periods on just plain water and air; but most of them require a soil high in humus and rich in minerals.

Soils for the window garden are formulated by mixing together in suitable proportions such ingredients as loam, sand, pulverized rocks, and organic matter in the form of compost, leaf mold, muck, and peat. Some suggested potting mixtures are given below:

1. General Potting Mixture

2 parts good garden loam.
1 part compost, leaf mold, or other fermented organic matter.
1 part clean coarse sand.
To the above mixture, add pulverized phosphate rock and potash rock (granite dust or greensand), each at the rate of a tablespoon for each potful of mixture.

2. Potting Mixture for Seedlings

1 part good garden loam.
1 part compost, leaf mold, peat, or other form of humus.
2 parts clean coarse sand.

3. Potting Mixture for Humus-loving Plants

1 part good garden loam.
2 parts compost, leaf mold, peat, or other form of humus.
1 part coarse, clean sand.
To this mixture should be added pulverized phosphate rock and potash rock (granite dust or greensand) at the rate of 1 tablespoon of each for each six-inch pot of mixture.

Re-potting is a must where house plants are concerned. The new, larger pot will give the crowded root-ball extra space for new growth.

4. *Potting Mixture for Cacti*

1 part good garden loam.
2 parts coarse, clean sand.
1 part broken pots, coarse gravel or small stones.
To this mixture may be added pulverized rock phosphate and potash rock (granite dust or greensand) at the rate of one tablespoon of each for each six-inch potful of mixture.

These potting mixtures represent various soil types which must be considered in the window garden. Potting mixture 1 will best meet the requirements of many house plants, and particularly those which occur naturally in mineral rather than in organic soils. For woodland plants, as ferns, African violet, primroses, and azaleas in the window garden, use potting mixture 3. The potting mixtures given above may be modified in one way or another to still better meet the requirements of special plants. In the case of acid-loving plants, for instance, acid peat may be added to give the soil an acid reaction, and lime may be added to make a soil mixture neutral or slightly alkaline.

By adding compost and such insoluble but plant-available minerals as phosphate rock and potash rock, the soil in the window box and flower pot will have the capacity of supplying the essential plant nutrients for a relatively long period of time, or until the plant needs to be repotted. This makes unnecessary the feeding of the plants in the window garden with manure water which gives off an unpleasant odor or with soluble chemical salts which usually make the plants susceptible to insects and diseases.

The best forms of humus in making up the potting mixtures are compost and oak leaf mold. If compost is not available, use the leaf mold. This can be collected in almost any woodland, or it can be made from autumnal leaves. If the leaves are shredded and then put in heaps mixed with a small amount of soil, leaf mold can be made in a comparatively short time.

DRAINAGE: One of the most important things to provide for in a soil is drainage. This is best secured by adding sand. Use a clean, sharp sand such as a mason would use for making mortar. If sand from the seashore is used, get it from the shore side of the sand hills, and wash it thoroughly before using in order to remove any salt. If the plants are to stay for a year or so in single pots without repotting (as is the case with palms), charcoal is a distinct advantage, not only because of the better drainage it affords, but also because it prevents the soil from souring.

It is very important to have on hand at all times the ingredients necessary to make up a good potting soil, so in an out-building away from the weather, or in the cellar, have bins in which a six months' (if not a year's) supply, of the articles just mentioned may be stored. Even manure may be stored in the cellar, if it is well decayed, without the least inconvenience.

Mix the soil thoroughly before planting. The best way to do this is to layer the component parts together and then throw the mass over to make a new pile. Always shovel from the bottom of the pile, and always throw the added matter on the apex of the new pile so that the soil can roll down the sides. If this is done, and the pile turned three or four times, the soil will be thoroughly mixed.

Before mixing the soil determine whether it is sufficiently moist. This may be told by taking a handful of the soil and pressing it firmly in the hand. If water can be squeezed out the soil is too damp, and ought not to be worked over until enough dry soil has been added to take up the surplus moisture.

If, after having been pressed in the hand, the soil remains together, but will break upon being lightly touched, it contains the proper amount of moisture. If it will not remain in a lump but breaks up immediately the pressure is released, it needs more water. Add it by means of a watering pot; the amount necessary can be judged better from experience than by any rules which may be laid down.

POTTING AND REPOTTING: The best time of year to repot house plants is in the spring (April or May), or when new growths start. Only in very exceptional cases do house plants need repotting during the winter; this is particularly true of palms, ferns, rubber plants, etc. These plants are then resting or are making very little growth, and meddling is positively dangerous to their lives. When a plant is resting it is unable to make a new root system rapidly, and so take hold of the new soil, so it may become sickly or die of shock.

To remove the plant from its pot, take the pot in the right hand and place the stem of the plant between the index and middle fingers of the left hand; then invert it and strike the edge of the pot sharply against the edge of the bench. The ball of earth and roots will slide out easily, unless the earth is dry; in that case, before attempting to remove the plant, immerse it in water until the earth has become damp.

Now, with the right hand, disentangle and spread out the lower half of the mass of roots. If part of the ball of earth crumbles away, it does not matter. Then place enough soil in the new pot to bring the plant in about the right position—that is, with the surface (which should be loosened up) of the old ball about half an inch to one inch, according to size, below the rim of the pot.

When removing palms, rubber plants and other comparatively large-rooted plants from the pots, the roots will be found matted together in circles. If possible, without injuring the roots, remove the old drainage. This will leave a large hole in the ball.

Before putting the plant in the new pot, fill up this hole with soil; otherwise it will allow the water to drain away too rapidly, and the interior of the ball becomes too dry. Sometimes the roots are so matted that it is impossible to remove the drainage.

Cuttings and seedlings are usually first potted up in thumb pots (two-inch), from which they are shifted to larger pots as soon as the pots have become filled with roots. The soil used in filling these small pots must be free from all lumps. The best way to pot these small plants is to hold the cutting with the left hand and with the right hand fill in the soil. When the pot is full, firm the soil with the thumbs and then give the pot a sharp rap on the bench to settle the soil. Or fill the pots with soil and then make a hole in the soil for the roots, after which the soil is firmed.

When potting plants in the fall which have been outdoors in the flower beds all summer, select only stocky, healthy plants.

Dig them carefully so as to secure as many roots as possible. If the soil is clayey, it must be neither so wet that it is muddy and the roots cling together, nor so dry that the dirt crumbles entirely away from them. The right condition of soil can be obtained by a thorough watering at least five hours before potting.

If the plants are growing in sandy soil, it is better to have it rather dry, for then more of the working roots can be saved than if it is wet.

After potting thoroughly water the plants and set them in a shaded place. Syringe the foliage several times a day until the roots have taken hold of the new soil; but under ordinary conditions, the soil will not again need watering until the new roots have been made. As soon as the plants have taken hold, gradually inure them to direct sunlight.

Potting is done best on a bench which is about waist high. For the window garden a portable affair will be found the most satisfactory. An old kitchen table on three sides of which some boards, about a foot wide, have been fastened to keep the soil from falling upon the floor will serve the purpose.

The best way to work the soil in among the roots is to hold the plant with the left hand, put a little soil around the roots, and work the plant up and down a little. Put in some more soil, and tamp it down with a potting stick. It is possible to get the soil too firm, so use the potting stick with moderation, and be careful not to strike the roots.

A potting stick is usually made from a piece of pine about a foot long, an inch wide, and an inch thick, with the corners and ends rounded off. A piece of a broom handle is sometimes used.

If the soil contains many lumps or coarse pieces of sod (as sometimes happens when the sod is not completely rotted), screen them out before potting. This will be necessary if the pots are small—six-inch and smaller—with larger pots it will make but little difference. Save the coarse material. It will be useful when potting.

In the bottom of each pot put some coarse drainage. Broken pots are usually used for this, but coal clinkers or stones are just as good. Broken charcoal is very good also. The larger sizes of pots—three-inch and up— need crocking; use from a quarter of an inch to two inches of drainage according to the size of the pot. If you use broken pots, put the pieces in with the convex side up; the crocks will fit better. Over this drainage put some of the coarse screenings to keep the finer soil from washing down through. If there are no coarse screenings, use sphagnum moss.

Any pot which seems to be in proportion to the plant, holding soil enough to keep it from being top-heavy, will be sufficiently large. A common mistake in the size of the pot is to use one a size or two too large. It is very easy to over-pot a plant, and

nothing in the plant's life can be more disastrous than an over-large pot. The plants will be over-watered and the soil become sour.

Pots may be obtained at almost any hardware store. Buy the heavier ones, as the very thin ones dry out too quickly. Soak new pots in water until they get through "bubbling"; otherwise, the soil of the newly potted plants will dry out too quickly. If the pots are old and green with algae, clean them by scrubbing them with sand and water, for the "green" makes them less porous, and old earth dried on the inside surface interferes with the new root-growth.

MULCHING: Plants may be mulched to prevent rapid drying from the surface, if desired. Sheet moss, commonly used to line hanging baskets, is recommended for the job.

Moss should be soaked 15 or 20 minutes in water before being placed on top of the soil. It will not pack down over the surface of the soil, but remains fluffy allowing sufficient aeration of the soil beneath. The moss is live, and will turn green and provide a growing cover for the soil. Water may be poured through it, or plants may be watered by plunging pots in a tub of water.

When used on African violets, gloxinias, or other flowers with succulent petioles the moss may be permitted to extend over the rim of the pot. This will prevent petiole-rot, which is a cause of high mortality among these flowers.

Plants may also be mulched with sphagnum or peat moss, though these are more likely to cause rot in certain soft plants than will live sheet moss.

RAISING PLANTS FROM SEEDS: Many of the best house plants can be raised from seed in the house where potted plants are grown in a window during winter.

Where only a few plants are to be started, unglazed pots or seedpans are often used, but "flats" are cheaper. To make these buy from a grocery store some soap boxes. A convenient size is 12 by 15 inches. Cut them into three-inch sections and nail bottoms on these, taking care to leave cracks between the boards or make four or five one-inch holes for drainage. The sides may be painted, if they are to be used in the house. These flats are better than pots both for starting the seed and pricking off, as they save care in watering, room, time, and trouble and the moisture in the soil is much more constant than in a small pot.

Over the holes or cracks in the flats put a one-half inch layer of broken potsherds, coal clinkers, or gravel for drainage. Then sieve part of the already mixed seed soil to get two lots of soil, one coarse the other fine. Spread a one-half inch layer of the coarse material over the drainage material that is already in the flat and on top of that fill the flat to within half an inch of the top with the fine, screened soil. Pack the soil in the corners and along the edges so it will not settle there more than in the middle. Watering then will not wash down the soil, uncovering and often taking the seed with it. Firm the whole by means of a damp brick or board.

Flats should be sterilized before sowing with a bath of boiling water, to cut loss from damping-off and fungus disease. Or they may be baked in the oven at 300° for one hour. In either case, the soil must be made moist, but not wet, before seeds are sown.

Make drills about two inches apart using a piece of narrow board as a marker, merely pressing it lightly into the soil for a quarter-inch or so. Sow the seeds thinly and evenly in the drills, and cover tightly; the best way to cover the seeds is to screen the soil on them, using a screen which has a mesh about the size of that in mosquito netting. A good rule to follow when covering seeds is to put on a layer of soil which is as deep as the diameter of the seeds. Sand, dry sphagnum, cocoanut fibre, or leaf mold which has

been rubbed through a fine screen, make very good coverings for seeds. They never get hard or bake, making an ideal covering—light, easily pushed through by the tender seed-shoots, and retentive of moisture.

Water the soil thoroughly after sowing. The best way is to set the flat in a large pan partly filled with water, allowing it to soak up from below. This is better than overhead watering because no matter how fine a spray is used it may wash the soil. Another way is to water through a sheet of blotting paper. Place the blotting paper on top of the seed bed and slowly apply the water, allowing it to soak through the paper. Drip is thus avoided.

Cover the box with a loose-fitting pane of glass to keep a more humid atmosphere, thus reducing evaporation from the soil. Every day remove the glass and wipe off any water of condensation which may be on it. Place the flat in a position where it will receive all the light possible, but shade it from the direct sunlight.

Pricking out is the first transplanting of the seedlings, and needs to be done tenderly. As a rule as soon as the seedlings have made their first two real leaves it is time to "prick out" into other flats, prepared similarly to the seed flat.

Do not try to take each single seedling from the seedbed. Take out a portion of soil which has a number of seedlings in it, lay it on its side and gently separate the soil.

The dibble is a very useful tool for this purpose. It is made from a small piece of wood one-fourth or three-eighths of an inch square, or round, and about four inches long. Make a tapering point—two inches long—on one end; the other should be drawn down to an edge. This latter will be very useful in separating the plants and firming the soil about the seedling when it has been set in the new soil.

Put the little plants in rows an inch or two apart, water thoroughly, and shade for several days from hot sun with newspapers. Do not water again until the surface begins to dry. Do not delay the pricking off. Do it just as soon as the little seedlings can be handled, for they may all be lost by "damping off," or they may become drawn. Should the seedlings begin to damp off apply some hot sand, sprinkling it on with a fine-meshed sieve.

As soon as the plants need still more room prick them out singly into thumb (two-inch) pots. When transplanting insert the plantlet a little deeper than it was in the old bed.

GIFT PLANTS: Because most gift plants got their start in life in the close-to-ideal environment of a greenhouse, they must be pampered more than plants raised from seed or cuttings in a house. The nearer greenhouse conditions they find in their new homes, the longer they will thrive.

Dry, over-heated rooms, for instance, are fatal. So are chilling drafts. The ideal place for most gift plants is in a large picture window or an enclosed, heated porch. In an apartment, the best choice is a window with morning or afternoon sun. It's generally quite a bit cooler near a window than in the rest of a room. And they must not be put anywhere near a radiator.

Here are the basic rules for maintaining Christmas poinsettias: give them constantly moist soil, a humid atmosphere, and a draft-free location. Any bright window, with no more than two hours of direct sun a day, will do. The temperature should range from a high of 65° during the day to no lower than 55 at night. It may need water daily.

After the blooms wither, reduce watering gradually until the plant is leafless. Then store it in a cool, dim place, such as a dry basement. In May, when all danger of frost is past, cut the stems back to four inches and repot in fresh, humusy soil. One part each of loam, sand and compost is best. Set it in the ground in a semi-

shaded spot for the summer. Cuttings taken in June, by the way, will root in two weeks and can be potted up then.

By late August, the poinsettia will be very luxuriant, so cut back the stems by one-third and pinch some out so that only a few stout ones will develop. Bring it into the house before frost, water abundantly—twice a day if necessary—and feed with weak manure tea. It needs plenty of sun at this time to form the bracts or flowers.

If the bracts don't start turning red (or white, if you have that variety) by early December, start keeping the plant in complete darkness for 14 to 16 hours out of every 24. It can be covered with a black hood for these hours to simulate the natural outdoor conditions. Some experts recommend doing this as early as late October to insure bloom by Christmas.

The popular Christmas cactus is very easy to make into a permanent member of a window garden collection. It will bloom every year from December into February. Any bright window sill is fine, and it is especially pretty in hanging baskets. One caution: the Christmas cactus needs more water than other cacti, but still far less than the majority of house plants.

Cyclamen likes to be kept cool and fairly moist. Feed it every two weeks when in bloom with dilute liquid manure, and give it a couple of hours sun a day. The temperature should range from 60° during the day to 45° at night.

After bloom, let cyclamen rest in a cool, dark place, watering sparingly. Then repot it into a larger pot, using a mixture of equal parts loam, leaf mold, sand and compost or well rotted manure. Put it in a sheltered spot outdoors for the summer. It must come indoors again before frost. The lovely blooms will appear in December and last into March or even April if the plant is kept healthy and vigorous.

Azaleas prefer the same temperature

range, light and moisture conditions as cyclamen. Remove faded blooms daily. Repot azaleas every two or three years immediately after blooming, using acid compost in the soil mixture. When bloom stops, continue watering until late spring, then sink the pots outdoors in partial shade. They can be brought indoors in late September and may bloom for Christmas. Some varieties, however, are best planted permanently in the garden, where they will bloom every spring.

It is difficult to keep over a Christmas begonia. But other varieties, like the Chatelaine, will last from year to year with good light, moderate watering and temperatures from 55 to 60°. The Chatelaine begonia should be planted outdoors in late spring in a fairly open spot. It will bloom there all summer and may be lifted and potted again in September.

The primroses florists bring into bloom for Christmas need bright light, 40 to 65°, and moist conditions. They benefit from bi-weekly liquid manure feedings. If these needs are met, they will bloom until May or later. But they will not keep for another year.

Christmas cherries and peppers are very fussy plants. They lose their fruits rapidly if not given a sunny but cool location, a humid atmosphere and complete freedom from drafts. Heather, too, needs a cool spot and won't last unless kept in a window or porch that is as light as a greenhouse.

The pretty kalanchoe, on the other hand, is wonderfully easy to keep for years. Now a favorite gift plant, this bushy little succulent rewards with long-lasting clusters of salmon-red flowers if given a sunny window, fresh air without drafts, and moderate watering.

Combination pots or dish gardens containing small-leaved ivies, peperomia and cacti may be kept in their original containers for perhaps two weeks, watering sparingly because of the poor or non-existent drainage. Then dismantle them and pot up the plants singly. Some of them may grow into beautiful specimens giving years of pleasure. Dilute fertilizer, plus occasional spraying of their foliage with clear water, will help get them settled comfortably in their new environment.

Certain of the spectacularly beautiful gift plants, such as paper white and *Soliel d'or narcissuses*, Roman hyacinths and lily-of-the-valley, must be discarded after bloom. Others— some of which are sold as Easter and Mother's Day plants — can become permanent indoor or outdoor garden guests. Gardenias of the *veitchi* type, for example, will flower for weeks if the night temperature is kept around 60°. Spray the foliage daily with water. These can spend the summer sunk outdoors. Gardenias should be repotted in spring, pruned lightly if necessary, and kept in a very moist atmosphere.

Hydrangeas, forced hardy narcissuses and daffodils, hardy hyacinths and Easter lilies may be kept for planting in the garden. They are not suitable for indoor growing again. To help the hardy bulbs do well outdoors, let them keep their foliage until it dies off naturally. The Easter lilies will usually bloom again in the garden in autumn, but hard winters will kill them off.

Some of the newly popular gift plants are the red-berried ardisia, Otaheite orange, Ponderosa lemon and the berried pyracantha. All of these are quite easy to handle, long-lasting and make fine tenants for a window garden.

ENEMIES: Perhaps the greatest enemy of plants grown in houses heated by hot air furnaces or coal stoves is coal gas. An otherwise imperceptible trace of it in the air will cause the leaves of some plants (as Jerusalem cherry) to drop off promptly. With a good chimney draught and with proper regulation of the dampers when attending to the fire there should be no trouble from this source.

Illuminating gas is almost as bad as coal gas. The slightest trace will retard the development of new leaves on all but the toughest-textured plants, like rubbers and palms. Such thin-leaved plants as geranium, coleus, heliotrope, and begonia succumb quickly. When gas is present in very small quantity the plants do not necessarily die but growth is stunted and the flower buds wither when beginning to show color, looking much as though they had been chilled.

The commonest insect enemies of house plants are plant lice or aphids. Look for these pests on the under side of the leaves where they suck the sap. Against them use tobacco water or soap suds. Tobacco water can be made from tobacco "stems" which can be bought from almost any florist or seedsman. Put a large handful into a gallon of warm water and let it stand for 24 hours, then dilute it to the color of weak tea and syringe the foliage, being careful to hit the under side of the leaves. A simpler way is to buy a tobacco extract and follow the directions on the package.

If soap suds are used, rinse the plants with clear water afterward.

An aphid sometimes attacks the roots, causing the plants to take on a sickly or yellow color. It is easily found by digging down near the base of the stem, and is attacked by watering with the tobacco water already described. If this does not kill the aphids the plant must be removed from the soil, the roots washed with whale-oil soap (one-quarter pound to two gallons of water). Then rinse and re-pot in fresh, clean soil.

Next to the aphids in destructiveness is the red spider, a very small red mite which can scarcely be seen by the naked eye. It lives on the under side of the leaves, but its presence can be readily discovered by numerous minute yellow spots on the upper side. Like the aphid, the red spider subsists on the plant's juices. It thrives in a hot, dry atmosphere, and its presence is a sure sign of insufficient moisture. The conditions ordinarily found in living rooms are very favorable for this pest. The remedy is obvious: syringe the plants with water, applying it on the under side of the leaves, and with considerable force because the spider is protected behind a web.

Mealy bug, which is almost always present in the greenhouse, sometimes infests house plants, too. This insect looks like a small tuft of white cotton, and is found on the under side of the leaves and in the joints. A strong stream of water will usually wash it off, but if that fails use kerosene emulsion or fir tree oil, which must be diluted according to the directions on the package, and applied as a spray or with a feather. Alcohol has also been successfully used when there are only a few mealy bugs. With a feather or small stick put one drop on each bug, and he will immediately succumb.

Very often scale insects will be found on the leaves of palms, ferns, rubber plants and cycads. The commonest one is the brown scale. It is one-quarter to three-eighths of an inch long, and nearly as wide, and its hard, convexed shell is dark brown in color. The other scale commonly found on greenhouse plants is white, and about the size of the head of a pin.

Both these scales can be removed easily by spraying with whale oil soap, kerosene emulsion, or fir tree oil.

Sometimes plants are infected with thrips, which eat the epidermis of the leaves. They are small, slender, brown or black insects, about one-quarter of an inch long, and are easily controlled by any of the remedies already mentioned.

Here are some general rules for protecting house plants from insects: Each month dust plants with a soft cloth, as dust cuts down on light that the plants receive. Clean leaves with warm water also, supporting leaves from bottom as you work. Bathing leaves in warm, soapy water is effective in protecting plants from red spiders and mealy bugs. Make a regular practice of turning the leaves over and checking underneath, since that's where most insects do their work.

PLANTS AS DECORATION: House plants may serve as decoration in a room when the window in which they grow best is in that room. Or they may be grown in a window of a little-used room and moved into other positions in the house when their flowers or foliage are at their best, as spot decoration. After flowers or foliage fade, or when another plant in the plant window surpasses the one being used for decoration, the first plant is returned to the plant window for its share of sun and moisture. While the decorative plant is being given its honored place in a living room it may suffer from dryness of the air. Daily spraying of the foliage, or a saucer of moist gravel under the pot, will help it to survive.

FLOWERING PLANTS: Begonias are one of the easiest house plants to raise and to bring into bloom. Most universally successful is *B. semperflorens*, in the single varieties. The doubles are attractive, but not so easily raised. Grown in sun, begonias bloom freely through most of the year. If they do not receive sun they will thrive, but as foliage plants. Propagation is by cuttings rooted in sand. They should be pinched back when three inches tall.

African violets respond well to organic culture when they are given a light window where direct sun is slightly screened, as through a curtain. They need plenty of water, and a moist atmosphere. They are propagated by rooted leaf cuttings, and bloom six to eight months after propagation.

Geraniums will flower well indoors only when they receive plenty of sun. During the shortest days, or during a cloudy winter, they will not bloom at all. Some varieties are grown for their spicy scented foliage. Winter plants are grown from cuttings made in the garden in June. All buds should be pinched back to promote winter bloom. Geraniums do best if pot-bound, kept cool and somewhat dry.

Primroses will bloom all winter if they are kept in sun, moderately cool, and are never allowed to dry out. They are propagated by seed which must be planted in a cool place, and will take several weeks to germinate. Seed is very fine and must be kept moist. This is most easily done by covering the seedpan with a pane of glass, which must be removed as soon as germination has taken place.

Cyclamen, a member of the primrose family, *primulaceae*, will bloom for about three months during the winter in a cool corner of the window where it is protected from direct rays of the sun. Watering should be done carefully to avoid wetting the heart of the plant or the foliage. Manure water should be given every two weeks. When leaves begin to turn yellow and new leaves cease to appear, the growing season is over, and the plant will rest. All water should be withheld until the leaves and stalks die and can be removed from the corm. The pot may then be removed to a cool cellar, where it is watered only about once in two or three weeks. It should be placed in the garden in May, and repotted after new leaves have appeared in August. It should be returned to the window by mid-September and given weekly feedings until it begins to bloom.

Fan iris or apostle plant, *Marica northiana*, bears three to four inch flowers midway along leaf-like flower stalks late in winter. Given plenty of water and sun, it will adapt to any temperature. Embryo plants appear after flowers have faded on the flower stalks, and may be picked off and rooted. Parent plant should be repotted in spring.

Azaleas will bloom in a window with partial sun if kept constantly moist and watered daily throughout the year. When repotting is necessary, only very acid soil and humus should be used. Well-rotted manure and bone meal may be sprinkled over the top of the soil for additional feeding. Foliage should be sprayed often. Pot may be sunk in the garden during the summer, but should never be allowed to dry out. Propagation is difficult, but is accomplished by rooting cuttings.

Shrimp plant, *Beloperone guttata*, takes its name from its shrimp-pink terminal bracts which resemble cooked shrimp. The bracts enclose inconspicuous white flowers. Shrimp plant needs full sun, plenty of water, and frequent feeding. Leggy tendencies may be controlled if side shoots are pinched back. Plant may be removed from pot to summer in the garden. Cuttings are made early for following winter's plants. If original plant is repotted, it should be cut back to five inches.

Many flowering annuals may be potted in the fall to continue their bloom in the house. Among them are marigolds, torenia, heliotrope and clarkia. Other flowering plants recommended for window gardens are the bromeliads, autumn crocus, euphorbia, kalanchoe, lantana, oxalis, patience, sweet olive, flowering maple, and roses. Flowering vines which may be grown indoors include passion flower, cup-and-saucer vine, flowering jasmine, wax plant, rosary vine, plumbago, and some of the annual garden vines, such as morning glory, nasturtium and petunias.

Foliage Plants: *Philodendron cordatum* and English ivy are hardy foliage plants which may be grown in the sun, in partial shade, or without sun at all. Both philodendron and ivy are now available in many other varieties, some climbing and some erect.

Philodendron in non-climbing species used for decoration in modern interiors include *P. bipinnatifidum,* with feathery foliage; *P. wendlandi,* with shiny oblong leaves; *P. undulatum* with wavy erect heart-shaped leaves;

P. selloum, with deeply cut foliage. All should be kept moderately moist, and foliage sprayed or sponged to keep it dust-free. Acid soil should be used for repotting.

Similar to philodendron in its response to neglect in the house is nephthytis, which may be kept in any window, with or without sun. The large, variegated, arrow shaped leaves should be kept clean by sponging or spraying. Nephthytis may be summered in the garden.

Dracaenas belong to the lily family, but are grown indoors for their ornamental, often variegated long narrow leaves. To keep their leaf markings, they must be kept in at least part sun, and they grow best when kept warm and well watered. An acid soil should be used for repotting.

Chinese evergreen, *Aglaonema commutatum,* with its shiny pointed leaves arising from a central stem, may be grown anywhere in the house, from the window to the coffee table. It may be grown in water, but is more prosperous in soil. If grown in water, the water should be changed often, and may be kept sweet with a piece of charcoal. Propagation is by means of cuttings.

Varieties of coleus are among the most colorful of foliage plants, but must be kept in the sun to keep their color. Culture is very easy, and propagation is accomplished through cuttings, which root quickly in any potting mixture.

Ferns require a moist atmosphere and weak sunlight for best growth. Varieties which may be grown indoors include bird's nest fern, *Asplenium nidus;* Boston fern, *Nephrolepis exaltata bostoniensis;* gold fern, Pityrogramma chrysophylla; hare's foot fern, *Polypodium Aureum Mandaianum;* maidenhair, *Adiantum cuneatum;* and staghorn fern, *Platycerium alcicorne.*

Summer Care: When the sun first becomes warm, plants must be moved from their customary windows either back into the room, or into another window, where they receive less sunlight. An east or west window in summer is equal in sunlight, to a south window in winter while a north window in summer is equivalent in sunshine to an east or west window in winter.

Give the plants plenty of fresh air, but keep them out of drafts. Plants dry out more quickly in summer and require more frequent watering. A mulch of grass clippings, peat moss, leaves, hay or buckwheat hulls will help keep moisture in the soil and the roots cool.

Very few house plants can take the full sun of a south window in summer. If you cannot move them, a shade or tinted glass curtain will give some protection from burning. The following plants will grow in such a window, or better still (in summer) in an east or west location:

African violet	patience plant
amaryllis	pothos
artillery plant	prayer plant
asparagus fern	screw pine
begonia	geranium
caladium	lantana
Christmas cactus	oxalis
coleus	shrimp plant
coral berry	strawberry begonia
corn plant	succulents
croton	sweet olive
crown-of-thorns	wandering Jew
grape ivy	wax begonia
flowering maple	wax plant

Some plants do not need sun in order to live and thrive. A north window or even a location near the source of light will do. From such a list as the following we can draw favorites for a cooling mass of green to decorate our summer living quarters:

African evergreen	ivy
Apostle plant	jade plant
cast-iron plant	philodendron
Chinese evergreen	pick-a-back plant
dumb cane	snake plant
ferns	spider plant
fig family	Swiss cheese plant
	watermelon begonia

MOVING OUTDOORS: Indoor plants are too tender to be placed out in the garden until all danger of frost is past, and a few very delicate ones should, even then, go no farther than a sheltered porch. But the majority of them will enjoy being out. First, select a sheltered place, receiving only filtered sunlight or perhaps just early morning sun. This spot may be under a low, spreading bush, or in the lee of a hedge, or perhaps between bushes close to the house.

If the ground is hard, dig it over and incorporate into it some compost, removing all grass, weeds and large roots as you work it. It is sometimes recommended that the plunge-bed be dug out to a depth greater than that of the tallest pot, and a layer of cinders or gravel be placed in the bottom for drainage. Unless drainage is a real problem in your area, this is not necessary.

Be sure that the plunge-bed is well-protected from children and dogs. A few small barberry bushes set in front of it, or a low picket fence will usually suffice. Even a few lengths of cord strung between stakes may be enough to deflect the "traffic" from your prized plants. If your section of the country is apt to have summer hail storms or extremely heavy rains, it is wise to guard against possible damage from these by making a cloth-covered frame to set over the plants on stakes when necessary.

Before placing the plants, knock them out of their pots to see if they are root-bound. Plants "on vacation" will grow at a great rate, and will derive the most benefit from their summer out if they have ample root room. Repot those that need it in a mixture of sand, humus or leaf mold, and compost. Water thoroughly and keep sheltered for a day or two before setting out.

When placing the plants, put them into the soil up to the pot rims. Then mulch thoroughly around each plant and between the pots with dried grass-clippings, until nothing can be seen but the plant tops. The grass-clippings will conserve moisture and, as they break down, will add nutrients to the soil. During the summer, replenish the mulch as necessary. Even with such a mulch, it is doubtful that the normal rainfall will be adequate for your potted plants, so check them at intervals to determine their need for an extra soaking.

HERBS: A sunny kitchen window sill may contain pots of herbs which are used in cookery throughout the winter. Most herbs are very hardy, and like fresh air directly from the outside on warm winter days, but at night they should be protected from cold drafts through window chinks. Most herbs are best in glazed pots or metal containers. Tops should be sprayed often in room-temperature water. Generally, leaves should be used from the outside, to encourage bushy growth.

Herbs may be potted and brought in from the garden in the fall. Seed of the annual varieties may be sown indoors and started directly in the window.

Especially recommended for window gardens are parsley, chives, basil, summer savory and rosemary. Perennial herbs which may be brought in from the garden include sage, thyme and mints.

See also FLUORESCENT LIGHT; FOLIAGE PLANTS; FLOWER GARDENING; BULB, FORCING.

HOWARD EXPERIMENTAL CYLINDERS:
Sixteen experimental plots, each exactly 1/1000th of an acre. The Howard Experimental Cylinders were built under the auspices of the Soil and Health Foundation in 1950, and experiments have been conducted each year, comparing different fertilizing and mulching methods. The cylinders are located at the Organic Experiment Farm in Allentown, Pennsylvania. *See also* ORGANIC METHOD, HISTORY OF.

HOWARD, SIR ALBERT: Sir Albert Howard, the first pioneer of organic

methods, was the greatest general in its campaigns. Although he was not the earliest critic of the ills of modern agriculture, he was the first to offer a remedy. His genius lay in his constructive approach. He saw the solution to the problem in the thorough study and application of the methods evolved by nature over the earth's lifespan.

Sir Albert Howard, son of a Shropshire farmer, worked in the West Indies, Africa and India. He drew conclusions from on-the-spot observation.

The most fruitful phase of Sir Albert's work is the period spent in India. His exacting scientific research there stands as his monument.

Albert Howard (knighthood was not conferred until later in England) came to India in 1905. He had already achieved recognition for work in the West Indies on sugar cane, hops and cacao. With him came his first wife, Gabrielle. Together they made a remarkable team: he had an "instinctive awareness of the importance of natural principles," and she "an enormous capacity for patient detail." *The London Times* paid tribute to their partnership by saying that "seldom in the sphere of economic investigation has there been a more fruitful collaboration between husband and wife."

Nearly 30 years were spent in India, years of the most painstaking research and slow building up of fact. In all their work, the Howards never lost sight of one fundamental principle: agricultural research must seek to solve the problems of both the land and the people. Their investigations were always practical, always keyed to an overall picture that gradually evolved into a *system* of farming. Sir Albert's most biting criticism was directed against "fragmentation"—the unnatural separation between the soil, crops, livestock and humans. He believed these all to be part of a natural complex, and research on each one without reference to the others was highly dangerous. In fact, he believed the dependence on chemical fertilizers, insecticides and drugs for human ills was directly caused by this fragmentation.

This was a novel approach. Abstract research, technical, hard to apply and generally confusing to the average farmer, was the order of the day. Sir Albert, however, had faith in the innate wisdom of the peasant and strove for a sincere relationship between experimenter and farmer. Only when an improvement was thoroughly integrated and adapted to the tools and ability of the Indian farmer did he release his findings.

India was probably the finest testing ground he could have for his ideas. The rigorous climate exacts a terrific toll on faulty practices, and thus was far more instructive than work in temperate climes.

Despite the low yields, Sir Albert found many commendable practices, particularly in the field of fertility maintenance. Rotations were widely used, wheat being grown with barley, peas, mustard, rape and linseed, and with some leguminous weeds which had enabled Punjab farmers to grow wheat continuously for centuries with no manure.

Some 12 years were spent in the breeding of wheats, during which time the very significant problem of plant disease arose. Indian wheats, even the new varieties the Howards developed, were very susceptible to rusts. Sir Albert soon saw that poor tilth, water-logging, packing and surface crusting went along with the disease, and he embarked on a long and fruitful study of soil aeration. To better control the terrific monsoon rains, he developed a system of contouring and terracing for the fields, but the real answer, he found, lay in using native deep-rooted plants to let air into the soil.

This led him to his first conclusions on soil fertilization. Sufficient air in the soil, he discovered, let its myriad organisms work to release plant foods like the nitrogen supplied by the green manures. Therefore the purchase of nitrates and phosphates was unnecessary, natural forces doing the job much better.

This was his first clue to the value of the soil's microbial life. Thereafter in all his work, with tobacco, fruits, fodder crops, vegetables and the rest, he followed up his theory that organic matter, the prime raw material with which these organisms worked, was the most important factor in crop success. A soil well supplied with organic matter, it became apparent over many years' experiments, grew bigger yields of healthier crops; these crops in turn were more attractive to animals and gave them outstanding health.

This, of course, is only the broadest outline of the evolvement of Sir Albert's system. Hundreds of acute observations, backed up by thousands of field trials, went into this work. Only the most open-minded investigator, one who was willing at all times to regard Nature as an infallible teacher, could have accomplished it. In this lies Sir Albert's greatness.

More than anything else, his personality led him to success. He could be, when necessary, an awe-inspiring antagonist. Appointed to the Botanical Section of the then new Pusa experiment station, he found no land appropriated for his work. He was deputed to work with plants, not with the soil, so his superiors considered only a laboratory necessary! His long fight for 75 acres for his experiments was characterized by a fierce obstinacy and an "amiable brutality" that came to be known and feared by many in officialdom.

On the other hand, his great honesty, cheerfulness and sincerity opened many doors to him. In the words of his widow, "It was because he was honest enough and humble-minded enough to note what the Bihar peasants were doing, what the Baluchistan tribesmen grew and how they grew it, because he loved talking to West Indian planters and Kentish hop growers, that all who cultivated the earth's surface, of whatever calibre or education or station, became his instructors; he was able to learn from all because he wanted to learn from all." More, he had great "respect for the empiric knowledge of cultivation methods accumulated in the course of several thousand years of tradition and experience."

That this marriage of Eastern wisdom and Western science would lead to an entirely new concept of agriculture the Howards were too busy even to suspect for a long time. Like much of their work, their earliest project, improving the Indian wheats, had to be started at the very bottom. They found practically no work had been done in classifying the myriad varieties of tropical crops. Plant breeding thus became the first consideration.

But Sir Albert was not content with this. He gave himself the added, unassigned task of growing all the crops to be studied on a field scale. The world is fortunate that he did so. The practical difficulties of cultivation brought up every crop-growing problem from drainage to disease to fertilization.

Here the Howards were breaking entirely new ground. Their work on irrigation alone was monumental. They developed a system of field contouring and drainage, all to be done by hand labor, that proved of enormous value to Indian farmers.

This led them directly into the question of poor soil aeration, a leading cause of low yields in tropic climes. From these studies their theory of soil conditions and disease resistance was formed. And by 1912, they were deep into a study of green manuring, which paved the way to the investigations of soil fertility. Each new problem they attacked led them to another. Most of this work was pioneering; their studies of root systems, for instance, were an entirely new idea. Up to that time, agricultural botanists had studied only the flowers, fruit and foliage of a plant, ignoring the roots. Sir Albert spent ten years, using equipment he made himself, examining the roots of several fruit trees as deep as 40 feet below ground.

This integration of research and the results it produced have had, and are still having, a profound effect. It led to a revolution in agricultural experimentation. The research station which Sir Albert later designed and built at Indore has become a model for present-day stations everywhere. He brought to agriculture a fresh outlook, saving it from the increasing stagnation that threatened to leave an ever-growing world population with ever-decreasing food resources. And the new—and yet old—system of farming he developed has proven universally valid, as farmers everywhere are finding today.

Following his return to England, he devoted the remainder of his life to perfecting and publicizing his ideas of good agriculture. All his life's work had shown him irrefutably that the only real basis of fertility was the return of all wastes to the soil; more, that plant, animal and human health were directly dependent on this waste return.

These were the qualities of Sir Albert Howard, founder of organics: a wholesale curiosity, allied with the most penetrating observation. A marvelous alertness of mind that saved him from the mental rigidity so prevalent among many of his colleagues. His shrewd insight led him to understand the qualities producing health in a plant from studying diseased plants, and his great store of common sense made him the champion of the despised earthworm. He unmercifully criticized contemporary research, but he also had a reserve of humility that made him prepared to learn from his failures. He was, in short, a kindly man, of huge intelligence and endowed with a capacity for work that was matched only by his willingness to learn from nature.

BIOGRAPHICAL SUMMARY: Born 8th December 1873, at Bishop's Castle, Shropshire, son of Richard Howard, farmer, and Ann Howard, nee Kilvert; died 20th October 1947 at Blackheath, London, S.E. Educated Wrekin College, Royal College of Science, South Kensington, and as Foundation Scholar, St. John's College, Cambridge.

Married, 1905, Gabrielle Louise Caroline Matthaei; 1931, Louise Ernestine Matthaei.

1896, 1897, First Class Natural Sciences Tripos, Cambridge, first in England, Cambridge Diploma of Agriculture, second in England, National Diploma of Agriculture; 1899, Lecturer in Agricultural Science, Harrison College, Barbados; 1899-1902, Mycologist and Agricultural Lecturer, Imperial Department of Agriculture for the West Indies; 1903-5, Botanist to the South-Eastern Agricultural College, Wye; 1905-24, Imperial Economic Botanist to the Government of India; 1914, created Companion of the Indian Empire (C.I.E.); 1920,

Silver Medal of the Royal Society of Arts; 1924-31, Director of the Institute of Plant Industry, Indore, and Agricultural Adviser to States in Central India and Rajputana; 1928, Fellow of the Royal Asiatic Society of Bengal; 1930, Barclay Memorial Medal of that Society; 1934, knighted; 1935, Hon. Fellow of the Imperial College of Science. *See also* ORGANIC METHOD, HISTORY OF.

HOW TO HAVE A GREEN THUMB WITHOUT AN ACHING BACK, by Ruth Stout. *See* BOOKS FOR ORGANIC GARDENERS AND FARMERS

HUBBARD SQUASH: *see* SQUASH

HUCKLEBERRY: (*Gaylussacia*) Frequently mistaken for the blueberry, huckleberry shrubs include both fruit-bearing as well as ornamental evergreen ones. Its fruit is generally considered not as tasty as that of the blueberry. High-bush or black huckleberry (*G. baccata*) is hardy throughout most of the United States, grows to about three feet high. Juniper orberry (*G. brachycera*), also known as box-huckleberry, is a low-growing evergreen, reaching about one and one-half feet, producing white or pink flowers. Dangleberry (*G. frondosa*) often grows to six feet, is a spreading type bush. Most huckleberries prefer a location which gives partial shade. Its culture is similar to that required for blueberries. *See also* BLUEBERRIES.

HULLS: Hulls are rich in potash and can be used for either mulches or compost. They decay readily and may even be spaded into the ground directly before the rainy season. Whether you prefer to apply the material in compost or as mulch will depend on the site of your garden. If it is dry, apt to bake, and lacks water-retentiveness, it may be wise to use the hulls for mulches. Hulls of rice, cottonseed, buckwheat, cocoa bean and oats are ones often used.

HUMIFICATION: *see* HUMUS

HUMUS: Humus is organic matter which is in a more advanced stage of decomposition than compost in its early stages. In a compost heap, some of the organic matter has turned to humus, but the remaining fraction will complete the decomposition process after it has been placed in the soil. Organic matter in the soil, in the early stages of decomposition, cannot be called humus. It must still be called organic matter. The process in which organic matter turns to humus is called *humification*.

The nature of humus will be more clearly understood by treating each of its defined, component parts in separate detail.

The great noticeable difference between humus and organic matter is that the latter is rough looking material, such as coarse plant matter, while in the humus form we find something that has turned into a more uniform looking substance. Humus, in scientific terminology, is called an amorphous substance, or something which is of no determinate shape. It is of no specified character. It is not organized. It has no regular or uniform internal structure. The word *amorphous* means more than merely being a fine material, not fibrous in texture.

Humus does not have any definite structure compared with ordinary substances which may have definite shape and size of particles and which have a specific make-up for each type of substance. The chemists call these substances *crystalline*. An example is common table salt, sodium chloride. It always has the same crystalline structure no matter where you may find it. A diamond is another example of a crystalline substance, made up of crystals.

Humus takes in a vast mixture of compounds, most of which are unknown in formula, broken down to a fine state, and its structure is not definite or uniform.

COLLOIDAL QUALITY: Humus to a certain extent is colloidal. For all practical purposes something is colloidal when it is in an extremely fine condition. But in more scientific terms the colloidal state of matter refers to substances which are in a state of subdivision which lies in a zone between the molecular and the microscopic size.

By definition, a colloid is: "A substance, ordinarily regarded as insoluble, in the form of particles so small as to be indistinguishable to the eye, which remain suspended indefinitely in a suitable medium." Colloidal particles are considered to be between one and 100 millimicrons in size.

Examples of colloidal matter are homogenized milk in which the butterfat is in the colloidal state, and silt, a component of soil, which is in a colloidal state. In this state, matter behaves entirely differently than when in the larger aggregates.

All portions of humus may not be colloidal. Dr. Selman Waksman, in his book *Humus* says that colloidal particles in humus "probably give rise to electrochemical phenomena through which the nutritive elements present in insoluble forms in soil are solubilized and rendered available to plants."

Note that in the dictionary definition a colloid is referred to as a substance which is ordinarily regarded as insoluble, but that Waksman indicates that the colloidal particles in humus, have an effect on nutrients present in the soil that transforms them into soluble substances.

By solubility is meant the ability of a substance to dissolve totally in water. Table salt and sugar are common examples of soluble substances. A chemical fertilizer is in a soluble form, which means it is "available" to the plant immediately through its roots. A plant feeds from the soil's solution, although some of its food supply comes from the air through the activity of soil organisms. Organic matter is said to be insoluble, but actual results show that as soon as it begins to decompose, a process takes place which brings nutrients into the plant's roots.

In review of the factors in the definition of humus covered thus far, we can say that humus is an amorphous, partly colloidal substance.

MIXED CHARACTER: Humus is a heterogeneous complex or aggregate which represents a mixture of a large number of different compounds. The word heterogeneous means *opposite* or *unlike in character, quality or structure*. It is the opposite of the word *homogeneous* which means uniform, or composed of similar parts. In other words humus is both *heterogeneous* and *amorphous*. Referring back to the definition of the word *amorphous*, it is something of no determinate shape. It must be of no specified kind of character and must not be organized. It must have no regular or uniform internal structure.

Humus is complex in its makeup. You can understand it more readily if we bring a substance like table salt into the discussion. This is a crystalline, non-amorphous substance. Table salt always has the same simple formula— namely sodium chloride, which means one part sodium and one part chlorine. But in humus there is a total lack of uniformity. It is truly a heterogeneous substance, and depends on the kind of materials out of which it is formed. And in this respect we must bear in mind that humus comes not only from the remains of plants or animal matter, but also from the dead bodies of the soil microorganisms — the bacteria, fungi, etc., that took part in its decomposition.

Although humus is extremely variable and heterogeneous, it has its own definitely defined characteristics which differ widely from other natural organic substances. It varies according to how the organic matter of which it is composed originated.

Modern research has shown that the following compounds, among others, may be found in humus:

Acrylic acid, acrotonic acid, a-mono-hydroxy-stearic acid, benzoic acid, agroceric acid, oxalic acid, succinic acid, lignoceric acid, humoceric acid, paraffinic acid, saccharic acid, di-hydroxy-stearic acid, resin acids, meta-oxytoluic acid, para-hydroxybenzoic acid, the aldehydes such as vanillin, tri-thiobenzaldehyde, salicylic aldehyde, etc. These are all known as organic compounds, consisting for the most part of variable amounts of carbon, hydrogen, oxygen, and sometimes nitrogen.

Let us examine the make-up of a few of the compounds mentioned above:

Acrylic Acid $= CH_2\ CH\ COOH$
Benzoic Acid $= C_6H_5\ COOH$
Oxalic Acid $= (COOH)_2 \cdot 2\ H_2O$
Succinic Acid $= COOH\ (CH_2)_2\ COOH$
Paraffinic Acid $= CH_3\ (CH_2)_{22}\ COOH$
Saccharic Acid $= COOH\ (CHOH)_4\ COOH$
    C stands for carbon
    H stands for hydrogen
    O stands for oxygen

These are all organic compounds which are in the carbohydrate group. Compounds which contain only carbon, oxygen and hydrogen are called carbohydrates. There are other organic compounds in humus, consisting of nitrogen, phosphorus and sulfur, in addition to carbon, hydrogen and oxygen, and these are usually proteins. The phosphorus and sulfur in them are minerals. But, although the carbohydrates in humus are not made up of minerals, and the proteins contain only the minerals phosphorus and sulfur, humus is never dissociated from minerals. Little is known about exactly how the minerals are interlocked with the organic compounds in humus, but there is evidence to show that each does not exist by itself in chemical purity. The following analysis appears in the book, *Green Manuring Principles and Practice,* by Adrian J. Pieters:

Carbon	44.12%
Hydrogen	6.00%
Oxygen	35.16%
Nitrogen	8.12%
Ash	6.60%
	100.00%

The ash, which results upon the burning out of the organic matter, consists of minerals—elements such as calcium, phosphorus, boron, zinc, magnesium, manganese, etc.

The analysis would tend to show that humus contains minerals. While they can isolate acids from the humus, the total humus is made up of both organic and inorganic compounds.

The term organic matter is a misnomer, in the strict sense. Corn cobs, pea vine residues, sawdust, etc., although referred to as organic matter, contain also inorganic matter. One would imagine that a pure product would result, that one would have a clear line of demarcation between organic and inorganic matter when the organic matter is finally refined into humus. But that does not happen. In nature, evidently, organic is never separated from inorganic. One needs the other, and is so saturated with the other that it takes the best skills of the chemist to separate them.

Millar and Turk state in their book *Fundamentals of Soil Science:* "Although humus is considered organic, it probably contains various inorganic elements which are an integral part of the complex."

The ash of humus consists of major and minor elements. If we remove such major ones as calcium, phosphorus, potash, iron, sulfur, we will find only the very tiniest fraction left—the trace mineral elements—the manganese, the zinc, copper, iodine, tungsten, molybdenum, etc. But we know how important each and every one is, even though it must be present in only two or three parts per million of matter. For example, if there is a manganese deficiency, and not much is required, tomato and bean plants will be dwarfed. A lack of zinc will produce mottled leaves on citrus trees. A want of copper will lower the sugar content of beets.

In review therefore, thus far, we find that humus is

1. an amorphous substance

2. some of which is colloidal

3. and is of heterogeneous, or complex make-up.

ORIGIN OF HUMUS: Humus consists of compounds that are of plant, animal or microbial origin. The source material out of which humus is synthesized is organic matter.

The process of decomposition from organic matter to humus is one of microbial and chemical action. The microbial process may be referred to as a biological one and includes action of bacteria, fungi, yeasts, algae, actinomycetes, protozoa, enzymes. The chemical action comprises hydrolysis: (a chemical reaction produced by decomposition of a compound, its elements taking up those of water), oxidation and reduction: (separating of an element from other elements combined with it). In this process, simple compounds are formed which can function directly or indirectly as nutrients. In organic matter, before its decomposition, there is nothing that can feed a plant.

The humus eventually becomes oxidized to carbonic acid, water, nitric acid and other simple substances serving as food for plants.

In the process of humification, the substances are undergoing decomposition, but true humus consists of those portions of the original organic matter which is resistant to further decomposition.

THE COLOR OF HUMUS: Humus is a dark substance, colored brown to black, and is the material that usually gives the soil its rich dark color. You never see light colored humus.

The chemical explanation is that in the plant and in the animal the chemical compounds are very complicated but as the matter turns to humus, these compounds resolve themselves into simpler ones. It is from the colors of these simple compounds that the ultimate darkness of humus is achieved. The extent of the color is in proportion to the extent of the decomposition, and the resulting extent of the exposure, so to speak, of these simpler compounds with their characteristic colors. The longer the decomposition, usually the darker the color.

A widely prevalent fallacy about the darkness of humus is that it is due to the presence of a large amount of carbon. Since coal is black and it contains a large amount of carbon, one jumps to the conclusion that carbon is always black. Actually, carbon has a wide range of colors. For example diamonds are pure carbon and can be yellow, blue, green, pink, etc. Carbon in the air is colorless.

The process of darkening in the gradual transposition of organic matter to humus can be illustrated by the manufacture of paper pulp from wood. The wood is first reduced in size to chips which are treated with chemical solutions. The wood chips and the cooking liquor mixtures are heated under pressure. As the process proceeds, the liquor assumes darker and darker colors which are due to the degradation of the lignin, and the cellulose, in part, into simpler substances, closely resembling humus which are in fact identical in chemical composition and structure with humus.

COLOR IN LEAVES: It is as if nature holds a paint brush and mixes colorful pigments. When the yellow of sulfur mixes with the black of carbon, a lighter black or dark brown might result. When you look at humus, or its effect in the soil, bear in mind that what you see is a mixture of ten or 20 or more simple compounds which are contributing their colors to the mixture.

In a plant, the green chlorophyl masks the other colors while it is alive, but when it dies and the chlorophyl is dissipated, the colors of the other compounds can show through as soon as a little decomposition takes place. This is what happens to leaves in the autumn. The reds and browns that seem to appear all of a sudden were there all of the time, but were masked by the chlorophyl, and were lost to view because they were part of more involved compounds. As soon as they "decompose" into simpler compounds, they show their color.

As we have already stated, the dark color depends on the simple compounds which are resolved out of the complex ones, but these depend on the nature of the organic matter from which the humus originates. Very little is known about this except that the dark colors arise mainly from the lignin, tannin and protein compounds. For example, therefore, if you are making compost from a lot of wheat straw, the resulting humus should be lighter in color than if alfalfa plant matter is used, for the latter is much richer in protein, which means that it contains a large amount of nitrogen. The lignins and tannins contain no nitrogen, being made up solely of hydrogen, oxygen and carbon.

Some persons think that the decomposition of animal matter would give a darker humus than that coming from plants, but that is not so. The lignins and tannins of plant matter are also responsible for the dark color factor.

Another determinant of color is the extent of the oxidation. The greater the degree of oxidation (and this is related to soil aeration), the lighter the color of any given soil or humus. In the case of soil where oxygen decreases, black turns to gray, while brown turns to yellow.

The tendency of increasing acidity does not necessarily reduce the color of humus, but the addition of lime flocculates the organic matter, reducing the loss of colloidal humus, thus deepening the color.

The use of chemical fertilizers tends to lighten the color of humus. It turns the soil to a grayish color, especially on top.

In review, here are the factors which make for darkness of color in humus.

1. Decomposition and reduction to simple compounds.

2. The nature of organic matter from which it originates—the lignin, tannin and protein making for the darkest colors.

3. The amount of oxidation (aeration).

4. The use of lime.

5. The concentration of chemical fertilizers.

THE COLOR OF SOILS: Can we always judge by the darkness of a soil as to its fertility? That depends whether the color is due to the humus, and the age of the humus. Where humus is extremely old, all the usable nutritional elements are out of it, and the mere blackness offers nothing

The color of soil layers is clearly shown here. Note the layer of topsoil half-way down; separate soil profiles stand out, sharply distinct.

exciting to plants. Old peaty soils are of this character.

Some soils are dark because they may be oversupplied with manganese. Others, because they may have originated from black rocks, and the dark color may be partly due to weathered rock fragments in the soil. We can safely say that yellow and gray topsoil indicates a soil deficient in humus. Red soils are more productive, the red oxide indicating the presence of iron. In volcanic soils dark-colored minerals will confuse the origin of the darkness. A soil may contain a large supply of old humus in an advanced stage of decomposition and not be as productive as one that is supplied with organic matter that has been applied to it only four or five months ago. The fresh organic matter is also more active in improving the physical condition of the soil. But this organic matter has little influence on soil color.

There are dark peat and muck soils which may be deficient in certain important elements. In the Everglade soils of Florida which are very dark, a project of raising cabbages many years ago failed because of such deficiency. Today they are using these soils successfully by providing the deficient elements.

One cannot jump to conclusions in analyzing the dark color of soils in judging its fertility, but in the great majority of situations the darker the soil the more fertile it is.

TEMPERATURE AND COLOR: The darker a substance the more heat it will absorb, also. That is why, in the tropics, white is worn so frequently. A white barn will be cooler inside than one painted red. A darker soil, therefore, has certain advantages. It may be five or six degrees warmer than a light colored one. This is of significance in the spring. In a dark colored soil seeds will germinate earlier and grow faster.

Another method of raising soil temperature is to improve its drainage. This is where the organic method is of great advantage, the humus preventing waterlogging. Too much water in the soil reduces its temperature.

THE DYNAMIC QUALITY OF HUMUS: To some persons humus is humus and that's all there is to it. But to know the true value of humus as a factor in making plants grow we must delve below the surface. Mere quantity may not mean too much; we do not want humus for its mere presence. We want it for what it can do for the soil and for plants.

When we place either raw organic matter, or what we term finished compost into the soil, decay begins to take place. If there was no decomposition these substances would be of little value in the soil. As they decay, nitrogen and other substances are released when there is sufficient organic matter for a continuous process of decomposition to go on. There is a dynamic quality, a movement from the organic matter that is required, if it is to be of any value. Were all the organic matter to be applied to the soil in the most advanced stages of decay, there would be no nitrogen available from this source.

Prof. Sidney B. Haskell, Director of the Massachusetts Agricultural Experiment Station, in his book *Farm Fertility* says:

"The benefit comes not so much from the character of the final product as from the process of decay taking place in the soil itself. Organic matter to be functional in the soil must decay in the soil; and decaying, the supply must be constantly renewed. Otherwise we either have a barren condition of the soil, brought about by too great a decay of this humus and failure to replace it, or an equally unfavorable condition in which the soil organic matter is dead and inert, like so much peat, or in extreme cases similar in its inertness to coal itself." Thus we have the terms living and dead humus.

A. F. Gustafson, *Nitrogen and Organic Matter in the Soil,* says:

"It is the newly decomposed organic matter on which crops depend mainly for their nitrogen."

He gives an interesting example of the difference between two soils. An Ontario loam contained three per cent organic matter. The Volusia silt loam had 5.2 per cent. But yet the latter, which had about 70 per cent more organic matter, yielded less in crops. The author says that one of the reasons is that the organic matter in the Ontario loam was more active. He states, "Much of that in the Volusia is so inactive that one might regard it as being in a sense embalmed." He advises the liberal addition to it of green manure, leguminous crops, the results of which should not be harvested, but plowed in.

Here we can see that if we wish to produce the most dynamic qualities in the new organic matter, much would depend on the kind of organic matter we plow in. If we put peat into the soil, the dynamic movement of nutrients from it will be very slow. Humus, whether it is in the form of coal or of fresh organic matter represents stored energy, but if it is to be of any value, it must give it off.

It has been found also that when fresh organic matter was added to a soil there was an acceleration in the rate of decomposition of the existing soil organic matter. It probably has something to do with the stimulation of the soil bacteria.

There are peculiarities in the rhythm and timing of decomposition. Another example is a virgin soil which is first put under the plow. The rate of decay of organic matter is very fast at first, but soon it slows down. Evidently the soil bacteria require continued stimulation. This stimulation brings about that dynamic quality which is so necessary.

In the tropics the movement is faster than in the temperate zone, and thus there is always an urgent call for fresh organic matter. The four conditions that make it ideal for microorganisms to do their share in the processes of decomposition are temperature, moisture, acidity and aeration. The higher temperatures in the tropics overstimulate bacteria.

Coming back to our general subject, here is an interesting quotation from *Farm Soils—Their Management and Fertilization* by Edmund L. Worthen:

"While the fresh, active organic-matter content of a soil is an important criterion of its degree of fertility, an unproductive soil may contain a considerable quantity of humus, even enough to produce a dark color. Organic matter in the form of humus contains a smaller proportion of the more essential plant-food elements than does fresh organic matter, and is in such an advanced stage of decomposition that it is very ineffective. It is sometimes referred to as the inactive form of organic matter. It not only has little chemical effect, but it is less beneficial than fresh organic matter in improving the physical condition of the soil or in stimulating activities of the beneficial soil organisms."

Degroff and Haystead (*The Business of Farming*—University of Oklahoma Press) say:

"The more there is of organic matter in the soil and the more rapid its decomposition, the more rapidly plants will grow." Note the expression "the more rapid its decomposition." There must be this dynamic movement for humus to exert its full value. It is of little use if it does not break down. Another writer refers to it as the organic balance—the balance between the constant addition and the constant subtraction of humus.

Bear in mind that organic matter as such is much more dynamic than the humus which it produces. When you apply fresh organic matter to the land there should begin at once a strong movement of decomposition if conditions are right. Of course, the rate for a thin-stemmed legume plant will be much faster than for a whole corn cob.

This process begins as soon as the organic matter is covered with earth. If left on the soil surface, the rate of decay will be much slower. When some of the organic matter turns to humus there will be a slower rate of decay. The humus much more slowly begins to break apart so as to give some of its nutrients to the soil solution.

OTHER NUTRIENTS: Adrian J. Pieters in his *Green Manuring* compares humus from a new and from an old soil. The new soil contained 8.12 per cent nitrogen, the old $6\frac{1}{2}$ per cent. The new soil also contained much more in the way of minerals, which indicates that it is not only nitrogen that is given off in the stream from fresh humus. The fact is that the whole array of minerals is held in the organic matter and a fast decomposition releases more of it for use by plants. A great part of the soil phosphorus, for example, is held in the organic matter. In a study of *Iowa Soils* (Pearson and Simonson), it was found that between 27 and 72 per cent of the total phosphorus present was in the organic matter.

Quoting from Lyon and Buckman *Nature and Properties of Soils*—"In recent years, Baumann by his researches has shown freshly precipitated organic matter to possess properties which are largely colloidal in nature (very fine). Among these characteristics are high water capacity, great absorptive power for certain salts, ready mixture with other colloids, power to decompose salts, great shrinkage on drying, and coagulation in the presence of electrolytes." These characteristics would not be present, or would be present to a much lesser extent, in older humus. All of these powers are part of the formula of dynamism. It speaks of action and fast movement.

WHAT HUMUS DOES: During the decay of organic matter certain acid substances are produced which have a solvent action on minerals, thus making them more soluble, and available to plants. One of the principal acids is carbonic acid. These acids are produced with the aid of microorganisms —bacteria, fungi, etc. A certain amount of carbon dioxide is important to the production of crop yields. It saturates the soil water, forming an acid solution which has a solvent action on the minerals in the soil, making them available for plant use. Thus we see the principal reason for keeping a fresh supply of organic matter on hand in the soil.

RESISTANCE TO DECAY: In the process of humus formation when the decomposition gets to a certain point it slows down. A certain portion becomes resistant to the activities of microorganisms, and remains in an undecomposed state. There is a point then where there is a hold-up in the composition for a period of time. Under some conditions the decomposition process stops altogether and eventually peat or coal is produced. This is where the soil becomes more or less permanently covered with water, and asphyxiation occurs. If there is little addition of organic matter from year to year in a soil, after a while, it will contain humus that is old and which lacks the required dynamic quality. That is what happens in farms and gardens where too much dependence is placed upon chemical fertilizers.

ANAEROBIC CONDITIONS: In cases where anaerobic conditions exist, that is, where air is lacking, there is a slower decomposition, but in considering this point there is a difference whether the anaerobic conditions exist in a composting process outside of the soil, or whether it is in the soil itself. In an aerobic decay there is an oxidation which, roughly speaking, is a "burning out" process. If it occurs in the soil, as the nutrients stream out of the humus, they are captured and held to a certain extent by the soil. But if this oxidation occurs in an ordinary compost heap, much of it dissipates itself into the atmosphere. In analyses of compost made by both processes it never fails that the anaerobic compost has much more nitrogen and other nutrients.

But in the soil, we want an aerobic condition. Anaerobic decomposition in composting destroys less, so that more is available for dynamic decay in the soil. But of course it is more difficult and costly to maintain anaerobic conditions in a composting process, although much progress has been made in this direction through the use of black polyethylene plastic tarpaulins over the compost pile. Ideally, anaerobic conditions in compost making are the best. In the soil, conditions should be aerobic.

NITROGEN IN HUMUS: Nitrogen is an extremely important element in farming and gardening. Without it, productivity of the soil will decline. High productivity is interrelated with the supply of organic matter in a soil. A deficiency of one usually indicates a deficiency of the other. Nitrogen is necessary to the functioning of every cell of the plant, and is needed for rapid growth. It is directly responsible for the vegetative growth of plants above ground. And with a good supply of it, maturity of the plant will come earlier. A lack of nitrogen is indicated by a lightening of the green color of leaves. A great lack of it will show up in the yellowing of the leaves. Of all nutrient deficiencies in arable soils, that of nitrogen is most common. But an excessive supply of it will not only retard the growth period but will reduce the plant's resistance to disease, and produce an inferior quality of crop, which will show up in poor keeping and shipping abilities. It waterlogs the plant, causing an over succulency. This is where the organic method is superior. The organic matter, unless a tremendous excess is applied to the soil, gradually feeds the nitrogen to the plants as required, rarely overfeeding them. It is a known fact that organic matter decays slowly, thus not releasing the nitrogen too quickly. The organic matter thus is a valuable storehouse of nitrogen, maintaining an automatic supply for the entire growing season. But with chemical fertilizers, a too enthusiastic hand can sometimes give the soil an oversupply which will lead to all the troubles described above.

PERCENTAGE OF NITROGEN: A very common error is found in most agricultural textbooks and publications dealing with the subject of organic matter. They usually state that on the average, five per cent of organic matter consists of nitrogen. At the most, organic matter contains up to two per cent of nitrogen. The basis of this error is that *humus* contains five per cent nitrogen, but there is a big difference between organic matter and humus. It is due to a loose and careless handling of the terms *organic matter* and *humus* that this error occurs again and again.

Here, therefore, is a general rule: no matter how much or how little nitrogen there is in any kind of organic matter to begin with, when it turns to humus, the latter's nitrogen content will be about five per cent.

PROTEIN: Nitrogen is not present, either in the soil or in humus in a free condition. If it were, it would be rapidly decomposed by soil organisms and much of it become lost to growing crops. Nitrogen is present in humus in the form of protein compounds which are highly resistant to microbial dissolution, thus releasing its nitrogen slowly. In raw organic matter, if not carefully handled, much of the nitrogen can become dissipated into the atmosphere in the form of ammonia, which is a compound of nitrogen and which results from the first stage in the breakdown of protein. This is the great value of humus—its ability to hoard its nitrogen for release to plant roots as needed.

About 30 to 35 per cent of humus consists of protein. Proteins contain about 50 to 55 per cent of carbon, 15 to 19 per cent of nitrogen, 6 to 7 per cent hydrogen and 21 to 23 per cent oxygen, with small amounts of sulfur and occasionally some phosphorus. (Carbohydrates, that is, sugars starches and cellulose, contain only carbon, hydrogen and oxygen.) In other words, proteins containing all the elements of carbohydrates plus nitrogen, sulfur and sometimes phosphorus.

Generally speaking it is considered that about 16 per cent or one-sixth of protein is nitrogen and therefore when the amount of nitrogen in a substance is known, the protein is figured out by multiplying it by 6.25. (16 by 6.25-100.) Not all the nitrogen is in the protein. Small quantities are found in other compounds contained in humus, but these are small in amount.

The release of nitrogen in humus is effected as follows: The protein first decomposes into its amino acids. The next step is the formation of ammonium compounds. Then bacteria break these down into nitrites. There are certain bacteria whose function in the soil is to do this, and only *they* can do it. Then other groups of bacteria turn the nitrites into nitrates, which is the form of nitrogen that plant roots can take in. Sometimes where air is lacking and the decomposition is anaerobic, other compounds besides amino-acids form, which give off putrefactive odors. This usually occurs in protein-rich materials.

PROTEIN: Protein is like humus. It has no uniform formula, but varies according to origin. It has an artificial chemical origin, it is greatly possible that the atoms may arrange themselves differently within the molecule than if the nitrogen is of organic origin. Nature has a way of arranging them based on an evolution of millions of years. Man, who only recently came upon the scene, cannot hope to duplicate the chemistry of Nature. In fact no man in any laboratory has ever been able to make protein—even an inferior kind. He has been able to extract nitrogen from the air. But protein is the beginning of life. It is protoplasm and the making of it is in the hands of a power higher than man's.

Dr. Selman Waksman, in his book *Humus* cites three researches to show the importance of the nature of protein in the soil in improving its ability to feed plant roots. It would seem logical that given defective protein we will have defective plants. In a recent ten year period in the Middle West the protein content of the grains declined ten per cent. This is a terrific reduction for such a short period of time. The question is—did the quality of the protein also decline? If it did, it might be an explanation for the alarming recent increases in the degenerative diseases, for protein builds body tissue. Defective protein—defective body tissue. Defective body tissue may be more susceptible to cancer.

Nitrogen is important, but the way it is held in the protein molecule may be *the* one factor which may control the fate of mankind.

Dr. George D. Scarseth of the American Farm Research Assoc. of Lafayette Indiana, in a bulletin entitled *Organic Matter and our Food Supply,* observed:

"Protein foods are nitrogen carrying foods. Every farmer knows that nitrogen and soil organic matter are closely related. Every farmer knows that a soil high in organic matter is also a very productive soil. Every farmer also knows that legumes like clover, alfalfa and sweet clover add valuable organic matter to the soil. The farmers also know that the organic matter from these legumes is better than the organic matter from non-legumes, because clover makes nitrogen into chemical compounds out of the free nitrogen in the air."

Nitrogen in Composting: Materials high in nitrogen content are extremely important in composting, for nitrogen (protein) is the principle food of the bacteria which engage in the decay processes. Their bodies are highly proteinaceous. When the raw materials of composting include highly nitrogenous materials such as hen manure and alfalfa hay the composting is accelerated and the quality of the compost better.

See also ORGANIC MATTER; COMPOST.

HUMUS AND THE FARMER, by Friend Sykes

See BOOKS FOR ORGANIC GARDENERS AND FARMERS.

HUNGER SIGNS IN PLANTS: *see* DEFICIENCIES, SOIL; FERTILIZING; TRACE ELEMENTS

HUNNEMANIA: (*H. fumariaefolia*) Sometimes called tulip poppy, it resembles a sulfur-yellow California poppy of giant size, coarser and of greater substance. The plants, about two feet in height, are very prolific, hardy and easy of culture after germination. Difficulty in getting a good stand is the general rule. Like the poppies, the seedlings do not transplant readily and for this reason the seeds should be sown where the plants are to bloom. Hunnemania is an excellent source of sulfur yellow color in the late spring border and as a cut flower it excels because of its attractive tulip form.

HUNZA: The sturdy, mountaineer Hunzas are a light-complexioned race of people, much fairer of skin than the natives of the northern plains of India. They claim descent from soldiers of the armies of Alexander the Great who lost their way in the precipitous gorges of the Himalayas.

Up until the end of the second World War, the people of Hunza were known to explorers as the most healthy of peoples. For this reason, and because they achieved their remarkable health through completely natural living, the Hunzas were of special interest to adherents of the organic method and to nutritionists.

The Hunza country is at the nor-

The health of the Hunzas, once splendid, has deteriorated as the people abandoned formerly simple and organic diets for modern foodstuffs.

thernmost tip of India, lying just south of the Soviet Union between Afghanistan and Sinkiang. It comprises several valleys in perhaps the most mountainous country in the world, the average range being 20,000 feet.

Until recent years, sickness was practically unknown in Hunza. Fatigue, too, was rare, for the Hunzas have no word for "tired" in their language. It was not uncommon to see a cheerful man of Hunza walk 60 miles over the mountains barefoot or plunge naked into a glacier-fed river through a hole cut in the ice.

For years, the Hunzukuts have attracted the attention of men of science. Sir Robert McCarrison, prominent English physician, has made perhaps the most extensive first-hand investigation of the health of these people. He gave as one of the prime reasons for their strength of body the fact that "The people live on the unsophisticated foods of Nature: milk, eggs, grains, fruits and vegetables. I don't suppose that one in every thousand of them has ever seen a tinned salmon, a chocolate or a patent infant food, nor that as much sugar is imported into their country in a year as is used in a moderately-sized hotel in a single day."

It should be stressed that this was written before World War 2 opened up this hitherto inaccessible region to a steady interchange of commodities and ways of modern living.

The health history of this once isolated people has been brought up to date by the publication of "Hunza —Lost Kingdom of the Himalayas" by John Clark. Mr. Clark, a geologist who lived for 20 months among the Hunza, clearly states in his book how civilization has encroached upon the Hunzas and brought about a corresponding undermining of national health. The second World War saw many young Hunzakuts leave the homeland for India, Pakistan and elsewhere in search of work. It is supposed that, on their return to Hunza, they brought back with them infections of various kinds. In addition, various civilized foods have been finding their way into the once-sheltered land, and today it is not unusual to find shipments of candy coming from well-meaning American groups, packages of sugar, white flour and chocolate brought in by visitors, and even patent medicines from the Western world. The resulting decline in Hunzakut health is evidenced by Mr. Clark's reports that the Hunzas now suffer from malaria, dysentery, ringworm, bronchitis, beri-beri, goiter and pneumonia—diseases not reported by earlier explorers.

The lesson taught by the Hunza story is obvious. The over-refined foods of western civilization have once more upset the ageless, traditional diet of a comparatively uncomplicated people, bringing about "civilized" diseases with which they are unable to cope. *See also* APRICOT, HUNZA.

HYACINTH: The hyacinth—fragrant and colorful—is fast becoming one of the important early spring flowers. It takes an early spot in the spring garden, often blooming before the daffodils are under way. Although the hyacinth doesn't have a big range of color there are several pretty shades of purple, blue, pink and rose, and there are both single and double-flowered forms.

For subtly appealing shades of blue and purple, plant bulbs of the above Grand Maitre variety. Hyacinths do not require planting in formal beds.

CULTURE: Many gardeners are under the impression that hyacinths must be planted in formal beds. This is not so. Many garden positions suit them. Plant them informally throughout perennial beds, along a picket fence or by a stone wall. They also look well in a single line or massed in groups in front of low shrubbery. You may even wish to raise them for indoor beauty during the winter months.

Hyacinths prefer light, sandy soils which drain easily and warm quickly in the spring. They root deeply so the soil should be cultivated and fertilized at least two feet deep. Thoroughly incorporate a generous amount of compost, well-rotted manure and bone meal.

The bulbs should be planted four to six inches deep and six to eight inches apart. Be sure to plant the bulbs at a uniform depth to have them bloom at the same time. The actual depths depend on soil conditions. In light soil plant deeper than in heavy clay.

The planting period starts about the first of September and extends until the ground freezes hard, but best results are usually obtained from early planting. September or early October gives the bulbs a good start.

In sections of the country with severe winters, mulch the bulb plantings with a loose covering of hay, straw, leaves, or evergreen boughs. Remove this covering early in the spring after the ground begins to thaw and there is no danger of refreezing.

After blooming is over, let the foliage continue growing until it turns yellow and withers of its own accord. Good leaf growth is important for the development of the bulbs for the next spring's performance. Begin to plant annuals as soon as the hyacinths stop blooming, and by the time their foliage becomes unsightly the annuals will take their place. The leaves of the hyacinth may be bunched together and tied loosely to allow more room between the bulbs for planting annuals.

FALL CARE: Hyacinths tend to "run out" and bulbs have to be replaced more often than other spring bulbs, but satisfying results can be obtained for several years by fertilizing the plantings each season and by resetting bulbs every two to three years. Take up the bulbs after the leaves have died down, spread in baskets or flats, and store in a cool dry place until fall.

VARIETIES: Enticing scent and vivid colors combine for a wonderful effect next spring when you plant hyacinth bulbs this fall. For blue and purple shades try planting Bismarck, Forget-me-not, King of the Lilacs, or Grand Maitre. Or, for pinks and reds try La Victoire, Marconi, Robert Stieger, or Roi des Belges. Among the desirable white varieties are Albatros and L'Innocence. For mixed plantings yellow varieties should be included such as King of the Yellows or Yellow Hammer.

See also Bulbs, Forcing; Bulb Garden; Flower Gardening.

HYBRID: Plants which result from the crossing (cross-fertilization) of species or varieties. Cross-breeding has become a basic means of causing slight variations and a way of improving a type. Disadvantages are that often hybrids do not breed true, in some cases are sterile. However, in many cases, crossing has resulted in higher nutritive quality plants, better-yielding, and ones with more disease-resistant properties.

HYDRANGEA: Highly ornamental, deciduous shrubs producing showy pink, blue and white flowers. Doing well along the shrub border, hydrangeas grow best in rich, well-drained soil. While they grow satisfactorily in a location that is part-shaded, they bloom most abundantly if placed in full sun and given sufficient moisture. Pruning is generally done in fall or early spring, the branches of the previous year's growth cut back to a single pair of buds; some gardeners cut shrubs back to ground annually to produce vigorous growing plants. Weaker branches are always cut off, and the less hardy varieties should be given protection during winter. Hydrangeas can be propagated by cuttings of fairly ripe wood, by layers or division.

Common hydrangea (*H. paniculata grandiflora*) is hardy throughout the United States, a very common sight in lawns, grows from six to 25 feet high. Insect and diseases rarely trouble them. Hortensia (*H. macrophylla*) much grown outside in the South, as tubbed plants, and in greenhouses, have been tried successfully outdoors in Northern gardens. It usually grows to ten feet. Give them winter protection by mounding the soil about the stems in the same way as roses. A slightly acid soil is recommended.

Since flower heads are quite heavy, it is often necessary to support plants. This should be done in early spring before buds swell. Place three or four stakes in a circle around the outer edge of the plant and ties heavy string around them. Later the foliage will cover the stakes, so that they will not detract from the attractiveness of the blooms.

Wild hydrangea (*H. arborescens*) reaches three to five feet; its variety *grandiflora* is called hills-of-snow. Climbing hydrangea (*H. petiolaris*) is a woody vine sometimes going up as high as 50 feet, is hardy in the South. Tea-of-heaven (*H. serrata*) grows to five feet, is also relatively tender.

HYDRATED LIME: *see* Lime

HYOSCYAMUS NIGER: *see* Henbane

HYDROPONICS: Hydroponics is the method of growing plants in a water solution without soil. The plants are supported in an inert, non-organic medium such as sand, fine gravel, or mica compositions; which are saturated with prepared "nutrient solutions" for various periods of time. All of the essential inorganic plant foods are available to the roots in great quantities.

The plants are forced far beyond their natural capacities; and upon this alone it would be unreasonable to expect super production.

Hydroponics is quite expensive and the most chemicalized method currently practiced. Plants cannot absorb the necessary minerals in the proper balance from chemical solutions and are bound to be unbalanced nutritionally.

HYPERICUM: *see* Saint John's Wort

HYSSOP: *see* Anise Hyssop; Honey Plants

I

IBERIS: *see* CANDYTUFT

ICELAND POPPY: *see* POPPY; FLOWER GARDENING; PERENNIALS

IGNEOUS: "Fire formed" rock, the result of the cooling of molten rock below the earth's crust. *See also* MINERAL ROCK.

ILEX: *see* HOLLY

IMPATIENS: Comprising both tender annuals and perennials, this family of plants includes some very popular garden and greenhouse flowers. The plant gets its name from the Latin, which refers to the tendency of the ripe pods to burst open at the slightest pressure. Touch-me-not (*I. biflora*) is an annual, with orange flowers, that prefers moist, shady areas, grows two to three feet high. Garden Balsam (*I. balsamina*) is another tender annual, with brilliant-colored flowers. Also growing two to three feet high, it does best in a rich soil, seed sown in May, and plants spaced about 1½ feet apart. The pale touch-me-not (*I. pallida*), called Jewel-weed, is larger than the *biflora* type, has light yellow flowers; likes moist, shady locations.

IMPORTED FIRE ANT: *see* FIRE ANT

INCH WORM: A form of caterpillar, often called canker-worm. Banding trunks of trees with a sticky compound is effective, since these worms crawl slowly, arching the middle of their bodies and forcing themselves ahead. *See also* INSECT CONTROL.

INCOME, GARDEN: Every gardener has many opportunities to supplement his income. For ways to make money through part-time gardening and homesteading activities, *see* HOMESTEAD.

INDOOR GARDENING: *see* HOUSE PLANTS; FRUITS, GROWING INDOOR

INFECTION: *see* DISEASE

INFORMAL GARDEN: Referring to a more natural, irregular form of garden landscaping, where the objective is to achieve the free-flowing lines of nature. Many organic gardeners, trying to capture the spirit of nature in their own plantings, maintain the original landscaping features of their grounds as they first found them. Their goal is to accentuate the most beautiful elements in this setting, rather than to introduce a new design. Paradoxically, to obtain this effect, often as much time is spent in careful study as is spent on many formal gardens. However, the final effect should be one that is almost completely devoid of artificiality and intrusion by man. *See also* LANDSCAPING.

INNOCENCE: *see* QUAKER LADIES

INOCULATION: *see* LEGUME INOCULATION

INSECT: All insects belong to the large group *Arthropoda*, which is broken down into five classes: *Insecta* (insects), *Crustacea* (crayfish, sowbugs, fairy shrimps, lobsters, crabs, etc.), *Arachnida* (spiders, ticks, mites, scorpions), *Diplopoda* (millipedes) and *Chilopoda* (centipedes). The animal members of these five classes are alike in certain ways—they have segmented bodies, jointed legs, antennae and other appendages, and a hardened covering over their bodies called an exoskeleton. Following is some general information about insects made by University of Illinois entomologists:

GENERAL CHARACTERISTICS: All insects have a total of six legs, or three pairs, at some time during their development—usually when they are adults. The body of an insect has three main parts—head, thorax and abdomen. In certain stages of growth, however, these parts cannot always be clearly distinguished. The eyes, antennae and mouth parts are in the head. The three pairs of legs (and the wings, if any) are attached to the thorax. In the abdomen, which is directly behind the thorax, are tiny air openings or pores, called spiracles. Sometimes prolegs or leglike projections, called claspers or filaments, are found on the abdomen.

As already mentioned, the body of an insect has a hard outer covering called an exoskeleton, which protects the fleshy internal organs against injury and loss of moisture. The material making up this exoskeleton is called chitin. The wings and breathing tubes are formed from extensions of this covering. The breathing tubes open through the air openings, or spiracles, which are arranged along the sides of the abdomen.

LIFE CYCLE: Most insects start from eggs laid by the female. In general, the insects develop from the eggs in two different ways. One group, which is said to have a "complete life cycle," goes through four stages of development—egg, larva, pupa and adult. The larva is a tiny worm which hatches from the egg. It grows steadily larger and eventually changes into a motionless, resting stage (pupa). In this stage an insect is best able to resist an adverse environment. The adult insect emerges by splitting the pupal skin. Beetles, flies, bees, butterflies and moths are examples of insects which have a complete life cycle. The other group has an incomplete life cycle, and goes through just three stages of development. When the young hatch from the eggs, they look like adults, except that they are smaller. They are called nymphs, and shed their skins as they grow larger, finally developing wings and becoming adults. Grasshoppers, crickets, roaches and true bugs are examples of this group. *See also* INSECT CONTROL.

INSECT CONTROL: There are some 86,000 different species of insects in the United States. Seventy-six thousand of these are "friendly" or beneficial to the gardener.

Many successful organic gardeners have found little cause to worry about insect control. A little know-how has helped them to control most of the troublesome bugs—without involving a lot of time, expense or any poisons.

By concentrating on improving their soils, organic gardeners have proven that they can produce vigorous plants with real resistance to pests and disease. Although organic methods sometimes don't provide 100 per cent control, organic gardeners are content to let the few pests they may find in their gardens have a small share as long as the major portion is left—healthfully—for them.

At the same time, there are important insect control methods that should be learned and used. Knowing just what a certain bug likes to eat and where the adult female lays her eggs goes a long way in ridding your garden of that enemy.

RECOGNITION: The first step in any control program is knowing the culprit. With a little practice, you can learn to recognize at a glance the signs and symptoms of common pests.

The various chewing insects make their own patterns. Flea beetles make tiny round perforations; weevils produce rather typical angular openings; beetle larvae (grubs) "skeletonize" leaves, chewing everything but the epidermis and veins.

Sucking insects cause leaves to be yellowish, stippled white or gray. These insects, as well as their brownish eggs or excrement, can often be seen on the underside of foliage. Red spider can be spotted by yellowed leaves that are cobwebby or mealy underneath; whitish streaks mean thrips. When leaves are curled up, or cupped down, look out for aphids. Deformed leaves may be caused by cyclamen mite; blotches or tunnels by leaf miners; round or conical protrusions by aphids, midges or gall wasps.

The partial collapse and dying of a plant, termed *wilt,* may result from a number of causes—very often nematodes or grubs.

Once you've found out what the destroyer is, concentrate on methods to eradicate it. The four main types of control are using resistant seed varieties, quarantine, destruction and prevention.

RESISTANT VARIETIES: The first and simplest method to try is using seed varieties which are most resistant to diseases in your region. Before investing in any special seed, however, it is important to make certain that the variety will grow well in your type soil.

The list of vegetable varieties, resistant to one or another disease or pest, is growing all the time. To prove this, compare the latest edition of a vegetable seed catalog with one printed five years ago. In many cases, $\frac{1}{3}$ to $\frac{1}{2}$ of the varieties available today are resistant to a specific trouble. For information on insect-resistant vegetable plants, check the seed catalog, visit the local seed store or write your agricultural college.

Plant pathologists throughout the nation are aiding this phase of insect and disease control by developing healthier vegetables. Just how well new resistant varieties are accepted by growers is evident by the new potato varieties released since 1932. They account for approximately 50 per cent of all the certified seed grown in 1951. The wilt-resistant Rutgers tomato was introduced in 1934; in 1951, about 50 per cent of all the tomato seed raised in this country was Rutgers.

This first step—using resistant varieties—in the control of insects and disease is very important. Of course, the basic rule still holds true . . . a healthy soil rich in humus and minerals will make any vegetable variety healthier, but there's little sense in assuming a handicap by not using varieties known to be resistant.

QUARANTINE: The second technique of insect and disease control is *quarantine.* No one would think of going out of his way to visit someone who has a contagious disease. Yet this phenomenon occurs daily in gardens everywhere. The amusing hobby of keeping a "pet" diseased plant for anyone to handle should not be tolerated; it is very dangerous. Everyone who enters the garden is shown it and asked if he or she knows what the trouble is. While giving an opinion, the visitor does the natural thing —turns up the leaves to see the disease underneath, later examining plant after plant in similar manner, thereby infecting the entire garden.

There is a strong case for isolation and destruction of diseased and insect-ridden plants. Recent experiences show that it is not a good practice to use such plants as a mulch or, in fact, in sheet composting. It's risky trying to use infected plants, except in the compost heap, and even then, be careful. When in doubt, it's better to destroy such material, and so make certain of not spreading the trouble.

"All gardeners should become health-minded and not worry too much about disease. If it comes, act promptly and destroy the first specimen. Feed the soil so that plants are in sturdy health, because all the remedies in the world are useless if the underlying cause is repeatedly neglected," writes the English authority, E. R. Janes, in his book, *The Vegetable Garden.*

DESTRUCTION: The third method of control is the destruction of a pest after it gets established in an area. This method employs the use of traps, parasites, safe inoculants, and other natural methods of getting rid of pests.

Here are some practices which organic gardeners have found effective:

For the small garden, insects on potato and other plants can be easily and effectively removed by holding plants over an ordinary pail half full of kerosene and brushing the leaves carefully, so that the bugs fall into the pail. Four or five days of this practice will rid plants of a heavy accumulation of the pests.

Flies, wasps and other beneficial insects—probably the best known is the ladybug—have been used to good advantage. *Lydella stabulans grisescens,* a parasitic fly, has eliminated corn borer infestation; insect parasites imported from India and Pakistan do a good job on olive scale; a species of ladybird beetle from Australia wages war on mites; parasites from France fight elm and fig scale; the hornet or yellow jacket thrives on cabbage worms. Praying mantids are also famous for their work. The list keeps growing, and biological control methods keep offering more and more solutions to the insect problem.

Japanese beetle grubs have been destroyed by 80 per cent with applications of milky spore disease. Acceptable to organic gardeners, this milky spore disease powder infects the Japanese beetlegrub, making its blood a milky color. As the disease advances, the grubs die, but the spores within their bodies remain in the soil. Thus one application is said to last as much as seven years.

Some types of traps are not overly desirable, because they work too indiscriminately; that is, destroying helpful insects along with harmful ones. One such trap is the outdoor shaded light bulb with the kerosene filled pan underneath. Flying insects go toward the light, then are killed when diving into the pan. Try some specialized treatments before resorting to this type bug trap.

Entomologists have found that blue and blue-white lights attract the most insects; yellow is less attractive, and red seems to be least visible.

Hanging a couple of large mouth pickle jars, half full of a weak mixture of molasses and water in plum trees, has been found an effective way for eliminating black-knot. Very little molasses is needed, just about one-half cup to one gallon of water. This same plan has also worked on apple and pear trees.

Japanese beetles have been caught in traps filled with geranium oil, while sassafras oil is used to attract the codling moth. A solid bait for codling moth may be made by filling a small ice cream cup $\frac{2}{3}$ full of sawdust, stirring into the sawdust a teaspoonful of sassafras oil and another of glacial acetic acid. Then add enough liquid glue to saturate completely the sawdust mixture. When the cup is dry, after a day or two, suspend it in a mason jar partly filled with water.

Mealy bugs may be cleaned off special plants with a cotton swab soaked with alcohol.

An inverted cabbage leaf makes a good trap for snails and slugs, along with other pests which hide during the day but forage on garden plants at night. Cut worms can also be destroyed by this method.

CULTIVATION: Cultivation is also very effective against the destructive grasshopper. Most species of grasshoppers lay their eggs in late summer, depositing them in shallow burrows in the ground. These insects spend six to eight months as eggs in the upper three inches of soil. In early spring they emerge as adults.

A fall plowing, or tilling, of the garden will destroy all burrows, preventing the hatched grasshoppers from coming up in spring, thus destroying them by the thousands.

Clean cultivation is a measure necessary only where a severe infestation is present. It can be used temporarily to help overcome this, and then be replaced by thorough mulching, a method usually effective in keeping insect damage to a minimum and one that is also very beneficial to the soil and plants.

In the Lake Erie region, many gardeners are pestered by the grape berry moth. Once these moths emerge from the soil, they are hard to control, and cause considerable damage to grape vines and berry patches.

The cocoons of the grape berry moth hibernate through winter in the upper two inches of soil around the base of plants they later feed upon. Cultivation in early spring will bury and destroy most cocoons, and prevent the adult from emerging from the soil. A rotary tiller is especially effective in destroying a great number of the cocoons.

Another very destructive insect that can readily be controlled by good tillage is the western cutworm which is a menace throughout the Great Plains region. Because it never surfaces, it is almost impossible to control by methods found effective against the more common cutworm found in the East.

These western worms hatch in early spring, and feed greedily on newly sprouted plants. They can survive for some time without food if they, as yet, have not eaten. But once they have feasted, they die quickly if their food supply is suddenly cut off. The secret here is to allow the worms to feed for a short time in spring, then destroy all vegetation by plowing it under. The garden should be kept free of all sprouting vegetation for at least three weeks in order to starve the worms. After that time, the garden will be safe for vegetable planting.

The more common cutworm that feeds above ground can be controlled in early fall by ridding your garden of as much of the vegetation as possible. This should be done during the month of September for that is when the adult moth comes to lay her eggs on tall grass and plant stems. Any plants that must remain well into fall should be removed to the compost heap as soon as possible to prevent the eggs from hatching. The larvae that manage to hatch and burrow into the soil can be controlled in spring by placing a heavy paper tube around each transplant during May and June. The tube should extend from just above the roots to $1\frac{1}{2}$ inches above the ground.

An application of wood ashes around the base of newly set plants is also effective. Toads, too, destroy great numbers by feeding upon them.

The cabbage worm, which causes considerable damage in the garden to radishes, turnips, cabbage, cauliflower, kohlrabi, Brussels sprouts and collards, is a queer one. These vegetables have a pungent odor and taste caused by a chemical known as mustard oil which is secreted by the plants. The white cabbage butterfly is attracted by this strong odor, and comes to lay her eggs upon the broad leaves. The caterpillars hatch, then feed to maturity on the plant selected by the parent butterfly. If, for any reason, the caterpillars are placed upon a different kind of plant to which they are not accustomed, they will stop eating and starve in the midst of plenty.

They can be controlled by covering such plants with cheesecloth to prevent the laying of eggs by the adult moth, or by sprinkling rye flour over and around the plants wet with dew. The dough will cling to the bodies of the moths and worms causing them to eventually bake in the sun and die. Yellow jackets are the natural enemy of the cabbage worm, and should be tolerated if they cause no pain to the gardener.

GARDEN SANITATION: It is very important to keep your garden as clean as possible. If piles of decaying garden refuse, or trash, are left around, sowbugs and earwigs will soon find them and use them as breeding places. Also remove old boards, bricks and logs under which they may hide and multiply. If either insect takes refuge under low-growing shrubs, place hollow tubes painted green, side by side, under the shrub. In the morning shake tubes into kerosene or boiling water. Hens are especially fond of these two bugs, and can destroy hundreds in one day.

CROP ROTATION: Rotation of crops can play a very important part in ridding the garden of such pests as the white grub. It is the larvae of the June beetle. The restricted food habits of the grub enable it to feed only on the roots of the grass family. It will destroy forage grasses or grain crops grown on land that had been in sod. If a patch of lawn has been converted into a garden plot, it should first be planted in a legume such as beans or clover. Since grubs will not feed on the roots of legumes, they will soon perish, leaving the soil safe for vegetable planting.

ENRICHING SOIL: Soil rich in humus proves its value in the control of aphids, or plant lice. These tiny creatures detest plants grown in an organically fed soil. To better understand this green demon, it has been found that in early summer, several generations of wingless females rapidly succeed one another. They, in turn, are followed by a generation of winged females who migrate to other types of plants to feed. (These, by the way, are among the very few insects that alternate their feeding habits.) In time this generation gives rise to another which comprises both sexes. This last generation produces eggs that over-winter on branches upon which the parents had been feeding.

In spring, the new brood of winged aphids migrate back to the plants upon which the very first generation fed, thus starting the cycle all over again. Extensive damage is caused by these many generations in one season, so their control is vital.

The first step in destroying the aphid, of course, is to enrich your soil organically, and to grow nasturtiums, which repel aphids, between your

vegetable rows, and around fruit trees. Remove them by hand wherever they appear. A dormant oil spray applied in early spring or fall also aids in the control.

CORRECT PLANTING DATES: Many times, the correct planting time has much to do in preventing serious damage by insects who feed on just one particular type of plants. Take the Mexican bean beetle, for instance. It feeds on nothing but the bean family. If beans are planted as early as possible, they will mature before the beetle appears later in the season.

To control them, pick beetles by hand and drop into kerosene. All egg masses should be destroyed.

By combining two or more of the following: cultivation, garden sanitation, crop rotation, organic fertilizers, early planting dates, hand picking, and hens, most of the following garden pests can be reasonably controlled without the use of chemicals.

ANTS: They spread aphids to other plants. They can be controlled by placing sticky bands of roofing paper around trees to prevent their ascent, and by sprinkling steamed bone meal around their mounds in lawns.

BLISTER BEETLES: Blister beetles are slender cylindrical insects ½ to one inch long with relatively soft bodies. They may be gray or black, or yellow striped with black. They usually occur in colonies or swarms. Although they have wings, they are very clumsy fliers.

BLISTER BEETLE

Blister Beetles are chewing insects, feeding on blossoms and foliage. They seem particularly fond of potatoes but also attack beans, beets, cabbage, corn, onions, peas, tomatoes, and other garden crops as well as legumes and other field crops.

Wear gloves to handpick these as they leave a blister. Pick as soon as detected to prevent serious damage to foliage and blossoms.

CABBAGE MAGGOT: The cabbage maggot is a white soft-bodied larva found on the roots of cole crops. The full-grown maggot is about ⅓ inch long.

Cabbage maggots attack the fine roots of cabbage, cauliflower, radish, turnip, and related crops. Later they make slimy tunnels just under the bark of the main stem or larger roots of the plants. The injury is almost entirely underground although the maggots sometimes work up into the stems above ground.

The most severe injury usually occurs during the early spring when the weather is cool and the soil moist. Occasionally weather conditions in the fall are favorable to the development of cabbage maggots, resulting in damage to late crops of the cabbage family. One of the first signs of injury is the wilting of plants during the heat of the day. Further evidence of maggot feeding is the discoloration of the foliage.

Side-dressing a crop with an organic nitrogen fertilizer and otherwise keeping it in a good, thrifty growing condition will help offset maggot damage when the attack is light.

Screening hotbeds and cold frames with cheesecloth will prevent egg laying before the plants are transplanted. *See also* CABBAGE.

CARROT WEEVIL: The carrot weevil is a coppery-colored snout beetle about ⅛ inch long. The larvae are small dirty-white grubs and they are found in the soil or in the roots of infested crops.

The larvae, or grubs, of the carrot weevil tunnel into the roots of carrots and to some extent in parsley. Early carrots are usually most severely injured.

The carrot weevil spends the winter in the adult stage in any weedy or grassy area immediately adjoining an old carrot field. The adults reappear the following May and move to the nearest host plants, mostly by walking. Because they migrate such a short distance, it is possible to prevent part of the damage by rotating the fields where carrots are grown.

CHINCH BUGS: These little black sucking insects can cause large brown patches in your lawn, and all but destroy the sweet corn. If present in your lawn, remove the soil from the spot, and replace it with ⅓ crushed rock, ⅓ sharp builder's sand and ⅓ compost. If they show up in the corn patch, plant soybeans as a ground cover as chinch bugs dislike shade.

CODLING MOTH LARVA: ¾ inch long; pinkish white and brown heads; the larvae winter in cocoons in the crotches and under bark of trees; moths emerge to lay their eggs in warm dry weather about a week after petals have fallen.

To control these use a dormant oil spray in spring, or make a trap by filling a small can ⅔ full of sawdust to which add one teaspoonful of sassafras oil, and another of glacial acetic acid. Add enough glue to saturate, then let dry for two days. When ready, suspend in a mason jar partly filled with water, and hang in the tree.

CUCUMBER BEETLES: adult: yellow to black; three black stripes down back; larva: white; slender; brownish at the ends; adults feed on leaves and spread bacterial wilt; larvae bore into roots and also feed on stems.

To drive these away, spray upper and lower sides of leaves with a mixture of one handful of wood ashes and one of hydrated lime mixed in two gallons of water. Marigolds also repel this pest.

CUTWORMS: Cutworms are plump soft-bodied worms, usually dull-colored and scantily covered with coarse bristles or hairs. The full-grown worms are one to 1½ inches long.

They are usually found in the soil at the base of plants on which they feed. When disturbed, they commonly coil their bodies.

WORM

Cutworms are chewing insects and as a rule destroy more of a plant than they eat. They attack nearly all garden crops.

Young plants are cut off near the soil line; this type of injury is most prevalent in hotbeds, cold frames, and in the garden during the early part of the growing season.

Land on which garden crops are to be grown should be kept free of weeds and grass, especially during the fall months, in order to prevent egg-laying by cutworm moths. Crops planted on sod land are especially subject to severe damage unless the land is plowed during the late summer or early fall and is kept free of weeds and grass during the rest of the growing season.

To control, place a stiff three-inch cardboard collar around the stems allowing it to extend about one inch into soil and protrude two inches above the soil; clear the stem by about ½ inch; another suggestion is to put a ring of wood ashes around the plants and soak the ashes. Keep down weeds and grasses on which the cutworm moth lays its eggs. Toads consume cutworms.

EARWIGS: adult and nymph: reddish-brown; prominent forceps at tail end; up to ¾ inch long; earwig hides during day and forages at night; discharges foul odor; seldom causes severe damage to vegetables, but is chiefly a health hazard.

To control, use of traps has been found very effective; here is one trap used: take four pieces of bamboo a foot in length—each piece open at both ends and tie with nylon yarn into a bundle at both ends. Lightly paint them with a green paint and when dry, put under bushes, against fences and any place where earwigs are likely to gather; leave them there

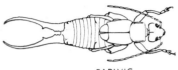

EARWIG

for a few days; early one morning, shake earwigs out of holes into bucket of hot water or kerosene; bantam hens have also been reported as an effective control against earwigs.

EUROPEAN CORN BORER: The European corn borer is a small, slender, white caterpillar spotted with black and is about one inch long when full-grown. It is especially abundant in the northern half of Illinois.

The injury inflicted by the corn borer is done entirely by the larvae, or worms. Corn is the principal garden crop injured although potatoes and tomatoes may sometimes be attacked. The larvae bore into all parts of the cornstalk and ear, interrupting the normal growth of the plant, weakening the stem, and allowing organisms of decay to enter. Infested stalks fail to produce good ears. The stalks break over in heavily infested fields, and the corn may be a complete loss.

To avoid serious losses, use varieties that require 80 or more days to mature, or delay plantings until the last half of May.

FLEA BEETLES: Flea beetles are usually small (about the size of a cabbage or turnip seed), very active, and hard to see. Although the different species differ in size and color, their feeding habits are very similar. One of the most common species found in gardens is the potato flea beetle.

Flea beetles eat small holes in the

leaves of cabbage, cauliflower, egg-plant, potato, turnip, and most other garden crops. Young plants are damaged severely while still in the hotbed or soon after they are transplanted.

FLEA BEETLE

Young flea beetle grubs attack the underground stems and tubers of potatoes and other vegetables.

Clean culture, weed control, and removal of crop remnants will help to prevent damage from flea beetles. Weeds should be controlled both in the garden and along the margins. Since flea beetles are sometimes driven away by shade, interplant susceptible crops near shade-giving ones.

GARDEN WEBWORM: The full-grown garden webworm is a yellowish-green caterpillar about one inch long, covered with numerous black spots along its back and sides.

A chewing insect, the webworm, eats holes in the leaves and stems of beets, beans, and other cultivated and wild plants. It is usually protected by a thin silken web which it spins about the food plant. Keeping down weeds and other wild host plants along the margins of gardens or fields helps to prevent injury.

GRASSHOPPERS: Grasshoppers vary considerably in size and color. The most common species are dull gray, olive, or reddish brown with markings of yellow and black. Those most likely to cause trouble in the garden are one to 1½ inches long.

No garden crop is immune to attack by grasshoppers. They are typical leaf-eating insects. They have chewing mouthparts and can devour a crop in a very short time if present in large numbers.

Injury is most likely to occur in gardens surrounded or bordered by meadow or wasteland, and may continue from late spring until frost in localities where grasshoppers are abundant.

The common species of grasshoppers overwinter in the soil in the egg stage. The eggs are deposited singly or in clusters, usually on sodland or

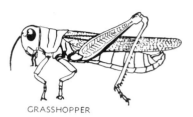

GRASSHOPPER

on areas adjoining sod. The young grasshoppers hatch in the spring and reach maturity during the late summer or fall. For control, *see* GRASS-HOPPER.

HORNWORMS: Full-grown hornworms, the largest insects attacking truck crops in Illinois, are three to four inches long. They are green to brown and have a series of diagonal white bars or V-shaped markings along each side and a prominent "horn" near the rear end of the body.

Hornworms are ravenous chewing insects. They feed on tomato, tobacco, and occasionally on pepper, eggplant, and potato. Although they feed chiefly on foliage, they will also feed on green tomatoes.

Hand-picking is an effective method of ridding a small garden of hornworms.

Hornworms are attacked by a tiny wasp parasite which is commonly seen attached to the body of infested worms. Worms bearing the cocoons of this parasite should not be destroyed, for they do no further damage and the immature parasites on their backs, if undisturbed, emerge later to infest other worms.

JAPANESE BEETLES: adult: shining metallic green; oval; coppery-brown outer wings; about two inches long and ¼ inch wide; larva: white body;

brown head up to one inch long when full grown; attack foliage of such crops as raspberry, beans, asparagus and sweet corn.

JAPANESE BEETLE

To control, beetle grubs have been destroyed by 80 per cent with applications of milky spore disease; one application is said to last as much as seven years; beetles have also been caught in traps filled with geranium oil. *See also* JAPANESE BEETLE.

MEALY BUGS: oval with short projections from the body; often looking like bits of cotton fluff because of the eggs carried by the females in a cottony sac; sluggish and do not move much; attack many house plants.

To control, mealy bugs may be cleaned off special plants with a cotton swab soaked with alcohol; oil sprays have also been found effective.

MEXICAN BEAN BEETLE: adult: copper-colored; oval; 1/4 inch long 16 black spots on back. Larva: orange to yellow; fuzzy or spiny up to 1/3 inch long; adults and larvae feed on pods and on underside of leaves, causing lacy appearance.

To control, handpick beetles and crush egg mashes (effective if done often); plant bean crop very early; praying mantids effective in controlling beetle.

NEMATODES (OR EELWORMS): mi-nute, eelshaped organisms; cause stunted plants; galls on small roots are tiny; compound galls on large roots may be an inch in diameter; attacks nearly all vegetable plants; some nematodes cause a disease called root knot.

To control, rotary tilling sweet clover or some other green manure crop into the soil has been found effective in fighting nematodes; gas from the decaying material kills large numbers of nematodes; heavy mulches effective in reducing injury to plants by nematodes. *See also* NEMATODES.

POTATO BEETLE: (known as Colorado potato beetle) adult: yellow; black-striped; 3/8 inch long; larva: brick-red; humpbacked; up to 3/5 inch long; defoliate plants; especially destructive to small plants.

To control, handpick beetles and crush egg masses (especially effective when done often); scatter common wheat bran in early morning over dew-covered vines; bugs will eat bran and swell up like ticks and fall dead.

RED SPIDER MITES: minute red mites; feed on undersides of leaves; web the leaves to give silvered appearance.

SPIDER MITE

To control, wash off plants with a stream of water from a pressure tank or ordinary sprayer; (generally, spiders washed off plants do not return); three per cent dormant oil spray also found effective.

SLUGS: grayish, wormlike, legless bodies; 1/2 to four inches long when full grown; hide in damp, protected places during day and feed at night; feed on leaves, leave a glistening trail of slime.

An inverted cabbage leaf makes a good trap for both slugs and snails;

spread wood-ashes on the ground; toads consume them.

SOWBUGS, OR PILLBUGS: several species, dark-gray; oval; flattened bodies; seven pairs of legs; up to ½ inch long; sowbugs hide under logs, boards, crop refuse and other damp places; they roll up and look like pills when disturbed; they feed on roots and tender parts of plants.

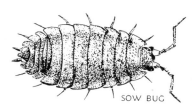

SOW BUG

Look for and eliminate hiding places; best control is prevention— make certain that garden area is cleaned of logs, boards, etc.

SQUASH BUGS: adult: brownish, flat-bodied bug about ⅝ inch long; young; greenish-gray with black legs; cluster on runners and fruit; suck sap from stem; plants wilt and die.

Trap bugs under boards placed on soil around plants; collect and destroy bugs every morning; handpick adults and eggs; plant squash early, as the borer lays eggs in July; by that time, an early grown plant has vines so large that it can do little damage.

WHITE GRUBS: white or light yellow; hard brown heads; curved; ½ to 1½ inches long when full grown; white grubs live in soil and are larvae of common brown May beetles; feed on roots and underground stems of many plants; also attack potato tubers.

Grassland is likely to be infested with white grubs; try to avoid planting vegetables in newly plowed grasslands; rotary tilling and plowing often destroys large numbers of grubs.

WIREWORMS: These insects live in acid soils which are not properly aerated. They are good indicators that the soil has become acid through improper aeration, and often occur in great numbers in an old sod where they live on grass roots.

To control wireworms, aerate the soil and enrich it with compost. It is poor practice to plant a cultivated crop in a field that has had sod on it for a long time, as wireworms will probably cause trouble under this practice.

INSECT CONTROL FOR FRUITS: One of the problems about which organic gardeners are frequently concerned is that of obtaining control over insects and diseases in their fruit plantings. Fruit trees are subject to attack by insects, fungi, bacteria and viruses, but before any of these pests become a problem, certain conditions must exist: (1) the responsible pest must, of course, be present; (2) a favorable environment for its growth is essential; and (3) the fruit crop must be susceptible.

Granting these prerequisites, it follows that we may control insects and diseases by practicing certain measures designed to eliminate the causal organism. These may include maintaining an unfavorable environment for the development of the organism, growing resistant varieties of fruits, and maintaining the health and vigor of the crop. Some of the methods which are discussed here will not afford complete control. However, they should assist the home gardener in keeping check on undesirable pests.

Making an unfavorable environment for growth of these unwanted intruders in the orchard as well as getting rid of them usually consists in the use of chemicals. One of the spray materials which is easy to apply, and which is not poisonous, is an oil spray, which may be applied during the dormant season. This material will help to control most of the common chewing and sucking insects, including red mite in the egg stage.

There are other natural means of establishing unfavorable conditions to pest growth, also. Some examples include proper pruning. Using the clover leaf method to open up a tree will allow movement of air and provide good drying conditions. This procedure assists in cutting down some of the fungus which demands moisture for growth.

In addition, pruning can be used to remove diseased parts as in fireblight, a bacterial disease. The removal of water sprouts will help in the elimination of countless aphids which attack this young succulent growth.

An investigation of the life history of some of the fungus diseases reveal that these may be reduced if apprehended during certain phases of the life cycle. Apple scab, for instance, overwinters in fallen leaves. By raking these leaves, scab will not be completely eliminated, but may be reduced. Peach brown rot, which is carried over mainly on mummies, or the dried peaches, can be partially controlled by the removal of these mummies from the tree and ground.

The control of plum curculio may be accomplished by cleaning up all areas near the orchard that provide places where the beetle might winter. This is followed by discing under the trees to break up and kill the pupae in the ground. During early morning, trees may be jarred so that the beetle will drop on to sheets spread underneath. From here they may be gathered and destroyed. Finally, it is suggested that drops found beneath the trees should be gathered and destroyed while the larvae are in them.

Codling moth, which is one of the most obnoxious pests to attack the apple can be partially controlled by removing loose bark on the trees and wrapping a loose band of cloth, burlap or tar paper around the lower part of the trunk. The larvae, on leaving the fruit, will seek a place in which to transform into adults. Finding no loose bark under which to hide, they will crawl under the band. By turning this band over, large numbers can be destroyed, thus cut-

ting down the next generation. Bins, barrels and other containers where fruit has been stored should be cleaned out and all insects found in these areas eliminated.

The female canker worms, which cause so much trouble, fortunately do not have wings. This makes it necessary for this sex to crawl up the trunks to reach a satisfactory place in which to lay eggs. There are two types, the fall and spring canker worm. By placing a sticky band around the tree trunk in the fall and spring, many of these insects can be eliminated. However, care should be taken that the bands are fresh and that there are no gaps or bridges over which the insects can cross.

The tent caterpillar can be controlled by burning with a torch, if care is taken not to injure the trees. It is also possible to remove egg clusters before they hatch. If the caterpillars have spread throughout the tree, they can be shaken off and also prevented from returning by the use of a sticky band.

The examples given are but a few of the many means of control for any individual pest. It should be remembered that besides traps, scientists have been working on lights, colors and odors which may attract insects from the trees to areas where they can be controlled easily either by electrocution or other means.

It is also important to remember that pests have natural enemies including birds, reptiles and beneficial insects, such as the ladybeetle. The latter are carnivorous, feeding on both larvae and adults of the scale insects, plant lice, and other important pests. Additional examples of the natural enemies could be given. But the important factor is to make conditions so pleasant that these predators will remain to help the orchardist control his harmful pests.

Further, by controlling insect carriers, the spread of viruses which cannot be controlled by spraying, may be reduced. However, when viruses get out of hand, either resistant varieties or the destruction and burning of plants is needed.

A final method for controlling pests is the maintenance of a healthy plant. Vigorous plants, like healthy animals, possess the strength to ward off insects and disease. Maintaining healthy specimens can be accomplished by cultivating in a favorable environment. If for any reason the environment retards growth, plants become weak and organisms can attack the plant more successfully. One of the many examples is that of powdery mildew. Where plants have been checked in growth due to improper watering, excessive heat or cold, or lack of nutrients, the plants become susceptible to the spores of this fungus.

No one of these methods is guaranteed to give 100 per cent control, or even that control demanded by a commercial grower. But for the organic gardener, it offers the possibility of lessening those diastrous results of the more harmful pests.

The importance of further study into the life cycles of indigenous insects and disease cannot be overemphasized, since by these means individual natural controls can thus be worked out and applied.—*Prof. Stephen Patronsky.*

See also listings under insect names; ORCHARD; FRUIT TREES; BRAMBLE FRUITS.

INSECT CONTROL ON FARMS

By following good practices in tillage, crop rotations, planting dates and field sanitation, organic farmers attain much control over pests without extra costs in time, money or convenience.

For example, legumes in a rotation will protect grain crops as well as forage grasses from white grubs; the corn rootworm can also be defeated by suitable rotations; the shade of soybeans grown as a companion crop with corn is used to keep chinch bugs away from the bases of corn plants; flea beetles also dislike shade and damage from them can also be kept little by this method.

Another course of action is to use self-made traps to control insect enemies. Often it is possible to stop army worms in this way. When the worms are moving from one field to another, they can be halted by deep, dusty-sided furrows across their path. The loose dirt keeps them from escaping, and the insects will fall into post holes dug at intervals along the bottom of the furrow. Then they can be destroyed by crushing them with a heavy stick.

Here are some of the specific practices which have helped farmers throughout the nation gain a good degree of control over harmful insects.

CONTROL METHODS: Delaying the seeding of winter wheat until after the fly-free date gives protection against the hessian fly. Fall seeding is deferred so that the wheat does not come up until the fall flight of the insect is past.

Moderately late plantings of corn are damaged less than early plantings by the corn rootworm, or budworm, in the Southeast and by the European corn borer in Northeastern and North Central States. Midseason plantings of corn in southeastern Texas can better survive attacks of the sugarcane borer than can early or late plantings. The corn thus escapes the first brood but attains enough growth before the appearance of later broods to withstand the pest more successfully than do late plantings.

Adjusting the time of planting of field dry beans, snap beans, and lima beans in upper New York State so that the beans do not sprout until the larvae of the seed-corn maggot are no longer active in the soil is highly important in avoiding damage by it. Usually that is accomplished by midseason planting, but it is best to delay planting to avoid maggot injury until information is available as to maggot-free dates. Safe dates vary from year to year and the information can be had from county agents.

These measures listed above go a long way in controlling damaging insects. All of them—plus many others that organic farmers across the country have come up with—show that there's no need to depend mainly on chemical products for insect control on a farm scale.

INSECT CONTROL, BIOLOGICAL: Biological control is the practice of reducing the numbers of a pest by the use of natural agencies such as parasites, predators and diseases. The aim of biological control is to achieve the most practical means of pest control. The fundamental basis of such control is the fact that life in nature exists in a state of balance which is maintained by the competitive interaction of various forces. However, man through his diverse activities frequently disturbes this natural balance, often with disastrous results to his own well-being.

For example, plant-feeding insects are seldom serious pests in their native environment where they have natural enemies that prey upon them. However, when such plant-feeding insects are transported to new areas, and their natural enemies are left behind, they may become extremely numerous and cause serious damage to agricultural crops. For this reason introduced species probably comprise more than $2/3$ of the major insect pests of agricultural crops in the United States.

When such a change occurs in the natural balance of an insect it becomes the business of those concerned with biological control to re-establish a satisfactory balance through the introduction of such control agencies as may be available regionally.

A brief review of the biological control of the cottony-cushion scale in California will serve to exemplify some of the principles involved in achieving this type of pest control. About 1869, the cottony-cushion scale entered California on some acacia trees brought from Australia. Since this scale also feeds on citrus and had no natural enemies here to keep it in check, it spread rapidly throughout the citrus orchards of southern California. No effective insecticides could be found to control this pest and by the early 1880's it was on the verge of destroying the entire citrus industry of California. However, in 1888 an entomologist was sent to Australia, the native home of this scale insect, to determine why it was not a pest there. It was soon found that there were beneficial insects there which fed on the cottony-cushion scale. These natural enemies, being good searchers, could seek out and destroy the cottony-cushion scale in such low infestations that the scale was seldom seen in the citrus groves of Australia. Several species of these beneficial insects were shipped to California. The most effective one proved to be a lady-bird beetle known as the Vedalia. In November of 1888, 129 of these beetles were received and propagated in California on enclosed citrus trees infested with the scale. The following June over 10,000 of their progeny were released. Within a few months the groves in which these beetles were released were practically free of the pest and one year later, due to the distribution and activity of this beneficial insect, the cottony-cushion scale was of no economic importance in California.

The successful solution of the cottony-cushion scale problem by the importation of its natural enemies gave the biological method of control such prominence that its use soon spread throughout the world.

SOME SUCCESSFUL CASES OF BIOLOGICAL CONTROL: Serious agricultural pests that have been brought under control by the biological method include the cottony-cushion scale in California, the sugar cane leafhopper and the sugar cane borer in Hawaii, the citrophilus mealybug in California, the cocoanut moth and cocoanut scale in Fiji, the citrus blackfly in Cuba, the spiny blackfly in Japan, the wooly apple aphid in a number of countries, the black scale on citrus in California, the Comstock mealybug in eastern United States, and more recently the oriental fruit fly in Hawaii.

It should be noted that these successes in the control of pests through the biological method are all concerned with food crops and that the benefit to agriculture from any one of these projects has amounted to millions of dollars.

THE RELATION BETWEEN CHEMICAL AND BIOLOGICAL CONTROL: Insecticides used against a specific pest all too frequently destroy the natural enemies of other plant-feeding insects. An effective natural balance may thus be destroyed. At times the damage resulting from such upsets may far outweigh the benefits gained by the chemical control of the original pest. The destruction of the Vedalia beetle by the use of DDT is a good example of this type of balance destruction.

In the Central Valley of California, after widespread applications of DDT to citrus and other crops in 1946, the Vedalia beetle which preys on the cottony-cushion scale was practically eliminated. Since the DDT applications did not control the cottony-cushion scale in numerous citrus groves but did destroy its natural enemies, the scale increased greatly, becoming a serious pest. When the Vedalia beetle was reestablished in the groves after the DDT residues were no longer toxic to it, the natural balance was again restored.

Other examples during the past few years of natural balance destroyed by the use of DDT are the increase in scale insect infestations on walnuts and citrus, and the increased infestation of various mites and aphids on walnuts, avocados, apples and pears, and a number of field crops. The use of parathion on citrus has resulted in serious infestation of soft brown scale. Many other such upsets between pests and their enemies have occurred on fruit, field, and truck crops throughout the United States during the past few years.

EFFECT OF CULTURAL METHODS UPON THE NATURAL ENEMY POPULATIONS: Certain cultural methods at times may have a pronounced bearing upon the effectiveness of natural enemies.

It has been shown that dust deposits on plants in some cases inhibit the activity of natural enemies and favor the increase of pests. In such cases any practices which tend to eliminate the dust, such as the oiling of field roads, non-cultivation, overhead sprinklers, etc., will tip the balance in favor of the natural enemies.

The control of ants which seek the honeydew secreted by aphids and various species of scale insects is in certain instances of marked importance in the maintenance of a biological control program. This is especially true when ants are numerous on tree crops and ornamentals. The ants which seek insect honeydew actually guard and protect a portion or all of the insect population which produces it. In so doing they not only drive away natural enemies of the honeydew-producing forms but also natural enemies which prey upon mites and other species of scale insects. This interference of ants with the activity of natural enemies occasionally results in serious economic loss to growers.

OTHER PHASES OF BIOLOGICAL CONTROL: A great deal of progress is currently being made in the use of disease organisms in biological control projects. Well known examples of control of insect pests by this means are the natural control of the European spruce sawfly in Canada by a virus disease and the control of the Japanese beetle in eastern United States through the use of "milky disease," caused by a spore-forming bacterium. In California, satisfactory control of the alfalfa caterpillar has been achieved recently by the use of spray suspensions of disease-producing bacteria and viruses. The indications at present are that the utilization of disease organisms as a means of pest control will be especially applicable to vegetable and field crops.

Another phase of biological control which may be economically important will be discussed briefly; that is the mass production, production by millions, of beneficial insects to be released periodically for pest control. Such measures become necessary when the life history of the destructive insect is unfavorable to the natural enemy in the seasonal development of generations or when the natural balance has been disturbed by climatic extremes or by the use of insecticides. Insectaries are maintained in most of the citrus producing counties of California for the production of beneficial insects.

SOME ADVANTAGES OF BIOLOGICAL CONTROL: The advantages of the biological control of pests are so striking that every effort should be made to expand this means of pest control as rapidly as possible. Some of the outstanding advantages of the biological control method are as follows:

1. The biological method is the most practical means of pest control. After the initial cost of the importation and distribution has been paid there is no further expense.

2. The prevailing natural balance of potential pests in the area is not destroyed. In all agricultural areas there are many potential pests under natural control; the establishment of introduced enemies of a specific pest does not interefere with this natural balance of other and minor pests of the same crop.

3. There are no harmful effects to the health and well being of plants protected by this method.

4. There is no development of pest resistance to biological control.

5. The biological method can in no way jeopardize the health of human beings or livestock.

This last mentioned advantage of the biological method of pest control is one of the most important and should be of especial interest to medical practitioners. The possible menace of insecticidal residues to public health is receiving considerable attention at the present time.

DANGERS OF INSECTICIDES: The harmful effects of insecticidal materials to human health may be due to the toxic residues on the plants or they may be due to secondary effects of such residues. Moreover, these secondary effects may be obtained from the treated plants themselves or they may be obtained from animals fed on the treated plants. The secondary harmful effects resulting directly from the insecticide-treated plants may occur through the translocation within the plant of toxic materials from nonedible to edible portions of the plant and thus to the consumer. In cases where the health of human beings may be endangered through livestock which has been fed insecticide-treated plant material, the toxic substances may be obtained from the flesh of the animal or from some product of its body such as eggs, milk, cream, butter, etc. It is a matter of record, for instance, that butter fat from cattle fed DDT-treated hay may contain a relatively high concentration of DDT. The health of persons consuming butter or cream with such a DDT content may be endangered.

NATURAL INSECT ENEMIES

The bald-faced hornet is one of the thousands of insects that live at the expense of other insects. Its life and activities exemplify a mechanism whereby nature keeps a species in check. Many insects often do become disastrously plentiful, but no species has yet even remotely approached the number of individuals it theoretically could, simply because no insect ever gets the chance to continue multiplying as fast as it can. Like most living things, insects are susceptible to bacterial and fungus diseases. Another ever-present control is their enemies.

The adult bald-faced hornets ordinarily feed on the nectar of flowers, but will take only liquids because their mouth openings are so small they cannot swallow solids. The food of the adults is mainly carbohydrate, but the growing brood back in the nest require proteins. To get that the hornets capture caterpillars.

The horse guard is well known in rural districts of the South. It is a large, aggressive, loud-buzzing, black-and-yellow wasp. Farm animals which are distressed by the relatively modest humming of the horse flies and bot flies, will stand quietly while the horse guards drone loudly all around them—they learn quickly that the wasps are catching the flies that are tormenting them. It is a mutually beneficial relationship. The animals attract the flies so that hunting for flies is easy around them, and the wasps, in catching the flies, help rid the livestock of the pests.

In April and May the asparagus beetle comes out of hibernation in asparagus beds. However, many of the eggs—sometimes nearly all—will not hatch. For scarcely has the asparagus beetle finished her laying when her chief enemy appears. It is a minute wasp, which is smaller than the asparagus beetle's egg itself. The wasp sets to work at once to destroy the eggs.

When the Japanese beetle became established in the United States, it multiplied rapidly because it was living here without the enemies that keep it in check in the orient. An intensive research was made in Japan, Korea, and eastern China for native parasites of the beetles. One of the most promising was *Tiphia popilliavora*, which has been established from Connecticut to Virginia.

The adults of Tiphia are shining black wasps, each about three-fourths of an inch long. They emerge in August to mate and feed on the nectar and pollen of flowers. Then when a female is ready to begin laying her eggs, she flies to an area infested with Japanese beetle grubs and burrows under the sod to find them. When she locates a suitable one, she approaches it from the rear, grasps it firmly, and crawls over its back until her head is level with his head. The grub does a good bit of squirming, but seldom succeeds in escaping from this determined wasp. Thrusting the end of her abdomen around the side of the grub's body and between its legs, the Tiphia stings it several times on the ventral side of its thorax. As soon as she strikes the vital thoracic nerve center, the grub ceases its struggling and becomes inert.

The Rove beetle is the main enemy of the cabbage maggot and is less than a $\frac{1}{4}$ inch long having a slender black body and brown legs. In the soil these little creatures construct a series of interconnecting tunnels between tiny subterranean chambers. In this cozy labyrinth, the beetles carry on their affairs.

The adult beetles feed on cabbage maggots or on any other fly maggots in the soil. They are ruthless predators and will attack and eat maggots much larger than themselves. They hunt singly or in small groups through the soil, and when they find a maggot they attack it and tear open its sides and feed upon it.

In a season as many as 80 per cent of the cabbage maggots in a field may fall victim to the aggressive beetles.— *Barnard D. Burks, From the* 1952 *U.S.D.A. Yearbook.*

See also INSECT CONTROL.

INSECTICIDES: Gardeners and farmers have for centuries used poisonous substances to kill insects attacking their plants. Practically every common toxic substance has at one time or another been used as an insecticide. Some, like pyrethrum, derris dust and rotenone are primarily toxic to insects and cold-blooded organisms like fish and earthworms. Other early insecticides were general toxic substances like mercury, arsenic and nicotine. The introduction of DDT during World War II provided a much more potent weapon against many insects than had previously been available, and opened the door to a whole family of new insecticides based on German nerve gases and "organic" phosphates.

Despite the fact that DDT and the other new insecticides are many times more toxic than older materials, farmers and gardeners are still not able to attain a completely satisfactory degree of insect control. There are several difficult problems that complicate the use of insecticides, no matter how powerful:

1. Because insects multiply rapidly and mutate freely, new generations become immune to the powerful new poisons within a few years of their introduction. Some species, like mosquitoes and house flies, develop immunity quicker than others.

2. Insecticides usually kill insects indiscriminately, destroying both the harmful and harmless species. Even birds are often killed. The balance of nature thus being disturbed, harmful insects are often free to multiply even more rapidly than before. Or, insects that formerly were not troublesome multiply quickly and begin destroying crop plants.

3. Insecticides impart toxic residues to treated plants and the soil on which they are grown. There is much concern that sprayed and dusted foods are harmful to human health. DDT, for example, accumulates in the fatty tis-

sue of the human body and can build up in strength to the point where it can cause cell degeneration.

Despite the obviousness of these three weak points of insecticides, there is a tremendous demand for them by farmers and gardeners. The farmer who sees his crops being attacked, his yields reduced and his profits eliminated by insects wants an immediate weapon of retaliation. His first and only thought is to kill the insects that are attacking his plants. This dependence of the farmer on insecticides exclusively is in direct contrast to the techniques of the professional entomologists. They consider insecticides only as a last resort measure, to be called into play when the more constructive insect control methods have been found unable to handle the problem.

OTHER METHODS: What are those more constructive insect control methods? First, there is the selection of plants that have greater resistance to insect attack. It is a fact that some varieties of plants are better able to resist insect attack than others, and the techniques they use to fight off insects are sometimes quite unusual. Some years back it was found that some types of wheat could actually kill the Hessian fly because their stalks suddenly became stiff, and the flies, which had punctured the stalks with their probosci, were unable to extricate themselves.

Another constructive method of fighting insects is biological control—primarily the introduction of natural enemies of troublesome insects. Crop rotation, proper tillage and the addition of humus to the soil are other methods of controlling insect populations without the use of dangerous poisons. Organic gardeners and farmers have long noticed that humus-rich soil with an ample supply of minerals grows plants of such health that they are either unattractive to insects or are better able to withstand insect attack. Some insects are considered to be nature's censors—consuming and destroying weaker plants.

MASS SPRAYING: Much public concern about the harm insecticides can do has been engendered by the campaigns to attempt to eradicate the gypsy moth in New England and the imported fire ant in the South through aerial spraying with DDT and Dieldrin. Both of those insects were introduced into the U. S. from foreign countries, and because they had no natural enemies in this country they multiplied rapidly and became pests. The U. S. Department of Agriculture has attempted to eradicate them by spraying whole counties and even states from the air. As a result, almost all insect life in the sprayed area was killed—both good insects and bad ones. Birds, small animals and even deer were killed in large number. Crops meant for human consumption were tainted by insecticide residues above the legal tolerances. In short, the balance of nature was disrupted and harm was done to human and animal life. Equally tragic is the fact that the mass eradication campaigns do not really eradicate the pests. There are always some that can't be reached by the poison and continue to multiply. Man has never succeeded in eradicating any insect.

People who formerly considered insecticides a necessary evil—or even a harmless tool of farming—have been shocked by the mass aerial spraying programs and have created a new public relations problem for the chemical industry. Wildlife conservation groups have become concerned that spraying may cause widespread lowering of game populations. George J. Wallace, professor of zoology at Michigan State University has reported that "robins are dying like flies" on his campus because of spraying with DDT. Earthworms accumulate DDT in their bodies by eating leaves and litter that has been sprayed, and the robins are poisoned when they eat the affected worms.

SYSTEMICS: Systemic insecticides—those that are absorbed into the sap stream of the plants—are also creating public health concern. Peeling or washing food treated with systemic insecticides does not reduce the poison concentration, as the poison is absorbed into every cell of the plant.

The U. S. Department of Agriculture sets tolerances for insecticide residues, and sometimes shipments of foods with excess residues are seized. However, there is much doubt that the U.S.D.A. tolerances are adequate to protect the public's health. First, the government is not able to test more than a minute percentage of all food shipments. Second, even farmers who mean well are unable to follow the complex instructions for application of the poisons. They may apply the correct dose to an *average* of all plants, but some sections of a field may get many times as heavy an application as others. Third, residue tolerances cannot take into consideration the fact that the consumer ingests pesticide poisons from many different foods, thereby increasing greatly the total that is consumed. Some of these poisons may potentiate, or react together in such a way as to multiply their poisonous effect many times.

Many people become organic gardeners and farmers because they want food that is not contaminated with insecticides or poisons of any kind. Eating food that has *any* insecticide residue is a compromise with perfection, and most people are satisfied only with perfection when their health is concerned. As concern about insecticide poisons becomes greater, pressure on the chemical industry and on Congress for protective legislation will become greater. The chief evil of our present insecticide policy is that it is dictated primarily by the farmer's need to make a profit, and only secondarily by public health considerations. Farmers want complete crop protection, and continually pressure the chemical industry and the government to that end. It is necessary that consumers exert equal or greater pressure for an insecticide policy that is dictated first by everyone's need for pure food. *See also* INSECT CONTROL; GYPSY MOTH.

INSECTIVOROUS PLANTS: *see* CARNIVOROUS PLANTS

INSECT-RESISTANT FRUITS: *see* FRUIT TREES, RESISTANT VARIETIES

INSPECTION, PLANT: *see* INSECT CONTROL

INTERRUPTED FERN: *see* OSMUNDA

IODINE: This element has recently become recognized as a valuable trace mineral. An iodine deficiency is known to cause the development of goiter. This deficiency in plant materials can be corrected by using organic fertilizers containing iodine, such as seaweed and kelp, and also rock phosphate.

IPOMOEA: *see* SWEET POTATO; MORNING GLORY

IRIS: A genus of perennial herbs belonging to the family *Iridaceae,* native to the north temperate zone.

CULTURE: The rhizome-rooted irises, such as the Tall Beardeds,

Any good garden soil that will grow petunias or zinnias will grow iris but the soil should have a good supply of nutrients to grow the best flowers.

Japanese and Siberians are set into the soil one foot apart, with barely an inch covering of earth. In heavy soil, some experts feel that the rhizome, or swollen rootstem, may be left slightly exposed. Since irises are not replanted more than every three years, prime the planting hole with compost about one foot below the rhizome. Avoid fresh manure near the root. Water thoroughly. Planting time for Tall Beardeds is in late June or July, for Japanese and Siberians in early spring and September or October.

Mass plantings of the bulb irises (Dutch, English and Spanish) is by far the most effective. In September, set from three to six inches deep, depending upon the particular variety.

Irises grown in the northern states ought to be provided with a mulch over the winter, chiefly to avoid heaving. Leaves or hay are easy to apply and do the job well.

PLANTING: First of all, lift the entire clump with a spade and tear the clump apart into small divisions. Choose only the largest and healthiest looking ones for transplanting. Let the hose run gently over these while you spade the soil deeply for the new plantings. Sprinkle bone meal over the spots and spade in. Irises demand plenty of rich soil so mix in a generous portion of rotted manure or compost. Good drainage is a must too.

Place one or several of the divisons into the prepared soil. If several are planted together, space them in a circle, leaves turned outwards. If leaves turn inwards the growth will soon center and become crowded. Make each hole deep and broad enough to take the roots without crowding and adjust the height of the plant so that the rhizomes are barely covered. (Rhizomes are the fleshy roots of the plant.) Tamp the soil firmly.

During the rest of the year there is little to do for these hardy perennials outside of the usual maintenance job. This will begin in November when you should mulch all new plantings with straw.

In January and February sometimes it is necessary to tramp over an old iris bed to push down the rhizomes which have sprung up during a thaw. In the middle of March give the beds a dressing of bone meal and lime, using equal parts of each. This mixture should be distributed evenly and thickly. The heavy spring rains—or March snow—will carry this down into the ground to feed the plants.

BLOOMING SEASON: During the blooming season in April, May or June pick the faded flowers from their stems every day and guard against other plants in the bed or border pushing up too closely. This is especially important for the bearded species—they need all the sunlight they can get.

As soon as all the blossoms on the stems have faded, cut the flower stalks down, but the stumps should still be hidden by the foliage. If cut too close to the rhizomes, the stems may rot.

During July the first dying leaves of the bearded iris will droop. Remove these. They will be a good addition to the compost pile, while if left on the plant they will shut out the sunlight from the rhizomes, and give the plant an unkempt appearance too.

The lovely flowers of the iris spring from two types of rooting systems—the bulbous and the non-bulbous, or rhizomatous. These are the most commonly planted, though the bulbous are increasing in popularity.

DISEASE AND INSECT PROTECTION: The following rules may be of help in controlling the troubles which sometimes attack irises:

1. Avoid excess watering and rich nitrogen fertilizers for the Tall Beardeds. Lush growth encourages disease and follow-up borers.

2. When replanting, examine each plant carefully, throwing diseased specimens and leaves into the compost heap. Constantly pick off diseased foliage. Cut away any borers found.

3. Cut back leaves six to eight inches after flowering to keep down excess growth.

4. Handle plants very carefully. Each wound may provide an entrance for the iris borer.

5. Keep the soil supplied with compost.

IRIS GROUPS: New varieties of iris are constanty being sought. The soft pink and clear red varieties in the Tall Bearded class have caught the imagination of iris beginners and enthusiasts. The frontier for breeders includes every conceivable iris type, of which the choice is bewildering.

The deep, rich purple tones of the Siberians are very much in demand for the dramatic setting. The new Japanese types have spread out to showy widths of almost a foot. The South has yielded great numbers of the orchid-like Louisiana iris. The end is hardly in sight.

Along with the first crocus sprouts up the dwarf iris, earliest of all varieties. Iris *cristata* or *statellae* is charming in a well-drained rock garden setting planted in patches or as a border edging in shades complimentary to its neighbors. Avoid any shading by taller plants, a foible of almost all the irises.

The Intermediates come into bloom in early May, bridging the gap between the Dwarfs and the Tall Bearded varieties. Strong on purples and whites but lacking in the pinks, they are useful to blend with bright tulips. Height averages from one to two feet with moderate-sized flowers.

BEARDED TYPES: The stately bearded types carry the blooming season into June. The riot of color is boundless, particularly in the bold and brilliant shades of yellow, blue and purple. The following list of great performers in the selfs (uniform colors) can be a general guide for your selection:

1. Yellow: *Ola Kala, Berkeley Gold Sovereign.*
2. Orange-copper: *Arab Chief, Argus Pheasant, Russet Wings.*
3. Pink: *China Maid, Pink Satin, Pink Formal, Pink Cameo, Cherie.*
4. Red: *Casa Morena, Ranger, Solid Mahogany.*
5. Blue: *Great Lakes, Blue Rhythm, Pierre Menard, Azure Skies, Super Autumn King, Black Forest.*
6. Purple: *Master Charles, Elmohr, Tournament Queen, Sable.*
7. White: *Gudrun, New Snow.*

Amoenas (white standards and colored falls):

1. *Wabash*—purple falls.
2. *Extravaganza*—red-violet falls.

Plicatas (white or yellow ground with colored edges):

1. *Port Wine*—purple edges.
2. *Signal Flare*—copper-brown edges.

The clear shades of the selfs, however, seem more popular at the moment than the busy patterns of amoenas and plicatas.

Try combining the Tall Beardeds with bright yellow daylilies, oriental poppies, or painted daisies in a well-drained spot.

The bulb irises (Dutch, English, and Spanish) arrive in bloom during the middle and end of June. Although mainly a hothouse class, they can be extremely useful for the cutting garden given a moist location. The Tall Beardeds last only for a single day when brought indoors. *White Excelsior, Yellow Queen* and *Imperator* (deep blue) are superb.

State flower of Tennessee, the Siberian iris has easy upkeep, blooms in June with a great abundance of medium-sized flowers. Popular varieties are *Perry's Blue, Eric the Red,* and *Snowcrest* (white).

Following the Siberians is a race of exotic irises known as the Spurias,

which harbor the tallest varieties. The gold-banded white *Ochroleuca gigantea* can grow over five feet, if nursed along with plenty of water. One of the largest flowers in the group is borne by *Wadi Zem Zem,* in a soft yellow.

JAPANESE TYPES: The giant among iris blooms is, of course, the lush Japanese type, flowering until late in July. They excel in shades of blue, purple, and violet, especially with fine speckling or veining. The newest introductions, working toward the clear colors of the Tall Beardeds, often extend a luxuriant eight to 12 inches in width. These varieties must have plenty of moisture and even appreciate a waterlogged soil (they tolerate a dry resting period after blooming). Well-rotted compost is the ideal food.

The unusual late bloomers finish off the season. Each *Vesper* iris flowers in August only for a day, opening at four o'clock in the afternoon. But the masses of blooms on each stem continue for several weeks. A few intermediates bloom both in spring and fall, like the lovely violet *Dorcas Hutcheson,* or *Autumn Queen.*

IRISES FOR LANDSCAPING: Light, cheerful colors are ordinarily most successful in the over-all garden scene. Save the deeper shades for bold accents, used sparingly. The modern setting takes extremely well to the vivid, primary tones, since our picture windows unite the outdoors with the interior decor. When you order your plants, however, keep in mind the color and texture of the house facade if it acts as a backdrop. *See also* PERENNIALS; FLOWER GARDENING.

IRON: This element has long been recognized as important to proper plant growth. Iron is a major factor in chlorophyll development and carbohydrate production. A deficiency of iron in plants causes chlorosis, resulting in the same symptoms as those for nitrogen or magnesium—namely, sickly yellow color. Contrary to many other elements, when iron becomes fixed in a plant, it is not readily sent to another part. Studies have indicated that more iron is necessary when plants are grown in light of high intensity than in light of low intensity.

Soils generally contain sufficient iron but most of it is in an insoluble form. Deficiencies often occur in alkali soils. Also iron deficiency is particularly common in the major fruit-growing districts of the country, as Florida and California. In many cases, the spraying of solutions of iron sulfate, iron oxide or iron chloride on iron-deficient citrus trees has resulted in the formation of soluble salts as ferrous sulfate which are toxic to many plants. Therefore the use of these materials to correct an iron shortage is not recommended.

HUMUS RELEASES IRON: Most of the soil iron is in the form of rather insoluble rocks and minerals, and as such it is unavailable to plants. Some of this iron may be brought into solution by the carbonic acid that is given off as an end-product of respiration by plant roots and microorganisms. But most of the iron that dissolves in the soil solution is probably made to do so by the action of organic chelating (pronounced kee-lating) agents. Soil humus is very likely the most abundant chelating substance found in nature. In addition to humus, the microbial cells themselves, many organic products that result from the biological activities of bacteria, actinomycetes, and fungi in the soil, and fresh and decomposing organic matter serve as chelators to bring iron and other important trace metals into solution where they can satisfy the nutrient needs of growing plants.

These chelators are substances that help dissolve insoluble inorganic salts such as soil and other minerals. They do this by forming water-soluble complexes, as they are called. Chemically,

this method of dissolving iron compounds is entirely different from the way in which acids do the job. For one thing, some chelators accomplish their dissolving action even under neutral and alkaline conditions. They do not require the low pH of acid solutions.

As a general rule, the small amount of iron needed by plants is made available by the action of humus. *See also* DEFICIENCIES, SOIL; TRACE ELEMENTS; CHELATORS.

IRON SULPHATE: *see* FERTILIZERS, ARTIFICIAL

IRONWEED: *see* VERNONIA

IRRIGATION: The objective of irrigation is to keep a readily available supply of moisture in contact with plants' roots at all times. But all too often farmers and some gardeners depend on irrigation to the exclusion of soil building and management practices. Their soil is not in condition to receive and properly utilize the water falling upon it as rain or applied by irrigation.

Experts say the correct treatment of land will insure that 90 to 95 per cent of irrigation and rain water will be used for crop benefit. The average in both irrigated and non-irrigated areas is under 50 per cent.

In New Mexico, for instance, only three of the average 12 inches of rain soak in. The soil is rich in minerals from centuries of weathering, but there is almost no organic matter. The lack of water, however, is much more obvious, so the farmer is led to believe that all he has to do is apply water to get good crops. But the water runs off or leaches away—taking huge amounts of minerals with it—and the soil becomes packed.

CULTURAL PRACTICES: The first thing a farmer should do when bringing semi-arid land under cultivation is to institute practices—green manuring and the like—to build up its organic matter content. Irrigation

Irrigation when seeding a cover crop means a heavier growth and more humus to add to the soil to retain moisture for the growing plants. This sprinkler system was set up on an alfalfa field in Washington.

should be held to a minimum necessary to grow the green manure. Too much water can make machinery contribute to soil compacting. Only three passes over a field a week after heavy irrigation can pack the soil enough to make crop roots grow sideways instead of down.

A soil rich in organic matter will catch and hold nearly all the rain falling on it. Thus much less irrigation water will be needed, and what is applied will be held better, too. Mulching, green manuring, strip cropping, contour plowing and terracing are vital to cut irrigation costs and save the underground sources from going dry.

Another disadvantage: the farmer with an irrigation system is often tempted to use it more than necessary. A heavy supply of water when crops are establishing their roots, for instance, will tend to make the roots stay in the upper layer of soil, instead

of reaching downward deeply. Thus the plant becomes dependent on irrigation, for when drought hits, it has no deep roots to seek out subsoil moisture. And thin, surface roots mean the plant can't pick up rich subsoil minerals for optimum growth. Too, experts say that rainwater that has been in the soil for months will be laden with more minerals than irrigation water. And if irrigation water is applied constantly, it will prevent nutrient-laden capillary water from rising to the root zone.

Better management practices to build the soil and hold rainwater are a lot less costly than irrigation.

Properly used, however, irrigation can be a valuable tool. Water is often a limiting factor in crop growth. In very dry seasons, irrigation may make the difference between crop success and failure.

Light irrigation at planting time on many crops will give earlier start-

Adding compost to irrigation water is an excellent way to fertilize fields, providing irrigation system works efficiently. The compost pile is to the left of the pump. Siphons are used to let water in channel.

ing, more even growth and earlier maturity and harvest.

In the orchard, irrigation can be an adequate stand-by measure—if done correctly. Don't spread out the water: it's better to water a few trees with 1,000 gallons each than to "tease" many trees with 100. Sods or mulches are vital to prevent run-off when these large amounts are applied.

COMPOST IRRIGATION: Some farmers have successfully coupled irrigation with organic fertilization. They run their irrigation water through compost piles, where it picks up billions of tiny particles of rich, bacteria-laden compost and carries them to the fields. The soil stays friable and highly fertile, always loaded with earthworms. Irrigation farmers in the West are increasingly turning to this practice. Many of them use no other fertilizers.

In some areas, sludge from canneries as well as municipalities is being piped directly onto farm fields, and results have been very good.

A fig grower, incidentally, who mulched his trees with manure and sawdust, found he could cut his irrigation from once in ten days to once in 30. His yields rose $\frac{1}{3}$, too, and no more plowing or cultivating was necessary.

Land leveling is another practice that goes hand-in-hand with irrigation. It can save 50 per cent of the water formerly used, and insure so much better utilization of the water applied that crop yields are often doubled. Where the subsoil is exposed by the leveler blades, feedlot manure plus working with a chisel or Graham plow has made it produce a good crop the first year. Leveling is expensive, but it can pay for itself quickly in lowered water costs.

INSTALLATION: Here are a few

tips if you are thinking of installing an irrigation system:

Get competent help from an equipment company. One farmer who worked out his own system found he would have to keep it going day and night for two weeks to apply an inch of water on ten acres.

Check your water source first. A good-sized pond or a stream that won't run dry is best—infinitely cheaper than digging a well. When buying equipment, look for simplicity, portability and coverage to fit the land and crops.

Water should be applied at the time when the crop normally makes its most rapid growth, if the soil moisture is low then. Check with a soil corer to a depth of eight inches. Don't apply water faster than the soil can absorb it, but be sure to wet it to the lower levels. Watch the weather forecasts—a heavy rain following irrigation can drown out the crop.

Irrigation can be worthwhile if it is not used as a substitute for rain wasted through lack of soilbuilding practices. It is most successful when installed after a complete organic program has been put into practice.

ITALIAN RYE GRASS: (*Lolium multiflorum*) This member of the rye grass family sometimes known as Australian rye, is a perennial that grows 12 to 30 inches high. Seldom grown in gardens, its flower clusters are most often seen in fields. *See also* RYE.

IVY: This name alone usually is used to signify *Hedera helix,* though any member of the genus *Hedera* of the *Araliaceae,* the ginseng family, may be called ivy. Other ivies not *Hedera* are: American or fine-leaved ivy, *Parthenocissus quinquefolia;* Boston or Japanese ivy, *P. tricuspidata;* Cape ivy, *Senecio macroglossus;* German ivy, *S. mikanoides;* ground ivy, *Nepeta hederacea;* Kennilworth ivy, *Cymbalaria muralis;* marine ivy, *Cissus incisa;* poison ivy, *Rhus toxicodendron;* and ivy geranium, *Pelargonium peltatum.*

Species of hedera, or ivy, are evergreen shrubs that climb by rootlets which fix themselves in cracks in the support over which they form a cover. They are planted as wall cover, ground cover, sometimes against buildings, and are grown as house plants.

Ivy thrives in rich, moist soil containing plenty of humus. It is propagated by cuttings which easily root at the leaf nodes where its climbing roots are already formed.

Hedera helix, English ivy, is the species most often grown as a climber. It is hardy to New England. It clothes its support in a thick cover of green which, in some varieties, becomes scarlet to rust-red in autumn. Its drawback is that the small rootlets may hasten deterioration of brick or masonry walls.

Some outstanding varieties are: *arborescens,* a shrubby non-climber; *baltica,* a very hardy variety with small leaves; *conglomerata,* with many small wavy leaves crowded on its stems; *gracilis,* whose leaves turn bronze in fall; and variegated leaf forms which are less hardy. *See also* HOUSE PLANTS; FOLIAGE PLANTS.

J

JACK BEAN: (*Canavalia ensiformis*) A vine that is often grown for food in tropical countries, it grows two to four feet high. Plant seeds about one foot apart in rows three feet apart.

JACK-IN-THE-PULPIT: *see* ARACEAE

JACOB'S LADDER: (*Polemonium caeruleum*) A hardy perennial that grows up to three feet high. Also known as Charity, it makes a fine blue-flowering border plant. Plant seeds in a coldframe in early spring, preferably in a sandy soil mixture; transplant about ten inches apart when plants are several inches high. The plant gets its name from the fact that the alternating leaves give a ladder-like effect.

JANUARY GARDEN OPERATIONS: *see* GARDEN CALENDAR

JAPANESE BEETLE: The Japanese beetle was accidentally introduced into this country in 1916. From that time, their numbers grew until the beetle assumed the infamous distinction of public enemy number one in the garden.

In 1933, government entomologists at a research laboratory in New Jersey isolated a handful of sick beetle grubs —and discovered biological means of controlling the beetles, at the same time discovering why Japanese beetles are not a problem in their homeland.

What they found was the first-line natural enemy of the beetle, a bacterial organism that produces a fatal blood disease in the grub. Since it brings about an abnormal white coloring in the infected insects, this was dubbed "milky" disease. And because it is present naturally throughout the soils of Japan, this milky disease germ is the main reason that Japanese beetles are kept fully in check in their native territory.

As with scores of other destructive pests, the beetle became a problem only when brought accidentally to areas devoid of its natural enemies, areas lacking the predators, parasites and insect diseases designed by nature as an ever-present, effective counterbalance. Fighting them with their own deadly ills and with hungry, pest-consuming insect foes is the basis of biological control.

MILKY SPORE DISEASE: After several years' work, the control specialists tackling the Japanese beetle enigma came up with a method of producing the milky disease organism in the laboratory. When it was added to the grub-infested soil in 14 states in an initial testing, the beetle-killing results proved astonishing. Local and federal governments since then have started over 150,000 "colonies" of milky disease in the Northeast alone. The most significant fact, though, is that wherever the milky disease has

The Japanese beetle, once feared for its seeming invulnerability coupled with its voracious appetite, can now be controlled by biological means.

been established, the Japanese beetle no longer rates as a serious pest.

Effect of milky disease on Japanese beetle grub. As the grub succumbs, the blood turns white. Infestation was reduced 95 per cent by inoculation.

The spore powder—a standard mixture of the germ spores, chalk and filler—is produced commercially under a process patent owned and licensed by the Dept. of Agriculture. Since its introduction, groups of homeowners and whole communities, along with individual gardeners, have joined forces and efforts successfully in eliminating the beetle in their sectors.

BEETLE GRUBS: Grubs of the Japanese beetle are hatched and live in the ground—frequently in lawn turf—until they mature into adult, winged beetles. All through their lengthy grub stage, however, they are subject to attack by several of the milky diseases. The most important of these is known as type A, caused by a germ organism technically termed *Bacillus popilliae*.

As the grub feeds where this is present, it ingests some of the spindle-shaped disease spores, which are 1/4600th of an inch long—so small that billions may exist in one infected grub. The spores form slender vegetative rods in the grub's blood, and these grow and multiply, developing in a few days into the milky spore.

When the affected grubs die (as they invariably do), the spores which fill the body cavity are left in the soil. They are taken up by other grubs as they feed, and these in turn become diseased. As the cycle goes on, the number of spores in the soil increases, more and more grubs are killed, and fewer beetles emerge.

Here are some important facts on the milky spore disease treatment:

It is cumulative; that is, it continues and spreads itself;

Ordinarily, only a single application is required for lasting control and protection;

The disease powder kills only Japanese beetles and a few of their close beetle relatives. It is totally harmless to the soil, to beneficial insects, bees, earthworms, all plants, animals and humans.

It is not affected by weather extremes, by cold, heat, rains, drought.

APPLICATION: All the gardener does is apply a teaspoonful of the spore disease powder on his grass or sod in spots three to four feet apart and in rows the same distance apart.

It can be applied at any time except when the ground is frozen or when it is windy. Recommended for treatment are only mowed or cropped grass areas. A pound of the spore powder will treat about 4,000 square feet of turf for moderately good results (up to 60 per cent kill within 12 months)—and, of course, continued and increasing protection. Higher application rates bring even greater results in less time. Authorities agree that the spore disease control averages 80 to 90 per cent in over-all effectiveness. *See also* INSECT CONTROL.

JAPANESE CHERRY: *see* TREES, FLOWERING; CHERRY, FLOWERING

JAPANESE QUINCE: *see* QUINCE

JAPANESE SPURGE: *see* GROUND-COVERS

JAPANESE WALNUT: see HEART-NUT; WALNUT

JAPONICA: Often used as an alternate term for the camellia (*C. japonica*), the very showy evergreen shrub that grows to 30 feet. Sometimes japonica refers to the Dwarf Japanese Quince (*Chaenomeles japonica*), an early-blooming shrub that grows to three feet. Its red flowers and yellowish-green fruit add to its usefulness as a hedge. *See also* CAMELLIA.

JASMINE: These handsome, flowering shrubs, often called Jessamine, are popular greenhouse plants. Hardy types are favorites for outdoor planting in the milder climates of central and southern states. Jasmines do best in a sunny location and in a well-drained loam. The fine fragrance of their flowers add to their popularity. They can easily be propagated by layers of cuttings of nearly ripe wood.

Spanish jasmine (*J. grandiflorum*),

The Star jasminum gains its name from a sharply defined flower formation. They do best in a sunny location and are popular greenhouse plants.

also known as Catalonian and Royal jasmine, is a nearly erect-growing shrub; reaching four feet high; a fine greenhouse plant; white-flowering. Set young stock out in spring.

Italian jasmine (*J. humile*) is evergreen or half-evergreen; can grow as high as 20 feet; yellow-flowering; hardy as far north as Maryland; blooms in summer and fall.

Primrose jasmine (*J. mesnyi*) is another evergreen type; five to ten feet high; spring-flowering; yellow-blooming. The common white variety (*J. officinale*) is a tall-growing (40 feet) deciduous shrub; summer-flowering. Winter jasmine (*J. nudiflorum*) has yellow flowers; grows upright; and often blooms all winter in mild climates.

JASMINE, RED: see PLUMERIA

JERUSALEM ARTICHOKE: see ARTICHOKE

JERUSALEM CHERRY: see CHRISTMAS CHERRY

JEWEL-WEED: see IMPATIENS

JIMSON WEED: (*Datura stranonium*) An ill-scented, dangerously poisonous weed, this plant is a rank-growing annual that produces both a nerve and stomach poison called hyoscyamine. Botanically, it is in the same family as nightshade, potatoes and petunias.

Domestic animals are poisoned by feeding on the tops of the plant; children, by eating the unripe seed pods, which are sometimes called thorn apples. Some people are especially susceptible and get a skin rash from touching the leaves. The nervous form of poisoning is the most common, its symptoms including headache, nausea, extreme thirst, burning sensation of the skin, dilated pupils and loss of sight and control of limbs. In extreme cases, mania, convulsions and death may occur.

A bushy weed, jimson may grow six feet tall on smooth stems that are either green or purple. Leaves are alternate, unevenly toothed and strong-scented. The large, trumpet-shaped flowers are white on the green-stemmed variety, violet or purplish on the purple-stemmed type. Fruit consists of a hard, prickly, four-parted capsule containing many large, flat, dark brown or black seeds. At maturity, the capsule splits open into four parts.

Jimson weed grows in fields or waste places, mostly on rich, gravelly soils. It should be mowed before seeds are produced, but if mowed after fruits are ripe, the plants should be burned. *See also* WEEDS.

JOE-PYE-WEED (*Eupatorium purpureum*): Also known as purple bone-set, it is a perennial herb three to eight feet tall with large clusters of composite heads and tubular, purple flowers. Of some value as a honey plant, Joe-pye-weed is common in low, damp ground in the eastern states during late summer, and is found in most parts of North America. It generally blooms in late summer or early fall; propagated by division in spring.

JOHNSON GRASS (*Holcus halepensis*): Also known as Means grass and Aleppo grass, it is a stout, perennial forage grass of agriculture value, but tending to become a weed in the garden.

In these days of very necessary emphasis on conservation crops to save blowing, washing soil resources, many crops get their start on farms as agents of conservation. Crops with thick, deep root systems that bind the soil against rain and wind are highly valued. And the organic farmer goes one step further, treasuring these crops for their production of humus and aerating, water-conserving qualities. Such a crop is Johnson grass.

Johnson grass was long considered one of the biggest plant pests in the lower half of the United States. Since it was first introduced into this country in South Carolina around 1850, and spread to large areas of the South and West, farmers fought its encroachment into their good cropland —often losing the battle to its rugged persistence.

But Johnson grass suddenly came into its own. In the Dust Bowl days of the thirties, farmers on the Central Plains found that Johnson was the best soil holder they had ever seen. It licked wind erosion completely.

Farmers have found that the qualities for which they once despised it are now making it a dependable, profitable crop: Johnson is hardy, grows fast, resists drought, and is high in protein and so palatable all livestock relish it. It yields well with little attention—up to five tons an acre of hay (six or seven when irrigated), 200 to 500 pounds of seed, and it will pasture one animal unit per acre for six months.

Johnson grass needs a fairly rich soil, but it also grows well on fine sandy loams. It will grow as far north as central Illinois, but agronomists do not recommend it as a perennial north of southern Tennessee. It spreads by vigorous underground rootstocks as well as by seed.

It is a good ground cover, growing thickly three to seven feet high. The grass grows well along basins and terraces, on steep slopes and in waterways. It can be started where it is practically impossible to get a stand of other grasses.

Plant Johnson grass any time after the soil gets warm until the end of June. Early plantings yield the most. Thorough disking well in advance of planting will give you a firm seedbed. A legume before the grass will supply ample nitrogen, but apply rock phosphate and potash as dictated by your soil test. Three to five tons per acre of manure are good, too, if available.

The seed may be broadcast at the rate of 20 to 35 pounds per acre, or drilled in four to six pounds per acre. Always drill it in one to two inches deep, on the contour. When mixed with legumes, 15 to 20 pounds of grass seed are usually used, but some farmers recommend more.

JONQUIL: *see* NARCISSUS

JUGLANS: The family of woody plants with attractive foliage that includes the walnut and butternut. Walnuts have massive straight trunks, large leaves, small green flowers, in addition to their edible nuts. They are hardy and fairly insect and disease resistant, generally preferring moderately moist, rich soils. Varieties include the English or Persian walnut (*J. regia*)—up to 70 feet tall; black walnut (*J. nigra*)—up to 150 feet; *J. californica*—40 to 50 feet high; and the butternut or white walnut (*J. cinerea*)—up to 100 feet with grey bark. *See also* WALNUT; BUTTERNUT; NUT TREES.

JUJUBE: (*Zizyphus jujuba*) Belonging to the family *Rhamnaceae*, jujubes are a little-known fruit, mostly grown in the warmer sections of the United States, especially in California. Growing up to 30 feet high, the trees should be planted 20 feet apart. They usually grow well in ordinary garden soil, and are quite resistant to insects and disease. Sometimes known as Chinese date, jujubes have become a popular candied fruit. The fruit is egg-shaped or oblong, about one inch long and brown when ripe.

JULY GARDEN OPERATIONS: *see* GARDEN CALENDAR

JUNEBERRY: The edible fruits of over 25 species of Amelanchier, also known as service-berry, grape-pear, and shadbush. Juicy and sweet, the juneberry fruits vary in size from a pea to a small crabapple, and from dark red to black. Better than the fruit of the hawthorn, juneberries years ago served as a prime source of nourishment to explorers and American Indians.

CHARACTERISTICS: The juneberry varies from dwarf shrubs to 30-40 foot-growing trees. Many species are highly resistant to insects and disease, besides being quite hardy in areas too cold for many other fruits. Their culture is similar to that required for apples.

Attractive as ornamentals, juneberries are highly recommended as an edible-berried shrub and tree. *See also* AMELANCHIER.

JUNE GARDEN OPERATIONS: *see* GARDEN CALENDAR

JUNIPER: (*Juniperus*) A large genus of evergreen trees and shrubs belonging to the pine family. Many of them are well suited to the small garden. The tall, pyramidal types are conspicuous planted singly or in groups; the low, spreading forms are excellent for foundation plantings and in a rock garden.

Junipers can grow satisfactorily in slightly dry, gravelly soil, but prefer a sandy loam with sufficient moisture. They do best in an open, sunny location.

Their gray-green needle-shaped leaves are usually borne in threes. The short, prickly ones stand out from the twigs, forming what is called whip-cord foliage, because it resembles a braided cord, while the scale-like leaves press closely against the many slender twigs. Generally, junipers with needle-shaped leaves can be propagated more easily than those with scale-like leaves.

VARIETIES: Its many forms differ widely in shape and height. The dwarf variety (*J. depressa*), known as the prostrate juniper, can grow well in poor soil and any exposure. Although it reaches a height of only two or three feet, this wide-spreading form may exceed five feet in width. Its color in winter is grey-green, and it is excellent as a low wall plant. One variation of the dwarf form, Irish juniper (*J. hibernica*) is often recommended as an accent plant.

Creeping juniper (*J. horizontalis*) is another low-growing type, hardy throughout the United States, and doing best in a sandy, rocky soil.

Common juniper (*J. communis*) grows to 12 feet, sometimes as high as 40 feet. It makes a fine upright shrub, has needle-like leaves, black fruit, is also hardy throughout the United States.

Western juniper or yellow cedar (*J. occidentalis*) is actually a tree, growing 40 to 60 feet high, with needle-like leaves and black fruit. Red cedar (*J. virginiana*) grows as high as 100 feet, usually about 50 feet. Its varieties have foliage varying from dark green and gray to ones with branches that have yellow tips.

Junipers are excellent choices for hedges and windbreaks, often making the most outstanding plants in the formal garden. Certain varieties are well adapted to sandy banks along seaside locations. Propagation can be done with seeds, but most often by cuttings of nearly ripe wood in autumn. *See also* EVERGREENS.

JUSSIAEA: *see* PRIMROSE WILLOWS

JUTE: (*Corchorus capsularis*) A fiber plant grown in the United States in the Gulf states. Belonging to the tropical family *Tiliaceae,* jute is fast-growing. The stems, up to 15 feet high, yield the fiber.

K

KAKI: *see* PERSIMMON

KALE: (*Brassica oleracea acephala*) Kale, or borecole, is hardy and lives over winter in latitudes as far north as Pennsylvania and in other locations where similar winter conditions prevail. It is an all-year plant since it is also resistant to heat and may be grown in summer, but its real merit is as a cool-weather greens. In northern regions where it lives over winter the last sowing should be about six weeks before frost in order that the plants may become well established. It may well follow green beans, potatoes, peas or some other vegetable that has occupied the soil during the summer and early fall.

Healthy kale will grow in almost any soil, and it may be seeded any time between early spring until a few weeks before hard frost. For these very reasons, it is probably often planted in the place in the garden which green beans and peas have occupied in the early part of the summer, and little if any additional food given to it for its own sake.

This method of planting ignores the fact that kale is a member of the cabbage family, all of whom are good feeders and need very fertile soil of a fine texture. The quality of the entire cabbage group is closely associated with quick growth. For this they need both rotted manure or compost at planting time, and a side dressing of organic nitrogen—about $\frac{1}{3}$ of an ounce to a foot of ground—at intervals of three weeks during the summer. Lime is essential for all members of the cabbage family. A liberal application of crushed calcium limestone or shell limestone should be applied to the area at the time of preparing the ground to assure good growth and make the plant food supplied by the previously applied compost readily available.

Like all leafy, green vegetables, kale develops best in deeply-prepared, loamy soil. It will have neither good flavor nor texture if grown in either light, sandy or heavy, clayey soils. A cool weather green, it is as hardy as spinach. It is also resistant to heat, so may be grown in summer, if desired, and if precaution is taken not to sow the seed in hot weather. Failing this, the crop will seldom mature.

The best garden varieties of kale are low-growing, spreading plants with thick, crinkled, curly leaves. They may be sown in the Middle States from early spring on until a few weeks before the first hard frost. If the time chosen is in the fall, the seeds may be broadcast like those of turnips. If sown in the spring, when weeds are especially active, seed the plants in a row. If this latter method is used, place the rows 30 inches apart and have the plants 16 inches apart. One packet of seeds will be enough for a family of four or five persons.

In preparing this row, dig in small amounts of lime, and liberal amounts of well-decomposed manure or other types of organic matter. Once they are in the ground, cover the seeds lightly by raking the soil over them. When the sprouts are two or more inches high, scatter humus lightly along the sides of the row, and around the individual plants, but do not allow it to go nearer than three inches from the stems of the plants.

It will bear repeating that, like all other members of this cabbage family, one cannot expect to obtain top quality in kale if the growth of the plants is hindered by lack of nutrients and water, and so are unable to make the rapid growth necessary for their highest development. If this growth appears to be slow, side dress the plants with the following application: Dissolve two teacupfuls of stable manure in 12 quarts of water and let the solution stand for 24 hours. At the end of this time, make a narrow furrow, also three inches away from the plants, and pour into it one cupful of the liquid for each foot of the row. Two weeks later, make a similar application, this time placing the solution six inches away from the plants.

Mulches are especially valuable in the growing of kale, for a large part of the root system develops near the surface of the ground, and runs through the soil almost horizontally across the rows. For this reason cultivation should be shallow and a mulch will not only conserve moisture and keep the soil cool in the heat of summer, but will also make it possible for the kale roots to feed on the topmost two or three inches of soil. Place your mulch during the latter part of May or early in June.

Kale may be harvested either by cutting the entire plant, or by taking the larger leaves while they are still young. Old kale will be found stringy and tough and of little use in the diet. Good seed is essential, and so should be one of the first considerations. Harvesting from the first planting in the spring should begin the first week in June. A crop planted near the middle of August should be ready for cutting by the middle of October.

The worst enemies attacking this vegetable are the flea beetles, which eat holes in the leaves; aphids, which suck the juice of the plant on the undersides of the leaves and stems; and the Herculean beetle which, with its masses of eggs, is easily seen and may be exterminated by picking off with the hand. As for the other two pests, there can be no better methods for these than attention to choosing healthy seed for the kale bed, proper bestowing of soil enrichment at stated times with organic matter, and careful mulching. This, as is the case with other home grown vegetables, will produce a well nourished plant,

healthy enough and strong enough to defend itself from marauders.

Kale is rather coarse for salads, but as it is valuable in its vitamin C content, it may well form an ingredient among mixed greens used in this manner, and also may be used as a garnish. Its best table use, however, will be to boil it as one would spinach. Sometime, we suggest that when you do this, you save the water in which it has been cooked; add to this, water in which a bunch of celery has been boiled; blend the two liquids, bring them to a boiling point, and let this mixture stand until it is cool enough to drink. The result will be a healthful beverage permeated with mineral and vitamin content.

There are three popular types: Blue Scotch or Dwarf Curled; Dwarf Green Curled Scotch; and Siberian; the latter is the most tender and of the most delicate flavor. *See also* COLLARD.

KALMIA: Family of evergreen shrubs that includes mountain laurel (*K. latifolia*), swamp laurel (*K. polifolia*) and sheep laurel (*K. angustifolia*). Belong to the heath class, kalmias have showy pink, white or purple flowers; prefer a shady location in a humus-rich, moist acid soil. If planted in a dry or wind-exposed location, be sure to keep mulch of oak leaves, or similar acid organic material.

Sheep laurel, also known as dwarf laurel, grows two to three feet high, is hardy throughout the country; its leaves are considered poisonous to animals. Swamp laurel is a two-foot high shrub, grows mostly in meadows and bogs. *See also* MOUNTAIN LAUREL.

KELP: A loosely-defined group of large brown seaweeds, especially the families *Laminariaceae* and *Fucaeae*. Kelp has been found valuable as a soil conditioner. It is rich in potash—2.25 to 6.25 per cent—and nitrogen—1.7 to 2.5 per cent and about .5 per cent phosphoric acid. *See also* SEAWEED.

KENTIA: *see* PALMS

KENTUCKY BLUEGRASS: *see* LAWN

KIDNEY BEAN: (*Phaseolus vulgaris*)
More commonly known as string or
snap bean, this refers to the bushy
annual variety. *See also* BEAN, BUSH.

KITCHEN GARDEN: *see* VEGETABLE
GARDEN; PLANNING

KITCHEN WASTES: Kitchen wastes
represent a tremendous potential of
organic matter which can be returned
to the soil. Reports show that the
average person is responsible for from
150 to 300 pounds of garbage a year.
At present, most cities destroy garbage, burning it, burying it or dumping it into the sea. In recent years,
however, some cities have been adopt-
ing various methods of municipal
composting, whereby all the city's
garbage is composted and reduced to
a fine material suitable for garden
and agricultural use. *See also* COM-
POST; GARBAGE.

KNOTWEED: (*Polygonum*) *see* BUCK-
WHEAT

KOHLRABI: (*Brassica caulorapa*) It
must be admitted that nobody seems
to know where the kohlrabi comes
from and how it got to be the way
it is today. It has been called "the
mongrel of the vegetable kingdom"
because it is like a "turnip growing
on a cabbage root."

CLIMATE AND SOIL: Kohlrabi
grows equally well in hot or cold
weather but, for best results, grow
your plants in the cool days either
of the spring or the autumn. The
species is naturally a cool-weather
plant which matures rapidly within
a period of twelve weeks. It will grow
well in high country—provided you
have a growing period of at least 80
days.

Soil should be rich loam, well-
drained to permit early planting. It
should contain plenty of humus;

green manure previously turned under
gives good results. Compost, barnyard
manures and old mulches are also
very satisfactory.

Make sure that your soil is not
too acid. Lime should be added when
the pH reading falls below 5.5. Fine-
ground limestone is best for long-
lasting results.

Hardy and fast-growing, kohlrabi does best in a
humus-rich, well-drained loam. Plant it as soon
as the ground permits working in early spring.

PLANTING AND CARE: Because
kohlrabi is very hardy and a fast-
growing vegetable you can make three
sowings in this temperate zone; in
April, toward the end of May and in
early July. The two recommended
varieties for garden growing are Purple Vienna and White Vienna. The
former is outstandingly hardy and
should be sown late for winter maturing. The White Vienna is highly
esteemed for its tenderness and sweetness and its "accommodating" nature.

You can start your plants in the
house or in a coldframe and transplant subsequently. But, for the best
results, sow your seeds directly into
the rows where they will attain maturity. Make a shallow furrow and
drop about ten seeds to one foot of
row, or about $\frac{1}{8}$ ounce of seed to
100 feet.

Cover the seeds with almost an inch
of soil. Firm with your foot and mark

the row which should be 15 to 18 inches apart from its neighbor.

When thinned, the plants should stand about four inches apart. The culls can be transplanted in another section of the garden, thus extending your harvest season. The shock of transplanting retards the growth process and the thinned-out plants come to maturity later than the original stand of kohlrabi.

Rapid growth is a must if you want tender, succulent bulbs. Slow-growing plants are tough and the flesh is strong. So your kohlrabi should grow in soil that is always "moderately moist." Shallow cultivation is also important because the young roots spread out just under the soil surface. Until the plants are tall enough for mulching, just scrape between the rows with a sharp hoe.

If you want to give the plants a booster feeding, side-dress them with an organic fertilizer equal to 4-12-4 after they have been thinned. Loosen the soil between the plants and in the rows before putting on a thick mulch, making sure to keep the cultivation shallow.

Keep the soil under this mulch moderately moist at all times. The proper amount of water is very important as far as good bulb texture and flavor are concerned. Quick growth means quality and while the kohlrabi has the reputation for standing up well to drought, the price for survival is tough, woody, "strong-flavor" bulbs. Don't starve the plant for water while it is growing; kohlrabi is much more succulent when plentifully watered.

HARVESTING: Many gardeners give up on kohlrabi because they don't harvest at the right time. The right time is when the plants are young and tender—not old and tough. Maturity time is about 80 days. Some people feel the right time to pick is when the bulb is the size of a baseball. You will probably be happier if you pick when it is the size of a golf ball—1½ to two inches in diameter. Don't give your kohlrabi a chance to grow old and stringy—start picking them early and enjoy them.

If they're growing faster than you can use them—pick them anyway. Pull them up at the right time and store them in a cool basement. Or you can bury them deep in the soil and cover them with straw or hay. They will keep crisp and fresh well into the winter.

If your kohlrabi has had plenty of water and you have picked it in good time, it is tender and succulent and has a good flavor. You can pick it and eat it raw. You can slice it into midsummer salads.

Always cook the kohlrabi in its skin to preserve flavor. The sliced root may be simmered and the bulb served steamed or boiled for winter meals.

Remember how-to rules:

1. Plant as soon as the ground can be worked in the spring—they are cool-weather growers;

2. Thin to four inches apart and cultivate lightly;

3. Mulch heavy and give plenty of water—keep the soil moderately moist at all times;

4. Grow them fast and pick them early—within 80 days.

It's a good practice to keep the ground working and improving after you have gathered kohlrabi. Plant it to snap beans and then turn them under when they begin to form pods. They will release plenty of nitrogen right into the soil as they decay. In this way you will fertilize your garden and get it ready for the following year with very little extra effort.

KOLKWITZIA: A particularly beautiful flowering shrub, sometimes known as "beauty-bush." There is only one species—*K. amabilis.*

It is a slender shrub with a graceful, arching, elegant habit of growth reaching a height of probably six to eight feet when fully matured and a spread of almost as much. The flowers are sort of tubular with a very lovely fragrance and with a white to pinkish cast.

The flowers just cover the plant from stem to stern and from leeward to windward or fore and aft or whatever other description a sailor might use. It is not a rampant grower and doesn't grow quickly either. It takes about three years in the nursery to get a decent-sized plant.

KUDZU: (*Pueraria thunbergiana*) Kudzu has been drought insurance for wise farmers in the southeastern "disaster area" in past summers. While other crops, notably corn, withers and dies under the blistering sun, kudzu is almost startling in its greenness and rank growth.

Although kudzu has been a special blessing to the eroded southlands, it also grows well in Pennsylvania, New York, Illinois, Ohio and Nova Scotia, according to reports from those areas. Its uses in agriculture are many, including erosion control, as permanent pasture, for hay making and as a soil improver in rotations. The organic farmer would find other uses not common to the traditional farm. Kudzu hay makes a mulch equal in value to alfalfa; it could be profitably used in orchards, spread over fields in sheet composting, or mixed in the compost pile.

Propagation is by seeds, cuttings and root-division. It shows large three-part lobed leaves, spikes of fragrant, purple flowers and flat, large, hairy seed pods.

Kudzu is a legume, a member of the bean family, with all the desirable qualities of that plant group, including nitrogen fixation. Kudzu is a deep-rooted perennial. Its roots go beyond the farmed-out top inches of soil to eight feet and more to utilize minerals previously of no value to the farmer. Once planted and cared for properly it lasts a lifetime. It does have limitations of climate—a severe

This three-year-old kudzu grew successfully on a worn-out portion of a Georgia dairy farm. A deep-rooted, drought-resistant legume, kudzu roots often reach down eight feet or more for nutrients.

winter of temperatures of 20 below will probably kill the roots, and it needs irrigation where rainfall is under 20 inches a year.

Kudzu resembles a grapevine; its large leaves protect the soil from torrential rains during the growing season, and after frost has killed the tops these leaves form so perfect a mulch that water loss on steepest slopes is only two per cent. Kudzu is well liked by all forms of livestock, including cattle, horses, sheep, hogs, goats, rabbits, and poultry. Kudzu is a high protein feed, testing as high as 18 per cent and comparing favorably with alfalfa in every respect, except that it is lower in calcium when grown on acid soils.

The Georgia Experiment Station gives this analysis of the cured Kudzu hay: 11.3 per cent protein, crude fat 2.2 per cent, crude fiber 35.1 per cent, nitrogen free extract 39.2 per cent, calcium 1.4 per cent, phosphorus .2 per cent, other minerals 5.3 per cent and moisture 5.3 per cent.

Kudzu made its debut in the United States in 1876, when it was used as a porch vine by the Japanese for their exhibit booth at the Centennial Exposition in Philadelphia.

The Soil Conservation Service began championing kudzu in 1934, going from farm to farm, showing men just what it would do. It is excellent for gullies and steep slopes because it can be planted here and there on fields in spots impossible to cultivate or prepare properly for any other crop, and in a few years its long vines have stretched along the bare ground, taking root wherever they touch soil. A ground cover of kudzu brings the return of dried up springs and ponds and neighboring streams soon run clear, because kudzu so perfectly prevents water loss and silting.—*R. W. Stephens.*

KUMQUAT: (*Fortunella*) Actually Chinese evergreen trees that are closely related to the orange. They have blossoms similar to oranges. Culture is also like that required by citrus trees. Meiwa kumquat (*F. crassifolia*) grows eight to 15 feet high; the ground kumquat (*F. japonica*) reaches ten feet. *See also* CITRUS.

L

LABURNUM: A genus of small ornamental trees of the *Leguminosae,* the pea family. Flowers, borne in May or June, are long hanging clusters of yellow pea-like blossoms, which give the trees their common name, golden chain trees. Leaves are light green to yellow. Thrives in any soil if it is well drained, and may be planted in full sun or part shade. Can be successfully used in city plantings. Propagation is by seed, which germinates easily, by layering, or grafting. Fruits of all species are poisonous.

Common laburnum, *L. anagyroides* or *L. vulgare,* is the less hardy of the two principal species, but it can be grown to central New York state, the southern New England states, and along the Pacific coast. In the colder regions its flower buds may be frosted in spring. Its flower clusters are about eight inches long, opening in May. Two interesting varieties are *aureum,* which has yellow leaves, and *autumnale* which flowers a second time in September.

Scotch laburnum is a more hardy species, and because it blooms two weeks later, its buds are not so likely to be frosted. It is stiffer and more upright than the common species, which has a tendency to droop, and its flower clusters are longer. Scotch laburnum is hardy as far north as Massachusetts.

LACEWING FLY: (*Chrysopa californica*): A natural insect enemy of the mealy bug. *See also* INSECT CONTROL; MEALY BUG.

LACINARIA: *see* LIATRIS

LACTUCA: *see* LETTUCE

LADINO CLOVER: *see* CLOVER

LADYBUG: (*Hippodamia convergens*) Ladybugs, sometimes called lady beetles or lady birds, now are annually harvested in eight western states and shipped all over the country to help check certain types of insect pests. Fortunately the ladybug is no vegetarian, her diet being strictly confined to soft-bodied insects such as aphids, mealy bugs and their kin which are so destructive to crops in many localities. Moreover she and her larvae do triple duty by feeding on eggs and larvae of these insect pests.

Of some 300 species of lady beetle the ladybug is found the most beneficial in habit, number and adaptability. She is about $\frac{1}{4}$ inch in length and has a shiny, hairless shell back of orange or reddish color with dark spots, an ornament at sight but really a cannibal at heart. Armed with stout jaws her diet is solely insect, never herbaceous. The larvae are almost as voracious as parent.

When entomologists made serious study of the beetle, they came up with a startling economic fact: it lives on scale, soft-bodied insects and their eggs and larvae, but it never damages plants, truly one of Nature's gifts for man's benefit. That finding doubtlessly saved the California orange industry some years ago. Mealy bugs were threatening the trees to extinction and in the crisis, lady beetles were imported from Australia to make a Roman holiday of the pests.

WHERE FOUND: With the advent of warm spring days, ladybugs emerge from protective rock crevices. In some mountainous sections of eastern Washington, ladybugs have been found so thickly clinging to warm ledges that they were literally scooped up. The warmer the weather the more the beetles scurry around for food, even winging to distant points. With the coming of cooler weather in fall the beetles tend to mobilize in swarms and seek protective shelter from the colder days.

After collection in mountainous regions, predatory ladybugs are packaged and kept at a cool temperature (32 to 60° F.). Gathered in the hibernation or non-eating stage, they are found to be fully active and effective when returned to warm temperatures following this cooling process. They should be released in the garden in the spring when warm weather has begun and when the soft-bodied insect pests which they eat in considerable numbers each day start appearing. Ladybugs are especially helpful in controlling aphids, Colorado potato beetles, alfalfa weevil, scale and other soft-bodied insects.

The matter of food supply is the big drawback to raising ladybugs in commercial quantity. They insist on taking their vitamins and proteins in the raw, soft-bodied insects, their eggs and larvae in the open.

The ladybug carries an unmistakable tag of identification—a white, V-shaped mark on its thorax, or joint between head and body.

CHARACTERISTICS: Its orange or reddish wing plates are veinless and thickened, forming a pair of convex shields which the entomologist calls *elytra*. When the beetle is at rest the shields form a straight line down its back, covering the folded flying wings which are veined and membraneous. When flying the shield wings stand out at right angles like the wings of a monoplane.

The larvae of the convergent ladybug is from 1/16 to ¼ inch in length, flattened, tapering, and of dark brown color with a bright orange spot on their backs. Under a reading glass the larvae appear warty, somewhat resembling the gila monster, a poisonous desert lizard of southwestern United States. The appetite of larvae is almost on par with that of the adult. Normally the adult consumes about 45 insects daily; each of the larvae takes on about 36 insects.

With both adult and larvae temperatures influence eating. In hot weather they scurry around more to take on more rations. On cool days, activity slows down and so do appetites. But nothing short of a freeze keeps the friendly little predators from foraging at all.

The adult lays orange-colored eggs in clusters of 15 to 30, depositing them on under side of leaves. In a full season the egg total runs around 350. So small they scarcely can be seen with naked eye, the eggs hatch in about 15 days, hence every month there should be about 30 times more ladybugs on the premises.

HOW TO USE: Care must be taken in "planting" ladybugs in an infested field. They should not be scattered like sowing grain, but carefully placed in a handful lot at the base of plants, usually a handful every 20 or 30 paces. The beetle's instinct is to climb up the nearest plant, seeking food on foliage. If handled too roughly, especially in warm weather, the beetles become excited, often seeking safety in flight. During summer months it's better to "plant" them during early morning or evening when cooler temperatures lessen their flying inclination.

Like birds and other forms of wildlife beneficial to man ladybugs ask only protection and food. When fall comes some of them may seek the sheltered nooks of a house to winter through, then emerge during the first warm days of spring.

Biggest enemy of the ladybug is the poisonous insecticide. Like all other forms of plant and soil life the ladybug just can't take a lethal spray.

Due to climatical condition and degree of infestation no standard formula has been worked out for quantity distribution of ladybugs but the following amounts based on study and experiment with different crops are recommended by G. C. Quick, entomology dealer of Phoenix, Arizona.

Cotton—16 gallons of ladybugs per acre.

Spring Wheat—Six gallons per

100 acres for aphids and green bug control.

Sorghum, in boot stage—16 gallons per 100 acres.

Trees, fruit and nut in heavy foliage—Two gallons per acre.

Truck Garden—One gallon per five acres.

It has been estimated that there are about 30,000 ladybugs in one gallon.

Ladybugs have been effective in helping control corn borer and even will eat roaches. Should infestation be critical a second application may be made; however this is necessary only in extreme cases.

And best of all the employment of ladybugs can be a long-term investment. Some of them winter through and are on hand to help Nature strike a balance next season. At any rate they have three distinct advantages over poisonous sprays: They are cheaper, they're natural, and they're safer to use.—*Jack Van Clute.*

See also INSECT CONTROL, BIOLOGICAL.

LAGERSTROEMIA: A genus of shrubs and small trees of the loosetrife family, *Lythraceae.* Flowers with fringed petals grow in loose terminal clusters, and may be white, pink, red, or purple, depending on variety. Blooming period lasts for several months in summer. Propagation is by seed or cuttings, which are easily rooted. Seedlings often produce bloom the first year, cuttings either the first or second year.

Crape myrtle, *L. indica,* is the principal species grown in the United States. It is hardy only in the South and as far north along coastal regions as Maryland. North of that area it is root-hardy to Massachusetts, if the roots are protected, but the tops will die back each year. Vigorous growth and bloom will follow the next spring. It is known in the North principally as a greenhouse subject. When grown indoors in a pot or tub, it is cut back severely each fall, and will bloom several times during the year. Young plants grown outdoors in the south must also be cut back almost to the ground after blooming, otherwise growth the following year will go into foliage, and bloom will be sparse. A dressing of manure or compost should be spread around it in spring. After root systems have become large enough to supply food for both foliage and flowers, the pruning may be continued if a shrub is desired, or may be somewhat lighter if it is to be allowed to become a flowering tree. Trees attain a height of about 20 feet.

Queen's flower, *L. speciosa,* is a tropical tree growing to 50 feet, a native of India and Australia, which can be grown only in southern Florida and southern California. Its mauve to purple flowers grow to three inches in diameter, and its leathery leaves to one foot long. It is extremely showy when in bloom.

LAMB'S-QUARTERS: *see* WEEDS

LAND CLEARING: Land clearing is perhaps the most fundamental of all farming work. The pioneers had to strive mightily with sweat and axe to wrest land from the forests before they could plant crops to sustain them in the wilderness.

Today many farms have one or more patches of overgrown land that could be put into pasture or crop production. Their owners, however, often hesitate to tackle what looks like a back-breaking and maybe expensive job. "Where's the profit," they say, in spending hours of hard work or hiring big, expensive equipment to clear out a few acres of brush and wood?"

If the land has a good production potential and can be cleared at reasonable cost, it's worth the time and work, as farmers who have recently cleared land in their spare time can attest. New tools—especially one-man chain saws—have cut the labor and time to a fraction of what it used to take.

There's another angle, too: organic methods and machines like wood chippers and shredders make valuable soil-building material from the brush, branches and leaves that once had to be burned to get rid of them during clearing operations.

You can do land clearing any time of the year that other work is not pressing. Winter used to be the traditional season for this job, but farmers today have found they can do it any time it will fit into their work schedules. In fact, after a hard day's work on other chores, using a motor saw to zip through big trees can be a pleasure—certainly more of a pleasure than swinging the old-time axe on trees that seem to get tougher with every stroke.

There are two principles, however, which must be considered before attacking any overgrown land:

First, to what use can the land be put. Many a farmer has regretted letting a custom operator talk him into having land cleared haphazardly. Some wooded land, for instance, with careful thinning and selective cutting thereafter could be built up into a fine woodlot that would yield steady income for decades. Other land, because of its steepness, stoniness or bad drainage, would be best left merely as a wildlife refuge; put into pasture or crops, it might well deteriorate to desert conditions in a very short time.

If you have any doubts as to the advisability of clearing any wasteland for production, let an expert decide. Your county agent will help you figure out whether a given piece of land is suitable for development without requiring stringent conservation measures, intricate drainage systems or other practices that might be costly. Your soil surveyor who draws up a soil map of your farm, or the Soil Conservation Service technician who makes up a complete conservation plan for the farm, are excellent men to consult. You may find that some overgrown land you had thought practically worthless can grow crops with a suitable rotation, or will make permanent pastures as good as any you already have.

The second principle—fully as important as the first—involves fertility and its maintenance. The soil of the land under consideration may be deep and rich as virgin prairie—or it may be thin and infertile. To the cost of the clearing job itself must be added the cost of the lime, rock fertilizer, manure and whatever else may be needed to bring the soil up to satisfactory fertility and organic matter levels. Even if you plan to grow soil-building legumes, it will probably require some lime, rock phosphate and/or manure to establish them, and soil tests may even show the soil to be lacking in a vital trace element.

So have the soil tested before clearing, and use a soil corer to study its depth, structure and subsoil characteristics. Knowing these facts, plus its degree of slope, will help you make a rough estimate of the total cost of conservation and fertility measures necessary to put the land into production.

Will the profit from the crop you intend to grow pay back the cost of clearing and fertilizing within a reasonable time—say two to three years? If so, lay out a plan for clearing the land.

The costs of clearing may vary greatly for different types of land and different methods. You may find, for example, that there are enough large trees on the area to pay for clearing it, if they are cut and sold as cord or pulp wood.

For about $300 you can buy a one-man chain saw, or get a self-propelled circular saw for $200. A chain saw can be used for many other jobs around the farm, and most of them are light enough to be held over your head to get high branches. Some circular saws have their own wheels, others are hand-carried and some work from the power take-off of a tractor.

A couple of swipes with an axe may be the most practical way to take out saplings and shrubby stuff. But sometimes a patch is so overgrown with briars and saplings that it is wiser to have a custom man come in and go over it with a bulldozer. Some have serrated blades that slice off roots below the ground, and many custom men use root rakes to collect the heavy roots that would take too long to rot in the soil.

Costs for 'dozer work ranges from $25 to $60 an acre, depending on how thick the growth is. A farmer who has little time to spare and wants the land in production in a hurry will probably find hiring a bulldozer man worth while. But check around with other farmers to make sure you're hiring a good 'dozer operator: you don't want your top-soil all ripped off and left to wash away with the first rain.

A bush-and-bog harrow is an excellent tool for cutting up brush and small saplings and working them into a mulch. It's particularly good for hillside work, where a bulldozer would have to back up steep slopes for each pass.

Don't burn the brush! Farmers and custom men have worked out all sorts of flame throwers and rigs to burn up this valuable material. Far better to use a wood chipper (farmers often get together and buy them cooperatively) to chew it up for mulch material. The plant food and organic matter in an acre of brush and branches can be worth a good piece of change, if used for soil building and protection. Brush can also be used, along with corn cobs and other organic materials, to fill gullies; it will catch eroding soil and also rot to gradually seal the gully.

Wood chips make fine bedding—in some respects, better than straw—and are also good for poultry litter. You may find a ready market for chips if you live in a dairy or poultry section. Deep mulches of wood chips are fine for orchards and berry bushes, too, as well as for vegetables and other crops. But don't work the material into the soil unless it's well rotted, or it will temporarily tie up nitrogen needed by crops. A wood chip mulch will hold moisture in the soil, help stabilize its temperature, and greatly increase bacterial activity. Custom work with their chippers, incidentally, has proven a profitable sideline for quite a few farmer-owners.

Get some kind of cover on the soil as soon as possible after the clearing is done, so erosion cannot steal your newly-won topsoil. Mulch the soil with organic materials or plant a green manure crop on it until you're ready to seed it to pasture or row crops.

LANDSCAPING: The gardener planning the composition of a landscape, and seeking to insure the best possible visual, productive, and soil-conserving results must use a sensible plan or blueprint. Of fundamental importance, if a completely satisfying effect is to stem from the composition, is the definite and concrete recognition of form, texture, and color. Heeding these three basic elements of landscaping is a necessity in successful composition.

Form, color, and texture have often been referred to as "The Unholy Three" because of the fact that all three must be present in balance to obtain good composition of a design. They are so closely allied that the line of demarcation between any of them is frequently difficult to distinguish.

Most forms are thought of as the flat surface of lines on a blueprint of the design we are drawing. For instance, a horizontal line suggests quiescence, a vertical line, ecstasy; but opposed to each other they convey power. A curved line suggests energy.

Now, if we combine these forms into the following designs, we have geometric solids which closely correspond with plants produced in nature:

To achieve the best results in using these line forms in the composition of a landscape think of them in a three-dimensional perspective. In other words, how they will look after they are growing in that part of the garden which is to be their permanent location.

are built into particular groups and masses. In other words, in the development of a satisfying effect in the garden one should not have dissimilar collections of flowers or plant forms, but should use a repetition of form character with just enough contrast introduced to lend variety and subdued points of interest.

Consider a rose garden. If it were planted in a manner which produced all the colors in one group we would have a monotony of color and all of the same form. The form would be all right as it is not dissimilar, but it

Beauty in a landscape or flower garden depends partly on the variations in forms of plants used, as well as resulting color and effect when plants mass together. Wall gardens add variety to design.

One should know what line forms to choose for any composition to be designed. Among the most common are: Cushion form—an effect obtained by using the prostrate junipers; Mound form—obtained by using boxwood or the barberry or privet; Egg form—obtained by using the maples; Matt form—by using creeping myrtle; and Columnar form—by using poplar.

Beauty in a landscape or flower garden is partly determined by the form type of the various plants that make up its composition, as well as the resulting effect when these plants

is the color which calls for attention. If we planted the rose garden in a prearranged pattern, with the various colors in their respective places, and then planted a subdued variety of another plant around the edges of the rose beds, we would have both a repetition of form character and a subdued point of interest. Height must be given every consideration in a composition. It regulates the size of planting in comparison to the scale. If height is forgotten, the result is flat, uninteresting, and out of proportion to the inside pattern.

SCALE: Scale is another important

factor to consider. By scale is meant the size of the landscape to be used in comparison to the size of the trees or shrubs employed. There are people who insist on planting five or six of the larger elm, maple, or oak trees on a lot fifty feet wide by one-hundred fifty feet long. This is considerably out of proportion to scale as regards the number and size of the trees on such a small piece of ground. There are so many attractive forms of trees and shrubs which could be used for the small lot situation which are more fitting in size and proportion.

In the expanded estate-type plantings, the larger forms such as the elm, red oak, black ash, and hickory can be used effectively to obtain a desired result or to frame a smaller scaled perspective.

Examples among the larger trees include: Cylinder type—tulip tree; pear type—hickory (both pignut and shellbark); vase type—Chinese elm and hackberry; spiral type—all larger conifers.

Plant forms are indicative of character, moods, and personalities, and should be chosen for a particular location with this in mind. Take, for instance, the delicacy of the beech tree. Its graceful lines indicate a gay personality which will create a mood of cheerfulness in any composition. Then there is the quiescent personality of the weeping willow. The rugged individualism of the sturdy oak gives an air of towering strength. Compare a group of birch trees with an oak grove. Here you will find a similarity of traits. Airiness, grace, delicacy, trimness, power, strength—these traits are the outcome of line and shadow in the plants and give the entire composition personality and character.

Vertical and horizontal-lined composition of form in the garden are the dominant and recessive characters which will determine the effectiveness of the plan.

Vertical-lined forms such as hollyhock, delphinium and fox-glove, contribute to development of vertical or horizontal effects made in the garden. They are at their best when planted in groups located at the back margin of the group and occasionally allowed to extend toward the front.

Horizontal-lined forms which are not defined sharply produce a restful and quiet effect. Sweet William, iris and peonies are representative of these, and should be planted in masses which are longer than wide, rather than in groups or as single specimens.

Winter study of various deciduous trees and shrubs will give the potential landscaper a better idea of the shape and lines of trees, for they are bare at this time of year. Of course, one must imagine how the trees will look when they are clothed with summer foliage. Evergreens, green through all seasons, can be studied at any time for their form.

The contour of the land where the planting is to be made will have a modifying effect on the forms of plants and trees, and controls the direction in which they are laid out. Gardens and landscapes laid out informally will take more study and planning than a formal design.

We can vary from the dominant forms to prevent the planting from becoming monotonous or to create an accent. By dominant forms is meant the basic plants used in largest amounts. Varying these should be done gradually. If we vary the dominant forms to create an accent, it must be remembered that the more sudden the variation, the stronger the contrast.

ACCENT: Accent should be judged on its merits for the particular location in which it is to be used. It should also be employed sparingly and with special care. Too many accents, a very common fault with amateurs, will cause a landscape to become wearisome. If accents are not placed properly they will destroy the balance of the landscape, and the harmonizing effect we have been looking for will be destroyed. An accent is to be a point of attention which will catch the eye momentarily, then allow it to pass over the remainder of the picture. This can be compared to the art of flower arranging, for each flower arrangement must have an accented center of attraction to make it a perfect composition.

Good composition of form includes simplicity, sequence, balance, and scale similarity. These are the main factors of form and will be applied best by experience and observation. Skill and good taste are obtained through comparison of plans, ideas, reading and experience.

COLOR CHARACTER: The beauty of a garden is in large part dependent on the use of good color combinations in bloom, foliage and bark. Using one of the standard color charts it is comparatively simple to determine what plants to use and where to place them in order to obtain proper color balance in the garden.

Design should include the complete garden lay-out such as size of flower beds, shape, and their location. Next, consideration should be given to what kind of a garden motif we wish, whether formal or informal, Chinese, Japanese, etc. Foliage and flower color is perhaps the most difficult consideration in planning a garden, for the foliage color has to be taken into consideration with the actual bloom color of the same plant.

Color, with its many hues, tints and shades, affects form and texture, in the composition of a flower garden. Hence is seen the need for good color harmony in order to have a balanced landscape picture.

In drawing the design of a flower garden, one must exercise care that too much ground is not embraced. It looks quite easy on paper to put in a lot of plants, but it is not as simple as it appears and it is better to have fewer flowers than to have a lot of them cared for improperly. This is a common fault with most beginners and of all things it happens most with annuals as they are the hardest to keep free of weeds and are difficult to transplant to their permanent beds.

Good soil and drainage are a necessity to growing flowers. Good soil containing the proper organic food elements will give the flowers and leaves the color Nature intended. Lack of good soil will keep the plants from their maximum leaf and bloom color. There are a number of other benefits which good soil will contribute in giving the plants the necessary elements to grow. Height, strength of stem, large root system, brittleness of stem, are but a few.

While we are talking about flower color, we cannot forget our garden accessories. Bowls, pergolas, vases, fountains, pools, walks, and other structures are all considered in the color composition of a garden, and they should be given every consideration. If the original garden plan is changed after the first year and the accessories do not fit in with the new scheme, it is no big job to use the desired color of paint and refinish them in colors to harmonize with the new planting.

The garden color guide will give you a good idea on mixing colors in a garden. Variation of color combinatins which will blend together in harmony can be obtained by simply using the different shades of the primary colors.

One thing we have to watch very closely in Mother Nature is her preference for green. She will provide so much of it, that unless you make compensations, it will throw your complete color scheme out of balance.

You do not need to have plants in the garden you do not like just to keep a particular color scheme. There are so many kinds of plants available that it would be hard not to be able to have one the same color as your own particular choice.

GARDEN COLOR GUIDE: Use deep blues with clear, soft yellows. With scarlet use clear white in the combination, as a rule.

Clear pale blues with clear pale pink; creamy white or blue-white or pale yellow, or all together.

No clear blue near a violet blue. Lavender blue near a violet blue may be used with pale yellow and pale rose pink. Deeper, brighter, warmer yellow with deeper or bluer violet.

An unusual combination, which should be used carefully is pink and blue-violet. With deeper purple very little is good save paler tints of the same, cream-white, or pale yellow.

Paler lilacs with white, pale yellow, and pale rose-pink.

Magenta is difficult, best alone or with white or palest yellow.

Deep blue-reds and blue-pinks will look well with practically nothing but each other; pale rose and creamy white are greatly improved by garden green.

Use rose-pinks of all tones together with or without white.

Use rose-pinks with deeper reds of the same tone combined with white.

Clear rose-pink with gold-lavender, pale yellow, not bright or clear, but creamy, or pale blue, or all together.

No scarlet near blue-red or purple. Soft creamy pinks are good with softest creamy yellows and white.

Scarlet with clear blue, or clear yellow, or both, with or without white.

Flame pinks with coldest gray-blue or with cream-white, or both alone with a deep green or gray-green foliage.

Use browns and tawny oranges only with each other, with cream white, or with any yellow.

Blue is bad with bronze tones.

Creamy orange with clear blue, gray-blue, some lavender-blue, and deep purples or violet blues.

Pure orange with brown and bronze, and yellow with softest gray-blue or cream white.

Pure orange with flame orange.

Use pale straw and creamy tints anywhere just as you would use white.

Pale creamy yellow with deep red or deep pink.

Clear yellow with most blues, using cream white freely.

Use clear bright yellow of any tone seldom with pale violet-blue, and not at all with pink.

TEXTURE: Texture has been, and is, one of the most discussed and misunderstood words in the landscaper's vocabulary. It is one of the three basic factors which we must consider in the composition of a beautiful landscape. Basically, texture includes the appearance of trees, shrubs and flowers as they will look in their permanent places in the completed landscape. Some trees, shrubs and flowers have a smooth appearance, while that of others is rough. These smooth and rough appearances are the direct result of the various sizes and shapes of the plants. The variations of size, appearance and shape among the parts of the plants produce texture. In our minds, we are aware of these various textures only by seeing them, and if we are to produce a unified composition, we must use these variations of plant textures and arrange them into a gradual change from tall, coarse-textured plants, to low, fine-textured plants. It is customary with most landscapers because of scale relations between the shape, size and texture of plants, to use the tall, coarse-textured plants for backgrounds, accent points, and distant planting effects; and, to use the low, fine-textured plants for close-up plantings.

Texture can mean more than just smooth and rough appearances. To the gardener just beginning, these two basic factors are a must in starting the landscape picture. By using these two and adding a lot of experience with the various plants, he will gradually become acquainted with other factors, such as: fineness and coarseness, lightness and heaviness, denseness and thinness, flexibility and stiffness.

We shall have to take into consideration the seasonal variations of the plants. Take, for instance, the dogwoods. In the spring their red, yellow and gray bark, makes a beautiful background, and as the summer brings on the green foliage there is still a hint of these shades of bark showing through the green leaves, providing another type of texture. Dogwoods are just one of many such examples of seasonal texture variations.

The location, soil, and moisture content of a soil are three factors which do a lot in regulating the quallity of the texture in plants.

Plants constantly change their characteristics with age. For instance, when young, the bark will be of a soft texture increasing to a more coarse texture as they become more mature.

Paths are another small but important texture factor in composing a good design. These little paths which wind in and out among the trees and shrubs should harmonize in their texture with that of the surrounding landscape. With the exception of large landscaped estates, it is my contention that it is a very bad example to use cement walks. If cement walks have to be used, soften their glaring effects by coloring them a soft green, red or blue. This can easily be done by using concrete color dye.

It is well to remember to avoid too great a contrast as well as too great a variety of textures, for too sudden and too strong a contrast will bring a discordant result. Let us take for an example a beautiful lawn of creeping bent or Kentucky blue grass. A lawn of this type by itself has unity and produces a beautiful picture. Now, if we were to allow dandelions to infiltrate into the lawn, we would have too great a contrast, and a resulting discord. We would also lose the fine soft-textured effect produced by the grass alone.

One thing we must remember when we use the various textures in our landscape design is that the resultant effect must be simple; it must have scale relationship, sequence and balance. If we keep these in mind we shall produce a garden composition that will be pleasing and acceptable, not only to ourselves, but also to all who view it. Texture applied by following these simple rules will stimulate the imagination and create an effect of character. It will give a symbolization of power, strength, refinement and good taste to our composition.—*Myron Parish.*

See also FLOWER GARDENING; FOUNDATION PLANTING; ROCK GARDEN; WILD GARDEN; SHRUBS; TREES.

LANDSCAPING PLANTS, GROWING:
see NURSERY, HOME

LANTANA: A tropical shrub that is often grown as a potted plant indoors. Red or yellow sage (*L. camara*) is a very popular showy shrub grown in the South; in the northern parts of the country, it is usually grown as a cool greenhouse plant. It grows to about four feet high, has yellow flowers that change to red. *L. montevidensis* is more of a vine, generally used as a trailer.

LANTERN-PLANT: *see* BRYOPHYLLUM

LARCH: Common name for any tree of the genus *larix* of the pine family. Larches are deciduous conifers, that is, cone-bearing trees which shed their needle-like leaves each year. The common larch is native to Europe and Asia, where it is hardy up to the area of perpetual snow. It attains a height of 60 to 100 feet, and lives as long as 200 years. It is of an elegant conical growth, which makes it valuable as a stately ornamental in large landscaped areas. It is also of value for its lumber, which is tough, elastic, and extremely durable. The tree yields Venetian turpentine, and its bark is used in tanning.

Leaves of the larch are narrow,

one to 1½ inches long, growing in pine-like tufts on short spurs, or distributed spirally on rapidly growing branches. When the young growth appears in spring, the effect is misty-green, and very pleasing. Male and female flowers grow on the same tree, and cones grow to one or 1½ inches, with woody persistent scales.

The European larch will grow in almost any soil in an open situation, with sufficient moisture. The American variety seems to prefer acid soil, and frequently is found in marshy bogs. Propagation is principally by seed, sown in fall or spring in shaded beds. They may be transplanted to their permanent sites after they are two years old, or may be transplanted to stand three to six feet apart in the nursery at that time.

Principal enemy of the larch is the larch saw-fly, whose black-headed larva attacks the leaves. The fly hibernates over the winter in surface litter, and lays its eggs in spring on new shoots. Best preventive is to remove all litter from below the trees in the fall.

The European larch, *L. decidua,* is distinguishable by its yellow-gray smooth shoots, and oval cones with downy scales on the backs.

American larch, *L. laracina,* is also sometimes called the tamarack or hackmatack. It grows to 60 feet, and is native from Labrador to the northern states, with extensive tracts in the Allegheny mountains, in swampy locations.

More often planted as an ornamental is the Japanese larch, *L. leptolepis,* a fast-growing species which grows farther south than the European or American larches. It will grow to 90 feet, has a scaly reddish bark, with oval cones.

The Dahurian larch, *L. gemlini,* attains a wider spread than the other species. It is also a northern species, native to Asia. Its shoots are brown, and small pink cones grow no more than an inch long.

LARIX: *see* LARCH

LARKSPUR: The stately spires of the larkspur will add a full measure of beauty to any garden composition. They are very nice for cut flowers, too.

CULTURE: Since larkspur is an exceedingly hardy annual you may plant seed in the late autumn. The seeds should be sown just before the ground is expected to freeze. The purpose of fall sowing is not to have the seeds sprout in the fall, but to have them in the ground and ready to germinate when conditions are favorable in the spring.

Thoroughly prepare the soil by incorporating compost, well-rotted manure and peat moss in light or sandy soils. If your soil is heavy, add a one-third portion of sand to the formula to help lighten it. This will help insure better drainage. The soil shouldn't be too rich, so you can be a little on the stingy side with the compost and manure. A moderately fertile soil gives best results.

Plant the seed in a location where the plants will receive full sun or light shade. Press lightly into the ground and cover with a light layer of pulverized soil. After the ground has frozen hard, mulch the bed with a loose covering of straw, grass clippings, leaves, or evergreen boughs. This will prevent alternate freezing and thawing of the ground. Remove the mulch in the spring after danger of frost has passed or when the seeds start to sprout.

VARIETIES: The Giant Steeplechase Larkspurs have big, double, compact flowers on long spikes. Color range in this variety includes blue, sky blue, pink, white and red. Giant Imperial Larkspurs grow upright like delphinium. They aren't as tall as the Steeplechase, but come in a range of the most desirable colors. The Branching Larkspur varieties produce many spikes and are free blooming.

These also come in a wide color range.

LOCATION: Larkspur should be planted where they will have full sun; however, they will do well in a lightly shaded area also. The most common use is as a background or tall border flower. The plants grow from three to five feet tall, and the massive spires of bloom are very beautiful. They look very well against the modern high wooden fences, erected as a windbreak or for privacy, where their tall spires of white, rose, pink, lavender and blue add a touch of color to the natural wood hues of the fence. A few spires of larkspur scattered here and there lend true beauty and height to any garden. *See also* DELPHINIUM.

LARVA: Plural, larvae. The early form of any animal in which it is unlike its parent, as, the tadpole is the larva of a frog. Specifically, the first stage after the egg of any insect in the caterpillar, maggot, or grub state before it enters the pupa or chrysalis and emerges with wings. The larval state is completely different from the adult state, which is attained during the pupal, or rest state. In this respect it differs from the *nymph* state of some insects which undergo a gradual change to the adult without going into a pupal state.

LATANIA: A genus of fan-palms native to the Mascarene Islands in the Indian Ocean, with two species occasionally grown as ornamentals in the warmer sections of California and Florida. In the north they are known as potted subjects, being grown in greenhouses sheltered from the sun. All of the several species known in this country are remarkable for their ornamental leaf growth, the fans attaining a diameter of five feet on fully grown subjects, with red or orange stalks and midribs. All species grow with stout, ringed trunks, and are not prickly or barbed except along the new growth and young leaves.

L. commersoni, which attains a height of 40 feet, is most commonly planted outdoors in the south. It is a handsome species, with deep red ribs, and leaf segments three inches wide at the base. Its fruit is nearly round, with ribs.

L. loddigesi is also occasionally planted in Florida, where it seldom reaches a height of more than 20 feet, though it grows in Mauritius to 50 feet. It has attractive blue-green fans, whose individual segments measure two feet in maturity. Young leaf-stalks are barbed and are reddish, fading to green as they get older, and the barbs becoming hairy bristles.

Hothouse plant seed offered as *L. borbonica,* the Bourbon palm, are usually *Livistona chinensis,* an entirely different plant. *L. commersoni* is sometimes also sold as Bourbon palm, though the true *L. borbonica* is seldom cultivated.

Like all palms, the *latanias* need manure or leaf mold-enriched soil, whether they are planted indoors or out. They want a reasonable amount of moisture during their growing periods, April to October, after which they are practically dormant, especially when grown indoors. At this time the potted specimens should be allowed to become almost dry.

Potted latanias may be placed in the border, with their pots sunk deep in the earth, after nights have become warm. They should be given a protected position, with partial shade. A feeding of manure water about every second week during the growing season will promote general health. Before the nights turn cool in September, the pots should be returned to indoor positions, and water gradually withheld. *See also* PALMS.

LATERITE: The word *laterite* comes from latin—*later,* meaning a brick. In some laterite soils there is a softness that can be cut with a knife. Sections so cut are made into blocks which when dried harden into stone.

In Indo-China, India and many other laterite soil countries such soil is commonly used as a substitute for brick and stone in making houses, temples and statuary.

Laterite soils are located under heavy tropical forests in hot, humid countries. But there are various degrees of laterization depending on certain conditions. The highest degree of it is in the tropical rain forest regions. Laterization lessens in the grassy or savanna region of the tropics, becomes still less in the tropical highlands and is weakest in the hot steppe country.

CLIMATE: The common denominator, as one can see, is heat. There also must be fairly abundant rain. The rain at least must be moderately high. Under podzolization we have high rainfall and temperate climate. Chernozem soils occur in sub-humid regions, with a cool climate, sometimes being very harsh. There are cold winters, hot summers, high winds in chernozems, and the rainfall which is only between 16 to 28 inches, can bunch itself in the spring in sharp showers. Water is usually scarce in chernozem regions and there is always a threat of drought.

LATERITE COLOR: The laterites are in the red family due to the presence of large amounts of iron oxide. The subsoils are always red and bright yellow, but topsoils are often brown or gray. In some regions reds or yellows come into the topsoil due to erosion. This is usual when the parent rock material is basalt. Podzols are usually ash-colored while chernozems are black.

GEOGRAPHY: In the United States there are over 460,000 acres of lateritic soils, which occur in Mississippi, Alabama and Georgia, but there are also red soils in Northern California and Oregon. There are laterites in Southern France, Italy, Spain, Greece, Central America, northern South America, Puerto Rico, Cuba, India, Burma, Thailand, Java, Borneo, Sumatra and Hawaii. Sometimes podzols and laterites overlap.

MINERALS: A laterite soil is very high in iron and aluminum, and is very low in silica. The heavy rains, helped along by the extreme heat, leach out the latter. The pH, or acid-alkaline measurement index, is usually high, thus precipitating the iron and aluminum, which means that it makes them insoluble. The term laterization means a soil low in silica and very high in aluminum and iron. Some soils that have turned into laterites may have once had originally about 40 per cent of silicates. Now they may be down to perhaps two per cent. The reverse is true of iron and aluminum. Where once a soil may have consisted of two per cent iron, in the process of laterization, it now may have over 70 per cent of it. One can observe iron concretions and in many laterite soils iron ore has formed.

Since the iron and aluminum are high, so is the phosphate, because the latter has a ready tendency to combine with iron and aluminum. But the phosphate is rendered insoluble. Therefore when the chemical fertilizer—superphosphate is used in laterite soils its phosphate portion becomes unavailable to plants. Lyon and Buchman in their textbook *The Nature and Properties of Soils* state, "For this reason rock phosphate, which is not so readily affected, can be used to advantage." Jacob S. Joffe in *The ABC of Soils* says, "It has been found that on podzol soils or on acid peats and mucks, finely ground phosphate rock does give good results." It is interesting to note how agronomists in isolated references, are caught off base, and will recommend phosphate rock which is such an essential part of the organic method. But when they write articles attacking the organic method, they will insist on saying that phosphate rock is as a rule an insoluble fertilizer and not to be recommended.

On a laterite soil calcium, potassium, magnesium and sodium are easily removed by leaching. Therefore, granite rock powders, which are usually rich in potassium could very well be used in such soils, for the same reason that phosphate rock is recommended. Also dolomitic limestone. Leaching in laterites is much more pronounced than in podzols. Lime should be used freely. It raises the pH, thus reducing the activity of the iron and aluminum.

Usually the fertility level in laterite soils is at a low ebb and the tendency is to lean heavily on chemical fertilizer.

In review on the question of iron and aluminum, podzols usually leach them into the subsoils whereas in laterites they are both in the subsoil and topsoil and in much larger quantities than in the podzols.

SILICA: We have said that laterite soils are unusually low in silicates. What is the significance of this fact? The dictionary refers to silica as a hard, white or colorless mineral subtance occurring as quartz, rock crystal, chalcedony, onyx, agate, flint, etc., and as sea sand. It is used in the manufacture of glass, as a flux in pottery making, as a refractory in steel furnaces, and in admixture with paints and rubber articles. Oxides of silica are the most prevalent substances in soil, some sandy soils containing over 90 per cent and loams—60 to 70 per cent. But in the laterite soils, the silicate is down to as low as two per cent. There must be some significance to this fact.

However, very little is known about the functions of silica in the soil. Some say it gives strength to the straw of the grains. It certainly is not an inert substance, for researches prove that growing plants take it up in liberal quantities from the soil. One experimenter found that where soluble silica was not given to growing plants more mildew developed. In another it was found that where the silica was kept low, the yields were depressed, and where the soil is low in phosphate the

addition of a silicate gave higher yields. It seems to be definitely known that silicates cause an increased absorption of phosphorus by plants.

In the studies of the organic method no attention has been given to the part played by silica. This may later lead to interesting interpretations and observations. Surely in the laterite soils which are so low in silica there is a field for experimental research. The dearth of silica in such soils may be one reason why the phosphorus is so easily rendered insoluble. Rock powders rich in silica may be found and applied to laterite soils with good results.

SILICA CONTENT IN
ROCK FERTILIZERS

Name	Silica SiO_2
Illite	51.47
Glauconite	45.71
Rhyolite	72.88
Granite	67.33
Wyomingite	50.94
Orendite Pumice	53.61
Feldspar	63.19
Orendite	50.00
Basalt	43.77
Alunite	0.69
Limestone	5.20

LATERITE SOIL: The upper part of the laterite soil, including part of the subsoil is loose, porous and friable, the latter meaning readily crumbled or reduced to powder. It has a decided granulation which allows water to enter freely and therefore reduces the hazards of erosion, although under careless farming methods there is much erosion in these soils. This granulation permits laterite soils to be plowed right after a heavy rain. In some cases such soils can be actually plowed during a heavy rain. If this were to be done to a podzol soil it would puddle and bake into a hard mass as soon as it dried. As we have said before, chernozem clays do not puddle as easily as podzolic clays because the former are not acid, but you cannot do with a chernozem in this respect what you can do with a laterite. In many laterites which have over 90 per cent fine clay, the soil is as loamy and friable as podzols that have less than 30 per cent of a similar type of clay. A typical laterite soil does not swell when it becomes saturated with water, neither does it shrink when it dries out. The result is it does not crack when it dries. It becomes as hard as stone, true.

ACIDITY: Laterite soils are usually only slightly acid, although under some conditions the acidity can become stronger. Part of this is due to the fact that on account of the rains, cal-cium and other alkalizing substances (bases) easily leaches downward. The use of lime, blast furnace slags, and ground phosphate rock is suggested to immobilize the acidity. Basic slag is a product which may safely be used by organic farmers.

CROPS: Laterite soils are best adapted for high carbohydrate crops like sugarcane, pineapple, bananas, rubber, coffee, cocoa, coconuts, etc. Corn, tubers, cotton, hemp and jute are also raised but not with optimum results. The extreme heat, and low efficiency encouraged as a result, prevents the intensive activity needed for raising dairy cattle, poultry, etc. Heavy applications of fertilizer are required.

ORGANIC MATTER: On account of the heat and ease of leaching due to heavy rainfall the organic matter content is low. Organic matter decays rapidly under these conditions. Termites and ants are extremely active in breaking down dead organic matter. In no time at all large dead trees are completely consumed and turned to humus by these insects. The question is, can the organic method be practiced in the tropics? The books of Sir Albert Howard give ample evidence that it can. Plants grow so luxuriantly there that much organic matter is available. Sir Albert gives concrete illustrations of higher yields

and less disease obtained by the organic method on tea estates, sugarcane plantations, rice paddies, etc. See also CHERNOZEM; PODZOL SOILS; SOIL.

LATH HOUSE: Used to give plants more shade, a lath house has been described as a greenhouse without glass. The strips of wood are placed about one inch apart to allow sufficient circulation of air with less than half the usual amount of light.

LATHYRUS: A genus of plants of the pea family, *Leguminosae*, which includes 200 species, including *L. odoratus*, or sweet pea. Representatives of the genus are found throughout the world, but occur most often in the north temperate zone. Annuals and perennials are included in the genus, growing erect or in vines, some climbing by means of tendrils which are extensions of the main leaf stalk. Showy flowers of the cultivated species come in colors ranging from white through yellow, pink, blue, purple, and red. Most species are cultivated for their flowers, but at least one species, *L. sativus*, the grass pea, is grown in the south of Europe for its edible lentil-like seed. Flowers are typical pea flowers of the *Leguminosae*, with an upstanding petal, the standard; two lateral petals, the wings; and two lower ones joined to form a keel. Leaves are compound and pinnate, with few leaflets in most species. Stems are either winged or angled.

Most important species is *L. odoratus* or sweet pea, an annual vine climbing to six or eight feet, with showy fragrant flowers growing as many as six to a stalk, which under intensive cultivation can be made to grow 18 inches long. Many hundreds of ruffled hybrids are now in the seed catalogs, and many hundreds more have been developed and dropped for newer varieties. The annual vines require full sun, deeply prepared rich moist soil, and cool temperatures for growing and flowering. The present varieties were probably developed from a much smaller vine with smooth-petalled flowers which were possibly all pinkish-lavender.

The everlasting pea, *L. grandiflorus,* is a perennial which bears two or three rosy lavender flowers on a stalk. Its cultural requirements are simple, growing as it does in any good garden loam, and in partial shade. It blooms continuously through most of the summer. It can be propagated from either seed or cuttings, and grows luxuriously when once established.

Also known as everlasting peas are *L. latifolius,* and *L. sylvestris,* both perennials with habits similar to that of *grandiflorus.* Flowers are rose pink to white and a few cultivated forms are dark red. Vines grow somewhat taller than *grandiflorus,* and may be trained to cover porches or to trail over banks.

Two species of perennial peas used to bind sand in seaside gardens are *L. littoralis,* on the Pacific coast, and *L. maritimus,* on the Atlantic coast. Common name of each is beach pea. Plants are quite similar, except that flower clusters of *maritimus* are usually larger and darker.

The edible grass pea, *L. sativus* also called chickling vetch, is an annual which grows no more than two feet high. Flowers are white tinged with blue. *See also* SWEET PEA; PEAS.

LAUREL: The genus *laurus* of the laurel family, *Lauraceae.* Also called sweet bay. The genus *laurus* is the true laurel of the Greeks. *L. nobilis,* originally a native of Asia minor is now found throughout the Mediterranean area. Sometimes a shrub to 15 feet, sometimes a tree to 50 or 60 feet. Commonly grown as a large potted plant, pruned and trained for use as ornamental accent, as on terraces, where it will thrive if provided with humus-rich soil and sufficient moisture. Dark green glossy leaves much used by florists in foliage arrangements. Small yellow flowers are in umbels, followed by dark purple or blackish berries. Propagated either by cuttings or seed.

Other plants called laurels include Alexandrian laurel, *Danae racemosa;* California laurel, *Umbelularia californica;* laurel cherry, or cherry-laurel, *Prunus laurocerasus* and *P. caroliniana;* Portugal laurel, *P. lusitanicus;* mountain laurel, *Kalmia latifolia* (which see); sheep laurel, *K. angustifolia;* ground laurel, or trailing arbutus, *Epigaea repens;* laurel oak, *Quercus laurifolia;* spurge laurel, *Daphne laureola;* laurel willow, *Salix pentandra;* and laurelwood, *Arbutus menziesi.*

LAVATERA: Also known as tree mallow, this genus includes annuals, biennials and perennials, that produce showy pink or purple flowers. *L. trimestris* is a fairly popular hardy annual that grows to six feet high, blooms in summer. *L. assurgentiflora* is a tall perennial that reaches more than ten feet high, often used for a temporary screen in warmer climates. *L. arborea* is a biennial, growing to ten feet.

LAVENDER: (*Lavandula*) The true lavender is a small shrubby plant native to southern Europe and widely cultivated for its fragrant flowers and for the oil distilled from the fresh flowering tops.

The plant thrives best in light and rather dry soils well supplied with lime, but can be grown in almost any well-drained loam. On low or wet land it is almost certain to winterkill. The plant can be grown from seed, but is more readily propagated from cuttings or by division. In cold climates the plants must be well protected in winter. Early in spring the seedlings or rooted cuttings are set in well-prepared soil, 12 to 15 inches apart in rows spaced to suit the cultivation intended. Frequent and thorough cultivation is desirable.

Growth is slow, and the plants do not produce any considerable quantity of flowers for several years, but full crops may be expected for sometime thereafter if the plants are given proper care. The flowering tops are harvested when in full bloom, and if used for the production of oil are distilled at once without drying. If the dry flowers are wanted, the tops are carefully dried in the shade and the flowers later stripped from the stems by hand.

Lavendula is a much-branched, somewhat woody perennial, that grows from 1½ to three feet high. Its narrow leaves are about two inches long, grayish-green in color. The small flowers are borne on stemmed, slender spikes. Smaller varieties are often used in the border, while the taller-growing ones are recommended for informal hedges. Protect plants during winter with a deep mulch. Known as common or French lavender, it is listed both as *L. officinalis* and *L. spica*.

LAVENDER COTTON: (*Santolina chamaecyparissus*) A tender shrubby perennial that is not consistently hardy in states above New York. Its striking gray color is often used as an accent plant in the flower or herb garden. Flower heads are yellow buttons on long stems. It grows well in rather poor soil and full sun; can be propagated by division. There is also a green-flowering species, *S. virens*. Both varieties can be clipped, are useful as borders or low-growing hedges.

LAWN: Perhaps no other item receives more attention and gives more trouble to the homeowner than the lawn. A good, lush, green lawn is a source of pride and satisfaction, and is not impossible, except under extremely adverse conditions. As in most gardening operations, the secret of success in lawn management is the ability to gear all operations to suit the individual climatic and geographic conditions. This involves quite a bit of study even before seed is purchased, and should be the first item on the list of any homeowner who wants to understand the basic principles of lawn management. The "what kind of a lawn?" question must be answered first.

The homeowner should know the three basic types of lawns listed below and be able to recognize each of them when he sees them. He should also decide what kind of lawn he wants to grow on his property, making sure that local conditions will permit him to do this successfully. Different kinds and combinations of grasses make different lawns and the soil is obviously suited better to one type of lawn than another. The home owner should know what that lawn type is before he starts ordering seed.

1. *The All-Purpose Lawn* is a compromise lawn which does equally well in sun and in moderate shade. It asks few favors and is usually the best choice.

2. *The Elegant Fine-Bladed Turf* is the show-place kind of lawn and everybody, for obvious reasons, can't have one. It calls for extra care and the grasses, mostly the bents are shallow-rooted and discourage easily.

3. *The Extra-Sturdy Working Lawn* for the growing family with plenty of children and pets who want to romp and play all during the hot summer when the grass is most vulnerable. Remember no grass is indestructable, but the tough, fescues will take considerable punishment—providing they get adequate care.

These are the three main types of lawn. There are subdivisions in lawns: partial shade, poor drainage, or extra-sandy areas all of which call for different grasses or mixtures. But the one big fact is the geographical location of your house and grounds.

The accompanying map clearly indicates the two main climate zones of the country. Most important to the lawn is the dividing line which

Bluegrass thrives and makes a good lawn north of the Bluegrass Line while Bermuda grass is recommended below it. The line indicates the transition from the cool to warm season grasses.

runs from east to west—the Bluegrass Line.

Dr. Ralph E. Engel, research specialist of the Agricultural Experiment Station at Rutgers University, New Jersey, in reviewing the importance of the Bluegrass Line, has this to say:

"The line indicates the transition regions between the cool season grass area of the northern United States where Kentucky bluegrass usually dominates and the warm season grass region where Bermuda grass dominates in the South. The imaginary line is not a sharp dividing zone; either type of grass may be found growing 200 miles north or south of it, according to local conditions and needs."

But essentially, bluegrass is the dominant lawn strain north of the line and Bermuda grass is the main lawn grass in the Deep South.

Zones One and Five favor the growth of the same grasses: colonial bents, common Kentucky bluegrass, also the Kentucky Merion bluegrass, the red fescues and the Chewing's fescue. Bermuda grass and the Meyers zoysia can be grown in certain limited areas.

As those residing in the Deep South know, the Bermuda grasses prevail there, also the zoysia. In limited areas, Carpetgrass, centipedegrass, St. Augustinegrass do well, also the common and Merion Kentucky bluegrasses.

Moisture assumes real importance in the Great Plains—Zone Three—where only the two bluegrass strains can be grown in the irrigated sections. In the non-irrigated areas plant blue gramagrass, hardy buffalograss and crested wheatgrass.

In Zone Four—the Southwest—Bermuda grass and the zoysias have a good chance of success. In limited areas with great care try the bluegrasses, Chewing's fescue and red fescue.

Adaptation of the proper grass to the climate is most important. Dr. Engel stresses that a good rule to follow is "to avoid taking a grass too far from its natural growing area." Neglect of this principle may "not always lead to failure but it makes lawn culture unnecessarily difficult."

Choosing a grass in the middle latitudes (near the Bluegrass line) may be "confusing," he notes. Because "elevation, turf need, soil conditions and maintenance potential influence the choice in this region where neither the cool season nor the warm season grasses are ideal at all times. If conditions are very severe (cold rather than hot), winter-hardy warm season grasses" should do better than other varieties.

THE NORTHERN GRASSES—BLUE-GRASS: Dr. Engel's ratings of the most important northern grass strains is of great value. He pays tribute to the Kentucky bluegrass as the most useful lawngrass for northern United States. Sunshine, good soil fertility or fertilization, a mowing height of 1½ inches, and a moderate amount of moisture in the growing season permit this species to be aggressive and attractive.

"There are a number of types and sources of Kentucky bluegrass. Merion is the superior type. Its principal advantages are tolerance of a closer cut and good resistance to leaf spot disease. This type is troubled more by rust, especially in the more southerly sections of the Kentucky bluegrass region. However this disease usually is not fatal and it appears at its worst when the grass is growing with a low level of nitrogen.

"Kentucky bluegrass is a persistent and aggressive species. It should be a component of most all mixtures in the northerly areas."

It will also be well to keep in mind that bluegrass is dormant during the summer which is the way it weathers the heat. It appears a dry, wiry turf, rather brown. But with the cool days it resumes its normal green, holding its verdure until the ground freezes.

Because the bluegrasses are slow in taking hold, they should be mixed with redtop when seeding. But blue-grass does well on a sweet, loamy soil with a pH rating of 7.5. When seeding use six pounds to 1000 square feet.

Bluegrass does not grow well in shade or on infertile, dry or poorly-drained land. It does not fight weeds too well at the beginning because its turf is not as dense as a lawn of bent grasses. But with time and proper management it will build up a healthy green carpet that will keep the weeds down.

This calls for high mowing—between 2½ and three inches, particularly, in June, July and August. But don't go into the winter season more than two inches high. Fertilize in the spring and fall and soak the soil to a depth of six inches when watering.

THE FESCUES: If the lawn is on the shady side, rather dry or even sandy, the fescues will do well. Dr. Engel advises that "red fescues are an excellent shade grass for the northern areas, especially where the summers are not too severe. They are intolerant of close mowing, but their tolerance of poor soil and shade makes them very useful. Red fescues may be listed as Chewing's fescue, Illahee fescue, Pennlawn fescue, certified creeping red fescue, and others. Most lawn seed mixtures for the cooler, mild climates of northern United States should contain red fescue."

The bents are vulnerable to fungus when the weather is humid and require hand-weeding at least once a week until the lawn is well established. They do best on a medium loam with a pH of 6.7 that is well-drained. Colonial bent mixed with Kentucky bluegrass will make a lasting and beautiful lawn although it requires an investment of money, time and extra work.

TEMPORARY, 'NURSE' GRASSES: These are the grasses, the "ryes" and "redtops" which will start the lawn off quickly and keep the weeds in check until the permanent varieties mentioned above come into maturity.

They are included in most of the seed mixtures below for this reason.

Redtop is perhaps the most popular of the nurse grasses. It works well with bluegrass, particularly on a sunny lawn, germinating within a week. It has a Jekyll and Hyde character; during its first season it makes a most attractive lawn, is fine-bladed and light green. But it is entirely different next year when it grows long stems, coarse leaves and sprawls out although very heavy seedings may prevent this tendency. But the lowly redtop does well on acid soils that are poorly drained and it resists drought well.

Ryegrass is another fort-holder until real help arrives in the form of a permanent lawn. It is also fine for slopes, helping to hold the soil together until the turf really goes to work. It also curls up in the heat and turns brown and is hard to mow and tends to grow in clumps.

In general, the fescues are fine-leaved, bluish-green and make few demands for extra feedings or moisture. They will give, even under adverse conditions, a thick, close turf of good color and texture. A family with a shady homegrounds and active children should consider this the answer to their grass problems.

On the debit side; fescues cannot be mixed with the bluegrasses because their habits of growth are different; they stand the heat poorly which causes them to grow in wiry clumps. Fescue seeds are also rather expensive. But they make a shady lawn that stands plenty of abuse.

THE BENT GRASSES: Properly handled they give the most elegant, fine bladed, closely cropped turf. Dr. Engel notes that Colonial bentgrass has "high quality and tolerates close cut," but adds that "its inability to resist severe disease injury limits its usefulness."

Close seeding is a must—a minimum of three pounds to 1000 square feet. While it is more expensive to maintain than ordinary lawn grasses,

it grows well in hot weather and will grow a dense turf. It should be trimmed less than three-fourths of an inch. It is deservedly popular in New England and the Northwest.

Because the bents are shallow rooted, they need more water. They should be fed twice a year, in September and March with a complete fertilizer. Be sure the formula gives twice as much nitrogen as phosphorus. Water copiously every two days preferably early in the morning so the grass is dry by evening.

There is no 'ideal' soil for lawns but the best growing medium is a porous, self-draining, moderate loam. It is made up of two parts of clay, one of silt (particles midway between fine sand and clay), one each of coarse sand and fine gravel, two of decaying organic matter. This is topsoil and it is the result of weathering under natural conditions over a period of years. It most definitely is not an overworked, neglected bit of soil which has been given a "shot-in-arm" with some inorganic chemical compounds.

NORTHERN SEED MIXTURES FOR VARIOUS LAWN TYPES

Sunny:

	Per cent
Bluegrass, Kentucky or Merion	45
Redtop	25
Rhode Island Bent	10
Ryegrass, perennial	15
White Clover	5

Partial Shade:

Bluegrass, Kentucky or Merion	10
Redtop	10
Rhode Island Bent	5
Velvet Bent	5
Rough-stalked bluegrass	10
Meadow fescue	10
Chewings fescue	50

Fine Turf:

Bluegrass, Kentucky or Merion	35
Redtop	15
Rhode Island Bent	15
Chewings fescue	35

Poor: Sandy: Banks:	Per cent
Bluegrass, Kentucky or Merion	10
Redtop	20
Rhode Island Bent	10
Ryegrass, perennial	15
White clover	5
Chewings fescue	40

General:

Bluegrass, Kentucky	40
Redtop	20
Creeping bent	10
Ryegrass, perennial	10
White clover	10
Red fescue	10

The chart on the previous page gives the most recommended northern seed mixtures, *balanced according to the type lawn desired.* When you have decided what kind of lawn you are going to have, be sure to check the seed mixture you buy against the proportions given here.

The box below should also help in determining soil types. It provides a sure indication of possible soil needs by noting which weeds grow on the various soils. It is not infallible but —it will give some indication of the nature of the particular soil problem and it is worth studying.

THE SOUTHERN, WARM-SEASON GRASSES: While "Bermuda grass is the best known and most used grass in the south," Dr. Engel notes that "there is also considerable interest developing in more northerly regions." Our gradually warming climate, plus "very severe summers" are reasons behind this.

But the Bermuda grasses are to the South and the Southwest what the bluegrasses are to the north. Given adequate moisture and feeding, they take hold firmly and resist drought. They are tough and can be shaved close but can get out of hand and become a weed nuisance if and when they invade the flower beds. They will not thrive in shady, poorly-drained land with an acid pH factor.

Dr. Engel advises contacting local turf experts when choosing varieties of Bermuda grass. It must be noted here that the common Bermuda is the only strain which can be planted from seed; the other varieties are grown from stolons or sprigs.

Among these is *Tiflawn* which, finer in texture than the common Bermuda, is deep green. It is very disease-resistant, a vigorous grower which must be mowed closely and often or it will form a heavy mat.

TYPES OF SOIL AS INDICATED BY WEED GROWTHS

1. **WET LAND:** ferns, horsetail, sedge, rush, cattail, buttercup, pennywort. *The surface may be dry but these weeds are a sure indication that the land is wet below. Drainage may be necessary.*

2. **SOUR LAND:** (ACID) sorrel, dock, wild strawberry, bramble. *The soil should be limed.*

3. **POOR, DRY:** Devil's paint brush, spurge. *Manures and sludge are needed.*

4. **TIGHT, COMPRESSED:** knotwood, poa annua. *Perforate surface, work in sand and peat moss dust.*

5. **DEEP CLAY:** self-heal, wild onion.

6. **LIMESTONE:** chicory, teasel.

Everglades No. 1 is finer and greener than *Tiflawn* but tends to grow prostrate. *Ormond* is coarser and more upright than the *Everglades* which, however, requires the least maintenance of the three varieties.

Three other varieties, *Tiffine, Tifgreen* and *Bayshore,* are used in fine lawns and golf greens. All are fine in texture, a medium green and require maximum maintenance.

Bermudagrass grows vigorously, spreading by runners above the ground and by rootstalks underground. It needs frequent and heavy applications of nitrogen. One variety, U-3, has been grown successfully as far north as Philadelphia, Cleveland, and St. Louis. It has finer blades than common Bermudagrass, is disease and insect-resistant and holds its color late into the fall when properly fertilized. It grows well in hot, humid weather.

When seeding, spread two pounds to 1000 square feet. Hulled seed means faster germination. If growing from sprigs, set them two feet apart. Bermudagrass stays green all winter in southern Florida but turns brown elsewhere. To try for a green winter lawn, oversow with domestic ryegrass in the fall. Rake and topdress when the ryegrass is killed by the hot weather. Mow close—from ½ to ¾ of an inch.

Carpetgrass does well on moist, sandy and poor soils. It has some tolerance for shade but winter-kills north of Augusta, Georgia. Sow two pounds to 1000 feet. While it requires little care, it turns brown in the winter. Mow one inch high.

Centipedegrass is considered the best low-maintenance lawn grass in the South. It requires less mowing, watering and fertilizing than other southern grasses. It resists insects and disease well but is vulnerable to salt water spray and sensitive to a lack of iron.

While drought-resistant, it should be watered during dry periods. Do not plant it on a farm lawn; it may escape into nearby pastures and destroy their grazing value. It spreads rapidly by short, creeping stems that form new plants at each node. It is established mostly vegetatively, but some seed is available; it should be sown two pounds to 1000 square feet.

St. Augustinegrass is rated the number one shade grass of the southernmost states. A creeping perennial, it spreads by long runners that produce short, leafy branches. It does well south of Augusta and Birmingham and westward to coastal Texas. It is propagated from sprigs.

St. Augustinegrass withstands salt water spray but is vulnerable to the chinch bug and army worm. It grows best in moist soils of high fertility and produces good turf in the muck soils of Florida. It needs a lot of nitrogen, particularly in sandy soils. Forming a coarse, dark-green sod, it should be mowed one inch high.

Zoysia matrella is reputed to be hardy as far north as Washington. It is a Manila grass but with texture of Kentucky bluegrass and is propagated by sprigs set six inches apart. It requires close mowing, well-drained soil of high fertility but is shade tolerant and disease and pest-resistant. It is brown in the winter and spreads and forms into a good turf rather slowly.

Zoysia japonica, another of the plug or sprig grasses has all the virtues of *Zoysia matrella.* It also forms a fine-textured turf, resists drought and requires a soil of moderate fertility. Mow between one and two inches.

STARTING THE NEW LAWN

Fall is a good time of year to start the new lawn because the weather is settled, which means the ground is neither too wet nor too dry. Don't work with wet soil or soil that is powdery. Seeding is best done in the fall, since the new grass has less competition from weeds.

In the case of a new home where the building crew has just moved out, the first job is to clean up. Get all the trash left by the builders off the place. If any is buried in the soil, dig it up and get it out.

Hard, packed soil that won't let water through and restricts root growth is probably the most common cause of lawn failure. At the very beginning do everything possible to aerate the soil and improve drainage. The best way to do this is to work in organic materials as you break up the clods of earth. This will speed and ease the job of making a proper grade also. A rotary tiller makes the job much easier.

At this stage, if it is evident that the land will not drain adequately, seriously consider putting in underground drains. Don't do this without professional advice. Call in the tile dealer who will supply the pipes and drains, and check with the local county agricultural agent.

GRADING: Try to avoid steep grades. A drop of more than 25 per cent, one foot in four, will be hard on future lawn maintenance—the soil will simply wash away. If faced with this problem, try terracing or breaking the slope with retaining walls.

If the land is almost dead level around the house, make a slight grade away, so that water will tend to flow from the foundations.

A weathered, sturdy leveling board with a spirit level securely and accurately attached will simplify the task while ensuring accuracy. Work with a leveling board ten feet long, six inches wide and one inch thick. The ideal lawn grade is $\frac{1}{8}$ of an inch to the linear foot.

LIMING: Most of the grasses do best on very slightly acid, almost neutral soil. Use very finely ground limestone which is long-lasting. Ground limestone does not destroy the humus and does not cake on top of the soil when used as a top-dressing.

To find the acidity-alkalinity of lawn soil, either send a soil sample to the state experiment station or make the test personally. All you need is some litmus paper, generally available at a drugstore.

Take a piece of litmus paper and press it with the thumb, down into the moist soil after a rain. If the test paper doesn't change color, other than getting wet, the soil's pH is approximately 7.0. If the test paper turns pink, the soil is acid. If the test paper turns blue, the soil is alkaline. It's best to test the soil in several places.

If tests show soil that is quite acid, you can raise it one full unit—from pH $5\frac{1}{2}$ to $6\frac{1}{2}$, by liming as follows:

Sandy soil ....35 *lbs. per* 1000 *ft.*
Sandy loam ...45 *lbs. per* 1000 *ft.*
Medium loam 70 *lbs. per* 1000 *ft.*
Silt or Clay ...75 *lbs. per* 1000 *ft.*

Sprinkle the lime in by hand or with a cart-spreader, but be sure to work from two different directions at right angles. This is the way to seed and spread fertilizer, because it guarantees even distribution. It is also wise to do these operations on comparatively windless days.

Although the general word on liming is to go slow and only when the soil is overly acid, liming has definite value to the lawn-maker. When soil is too acid, it impedes the growth and activity of bacteria necessary to convert raw fertilizing substances into forms the grass can absorb.

When this happens, the grass is literally starving in the proverbial land of plenty. More fertilizing will not correct this as it will in a soil with a pH of six or better.

The situation worsens in really acid soils because organic matter does not decay at a normal rate and roots tend to congest the turf. This prevents air and water from getting into the topsoil which further aggravates the acid condition.

But, caution is advisable where liming is concerned. Do not spread lime when the grass is wet and be sure to water it in immediately after it is spread.

ORGANIC FERTILIZERS: Spread, mix and get organic fertilizers right into the topsoil while it is in the topping-off phase. Again, spread and mix from opposite directions at right angles to insure uniformity.

Fertilizer preferences include processed sewage sludge which yields two pounds of nitrogen for each 34 pounds spread to the 1000 square feet. Check with the local sewage disposal plant; often sludge is free for the hauling.

When using manure, compost or bone meal, 100 pounds per 1000 feet will add two pounds of nitrogen to the soil.

Cottonseed meal is recommended for its high nitrogen count. It is obtained from the local feed mill, although it is comparatively expensive—about $4.00 per 100 pounds. Tobacco stems are excellent for potash in addition to nitrogen, while bone meal provides phosphorus and nitrogen.

Be guided by what you can get locally at the best price. Don't hesitate to substitute soybean meal for cottonseed meal if you can get lots of it cheap. And, don't forget to check with the local authorities about sewage sludge—it's ideal for lawn building.

Whatever is used should be worked into the topsoil thoroughly. The soil should be well mixed and loose to a depth of six to ten inches.

Be sure the ground is fairly dry when rolled and follow this operation by a light raking until the surface is very smooth and quite fine in texture. This should be done almost immediately before sowing so that rain will not interfere to cake the surface. If this happens, rake the surface again and then sow.

LAWNS WITHOUT TOPSOIL: Maybe the builders took away the topsoil or buried it so deep it can't be found. Don't buy topsoil which is full of seeds and of dubious fertility. Instead, start a lawn and build topsoil

ORGANIC LAWN FOODS

BONE MEAL: A stockyard by-product particularly rich in nitrogen, phosphoric acid and calcium. It is excellent for preparing land for a new lawn or for top-dressing old turf. The coarser ground meal is slower-acting while the finer grinds are quick to act, often producing greener grass when spread on turf within two weeks. A mixture of coarse and fine is recommended for all-around performance.

CASTOR POMACE: The ground remains of castor beans after oil has been squeezed out. An excellent and slow-acting plant food, castor pomace should be used in combination with other organic soil nutrients.

COTTONSEED MEAL: The squeezed fibrous residue of the seeds of the cotton plant is, like castor pomace, slow-acting but an excellent source of nitrogen. Like it, cottonseed meal should be applied with other foods.

CATTLE MANURE: Cleanings from cattle pens, good to work into soil a season before planting if fresh or should be weathered before being applied as a fertilizer. Dehydrated manures can be applied directly to the soil.

SHEEP MANURE, PULVERIZED: Suitable for mixing as top-dressing with other foods. The drying process destroys most weed seeds which tends to keep down the amount of weed growth on lawns top-dressed with this manure.

TOBACCO SCRAP: Stem and leaf fragments from tobacco factories. Excellent, long-acting source of potash and other nutrients because stems and veins decay slowly. Also ward off many insects which dislike tobacco.

as you go. It's not too hard but it takes time—at least a year. Here's how it's done: sow a green manure cover crop right into the subsoil after you have enriched it with sludge, cottonseed meal, tobacco stems and bone meal. This is the advice of Thomas H. Everett, Curator of Education and Horticulturist, New York Botanical Garden. In his handbook on lawns, Mr. Everett makes this sound suggetion: after liming and fertilizing the subsoil, sow two quarts of winter rye to each 1000 square feet of soil or the same quantity of Canada field peas.

"Green manuring means growing cover crops especially for the purpose of turning them under and converting in the soil to humus," notes Mr. Everett, adding that "humus is formed by the decay of the extensive root systems as well as the tops. . . . When top growth is six to 12 inches tall, spade the cover crop under or bury it with plow or rotary tiller and immediately refertilize and sow another cover crop. Don't turn the last of the cover crops under later than six weeks before sowing the permanent grass seed." In other words, give the cover crop at least six weeks to decay and form humus.

To this sound counsel to lawn builders who are willing to build their own topsoil from scratch, this word to residents of the Deep South should be added. The fall is an excellent time to plant crimson clover, hairy vetch, winter rye or ryegrass. This means providing excellent green manures which can be turned under prior to spring lawn planting. These crops also provide a cover for the soil during the fall and winter.

PLANTING: You already know what kind of grass you are going to sow because you have decided what kind of lawn will do best on your land. Select a seed mixture for either a shady or sunny lawn, or for a show-turf or play-area.

Whatever seed is used—don't sow it on a windy day. This is a good way to spoil the entire operation from the beginning. A good lawn requires even, uniform distribution of seed.

Divide seed into two equal parts on a minimum basis of three pounds to 1000 square feet. Check with the local dealer; he will probably advise planting four to five pounds to the 1000 feet. Sow half of the total seed in one direction, then sow the second portion crosswise to the first sowing.

Do this by hand or with a seed-sowing cart, which probably can be rented from the local garden supply dealer at reasonable rates.

Next, cover the seed lightly by hand raking. Large seeds should be covered ¼ to ⅜ inch and small seeds ⅛ to ¼ inch. Firm the seed under with the light roller. This brings the seed into close contact with the soil and speeds germination. Be sure the roller is dry so it doesn't pick up seeds. The roller, like the seed cart, can usually be obtained at a modest rental from the dealer.

SPRIGS, STOLONS AND PLUGS: Many grass varieties, particularly those flourishing south of the Bluegrass line, are best grown by the vegetative method. This is done by planting units of the grown grass and literally represents a transplanting process. Grasses thus planted include zoysia, Bermudagrass, St. Augustinegrass, centipedegrass, creeping bentgrass and velvet bentgrass. Grasses planted this way must be kept moist until they really take hold.

Of these varieties, only the last two should be propagated in the autumn. Both of them, creeping bentgrass and velvet bentgrass, can be stolonized (a stolon is a branch or shoot at the summit of a root). This calls for ten bushels of stolons to 1000 square feet, top-dressing with topsoil ¼ inch deep and then rolling to firm the stolons into the topsoil.

But the creeping bent lawn is more

laborious to create than one made from seed and the stolons themselves are more expensive. In addition, creeping bent lawns require considerable upkeep: frequent watering, mowing, fertilizing and top-dressing. Essentially, this type lawn is for the specialist.

MAINTENANCE; MULCHING: Mulching with a light cover of straw or hay will help hold moisture in the soil and also prevent washing away of seeds by rain. A single 60 to 80-pound bale of hay will adequately cover 1000 square feet. The evenly and lightly applied mulch can stay after the grass comes up through it and will eventually break down into compost.

Pin the young lawn down with cheesecloth if it is on a steep slope or bank. Use thin young twigs to fasten it to the ground. Do not remove the cover when the grass comes up but leave it in place to rot. Don't worry about watering at this time. The grass will do all right in the cooler days of autumn and the roots will go deeper into the soil after moisture—which is a sure way to build a really sturdy lawn.

MAINTAINING LAWN SOIL FERTILITY: If the lawn cover is thin, yellow, or weedy, improve the soil fertility. Adequate fertility will solve more lawn problems than any other treatment. *Maintain the right pH.* The proper pH is a first step in developing good fertility. Excessive acidity discourages desirable bacteria and gives rise to toxic quantities of iron and aluminum. A high pH, or excessive alkalinity, also interferes with natural functions of the soil. The heavy rainfall areas of the Eastern sections and other locations may require frequent use of ground limestone. In northeastern United States, 50 pounds of ground limestone per 1000 square feet is usually required every two or three years. If you are in a region of excessive alkalinity, careful measures must be taken upon advice of turf specialists.

FEEDING: Lawn should get a thorough feeding each spring. Skipping makes for bald spots and weeds.

Of three major nutrients—nitrogen, phosphorus and potassium—nitrogen is the most important. Organic lawn fertilizers will not 'burn' the lawn because they are slow-acting. But apply plenty of organic fertilizer. Good sources of nitrogen are cottonseed meal and sewage sludge. Cottonseed meal is excellent lawn top dressing. It analyzes seven to eight per cent nitrogen, three per cent phosphoric acid and two per cent potash. Top dress 12 *pounds per* 1000 *square feet* right on grass and then water in with a hose. Bonemeal is very good for phosphorus which makes good stiff growth. Top dress *five pounds to* 1000 *square feet.*

MOWING: The Kentucky bluegrass—red fescue type lawn is more drought tolerant and weed free if it is cut 1½ inches or higher. Bentgrass and Bermuda grass lawns can be cut closer than one inch. Merion Kentucky bluegrass might be cut as close as one inch if conditions are favorable.

If the grass is growing with vigor, mowing can seldom be less frequent than once per week, and as many as two or three mowings per week may be required.

Excessive growth between clippings makes for more open, stemmy turf, and it may necessitate removal of clippings to avoid smothering the grass. The clippings provide valuable quantities of plant food and help control weeds such as crabgrass.

Either the reel type mower or the horizontal blade type can be used satisfactorily for most lawns. However, the reel type is better adapted to closer mowing, while the blade type is better for the higher cuts.

CONTROL OF WEEDS: A dense turf is recommended universally as the all around weed control measure. Grass is very aggressive when fertilized generously. If weeds continually trouble the lawn, increase the use of fertilizer. Other factors such as insect damage, disease, excessive watering, and close mowing of the Kentucky bluegrass— red fescue lawn all increase the number of weeds.

Unfortunately man's efforts at management are never perfect enough to control all weeds. This creates the necessity to attack the weeds directly. The secret of controlling annual lawn weeds is to prevent seed development. Crabgrass is no exception. Preventing seed set for several seasons and simultaneous development of a dense turf gives certain success. Persistence is a necessary virtue when eliminating weeds from the lawn. If the lawn is not too big, hand weeding may be practical. It may be a tremendous job at first. However, use of fertilizer in conjunction with weeding will thicken the turf and greatly reduce the amount of weeding required the next season. If hand weeding is started, good dividends are paid to those who follow through and eliminate those few scattered weeds at a later date.

WATERING: Some gardeners advise that watering is not "critical" or as "crucial" as most of us believe. The well planned and created lawn will, they stress, stand the mid-summer strain of great midday heat and little water with surprising success. Again, it is a matter of having a lawn with deep grass roots.

It is better not to water at all, than to water lightly or to sprinkle during periods of drought.

But when watering, be sure enough is available for regular, weekly use. It's best to water once a week, soaking the soil to a minimum depth of four inches. If you don't have enough water to maintain this program, it is better not to water at all.

The deeper the water penetrates, the better the root development. A healthy, sturdy system of roots gets all the food value from the surrounding soil, *as far down as possible*. Shallow sprinkling forces the roots to spread out near the top of the soil where they will later be baked by the

hot summer sun and rendered unable to withstand drought.

Any discussion of lawn watering must take into consideration the fact that the soil with the most organic humus will hold the most water in suspension so it can be readily absorbed by the grass. A lawn with plenty of organic humus that is thoroughly watered at regular intervals will stay sound and drought-resistant during the summer.

Watering should also be conditioned by the type of soil. Light soils need more water because they drain readily. Heavy, clayey soils obviously need less water.

REBUILDING BARE SPOTS: Rake out all dead grass and break up the surface thoroughly, even though some good grass plants may be dislodged in the process. Re-establish the even contour of the surface by careful raking, then follow the instructions given for starting a new lawn. In small areas, even seeding can be accomplished with the use of a flour sifter. In larger areas, revert to the standard grass seeder.

A SUBSTITUTE: Dichondra or lawn leaf is a very satisfactory substitute for lawn grass. It requires no mowing or reseeding, thrives in either sun or shade, is tolerant to a wide variety of soil conditions, and is very resistant to rough usage. Moths and beetle larvae do not injure it. Best of all, particularly in arid regions, it remains vigorously fresh during dry spells that ordinarily kill grass.

To prepare a dichondra lawn, work up the soil thoroughly with well rotted compost. Chicken droppings, bone meal and dried blood are excellent ingredients. After mixing, rake the earth level and smooth.

Seed should be broadcast, not too thickly, as each plant will spread over about four square inches. Cover seed with a thin layer of finely screened compost mixed with ground phosphate rock, and water liberally during the first week. Germination takes about ten days.

Sometimes the seed is mixed with white clover or a short-lived grass. When this is done the new lawn will need mowing and it is necessary to rake off all the clippings as these will harm the dichondra seedlings. The young plants gradually replace the clover or grass.

Although grown mainly for lawns, dichondra makes an excellent ground cover around shrubs or a filter between flag stones. When allowed to spread, it chokes out noxious weeds and covers unattractive bare places. It can even be used in rock gardens where its gay patches of green produce a decidedly ornamental effect.

CONCLUSION: A good lawn is one of the finest ingredients of a pleasant home grounds. Be faithful in maintaining the proper pH, fertilize regularly and adequately, avoid close mowing, water wisely if necessary, and choose the best grass. If this is done, a good lawn will exist most of the time. While lawn grasses are tender, herbaceous plants liable to setbacks, they have great ability to compete, endure, and recover if given a chance. *See also* CRABGRASS; GRASS CLIPPINGS; FERTILIZER.

LAWN CLIPPINGS: *see* GRASS CLIPPINGS

LAWN MOWER: *see* MOWER, POWER

LAWN MOWER, CARE OF: *see* MACHINERY, CARE OF

LAYERING: This refers to a method of plant propagation in which the rooting of branches of woody plants takes place while they are still attached to the parent plant.

AIR LAYERING

Air layering is a method of propagation which is also called pot, or Chinese layering. These names all

Simple layering can be done by bending branches to ground, burying them a few inches deep. Multiflora roses tend to layer naturally.

have simple explanations—the Chinese have been expert for centuries on certain phases of propagation—this type of propagation sometimes makes use of pots to help roots to form—and it is performed on the plants without burying any part in soil, as is true with other types of layering.

This method of layering is used on certain woody plants, usually, which have become too "leggy," that is, too tall and gangly, with a few leaves growing at the end of the long stem. Its purpose is to produce shorter, stockier, more robust looking, and better foliaged plants.

Another object is to increase the number of shrubs and trees in the home landscape at practically no cost.

PRINCIPLES: When tree branches have been damaged, either intentionally or by accident, the bark and the cambium soon begin the process of healing the wound, by gradually growing over the exposed wood. Here then is Nature's secret to successful propagation by air-layering—taking advantage of the efforts of the branches to continue to live.

There are two methods of air-layering. The first method is often used in England. Select a twig or branch about the size of a pencil in circumference, and with a sharp knife, make an incision in the branch center and continue the cut upwards for about two inches. This cut should be made just below a dormant bud situated not more than 12 inches from the tip of the branch. Now, carefully bend open the incision or open it with the aid of your knife and keep it open until you have inserted in the incision, a tiny pebble or stone, or better still a small piece of sphagnum or other moss. The object of this is to prevent Nature from healing the wound by contact.

You now envelop this incision with a good-sized handful of sphagnum moss, compost, crushed straw or hay—all of which must be moistened—pref-

may carefully untie the "shroud," but be sure to again properly wrap to prevent drought.

The importance of the "shrouds" and their proper application to the location of the incision or removal of bark is so important that it must be emphasized. It is the "shroud" which prevents the rapid evaporation of the essential moisture and once you have properly moistened the enveloping materials in which the roots actually will form, the materials will thereafter be kept properly moist and there will be no need to add additional

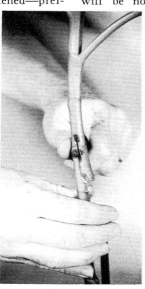

Left—Air layering saves best part of a defoliated plant. *Center*—Cut half through stem below the lowest leaf axil. *Right*—Wedge wound open, and tie on split bamboo brace firmly in place.

erably in rain or pond water—to the consistency of a squeezed-out sponge. To keep the material properly moist, cover with a wrapping of polyethylene film or aluminum foil, completely enclosing the moistened moss and securing each end of the "shroud" with string, tape, etc. In four or five weeks, depending on the type of plant you are air-layering, roots should develop.

If you are anxious to take a peep to see how Nature is progressing, you

moisture at any time the roots are forming.

Here is the second method: it is not necessary to be too precise about the size of the plant stem or branch that you wish to make produce roots. Many gardeners have actual rooted specimens varying from one inch to three inches in circumference. The length of the branch may also be approximate—from six inches to a couple of feet long. In any case, you circle the bark and cambium with a cut from your sharp knife and down to the actual hard wood. In the case of the smaller branches, another similar cut is made one inch away from the first cut.

Allow a space of up to 1½ inches between cuts in the larger branches. Now, entirely remove all the bark and cambium—down to the white wood stem—between the two cuts made with your knife. You have entirely severed the sap flow, the life line, from the mother plant. If the

cut to about eight inches in length.

The successfully rooted branches are now on their own and entirely separated from the Mother plant. In starting life on their own, they must be handled with some care until they gain experience in this life. Remove the "shroud" and soak the roots in tepid water for an hour. Discard the moss or other rooting media. The newly formed roots must now supply life-giving liquids to the plant. To give them a hand, it is necessary to reduce the volume. Therefore, prune

Left—Tie wrapping of moist sphagnum moss about area. *Center*—Tie plastic loosely at top, and securely at the bottom. *Right*—When roots appear, cut new plant, and repot without any delay.

branch is left like this and uncovered, this branch ahead of the wound will die. To complete this operation, all you have to do now is cover the wound with sphagnum moss, moistened, and tie it with the "shroud" of your choice. It should look like the bulge of a sweet potato with tapered ends. Roots may be formed in from one to two months' time. When roots are well established and several inches long, the branch may be severed by a saw or clean cutting shears, immediately below the bottom end of the "shroud," which is conveniently

the entire branch at least one third of its stature.

These rooted branches may now be set out in suitable sized pots or planted directly into the garden soil. They must be kept damp and shaded for several months; then transfer them to the permanent quarters that you have selected.

The ambition of all plants is to live healthily and to reproduce its kind. In this instance of air-layering, we so treated the branch that something very serious would happen to it; it would die for its vital source of life supply had been cut off from it. You might say then that it has a burning desire to live and so it will do one of two things: (1) it will attempt to heal the wound, by growing the bark and cambium together and so once again establish a life line for the sap to proceed to the branch, and so continue to live, or (2) it will set up its own housekeeping by sending out roots for sustenance and so continue to live. What man has done is to make the gap of the bark and cambium cut wide enough to prevent the branch from being bridged over again. The roots are then formed as a result of the ideal conditions which we have set up.

You may try the system on any tree you wish and remember that your rare trees and shrubs will always, when so rooted, be absolutely true to the mother plant.

Air Layering House Plants

House plants which are especially adapted to air layering include rubber plants, croton, oleander, dracaena, philodendrons, and fiddle leafed figs. These are plants which tend to grow with slender, long stalks, and most of them have a single stem.

As with the other methods of layering which are used to propagate plants (these other methods are used out of doors where the propagating points can be covered with soil) air layering reproduces a plant exactly—without any variation at all, such as might occur with seed-raised plants.

The steps in air layering house plants are easy to follow. The stem is wounded at a point near the leafy top of the plant by girdling, notching, or by simply cutting in at a slant about ¼ to ½ of the way through with a sharp knife. The pot method calls for using a 2½ or three inch pot, the bottom of which has been nearly or entirely knocked out. The leaves of the plant are folded up so that the pot can be slipped down over them. Then the pot is placed at

the point where the stem has been wounded, and it is filled with sphagnum or peat moss. A stake is used for support and tied securely to the pot. After the roots are formed, the new plant is cut from the old stem and repotted.

Growing tip, after it was re-rooted, was potted in mixture containing one-third peat moss, one-third leaf mold and one-third sharp, clean sand.

The wound must be wedged open, of course, by using a stick, pebble, or any other small object for that purpose. There are special pots which can be bought for this pot technique. However, burlap or any strong cloth can be used instead of a pot.

However, perhaps the simplest and best method to use in air layering is the plastic wrap. The slanting cut is made with a knife on the stem a short distance below the foliage, then the wound is wedged open and the cut spot supported with bamboo splints or any other thin but strong splices. The next step is to fasten sphagnum moss (moistened) around the wounded area (using a layer of moss two or three inches long). Then place a piece of plastic (either transparent or not) around the moss, tying the plastic tightly at the bottom of the moss and loosely at the top of the moss.

If transparent plastic is used it will be possible to see when the roots have developed. However, ordinarily from six to eight weeks will be long enough to develop healthy roots at the wounded section of the stem. Then the stem is cut below the new roots and this top part of the plant is repotted at once. A good potting mixture is ⅓ peat moss, ⅓ leaf mold, and ⅓ sand.

Rubber plants on which air layering has been done sometimes send out side shoots and develop new heads down low enough to make attractive plants below the point where the new plant has been propagated and cut off the old plant.

Air layering is convenient and simple for anyone who likes to keep shapely, good looking plants around the home.

Simple Layering

Simple layers are made by bending branches to the ground and covering a part of their length three to six inches deep, so that the buried portion will remain in moist soil during the process of rooting. Generally this is done in the spring before growth begins. The tip ends of the layered branches are left exposed to form the tops of the new plant. Frequently rooting is stimulated by making a slanting cut into the branch on the lower side at the point where roots are desired. Many trees and shrubs so treated will strike roots the first season, whereas others may require two seasons. When well rooted, the layers are severed from the mother plant during the dormant season and treated as independent plants.

The propagation of rhododendrons exemplifies one of the applications of this method. The varieties desired are planted several feet apart to allow space to bend all of the branches to the ground. Previous to layering, the plants are allowed to become well established and are headed low to induce vigorous shoots to start near the ground.

During March or early April is the usual time for putting down rho-

dodendron layers. The growth made the preceding season is the best, but old wood will form roots. The branch is prepared by stripping off a few leaves from the portion of the stem to be buried and by removing any flower buds. At the point where the roots are desired on the branch, a cut is made about 1½ inches long, running upward and slanting toward the center of the branch, thus forming a "tongue." The shoot is then gently bent over to avoid breaking and is so buried in the soil that the tongue points nearly straight downward and is several inches below the ground level, with six inches or more of the tip of the shoot nearly erect above the ground. The branch is held in this position by wooden pegs or stiff wires, and the soil is pressed firmly around it. All of the vigorous branches of the mother plant that can be brought to the ground may be treated in the same manner.

The soil around the buried portion should be moist all through the season. A heavy mulch of oak leaves for rhododendrons and other plants requiring acid soils helps to retain the necessary moisture and also improves the soil as the leaves decay.

Rhododendron layers make the best plants if they are allowed to remain two years, although some roots may form the first season. The second spring they are severed from the mother plants and carefully transplanted into beds of especially prepared soil. The first year these beds should have lath shade and facilities for watering. The second season they are ready to be transplanted to the open ground.

Mound or Stool Layering

Stool or mound layering is well adapted to plants that form shoots freely near the ground level. It is the method often employed for the propagation of the quince and gooseberry.

Fertile sandy loam which is easily

worked and in a situation that is nearly level to avoid washing should be selected for mound layers. After the beds are established, yearly crops of rooted shoots can be obtained from them without renewing the mother plants; hence special consideration in the choice of a favorable site is important.

The plants to be propagated are spaced four to five feet apart each way, a sufficient distance to allow ample room for root development and to permit a mound to be made several inches high around each plant. They are grown a year before layering to become well established, during which time they are given care to encourage as much growth as possible.

Before growth starts the following spring the plants are cut off at the ground level. When the shoots growing from the stubs are four or five inches high, soil is drawn up leaving only the tips exposed. It is advisable to spread the shoots a little apart when hilling the first time, to give each shoot more space and to induce uniform growth. Root formation is aided if the hilling is begun while the shoots are still small. As growth progresses, from four to six inches of soil are drawn up around the shoots at intervals during May and June. The rooted shoots can be cut off in the late fall or early the next spring. The stubs or "stools" are left undisturbed, to produce another crop of shoots the following year.

Trench Layers

Instead of cutting back the mother plants to form stools, the stems may be brought down into a furrow made four to six inches deep beside the row (trench layering). This is done early in spring before growth starts. Care should be taken to peg down the branches horizontally in the bottom of the furrow at the same distance below the ground level. Two or more stems may parallel and overlap each other, thus providing for a close stand of new shoots in the row. When the new growth is two to four inches long, soil is brought in to cover the lower part of the new growth, leaving only the tips exposed, and, as growth develops, more soil is brought around the stems. Roots ordinarily form most readily near the base of the shoot, hence this portion should be sufficiently covered by the soil that is constantly moist. As rooting may frequently take place most freely in fall, it is advisable to postpone removing the rooted layers until very late in fall or early the next spring.—*Guy Yerkes.*

See also Bramble Fruits; Cuttings; Division.

LEACHING: Rainwater and irrigation is known to dissolve a certain amount of plant food elements from the soil, carrying them down to greater depths where they will be lost by roots. This leaching is inevitable and should be remembered when fertilizing. Leaching also occurs in house plants, but this kind of leaching can be prevented by not overwatering plants. Remember that every time water runs out of the drainage hole and is thrown away as excess, it carries with it some soil nutrients.

There has been relatively little research on the exact amount of nutrients lost by leaching. In experiments at Michigan State University, however, it was found that the nutrient content of the plant, the plant species, sunlight, maturity and the amount and duration of rainfall are among factors which determine loss.

LEADWORT: *see* Plumbago

LEAF FEEDING: *see* Foliar Feeding

LEAF HOPPER: Beginning in August, small greenish wedge-shaped leafhoppers are often present in home gardens in great numbers. Leafhoppers are about ⅛ inch long and fly away actively from the plant on which they are feeding if disturbed. The immature leafhoppers run actively over the surface of the leaves and are usually found feeding on the under-surface of beans and other garden plants.

Not only do leafhoppers cause the so-called "hopper burn" of many plants and a crinkling distortion of the leaf, but the six-spotted leafhopper spreads the aster yellows disease, which affects many vegetable and flowering plants. *See also* INSECT CONTROL; BRAMBLE FRUITS.

LEAF MOLD: *see* LEAVES

LEATHER DUST: Leather dust makes an excellent fertilizer material, high in nitrogen. The nitrogen content varies from 5.5 to 12 per, cent, and it also contains considerable amounts of phosphorus.

LEATHERWOOD: (*Dirca palustris*) An early, choice native shrub which blooms before leafing out in the early spring. Reported as hardy as far north as Minnesota, it grows to about five feet and remains shapely at all times.

Its great number of small, yellow blossoms make it showy and beautiful when there is little or no other color in the border. Growing best in the shade, its light yellow autumn foliage gives a second bonus of color towards the end of the year. It is wild in the eastern parts of the country, growing in moist places, but can be cultivated in ordinary garden soil.

LEAVES: The foliage portion of a plant where the manufacture of sugar and starch takes place. Each leaf on every plant functions during its entire life as a factory, where the energy of the sun, the carbon dioxide of the air, and the minerals and water of the earth are converted into carbohydrates—food for the plant and for animals.

All living things—plant and animal —are composed of carbon compounds. These compounds are in constant

process of change, of breaking down to yield heat and energy, or of building into more and more complex carbon compounds in the form of fats and proteins. Each of these changes

Leaves may be used as a mulch to protect plants during winter or summer, may be added to the compost heap, or made into leaf mold.

takes energy to accomplish. Some of the original carbohydrates are burned to provide this energy. One of the by-products of burning a carbon compound is carbon dioxide, in which carbon is returned in its mineral state to the atmosphere.

Green leaves are the only known organs that can take mineral carbon from the carbon dioxide in the air and combine it with water and other minerals to build carbohydrates. Without this synthesis of carbohydrates by leaves the world's supply would soon run down and life could not continue.

Leaves are in constant process of replenishing the layer of organic matter which lies on the surface of the earth. Other living things are just as busy breaking down this layer into its component minerals and gases, which escape into the air or are washed by the rains into the earth. Only the roots of the plants can reach deep into the earth to bring back this lost material, and only the leaves can return it to usefulness.

Minerals from the earth are carried up into the leaves through the trunks of trees in water. The more water the tree uses, the more is transpired through the leaves, and the more mineral will be found in the leaves. Thus it will be found that leaves of ash or willow or other trees growing in wet places will contain up to seven per cent mineral, while pines, which transpire little, contain no more than 2.5 per cent.

STRUCTURE: Cells of a typical leaf are specialized, just as organs of the human body each has its special job to do. A thin layer of transparent cells on the surface of the leaf acts as a skin protecting more tender cells inside. Beneath this skin, or cortex, are the chlorophyll cells, where the energy from the sun is used as fuel to spark the complex chemical processes of building food. Veins in the leaf carry water and plant nutrients into the leaf by day, and when the light fails, the same veins reverse their flow to carry away the completed foods to be used for root storage, for building growth of the plant, or for producing flowers and fruit. Leaf pores, or stomata, open to admit carbon dioxide, and to release oxygen freed from the carbon which is being used in the leaf process.

From the importance of its leaves, it can be inferred that the health of the whole plant depends upon the health of the leaves. When leaves are sprayed and stomata are clogged with spray materials, the cycle of building and producing must stop until the leaves are clean again. If roots are injured, supplies cannot reach the leaves and the injury to the plant will result in the death of some leaves, which turn yellow and drop off the plant. On the other hand, a plant with robust, deeply colored leaves is a healthy plant.

As FERTILIZER: In the autumn when the plants enter their winter rest period, leaves which have finished their jobs fall to the ground. In them there still will be some remnants of the products they have manufactured through the year. If they are in the forest, the leaves will lie at the foot of the tree on top of those which fell the year before, and the year before that. Insects and bacteria living in the leaf mold layer will work up through the new layer, wet with fall rains, and by spring it will be difficult to separate this years' fall of leaves from last. Beneath the surface, organisms of all kinds are at work making the leaf mold palatable for the roots of smaller plants on the forest floor.

No chemical fertilizers are added to leaf mold in the forest, and there is no need of them, because there nothing is wasted. Plants and leaves

NUTRIENT CONTENT OF POPULAR LEAF VARIETIES

NAME	CALCIUM	MAG-NESIUM	POTAS-SIUM	PHOS-PHORUS	NITRO-GEN	ASH	pH
Balsam fir	1.12	0.16	0.12	0.09	1.25	3.08	5.5
Red maple	1.29	0.40	0.40	0.09	0.52	10.97	4.70
Sugar maple	1.81	0.24	0.75	0.11	0.67	11.85	4.30
American beech	0.99	0.22	0.65	0.10	0.67	7.37	5.08
White ash	2.37	0.27	0.54	0.15	0.63	10.26	6.80
White oak	1.36	0.24	0.52	0.13	0.65	5.71	4.40
E. hemlock	0.68	0.14	0.27	0.07	1.05	—	5.5

which fall become part of the food for next year's growth.

Unfortunately, this is not always what happens in a cultivated area. In an excess of zeal to be tidy, gardeners are too often guilty of destroying one of their most valuable sources of fertilizer.

The leaves of one large shade tree can be worth as much as $15 in terms of plant food and humus. Pound for pound, the leaves of most trees contain twice as many minerals as manure. For example, the mineral content of a sugar maple leaf is over five per cent, while even common pine needles have 2.5 per cent of their weight in calcium, magnesium, nitrogen and phosphorus, plus other trace elements. See the accompanying chart for an analysis of the nutrient elements in fallen leaves.

Actually these multi-colored gifts from above are most valuable for the large amounts of fibrous organic matter they supply. Their humus-building qualities mean improved structure for all soil types. They aerate heavy clay soils, prevent sandy soils from drying out too fast, soak up rain and check evaporation.

A lawn sweeper is a good machine to use for collecting leaves. Using a sweeper is much faster than hand raking, and a better picking-up job is done.

After the leaves have been collected, they may be used directly on the soil as mulch around plants during the winter, after which they will be cultivated into the soil in the spring. Or they may be stored and dug into the soil in preparation for the spring garden. Or they may be made into leaf mold, which will be used as a summer mulch and fertilizer. Or they may be used to make compost.

As MULCH: Leaves provide excellent winter protection for perennials, provided care is taken to avoid matting. They may also be spread over the strawberry bed, if coarse material such as cornstalks, bean plants, or tomato stalks are first scattered over the bed. This coarse material will hold leaf blanket away from the strawberries enough to prevent smothering. In the spring, after the stalks have been removed, the leaves may be worked into the soil to add to its humus content.

Plants which require special acid soil, such as azaleas, rhododendrons, holly, and magnolia, will welcome a mulch of acid leaves. Oak leaves or pine needles spread around their roots in fall or early spring will not only add humus and acid to the soil, but will increase the capacity of the soil to hold the moisture which all of these shrubs need.

Leaves may be used just as they fall from the tree, or they may be shredded before they are used as mulch. If they are first shredded they will break down more quickly to humus, and they will not blow and scatter as much as if they are left whole, nor mat so compactly when wet.

How TO SHRED: There are a number of compost shredders on the market which will shred leaves for composting and for mulch. A rotary mower may also be used by running it over the leaves if they are dry and crisp. If the mower has a special leaf-mulching attachment, the leaves will be ground to a powder.

Home-made leaf shredders have been successfully made from both reel-type mowers and from rotary power mowers. The basic idea behind each kind of shredder is to bring the material to the machine, rather than running the mower over the material.

Since the machine is to be stationary, a frame must be constructed on which the mower will stand, either temporarily if the mower is also to be used for cutting grass, or permanently, if it has been retired from its original purpose. The frame must be strongly constructed to take the vibration, and provision must be made to lock the machine to the frame while it is in use. The frame must be high enough to raise the machine a foot or more above the ground, in order to permit ground leaves to drop in a heap below it.

A screen of ⅝ inch mesh hardware cloth is stretched across the frame below the mower to make a sifter-floor through which finely ground leaves will drop. A hopper or trough is attached above to conduct the leaves to the cutter blades. If the mower is the old style reel type, the hopper may be placed directly over the blades. If it is a rotary power mower, the hopper will be attached to the vent where grass clippings are ordinarily ejected. The latter hopper will need to be angled so that leaves will tend to drop under the mower. It is advisable with either machine to provide the operator with a wooden pusher which will be used instead of his hands to push the leaves through the hopper.

If a reel mower is used, the reel holding the blades must be attached directly to the frame by removing the wheels and pushing their axle through holes in the side of the support. In this case the wire mesh will be shaped to fit closely around the reel, in order that the leaves will be ground by being caught between blades and mesh. The reel mower may be powered by a ¼ H.P. motor which is belted to the cutter shaft. Such a machine will cut dry leaves into pieces ½ inch square and finer, though some leaves will be only partially cut. It will also cut wet leaves, but they will not drop through the screen. The product will be ready to use as mulch, to be stored for leaf mold, or to be composted.

LEAF MOLD: Leaf mold is not as rich in plant foods as composted leaves, but it is easier to make, and is especially useful as a summer mulch.

A bin of snow-fencing, wood, or stone may be made to contain the leaves. As the leaves are placed in the enclosure—shredded, if possible— they are damped down and tamped to pack them. If they are intended for any except acid-loving plants, they will probably need an application of ground limestone, since most leaves are somewhat acid. Liming will also help speed bacterial action.

These leaves will not break down in the course of one winter into the fine black leaf mold found on forest floors. Such black mold is the result of several years' decomposition. But with the assistance of shredding, the bin full of leaves will be broken down enough to make excellent mulch. The ability of such leaf mold to hold moisture is five to ten times that of ordinary topsoil.

Freshly fallen leaves pass through several stages from surface litter to well-decomposed humus partly mixed with mineral soil. Leaf mold from deciduous trees is somewhat richer in such mineral foods as potash and phosphorus than that from conifers. The nitrogen content varies from .2 to 5 per cent.

COMPOSTING LEAVES: Two steps are necessary to assure success in composting leaves.

1. Extra nitrogen must be added. Manure is the best nitrogen supplement. A mixture of five parts leaves to one part manure will break down quickly. Nitrogen supplements like dried blood, cottonseed meal, bone meal, and Agrinite will work almost as well as manure. Nitrogen added to the heap will speed the heating process, because leaves alone do not contain enough nitrogen to supply food to the bacteria. The proportion of such supplements would be two cups full to a wheelbarrow of dried leaves.

2. Grind or shred leaves for composting. This makes the material easier to handle, prevents matting, and helps to start the process of decomposition.

A compost pile may be made in any shape, but usually for ease of handling it is made rectangular in a bin where it can be turned into a second bin. On the bottom of the bin is spread a six-inch layer of leaves, shredded if possible. Over this goes a two-inch layer of high-nitrogen materials, such as manure, garbage, green weeds, grass clippings, or old leguminous vines. These layers are mixed, and water is added to make the heap moist, but not soggy. The layers are repeated until all leaves are used. The heap is turned every three weeks, or a total of three or four times before late spring of the following year, when it will be ready to use as mulch.

Compost may be made from leaves in as short a time as 14 days if the following steps are taken:

1. Leaves are shredded.

2. Four parts of leaves are mixed with one of manure or nitrogen-enriched supplement.

3. The heap is turned every three days.

A plastic sheet used to cover the heap will protect it from rain and drying winds. Unless it is raised slightly by a layer of coarse material, however, the plastic may cut off a necessary supply of air. After the heap has cooled down, it may be inoculated with earthworms to speed the churning action which makes it friable and homogenous.

LEAVES FOR LAWN BUILDING: If leaves are not needed to produce compost for the flower or vegetable garden, they may be shredded where they fall on the lawn when the mower is run for the last time in autumn. A fast rotary mower will make leaves disappear like magic, with half the expenditure of energy needed to rake and burn them. The result of such treatment will be the enrichment of the lawn, which will have humus sifted over grass roots to hold moisture against the next summer's drought.

Low spots in the lawn may be suc-cessfully corrected by spading under as much leaf mold or compost as is needed. Cut the sod with a sharp spade, fold it back gently, work the leaf compost into the soil thoroughly until the desired level is attained, fold the sod back, pack freely and water. The satisfaction from a job like this will be felt every time the mower rolls over it. *See also* COM-POST; MULCH.

LEBBEK: (*Albizzia*) Closely resem-bling the acacia, Albizzias are tropi-cal trees that can stand much dry weather as well as some cold weather. They bear flowers in pompom-like masses, greenish-yellow in color, and with a pleasant fragrance. The silk tree (*A. julibrissin*) grows to about 30 feet, is a favorite ornamental in southeastern states, produces great masses of pink flowers in June. The lebbek tree (*A. lebbek*), also called siris, grows up to 80 feet high, is a fast-grower, easy to transplant. It also goes under the name of woman's tongue, a name which is attributed to the rustling of its dry pods in the wind. *A. lophantha* is a 20 foot shrub often grown in Florida.

LEEK: (*Allium porrum*) An onion-like plant, which is used much like the onion, but is milder in flavor. Leeks like a rich, deep loam, but are not too particular about soil requirements. They respond readily to heavy appli-cations of mature compost; well-rotted manure may be substituted if necessary, but avoid the use of raw manure. Leeks will tolerate a mod-erately acid soil, but it must be one rich in nitrogen. This is especially essential during early growth.

CULTURE: Seed is planted thickly, 1/2 inch deep. When the seedlings are eight inches high they should be carefully dug up, about half the tops removed, and replanted six inches apart. Trenches six inches deep and three or four inches wide should be dug and the seedlings planted in the bottoms of these trenches. As the

Large, onion-like plants, leeks do best in areas of cool to moderate temperatures; applications of compost or rotted manure aid early growth.

plants grow the sides of the trenches should be broken down to blanch the edible stems. A heavy supply of sifted compost humus should be incorporated with the soil in the bottoms of the trenches. During the early stages of their growth, leeks require an abundance of plant food. A plentiful supply of moisture is necessary to make this available to them.

There are two types of popular, cultivated leeks: the Broad London and the Elephant take 130 and 125 days to mature. *See also* ONION.

LEGGY: A term used to describe a plant, usually a seedling, which has grown a long stem out of proportion with its foliage. In seedlings, this results from having the seed flats too crowded, from giving the plants too little sun, or from making the soil too rich in the seed germinating flat. In older plants, it is usually a result of crowding or of lack of proper pinching back or pruning. Thus, zinnias may become leggy, or grow one long central stem if not pinched back early. Or forsythia may grow to 12 feet, with bare leggy wood at the base, through lack of pruning.

LEGUME: A member of the plant family *Leguminosæ* characterized by their fruits as having a single-cavity ovary splitting when dry along two seams (pod-bearing plants such as peas, beans, and clovers). Leguminous plants are also unique in functioning with nodule bacteria to fix nitrogen from the air for plant use.

Legumes are our best soil building and forage crops. Properly grown, legumes supply more protein, calcium and vitamins A and D per acre than any other roughage. Legume feed, as hay, pasture or silage, is the cheapest source of total digestible nutrients and protein you can grow.

The ability of legumes to improve fertility and soil structure is rightly famed: with deep, subsoil-probing roots—alfalfa often goes down over 30 feet—they facilitate drainage and bring up nutrients from the subsoil's hidden storehouse. Plowed down, a good legume stand adds all this plant food, plus tons of organic matter, to the soil.

But it's in nitrogen production that they really excel. An acre of inoculated legumes will take as much nitrogen from the air as is contained in *10 tons of manure.* Much of this is stored up in the soil, and much or all of the rest is returned to the soil when the plants or their residues are plowed down.

Leguminous crops are active nitrogen gatherers. According to Dr. Parker, Assistant Chief, Bureau of Plant Industry, United States Department of Agriculture, legumes furnish far more nitrogen to our crops than farm manures and fertilizers combined. This nitrogen comes largely from the air, mainly through the action of a group of bacteria called Rhizobia. Because of the high nitrogen content, plowing under of green manure crops of clover, alfalfa, peas, etc., is no shock to the soil. The best time for incorporating them in the soil is before blooming time, because then the plants are most leafy and richest in nitrogen. It is usually more economical to cut established legume fields for hay and to let the plants become well established. As they sink their roots down, they not only aerate the soil, but add valuable organic matter to it, beside bringing minerals to the surface.

A number of legume crops are suited to special conditions. Some mixed crops are practical, for instance, a winter grain with vetch, sown at about 20 pounds per acre; spring oats and alfalfa; spring oats and field peas; sudan grass and soybeans or cowpeas; white clover, a very reliable perennial, had best be incorporated in mixtures for pastures. Sometimes it is practical to sow forage crops for hogs, for instance cowpeas, soybeans, field peas, vetch, and even crimson clover. All of these can be pastured for at least four weeks, and the residues will mean a more fertile bit of ground in the end.

With all legumes, adaptation to soil, moisture, and temperature conditions is essential, and the origin of the seed may furthermore seriously affect the success, especially with alfalfa. Alsike clover, for example, can stand heat better than red clover, but likes a cool, moist climate. It is, to all practical intents, a biennial. Crimson clover, a winter annual, will not do well in cold, water sogged soils and regions, but still requires rains and moisture. It must be cut young, but does not develop an extended root system and is therefore not so valuable for its residues as red clover. Lespedeza is grown in the warmer regions, both for hay and for pasture. It has deep roots, but is not so nutritious as the clovers. It is an annual. So is burr clover, another warm weather crop suited mainly to green manuring. The vetches are also warm region plants, though the hairy vetch extends farther North than the common vetch. Soybeans and cowpeas, velvet beans and field peas, field beans and peanuts are rarely grown for manuring purposes, because their seed is valuable and because they are annuals and therefore do not develop deep root systems.

A few typical analyses follow:

	Nitrogen	Phosphoric Acid	Potash
Green cowpeas	.4	.1	.4
Cowpea hay	3.0	.3	2.8
Pea forage	—	.3	1.4
Pea hay	1.5—2.5	—	—
Soybean hay	1.5—3.0	.3—.5	1.2—2.3

In addition to use as soil builders, legumes also include edible plants as peanuts, lentils and carob; shrubs and trees as the locust, mesquite and broom; flowers as baptisia, anthyllis and lathyrus; and tropical plants as acacia, derris and mimosa. *See also* GREEN MANURE; COVER CROPS.

LEGUME INOCULATION: Legumes are actually nitrogen factories, and growing inoculated legumes is the simplest and most economical way to put this vital plant food into your soil.

Seed inoculation is not something new and mysterious; some European farmers have practiced it for centuries. They knew that clover, for instance, grew better if the seed was first well-mixed with some soil from

Inoculating legumes encourages greater root nodule development as shown by highly effective nodulation on soybean clusters around taproot.

a field that had just produced a good clover stand.

What they were doing was coating each seed with a strain of nitrogen-fixing bacteria especially suited to living with clover. As the seed sprouted, these bacteria entered the root hairs, forming nodules in which they lived. There they took nitrogen from the air and "fixed" it in compounds usable by the plant.

Just how these species of bacteria fix nitrogen is not known, but their activities show up in increased crop yield and quality. Inoculated alfalfa, for example, may contain over 16 per cent protein, as against ten per cent for non-inoculated (which has had to depend on the soil supply for the nitrogen with which to manufacture its protein). Soybeans when inoculated have raised their yields by more than 12 bushels per acre, with nine per cent more protein and a comparable rise in oil content.

Often the difference between inoculating and not inoculating is the difference between a healthy profit from the crop and not getting enough to bother harvesting. Given good weather, organic soil and proper fertilization, legume seed that is inoculated by the correct strain of bacteria will outyield the same seed, not inoculated, by 15 to 25 per cent.

Sometimes a farmer will show you a clover plant from a fine stand that has plenty of nodules on its roots, and tell you that he has never inoculated his seed. This is more often the exception than the rule. There are always some of the right bacteria in the soil, of course, but their numbers are rarely sufficient to do the job well. Even when the same legume was grown on the field the previous year, most of them will have died out or lost their efficiency in the intervening time. Too, the inoculants sold commercially contain improved strains of bacteria that do a better job than those occurring normally in most

soils—and this shows up in better yields.

Inoculants are very inexpensive and easy to use. Be sure to buy the right inoculant for the seed you are planting. Most states have laws regulating the quality of inoculants on the market, so you can be sure of getting one that will perform as expected. Use it fresh, however; the bacteria may become inactive if kept from year to year. Cold has no effect on inoculant bacteria, but never store them in the sun or near a hot stove.

Legume bacteria come either packaged in moist humus or in bottles of nutrient agar (a breeding solution made from seaweed). Add a little water to the inoculant and pour it over the seeds which have first been moistened slightly in a tub, on the floor or in the wagon. Mix it in well with a shovel, paddle, or your hands—the bacteria are completely harmless even if you have cuts in the skin. Soybeans can be inoculated right in the drill. If you're planting a meadow mixture that calls for several types of inoculants, mix them all together and apply them the same as you would a single inoculant.

Plant the seed immediately after inoculating, as any long exposure may reduce the efficiency of the bacteria. Reinoculate any seed kept overnight.

And if you want your bacteria to live to do the job you bought them for, don't use any chemical fertilizers or seed treatments when planting. Like nearly all beneficial soil organisms, they are sensitive to these foreign substances.

An acid soil will not support the growth of legume bacteria. A pH of 6.5 is best for them, so lime the soil as needed. Both the bacteria and the legumes themselves will benefit from the calcium, which they need in large amounts for growth.

Humus provides the ideal living conditions for all beneficial bacteria, and the nitrogen-fixing species are no exception. Soil with plenty of organic matter suffers less from moisture loss, hot sun, lack of aeration and all the other organism-killing ills that chemically-fertilized or worn out soil is heir to. Don't expect even the best inoculated seed to "catch" on severely-eroded, badly-packed or dried-out soil. Work in some manure or organic materials first, well in advance of planting. Subsoiling with machinery may be necessary if the soil is extremely packed.

Legumes are top soil builders, but like any crop they require plant food to grow. Soil tests and applications of rock fertilizers are just as necessary to them as to corn or cabbage. Liberal applications of rock phosphate in particular produce strong, vigorous growth in legumes.

The symbiotic (mutually beneficial) relationship between legume roots and nitrogen-fixing bacteria is very much like that between bees and honey plants. Bees pollinate the flowers so the plant can reproduce itself, in return for the nectar. In the same way as we supply bees to aid pollination, so we can help legumes by supplying bacteria. There is nothing artificial about either process. In inoculation, man helps out Nature because his system of crop rotation does not allow her to constantly have large enough population of the right bacteria in the soil to do the legume production job well.

PREPARATION: Laboratories prepare inoculants by taking bacteria from a healthy legume root nodule. Technicians study them for vigor and efficiency, and the best strains are painstakingly reproduced in cultures of nutrient agar. The process is entirely natural.

One more important point: just as inoculated legumes make better aboveground growth, so too do they develop more vigorous root systems.

This is an advantage that is invaluable. Good tilth, produced by strong roots breaking up the soil deep down,

then adding organic matter to it when they decay, is something no chemical fertilizers or soil conditioners can bring about. The soil's physical condition determines the amount of water it can hold to keep plants growing well in dry weather. It also insures the aeration necessary for plant roots and for the bacteria that work to make nutrients available to them.

LEMON: (*Citrus limonia*) A small evergreen tree grown commercially for its oval or oblong fruit primarily as a source of the important acid citrus juice. Originally from Asia, the lemon spread west to Europe and then to America about the time of Columbus. During the 17th century, the first extensive plantings were made in Florida. Today, California is the center of our lemon growing, and the trees there are generally everbearing.

Decorative as well as productive, lemon trees are grown mostly in California. They do well in heavy soils, but are very susceptible to frost.

Lemon trees respond well to heavy soils, and can tolerate the occasional colder temperature that hits the sectors in which they are usually grown. For planting, it is best to use rootstocks particularly adapted to the local soil, although seedling trees may also be planted. The lemon is most frequently grafted to the stock of the sour orange.

Beyond the recognized citrus areas, success with lemon trees is a risk. Single trees may be tried in uncertain locations. Provide protection by placing these on the south side of a house or other building. Since the lemon is seldom without either fruit or flowers, a frost will usually destroy its crop, although an established tree probably would not be killed.

Perhaps the best variety for home planting is the Lisbon, which is hardy, disease resistant and vigorous. Also adaptable are the Villa Franca and Eureka. A hybrid lemon, the Perrine, is quite resistant to citrus scab, grows quickly and produces good-quality, medium-sized fruit.

Most suitable for cold areas is the Meyer lemon, which can withstand temperatures down to 10 or 15° F. without being killed. Propagated by cuttings, the mature tree reaches a six to ten-foot height, bears prolifically a more oranged-shaped fruit that has a very thin skin and lots of juice.

The Meyer lemon used in the bush form makes a most acceptable medium-sized hedge. Coming to us from the colder sections of temperate China, this lemon has proved frost-resistant even in California's occasional cold winters. Fruits ripen throughout the year, big luscious lemons which make the most delicious lemon pies. The shrub is beautiful in appearance with its glossy green leaves and its fragrant citrus blooms which are tinted pink. From the seacoast to the hottest interior valleys, this hardy, lemon adapts itself to all sorts of growing conditions, and always produces heavy crops. For hedges always plant the bush type, spacing so that there is room for a full, rounded development. You will not be troubled with endless pruning and shaping entailed by ordinary hedges.

Other cultural requirements are similar to all citrus fruits. *See also* CITRUS; FRUIT, INDOOR.

LEMON BALM: *see* MELISSA

LEMON THYME: *see* MOTHER-OF-THYME

LEMON VERBENA: The most widely grown species *lippia,* a genus of the verbena family, *Verbenaceae. Lippia* is a large genus of mostly aromatic herbs and shrubs, native to the warmer parts of America. Flowers are small, generally in clusters, either umbel or raceme. Flower parts are in pairs and fours, with fruit in two inconspicuous nutlets. Beside lemon verbena, the only other cultivated variety is the carpet grass or fog fruit of southern California, a creeping form used on dry poor soils as a ground cover.

Lemon verbena, *lippia citriodora,* is a shrub from South America, where it grows six to ten feet. In this country it is grown mostly as a potted plant, and pruned to smaller size. Its foliage has a strong lemon scent, which made it an old-time bouquet favorite. Flowers are small white spikes, leaves are long and narrow, and grow in whorls. Grown as a greenhouse subject, pots should be wintered at cool house temperatures, about 55°. In summer it may be planted in the garden or placed in a protected position in its pot. Potting soil should be a mixture of sand, loam, and leaf mold, with additions of a small amount of manure and bone meal. Propagation is by greenwood cuttings rooted in sand. In frost-free climates it may be grown outside year round, and pruned to a small standard tree shape.

Carpet grass, *l. canescens,* sometimes called *l. repens,* is also from South America. It spreads from creeping stems, and can be kept mowed to remove seed heads which prevents it from becoming a pest. Flowers are small lilac colored heads, leaves are long and slender. Best means of planting is by clumps spotted at intervals, from which it will spread rapidly to cover entire area.

LEMON WASTES: *see* CITRUS WASTES

LENS: *see* LENTIL

LENTEN ROSE: (*Helleborus niger*) *see* CHRISTMAS ROSE

LENTIL: (*Lens esculenta*) An annual of the pea family, *Leguminaceae.* The lentil grows on a straggling 12 to 18 inch vine, and produces inconspicuous whitish to lavender pea-like flowers, which are a good source of honey. They are followed by flat pods containing two seeds each, in three varieties, small flat brown, small yellow, or larger pea-shaped. Lentils have been used as food in Mediterranean countries from antiquity. They are used for soup, as beans, or the larger pea shape which is grown in Provence, as fodder. Seed is sown in early spring in sandy soil, the rows 18 to 30 inches apart. Seed keeps best when left in the pod.

LEOPOLD-PLANT: *see* LIGULARIA

LEPACHYS: A genus of annuals and perennials of the daisy family, *compositeae,* and one of the several genera known as coneflowers. The flowers closely resemble black-eyed Susans, having yellow ray-flowers and brownish or purplish disks, but the disks are higher than those of *rudbeckia,* and the foliage is finer cut.

Two species, both natives of the American prairie states, have been taken from their wild state into the garden. Both are easily raised from seed in any good garden soil. The seed of the annual, *l. columnifera,* (sometimes called *rudbeckia columnaris*) is sown where the plants are to stand early in spring. *Columnifera* grows to 2½ feet, with hairy somewhat coarse foliage, flowers two to three inches in diameter, rays yellow with columnar disk. A variety, *pulcherrima,* has brown-purple rays, and another, variety has double flowers.

L. pinnata, the perennial species, grows to five feet, with larger, coarser foliage. The flower, which is like a sunflower except for its raised cone, grows to five inches in diameter, with yellow rays and brownish disk. Seed started early indoors will bloom the same year.

Lepachys is also sometimes called *ratibida. See also* CONEFLOWER.

LEPTOSPERMUM: Tea tree or sand stay. A genus of about 25 species of evergreen shrubs and trees of the myrtle family, *Myrtaceae.* Natives of Australia and New Zealand, they are warm-climate plants, and can be grown only in the southernmost portions of the United States. Several of the most freely blooming species have been developed as greenhouse plants. They are kept in a cool house throughout the winter and gradually brought up to 60° in February or March, when they will bloom.

Leaves of *leptospermum,* which are sometimes used as substitute for tea, are stiff, small, growing ½ to one inch long. Flowers are white, pink, or red, growing in the leaf axils. In spring the plants are most attractive, with quantities of bloom. They are easily grown in warm climates, and are used in Australia and in California to bind loose sandy soils. Propagation is by seeds in spring, greenwood cuttings early in spring under glass, or mature cuttings in sand in the fall.

Most commonly planted in California is *l. laevigatum,* the tea tree. It will grow to 30 feet, but is also pruned to a shrub, the form most often seen in California. Leaves are one inch, flowers white and ¾ inch. With similar flowers but much shorter, silkier leaves is *l. pubescens.*

Some varieties of *l. scoparium* are grown in this country as greenhouse plants, but not many are cultivated outdoors. They are shrubs or small trees 12 to 25 feet tall, but may also be found in dwarf forms one to two feet, more acceptable for indoor culture. Flowers of the type are white, but varieties have colored blossoms—

Chapmannii, bright rose; *grandiflorum,* pinkish white; *Nichollsii,* carmine; *roseum,* rose-pink; and *rubrum,* dark red.

LESPEDEZA: Also known as bush clover, common lespedeza (*L. striata*) is an annual spreading or upright legume that reaches a height of one to 1½ feet on fertile soils, about six inches to one foot on poorer ones. It is well-adapted to the Southeast, where it is used for green manure, hay or rotating with cash crops. Sericea lespedza is a hardy perennial plant similar in growth to alfalfa. It can grow fairly well on acid and poorer soils. Korean lespedeza is similar to common lespedeza but grows best somewhat further north.

Branches of common, Kobe and Korean lespedeza. Leaflets of Kobe are larger than common; Korean leaflets have more prominent stipules.

L. bicolor and *L. formosa* are late-blooming ornamental shrubs. They do best in a sandy soil and open location, are propagated by cuttings. *L. bicolor* grows six to ten feet high, has purple flowers, while *L. formosa* or *thunbergi* grows three to eight feet, also with showy purple flowers. *See also* GREEN MANURE; LEGUME; COVER CROP.

LETTUCE: (*Lactuca sativa*) Few salad vegetables exceed lettuce in popularity, and you should have little difficulty in growing it. But success in producing a steady supply of fresh, crisp leaves depends to a great extent upon an understanding of the habits of this plant.

Lettuce grows readily probably because all cultivated strains were obtained originally from the prickly lettuce (*L. scariola*), an Asiatic weed. Prominent among other wild forms are Sleepwort (*L. virosa*) and the familiar wild lettuce (*L. canadensis*) a tall, yellow-flowered herb which is often a troublesome weed.

Almost any fairly good garden soil that is well-drained, not excessively acid, is suitable for lettuce. The only real secret about growing fine plants is to keep them uncrowded and growing rapidly. Rapid growth demands an abundance of moisture plus an abundance of natural plant nutrients. Mature compost humus or old, well-rotted manure should be dug in along the row before the seed is sown. In transplanting, a generous amount of organic humus should be worked into the hole before the plant is set out.

Wild lettuce prefers a temperate climate and its cultivated descendants naturally thrive best during cool weather although some loose-leafed strains are notable for their ability to grow during summer heat.

FOUR TYPES: Cultivated lettuce may be conveniently divided into four types.

1. Loose-leaf, non-heading. Probably the easiest of all to grow. Leaves may be harvested by stripping, much as Swiss Chard is gathered, while the plant continues to grow. Grand Rapids, a crumpled-leaf variety which matures in around 45 days, is an excellent example. It withstands summer heat and its green leaves are believed to have a higher food value than any of the blanched types.

2. The Butterheads. These form a soft, buttery head, yellow almost to the center with dark outer leaves. Mignonette, which matures in 80 days is a favorite, Big Boston is another.

3. The Cabbageheads. These offer quite a challenge. If you can produce a good stand of fine heads your repu-

tation as a gardener is secure. Not that this is so difficult if you know how but certain elements have to be kept in mind. New York (Wonderful) and Imperial, 84 days to maturity, are typical. But before going into more detail regarding the cabbageheads you will like to remember that fine strain, the Cos lettuce.

4. Cos (or Romaine). These form a tall, elongated head and have a leaf shaped somewhat like the bowl of a spoon. They have an elegance and fineness of flavor that brings them distinction. Paris White, 83 days to maturity, is matched with Trianon for honors. The outer leaves are sometimes gathered up and loosely tied so that the interior of the head will be surely blanched although the plant usually does a good job of self-blanching. In spite of their refinement, the Cos strains are excellent for summer use.

Whether you grow a row of the loose-leaf type or a few Cos, you will naturally like to grow many large heads of the fine varieties you see in the stores, usually one of the Cabbageheads. In general this form will not head during hot weather. That means that the transplants have to be set out very early, even before danger of frost is past. Delicate as the lettuce plant may seem it is really hardy.

PLANTING: Heading lettuce may be planted to head-up either during the early summer or the fall. For the early crop the seed should be sown about $1/4$ inch deep in flats or similar containers and placed in a sunny window or a cold frame about the beginning of March. The young plants should be ready to set out early in April. In the flats, the seed should be thinly sown and the seedlings thinned just as soon as the leaves touch. Probably no fault is more universal than the common practice of sowing lettuce seed, which is fine but almost always of good quality, too thickly.

For the spring crop, many gardeners start seeds indoors in flats or pots in a sunny, cool (50-60 degrees) location, or outside in a hotbed or coldframe, about four to six weeks before the last severe frost. For a good potting mixture, sift together one part sand, one part good loam and one part compost. Keep moist until germination and the young plants are growing well. When the seedlings have at least their first set of true leaves, transplant to plant bands or flats. Gradually harden off the plants by setting them outdoors during the sunny part of the day.

TRANSPLANTING: Setting the transplants out very early is essential. In fact, some gardeners make a practice of sowing their lettuce seed in the fall in a carefully prepared area. The seedlings become fairly large before severe frost. As cold weather approaches the seedlings are covered with a gradually increasing layer of loose straw, leaves, twigs, and the like. Under this, the small plants survive the winter easily and the gardener has a heavy supply of sturdy, very early seedlings upon which to draw.

In setting out the transplants, they should stand about 15 inches apart in the row and the rows should be about two feet part. When seed is sown directly into the garden, the seedlings should be ruthlessly thinned to stand at least a foot apart to prevent overcrowding.

In the early stages of its growth the plant has a cluster of shallow feeding rootlets. This condition makes it ideal for transplanting but renders it while small an easy prey of weeds. A light mulching of compost humus sifted around the plants will do much to keep down weedy growth and later supply easily available plant nutrients.

Lettuce plants will not do their best unless they have a very liberal supply of moisture. Normally the supply of rainwater is insufficient, often inopportune. It will aid your plants to continue rapid growth during dry weather if you water them liberally with compost water-rainwater which has filtered through a container holding a quantity of fertile compost.

It may be that for one of many reasons your plants do not reach the heading stage before the arrival of hot weather. Many gardeners have had this experience. The most popular solution to the problem consists in covering the plants so as to give them partial shade. A few stakes driven into the ground along the sides of the rows may be used to support a length of cheesecloth stretched upon them. A slightly heavier framework may be made to support a thin layer of brush, or a slat roof in which the slats are altered with spaces about equal to the width of the slats. Any such arrangement which excludes excessive sunlight will usually produce the coolness necessary to the plants if they are to form satisfactory heads. Some gardeners make good use of a partially shaded spot in the garden as a favored site for lettuce.

Lettuce usually suffers little from insect pests, but because of the necessity for growing large, crisp leaves on a plant which in its wild state develops rather small leaves, the gardener must supply rather moist conditions. Because of this, the lower leaves— especially if the plants are overcrowded at maturity—are somewhat subject to attack from a form of rot. If this is not checked it will destroy the heart of the plant. A layer of clean sand spread around the plants will prevent the lower leaves from coming into contact with the soil and do much to prevent lettuce rot.

You may have found in your garden some lettuce plant which seemed to you to have exceptional qualities. Its flavor may be quite different—the degree of bitterness natural to this plant is a very elusive quality. The plant may be allowed to run to seed and if you save the seed your chances are very good that the following season you may be able to grow many similar plants.

But you will enjoy growing lettuce and you may be sure that what you grow will far exceed in flavor and food value the wilted heads you had formerly purchased in the stores. You will find that different strains of lettuce taste differently. And you will enjoy most of all that moment when, for the first time, you cut and take into the house a couple of fine, firm heads of crisp, fresh lettuce; when, for the first time, you discover the fine flavor that was their inheritance from the compost humus incorporated soil in which they thrived.—*Roger Smith*.

See also FERTILIZER.

LEUCOJUM: *see* SNOWFLAKE

LEUCOTHOE: Fairly small, ornamental shrubs with white, bell-shaped flowers produced in dense, racemes. They are grown mainly along the east coast, bloom in April or May. Leucothoes have attractive foliage as well as flowers and make good foundation and border plantings. They grow best in humus-rich moist soil that is fairly sandy. Fetter-bush (*L. catesbaei*) is an evergreen shrub that grows to about six feet, is the hardiest of the leucothoes. Pepperbush (*L. racemosa*), also known as sweetbells, is deciduous, sometimes reaching 12 feet high.

LEVISTICUM OFFICINALE: *see* LOVAGE

LEWISIA: A genus of the portulaca family, *Portulacaceae,* native to the northwestern American continent. Low-growing evergreen and deciduous perennial herbs, with starchy, fleshy roots which, in the species *l. rediviva,* are used as food by Oregon Indians. The genus was named for Meriwether Lewis. Most species are hardy throughout the United States.

Lewisias grow close to the ground, forming rosettes of leaves one to three inches long. Satiny cactus-like flowers grow sometimes singly and sometimes in loose clusters on short stems seldom more than eight inches high. Flowers are about two inches across, in shades of pink, lavender, orange, red, and white marked or tinged with the above. They are suited by their form and cultural requirements both to the rock garden, rather than to the open border. All varieties must have well-drained soil for their fleshy roots, most preferring abundant moisture early in spring, when leaf and flower growth is made, and dryness during the summer. Full sun is needed by all deciduous varieties. Evergreens which need more moisture may require partial shade in summer.

Soil for both types of lewisias should be composed of at least half coarse gritty sand, and half leaf mold or compost. The soil should be deeply prepared. Seed germinates best if sown very early in spring, or in fall. If it must be sown in warm weather, it should be refrigerated for several weeks first. Evergreen species should be grown in a bed mulched in the top inch with fine gravel, to permit water to drain easily from the axils of the leaves.

L. rediviva, or bitter root, covers acres with its bloom in spring in Montana, where it is the state flower. White to rose flowers are 1½ inches across on two inch stems. Deciduous.

L. brachycal has oblong, light green leaves, flowers two inches across white veined with rose on two inch stems. Deciduous.

L. oppositifolia has fewer leaves, and raises its rose-tinted flowers from six to 12 inches high. Deciduous.

L. nevadensis has a fleshy root that might almost be considered a tuber. Lavender-tinted white flowers are raised singly on four inch stems. Deciduous.

Especially recommended of the evergreen species are: variety *roseum* of the *l. columbianum,* with clusters of deep rose flowers on six to nine inch stems above a dense rosette of green leaves; *howelli,* with leaves with wavy margins, sometimes tinted

red, and numerous clusters of pink flowers striped with violet and with white margins, on six inch stems; *tweedyi,* whose showy salmon-pink flowers are two inches across, one to three on a stem which rises just above the thick, somewhat fleshy leaves; and *heckneri,* whose broad dark green leaves are purplish underneath, with panicles of rose-pink flowers on four inch stems.

LEY: A term mostly used in England, this refers to the duration of a meadow or pasture; thus a two year ley or four year ley.

LIATRIS: (*Lacinaria*) A genus of the daisy family, *compositeae,* comprising about 20 showy flowering perennials native to N. America. Common names for the various species are gayfeather, blazing star, button-snakewood, and devil's bit. They are characterized by their stiff narrow leaves that grow around central stems to six feet, topped by spikes of racemes of purplish flowers composed exclusively of the typical *compositeae* disks. Flowers bloom from the top of the spike down, rather than blooming from the lowest buds and continuing toward the top. Blossoming time is late summer and early fall. Flowers attract many butterflies and bees.

Liatris will thrive where few other flowers will grow, in almost any soil or shade, but they prefer a light soil with a good amount of humus and partial shade. They are propagated easily by seed sown in the fall, by division of the tuberous roots, or in some species by offsets. They are good subjects for the wild garden, some species being difficult to combine with other colors in the flower border.

Blazing star is *l. squarrosa,* also sometimes called rattlesnake master or colicroot. It grows to two feet, with flower heads 1½ inches long, purple.

Button snakewood, sometimes called prairie button snakewood, is *l. pycnostachya,* growing five feet tall, with dense purple spikes of flowers up to 1½ feet long. They are excellent when planted in masses in an open situation.

The name gayfeather is applied to two species, *l. spicata* and *l. scariosa,* both growing to six feet, the former with rosy-purple, the latter with bluish-purple flowers.

L. gramifolia grows about three feet high, with leaves up to one foot long, and purple flowers sometimes branched.

LICHEN: Lichens are actually flowerless plants, active in the initial stages of soil formation.

"Eternity's soil maker," you could call him. Long before your ancestors and mine appeared on earth, he was laboring endlessly on flinty rock and sterile sand, in steaming tropics and icy tundra.

He is perhaps the best example of the teamwork that is the very cornerstone of Nature. Other organisms work together to build soil from the inert substances of the earth's crust— aerobic bacteria and anaerobic, earthworms take over where fungi and molds leave off. All these tiny creatures form links in a chain, the end product of which is life-sustaining fertile soil.

But the lichen is the indispensable "starter" link in the chain. He is a very close-knit team, thanks to the process of *symbiosis*: a lichen is two separate and different plant forms, joined together in *a partnership keyed to mutual survival and benefit.* He is a composite organism made up of an alga and an ascomycete (a higher type fungus).

The fungus' role is to absorb and conserve moisture, without which the alga, a water plant, cannot live. The alga, in turn, shares with the fungus its food products which it is able to fabricate from the raw materials around it. The fungus has no such food-producing ability.

Thus the lichen can thrive in deserts and sub-freezing climes, where neither alga nor fungus could exist alone. The oldest living things on earth, they are found everywhere. They live on the scorched rocks in the desert, flourishing on the night dews. Some are frozen solid, others baked into a crumbly dust that miraculously springs into bright spots of living color after a shower. One species on volcanic islands establishes itself on the streams of lava as soon as they begin to cool. Any damp rock, tree trunk or clump of sterile soil where the right algae are present becomes lichen-covered when ascomycete spores alight there.

Then the soil-building work begins. The lichens weather the rock, their cobwebby threads prying loose particles, then dissolving them. The sheerest cliff that can support no other plant life becomes matted and creviced with their strange jewelry. The lichen is a farmer who farms with self-made soil, building a kind of fertile leaf mold from pure rock and atmospheric gases, aided by the algae's process of photosynthesis. Soon the lichen dies adding its own body as a green manure to the deposit of soil already formed. Higher types of lichen follow, then mosses, ferns, and finally seed plants.

The first lichen to appear on a bare surface is usually a crust form, the latter ones being leafy or even shrublike, growing with a tiny "trunk" and branches. Their one absolute requirement is pure air—a smoky or chemical-laden atmosphere spells death.

A rich variety of lichens—some 6,000 different kinds—is found throughout the world. California's oaks are famed for their "old man's beard," a blue-green epiphyte that hangs from their trunks and branches in rich profusion. The lichens on rocks and walls are usually bright orange, while "cup" or "trumpet" lichens are a lively red and often have a shrubby growth. Flint pebbles are covered with a black crust form.

"Dog's-tooth" lichens, once used as a specific for hydrophobia, are a gray-green variety that appear on soil.

You can often find hundreds of lichens making a woodland floor bright with their hues, and humming-birds' nests may be so covered with a lichen camouflage that they resemble just another bump on a branch. Lichens change colors like chameleons —on damp days, the strands of fungus become translucent, and the green of the alga shows up brilliantly.

Brown "Iceland moss" has long provided both animal fodder and food for the Lapps and other Northern peoples. Eskimos have winter pastures: their reindeer fatten on field and rock lichens, and especially prize the bearded forms on trees. Raked up during wet weather, Iceland moss can be dried and fed to all kinds of animals. Containing five per cent protein, it gives a marvelous richness to the milk of Northern Scandinavia. Powdered, it is made into excellent breads, cereals, jelly and salads. A similar variety is believed to be the "manna" that fed the starving Israelites in the wilderness.

In ancient times, lichens were used for everything from dyes and pigments to perfume and hair tonic. Tanners, brewers, distillers and medical men found them highly useful. At one time, various lichens were recommended as cures for dozens of ailments, and as a narcotic and even an insecticide.

Recent research has shown them to contain one or several antibiotics. The Smithsonian Institution reports that one common species shows considerable promise as a cure for anemia.

LICHENS IN THE GARDEN: You can have a lot of fun with lichens in both your indoor and outdoor gardening. Lichen-covered twigs and pebbles dress up an aquarium, and you'll find the brilliant red-crested lichen, or "British soldier," that grows on sterile soil, a delightful decoration for dish gardens.

Outdoors, lichens will add natural loveliness to retaining walls, stone pavements, ornamental rocks and rock gardens. Give Nature a little help, and the most unpleasing face of stone can be beautified with them.

Collect some lichens in the country. Look for old rocks and tree trunks overgrown with them. A knife can be used to scrape them off. After a few hours drying in the sun, they can be crumbled and rubbed into the surface of a rock freshly sprinkled with water. This moisture is very important— sprinkle the rock two or three times a day. In a few days, a gentle green will appear, gradually deepening until the whole surface is carpeted. Granite is slower to respond than sandstone, shale or limestone, but the result is equally pleasing.

We have found that lichens, and algae alone, can be made to increase very rapidly by fertilization. Lichens respond well to nitrogen: in the Arctic, they grow richly outside marmot burrows, where they are fed by the manure. Algae, we know, multiply with astounding speed upon the application of phosphorus.

Algae-mold crusts have recently been discovered on vast areas of badly eroded farms and rangeland in the Southwest. Holding down the barren dust and blow-sand, they halt erosion and produce organic matter and nitrogen. Even tough Dust Bowl land soon begins the succession to grass cover after the lichen crust is established.

The algae and molds that compose lichens are floating everywhere in the air. Given the surface best suited to that variety of lichen, plus the essential moisture, and soil will replace dead matter. Lichens, incidentally, collect additional organic matter besides that which they make themselves —they are natural "dust traps," and even dead insects are incorporated into their compost manufacture. Too, lichens are eaten by snails, mites, caterpillars and the like, and these creatures supply manure to further the soil making.

LICORICE: Licorice is derived from two closely related perennial herbs (*Glycyrrhiza glabra* and *G. glandulifera*) native to southern Europe, northern Africa, and western Asia. The rhizome and root are used in medicine, confections, and to a larger extent in various tobacco products.

Licorice thrives best in warm regions where the growing season is sufficiently long to promote strong growth. The plant requires deep and sandy soil of good fertility and does not thrive on heavy soil in which the rhizomes cannot penetrate easily to considerable depth. It may be grown from seed, but the usual practice is to propagate it from cuttings of the younger parts of the rhizomes, from suckers, or by crown divisions. These are planted in spring about 18 inches apart in rows spaced to permit cultivation necessary for weed control.

The sandy and sandy loam river valleys in the Southwestern states and in Texas are believed to be well adapted to licorice growing.

LIEBIG, JUSTUS VON: The father of chemical fertilizers was born in 1803 and died at Munich in 1873. He was the originator of the laboratory method of teaching chemistry. He was the discoverer of chloroform and other chemicals. He isolated the first amino acid, tyrosine, and was the developer of baking powder.

For 28 years Liebig taught at the University of Gressen where he saw to it that every chemistry student worked in his laboratory. From this he developed the first textbook on qualitative analysis, which enabled students to analyze minerals and to determine their chemical composition. This was to be very important in the field of geology.

At this time the agriculture world believed in the humus theory. Agriculturists were certain that plants "ate" humus, but when Liebig published his *Chemistry of Agriculture and Physiology* he dealt a death blow to this idea. This book was the beginning of agricultural science as we know it today. In it Liebig asked, "If plants get all of their food from humus, then where did the first plant get its food—since humus is composed of decayed plants?" But Liebig overlooked the fact that the first plant was only moss or lichen that grew on rocks, and that at the beginning of the world, nothing grew but this moss which received its nourishment from the air and the rock. The decaying lichen, plus admixtures of rock pulverized by the elements, made the soil in which plants began to grow—first ferns, then the higher developed ones. The original lichen could not produce seed but reproduced by spores flying in the air.

Sir Albert Howard in his *Agricultural Testament,* regarding Liebig, said, "He followed the science of the moment. In his onslaught on the humus theory he was so sure of his ground that he did not call in Nature to verify his conclusions. It did not occur to him that while the humus theory, as then expressed might be wrong, humus itself might be right. . . . He was unable to visualize his problem from two very different points of view at one and the same moment—the scientific and the practical. His failure has cast its shadow on much of the scientific investigation of the next hundred years. . . . During the period (1840-1900) . . . the use of artificial manures became firmly welded into the work and outlook of the Experiment Stations; the great importance of nitrogen (N), phosphorus (P), and potash (K) in the soil solution was established; what may briefly be described as the NPK mentality was born."

Dr. Selman A. Waksman in his book *Humus* says in regard to Liebig: "—in the absence of oxygen, the organic substances interact, giving rise to reduction processes, namely, those of 'putrefaction,' as a result of which there is a greater amount of residual organic matter than by the aerobic process. The two processes were believed to exclude one another. With such primitive ideas concerning the decomposition of organic matter in nature and without the proper recognition of the activities of living organisms in these processes, it is not surprising that the importance of humus in the soil was not sufficiently appreciated. Liebig's influence upon the subsequent development of the science of plant nutrition was so great that even at the present time many chemists have not freed themselves from some of his opinions on this subject."

LIFE-PLANT: *see* BRYOPHYLLUM

LIGHT: Light plays so prominent a part in plant growth that the scientific name for the process is called photosynthesis from the Greek word, photos, meaning light. To a plant, natural or artificial light is its principal source of energy. Other important factors necessary for plant growth include the soil, fertilizer, moisture, temperature, air and humidity, and the characteristics of the plant itself.

Plants differ in their appetite for light; some love bright sunshine, others grow best in the shade. However, all plants take carbon dioxide and water and certain chemically inorganic minerals and by means of light from the sun or electric lamps transform these into living organic matter and oxygen, which they give off as long as the light is present. At night, photosynthesis stops and the plants absorb oxygen, give off carbon dioxide.

According to a report by General Electric, plants have to grow to a certain stage of development before they mature and can reproduce. A prominent factor in the timing of plant maturity is the length of days and nights in the spot on the earth in which it is planted. The number of hours of uninterrupted darkness in a 24-hour cycle is the important factor

in determining the blossoming time. It also triggers tuber and bulb formation and other growth characteristics such as the color and formation of the leaves and the branching of the stems.

This light-rhythm characteristic is called photoperiodism. The world's knowledge of photoperiodism is relatively new. Its important role was discovered in Washington, D. C., by two U. S. Department of Agriculture scientists who were investigating the flowering of tobacco plants about 35 years ago. Their findings resulted in extensive knowledge of the limited range of plants, that is, the boundaries (north and south) in which a particular species could mature.

Another branch of knowledge which their work promoted was the classification of plants according to their day-length characteristics.

Some plants like long days and short nights; these are called long-day plants. Others flower under short days and long nights; these are short-day plants. Still others seem to be independent of the relative light-and-dark periods in each 24 hours; these are called indeterminate. *See also* FLUORESCENT LIGHT; HOUSE PLANTS.

LIGHTNING: Nearly half of all farm fires occur during July and August—and over two-thirds of these are caused by lightning. Nature's bad actor kills 500 farm people every year and injures or cripples another 1,300. And you can add to that a toll of suffering and hardships, and the loss of possessions and equipment it may have taken lifetimes to accumulate, and that no amount of insurance can fully replace.

Oddly enough, lightning's great destructive ability is to a great extent man's fault. He builds structures of concrete, wood, brick and glass—all poor conductors of electricity. When an electrical charge hits one of these materials, it has so much trouble going through it that terrific quantities of heat are generated. Result: explosion and fire.

But metal is a good electrical conductor. So if we make a path of metal from a high point on a building—lightning is lazy and always seeks striking places nearest the clouds where it was born—to the ground, where it can release its energy harmlessly, no destructive heat will be built up.

Hence the need for lightning rods. Statistics show that a properly installed and maintained lightning protection system is an absolute guarantee against damage from lightning. Insurance companies, checking on reported "failures" of rod systems, found that in every case the damage was the result of inferior workmanship or carelessness in installing the system, letting it get run down, or changing the building without revising the system to provide adequate protection.

Lightning protection, incidentally is good business. Besides the safety, it affords a good protection system on farm buildings, often means reduced insurance premiums on those buildings.

It's a good idea to check your system and make sure it's doing the job it was meant to do.

Old, unlabelled systems will probably require the services of a reliable installer for checking.

Lightning rods, or air terminals, must be at least ten inches higher than the elevation they protect. They should be placed not more than 20 feet apart (25 if they are more than 30 inches high) at or within two feet of the ends of all ridges, gables, chimneys or large dormers. Terminals higher than two feet should be braced halfway up.

Many lightning systems use a compact ⅜-inch solid copper rod ten to 15 inches high, and have all conducting cables on the inside of the building, giving a neat, efficient appearance.

An improperly grounded system won't stop any lightning bolts. Make sure your ground connections are tight in the earth; they should go down at least ten feet to permanently moist earth. Then follow the conductors over the building. There should be at least two conductors ending in grounds for a building 80 feet long or under, and one more for each additional 60 feet.

Check the conducting cables to see that they are continuous, and that all connections to parts of the building are tight and made with clamps or cleats of the same metal as the conductor. If a down conductor is torn away from the side of a building, put copper clamps over it every few feet and nail them down with copper nails.

All metal objects in the building—ventilators, door or hay carrier tracks, eave troughs, stanchions, water pipes—should be bonded to the roof or down conductors.

Buildings with metal roofs or siding, contrary to general thought, are not invulnerable to lightning bolts. They need a full protection system just like wooden or concrete structures. Use conductors of the same kind of metal as the roof or walls.

Cattle often seek shelter under isolated trees during storms. To protect them, rod these trees by wiring a copper down lead from the rod underground out from the tree's base through a brass or copper-coated pipe to an electrode driven at least six feet into the ground. And all wire fences should be grounded, those attached to buildings at the post nearest the building.

Every farm building 12 by 14 feet or larger should be rodded, unless directly attached to a rodded stucture. The farm with the best lightning protection is the one that never discloses a need for protection.

LIGHTNING BUG: *see* FIREFLY

LIGNIN: A major constituent of wood, lignin has been classed as the largest waste in industry, pulp and paper mills alone discharging two million tons of it annually. Sawmills and other woodworking plants scattered throughout the nation can make readily available another ten million tons of wood waste, while forest and agricultural wastes have many times that amount potentially available.

In recent years much research has been done to determine if lignin could be successfully used for a fertilizer. The results have been most promising; they have indicated that lignin is of special importance to soils as a supplier of humus and organic matter. Reported Robert Aries, field director for the Northeastern Wood Utilization Council: "If lignin is used on presently-fertilized soils which need humus and organic matter, it is estimated that the efficiency of these soils would be raised about 20 per cent."

Experiments at the University of New Hampshire showed that the addition of lignin to the seed bed produced a better and greener growth. Where available, it should be used for compost-making and in mulches. The lignin content of cornstalks is 11 per cent, that of oak leaves 30 per cent, of old pine needles 23 per cent, and of dry alfalfa plants 11 per cent. A forest humus has about 48 per cent lignin in it.

LIGULARIA: A genus of hardy and half-hardy perennials of the composite family, some growing to six feet with showy flower heads, and some grown in window gardens for their variegated foliage. Formerly they were included in the genus *senecio,* to which they are closely related. Basal leaves are broad, sometimes marked, and flower heads with long yellow ray flowers are usually nodding. Originally from Europe and Asia, some species may be grown outdoors only south of Washington, D. C. They may be grown in the flower border in ordinary soil from seed

planted out in April, or may be propagated by root division or cuttings.

L. clivorum is a hardy four-foot species with basal leaves that sometimes grow as much as 20 inches across. The flowers have yellow-orange rays and dark brown disks, in heads four inches across.

Leopard plant, *l. kaempferi* variety *aureo-maculata* is one of the more tender species, grown mostly as a house plant. Leaves are up to ten inches across, are blotched with yellow, white, or light rose. In the variety *argentea* markings are cream colored on green leaves which show a whitish bloom. Flowers are light yellow, in heads two inches across.

Giant groundsel, *l. wilsoniana,* and *l. japonica* are hardy to New York, and grow to a height of five feet. Groundsel is distinguished by its elongated spikes of yellow flowers, and basal leaves 20 inches across. The Japanese species' basal leaves are palmate divided into seven to 11 narrow divisions. Three inch flower heads are on branched stalks, and are orange.

LIGUSTRUM: *see* PRIVET

LILAC: (*Syringa*) A group of shrubs and small trees belonging to the olive family.

There is an old saying about lilacs: "A little sun, a little soil, a little rain, and little toil." Lilacs are hardy and can withstand all sorts of ill treatment, but the blooms you prize will be picked from the shrubs that have had a little care.

Lilacs need full sun. They acquire mildew very easily in a shady site. Incidentally, this unsightly affliction of the lilac does not seem to do it permanent harm. The soil should be loamy and well drained. Never allow a lilac to have wet feet.

Since it is a heavy feeder, a course of fertilizing is called for every other year at least. In the spring spread a six-inch layer of well-rotted compost around the bush and out far enough to take in most of the branch spread. Dig this in well, being careful not to injure the roots, and cover with a mulch of hay or leaves, wood ashes, or pine needles if the soil is not acid

Members of the olive family, lilacs produce loveliest blooms when grown in full sun and a well-drained loam, blooming on previous year's wood.

enough. Lilacs, like most shrubs, grow best in slightly acid soil. If it is too acid, an application of agricultural lime is recommended. In the late fall, work this mulch into the soil and re-mulch with leaves or grass clippings for the winter. This will prevent heaving of roots when the ground freezes and thaws.

Lilacs bloom on last year's wood, so spare as much new wood as possible when gathering the flowers. Ideally, one should pick off the faded blooms to conserve the energy of the shrub, but on a tall specimen this is a chore indeed. Healthy plants seem to produce blooms year after year without this precaution, but if your lilac is not flowering the way it should be, by all means, take the trouble to cut off each faded truss (blossom).

Pruning is mostly a matter of removing weak ungainly branches and keeping down over-abundant sucker growth. It is best to loosen the soil and pull up these unwanted sprouts.

If you cut them off at ground level the roots may send up new growth.

PROPAGATION AND TRANSPLANTING: Perhaps you will wish to begin a new plant from one of these suckers. This is a simple process, but to be used only if the lilac is one of the common, or New England species (*S. vulgaris*). Select a shoot farthest from the parent bush. Dig it out gently, getting the root, and plant in a hole wide enough and deep enough to take the root without cramping. Now fill the hole with a mixture of topsoil and well rotted compost, adding a few handfuls of bone meal. Water generously throughout the first season. When the shoot has made some growth, lay a mulch of finely chopped grass clippings around it.

The propagation of the hybrid lilac is a bit fussier, but the results are as successful. The method here will be to take cuttings or slips from a mature bush. These are cut in late June from soft new growth, and set in sand. Keep under glass until they have taken root. In September plant in their permanent position, and in November mulch them heavily for the winter.

Unless your winters are very severe, it is best to transplant a well started shrub in the fall. Dig a hole two feet deep. Layer the hole with a mixture of compost and topsoil, and again, bone meal, setting the roots on this. Fill in the hole with the same mixture and water generously.

VARIETIES: There are about 500 varieties of lilacs. There are single florets with simple charm, or opulent double ones; drooping sprays or upright panicles; the tiny lace-like florets of the Persian lilac, or the long narrow trusses of *S. sweginzowi*.

Very Early Bloomers: *S. oblata*—lilac-colored blooms; compact shrub. *S. persica* (Persian)—pale lilac flowers; graceful, slender branches. *S. vulgaris* (common)—usually lilac-colored blooms; French lilacs popular.

Early Bloomers: *S. chinensis* (Chinese)—reddish-purple flowers; wine-colored foliage in fall; fast grower.

S. josikaea (Hungarian)—deep lilac flowers; dense shrub.

S. pubescens—very fragrant flowers.

Midseason Bloomers: *S. amurensis*—yellow-white flowers; tree-like shrub.

S. japonica (Japanese)—yellow-white flowers; tree-like shrub.

Late Bloomers: *S. pekinensis*—yellow-white flowers, flat clusters; tree-like shrub.

S. reflexa (nodding)—flowers red in bud, turn rose when opening in drooping clusters; no scent.

S. sweginzowi—long, narrow, pale pink clusters of flowers.

S. villosa—lilac-colored, profuse clusters of flowers; dense shrub; very hardy.

Double Bloomers: *S. microphylla* (Daphne)—small pink, very fragrant flowers; graceful, spreading shrub; blooms in May and late summer.

S. meyeri—magenta flowers; bears very young; blooms in May and late summer.—*Leonora Sill Ashton.*

LILY: The order *Liliaceae,* the lily family, is divided into 200 such widely varying genera as the true lilies, asparagus, garlic and onions, smilax, tulips, yucca, aspidistra, Star of Bethlehem, grape hyacinth, and trillium. Almost all are native of the northern hemisphere, and most are hardy perennials growing from bulbs or tubers.

Many so-called lilies do not belong to the lily family at all, but to families closely related. Among these are members of the amaryllis family, such as rain lily, prairie lily, fairy lily, torch lily, amazon lily, spider lily, St. James or Jacobean lily, zephyr lily, and blood lily. Water lilies are all members of the water lily family, the *Nymphaeceae.* Calla lilies belong to the arum family, butterfly lilies to the ginger family, and blackberry lilies to the iris family.

Several genera of the lily family, along with Easter lilies, or the tender true lilies, are known in the north only as hothouse plants. These include the African lily, *Agapanthus africans;* triplet lily and snake lily, both of the genus *Brodiaea;* and glory-lily, the showy *gloriosa* vine.

Somewhat hardier, but requiring protection in the colder latitudes are the St. Bernard's lily, *Anthericum liliago;* globe lilies and Mariposa lilies, both sometimes called tulips, and both species of the genus *Calochortus;* and the checkered lilies or tulips, the *fritillarias.*

Several of the trout lilies, *Erythronium,* are shy woods natives that can be transplanted to the garden only if their woodland surroundings are duplicated there. These include dogtooth violet, avalanche lily, spring or fawn lily, and chamise lily.

The horticulturally most important flowers of the lily family are tulips (which see); day lilies, genus *Hemerocallis;* lily-of-the-valley, genus *convallaria;* plantain lilies, *hosta;* and the true lilies, genus *lilium.*

DAYLILIES: Members of the genus *hemerocallis* are properly called daylilies, though sometimes some of the *hostas,* the plantain lilies, are also so-called because their blooms last one day as do the daylilies.

About a dozen basic species comprise the daylilies proper, from which many beautiful hybrids are being developed each year. Perennials, they grow from fleshy roots, and must be propagated by root division if they are to come true to type. Flowers are yellow and orange, with hybrids in shades of pink and red. There are no true blues. Average height of the cultivated varieties is about three feet, though some species grow to eight feet. Flowering period is spring and early summer. No more than one blossom on each stalk opens each day during the period of bloom, which lasts for two to three weeks as different stalks come into bloom. By planting a variety of kinds, a gardener may keep his daylilies blooming from the first of June until late in the summer.

Members of the *Lilium* family produce showy flowers in a great variety of colors, singly or in clusters. Lilies should have a well-drained site.

Daylilies are easy to grow, being very hardy and relatively unmolested by either insects or disease. They will grow in any ordinary garden soil, with no special requirements as to sunlight or moisture. A dry hillside in full sun will produce quantities of flowers, and so will a moist partially shaded bank of a stream. In extremely hot climates a partially shaded spot will produce the best results.

Few seeds are produced by daylilies. They are almost entirely propagated by root division. The best time for division is early spring, before growth has started, or after the blooming period is finished. Division every three or four years insures maximum bloom, which may slacken off if the roots are left too long in one place. Being strong feeders, the fleshy

tubers in the center of a clump may crowd each other and exhaust soil nutrients after a few years, so that the clump will spread laterally, with bloom only around the outside and matted foliage in the center. Clumps of foliage of *H. fulva,* the most common orange daylily, may often be found along roadsides or under trees which have cut off all of its sunlight. The foliage will persist for years without any encouragement.

Roots of *Hemerocallis* varieties and hybrids are listed under summer bulbs in most nursery catalogs. The small clumps purchased from a nursery will usually bloom the first year, if they are planted early enough. Hybrid varieties are developed from *clones,* that is, from plants all of which have been rooted from a single seeded parent.

H. fulva is the most common daylily in the northeastern states, growing wild along roadsides where it was spread from gardens. It is native in Japan, China, and Europe. Flowers of the type are large orange trumpets, sometimes marked with brown. A pink variety, which originated in the Orient, has been used in the development of many pink, rose, and red hybrids.

Slightly less hardy, but also to be found naturalized in many parts of the East are the lemon lilies, *H. flava,* also known as custard lilies and tall yellow daylilies. They send up masses of lemon yellow, fragrant blooms early in June north of Philadelphia, somewhat earlier farther south.

Still earlier and more tender are the narrow dwarf or Dumortiers daylilies, *H. dumortieri.* Leaves and flowers of this species grow to about two feet, opening pure orange blossoms in May. These are valuable especially in the rock garden.

The broad dwarf daylilies, *H. middendorfi,* grow somewhat taller, raising orange flowers above the leaves to reach about three feet in height. Roots of this species are less fleshy than most daylilies, and foliage is evergreen in the south, where they prosper best.

For late bloom, *H. thunbergi,* the late yellow daylily will bloom in July where the summers are not too hot. Blossoms open in the evening and lose some of their color during the day if planted in full sun. *Thunbergi* grows to about three feet, with flowers two to three inches long.

H. citrina, the citron daylily, is a larger night-blooming species, its pale yellow flowers attaining a length of five inches. This is also a late bloomer, coming about the end of July.

New varieties are being offered each year, some of which extend the period of bloom into August and almost up to the end of summer. Varieties of dark red, rose, and pink are listed.

Lily-of-the-Valley: The only species of *convallaria* which is cultivated is lily-of-the-valley, *C. majalis.* Other members of the genus, which are distinguished by their pips or buds that arise from creeping rootstocks, include wild solomon's seal, *C. polygonatum.*

Lily-of-the-valley is so easily grown that it can spread to become a nuisance unless it is planted where it will be held within bounds. It will grow in almost any situation, but prefers the shade of trees during most of the day. It is useful on the north side of buildings where few other flowers will grow.

Pip: Pips, which may be purchased from a nursery, may be planted in early spring or late fall. They are buried under about an inch of soil. The graceful, fragrant sprays of bride's bouquet blossoms will be sent up the first year, being already in embryo in the pips. If flowers in the bed become smaller or fewer in number after they have occupied one position for a long time, they should be dug and divided in the fall. Pips removed at this time may be stored for winter indoor forcing, or may be planted in new positions.

Pips may be purchased for forcing, or may be dug from the border and stored outside until blooms indoors are wanted. When a mass of roots are dug in the garden, some of the pink pips will be found to be rather blunt and plump, and some will be slenderer. In an old bed where bloom has decreased, the plump pips will be about as numerous as the previous spring's blossoms. These are the pips which contain flower embryos. The slender pointed pips will produce only foliage.

Lily-of-the-valley must be frosted each winter before it will bloom, whether it is forced or remains outdoors. Flower pips dug from the border should be wrapped in sphagnum moss and stored under a loose mulch until the middle of the winter. When they are dug out and brought indoors, they must be thawed gradually at 55 to 60°. They may then be planted in pots of sand, placed in bowls of pebbles which will be partially filled with water, or surrounded with damp sphagnum moss in a decorative container. The container may then be set in a cool cellar until buds begin to rise, when it is brought into a warm light room, but protected from direct sun. Or it may be immediately placed in a light warm room. Plants grown in a cool place will take longer to bloom and have fewer leaves, but the blossoms will last longer. Less foliage should also be expected from pips forced during the early part of the winter. Later, toward spring, more foliage will develop. Blossoms can be expected in three or four weeks.

Plantain Lilies: The genus *hosta,* formerly called *funkia.* Similar in habit of growth to the weed, plantain, the species of *hosta* are almost as much valued for their rosettes of large glossy, deeply veined leaves as for the blue, lavender, or white clusters of lilies that they send up in spring, summer, or autumn. The foliage is handsome, especially when used as an edging, and grows more luxurious each succeeding year.

Plantain lilies are easy to grow in almost any position in the garden, but prefer some shade and moist soil. Some species will grow in dense shade under trees where few other flowers thrive. Others will tolerate full sun, when they are used as a border along a drive or walk. They may be divided and transplanted in early spring or late fall. They will do best in a bed deeply prepared and enriched with compost.

Blue plantain, *H. caerula,* grows to three feet, lavender-blue flowers which open in mid-summer. Leaves are large and deep green.

Midsummer plantain, *H. erromena,* is an old-fashioned garden variety, with pale lavender trumpet-shaped flowers growing to three feet. Leaves are not quite so large as those of *caerula,* but grow to two feet. Blossoming period is late July and August above Philadelphia.

Tall-cluster plantain, *H. fortunei,* sends up two-foot clusters of small pale lilac flowers above low clusters of five inch leaves. In the variety *gigantea* the leaves are larger and the flowers are not quite so tall.

H. lancifolia, or *H. japonica* is a species with long narrow leaves, which are white bordered in the variety *albomarginata.* One variety, *tardiflora,* blooms late in the fall. Flowers are two inches long, pale lilac.

The fragrant plantain, *H. plantaginea,* is one of the best shade lilies, with flowers that grow five inches long opening in late summer and early fall. Leaves are as large and decorative as those of the blue plantain. Flower stalks rise to 2½ feet.

The wavy-leaved plantain, *H. undulata,* is notable chiefly for its foliage, which is not only wavy along its margins, but is also marked with white in some varieties. The pale lavender flowers rise to more than two feet, well above the foliage clusters.

LILIUM: The true lilies. Plants of this genus are distinguished by the fact that all grow from deep, scaly bulbs. Flowers are the most showy of all the lilies, and come in all colors except pure blue. Many of the blooms, which may occur singly or in clusters, are very fragrant. All are perennial, but some, which have been classed as Easter lilies because of their reputation as hothouse subjects, are tender and cannot be grown outdoors except in the far south.

Lilies, with their fleshy open bulbs, must have good drainage above all else. If water is allowed to settle among the scales of the bulb, which in some cases are as loose as leaves of an artichoke, the bulb will rot, and the plant die. A bed on a hillside, where good drainage is assured, is safest for most varieties. In addition, some gardeners make a practice of tilting the bulbs slightly when planting them, to allow water to run out away from their centers. Exceptions are *L. canadense* and *L. superbum,* which thrive in damp situations.

While the bulb must be kept well drained, it must also be kept cool and moist. A bed deeply prepared with compost, mixed with a large percentage of sand, is ideal. No manure should be permitted to come in contact with the bulbs, but manure may be used in the mulch over the top of the soil, if it is sufficiently decayed. A deep mulch of leaf mold over the lily bed will be appreciated during the hot weather. Or the lilies may be planted among low-growing annuals or shrubs which will keep the soil shaded. All lilies prefer slightly acid soil, and few will tolerate lime.

Most lilies prefer to grow in full sun, even though they like to keep their feet cool. There are some exceptions to this rule. A little shade during part of the day will be tolerated by madonna lilies, Martagon lily, regal lily, Sargent lily, and tiger lily. Lilies which actually prefer partial shade are the goldbanded lily, orange lily, Hanson lily, Henry lily, and Japanese lily.

LILY . BULBS: Lily bulbs are planted in summer or fall when they are dormant. *L. candidum* should be planted no later than September, while *L. auratum* and *L. speciosum* may be planted late in November, or even in December, if the ground can be kept thawed that late. Bulbs dry out quickly, and should never be kept out of the soil longer than is absolutely necessary. When it is impossible to plant them immediately upon receiving them from the nursery, they should be stored in sand or soil until the planting time arrives.

Depth of planting depends on the type of lily bulb being planted. Some lilies produce roots only from the base of the bulb, which supply food and moisture to the plant. These bulbs should be planted no more than four inches below the surface, with 12 or 18 inches of rich loam beneath them. Usually the roots of these bulbs will have been damaged in transport from the nursery, and they will have to grow a large and strong tuft of roots before blooming, possibly not blooming the first year at all. Lilies of this type include the madonna lilies, scarlet turkscap lily, *L. giganteum,* Martagon lily, Caucasian lily, *L. superbum* or the American turkscap, and Nankeen lily.·

Other species of lilies produce roots along the stems which arise from the lily bulb. These bulbs must be planted deep, to allow plenty of room for the development of roots. The rule for planting these is to sink them three times their own depth, that is, the top of a three-inch bulb will be planted nine inches below the surface. For these bulbs a good mixture of bone meal in the top 18 inches of soil is recommended. Among the stem-rooting varieties are many of the most beautiful garden specimens, such as

goldbanded, Batemann, Brown, morningstar, orange, Hanson, Henry, Japanese, Easter, royal, speciosum tiger, and yellow Martagon lilies.

Propagation of true lilies may be accomplished in a variety of ways, but in most cases several years will be required to grow flowering bulbs. Seed germinates readily if it is fresh, but the seedlings will be slender and will provide very small bulbs during the first year or two. Some variation from the parent must be expected from seed also, so that the gardener may be disappointed with his crop after waiting as much as four years to find out what his blooms look like. Regal lilies are an exception, producing flowers in nine to 15 months from seed.

A more certain method of growing plants true to type is by separating the scales from the bulbs and planting them in moist sand. This is the only method recommended for reproducing hybrids. After a time in the sand, each scale will grow a small bulb, which may then be planted in the garden bed in a protected position. Each year the bulb will be lifted, and planted a little deeper, until it has attained flowering size, when it will be placed in its permanent position. In some cases this may take no more than two years, in others it will take longer.

Some lilies spread by sending fleshy rootstocks out in runners from the original bulb. New bulbs will form possibly two feet from the original plant, and a new shoot will come up. Turkscap lily and meadow lily both multiply in this way.

Easter lilies are various, though the blossoms will appear similar to the amateur gardener. They are listed as forcing bulbs in seed or nursery catalogs. Most varieties have been developed from *L. longiflorum.* Bulb is planted in six-inch pot and placed in a cool greenhouse away from sun, or outdoors in a protected position where it will not be touched by frost until a root system develops, and growth appears above the soil. They are then brought into the light and gradually warmed to 60 to 70°. Flowers open approximately three to four months after forcing begins.

Easter lilies may be planted in the open during the summer, in northern states, but they must be lifted in the fall. In the south and in California they may remain outside all year.

Following is a partial list of the many species of hardy lilies suitable for planting in northern gardens:

Regal lily, three to four feet tall, white trumpets with lilac shadings outside, yellow shadings inside. Adapts well to most gardens.

Speciosum lily, four feet tall, white flushed with pink or rose, pink, or deep rose. Flowers droop slightly, petals are reflexed. Grows well among small shrubs.

Madonna lily, three to four feet, pure white horizontal trumpets from stems which appear in fall and persist through the winter.

Goldbanded lily, grows to six feet, fragrant, ivory-white with gold bands down the center of each petal, and purple blotches. Will not tolerate lime, but does well in rich humus. Var. *rubrum* is banded with crimson instead of yellow.

Tiger lily, three to four feet, orange-red flowers with black dots. Easily grown in good garden loam, and will spread if well content.

Brown lily, name referring to a man, not the color of the flower, which is white inside and rose outside. Should be planted on its side deep in a bed of sand.

Hanson lily, five feet, bright yellow-orange with brown dots. Should be planted in partial shade.

Henry lily, a spectacular species that sends up as many as 20 blooms on a nine foot stem. Best grown among loosely branched shrubs, which will help support it. Flowers are golden yellow, with reflexed petals.

Orange lily, to six feet, yellow or orange flowers spotted with red. Grows well and spreads in good garden loam.

Nankeen lily, flat slightly reflexed apricot flowers. Best planted among perennials.

Coral lily, 1½ to three feet, scarlet, good for rock gardens.

Scarlet turk's cap lily, four feet, scarlet with reflexed petals, grows easily in full sun.

Martagon or turk's cap lily, six feet, drooping purplish to rose flowers with deep red dots, reflexed petals. Will grow in sun or partial shade.

American turk's cap lily, orange-spotted purple. Should be grown in a moist position, preferably near water.

Japanese lily, two feet, pale pink to rose. Needs acid soil, and winter protection in the north. Too tender for very cold winters.

Meadow lily, three to five feet, gold to red, will tolerate a more damp location than most lilies.

Leopard lily, to eight feet, drooping orange-red flowers, reflexed, require full sun. Grows best on the Pacific coast.

LILY-OF-THE-VALLEY: *see* LILY

LILY POND: The garden landscape can often be enhanced by the construction of a lily pond. If you have limited space for your project, perhaps the tub pond will be most suitable. It is definitely the easiest method of creating a small pond and requires practically no up-keep once constucted.

Merely sink a wooden tub halfway into the ground. Then fill it about halfway with good, rich soil. Put about six inches of water over the soil. Plant the hardy water lily horizontally, about one inch deep, with the crown exposed. After planting, a one inch layer of sand is recommended to keep the water clear. Next, tie a bag over the end of a garden hose and gradually fill the tub. At first, some water will be lost due to leakage, but in a few hours the boards will be swollen and permanently watertight.

A few rocks, boulders or other plants placed around the pond will add a great deal of interest and beauty. Your pond is an individual thing and should be planned as such. There is no limit to the various effects which can be created with a little touch of imagination. Various shallow water and bog plants will help give your pond a natural appearance. The same is true of floating water plants.

If you are not satisfied with the small tub-type pond, you may want to go in for the larger cement pool.

Select a sunny location if possible, although many lilies will bloom in partial shade. Build your pool of concrete with sloping sides. No special form is required. Use a three-two-one mixture (three parts gravel, two parts sand, one part cement). It should be six inches thick, two feet deep, and should be reinforced near the top with a few strands of heavy smooth wire placed in the center of the concrete. Pockets can be built along the sides for shallow water plants by pressing bricks into soft concrete. Fill with water and drain twice before planting lilies or adding fish. When dry, paint with underwater enamel to add the beautifying touch.

FERTILIZING: Rotted cow manure, placed near the bottom of the tub, is a very good fertilizer for water lilies. Be sure to put it near the bottom to prevent the manure from turning the water green. A ratio of three parts soil to one part manure is recommended. Chemical fertilizers are especially dangerous to fish and other water life in your pond. Cow manure will do the job very adequately. Also, in the spring, it would be well to add ground blood to each tub. Small pots require one tablespoonful, while large three-foot tubs require one full pint.

FISH: The graceful goldfish, darting back and forth beneath the lily pads, add the finishing touch to the perfect pond. There are many types of goldfish, and here again, your personal taste is your key to success. The fish will more than earn their keep by eating mosquito larvae and insects. For this reason, they are an absolute necessity in the pond.

Water scavengers are the housekeepers of the pond. They keep plants free from disease as well as clean up the pond. Snails eat the green scum and algae; tadpoles live on decaying lily leaves and fish excrements; frogs live on mosquitoes, flies and other insects; salamanders aid also in the pool janitorial work. Use plenty of scavengers and your pond will be crystal-clear. Scavengers are very fascinating to observe, too. Every pond should allow two scavengers for every square foot of pool surface.

Oxygenating plants are absolutely essential for fish life. These plants absorb the carbon dioxide which the fish give off and liberate oxygen which the fish must have to live. Fish need oxygenating plants in which to spawn and lay their eggs. Baby fish need them to hide in, lest they be devoured by their own parents. These plants and other pond materials can be obtained at many pet stores or may be ordered by mail from firms specializing in pond supplies.

WINTER CARE: Cover your pool or tub with boards and leaves, hay or straw when the wintery season blows in. Hardies can remain undamaged in the pool over winter. Tropical plants, however, should be replaced each spring, unless a greenhouse is available. Goldfish may be left in the pool providing the water is about two feet deep. Otherwise, transfer them to the house until the freezing weather is past. *See also* WATER GARDENS.

LILYTURF, CREEPING: *see* GROUND COVER

LIMA BEAN: (*Phaseolus limensis*) Perennial vine in its native tropical climate, but grown as an annual in vegetable gardens of the temperate regions. Flowers are yellowing white, growing in loose spikes or clusters, leaves of three leaflets, pods flat and up to five inches long, with two to six seeds which are ¾ to one inch across. Bush varieties are from var. *limenanus.*

Lima beans should be planted when the soil is thoroughly warm in a location that has full sun. Mulch is important, as they need much moisture.

Soil for lima beans should be well-drained loam, with a moderate amount of ground limestone and some compost dug in. Planting should be in full sun, with no shade in any part of the day. Pole limas may be trained along a fence on the north side of the vegetable garden, or the poles should be placed on the north side, to give the garden protection from winds, and to avoid shading lower-growing plants.

Seed should be planted after the soil is thoroughly warm, late in May in areas around New York City, or about two weeks after the first string beans are planted. Seed planted too early will rot in the cold soil. After compost has been mixed with soil, a two-inch trench is dug, and seed placed, eye down, about four inches apart. A fine sifting of soil is used to cover seed, and is firmed down. Unless beans or peas have recently been grown in the same soil, it is advisable to inoculate the seed with

nitrogen-fixing bacteria, which may be purchased from seed houses. The seed is dampened, and the black powdery inoculant stirred into it before sowing. After germination, bush limas may be thinned to stand eight inches apart in the rows, which should be 24 to 30 inches apart.

Pole limas are planted around rough ten-foot poles which have been sunk in the ground three feet before beans are planted. Or the poles may be sunk one foot if placed in threes, and tied together at the top to form a tripod. Six or eight seeds are placed around each pole, and the seedlings are thinned to leave the three or four strongest to climb each pole.

Limas need plenty of moisture after the blossoms have fallen, in order to produce large tender beans. A heavy straw mulch is helpful, assisted in a drought by a weekly irrigation along the roots of the plants.

LIME: Chemically, lime is the oxide of calcium, with a chemical formula CaO. It occurs in limestone, marble, and chalk as calcium carbonate, $CaCO_3$. If these substances are heated carbon dioxide, CO_2, escapes as a gas and CaO, or quick-lime, remains. If the quick-lime is now combined with the correct amount of water, slaked lime or hydrate of lime, $Ca(OH)_2$, results.

Any of these three substances may be used to alkalize soil. At various times each of the three has had a vogue. The difference in their action relates to the organic life of the soil, rather than to the chemical change, which is the same in each case.

Quick-lime, CaO, will unite with water in the soil to form a hydrate. If enough actual water is not available, as it seldom is, the quick-lime wrenches water from living organisms in the soil, such as bacteria, fungi, or plant roots, usually burning them enough to bring about their death. If manure or other nitrogenous fertilizers are present, the quick-lime will unite with the nitrogen compounds they contain to rob them of their water, and will free the nitrogen as a gas, lowering the amount of nitrogen in the soil in compounds which can be used by plants.

Hydrate of lime has already united its calcium with water, so it will not have the burning effect of quick-lime. However, hydrate of lime is lime in readily available condition, ready to be used immediately in the soil. When rain water washes through the soil, it dissolves the hydrate of lime, which can quickly leach down to soil levels where it cannot be reached by plant roots.

Ground limestone is the form in which lime is best applied to soil to provide lime in a beneficial form which will be available over a long period of time. In order to be of use immediately and to continue to break down for gradual use over a period of years, limestone should be ground fine enough to sift through a 100-mesh sieve. In this form the lime will be exposed to water in the soil in sufficient quantities to dissolve slowly, but the entire application will not have dissolved for several years.

Lime is seldom used as a fertilizer, although its calcium content is very important to plant life as it is to animals. However, most soils contain enough calcium in one compound or another to supply all that plants need.

The primary use for lime in the garden or farm is as an alkalizer, to raise the pH factor of the soil. To understand this it is necessary to understand the chemical difference between acidity and alkalinity.

The acidity or alkalinity of a mixture of soil and water is determined by the number of free hydrogen or hydroxyl ions. If there are more hydrogen ions, the mixture is acid. If hydroxyl ions predominate, the mixture is alkaline. If they are balanced, with the same number of each, the mixture is neutral.

pH is a measure of the number of free hydrogen ions. The initials are derived from German, H standing for hydrogen, p for a term meaning the negative logarithmic value. pH values run from zero to 14, and soil pH factors fall somewhere between four and nine. Neutral soil has a pH factor of seven. Soil with a pH of four contains ten times as many free hydrogen ions as soil with a pH factor of five, that is to say it is ten times as acid.

Application of lime to soil raises the pH factor by replacing free hydrogen ions with calcium ions.

Free hydrogen ions are carried in solution in rain water, which is constantly washing through the soil; therefor rain water is generally acid. The presence of slowly breaking down limestone in the soil provides a steady source of calcium ions to replace the hydrogen ions; hence liming is usually unnecessary.

The solubility and availability of many important nutrients in the soil are affected by pH. In soil ions of aluminum, iron, manganese, copper, and zinc increase with increasing acidity. In very acid soil these substances may be present in ionized form in quantities which are toxic to some plants, causing them to become sickly and die. As the pH is raised, these ions become inert, and cannot affect plants. Neutralizing soil also makes conditions more favorable for useful soil bacteria.

PLANT PREFERENCES: The following garden plants prefer soils which are approximately neutral: abelia, alyssum, anemone, arborvitae, aster, barberry, begonia, clematis, columbine, coreopsis, cosmos, dahlia, deutzia, forsythia, larkspur, lilac, mock orange, narcissus, pansy, peony, poppy, bell flower, box, bittersweet, butterfly bush, calendula, canna, carnation, chrysanthemum, geranium, gladiolus, hibiscus, honeysuckle, hyacinth, hydrangea, iris, ivy, primrose, privet, rose, spirea, tulip, violet, wisteria, and zinnia.

Some plants which prefer slight to medium acidity are: some vaireties of aster, bunchflower, fir, heather, holly, huckleberry, juniper, lily, lily-of-the-valley, magnolia, red oak, phlox, pine, spruce, creeping willow, and wintergreen. Medium to strongly acid soils are required by the following: arethusa, arnica, azalea, most varieties of ferns, galax, gardenia, orchid, ladyslipper, pitcherplant, rhododendron, rose pogonia, sandmyrtle, sundew, trailing arbutus, wild calla.

Most vegetables prefer lime, and dislike acidity. Carrots and tomatoes are only slightly affected by acidity, but only potatoes, radishes, and watermelons positively dislike lime. Fruits which prefer acid soil are blackberry, blackcap raspberry, blueberry, cranberry, huckleberry, and strawberry.

The only field crops which prefer acid are flax and velvet bean, while flint corn, millet, and rye are only slightly affected by it. All others prefer limed soils.

Leguminous crops—peas, beans, vetch, clover—increase their yield to a remarkable degree in the presence of sufficient lime. Beans, sown in the open field, have been known to yield ten times as much as formerly after the field was limed. The reason for this is that nitrogen-fixing bacteria, which live in the root tubules of legumes, thrive in alkaline soils.

PHYSICAL EFFECT: Lime has a physical, as well as a chemical, effect upon soil. When spread upon clay soils, lime flocculates the clay, that is, it causes particles to gather in groups to make larger physical units in the soil. Water and air more easily penetrate such a soil than a soil composed of fine clay particles. On the other hand, in a sandy soil lime has the effect of holding the particles more closely together, so that water is held for a longer period.

One other function of lime in the soil is to release some of the phosphorus and potash from their insoluble compounds, making them available for plant use. Thus, though lime is not itself a fertilizer, it has the effect of increasing the fertility of the soil.

APPLICATION: General advice is about one ton of ground limestone per acre every three or four years. On most soils, this rate will be effective, although soil testing is always advised to avoid unnecessary liming. Since ground limestone becomes available slowly, dangers of overliming are lessened. For the garden, the rate would be about 50 pounds for 1000 square feet every three or four years, unless tests indicate differently. Fall or early spring applications are satisfactory. Liming is usually done on freshly cultivated soil, preferably on a windless day. Make sure that the lime is spread evenly and thoroughly to avoid skipping areas. Unlike fertilizers, lime does not spread over adjacent areas, but works itself down into the soil.

OTHER SOURCES: Beside limestone, other sources of calcium which may be used in the garden include bone meal, chalk, dolomite, gypsum, marble dust, marl, oyster shells and wood ashes.

Bone meal contains approximately 30 per cent calcium, to 20 per cent of phosphorus, $1\frac{1}{2}$ per cent nitrogen, and .2 per cent potash. Care must be exercised in its use as a source of phosphorus for plants that prefer acidity. For alkaline-preference plants, however, it is strongly recommended, because it breaks down slowly and provides phosphorus and calcium over an extended period.

Chalk is widely used in England as an alkalizer. It is composed of fossilized shell particles, and is bulky by comparison with limestone.

Dolomite is a form of limestone rich in magnesium, which may be present in amounts up to 40 per cent.

Magnesium in itself is necessary to plant life, and it also has the effect of cutting the plant's potash requirement.

Gypsum, sometimes called sulfate of lime, contains about 23 per cent of calcium oxide. It helps liberate potash for plant use, but its sulphur content tends to make the soil acid, so its effect is opposite to that of lime. It has special uses, such as in reclamation of alkaline soil. Gypsum forms up to 50 per cent of superphosphate fertilizers. *See also* GYPSUM.

Marble is a crystallized form of limestone. If it is not burned to form quick-lime, it is as satisfactory as limestone. Like limestone, it must be finely pulverized.

Marl is a crumbly lime-clay deposit found under the organic deposits in the beds of streams and other bodies of water. It can be used to supply lime to soil, but it is more slowly available than limestone.

Oyster shells have, in addition to a large percentage of calcium carbonate, about ten per cent phosphoric acid, which makes them valuable sources of both lime and phosphorus. They should be used, in flour form, whenever available.

Wood ashes are a rich source of potash, as well as of lime. Percentages of each vary with the kind of wood that was burned to make the ash. In addition, phosphoric acid and magnesium are found in ash residues. Rain quickly leaches out all the plant food in ash, so it becomes quickly available. By the same process, it is quickly leached down through the soil, beyond the reach of plant roots. Wood ash should never be used on soil in which acid-loving plants are grown, unless the soil is extremely acid.

Other ashes—from paper, leaves, or coal—are not particularly useful for their calcium content. Paper ash contains much acid used in the manufacture of paper, which may be injurious to plants. Leaf ash contains almost nothing except charcoal or carbon. Coal ash does not contain valuable lime or other nutrients, but may be useful in some cases to lighten heavy clay soils.

Pulverized limestone added to a compost heap helps speed the bacterial process of breaking down green manures. Calcium carbonates are also useful in the process of nitrogen fixing, in stable manure. The limestone may be mixed with soil, or sprinkled over the soil layer in the heap.

INDICATIONS OF SOIL ACIDITY: If soil has poor drainage, and if it is known not to be underlain with limestone, it is probably acid. Most forest soils are acid, and eroded soils or those depleted by cultivation also show an acid pH factor.

Vegetation which indicates the presence of acid soil includes conifers, sassafras, oak, wintergreen, blueberries, mosses, horsetail rush, sorrel, and spurry.

In order to discover the exact degree of acidity of the soil, it is necessary to make a chemical test. Before application of lime, such a test should be made. Soil testing kits may be purchased which contain colorimetric tests sufficiently accurate for the home gardener. Or soil samples may be sent to State agricultural colleges, where the tests will be made free or at nominal cost. Application to the college should first be made for instructions in gathering soil samples. Instructions are included in the kits.

Different kinds of clay found in cool-temperate and in warm-temperate to tropical regions require different amounts of lime to neutralize their acidity. Also, sandy soils in general require less lime to neutralize them than do heavy clay soils. The following table is given in the Department of Agriculture yearbook for 1957 for the approximate number of tons per acre of finely ground limestone needed to raise the pH of a seven inch layer of soil, as indicated:

TONS OF GROUND LIMESTONE NEEDED TO RAISE pH

Soils of warm-temperate and tropical regions:	From pH 3.5 to pH 4.5	4.5 to 5.5	5.5 to 6.5
Sandy and loamy sand	0.3	0.3	0.4
Sandy loam	...	.5	.7
Loam	...	.8	1.0
Silt loam	...	1.2	1.4
Clay loam	...	1.5	2.0
Muck	2.5	3.3	3.8
Soils of cool-temperate and temperate regions:			
Sand and loamy sand	.4	.5	.6
Sandy loam	...	.8	1.3
Loam	...	1.2	1.7
Silt loam	...	1.5	2.0
Clay loam	...	1.9	2.3
Muck	2.9	3.8	4.3

See also ACIDITY-ALKALINITY.

LIME: (*Citrus aurantifolia*) Another small evergreen citrus, the lime is, as the lemon, grown principally for the juice of its fruit. These are round or oval, quite small and greenish-yellow when ripe. Peels are thin and both the pulp and juice are distinctly acid.

Since it is the most sensitive of the citrus group, limes are grown almost entirely in semi-tropical areas. Production in this country is held principally to the southernmost parts of Florida and to the Keys off the tip of the state.

Among the varieties, the West Indian and Tahiti limes are both popular for their quality. Rangpur is a tangerine-like type that is hardier and bears heavily during a longer period of the year. Although the Tahiti and other species are extremely tender, they are quick to revive after being frozen back if grown from cuttings. *See also* CITRUS.

LIMESTONE: *see* LIME; MINERAL ROCKS; DOLOMITE; ACIDITY-ALKALINITY

LIME TREE: *see* LINDEN

LIMONIUM: More commonly known as statice, limonium is the sea-lavender or sea-pink genus of the order *Plumbaginaceae,* the plumbago family. Of the more than 180 species, perhaps a dozen are grown as garden flowers, or in greenhouses, many of them used as cut flowers for their feathery heads and some treated as everlastings, because they retain their color well when dried. Native of the Pacific islands, Asia, and Europe, the limoniums were originally marsh flowers, but many of them have been successfully grown under garden conditions, where they prefer a sandy soil. Flowers are small but profuse in loose panicles or branching spikes, in colors ranging from white through silvery gray, blue, lavender, to rose, purple, and yellow.

Species of limonium are annual or perennial, but mostly grown as annuals in northern gardens. Any open, sunny garden position is acceptable to them. Annuals should be sown where they will bloom in late summer. Perennials may be propagated by seed or by division.

L. sinatum is most frequently offered as statice in seed catalogs, with many handsome varieties in apricot, lavender, blue, rose, or a combination of rose to lavender in one plant. It may be grown as a perennial or biennial, and is often used by florists for feathery material in arrangements. It grows to two feet.

L. bellidifolium, or statice caspia, is grown in a blue dwarf form, var. nanum, as a rock garden perennial.

Bonduelli is a clear yellow form, growing two feet high, that may be grown as an annual or a perennial.

Gmelinii is a two-foot perennial with large branching violet-blue panicles, good in the border.

Another dwarf form is *tataricum,* var. *nanum,* which may be either white or rose, and makes a good rock garden plant. It is perennial.

L. suworowi has more compact spikes, finger-shaped and lilac colored. Sown indoors in January, it will provide flowers in the house for a long time, because the spikes do not fade easily.

LINARIA: A genus of the *scrophulariaceae* or figwort family, containing a number of annual and perennials which resemble miniature snapdragons, and are suitable for rock gardens. The genus is most commonly known for toadflax or butter-and-eggs, *linaria vulgaris,* a native of Europe and Asia which may be found on every roadside in America.

Annuals are usually started early indoors. Perennials may also be started from seed, but will usually not produce flowers the first year. They may also be propagated by division. They prefer a light soil.

Toadflax, the common roadside variety, has been improved and is now sold as a garden annual. *Marocanna,* another annual, grows to about 15 inches in orange, blue, and crimson. It is also offered by seedsmen in a large variety of colors in a compact variety, called fairy bouquet, fairy bridesmaid, etc.

L. alpina is a perennial dwarf rock plant, growing six inches high, with blue-violet flowers with an orange palate, and is also offered in a rose variety. *L. anticaria* is a low branching plant which does well in part shade, with blue and white lilac-spurred flowers, also a good rock garden subject.

L. dalmatica and *l. macedonica* are both yellow and orange species similar to butter-and-eggs, but grow taller and showier. Both are perennials.

LINDEN: Common name for the genus *Tilia,* the only northern representative of the *Tiliaceae,* the jute family. Also called lime tree or basswood, formerly bastwood, from the bast fiber obtained from inside the bark. About 30 species of linden are native to the north temperate zone. They are deciduous, are grown for timber, for ornament, for bast fiber, and an oil is extracted from their flowers for use in manufacture of perfumes. Their numerous clustered yellow blossoms attract bees in June.

Lindens thrive in a rich, moist soil, which must be well-drained. A heavy mulch over the roots in hot dry weather would help protect the tree from drought, which affects it adversely.

Lindens are used extensively in formal plantings because their regular pyramidal shape adapts itself well to driveway borders. They are also used extensively here and abroad in city street plantings. Their dense foliage gives good shade.

Propagation may be from seed, which requires two years to germinate, from layers, cuttings, and grafting. Young trees are best set out in early spring, rather than in fall.

American linden, *T. americana,* is one of the most stately lindens, growing to 120 feet. Leaves are heart-shaped, toothed, four to eight inches. Variety *dentata* has irregularly toothed leaves, and variety *macrophylla* has larger leaves.

Small-leafed linden, *T. cordata,* has leaves under 2½ inches. Tree holds its shape well as it grows to 90 or 100 feet. Clusters of fragrant yellow blossoms in early summer.

T. dasystyla has broad shiny leaves growing to six inches.

Crimean linden, *T. euchlora,* is one of the handsomest lindens, a hybrid of *T. cordata* and *T. dasystyla.* It grows to about 50 feet, and its four-inch leaves are glossy dark green above, paler green below, heart-shaped and sharply toothed. Flowers hang in pendulous clusters in June. *T. europeae* does well in city streets. It is a hybrid of *T. cordata* and *T. platyphyllos.* Four inch leaves, dull green above.

Japanese linden, *T. japonica,* grows to 60 feet, with three-inch leaves which are bluish-green beneath when young.

Mongolian linden, *T. mongolica,* is a comparatively short linden, growing to only about 30 feet, but its foliage is handsome, 2½ inch leaves being glossy, coarsely toothed, and three-lobed.

The large-leaved linden, *T. platyphyllos,* grows as large as the American linden, with four-inch leaves heart-shaped at the base, light green, three whitish flowers in a cluster blooming in June. In variety *aurea,* branches are yellow when young; in *rubra* they are red. Variety *laciniata* has more deeply toothed leaves. *Vitifolia* leaves are somewhat three-lobed.

White or silver linden, *T. tomentosa,* is also a tall pyramidal tree, growing to 100 feet. Leaves are broad, to five inches long, dark green above and slightly downy below, some bases heart-shaped, some straight.

LINDERA: *see* SPICEBUSH

LINNAEA: *see* TWINFLOWER

LINNAEUS, Carl Linne (b. 1707, d. 1778) or Carl von Linne after 1761, when he was granted a patent of nobility. Swedish botanist and author of the first practical classification of the plant kingdom. His name was latinized as Carolus Linnaeus on the books which he published, all of which were in Latin.

Linnaeus' most important books on the classification of plants were his *Systema Naturae, Fundamenta Botanica, Genera Plantarum, Classes Plantarum,* and *Species Plantarum.* The last named was published in Stockholm in 1753, setting forth for the first time specific names for all the plants known at that time.

Linnaeus' system of classification was based upon the sexual characteristics of plants, a fundamental system which is used to the present time, although many of the principles have been re-arranged. His first work in the field was inspired by a review of Sebastien Vaillant's *Sermo de Structura Florum,* which set him to examining the structure of flowers.

Though much of Linnaeus' work has been modified and changed from his original plan, his system of defining genera and species, and his uniform use of descriptive terminology is retained in modern classification.

LINSEED MEAL: An excellent source of nitrogen. Only the high price of this meal possibly prevents an extensive use of it, except for fertilization of wrapper tobacco. When part of the nitrogen is taken from this source, a better "finish" of the wrapper leaf is obtained.

The rate of nitrification is similar to that of cottonseed meal but the material is slightly more "efficient" than the latter.

LINUM: Flax, a genus of the *Linaceae,* the flax family, comprising about 100 species, all flowering and cultivated for ornamental purposes with the exception of *l. usitatissimum,* the commercial flax from which linen and linseed oil are derived. See FLAX.

Foliage in all the species is very similar. Leaves are narrow and stalkless, mostly small. Flower parts come in five's and multiples of five. Colors are red, yellow, blue and pink.

Flowers bloom profusely if planted in full sun. Average garden soil is sufficiently rich for their requirements. Annuals may be planted where they are to stand, or started early under glass and transplanted when weather is warm. Frost will kill plants.

L. grandiflorum, called flowering flax, is most often grown. An annual, it grows to two feet, with red to purplish blue flowers 1½ inches across. Varieties include scarlet, pink, and reds.

Golden flax, *l. flavum,* is a two-foot perennial, half-hardy, with bright yellow flowers. A variety, *compactum,* is recommended as a dwarf form.

L. monogynum and *l. salsoloides* are hardy showy forms not generally grown, growing to two feet, with large white or white tinted flowers.

The most dependable perennial is *l. perenne,* whose bright blue flowers are in pannicles. A white variety is also available.

For rock gardens, *l. narbonnense* is recommended, a perennial with azure blue flowers with white eye.

LIPPIA: *see* LEMON VERBENA

LIQUID MANURE: Often recommended for fertilizing house plants as well as outside plantings.

There are several ways of making liquid manure, but the following method is easy, economical and not a bit messy.

As soon as the weather is warm enough to keep water from freezing, get three large 100 pound sugar sacks and fill each one with a mixture of fresh cow, horse and chicken manure in equal parts. These are then suspended in 60-gallon steel drums, one to each drum, and then the drums are filled full of warm water. Be sure the sacks of manure are under water. Some gardeners "bury" the drums in an inconspicuous place.

After you have made sure that the bags are under water, cover the drums and let the manure steep in the water for 30 to 45 days. At the end of this time, remove the manure sacks and add enough water to the liquid manure so that it is about the color of weak tea. By filling the drum to within one inch of the top, the strength of the solution is generally right for all general purposes. The main purpose of the liquid manure is to give plants a boost just before they start to bloom, so the liquid manure can be made up at any time in order to be ready in time for the flowers and shrubs as they come into bloom.

Liquid manure should be applied to the ground around the particular plants which are to receive it; then washed in with water. One can save a lot of steps and labor if he can apply the manure just before a good rain, but by all means, see that it will do the good for which it was intended.

Many gardeners give plants three applications a year in the proportion of one gallon to five square feet of plant bed. For shrub groups use the same proportion.—*Myron Parish.*

See also MANURE; COMPOST WATER.

LIRIOPE SPICATA: *see* GROUND COVER

LITCHI: Common name for Chinese evergreen, *L. chinensis,* popular in warm Oriental countries for its fruit, which is eaten fresh or dried. In this country it can be grown only in the warmest sections of Florida and California. Fruit of the litchi is known in the North only in its dried state, when it is a prune-like fruit, surrounded by a thin, papery shell. When fresh, it has a red skin and sweet white flesh.

The litchi tree is round-topped, to 40 feet with 30-40 foot spread, with compound leathery leaves and one-foot panicles of small yellowish flowers. Considered an ornamental in some places because of its bright red fruit. For best growth, it needs a fertile acid loam with plenty of moisture. Propagation may be accomplished by seed, cuttings, layering or grafting.

LITHOSOL SOIL: *see* AZONAL SOIL

LIVESTOCK: *see* GOAT; COW; POULTRY; GEESE

LIVING SOIL, THE: *by E. B. Balfour.* See BOOKS FOR ORGANIC GARDENERS AND FARMERS.

LOAM: Soil which is composed of a friable mixture of clay, silt, sand, and organic matter is called loam. The mixture of mineral and organic material in a good loam should be of such a proportion as to provide 50 per cent solid matter and 50 per cent space between the solids. Of the space, about half should be filled with water and half air for optimum plant growth.

Clay, silt, and sand are particles of rock, usually of the rock which underlies the field on which they are found. Silt is composed of rock particles of less than 1/16 mm. in diameter which is or has been deposited on the bed of a body of water. Sand is coarser rock material, clay is finer.

If the mineral content of a loam is composed of more than half sand, it is said to be a sand loam. If clay predominates, it is a clay loam, or if it is mostly silt, it is a silt loam.

If the rock underlying the soil is limestone, the soil above will probably have a neutral or slightly alkaline pH. If the mineral content of the soil does not come from limestone, the pH will probably be acid, except under unusual conditions.

Amounts of organic matter in loam vary from a trace to about 15 per cent. Good loam contains at least five per cent organic matter, which helps the soil to retain its moisture, and contributes to the never-ending process of decomposition and growth which goes on in the soil. *See also* SOIL; COMPOST; HUMUS.

LOBELIA: Perennial or annual herbs of the family *Lobeliaceae*. Flowers are usually blue or red, and are formed in long, spike-like clusters.

Edging lobelia, *L. erinus* in its beautiful shades of blue, may be had in dwarf compact forms, which are used in pots, boxes and baskets. The charming much-branched dwarf plants, under six inches in height, are covered with tiny blue flowers throughout the blooming season. Unfortunately, they demand cool weather but cannot stand freezing, so they must be grown during the winter in most nearly frost-free sections and receive protection on cold nights. The seeds germinate well and quickly produce good stands of robust plants.

L. cardinalis, is an erect perennial with bright scarlet flowers.

L. fulgens, a perennial hairy herb grows to three feet and produces deep red flowers, but is hardy only in the deep South.

L. syphilitica, or blue lobelia, sometimes known as great lobelia, is a hardy perennial growing to three feet with blue-purple flowers. It is a good late bloomer in the East. *See also* CARDINAL FLOWER.

LOCO WEED: *see* WEEDS

LOCUST: Common name for the genus *Robinia,* a small group of deciduous pea-family trees and shrubs, native to North and Central America. Locusts are mostly hardy, and are grown both for ornament and timber. They have feathery foliage and in spring the blossoms are in long drooping clusters of pink, white, or purple pea-like flowers. Flowers are fragrant, and attract the bees. Seedpods are brown and leathery, some persisting through the winter to make a dry, rustling noise in the winter winds.

Locusts thrive in any soil, even sand. They transplant well, and may be propagated by root cuttings, suckers, division, cuttings, as well as by seed.

Most common species is the *R. pseudoacacia,* black locust, yellow locust, or false acacia, a tree which sometimes attains 70-80 feet. Leaflets are one to two inches long, with nine to 17 in a pinnate leaf. Flowers are white and fragrant in pendulous clusters up to five inches. Bark is brown and furrowed, and the wood is strong and resists decay from moisture.

Rose-acacia, *R. hispida,* also called pink locust, is a shrub growing to nine feet, hardy only in the South, where it is sometimes trained as a standard. Drooping clusters of pink or rose flowers in May or June are followed by two to three inch pods covered with red bristles. Suckers freely, and may be propagated by severing and transplanting suckers.

The clammy locust, *R. viscosa,* is grown as an ornamental in the South and some intermediate areas for its feathery foliage and pink flowers. It grows 30-40 feet, but seldom attains that height because it is usually attacked and killed by borers, as are the black locusts. Both of these species should be watched for signs of sawdust around their trunks. When found, the hole of the borer must be sought somewhere above, and the borer dug out and destroyed. If not destroyed, wood decay will follow the borer's tunnel, and will leave ugly scars on the tree.

The thorny locust, *R. neo-mexicana,* is a native of the Southwest, and is not hardy north of Washington. It grows as a spiny shrub or sometimes a small tree not over 30 feet. Rose-colored flowers are borne from June through August. Leaves are feathery, the seed pod about four inches long and smooth.

LOCUST: A common name applied to a family of insects closely allied to grasshoppers, sometimes called shorthorn grasshoppers. They are eaten in many countries—roasted, fried, preserved in lime, or dried in the sun. One of the most destructive forms is the Rocky Mountain locust. In Asia and Africa they sometimes swarm in clouds, destroying all vegetation wherever they alight. In 1931, thousands of square miles of the midwestern states were ravaged by locusts.

LOESS: A fine grained, erosional sediment, deposited by wind, covering vast areas in Asia, Europe and North and South America. Often it contains snail shells. Largest deposit in the United States is in the drainage basin of the Mississippi River. *See also* ALLUVIUM.

LOGANBERRY: (*Rubus loganobaccus*) A popular bramble fruit resembling the blackberry, except in color. The loganberry is red, and thus is often called the red blackberry. It is a trailing variety, not hardy in the Northeast, but can be grown with winter protection in places where temperatures do not drop to zero.

Loganberry canes can be woven over a four-wire trellis, so that each flower and fruit cluster will receive as much light as is available.

Ninety per cent of the fruit is grown on the west coast. The loganberry is self-fertile, not requiring a pollenizer. The fruit was discovered in 1881 by Judge J. H. Logan, Santa Cruz, California, from seed planted in his garden. Actually, it is a form of trailing blackberry, a red fruited (sport) form. *See also* BRAMBLE FRUITS.

LOLIUM: *see* RYE

LOMBARDY POPLAR: *see* POPLAR

LONG-LEAVED MINT: *see* MINT

LONICERA: *see* HONEYSUCKLE

LOOSESTRIFE: *see* LYSIMACHIA; LYTHRUM

LOQUAT: (*Eriobotrya japonica*) An evergreen fruit tree of the rose family, widely grown in China and Japan and less popularly in the warmer sections of California for its apple- or pear-shaped small fruits. The fruit is also called the Japanese medlar, and in the Orient, the biwa, lukwati, and pipa. The tree, which will not be killed by occasional drops to 10 to 15°, is sometimes grown as an ornamental in the less tropical areas of the southern states. One or two degrees of frost are sufficient to kill blossoms or fruit, and since the tree blooms in fall and ripens its fruit through the winter, it does not make a dependable crop in this country.

Tree grows to 25 feet, but usually not more than 15 feet when grown as an ornamental. It may also be grown as a greenhouse subject. Leaves are stiff and shining, to one foot long, flowers are white, fragrant, ½ inch across, borne in six-inch clusters. Fruits are yellow to orange, one to three inches long.

Soil requirements are not rigid, though the loquat seems to prefer clay, well drained, and appreciates mulch. In orchards these are planted 20 to 25 feet apart, or may be somewhat crowded to increase fruit size. Propagation is by seed, grafting, cuttings, or shield budding. Ornamentals are usually grown from seed.

LOTI-BUSH: (*Zizyphus obtusifolia*) Sometimes known as Texas buckthorn or buckthorn, the Loti-bush or Lote-bush is a thorny shrub with greenish flowers found from southeastern Texas to Mexico and Arizona.

LOTUS: Common name for water lilies of the genus *Nelumbium;* also properly applied as name of a genus of leguminous shrubs and herbs of the pea family; also in antiquity lotus of the lotus-eaters the *Zizyphus lotus,* a tree whose fruit is a jujube.

NELUMBIUM: Large water lilies with shield-shaped leaves standing above the water. Flowers usually rise several feet above the surface, opening three successive days before fading. Can grow in any climate where roots will not freeze. Usually grown in the South of the United States, native to Mediter-

ranean and Indian Ocean areas and Australia. Seeds are large and very tough—sometimes filed or bored to aid germination. Planted in shallow pans outside, or rolled in clay and dropped into ponds. When grown in pans, roots not planted in ponds until well developed. Require rich bed and full sun.

East Indian lotus, *N. speciosum,* leaves one to three feet in diameter which rise above the water three to six feet, flowers four to ten inches, pink or rose and fragrant. The sacred flower of the Egyptians. Long fleshy rootstocks used in some countries for food. Varieties include white, red, dwarfs, and doubles.

American lotus or water chinkapin, *N. luteum,* has smaller and lower leaves, one or two feet, cup-shaped, and ten-inch yellow flowers.

NYMPHAEA: Flowers and leaves of these water lilies stand or float on the surface of the water. Included in the genus are three species known as lotus.

Blue lotus of Egypt, *N. caerulea,* tender, with leaves 12-16 inches in diameter, light blue flowers with white centers, three to six inches.

White lotus of Egypt, *N. lotus,* tender, has leaves 12-20 inches across and white flower with pinkish outer petals five to ten inches. Opens in the evening and remains open until nearly noon next day.

The blue lotus of India is *N. stellata,* a smaller variety than either of the two above, pale blue petals with white bases, some varieties pink.

LOTUS: Genus of the pea family composed of herbs and prostrate shrubs of little horticultural importance, except a few species which are cultivated in a few places as ornamentals, fodder, or edible peas.

Bird's-foot trefoil (*L. corniculatus*) is a perennial which is sometimes grown for forage. It is a sprawling plant, or can grow to two feet, with small yellow flowers from red buds. St. James trefoil (*L. jacobaeus*) is

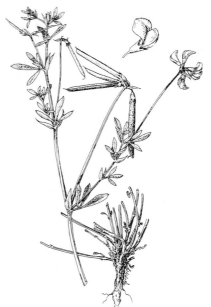

A perennial plant, recommended for forage and as a soil building crop, bird's-foot trefoil is often a sprawling plant with small, yellow flowers.

grown as an ornamental, having yellow and dark purple flowers, sometimes both at once, on three foot plants.

L. Berthelotii is a small shrub grown in California and sometimes under glass for its odd scarlet flowers.

Winged pea (*L. tetragonolobus*) is a trailing annual grown in the south of Europe for the seed and pods, which are edible when young.

LOVAGE: (*Levisticum officinale*) A perennial plant introduced from Europe. It has been grown occasionally as a garden plant. The root has long been supposed to have medicinal properties and is in some demand in the drug trade. The flowering tops yield a volatile oil, but there is little demand for it. The seed, leaves, and roots are also used for flavoring foods.

Lovage grows well in almost any deep well-drained soil that will produce a fair crop of corn or potatoes and is benefited by the liberal use of fertilizer, although heavy applications of manure tend to produce excessive top growth. It is propagated from seed or by root divisions. The seed may be planted in the field in fall and lightly covered in rows 18 inches apart or sown in early spring in a hotbed, greenhouse, or well-prepared seedbed in a sheltered part of the garden and covered very lightly with sand or fine sifted soil. It is advisable to spread old burlap or other sacking over the bed and sprinkle it occasionally in dry weather. When the first seedlings break the soil the cover should be removed. The plants reach a size suitable for transplanting by the end of May, when they are set eight inches apart in rows spaced for convenient cultivation.

The roots may be dug in October of the second or third year after setting the plants. Numerous offsets will generally be found, and if these have good roots they may be reset at once to renew the planting without recourse to seed. The freshly dug roots are washed, cut into slices about ½ thick, and carefully dried. Artificial heat, not to exceed 125° F., may be used to hasten the drying.

LOVE GRASS: *see* GRASS, ORNAMENTAL

LOVE-IN-A-MIST: *see* NIGELLA

LUCERNE: *see* ALFALFA

LUDWIGIA: *see* AQUARIUMS

LUFFA: A genus of tropical gourds belonging to the cucumber family. There are two species—*L. acutangula*, the fruits of which grow to 12 inches, and the more popular *L. cylindrica*, the fruits of which grow to 20 inches and weigh up to five pounds.

Luffa makes such good towels and sponges that it has even been named "towel gourd" and "vegetable sponge." Its fibrous interior after processing makes excellent pot holders, door mats, table mats, bathroom rugs, gloves, sandals, and sun helmets, and is used for stuffing pillows and mattresses.

The U.S. Navy used luffa for filters in steam engines in preference to any other material during the last war.

The Army used it for wiping the windshields of jeeps. It was even used in surgical operations.

In many parts of the world luffa is esteemed as a medicine. It has been used for treating every ailment from intestinal worms to hemorrhage, hernia, scarlet fever, small pox, aching teeth, and parasitic infections, and as a tonic for the genital organs.

The fresh fruits of the sweet variety are sliced and eaten like cucumbers. Or they are good in soups, used like okra. They can be cooked in any way that squash can. The pure seed oil has been suggested as a substitute for olive oil.

The Japanese slice the young fruits and dry them in the sun, like dried apples, for future use. The Malayans relish the young leaves, while the Annamites like the male flowers and flower buds.

The inside of this amazing vegetable gourd is a mass of spongy tissue, with large seeds in the center. Although it is a tropical plant, it grows well and produces fruits over two feet long in temperate climates, growing as far north as Connecticut.

The usual practice is to start luffa in March or April in a hotbed or indoors in pots placed in a warm, sunny window. About three seeds to a pot is plenty.

The started plants are transplanted to the garden on a cloudy day after all danger of frost is past. This is usually about the time the sweet corn starts coming up.

A good organic soil, with plenty of humus and, if possible, well-rotted manure well-worked in, is best for growing luffa. The plants should be set out about four feet apart, with four feet between rows.

The young leaves may be eaten at any time, and the young fruit used until it gets as large as cucumbers. If grown on a good soil the fruits will grow to be over two feet long and will mature before frost. The mature fruits are the ones used for mats, sponges and sandals since they have developed the desired coarse fiber.

As many as 25 gourds grow on a single vine, and the gourds may weigh as much as five pounds each. Under experienced management with optimum conditions, it is estimated that 24,000 gourds can be grown per acre.

Better fruits can be had if care is taken in pruning off all of the first flowers and any newly-formed gourds which are deformed, pear-shaped, or coarse. Also, fruits should be kept off the ground by placing a flat stone under the fruit or providing a trellis for the vines to climb. *See also* GOURDS.

LUNARIA: *see* HONESTY PLANT

LUPINE: (*Lupinus*) A genus of the pea family.

Lupines grow as high as five feet, producing blooms one foot long in many colors. The plants do best in a light soil with plenty of moisture.

Lupines bear pea-shaped flowers closely placed on long, hollow, stiff spikes. Practically all the flowers open at one time and make a gorgeous showing. They reach a height of from three to five feet with the blooms over a foot long. They come in many colors of white, maroon, purple, yellow, red, pink, and blue, and with combinations of colors.

The general soil recommendation calls for a sandy or light soil. In the heavy clay the roots rot frequently. The plants like plenty of moisture with good drainage.

It is easy to save a lot of ripened seeds. Before sowing in the spring, soak the seed in some water overnight to soften the shells. Sow the seed ¼ of an inch deep in specially prepared soil that will not bake. Put a piece of wet burlap over the area and keep it moist. When the plants appear above the soil remove the burlap. Lupines have a wonderful root system, a taproot with a few big prongs. They resent transplanting, therefore plant small plants at a favorable time and see to it that there is plenty of earth adhering to the roots.

Quaker bonnets (*L. perennis*) is the common wild lupine prevalent in the eastern states. It prefers a sandy soil; grows one to two feet; has blue or white flowers. Tree lupine (*L. arboreus*) grows four to eight feet, has fragrant yellow flowers. Bluebonnet (*L. subcarnosa*) makes an attractive spring-blooming annual, growing to about a foot high. It is the state flower of Texas.

LYCHEE: *see* LITCHI

LYCHNIS: A genus of the pink family, *Caryophyllaceae,* comprising a large number of annual, biennial, and perennial flowers most of which have been cultivated in their present forms for many years. All are in shades of white, pink, rose, scarlet, or magenta, many with wooly or hirsute foliage. Several species are commonly called campions, a name also applied to some closely related species of the genus *silene.*

Most species like full sun, and will do well in any good garden soil, even if somewhat sandy. Seeds of all are easily germinated, the perennials giving a light bloom the first year if sown indoors very early. Perennials may also be propagated by division of clumps early in spring.

Flowers are characterized by a tube, from which five petals expand at top, most of the petals either notched or divided in the center. Bloom starts in June and lasts through August.

Evening campion (*L. alba*) has fragrant white flowers one inch across that open each evening in loose clusters. Foliage is somewhat hairy and sticky. Biennial or perennial. Similar in growth is the red morning campion (*L. dioica.*) which opens its flowers early in the morning. There are also white varieties of *dioica.*

Arctic campion (*L. alpina*) grows only one foot high, and makes a good rock garden plant. The type has dense heads of rose-pink flowers, but there are varieties in white and red. Perennial.

Rose campion (*L. coronaria*) is also called mullein-pink, or dusty miller, has wooly gray-white leaves on wooly branched stems, each tipped with a magenta flower one inch across. White varieties, as well as bicolors, are also known.

Perhaps the most showy *lychnis* is *chalcedonica,* called Maltese Cross, Jerusalem Cross, and scarlet lightning. It is a two to three foot perennial with somewhat coarse, hairy foliage, and large umbels of scarlet flowers raised above the foliage in spring, followed by smaller heads from lower leaf axils later in summer. There are also varieties in white, pink, salmon, and doubles.

Rose-of-heaven (*L. coeli-rosa*) formerly *agrostemma coeli-rosa* is a one-foot annual with solitary one-inch rose flowers at the top of each stem.

White, red, purple-eyed, and toothed-petal varieties have also been listed.

L. coronata is an annual, or a tender biennial blooming the first year from seed sown early. It bears loose clusters of salmon-pink, brick-red, or cinnabar flowers early in summer.

Cuckoo flower (*L. flos-cuculi*) or *Agrostemma cuculi*, is a hardy rapid-spreading perennial with loose panicles of pink, red, white, and some double one-inch flowers.

Flower-of-Jove (*L. flos-jovis* or *A. flos-jovis*) is a 1½-foot perennial with dense umbel heads of rose-pink blossoms.

German catchfly (*L. viscaria*) so-called because of the sticky patches below the red or purple clusters of flowers. Varieties are *alba, grandiflora alba, nana, rosea, splendens,* and *splendens flore-pleno.*

A delicate rock-plant is *L. pyrenaica,* about four inches high, with a basal rosette of club-shaped leaves from which rise stems with heart-shaped leaves terminating in single ¼-inch solitary pink flowers. Perennial.

LYCIUM: *see* MATRIMONY VINE

LYE: Lye, which is crude sodium hydroxide, should not be used in the compost heap to speed decay. It will kill soil organisms. The lye is so strong that it can dissolve an iron pail. If put with garbage it would dissolve all the tin cans, but the resulting product would not be good biologically.

LYGODIUM: A genus of climbing ferns mostly from warm or tropical climates, only one, the Hartford fern, being native to United States. This species has been so much sought for ornamentation that it is almost extinct in New Jersey and Connecticut, where it formerly grew along river banks. Most species are grown in greenhouses for their graceful habit and finely segmented and re-segmented fronds, some of which terminate in palmate-type forms. Some species in their native surroundings grow to 30 feet, but in greenhouses seldom attain more than eight. Fronds grow at intervals from creeping stems.

Lygodiums grow best in very acid soil, and prefer a mixture of loam, peat moss, and leaf mold. They climb best on other plants, or on twigs, rather than on artificial supports.

L. dichotomum is a robust and long-lived species in a warm greenhouse, with bright green deeply divided palmate leaflets to one foot.

L. japonicum is lighter green, with feathery pinnate foliage, finely divided. The most popular greenhouse species.

Hartford fern (*L. palmatum*) grows to three or four feet and needs the support of other plants, and partial shade. Fronds are palmate, almost round, about four inches with five equal radial lobes.

LYONIA: A genus comprising about 30 shrubs of the heath family, *Ericaceae.* Most are not hardy in the North, and only a few are cultivated as ornamental shrubs.

Mostly deciduous, with only one, the fetter-bush, an evergreen, they have small alternate leaves, small white or pink flowers in clusters either from the leaf axil or from the ends of branches.

Lyonias are propagated mostly from cuttings, and are grown in rather sandy soil with a pH around five, distinctly acid. They need a heavy mulch, preferably of oak or other acid leaves, and do not like to be disturbed.

Swamp andromeda (*L. ligustrina*) also called male-berry and he-huckleberry, is a hardy deciduous shrub growing to 12 feet. Spring flowers are in six-inch racemes. Foliage changes color in fall.

Fetter-bush (*L. lucida*) is the evergreen of the genus, found only south of Washington, D.C. It grows to six feet, with shining leaves and flowers early in spring in pannicles. Native in low-lying woods.

Stagger-bush is hardy to Rhode Island. It grows six feet tall, and has pink or white nodding clusters of flowers in May and June.

LYSIMACHIA: A genus of the primrose family, commonly called loosestrife, though not belonging to the loosestrife family. Very few cultivated, though one species, moneywort, is used as ground cover. Perennial, they are mostly hardy throughout the eastern seaboard. They need a moist spot in the garden, partially shaded. Propagation is by division.

Moneywort (*L. nummularia*) is also creeping Charlie and creeping Jennie. Its trailing stems send out roots from joints. Inconspicuous flowers are yellow, and leaves are round, about ¾ inch in diameter. Will grow in sun, but prefers shade. Can be used under trees for ground cover.

Golden loosestrife (*L. vulgaris*) is also called willow-wort. It grows three to five feet high, with yellow flowers in leafy clusters, and bushy foliage dense at base.

LYTHRUM: Loosestrife, a genus of the loosestrife family, *Lythraceae*. Annuals and perennials, some native to northeastern America, some Eurasian. Mostly marsh plants, and under cultivation do best naturalized along a stream or next to a pond. Soil must be moist. Showy, with pink or magenta flowers singly or in clusters. Perennials all propagated by division.

Purple loosestrife (*L. salicaria*), a perennial that grows to four or five feet, sometimes known as the willowherb because of its willow-like foliage. Originally introduced from Europe, it has naturalized in marshes throughout the East, where it blooms in late summer. A rose-purple variety is *superbum*.

L. virgatum is similar, but has smaller flowers in leafy racemes. A horticultural variety is Rose Queen, with bright rose spikes.

M

MACADAMIA: *see* QUEENSLAND
NUT

MACHINERY, CARE OF: The general
rule to follow is—follow the manufacturer's instructions. These come, or
should come, with every piece of
equipment sold. Look for them when
making any purchase and keep them
handy in a place where they can be
readily consulted.

Power tools range from one-cylinder mowers, tillers and shredders to
four-cylinder tractors. Principles of
good care and management are practically identical for any powered
metal tool whose moving parts operate
at high speed and depend on proper
lubrication to overcome heat and friction.

Cleanliness is the obvious base rule
which should be applied. After a machine has been used in the field, it
should be cleaned and inspected before
being put away. Before a machine is
taken out of the shed or barn to be
used it should be checked for over-
all tightness and for proper lubrication.

In addition to the daily or weekly
inspection-plus-cleaning, these are the
seasonal check-ups which in the spring
and late fall can prevent much
trouble:

1. Using a kerosene soaked rag,
wipe off excess grease and oil from
drive chain, flywheel, axle, wheels, etc.
2. Drain dirty oil from engine.
3. Add clean oil of proper consistency for warm weather operation.
4. Put a few drops of light machine
oil on all drive chains.
5. Using grease gun, grease all
lubrication points on the power appliance with heavy lubricating grease.
6. Tighten all nuts, bolts and
screws.
7. Clean off rust spots with emery

cloth and touch up with good quality
paint.
8. Sharpen and clean cutting edges
of attachments; lubricate moving
parts where specified.
9. Check rubber tires on power
units for cuts, nicks and proper air
pressure. The proper pressure is
usually indicated by the manufacturer.
10. Fuel the appliance with regular
gas and the equipment is ready to
operate. High test gas is not recommended.

Following these principles should
keep breakdowns and poor performance in the field to a minimum. To
these, however, can be added the cau-
tionary admonition to run the machine
in the way it was intended. Don't
overload it, don't give the tool tasks
it was not designed to do, thus inviting
the grave danger of a serious breakdown ending in an accident.

A good operator knows when a machine is running well from the way
it sounds, also its general "feel" and
the vibrations. An immediate check is
called for if the machine does not
sound or "feel" right.

WINTER STORAGE: The common-
sense rules of cleaning and checking
for excessive wear and tear must be
followed. Before starting out, disconnect the spark plug lead-in wire to
avoid the danger of any unintentional
starts.

Give the undercarriage of the machine and all joints an extra-special
cleaning. Lubricate with the proper
oil. Repaint parts where the manufacturer so advises. Coat all machined
parts that are not otherwise covered
or protected with heavy oil.

Drain oil from the crankcase and
replace with clean oil. If possible,
flush interior with clean gasoline and
rinse before filling with fresh oil. Re-

move the air filter over the carburetor, wash the mesh screening in clean gasoline, drain the oil out of the cup and refill with fresh oil and reassemble.

Remove the spark plug and clean the terminals with emery cloth. Check the gap and reset for correct aperture if necessary. Replace the plug if it appears badly pitted or damaged.

Drain the gas tank to prevent the gasoline from forming lead deposits. Pull the starter rope a few times to empty the carburetor and exhaust. The extra meticulous will also cork the exhaust and fill the cylinder with light machine oil for the winter. This should keep rust out of the interior and effectively seal out the damp. To fill the cylinder it will be necessary to remove the spark plug, pour in the light oil and then replace the plug. The cylinder will have to be emptied in the spring and flushed with clean gasoline and the plug terminals cleaned and dried.

It should be stressed that farm and garden equipment is called upon to work in a hard terrain under conditions which frequently are far from ideal. The automobile operates over a smooth surface but agricultural tools literally work in dirt, mud and mire. The need for extra care and cleanliness in their use is manifest when the circumstances are soberly considered.

MADONNA LILY: *see* LILY

MAGGOT: *see* INSECT CONTROL

MAGNESIUM: An element important in the composition of chlorophyll, the green part of leaves. Magnesium is essential for plant utilization of nitrogen, phosphorus and sulfur; it aids in protein formation and is capable of correcting acidity in plants and soils. A magnesium deficiency will cause lower leaves to turn yellow between the veins, which remain green. Leaf edges turn first; the color changes to orange and brown in later stages, after

which the leaf soon dies. An excess of magnesium is rarely encountered, but can cause calcium deficiency.

Magnesium occurs in all plants and farm crops in somewhat smaller amounts than calcium, but in the seeds of grains it is stored up three times more than calcium. Magnesium is assimilated more slowly than calcium; in fact, it is assimilated as a rule more slowly than any other ash element. The plant does not require magnesium until the approach of seed formation, although a small amount is necessary for perfect leaf action, as it enters into the chemical composition of chlorophyll. *See also* DEFICIENCIES, SOIL; FRUIT TREE, DEFICIENCIES; TRACE ELEMENTS.

MAGNESIUM SULPHATE: *see* FERTILIZER, ARTIFICIAL

MAGNOLIA: Magnolias are among the most beautiful trees and shrubs for the garden. They fit into formal and informal plantings and dominate their surroundings when in flower.

The Chinese Magnolias bloom before the leaves appear, and the flowers show to great advantage if given a background of evergreen trees. They are not difficult to grow, prefer a sunny location, and like a rich, deep, sandy loam with plenty of humus that will hold moisture around the roots. While they like this moisture, the roots must not be waterlogged, and good drainage is essential to carry off any excess moisture. During the active growing season in spring, water them once a week if the weather is hot.

Magnolias rarely require pruning, but if it is necessary at any time, do it immediately after the shrubs have finished flowering. Usually by July buds are found for next year's flowering, and cutting of the branches must not be done after this date.

PROPAGATING: Stock is increased by cuttings made from mature wood and by layering. Put down the branches for layering in June and July. After the layered branch has rooted it may be cut from the parent stock and grown on its own roots. When the layered branch is cut from the shrub, do not move it until the following spring. Allow the layered branch to become well established on its own roots before lifting it to plant in some other section of the garden. A mulch of manure or compost is beneficial for magnolias during hot weather.

SPECIES: There are many outstanding species and hybrids. The lovely *M. denudata,* also known as the Yulan and Conspicua, is one of the chief glories of the garden when covered with its large, white, cup-shaped flowers. The beauty of the flowers has made it a universal favorite.

The Star Magnolia, the first of the deciduous ones to bloom, produces pure white, fragrant long-lived flowers to beautify the homegrounds.

M. liliflora has a charming, large, lily-formed flower. It is one of the purple-flowered magnolias and is sometimes sold as *M. obovata,* and *M. purpurea.* A handsome shrub of erect growth it also has several hybrids.

The magnolia most generally grown is *soulangeana,* which makes a large shrub, and if grown to one stem will form a tree. The flowers are white with pink and lilac shading.

M. lennei is a hybrid with large, dark, reddish-purple flowers, and is one of the last of the Chinese magnolias to bloom.

Another lovely purple-flowered magnolia with rich color and fine form is Alexandrina. These magnolias are specimen shrubs sufficiently beautiful to stand alone in the lawn or where they will add distinction to the scene.

M. stellata, the Star Magnolia, is the first of the deciduous magnolias to bloom, and the pure white flowers are delightfully fragrant. The starry white buds open in January and continue to flower for a long time, each flower being about three inches across, and composed of many petals. *M. stellata rosea* is the pink form of this, and makes a good companion to the white one. They should be given a choice place in the garden. In growing magnolias, plant the tall-growing ones behind *stellata,* as this shrub ultimately grows wider than it is high.

There are three Indian species, *M. globosa, M. sphenocarpa,* and the magnificent *M. campbellii* of the Himalayas. The last mentioned is a large forest tree which grows 80 to 100 feet high, some even higher. The flowers are six to ten inches across, lending a glorious rose-coloring in the spring.

The delicate diversity of color, the wide range of flowering seasons, and the ample adaptability in landscaping arrangements for gardens and lawns have multiplied the appeal and beauty of magnolias, making them a gardening favorite across the country. Within the last two decades, the deciduous tree and bush varieties have expanded their understandable popularity in the Southwest, while maintaining their enhancingly attractive status throughout the eastern and central areas.

There are 35 American and Asiatic species as well as many hybrids of the magnolia which is named in honor of Pierre Magnol, an eminent seventeenth century French botanist.

CULTURE: Species and varieties may be chosen which provide colorful blooms from March until July or even

August because certain members of the genus produce flowers before the foliage is fully developed.

Earliest to show color is *M. stellata,* a shrubby plant hardy north of Boston which blooms at the end of March. It is followed by *M. salicipolia, kobus, denudata, soulangeana,* and *liliflora* all of which produce flowers before leaves.

At about mid-June the following varieties come into bloom: *M. acuminata, obovata, fraseri, macrophylla, sieboldi* and *tripetala. M. grandiflora,* among the evergreen species, is hardy only south of Washington, D.C., while *M. virginiana,* although hardy throughout the country, retains its foliage only in the warmer regions.

Good drainage is more essential than a rich soil to successful cultivation. For best results, apply a natural fertilizer or compost such as well-rotted stable or cow manure around the plant's base every two or three years. Wherever possible, magnolias should not be transplanted but left where they are. If moving is imperative, ball and burlap the roots with great care and do not permit them to dry out.

Magnolias can be grown from seed but the hybrids and varieties are veneer-grafted on *M. kobus.* This is done in the greenhouse during January. Layering is recommended to the enthusiast. Vigorous shoots are pegged into the ground after the bark is scarred with a knife to stimulate new growth and covered with a few inches of soil. After one to two seasons, those shoots which have taken good hold are severed from the parent plants and set out in good soil. Budding is also practiced. *M. kobus* is used for the stock; the buds are tied from the tops down, a reversal of the usual procedure.— *E. Hamilton Fairley.*

MAHOGANY: (*Swietenia mahagoni*) The true mahogany is a tall, slender, tropical evergreen tree grown in extreme southern Florida as an ornamental and shade tree. In the West Indies and Central and South America, it is a valuable timber tree and the world's foremost cabinetwood. African and Philippine mahogany are not as high-grade. The mountain mahogany (*Cercocarpus*) and varieties of eucalyptus sometimes called red, swamp or bastard mahogany, are not related to the true mahogany.

MAHONIA: These spring-blooming shrubs bear fragrant yellow blooms in pretty racemes, and are fine specimens for foundation plantings and shrub borders. They like shelter from the winter sun and wind, and a medium-fertile soil. *M. bealei* is the tallest of the mahonias, reaching 12 feet. The Oregon grape, *M. aquifolium,* grows up to eight feet or so in height, is quite hardy and has small, blue, edible berries. *M. nervosa,* the water holly, is sometimes called Oregon grape and bears similar edible berries, but it rarely grows over two feet high. California barberry, *M. pinnata,* grows about ten feet tall, and creeping barberry, *M. repens,* is a ground cover under a foot in height, with creeping roots. Agarita, *M. trifoliolata,* a six-foot shrub, is grown occasionally in the Southwest and is not hardy north of there. All the mahonias can be propagated by seeds and suckers, and by layers and cuttings of half-ripened wood under glass.

MAIDENHAIR FERN: *see* FERN

MAIDEN PINK: *see* DIANTHUS

MAJORANA: *see* MARJORAM

MALABAR: The well-known farm of the late Louis Bromfield. Located in Pleasant Valley near Mansfield, Ohio, this thousand-acre expanse of worked-out soil was chosen by Bromfield in 1939 when he returned to the U. S. after nearly 20 years in India and France.

He did not believe in the use of agricultural chemicals but with grasses and legumes, soil-building crops, rotation, return of organic matter and other natural farming and conservation practices rebuilt a topsoil three to seven inches *deeper* than the original virgin soil had been.

As Bromfield himself pictured Malabar: "It might be described as a gigantic test plot in soil and water management ... We are primarily interested in what works and what is permanently good for the farmer, his soils, his crops and his animals and what gives him the highest production and the best nutritional quality."

Since Bromfield's death in 1956, diligent effort by The Friends of the Land organization has established an ecological research, testing and instruction center at Malabar. (Ecology is the study of the relation of organisms to their environment.) Called the Louis Bromfield Institution, this center, directed by 100 conservationists under the chairmanship of Cleveland Press editor Louis B. Seltzer, will carry on the ideas and projects that Bromfield started in his lifetime. *See also* BROMFIELD, LOUIS.

MALLOW (*Malva*) These annual or perennial herbs are easily grown in ordinary garden soil. The annuals are hardy and can be sown where they are to grow, and the perennials are easily divided in spring or fall. Mallows are related to *Hibiscus* but not nearly as popular. *M. moschata,* musk rose or musk mallow, and *M. alcea,* the vervain mallow, grow up to two feet tall and have white or pink flowers. Curled mallow, *M. crispa* or *M. verticillata,* may grow over ten feet high, with thick clusters of white blooms. Another variety, common mallow, *M. rotundifolia,* a low plant sometimes called cheeses because of the shape of its fruit, is one of our worst garden weeds and must be cultivated out strenuously. With the others, there is danger that they will spread into other areas of the garden, but they are not so difficult to eradicate.

MALNUTRITION: *see* NUTRITION

MALPIGHIA GLABRA: *see* ACEROLA

MALTESE CROSS: *see* LYCHNIS

MALUS: *see* APPLE

MAMMILLARIA: *see* PIN-CUSHION CACTUS

MANDARIN: *see* CITRUS; ORANGE

MANGANESE: One of the minor elements, which in recent years has been shown to have important functions in the economy of soils, plants and animals. Because of its manganese content, manure has effectively been used to correct manganese deficiencies.

Some areas of soil are deficient in manganese and therefore produce crops inferior in quantity as well as in food quality. Manganese may be made unavailable in some soils by the application of an excess of basic materials, including calcium carbonate, in the form of ground limestone or marl. When some soils are made alkaline with a basic material, the active compounds of manganese are rendered so inactive or unavailable that growth of the crop is retarded, yields are diminished, and the quality of the harvested product is inferior.

The condition on oats known as "grey speck" is due to manganese deficiency or unavailability in the soil. When different species of plants are grown on the same type of soil they show a considerable range in manganese content. The leguminous plants usually contain the least amount of manganese, and the grasses the greatest amount. *See also* TRACE ELEMENTS; DEFICIENCIES, SOIL.

MANGANESE SULPHATE: *see* FERTILIZERS, ARTIFICIAL

MANGO: (*Mangifera*) Fruit trees of great antiquity from Southeast Asia, comprising approximately 30 species of the sumac family. Of these, the common mango (*M. indica*) is cultivated throughout the tropics in both the eastern and western hemispheres.

Attaining a height of 90 feet, it is a handsome, round-topped tree with lace-shaped, alternate leaves, eight to 14 inches long. The flowers are small, pinkish-white and usually in terminal clusters. The fruit is large, fleshy and aromatic, drupe-like, red or yellow-orange. It is very juicy but extremely perishable.

CULTURE: The mango has been called the "apple of the tropics" because of its universality there. It is strictly tropical in its requirements and can endure but little frost. It is grown in southern Florida and California in this country, having been introduced into the former over 100 years ago.

The oval-pointed fruits are quite handsome. Many grafted varieties are rich, sweet and spicy, with agreeably textured flesh, free of tough fibers. The more common "turpentine" variety has a fibrous flesh and strong flavor although it is edible.

Ripe fruits contain 11 to 19 per cent sugar in the form of sucrose, $\frac{1}{2}$ to one per cent protein, practically no starches and are a good source of vitamins A and C.

Most popular varieties grown in Florida include the *haden, paheri, pico, amini, langra benarsi, cambodiana, cecil,* and *sandersha.* Maturity begins in May and extends with some varieties well into the autumn.

The mango can thrive on some poor and sandy soil, but the trees do their best on better ground. In addition to their fruit, they are also planted for shade and ornamental value. The large varieties demand wide spacing in maturity; a minimal 30 by 30 feet. Fertilizers will help but excess nitrogen will stimulate vegetative growth at the expense of the fruit. Bearing age is reached in five to seven years; the trees are extremly long-lived.

Propagation is mostly from seed; those of most of the Philippine varieties will come true. Shield budding and crown grafting are also employed.

MANGROVE, BLACK: (*Avicennia nitida*) Shrubs or small trees with small white flowers and evergreen leaves, found along the coast of South Florida, north to New Smyrna on the east coast and to Tampa Bay on the west coast. Black mangrove usually grows a little back from the water rather than in it, as in the case of the red mangrove. Black mangrove is of some value as a honey plant, surpluses of 50 to 75 pounds being reported.

MANIHOT: Cassava or manihot, occasionally called manioc or mandioca, is a shrub whose edible rootstock yields a nutritious starch. Cultivated throughout the tropics, it is a source of tapioca. The huge roots, often weighing more than 20 pounds, are poisonous until the juice is extracted by pressing and heating. *M. esculenta* grows about eight feet tall, with yellow-green flowers. In Florida, it is grown as a food for livestock, and in the north it does well in a dry, warm greenhouse. Sweet cassava, *M. dulcis,* is a similar plant, but its roots are not poisonous when young. Other varieties are trees that yield a poor kind of rubber. Yuquilla, *M. carthaginensis,* is a tree found growing wild in the desert of the Southwest. All varieties can be increased by cuttings rooted over bottom-heat.

MANNA GRASS: *see* GRASS, ORNAMENTAL

MANTID, PRAYING: Praying mantids are odd-looking relatives of the grasshoppers. Their name stems from the unusual way they hold up the forepart of the body and stout front legs, as if in prayer. This stance, however, is one of anything but pious reverence. "Preying" would be more descriptive. Actually, what the mantid is doing is holding itself in poised readiness to capture and consume insects. This is accomplished by a lightning-fast movement of the forelegs, equipped with rows of sharp teeth for holding victims.

These devout-looking benefactors are especially valuable because they have very selective diets coupled with voracious appetites. Their daily menu consists entirely of destructive garden insects—just about all kinds. Particularly fond are they of the sucking and cutting varieties—those that do greatest damage to food crops, trees and flowers.

Maintaining a posture of poised readiness, the praying mantid uses lightning-fast movements of its forelegs to capture aphids and other insects.

Young mantids feed on aphids, caterpillars and other soft-bodied insects, while the older ones are able to capture and consume many additional, larger pests. At the same time, both young and old mantids are completely harmless to plants and people. As carnivorous predators, their bill-of-fare is limited strictly to insects.

Most important to the gardener seeking their natural protection talents, mantids are surprisingly easy to introduce into any pest-packed area. All there is to it is tying a few egg cases where their services are needed. After that, the hungry mantids—and nature—take over. Each female deposits several egg masses in a season. These masses, or egg cases as they're called, form a hardened, rough-textured covering which protects the dormant life inside through the winter. Then, as spring appears, so do the young mantids—anywhere from 50 to 400 from each egg case—to start their season of gluttonous garden care.

How many cases are needed for adequate protection? One egg case for each major shrub or tree; four cases per quarter acre without shrubbery. These cases need no special care. You merely tie them outside where they are to hatch. They're extremely winter hardy, able to stand sub-freezing temperatures safely. Good for greenhouses, too. And what's more, once they are introduced, they will remain in your immediate area or near vicinity, and continue their protective cycle by depositing their eggs in the fall for the next year.

Mantid egg cases, it should be noted, can be sent only during the dormant period—approximately November 1st to May 15th. Since it is recognized as a beneficial insect, there are no restrictions on its being sent through the mails and it is exempt from insect control laws. *See also* INSECT CONTROL, BIOLOGICAL.

MANURE: The excreta of agricultural animals, along with stable litter, constitutes one of the oldest and most effective fertilizers known to man. The rise of chemical fertilizers in the 20th century has led to a decrease in the amount of manure utilized by world agriculturists. This wasteful misuse of natural fertilizer is often rationalized by farmers and agriculturists, who allege that the supply is not adequate for the need for fertilizers. This is faulty reasoning. In 1889 there were 13,663,000 horses in the United States and 50,331,000 head of cattle. Today there are fewer horses—about 3,000,000 total—but almost one hundred million head of cattle. There has also been a subsequent rise in the number of other livestock. The problem is not insufficient manure, but its misuse.

It has also been calculated that a farmer by wise management of his animal manures can return to the soil 70 per cent of the nitrogen, 75 per cent of the phosphorus, and 80 per cent of the potash which was taken out by the home-grown plants his animals eat. This is a considerable saving when it is realized that a dairy cow gives 27,000 pounds of manure annually and a horse, 18,000.

Actually only a small fraction of the potential crop producing and soil-conserving value of manure is used. Approximately half of the excrements from farm stock is dropped on pastures and uncultivated ground. Vast amounts of manure in stockyards, piggeries, poultry farms, and other animal industries are considered worthless wastes and are dumped on uncultivated lands. On most farms the manure is so badly handled that it suffers enormous losses of nitrogen through improper fermentation and drying, and of nutrients due to the draining off of the urine and leaching of the solid portion of the manure by rain and surface water. Fermented manure loses ammonia if allowed to dry on the field before it is worked into the soil. There is also a loss as a result of the inefficient use of manure as, for instance, when it is not applied at the season, in the manner, at the rate, or to the crop which would give the greatest return. In view of these facts it is safe to assume that only from a third to a quarter of the potential value of the manure resource of the country is now realized. The present wasteful and inefficient methods of using manure seen in all sections of the country are sufficient evidence that many farmers do not understand the true nature of manure, the perishable character of its most valuable constituents, and the direct money loss incurred through its improper treatment. This situation is doubtless due in large part to the increased use of artificial chemical fertilizers during the past 25 or 50 years.

VALUED BY GREEKS AND ROMANS: Tradition has it that King Augeas was the first in Greece to make use of manure, and that Hercules introduced the practice into Italy. M. Varro assigns the first rank for excellence to the dung of thrushes kept in aviaries, and praises it as being not only food for land, but excellent food for oxen and swine as well. Columella gives the second rank to pigeon manure, and third rank to poultry manure. Next to these, the dung of swine was highly esteemed. Dungs rated less in quality were, in order, goats, sheep, oxen, and last of all, beasts of burden. The ancients also doubtless composted their manures in some regions, for we read, . . . "In some of the provinces, too, which abound more particularly in cattle, by reason of their prolific soil, we have seen the manure passed through a sieve like so much flour, and perfectly devoid, through lapse of time, of all bad smell or repulsive look, being changed in its appearance to something rather agreeable than otherwise."

Varro believed that corn (small grains) land should be manured with horse-dung, that being the lightest manure of all, while meadow land, he said, thrives better with a manure of a more heavy nature, and supplied by beasts that have been fed upon barley.

CONTENT AND VALUE OF MANURE: The most common domestic animals which are a source of manure are horses, cattle, goats, sheep, pigs, rabbits, and poultry. The dung consists of the undigested portions of the foods which have been ground into fine bits and saturated with digestive juices in the alimentary tract. It also contains a large population of bacteria which may make up as much as 30 per cent of its mass. Dung contains, as a rule, one-third of the total nitrogen, one-fifth of the total potash, and nearly all of the phosphoric acid voided by the animals.

The urine contains compounds from the digested portion of the foods and secretions from the animal body. The urine usually contains about two-thirds of the total nitrogen, four-fifths of the total potash, and but very little of the phosphoric acid voided by the animal. Because they are in solution, the elements in the urine are or become available as plant nutrients much more quickly than the constituents found in the dung.

The value of animal manure varies with the food eaten by the animal, the age of the animal, the products yielded (as milk, wool, or meat), and the physical condition and health of the animal.

The richer the food is in the elements which are essential to plant growth, the more valuable will be the manure. The manure of animals fed on wheat bran, gluten meal, and cottonseed meal, for instance, will be much richer in nutrient elements than from animals fed with straw or hay without grains.

The manure of young animals, which are forming bones and muscles from their foods, will be poorer in nutrient elements than the manure of mature animals.

The value of the manure varies also according to the animal products which are made, as milk which contains considerable amounts of nitrogen, phosphorus, and potassium; wool which contains a large amount of nitrogen; and beef which contains practically all the elements necessary for plant growth.

Sometimes cattle are grown in regions with mineral-rich soils and fattened in regions where carbonaceous foods are abundant and cheap. The manure from mature animals which are being fattened is relatively rich in minerals, as fat contains little or no minerals.

Unfortunately the values of manure and fertilizers in general have been, in the past, based on the relative amount of nitrogen, phosphoric acid, and potash which they contain. While these are major elements and doubtless affect the values of manure to a greater extent than the proportion of any other constituents, it is misleading to make a direct comparison be-

tween farm manures and artificial chemical fertilizers on the basis of the relative amounts of N, P, and K. Soil needs organic matter to keep it alive. Organic matter in the soil is converted into humus, and humus plays an important role in making the nutrient elements in the soil available to the higher plants.

The average composition of farmyard manure, based on many analyses made at the Experiment Station, Amherst, Massachusetts, was found to be water, 67.7 per cent; nitrogen, 0.465 per cent; phosphoric acid, 0.326 per cent; and potash, 0.485 per cent.

It has been estimated that 80 per cent of the manurial constituents found in the food of milk cows will be voided in the excrements. In fattening cattle and hogs, as much as 90 per cent of the nutrient elements in the food are voided. By keeping these percentages in mind, it is not difficult to calculate the amount of nitrogen, phosphoric acid, potash, and other elements in the manure when the composition of the feeds is known.

As a rule, horse manure is more valuable than the manure of other farm animals. This doubtless varies with the amount of grain which is included in the diet. Grains are relatively high in all plant nutrients. Horse manure is richer in nitrogen than either cow or hog manure and is much more liable to fermentation. For this reason it is frequently referred to as a *hot manure*. Another hot manure is that of sheep which is generally quite dry and quite rich. Cow manure and hog manure are relatively wet and correspondingly low in nitrogen. Because of their high water and low nitrogen content, these manures ferment slowly and are commonly regarded as *cold manures*.

It is worth noting that the urine of most animals contains more nitrogen and more potash than the solid excreta. Unfortunately farm manures are handled in such ways that most of the urine is carelessly allowed to escape into drains which lead it off the farm. Urines are especially valuable as activators in converting crop residues into humus.

FRESH VS. ROTTED MANURE: Assuming that fresh manure is a normal mixture of urine and feces and that conditions have been controlled, fresh manure differs from rotted manure in composition as follows:

1. Rotted manure is richer in plant nutrients. This is a result largely of the loss in dry weight of the manure. One ton of fresh manure may lose one-half its weight in the rotting process.

2. The nitrogen in the composted (rotted) manure has been fixed by microorganisms while nitrogen in fresh manure is mostly soluble. These organisms build the soluble nitrogen compounds into their own bodies. The nitrogen in the urine is used in the formation of complex proteins during the decomposition of the manure.

3. The solubility of the phosphorus and potash is greater in the composted manure. If leaching can be prevented, there is no change in the total amount of phosphorus and potassium. Precautions must be taken to prevent the loss of nitrogen in the composting process.

HANDLING MANURE: Manure can be handled several ways. It can be hauled out directly to the fields as it accumulates, or it can be stored or composted. If it is spring or summer and there is a proper place for it in a field, it should be applied directly, and then disced or plowed right in. *If even one day goes by between applying the manure and discing it in there is a great loss which will be reflected in a lower yield.* Experiments were done where manure was left lying on the soil for about a week before being plowed under and the resultant yield of the plant went down by almost one-half. Organic matter is closely tied in with the general process of the release of nitrogen in the soil and the more organic matter is properly applied to the soil, the more nitrogen will be available to the growing crop and the greater the yield.

Some farmers haul their manure out to the fields daily and, during the winter, put it on top of snow. Especially on a farm that has rolling land there will be disastrous losses where this method is followed.

Spreading manure on land and working it into soil immediately is the farmer's ideal method of preventing nutrient losses through leaching.

STORING MANURE: Unless manure can be properly stored and protected without loss through oxidation and leaching, it should be spread on the land, winter and summer, as soon as possible. In no case should it be applied on land with a considerable slope so that it is washed off during the winter months.

The methods by which manures are stored and kept affect their value to a greater degree than any other one factor. It is almost impossible to prevent loss of nutrients entirely. Sources of loss are (1) escape of the natural drainage occurring in manure, (2) leaching caused by soaking of water through the manure, and (3) losses of the gases of fermentation into the air. Perhaps the best storage is in watertight, covered pits. If stored in the open, manure should be heaped on a level or slightly concave place with a clay base to prevent seepage of the juices into the soil. The heap should be made so high that rain will not soak through from top to bottom, and the top of the heap should be slightly concave to catch rain water. It is well also to cover the heap with a thin covering of topsoil if it must stand for a long time.

In the enclosed pit, the manure soon becomes impregnated and completely enclosed by an atmosphere of carbon dioxide having also a relatively high humidity. Under these conditions manure breaks down semi-anaerobically to form a product that is unusually high in the important nutrient elements. *There seem to be very little or no losses of nitrogen or other elements when manures are fermented in a properly constructed enclosed pit.* The conditions which affect the fermentation or other decomposition of manures are temperature, degree of compactness of the manure, degree of moisture, and the composition of the manure itself. It is especially important to prevent the manure from drying out. When too dry the manure turns white and is said to be "fire-fanged." In this condition manure has lost a considerable portion of its nitrogen, and some of its organic matter which has escaped into the air as carbon dioxide.

The amount of manure that can be produced by various animals can be determined by multiplying the dry matter consumed in the foods by an appropriate factor. For the horse, multiply the weight of the dry matter consumed by 2.1; for the cow, the factor is 3.8; for the sheep the factor is 1.8; and for poultry, the factor is 1.6. To the product of each of these weights, add the weight of the bedding or litter to determine the total amount of manure that will be made.

NUTRIENT LOSSES: The loss of the urine rich in nitrogen and potassium has already been mentioned. Other losses occur as the result of leaching, scattering, and volatilization. Commonly manure is thrown in the barn-yard or other exposed place where it is unprotected from rain. Not infrequently the rain water from the barn roof drains into the manure. If the manure is thrown in small, loose, open piles and exposed to rains, it may, in the course of six months, lose more than half of its fertilizing value. Leaching losses include the nitrogen, phosphorus, and potassium from the solid portion as well as from the urine.

Organic matter and nitrogen in some volatile form are lost by passing into the air in gaseous form. In the decomposition of the manure, the ammonia produced combines with carbonic acid to form ammonium carbonate and bicarbonate. *Losses may be prevented or reduced by the direct hauling of the manure to the field or by protecting it from the various factors which are responsible for the losses. Manure spread on the land and worked into the soil is perhaps in its safest place. The soil has the capacity to rapidly fix large quantities of the plant nutrients carried in the manure.* Very little loss as a rule occurs when manure is hauled directly to the field, except when it is spread on hillsides or on frozen ground, where it may be washed down the slope. In any case, it is better to have the liquid go into the soil where plants are to be grown than to allow it to be absorbed by the barnyard soil or to be washed away in surface drainage.

Leaching by rain may be even more serious, as the total soluble matter is thus removed. A single heavy rain of $1\frac{1}{2}$ inches is equivalent to about one gallon of water per square foot, most of which will percolate through manure in shallow piles and remove a large part of the soluble material in doing so.

AMOUNT OF MANURE: The amounts of fresh excrements produced by farm animals are subject to wide variations, being governed by the kind of animal, age, amounts of food, activity, and other factors. How much is produced annually is given in the following table:

Annual Excrement Per 1,000 Pounds Live Weight

KIND OF ANIMAL	TOTAL EXCREMENTS POUNDS	SOLID POUNDS	LIQUID POUNDS
Horse	18,000	14,400	3,300
Cow	27,000	19,000	8,000
Pig	30,500	18,300	12,200
Sheep	12,000	8,300	4,200
Hen	8,500		

DECOMPOSITION CHANGES: The decomposition changes which take place in manure are briefly:

1. Decomposition of urinary nitrogen. The first change is the formation of ammonia in urine which is lost unless the manure is kept moist and compact.

2. Decomposition of insoluble nitrogen. Next the insoluble nitrogen contained in the solid parts of the excrement undergoes putrefactive changes with the formation of ammonia.

3. Conversion of soluble into insoluble nitrogen. The ammonia and other soluble compounds of nitrogen are used in considerable amounts as food for the bacteria in the manure and are stored in their bodily substance in insoluble form. This nitrogen becomes available when the bacteria die and undergo decomposition.

4. Formation of free nitrogen. Under certain conditions ammonia and nitrates are decomposed with the formation of free nitrogen which escapes into the atmosphere and is thus lost permanently.

5. Decomposition of nitrogen-free compounds. The fibrous parts of the manure which are made up largely of cellulose, lignin, and other complex carbohydrates are eventually broken down with the escape of the carbon into the atmosphere in the form of carbon dioxide, and hydrogen in the form of water. These elements, carbon and hydrogen, escape in such amounts that from $\frac{1}{4}$ to $\frac{1}{2}$ of the original dry matter in the manure is lost. This is the reason for the great shrinkage in bulk during decomposition.

BENEFIT TO CROPS: Some crops are benefited by the application of barnyard manure, while others are damaged or produce crops of poor quality. A good practice is to add manure to the soil for the growing of crops which are benefited by manure, while the unused residue is left for manure-sensitive crops the following year.

1. Grass-lands are generally much benefited by top-dressing with farm manure, either fresh or fermented.

2. Root crops usually respond most satisfactorily to generous applications of stable manure. Some precautions, however, must be taken in the case of potatoes and sugar beets. Excessive amounts of fresh manure on light soils and loams cause the beets to become very large but with a low sugar content. Fresh manure can result in leggy plants.

3. Corn, millet, and leafy crops in general respond favorably to manure, fresh or decomposed.

4. Garden crops in general respond quite favorably to generous applications of manure.

Approximately 25 pounds of manure, to which has been added ten pounds of rock phosphate, per 100 square feet of garden will enrich and condition soils. If it is not well-rotted and larger quantities are used, apply it three or more weeks before planting and incorporate the manure into the soil.

5. Young deciduous trees and shrubs respond favorably to manure, but prefer the decomposed manure.

6. Cereals are injured by large applications of manure. The straw of wheat and barley in particular grows

Percentages of Nitrogen, Phosphate and Potash in Different Manures

Kind of Animal Manure	% Nitrogen	% Phosphate	% Potash
Rabbit	2.4	1.4	0.6
Hen	1.1	0.8	0.5
Sheep	0.7	0.3	0.9
Steer	0.7	0.3	0.4
Horse	0.7	0.3	0.6
Duck	0.6	1.4	0.5
Cow	0.6	0.2	0.5
Pig	0.5	0.3	0.5

very large at the expense of the grain. This condition favors lodging.

7. Tobacco develops large leaves of coarse texture and poor quality when treated directly with large amounts of stable manure.

MANURE, POULTRY

The average hen gives off about 140 pounds of manure a year, or every hundred birds produces about seven tons of manure. It was estimated that a mixture of a winter's accumulation of dropping board and floor litter manure, without adding any other fertilizers, contained two per cent nitrogen, two per cent phosphoric acid and one per cent potash, the three essential elements needed for plant growth. This would mean that each ton of chicken manure would contain 40 pounds of nitrogen, 40 pounds of phosphoric acid and 20 pounds of potash.

Studies of poultry manure made at the Pennsylvania State Agricultural Experiment Station indicate that laying hens, on the average, produce 138 pounds of fresh manure annually having a moisture content of about 76 per cent. A turkey produces 339 pounds of fresh manure with a moisture content of 74 per cent. The N-P-K- composition of fresh hen manure was found to be 1.48 per cent nitrogen, 0.96 per cent phosphoric acid, and 0.47 per cent potash. Fresh turkey manure contains 1.31 per cent nitrogen, 0.71 per cent phos-

phoric acid, and 0.49 per cent potash. Both hen manure and turkey manure tend to lose nitrogen as they age. The loss of nitrogen may be reduced by drying or other methods the simplest and most efficient of which is the dropping pit. The henhouse should contain a brick-sided compost pit large enough to accommodate the bird population. Over the pit are placed coarse wire screening and roosts. The hens loaf and sleep over the pit and the droppings fall into the pit and are immediately composted so that the nitrogen is fixed and unable to escape into the air. Such composted poultry manure can be applied to the soil immediately before seeding or transplanting vegetable crops.

Further experiments with poultry manure on crops showed the following results:

On a hay field of mixed grasses that has been run down, the yield per acre was 1.4 tons. When two tons of chicken manure were spread per acre, the yield rose to 2.4 tons. With four tons of manure, the yield went up to 2.9 tons, and with eight tons per acre, 3.3 tons of hay were cut. There was some lodging of the first cutting when the eight-ton-per-acre rate was used. It was also shown that fall manuring gave 12 per cent larger yields than spring treatments. When the same number of pounds of the three essential nutrients were used, poultry manure produced the same yields as commercial fertilizer, but with a better showing of clover on the manured fields. Because of its high nitrogen and low potash contents, poultry manure is not recommended for legumes such as alfalfa and clover.

When a plot of silage corn was treated with two tons of chicken manure, an acre yielded about 12 tons. Four tons of manure per acre yields about 15 per cent more corn than the two ton application, while eight tons yielded 25 per cent more, and 16 tons yielded 27 per cent more. "The protein content of the silage increased with increasing rates of poultry manure," the experimenters comment.

Adding potash or superphosphate to four tons of poultry manure per acre did not give any significant increase in yields over manure alone. Also there were no noticeable increases in yields when 1,000 pounds of 10-10-10 were added along with four tons of manure. It was also shown in these experiments that two tons of poultry manure were as effective as ten tons of cow manure, on the corn fields. *See also* LIQUID MANURE; COMPOST; FERTILIZER.

MANURE, GREEN: *see* GREEN MANURE

MAPLE: (*Acer*) There are well over 100 different species of maples, almost all of which make handsome ornamental, shade or street trees. They range in height from ten to 120 feet. Many of them are prized for the magnificent coloring of their leaves in autumn. They also have interesting winged seeds or "keys" which spin lazily to the ground.

Some of the most popular maples are:

The red maple, *A. rubrum,* is one of the tallest maples and has blossoms that look like tufts of rich red fuzz instead of flowers; it is often called the swamp maple because it grows wild in wet places. *A. saccharinum,* the sugar maple, is also very tall and is perhaps the most popular species in the East

for lawn and tree planting. The silver maple (also *A. saccharinum*) is extremely hardy and grown from Canada to Florida and west to Nebraska. Norway maple, *A. platanoides,* another tall one, has a variety called Schwedler's maple that has foliage that is bright red in the spring, later turning green. The Oregon or big-leaf maple, *A. macrophyllum,* is hardy only to southern Pennsylvania.

In the medium-size class there are the box-elder, *A. negundo,* a rapid grower to about 60 feet, and very good for shelterbelts; the vine maple, *A. circinatum,* a handsome large shrub or small tree; *A. ginnala* and *A. tataricum,* both 20 feet high; the striped maple or moosewood, *A. pennsylvanicum,* an acid lover reaching about 40 feet; and *A. cappadocicum,* which grows to 50 feet but is not as hardy as the others. The Japanese maples, *A. palmatum,* grow as shrubs or 25-foot trees, and can be grown as pot plants. The mountain maple, *A. spicatum,* is a dwarf about ten feet tall; it does well in rather dry, acid places, and has showy yellow blooms borne in spikes in early spring, followed by drooping reddish seed-clusters.

The vast variety of maples makes it easy to find ones to fit any particular situation. The maple suffers from few diseases in good organic soil, and is virtually immune to insect pests. *See also* TREES.

MAPLE SUGAR: The homesteader or farmer who has some sugar maples can home-produce a fine sweet, or perhaps even earn sizeable extra income from making and selling the syrup and sugar. Several other varieties are also fair to good producers.

March and April is sugaring time from Maine to Minnesota and as far south as Kentucky. Maple sugar, incidentally, was the only sweetening agent the early Americans had, besides wild honey; they produced some 7,000,000 gallons of syrup in 1860. Oddly enough, nobody knows what makes the distinctive maple flavor—as it comes from the tree, maple sap has no flavor. It is acquired in the process of heating the sap to lower its water content.

A tall and very popular tree in the East, the sugar maple—like other maples—suffers little from disease when grown in a humus-rich soil.

The average sugar or black maple tree produces sap with a two to three per cent sugar content. However, sap may contain as little as one per cent sugar, in which case it takes 86 gallons of sap to make one gallon of syrup, or as much as nine per cent. Soil conditions are often responsible for this. Deep, moist soil, loose and mellow with abundant leaf litter and organic matter, produced the most and richest sap in Ohio tests. Even red, silver and Oregon maples, generally poor yielders, gave better-than-average sap under these conditions. These facts indicate that we may someday be managing our sugar trees like regular orchards, feeding with rock fertilizers, mulching, planting cover crops and using other organic practices to raise yields.

A few trees are worth tapping to provide syrup for your family, but for a profitable selling operation you should have at least 30 to 40 mature maples. Sometimes woodlots can be thinned out, cutting all other species for lumber or fuel, to achieve this. Uncrowded maples develop thick crowns that keep down the growth of useless briars and weeds by excluding sunlight. Any grazing on the woodlot should be light.

Cold, brisk nights, with unusually warm days, are "sap weather." Prompt gathering and boiling, plus clean equipment, will insure light-colored, high-quality syrup with fine flavor. Covered buckets that keep out rain or dirt are best. Small amounts of syrup can be boiled on the kitchen stove, but bigger lots call for a roaring fire and a flue-type evaporator, preferably set up in a well-built sap house. Boiling, filtering and packaging all require care, but they can be as much fun as gathering the buckets on a brisk end-of-winter day.

Bulletin No. 38 of the Vermont Agricultural Experiment Station, Burlington, Vt., and Bulletin 397 of Cornell University Agricultural College, Ithaca, N. Y., give excellent information on all aspects of maple sugaring.

MARANTA: The fleshy rootstock of *M. arundinacea,* grown in the tropics, yields arrowroot, a nourishing starch. It survives outdoors only in Florida, but elsewhere it is a handsome subject for greenhouse cultivation, sometimes having variegated leaves. Other beautiful varieties are *M. bicolor* and *M. leuconeura,* both of which have purple, red-spotted or white-banded leaves and do not grow over a foot tall. They are sometimes sold by florists as calathea, and vice-versa. In the greenhouse, marantas need very rich organic soil, biweekly feedings of liquid manure, and ample moisture both in the soil and in the air. A constant temperature of 75 degrees or more, and some shading from the hottest sun, are also recommended. Maranta is often called the prayer plant because its leaves turn up at night like praying hands.

MARCH GARDEN OPERATIONS: *see* GARDEN CALENDAR

MARIGOLD: (*Tagetes*) One of the most easily grown and widely popular annuals, marigolds come in varieties from six inches to four feet tall. The colors range from bright yellow through orange and pure red. Most varieties have strongly scented foliage. All of them flower freely from mid-June until frost, and are excellent for cutting.

The French marigolds are the lowest-growing, and feature single- and double-flowered types. They are fine for bedding. The dwarf forms make good edgings and window box subjects. The taller African marigolds are less bushy and suit the open border. There are chrysanthemum-flowered and carnation-flowered varieties. In addition, many new types appear every season, like the red-and-gold African-French hybrids, and dwarf hybrids which bloom so profusely they are a solid mass of color for weeks on end. There is even a new winter-flowering marigold for greenhouse culture.

CULTURE: All marigolds are good for cutting, *excepting T. Lucida.* This bears a pleasantly-scented foliage although its blooms are less showy than the other varieties. Because of its strong scent, the French or African marigold is not esteemed as a cut flower.

The most rewarding bloom is achieved in hot, sunny, southern exposures. Treat marigolds as a tender annual and sow the seed indoors early to get bloom several weeks in advance of outdoor-planted seed. Set the young plants out when the soil is thoroughly warmed up. Marigolds will give more and better bloom in poor soil than in rich. *See also* ANNUALS; FLOWER GARDENING.

MARINE PLANTS: *see* AQUARIUMS; WATER GARDENS

MARJORAM: (*Origanum majorana*) A widely cultivated perennial plant native to the Mediterranean region. It is commonly known as sweet marjoram, as distinguished from a related species, and is characterized by a pleasant, fragrant, spicy odor and flavor that makes the herb very popular for seasoning soups, stews, dressings and similar dishes.

CULTURE: The plant grows well in any well-drained fertile garden loam. Although primarily a warm-climate plant, it makes good growth in cooler regions but is very subject there to winterkilling unless well mulched with straw or leaves. For this reason it is often grown as an annual. The seed is small and is best started in the greenhouse, the seedlings being transplanted to the field after all danger of frost has passed. Propagation by cuttings is also entirely practical. Marjoram can be grown in many sections of this country, as an annual in the northern states and as an annual or perennial in the South and on the west coast.

Pot marjoram differs from sweet marjoram in being hardier and in having slightly larger leaves without stalks. The scent and flavor are somewhat more thyme-like than those of sweet marjoram. Pot marjoram is harvested and used in the same way as sweet marjoram. Pot marjoram grows best in a light limestone soil. Hardy in the vicinity of New York City, it should be taken indoors where winters are very severe. Propagation is from seed or by division.

MARJORAM, WILD: (*Origanum vulgare*) A hardy perennial with sprawling stems which may become two feet high. Much coarser than sweet marjoram, it smells more like thyme. Small pink or white flowers. Its leaves are used as a flavoring in cooking, but most people do not consider them as good as sweet marjoram leaves. Other than for flavoring wild marjoram is of little horticultural value, except perhaps that its flowers are pleasantly fragrant, making it an attractive honey plant. Beekeepers sometimes plant wild marjoram on run-down land as a honey crop. A surplus of up to 50 pounds may be obtained, according to Vermont beekeepers.

Wild marjoram grows well in poor soil, is propagated by seeds or division.

MARKET DISEASES: Market diseases of fruits and vegetables are those that develop during the process of marketing. This process should be understood to include the harvesting, grading, and packing of the crop, its transportation to market, its storage at shipping point or at the market, and the various handling operations required to move it from the wholesale dealer to the retail store and the ultimate consumer. During any of these operations the product may be subjected to conditions that impair its appearance and food value and render it liable to attack by decay-producing organisms.

Fruits and vegetables are susceptible to invasion by bacteria and fungi at bruises and skin breaks. Hence, it is of prime importance that they be handled as carefully as possible at all times. Clipper cuts, fingernail scratches, injuries caused by packing-house machinery, packing bruises, damage caused by rough handling in transit and on the market are all sources of danger, especially if the places where the fruit is packed, or stored, or offered for sale are not kept free of rotting fruit and other infectious material. These, as well as insect injuries, must all be considered by anyone attempting to judge the storage or shipping quality of the fruit or its ability to hold up well until it is consumed.

Temperature and humidity have a direct effect on the development of decay in fruits. They should have the critical attention of those who wish to ship or store fruits and of those who attempt to determine why a given lot, at any stage in the marketing process, shows decay or other deterioration. Too low temperature may freeze the fruit, or it may cause only chilling injury; subtropical fruits are particularly susceptible to such injury. Too high temperature favors decay and may cause undesirable color changes. High humidity favors the growth of fungi, and low humidity causes loss in weight and possibly shriveling, especially if combined with high temperature. For all of these reasons, the management of storage rooms for citrus and other subtropical fruits and the choice of conditions under which to ship them to market, whether under refrigeration or under ventilation, are not likely to give the best results unless based on an intelligent use of all available information concerning the market diseases of those fruits. *See also* DISEASE.

MARKETING: *see* ORGANIC FOODS, MARKETING

MARL: An oceanic deposit, marl is usually a mixture of lime and fine clay. Greensand marl, for example, is found in New Jersey and has been called excellent as a soil builder. *See also* GREENSAND; MINERAL ROCK; LIME.

MARRAM GRASS: *see* GRASS, ORNAMENTAL

MARSH MARIGOLD: Popping up brightly in swampy areas and along brooks all over the country, marsh marigold provides fresh green food for health-conscious people in the spring. Often called cowslip, it is a member of the buttercup family and one of the tastiest of all the spring greens. Marsh marigold is a strong-growing perennial that thrives in wet spots and will do well in the wild garden, to which it is easily transplanted. Or it will grow nicely in the border if the soil is moist and rich and partial shade is provided. Other suitable growing spots are along shallow streams, around springs and even in roadside ditches. Pick it for cooking just as the first flower buds begin to burst into golden bloom. Marsh marigold grows up to two feet tall and is easily propagated by seeds and division.

MARSILEA: *see* PEPPERWORT

MAST: Forage derived from the fruits of oaks, beeches, and some other trees.

MATHIOLA: *see* STOCK

MATRIMONY VINE: (*Lycium*) Also called box-thorn. Deciduous or evergreen shrubs from the warmer regions of both hemispheres, a genus of the nightshade family. They are often spiny, and tend to become rampant. Most may be propagated from suckers, which tend to be a nuisance. Also propagated from seed, layering, and cuttings. Thrive everywhere, even in sandy soil.

L. *chinense* is not evergreen, but holds its leaves late. It is a shrub with branches often prostrate to 12 feet. Many small purple flowers are followed by one-inch orange-red berries.

L. *halimifolium* is upright or spreading, with curving spiny branches to ten feet. Flowers are dull lilac, fruit red-orange berry about ¾ inch long.

L. *horridum* is a three-foot, much branched, spiny shrub used in South Africa for hedges. Leaves and flowers are small, berries are scarlet.

MAYAPPLE: (*Podophyllum peltatum*) This woodland perennial has a creeping

A fine plant for the wild garden, the Mayapple or Indian apple grows to 1½ feet. A winter mulch of hardwood leaves helps prevent heaving.

rootstock, and is easily propagated by division of this. Its green leaves are often a foot wide, and in May it bears pinkish or white, waxy, cup-shaped flowers, which have a somewhat unpleasant odor. The yellow berries are edible, and the rootstock is used in medicine.

Mayapple is an interesting plant for the wild garden, growing about 18 inches high in rich, well-drained woods soil. It will do well in full or partial shade, and appreciates an annual feeding of bone meal. A winter mulch of hardwood leaves is recommended to prevent heaving. Mayapple is sometimes known as the Indian apple.

MAY GARDEN OPERATIONS: *see* GARDEN CALENDAR

MEADOW: A field or area covered with fine-stemmed forage plants, wholly or mainly perennial and used to produce hay.

MEADOW-BEAUTY: (*Rhexia*) These pretty little perennial wild flowers need wet, acid, sandy soil. The two common varieties, *R. mariana* and *R. virginica* (also called deer grass and handsome Harry), grow from one to two feet high, with purple flowers in clusters. They are found in sandy or pine-barren bogs along the East Coast and west to Texas.

Meadow-beauty is transplanted fairly easily from the wild into boggy sites along the edges of ponds or streams. Naturally boggy soil usually contains large amounts of humus and fiber. Acid peat, decayed hardwood leaves or sawdust are excellent for providing this requirement when making an artificial bog garden. Dig them in or use them as a mulch.

MEADOW PINK: *see* CUCKOO FLOWER

MEALY BUG: (*Pseudococcus maritimus*) These horticultural pests are particularly annoying and harmful on house plants. They are oval with short projections from the body. They often look like bits of cotton fluff because of the eggs carried by the female in a cottony sac. Mealy bugs are sluggish and do not move much.

CONTROL: Mealy bugs may be cleaned off special plants with a cotton swab soaked with alcohol; oil sprays have also been found effective.

A useful method of controlling the mealy bug on pears is reported by the University of California. In the Santa Clara valley, it appears, the natural enemy of this pest is the lacewing fly *Chrysopa californica*. Complete control was obtained by supplying artificially produced eggs to pear orchards.

It was found that the time of egg colonization was extremely important if effective control was to be obtained. The usual routine was to place a batch of about 250 eggs in the crotch of each tree at a time so that the larvae would develop while the immature stages of the first generation of the pest were on the trees. This treatment gave best results when repeated at two successive intervals.

Another interesting facet to this research is that once the mealy bug is suppressed by *Chrysopa californica,* the pest population remains economically low for about two years. *See also* IN-SECT CONTROL.

MEANS GRASS: *see* JOHNSON GRASS

MEDICAGO: *see* ALFALFA

MEDICINAL PLANTS: *see* HERBS; ACONITE; HENBANE; GOLDENSEAL; GINSENG; LICORICE; MELISSA

MELALEUCA LEUCADENDRON: *see* CAJEPUT

MELISSA: (*Melissa officinalis*) Also known as lemon balm, it is a perennial herb native of Southern Europe and has long been cultivated in gardens in this country. In many places in the Eastern States it has escaped and is now growing wild. The leaves are widely used for culinary flavoring, and the leaves and flowering tops are used in medicine. The volatile oil distilled from the plant is said to be used in perfumery and also for flavoring.

CULTURE: Balm grows readily on any good garden soil and is easily propagated from seed or cuttings or by division. The seed is small and is best sown thinly in shallow flats in a greenhouse or in a hotbed on the surface of fine soil, which is then firmed. The seedlings are transferred to deeper flats when small and when four or five inches high are set in the field about one foot apart in rows spaced to suit cultivation, which should be frequent while the plants are small.

MELON: Melons are the fruit of two members of the *Cucurbitaceae* family—the cantaloupe or muskmelon, *Cucumis melo,* and the watermelon, *Citrullus vulgaris.* In the cantaloupe category are included the winter melons, casaba and honeydew; the snake melon used for preserves; the melon-apple or mango melon used for pickling; and a purely ornamental variety, the pomegranate melon. The citron or preserving melon is a variety of watermelon. *See also* CANTALOUPE; WATERMELON.

MENDEL, GREGOR JOHANN (1822-1884), an Austrian botanist and monk, is recognized as the father of genetics, the modern science of heredity. His work with peas, conducted over eight years in an Augustine monastery, resulted in what we call Mendel's laws.

Mendel discovered that plants transmit their characteristics to their offspring in a predictable, mathematical way. He found that crossing a purebred red-flowered pea, for example, with a purebred one with white flowers, produced seeds that all grew into red-flowered plants (F1). He called red-floweredness the "dominant" characteristic. The white-floweredness, however, was still there and so was called "recessive." (Dominance, we now know, is rarely total, the recessive trait expressing itself to some degree, usually in a modification of the dominant.) This, he concluded, was due to a special factor—now known as genes—in the reproductive cells of the plants. Mendel then followed up by self-pollinating his red-flowered hybrids, and obtained seed that gave three red-flowered plants to one white-flowered one (F2). When these in turn were self-pollinated, the white-flowered peas were seen to give only white-flowered plants, while of the red-flowered varieties, one out of three bred true, and the other two produced three red-flowered varieties to one white-flowered variety (F3). Mendel's work thus proved that a minute mechanism within the cells of plants regulates the traits of their descendants in accordance with precise mathematical laws. All further work on heredity has been based on the solid foundation of his discoveries.

Thanks to Mendel, today plant breeders can predict quite exactly the results of dozens of crosses. This has helped them immeasurably to develop plants with specific desired traits valuable to gardeners and farmers.

MENTHA: *see* MINT

MENTHA PIPERITA: *see* PEPPERMINT

MERCURY: see FUNGICIDE

MERTENSIA: Sometimes called lungwort or bluebells, mertensia is a handsome perennial that grows about two feet tall. Its two common varieties are suited to the wild garden and can be easily transplanted there from the wild. *M. ciliata* is found mostly in the Rocky Mountain region, while *M. virginica* is a native of the East from Tennessee northward into New England. The latter is often known as Virginia cowslip. Both have brilliant blue flowers borne in racemes, and *M. virginica* has a variety with pink blooms. They like a moist, rich, humusy soil and semi-shade, imitating the conditions in the woodlands where they are found, but *M. virginica* will do well in the open border if mulched. Because they are hard to divide successfully, new plants should be grown from seed; sow the seed immediately after harvesting it.

MESCAL BEAN: (*Sophora secundiflora*) This handsome, free-flowering evergreen shrub or small tree is hardy in the deep South and along the Pacific Coast. The flowers are showy and fragrant, blue-violet, and borne in panicles. The plant has feathery foliage and bears pods six to eight inches long. Mescal bean does well on practically all types of soils. It is propagated by the seeds, which germinate very slowly, or by greenwood cuttings or layering.

MESEMBRYANTHEMUM: These fleshy-leaved succulents, often called fig-marigolds, bear big, gorgeous flowers which close up at night. Desert plants, they can grow in pure, hot sand; the annuals do best where there is a long growing season and little moisture. Outdoors the perennials can be grown only in dry areas of California and the deep South. They are also popular greenhouse plants, given a sandy soil with a little humus, bone meal and lime. Keep the temperature around 55 to 60° in winter, and plunge the pots outdoors in a bed of sand in full sun for the summer. Be very careful not to overwater. A few days exposure to cold—but not freezing—plus withholding the water, will usually force them into bloom. Propagate by division.

There are hundreds of species. Some of the most popular annuals are *M. crystallinum,* the ice plant, which has white or pink flowers and leaves covered with glistening dots; the leaves are edible and often used like spinach. *M. lineare* is a densely clumped plant with comparatively large red or pink flowers, while the similar *M. criniflorum* has bigger, daisy-like flowers in shades from apricot and buff to crimson. Vetkousie (*M. pomeridianum*) has large yellow flowers and is also edible.

Of the perennials, *M. aureum,* 18 inches high and yellow-flowered, and *M. cordifolium,* with purple flowers, are grown in window gardens. The Hottentot fig (*M. edule*), a sprawling plant with very handsome yellow blooms, is used to cover banks in California, and bears edible fruit.

MESQUITE: (*Prosopis*) A dwarfed, thorn-studded tree averaging 12 feet high that grows abundantly on Southwestern prairie lands. Often considered a pest by some ranchers, research is being done to check the value of ground-up mesquite as a garden fertilizer. It also makes an inexpensive nutritious feed for livestock.

Mesquite beans are similar to those of carob in analysis, and often have served as a human as well as animal food. The beans ripen in August. Plants grow in all types of soil, with the exception of wet ones. The massive root system enables it to grow even in periods of great drought. It produces small, green flowers on rounded spikes.

Honey locust (*P. juliflora*) makes a thorny shrub, growing several feet high. The variety *glandulosa* is useful as a honey plant in the Southwest.

MEXICAN BEAN BEETLE: *see* INSECT CONTROL

MICE: *see* MOUSE

MICHAELMAS DAISY: The late-blooming, hardy perennial asters are known as Michaelmas daisies. They come in a vast number of varieties, most of them hybrids of native wild asters. Their colors range from white and red through the deepest blues and purples, and they vary from one to six feet in height. All of them grow and spread rapidly. Their beauty makes them an excellent subject for massing in beds or for the perennial border, and many of them make fine cut flowers.

A rich soil, moist and deep, is vital for really fine bloom. The soil should be in good tilth for three feet down, and fertilized with compost or manure and bone meal. Every fall or spring, divide the clumps, planting only the strongest divisions from the outside of each clump. Each division should have two or three shoots. With small varieties, set the divisions at least 24

inches apart; with vigorous ones, set them 36 inches apart. Spring bulbs can be interplanted to fill in the spaces until the daisies spread out. Cuttings may also be made in the fall and carried over the winter in the cold frame. You can keep Michaelmas daisies at virtually any desired height by cutting them judiciously in June. Winter mulching with leaves or hay, held down with evergreen boughs or cornstalks, is a sound practice.

MICROBES: *see* MICROORGANISM

MICROBIAL ACTION IN HUMUS: *see* HUMUS

MICROBIAL CONTROL OF INSECTS: *see* INSECT CONTROL, BIOLOGICAL

MICROMERIA: Fine plants for the rock garden or border, both *M. piperella* and *M. rupestris* are low-growing or sprawling perennials of the mint family. They are worth featuring for their fragrant foliage, which smells something like pennyroyal. The tiny flowers are reddish-purple in the first variety, white and lavender-spotted in the second, and appear from July to frost. Micromerias like a well-drained, not very rich, nearly neutral soil. Propagate them by division of the roots in spring. Another variety, the yerba buena, *M. chamissonis,* does not stand cold, wet winters, and is generally grown only along the Pacific Coast.

MICROORGANISM: There are many kinds and weights of microorganisms in the surface foot of soil and there are large numbers of each kind. Each kind of organism plays some significant role in the decomposition of plant and animal residues, liberation of plant nutrients, or in the development of soil structure. Many groups are dependent on each other; consequently one kind may tend to follow another.

According to Nebraska Agronomists T. M. McCalla and T. H. Goodding in their report, "Microorganisms and their effects on crops and soils," they set up a series of reactions in the soil that follow one another in an organized sequence. In size the organisms vary from forms invisible with the ordinary microscope but visible with the electron microscope to those that can be seen with the naked eye. In shape they vary from tiny dots to weird twisted forms. They have the capacity to digest the materials in the soil because they produce enzymes which in different microbial groups form a gigantic, complex enzymatic system that extends throughout the soil. There are few things in the soil—even such resistant materials as hair and horn— that escape digestion.

PHAGES AND VIRUSES: These are the smallest forms of living matter in the soil. Some investigators do not class viruses as living. These minute organisms are so small that they are in the twilight zone between the living and the non-living materials. The phages cause diseases of bacteria and the viruses in the soil cause diseases of higher plants.

get their energy from carbohydrates, fats, proteins or other compounds sythesized in plants or bodies. In the process of obtaining their food from plant and animal residues, bacteria in the soil bring about the decomposition of these materials.

Some of the important soil bacteria are the ones that convert unavailable nitrogen of the soil organic matter to ammonia, and those that convert ammonia to nitrites and then to nitrates. Others are the bacteria in the root nodules of legumes that fix nitrogen. Most of the nitrogen that is returned to the soil from sources outside the soil is fixed by the legume bacteria. Many other bacteria play important roles in the soil. They make nutrients available or unavailable, modify soil structure, and change the air relations of the soil.

The microorganisms in the soil may vary from a very few up to very large numbers in some cases. Certain organisms occur in relatively small numbers. —*Elizabeth McCoy, University of Wisconsin.*

Quantities and Weights of Microorganisms in Soil

Kind	Average number per gram of soil	Average weight in pounds per acre-foot of soil
Bacteria	1,000,000,000	500—1,000
Actinomycetes	10-20,000,000,000	800—1,500
Fungi	1,000,000	1,500—2,000
Protozoa	1,000,000	200— 400
Yeasts	1,000	—
Algae	100,000	200— 300
Worms and insects		800—1,000

BACTERIA: These are the microorganisms that account for the largest numbers in the soil. There are many different types. In shape they resemble balls, cylinders, or corkscrews. Bacteria in the resting stage are resistant to heat, dryness, and other adverse environmental conditions. The spore formers, which constitute about ten per cent of the soil bacteria, are highly resistant when in the spore or resting stage. Higher plants can combine carbon dioxide and water in the presence of sunlight and chlorophyll to make their own food, but bacteria are much like animals in that most of them must

ACTINOMYCETES: Closely related to the bacteria. These organisms are more complicated in structure than the bacteria. The characteristic odor that is evident in newly plowed soil in the spring is due to substances produced by the actinomycetes. Some of the organisms belonging to this group produce plant diseases, such as potato scab. Many carry on the essential activities of decomposing organic matter and making mineral nutrients available for higher plants. A good soil may have 100 to 1000 million bacteria in a gram of soil. Five per cent or more of this number are generally actinomycetes. The growth of actinomycetes on a cultural medium in the laboratory is usually of a leathery nature.

YEASTS: These single-celled organisms are like bacteria except they are larger and their structure is more highly developed. The yeasts make up only a small per cent of the total organisms in the soil. The importance of yeasts in the soil is not known.

FUNGI: The fungi are an essential part of the soil microbial flora. Although fungi may be outnumbered by bacteria per gram of soil, they have a greater mass of growth. These organisms form a maze of tiny threads called mycelium that may enmesh soil particles into granules. Fungi grow best in an aerated soil. Many of them cause plant diseases. However, they decompose organic matter mainly and during the decomposition of plant and animal residues they synthesize some organic matter as cell tissue.

ALGAE: These are microscopic plants that form chlorophyll in the presence of sunlight. They are found in surface layers of soil that is moist, and where light is available they grow as green plants. In the absence of light they grow as other soil microorganisms. Algae change carbon dioxide from the air into organic matter in the presence of sunlight. They take their nitrogen and mineral nutrients from the soil. There may be as many as 100,000 algae per gram of soil under optimum conditions. The development of algae may result in the soil turning green at the surface in moist, shady areas. This is not injurious to plants.

PROTOZOA: These organisms are the simplest form belonging to the animal group. Although they are unicellular and microscopic in size, they are larger than most bacteria and more complex in their activities. Soil may contain as many as 1,000,000 per gram. Protozoa obtain their food from organic matter in the same way as bacteria.

In addition to these microscopic forms there are larger organisms in the soil such as nematodes, earthworms, and insects. All of these play an important part in changing the soil condition and in promoting or hindering crop production.

SOIL ENVIRONMENT: Many factors in the soil environment influence the number and activity of soil microorganisms. Factors of considerable importance are temperature, moisture, aeration and acidity or alkalinity.

Temperature: During a Nebraska winter microbial activity in the soil is largely at a standstill. In the spring, after temperatures reach 50 to 60°F., microbial activity begins to pick up. The optimum temperature for a high state of activity is about 85 to 90°F. In order for microorganisms to decay plant material and develop nitrates at a rapid rate the soil must be warm. Microbial growth is retarded at high as well as at low soil temperatures. Temperatures higher than 100°F. retard or stop the activity of many soil microorganisms.

Moisture: Moisture influences the decomposition of plant and animal residues. When the soil is too dry there is little or no microbial activity. When the soil has optimum moisture the beneficial groups of microorganisms are most active. In a wet soil unfavorable groups such as anaerobic organisms may be active. (Anaerobic refers to microorganisms that grow in the absence of atmospheric oxygen.) They may convert nitrates to gaseous nitrogen sulfates to sulfides, and use up all the oxygen in the soil. Sometimes wet soils are unfavorable for certain plants because of this type of undesirable microbial activity.

Aeration: Generally a well-ventilated soil supports the growth of beneficial microorganisms that convert nutrients to available forms essential for high crop productivity. Soils possessing good structure are usually well aerated. Soil aeration may be improved by good tillage practices. In a soil not adequately aerated, microorganisms compete with each other for the oxygen and some may convert oxidized compounds such as nitrates into a form not available to plants. Sulfates may be converted to hydrogen sulfide, and iron may be converted to a reduced form. Too much moisture may intensify the shortage of oxygen by slowing down the movement of air through the soil.

Acidity or Alkalinity: Certain organisms become inactive in acid soils. The bacteria that occur in the root nodules of legumes and azotobacter which fix nitrogen in an acid soil. Where lime is deficient, nodulation of legumes is often difficult to obtain until lime is added to the soil. In general, fungi are more active in acid soils than are bacteria. In more alkaline soils the actinomycetes become active. Soils that are excessively alkaline may be devoid of the proper kinds of microorganisms or the activity of the microorganisms may be limited or directed along lines that are unfavorable for plant growth. *See also* ACTINOMYCETES; SOIL; FUNGUS; ALGAE.

MIGNONETTE: (*Reseda*) Because of its delightful fragrance, the chief value of mignonette is its use in bouquets of flowers which have no odor of their own. Difficulty is often encountered in getting the seeds to germinate and hot weather is often fatal to plants.

CULTURE: Mignonette is very difficult to transplant, so seeds are always sown where plants are to grow, after which seedlings are thinned. In the North, seeds may go out in late April. Many people, to extend the blooming period, make subsequent sowings into July. When flower-shoots are well set, an application of liquid manure may be applied.

There are many species of mignonette; *M. odorata* is the common one. One of its many varieties, *grandiflora arborea* is quite large and is often grown as an annual. They are also useful in the greenhouse, especially for their cut flowers in winter.

MILD WATER PEPPER: *see* BUCKWHEAT

MILDEW: A fine cobwebby-like growth produced on many plants by a white fungus. The fuzzy growth occurs most abundantly on the top surfaces of leaves and especially in wet seasons. Practically the entire fungus is on the exterior of the plant. Control is by the collection and destruction of affected parts. Thin out the plants to let in sun and air; try to keep plants dry. *See also* DISEASE; FUNGI.

MILKWEED: *see* WEEDS

MILKWORT: *see* POLYGALA

MILKY SPORE DISEASE: One of the few beneficial diseases, only because it has been found to be particularly effective in controlling Japanese beetles. Some time ago, a fungus disease was discovered on the bodies of some of the Japanese beetle grubs which effectively destroyed them. As a result, the milky spore disease, treated with talc, is now sold commercially and is doing yeoman service in destroying the grubs of this pernicious pest. While the mere statement "treated with talc" may make this sound simple, it is in actual practice, a long, complicated, and highly technical process.

Actually, the disease is caused by any one of several milky diseases. Type A, caused by *Bacillus popilliae,* is the most widespread. The germs are taken in by the grubs during their life in the soil and once in the grub they multiply rapidly until millions of spores are formed. These are able to withstand all conditions of moisture or dryness, and are so rugged that there is no known adverse condition which will kill them off. Once in a soil they'll stay there for years, and even spread to new areas as well.

The blood of the Japanese beetle grub is normally clear in color, but once infected with the milky spore disease, the spores make the blood appear milky, hence the popular name of the disease. As the disease advances (which is actually the rapid multiplication of the spores), the grubs die, but the spores within their bodies remain in the soil. Obviously they are taken up by other grubs in the course of their feeding on plant roots and their general life in the soil, and so the disease spreads its death-dealing punch to all Japanese beetle grubs and those of a few closely-related species. This, in turn, leads to a considerable reduction in the number of beetles which emerge from the pupal stage and, therefore, a lessening in the number of eggs which are laid. *See also* JAPANESE BEETLE; INSECT CONTROL.

MILLET: Also known as grain sorghum, produces small, round seeds which bear resemblance to corn in chemical composition, both being richer in fat than most other grains, the fat content of millet being 3.5 per cent. It is also richer in protein, of which it contains 9.0 per cent. Since corn germ has recently been found to contain all the essential amino acids of meat, soy beans and other complete proteins, we may assume that the same should be true of millet. That this is so, is indicated by the experiments of Osborne and Mendel of Yale University, who found that millet, when served as an exclusive food, is able to supply all essential amino acids necessary for normal growth and maintenance, which would indicate that it contains a protein of high biological value.

The grain sorghums comprise three varieties: the *Dwarf* and *White Milo* (to which milo maize belongs), which is the best variety for grain; the *Kafirs,* a sorghum with a more juicy stem, which is better adapted for forage purposes; and the *Kaoliangs,* a sorghum grain which has been used as a human food in India and northern Africa since time immemorial.

The sorghum grains were first introduced into this country in 1874, when they were brought over from Egypt and first planted in California. As they can withstand more drought than other field crops they did very well

in this part of the country. In the Imperial Valley, in Southern California, 150,000 acres of milo maize were cultivated in 1918, yielding on an average a ton an acre.

Grain sorghums, or millets, served as a basic food in southern Egypt for many centuries. In fact, millet is one of the oldest foods of the human race; and was grown as a grain crop since man first commenced to cultivate the earth. Since that time it has constituted a basic food of a considerable percentage of the world's population. At present one-third of the human race living in the Orient uses millet as a daily food. In China millet has been cultivated for at least 5000 years; and in India the consumption of millet is greater than that of wheat. Contrary to popular ideas on the subject, the Japanese, like the Chinese, are millet-eaters as well as rice-eaters.

CULTURE: Sorghum should be grown in regions with hot, extended summers. It is most successful in areas below Virginia, Tennessee and Oklahoma. Sorghum thrives best on a sandy loam and is cultivated much the same way as corn, except that hilling is not necessary.

MIMOSA: A quick-growing and blooming tree, with as fragrant a blossom as any except possibly the magnolia. Given ordinary care, it is quite hardy and grows fast. It makes fine shade and has the added advantage in normal seasons of shedding leaves which are so tiny and brittle that they go into the ground and do not have to be raked.

It often occurs that once two or three trees start to bloom and the seed pods fall on the ground in winter, in the spring there are many new mimosa plants.

CULTURE: If you are planting the seeds or seed pods, they should be given the same care and rich soil that you give any vegetable or flower that you grow in a bed to transplant later.

The seeds, by the way, look very much like apple seeds and are about the same size. When the plants come up, they can be transplanted to the garden until they grow a little larger, or put where you want them to grow permanently. If you are putting them out in their permanent place, follow the same procedure as for larger plants but be sure to fill in with rich soil and keep them watered and mulched well until they begin to grow.

If setting out large plants, you will need a hole from one to two feet deep, depending on the length of the root. The roots of a mimosa generally grow almost straight without much branching out until they get older. When you are transplanting, be sure to get the tap root or the main stem. The smaller roots are not too important. Be sure the hole is several inches deeper than the length of the root as it should be planted straight down. If the subsoil is very hard and dry, fill in the hole with richer soil and compost. In ordinary soil which will grow vegetables like corn or tomatoes or beans, this is not necessary. Just cover with the soil removed from the hole.

While the plants are young and until they get a good start (a year or two) they should be mulched and kept watered. Watering is the most important step in getting a good start of mimosas. In selecting plants, you will find that the small ones, one to two feet high, may grow faster than the taller ones, and if you find it necessary to brace them to straighten them, you can do that much more easily when they are small. After they get a good firm root and are a few feet tall, you can forget them. They will not require any more attention except pruning at times.

GROWTH: If you plan to have several in your yard, set them out about ten or 15 feet apart. Even at that after several years, they will probably touch each other. At that distance apart they make a good shade but still let in plenty of light and air.

The growth of the tree depends a lot on the moisture and mulching you give it for the first two or three years. Under normal conditions, it will grow about two to four feet a year in height, and bloom in about four years. That is not an exact figure as some trees bloom much earlier than others. To insure blooms, you will find that mimosas are like holly and many other trees—you will need two or more. Sometimes single ones bloom and sometimes they do not.

In a tropical climate, mimosas are considered as shrubs and do not grow very large, but in a moderate climate, they grow from ten to 20 feet tall in about ten years. The blooms come in clusters and look very much like pink and white silk threads fitted into a yellow pincushion. Blooms usually are light or dark pink which fades into white at the base. Mimosas are sometimes confused with the acacia. It is true that the acacias are of the mimosa family but those in the United States grow mostly in the Southwest, or in greenhouses, and have yellow blossoms somewhat similar to our native mimosas but not exactly like them.

TRIMMING: Trimming is important in getting a well-shaped tree. After a few years, the branches will begin to grow so thick and fast you will have to trim them back to keep your tree growing upward instead of branching out too far down. If the lower branches are not kept trimmed off, they hang too close to the ground and break off. The trimming every two years sounds like a great deal of trouble but it is well worth it in the beautiful well-shaped trees you have when they are grown. When trimmed in this way, the trees will be something of the shape of an umbrella, being widest across the top, which is where most of the blooms are.

In the spring when the mimosas are late coming out and other trees are already in full leaf, you may have a tinge of regret about mimosas but later on in the year you will be doubly glad you have them. The lovely fragrant blossoms cover the trees; the scent of the blossoms fills the house and yard all day and all night long. Also if you live in a part of the country where there are humming-birds, you will find that they will flock to the mimosa blossoms just as they do to petunias and honeysuckle.

If you are wondering if mimosas will grow in your part of the country, remember that if you can grow ordinary garden vegetables and flowers, and can keep them watered, you can probably succeed with mimosas.

Sensitive plant (*M. pudica*), also known as humble plant, is a low-growing perennial with purple flowers. It is mainly grown in Florida and the Gulf states.—*Jean Bible.*

MIMULUS: *see* MONKEY-FLOWER

MINERAL ROCKS: Every alert farmer and gardener is a practical geologist. Some may disclaim any knowledge of geologic science, especially if they have not made a formal study of it. However, casual inquiry will reveal that most farmers have discovered, through close observation of the earth, many of the principles of geology.

One fact about which there is no doubt—every grower should be interested in the geology that applies to his own farm and soil.

The popular idea of geology is that it is a science of rocks, but the study of rocks and soil is only one segment of a broad field. Equally important are such topics as land and soil erosion, the silting up of low places, the occurrence of artesian and spring water, and the formation of coal, oil, and metallic ore deposits.

Furthermore, the rise of mountain ranges and their reduction by wind, water, and glacial ice; caves, dunes, river flood plains, wind-blown loessial and glacial deposits, geysers, earthquakes and volcanoes are all the concern of geology. Even the principles involved in the artificial terracing of fields are geological.

THE ROCK CYCLE: Solid rock underlies every part of the earth. Although not even a boulder may be in sight on a river flood plain, on the ocean beach, or amidst thick deposits of loessial soil, if a drill bit is sent down, it will sooner or later encounter hard, solid rock.

All solid rocks are classified by geologists into three major groups: *igneous* or formerly molten rocks, *sedimentary* or layered rocks, and *metamorphic* (changed) rocks. Besides having different origins, certain mineral and chemical compositions characterize each group. Because the different compositions influence soil types, erosion, and economic products their differences are of practical importance.

Igneous rocks (they have also been called the primary rocks) are those which solidified from hot, molten, liquid rock material. Lava flows which emerge from volcanoes, and volcanic cones which rise as mountains are composed of igneous rock. For example, Mt. Rainier, Shasta, Paricutin, Lassen and others in the U. S. are built of volcanic igneous rocks. Much of Oregon and Washington in the Columbia River region are surfaced by huge black lava flows. All of the occurrences of igneous rocks mentioned so far have solidified outside or on top of the earth's surface. The igneous rock called basalt is common in flows.

Long after solidification has been complete, the originally subsurface igneous body may be exposed by prolonged erosion and removal of the rock cover. Alternatively, earth movements (from which earthquakes are generated) may break the outer earth's crust and push the solidified igneous mass outward until it is exposed. By these ways, granite comes to the surface and becomes patent rock for soil or available for quarrying. Large parts of the Appalachian Mountain chain, the eastern Ozarks, cores of the Rocky Mountain ranges, parts of the Great Lakes region, and the central portion of the Sierra Nevada range are examples of raised and exposed intrustive igneous rocks.

If we examine closely the igneous rocks of these mountain cores we find most of them to be granites, or granite-like rocks. Granites are coarse grained; that is, the grains are coarse enough to be distinguishable with the unaided eye. They are hard, and are glassy in luster. Usually granites are gray, pink or red. If we examine the grains of the rock closely we see at least two different kinds of mineral grains. Minerals are the unique constituents, relatively constant in composition, which are intergrown to give rise to rocks.

THE MINERALS IN GRANITE: One variety of the mineral grains in granite is white or pink, semi-opaque, and breaks so as to leave tiny flat-surfaced faces. This is potash feldspar which contains about 16 per cent potash. Other feldspars contain calcium and sodium, but the feldspar of granite is characteristically a potash feldspar. Upon weathering, it will release potassium—somewhat grudgingly, however The release of potash from feldspar is facilitated to a practical degree by pulverizing. It is recommended to organic farmers.

Granite also contains clearer, harder, and more glassy mineral grains. These are quartz, whose composition is silicon dioxide. Quartz when reduced to sand size comprises most of the sand in soil, and bars, beaches, dunes, and standstones. Quartz has no nutrient value to plants.

Granites commonly contain also tiny flakes of mica, which is usually green to black, but may be colorless or water-white. Mica can be identified by its habit of flaking off, or cleaving, and because it is relatively soft.

Soils which have been derived from the weathered products of granite are usually gravelly or sandy because of the abundance of quartz (silica). Their clay comes from the weathering of feldspar. Pulverized granite when used as an agstone carries the excessively high content of silica shown above, and tends to weather slowly. Usually volcanic ash or leucite-containing igneous rocks which run higher in potash and lower in silica than granite, decompose more readily than does granite.

BASALT AND ITS MINERALS: We have mentioned the black lava flows which occur in Washington and Oregon The igneous rock which makes up the black lava is called basalt. Basalt is simply a rock name like granite, except that basalt is fine-grained, dark-colored, and contains a different assemblage of minerals (and therefore a different chemical composition) than granite. The fineness of grain is due to rapid cooling and solidification on the earth's surface. Where basaltic lava solidified below the surface (and therefore more slowly) it gives rise to coarse-grained, dark-colored rock which is called gabbro or diabase.

Basalts are more susceptible to weathering than are granites. They contain less silica and more calcium and magnesium. Hence, pulverized basalt may be preferred as an agstone over granite. Soils derived from basalts are rich in clay and iron oxides. Iron oxides are deep red, yellow, and brown in color, except where abundant organic matter is present to reduce the oxides to compounds which are on the dark gray, to greenish black side. Soils from basalt may be fertile as far as inorganic elements are concerned.

The basalt group of rocks contains several varieties which make them especially valuable and desirable as agstone because of their mineral and chemical compositions.

WEATHERING: The next logical step in the geological story of the rock cycle is that of weathering, followed by the eventual formation of sedimentary rocks. Weathering slowly but surely attacks and reduces even the hardest of igneous rocks. It is well that it does, otherwise there would be no soil. The agents or forces of weathering include the rain and ground (soil) water, acid clays, soil humic acids, plant roots, bacteria, oxygen, carbon dioxide, the atmosphere, freezing and thawing, glaciers, and others.

The net result of weathering on rocks is to convert them into groups of weathered products: the insoluble soil material, and the soluble substances that are leached away in clear (and muddy) spring or stream water.

Clay minerals are developed from weathered feldspars, and the dark minerals which are present in basalt. Quartz sand comes from the quartz in granite. Red and brown iron oxides result from the weathering of iron-containing minerals. The clay, the quartz sand, and the iron oxides are insoluble; therefore they remain behind as a soil-forming cover or mantle, or they may be eroded or washed away in suspension as muddy stream water.

The calcium, magnesium, and sodium are easily dissolved in ground water during the weathering of rocks and are thereby quickly leached away. That explains why the calcium of even a soil derived from limestone (rich in calcium) may be entirely removed in a region of humid climate. Water containing abundant calcium and magnesium in solution is hard water.

Potassium may be leached only partly. Because of its ionic size and chemical properties it is usually held rather firmly on to the clay. It may be semi-permanently fixed on the clay.

The residuum of weathered rock products, which accumulate as soil represents only a temporary halt in its march to eventual deposition in the sea as sedimentary rock. We prolong its stay as soil by terracing and control of erosion. The control of erosion is an interesting application of geological principles.

During the time we preserve the weathered rock products from an early removal by erosion and hold them as soil material we try to extract as much of the plant nutrients as possible.

After we have robbed them of as much nutrient as we can, we add new reserves in the form of pulverized, unweathered rock (or fertilizers) and employ the soil further as a support for and transfer of nutrients to plant roots. The soil mantle is being thickened slowly by Mother Nature as she weathers the soil rock beneath the subsoil, but that weathering proceeds at only a tiny fraction of the speed by which the loosened surface soil can be removed.

From the viewpoint of the strict geological process, the fate of the weathered products is movement toward a lower resting place, the sea floor. Suspended sand and mud, and the dissolved calcium, sodium, magnesium, etc., are poured out into the ocean. Gravel, sand, silt, and clay mud progressively, settle out in the quiet water. They are sorted (imperfectly) as to particle size, the coarser being deposited first, and the finer mud in quieter water. They become sedimentary rocks.

The sodium remains in solution in the ocean. The brine of the ocean is a solution of sodium chloride.

The calcium, however, does not long remain in solution but ends up as deposits of limestone on the sea floor, like lime scale on the bottom of a tea kettle. Several processes contribute to the deposition of limestone. For example, the ocean water evaporates (which moisture blows back in clouds over the continents and falls again as rain on the land) and leaves after evaporation the beds of calcium limestone on the shallow portion of the ocean floor. Furthermore, many marine animals, such as oysters, extract the calcium from the water to make shells which accumulate into fossiliferous limestone beds. This explains the source of calcium in oyster shell grits which are fed to chickens, providing calcium for egg shells.

SEDIMENTS: The sediments which are brought to the ocean by streams are consolidated as more and more sediment is piled upon them, and eventually they become solid, firm rock. These sediments were deposited in thin to thick beds or layers of mud, of sand, or of lime. Hence they become layered or stratified rocks. Strata, beds, or layers distinguish sedimentary rocks, and often furnish a clue to that kind of rocks which may be seen far off in an exposed cliff, mountain, or bank of a stream.

Wide deposits of sand, as on beaches, dunes, river bars, or in important offshore sand deposits in the ocean, will become formations of sandstone upon being consolidated. Indeed, most of the sandstones now found on land, and cemented, even in high mountains, were once sand deposits beneath the sea. The hard, relatively insoluble quartz grains which predominate in sandstones were originally derived from granite. A sandstone represents a segregation of sand, one of the "refined or purified" weathered products of granite. The purer the sandstone, the richer it will be in quartz, but thereby the leaner in nutrient elements. Fertility in a soil derived from sandstone arises only from non-quartz "impurities" and organic matter.

The mud which settles to the bottom of the near-shore ocean floor gives rise to layers which form rock called shale. It is really a compacted mud rock, which usually contains accessories of sand, lime, iron oxides, organic matter and a wide variety of chemical compounds and mud. We know from general experience that clay is a greedy absorbent for almost anything it contacts, and natural, shale-forming clay is no exception. Therefore, shales are rich in a variety of elements.

Shales, after being raised to land above sea level and upon being subjected to weathering, return to a clay-rich soil. The soil is relatively heavy if the shale source is rich in clay, but a sandy shale weathers to a sandy soil.

The calcium which was deposited from sea water through the ways described previously becomes layers of limestone (calcium carbonate). Some limestones, the dolomites, may contain magnesium in varying quantities.

A few limestones are slightly phosphatic. Some limestones in Arkansas contain "impurities" of manganese carbonate which is readily soluble and is an available source of the trace element manganese. Some limestones and dolomites carry green glauconite, the mineral of greensand, which contains potassium. Limestones may be sandy, or clayey, because sand and clay mud were mixed with the lime on the muddy ocean floor. The impurities, or better, the accessories, of limestone and dolomite provide another source of fertility and a source of trace elements in limestone used as agstone. Previous emphasis on high purity of agricultural limestone has been misleading.

Besides the big three of sedimentary rocks (sandstone, shale, and limestone), several others are interesting to farmers because of their special compositions and potential uses.

ROCK PHOSPHATE: Raw rock phosphate is a sedimentary deposit which may represent an accumulation of phosphatic organic residues, or a replacement of an earlier calcium limestone by phosphate. It may originate also as a direct precipitate in the ocean. Besides the phosphate deposits rich enough to be exploited at a profit, there are countless tons of lean phosphatic limestones and phosphatic shales which would be most valuable as soil replenishers. Besides their phosphate, they contain many other naturally deposited trace elements.

Farmers should be strongly urged to make intensive inquiry from their local geologists and state geological surveys as to the location of accessible phosphate-bearing rocks which have been too low in phosphate to attract commercial production. Many of these can be worked locally and during spare times by farmers to their own benefit.

POTASH ROCKS: The beds of salt (rock salt) and potash minerals (like those in the New Mexico-Texas region) represent mineral residues of evaporated salt lakes and cut-off arms of the sea. Suppose, for instance, that the narrow Straits of Gibraltar were to be uplifted by earth movements, and that no artificial Suez Canal had been constructed. The Mediterranean would become by such earth movement a salty body of water isolated from the ocean and located in a warm part of the earth where evaporation would exceed rainfall. Within short geological time the Mediterranean would evaporate until a shrunken lake would result, and which would be so concentrated by evaporation that ordinary salt, potash, magnesium, boron and other minerals would be deposited. That is the way by which most gypsum, salt, potash, and borax deposits originated.

Glauconite, a soft green mineral composed of potassium, iron and silica, forms under special sedimentary conditions in the ocean. The New Jersey greensands contain mainly glauconite. Trace elements are also associated with the glauconites. Fortunately, dolomites and limestones which contain sparse to rich streaks of glauconite occur in many states in our Union. A glauconite dolomite will contribute calcium, magnesium, potassium, and trace elements to the soil when used as agstone.

Flint or chert pebbles and gravel are abundant and common over many miles of land. This rock is a solid variety of silica. It has the same chemical composition as quartz, and is almost as resistant to weathering as is quartz. No wonder it remains in the soil, in stream beds, and lasts long as road gravel. Chert originates from the small amount of soluble silica which is liberated during the weathering of feldspars, and which later is deposited in solid form. Obviously, it does not contain useable plant nutrients.

Sedimentary rocks, those discussed above, cover something like 75 per cent of the land on our earth, hence they are exceedingly important to farmers.

METAMORPHIC ROCKS: Rocks whose characteristics show them to have been later impressed with a secondary origin are the metamorphic rocks. As their name indicates, they are changed rocks —changed from the original. We have noted before that sedimentary rocks may be piled up thickly so that the lowest ones become deeply buried and heavily weighted. Igneous rocks may solidify beneath the earth's surface. All of these rock areas may be violently upheaved or depressed, crushed or squeezed by mountain and continent making earth movements. They may be baked or heated by various sources of heat.

Under the stress of the tremendous forces of mountain making, and under the conditions of high temperature due to deep burial or frictional movements, augmented by the heat of igneous action, rocks may be changed. Despite the rocks being as strong as they are—and as inert chemically as we know them— under the severe conditions of metamorphism they actually flow like taffy candy or "marbelized cake dough," and recrystallize like a squeezed snow-ball recrystallizes to ice. The changes produced during metamorphism are startling, and at first almost unbelievable. However, the evidence is sound and unquestioned. Indeed, metamorphism has been partially duplicated on a small scale in furnaces and under terrific laboratory pressures. No scientist questions for a moment the validity of the metamorphic process.

The detailed mineralogical and chemical changes which rocks undergo during metamorphism are highly technical. The broad changes are easily recognized and understood, and will be described below. Pre-existing igneous, sedimentary or metamorphic rocks may be metamorphosed to produce thick or coarsely banded, thinly banded to slaty rocks, marbles, and less well defined varieties.

GNEISS: Coarsely banded metamorphic rocks usually appear like banded granites, and are called gneiss (pronounced "nice"). The minerals in the gneiss are usually feldspar and quartz, with dark minerals like those which occur in basalt. Therefore, their response to weathering and other erosion is similar to that of granite.

Thinly banded metamorphic rocks may be of parallel aggregates of platy mica, or of microscopic parallel bundles of dark hornblende needles (like the horneblende in basalt). These thinly banded metamorphic rocks are called schists: mica schists, or hornblende schists. Mica schists weather and respond much the same as the mica of granite, which is resistant to weathering and exceedingly scanty in delivery of nutrients. Hornblende schists weather to form clay, iron oxides, and liberate calcium and magnesium compounds.

Slate, the rock which is split into roofing material and blackboard panels, is the metamorphosed product of shale. The clay minerals in shale have been converted during metamorphism into tiny parallel mica flakes which shed rain or snow without slaking as shale would do. Because of this ability to resist the action of the weather, well metamorphosed slate is not readily converted into fertile soil. Weakly metamorphosed slate, however, may be decomposed and weathered similarly to shale.

Metamorphic rocks tend to respond to geologic process in much the same way as their igneous and sedimentary heredity would suggest. Gneisses and schists, because they contain igneous-type minerals, behave like igneous rocks.

EVOLUTION OF ROCKS: The course of rock alteration and evolution has been traced from igneous to sedimentary and metamorphic rocks. All three types, igneous, sedimentary, and metamorphic, may undergo more weathering and then become new sedimentary rocks, or all three may be further metamorphosed. Furthermore, under certain conditions they may be redissolved by the action of hot mineralizing solutions and revert to igneous rocks. Thus rock changes are potentially cyclic, and geologists regularly refer to the entire series of changes as the Rock Cycle. The story of the rock cycle organizes in a broad way our knowledge of the major earth materials.

Farmers and geologists will never run out of rocks. Neither is there serious prospect of new types developing. If one familiarizes himself with the important types covered in this article, he will be prepared to recognize old rock friends anywhere on the globe, even if he does not fully understand the work of the man who lives on them. Agriculture and geology are cosmopolitan sciences, indeed.—*W. D. Keller, Professor of Geology, University of Missouri.*

See also PHOSPHATE ROCK; POTASH ROCK; BASALT; GREENSAND.

MINERALS IN FOOD: *see* NUTRITION

MINIATURE GARDENS: *see* TERRARIUMS

MINIATURE PLANTS: In recent years, botanists have discovered, and plant breeders have developed, numerous smaller varieties of favorite garden plants. These can be used to advantage in many situations, for special effects, or to make the most of cramped space.

The miniature flowers are especially enchanting, their form and blooms perfect replicas of their bigger prototypes. Among the most delightful are the miniature daylilies (some of which grow only eight inches tall), the English lilliput chrysanthemums, dwarf dahlias, miniature gladioli and dwarf Oregon asters. The tiny irises, *Iris pumila* and *I. chamaeris,* are miniatures of bearded iris. Dwarf bleeding heart is another recent one. As with all classes of plants, the list of miniature varieties—of which we can name here only a few—grows longer every season.

Some of the best new varieties of flowering shrubs which might be loosely called dwarfs are the White Hedge snowberry, hybrid daphne Hever Castle, dwarf pearl bush The Bride, Frosty Morn mockorange, Gold Drop potentilla and Swan Lake spirea. Several of these stay under three feet, while their relatives are double that. Little Gem arborvitae and Crimson Pygmy barberry, for instance, never grow over a foot tall.

The dwarf fruit trees that so often serve as the backbone of the organic gardener's food production scheme are, of course, well known. But there are also many valuable miniature vegetables. Many of them grow less than half the size of the standard species. Golden Midget sweet corn, for example, is only two feet tall, but the ears have delicious, full-sized kernels. Some other miniatures are Tiny Tim and Window Box tomatoes; Tom Thumb lettuce; Mincu baby cucumbers; New Hampshire midget watermelon; Little Marvel peas; and Minnesota midget muskmelon. You can get sweet potatoes with vines that spread only three feet, bush squashes with short runners, or peas which grow only 15 inches high. There is even a miniature popcorn! All of these space savers are valuable to the organic gardener who aims to get the biggest possible yields from his vegetable plot.

These, of course, are only a few of the new plants that can be called miniatures. Hunting through the catalogs will produce a much more comprehensive list. Such a hunt can be fun and rewarding, particularly if your garden is small. But even in the larger garden, miniature plants used with ingenuity can produce interesting effects not possible with their bigger relatives.

MINT: (*Mentha*) The mint family is outstanding for the fragrance of its foliage. The mint family is large and is divided into 160 groups. Many herbs, for example, thymes, sages and marjorams, are also in this family.

The value of the useful mint lies in volatile oils produced on their leaves and stems. These oils are found in tiny glands which can be seen with a magnifying glass. If a hand is brushed against the plant some of the oil is released and clings to the skin.

Peppermint (*M. piperita*) is a hybrid—a cross between spearmint (*M. spicata*) and water mint (*M. aquatica*). Even spearmint itself is thought to be the result of a cross between apple mint (*M. rotundifolia*) and long-leaved mint (*M. longifolia*). There are many other hybrid mints and even the true species are highly variable, so the naming of the many kinds of mints has become involved and uncertain.

Despite the confusion in naming many of the mints, some of the most commonly grown ones are reasonably definite and can be recognized. Among these are four which produce their flowers in slender spikes. These are peppermint, spearmint, apple mint and long-leaved mint. Peppermint can be distinguished from the other three because its leaves are on small stalks; the leaves of the others have very short stalks or none at all. Of these, spearmint can be recognized by its almost hairless leaves. Apple mint and long-leaved mint have hairy leaves, but those of apple mint are quite rounded, the leaves of the other longer and more narrow.

When "mint" is spoken of, usually spearmint is the one being referred to. It is the one most often used in making mint jelly, sauce, juleps and so on. Apple mint and long-leaved mint are probably just as useful, but their wooliness has kept them from becoming so popular. Another mint, *M. niliaca,* has leaves that are so velvety that English children call them "fairy blankets." This is a tall mint, growing to three or four feet in height, and it is thought to be a hybrid between apple mint and either spearmint or long-leaved mint.

Water mint (*M. aquatica*) bears its flowers in little rounded balls at the tips of the stems and in the axils of the uppermost leaves. The leaves are egg-shaped, have stalks, and are somewhat hairy. One well known variety of water mint has crisped or crinkled leaves and is sometimes called *M. crispa*. There are also forms of other mints that have crisped leaves. Bergamot or lemon mint is very likely also a form of water mint with smooth, hairless leaves.

Pennyroyal (*M. pulegium*) is quite different in appearance from the other mints. It is a much-branched, prostrate perennial with its flower heads in the axils of rather long leafy stalks. Its delightful fragrance was believed to drive away fleas, hence its scientific name which is derived from "pulex," the Latin for flea.

Mountain mint (*Pycnanthemum tenuifolium*) is a very fragrant mint with very slender leaves. It is common in the eastern states west to Minnesota and Texas in old pastures and fields.

Corsican mint (*M. requieni*) is a delightful little creeping plant with minute, rounded leaves, forming an almost moss-like mat. When lightly brushed it emits a very strong, pleasing odor of mint. It is sprinkled in late summer with little lavender blossoms. Corsican mint reportedly is used to flavor liqueurs, and is delightful as a ground cover for small spots.

It thrives in moist shade, but will also grow in sun. Since it does not survive cold winters unless well covered by snow, it is better to keep indoors in pots over winter. Propagation is by division.

M. viridis, known simply as mint, is a hardy perennial plant, found growing in abundance along the roadsides in many places. It is often grown in gardens, however, and is used in soups, sauces, salads, etc., very generally. It is of the easiest culture. It is increased by divisions of the root, and planted at distances of a foot apart; it quickly forms a mass, which may be cut for many years without renewal. It is grown to a considerable extent in hotbeds and forcing pits, in the same way as lettuce. Its treatment there is very simple, being merely to lift up the roots in solid mass, placing them on the three or four inches of earth in the hot-bed

or bench of the forcing house, and water freely as soon as it begins to grow.—*George Kalmbacher.*

See also HERBS; SPEARMINT; PEPPERMINT.

MINT GERANIUM: *see* COSTMARY

MIRABILIS: *see* FOUR-O'CLOCK

MIST: *see* GYPSOPHILA

MISTLETOE: The pretty mistletoe that brightens our Christmases is not strictly a garden plant, but a parasite that grows on trees. Common mistletoe, *Phoradendron flavescens,* grows from New Jersey southward, while in the West there are several other species.

The Western dwarf mistletoes, *Arceuthobium,* are called "slow killers" because their roots invade the bark and wood of the host tree, stealing water and nutrients and eventually destroying it. The plant can be removed by pruning out the branch on which it is growing 18 inches back of the shoots, but where the shoots are closer than this to the trunk, it has usually invaded the trunk and nothing can be done. Dwarf mistletoe attacks conifers, and has done more damage in Western coniferous forests than any other pest or disease except heart rot. Unlike common mistletoe, which is spread only by birds, it has an "explosive" seed, which is shot out of its casing as far as 60 feet. If it lands on a young, healthy branch of a suitable host, a new plant soon appears. Dwarf mistletoes have recently been found as far east as Connecticut.

The common mistletoe is less damaging and is generally found on deciduous trees, particularly the oak, and on junipers. Contrary to common belief, it can be cultivated as follows:

Save holiday mistletoe, or gather fresh berries in the spring which will have more germinating power. Squeeze the berry until it bursts, then simply stick the seed to the underside of a young twig by means of its gummy coating. Sometimes it helps to scrape the twig lightly first, or make a cut in the bark—birds usually push the seed into a crack while trying to rub off the sticky juice. To be sure of getting more than one plant, necessary for germination, stick on at least half a dozen seeds. It takes about a year before the first leaves appear, but thereafter growth is rapid. Apple, poplar and hawthorne are among the best host trees. An enterprising homesteader or farmer can make extra income by doing this in an old orchard.

MITCHELLA REPENS: *see* GROUND COVER

MITES: *see* INSECT CONTROL

MOCK ORANGE: (*Philadelphus*) Shrubs of the Mock Orange family are among the most desirable flowering shrubs for the garden. They are easily grown and maintained, and in recent years many new hybrids have been introduced. Some of these are not as tall growing as the older varieties, and are useful in many positions in the garden, where they will add interest and beauty.

The *Philadelphus* is one of the oldest shrubs in cultivation, having been grown in gardens for the past three or four hundred years. In olden times both the Mock Orange and Lilacs were known as *Syringa*. Linneaus separated them, keeping the Lilac as a true *Syringa,* and he gave the Mock Orange the name of *Philadelphus*.

Lemoine of Nancy, France, hybridized many of these shrubs. In 1883 he developed one which was known as *P. lemoine* and was extensively planted for years.

P. coronarius is an old garden favorite and the common Mock Orange, growing to ten feet high. It forms a large dense shrub with fragrant white flowers. There are a number of hybrids of this and other species.

A shrubbery might be composed en-

Mock Orange *(Philadelphus virginalis)* offers a fine display of flowers in late spring or early summer. A most popular shrub for lawn, border or foundation plantings, it has large, semi-double flowers.

tirely of Mock Oranges, using several of a kind, the tall ones at the back and the lower growing ones in front.

P. virginalis presents a fine display of flowers in late spring or early summer, and is a popular shrub with large semi-double flowers. It is often used for forcing.

P. Belle Etoile is a Lemoine hybrid of which the single white flowers have a purple blotch at the base of each petal.

PLANTING: In planting these shrubs prepare the ground well for them. Dig the hole three times as deep and wide as the ball of roots. They thrive in a sandy loam. In the bottom of the hole place some well-pulverized compost and mix with good soil. Set the shrub in the center of the hole and be sure it is straight. Fill in around the ball of roots and when the hole is three-quarters full of soil, run water in to settle it, being sure to give enough water to reach down below the roots. Fill in with more soil and make a basin around the shrub to hold water.

PRUNING: Immediately after the flowering season is over is the right time to prune these shrubs. The new shoots produced during the summer will carry the flowering wood for next year. If the shrubs are not pruned till autumn or winter, there will be few if any flowers, for the flowering shoots will have been cut off.

To keep Mock Orange bushes in good condition and flowering freely, some of the old wood should be thinned out when the main stems become congested, as they usually do on old specimens. Cut them at ground level. This should be done immediately after the flowering season is over so new growth may be produced while the weather is warm and growth is active. The flowering branches for the following year will have more space in which to develop.

A fine hybrid is *P. atlas,* which grows upright to a height of four or five feet, and has crisp white flowers.

P. innocence has graceful, arching branches, covered with delightfully fragrant single white flowers. Stock may be increased by cuttings or layering.

P. mexicana, the evergreen Mexican Mock Orange, may be grown as a shrub or a vine and trained against a building, garden wall or fence. The double white flowers are very fragrant.

Newly planted shrubs have to be watered regularly until they are established. Deep watering is what shrubs and plants require to keep the roots down where they belong and not allow them to come up near the surface of the ground in search of water, where the suns rays bake them.

MULCHING: During the hot days of summer it is well to use a mulch three to four inches thick. Put it on after a thorough watering. Different materials may be used for this purpose. Well decomposed vegetable matter from the compost pile, manure or leaf mold, will be suitable. As it is washed into the soil, a fresh application has to be applied. Although some mulches are at the same time top dressings, these two preparations are applied for different purposes. Mulches are used primarily to prevent over-rapid evaporation, and the aim of the top dressing is to enrich the soil and furnish new food for the shrub. Top dressings are used to augment the plant food supplied by manure at time of planting, or when it is not feasible to disturb plants so that manure may be dug in.

Water is drawn up by the roots passing through a series of cells, except in a few rare cases where it is taken up only at the tip of the roots. This is why deep watering is so important. If drainage is good, any excess water will be carried off.— *E. Hamilton Fairley.*

MOISTURE-LOVING PLANTS: Although most garden plants like a well-drained soil, there are many attractive varieties that will do well in damp soil. Included in this list of moisture-loving plants are the primroses, polyanthus

(*Primula polyantha*), oxlip (*P. elatior*), marsh-marigold (*Caltha palustris*), meadow-beauty (*Rhexia virginica*), umbrella plant (*Peltiphyllum peltatum*), sweet flag (*Acorus calamus*), *Acorus gramineus,* star-grass (*Aletris farinosa*), swamp-pink (*Helonias bullata*), purple loosestrife (*Lythrum salicaria*), cardinal-flower (*Lobelia cardinalis*), Carolina Grass-of-Parnassus (*Parnassia caroliniana*), the various astilbes (*astilbe*), *Aronia arbutifolia,* black chokeberry, spicebush, and cornelian cherry.

Most of these plants actually like very damp soil, but most will not tolerate a heavy clay, which often causes poor drainage. A sound organic program of soil building will cure most heavy soils by the incorporation of organic matter. *See also individual varieties;* SOIL; CLAY; DRAINAGE.

MOISTURE, SOIL: *see* SOIL; MULCH; AERATION

MOLD: *see* FUNGUS

MOLE: The presence of moles is often an indication that your soil is good—that you have plenty of earthworms to keep it well worked up—as earthworms are the choicest food for moles.

The best solution to your problem is to kill the moles in a way that won't kill your earthworms—with a mole trap, instead of poisons.

Moles live under the ground. They build vast networks of tunnels out from their nests. You never see their permanent "galleries" but you do see the runs, just under the surface of the ground, which they use for hunting food, principally earthworms and white grubs, plus the larvae of ground-inhabiting insects. In fact, a mole will often eat more than his own weight in a day. It is no wonder they can destroy lawns so quickly.

Moles breed in the spring—usually produce four young, sometime late in March or early April. The youngsters grow rapidly, spend only about a month in the nest, and by early June are practically as large as their parents.

DAMAGE TO AVOID: Although stomach-content checks of hundreds of moles clearly indicate that earthworms and insects are their natural food, they are also known to cause serious damage in cornfields, gardens, and flower beds by damaging roots, or carrying disease organisms from one diseased plant to the others. In addition, shrews, meadow mice, house mice, rats, and pocket gophers often use mole runways to do more damage than the moles themselves, particularly in orchards and large fields. It's a good idea to get rid of moles—promptly.

TRAPPING MOLES: Conservation Bulletin 16 on Mole Control, published by the Fish and Wildlife Service of the U. S. Department of Interior (sold by the Superintendent of Documents, Washington, D.C. for 10 cents) says this:

"Trapping is the most universally applicable and satisfactory method of mole control, but it is successful only if the habits and instincts of the mole are carefully considered. The suspicion of the mole . . . is aroused when its sensitive nose encounters anything foreign in its runways, and it will immediately back up and burrow around or under an ordinary trap set in its tunnel. It is not suspicious of dirt blocking the runway . . . as its burrow is frequently closed by farm machinery, man, and large animals. The mole will immediately push its way into such a dirt blockade, reopen it, and continue on its way.

"This habit provides opportunity for using a specially designed trap that straddles, encircles, or is held suspended above the runway, the trigger pan resting on or hidden in a dirt blockade. Under such a condition the unsuspecting mole cannot detect the presence of the trap, and in pushing into the dirt obstruction . . . releases the trap spring.

WEST COAST HINTS: The Townsend moles of the West Coast are

larger and travel in much deeper, unseen runways. Runways can be located by probing with a one-fourth or three-eighths inch metal rod around the mounds pushed up, first three or four inches from the mound, then a foot away to determine the direction of the runway.

MOLYBDENUM: An important trace element, molybdenum deficiencies most often occur in plants grown on soils below pH 5.2. Applications of ground limestone will often alleviate the deficiency. Tests indicate that of all the trace elements, molybdenum is taken up by plants in the smallest amounts. It is believed that molybdenum is closely associated in some way with the nitrogen cycle, that is, it acts as a catalyst in the reduction of nitrates to ammonia in non-legumes. Molybdenum also is used similarly by legume bacteria to reduce atmospheric nitrogen to ammonia. *See also* TRACE ELEMENTS; DEFICIENCIES, SOIL.

MOMBIN: *see* OTAHEITE APPLE

MONEYWORT: *see* AQUARIUMS; LYSIMACHIA

MONKEY-FLOWER (*Mimulus*) Monkey flowers are perennial herbs or subshrubs of the figwort family. Only one variety, *M. ringens,* is found in the East. It is an easily grown wild garden plant one to four feet high, thriving only in moist places. The other varieties are garden plants in the West, usually treated as annuals, or are grown in the greenhouse from seed sown in January in a general-purpose soil mixture. Outdoors they need decidedly moist, cool conditions in semi-shade. They can also be propagated by division and cuttings. Most of them have yellow flowers, sometimes spotted red or brown, but there are some with white, red or violet blooms. *M. cardinalis* and *M. lewisi* have hairy, sticky foliage. *M. primuloides* is a low ground cover two to four inches tall, with bright yellow flowers.

MONKSHOOD: (*Aconitum*) Often called aconite, these are attractive perennials belonging to the buttercup family. All of them are poisonous. Late-blooming, they do best in a humus-rich soil and a part-shady location. Varieties include *A. autumnale*—about five feet high with blue flowers; *A. anthora*—two feet high with yellow flowers; wolfsbane (*A. lycoctonum*)—about five feet high with white or yellow flowers; common monkshood (*A. napellus*)—reaching four feet with blue flowers; wild monkshood (*A. uncinatum*)—five feet with blue flowers; and *A. fischeri*—reaching six feet with blue sometimes white flowers. *See also* ACONITE.

MONTMORENCY: *see* CHERRY

MOON PLANTING: Referring to the idea that the moon, in its monthly trip around the earth, exerts an appreciable amount of influence on the activities of growing plants—appreciable enough to schedule crop plantings at times when the moon is in a "favorable" position. The two main tenets of moon planting are that (1) plants that produce the eaten or desired part above ground (corn, tomatoes, flowers, etc.) should be planted in the waxing moon (the period of increasing between a new and full moon), and that (2) plants which produce the eaten or desired part below ground (rootcrops, flowers grown especially for bulbs or tubers) should be planted in the waning moon (the period after the full moon and before the next new moon). There are other tenets of the moon planting school, most of which depend upon the exact position of the moon, calculated in terms of the 12 zodiac signs.

The belief in moon planting is wrapped in an ancient and obscure history. In modern times it is interesting to note that the strongholds of belief in the system have always come from practical farmers, and the doctrine has always been scoffed at by scientists and other academics. There have actually been very few closely-supervised experiments made upon the moon planting idea, and those that have been made usually show that there is little or no difference resulting from plantings made at different times of the month.

From a top agronomist comes this sage explanation of the moon planting idea. Dr. William A. Albrecht, chairman of the Department of Soils at the University of Missouri, admits that faith must take up where science leaves off. He says, "While the word 'moon' was the origin of our calendar division 'month' we are too apt to forget that the seasons were not always tabulated to such a fine degree of accuracy as :hey now are. To man as a primitive the moon in its cycles may have been the only calendar and in speaking of planting according to the season, he was planting according to the moons. Now that persistence may have held on and come down to us so that some people still think they are planting according to the stage of the moon as we outline it by quarters as waning or waxing.

"However, some interesting research at Missouri considered the reflected light of the moon as it might be of significance in starting seeds. Many years ago some studies were carried on here which showed that tobacco seeds must be exposed to light if they are to germinate. Should they be harvested without having exposure to light they would not germinate. But by exposure to light as small as that reflected by the moon they will germinate and go forward. That work was done in the Department of Botany by R. R. Kincaid.

"That is cited to you to point out that hidden in the biological performances about us there are many factors with which we are not familiar. Then because of our ignorance we are apt to be 'down on what we are not up on.' Keeping one's mind closed is an easy performance but keeping it open and handling all that may come into it is something quite different. It is regrettable that in education we have not invented a can opener for the closed mind.

"So there is much empiricism in any profession including some of those standing most high in public estimate which carries the profession on much farther than we move by all the science and knowledge we generate ourselves.

"As a consequence I like to study some of these items which might be considered witchcraft or things of that kind. There was a time probably when things that are now included in the results of thinking about 'relativity' might have been considered witchcraft not too long ago. It would have been that especially when we discovered that it was coming in from the heavens as it were and we called it cosmic rays."

More than one scientist suggested that if there were anything in moon planting at all, it might be caused by the tidal powers of the moon. They explain that tides occur on dry land and in the atmosphere as well as on the sea. Land tides bulge the earth upward four inches in north central U. S.

MORAEA: *see* PEACOCK IRIS

MORAINE LOCUST: This variety of honey locust has two advantages: it stands city smoke and dust very well, and it has no thorns. Its hardiness range is the same as that of the common honey locust. but it is somewhat more tolerant of alkaline soils. A rapid grower, moraine locust attains 50 to 75 feet, and is a vigorous, wide-branched tree. It is often used for street planting, as well as for fast-growing shade trees on the home grounds.

MORNING-GLORY: (*Ipomoea*) The annual morning-glories are popular both for their beauty and for their ability to clamber quickly over porches, fences and such unsightly objects as stumps. Some varieties grow to a height of 25 feet. They bloom from early summer until frost, and self-sow readily. Give them full sun, but the soil should not be too rich in nitrogen or few flowers will result. Small amounts of bone meal and manure are helpful, as is a mulch of several inches of peat moss or similar material. The seeds are hard and should be soaked overnight or notched with a file to aid germination.

The most common variety is *I. purpurea,* which is often seen growing wild in fields and roadsides. It has large, heart-shaped leaves and big, delicate pink, blue or purple flowers. There are other varieties with double flowers and white or red flowers. Dwarf morning-glory, usually sold as *Convolvulus tricolor,* grows only a foot tall and has bright blue flowers. It is very resistant to sun and heat. A Mexican variety that blooms in the evening, and the spectacular Heavenly Blue Japanese morning-glory are two other favorites.

The morning-glories make attractive house plants for sunny windows. Soak or notch the seeds, and plant five to a six-inch pot. When they come up, pull out all but the three strongest plants, and provide supports. The dwarf morning-glory is especially good for hanging baskets and window boxes. It blooms in ten weeks from seed, and should be pinched once to make the plants bushier.

There are perennial species of morning-glory that are not always hardy in the North. Their roots should be dug up before frost and stored in a cool cellar for replanting the following spring. *See also* IPOMOEA.

MOROCCAN TOADFLAX: (*Linaria maroccana*) A dwarf grower of exceeding hardiness that bears its spikes of tiny snapdragonlike flowers throughout the winter and early spring. The small dark green leaves are narrow, delicate in texture; the flowers are white, lemon, pink, blue and purple. Toadflax self-sows and volunteers most readily, the seedlings being used as planting stock year after year.

Blooming profusely, even during frosts, in poor sandy soil, the toadflax is recommended for edgings, borders and rock gardens in Florida.

MORUS: *see* MULBERRY

MOSAIC: *see* DISEASE; BRAMBLE FRUITS

MOSS: Common name for many small, flowerless plants. In North America there are about 1,000 species, distributed in various families. Moss thrives in a very moist, acid soil, in heavy shade. In some places in the garden—particularly in rock gardens—moss is very attractive, but in spots where it is undesirable, it may be prevented by incorporating dry, bulky organic matter in the soil, along with heavy additions of lime.

SPHAGNUM MOSS: Sphagnum moss, which is collected from bogs, has found a place in the nursery. Its excellent moisture-holding properties lend it to use as packing for plants which are to be shipped through the mails and as a medium for seed germination. In germinating seeds, use of sphagnum moss obviates the need for applying chemical protectants to the seeds or the seeding medium to avoid attacks of damping-off; it reduces the need for constant watchfulness and for expert judgment; and it prevents harm from overwatering. *See also* PEAT MOSS.

MOSS VERBENA: (*Verbena pulchella*) A perennial plant for the rock garden. It has a somewhat woody base and is decumbent or sprawling in habit. The hairy to nearly smooth stems are sometimes 20 inches long and strike root readily where they come in contact with the soil. The leaves are small and finely dissected into linear, acute lobes giving a mossy appearance. The flowers are a solid blue or lilac, borne in terminal, dense, conspicuous heads that elongate when in fruit. The species is native to southern South America but now is becoming widely naturalized.

CULTURE: The propagation of the species and the variety is not considered too easy; thus it is a challenge to an enthusiastic gardener. They are usually grown by seed and treated like annuals although they are both perennials. The seeds should be sown in flats about March 1st in light sandy soil. The flat should be set out in a cool greenhouse or in a cold frame with a temperature of 60° at night and 70 to 75° during the day. When the seedlings are large enough to handle they should be transplanted into flats or small pots and kept in the same temperature until growth starts, which is normally in about 10 days. After danger of frost is past the plants may be set into their permanent beds in the garden. Cuttings may also be made in early September when young shoots develop in the established summer growth. These young shoots can be easily rooted under glass and then kept in protected cold frames or in cool greenhouses over winter.

The bright, vivid color of the flowers is ever present throughout the summer months and it is particularly valuable when most of the rock garden plants have either completed their bloom or are developing for fall flowers.

MOTHER-OF-THYME: (*Thymus serpyllum*) Prostrate, spreading, shrubby perennials, usually only a few inches in height. They have small oval leaves and purple flowers, and there are varieties with white, rose or crimson flowers, others with yellow- or white-variegated leaves. Lemon thyme (*T. serpyllum*) has lemon-scented foliage.

Mother-of-thyme is grown, harvested and used the same as common thyme. *See also* THYME.

MOTTLING: *see* DISEASE

MOUND LAYERING: *see* LAYERING

MOUNTAIN-ASH: (*Sorbus*) Its dense clusters of showy white blooms in spring and its bright red berries make mountain-ash a favorite tree for the home grounds. It is quite hardy and many beautiful specimens are seen in New England. These are mostly the European mountain-ash, or rowan tree, *S. aucuparia,* which reaches a height of 50 feet. It was brought here in colonial days. The American species, *S. americana,* grows 30 feet tall and is seen commonly growing wild in the woods. Both have a somewhat open to round-topped crown, are fairly slow in growth and comparatively short-lived. Their chief value lies in the large clusters of berries, which remain over the winter and provide food for the birds when other supplies are short. Mountain-ash isn't really an ash, although its leaves, like those of the true ash, are made up of long stems with leaflets strung along both sides of them, giving the tree a feathery appearance. The true ash, however, has winged seeds, not berries.

There are several other varieties: the whitebeam, *S. aria,* which grows 50 feet tall but tends to remain a shrub on poor soil; *S. decora,* a shrubby tree 30 feet high; the service tree, *S. domestica,* 60 feet tall, not so hardy as the others, and with pear-shaped yellow-green or brown fruits; and *S. hybrida,* a 40-foot tree.

Mountain-ash is easily grown even in dry soils. It is propagated by seeds and layering. The berries, incidentally, can be made into preserves.

MOUNTAIN FETTER-BUSH: (*Pieris floribunda*) A shrub which grows natively on moist hillsides and mountains from Virginia to Georgia. It is a slow-growing evergreen shrub with dull green leaves and nodding white flowers borne on dense upward pointing panicles. The flower buds remain conspicuous all winter.

This shrub belongs to the heath family and thrives best in a sheltered position, and a rather moist sandy soil with plenty of peat or leaf mold. It blooms very early in the spring, and is an excellent shrub for planting with azalea, laurel and rhododendron. It reaches an ultimate height of about six feet.

Pieris is adapted for many uses in the garden. They are fine for gateway plantings, as accent plants in the shrubbery, and for the rock garden. They may be propagated by layers or by seeds. They should be kept mulched with shredded leaves at all times.

MOUNTAIN LAUREL: (*Kalmia latifolia*) Also called calico bush, mountain laurel is a beautiful round-topped shrub growing four to ten feet high. In the wild, it favors rocky hillsides and acid swamps, and it is extensively planted in gardens from Maine through the central states and in elevated sections of the South. The leaves are thick and evergreen, the flowers white to rose-pink and borne in large clusters in May and June. Each flower has ten explosive stamens that shower bees with pollen. Mountain laurel is one of the finest shrubs for specimen planting or massing. It is sometimes forced.

Either sun or shade will suit it, although it does best in partial shade. Plant it on the north side of the house, or in a spot where the hot summer sun will be tempered by the open branches of nearby trees or shrubs. Ordinary garden soil, if not too clayey, is satisfactory, but for finest growth give it a moist, peaty, humus-rich loam. The soil should be definitely acid. Mountain laurel requires plenty of moisture and will do well even in marshy soil. If grown in comparatively dry, exposed places, it will need heavy watering and a permanent mulch of, preferably, oak or beech leaves. Propagation is generally by seed.

Among the other varieties are *K. microphylla,* a charming dwarf less than a foot high, with pretty rose-lilac flowers. *K. polifolia,* the swamp laurel, is a low shrub about two feet high, useful in the wild garden in moist or wet, acid ground. *K. hirsuta* and *K. cuneata* are deciduous species grown

mostly from North Carolina southward. Sheep laurel, *K. angustifolia,* is sometimes called lambkill because its leaves poison grazing animals. Mountain laurel honey, incidentally, may contain this poison, andromedotoxin, which can cause a person to become numb and even lose consciousness for several hours. *See also* SHRUBS.

MOUNTAIN MINT: (*Pycnanthemum pilosum*) Grows wild from Pennsylvania to Kansas and Arkansas. It grows in half-shady locations in woodland borders, usually near the top of rather poor hills on north or west exposures.

The plant comes into bloom in late July and lasts over a period of several weeks. The bees work the flowers eagerly and in favored localities get a fair crop of rather strong, amber honey. A single clump when well grown will have about a dozen stems with dozens of heads on each stem. *See also* MINT; HONEY PLANTS.

MOURNING BRIDE: (*Scabiosa atropurpurea*) The globular, tufted flowers of the mourning bride or pincushion flower furnish a range of color found in no other annual. From white, through yellow, blue, rose, red, maroon, to black purple, the colors are most charming and are, of course, always harmonious. The plants, which attain a height of about three feet when well grown, are prolific, thrifty and hardy. The keeping quality of the blossoms is good, the long stiff stems make for artistic flower arrangements.

MOUSE: Mice occasionally do damage in the garden. Most often mouse injury is correlated with moles. The moles provide the underground tunnels which the mice invade, thereby finding access to plant roots and bulbs. If the moles are properly controlled and the runways destroyed by rolling the ground or filling in, the mouse problem will be eliminated.

MICE IN THE ORCHARD: Mice that occupy the orchard and do damage are most often of two kinds, the field mouse and the pine mouse. The field or meadow mouse is rather thick-set, short-legged, short-eared, usually blackish, grizzled with grey. The pine mouse is generally much smaller in size, having a very short tail. The fur is uniform dull chestnut, and of very soft texture.

Field mice are not difficult to control in the orchard. They rarely burrow below the ground. They often feed on the trunk but not on the roots. If mulch is used in the orchard, be sure to pull it away from the trunk in the fall. Field mice often build nests in such mulch, but are rather hesitant in running around in the open once cold weather sets in. A space of at least three feet between the tree trunk and the mulch is desirable. The same general control measure as described for rabbits, that of placing a wire cylinder around the trunks of the trees, is also effective against field mice.

Pine mice are often very difficult to control. Persistence is very necessary.

One method is to dig some of the soil away from the base of the tree in the fall and fill it in with cinders. Also, spread cinders in a circle to at least three feet from the trunk. These cinders are sharp and will help prevent the rodents from tunneling in the soil. Regular, snap-back mouse traps can be effective if carefully set in the runs.

MOWER, LAWN: There are three types of mowers: rotary, reel and sickle bar. The first-named is the most popular and serviceable. Not only will it cut grass and do a good job, but it also mulches leaves, hay, straw and light compostable materials.

The *rotary mower* is usually powered by a one-cylinder, four-cycle gasoline engine. This engine is recommended over the two-cycle motor which emits heavier fumes because it consumes oil mixed in with gasoline. Power mowers are also electrically driven. While these are quiet and smooth-running, their radius of activity is lim-

ited by the length of the electric cable which can also get in the way of the operator.

The *reel mower* is mostly used for the smaller, finer lawn. It requires a smooth, well-graded surface from which all obstacles and uneven planes have been removed. Within these limitations it is a most efficient power tool which will do a first-rate job. Reel mowers are also used in gangs on golf courses, attached to small tractors. Here their ability to create a smooth, well-shaved lawn is appreciated.

In the *sickle mower,* cutting is done by a pair of steel-toothed bars, one rigidly fixed over which the other slides. The principle is the same as that of the barber's clippers.

Consider personal needs carefully when buying a mower. Except for a very smooth terrain planted to bent grasses, the rotary mower is best all-around. Get a mower with good, sturdy wheels that are readily adjustable for cutting height. It is good to have a motor with a high horsepower rating; three is excellent while two should be considered the minimum.

A self-powered mower is a much more complicated piece of machinery than the relatively simple rotary tool. The motor, in addition to turning a steel blade, must also drive the entire mechanism through the grass. Be sure to get a powerful motor; two and one-half horsepower is the absolute minimum here.

CARE OF THE MOWER: Clean the mower after using it. The bits of grass adhering to the undercarriage and housing heat up like all compostable materials and cause rapid deterioration. Disconnect the sparkplug and jack up the machine to permit easy and thorough scraping of the undercarriage. Check all nuts and bolts and the oil level. Neglect of these little details not only means less efficient operation but a possible breakdown which can be dangerous. Always make sure the blade is well balanced on the shaft. *See also* MACHINERY, CARE OF.

MUCK SOILS: Muck lands have been called our "last virgin agricultural frontier." Potentially high producers, they have long been ignored, the few in production, until recently, yielding poorly and wearing out quickly.

Properly managed muck soils will grow practically any crop, with the possible exception of canteloupes (muck-grown canteloupes taste like pumpkin). Truck crops, sweet corn, raspberries, soybeans and grasses of all kinds are grown with outstanding success. Potatoes have yielded up to 800 bushels per acre—four times the national average — on Wisconsin muck, and nearly 600 bushels is the recent record for onions. Prize celery, beets, popcorn and mint hay are chief crops on Indiana's 300,000 acres of muck soils. Chinese cabbage, carrots, horseradish, lettuce and spinach do well on muck.

Muck lands are vast natural compost heaps. Over the ages, they were formed by the decomposition of aquatic plants growing in poorly drained areas. First peat formed, then as the amount of material increased, rising above the water, aeration and drainage improved and the deposit changed to muck, a more completely decomposed organic material. In some states, muck occupies one out of every eight acres of total land area. Ranging from three to 90 feet deep, muck deposits were valued at $10 an acre only a few years ago. Today such land brings $300 an acre.

DRAINAGE PROBLEM: Drainage is the muck farmer's biggest problem. Dams and ditching are necessary to lower the water table so crops won't be drowned out. The ideal water table is about $2\frac{1}{2}$ feet below the soil surface. Lowering it more than this will let the muck dry out and become powdery.

Some muck soils are highly acid, others are close to neutral and a few are alkaline. The last is rare, while the first can be corrected by the application of two to three tons of dolomitic limestone, added every four to six years.

Because it is very high in organic matter, muck contains abundant nitrogen—generally two to four per cent. For the same reason, it is also highly workable, with good structure and aeration. However, the organic matter of muck is a slow decayer. Therefore it is very beneficial to regularly add fresh green material, which decomposes more readily. This should preferably be leguminous. Rotations, while not needed to maintain good tilth, are necessary to hold down plant disease, insects and weeds. Muck, like any other soil, should not be "mined"; onion farmers, particularly, have found that continuous cropping exhausts some ingredient that no amount of fertilizer can replace. Diversification produces the greatest long-run profit.

DEFICIENCIES: Muck soils are low in minerals. A newly broken muck may have a phosphorus content adequate for several years. However, organic muck farmers have found a program of phosphorus build-up pays off very well. Potash is needed, too. Most farmers use 1,500 pounds a year of rock phosphate and a like or larger amount of granite dust or greensand. *High fertilization rates mean high production on muck*. If your soil tests show deficiencies of trace elements, these should be applied as needed.

Green manuring is a vital part of muck farming. Record crops follow heavy crops of rye, vetch or oats. The more powdery and decomposed the muck, the more green manures are needed. On newer mucks, fibrous, woody organic materials bind the particles together, preventing powdering and blowing. Cover crops of oats, corn or soybeans yield considerable woody straw, as do many crop residues. Mulching is also good where practicable. Rotary tilling is usually preferable to plowing, due to the sponginess of the soil.

Windbreaks of blueberry hedges, sunflowers or trees like willows or pines, aided by strip crops of rye, barley or corn, will prevent muck blowing, which can be highly damaging to crops. Water erosion is rarely more than negligible, although older mucks may need some sodded waterways or diversion ditches for protection.

One caution: if spring in your area is usually wet, the muck may be cold and should not be planted to crops like beans, eggplant, peppers, melons and tomatoes, which need a long, warm growing season. Also, in wet spring weather, tillage implements should be kept off the muck until they can be used without clogging up with soggy soil.

One way to tell if muck is worth putting into production is to observe what is already growing on it. If there are no trees, or only a few black spruces, arbovitae and tamarisks, it may not pay to reclaim it. But if there are hardwood trees, the cost should not be too great.

Sometimes muck areas can be made into wild gardens. Many shrubs, ferns and trees will be happy here. Common garden asters and sweet peas do well on muck, and many wild plants can be taken from nearby areas that are similarly swampy. Drainage should be fairly good and the muck nearly neutral in reaction.

Muck soil can also be useful as a soil amendment. And if the muck overlies a marl deposit, mix the two together and you have a fine fertilizer. If you have a sufficient area of such soil, it may be worth selling locally by the bag or truckload.

MULBERRY: (*Morus*) While most of us think of the mulberry as a bush, usually not very good-looking and troublesome to prune, these shrubs are actually a very small part of the mulberry family, a family of hardy, useful *trees*.

One variety of the mulberry grows to over 60 feet tall, and other common, easily-raised types grow 30 or more feet.

Full-sized mulberry trees draw wildlife, birds in particular. In turn, these patrol the orchard, consume thousands of insects, pest eggs, etc., and help maintain a desirable natural balance.

Its berries are also a favorite with all poultry, and serve as a nutritionally-rich feed in the chicken pen. Here, again, the berries are readily accessible, since the ripe fruits drop to the ground. It also makes a good feed for hogs.

VARIETIES: The low, wide-spreading white mulberry (*M. alba*) casts a dense shade. Familiar along the roadsides of old New England towns, this type produces fruit like white blackberries that ripen a few at a time over the entire summer, rather than maturing and falling all at once as do most tree fruits. In addition to this variety's berries being a great attraction for birds and good for fattening poultry, it is the silkworm tree. (Many early Americans, including Washington and Franklin, planted it liberally in the hope of starting a domestic silk industry.)

Next, there's the Paper Mulberry (*Broussonetia papyrifera*) which is common throughout the South where its frequent abnormal trunk growth is a colonial landscape feature always marveled at by visitors.

The Red Mulberry (*M. rubra*), our native American tree, reaches tall, straight heights of 60 feet or more amid the southern Appalachian woods. Farmers in the Midwest and South like it for fence posts because its wood is hard and doesn't decay on contact with the soil. Its tart, dark-red to blackish fruits are probably the best flavored of the mulberries, and it makes a fine shade tree to plant beside the poultry yard.

Other types include the Asian Black Mulberry which has large, thick, dark fruits, but is not hardy in the North; and the Russian Mulberry, widespread throughout the West, which is very hardy and resistant to cold and drought, but of much less value for its fruit.

In his book on *Tree Crops*, J. Russell Smith cites a lengthy list of unusual advantages for the Mulberry.

Among these are its ease of propagation and transplanting; rapid growth, early bearing and long fruiting season; its power of recovery from frost, comparative freedom from most tree pests and diseases.

Mulberries grow well in a wide range of soils. In orchard plantings, space trees about 30 feet apart. Varieties recommended for fruit-bearing include Downing, Hicks and Black English. *See also* FRUIT TREES.

MULCH: A layer of material, preferably organic material, that is placed on the soil surface to conserve moisture, hold down weeds, and ultimately improve soil structure and fertility. As with composting, mulching is a basic practice in the organic method; it is a practice which nature employs constantly, that of always covering a bare soil. In addition, mulching also protects plants during winter, reducing the dangers of freezing and heaving.

Straw is being applied evenly four to five inches deep between plants and rows. Many other easily available materials are effective as a mulch.

Experiments have shown these advantages:

1. We know that a mulched plant is not subjected to the extremes of temperatures of an exposed plant. Unmulched roots are damaged by the heaving of soil brought on by sudden thaws and sudden frosts. The mulch acts as an insulating blanket, keeping the soil warmer in winter and cooler in summer.

2. Certain materials used for a mulch contain rich minerals, and gradually, through the action of rain and time, these work into the soil to feed the roots of the plants. Some of the minerals soak into the ground during the first heavy rain. Therefore mulch fertilizes the soil while it is on the soil surface as well as after it decays.

3. For the busy gardener mulching is a boon indeed. Many backbreaking hours of weeding and hoeing are practically eliminated. Weeds do not have a chance to get a foothold, and the few that might manage to come up through the mulch can be hoed out in a jiffy. And since the mulch keeps the soil loose, there is no need to cultivate.

4. The mulch prevents the hot, drying sun and wind from penetrating to the soil, so its moisture does not evaporate quickly. A few good soakings during the growing season will tide plants over a long dry spell. It also prevents erosion from wind and hard rains. Soil underneath a mulch is damp and cool to the touch. Often mulched plants endure a long dry season with practically no watering at all.

5. At harvest time vegetables which sprawl on the ground, such as cucumbers, squash, strawberries, unstaked tomatoes, etc., often become mildewed, moldy, or even develop rot. A mulch prevents this damage by keeping the vegetables clean and dry. This is the season when most gardens begin to look unkempt. But the mulched garden always looks neat and trim, no matter what the season. In addition, mud is less of a problem when walking on mulched rows, and low-growing flowers are not splashed with mud.

DISADVANTAGES: Here are some potential disadvantages of mulching:

1. Seedlings planted in very moist soil should not be mulched immediately. The addition of any organic matter

which keeps the soil at a high humidity encourages damping-off of young plants. Damping-off is a disease caused by a fungus inhabiting moist, poorly ventilated soil, and can be 90 per cent fatal. Allow seedlings to become established then, before mulching.

2. It is wise, too, to consider the danger of crown-rot in perennials. This disease is also caused by a fungus. If there has been especially heavy rains, postpone mulching until the soil is no longer water-logged. Do not allow mulches composed of peat moss, manure, compost, or ground corn cobs to touch the base of these plants. Leave a circle several inches in diameter. The idea here is to permit the soil to remain dry and open to the air around the immediate area of the plant.

3. Do not mulch a wet, low-lying soil, or at most, use only a dry light type of material, such as salt hay or buckwheat hulls. Leaves are definitely to be avoided as they may mat down and add to the sogginess.

With the instructions given above, it is simple enough to know when and where not to mulch. Except for these instances, the gardener really can't do without mulching as a wonderful, labor-saving helpmate.

MULCHING MATERIALS: Practically any organic waste material can be used

Grass clippings are excellent for use as a mulch to keep soil cool, hold down weeds, and retain more moisture in ground for better plant growth.

for mulching. However, since different materials have different textures and other properties, they differ in suitability. Here are listed the most common mulch materials.

Grass Clippings. A commonly available and excellent mulch material. *See* GRASS CLIPPINGS.

Corn Stalks. To the depth of three or four inches, they provide a well aerated winter mulch, but do not use stalks from a field which was heavily infested with borers. Lay the stalks criss-cross with tops and butts alternating. Shredded, the stalks make a fine garden mulch.

Straw. This is clean, contains no weed seeds, is inexpensive, quick and easy to lay down, and it looks presentable. Once it has been applied it remains in place an entire season. In fall, dig it in, and by spring it will have become an indistinguishable part of the soil. It is estimated that one ton will give a one-inch mulch on an acre of land.

Shredded Leaves. An excellent mulch. They do not mat down and they enrich the soil more quickly than whole leaves. There is rarely any nitrogen deficiency in leaves.

Unshredded Leaves. Should be mixed with straw or some other light material so that they do not become a soggy mass. With a mixture, the mulch can be spread eight to 12 inches deep for winter. *See* LEAVES.

Sawdust. For blueberries use a softwood mulch. There will be less packing down and better aeration, and the blueberries prefer an acid type. Try banking sawdust (hardwood type) around the base of old apple trees. New bark will appear, the old gradually peeling off.

A six-inch layer will smother weeds effectively. If there is quack grass in the soil, their roots will soon lie at the surface just under the mulch. It is easy to run your fingers under the roots and pull them out.

To counteract the nitrogen deficiency in sawdust, add soybean meal, cotton seed meal, or compost. *See* SAWDUST.

Cocoa Bean Hulls or Shells. Excellent as a mulch. They absorb $2\frac{1}{2}$ times their weight in water.

Corn Cobs. Ground into one-inch pieces, they have many uses. The sugar content will help to increase the microorganisms in the soil, and these will give a better soil granulation.

Finely ground corn cobs are highly recommended for seed flats. Use lightly here as a protection against too much nitrogen which forces premature growth in seedlings. It is interesting to note that florists using this material claim 100 per cent more production and 30 per cent saving on operating costs as germination takes place more rapidly and there is not the need for frequent watering.

In the opinion of L. C. Chadwick, Professor of Horticulture, Ohio State University, a ground corn cob mulch helps to prevent black spot on roses.

Pine Needles. Good for strawberries the year around. Keep in mind that they can be a fire hazard when dry. Use a two to four inch mulch and renew every year.

Peat Moss. An old standby. As a bale it is greatly compressed and very dry, you'll have to give it a good soaking after it is applied. Sometimes it will form a crust over the beds, but it can be easily broken up with a rake.

Alfalfa Hay. Coarse and ragged in appearance, it is most easily handled when green and freshly cut. It contains a high nitrogen content and will supply the requirements of fruit trees. Rain-spoiled hay can always be used as a mulch material, so there need be no waste here.

Oak Tow. Like sawdust, but contains coarser wood strings. It is made by tearing the wood lengthwise in sawing stave bolts. If you can get this material from a saw mill you'll find it does not compact or blow as readily as sawdust.

Rotted Pine Wood. Like pine needles, these materials are excellent for mulching such acid-loving plants as azaleas,

camellias, and rhododendrons. Before being used for plants that require a neutral or slightly alkaline soil, these materials should be composted.

Packing Materials. Trees and plants ordered from nurseries usually come packed in sphagnum moss or redwood shavings. Breakables shipped from out of town arrive packed in excelsior or shredded paper. Save these materials and use them as mulches, alone or mixed with other materials.

Weeds and Native Grasses. These make an excellent mulch around trees, where it is important to build a deeper covering than we use in the gardens and where this sort of mulch does not look out of place. They should be exposed to the air before applying to prevent rooting. They may be shredded to make a neat appearance, and can be mixed with grass clippings.

Buckwheat Hulls. Can be spread one or two inches deep in summer and a little deeper in winter. They make a clean, attractive mulch.

Salt Hay. According to the Wisconsin Experimental Station, it makes the best mulch for strawberries. Use a $1\frac{1}{2}$ to two inch layer here, for other uses, three inches. This straw is usually cheap and easily obtained. It does not mat down, and remains stiff and firm throughout the season. If used as a winter mulch, it can be taken off in the spring and stacked in corner of the plot to be used again the following winter. However, it is recommended as an all year round mulch too.

Dust Mulch. This is actually fine soil. The principle is to break the capillary action of water rising to the soil surface and then evaporating by frequent shallow cultivation. A layer of "dust" is then formed on top of the soil; when moisture seeps up toward the surface of the soil, the dust mulch stops the upward progress. However, organic materials do this more effectively. The main disadvantage of the dust mulch is that the soil surface is subject to loss by blowing; therefore it is not recommended.

Stones. Stone mulching consists of placing rocks between and around growing plants. The flat stones are placed close enough along the rows so that little soil area is exposed. *See* STONE MULCHING.

Other Mulches. Other materials which have been used with more or less success are aluminum foil, glass wool, and dust. These materials perform some of the functions of an organic mulch but cannot be used as food by living organisms.

WHEN TO APPLY: In some crops, at least, the mulch may be applied immediately after planting the seed. This is especially true of potatoes, and gardeners report success with most vegetables. A suitable mulch for potatoes consists of a foot of straw or hay applied immediately after planting. The potatoes should be only lightly covered with soil. If beans, corn, peas, carrots, beets, and similar vegetables are to be mulched immediately after the seed is planted, the mulch over the row should be loose and not thicker than from four to six inches.

Transplanted tomatoes, cabbages, cauliflower, peppers and other vegetables may be mulched immediately after the plants are set out. A circular area around each plant should be kept unmulched until the plant is well started when the mulch may be pulled up close to the stem of the plant.

HOW TO MULCH: The gardener must keep in mind the purpose or purposes of the mulch. After the soil is prepared and planted, level the soil with a rake. Then apply the mulch over the soil without mixing it with the soil. The thickness of the mulch should be sufficient to prevent the growth of weeds. A thin layer of finely shredded plant materials is more effective than a similar layer of unshredded loose material. If mulches are put down immediately after sowing the seeds, the mulch should be loose over the row area and more compact in the spaces between the rows. — *Virginia Brundage.*

HOW TO FIND MULCH MATERIALS: Here's a system used successfully by a great many gardeners: First, page through the classified section of your telephone directory; make a list of a few promising firms (lumber companies, mills, meat packing houses, quarries, dairies, leather tanneries, city park departments, riding stables, wholesale food companies, etc.). Then you are ready to embark on a most rewarding collection trip. If you can't borrow a pick-up truck or small trailer, you most likely can rent one for a few hours at a nominal charge. Or else, you can always use the trunk of your car to haul materials back to your garden.

ORCHARD MULCHING

Mulching in the orchard is an attempt to imitate nature and allow litter to accumulate in increasing proportion beneath the trees and thus conserve moisture and add nutrients to the soil. When one observes the trees that grow in forests where natural mulch materials are constantly being built up on the soil, it is not difficult to understand that this type of ground cover is extremely important.

The term "mulch" as applied to the orchard has taken on a very wide interpretation so that anything from mowing a sparse grass and allowing it to decompose where it falls, to spreading straw or other materials to a depth of several feet, has been designated as mulch. The first example cited is not truly mulching and should be considered but a poor excuse which provides only to the smallest extent the desirable effects obtained by a good mulch.

The age-old problem in orchards is to maintain the organic content of soils. Organic matter oxidizes giving up many of its nutrient substances for plant growth and therefore needs to be replenished each year. Cultural systems that do not provide for this return will, in time, devitalize the soil of its organic content and result in poor tree growth and response. An example of such a system that greatly reduces the vigor of trees is clean cultivation.

CLEAN CULTIVATION: Clean cultivation systems were practiced by orchardists when it was found that sod orchards did not do well because of the competition between trees and ground cover. The conversion to clean cultivation was rapid and during the early part of the century it became the accepted practice. The immediate effect of clean cultivation was an invigoration of trees and stimulation of growth. The more frequent and thorough the cultivation, the better the results appeared to be. So complete was this shift to cultivation that in many localities an orchardist who permitted even a few weeds to develop was considered to be an unworthy member of the fruit-growing profession. It was not known at that time that the reason the trees grew so well was because the vegetation present on the soil had been turned under and decomposition resulting in organic materials had taken place. Continual cultivation placed these materials near the surface of the soil where oxidation and decomposition could take place rapidly.

During the time that the organic matter persisted and continued to break down, good results were obtained. This method not only accelerated the utilization of organic matter, but left the soil unprotected from erosion. The organic matter became exhausted resulting in a breakdown of the soil structure. Soils that had originally been friable and retentive of moisture were found to run together into a sticky mass when rain fell. As the soil became wet with the first few minutes of a shower, impervious layers formed on the surface and heavy runoff caused severe erosion. Such soils store little water and when dry weather comes, the soil turns to a dusty powder and the trees suffer for lack of moisture. Many orchardists still follow clean cultivation although all evidence points to the soil depletion effects of this system.

MULCH DIFFERS FROM SOD: Orchardists, in their argument for clean cultivation, claim that mulching is not unlike sod culture and would appear to them to be only a glorified modification of the same procedure. This is not true, for a good mulch system is as different from sod in its biological effect as sod is different from tillage. The fact that all the surface growth beneath the trees is destroyed or suppressed, together with other physical and biological results, places this system in a category by itself.

As compared with sod, a mulch eliminates the competition between trees and ground cover for water and nutrient materials. It increases the penetrability of water and retards runoff. Evaporation of moisture from the soil is reduced to a minimum. The organic mulch materials gradually break down and humus is formed. Besides the addition of organic matter, substantial amounts of potash, lime and many mineral trace elements are added to the soil. The soil does not become compact, thus facilitating aeration. Mulching prevents the soil from getting too hot in summer and too cold in winter.

Of special interest to growers are the higher yields through mulching which result from improvement of the soil structure, increases of moisture, and plant food, and the lower summer temperature of the soil. These factors increase fruit bud formation, leaf area, and size of the tree.

Apart from the advantages in better soil conditions there are economic advantages of the mulch system. Mulch reduces to some extent the amount of bruising of the windfalls and fruit which falls during the picking operation. This fruit is also cleaner than where clean cultivation is practiced. Trees under mulch have been known to come into bearing somewhat earlier than trees under clean cultivation and sod. Also, the color of the fruit is somewhat improved.

Some of the results performed by agricultural investigators have been quite revealing. For example, yields from cherry trees have been increased 100 per cent in experiments at Michigan State College. It was done by mulching the trees with straw or legume hay, in tests by Dr. A. L. Kenworthy, horticulturist. The increase came on trees receiving only mulch and no fertilizer, as compared with trees which received complete fertilizer but no mulch.

It is reported from New Zealand that excellent results have been secured by mulching citrus trees, as indicated by the dark green foliage and the smooth clear skin of the fruit. Since mulching has been undertaken, the quantities of artificial manures have been reduced by nearly half. The practice is to grow clovers or grasses in adjacent fields and place the cut materials in the late summer around the trees out to the limit of the branch spread.

PRODUCTION OF MULCH MATERIALS: One of the problems in a large mulch orchard is to secure sufficient litter. There are three common sources of such material. It may be grown within the orchard, produced elsewhere and hauled into the orchard or purchased from an outside source.

Mulching materials that may be utilized include a wide variety of substances. The cut plant material of a large group of field and cover crops are available. Summer cover crops that may be planted in the orchard and cut for mulching material include soybeans, cowpeas, millet, sudan grass, buckwheat, lespedeza, crotalaria, and sesbania. Orchard winter cover crops that may be cut for mulching purposes include rye, wheat, vetch, crimson clover, sweet clover, alfalfa, and kudzu beans. Besides these materials, many other substances are often available, including weeds, sawdust, seaweed, peat moss, peat, whole or ground corn cobs, stones, rotted wood, leaves, pine needles, waste products such as apple pomace, pea vines, brewery and canning wastes, etc. When one considers the vast store of organic materials nature provides, it should not be difficult to procure sufficient mulching material.

ALL FRUITS BENEFIT FROM MULCH: Although mulching was originally developed as a cultural practice for apples and pears, experiments in several states have shown that peach and other stone fruit trees can be profitably grown in sod areas if adequate mulch is provided about the trees. For a long time it was considered that the only way to grow stone fruits profitably was through clean cultivation. The results of more recent experiments have disproved this. The peach and stone fruit problem was the last stronghold of the clean cultivation advocates. Now this too has broken down and with it has evolved the practicality of growing stone fruits on rolling terrain where it was previously considered unadvisable.

Another old cry in opposition to mulching has been the depletion of nitrogen from the soil because it is used up by the soil organisms in their effort to break down the organic materials. Because the mulch material is not mixed with the surface soil itself, but exists only as a cover, decomposition is not rapid and takes place primarily at the interfacial layer where soil and mulch are in contact.

Temporary nitrogen deficiency does occur when mulches are used improperly, but for the individual who does not go overboard in the use of low-nitrogen materials, there is little danger. If straw, corn cobs and sawdust, which are low in nitrogen content, are mixed with other mulching materials such as legume residues, felt or wool wastes, hoof and horn meal, cottonseed meal, castor pomace, etc., which are high in nitrogen content, little difficulty should be encountered with nitrogen deficiency.—*William Ackerman.*

YEAR ROUND MULCHING: In 1955, Ruth Stout of West Redding, Connecticut, has written a book, *How to Have a Green Thumb Without an*

Aching Back. In it, she described her own personal method of mulch gardening, which, according to Miss Stout, eliminated completely spading, hoeing and weeding. What Miss Stout did, essentially, was to carry the logic of the mulch to its fullest extent.

Actually a practice of constant deep mulching that has been used by some gardeners for many years, year-round mulching can work well in many fertile, well-aerated soils. "Just push the mulch aside and plant" is the motto. For a detailed description and evaluation of year-round mulching, *see* No-Digging Method.

Vertical Mulching

One of the best ways you can protect your garden against drought damage is to build fertility deep down in your soil where your plant food will stay moist longer. In the garden, this can be done by vertical mulching, or more accurately, vertical *composting.*

Many soils have only a thin layer of fertile matter over a bed of clay and therefore have no built-in drought protection. During dry periods, roots have no place to go to look for nutrients. If you have a soil with only a shallow fertile layer, you'll be especially pleased with the results of vertical composting.

Here's how to do it:

1. Spread compost, natural rock fertilizers or bagged organic fertilizer on the surface of your soil—then plow deeply to get the plant food to a depth of six or eight inches. This method has the disadvantage of requiring a deep turnover of soil, so the result might be clay on the soil surface and topsoil underneath.

2. If you are mechanically minded, you can build an attachment for your garden tractor or rotary tiller that will place compost or other organic fertilizer deep down in the soil without disturbing its normal layers.

This "deep fertilizer sower," as we call this machine, can be made by combining a chisel attachment for your tractor with the hopper of a fertilizer

side dresser. It is necessary to connect the two parts together with a drop tube long enough to reach at least a foot into the soil.

Some of the smaller tractors may not have sufficient power to pull a chisel that penetrates eight or ten inches. Even when using a larger tractor it may be necessary to first loosen the soil. But on light or sandy soils, deep penetration will not be a problem.

The basic purpose of vertical composting is to put nutrients down into the soil—where they will help retain moisture and remain useful longer. *See also* No-Digging Method; Compost; Flower Gardening; Vegetable Gardening; Drought Gardening; Stubble Mulch.

MULCH TILLAGE: *see* Stubble Mulching; Rotary Tilling

MULDER, GERRIT JAN: Born in 1802, died in 1880. Mulder was a Dutch professor of chemistry who was opposed to Justus von Liebig's chemical conception of agriculture. He is famous for his protein theory, for which he is given credit in scientific literature. It was Mulder who gave the name *protein* to the albuminous substances he had isolated. He was of the opinion that protein was the foster substance of the entire animal kingdom.

It was Mulder's work with protein that caused scientists to consider the nitrogen content of farm feeds as the basis of the ration's nutritional value, there again illustrating the basic fact that protein is of first importance, because it is very rich in nitrogen.

Mulder had discovered that in all protein compounds, nitrogen makes up 16 per cent. This is a figure still used by scientists today for calculating the protein content of a substance when its nitrogen content is known.

In 1846 Justus von Liebig began to question the exactness of Mulder's analyses. No doubt, von Liebig was the better chemist as far as techniques and knowledge of the exact methods of making analyses were concerned.

There followed a stormy dispute and Mulder was defeated. The scientific world believed in von Liebig, and lost faith in the protein theory. As a result, Mulder's reputation was greatly injured, while Liebig's star rose to higher heights.

Regarding Mulder's views on the subject of chemical fertilizers, one recent biographer has said, "In his restless activity he made an extensive study in the field of agricultural chemistry, evidenced by *'De scheikunde der bouware aarde'* ("The Chemistry of the Cultivable Soil," 1860, 4 volumes). Mulder defended the old humus theory against the mineral theory of Liebig. According to Mulder, it is the soil that regulates the reaction of the plant to fertilizers. The well-known conception that not the plant should be fertilized but rather the soil, originated in his mind. In brief, the ideas in the above-mentioned book are of such stature that Van Bemmelen, the famous father of colloid chemistry, regretted in 1901 that this book did not meet with more success, because it would have given a much better basis for further research than the theory of Liebig.

MULLEIN-PINK: *see* Lychnis

MULTIFLORA ROSE: (*Rosa multiflora*) Multiflora is a fast-growing rose variety which will reach a height of five to seven feet in three or four years. Therefore, you should select a site where there is plenty of room for this ambitious hedge. The multiflora will grow into a dense thicket, sprinkled with a profusion of small, white flowers in June and July and, later on, will provide thousands of red, pea-sized berries, on which birds and other wildlife will feast throughout the winter. The canes grow very rapidly and tend to tip, the ends of which root in the ground and start new plants. In this way, the multiflora will propagate itself until you decide to halt its progress. Control is easy, however. The tipping canes will not root too well in sod,

and those which do root may be mowed down right along with the grass.

Culture: Planting is relatively simple, not requiring much soil preparation. Multiflora grows in practically any type of soil, except very poorly-drained ones. Fertilizing will give plants a good start, but very little is actually necessary for normal growth. If your soil is very poor, dig in plenty of compost—or another balanced organic fertilizer — before planting. Multiflora will grow even on deficient soils, if there is little competition from other plants. To plant the row, dig either a furrow or individual holes—one foot apart, and deep enough to generously accommodate the root depth. There should be no sod or other growth within a foot of each plant. Working the soil deeply before planting will help plants but, again, is not necessary for normal growth. A good way to set in plants is to put about a dozen at a time in a bucket of water (plants are small, twig-looking, with short roots), set into the soil at about the level to which they were planted in the nursery (you can tell by the difference in color), and firm the soil around each plant. After all 12 are set in, pour the bucket of water over the plants.

At one time, the Soil Conservation Service promoted multiflora to farmers at a very low cost as a conservation measure.

Maintenance: Multiflora is a lazy gardener's dream. After planting, a straw mulch will eliminate the need for cultivation throughout the season and, after two years and plants are on the way to maturity, you can discard the mulch altogether. Pruning? Forget it! The only pruning you need on the multiflora is when the canes get too unruly for your needs. Multiflora is subject to some diseases, as are other roses, but no serious trouble has been experienced from diseases or insects.

MUM: *see* Chrysanthemum

MUNICIPAL COMPOSTING: *see* COMPOST

MURIATE OF POTASH: *see* FERTILIZER, ARTIFICIAL

MUSA: These giant tropical herbs include the banana and several other edible and ornamental plants. *M. paradisiaca,* the plantain, closely resembles the common banana, growing up to 30 feet tall, with leaves as long as ten feet. Its fruit, cooked, is a staple food for millions in the tropics. The Abyssinian banana tree, *M. ensete,* is even bigger, but its fruits are inedible. A much smaller variety, the dwarf or Chinese banana, *M. cavendishi,* grows about six feet tall with four-foot-long leaves. It is the most tolerant of cold and wind of all the bananas and produces good quality fruit, but it is most often grown solely for ornament in Florida, parts of the Gulf Coast and Southern California. The fruits are fragrant and numerous, often 200 in a cluster. It likes a friable, loose and fertile soil, with full sun and plenty of moisture; heavy mulching is beneficial. Another variety, the abaca, *M. textilis,* has stalks that yield the strong cordage fiber, Manila hemp. Its fruit is not edible, and it is rarely grown outside of the Philippines. *See also* BANANA.

MUSCARI: *see* GRAPE-HYACINTH

MUSHROOM: (*Agaricus campestris*) The common mushroom is the only cultivated fungi in common usage. Although it grows wild in many places, it is safer to purchase or cultivate the mushroom rather than try to differentiate *A. campestris* from its many poisonous relatives.

For your winter-time gardening pleasure, you'll find mushroom growing just the thing. All you need is a place—a very small one—that is dark, moist and cool. For most homeowners, that place will be in the basement; even the area under the kitchen sink might do.

It is not necessary to make an absolute "dark room" out of your entire basement; a certain amount of light will not hurt mushrooms. But they do need controlled humidity and temperature. Strong drafts and dry air are fatal, as is a temperature that ranges much above 60° or below 55°.

Mushroom spawn, similar to bread mold, works its way to the surface. It appears above as white, stringy matter and little white dots.

In order to find a place that maintains the proper temperature range both day and night, make some tests by placing a few thermometers in various spots of your basement. Since temperatures can vary as much as ten degrees at different levels in the same location, make certain you put the thermometer at about the level where the mushrooms will be growing.

Once you've selected the spot for your mushroom garden, the next step is to decide how you're going to grow them. If you use the tray method, a bench or hanging shelves on tiers will do the job. Generally, you can estimate that the trays will weigh about 25 pounds when ready for growth.

Prepared trays, already filled with the growing medium and inoculated with the mushroom spawn, can be purchased. Constructed like seed flats, they measure about six inches deep and 14 by 16 inches in size. They contain compost covered with heavy paper and loose topsoil. Spawn is already planted in the trays, so all you have to do is remove the paper, add an inch of topsoil and water thoroughly. If the conditions are right, you'll be harvesting your crop in about four weeks.

GROWING MEDIUM: Mushrooms grow in organic material containing carbohydrates such as sugar, starch, cellulose or lignin, as well as the nitrogen required by all green plants. However, mushrooms cannot manufacture these products the way other plants do because they have no green color in their tissues. They develop their full root system, a network of fine white threads called mycelium, before any part of the plant appears above the soil. Fresh strawy horse manure is excellent for mushroom growing. It should be composted by turning it every four or five days, shaking thoroughly and watering well each time. Keep it moist, but not saturated. After three or four turnings, it should be a rich dark brown, with no odor. It can then be put in trays of any convenient size and allowed to "sweat out"—heat to 140°. After about a week, this should be ready for planting.

Many growers do not use horse manure as their special mushroom compost, but instead find it more practical to make compost using materials more readily available. Here is how to do it:

Mix together in a heap about 100 pounds of corn fodder or finely ground corn cobs and an equal amount of straw. Water and firm this well and let it stand a few days. Then mix in thoroughly 20 pounds each of leaf mold or peat moss, tankage, and either greensand or granite dust. Some well-rotted compost can be added to aid decomposition. About 30 pounds of whole grains completes the mixture.

After a good watering, let it stand five or six days before turning. A second turning a week or so later should be enough before setting in the trays and planting. Plant the spawn as soon as the temperature of the beds reaches about 75°.

SPAWN: You can purchase spawn, which is much like a cheese or bread mold, from most seed companies. Bottle spawn is the purest form of culture. Break it into pieces a little smaller than a golf ball and plant them eight to ten inches apart, about two inches deep.

To get a good run of spawn, keep the room as dark as possible and the temperature about 70° for the next 21 days. At the end of that time, the threadlike filaments (mycelium) from adjacent plantings should meet. The temperature should then be dropped to about 60° and the beds "cased"—covered with a one-inch layer of good garden soil. (Many home growers keep their beds near the heating plant for the sweating out and spawning periods, then move them to the 60° spot at casing time.)

Water well with a gentle spray; the medium should be moist and crumbly, but not so moist that water can be readily squeezed out of it. Most mushroom diseases and pests—fogging off, sow bugs, and black spot—will never make their appearance if moisture and temperature conditions are carefully tended. Any snails and slugs can be trapped with lettuce or cabbage leaves. If the air in your cellar is on the dry side, a layer or two of moist burlap over the trays will maintain the proper humidity. Water whenever the topsoil feels powdery.

In approximately three weeks, tiny white dots will appear. You'll find these clustered together in groups, called a "flush" or "break." In another ten days, the largest will be ready for picking, but don't rush the harvest. Pick only those whose cap has split away from the stem. These ripe ones will taste much better than the "green," immature ones commercial growers must ship to avoid bruising.

HARVESTING: Careful picking of the tiny buttons or the giant-size ones is the order of the day. Don't pull them up—you may injure others just breaking through. Press the soil down around the bottom of the stem with one hand and twist it off at soil level with the other. Or use a sharp knife to cut the stem at its base.

Practice selective harvesting, picking every day if possible, and your beds will crop up to six months. After each "flush" is completely picked, clean out the remaining ends and diseased or underdeveloped mushrooms.

When the entire bed is cropped out, the compost will make a fine soil conditioner. Most gardeners don't try to grow mushrooms during the summer—it's too hard to maintain a 60° temperature — so you can set up a profitable schedule: fall preparation of compost, winter cropping, and spring fertilization of your garden with the used compost.

The wonderful flavor of cultivated mushrooms and their ability to elevate any dish from the mediocre category is enough to make them a valuable part of the diet. But cultivated mushrooms also contain valuable nutritive elements. Nutritionists have found them to be a good source of extra protein, iron, vitamin C, riboflavin and niacin.

MUSKMELON: *see* CANTALOUPE

MUSTARD: (*Brassica*) Commercial mustard seed is obtained from several closely related species and varieties of *Brassica,* which are annual plants of wide geographic distribution. The seeds of these varieties differ slightly in size and range in color from pale yellow to black. The most important varieties are the yellow (sometimes referred to as white mustard), the brown, and the oriental types, all of which are produced under cultivation. The principal use of the seed is as a condiment; however, it is also used medicinally. For this use the brown is preferred to the yellow, because it is more pungent. The several types differ in color of their seed coats only. When these are completely removed from the ground seed the flour of any of them may be used for prepared mustard and other seasoning preparations. The yellow seed, unground, is used in pickling, especially in sweet, mixed pickles.

CULTURE: Yellow mustard is best adapted to a rather heavy type of sandy loam and light adobe soil, whereas the brown requires a lighter sandy loam.

The crop requires only limited rainfall, preferably so distributed that the seed can mature during a period of dry weather. These conditions prevail in the principal producing regions. In the Lompoc Valley, in Santa Barbara County, Calif., the crop is also said to be favored by cool west winds and fogs. The land is best prepared in fall, the method depending on the cultural practices used with the preceding crop. Seed is broadcast in spring, using an alfalfa or grain seeder, after which the ground is harrowed. In California the brown seed is sown from January to March and the yellow seed near the end of this period. In Montana, seed is sown from early spring to the first of June. About three pounds of brown or four pounds of yellow seed are required per acre.

The crop is usually ready for harvesting in August. The seed shatters severely when it is fully ripe and the crop must, therefore, be harvested when the pods are fully grown but still closed. In California two methods are employed, depending on the equipment and facilities available. The crop is cut with a mower and allowed to dry in windrows, from which it is threshed with a pick-up harvester when dry; or it is cut and bound with a grain binder, cured in the field, and then threshed with a modified grain thresher. In Montana most of the crop is harvested with a combine.

The brown variety produces heavier yields than the yellow. In California the former is reported to yield from 1,200 to 1,500 pounds to the acre and the latter 800 to 1,000 pounds. In Montana the yields are dependent on the rainfall during the growing season. The average annual yields per acre in that State over a period of years have ranged from 115 to 548 pounds, but individual growers have reported yields as high as 1,500 pounds. Generally if the yields are good the quality also is good.

Mustard is definitely a crop for the Western States for climatic reasons.

Elsewhere frequent rains when the crop matures may interfere with proper and timely harvesting and result in loss of seed. It has been successfully grown in the Western States, since it is an annual crop yielding early returns, is not difficult to grow, and can be handled with equipment usually available on large farms. Soil and climate apparently have a pronounced influence on the quality of the seed. In new localities, especially where conditions are quite different, it is advisable first to grow a small trial acreage to determine whether the seed produced is of acceptable quality. The species and varieties of mustard grown can become established as weed pests.

MUTATION: Any change in the character of a plant not brought about by crossing it with another plant, is called a mutation. It may be a variation in color, size, flowering, yield, root or top-growth habit, or any other characteristic. Sometimes only a part of the plant, such as a single branch, may show the new trait, as happens often with roses and fruits. Cuttings of these branches will produce new plants having the alteration throughout. But generally mutations appear most often among plants reproduced by seed.

Mutations are the variations plant breeders spend their lives searching for, the off-types whose new characteristics may be valuable. When reproduced, a new variety joins the ranks of useful plants. Mutations are the source of disease-resistant varieties, higher-yielding crops, and hardier and more beautiful plants, and thus are of great interest to the gardener and farmer. Natural mutations are worth watching for in your plants. Plant breeders sometimes produce them artificially by means of chemicals or radiation, or by changing factors like temperature in the plant's environment.

MYCELIUM: Mycelium is the collective term which designates mold tissue or the mass of growth of filamentous (thread) fungi. Yeasts are in general unicellular fungi; that is, each individual yeast organism, as a rule, consists of a single cell. The molds, also called filamentous fungi, usually are made up of ramifying, branched, and multicellular threads, each thread, in general being, a chain-like arrangement of cells attached end to end. These threads or filaments (hence, the name filamentous fungi) are known as hyphae. Each individual thread is a hypha; the mass of hyphae is the mycelium.

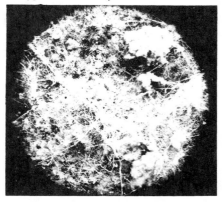

Mycelia (tiny, thread-like organisms) are formed from beneficial fungi growing in the soil. They serve to bind individual soil particles together.

In the production of penicillin, fumaric acid, citric acid, kojic acid, gluconic acid and other industrial processes which employ mold fermentations mycelium, is a by-product or a waste product. In these large scale industrial processes, tanks or vats containing thousands of gallons of corn mash, or some other suitable raw material, are inoculated with mold mycelium or mold spores (equivalent to "seeds"). The mycelium increases tremendously in mass as the mold grows and produces whatever product the fermentation is designed for.

These products, with the exception of some fats, are as a rule soluble in water. The recovery procedure therefore usually begins by a separation of the mycelium from the liquid in which it has grown. However, in some cases the entire contents of the tank (mycelium and liquid) are treated without preliminary separation. This mycelium has a rather high water content (it may be ninety per cent), although of course it can be dried. It may run about two to three per cent ash (mineral constituents), two and one-half to five per cent nitrogen, and 40 to 50 per cent carbon. There would also undoubtedly be a number of vitamins present in the mycelium. Some "lignin-like" material (perhaps ten to 20 per cent) and around three to five per cent fats would also be expected to be present.

As far as its stability in the soil is concerned, it would no doubt be quickly decomposed. Mushrooms and toadstools (which are very close in biochemical composition to mycelium) rot seemingly over night. Mold mycelium would behave in a very similar manner.

In the process of growth, molds respire; they derive their energy by oxidizing a large amount of whatever they are growing on to carbon dioxide which of course is lost as a volatile gas. There is always therefore much less organic matter in mold mycelium than was originally present in the organic matter on which the mold grew. This is because of the loss of some organic matter in the form of carbon dioxide. *See also* MICROORGANISM.

MYCORRHIZA: The association, usually symbiotic, of the mycelium of various fungi and the roots of seed plants.

Dr. William F. Ganung, in his *Textbook of Botany* describes the function of mycorrhiza: "Fungi develop in contact with the tips of many plants —particularly those living in much humus, weaving around them a close cover of threads which replace the root hairs. This mycorrhiza as it is named, absorbs water and mineral matters which it transmits to the roots, and it also absorbs soluble organic matters set free in decay of humus but useful again to the plants. We have here one of the cases where two differ-

ent organisms derive benefit from their association, a condition called *symbosis.*"

Or in plainer words, the mycorrhiza is not a parasite—it does not gain its sustenance from the roots of the plants which it covers, but rather it is in partnership with them. Together the roots and this covering of mycorrhiza are able to draw in sustenance from the surrounding soil. There are two large groups of mycorrhizas, those which encase the roots, and those which invade the root cells of the plants. Both are of beneficial and of unusual importance to agriculture.

Another noteworthy statement on the subject is to be found in Sir Albert Howard's *An Agricultural Testament*:

"The mycorrhizal association . . . is the living bridge by which a fertile soil (one rich in humus) and the crop are directly connected and by which food materials ready for immediate use can be transferred from soil to plant. How this association influences the work of the green leaf is now one of the most interesting problems science has now to investigate. Is the effective synthesis of carbohydrates and proteins in the green leaf dependent on the digestion products of these soil fungi? It is more than probable that this must prove to be the case. Are these digestion products at the root of disease resistance and quality?"

Since the great pioneer of the organic method in agriculture posed these questions, more than ten years ago, no scientific researcher has brought forth a specific answer.

Practical experience has nevertheless proved that the answers to Sir Albert Howard's questions are, *yes*.

Sir Albert Howard went on to say that "On efficiency of this mycorrhizal association the health and well-being of mankind must depend. In a fertile soil, the soil and the plant come into gear in two ways simultaneously. In establishing and maintaining these contacts, humus is essential. It is therefore a key material in the life cycle. Without this substance the wheel of life cannot function effectively." *See also* MICROORGANISM.

MYOSOTIS: *see* FORGET-ME-NOT

MYRICA: These shrubs are often called bayberry, but they are no relation to the true bayberry. *M. pennsylvanica,* a semi-evergreen shrub three to eight feet tall and popular in the East, is very commonly called bayberry. Its waxy gray berries are highly aromatic and are used to make bayberry candles. *M. cerifera,* the wax myrtle, is a large evergreen shrub or small tree about 30 feet in height. It also bears waxy, scented fruit, and is grown from New Jersey southward. Both of these varieties thrive in sandy, very dry places. A third variety, the sweet gale or bog myrtle, *M. gale,* is deciduous, about three feet tall, and carries its fruits in heavy catkins. It likes acid, boggy situations from Virginia to the far North, and is a good subject for the bog garden.

MYRTLE: (*Myrtus*) The true myrtle (*M. communis*), is an evergreen shrub that grows to a maximum height of ten feet. It is widely grown for ornament in the South and on the West Coast, and above Richmond, Va., is a popular pot plant for the cool greenhouse. Myrtle has bright green, scented leaves, and creamy-white or pink flowers in July, followed by purple-black berries. There are smaller varieties and ones with double flowers and variegated leaves. In Greek festivals, myrtle was used as a symbol of youth and beauty. The leaves and berries are still used in some parts of southern Europe as a medicine, and the bark for tanning. Myrtle prefers a light, sandy, humusy soil, and is propagated by seeds or by cuttings of half-ripened wood under glass. Other varieties include a tall shrub or small tree, the luma (*M. luma*), and the Chilean guava (*M. ugni*), both of which are grown in South America and occasionally in California for their sweet, edible fruits, which taste like wild strawberries.

N

NAEGELIA: Perennial tropical American herbs of the *Gesneria* family. Raised in a warm greenhouse in the north, it usually grows to two or three feet, with soft heart-shaped leaves, and clusters of tubular flowers about 1½ inches long, colored red, yellow, purple, and white.

Propagation may be by seed, division of tubers, or by offsets. Soil must be rich in humus and well-drained. In the greenhouse the plants, especially when flowering, should be slightly screened from the full sun. After flowering the pots with tubers are placed below the bench, and allowed a period of rest where they are kept almost dry. Seed is sown in well-drained peaty soil in late winter to early spring. Cuttings may be rooted at the same time. Blossoming period will be in September to November.

Difference between species is mainly a matter of size and color. *N. cinnabarina* is two feet high, with leaves covered with reddish hairs, flowers cinnabar-red spotted with white and swollen toward the base. *N. multiflora* grows to about 1½ feet, and has white flowers with a barely swollen tube. *N. zebrina* is taller, growing to three feet, with hairy leaves red or brown along the veins, flowers red with yellow spots and contracted at the base. *N. hybrida* is a hybrid of *zebrina* and *multiflora,* a short plant with hairy leaves and creamy blossoms.

NARCISSUS: Bulbous plants of the *Amaryllidaceae* family, including daffodil, jonquil, paper-white, Chinese sacred lily, and poet's narcissus. In Greek mythology, Narcissus was a youth who, for his indifference to the nymph Echo, was doomed to pine away for love of his own image, until he was finally changed into a flower. The flower today represents the rebirth of spring in many gardens throughout the country and is one which can be easily grown by any gardener. Many land owners with acres of rolling hills scatter the bulbs on hillsides, merely planting them about six inches deep and leaving them to grow and reproduce by themselves. In this way, each spring will be greeted by more and more blooms to grace the countryside.

Symbol of the start of spring in many gardens, narcissus should be planted in September or October in a deeply-spaded, humus-rich soil.

In the well-planned home garden you may want to take more time and trouble to insure large and perfect blooms. The big secret in attaining this goal is in proper planting in the fall.

FALL PLANTING: September or October is about the best time to plant narcissus bulbs, although they may be planted as late as December first. An early planting will insure the plant's early blooming next spring (about the latter part of April).

Narcissuses can be grouped in beds, in borders along driveways or walks, or they may simply be scattered through a lawn, for they require little care after planted.

When planting in groups, spade the soil deeply to allow for plenty of root action in the spring. Work in plenty of rotted manure throughout the planting area until the soil assumes a good, crumbly structure. A light application of bone meal and wood ashes will give the bulbs a good potassium and phosphorus balance for a good spring start. Remove about six inches of the soil to form a trench. Then mix the bone meal and wood ashes with the soil you removed and set the bulbs in a one-inch layer of sand. Apply more sand until the bulbs are covered up to their necks. Then replace the soil you removed. The bulbs should be about three inches below the surface and at least six inches apart.

Scatter the bulbs at random and plant them where they fall. Of course they look lovely in more formal beds, too, but keep them in clumps or groups, not in rows. Once planted, narcissuses may remain several years before you need to replant them. Be sure they get a top dressing of compost each year to insure a good display of flowers. When the plantings become too crowded and blooms are small, it is time to dig up the bulbs, separate them, enrich the soil, and replant.

WINTER CARE: If you live in the North, a winter mulch will protect the bulbs from alternate freezing and thawing periods which can heave the soil and harm the bulbs. A layer of straw, hay or evergreen boughs will serve the purpose adequately. Let the mulch on the bed until the plant pushes through the soil in spring. Then uncover, unless you expect more frosts.

AFTER SPRING BLOOMING: When the bloom begins to wither in spring, pinch it off at the base to preserve nutrients which would otherwise be wasted on forming seed pods. The plant should be allowed to wither before it is cut off at its base. Narcissuses, like other bulbs, can be left in the same location for a number of years. If the growth becomes too thick, bulbs may be transplanted elsewhere. *See also* BULB; BULB GARDEN; FLOWER GARDENING.

NASTURTIUM: (*Tropaeolum*) Including about 50 annual or perennial plants, mostly climbing. Common nasturtium (*T. majus*), also called Indian cress, is a tender annual with climbing stems and round, green leaves. It is one of the most popular annuals because of its showy flowers in many shades of yellow, orange and red. Large varieties climb as high as ten to 12 feet. Dwarf varieties include Tom Thumb types (*nanum*), which grow in low, compact, rounded bushes slightly less than one foot high and about a foot in diameter. These forms are excellent for bedding.

CULTURE: Nasturtiums do best in a sunny, well-drained location. When planted in a shady site or in wet ground, they tend to produce a large growth of foliage with relatively few flowers. Cultivate soil well before planting seed in spring after danger of frost is over. Cover seed with about one inch of soil, and firm well. Thin plants to about one foot apart. If soil is poor and hard, spade deeply and add several inches of finished compost to the soil surface.

USEFUL IN COOKING: The entire plant of nasturtium—both flowers and young tender leaves—have a spicy, yet delicately pungent flavor similar to cress. They are fine for salads and sandwiches in the same way as lettuce. Seeds also make a fine snack in winter. Gather seed clusters when about half grown with some of the stem still attached. Clean and put them in a jar, covering with freshly boiled cider vinegar. Close lids tightly and store in cool place.

Other varieties include the Canary-bird flower (*T. peregrinum*), a tall-climbing annual with light yellow flowers, and dwarf nasturtium (*T. minus*), useful as a border plant.

NASTURTIUM OFFICINALE: *see* WATER CRESS

NATURAL CONTROL OF INSECTS: *see* INSECT CONTROL, BIOLOGICAL

NAVEL ORANGE: *see* ORANGE; CITRUS

NAVELWORT: (*Omphalodes*) The annual species of navelwort (*O. linifolia*) grows about a foot tall and has white flowers. It thrives in moist fairly fertile soil in part shade. Sow the seeds, 1/8-inch deep, where the plant is to grow, in spring for summer bloom; if sown in the fall it will flower early the following spring. A variety, *O. linifolia caerulescens,* has blue flowers and is suited to dry, stony soil.

There are also two perennial species that grow about eight inches high, with bright blue flowers. *O. cappadocica* is a fine subject for a shady spot in the rock garden, while *O. verna,* the creeping forget-me-not, is grown most often as a ground cover. Sow the seeds in the spring, or divide the roots in spring or fall. These, too, like a shaded position and moist, neutral or slightly alkaline soil.

NECROSIS: The dying of plant tissue, a common sign of disease, which results in such conditions as rot, canker, blight and wilt. *See also* DISEASE.

NECTAR: The sweet secretion of the *nectary* of plants which is collected and partially digested by bees to form honey. Nectaries are usually located deep in the center of flowers, where the bees will be forced to brush past stamens and come in contact with the pistils, thus cross-pollinating as they visit flower after flower. Sometimes the nectary is located in the calyx, as in nasturtiums; sometimes deep

in the spurs, as in columbine; sometimes in furrows through the petals, as in lilies; sometimes in scales in petals, as in ranunculus. Occasionally nectaries are found in leaf axils, or in parts of the plant not associated with fertilization. In this case, they may attract insects which will protect the plant in some way. *See also* POLLINATION.

NECTARINE: A smooth, firm, flavorful peach. *Prunus persica* variety *nectarina.* Nectarines may be freestone or clings, like peaches. Their culture is the same as peaches. Nectarines are grown more in California than in the East, and seem to do somewhat better west of the Rocky Mountains.

Nectarines may be grown from seed or from buds, though the seed sometimes produces peaches instead of nectarines. Sometimes both fruits are found on one tree, without cross-pollination, a phenomenon which has mystified growers for hundreds of years. Darwin called this strange, unpredictable behavior a bud mutation, known also as a bud sport, which labels but does not explain it.

Most popular varieties are Hunter, Kentucky, Quetta or Persian, Red Roman, and Sure-crop. Dwarf varieties are also offered for backyard gardening. *See also* PEACH; FRUIT TREE, DWARF; ORCHARD.

NELUMBIUM: *see* LOTUS

NEMATODE: Nematodes or eel worms are quite minute—being as small as 1/125 of an inch in length but also measuring up to a yard long as in the case of certain animal parasites. Although most abundant in tropical areas, they nevertheless occur in sizable numbers in all other parts of the world.

Without brains or eyesight, these minute, eelshaped organisms move around in the soil in what appears to be an aimless pattern. The pattern, however, does have a direction, for they will head straight toward any root that is near them. Once they arrive, the nematodes pierce the root and feed on it, or lay their eggs in it, causing knots to form. Result—the plant loses nourishment from the roots, becomes stunted or dies.

Infesting roots and causing knots to form, as shown above, nematodes can be controlled by beneficial fungi which grow in decomposing humus.

Scarcely any crop is free from nematode attack, whether in home garden, orchard, greenhouse or field. Investigation has shown that almost every acre of land in this nation is infested with them. In stressing the seriousness of the nematode problem, Dr. Gerald W. Thorne, plant pathologist at the University of Wisconsin writes:

"Because of nematodes, we have not realized the fullest possible production from many of our fields. Our successful control of them would help guarantee adequate food supplies for the world's ever-increasing population."

ROOT PARASITES: The greater majority of plant-parasitic nematodes are root parasites and do not cause specific symptoms of injury on above-ground parts of plants. These symptoms are usually an unhealthy condition in which plants grow poorly and frequently have a stunted appearance. On hot summer days nematode-infected succulent plants tend to wilt more rapidly than healthy plants but usually recover when temperatures become cooler. Yellowing of foliage and "die-back" of branches or shoots may also be a common occurrence with such infections. Since there are also a number of free-living, non-parasitic nematodes usually associated with root systems of many plants, the finding of a number of nematodes is not always an indication that plants are suffering from nematode injury. Along the same lines, the presence of root-pathogenic nematodes is not always an indication that plants are suffering solely from nematode injury since many other microorganisms, especially root-pathogenic fungi, can cause serious root injury.

In any consideration of plant-parasitic nematodes it should be pointed out that these creatures are capable of causing their greatest damage to plants when conditions of moisture and temperature are favorable. Whereas nematodes are most active in soil suitable for germination of seed and subsequent growth of plants, considerable numbers of some of them may be killed by flooding the soil for extended periods or by permitting soil, such as on greenhouse benches, to dry completely. Nematode activity diminishes rapidly as temperatures are lowered. This is the principle under which a profitable crop of lettuce, which can be grown in cooler temperature, is cultivated on root-knot nematode-infested soil. Freezing of the soil is of little value for reducing the nematode population contained within.

Higher temperatures on the other hand, can be extremely detrimental to nematodes. Without a doubt, the sun often plays an important role in eliminating a considerable number of nematodes by continued baking of the upper soil layer. Some nematodes, however, are prepared for adverse conditions and go into a resistant stage or live over in protective egg shells. Even among those nematodes which are not adapted to survive adverse conditions a few usually escape death among the many that perish, and these multiply rapidly once conditions again become favorable.

CONTROL: Methods of controlling nematode parasites of plants are constantly being improved. The continued recommendation for use of nematode-free planting stock may be extremely effective in reducing the introduction and spread of plant-parasitic nematodes, but is little consolation to growers who own fields infested with these parasites. Crop rotation is perhaps one of the most inexpensive yet effective measures on which we can rely. Nematodes, like other parasites, prefer certain types of plants to others. If a crop which is undesirable to plant-parasitic nematodes is planted, the parasites are starved and their populations in the soil reduced accordingly. Since certain types of nematodes thrive on several different crops, however, the grower should be certain that the substitute crop is not another on which the nematodes can feed and reproduce. This can be accomplished only by sending plant and soil samples for examination by competent personnel located in federal and state laboratories throughout the country.

Fertilization of infected plants induces the formation of roots and improves plant vigor thus masking the deleterious effects of nematodes feeding on the roots. Such improvements in plant growth are relatively short-lived, however, since root-parasitic nematodes can multiply rapidly and again cause plant decline once conditions become adverse for the plant.

ORGANIC FERTILIZING: When quantities of organic fertilizers are added to the soil around plants with roots parasitized by nematodes, growth of insects, nematodes, and fungi which prey on plant-parasitic nematodes is often encouraged.

Research by English scientists in London several years ago has given new support to an all-important organic gardening concept—adding humus to soils will help control nematodes.

The man most responsible for this important research is Dr. C. L. Duddington, senior lecturer in botany at the Regent Street Polytechnic in London. In 1951, he made his first experiments, conducted in flower pots on a roof in central London, to learn the value of a combination of organic materials and fungus cultures to stop nematode destruction. Later he made field tests with farm crops (mostly cereals and potatoes).

All experiments clearly showed that nematodes could be controlled by building up concentrations of beneficial fungi and organic matter in the soil!

BENEFICIAL FUNGI: The fungi are closely related to the blue mold penicillium but are invisible to the naked eye, so microscopically small are their threads; and they achieve their results by virtually eating nematodes alive.

Botanists refer to them as predacious fungi, and also as "fungi imperfecta" (having no sex life); 48 different species of such "nematode eaters" have been isolated. They can be grown artificially in the laboratory with considerable ease if proper facilities are available.

In their natural state, these fungi grow in decomposing vegetable matter and farmyard manure—and wherever there are nematodes. They are extremely widespread, easily isolated, harmless to crops, animals and human beings. But to nematodes, they are killers.

HOW THEY WORK: The fungi do their work of destruction in a number of ways. In some cases, the fine threads of the fungus have branches which form loops, and these loops in turn form three-dimensional networks something like crumpled wire netting.

The networks secrete a sticky fluid when they come into contact with the nematode, and the nematodes are caught as effectively as a fly by fly-paper. After the fungus catches the nematode, it then sends branches into its body, or grows into itself; and simply absorbs its tissue.

Another way in which fungus traps nematodes is by sticky branches which reproduce rapidly and form little circular loops in which the worm is trapped.

A third mechanism consists of sticky knots at the end of stalks. These knots hold the nematode and form a structure inside which spreads out; and thus destroys the worm.

Still another way in which nematodes are trapped is by the formation of a constricting ring to three cells on a stalk. The nematode puts its "nose" into the ring accidentally; the cells swell; and the ring closes.

BENEFITS OF METHOD: The advantages of controlling nematodes by fungi and organic matter are obvious. Plenty of chemicals are known which will kill nematodes; but they are mostly harmful to the soil and either expensive to produce or expensive to apply. They must always be mixed thoroughly with the top soil; since the weight of the top nine inches of soil on an acre of farmland is something like 1,000 tons, the difficulty is evident.

MULCH AGAINST ROOT-KNOT: Here's a report from the University of Florida's Agricultural Experiment Station, issued some 15 years ago, which also reveals the value of humus against nematodes and root-knot:

"Among the plants which are susceptible to nematode injury and consequently which may be greatly benefitted by mulching, are . . . okra, tomatoes, peppers, eggplant, squash, cantaloupes, watermelons, beans, celery and lettuce.

"Like practically all forms of animal life, nematodes have their enemies. Among the most common and efficient of these enemies are certain kinds of fungi which live in decaying vegetable matter. This doubtless accounts for much of the importance and advantages of a mulch.

"Rotting vegetable matter piled around the plants has a very marked effect in checking the development of root-knot and in enabling the plants to withstand the disease. In practice, one piles around the plants to the depth of many inches or even a foot any available vegetable matter that will decay. Dead grasses, weeds and leaves are excellent. Persons living near a stream or lake with water hyacinths will find these plants particularly suitable for a mulch, since they hold water for a long time. Fungi developing in this rotting vegetable matter have been seen by a number of investigators to trap nematodes and to enter their body."

ORGANIC MATTER VITAL: When first developing the fungi, Dr. Duddington spent some time in studying the various ways of growing these particular types, mainly to encourage their optimum growth. Early experiments were with potatoes in pots. One thing of fundamental importance resulted from these tests:

Positive results in controlling nematodes were achieved only in the presence of added organic matter such as compost or leaf mold. Where fungus was tried without organic matter, the results were negative.

The first field experiment was with cereal root nematodes. Small plots which previous tests had shown to contain suitable fungi were artificially infested with nematodes by adding infested soil. Half the plots were then treated by digging in chopped cabbage leaves, while the other half were left untreated as controls; no inoculation was given to any plots.

DRAMATIC RESULTS: The result of this test was, in Dr. Duddington's words, "quite dramatic." A perfectly healthy crop was reared in the treated plots, but in the untreated plots there was severe nematode damage.

As a further check, the plots were sampled by taking plants at the seedling stage and counting the nematodes in the roots, while soil samples from the plots were also tested for fungus activity. These samplings showed far fewer nematodes in the treated roots, where the activity of fungi was correspondingly greater.

But perhaps the most decisive of all the trials were those held in Lincolnshire with farmyard manure. The land concerned, heavily affected by potato root nematode, had been officially scheduled as unfit for potatoes as a result of infestation. Nevertheless, the plot treated with manure and fungus produced an excellent crop of potatoes, while an untreated plot was a complete failure.

OTHER CONTROLS: Two other methods of controlling plant-parasitic nematodes are by trap cropping and by the use of resistant plant varieties. The former method involves the planting of a crop, roots of which nematodes will penetrate for purposes of feeding and reproduction. Since certain nematodes cannot leave roots which they have entered once they have started to complete their life cycles, plowing the crop thus killing the plants likewise kills the nematodes in the roots. Considerable work on the breeding of nematode resistant plants is now in progress. To date, advances have been made in the breeding of resistant tobacco and fruit trees.

Despite the large number of nematode diseases that currently are recognized and being discovered continually, more scientific research is being conducted on them and their control than ever before. The future holds promise of new developments in disease control that will benefit producer and consumer alike.—*A. C. Tarjan.*

See also INSECT CONTROL.

NEMESIA: Half-hardy annuals of the snapdragon family, grown successfully as annuals in England and in this country where the summers are very cool. Where summers are hot they are started in January or February indoors, and are hardened off to transplant to the flower border as soon as early seed is planted, preferably by April 1, when they will bloom through May and June, and then succumb to the summer heat.

Flowers somewhat resemble snapdragons in white, yellow, or purple, with improved varieties of pink and orange. Leaves are small, opposite, and stems are not very strong, so plants should stand about six inches apart, for mutual support.

The most frequently grown species is *N. strumosa,* growing to two feet, with slender three-inch leaves and flowers in clusters to four inches. Flowers are white, yellow, or purple, with spotted throats and orange or white beard. Variety *grandiflora* has larger flowers; *nana compacta* is dwarfed; and *suttonii* has flowers in yellow, rose-pink, orange, crimson, and scarlet.

NEMOPHILO: A genus of exquisite small annuals of the *Hydrophyllaceae,* native in California. Leaves are hairy, narrow and squarely notched on each side almost to midrib. Flowers are wide-open bells, white, blue, or purple, mostly single, some margined, veined, or blotched.

Seed may be sown early in spring where plants are to stand. Sometimes self-seeding. Usually planted as edging, or in low masses, in partial shade, with plenty of humus but not necessarily rich soil.

Cultivated species include baby-blue-eyes, *N. menziesii,* variety *insignis,* a low sprawling plant whose stems may grow to 20 inches, prostrate, raising white-margined blue flowers six inches above the ground; five-spot, *N. maculata,* similar growth habit, white flowers with deep purple spot at tip of each petal; and *N. aurita,* fiesta flower, which climbs three to six feet over twigs or other plants by means of prickles at base of leaves, flowers blue or light violet, lighter outside, with darker markings in the throat. Sometimes classed as genus *pholistoma.*

NEPENTHES: *see* PITCHER-PLANT.

NEPETA: Genus of aromatic annuals and perennials of the mint family, *Labiate,* some grown for medicinal purposes and many naturalized in the United States. Best known species are catnip, *N. cataria,* and ground-ivy, *N. hederacea.* Flowers of the genus are blue or white in whorls in clusters and spikes, leaves cut and sometimes toothed. Grown in almost any soil in part shade, used as ground cover under trees.

Catnip, or catmint, is one of the sweet perennials, grows to three feet, with downy foliage, pale green, and pale lavender small flowers growing in spikes to five inches. Ground ivy is a mat-forming perennial which naturalizes in the lawn under trees and gives off an aromatic scent when the lawn-mower is run through it. Leaves are roundish with scalloped edges, blue flowers are in sparse clusters. *See also* CATNIP.

NEPHROLEPIS: Sword fern or ladder fern. A genus of the family *Polypodiaceae* of tropical and sub-tropical ferns, most important of which, horticulturally, is the Boston fern. Fronds are usually long and narrow, many drooping, with feathery pinnate segments. They are grown in a rich mixture of sand, leaf mold, and loam, and are propagated by division or runners. Cultivated species seldom produce spores. They are easily grown, and make good house plants.

Tuber fern, *N. cordifolia,* grows from a rhizome bearing tubers, and has fronds up to two feet, erect, with bright green sharply toothed segments.

Basket fern, *N. pectinata,* is so-named because it is well adapted to culture in hanging baskets. Fronds are about 1½ feet, one inch wide, with fine, toothed segments. Habit of growth is compact.

Boston fern is a variety of *N. exaltata,* which was developed from a single plant in Boston some time in the 1890's. Fronds of the species grow long and graceful, to five or six feet, with segments close together and up to three inches long. Many forms have been developed from the original

Boston fern, which is an easily grown subject for greenhouse, window garden, or table. With neglect it will produce a creditable plant, and with proper treatment will proliferate. Some of the mutations which have arisen have crested or compound fronds with very fine segments. Propagated by runners. *See also* FERNS.

NERIUM: *see* OLEANDER

NETTLES: *see* STINGING NETTLE; WOOD NETTLE

NEUTRAL: Referring to soils that are in proper balance between acidity and alkalinity, having a pH of about seven. *See also* ACIDITY-ALKALINITY; LIME.

NICHOLS, JOE D., M.D.: Dr. Joe D. Nichols has been president of the Natural Foods Associates, Atlanta, Texas, since 1953. He has helped organize a number of regional chapters of Natural Foods Associates in various states.

NICOTIANA: Tobacco. Genus of mostly native American annuals, perennials, and shrubby perennials of the nightshade family, *Solanaceae.* Most are tropical plants and are grown as annuals throughout the United States, because they bloom freely the first year from seed. Included in the genus is commercially grown tobacco, *N. tabacum,* Indian tobacco, *N. bigelovii,* and several species called flowering tobacco which are used for ornament. Flowers are fragrant, tubular, mostly opening at night, in white, yellow, red, and purple. Leaves are usually large, hairy, and poisonous or narcotic. Ornamentals are usually started indoors in flats, or the fine seed may be planted directly in the garden. Also self-seeds. Prefers rich, moist loam in full sun, but will tolerate acid soil and partial shade. Sometimes grown as pot plants, and will remain open all day when cut.

Commercially grown tobacco is an annual growing to six feet, with leaves a foot long, rose or red funnel-shaped, woolly flowers opening at night. Variety *macrophylla* has larger leaves, and is called Maryland tobacco. Virginia tobacco is variety *angustifolia*. Indian tobacco grows to two feet, with leaves seven inches long and white flowers.

Flowering tobacco or jasmine tobacco, used for ornament, is *N. alata,* variety *affinis*. The type grows to five feet, with white night-blooming flowers, their tubes slender and lobes two inches across. A species which stays open all day but is not quite so fragrant is *N. sylvestris*. The red-flowered species grown in the garden are not so tall, growing to three feet, their rose or crimson flowers staying open in the daytime. Many hybrids have been developed.

An ornamental tree, tree tobacco (*N. glauca*) grows to 20 feet, with soft blue-green foliage and yellowish flowers. It is naturalized in Texas and California, but is not hardy North.

NICOTINE: An extract of tobacco used as a poison contact spray for sucking insects such as aphids. In the concentrated form in which it is sold it is highly dangerous to human beings, who may be poisoned even by contact with the thick brownish liquid. Also sold in powder form for dusting the same insects. Not approved in any form by organic gardeners, who believe that aphids are a symptom of trouble in the garden, and will usually disappear if the trouble is found and corrected. *See also* INSECT CONTROL.

NIEREMBERGIA: *see* CUP-FLOWER

NIGELLA: A genus of hardy annual herbs of the buttercup family, *Ranunculaceae*. Flowers blue or white, foliage misty-fine with pinnate leaves. Seed enclosed in a horned pod which is attractive in arrangements. Nigella prefers an open, sunny spot in the border, but are not particular about

soil. Seed may be planted in fall for early bloom, and again in spring to prolong blooming period.

Love-in-a-mist (*N. damascena*) is the airiest species, the blue flowers blossoming separately in a cloud of fine green foliage. Plants grow 12-18 inches high.

Fennel-flower (*N. sativa*) has less finely divided leaves which are slender but not thread-like, and do not surround the flowers. Flowers are blue, and seeds, which are used like pepper, are enclosed in an inflated pod.

NIGHT-BLOOMING FLOWERS: A garden of night-blooming flowers could be planted, composed of some flowers that open when the sun leaves' them, some that open at midnight, and others that are open on any cloudy day. Though many of the night-bloomers are tropical, and possibly open late in the day to escape a searing sun, there are enough such temperate zone natives to fill a border for the pleasure of sunset gardeners.

Most night-blooming flowers are very fragrant, and many of them are white. Such exotics as night-blooming cereus, lotus, which opens at dusk and closes the next noon, or night-blooming jasmine, which is grown only in tropical climates, must be grown in the greenhouse in the north. Lady-of-the-night or Franciscan nightshade, evening star, and false aloe are also very tender night-bloomers.

Northern gardens may contain the following, which are all night-blooming and mostly fragrant: gladiolus tristis, Thunberg daylily, gillyflower, honeysuckle of the *heckrotti* species, evening campion, evening stock, four o'clock, soapwort, night-blooming silene, night phlox, and flowering tobacco.

NIKKO FIR: *see* FIR

NINEBARK: (*Physocarpus opulifolia*) An eight-foot flowering shrub, ninebark or opulaster is commonly grown in the eastern or central states in the shrub border or as a specimen plant. It has peeling bark and very dense clusters of white blooms in June. Ninebark makes a handsome deciduous hedge when sheared. It thrives in ordinary garden soil in country or city, in sun or shade, and is quick-growing. Dwarf ninebark, *P. monogynus,* grows three feet tall and has white or pinkish flowers. *See also* SHRUBS.

NIOBE: *see* HOSTA

NIPPON BELLS: *see* OCONEE BELLS

NITRATE OF SODA: *see* FERTILIZER, ARTIFICIAL

NITROGEN: Nitrogen is one of the most vital elements in farming and gardening. When there is too much or too little of it in the soil, productivity declines. There must be a constant renewal of nitrogen in the soil.

Nitrogen is directly responsible for the vegetative growth of plants above ground. With a good supply of it, the plant grows sturdily and matures rapidly, its foliage a rich, dark green color. A lack of nitrogen is indicated by a lightening of the green color, by yellowing in cases of considerable lack.

Excesses of nitrogen can be even more harmful. These commonly result when concentrated chemical forms of the element are applied to the soil. They give crops a "shot-in-the-arm" treatment, which causes weak, watery growth. The plant's resistance to disease is lowered because the excess nitrogen has displaced other nutrients it needs. Flavor, color and food value also decline. And if a sudden rainstorm should drench the field, the chemical nitrogen is largely washed out and the plants become starved for this element.

Organic forms of nitrogen, on the other hand, are more stable and become available for plant growth more gradually. Organic matter holds nitrogen in the form of protein compounds, which give it up slowly under the pressure of microbial dissolution.

The release of nitrogen from organic matter is affected as follows: The protein first decomposes into its amino acids. The next step is the formation of ammonium compounds. Then bacteria break these down into

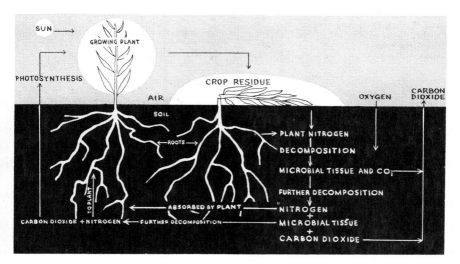

Shown above is the transformation of nitrogen and its movement through the soil and into the plant. The drawing, prepared by the Arizona Experiment Station, also shows the value of crop residues.

NITROGEN CONTENT OF ORGANIC SUBSTANCES

The following is a list of representative classifications of organic matter and typical analyses with respect to their nitrogen content:

MEAL

Bone Black Bone Meal	1.5
Raw Bone Meal	3.3 to 4.1
Steamed Bone Meal	1.6 to 2.5
Cottonseed Meal	7.0
Corn Fodder	.41
Oats, Green Fodder	.49
Corn Silage	.42
Gluten Meal	6.4
Wheat Bran	2.36
Wheat Middlings	2.75
Meat Meal	9 to 11
Bone Tankage	3 to 10

MANURES

Cattle Manure (fresh excrement)	0.29
Cattle Manure (fresh urine)	0.58
Hen Manure (fresh)	1.63
Dog Manure	2.0
Horse Manure (solid fresh excrement)	0.44
Horse Manure (fresh urine)	1.55
Human Excrement (solid)	1.00
Human Urine	0.60
Night Soil	0.80
Sheep Manure (solid fresh excrement)	0.55
Sheep (fresh urine)	1.95
Stable Manure, mixed	0.50
Swine Manure (solid fresh excrement)	0.60
Swine (fresh urine)	0.43
Sewage Sludge	1.7 to 2.26

ANIMAL WASTES
(Other than manures)

Eggshells	1.00+
Dried Blood	10 to 14
Feathers	15.3
Dried Jellyfish	4.6
Fresh Crabs	5
Dried Ground Crabs	10
Dried Shrimp Heads	7.8
Lobster Wastes	2.9
Shrimp Wastes	2.9
Mussels	1
Dried Ground Fish	8
Acid Fish Scrap	4.0 to 6.5
Oyster Shells	.36
Milk	.5
Wool Wastes	3.5 to 6.0
Silkworm Cocoons	10
Silk Wastes	8
Felt Wastes	14

PLANT WASTES

	% Nitrogen
Beet Wastes	.4
Brewery Wastes	1.0
Castor Pomace	4.0 to 6.6
Cattail Reeds	2.0
Cocoa Shell Dust	1.0
Cocoa Wastes	2.7
Coffee Wastes	2.0
Grape Pomace	1.0
Green Cowpeas	.4
Nut Shells	2.5
Olive Residues	1.15
Peanut Shells	3.6
Peanut Shell Ashes	.8
Pine Needles	.5
Potato Skins	.6
Sugar Wastes	2.0
Tea Grounds	4.1
Tobacco Stems	2.5 to 3.7
Tung Oil Pomace	6.1

LEAVES

Peach Leaves	.9
Oak Leaves	.8
Grape Leaves	.45
Pear Leaves	.7
Apple Leaves	1.0
Cherry Leaves	.6
Raspberry Leaves	1.35
Garden Pea Vines	.25

GRASSES

Clover	2.0
Red Clover	.55
Vetch Hay	2.8
Corn Stalks	.75
Alfalfa	2.4
Immature Grass	1.0
Blue Grass Hay	1.2
Cowpea Hay	3.0
Pea Hay	1.5 to 2.5
Soybean Hay	1.5 to 3.0
Timothy Hay	1.19
Salt Hay	1.06
Millet Hay	1.22

SEAWEED

Fresh Seaweed	0.2 to 0.38
Dry Seaweed	1.1 to 1.5

nitrites. There are certain bacteria in the soil whose function it is to do this, and only they can do it. Then other groups of bacteria turn the nitrites into nitrates, which is the form of nitrogen that plant roots can take in. It is virtually impossible for too much nitrates to be released at once. (Another dangerous effect of concentrated chemical nitrogen is a build-up of nitrates in the plant, which can poison people and animals eating the crop.) Then, with the addition of certain other elements, protein is produced in the plant. This protein, many experts believe, is a superior kind of protein to that produced when chemical nitrogen is used. Inferior protein is thought to be an important factor in diseases and reproductive troubles in livestock, and the cause of the "running out" of plant varieties.

SYNTHETIC NITROGEN: Urea is a synthetic containing 45 per cent nitrogen (as compared to 33.5 per cent for ammonium nitrate, formerly the chemical fertilizer highest in nitrogen). Composed of two parts of ammonia and one part of carbon dioxide, urea is a solid material manufactured from air and natural gas or coal. It can be dissolved and used as leaf spray.

Along with urea goes urea-form, a derivative which contains 37 to 39 per cent nitrogen. It is a combination of urea and formaldehyde, a powerful disinfectant and preservative used in embalming fluids.

Another synthetic is anhydrous ammonia, a by-product of the oil industry. The most potent of the high-nitrogen fertilizers, it is 82 per cent nitrogen. Anhydrous comes in bottle-gas cylinders under high pressure for direct injection into the soil or for mixing with irrigation water.

There is also aqueous ammonia, popularly called "aqua ammonia." When anhydrous ammonia gas is dissolved in water, the resulting solution is sold as aqua ammonia, which contains 20 to 24 per cent nitrogen. Synthetic urea is similar to the natural urea in animal urine. However, it generally has a higher nitrogen content. Like animal urine that is not handled very carefully, it can easily burn plants. Severe burning of vegetation occurs when as much as 400 pounds per acre of nitrogen are applied in the form of urea.

Too, synthetic urea contains biuret, a compound toxic to many plants when applied to the soil or sprayed on their leaves. In a recent study, Department of Agriculture researchers in Gainesville, Fla., reported mild to severe leaf necrosis on mature tung trees after five years of treatment. Other crops have also been affected by the toxic accumulations in the soil.

Urea-form has an additional strike against it: the formaldehyde it contains is a powerful bactericide. It will kill off all kinds of soil life.

Anhydrous ammonia is extremely caustic—as witness the fact that men who apply it are cautioned to wear goggles, masks, rubber gloves and rain gear. Inhalation can cause death, and frostbite and extreme burns follow getting it on your skin.

It is so caustic that agronomists recommend that it be banded deeper and farther away from crop roots than any other chemical fertilizer. Put it too close to the plant row, and roots will be severely injured. The same goes for aqua ammonia: in California, when liquid ammonia was applied in an irrigation system, thousands of earthworms came to the surface and died in a few minutes.

Anhydrous ammonia gas is in such a "free form" that unless the soil has just the right moisture conditions, most of it will be lost into the air in a very short time after you apply it.

Synthetic nitrogen fertilizers are poor substitutes for organic sources, which are safe, long-lasting and more economical in the long run. *See also* DEFICIENCIES, SOIL; FERTILIZER; LEGUMES; HUMUS; COMPOST; CARBON-NITROGEN.

NITROGEN IN HUMUS: see HUMUS

NODE: The point on a stem at which a leaf, or sometimes a flower stem, is borne. The space between nodes is called the internode. The presence of nodes distinguishes an underground stem from a root. New plants arise from nodes in propagation by suckers, stolons, rhizomes, and runners.

NO-DIGGING METHOD: There is a school of gardening which adheres to the belief that no digging or soil spading is necessary to achieve best garden results. In 1946, F. C. King, an Englishman, published a book entitled *Is Digging Necessary?* which set forth a no-digging method dependent on optimum soil life activity and heavy composting. In 1949 another Englishman, A. Guest, published *Gardening Without Digging,* setting forth essentially the same principles as Mr. King.

In the No-Digging method, seeds and seedlings are planted merely by pushing the mulch aside. Neither spading, hoeing nor weeding is done.

Here are the basic principles:

1. to imitate nature closely by not inverting the soil;

2. to economize on compost and other organic materials by using them as a surface mulch, where nature keeps her fertility promoting materials;

3. to reduce weed growth by not bringing more and more seeds to the surface;

4. and, by all these methods, to maintain a balance of air, moisture, biological life and plant foods.

Not everyone who has experimented with the no-digging method has had success stories to rave about, so try it out with some caution. For example, one grower found that after a few years, soil fertility seemed to decline; he also was unable to get good yields of root crops (especially radishes) on his undug plots.

RUTH STOUT: The foremost exponent of the "no-digging" or "year-round mulch" system of gardening in this country is Ruth Stout of West Redding, Connecticut. Here is Miss Stout's description of how she got started in mulch gardening:

"One maddening thing about gardening is the plowing or spading, whichever one you do. If you hire someone to plow and harrow, it is not possible to have it done piecemeal. This means that the whole plot should be plowed early in April in order to get the peas, spinach, lettuce and parsley started on time. But if you do that, the part where you will put your late crops is lying idle through April, May and part of June. No, not idle, that's the trouble; it is growing a fine crop of weeds if there is rainy weather. And if it is dry the sun is baking the soil.

"If you spade your garden, of course you can dig up just as much as you are ready to use. However, that means that the rest of it is producing weeds, some of them perennial and mean to handle."

Each year—for 14 years—Miss Stout had her large (240 feet by 100 feet) garden plot plowed by a neighboring farmer. Then in April of 1944, the inevitable happened: the farmer was ready to plow, but the tractor wouldn't go.

"So now on this perfect morning I stood there in the garden, longing to put in some seeds. I wandered over to the asparagus bed and said to it affectionately: 'Bless your heart, you don't have to wait for anyone to plow you. You merely . . .'

"I stopped short as a thought struck me like a blow. One never plows asparagus and it gets along fine. Except for new sod, why plow anything, ever? Why turn the soil upside down? Why not just plant?

". . . It was my good fortune that, in spite of all warnings against it, I had formed the habit of leaving all the vegetable waste, such as corn stalks, right there in the garden and had spread leaves all over it in the fall and vegetable garbage all winter long. Now, when I raked this mass of stuff aside to make a row for the spinach I found the ground so soft and moist that I made a tiny drill with my finger.

". . . If it really worked, in May and June the ground would surely be soft enough to put in corn, beans and the other late things. With all these leaves no weeds would come through. Some did, however. The mulch wasn't thick enough.

". . . Even that first year I began to visualize the utopia I had thought up for everyone who wanted to grow his own vegetables. Besides the expense, it is not easy to find someone to plow and harrow for you and often impossible to get it done just when you want it. The alternative, spading, is quite a job. Eliminate these things and eliminate also hoeing, weeding, cultivating—it sounded like science fiction and yet I believed in it."

INITIAL STRUGGLE: ". . . The first three years were a struggle and a mess . . . but I must reassure all prospective mulchers; those first years needn't have been difficult. Once you get it into your head that you have to put on enough mulch, six or eight inches deep, you do it, relax and enjoy your leisure.

"It took me a long time to realize how much was necessary. It was hard to find enough; then I remembered that I had heard farmers talk about spoiled hay and I asked a neighbor-

ing farmer if he had any. He did and said if I could get someone to bring it down to me I was welcome to it. I got a great load of it, and that autumn I covered the whole garden thickly with leaves and hay to lie there over the winter. . . ."

Whenever Miss Stout wants to put in some seeds, she rakes the mulch back and plants; later when the seeds have sprouted, the mulch is pulled close around the plants, thereby keeping the ground around them moist and outwitting the weeds.

Now, after some 15 years of gardening according to her "over-all year-round mulch" system, Miss Stout says emphatically: "I know it works. I know that it saves at least nine-tenths of the labor of gardening. I know the results are splendid and the other advantages tremendous."

UNDISTURBED MULCH: Every organic gardener is well aware of the virtues of mulching, and is, undoubtedly, using mulches to some degree. However, Miss Stout's method calls for a thick mulch to be used for every flower and vegetable, shrub and tree. It is never turned under, never disturbed; it is, in effect, "a constantly rotting compost pile" spread over all the places where you want rich earth to abound.

"Some people hesitate to adopt over-all mulching because they prefer the looks of a neatly cultivated garden. I used to," Miss Stout points out, "but now a garden with the earth exposed to the burning, baking sun looks helpless and pathetic to me. It looks fine if someone has just cultivated it after a good rain, but how often is that the case? At all other times an unmulched garden looks to me like some naked thing which, for one reason or another, would be better off with a few clothes on."

After reflecting upon the droughty summers we've been having in recent years, I can't see how anyone could find fault with the above analysis.

Actually there is no reason why a

mulched garden should appear ugly. For example, Miss Stout has a row of mulched rosebushes which look exactly like any other well-kept row of roses. As she observes, "a flourishing garden with clean hay spread neatly between the rows looks attractive to me, and comfortable."

ENGLISH PRACTICES: In England, the "no digging" technique has been advocated for a number of years by several persons; F. C. King has been the foremost spokesman. He is "firmly convinced that if two gardeners of equal skill were to cultivate two plots of equal size and comparable fertility, one digging and trenching and the other practicing the principles of surface cultivation . . . it would be possible for the no-digger to secure the best results at less cost in time and cash." Mr. King also cites his own experiences as head gardener at Levens Hall, South Westmoreland to prove that crops grown by the no-digging method have greater resistance to insects and disease.

The primary difference between Miss Stout's over-all mulch program and Mr. King's no digging method is the use of compost. While Miss Stout believes that any organic material such as hay will suffice to cover the soil and provide fertility, Mr. King writes: "one can hardly think of no-digging without at the same time associating in one's mind the necessity for composting; indeed, success with the no-digging technique is quite impossible unless and until the soil has previously received generous applications of properly made compost —say a pailful to the square yard as an initial top dressing—on any kind of soil, sandy or clay, heavy or light, shallow or more or less exhausted. The first step, then, to be taken to ensure an adequate supply of compost for use during September is to make a thorough collection of all organic wastes during the spring and summer months."

SURFACE PLANTING: In addition, under the English system, the seeds of some plants can be placed directly on the surface of the soil and then covered with an inch or more of compost.

Another staunch advocate of no digging, A. Guest of Yorkshire, England, describes his own experiences in the pamphlet, "Gardening Without Digging." At the request of The (English) Soil Association I took, on their plot, two strips separated by a narrow path and removed 1½ inches of turf from each strip. One I dug and composted in the ordinary way; the other I left undug and applied compost on the surface. . . . The two plots were sown with identical seeds at the same time and the results showed a vast superiority in favor of no-digging."

DISADVANTAGES: However, not everyone who has tried no-digging in England speaks of it in only glowing terms. For example, Ben Easey, a noted English gardening authority, points out that although much work is eliminated by not cultivating, there is a lot of heavy weeding to be done the first two or three years. He also emphasizes that "the supply of enough compost is the biggest snag, for surface cultivation will not work without it."

Mr. Easey estimates that it is necessary to apply an autumn mulch of compost, two inches thick, and another inch as a spring dressing to cover seeds—"this on soil already of high organic matter content."

Although the no-digging method has been tried out in many countries, there are few records to show comparative yields of crops grown on experimental dug and undug plots. The only comprehensive set of figures available to date has been provided by J. L. Chase of England.

COMPARATIVE TEST: In order to compare the two methods, Mr. Chase began an experiment in 1947 on his trial grounds in Chertsey. In general, the test, which ran for seven years, showed that most crops yielded more on the dug plots than on the undug ones. (Mr. Easey points out that the Chase experiment is an isolated one, on one type of soil and that results are measured by weight, not quality or freedom from disease.)

Here is an excerpt from Mr. Chase's report:

For the first three years, it was difficult to distinguish any "pattern" in the results. All that could be said was that there was little difference between the plots as a whole, though some crops did better on one plot and some on the other. Out of nine crops of peas and beans, eight did better on the dug plot. Root crops were always better on Dug, particularly in the case of the radish.

Lettuce, on the other hand, were better five times out of six on the Undug plot, and sweet peas and sweet corn were also better on Undug. Cucumbers and marrows varied a good deal, but in some years were considerably better on Undug, while tomatoes were remarkably even on the two plots.

In 1951, the fourth year, however, there was a change. What could almost be called a breakdown of the Undug plot occurred, and this could be observed visually throughout the season. Spring cabbage was a freak exception, but the figure is perhaps misleading as the whole crop was poor. Sweet peas in 1951 were spring planted instead of autumn sown, and were better on the Dug soil than the Undug. Throughout the experiment the autumn-sown clochard (glass protected) sweet peas were both earlier, of better quality, and more numerous on the Undug plot.

In 1952 the deterioration of the Undug plot continued, and results became progressively worse until, in 1954, only one crop, sweet peas, did better on the Undug plot than on the Dug. Until the last three years of the experiment, one could say quite fairly that good crops were grown on

both plots. But from 1952 onwards, and particularly in 1954, some of the crops on the Undug plot failed. Tomatoes and lettuces, which had previously done well on Undug, now no longer gave a good crop.

Mr. Chase concludes: It does seem that, on our soil, surface cultivation without digging for three years is quite satisfactory and even advantageous for all crops except legumes and root crops. After three years it is advisable to dig the ground, and perhaps triennial digging is the answer.

OBSERVATION: No-digging methods appear to have the following weaknesses:

1. No-digging does not place nutrients deep in the soil, where plants can make the best use of them; and

2. Over a period of no-digging years, the soil may suffer from lack of aeration.

A combination of heavy mulching and tilling once a year for aeration purposes seems to be the best course of action. *See also* MULCH; AERATION.

NODULE: A rounded mass of irregular shape, such as the tubercle found on the root of a legume, which contains colonies of nitrogen-fixing bacteria. *See also* LEGUME.

NORWAY SPRUCE: *see* SPRUCE; CHRISTMAS TREE FARMING

NOVEMBER GARDEN OPERATIONS: *see* GARDEN CALENDAR

NPK: Abbreviation for nitrogen, phosphorus, and potash, the major plant nutrients. The NPK ratio is understood to mean the proportion of these three ingredients in a fertilizer. *See also* FERTILIZER.

NUBIAN GOATS: *see* GOAT

NURSE CROP: Referring to a crop that is sown to give protection to another. For example, crimson clover is often sown with a nurse crop of buckwheat or cowpeas to protect it from the sun. Usually the nurse crop is rather thinly sown and is cut as soon as its protection is no longer needed. *See also* COMPANION PLANT-INGS.

NURSERY, HOME: A spare corner near the garden can become a little home nursery for plants, a propagating and proving ground, a catchall for odds-and-ends of garden landscape problems.

Any spare corner will do—even a five by ten foot plot, since wide gardening rows are not necessary. Ordinary garden soil enriched with compost is satisfactory, and a small section of sand mixed with peat moss is recommended.

IMPORTANCE OF SHADE: Plants in the home nursery should be given ample shade, easily provided by placing slats over the beds. Some gardeners provide shade with old crates of about ⅛ inch slats, four inches wide that are interwoven with wire. A strip of scrap wood on each side and a stake at each corner will brace and support it well.

Wood laths or any scraps similar to them are ideal and should be spaced to exclude about half the light. These beds may be weeded but should not be cultivated. Mulching around the plants is the best way to stifle weeds; pine needles, leaves, sawdust, leaf mold, grass clippings—all make excellent mulch materials.

Some plants, such as flowering shrubs and trees, need sunlight once they are established. Set these out in rows in the garden, and cultivate them just as commercial nurseries do. *See also* CUTTINGS; DIVISION; COLD FRAME.

NUT GRASS: Nut grass is very difficult to eradicate once it gets beyond the hand-picking stage. Trials have shown that it is severely discouraged by growing a heavy cover of cowpeas on the plot for one or more summers. As soon as possible, in early summer,

sow cowpeas thickly, apply a large amount of compost, and allow them to become heavily matted to shade the soil. The vines should be plowed or dug into the soil in October.

NUT SHELLS: Often used as a mulch or for composting. The composition of nut shells varies according to the nuts. Almond shells and pecans decay readily, black walnut shells which contain greater amounts of lignin, take longer; filberts and English walnuts decompose without trouble. Analysis of coconut shells is given as 2.5 per cent nitrogen, one per cent phosphoric acid and 2.5 per cent potash. *See also* MULCH.

NUT TREES: Nut trees have so much to recommend them that they should be more widely utilized in home planting. These trees are beautiful, having most attractive foliage and a delightful autumn coloring. Furthermore, they produce crops of the highest value.

There are nut trees that range in size from small, bushy plants to towering giants and so meet any purpose on the home grounds.

Either the Black Walnut or the Pecan—northern varieties for cooler areas—become large spreading trees that can add that indefinable touch of a home that is cradled beneath protective trees which also make beautiful growths with which to adorn the lawn.

Where smaller trees are desired, the Heartnut, the Chinese Chestnut, the Persian (or English) Walnut, or the Hickory fill the need. As for low, bushy growths, the Chinese Chestnut, left unpruned; the Filbert, grown in bush form; or the Chinkapin meet the need exactly.

PLANTING NUT TREES: Here are some places where nut trees will grow and yield:

1. About the home as shade trees and ornamentals;

2. Along roadsides for the same reason, also to put land to work:

3. As shade for poultry and animals;

4. To fill in odd spots, otherwise unproductive;

5. Along permanent fence rows;

6. On steep hillsides, to prevent erosion. The trees will not hurt grass production and will provide shade for livestock;

7. Along stream banks, providing the land is well drained;

8. On land too stony or rough to be tilled.

Before you plant, consider this:

Are you trying to beautify the home grounds, provide shade for humans and animals and prevent soil erosion?

Or are you trying to get an income out of land which is otherwise unproductive?

If it's income you want then you must:

1. Plant on well-drained land, fertile or where you can supply fertility;

2. Avoid frost pockets, plant on hillsides or places with good air drainage;

3. Avoid late spring frosts by planting the latest varieties;

4. Avoid southern exposures unless they are near the hilltop;

5. Plant on northern and eastern slopes to help the trees escape winter and late spring frost injury.

It must be stressed here that, despite all reasonable precautions, there are temperatures that will kill a tree, no matter where you plant it. But the coldest air stays in the low spots on your land where the air drainage is bad. Don't plant your trees in these places.

Wrapping the trees during the first winter is another must. This includes the tops, particularly of Persian Walnut, which may sunscald. Regular tree wrapping paper or burlap bags are good. Wrapping also prevents drying out. And be sure to remove wrapping only when all danger of a late spring frost is safely past; also

before the spring growth begins. This is very important.

SPACING: Give your trees plenty of growing room. A safe rule is to plant them 50 feet apart in all directions. You may plant your pecans 35 feet apart in rows spaced 70 feet apart and your chestnuts 30 feet apart. Walnuts, chestnuts and hickory trees are all big fellows towering 50 to 100 feet above the ground with diameters of ten to 12 feet. They will need plenty of sunlight and air, not only on their tops but on the lower branches as well.

The pecan is only one of the many valuable nut trees which offer the home gardener attractive foliage as well as a valuable harvest.

Underground your trees will be competing with each other for soil nutrients. Their roots will stretch out in the search for food which goes on at all times in the plant world.

Their root systems will equal, approximately, the size and extent of their branch-and-leaf areas.

SIZE AND AGE: Many people believe the smaller the tree when it is transplanted—the better. This is partly true. The younger trees will sustain the shock of transplanting better. But it is also true that the root stock must be one year old before it can be grafted. It is also true that the graft or scion must have one full season's growth before it can be transplanted. The youngest tree that can be bought from a nursery is a one-year whip (scion or grafting) on a two-year-old root.

There are tree planters and growers who favor the older tree for transplanting. These often make a good recovery and start growing before the younger trees catch up with them.

But it is also true that the rate of loss from the older trees is much greater than from the younger.

You will also find that the price of the tree increases with the size. Trees range from two to eight feet. Experts advise that those five feet and more are the most economical in the end.

When the Trees Arrive: Planting holes should be wide and deep enough to accommodate the roots without bending. Make sure the roots are not dried out.

They should be kept moist from the time they are dug until they are safely planted. Carry the trees to the planting site with the roots wrapped in burlap bags. Do not try to carry too many at one time. Keep the roots of all trees except the one you are planting covered with wet burlap.

If trees cannot be planted right away, keep them in a cool place and don't unpack them. They'll stay moist that way. But if you must wait a week or so—plant them in a shallow trench making sure the roots are covered with damp soil.

Holes for walnut trees should be three feet wide and 18 inches deep. Hickories need holes two feet wide and 1½ to two feet deep. Sometimes it may seem that the hole is much too large for the tree but nurserymen have a saying which bears repeating: "Better to set a ten-cent tree in a dollar hole than a dollar tree in a ten-cent hole."

In fact you will frequently find it necessary to make the holes larger. Be sure to keep the roots of the tree covered with wet burlap. Never forget this: Exposure of the roots of your tree to the sun or wind for only a few minutes can spoil your tree beyond all cure.

Filling Hole: Use good, rich topsoil when filling the hole. This gives your tree a real chance to get started. Later when the roots extend out into the poorer surrounding soil, it will not matter so much. But it is obvious that lack of fertility during the critical starting period can result in loss of the tree.

Remember, the hole must be large enough to take the roots of the tree without bending them too much. Make a mound of the topsoil at the bottom of the hole and set your tree on this mound with the sideroots running down its sides.

Be sure not to leave air pockets when tamping soil over and around the roots. You cannot have these if the tree is to flourish and produce. Some experts stress that only a skilled, experienced tree planter can be trusted with the proper setting of a tree. Other experts merely advise you to "pack the soil firmly about the roots, being careful not to injure them." You can use a stick with a rounded end for poking and tamping the earth into place.

Tramping the soil down, layer by layer, is also recommended. Wear rubber soled shoes or boots so you won't injure the delicate roots. The experts also say you can't tramp hard or long enough.

Here is another way to avoid air pockets. Fill the hole with earth to within six inches of the top. Then pour water up to the rim. Hold the tree trunk and rock and jar the tree gently as the earth settles with the water. After this use more topsoil to fill the hole.

Care of Roots: Change root positions as little as possible while planting the tree. Try to keep as they were before transplanting. Hold the side roots up as the soil is placed around the tree. Let go of the roots one by one as the hole fills up.

The place for manures or fertilizers is on the top of the soil, around the tree, after it is planted.

Don't mix them with soil when filling up the hole. During the first growing season keep all compost material on top of the ground, close to the trunk of the tree.

Set the tree deep enough in the hole to cover it adequately without filling the hole all the way to the top. Leave a space of three to four inches to act as a basin for holding water during the first critical years. Later it will gradually fill up by itself.

While setting the tree deeper be careful to keep the grafting point uncovered. It it vitally important not to set the tree as deep as the grafting point.

After planting, set a strong stake or post next to the tree. It will keep the tree growing straight and prevent its falling over. Your string around the tree must be loose, but tight around the post. If you tie a tight loop or knot around the tree, it will girdle the planting and kill it above that point. Also be sure to remove all identification tags from the tree and attach them to the stake.

Make notes of each tree, their variety and kind, also a clear, simple map of the grove, showing the place of each tree. File this for future reference.

WATERING THE TREE: By now, you're practically on your own. Your trees are all in the ground on good planting sites; their roots have not been damaged in transplanting and you're getting ready to make a map of the orchard.

But you're not through with your initial chores. You must water the trees—thoroughly—as soon as they are planted. We mean thoroughly water them—several pails to the tree. Soak the ground so that the water remains on top for several minutes. This thorough soaking once again helps settle the soil around the roots. So add more topsoil if necessary. But don't fill up the hole; remember to leave three to four inches for water storage.

Water the trees once a week after growth starts in the spring. Do a thor-

Nutritional Values of Nuts

NUTS	MEASURE	Calories (Energy Value)	Protein gm.	Fat gm.	Calcium mg.	Iron mg.	Vitamin A International Units	Thiamine (B.) mg.	Riboflavin (B.) mg.	Niacin mg.	Vitamin C (Ascorbic Acid) mg.
Almonds (unblanched)	1 cup, shelled	848	26.4	76.8	361	6.2	...	.25	.67	4.6	Trace
Brazil nuts	1 cup, shelled	905	20.2	92.3	260	4.8	Trace	.86	...	...	...
Cashew nuts (roasted)	1 cup, shelled	1312	41.0	109.6	104	11.2	...	1.4	.40	4.8	...
Coconut meat	1 cup, shelled	359	3.4	34.7	21	2.0	...	.10	.01	.2	2
Filberts	1 cup, shelled	1520	28.8	138.4	656	8.8	224	.88	...	...	...
Hickory nuts	1 cup, shelled	1616	35.2	152.8	...	...	...	...	...	...	...
Peanuts (roasted)	1 cup, shelled	1272	60.8	100.8	168	4.0	...	.72	.32	36.8	...
Pecans	1 cup, halves	696	9.4	73.0	74	2.4	50	.72	.11	.9	2
Walnuts, English	1 cup, halves	645	15.0	64.4	83	2.1	30	.48	.13	1.2	3
Walnuts, Black	1 cup, shelled	672	18.3	58.2	83	2.1	70	.33	.11	1.2	...

ough job. If enough rain falls to fill the depression about each tree you can omit watering that week. Watch the topsoil around the tree and replenish it if and when necessary.

But—water once a week only. Nut trees will not grow in a swamp. Standing water in the soil keeps the air out. The proper amount of air in the soil is just as important to the health of the tree as the moisture.

The water that should always be in the soil is the film that adheres to each soil particle. As trees and other plants take up this film of moisture from each soil particle, it is replaced through capillary action by water deeper in the soil.

It is this water that dissolves the plant-food elements and holds them in solution for the tree roots to absorb. This is the only way that trees and other plants can take food up and out of the soil.

COMPOST: Use compost to start and nourish your tree.

Use compost as a mulch around each tree. Your trees need nitrogen, phosphorus and potash and your compost pile should contain these nutrients in good proportion. Take a series of soil tests in the orchard to determine soil needs.

PRUNING: Your trees should be pruned when planted. Check with the man who sold you the trees; maybe it has already been done for you. If not, here are a few simple rules:

1. Don't cut back the tops of one-year grafts;

2. Cut the side branches of the older grafts close to the trunk but don't cut the leader;

3. Trees set in the spring should be pruned when set;

4. Trees set in the fall should be pruned in late winter or early spring.

It is often wise to place a protective band of wire mesh around each of your young trees. It should be sturdy and 18 inches high. Don't make it tight enough to strangle the tree; a cylinder nine inches in diameter will keep the mice away . . . if you press it firmly into the ground so they can't burrow under it.

FOOD VALUE: Nuts offer an important nutritional frontier to the American people.

English walnuts, shown growing above, contain 15 grams of protein, over 80 grams of calcium, and many other important nutrients per cup.

Raw nuts contain unsaturated fat. These fats are the best for our body. Lately, scientists who have investigated heart conditions advise that unsaturated fats are the least damaging to the heart and arteries, and this in itself is a very good reason why the American people should take advantage of the use of nut fats in their diet.

Another good reason for eating nuts is that their food quality is enhanced by the deep-rooting of the trees. Roots of trees like the hickory, walnut and pecan reach down as far as 15 feet or more into the mineral-rich subsoil for nourishment of the tree and production of the seed, which are the nuts.

See also names of individual nuts: ALMOND; BUTTERNUT; CHESTNUT; HEARTNUT; PECAN; WALNUT; FILBERT; HICKORY; HAZLENUT; ORCHARDING; INSECT CONTROL.

NUTRIENTS: *see* FERTILIZER

NUTRITION: Proper nutrition is an integral part of the organic method of gardening and farming. Aside from the many other advantages of the organic method of gardening, the sound nutrition that is achieved from eating naturally-grown foods is reason enough to follow the organic method. The relation between soil and health is as basic as the very processes of nature; the axiom "you are what you eat" assumes greater and greater impact as experiments show the wonderful results of eating carefully selected, organically-grown foods.

DEFICIENCIES: A great percentage of the public has been found calcium deficient. Over half of the American people are deficient in vitamin C. Startling though these facts may be to many, it is really a most conservative estimate. Actually, that percentage does not include the millions of people constantly courting borderline malnutrition—people whose condition hasn't quite reached an acute, clinically diagnosed stage of deficiency, and yet who are day after day weary, nervous and lacking in normal energy and vitality.

What's responsible for this nationwide unhealthiness? Why should so many—in the acclaimed "land of plenty"—go literally starved on full stomachs? The answer lies in a threefold cause: (1) The way in which our food is grown, the health of the land from which it comes to us. (2) The foods we actually eat, what they really contain and contribute to our well-being—and how our methods of processing and preparation affect these values. (3) The elements, aside from food, which through choice or habit we also put into our bodies.

We need to know how these basic factors influence our lives and our resistance to every type of illness. And we need to act to prevent the tragic spread of so many degenerative diseases, as well as the vast malnutrition —which, not-so-incidentally, almost always precedes the appearance of these. In particular, we need to expose and firmly plug those leaks through

which a great portion of our vitamins and other essential food elements are now disappearing.

SOIL HEALTH IS BASIC: Starting at the ground level, it's simple logic that a healthy soil is necessary to produce healthy food. Soils that lack vital plant nutrients cannot possibly give these food values to what is grown in them. Neither can a dead, constantly chemicalized soil continue to give full life-giving qualities to produce.

Comparatively few people appreciate the extent to which the condition and treatment of the soil govern the food value of what is taken from it. To most, a fruit or vegetable or grain is just that, and while there may be outward variations in appearance and quality, and perhaps some differences in taste appeal as well as in the price per pound or dozen, that's about all that is realized. But that is definitely not all. Nutritionally there are other, much more important differences. The mineral and organic content of a soil, its acid-alkaline status, and consequently the culture it receives determine the amounts of every food element, major and trace minerals, vitamins, carbohydrates, etc., in the produce taken from that soil.

In a review entitled *The Mineral Composition of Crops with Particular Reference to Soils in Which They Were Grown*, Kenneth C. Beeson of the Bureau of Plant Industry, United States Department of Agriculture, has stressed this fact, stating in part: "The inability of some soils to supply in proper amounts and proportions those elements essential to the well-being of man and animals has been known for more than a century. Investigations of certain nutritional diseases during the last 25 years have emphasized the importance of soils, for, throughout the world, the occurrence of bone diseases, nutritional anemias, or of the effect on animals of excessive quantities of some inorganic elements has been characterized by the interspersion of normal and abnormal areas. . . . It is believed . . . that many nutritional diseases are caused by deficiencies or excesses of particular minerals in food plants grown in different soils, in different localities, and with different cultural practices."

CONTENT VARIES: Do the amounts of essential minerals really differ much in foods grown on various soils and by different methods? Indeed they do. Noted soil scientist Firman E. Bear of Rutgers University recently prepared a report which includes the Variations in Mineral Content in Vegetables.

Tomatoes varied more than double the amount of phosphorus in the highest to lowest content comparison. The same vegetable showed differences of nearly three times the content of potassium, five times that of calcium, more than six times that of sodium, boron and cobalt, 12 times more magnesium, 53 times more copper, 68 of manganese, and 1,938 times more iron in the highest to lowest samples!

No wonder the Hunza people of India are invariably termed the healthy Hunzas. Their soils are as rich today as a thousand years ago; their native diet when fed to rats turns them into "veritable rodent Methuselahs," according to Stuart Chase in the foreword to the revealing book, *Tomorrw's Food,* and according to other researchers who have studied the Hunzas over half a century.

Thus, while volumes more might well be included on this aspect, the point is nonetheless clear: The way in which our food is grown, the health of the land from which it comes to us—this is the prime fundamental, the very foundation of good nutrition and health, or the lack of it. This, in essence, is the why of the organic method.

FOOD PREPARATION: Cause number two of our lack of good nutrition

is what is done to the food we eat. As important as good soil treatment and growing methods are, the worth of these is often obliterated in the name of modern processing and preparation. There is hardly an item of food in the American diet today which does not suffer from one to dozens of "preparing" steps before it is finally consumed, supposedly then to provide abundantly of all of Nature's nutritive values.

Knowing this, let's look again at precisely what happens to the vast bulk of our foods—both before and after we get them.

Our wheat has the germ—the very core of its life and food value—completely removed. It is ground, milled and processed until still less remains. It is chemically bleached, becoming a pure, practically worthless white. It is combined with substitutes for everything from eggs to milk and butter. Then it is "fortified" with a few synthetic B vitamins, stuffed with chemicals to retard spoilage (of the bread, not consumer), and baked. Finally it comes to the public as loudly proclaimed "enriched" bread!

Our other grains undergo similar treatment. Rice is polished, oats hulled—and all lose important mineral and vitamin values in the bargain. Our vegetables are blanched, which removes the natural chlorophyll along with part of the vitamins and minerals. Citrus fruits are picked before ripe, dyed or given gas treatments for coloring. Dried fruits such as dates, figs, prunes and raisins are accorded a sulphur treatment. Our milk is pasteurized, homogenized, irradiated and often combined with sugary or synthetic syrups. Our "refined" sugar, by the way, is a product of sugar cane or beet juice from which all minerals and vitamins are totally removed.

PROCESSING: To continue, many of our meats are salted, dried and pickled. Some are soaked in smoke solutions or injected with gelatin, fat, brine or chemicals. Our eggs are mass-produced, resulting in nonfertile, less nutritive eggs. Poultry is frequently injected with stilbestrol, a chemical hormone which has already caused sterility in animals, serious reactions in man, and which has been wisely outlawed in Canada—but not here. Our canned meats and other foods contain sodium nitrite and sodium nitrate, which are preservatives of salt and sugar uniformity and drugs about which there is still nothing but uncertainty as far as the cumulative effects on our health is concerned.

Other processing thieves of good nutrition include artificial coloring and flavoring of many products; lye-solution peeling of vegetables; use of excessive sugars and spices in pre-cooked, canned and jarred foods; preservatives, acids, drugs and caustic sodas in various foods and soft drinks —to name just a few. The point, once again, is clear: our science-stretched living modes and short-sighted commercialism (seeing nothing beyond the dollar sign, that is) have so molded our tastes and habits and economy that all these devitalized, mangled and patched up foods are the rule—while foods of wholesome, natural standing are the exception!

DIFFERENCES IN VEGETABLES: Chemists and nutritionists have analyzed green vegetables by the carload and have averaged and printed such data in easy-to-use form. Later, other scientists have looked for differences in chemical composition and have sought to explain the variations found.

For example, six southern states cooperated in a study of the iron content of turnip greens. They found that:

1. Turnip greens varied 400-500 per cent in iron content.

2. Nitrogen fertilizers increased yields but decreased the iron content by approximately 20 per cent.

3. The higher the organic matter in the soil, the higher the iron content of turnip greens.

Other researches point to the fact that the iron content of many vegetables such as cabbage, lettuce, carrots, spinach and tomatoes varies tremendously.

For example, the iron content of spinach varied from 1,750 to as low as 54 parts per million and lettuce from almost 5,000 down to 65 parts per million. This means that lettuce and spinach may be a good source of iron or they may not be, depending on many factors.

Varieties of lettuce and spinach, without a doubt contain different amounts of iron when grown under identical conditions, but very few studies have been made on this subject.

What we are absolutely sure of is that turnip greens contain more iron when the soil organic matter is high and when very little nitrogen fertilizer is used. From this information and from bits of other data available, we can reasonably assume that lettuce and spinach will also contain more iron under similar conditions.

And the story is similar but not as contrasting with the percentage of calcium and phosphorus in vegetables. Lettuce may contain only 0.33 per cent or as much as 1.38 per cent calcium. Spinach and other vegetables vary in calcium and phosphorus content about the same. There are many causes for the variations in calcium and phosphorus content of vegetables, but one thing is certain. When the garden soil is adequately supplied with these nutrients, the percentage in the vegetables will be higher.

Why so much stress and concern with iron, calcium and phosphorus? Because these three essential elements, together with iodine, are most frequently lacking in our diets. As proof of this statement, the 1939 Yearbook of Agriculture, *Food and Life,* states: ". . . of these (essential elements) only four . . . calcium, phosphorus, iron and iodine . . . are likely to be deficient in ordinary diets."

What to do?

Iodine deficiency can usually be satisfied by using iodized salt, especially in the "goiter belt" which is located in the humid regions away from the coasts.

This leaves iron, calcium and phosphorus to be concerned about.

In the first place, why be concerned? You may go back to sleep now, but if you do you may awaken with anemia (too few red blood cells) and weak bones and poor teeth.

Assuming that you are now interested in remaining healthy, what then?

It's really quite simple to be sure of having vegetables which are high in iron, calcium, and phosphorus, especially if you have a garden. Here are the steps:

1. Be sure that your garden soil has an abundance of organic matter. Manure, compost, crop residues, leaves, grass clippings, clean garbage, and a host of other organic materials should be used in liberal amounts. When should these materials be used? Whenever they are available! And the best time to put this organic matter on the garden soil is when you have it. Plowed under, spaded in, or used as a mulch on top of the soil, are all recommended practices.

2. To determine if your garden soil needs calcium and phosphorus, have your soil tested. As of 1953, all agricultural colleges in each of the 48 states provide a soil testing service available for a modest fee of approximately $1.00 a sample. To get in contact with this service, look in your telephone directory for the county agricultural agent. He will send you instructions on how to take a soil sample and where to send it for analysis. The results of these tests will be made available to you and if you follow the recommendations, your vegetables will contain sufficient calcium and phosphorus.

3. Supply your garden with only moderate amounts of nitrogen.

If you cannot raise a garden your-self, then perhaps you can help a neighbor to fertilize properly and then to sell you some vegetables.

By following these rather simple suggestions, the chances of having vegetables rich in iron, calcium, and phosphorus will be increased tremendously. But no good will come to you even then unless you eat large quantities of the vegetables that are properly raised.—*Prof Roy L. Donahue, U. of New Hampshire.*

SAVING VITAMINS IN COOKING: After you have put your time and energy into producing an abundant and attractive harvest from your garden, which is "chuck-full" of good vitamins and minerals, you won't want to lose this potential wealth by washing it down the kitchen sink. The principal weakness in American cooking lies in the preparation of vegetables. As they are usually cooked by boiling, 50 to 90 per cent of many nutrients and much of their flavor is lost before they reach the table. These losses are largely avoidable.

Three factors are important in evaluating prepared vegetables. First, they must provide nutrients; second, they must have a pleasing taste; and third, they must be eye-appealing. The homemaker must learn to prepare foods which incorporate these factors, as nothing could be more tasteless, less appealing, or less useful than eating waterlogged, overcooked, boiled vegetables.

RAW VEGETABLES BEST: First, a word about raw vegetables. Actually enough could not be said for the merits of eating fresh raw vegetables right out of your garden. There is nothing that could supply more vitamins and minerals than a fresh garden salad. Don't think you are limited to vegetables commonly used in salads such as lettuce, cabbage, tomatoes, radishes, onions, celery, parsley, green peppers, cucumbers, and carrots. This gives you a good list, but add to it by using raw shredded beets, chopped spinach, chopped cauliflower, chard, brussels sprouts, kohlrabi, and nothing is sweeter than a fresh raw turnip just pulled from the garden. Mix some of these raw vegetables in with your favorite vegetable salad.

Ideally your vegetables should be gathered immediately before using, but, if you must gather them some time before, wash and dry them immediately. Chill and put them into a dark place—your refrigerator—as quickly as possible to stop enzyme action. Make your salad just before serving.

Beyond a shadow of a doubt, the best way to insure your health with a daily dosage of vitalizing minerals and vitamins is to see to it that you eat a good part of your vegetables raw.

VITAMIN LOSSES: Vegetables to be cooked should be handled in the same manner as salad vegetables. Gather immediately before using or else wash, dry, and store in a cool place. If they are left at room temperature and in the light, much folic acid, vitamin B_2 and 50 per cent or more of the vitamin C in most fresh vegetables can be lost in a few hours.

The greatest loss of vitamins and minerals occurs in soaking and boiling vegetables. Vitamins C, P, and many B vitamins pass out of the vegetables and dissolve in water very quickly. Various studies made of nutrient losses, have shown that when whole vegetables are boiled four minutes, 20 to 45 per cent of the total mineral content and 75 per cent of the sugars they contain pass into the water. Since vegetables are often soaked before and during cooking for longer periods, as much as 75 to 100 per cent of the sugars, minerals, and water-soluble vitamins are often lost. The color of the water left after certain vegetables are washed or slowly boiled indicates how quickly these substances can pass out of vegetables, even though unpeeled. The losses are hastened when vegetables are soaked after being peeled, chopped, sliced,

or shredded, and especially after the cell walls are softened by cooking.

SAVE FLAVOR: Flavor is lost when nutritive value is lost. Vegetables contain aromatic oils which give them their characteristic flavor. These oils are not true oils, and they readily dissolve in water. Vegetables also contain minerals and sugars which add to their flavor. Minerals add a saltiness to the taste, and sugars cause them to be sweet. If you want your vegetables to be delicious, as well as nutritious, do not let them soak during washing and cook them by methods other than boiling.

If vegetables are not soaked, the saving of vitamin C and B_2 during preparation and cooking largely depends on preventing enzyme action and eliminating oxygen and light. Enzymes are known to be inactive when cold, and are destroyed by heat. It is important to exclude as much oxygen and light as possible as vitamin C is destroyed only in the presence of oxygen, and vitamin B_2 only in light. When preparing vegetables try not to let them reach room temperature, and if you prepare vegetables prior to cooking them, put them back into the refrigerator to keep them chilled. It is important to heat vegetables as quickly as possible to destroy enzyme action; therefore, preheat the oven or the utensil to be used so it is ready by the time your vegetables are prepared. Lift the lid as few times as possible during cooking. To insure flavor and the most nutrients, cook vegetables for the shortest time necessary to make them tender.

Salt draws moisture out of substances; consequently when a vegetable is salted at the beginning of cooking, its juices, carrying vitamins, minerals, sugars, and flavors, are drawn out. Do not use baking soda to intensify color in vegetables. This will still amplify vitamin and mineral losses. When you prepare and cook vegetables to preserve nutrients and flavor, their natural colors are

Nutritional Values of Common Fresh Fruits

Fresh Fruit	Measure	Calories (Energy Value)	Protein gm.	Fat gm.	Calcium mg.	Iron mg.	Vitamin A Internat. Units	(B₁) mg. Thiamine	Riboflavin (B₂) mg.	Niacin mg.	Vitamin C (Ascorbic Acid) mg.
Apples	1 medium	76	.4	.5	8	.4	120	.05	.04	.2	6
Apricots	three	54	1.1	.1	17	.5	2990	.03	.05	.9	7
Avocados	½ peeled	279	1.9	30.1	11	.7	330	.07	.15	1.3	18
Bananas	1 large	119	1.6	.3	11	.8	570	.06	.06	1.0	13
Blackberries	1 cup	82	1.7	1.4	46	1.3	280	.05	.06	.5	30
Blueberries	1 cup	85	.8	.8	22	1.1	400	.04	.03	.4	23
Cherries	1 cup	65	1.2	.5	19	.4	660	.05	.06	.4	9
Currants	1 cup	60	1.3	.2	40	1.0	130	.04	0	0	40
Dates (fresh or dried)	1 cup, pitted	505	3.9	1.1	128	3.7	100	.16	.17	3.9	0
Figs	4 large	79	1.4	.4	54	.6	80	.06	.05	.5	2
Grapefruit	½ medium	75	.9	.4	41	.4	20	.07	.04	.4	76
Grapes (American)	1 cup, raw	84	1.7	1.7	20	.7	90	.07	.05	.3	5
Guavas	one	49	.7	.4	21	.5	180	.05	.03	.8	212
Lemons	1 medium	20	.6	.4	25	.4	0	.03	tr.	.1	31
Limes	1 medium	18	.4	.1	21	.3	0	.02	tr.	.1	14
Loganberries	1 cup	90	1.4	.9	50	1.7	280	.04	.10	.4	34
Mangoes	1 medium	87	.9	.3	12	.3	8380	.08	.07	1.2	55
Oranges	1 medium	70	1.4	.3	51	.6	290	.12	.04	.4	77
Papayas	1 cup	71	1.1	.2	36	.5	3190	.06	.07	.5	102
Peaches	1 medium	46	.5	.1	8	.6	880	.02	.05	.9	8
Pears	1 medium, peeled	95	1.1	.6	20	.5	30	.03	.06	.2	6
Persimmons	1 medium, seedless	95	1.0	.5	7	.4	3270	.06	.05	tr.	13
Pineapple	1 cup, diced	74	.6	.3	22	.4	180	.12	.04	.3	33
Plums	1 medium	29	.4	.1	10	.3	200	.04	.02	.3	3
Prunes (dried)	4 medium, unsulfured	73	.6	.2	15	1.1	510	.03	.04	.5	1
Raisins (dried)	1 cup, unsulfured	429	3.7	.8	125	5.3	80	.24	.13	.8	tr.
Raspberries (black)	1 cup	74	1.5	2.1	54	1.2	0	.03	.09	.4	32
Raspberries (red)	1 cup	70	1.5	.5	49	1.1	160	.03	.08	.4	29
Strawberries	1 cup	54	1.2	.7	42	1.2	90	.04	.10	.4	89
Tangerines	1 medium	35	.6	.2	27	.3	340	.06	.02	.2	25

Vegetables Containing the Largest Amounts of VITAMIN C

(Average minimum daily requirement is 75 milligrams)

Vegetables:	Milligrams of Vitamin C:
Asparagus	20 in 8 stalks
Beans, green lima	42 in ½ cup
Beet greens, cooked	50 in ½ cup
Broccoli, flower	65 in ¾ cup
Broccoli, leaf	90 in ¾ cup
Brussels sprouts	130 in ¾ cup
Cabbage, raw	50 in 1 cup
Chard, Swiss, cooked	37 in ½ cup
Collards, cooked	70 in ½ cup
Dandelion greens, cooked	100 in 1 cup
Kale, cooked	96 in ¾ cup
Kohlrabi	50 in ½ cup
Leeks	25 in ½ cup
Mustard greens, cooked	125 in ½ cup
Parsley	70 in ½ cup
Parsnips	40 in ½ cup
Peas, fresh cooked	20 in 1 cup
Peppers, green	125 in 1 medium pepper
Peppers, pimento	100 in 1 medium pepper
Potatoes, sweet	25 in 1 medium potato
Potatoes, white, baked	20 in 1 medium potato
Potatoes, white, raw	33 in 1 medium potato
Radishes	25 in 15 large radishes
Rutabagas	26 in ¾ cup
Spinach, cooked	30 in ½ cup
Tomatoes, fresh	25 in 1 medium tomato
Turnips, cooked	22 in ½ cup
Turnips, raw	30 in 1 medium turnip
Turnip tops, cooked	130 in ½ cup
Watercress	54 in 1 average bunch

Vegetables Containing Largest Amounts of B-Complex Vitamins

	Milligrams of		
Vegetable:	**Thiamin (B$_1$)** (M.D.R. 1.8 mg.)	**Riboflavin (B$_2$)** (M.D.R. 2.7 mg.)	**Pyridoxine (B$_6$)** (M.D.R. 1.8 mg.)
ARTICHOKES, Jerusalem			
ASPARAGUS, fresh	.16 in 12 stalks		
BEANS, dried lima	.60 in ½ cup cooked	.24 to .75 in ½ cup	.55 in ½ cup
BEANS, dried soy		.31 in ½ cup	
BEANS, green			
BEETS			.11 in ½ cup
BEET TOPS		.17 to .30 in ½ cup	
BROCCOLI			
CABBAGE			.29 in ½ cup
CARROTS			
CAULIFLOWER	.09 in ¼ small head		
COLLARDS	.19 in ½ cup, cooked	.22 in ½ cup, steamed	
CORN, yellow	1.9 in 1 lb.	0.5 in 1 lb.	
DANDELION, greens	.19 in 1 cup, steamed		
ENDIVE (escarole)		.20 in 1 head	
KALE			
MUSHROOMS			
MUSTARD GREENS		.20 to .37 in 1 cup, steamed	
PEAS, green, fresh	.36 in 1 cup, cooked	.18 to .21 in 1 cup, steamed	1.9 in 1 cup
POTATOES, Irish			.16 in 1 medium potato
POTATOES, sweet			.32 in 1 medium potato
SPINACH		.24 to .30 in ½ cup, steamed	
TOMATOES, fresh			
TURNIPS			
TURNIP greens	.10 in ½ cup, steamed	.35 to .56 in ½ cup	.10 in ½ cup

Vegetables Containing Largest Amounts of B-Complex Vitamins

Milligrams of

Choline (M.D.R. not established)	Folic Acid (Micrograms) (M.D.R. not established)	Inositol (M.D.R. not established)	Niacin (M.D.R. 18-20 mg.)	Pantothenic Acid (M.D.R. not established)
				.40 in 4 artichokes
130 in 12 stalks	120 in 12 stalks			
	330 in ½ cup	170 in ½ cup	9.6 in 1 lb.	.83 in ½ cup
340 in ½ cup				
340 in 1 cup	71 in 1 cup			
8 in ½ cup	42 in ½ cup, diced	21 in ½ cup		
	25 in ½ cup			
	90 to 110 in 1 cup			1.4 in 1 cup
250 in 1 cup		95 in 1 cup		
95 in 1 cup	97 in 1 cup	48 in 1 cup		.2 in ½ cup
	44 in ¼ small head	95 in ¼ head		.92 in ¼ head
			7.8 in 1 lb.	2.3 in 1 lb.
	62 to 75 in 1 head			
	100 in 1 cup			.30 in 1 cup
	98 in ½ cup, cooked	17 in 7 mushrooms	6.0 in 7 mushrooms	1.7 in 7 mushrooms
252 in 1 cup				
260 in 1 cup	22 in 1 cup	80 in ½ cup		.60 in 1 cup
105 in 1 med. potato	140 in 1 small potato	29 in 1 med. potato		65 in 1 med. potato
35 in 1 med. potato		66 in 1 med. potato		.95 in 1 med. potato
240 in ½ cup	225 to 280 in ½ cup	27 in ½ cup		
	12 to 14 in 1 sm. tomato	46 in 1 sm. tomato		
94 in ½ cup		46 in ½ cup		
245 in ½ cup				

preserved also. Green vegetables contain plant acids which react chemically during cooking with the coloring matter. If the vegetable is cooked quickly and not over-cooked, little acid is freed, and the bright color you desire is preserved.

DON'T PEEL VEGETABLES: Another great cause of lost nutrients is the peeling of vegetables. The minerals in most root vegetables are concentrated under the skin and are discarded when the vegetable is peeled. Leave the skin on whenever it is practical. A good rule to follow is peel vegetables only when the skin is tough, bitter or too uneven to be thoroughly cleaned.

A good cooking method should meet the following requirements: the initial heating must be rapid to destroy enzymes; contact with oxygen

Vegetables Containing the Largest Amounts of VITAMIN A

(Average minimum daily requirement is 5,000 units)

Vegetables:	International Units of Vitamin A:
Asparagus, fresh	1,000 in 12 stalks
Beans, snap	630 to 2,000 in 1 cup, cooked
Beet greens	6,700 in ½ cup, cooked
Broccoli	3,500 in 1 cup, cooked
Carrots, fresh	12,000 in 1 cup, cooked
Celery cabbage	9,000 in 1 cup
Collards	6,870 in 1 cup, cooked
Dandelion greens	13,650 in 1 cup, cooked
Endive (escarole)	10,000 to 15,000 in 1 head
Kale	7,540 in ½ cup, cooked
Lettuce, green	4,000 to 5,000 in 6 large leaves
Parsley	5,000 to 30,000 in 100 sprigs
Peas, split	1,680 in 1 pound
Peppers, green	3,000 in 2 peppers
Peppers, red	2,000 in 2 peppers
Pumpkin	1,200 to 3,400 in 1 cup, cooked
Spinach, fresh	9,420 in ½ cup, cooked
Spinach, canned	5,500 in ½ cup
Squash, winter	4,950 in ½ cup, cooked
Sweet potatoes	7,700 in 1 medium potato, baked
Tomatoes, fresh	1,100 in 1 medium tomato
Turnip greens	9,540 in ½ cup, cooked
Watercress	4,000 in 1 bunch

should be avoided by leaving the vegetable unpeeled, by covering cut surfaces with oil, or by displacing the oxygen in the utensil with steam to prevent loss of vitamin C; the vegetable should be cooked in the shortest time necessary and all of the liquid which touches the vegetable should be used to prevent loss of other nutrients.

There is no objection to boiling vegetables if the water is rapidly boiling before the vegetable is dropped into it; if it is quickly reheated to boiling; if the vegetables is not overcooked; and if all the cooking liquid is used. But how often is all this liquid used?

WATERLESS METHOD BEST: The best method of cooking vegetables is probably the waterless method. Fresh vegetables contain 70 to 95 per cent water, which is sufficient for cooking them if the heat is controlled so that no steam escapes. The utensil must have a tight-fitting lid, and the heat should be evenly distributed to the sides and the lid. In this way the vegetable cooks by heat coming from all directions. Vegetables can be cooked without any added water by this method, but a tablespoon or two

should be put into the preheated utensil in order to replace oxygen by steam. The important thing to remember in this method is to keep the heat low after the first few minutes, so that no steam escapes. Waterless-cooking equipment pays for itself in saving fuel, and what is more important it pays for itself a hundredfold in promoting health.

Steaming in the pressure cooker is another good method, provided the cooking time is watched. Length of time for cooking each vegetable is included in the directions with the equipment. Only a few tablespoons of water need be used and the remaining liquid should be served with the vegetable. As soon as the cooking time is completed, the utensil should be cooled immediately. There is some controversy over this method. Some believe this method causes too much intense heat, thus destroying nutrients. There is no definite proof one way or the other so it is up to the individual's discretion whether to use this method or not.

BROILING TECHNIQUES: Another good method of cooking vegetables, and one which almost everyone would

---

Vegetables Containing the Largest Amounts of VITAMIN E

(Minimum daily requirements have not been established)

Vegetables:	Milligrams of Vitamin E
Beans, dry navy	3.60 in ½ cup steamed
Carrots	.45 in 1 cup
Celery	.48 in 1 cup
Lettuce	.50 in 6 large leaves
Onions	.26 in 2 medium raw onions
Peas, green	2.10 in 1 cup
Potatoes, white	.06 in 1 medium potato
Potatoes, sweet	4.0 in 1 medium potato
Tomatoes	.36 in 1 small tomato
Turnip greens	2.30 in ½ cup steamed

MINERAL CONTENT OF SEEDS AND GRAINS

Seed	Calcium %	Phosphorus %	Potassium %	Sodium %	Chlorine %	Sulphur %	Magnesium %	Iron %	Manganese Mg. per lb.	Copper Mg. per lb.
Barley	0.06	0.37	0.49	0.06	0.15	0.15	0.13	0.0008	8.0	5.8
Beans, field	0.15	0.57	1.27	0.09	0.04	0.23	0.17	0.0012	8.4	4.5
Beans, Lima	0.09	0.37	1.70	0.03	0.03	0.20	0.18	0.010	7.3	3.7
Corn, dent	0.02	0.28	0.28	0.01	0.06	0.12	0.10	0.003	2.6	1.8
Cottonseed	0.14	0.70	1.11	0.29		0.24	0.32	0.014	5.5	22.7
Cow pea seed	0.11	0.46	1.30	0.27	0.04	0.25	0.26	0.036	18.2	2.0
Flax seed	0.26	0.55	0.59			0.06	0.40	0.009	26.0	
Kafir grain	0.02	0.31	0.34	0.06	0.10	0.16	0.15	0.001	7.4	3.0
Millet seed	0.05	0.30	0.43				0.16			
Milo grain	0.03	0.28	0.36				0.22	0.005	5.9	7.8
Oats kernels	0.08	0.46	0.39	0.05	0.09	0.20	0.15	0.010	16.8	3.6
Oat grain	0.09	0.34	0.43	0.09	0.12	0.21	0.14	0.007	19.9	3.8
Peanuts—No Hulls	0.06	0.44	0.54	0.56	0.02	0.25	0.18			
Rice, brown	0.04	0.25			0.08		0.14	0.001	9.2	1.2
Rice, grain	0.08	0.32	0.34		0.09					
Rye grain	0.10	0.33	0.47	0.04	0.02	0.16	0.12	0.008	37.0	3.4
Soy bean seed	0.25	0.59	1.50	0.22	0.03	0.22	0.28	0.008	13.4	7.1
Sunflower seed		0.55	0.66	0.03	0.01	0.02		0.003	9.8	
Sunflower seed, Hulled	0.20	0.96	0.92	0.03	0.01	0.02	0.38			
Wheat grain	0.04	0.39	0.42	0.06	0.08	0.20	0.14	0.006	19.9	3.7

have equipment for, is to cook your vegetables in the top of a double boiler. A few tablespoons of water are put into the top of the double boiler and brought to a boil; the vegetables are added and steamed over high direct heat until the enzymes are destroyed. The vegetables are then placed over boiling water, in the bottom part of the boiler, to finish cooking.

Strange as it may seem, broiling is a good method of cooking vegetables. The important factors of a good cooking method are utilized in that the initial heating is rapid, no moisture is needed, and the vegetables cool quickly. If the cooking time is relatively long, the vegetable should be brushed or tossed with oil to prevent loss of vitamin C. It is important to keep the heat moderate or low after the vegetable is once heated through; otherwise you may end up with a shriveled and unattractive vegetable.

BAKING SUPERIOR TO BOILING: Baking is superior to boiling as a method of cooking vegetables, but vitamin C can be destroyed because of slow initial heating and long cooking. Vegetables to be baked should first be quickly steamed or put under the broiler until they are heated through and the enzymes destroyed. Then they should be transferred to the preheated oven to finish cooking. When vegetables are baked in a casserole, the liquid used should be hot, the casserole and the oven preheated, and a lid put on to hold in steam and prevent contact with oxygen.

To insure a year-round supply of vitamins and minerals in your diet, you will want to process your excess produce from your garden for winter use.

FREEZING PRESERVES NUTRIENTS: Freezing is probably the best and fastest method of preserving food. Frozen vegetables retain their nutritive value during freezing and storage, although 50 per cent of the vitamin C may be lost before they are frozen. The same rules apply for preserving nutrients and flavor in vegetables for freezing as in preparing them for cooking. Speed is necessary in getting the vegetables from the garden into your freezer. Only gather the amount you can handle conveniently at one time and process it immediately. If you have your own freezing unit you may want to gather the various vegetables at dusk after a sunny day when the vitamin content has been found to be at its highest, and pack and freeze them in the cool of the evening. Vegetables retain greater nutritive value if they are blanched to destroy enzymes before being frozen.

When you raise your garden organically so as to insure the maximum amount of nutrients being present in your produce, and you take precautions of safeguarding these nutrients till they appear on your table, you can be assured of getting out of your food what nature intended. *See also* FREEZING.

NYMPHAEA: Waterlilies. A genus of aquatic flowers of the waterlily family, *Nymphaceae,* consisting of about 40 species of showy flowers which float on top of the water, or stand near the surface. Flowers are white, pink, red, yellow, or blue, some open during the day and others during the night. Leaves are mostly round, large, dark green on top and liver-colored underneath, leaves and flowers both floating at the ends of long rubbery stems arising from rootstocks which may be tuberous, and are buried in mud at the bottom of the pond. All are perennial, but some tender in cool climates. Numerous hybrids have been developed.

CULTURE: *Nymphea* may be propagated by seed or root division. The seed is sometimes very hard, and will germinate more quickly if filed or sawed. It may then be started in a pot submerged in water indoors, or may be rolled in a ball of clay and dropped into the pond where it is to grow. Similarly, roots may be divided and started indoors in a submerged pot, or may be planted immediately in the pond, where they will need to be anchored with a weight. Tuberous plants are always started indoors until new tubers have developed. All need rich soil and full sun, and should be submerged under one to two feet of water.

Three *nymphaea* species are commonly known as lotus; they are *N. caerula,* the blue lotus of Egypt; *N. lotus,* the white lotus of Egypt; and *N. stellata,* the blue lotus of India.

European white waterlily (*N. alba*) is hardy, with flowers four or five inches across that are open all day. Variety *candidissima* has early spring blooms, and continues its bloom until frost. *Rubra* is a red variety.

N. capensis, the Cape blue waterlily, is a tender species with leaves that grow to 16 inches in diameter. Its large light blue flowers, six to eight inches across, open four days in a row, instead of the usual three.

A pale violet species (*N. elegans*) is grown in Texas and Mexico, with three to six inch blooms open only in the morning.

One of the largest is the Australian waterlily (*N. gigantea*) with leaves 18 inches across, and flowers growing to 12 inches. Flowers are light blue, with petals tipped with dark blue, and they open seven days each.

The yellow waterlily (*N. mexicana*) grows from a tuberous rootstock, which spreads by means of runners. Bright yellow four-inch flowers open for the afternoon, standing several inches above the water.

The fragrant waterlily (*N. odorata*) has small morning flowers, about three to five inches across. The type is white, but pink and yellow varieties are known to grow wild in the eastern United States.

A tender species which grows in Africa (*N. ovalifolia*) has elliptical leaves about six by ten inches, and deep blue flowers which will open only when the sun shines.

The red India waterlily (*N. rubra*) is almost as large as gigantea. It is a night-blooming species, open until almost noon of the following days.

Pygmy waterlily (*N. tetragona*) has flowers that are under two inches across, and leaves about three to four inches in diameter. It is a hardy species, growing as far north as Ontario. Flowers are white, and there is a yellow variety, all open in the afternoons.

Magnolia or tuberous waterlily (*N. tuberosa*) is one of the handsomest, with white flowers four to nine inches across, and in the variety *Richardsonii* having so many petals as to form a globe when open. Hybrids are pink, red, and yellow. *See also* LOTUS.

NYSSA: A genus of marsh trees grown in the southern United States for ornament. Deciduous, with simple alternate leaves, inconspicuous greenish flowers separately male or female. Leaves turn bright red in autumn. Grown from seed, and sold burlapped and balled, because the trees transplant very badly, unless roots are intact. Grow in moist situations.

Cotton or tupelo gum (*N. aquatica*) grows to 100 feet, has seven-inch, smooth edged leaves, dark blue fruits less than an inch long.

Pepperidge, also called black or sour gum (*N. sylvatica*) grows to about the same size, but has leaves about half as large.

O

OAK: (*Quercus*) The oaks are among the most beautiful landscaping trees in the world and a prized source of fine lumber. A few of them are evergreen, but most have leaves that last over winter only in a withered state. They flower early in the spring, and many of them have edible acorns, especially liked by squirrels, birds and pigs and once commonly eaten by people.

Oaks are very long-lived, but somewhat slow-growing. Specimens over 800 years old have been found. With a few exceptions (noted below), they prefer a rich, fairly heavy and damp clay soil. They are usually propagated by planting the acorns in the fall as soon as they drop from the tree. They can also be stored over the winter in damp moss or sand. Sometimes cuttings or layering are used to increase the evergreen species, and the hybrid oaks are propagated by grafting in the winter under glass. All except the white oak transplant easily.

There are over 200 species of oaks, ranging from the shrubby scrub oak, *Q. prinoides*, less than six feet high, to giants like the quercitron or black oak, *Q. velutina*, that reaches up 125 feet. Another scrub oak, *Q. ilicifolia*, grows about eight feet tall, is very hardy, and does well on sandy, dry soils.

Some of the medium-sized oaks are *Q. acuta*, the Japanese evergreen oak, hardy through the upper South; *Q. agrifolia*, the California oak, a shrubby southern tree 60 or 70 feet tall; *Q. bicolor*, a hardy specimen about 50 feet tall, called the swamp white oak; the canon live oak or maul oak, *Q. chrysolepis*, 60 feet tall and grown in the Far West and South; the scarlet oak, *Q. coccinea*, very hardy, tolerant of city conditions, with brilliant red autumn foliage and a preference for light soils; the evergreen white oak, *Q. engelmanni*, 40 feet tall, not hardy in the East; *Q. ilex*, a southern ever-

green called the Holm oak, with prickly holly-like leaves; the 50-foot shingle oak, *Q. imbricaria*, hardy from Pennsylvania southward; *Q. laurifolia*, the laurel oak, 40 feet high and grown in the South; *Q. nigra*, the water oak, from Pennsylvania southward; the pin oak, *Q. palustris*, a fine, hardy street or lawn tree about 70 feet tall, with spectacular autumn foliage; *Q. phellos*, the willow oak, usually under 50 feet tall and hardy up to lower New York; the English oak, *Q. robur*, which sometimes has variegated leaves and likes a light, sandy soil; and *Q. virginiana*, the evergreen live oak, grown from Virginia southward. The cork oak, *Q. suber*, whose bark is the source of cork, is hardy only in the South, and is becoming popular as a woodland crop.

The big oaks include *Q. alba*, the white oak, whose trunk may reach 20 feet in circumference over the centuries; the valley white oak, *Q. lobata*, hardy only in the South; the bur oak, *Q. macrocarpa*, and the crescent oak, *Q. montana*, both quite hardy; *Q. rubra*, the red oak, a popular, rapid grower; and *Q. stellata*, the post oak, often seen along the edges of marshes and on sand dunes in the East.

OAK TOW: *see* MULCH

OAT HULLS: *see* HULLS; MULCH

OATS (*Avena sativa*) Grown throughout the nation. In general, the spring oat crop is grown where the climate is cool and moist. The North Central states comprise the largest producing section of the country.

CULTURE: Oats will grow on any soil that can be plowed and harrowed. However, the best yields, other things being equal, are to be expected when the crop is grown on clay loams. Gravelly and sandy soils become too hot and dry too early for maximum yields.

SEEDING: Try to seed the crop at a time which will enable it to escape as much hot weather as possible, particularly during the period from flowering to ripening of the crop. Therefore, it is always a good practice to sow spring oats as early as possible. Experiments at the Illinois Station indicate that every day of delay in seeding oats after the first possible seeding date in the spring results in approximately a half bushel decrease per acre in yield.

PLACE IN ROTATION: Most cereal crops do well when they follow clover sod. Due to the fact that oats mature within the short space of 90 to 110 days not too much organic matter should be plowed under in the spring, unless it is well cut up and mixed with the soil by discing before plowing. This material does not have enough time to decompose before seeding. The best practice is to follow corn or soybeans with oats. The oats mature in time to plow and fit the ground for seeding wheat or rye.

OCIMUM: *see* BASIL; HERBS

OCONEE BELLS: (*Shortia galacifolia*) This attractive evergreen plant is suited to the rock or wild garden. Growing eight inches high, with shiny green leaves and nodding, bell-shaped white flowers, it is native to the mountains of North and South Carolina. It has underground creeping stems, and can be increased by division in spring. Give it a shady spot and slightly acid, well-drained soil rich in humus, peat and leaf mold. Shortia is not easy to transplant and once established, should not be moved. There is a Japanese variety, *S. uniflora,* called Nippon bells, that has heart-shaped leaves. Both are propagated by division and runners.

OCOTILLO: *see* VINE CACTUS

OCTOBER GARDEN OPERATIONS: *see* GARDEN CALENDAR

ODONTOGLOSSUM: Only three species of these epiphytic orchids are popularly grown here, in the cool greenhouse. They are natives of mountainous region in Central America. Their showy flowers are borne on long, slender stalks, usually in racemes. From one to three wide, slightly curled leaves rise from each pseudobulb.

O. grande, the tiger or clown orchid, has large, waxy, long-lasting flowers, yellow and striped with brown, the lip white. It blooms in late summer or early fall. *O. citrosmum* or *pendulum* bears drooping sprays of delicate violet and pink flowers in the spring. *O. crispum* has many variations, ranging from a pure white to yellow and rose, including various highly spotted forms. As many as 20 blooms may spring from each spike. It is sometimes called a perpetual bloomer, because it may flower at different times of the year as the bulbs are completed; most often, however, it blooms in early spring.

There are well over 100 species and many more hybrids of odontoglossum, of all habits and colors, but most of them are only rarely offered in orchid catalogs. *See also* ORCHIDS.

OIL SPRAY: *see* DORMANT OIL SPRAY; SPRAY, DORMANT OIL

OKRA: (*Hibiscus esculentus*) Primarily a hot weather tropical vegetable, that can be grown in northern as well as southern gardens. A tall-growing annual, often called gumbo, okra grows best in the warmth of the deep southern states, where two crops are often grown in a single year.

CULTURE: It can be planted as early as March 20 through May for the first crop and from June 1st to July 1st for the fall growing crop. The maturation dates are from 55 to 65 days according to the variety. However, there is a rule that must be followed in planting okra—always plant okra after all danger of frost is past and the earth will continue warm. For okra is a warm weather plant and, as had been said, is by nature a tropical plant and will not stand cool weather.

In North Carolina and Virginia the planting dates are later, but good results cannot be obtained there with a fall crop unless planted, as in the lower South, by July 1st, for the cool weather will catch it before the maturity date.

Fresh green okra, with pods in prime condition, is a rich source of vitamin A. This hot-weather vegetable thrives in well-drained soil in sunlight.

Okra may be planted as a midsummer crop almost anywhere, always abiding by the rule "after all danger of frost is past." It has been known to grow in Michigan when planted in late June.

PLANTING: Okra thrives in any well-drained, good garden soil in full sunlight. If the soil is wet, the seeds tend to rot, so good drainage is necessary. Okra is hard to transplant, but in very northernmost places the seeds can be started in cold frames or hotbeds and transplanted with precaution into the garden.

Thorough preparation of the soil before planting okra is very important, although it will do very well in any kind of ground. These woody plants can take on all the food that can be given them. Because okra is very rapid growing, nitrogen is particularly needed. Poultry manure is splendid material for the okra beds, but as it is very strong only about onetenth as much as other animal manures can be used. Compost, leaf mold, peat moss and wood ashes can be used to advantage to improve poor soil in the garden. Peat moss and leaf mold are usually acid and a slight amount of lime should be used along with either of these two materials. These soil builders should be plowed under in the winter awaiting the planting time, or in a small home garden can be spaded under in the early spring.

The rows should be at least three to five feet apart, for the stalks take on a bushy growth and can become quite large when well fertilized and during rainy seasons. Scatter the seeds in drills or plant loosely in hills and cover to a depth of one to two inches, according to the compactness of the soil. The seeds should be separated three or four inches to allow space for the development of the stems. If it is warm, germination should take place within a few days. But if there is a heavy rainfall in the meanwhile, the soil should be lightly cultivated between the rows and the crust broken up over the seeds by means of a garden rake. This is suggested where the soil contains clay or is heavy. Sandy loam will probably not need any such treatment as the seeds will come through when the soil has been drained or the water has been evaporated by the action of the sun.

When plants are well up, thin them to 18 or 20 inches apart. Then mulch lightly with available organic matter.

For continuous production, pods should be gathered every day when they are one to four inches long, according to the variety. They should still be soft and the seed should be only half grown for edible pods. If it is necessary to keep the pods over 24 hours, they should be spread out in a cool place and slightly moistened. They should not be kept without good air circulation as they have a tendency to become heated when in closed crates or boxes.

VARIETIES: The Early Dwarf matures in 50 days, as does also the Perkins Mammoth, sometimes called Long Green. White Velvet takes 60 days to mature but this is the standard okra for many markets in the South. The Clemson Spineless okra matures in 60 days also and has uniform dark green spineless, long pods. Lady Finger is another variety often planted.

INJURIOUS INSECTS: The okra plant is not subject to attack from many insects, but the bollworm is its most formidable pest. This bores into the pods and thus injures them for food. The stinkbug also attacks the pods, piercing the pods and extracting the juices. Since damage from the latter occurs late in the season, the loss is very little. Blister beetles and leaf beetles often feed upon the foliage of okra but these pests do little harm to the pod and scarcely influence the production of pods at all. Handpicking usually keeps these insects well under control.

FOOD VALUE: The principal use of okra is in soups, such as gumbo soups, and as a vegetable. It is valuable in the diet chiefly because of the nutritionally important minerals it contains. It is a good source of calcium and phosphorus and a fair source of iron. Fresh green okra is also a source of vitamin A. Drying okra reduces the vitamin A content by one-half. Another value is due to its indigestible residue, some of which is considered desirable to provide bulk in the digestive tract of persons in normal health. Okra contains 90 per cent water, two per cent protein, seven per cent carbohydrate and one per cent of mineral matter.—*Myra R. Myrick.*

OLD MAN: *see* ARTEMISIA

OLD-MAN-AND-WOMAN: (*Sempervivum tectorum*) The well-known hen-and-chickens, this succulent grows three inches high, with pink flowers. It has rosettes of thick, fleshy wedge-shaped leaves, which are colored at the base and sometimes covered with a cobwebby material. The most commonly grown species of houseleek, it is often called the roof houseleek, for its habit of growing profusely on thatched roofs in some countries. Here it is widely used in rock gardens, wall gardens and borders, and as carpet bedding plants and house plants.

Like the other houseleeks, it is best suited to fairly dry, sandy soils and sunny locations. Old-man-and-woman is easily propagated by offsets, or by seed when available.

OLD-MAN'S-BEARD: (*Chionanthus virginica*) Sometimes called the fringe tree, this exceptionally beautiful shrub of the olive family bears loose panicles of pure white, scented flowers in June, and egg-shaped dark blue berries. In autumn, the foliage turns a glorious yellow. It grows about 20 feet or so high in reasonably good, moist loam soils and full sun, and is hardy north in a sheltered position. A later-blooming variety, the Chinese fringe tree, *C. retusa,* is somewhat less hardy and grows ten to 12 feet high. Both are propagated by seeds, layers or cuttings, or by grafting or budding onto the ash. Two vines, *Clematis vitalba* and *C. virginiana,* are also sometimes called old-man's-beard because they have similar flowers.

OLD WOMAN: *see* ARTEMISIA

OLEANDER: (*Nerium oleander*) This spectacularly beautiful evergreen shrub or small tree is hardy in Florida and southern California, and sometimes grown in the deep South with winter protection. It grows from eight feet to perhaps 25 feet high, with white, pink, red or purple flowers, often double. The most popular variety is often called the rose bay, because of its rose-colored, long-lasting double blooms. There are deep cream and velvety crimson varieties, and an especially lovely one with single peach-blossom-pink blooms. A separate species, *N. indicum,* the sweet oleander, bears lovely vanilla-scented white or pink flowers. It grows about eight feet tall.

Beautiful evergreen shrubs or trees, oleanders grow from eight to 25 feet high, produce blooms ranging from white and pink to red and purple.

CULTURE: Oleanders are used outdoors for specimens, hedges and sidewalk plantings. The rose bay is a favorite street or avenue ornamental. Sunny locations are best, and the oleander is well able to stand hot, dry, dusty conditions. It likes a sandy soil, and will give an incredible profusion of blooms if fed abundantly with compost, rotted manure or other organic fertilizers. A mulch, plus heavy watering in drought periods, are also advised. A rapid grower, the oleander can be easily pruned to be a medium-sized or large, wide shrub or a handsome symmetrical tree. It blooms from May to October. Propagation is by layers, or by cuttings started in winter in porous soil.

Where it is not hardy, the oleander is often grown as a highly decorative tub plant or as a pot plant for the house. In tubs, it needs a soil made up of equal parts of sand, loam, peat moss, and leaf mold or humus. It can be sheared moderately into a pleasing shape in late winter. Give it a very sunny position in the summer. Just before frost, bring it to a cool spot indoors—a frost-free cellar is excellent. The less light there is, the cooler it can be. Keep it on the dry side, and don't fertilize. Then topdress with compost or manure before putting it outdoors in the spring, and water and feed regularly through the blooming period.

In the house, oleanders in pots will flower from the middle of spring to early summer, if they have been kept fairly dry and at a temperature of close to 50° during the winter. Put them in a sunny window and increase the watering about the first week in March. The plants should be plunged outdoors in full sun for the summer.

The sap of oleander is extremely poisonous, and small children should be cautioned against it. *See also* SHRUBS.

OLEARIA: *see* TREE ASTER

OLEASTER: (*Elaeagnus angustifolia*) Also called the Russian olive, the oleaster is a shrub or small tree growing ten to 20 feet high. It is hardy in the far North and is planted throughout the United States for its handsome silvery foliage and fragrant yellow, bell-shaped flowers. The sweet, mealy berries are edible. It is useful for wildlife plantings and provides bee homes and food. The dry, fallen leaves are sometimes eaten by cattle, goats and sheep. The shrub is highly resistant to drought and wind, and tolerant of alkali and city smoke. As a windbreak or shelterbelt, oleasters can be planted five to six feet apart. It is also good for seaside gardens.

Oleaster does well on many sites, from sandy and dry to alkaline soils, and will succeed in partial shade. But for best growth in the garden, it prefers a moist, rich soil and open sunlight. It makes a good street tree if the lower branches are pruned while the tree is young. Stratified seeds sown the second year will give new plants, or it can be propagated by cuttings, grafting or layering. It is sometimes called the Trebizond date.

OLIVE: (*Olea europaea*) The olive is a hardy evergreen tree of the subtropics whose fruit is made into olive oil and pickled. The flavor of the fruit is piquant and nutty, and it is high in food value, especially fat. In the United States, olives are grown commercially mainly in lower California and parts of Arizona. There the trees are generally about 25 feet high, with silvery foliage and fragrant panicles of white blooms, followed by the plum-like fruits in late autumn.

CULTURE: The olive tree likes heat, and needs a long, comparatively droughty season. Although it grows well in the lower South, it sets fruit only occasionally there because of the relatively high humidity. However, it is a very beautiful tree and exceptionally long-lived, some specimens in the Mediterranean areas where it originated bearing over 1,500 years. Of the hundreds of varieties cultivated here, most come from France, Italy, Spain and Tunisia. The main ones are Ascolano, Mission, Barouni, Manzanillo, Nevadillo, Redding Picholine and Sevillano. The big-fruited varieties, Ascolano, Barouni and Sevillano are usually known as Queen olives. Most species will stand temperatures as low as 15°, but the fruit is injured by frost.

Olive trees are propagated by seeds or cuttings. A common practice is to change the variety of older trees by top-grafting. They are not exacting as to soil requirements, providing they have good drainage. Open, sandy loams or clay loams are ideal. In poor soils, nitrogen is usually the crop-limiting element. Olives are moderately tolerant of salt and alkaline soil. Irrigation is practiced in most commercial groves, and the fruit is commonly thinned to overcome the trees' tendency to alternate bearing. Correct pruning and spacing of the trees are vital, as shade can considerably lower yields. The few pests and diseases are easily controlled by sanitation.

Planted from 25 to 40 feet apart, the trees start to bear in four to eight years, but 12 to 15 years are required for a full crop. Two tons to the acre is the average yield. The oil content of ripe California olives varies from 18 to 25 per cent. Between 50 and 60 gallons of oil of all grades are usually obtained from each ton of olives pressed.

Olives for pickling are usually gathered while still green, sometimes when ripe and black. They must be harvested by hand and handled carefully to avoid bruising. Some pickling is done in brine, but most methods involve the use of lye. When the olives are used for oil, cold and hot pressing methods are employed, the latter extracting the inedible oils which are used in soap-making and other cosmetic and pharmaceutical preparations.

OLIVE RESIDUES: The analysis of olive pomace is given as 1.15 nitrogen, 0.78 phosphoric acid and 1.26 potash, while some olive refuse showed 1.22 nitrogen, 0.18 phosphoric acid and 0.32 potash. It is not known how olive pits would show up from a fertilizer standpoint, but there is little doubt that they too should be used for adding fertility to the soil, since they not only contain phosphorus and nitrogen in higher amounts than mere refuse, but also lignin.

OMPHALODES: *see* NAVELWORT

ONCIDIUM: Numerous spectacular flowers on stems several feet long are the hallmark of these orchids. The long, branched clusters of *O. varicosum,* the most commonly grown type, are very beautiful, the blooms often being nicknamed "dancing dolls." Although the leaves may be only eight inches tall, the flower spray is frequently five feet in length with 250 bright yellow flowers the size of a fifty-cent piece. It is fall-blooming. Other varieties with somewhat shorter stems and larger flowers are *O. papilio,* the butterfly-orchid, which blooms most of the year in the greenhouse; *O. ampliatum,* a compact variety sometimes grown on a chunk of osmunda fiber wired to a slab of wood; *O. flexuosum, O. ornithorhynchum, O. splendidum, O. obryzatum* and *O. sphacelatum,* all rich yellow marked with brown or green. These are only the most popular of the oncidiums—over 300 species and many more varieties are known and occasionally offered by growers. *See also* ORCHIDS.

ONION: (*Allium cepa*) Gardeners have grown onions since anicent days. Egypt, in the days of the Pharaohs, was famed for the mildness of its onions. The choice of varieties extends from the satiny, globular-rooted "Bermuda" type to the pungent little garlic onion; from the very mild, thick-stemmed leek to the homely shallot.

Onions are relatively easy to grow provided the garden soil is rich, fertile and reasonably well-drained. The topsoil should be deep and contain an ample supply of humus. If the soil is exceptionally sandy or very heavy (clayey), this condition should be corrected the season before planting by the addition of well-rotted horse manure, leaves, or other organic material deeply dug in.

The use of lime may be necessary to offset excess soil acidity. If finely crushed limestone is used this may be incorporated in the soil at any time previous to planting. During the digging and pulverizing of the area in which the onions are to grow a generous application of fine compost should be made.

CULTURE: An easy way to become familiar with onion growing is to start by using sets. Sets are small seed onions commonly of the Ebenezer type, although they come in white-, brown-, or red-skinned varieties. The best sets to plant are those about the size of a dime. Those smaller than that are usually lacking in vigor. You will find that it pays to plant sets carefully in their natural position, two to three inches apart in the row. They should be covered with a quarter of an inch of sifted compost, watered and well

firmed. One pound of sets is enough for 50 feet of row.

Sown as early in the spring as possible, the sets will grow rapidly. They demand only shallow cultivation and necessary weeding. By five weeks the young plants should have made good growth. If pulled at this stage they are known as "scallions" or "early green bunching onions."

Onion sets mature in about 100 days and as the plants approach maturity, gradually the tops fall to the ground. When most of the tops are down the remainder are generally broken down by running the back of a rake over them. A day or two later the onions should be pulled and left on the surface of the ground for a couple of days to receive the drying, curing effect of exposure to sun and air. They are then gathered and the tops clipped off about an inch from the bulb. To complete their curing, they should be spread loosely in a shed or airy lean-to where they may remain drying until cold weather arrives. Then they should be placed in orange crates, net bags, or similar open containers and moved to a cool, dry storage cellar. Lacking a storage cellar, onions in open containers may be stored in some well-ventilated place such as an attic. Provided they are dry, slight freezing does not injure them although they should not be handled while frozen.

IMPORTANCE OF DAYLIGHT: Your success in growing a few bags of fine smooth onions might cause you to wonder how this satiny bulb came to be formed. In this connection, it is well to remember that though the health of the plant itself depends upon the liberal use of plant nutrients supplied by humus, good drainage and the like, the formation of the onion bulb is determined by the length of the daylight. The time when the formation of the edible bulb forms is determined by the amount of daylight the plant receives and not because of the maturity of the plant.

This explains why some types of

onions form bulbs in certain localities and not in others. There are onions which form bulbs when receiving only 12 hours of daylight daily (Yellow Bermuda, White Creole, etc.). Ebenezer and Yellow Danvers require 13 hours of daylight each day to bulb. Such types as Red Wethersfield require as much as 14 hours.

Onions grown from seed mature in about 130 days but offer a much wider range of varieties than those grown from sets. One ounce of seed is sufficient for 100 feet of row. Seed should be in the ground just as early as possible, even before danger of frost has passed. It should be planted thickly and evenly in a shallow drill and covered with a half inch of sifted compost and firmed. Careful weeding of the rows and the same general care should be given as for onions grown from sets.

Because of the necessity for an early start so that the plants may be benefitted by the long daylight hours and mature before the arrival of summer drought, many gardeners purchase young plants. But to obtain fine young plants, true to type and free from disease, you may decide to grow your own seedlings with the aid of a cold frame. You will then be in a position to transplant the seedlings to the garden the minute the ground is in a condition to receive them.

LEEKS: Leeks are quite easily grown, mild-flavored, and very bulky. They have much the appearance of giant scallions with stems over two inches thick on plants reaching almost a foot high.

Leeks will thrive under about the same conditions as globe onions. The seed is planted thickly in the same manner. However, its culture, after the plant reaches eight inches high, is quite different from that given the globe onion. When the plant has reached this height, the tops are cut back to about four inches high. A new area for them is prepared and a furrow five inches deep formed. The plants are then dug and carefully transplanted to the furrow in the bottom of which they are planted five inches apart and well watered. If another furrow is necessary to receive all the plants you have grown it may be formed parallel with and two feet from the first.

This shifting of the plants is done to give them more room and so that, as they grow, the sides of the furrow can be gradually broken down with a hoe to encourage the formation of long, thick stalks. This blanching of the stalks also makes them finer and crisper.

GARLIC: Quite different from either the globe onion or the leek is the garlic onion and the shallot. A very small planting of garlic will be adequate for the production of sufficient garlic "cloves" needed by the average family.

Garlic is usually grown from sets. The sets in this case are sometimes called "mother onions." They are really a cluster of "cloves"—more properly bulblets—held together in a membranous papery sac. At planting time the "mother onion" is separated into its component bulblets which are planted four inches apart in the row and covered with a half an inch of good compost. The rows are usually 18 inches apart, although you will likely find that one short row is more than enough.

Because of its persistence, garlic sometimes becomes a serious weed. Garlic grows in the wild and it is not unlikely that many of the varied types of cultivated onions were developed long ago by ancient peoples from such wild forms.

In garlic you will meet a plant that increases and multiplies through the "mother onion," i.e., a soft-shelled bulb around which grows a number of hard-shelled bulblets all of which are ready to form a new plant. The plant also forms aerial bulblets, that is, a cluster of small bulbs at the top of a stalk some two feet tall. Each of these aerial bulblets is capable of forming new plants. In addition, of course, the plant flowers and forms viable seed. Two types of onions are grown as ornamentals because of the beauty of their flowers.

SHALLOT: The shallot is an onion of the garlic type although it forms bulbs much larger and much less pungent. It is grown from sets in the same manner as garlic. Multiplier onions of the Egyptian type are often used as shallots. The shallot differs also from the garlic onion in that the "mother onion" is not held together by a papery sac. Altogether, the shallot is a sturdy, delightful garden plant, not too well appreciated. It is very resistant to plant disease and insect pests and for this reason much interest has lately been taken in work being done to cross this resistant plant with the more delicate, large bulbed onion types.

The average garden-grown onion is relatively free from plant disease and insect pests, although the onion root maggot can be troublesome in some localities until the garden soil has been properly conditioned by the liberal use of properly composted organic humus. As an emergency measure, some gardeners have found that radishes interplanted between rows of onions act as a very satisfactory trap crop. The onion root maggot prefers the radish root. They infest these to the exclusion of the onion roots, and the radishes are easily pulled and destroyed when they become infested.

ONION MAGGOT: The full-grown onion maggot is legless, pearly white, and about $\frac{1}{3}$ inch long. The body tapers to a point at the head. This insect is very similar to the cabbage maggot.

The onion maggot seldom attacks any crop except onions, but it will attack this crop throughout the growing season. Onions planted for sets are more susceptible than large onions; white varieties are more likely to be damaged than yellow ones; red varieties are least likely to be damaged. Damage is most severe when the

onions are small. One maggot is capable of destroying many seedlings by destroying their underground parts; whereas a single large onion may harbor several maggots, though larger onions are rendered unfit for use even if they are not killed. The destruction of onion seedlings not only reduces the stand but causes the remaining plants to be less uniform in size. This lack of uniformity is of considerable importance when onion sets are grown.

The maggots usually gain entrance to larger onions near the base where they attack the roots and may burrow upward as much as two inches. When damaged onions are put into storage, they decay and cause surrounding sound bulbs to rot.

Cull onions should not be dumped on fields and plowed under nor should they be piled in heaps near onion fields.

LIFE HISTORY: Onion maggots overwinter as brown puparia in the soil or in piles of cull onions and screenings. The flies that emerge are similar in size and appearance to those of the cabbage maggot. The female deposits her small white eggs singly or in groups on the base of plants or in the soil nearby. The eggs hatch in two to ten days. The maggots require two to three weeks to become full-grown. They transform to dark-brown inactive pupae which, during the summer, become flies after about two weeks. There are two or three generations each season.

ONION THRIPS: The onion thrips is slender, light yellow to brown, very active, and almost too small to be seen with the naked eye.

Onion thrips feed on onions, beans, cabbage, and a large number of other crops and weeds.

This insect, unlike most others, scrapes the surface of a leaf with its mouthparts and laps up the sap that flows from the wounded tissue. Small whitish blotches appear where thrips have fed. Heavily infested plants become stunted, the leaves become bleached and die back from the tips, abnormally thick necks are produced, and the bulbs fail to develop normally.

It is not uncommon for large fields of onions to be destroyed by onion thrips during July and August. Injury is most severe during hot dry seasons.

Spanish onions show considerable resistance to onion thrips. If the infestation is severe, even they will be destroyed; but the chance, during years when thrips are bad, of growing a crop of Spanish onions is much better than is the chance of growing the ordinary globe or flat onion.

Onion sets should not be planted next to a field of large onions. Thrips from the early-maturing sets will migrate to other onions in the vicinity and destroy the crop during hot dry summers.

Onion thrips overwinter as adults and nymphs on onions and other food plants, or under rubbish near the fields. They emerge early in the spring and feed on any of a number of plants. They migrate to onion fields during late spring or early summer. From ten to 15 days are required for this insect to develop from an egg to an adult during the summer.—*Roger Smith.*

See also INSECT CONTROL.

ONONBRYCHIS: In the Old World, *O. viciaefolia* is grown for forage for livestock, but here its lovely racemes of white, pink or rose blooms make it an attractive perennial for the border or massed planting. It is sometimes called saintfoin or holy clover, and grows two feet tall, with prickly pods. A smaller variety, *O. crista-galli,* is one foot tall. Both do well in sandy, poor soil. Sow the seeds in spring or summer for bloom the next year. They should be planted ½ inch deep where they are to flower.

ONONIS: *see* RESTHARROW

ONOPORDON: *see* SCOTCH THISTLE

OPHIOGLOSSUM: The adder's-tongue fern, *O. vulgatum,* grows about a foot tall, with narrow fronds. It is not an especially handsome fern. Damp meadows are its usual habitat, and it is grown occasionally in the wild garden or in fern plantings. *See also* FERNS.

OPHIOPOGON: This lily-turf is hardier than its relative, *Liriope,* surviving up to the latitude of New York. It is especially popular in California. An evergreen ground cover, it prefers sandy, moist banks and thrives under trees. There are two varieties, *O. japonicus,* ten inches high with underground stolons and small violet flowers in loose racemes, and *O. jaburan* (often sold as *Mondo jaburan*) with white blooms, leaves over a foot long, and a thick mass of roots. A variety of the latter has white-striped leaves. Both bear pea-sized blue berries, and are easily propagated by division. *See also* GROUND COVERS.

OPIUM POPPY: (*Papaver somniferum*) This herb has been grown for over a thousand years as a source of opium gum, a sleep-inducer found in the milky juice of the unripe pods. The seeds today are used for flavoring. Opium poppy is a vigorous annual about three to four feet high, with showy single or double, red, white, pink or purple blooms four inches across. The strain with fringed petals is sometimes called the carnation poppy. *See also* POPPY.

OPULASTER: *see* NINEBARK

OPUNTIA: *see* PRICKLY PEAR

ORACH (*Atriplex hortensis*) A plant of the spinach family; its leaves are used in the same manner as spinach. Orach succeeds best if sown where it is to grow, in rich, moist soil. Seed should be sown in rows eight inches apart; when plants are two inches high, they should be thinned to six inches apart in the rows. Orach foliage should be utilized when quite young, to enjoy the short-lived tenderness and flavor.

ORANGE: (*Citrus*) The Common or Sweet Orange (*C. sinensis*) has many popular varieties of commercial importance. The sour or Seville orange (*C. aurantium*) is used mainly as a rootstock. Although the orange can be grown commercially only in warmer parts of Florida, California, the Mississippi Delta and the lower Rio Grande Valley, many varieties are suitable for greenhouse growing in the North. Citrus fruits, including the orange, will grow readily in any well-drained soil, but prefer a medium loam.

Similar to other members of the citrus family, orange trees are evergreen. Producing small flowers, they do best in a medium loam soil.

CULTURE: Orange trees, like all other citrus trees, are evergreen and can be planted most any time of the year. However, in the colder months, December, January and February, it is not advisable to plant as they will not grow when weather is cold. For the best results plant in March, April or May as weather conditions are most favorable at that time.

When you are ready to plant your orange trees, dig a hole about three feet deep and two feet wide. Add enough good topsoil so that when you plant the tree it will be two inches above the bud union or the place where the tree was grafted onto the seedling. Place your tree upright in the center of the hole. Then fill in with soil, packing it tightly but gently around the ball, filling the hole to about one inch below the bud union. It is now ready for a good irrigation. Be sure to put in enough water to wet it right down to the roots.

PRUNING: Pruning causes new growth and this new growth produces better fruit. All old growth that has died back should be cut off, also any branches that cross each other and cause damage by rubbing should be thinned out to eliminate that condition.

OTHER VARIETIES: Mandarins as well as the tangerines are members of the species *C. nobilis*. The bergamot orange (*C. bergamia*) is more closely related to the lemon. There are early- and late-ripening varieties, as well as mid-season ones. For example, along Southern California coasts, Valencia which is a late-maturing type requiring high-heat, ripens during the second summer following bloom. Washington Navel ripens in fall or winter of the same year as bloom; it's grown in areas with hot summers. *See also* CITRUS FRUITS; FRUIT TREES; ORCHARD.

ORANGEBERRY: (*Triphasia trifolia*) Grown for ornament in the deep South and along the Pacific Coast, this spiny shrub has very fragrant flowers resembling orange blossoms. The berry-type red fruit has a spicy pulp, but it is not often eaten. Orangeberry is frequently used for hedges.

ORANGE GUM: (*Angophora lanceolata*) This medium-sized tree, also called the gum myrtle, is generally planted only in Florida and southern California. It is a relative of the eucalyptus, with showy white flowers in clusters. Propagate by seeds sown in flats in summer, and give it ordinary garden soil.

ORANGE WASTES: *see* CITRUS WASTES

ORCHARD: Fruit growing success in the home garden is not achieved easily or blindly. If the venture is to be enjoyable and profitable, planning and sound judgment followed by prompt and effective action is necessary. Of prime importance is the selection of nursery stock, procurement of varieties that are best adapted to your particular climate and soil and the proper arrangement, spacing and planting of these varieties.

Fruit trees may be planted in the spring or fall. In the milder parts of the United States where minimum temperatures are not likely to go below 0° F., they may be planted in the late fall before the ground is frozen. Peaches, apricots and other tender fruits often suffer considerable winter injury in more severe climates and should therefore be planted in spring. Spring-planted trees should be set as early as the ground will permit.

HEELING: When trees are obtained from the nursery, be sure they do not dry out at any time before planting. If not planted at the time they are received, the trees should be heeled in. Select a place that is protected from excessive exposure and where the soil is well-drained. Dig a trench deep enough to accommodate all the roots, throwing the soil in a mound along the south side of the trench. The boxes or bales in which the trees were shipped should be opened or heating may occur within the package and the trees injured. Cut the bundles and separate the trees from each other somewhat, making sure that the varieties are separated so they may be distinguished later. The trees should be placed close together in the trench row and slanted toward the south to prevent sun injury. Fill the trench with soil being sure all the roots are covered. Trees heeled in this fashion may be held for a considerable length of time before they are permanently planted in the orchard.

SPACING THE TREES: Assuming that the location of the orchard has

Apple and other fruit trees are most commonly spaced in a square, quincunx, or hexagonal arrangement. Planting distance depends upon the size at maturity; 30 to 45 feet is common for apples.

been determined, a plan must be decided on for the arrangement of the trees. Orchard trees are generally planted according to some definite system. The three most common arrangements of trees in an orchard are the square, the quincunx or diagonal and the hexagon or triangle. Where the land is rugged and steep a fourth system, the contour arrangement, is best.

The "square" system is the usual plan in most sections and makes orchard operations easy to handle. In this arrangement a tree is set in each corner of a square, whatever the distance may be. If filler, or temporary trees are used one may be set between every two trees in the row and another row of fillers set between each two permanent rows so that the permanent trees are twice as far apart as the filler trees. The filler trees are removed after the trees begin to crowd each other too much.

The quincunx system is very similar to the square, except that there is a tree in the center of each square. The center tree is considered semipermanent and is usually removed after the trees become very large. This method is particularly desirable when alternate rows are planted to different varieties. Generally more fruit can be produced over a longer period of time since a larger number of trees can be planted to the acre. A disadvantage is encountered with this system however, since cultural practices must be carried out on the diagonal.

When the hexagonal system is used all trees are equidistant from each other and a calculated 15 per cent more trees can be planted to the acre than with the square system.

The contour system is the most feasible arrangement for planting an orchard on a hillside. In contour planting on sloping land, all trees in any one row are in the soil at the same elevation. Obviously, the tree rows will not be equally spaced in all parts of the orchard.

The first step in laying out a contour planting is to decide upon a minimum allowable interval between rows. This distance will depend on the kind and varieties of fruit trees planted. The first contour line should be laid out at the highest elevation. From a given point, the line is projected on the contour in both directions to the limits of the area to be planted, by using an engineer's level and rod. Then proceed to the steepest slope in the orchard below the first line and establish a point at the minimum distance between rows below the first line. A line is then projected in both directions from this point in a similar manner as that in establishing the first line. If at any place in the orchard the distance between two adjacent lines becomes twice the minimum interval, a new line is laid out on the contour between them.

DISTANCE BETWEEN TREES: The planting distance must be determined principally by the size the trees are likely to attain at maturity. This is largely dependent upon the type of fruit, the variety, fertility and depth of the soil and amount of rainfall or available moisture. The trees must be sufficiently far apart to allow the sun to hit the lower branches if fruit of satisfactory quality is to be grown on the lower parts of the trees.

Although the matter has never been definitely settled the following distances are most frequently used:

Fruit	Distance in ft.
Apple	32 to 45
Pear	25 to 35
Apricot	20
Peach	20 to 24
Plum	20 to 24
Cherry, sour	24 to 30
Cherry, sweet ...	25 to 30
Quince	18 to 22
Dwarf trees	10 x 10
	10 x 15
	15 x 15

The variation in the planting distances for each type of fruit is largely dependent upon the variety. This can be illustrated in the example of apples. Vigorous apple varieties, such as Baldwin, McIntosh, and York Imperial, planted 25 feet apart in fertile soil, may crowd when only about 15 years old; planted 30 feet apart they will usually crowd when about 20 years old. Less vigorous trees such as Rome Beauty, Winesap, and Golden Delicious, planted 25 feet apart, would not crowd seriously until 18 or 20 years old.

CHOOSING A SITE: Orcharding is a long time investment, whether practiced on a large or small scale, and consideration should be given to all the factors involved in selecting a desirable site. An error in planting annual crops can be corrected the following year, but to the orchardist, site selection must be a rather permanent thing. The principal factors in choosing a site are soil and topography. Without a favorable combination of them, orcharding can be hazardous. Constantly lower yields may result with even slight deviations from the optimum site. Actually there are more favorable sites than will ever be needed in this country for orcharding, yet a surprisingly large number of our orchards, both of the commercial and home types, are on poorly selected land. The importance of proper selection of orchard sites cannot be over emphasized, because a mistake in this initial step often can never be remedied during the entire life of the orchard. In other words, conscientious management cannot profitably offset the natural consequences of frequent late spring freezes, water logged soils, poor fruit color and loss of trees caused by poor orchard location.

Before selecting a region for fruit growing the home orchardist should make a study of winter and spring temperatures, moisture, soil and site conditions and the suitability of a certain kind of fruit for a given region or site. The commercial grower must carefully study all of these above mentioned factors plus such things as transportation and marketing facilities.

Cover crops, as the vetch shown growing above in a California apricot grove, are an excellent source of mulch material around trees. Clover, soybeans, rye, kudzu, alfalfa and buckwheat are also grown.

CHECK WEATHER RECORDS: Temperature is the most important climatic factor affecting the geographic distribution of fruits and varieties of fruits. Man has little control over the temperature. Therefore, it is wise to check carefully with local growers, horticultural extension specialists, and the local United States Weather Bureau regarding frequency of frosts and extremes in temperatures in past years. Extremely cold winter of 20-40 degrees below zero or violent fluctuations of rising and falling temperatures in the winter can prove fatal to any orcharding venture. For profitable fruit production it is necessary that the trees experience an uninterrupted winter rest period when life processes are held at a minimum.

Spring frosts or freezes shortly before, during, or after the blossoming period constitute one of the most hazardous conditions in fruit growing. They are far more destructive to the fruit industry than early autumn frosts. There are few orchardists who are fortunate enough to be completely immune to even occasional late frosts, but to suffer from frost injury year after year is one of the surest signs of a fatal enterprise.

Heavy winds which blow more or less continuously over an area are undesirable from several points of view. Strong winds during the period of blossoming often reduce the fruit set with subsequent reductions in the crop. If the winds are prevalent from one direction young trees tend to grow onesided. This more or less throws the tree off balance and may cause it to break under the weight of its first heavy crop.

Hail is a hazard to fruit growing which, although less serious than spring frosts, can be destructive to the fruit reducing it in grade, or if the stones are large enough completely detroying a season's crop.

The amount of sunshine directly affects the rate of food manufacture by the leaves which, in turn, affects the size and color of the fruit and the regularity with which the trees in regions of Washington State bear from year to year. For example, where sunshine is relatively abundant, fruit production per acre is greater and alternate bearing of light and heavy crops of fruit is much less pronounced than in Eastern states where there is more cloudiness during the growing season. The amount of sunshine may also be affected to a greater or lesser degree from proximity of orchards to heavy industrial centers, where factory smoke constantly clouds the sky.

ELEVATION: The elevation of the site in relation to land immediately around it is especially important in the prevention of frost and freezing hazards. Upland rolling or sloping fields which are not too steep for efficient orchard operations, broad ridges or upland plains bordering depressions are the most desirable sites. River bottoms or flat valley floors are definitely undesirable. During still nights (especially important during blossoming time) the cold air drains from high lands into depressions and valleys, often resulting in damage to crops in these lower areas, while those on higher elevations may escape injury. Trees should not be planted lower than 50 feet above the base of the slope. A difference of ten feet in elevation may make a difference of five to ten degrees in the minimum temperature encountered. In some seasons, such differences would mean the difference between a full crop and a crop failure. These colder temperatures at the lower elevations may at first seem contradictory to some people, since it is true that air temperatures become lower with increased elevations. However, during clear, still nights there is a temperature inversion. This phenomenon takes place because the layer of air which lies next to the earth is cooler, and, as cold air is heavier than warm, it flows downward; warm air rises. Air stratification may at times be so critical that blossoms on the lower part of a tree may be destroyed while those in the upper part remain uninjured.

Placing an orchard on the leeward side of a large body of water is a good substitute for elevation. Such a site usually experiences slow changes in temperature due to the tempering effect of deep water. A body of water that is large enough not to completely freeze over during the winter maintains a more even temperature throughout the year than a nearby equal area of land. Consequently, air masses passing over large areas of water will not have as great a variation in temperature as those passing over land. Land on the leeward side of a body of water will therefore experience the following advantages: 1. In spring, the air temperatures will remain at a lower level and retard plant growth beyond the date of frost injury. 2. In autumn, the period for ripening of fruit will be extended due to warmer temperatures near the shore line. 3. During the winter, there will be a reduction of violent and sudden changes from warm to extremely cold temperatures.

SOIL TYPES: Fruit trees thrive over a wide range of soil types and the limits are not so exacting as with some other crops. However, experience indicates that soil alone may often cause a difference of 50 to 100 per cent in yield.

Often a very productive soil for farm crops may not be suitable for orchards and conversely, a less productive one in good physical condition may support an excellent orchard when properly managed.

The first requirement of a good orchard soil is proper water drainage permitting good aeration and extensive root development. Orchard trees are deep rooted when compared to most other crops. Consequently the subsoil is more important than the upper layer of soil in selecting a proper site. When the subsoil is hard and impervious, trees often grow satisfactorily for a few years, but become weak when they mature. If a severe winter occurs, they may die. Fruit trees will not tolerate wet soils during the growing season. After a rain the water table rises, but should recede within a few days after the rain. If it does not, and ground water persists within a foot or so of the surface during the critical blossoming and fruit setting period, many roots will die and the tree suffers accordingly. Submergence of the root system for even a few days during the summer growing season, when temperatures are high, usually results in eventual death of the roots. A soil on which water stands for more than a week after a heavy rain is unfit for fruit growing. In most orchards, it is not unusual to find isolated wet spots where there are small depressions in the orchard. These can be avoided, or drained by tile, if this procedure does not prove too expensive.

ROOT DEVELOPMENT: The rooting area for a fruit tree should be at least four to five feet in depth, but this depends somewhat on the region and soil type. Heavy compact soils are unfavorable since soil aeration is an important factor for deep rooted, well established trees. Under optimum conditions for plant growth about half of the pore space, which in the average soil comprises about 50 per cent of the soil volume, should be occupied by water and the rest by air. In compact soil the pores are very small and are filled with water so that the air is excluded.

The color of the soil gives an excellent index of its depth of drainage. Poor subsurface drainage results in inadequate aeration which causes mottling in the subsoil. These mottled colors are most usually brown and gray, yellow and gray, or yellow and brown. The depth of mottling corresponds to the depth of good subsurface drainage. If mottling occurs near the surface, such soils are usually too poorly drained for a good orchard site. A simple method of studying subsoil colors is through the use of a soil auger of the type that removes a continuous core of soil. A more difficult but better method is to dig a trench about two feet wide, several feet long and about six feet deep. This may seem like a lot of trouble, but when one remembers the years of work that may be wasted, every means should be used to insure success.

POLLINATION

Perhaps the most serious mistake and the one made most often by the small back yard orchardist is incompatibility between fruits and improper pollination.

In many cases where the space is small and the would-be orchardist desires to have as many kinds of fruit as possible, single trees of individual fruits are planted with no thought as to whether they will be properly pollinated and thus bear fruit. It is a sad experience when an individual buys the best trees from the nursery, prepares the soil with organic materials, carefully plants the trees and tenderly cares for them year after year, only to find out that although he has beautiful trees which blossom each spring, few, if any fruits develop. Then the question arises: "Why don't my fruit trees bear fruit?"

There are several factors which cause unfruitfulness among fruit trees. Several of them arise from a lack or unbalance of nutritional elements needed by the tree for fruit-formation. However, the most common factor in small backyard orchards is improper pollination.

IMPROPER POLLINATION: To explain this, it is necessary to start with some of the fundamental facts that influence fruit-formation. When fruit trees reach a certain age, depending on the variety and the nutritional status of the tree, flowers are formed. These flowers consist of two principal parts: the pollen-producers, *i.e.*, stamens and anthers, or the male part of the flower, and the pollen-receivers, *i.e.*, pistil and stigma, or the female part of the flower.

Pollination refers to the transfer of pollen from the anthers to the stigma of a flower. Self-pollination refers to the transfer of pollen from the anthers of a flower to the stigma of the same flower or a flower of the same variety.

Cross-pollination refers to the transfer of pollen from a flower on one fruit type to the stigma of a flower of a different variety. Pollination does not mean that fruit will be produced, since the pollen of many fruit trees will not fertilize the flowers of the same variety or those of some other varieties.

Self-unfruitfulness, in the strict sense, means the inability of a tree to produce fruit with viable seeds following self-pollination, while self-fruitfulness involves the production of fruits with viable seeds. Cross-unfruitfulness takes place if one fruit type, when used as the pollinizer of another, is unable to produce sufficient fruits for the production of a commercial crop. If fruits are produced readily through cross-pollination, the varieties are said to be cross-fruitful. Most of the fruit types display rather definite patterns of self-and cross-unfruitfulness among the different varieties.

Some fruit trees are sufficiently self-fruitful to be dependably productive if planted alone. However, there are many other fruit varieties that will not produce fruits if planted alone, nor will they bear if planted with some other varieties. It is therefore extremely important that the proper varieties are planted which will be either self- or cross-fruitful. When cross-fruitful types are planted, it is important that they be planted close enough to insure adequate transfer of pollen by bees and other insects. Orchard observations and experimental results indicate that to obtain the most dependable set of fruit, trees of different varieties should not be further apart than about 70 to 80 feet for apple, 40 to 60 feet for pear, 40 feet for peach, 30 to 40 feet for plum and sour cherry, and 40 to 50 feet for sweet cherry.

The value of a pollinizer, other than the ability of its pollen to fertilize other flowers depends on several factors. Certain trees are not cross-fruitful because their blooming seasons usually do not overlap sufficiently. Certain two-variety combinations may be unfruitful because of the difference in age at which they form their first flowers. Also, combinations that consist of annual and decidedly alternate bearing trees will not produce full crops year after year. The use of a third variety in such cases to supplement pollination of the annual bearing tree will remedy the situation. The most frequent reason for failure of cross-pollination between varieties is their close relationship. The unfruitful combinations in most instances are comprised of a fruit tree and its bud mutation or "bud sport."

Here are some facts about different fruits that should be considered before planting.

APPLE: Pollination tests have shown that cross-pollination is essential for a full commercial crop. It is now generally conceded that all apple varieties should be interplanted to insure the production of high yields.

A few fruits such as Jonathan, Baldwin, Rome Beauty, Gallia Beauty, and Yellow Newtown, will produce a partial crop when self-pollinated, but Baldwin is the only variety of any commercial importance which has been reported to produce a commercial crop under these circumstances.

Varieties which have proved to be ineffective as pollinizers in cross-pollination are: Arkansas Black, Baldwin, Blenheim, Canada Reinette, Crimson Bramley, Fall Pippin, Gravenstein, Red Gravenstein, Mann, Minkler, Paragon, Rhode Island Greening, Ribston Pippin, Roxbury Russet, Stark, Stayman Winesap, Staymared, Blaxtayman, Summer Rambo, Tompkins King, Turley, Hibernal, Virginia Crab and Winesap.

There are many apples which are cross-unfruitful with related varieties, mutations, or "bud sports." A few examples are:

Cortland and Early McIntosh
Rome Beauty and Gallia Beauty
Delicious and all its color strains such as Starking and Shotwell Delicious
Jonathan
Northern Spy and Red Spy

At least one case has been observed of the failure of a variety that normally produces good pollen, to fertilize the flowers of a distinctly unrelated variety. Such a case is that of Grimes Golden which will not pollinate Arkansas Black or Paragon.

PEARS: All of the European pears and those of hybrid origin such as Keiffer, have been found to be completely or partially self-unfruitful. Because of this condition, a single tree or variety of pear should never be planted. Several varietal combinations have been found by various investigators to be cross-unfruitful, probably because of close relationship. In most, if not all instances, these pears are related to Bartlett. Any combination of the following varieties will produce either a very poor, or no set of fruit: Bartlett, Seckel, Louise Bonne de Jersey, and Belle Lucrative.

QUINCE: All quince varieties grown in United States have been found to be self-fruitful. These include Orange, Rea, Champion, and Meach.

PEACH: The greater proportion of tested varieties are self-fruitful and may be planted singly or in blocks of one variety. The self-unfruitful types are: Candoka, Chili, Chinese Cling, Hal-berta, Hope Farm, J. H. Hale, Mikado, Pacemaker, Sargents, Tuscan Cling, and Vimy.

NECTARINES AND APRICOTS: All varieties of these fruits have been found to be self-fruitful.

SWEET CHERRY: All sweet cherries tested have been found to be self-unfruitful. Practically no fruits at all are obtained through self-pollination. Not only does self-unfruitfulness exist, but many varietal combinations are unfruitful.

More than a dozen groups are known which contain varieties reciprocally incompatible, and the number is being enlarged with further research. The fruits within any one group are all closely related, being either seedlings or bud mutations of some parent variety. A few such groups are as follows:

1) Napoleon, Bing, Lambert, Emperor Francis and Ohio Beauty
2) Early Purple and Rockport
3) Windsor and Abundance
4) Elton, Wood and Stark's Gold
5) Black Tartarian, Knight's Early Black, Early Rivers, Bedford Prolific and Black Eagle

SOUR CHERRY: Self-fruitfulness exists for such sour cherries as Early Richmond, Montmorency, Dyehouse and the Morello group. The varieties Chase, Homer, and Ostheim have been found to produce only a small set when self-pollinated and should be interplanted with other sour cherries. All sour cherries (with the possible exception of Wragg and Ostheim) produce sufficient viable pollen in abundance.

DUKE CHERRY: Duke cherries are the result of crosses between the sweet and sour cherries. They are, thus, hybrids which range in taste between sweet and sour, actually being neither. All Duke varieties have been found to produce full commercial crops only when cross-pollinated. Of the Dukes, the Royal Duke and May Duke are usually the most productive, with Reine Hortense producing somewhat lighter yields.

The late-blooming sweet cherries, such as Napoleon, Windsor and Wood are effective in cross-pollinating the earlier blooming Dukes. On the other hand, the early to midseason blooming sour cherries such as Montmorency and Early Richmond, are sufficiently effective pollinizers for the late-blooming Dukes.

PLUM: The group is represented by three distinctly separate groups: the European, Japanese, and Native American plum. The European plum exhibits a rather wide range of differences in the response of its varieties to set fruit through self- and cross-pollination. Among plums that were classified, differences of unfruitfulness have been claimed in different parts of the world. This has been explained by the fact that different strains of supposedly the same variety are grown in different regions. Under such circumstances, it would be difficult to list those that are self-fruitful, since, as an example, the results in California contradict those in New York, those in Washington, and so forth.

Pollination tests have shown that the greater proportion of varieties included in the Japanese group are self-unfruitful. The varieties, Beauty, Climax, Methley, and Santa Rosa, produce more fruits from self-pollination than the other Japanese plums, but it is recommended that even these be interplanted with other effectively pollinizing Japanese plums. In addition, this group is subject to a considerable amount of pollen sterility. The pollen of Apex, Apple, Combination, Eldorado, Formosa, Gaviota, and Kelsey is so low in viability that they are not recommended as pollinizers of any other plums.

Some varieties of the European plum will pollinize the Japanese types but not all are consistently effective in this role. It has been reported that Clyman, Ouillins, Reine Claude, Victoria and Yellow Egg give fair to good sets on Japanese varieties. Those native American species which possess viable pollen have been found to be the most effective pollinizers of the Japanese plums.

SUGGESTED PLANTING: Where cross-pollination is necessary and there is not room for more than one tree, trees may be top-worked to more than one variety. This is a grafting or budding procedure that involves the placement of two or more varieties on one tree. Many nurseries sell two-in-one, or three-in-one trees which contain selected varieties which are cross-fruitful in respect to each other. Information on how to top-work your trees may be obtained from your State Agricultural Experiment Station or the United States Department of Agriculture.

If more than one tree of a particular fruit is necessary and there is not room for the standard trees, it is possible to buy dwarf trees which may be planted much closer together.

Here is a guide for the minimum number of trees to plant:

Apple: A minimum of two cross-fruitful trees for all varieties except Baldwin, which may be planted alone.

Pear: A minimum of two cross-fruitful trees for all varieties with no exceptions. The Bartlett pear has been claimed to set a partial crop of fruit through self-pollination in some regions (primarily California), but it is not sufficient to be considered a recommendable practice to plant Bartlett alone. The Kieffer pear also sets a partial crop at times.

Quince: A single tree of one variety may be planted.

Peach: A single tree of one variety may be planted except for those fruits previously listed as being self-unfruitful. If one of this group of peach trees is planted, another variety must be planted also.

Nectarine and Apricot: A single tree of one variety of either of these two fruits may be planted.

Sweet Cherry: A minimum of two cross-fruitful varieties must be planted. For fruit-production it is necessary to have at least one tree of two or more different groups listed previously under sweet cherry.

Sour Cherry: A single tree for those varieties previously listed as self-fruitful. At least two trees of different types for those self-unfruitful.

Duke Cherry: A minimum of two cross-fruitful varieties unless a single Duke cherry tree is pollinated with a late-blooming sweet or early-blooming sour cherry, as previously discussed.

Plum: The minimum number of trees required will depend on whether the particular trees desired are self-fruitful or not.

WINTER CARE: To protect trees during fall and winter from rabbit and mice damage, use a screening about 18 inches high and five inches in diameter that is firmed into the ground. Aluminum foil is also effective around trees, prevent sun scald as well. Remove piles of brush and stones where rabbits often nest.—*William Ackerman.*

See also names of individual fruits; FRUIT TREE; MULCH; INSECT CONTROL; PRUNING.

ORCHARD GRASS: (*Dactylis glomerata*) Orchard grass is used in many pasture mixtures. A hardy perennial grass growing up to three feet tall in dense clusters, it is widely adapted in the North and upper South. It thrives in moderately acid to neutral soils, and prefers shallow to deep gravelly loams, but will tolerate poorly drained clay and very moist conditions. It is sometimes used to stabilize dunes in the Great Lakes region. A silver-margined variety is occasionally grown in the garden as an ornamental grass.

Another pasture grass, sheep's fescue, *Festuca ovina,* is sometimes called orchard grass. Useful in dry places, it grows about a foot tall, and is one of the most abundant and valuable grasses of the rangelands. As a lawn grass, it is suited mainly to shady spots in the northern states and higher latitudes in the South. It grows in highly acid to neutral soils, preferring gravelly loams and well-drained clays. The leaves are rolled or coiled and thread-like, and the stems very fine and slender.

ORCHIDS: Much conflicting information has been written about the orchid. Some people declare that "orchids are easy" to grow, while others bemoan their complete lack of success with these beautiful flowering plants.

The truth is this: you simply cannot

succeed with orchids unless you *choose those that will be at home in your particular situation, and give them correct care.*

A large-flowering, tree-perching orchid, Vanda caerulea grows about two feet high, has lovely light blue flowers, up to four inches in diameter.

The orchid is one of the most admired, most wanted and least understood flowers in the world today. There are over 15,000 wild varieties of orchids. They are scattered over the entire earth, from high on tropical mountains to the tundras of Alaska. Some are hardy, some tender, some have a dormant period, some are evergreen, some huge, some tiny, some are rapid growers, and others grow at a very slow rate.

Orchids are divided into two groups, epiphytic and terrestrial. Epiphytic orchids are those that live on trees, rocks or logs, but not upon the ground. Terrestrial orchids are those that grow in the soil. Many of the terrestrial orchids are native to this country and are valuable plants for special places in the outdoor garden.

HARDY TERRESTRIAL ORCHIDS: The rock, wild or bog garden is ideal for the hardy native terrestrial orchids.

Many of them can be purchased from wildflower nurseries, or you can transplant them from the wild. The best time for transplanting is in the fall, for spring moving is apt to injure the tubers which need to develop all season to be strong.

In general, they need a peaty, fibrous soil, moist and acid. The conditions in which you find them should be duplicated as carefully as possible. They all need partial shade, and benefit immeasurably from a winter mulch of several inches of leaves, or a couple of inches of peat moss.

The best of the native orchids are the familiar lady's slipper, *Cypripedium,* varieties of which are found in both bogs and woods; the fringe orchids, *Habenaria,* which grow in bogs, damp meadows and moist roadsides and range from less than a foot to nearly three feet high, with fragrant spikes of purple blooms; the orchis, *O. spectabilis,* a native of rich moist woods, with purple and white flowers in late spring; the little twayblades, *Liparis,* growing to eight inches tall; and the ladies' tresses, *Spiranthes cernua,* a fall-blooming, white-flowered orchid about a foot tall.

Others, a little more difficult to transplant but worth trying, are the rose pogonia or adder's-mouth, *Pogonia ophioglossoides,* a bog plant with rose-purple blooms in summer; *Aplectrum hyemale,* which grows in forests and has yellowish-brown flowers; *Arethusa bulbosa,* the dragon's mouth, growing eight inches tall in acid bog soil, with yellow-fringed purple blooms; *Calopogon pulchellus,* the swamp pink, very similar to the dragon's mouth but taller; and the rattlesnake plantain, *Epipactus pubescens,* and its related varieties, suited to dry, open sites in the wild garden.

For additional information on hardy orchids, see the entries under their names.

ORCHIDS IN THE GREENHOUSE AND HOME: There are over 500 genera of orchids suitable to greenhouse culture, and quite a few of them will do well if handled properly in the house. Most of the magnificently beautiful orchids for indoor culture are epiphytes, but a few terrestrials, notably cymbidium, calanthe, cypripedium and phaius also fall into this category.

GROWING MEDIUMS: All orchids need good drainage and an abundance of air about their roots. For this reason, the most commonly used potting medium is osmunda fiber, the coarse roots of the osmunda ferns. This loose material provides both the correct measures of aeration and drainage, and also feeds the orchids as it decays, making fertilization unnecessary.

In recent years, there has been a trend toward planting orchids in bark, either fir, cedar or pine. Orchids root well in this medium, but it has virtually no food value. This is a big drawback, for little is known about the exact nutrient requirements of many orchids, and a hit-or-miss feeding program can easily ruin the chances of bloom. Diluted manure water and organic fish fertilizer, however, seem to work out well. Bark also dries out more quickly, making more frequent watering necessary.

Other mediums, such as charcoal, vermiculite and certain gravels, have also been tested, but nothing has been found that is all-around better than osmunda. It is inexpensive and meets all the needs of the plants.

Terrestrial orchids are best potted up in mixtures of osmunda, woods soil or leaf mold, sand and manure. Compost can be substituted for the manure, and peat moss for the leaf mold. Brown osmunda, a more aged form, is usually considered better than regular osmunda, and terrestrial orchids are sometimes planted in it alone. In any case, the medium must be very fluffy and porous, like that offered by the forest floor where most of these orchids grow.

With all indoor orchids, the bottom one-third of the pot should be filled with gravel or broken crock to insure good drainage. Most orchids need repotting every two years.

LIGHT, WATERING AND HUMIDITY: Practically all indoor-grown orchids will benefit from as much light as you can give them. However, direct, hot sunlight can burn the plants, so some shading may be necessary during the summer from perhaps 11 a.m. to 3 p.m. A semi-shaded porch is a good summer home for them, or you can hang the plants from the limbs of trees in your garden. In the house, the roof overhang will usually shade out the hot midday sun. In the winter, give them every bit of sun you can, preferably in a southern window. You can judge by studying the foliage: if the growth looks dark green, weak and soft, your orchids need more light. If it is hard, yellowish and leathery, they are getting too much sun.

Proper watering is very important. Most orchids should be watered abundantly during vigorous growth, but the growing medium should be allowed to become almost completely dry between waterings. Once a week may be fine. During the winter, be especially careful not to overwater. Wait until the osmunda looks light brown and bone dry, then dip the plant in a tub or sink for a thorough soaking. The best rule is, when in doubt, don't water!

Humidity is not as critical a factor in orchid growing as many people believe. Placing the pots on a tray of pebbles and water, and spraying the foliage with a mist-type sprayer on bright days, will generally provide ample humidity. To make sure the roots never stand in water, the pots can be put on slats or mesh over the tray, or stood on inverted pots. If you grow your orchids in a glass or plastic-enclosed case, ventilate carefully so that the humidity does not remain constantly at a very high level. On cold, dark days of winter, fairly dry air is best. Try to give them some fresh air every day, but avoid drafts. As a general rule, the higher the light intensity and/or the temperature, the greater the humidity required.

TEMPERATURE: This, more than any other factor, will determine the kinds of orchids you can grow. There are three temperature classifications:

Warm—65 to 70° by day, 60 to 65° at night (cirrhopetalum, the mottle-leaved cypripediums, some oncidiums, phalaenopsis, pleurothallis, vanda);

Intermediate—60 to 70° by day, 55 to 60° at night (cattleya, coelogyne, cycnoches, some cypripediums, epidendrum, laelia, odontoglossum, oncidium, stanhopea);

Cool—55 to 60° by day, 45 to 50° at night (cymbidium, the plain-leaved cypripediums, dendrobium, miltonia, some odontoglossums).

These are *winter* temperatures. In the greenhouse, you may be able to grow species in all the classifications, by careful regulation of ventilation, placing the cool-loving plants farther from the source of heat than the warm-loving ones, and so on.

But in the home, the cool ones are generally out of the question because modern heating systems make it difficult to find spots cool enough for them. *These temperatures are critical with most species.* Even five degrees above or below them for more than very short periods can make the difference between good growth and poor growth, between flowers and no flowers.

However, the warm and intermediate types include such vast numbers of species that only the most rabid fancier will be disappointed if he cannot grow the relatively few cool ones in his home. Often varieties in a cool species can be found that will thrive under warm conditions. Some species, incidentally, like the cattleyas, are so diverse that it is possible to have different varieties in bloom every month of the year.

For descriptions of the species mentioned above, see the listings under their names. There are, of course, many, many more species, and a huge number of hybrids. The catalogs of orchid specialists often list up to several hundred and give specific directions for their culture.

STARTING WITH ORCHIDS: The beginner is advised to purchase as his first orchid, a blooming size plant of a popular species such as the cattleya. Many orchids take three to seven years from seed to bloom, and starting with seedlings can mean a long wait that could dampen your enthusiasm. Blooming size plants can be obtained for only a few dollars.

Study all the books you can get on orchid culture. Some good ones are *Orchids as House Plants,* and *Home Orchid Growing,* both by Revecca T. Northern; *ABC of Orchid Growing,* by John Watkins; and *Orchids Are Easy to Grow,* by H. B. Logan and L. C. Cosper. Visit orchid greenhouses in your area. The American Orchid Society, Cambridge 38, Mass., publishes a most helpful magazine.

And most important of all, study your conditions. Hang thermometers around and note the temperature and light intensity in various spots. You may want to experiment with artificial light, or build a homemade orchid case for better control of conditions. You can use simple plastic enclosures for humidity control, thin curtains for shade, and an inexpensive heating cable to take the chill off cold nights if you turn off your furnace.

ORCHID CACTUS: *see* EPIPHYLLUM

OREGON GRAPE: *see* MAHONIA

ORGANIC FARMING: *By Hugh Corley. See* BOOKS FOR ORGANIC GARDENERS AND FARMERS.

ORGANIC FERTILIZER: Referring to fertilizers derived from plant and animal residues. These may be fresh residues, or residues which have accumulated and have been preserved for long periods of time, as peat, marl and limestone. In the practice of the organic method, organic fertilizers also include such natural earth products as rock phosphate and potash. *See also* FERTILIZER; HUMUS; ORGANIC MATERIALS; ORGANIC MATTER.

ORGANIC FOODS, MARKETING: Demand for organic food is steadily increasing. There are more people than ever who want organic foods, and there are more people who are growing them and selling them. This mushrooming demand for organic foods is the direct result of the quickly-increasing chemicalization of the American food supply. New food processing chemicals are constantly being introduced; new drugs are added to animal feed rations; new poisonous insecticides are sprayed on crops; and more caustic artificial fertilizers are added to soils. People want more natural, untreated foods.

DISTRIBUTION: The most common way of selling organic food is through local retail stores or roadside stands. Next most popular method is by mail or express, while still others sell food wholesale to stores.

ROADSIDE SELLING: Here is some advice for setting up a roadside business:

The Stand—Keep it simple but attractive. Make plenty of open shelves, and perhaps you'll want to put some display counters out front for your most attractive products. A brightly painted stand—paint it fresh every year!—can be further dressed up with flower displays and bright baskets.

Signs—Make them neat, and legible at a distance. Five to eight feet square is a good size, and it will probably pay you to have them professionally painted. One a half-mile from the stand and another about 200 feet from it will give motorists ample time to slow down.

Stress the words, "Organically Grown," and put additional small signs explaining the value of chemical-free produce on the stand itself. Small cards bearing the same message and given out with each purchase are good advertising, too. Some roadside sellers keep a register book on the stand and encourage customers to write their names and addresses in it for possible mail-order business in the future.

Your Products—Always keep only the freshest produce on your stand, neatly and attractively displayed. Hay, straw or sawdust makes handsome bedding for many fruits and vegetables. Fresh, cold fruit juice, honey, homemade cider and milk from your cows or goats are good sellers and attract many customers who might not be enticed to stop for vegetables alone.

ORGANIC GARDEN CLUBS: *See* GARDEN CLUBS, ORGANIC

ORGANIC GARDENING: *By J. I. Rodale. See* BOOKS FOR ORGANIC GARDENERS AND FARMERS

ORGANIC GARDENING: Organic gardening or farming is a system whereby a fertile soil is maintained by applying Nature's own law of replenishing it—that is, the addition and preservation of humus, the use of organic matter instead of chemical fertilizers, and, of course, the making of compost and mulching. Organiculture is a vigorous and growing movement, one that is destined to alter our concepts of the garden and the farm and to revolutionize our methods of operating them in order to secure for ourselves more abundant and more perfect food. The seed sown by Sir Albert Howard, the great pioneer in organic farming, is beginning to bloom lustily and with such vim that it is already thriving and propagating by its own strength. Composters by the thousands are telling their neighbors of the wonders of this new, yet in reality age-old, method, and they in turn are listening and beginning to follow. Compost heaps are becoming an integral part of the farm, the garden, and the landscape. Organiculture is here to stay. When it is possible to see astounding results obtained by one's own hand, a quick good-by is said to groping and artificial test-tube methods.

PRACTICES: Human health is more precious than quick profits and insect-free crops. Any methods to bolster yields should be adopted only after we are thoroughly convinced that future generations will not be injured. Increased yields will come with the intense practice of the organic methods and the proper lapse of time.

The balance of Nature must be respected. Each part has its own sphere of activity as well as fusing with and complementing other related parts. A substance that alters one part, for instance, may affect half a dozen others —most often to our own disadvantage. Spraying, for example, kills off beneficial insects and birds, contaminates the soil, leaves poisonous residues on crops, and is a financial burden on the farmer.

The soil is a storehouse of living organisms which must be fed and cared for as any others. Bacteria, fungi, insects, and earthworms inhabit it by the millions, using organic matter as food and in turn preparing it for living plants. Concentrated chemicals, on the other hand, cannot be continually added to the soil to destroy harmful insects and disease organisms without harming the needed beneficial microorganisms.

The organic gardener, of course, realizes that fertilization is not the only measure for success. He must treat the soil as a living, breathing entity. Compost alone does not make a successful gardener any more than does gardening without compost. The organic farmer observes the law of return, restoring to the soil all plant residues that come from it. He does not burn leaves, spoiled hay, or other crop by-products, but often goes out of his way to retrieve organic matter that others throw away.

Relying on harsh chemicals year after year will produce nutritionally poor crops. Flooding plant roots with these chemical fertilizers may cause trace-element deficiencies. The soil becomes strongly acid, unless lime is contantly applied. Earthworms and beneficial bacteria and fungi are driven away or killed. Toxic residues, such as chlorides and sulfates, build up year after year. Lastly, organic matter is quickly depleted from chemically fertilized soils.

FERTILIZING: The organic gardener believes that only suitable organic matter should go back to the land, either by mulching or composting. A mulch is a layer of organic matter (plant or animal wastes), placed on the soil surface, which protects the land while fertilizing it. Only those materials which ordinarily are not applied directly to the soil (garbage, for example) need be composted. Organic matter can be piled in bins, pits, or open heaps to decay, or compost.

Besides compost made of plant matter, the organiculturist usually employs as fertilizers such substances as raw phosphate rock, dolomite, ground oyster shells, and miscellaneous ground rocks such as granite dusts and pulverized limestone. Quicklime, on the other hand, is much too strong in action and will destroy bacteria. Wood ashes may be used as a substitute for lime in making compost.

Raw ground phosphate rock and colloidal phosphate supply phosphorus, while glauconite marl and granite dust release potash. These fertilizers dissolve slowly, benefiting crops for several years. Rock fertilizers, in addition, do not leach quickly into the drainage waters. Millions of tons of natural rock fertilizers await further discovery by enlightened fertilizer companies. The supply of such rock materials is enormous and cheap, and recent experimental work has already demonstrated that, if ground fine enough, they become a quick-acting fertilizer. Many rocks contain plant nutrients in considerable amounts which are insoluble until they are pulverized and brought into contact with the soil, where they are rendered soluble by carbonic acid and other mild acids in the soil.

Another tenet of the organiculturists is the making of compost by Sir Albert Howard's Indore process, involving the ratio of one part animal matter to three parts of plant residue, a relationship which is found naturally in field and forest.

SPRAYS AND DUSTS: The use of poison sprays in orchards and on crops is taboo, for there is definite evidence to confirm the fact that the strengthening of a plant or tree by the use of compost makes the plant or tree much less susceptible to infestation by insects or disease than does recourse to sprays. The organiculturist believes that even on a commercial scale orcharding can eventually eliminate dependence on poison sprays.

It is interesting to note that a prominent scientist recently remarked that sprays and dusts which destroy insects certainly are not free from some toxicity for human beings. The same can be said about potent weed killers, fungicides, and other chemicals that violently disturb the natural functions of plant and animal life. The highly popular hormone sprays, for example, were given hasty official acceptance without thorough study of the side effects on fruits and vegetables. It is well to keep these facts in mind when tempted to invest in spray equipment. The least toxic of insecticides are plant extracts such as rotenone or derris dust, which should be applied only when absolutely necessary. A conscientious organic gardener, however, will try to avoid using them.

SAFE CONTROL OF INSECTS AND PESTS: It is true that some natural insect controls may be necessary until, and possibly after, the gardener has been practicing the organic method for several years. The soil must become rich and fertile; insect parasites and predators must be encouraged. Safe measures for control are handpicking of insect pests, encouraging birds, interplanting with crops that repel insects, planting resistant varieties, and setting out traps. Exterminating all harmful insects is not our goal; good yields, truly safe food, and sensible insect controls is the answer.

"CHEMICAL" AND "ORGANIC": Sometimes a chemist criticizes the inclusion of certain items in the organic arsenal of weapons. For example, he calls lime a chemical, yet we advocate its presence in the compost heap. Of course lime is a chemical. So is everything else. There is nitrogen, phosphorus, and potash in your tablecloth, in ham and eggs, and in your very own mother-in-law! So it is high time that we and our adversaries stop talking in elusive generalities and start to clarify our specific points.

In regard to the word "organic," Webster says, "Pertaining to, or derived from, living organisms." On the other hand—also according to Webster—when a chemist refers to the word "organic" he means "Pertaining to or designating that branch of chemistry which treats of the carbon compounds produced in plants and animals. . . ." It can be seen, therefore, that when we say "organic" we mean something different from what the chemist understands by that word, but these are mere technicalities resulting from professionalized word usage. We do not exclude a chemical simply because it is a chemical any more than we include an organism just because it is an organism. There are, however, some chemicals that try to upset everything that the organiculturist is attempting to achieve. Those saboteurs are the ones against which we discriminate. *See also* COMPOST; SOIL; FERTILIZER; HUMUS; INSECT CONTROL; INSECTICIDES; HOWARD, SIR ALBERT; NUTRITION; VEGETABLE GARDENING; FLOWER GARDENING.

ORGANIC MATERIALS: Organic materials, or organic matter, is any part of any substance which once had life. Organic matter, then, consists of any animal or vegetable waste or byproduct. Most all organic matter can be composted to return its nutritive substances to the soil, thus continuing the natural cycle of nature.

Occasionally, gardeners live close to processing plants which have enormous amounts of waste materials, free for the hauling. The wise gardener will avail himself of these various forms of organic matter and use them in the compost heap. Many gardeners get the names of the best sources of free organic materials, and make periodic trips, hauling several different kinds of materials in each trip.

Following is an extensive list of organic materials, along with the nitrogen, phosphorus and potash contents of each material. From these figures, the gardener can determine, roughly, the NPK ratio of his compost.

PERCENTAGE COMPOSITION OF VARIOUS MATERIALS

(Compiled by the U. S. Dept. of Agriculture)

Material	Nitrogen	Phosphoric Acid	Potash
Alfalfa hay	2.45	0.50	2.10
Apple, fruit	.05	.02	.10
Apple, leaves	1.00	.15	.35
Apple pomace	.20	.02	.15
Apple skins (ash)		3.08	11.74
Ash from Cana tree			15.65
Banana skins (ash)		3.25	41.76
Banana stalk (ash)		2.34	49.40
Barley (grain)	1.75	.75	.50
Bat guano	1–12	2.5–16	
Beet roots	.25	.10	.50
Brewer's grains (wet)	.90	.50	.05
Brigham tea (ash)			5.94
Ground bone, burned		34.70	
By-product from silk mills	8.37	1.14	.12
Cantaloupe rinds (ash)		9.77	12.21
Castor-bean pomace	5– 6	2–2.5	1.0–1.25
Cattail reed and stems of waterlily	2.02	.81	3.43
Cattail seed	.98	.39	1.71
Coal ash (anthracite)		.1– .15	.1– .15
Coal ash (bituminous)		.4– .5	.4– .5
Cocoa-shell dust	1.04	1.49	2.71
Coffee grounds	2.08	.32	.28
Coffee grounds (dried)	1.99	.36	.67
Corncobs (ground, charred)			2.01
Corncob ash			50.00
Common crab	1.95	3.60	.20
Corn (grain)	1.65	.65	.40
Corn (green forage)	.30	.13	.33
Cottonseed	3.15	1.25	1.15
Cottonseed-hull ashes		7–10	15–30
Cottonseed-hull (ash)		3.70	23.93
Cotton waste from factory	1.32	.45	.36
Cowpeas, green forage	.45	.12	.45
Cowpeas, seed	3.10	1.00	1.20
Crabgrass (green)	.66	.19	.71
Cucumber skins (ash)		11.28	27.20
Dog manure	1.97	9.95	.30
Dried jellyfish	4.60		
Dried mussel mud	.72	.35	
Duck manure (fresh)	1.12	1.44	.49
Eggs	2.25	.40	.15
Eggshells (burned)		.43	.29

Material	Nitrogen	Phosphoric Acid	Potash
Eggshells	1.19	.38	.14
Feathers	15.30		
Field bean (seed)	4.00	1.20	1.30
Field bean (shells)	1.70	.30	.35
Fire-pit ashes from smokehouses			4.96
Fish scrap (red snapper and grouper)	7.76	13.00	.38
Fish scrap (fresh)	2– 7.5	1.5– 6	
Fresh-water mud	1.37	.26	.22
Garbage rubbish (New York City)	3.4–3.7	.1–1.47	2.25–4.25
Garbage tankage	1 –2	.5–1	.5 –1
Greasewood ashes			12.61
Garden beans, beans and pods	.25	.08	.30
Gluten feed	4 –5		
Greensand		1 –2	5.00
Grapes, fruit	.15	.07	.30
Grapefruit skins (ash)		3.58	30.60
Hair	12 –16		
Harbor mud	.99	.77	.05
Hoof meal and horn dust	10 –15	1.5–2	
Incinerator ash	.24	5.15	2.33
Kentucky bluegrass (green)	.66	.19	.71
Kentucky bluegrass (hay)	1.20	.40	1.55
King crab (dried and ground)	10.00	.26	.06
King crab (fresh)	2 –2.5		
Leather (acidulated)	7 –8		
Leather (ground)	10 –12		
Leather, scrap (ash)		2.16	.35
Lemon culls, California	.15	.06	.26
Lemon skins (ash)		6.30	31.00
Lobster refuse	4.50	3.50	
Lobster shells	4.60	3.52	
Milk	.50	.30	.18
Mussels	.90	.12	.13
Molasses residue in manufacturing of alcohol	.70		5.32
Oak leaves	.80	.35	.15
Oats, grain	2.00	.80	.60
Olive pomace	1.15	.78	1.26
Olive refuse	1.22	0.18	0.32
Orange culls	.20	.13	.21
Orange skins (ash)		2.90	27.00
Pea pods (ash)		1.79	9.00
Peanuts, seeds or kernels	3.60	.70	.45
Peanut shells	.80	.15	.50
Peanut shells (ash)		1.23	6.45
Pigeon manure (fresh)	4.19	2.24	1.41
Pigweed, rough	.60	.16	
Pine needles	.46	.12	.03
Potatoes, tubers	.35	.15	.50
Potatoes, leaves, and stalks	.60	.15	.45
Potato skins, raw (ash)		5.18	27.50
Poudrette	1.46	3.68	.48
Powder-works waste	2–3		16–18
Prune refuse	.18	.07	.31
Pumpkins, flesh	.16	.07	.26
Pumpkin seeds	.87	.50	.45
Rabbit-brush ashes			13.04
Ragweed, great	.76	.26	
Red clover, hay	2.10	.50	2.00
Redtop hay	1.20	.35	1.00
Residuum from raw sugar	1.14	8.33	
Rockweed	1.90	.25	3.68
Roses, flower	.30	.10	.40

Material	Nitrogen	Phosphoric Acid	Potash
Rhubarb, stems	.10	.04	.35
Rock and mussel deposits from sea	.22	.09	1.78
Salt-marsh hay	1.10	.25	.75
Salt mud	.40		
Sardine scrap	7.97	7.11	
Seaweed (Atlantic City, N. J.)	1.68	.75	4.93
Sewage sludge from filter beds	.74	.33	.24
Shoddy and felt	4–12		
Shrimp heads (dried)	7.82	4.20	
Shrimp waste	2.87	9.95	
Siftings from oyster-shell mound	.36	10.38	.09
Silkworm cocoons	9.42	1.82	1.08
Soot from chimney flues	.5–11	1.05	.35
Spanish moss	.60	.10	.55
Starfish	1.80	.20	.25
String bean strings and stems (ash)		4.99	18.03
Sunflower seed	2.25	1.25	.79
Sweetpotato skins, boiled (ash)		3.29	13.89
Sweetpotatoes	.25	.10	.50
Tanbark ash		.24	.38
Tanbark ash (spent)		1.5–2	1.5–2.5
Tea grounds	4.15	.62	.40
Tea-leaf ash		1.60	.44
Timothy hay	1.25	.55	1.00
Tobacco leaves	4.00	.50	6.00
Tobacco stalks	3.70	.65	4.50
Tobacco stems	2.50	.90	7.00
Tomatoes, fruit	.20	.07	.35
Tomatoes, leaves	.35	.10	.40
Tomatoes, stalks	.35	.10	.50
Waste from hares and rabbits	7.00	1.7–3.1	.60
Waste from felt-hat factory	13.80		.98
Waste product from paint manufacture	.028	39.50	
Waste silt	8–11		
Wheat, bran	2.65	2.90	1.60
Wheat, grain	2.00	.85	.50
Wheat, straw	.50	.15	.60
White clover (green)	.50	.20	.30
White sage (ashes)			13.77
Wood ashes (leached)		1–1.5	1–3
Wood ashes (unleached)		1–2	4–10
Wool waste	5–6	2–4	1–3

ORGANIC MATTER: A term applied to both plant and animal matter, alive or dead. But regardless whether it is dead or alive, organic matter is the life of the soil. Plant and animal matter includes the bodies of bacteria, fungi, yeasts, protozoa, etc. Organic matter represents material that was living tissue or that has come from it. Examples are manure, plant sap, sawdust, olive oil, etc. It consists of matter that may have been alive hundreds of thousands of years ago, like peat or coal.

Organic matter represents the remains of all kinds of plants, animals and microorganisms in various stages of decomposition. But actually, the expression of organic matter, as we sometimes refer to it, is a misnomer, for it includes both organic and inorganic substances. A corn cob, for example, is usually referred to as representing organic matter. But, if burnt down to its ash, destroying all the organic matter, there will be an important residue, in that ash, of a significant amount of minerals. In

Nature all of what we usually consider organic matter contains some inorganic compounds. So we must be aware of this confusion when we use the term organic matter. Perhaps it would be more correct to say that corn cobs are a form of substance which contains both organic and inorganic materials. We might say that it is an organic type of material.

EXAMPLES: Typical examples of organic matter, in the common usage of the term, are leaves, weeds, grass clippings, manure, the bodies of cows or pigs, the human body, etc. A piece of stone would not usually be referred to as organic matter, although in extremely rare cases rock may be found that does contain some. A piece of cotton or woolen cloth might be termed organic matter, the way we usually use the term, because it comes from a plant and an animal respectively, although it usually has some inorganic minerals included in its makeup. Dirt as swept up from a floor would usually be a combination of organic and inorganic material. Hair is organic. Metallic iron is inorganic. Such substances as calcium, phosphorus, sulphur, etc., are inorganic.

Some organic matter is in a raw state; others are in an intermediary stage of decomposition. Those that are in a more advanced state are sometimes referred to as humus, but that is an inaccurate statement, as we shall see later. The raw materials usually placed in the compost heap, except the lime, are referred to as organic matter. To review the terms we might say that organic matter is placed in a compost heap to form humus.

To review the definition of organic matter, then, we find that it is a substance that is alive or that was once living. In the biologic field the dictionary will define the word organic as pertaining to or deriving from anything that has life. The only known substances that are alive are in plants, animals and man. Among the lower

forms of plants we find bacteria or molds. Many persons believe that germs are tiny animals. This is not so. They are bacteria or molds, etc., which are lower forms in the plant world. People confuse them with protozoa which are one-celled animals.

In the upper seven inches of an acre of soil the weight of bacteria might average 400 to 800 pounds. In the form of animals in the soil beside the protozoa, there are nematodes, rotifers, etc. Between both groups (plant and animal lower forms) their functioning and death furnish considerable amounts of organic matter.

GREEN MATTER: The term green matter, in the sense we use it, differs from organic matter in that it includes only plant materials. It is applied to any plant matter, regardless whether it is freshly cut or actually green. It would consist of fresh or withered lawn clippings or weeds, dry leaves, cured hay or sawdust.

LEAF MOLD: The term mold is often used in the expression leaf mold and, according to the dictionary, it is a soft, rich soil or an earthy material. Leaves decompose into a form of compost which is called leaf mold by normal decomposition.

ORGANIC RESIDUES: These terms indicate a vast array of decomposable materials which are in the category of organic matter (organic and inorganic). They include city garbage, leather dust of shoe factories, cannery wastes, apple pomace of cider mills (skins), spoiled milk, and hundreds of others. Much of this material today is wasted. By proper handling and quick decomposition processes, they can be turned into valuable organic, humus-containing fertilizers.

TOTAL ORGANIC MATTER: Sometimes we use the term total organic matter to refer to organic materials in general, using the term humus for the real organic fraction of it which is realized when the processes of decomposition go into action.

ORGANIC COMPOUNDS: The term organic has several meanings. One of them is in the sense that it is something living. It is the organic part of the expression organic matter. The other one is entirely different. It consists of anything containing carbon. This type of substance takes in carbon compounds. Since all organic matter contains carbon, the organic matter which the gardener and farmer uses must be considered carbon compounds also. But there is another class of carbon-containing compounds which we would not consider a type of organic material useable as a fertilizer. One of them is petroleum. Impregnate your soil with a fair amount of this oil and you will destroy its ability to raise crops for a long time.

There is an entire field of chemistry devoted to the study of this second type of organic substance, or carbon compounds. Examples of organic compounds of this type are alcohol, and many coal-tar derivatives such as aspirin, synthetic vitamins, etc. In our consideration of organic materials which are valuable as a fertilizer we must completely exclude these chemical carbon compounds.

COMPOST: Compost has two meanings. First, we give the general definition which is, a composition, mixture or compound. The word compote, which means fruit stewed in syrup, has the same origin.

The specialized meaning of the word compost as it applies to farming and gardening, according to Webster's Dictionary is, "a mixture for fertilizing or renovating land in which plants are grown; now, especially a fertilizing mixture composed of such substances as peat, leaf mold, manure, lime, etc., thoroughly mingled and decomposed, usually in a heap called a compost heap."

The important thing is that the material must be decomposed in order to be called compost, and it is not to be called compost until it is. There are two basic things about a compost heap. You must have organic materials and there must be the proper conditions to make them decompose. The degree of decomposition may be referred to in terms such as finished or unfinished compost. In a more or less finished compost the materials would be greatly reduced in the extent of their fibrous appearance.

In an agricultural textbook you may find the following type of definition: "A compost is a fertilizing mixture of partially decomposed organic materials of plant or animal origin, or both, and may include substances such as ash, lime and chemicals."

In the organic method we would exclude the ash, if it is from coal, and would also condemn the addition of the usual artifical fertilizers.

In review we can see that organic matter is the raw material of the composting process, which process hastens the formation of humus. Composting, then, is a process of making humus. *See also* HUMUS; COMPOST; SOIL.

STOREHOUSE: Organic matter has been called "the storehouse of the soil's nutrients" and rightly so. Briefly, the reasons it is so vital to soils are that it (1) improves tilth and structure, (2) improves water-holding capacity, (3) aids in nitrogen fixation and (4) makes nutrients available to plants.

Wesley Chaffin and Robert Woodward, agronomists at Oklahoma A. and M. College have written: "Nearly all of the nitrogen and sulphur, and more than one-third of the phosphorus that become available for plant use are supplied by the organic matter. Smaller quantities of the other plant nutrients also come from this source: consequently, an increase in the rate of organic matter decomposition likewise increases the quantities of nitrogen, phosphorus, potassium, calcium, magnesium, and other plant nutrients in the soil solution."

ORGANIC METHOD, HISTORY OF:
The history of the organic movement had its inception in the researches and experiments of Sir Albert Howard, in India, over a period of 40 years. Sir Albert Howard was a British Government agronomist whose mind integrated itself with what his eyes saw. He noticed that results on government farms did not compare favorably with those of neighboring native husbandmen from the point of view of animal and plant diseases. He noticed that the natives did not make use of artificial fertilizers. In order to develop a system of farming that would keep disease down to a minimum, Sir Albert decided to use the methods of the natives, but with scientific management.

In his experiment, Sir Albert broke away from the accepted research procedures. He shunned the fragmentized approach of the agricultural stations. Instead of growing plants in pocket-handkerchief-sized plots, he farmed for more than 25 years, like an ordinary farmer would on large acreage. He proved conclusively that the use of chemical fertilizers was degenerating plants, animals and people, due to the poor nutritional quality

of their food. This is caused by deficiencies and imbalances created by these too soluble and too toxic chemicals. His final findings had the strength of a heavily joisted and integrated structure, rather than the impotence of a shower of insignificant splinters.

In 1940, under the imprint of the Oxford University Press, there was published Sir Albert Howard's breathtaking book, *An Agricultural Testament*. Its general theme was that present-day agricultural research was obsolete and that the use of chemical fertilizers was far from the answer to the maintenance and perpetuation of soil fertility. The book brought neglected organic matter back into the limelight in the equation of soil functioning. But it created hardly a ripple in agricultural scientific circles.

"In the reading of *An Agricultural Testament,* I was affected so profoundly that I could not rest until I purchased a farm in order to assure for ourselves a supply of food raised by the new method. The reading of this great book showed me how simple the practice of the organic method could be."

That is how J. I. Rodale sums

These gardens are part of the Organic Experimental Farm located near Emmaus, Pennsylvania. Tests are annually made in the Howard Cylinders to evaluate the effect of fertilizing on the quality of food.

up his introduction to the organic gardening idea, and also how the organic experimental farm in Allentown, Pennsylvania came into being. In May, 1942 appeared the first issue of the magazine which was called *Organic Farming and Gardening*.

CHANGES: When it first began, the organic method consisted merely of making compost of animal manure, plant matter as weeds, leaves, sawdust, cannery wastes, or any other kind of residual plant matter that could be secured, including garbage.

In making compost, Sir Albert Howard found by experiment that the best compost consisted of three times as much plant matter as manure, for that is the way he found it when nature made her compost in the field and forest. After a few years, we began to recommend that ground raw rock phosphate be added to the compost or spread directly on the land.

From the very beginning we recommended green manuring and contour and strip farming. We also recommended the use of ground limestone and good crop rotations. In other words it is always advisable to be a good farmer.

In connection with plant matter to be used in composting, we insist that some of it should come from sources outside of one's own farm. Although it is surprising how much can come from your own place—such as corn cobs, leaves, roadside weeds, spoiled hay, table garbage and tree prunings —it is all the more surprising to see how much plant matter can be obtained free from outside sources. There is available sawdust, corn cobs, leather dust from shoe factories, cannery wastes, city garbage, poultry shop waste cuttings, apple pomace at cider mills, brewery wastes, spent mushroom manure, cocoa wastes and chicken hatchery wastes.

POTASH ROCKS: The next improvement in the organic method was to recommend ground up raw potash rocks, such as granites and glauconites. Here you have raw potash without the addition of any acid that you get in the muriate of potash. There are granite quarries and other rock quarries, the owners of which do not know that if their product were ground fine enough they have a wonderful fertilizer to sell. And finally the practice of sheet composting was another modification that made large-scale composting more practical. By this method, materials are spread directly on the fields instead of being piled in heaps first.

IMPORTANT ROLE: Since 1942 the organic method has been an effective force against the misuse of the soil and other natural resources.

During this period much evidence was discovered that would indicate that there is a relationship between a chemicalized soil and the increasing amount of human degenerative disease. Among our readers, thousands upon thousands began to raise their own vegetables organically and many of them have written expressing the improvement of their health in glowing words. Many of them have written to their local newspapers, describing how the organic method has produced fabulously bountiful growth in their vegetables and flowers, and thus the knowledge of the method has spread to every part of our country.

The organic method is known in every nook and corner of our land, from the halls of congress down to the smallest country town. It is discussed in all the government agricultural experiment stations and in many science courses in high schools and colleges.

The organic movement has been a godsend to the gardener. As regards farming, it is not quite as simple, but any gardener who has a little gumption will find that this method is exactly what he has been seeking. The continued application of organic matter from year to year will give him such a wonderful soil that he will not need any advice of so-called gardening experts to advise him that unless he uses chemical fertilizers he will not get the best results. He will see how easy it becomes to pull a weed out of the soil, how little disease his plants will have, how much larger his vegetables will be, and so many other advantages that will be apparent. The ranks are enlarging very year, and the day is not far off when the home gardener who uses chemical fertilizers will be a rarity. All over the country the compost heaps in the gardens are becoming an accepted part of the art of gardening. *See also* HOWARD, SIR ALBERT; ORGANIC GARDENING.

ORIENTAL POPPY: (*Papaver orientale*) The gorgeous Oriental poppy reaches a height of four feet and blooms in May and June. A vigorous, long-lived perennial, it springs from strong, deep-growing rootstocks. The hairy leaves are often 18 inches long, and the enormous flowers—from six to 12 inches across—are brilliant scarlet with purplish bases. There are hybrid varieties with white, salmon, crimson, orange, shell-pink, lavender and mahogany flowers, as well as shorter varieties good for the rock garden. Oriental poppies make magnificent spots of interest in the perennial border, and are fine for cut flowers. They have two disadvantages, however: the foliage dies down by midsummer, leaving gaps in the border, and the hybrid varieties are likely to self-sow, resulting in undesirable colors. *See also* POPPY.

ORIGANUM: *see* MARJORAM

ORMOND: *see* LAWN

ORNAMENTAL: Any plant that is used primarily for decoration, rather than for food, fodder, lumber or other purposes, is called an ornamental. Usually ornamentals have showy flowers, fruits or foliage. The category includes many shrubs, trees and annual and perennial flowers. *See also* FLOWER GARDENING; SHRUBS; ANNUALS; PERENNIALS.

ORNAMENTAL GRASSES: *see* GRASS, ORNAMENTAL

ORNAMENTAL TOBACCO: *see* NICOTIANA

ORNITHOGALUM: The tender species of these bulbs, often called chinkerichee or star-of-Bethlehem, are grown indoors, while the hardy ones are usually relegated to the wild garden because of their habit of spreading until they become serious pests. The most common hardy variety, *O. umbellatum,* grows to a foot tall, with green-edged white flowers in racemes. Two similar hardy ones, *O. pyramidale* and *O. nutans,* reach two feet in height.

CULTURE: The tender species are grown in the border in the South, in sunny windows or the cool greenhouse elsewhere. They do best in a mixture of two parts of loam and one part each of sand and leaf mold or peat moss, with some bone meal and dried manure added. Plant them one inch deep, anytime from September to February, six bulbs to a large pot. Water well after planting, then sparingly until growth begins. Thereafter, give weekly feedings of liquid manure and plenty of water until the foliage begins to die off. A temperature not exceeding 60 degrees is best. The bulbs can be dried and stored for the next year.

The best indoor varieties are *O. arabicum,* with two-foot-tall clusters of big creamy-white, black-centered flowers that smell like ripe apples; *O. caudatum,* three feet tall with green-centered blooms; *O. thyrsoides,* with pale yellow flowers; and *O. aureum,* popular for its bright golden-yellow flowers.

ORRIS: Orris root is obtained from three species of iris (*Iris florentina, I. pallida,* and *I. germanica*) perennials native to southern Europe and cultivated chiefly in Italy for their fragrant rootstocks. Powdered orris root is used principally as a scenting agent in perfumery and cosmetics. The plants grow well in a variety of soils and flourish in rich moist loam, but roots grown in rather dry, gravelly soil appear to be the most fragrant.

Orris is readily propagated by division of the old plants, which may be set either in spring or fall about a foot apart in rows spaced conveniently for cultivation. It requires three years to produce a marketable crop of roots. After the roots are dug at the end of the third season they are peeled and dried in the open air. The desired fragrance does not develop until after the dry roots have been stored for a long time, during which they are especially liable to the attacks of insects. The yield is from five to six tons of dry root per acre every third year under good conditions.

Orris grows best in full sun, is often used in borders.

OSAGE ORANGE: (*Maclura pomifera*) The osage orange has spiny branches and can be trained as a thick, impenetrable hedge. As such, it is an excellent wildlife plant. Left alone, it grows into a beautiful tree, 40 to 50 feet high, with very glossy foliage and dense heads of greenish flowers. The striking green fruits, up to five inches in diameter, look like big grapefruits, but are not edible. The trees are often used for shelterbelts.

Osage orange does well in ordinary or poor soil, and is hardy to southern New England. The wood is very elastic, and the Indians of the Southwest, where it grows wild, used it for bows. A strong fiber is obtained from the bark, and the bark of the roots yields a yellow dye. Propagate by seeds, soaked in water at least a day before planting, or by cuttings.

OSMANTHUS: *see* TEA OLIVE

OSMOSIS: The process by which solutions of different densities become of the same density by mingling through a permeable membrane. The less dense solution will flow into the more dense one. It is by this process that the soil's nutrient solutions are absorbed through the microscopic membrane in the root hairs of plants. As the solutions are absorbed, pressure is set up in the roots that is responsible in large measure for the rise of the sap in the stem. The same process occurs in the cells of the plant, nutrient solutions in the sap permeating through the walls of the cell.

OSMUNDA: These hardy ferns are very easy to grow. Both the cinnamon fern *O. cinnamonea,* and the interrupted fern, *O. claytoniana,* are good for massing in damp or wet, partly shady spots. The royal fern, *O. regalis,* likes sunlight and will thrive in very wet places, like bogs, meadows or the edges of a brook or lake, if its crowns are above the high water line. The soil should be rich, fertilized with manure or compost. The fruiting fronds of the cinnamon and royal fern resemble flower heads. All three species are propagated by spores, and grow two to three feet tall, occasionally much taller.

Both the cinnamon and the interrupted fern form large, fibrous root masses, often several feet square, above the ground. Called osmunda fiber or osmundine, this material is used to pot up orchids. Very rich, it will feed an orchid for up to five years. It is also extremely tough, and must be cut with a saw. *See also* FERNS.

OSTRICH FERN: (*Pteretis nodulosa*) A tall-growing, very handsome subject for the fern garden, ostrich fern has running rootstocks that send up new plants to give a dense, massed effect. The foliage fronds may be as long as ten feet, but more often about five or six feet, borne on short stalks. It grows wild in the East, and is easily propagated by division of the rootstocks. Plant it in partial shade in a deep mixture of good loam and swamp muck or leaf mold, with part of the crown left exposed above the ground. Mulch it lightly with leaves until it is established, and soon there will be a luxuriant thicket. *See also* FERNS.

OSWEGO-TEA: *see* BEE-BALM

OTAHEITE APPLE: (*Spondias cytherea*) A tropical fruit tree growing about 50 feet high, Otaheite apple bears clusters of white flowers and fruits that look like big yellow plums, used usually for preserves. It is very tender and grown only in the southernmost part of Florida. Two other varieties, the purple mombin, *S. purpurea,* and the yellow mombin or hog plum, *S. mombin,* are occasionally grown there, too, but their fruit is smaller; it is well liked, however, either raw or cooked, in the tropics. Both of these have greenish flowers. Otaheite apples are not particular as to soils, and can be easily propagated by seeds.

OTAHEITE GOOSEBERRY: (*Phyllanthus acidus*) The acid berries produced by this 20-foot tree, grown in Florida, are used for preserves. It has clusters of small red flowers, and is propagated by seeds or cuttings. Give it a somewhat sandy, medium fertile soil and full sun.

OTAHEITE ORANGE: (*Citrus taitensis*) This miniature orange tree is a popular, attractive plant for a sunny window or the cool greenhouse. It grows two to three feet tall with glossy leaves and waxy white, pink-tinted flowers. The fruits are very numerous, shaped like lemons but a bright orange in color. A plant in a five-inch pot may carry over a dozen of the fruits, which are smaller than the common oranges and not as tasty. Otaheite orange likes a humusy soil made up of equal parts of sand, loam and leaf mold or compost, with dried manure and bone meal added. Otaheite, incidentally, is an old name for

the Pacific island of Tahiti, but the plant is not grown there. *See also* FRUITS, INDOORS.

OVARY: *see* FLOWER

OVULE: *see* FLOWER

OXALIS: Often called wood sorrel, these perennial bulbous plants grow six inches or less in height, except for one variety, *O. ortgiesi,* over a foot in height. They have clover-shaped leaves that fold up at night, and abundant bright yellow, white, pink or red flowers.

O. acetosella, the common white-flowered wood sorrel, needs a rich woods soil and shade. A similar hardy perennial, violet or purple wood sorrel, *O. violacea,* likes the same conditions and is a good plant for the wild garden. *O. corniculata,* yellow sorrel, is a roadside weed, while *O. valvidensis,* also yellow, is a perennial that will bloom from seed in one season when treated as a tender annual.

The rest of the oxalis varieties are spring-blooming bulbs planted outdoors in the South in autumn, two inches deep and three inches apart. They like a sunny location and soil liberally enriched with compost. Also, they are grown in window gardens or cool greenhouses in the North for winter bloom.

Pot them in a soil mixture of two parts of loam to one each of sand and leaf mold or compost, with a sprinkling of bone meal added. Six bulbs can be fitted into a six-inch pot. Put them in a cool dark place, giving little water until growth starts. Then move them to a sunny window, water well and feed with liquid manure. When bloom is finished, reduce the water until the foliage matures. Store them in the pots until early fall, then divide and replant. The best varieties are *O. adenophylla,* pink; *O. bowieana,* rose-purple and summer-blooming (this one can be planted outdoors and treated like gladiolus); *O. cer-*

nua, the Bermuda buttercup, yellow; *O. enneaphylla* and *O. ortgiesi,* both white; and *O. rubra,* pink, lilac or white.

Oxalis is propagated by seeds, offsets or root divisions.

OXIDATION IN HUMUS: *see* HUMUS

OXLIP: (*Primula elatior*) A member of the primrose family, the oxlip thrives in any good garden soil. This low-growing perennial reaches eight inches, has yellow flowers about one inch in diameter in spring. It should receive sufficient shade and moisture during summer. *See also* PRIMROSE.

OXYGEN: The most widely distributed element in nature, oxygen makes up nearly half of all terrestrial matter. It forms approximately 21 per cent by volume of the atmosphere; 87 per cent by weight of all the water on the earth; and over 40 per cent of the human body.

Plants and soil organisms cannot live without oxygen. Plants get this vital element from the carbon dioxide of the atmosphere, from water drawn from the soil, and from numerous other substances. The roots need oxygen for their life processes, and release carbon dioxide, which is used by the above-ground parts of the plant (these in turn release oxygen to the air during photosynthesis).

In a well-aerated soil, the composition of the air is similar to that in the atmosphere above the soil.

When the oxygen supply is cut off to the roots of most plants, they suffocate and die, their intake of water and nutrients ceases, and the plant wilts and succumbs.

Plants that normally grow on well-drained and aerated soils usually are most sensitive to lack of oxygen. Even plants such as cranberries, which can remain largely under water during a long dormant period, will suffer from poor aeration in summer when the plant uses more water and nutrients.

By lowering the oxygen, compaction or saturation slows or halts the work of beneficial microorganisms, which break down organic matter and release fertility. Anaerobic bacteria, organisms that live without oxygen, are stimulated to destroy valuable compounds and produce toxic amounts of hydrogen sulfide gas. Denitrification also proceeds faster, showing up in the lowered content of crude protein in plant tissues.

Flooding or compactions caused by trampling, the pressure of machinery or certain chemical fertilizers all lower the oxygen content of the soil, and thus are harmful to plants. *See also* AERATION.

OYSTER PLANT: (*Tragopogon porrifolius*) Salsify or oyster plant gets its name from the delicious flavor of the cooked root. One of the most nutritious of the root crops, it is a biennial, growing three to four feet high, with a white-skinned, deep taproot.

CULTURE: A long season crop, its seeds should be sown as early in the spring as possible, in deep, rich, not too heavy soil. A sandy loam is best, and oyster plant responds well to generous applications of well-rotted manure. Plant the seed $\frac{1}{2}$ inch deep in rows 18 inches apart, and thin the young plants to four inches apart. One ounce of seed will plant a 50-foot row, sufficient for the average family.

Frosts improve the flavor and texture. Dig part of the crop in the fall, and store it like cabbage in the cellar for winter use. The remainder of the crop can be dug in the spring. If the winters are not too harsh, a mulch will let you dig the roots as needed all through the cold months. They are cooked like parsnips.

The Spanish oyster plant, *Scolymus hispanicus,* is often called golden thistle and is similar to salsify. Even better in flavor, some people say, is black salsify, *Scorzonera hispanica,* which has a black-skinned root. Its leaves are often used in salads.

OYSTER SHELLS: An excellent source of calcium (ranging between 35 and 55 per cent), oyster shells are often ground and marketed commercially. Ground oyster shells can be added to the compost heap to insure an adequate calcium supply, or they may be mixed in sparing amounts with other organic materials for direct application to soil. The shells also contain over 40 per cent carbon dioxide and lesser amounts of aluminum, copper, iron, magnesium, manganese, P_2O_5, silica, zinc, organic matter, chlorine, fluorine and nitrogen. *See also* ORGANIC MATERIALS, CALCIUM.

P

PACHYSANDRA: *see* GROUND COVERS

PACKING MATERIALS: *see* MULCH

PAEONIA: *see* PEONY

PAINTED-DAISY: *see* PYRETHRUM

PAINTED-TONGUE: (*Salpiglossis sinuata*) The striking, highly-colored, gold-banded and veined flowers of the painted-tongue resemble ornate petunias. A wide range of bright colors is exhibited by the funnel-shaped blossoms.

These tender annuals grow to three feet high. Their blooms make excellent cut flowers. Seed should be planted in the cold frame in March; in a greenhouse, sow in February.

PAK-CHOI: *see* CHINESE CABBAGE

PALM: Among the best all-round house plants, of a purely decorative nature, are the palms. In the sizes best adapted for house culture, the stem is short, but from it arises a cluster of long, slender, arching leaves which are bold and massive, yet, at the same time, light and airy. One great advantage they have over most plants is that they do not need a large amount of sunlight; in fact, the light of a north window is sufficient. If for purposes of decoration you wish to put them in a dark corner of the room or in a hall, they can stay there three or four days without injury; but they must then be put back in the light to recuperate, for no green plant can live long without light.

Many palms have similar characteristics. This is particularly true when in the young state; in most of them, the seed leaves show no distinguishing characteristics whatever, the characteristic leaves not being developed until the plants are nearly a year old. Even in some of the older plants, there is not much difference; some hundreds of species make up the host of palms.

Two fine palms for house culture are the curly palm (*Howea belmoreana*) and the thatch leaf palm (*H. forsteriana*). They are also known as *Kentia belmoreana* and *K. forsteriana*. They might be identified in popular terms as the erect kentia and the spreading kentia. Although very much alike, belmoreana can readily be told from forsteriana by the more upright leaflets, those of forsteriana have a decidedly, drooping tendency. Moreover, belmoreana has a more dwarf and spreading habit than forsteriana, while the latter is a stranger grower and has broader foliage. As ordinarily seen in the florists' shops, a kentia in a six-inch pot is two to 2½ feet high and has half a dozen leaves, two-thirds of the leaf consisting of a long, slender gradually tapering, arching stem surmounted by many broad, dark green leaflets set in two rows. Both these palms will succeed where no other palms can be grown.

CHINESE FAN PALM: Probably the Chinese fan palm (*Livistona chinensis*, but usually spoken of as *Latania borbonica*) is the most popular of house palms, and, to the eye, certainly the most beautiful. It does not grow nearly as tall as the kentia, but is much broader. In this palm the leaf stem is as long as the leaf, and for more than half the length of the leaf, its edges are covered with short, stout, sharp spines. The leaf is a foot or more in diameter, the outer edge being divided into long narrow segments. The foliage is a deep, rich green, and presents a more massive appearance than that of any other palm. This will succeed in any room where the temperature does not go below 45° at night.

GROUND RATTAN: A somewhat stiff, formal, but interesting palm is the so-called ground rattan (*Rhapis flabelliformis*). It is a slow grower and lasts very well indeed in the house. The rhapis seldom grows more than five or six feet high. The stem is ¾ of an inch to an inch in diameter and covered with a mass of dark brown threads which are the remains of the leaf sheaths. A cluster of very deeply divided dark green leaves is borne on the top of the stem, each of which is about a foot in diameter. The rhapis differs from most of the palms in that it produces suckers, each of which sends up a stem so that in time the plant will become as broad as it is tall.

The most beautiful dwarf palm in cultivation is *Cocos weddelliana,* and as a house plant it is extremely popular. The characteristic leaves are developed at a very early stage, and as the plant is a slow grower, it retains its beauty for a long time. The short stem of the *C. weddelliana* bears numerous gracefully arching leaves which are a foot or more long and three or four inches wide, and remind one of a feather. The leaflets are very slender, and silvery white on the reverse. It is particularly useful for table decoration in fern dishes as a center piece, small ferns, such as pteris, and selaginella moss being placed about the base.

This is often referred to as the cocoanut palm; that belongs to the same genus, but is quite different, however, in having large broad leaves in the young state.

Although of no value as a house plant, lots of fun may be had from growing the cocoanut palm from seed. To do this, secure a cocoanut with the husk on and place it on its side in a pot filled with soil. Do not bury more than ¼ of the nut. The germination is very interesting as a leaf will appear long before there is any sign of a root, which may not develop for a year. The cocoanut is easily injured by too much water; it needs practically none.

Date Palms: Other palms which succeed in the house are the date palms (*Phoenix canariensis, reclinata,* and *roebelenii*). These are all very much alike, the chief differences being the habit of growth. *P. roebelenii* is a real dwarf; the leaves gracefully curving, are only a foot or so long. It withstands the hardships of house cultivation equally as well as does the kentia and when small is as graceful as *Cocos weedlliana.* It is perhaps the most costly of all the house palms. *P. rupicola* is probably the hardiest. It seems able to withstand almost any hardship which may be imposed upon it. In the South and in California, *P. canariensis* is considered the handsomest of all the date palms. The leaves are more slender and graceful than in the other palms and it is also the fastest growing date palm.

Considerable fun may be had from raising date palms (*P. dactylifera*) from the dates of the grocery stores. The seeds will germinate in a few weeks, but the plant is not so graceful as the kinds just named.

Areca: The palm often sold by the florist is the areca (*Chrysolidocarpus lutescens*). This is easily distinguished from the other palms by its golden yellow leaf-stem and also by the little plants which may be seen growing around the base; like the rhapis, the areca sends out underground suckers. The leaflets are flat, long and narrow, and of a bright glossy green. The areca can be grown successfully in the house, but it requires some care and it will not stand hardships like the other palms already mentioned.

CULTURE

The plants must not be subjected at any time to sudden changes of temperatures, such as a draft blowing across them from an open window or door; and the sudden falling of the temperature of the room will cause a chill; the leaves then turn brown and possibly they will die in a short time. To recuperate such plants will need a year or so in a greenhouse under the care of a skillful owner.

Palms need lots of water, but the soil must never become waterlogged. If plenty of drainage is given in the bottom of the pot, and sand and charcoal added to the soil, there will be no danger of over-watering for the surplus will drain away quickly.

Keep the leaves of the palms clean by passing a damp sponge over the surface each day. If the plants are not too large to handle conveniently, carry them to the sink or bathtub and syringe them with clean water. Be sure to syringe the under side as well as the top, for this will prevent the red spider and the thrips from gaining a foothold on the plants.

A potting soil made up of two parts of peat, one of rich loam such as rotted sod, and one part of sand will give the best results. Leaf mold is too light for palms, but a little may be added to the rotted sod if peat is not available.

As the plants become older, a little well-decayed horse manure may be added to the soil with benefit. The best time to repot palms is in the spring or early summer—April to June—before much growth takes place, but they can be shifted at any time up to the first or middle of October without harm. After that date it is unsafe to disturb the roots; disaster is almsot sure to follow any meddling with the root system during the winter.

Never overpot palms, for the soil will become soured very easily. A shift of one size at a time is enough. When repotting be very careful not to injure the roots; but if any are injured, cut off the injured portion with a sharp knife, making a clean cut. If the roots have bound up the drainage, get out all that is possible without injury to the roots, and fill the hole with good soil before putting the plant back into the pot. The new soil must be firmly packed about the old ball. To do this, use a thin potting stick.

PAMPAS GRASS: (*Cortaderia argentea*) This South American grass grows in thick tussocks with slender, basal leaves. It sends up stalks six to 12 feet high crowned with ample, silky panicles. The Pampas (plains) part of its name is actually a misnomer, since in its native land this plant grows in mountainous regions.

Easy to raise from seed and equally as fast to mature as the castor bean, Pampas grass quickly attains sufficient height to fulfill its screening purpose. It's especially practical and attractive for those necessary but unsightly areas. Moreover, it serves handsomely as a decorative accent plant anywhere in the garden.

Although actually a perennial, Pampas grass is not reliably hardy in severe climates, and so must be treated as an annual in these regions. Sow seeds as early as possible in the spring (a box of rich soil on a warm, bright windowsill helps get a head start), and then place the seedlings in a sunny, open position.

Like all tropicals, Pampas grass loves rich, humusy soil with a little sand added for good drainage. So, if the site selected has heavy soil, be sure to incorporate a generous amount of organic matter to lighten and enrich it.

The beautiful silky plumes of Pampas grass reach full maturity in August (even in Maine where seasons are short), and remain lovely for weeks. They may be either white or pink, and make glorious additions to dried collections.

In warmer climes where Pampas grass remains a perennial, it may be used in small clumps for permanent screens or unique lawn accents. *See also* GRASS, ORNAMENTAL.

PANAMA-HAT PLANT: (*Carludovica palmata*) A tropical tree whose leaves are made into Panama hats, this palm-like plant grows six or eight feet tall in the greenhouse. It has no trunk, the fan-type leaves being borne on stalks. The pinkish or greenish-white flowers are borne in clusters, and the fruit is a berry which is ornamental for a short time after bursting open.

Sow the seeds in moist sphagnum moss, or propagate by division in early spring. The Panama-hat plant likes a humusy soil with excellent drainage, as it requires plenty of moisture while growing. Feed liquid manure once a month. It prefers nearly pot-bound conditions, and a night temperature of 55 to 60°. Some shading over the glass is recommended to prevent burning of the foliage by strong sun. A dwarf variety, *C. humilis,* is also grown occasionally.

PANAMA ORANGE: (*Citrus mitis*) This small tree is occasionally grown in the deep South. It bears small, orange-yellow flowers and fruit about an inch in diameter, with acid pulp. The fruit is used similarly to the common orange, and the tree is worth planting in those southern states where the latter is not hardy.

PANAX QUINQUEFOLIUM: *see* GIN-SENG

PANDANUS: The pandanus or screw pines are easy-to-grow tub and pot plants for the greenhouse and home. Where they grow outdoors in the tropics, they are huge palm-like trees, 50 feet tall or taller. In the South, handsome specimens in big tubs are used for lawn and terrace decoration. These have long, stiff, sword-shaped leaves, rising from a thick trunk propped up on aerial roots like stilts.

When they are grown as house or greenhouse plants, the trunk is very short, but the roots and leaves develop just as they do in the large tropical specimens. This makes them both handsome and interesting, and their cultural requirements are quite simple.

CULTURE: Two varieties are grown as indoor plants. *P. veitchi* has green, silver- or gold-banded leaves two to three feet long and two inches or more wide. It is a popular house plant, able to survive with little or no sun provided the temperature range is close to 55 to 70°. *P. utilis,* which in the tropics rises up majestically on prop roots as long as 20 feet, is a striking plant with blue-green leaves up to three feet long and numerous red spines. It is best suited to the tropical greenhouse, but will, however, do well in the home if given as much sun as possible. The fruits of *P. utilis* are eaten in tropical countries, and the roots and leaves furnish a fiber for ropes, baskets and hats.

Both of these should have a rich soil mixture of two parts of loam to one part each of sand, leaf mold or compost and rotted manure. Excellent drainage is essential—they need plenty of moisture, but too much water standing around the roots will quickly ruin a pandanus. The foliage should be sprayed daily with water at room temperature. Reduce the watering during the winter when the plant is relatively dormant. Liquid manure once a month during the summer growing period is helpful. *P. utilis* needs some shade over the glass when the sun is very strong and hot.

The screw pines are propagated by seeds, soaked overnight before planting, or by rooting the suckers in a loam, sand and peat mixture in late winter.

PANIC GRASS: (*Panicum*) There are many annual and perennial species of panic grass, adapted to a wide range of soil and climatic conditions. Most of them are grown for forage or grain, but gardeners plant them occasionally for their flowers which are borne in feathery clusters and make good dried flowers.

The seed is sown in early spring, 1/8 inch deep in patches, and the plants are thinned to three inches apart. The perennials can also be divided in the fall.

Blue panic grass (*P. antidotale*) is drought resistant, but not winter-hardy and is grown in the southern parts of the Great Plains and the Southwest. It prefers sandy loams to well-drained, fertile clays, moderately acid to slightly alkaline and of good depth. It is not as important a range grass as some of the other species.

Colorado grass or Texas millet (*P. texanum*) is a creeping annual with stems three to four feet tall and eight-inch leaves. It is not often grown, and suited only to the Southwest.

Guinea grass (*P. maximum*) a forage grass in the South, tolerates a high degree of acidity. A perennial, it has leaves up to two feet long but very narrow, and flower clusters 18 to 24 inches in length. It is a bunch-type grass.

Para grass (*P. purpurascens*) is another southern grass, a perennial that grows in neutral to highly acid soils. It requires very moist conditions and tolerates some flooding. A forage grass, it has erect stems up to ten feet high, and creeping stems that spread as much as 20 feet, rooting at each joint.

Proso millet or broomcorn millet (*P. miliaceum*) is an annual, grown for centuries for grain and fodder. It will tolerate moderate acidity and prefers deep, sandy loams and dry to moist conditions. It is most often cultivated in the Great Plains for its shiny white seed, and grows three to four feet high, with drooping flower clusters.

Switch grass (*P. virgatum*) a vigorous perennial, prefers sandy loams that are reasonably well supplied with moisture. It grows up to six feet tall, and is hardy from Maine southward. It is often grown as an ornamental grass, having flower clusters up to 18 inches long.

Vine mesquite grass (*P. obtusum*) likes sandy loams to well-drained clay, neutral to moderately alkaline. It tolerates slight salinity, and prefers dry

conditions. A drought-resistant perennial, it is grown mostly in the southwestern states.

PANICLE: A panicle is an elongated, pyramidal flower cluster with a single main stalk that itself bears no blooms, but that has numerous branched flowering stalks arising from it. Technically, it is a compound raceme. Panicles are a characteristic of plants like yucca, oats and catalpas.

PANSY: (*Viola tricolor hortensis*) The pansy is a wonderful flower for massing or edgings in borders and beds. It makes a lovely cut flower, too, to adorn your dining room table all winter if you live in an area where only slight frosts occur, or through the early spring, summer and fall.

There are varieties that grow over four feet tall, "jumbos" that have blooms four inches across, and special varieties for the cool greenhouse. You can have pansies in blue, apricot, white, purple, red or orange, all with fascinating markings and lovely velvety faces.

CULTURE: Pansies are quite hardy, withstanding temperatures down to 15° if given a light covering of salt hay, dry leaves or strawy manure through the winter. They want cool, moist soil and a rich mulch, for they are gluttons. Use manure, compost, woods soil, leaf mold, or sawdust and shavings mixed with sheep or poultry manure. The mulch feeds them richly —they are surface feeders—and keeps the roots cool in summer, warm in winter.

The pansy is essentially a cold weather plant, so if you want to keep them over the summer, plant them where they will have a few hours shade each day. They are best raised from seed every year, as old plants give disappointing bloom. Seeds can be sown in spring for fall bloom, or started indoors in January or February for late spring and summer bloom.

Most often, pansies are sown in August in the cold frame or seedbed for early spring bloom (they are particularly beautiful interplanted between tulips). Always purchase the best seeds obtainable, preferably from a pansy specialist—home-saved seeds soon degenerate. Sow them not more than ⅛-inch deep in rows, and keep them shaded and moist. Transplant as soon as they are large enough to handle to a nursery bed or permanent position, and mulch lightly. If you sow later than August in the cold frame, the plants must stay there over the winter in the North.

New plants are easily rooted from cuttings made from the side shoots in August. Set the cuttings out and treat them the same as seeds. Feedings of manure water will make them grow fast and healthy.

For biggest blooms, trim your plants to from four to six shoots after they start flowering, and if you wish to exhibit them, remove all blossoms up to three weeks before the show when your plants will be stronger and the flowers extra-large.

After hot weather sets in, the pansies bloom so fast you won't have the time to pick them from a large bed or walk. So another trick is to shear them, leaves, blooms and all. In other words, cut them in two. This will set them back for a while. The plants, now rid of the burden of producing so many flowers, will green up and start blooming all over again. Never allowing seed to form considerably prolongs bloom. *See also* BORDERS; FLOWER GARDENING.

PAPAYA: (*Carica*) Papayas are called the "melons that grow on trees." The fragrant yellow or orange fruit varies in size from two to 20 pounds, with a soft, melting texture when ripe. It is highly perishable. The flavor has been compared to that of peaches, canteloupes and strawberries. Papayas have a milky juice and black seeds, both rich in papain, an enzyme used to tenderize meats.

CULTURE: The papaya tree usually grows 15 feet or less in height, and the fruits ripen from midwinter to early spring. It is hardy only in the lower tip of Florida, sometimes in mid-Florida and southern California if protected. The trunk resembles that of a palm tree and is topped with a cluster of huge, deeply-lobed leaves. Usually papayas must be planted in a ratio of one male to eight female trees, but a self-pollinating variety is now becoming common. Wild papaya trees are found throughout the growing range, and must be grubbed out before planting the cultivated types to prevent undesirable crossing.

Papaya trees are planted eight feet apart, and like a rich moist soil. Compost made with seaweed, water hyacinths, residues of the ramie plant (used for fiber) and other wastes is often used as fertilizer. Papayas are propagated by seed, the trees beginning to bear about nine months after planting. A tree lives about four years, but it is a common practice to replant every year or two, as the fruits get smaller after this.

PAPER MULBERRY: *see* MULBERRY

PAPER-WHITE: *see* NARCISSUS

PAPRIKA: Paprika is one of the less pungent of the varieties of red pepper (*Capsicum frutescens*) and is widely used as a condiment. It has long been grown for export in eastern and southern Europe and successfully cultivated in the United States. The substance giving red peppers their pungent properties is produced almost entirely in the thin papery tissues of the placenta to which the seed are attached. Even in the mild paprika pepper this sometimes is somewhat pungent. The degree of pungency of ground paprika may therefore depend on the thoroughness with which the placentae are removed. Removal of the seed and placentae results in a mild product, while grinding the whole fruit results in a product of more pungency, but the seeds add a nutty, oily flavor. The so-called Spanish paprika is the milder type, the production of which calls for the complete removal of seeds and placentae.

The paprika pepper, like the related more pungent varieties, is well adapted to the warm areas in the southern states from the eastern coastal plain to California. The long growing season in that region is adapted to the habit of the plant to fruit over a long period. Moreover, sunshine during the fruiting period adds brilliancy to the color of the fruit and causes more uniform ripening. If there is much rainy and cloudy weather at the blooming stage, the plants sometimes fail to set fruit, and if such weather prevails late in summer the fruit will not color properly and may be much damaged by disease.

The paprika pepper grows on a large variety of fertile soils but thrives best on a warm mellow well-drained sandy loam or clay loam type. The plant is propagated exclusively from seed, which may be planted in seedbeds or directly in the field. In beds the seed is sown as early in spring as possible, and the seedlings are then ready to be planted in the field as soon as the danger of frost has passed. They are spaced 12 to 18 inches apart, in rows 30 to 48 inches apart. If there is favorable weather early in spring the seed may be planted directly in the field by drilling in rows three to four feet apart and covering with one inch of soil. When the plants are two to three inches high they should be thinned to stand 12 to 18 inches apart in the rows and missing places filled in as necessary. Frequent shallow cultivation is necessary, and this must be continued throughout the long growing period of the crop.

Fruits of various degrees of maturity are found on the plant in summer and fall because the flowers are produced over a long period. Only fully mature fruits should be picked. Therefore, the harvesting must extend over several months, and the field must be gone over at weekly intervals when good ripening weather prevails. *See also* PEPPER.

PARASITES: In Nature, there are two types of parasites. The first is a plant which attaches itself to another plant and steals food from the host. A good example is the mistletoe, which can kill a big tree in a few years by sending its roots into the sap of the tree and draining off nutrients for its own use. Certain orchids and other tree-perching plants, such as Spanish moss and some of the ferns, are often called parasites. But this is incorrect, as they do not steal food but merely seek a place to live near the light, rather than on the dark forest floor. They are properly called epiphytes.

The second type is a minute living organism which invades and grows within plant or animal tissue and obtains its nourishment from it. Some are external parasites, such as ticks and mites. These parasites interfere with the functioning of the host and disease is the result.

They are called pathogens and the diseases they cause are the pathogenic or parasitic diseases. Because the diseases are the result of infection that may be spread from plant to plant or animal to animal, they are also called the infectious diseases. This is in contrast to the non-parasitic diseases, which are due to environmental or nutritional factors unfavorable to the plant or animal, or to some abnormality in its constitution. Often the non-parasitic diseases, such as those caused by a deficiency or unbalanced supply of nutrients or factors like unfavorable weather, can weaken a plant so that it is more susceptible to damage by parasites.

Subclinical parasitism, a level of infection too low to cause obvious, easily recognized damage, is responsible for a vast amount of poor growth and unproductiveness.

Eradication or prevention of the

parasitic diseases is achieved by proper nutrition, sanitation, rotations, breeding for resistance, biological control and various measures affecting the soil and air environments of the host. *See also* DISEASE; INSECT CONTROL.

PARASOL TREE: (*Firmiana simplex*) Popular through the lower South to California, this handsome round-headed tree grows about 30 feet tall and has heart-shaped leaves a foot wide. The flowers are small and yellow-green, borne in clusters up to 18 inches long. Both these and the odd fruits, pods which split open to expose the seeds clinging to their leaf-like segments, make it a conversation piece for the home grounds. It is also called the bottletree and the Japanese varnish tree, and is widely planted along streets.

PARATHION: A synthetic insecticide of the highly toxic organic phosphate type, parathion is one of the deadliest and most dangerous sprays. Contact of any kind with it must be avoided. Parathion sprays must not be applied by hand equipment, or parathion dust spread by airplane. It is extremely toxic to bees and fish, and because it is lethal to warm-blooded creatures of all kinds, it may not be used against insects affecting man or animals, such as household or livestock pests. Regulations provide that treated grains should not be pastured or cut for hay or grain for at least two weeks after application, and many crops should not be harvested for three weeks after treatment. Parathion is sometimes applied to the soil as a fumigant or systemic insecticide. Instances of resistance to it have been noted. *See also* INSECTICIDE.

PARNASSIA: These low-growing hardy perennials, called grass-of-Parnassus, grow wild in damp or wet, shady places throughout the northern hemisphere. Good for the wild garden, they are best suited to the edges of bogs and ponds. Sow the seeds in peaty, very moist soil in spring or fall. They can also be propagated by division. *P. caroliniana* is common in the East and sometimes grows to 24 inches tall. Two less common varieties are *P. californica*, about 15 inches tall and confined mostly to the mountains of the Far West, and *P. fimbriata*, one foot or less high and found widely in the West. All are long-lived, showy plants, with white or yellow, green-veined flowers nearly two inches across, appearing from June to September.

PARROT'S BILL: (*Clianthus puniceus*) A very beautiful spring-blooming vine, parrot's bill is grown outdoors in Florida and southern California, in the cool greenhouse elsewhere. The flowers are red or white, three inches long and borne in clusters, and the plant will grow five feet tall or taller trained on a trellis. It is propagated by seeds or cuttings, and potted in a mixture of two parts of loam to one each of sand and leaf mold or compost, enriched with manure. Outdoors it does well in ordinary garden soil and full sun. Another species, *C. dampieri*, the glory pea, grows up to four feet tall and bears scarlet, purple-blotched flowers. It is propagated by grafting on the bladder-senna, *Colutea arborescens*, which, like it, is a member of the pea family.

PARSLEY: (*Petroselinum*) Grown extensively in many vegetable gardens and often considered to be an annual vegetable, instead of a biennial herb.

The uses of parsley are many in the culinary sphere. Its crisp green leaves add much to a salad nutritively as well as decoratively. Parsley is also used sprinkled over potatoes—whether mashed, whole, or salad style, and its use in flavoring sauces, soups and stuffings is extensive.

CULTURE: Any ordinary garden soil which does not dry out too rapidly and is not excessively alkaline is suitable for parsley. Parsley requires large quantities of nitrogen, and this is best supplied in two ways: Before planting the seed, a trench about three inches deep should be dug where the row is to stand. Fill the trench with sifted compost to which has been added some well-rotted manure. Sow the seed, firm and water. Later in the season a side dressing of sifted compost humus should be applied.

Since parsley seed germinates slowly, it is best to soak them in lukewarm water for 24 hours before planting. The seed usually requires four weeks to germinate. One packet of seed should sow 100 feet of row. Place seed in a shallow trench and cover with about 1/4 inch of soil. Plant rows about 12-16 inches apart. Parsley is usually planted in March or April. It is a biennial which does well either in open sun or partial shade. For a thick growth, unwanted seedlings should be thinned so that the mature plants stand at least six inches apart. The leaves also may be clipped.

Parsley, being a biennial, will overwinter if given the protection of a light mulch during severely cold weather, and be one of the earliest green plants to show in the spring. The plant blossoms during the second year. To prevent the herb from going to seed, the blossoms, which look like Queen Anne's Lace, should be cut off as soon as they appear.

In the fall the herb may be dug up and potted. The potted herb is as easily taken care of as any house plant, and one may enjoy its freshness through all winter months. Care should be taken to dig up as much of the root as possible, and some of the outside foliage should be cut from the plant. Potted plants may also be started from seed indoors.

The first tender sprigs may be cut as soon as the leaves are well formed. From then on, the leaves with a portion of the stem may be cut as needed. Customarily the outer leaves only are cut. This practice permits the hearts

of the plant to continue to grow and produce more leaves.

For use as flavoring, the leaves may be cut and dried. The tender parts of the stems are cut from the plants and placed on a screen in a shady, dry, well-ventilated location. When thoroughly dried, they may be crushed and stored in small, tightly-covered containers.

VARIETIES: Several cultivated varieties exist, the principal ones being the common plain-leaved, the curled-leaved, the celery-leaved, and the parsnip-rooted or Hamburg. The double-curled and the moss-leaved varieties are the most attractive for garnishing. Neapolitan, or celery-leaved parsley is grown for the use of its leaf-stalks, which are blanched and eaten like those of celery. Parsnip-rooted or Hamburg is grown mainly for the thick, fleshy roots which are used for flavoring soups, stews, etc.; however the leaves can be used like ordinary parsley. *See also* HERBS.

PARSNIP: (*Pastinaca sativa*) In the East and North parsnips can be left in the ground all winter and dug out when you want some for cooking. Freezing seems to improve them and gives them a more delicate taste. In southern and western states when winters are mild, spring-planted parsnips continue growing, become tasteless and woody, so they should be planted in these areas in fall and grown for a winter crop.

CULTURE: Parsnips are a long-season crop, so the seed is sown as early in the spring as possible. For all plants that have deep-growing roots as the parsnip, the soil must be deeply spaded. They grow best in a light, rich soil. A generous amount of compost, or humus in some other form, incorporated in the soil will help provide for soil aeration and a uniform distribution of moisture, besides the source of food supply for the plants.

Parsnip seeds germinate slowly and

have a very short vitality. For that reason, fresh seed should be secured each year. Soaking the seed overnight may help to hasten germination. It is wise to mulch the rows after planting as the soil must remain cool

Parsnips will grow best in a light, rich soil that has been deeply spaded and has received generous applications of compost to improve aeration.

and moist during the long germination period when the seeds are in danger of drying out. Plant the seeds thickly in rows about 18 inches apart. Plant some radish seed along with the parsnips. The radish will mark the row and keep the crust from hardening, making life a little easier for the frail parsnips pushing through. As the radishes become of edible size, use them and weed and thin the parsnip seedlings to stand six inches apart. Cultivate cleanly all season until the foliage touches between the rows.

VARIETIES: Hollow-crown is the all-time favorite variety. Guernsey and All American are also good. Early Round is a variety suitable for shallow soils.

HARVESTING: Parsnips may be harvested at times when the ground has little else to offer. They may remain in the ground over winter. Dig them during a thaw or when the spring thaw comes. They require a freeze to sweeten them. Just before the ground freezes hard, some may be dug and stored in a root cellar for winter use. In spring dig as needed until the new tops start to grow, then dig all that remains and store them in a cold place to prevent sprouting. After the growth of new tops begins, the roots lose flavor and soon become lean and limp as well as tough and stringy. Therefore, begin digging very early.

A good way to serve parsnips is to parboil them, slice them, turn them gently in butter to a golden brown and serve.

PARTHENOCISSUS: A genus of the grape family, *Vitaceae,* sometimes called *psedera.* Deciduous climbers native to Asia and North America, clinging to walls and tree trunks by means of tendrils with adhesive tips. Alternate leaves are lobed, or divided into leaflets. Inconspicuous flowers opposite the leaves are followed by a dark blue or black berry. Good for use as ground cover on banks, or form a dense cover, which is brilliant in autumn, on walls or trees. Will grow easily in any moderately moist soil. Propagated by layering, seeds, or cuttings.

Virginia creeper, sometimes called American ivy or woodbine, is a native of the eastern United States. *P. quinquefolia* is distinguishable from poison ivy, which it resembles, by its five-parted leaves, from which it takes another common name, five-leaved ivy. Native include a number of varieties—*hirsuta,* with hairy leaves; *St. Paulii,* with aerial rootlets; *vitacea,* which lacks the adhesive disks and does not cling well; and *Engelmanni,* with smaller leaflets.

Boston ivy or Japanese ivy, *P. tricuspidata,* which has glossy three-lobed leaves, is used as a wall covering. Autumn coloring is brilliant. Varieties have leaves purple when young, or purple below.

P. henryana is a tender vine growing to moderate size. Somewhat tender, it is best grown under glass in this country. Five ovate leaflets are marked white along the veins when grown indoors or in partial shade.

PARTRIDGE BERRY: *see* GROUND COVERS

PASQUE FLOWER: *see* ANEMONE; PULSATILLA

PASSION FLOWER (*Passiflora*) Attractive stem-climbing vines with beautiful flowers.

From a large family of over 400 species, the majority of which do not bear edible fruit, the purple passion fruit vine, (*P. edulis*) and a yellow passion fruit (*P. edulis f. flavicarpa*) are the two varieties considered worth commercial growing. The purple variety is used almost exclusively in Australia, New Zealand, South Africa, and in the U. S. The yellow strain is grown in Hawaii's lower elevations. The purple type is recommended for flavor and aroma.

Early Spanish Missionaries in South America gave much religious significance in the vine's distinctive purple

The very beautiful Passion Flower, with stem-climbing vines, includes some varieties which bear delicious edible fruit about the size of a plum.

and white flowers, and the plant's name is taken from this resemblance to the Passion of Christ.

FRUIT: The fruit has a thick, leathery, deep purple hull, and is about the size of a plum. Its flavor is described as a blending of the cling peach, apricot, pineapple, guava, banana, lemon and lime.

Fragrant golden pulp sacs containing edible black seeds fill the inside of the fruit. This pulp may either be scraped from the hull and served separately or spooned directly from the halved fruit. In Australia, New Zealand and Hawaii, quantities of passion fruit are grown yearly, and are extremely popular as flavorings and as pie or fruit salad ingredients. The fruit is also a great favorite in England, where it is imported mainly from Australia and New Zealand.

The passion fruit is never picked from the vine, but rather gathered from the ground, where it conveniently falls when ripe. Partially ripe fruits allowed to ripen off the vine have a woody off-flavor.

CULTURE: The plants respond well to barnyard or poultry manure, but are not particular about soil type, provided there is good drainage, as they use only a moderate amount of water.

The mature vines will stand cold only down to 28° without being affected, while the young one and two-year-old vines are even more tender. Besides the worry of heavy frosts or extreme heat, the vines are short lived and must be replaced with new stock every eight years.

Getting little plants started is a tedious task, with propagation by seed or cuttings.

Between the fourth and fifth year, a vine is in full production, and under favorable conditions, can produce up to 40 pounds of fruit yearly.

Passion fruit vines produce two crops a year. The winter crop, the smaller of the two, blossoms in October and ripens in March and April, while the summer crop blossoms in April and matures from July to September.

Numerous flowers will develop along a vine, but the last produced may not set fruit. When a number of fruits have set along a branch, there is a short cessation of fruit setting. Later, after the first set fruits begin maturing, flower setting may resume for the remainder of the flowering period. This alternation of setting and cessation of fruit setting results in several sections of a vine bearing fruit, with fruitless spots in between.

Other varieties include the Maypop or wild passion flower (*P. incarnata*), which also produces edible fruit. It is the hardiest of the *Passifloras,* often being grown in Virginia to Texas. A vigorous-growing vine, it dies down each year.

Passion flowers are often called granadillas, as *P. quadrangularis*—giant granadilla; *P. edulis*—purple granadilla; and *P. laurifolia*—yellow granadilla.

PASTURE: Field of vegetation (generally consisting of grasses and legumes) which is harvested directly by grazing animals. *See also* LEGUME; GRASS; HAY; FORAGE.

PATHOGENE: A living organism which causes a disease in plants. *See also* DISEASE.

PATIENCE DOCK: *see* BUCKWHEAT

PAULOWNIA: A small genus mostly tender trees of the figwort family, *Scrophulareaceae,* native to China. Foliage resembles catalpa, with large heart-shaped leaves, sometimes lobed, and clusters of showy lavender to white flowers. Fruit, which remains on the tree into the winter, is a large capsule with winged seeds.

Used mostly from Washington south as specimen trees, they are mostly root-hardy into the north as far as Montreal, sending up vigorous

shoots as much as 15 feet tall in a single season. Rich loam and protected situation preferred. Propagation is by seed, cuttings, or by rooting leaves cut when they are one inch long.

P. fortunei grows to 20 feet, with ten-inch leaves and showy clusters of flowers blooming before the leaves are open. Flowers are four inches, white with purple spots in the throats.

Empress tree (*P. tomentosa*) has large erect clusters of violet gloxinia-like flowers, panicles sometimes a foot long. Leaves to 12 inches. Hardy to New York state. Variety *pallida* has lighter flowers.

PAUNCH WASTES: In slaughtering cattle a great amount of paunch content accumulates. This material is purely organic and forms one of the richest sources of bacteria, since the intestinal flora of the bovine stomach is abundant enough to break up refractory plant matter that is indigestible by the human stomach. Paunch wastes are excellent materials to add to the compost heap, hastening the decomposition process. *See also* COMPOST.

PEA: (*Pisum*) Belongs to the legume family. Aside from being a comparatively easy crop to grow, green peas are highly nutritional, being rich in vitamins A, B, and C.

CULTURE: Cool weather is essential for the growing of peas. In fact, the cooler the summer, the longer the season for peas. They will not do very well in summer unless the roots are kept cool by a heavy mulch of organic matter.

The planting of peas depends upon many combined factors. Unlike beans, for example, peas do not usually grow well if planted in the same place two years in succession.

The pea-grower must regulate his planting according to the particular soil with which he is working. Heavy soil calls for shallow seeding, while a light soil calls for deep planting. On a heavy clay soil, if the peas are planted too deeply, heavy rain may fall before the plants are up. In this case, a hard crust will form and make it difficult for the peas to break through. The best way to prepare a seed bed in heavy soil is to work the soil rather deeply and produce a tilth which is quite flaky.

Should the ground be hard and dry, deep planting is essential in order to get down far enough to provide the necessary moisture to germinate the seed. Plenty of organic matter in the soil will greatly lessen the dangers of hardening. Weeds, old leaves and grass clippings are wonderful organic materials to work into the soil.

A good manure such as cow manure is a great help in growing peas. In using such a manure, if the garden has not been manured the previous fall, only well-rotted manure should be applied. If a fresh manure is used, it will prove too hot and as a result, will endanger the crop.

FERTILIZERS: The pea, being a legume, absorbs its supply of nitrogen from the air. This process does not however, take place until after germination. Bone meal is a fine source of nitrogen. It has a slow action in the soil and cannot harm any crop. Dried blood, usually obtained from slaughter houses, is another good fertilizer. Basic slags and ground phosphates supply phosphoric acid which helps in final crop production. From four to six per cent potash is found in ordinary wood ashes. A suggested organic fertilizer for peas consists of one part of dried blood, one part of bone meal, and one part of greensand potash mineral or granite dust. This fertilizer should be applied at the rate of from $\frac{1}{4}$ to $\frac{1}{2}$ pound per square foot of soil area.

INOCULATION: To give peas a good start in the garden, they should be soaked first in water. Cover only half the seed and watch constantly for the tiny sprouts; they appear over-night. A bacterial mixture is often used to coat the peas when the soil in which they are to be planted has not been used before for this crop. The mixture will aid the plants in gaining nitrogen from the air. Look for it in your seed store or write your seed house. *See also* LEGUME; INOCULATION.

With a little know-how, the gardener can choose the variety of peas which will fill his needs most exactly. In planting garden peas one should keep in mind that the seed of the finest-flavored varieties are very much shriveled or wrinkled when in the dried state, owing to the large percentage of sugar they contain. Be careful that the soil is dry and warm enough in the spring when using this type of seed because they are liable to rot in the ground.

Most gardeners are also vitally interested in the vitamin content of home-raised vegetables. Certain varieties will naturally manufacture nearly twice as much vitamin C as other varieties under the same conditions. In general, the early small-seeded varieties of peas are better sources of vitamin C than the late large-seeded varieties.

There are two distinct types of peas from which the gardener may choose. They are the low or bush peas (*P. sativum humile*) and the tall variety (*P. sativum*). By careful planting and good care, excellent yields can be expected from either type.

PLANTING: Low bush peas are planted in drills about two inches deep in light sandy soil; about one inch deep in heavy or clay-like soil. If later plantings are followed, they should be planted twice as deep. Late plantings are subject to greater heat when they come up and deeper planting and mulching will insure them more moisture and greater coolness, thus protecting them from the heat of the sun. The seed can be scattered freely in the drills and not less than one inch apart. As the plants come up, they can be thinned to two or three inches apart. One pound of seed is sufficient for a 100 foot row.

High varieties are planted somewhat differently. The seeds are planted in double rows 30 to 36 inches apart. Two parallel drills six inches apart, or one trench six inches wide and four inches deep are two common methods. In the drills, seeds are planted 2½ inches apart—in trenches, on the outer edges. The seeds are covered with enough soil so as to half-fill the drills or trenches. After the plants come up, the drills or trenches can be filled. Double-rows are used to good advantage. Wire or brush for the purpose of supports is placed between the rows and is set before the seed is completely covered. A pound to a pound and a half of seed is used to each double hundred foot row. The final stand is thinned to four inches apart. It is important to keep the space between the rows free from weeds. So by all means lay down a mulch either before or after you plant. The mulch can be pushed back while you put in the seeds and immediately replaced. It is good to make a daily inspection of the plants to be sure that the supports for the high types are intact.

When to Plant: Choose a time to plant peas when the last frost in your vicinity is expected. It is wise to gain an early start with this crop as it will not do well in hot weather. Check with the local weather bureau for information or with your state department of agriculture. The tall varieties will do better if they are planted about ten days later than the low bush.

Supports: No high variety peas will amount to much without proper supports for the plants. Placed at the time of planting, the best supports are those made of brush having plenty of twigs and with the bark intact. After fixing the stems of the brush firmly in the ground, the support should stand four or five feet high. It should be placed close together so that it can afford the greatest protection for all of the plants.

Many gardeners use fine-mesh chicken wire in preference to the brush because it may be used season after season. This should be tightly stretched and securely fastened to stakes placed at six foot intervals. Small-meshed wire is better than large-meshed because it will not sag.

Diseases and Pests: There are a few common diseases of peas. Their importance is usually determined by climatic conditions and where one may not be reason for any worry on the part of the gardener, another may be. In the northwestern states, these diseases are not nearly as common as they are in other parts of the country and, if possible, seed should be obtained from these states.

Such fungi which cause root rot, may destroy the entire pea crop. A good control is to rotate the crop each season with unrelated crops. Do not plant peas on low-lying spots where drainage is poor. The same measures prove valuable in controlling wilt, bacterial blight, and anthracnose. If you are having trouble with damping-off, you may be planting your peas too deep.

Varieties: Freezonian, Little Marvel, Thos. Laxton and World's Record are good varieties among the early peas. For the main-crop or mid-season varieties, Wando, Alderman, Mid-freezer and Lincoln are good varieties.

Harvesting: Green peas should be harvested when they are young and tender. The general tendency is to let them hang on the vines too long, and they become starchy and hard. They should be shelled and cooked within an hour or so after picking. The sugar in peas begins to turn to starch within two hours after picking. The peas are still edible, but they are not so sweet. Don't tear the pods from the vines. Tearing or jerking the pods from the vines injures the plants so much that they may either dry up partially or stop bearing pods. Since peas mature rapidly, plan to preserve your surplus by canning or freezing. Freezing is a good way of preserving peas.—*Charles E. Booth.*

PEACH: (*Amygdalus persica*) The popularity of peaches in this country goes back to colonial days, when they were first brought here and where they thrived amazingly well. Peaches in season are readily available and relatively cheap; the reason—peach trees can be grown almost anywhere, although chief commercial centers are in the Northeast, Southeast, Midwest and Pacific Coast regions.

As is the case with the apple and pear, peaches (and other stone, or drupe, fruits) have distinct winter and growing season temperature requirements. Where commercially grown, winter temperatures are sufficiently low and last long enough to bring the trees out of the rest period, without damaging the root or top system severely. Generally, an exposure of about 700 hours of temperatures below 45° F. is needed to break the rest period fully, depending upon the fruit and variety. For example, American plums need more cold than peaches, and Elberta, an important peach variety, requires more cold than the Babcock variety. (When selecting a peach variety for your home grounds, be sure to consider this factor.)

When it comes to minimum temperatures, peaches (and apricots) are the least hardy of the stone fruits, although well-hardened trees are most often able to withstand 10° below zero weather. This relatively lower hardiness of the peach explains why many northern commercial peach belts are on the leeward side of large bodies of water; for example, the southern shore of Lake Erie and Lake Ontario and eastern shore of Lake Michigan. Regarding temperatures during the growing season, the highest production and best quality of peaches are obtained in sections which have a mean summer temperature of 75° F.

CULTURE: Here's some advice on peach growing from Phil Arena, well-known organic orchardist from Escondido, California:

Young trees which you buy from nurseries should be fairly straight with good roots and, most important of all with good buds. When you're ready to plant the tree, cut it back to about 18 inches above ground level, providing you can see good healthy buds. After it sprouts in spring, the tree structure will be formed where you have left the bud.

As the tree grows in summer, water it every eight to ten days according to the heat. Keep weeds cleaned away; use plenty of mulch to save water. (In general, the root system of peaches is less extensive and less deep than that of the apple and pear, so peach trees suffer more quickly from drought and weed competition.)

Watch for sucker growth that will come up from the trunk. Be sure to clean them off using a sharp knife and make a smooth cut. If you don't cut them out, they will grow faster than the main trunk and soon your tree will turn wild. Also cut away limbs that are crossed or out of line. The tree will grow as well as you train it. Incidentally, by cutting it back when you prune it, the tree will grow wide instead of tall, so you won't need a ladder to pick the fruit.

The third year from planting, you should have a fine tree ready to give you lots of fruit. Fertilize well before the rains in the fall. Prune it before February and be sure to cut back enough, in many cases 50 per cent. You may wonder where the fruit will come from. However, you will be very much surprised when spring comes and the tree begins to bloom.

One of the biggest mistakes that people make is to leave all the fruit that sets on a limb. As many as 50 peaches can sometimes be counted on a small limb. These should be thinned to only ten or 12 inches apart leaving three peaches where the 50 were. You may leave the 50 and get poor quality and poor flavor, or you can thin out to improve both flavor and quality. In many cases the tree will even die when you don't thin at the proper time. You should thin the first time when the peach set is about the size of a pea and again when they are the size of marbles.

For best results, go over the tree three times and don't be afraid to pull the fruit off where it is too thick. Some winters are too mild and the deciduous trees don't go through a normal dormant period. This will throw them out of balance and when spring comes, they will bloom but fail to leaf out.

This is called delayed foliation, and it weakens the tree so much that sometimes they never come out of it. Strange as it may seem, they will bloom heavy and set heavy, but without leaves the tree cannot support the fruit. So it is best to take off most of the fruit and in most cases the leaves will finally come out in late spring, although the tree will still be left in a weak condition.

Sometimes they will come out too early if the winter is warm. Then a late frost will kill the bloom. Heavy watering will keep the ground cool and hold them dormant longer. Regardless of obstacles, you do your part by good fertilization, mulching, and plenty of water at the proper time: "The better the care, the better the results," concludes orchardist Arena about growing fruit trees.

COVER CROP FOR PEACHES: Extensive experiments involving 384 trees and ten years of study show that the best growth and vitality in peach trees results when a vigorous winter cover crop is employed. These experiments were conducted by the University of Delaware at the Research Station at Georgetown in southern Delaware.

Specifically, it was discovered that the most satisfactory cover crop appeared to be a mixture of rye and vetch, the proportion of each being, 70 pounds of rye and 30 pounds of vetch. This was sowed the first of September and disced under ground the middle of May.

One of the prime results reported in the use of this winter cover crop is, that it reduces competition for nutrients and moisture, which is a most important procedure during the growing season.

Also, during these years of research, combinations of cover crops throughout the entire years were studied. In this connection it was found that in addition to the double cover combination of rye-vetch in winter, a planting of soybeans in summer yielded the best growth of peach trees. However, the researchers do not recommend this for peach orchards, because of the additional expense of growing soybeans in the summer season.

As for the subject of soils, results obtained from this portion of the experiment show that for good growth for the cover crop as well as for the trees themselves, the ground should be well fertilized before sowing the crop. In some cases it was observed that the cover crop fertilizer was a more important stimulant to the growth of the trees than the crop itself.

The soil was limed as often as necessary for a good growth of the cover, and both organic and commercial fertilizers were used in the test.

Poultry manure—to the use of which as a fertilizer, the Delaware Experiment Station has given extensive study—is not recommended in these findings as a fertilizer for peach or other fruit trees. The reason for this is that its nitrogen content can vary widely from one application to the next. *See also* FRUIT TREES; ORCHARD; FRUIT TREES, DWARF.

PEACOCK-FLOWER: *see* POINCIANA

PEACOCK IRIS: (*Moraea pavonia*) A species of tender iris native to South Africa, but grown in this country only in California and Florida. One to two feet tall, with bright red one-inch flowers spotted at the base with blue-black or green-black. Varieties have unspotted yellow flowers, bright purple with blue-black spots, and white flowers with blue spots.

PEANUT: (*Arachis*) A low-growing herb. Usually grown in the warmer regions, they can mature as far north as New England in a soil that is rich in humus. Although semi-tropical, the light frosts of early spring, or late fall, do them little harm. What they do require, however, is a long growing season. That is why they have become one of the chief Southern crops. But, through special growing methods, they can be grown with reasonable success in the North as well. Very few places in the United States have a more severe climate than in New England. Yet, each summer, many gardeners there grow a bountiful winter's supply of peanuts in their gardens.

KIND TO PLANT: The Spanish red and the Mexican brown peanuts are the most commonly grown in this country. Both do equally well in the

Gardeners are discovering that peanuts can be grown in the North. Shallow planting encourages quicker growth, lessens danger of damp rot.

North. The Mexican peanut is the small variety used chiefly in making "salted peanuts." Although small as a pea, they produce heavily.

The Spanish red peanut is the larger one usually boiled in oils, or sold roasted in their jackets. They do not produce as abundantly as the Mexican variety, but their flavor is far superior. Both are planted and grown alike.

CULTURE: Growing peanuts is no more difficult than growing string beans or snap beans. And it's far more enjoyable. Work the soil deep and well, turning in compost, aged manure, or leaf mold if no previous organic materials have been added. In the South, the kernels are planted at least four inches deep. But, in the North, plant no deeper than 1½ inches. Shallow planting will encourage quicker growth, and prevent damp rot in case of a cold, wet spring. Plant four kernels to a mound, with mounds 18 inches apart in rows two feet apart. In the central part of Massachusetts, peanuts may be planted during the second last week of April. Subtract a week if you live a hundred miles further south, or add a week if that much further north.

CARE DURING GROWTH: If the sun isn't too warm, the peanuts will take some time to germinate and send up tender shoots. Do not be discouraged if plants fail to appear in seven days. If the weather is wet and cold, the kernels may not sprout for two weeks.

When the plants are six inches tall, begin cultivating. This will aerate the soil and keep down weeds. After plants have attained 12 inches, hill the rows as you would potatoes, hilling the soil high around each plant. This is very important, for, as the branches grow, their lower leaves drop off. In the place of the discarded leaf, a long, pointed peduncle appears. As it grows it will force its way into the mounted soil, and there form a peanut pot at its very tip.

After the plants have been properly hilled, mulch between the plants well with at least eight inches of straw or grass clippings. The decaying material will not only keep down weeds, but, each time it rains, their juices will be carried down to the hungry roots. Your peanut plants, thus treated, will require no more attention until harvest time.

How to Harvest: To get the most out of your peanut crop, allow plants to remain undisturbed until heavy frost completely destroys the tops. This will be around the last of October. Most of the pods are formed as early as the middle of September, but they are empty. The kernels will need another month or six weeks to develop fully. Early frosts may darken the leaves of the plants, but the stems will continue to provide food for the nuts to develop.

When harvest time arrives, lift each bush carefully out of the soil with a garden fork, and shake free of all dirt. You might run your fingers through the dirt left in the hole to rescue any peanuts that have broken off. Pluck the pods from the roots immediately, and drop into shallow trays for drying. Later, store these filled trays in the attic of your home or garage to dry. Never store in a cool, damp basement as the moisture still in the uncured pods will cause them to mildew and rot.

When and How to Prepare: Two months of drying time will render the peanuts fit for roasting. They are delicious roasted in their jackets in an oven preheated to 300°. Allow to roast for 20 minutes, then remove immediately and pour out of the hot pan. One thing must be remembered in cooking peanuts—the nuts will continue to cook for some time after they have been removed from the oven. For this reason, it is always best to undercook. By the time the nuts cool, they will be done.

Saving Seed: Before the family eats them all, pick out suitable seed for next year's planting. This seed is better than any you can buy for they have already become accustomed to your soil, climate and growing conditions. To pick out the best seed, choose pods that have a pleasing yellow color. These are the fully ripe ones. For further proof, shake each pod near your ear. If a good, loud rattle results, the nut is ripe. Allow seed to remain in the pods until planting time to prevent drying up.

Food Value: There are many people who wisely eat the raw centers of vegetable or fruit seeds for the large amount of vitamins they contain. Have you ever tasted raw peanuts? They have a delightful nut flavor all their own. One cup of roasted peanuts gives but 200 International Units of B_1. The equal amount of uncooked peanuts contains 50 units of vitamin A, 438 units of B_1, 240 units of C, and 200 units of G. So, you can readily see what an excellent source of health-giving vitamins raw peanuts are.

Peanut Butter: In making peanut butter, roast your peanuts in their shells in a 300-320° oven for about 20 to 25 minutes, turning occasionally. Then run them through the kitchen meat grinder three or four times for a fine, smooth butter.—*Betty Brinhart.*

PEANUT HULLS: Peanut hulls and shells are rich in nitrogen. They can be effectively used in mulching and composting. Here is an analysis:

	Nitrogen	Phosphoric Acid	Potash
Peanut shells	3.6	.70	.45
Peanut shell ashes	.8	.15	.50

PEAR: (*Pyrus*) The pear is one of the fruit trees that fits so well into an organic landscaping scheme. Pear trees are quite hardy and grow well on deep, well-drained loam soil with ample moisture. A heavy mulch or permanent leguminous cover crop produces the best growth. Lime is particularly important with pears, as the tree contains a high percentage of tannin. The only thing to avoid is excessive nitrogen fertilization—it encourages disease—but a mulch or barnyard manure is perfectly safe to use.

A cross between the Chinese sand pear and Bartlett, the Kieffer pear is remarkably resistant to disease and will even thrive in heavy soils.

Dwarf pears are generally planted 12 feet apart in each direction, full-sized trees 16 to 20 feet apart. Nearly all varieties require cross-pollination; any two varieties that blossom at the same time will cross-pollinate each other. Pear trees are well adapted to espalier training, and thus are a good fruit for small gardens.

Pears are generally planted as one-year-old whips, which are headed back to 30 inches. At the end of the first summer, all except three evenly spaced branches are removed. Each year, these are headed back moderately and three or four shoots are left to make secondary branches. Once the tree comes into bearing, the only pruning necessary is removal of enough wood to induce new shoot growth about 12 to 18 inches long over the periphery of the tree, and thinning to prevent overbearing.

Fire blight is the only serious disease of pears, and is controlled by pruning out and composting or burning the infected parts.

VARIETIES: Here are some of the best pear varieties:

Bartlett—the most popular variety in this country, Bartlett produces big, juicy yellow pears most delicious and used for eating fresh, stewing, canning and drying. The tree is quite large and extremely productive under organic treatment.

Gorham—very similar to Bartlett but ripening somewhat later, this variety is blight-resistant.

Seckel—these pears are not often seen as they are rarely grown commercially (orchardists find the larger pears sell better). But Seckel pears, though very small, are sweet, with a unique, almost nut-like flavor, and the tree is highly blight-resistant. It is one of the best pears for the home garden.

Cayuga—this is similar to Seckel, but with much larger fruits.

Clapp Favorite—producing a yellow pear with a bright red blush, this is a large, vigorous tree frequently planted in pear orchards in the Northeast. However, it is one of the most blight-susceptible varieties.

Tyson—a big tree that produces small but very luscious fruits, Tyson is highly productive and grows in the same areas as Clapp Favorite.

Winter Nelis—this is one of the best pears for winter storage. It is greenish-yellow, usually russeted, and tasty. The trees are slow growers but eventually reach a bigger size than any other pear variety.

Beurre Bosc, Beurre D'Anjou and Beurre Hardy—these produce greenish-yellow fruits on large, medium-productive trees. The first variety is the best for the East.

Kieffer—this interesting, comparatively new variety is a cross between the Chinese sand pear and the Bartlett. It is remarkably resistant to disease, and will thrive on very heavy loam or clay loam soils. Its roots plunge to great depths in search of subsoil minerals. In many areas, it is now the most commonly grown variety. *See also* FRUIT TREES; ORCHARD; FRUIT TREES, DWARF.

PEARL MILLET: *see* GREEN MANURE

PEAT MOSS: Peat moss is the partially decomposed remains of plants accumulated over centuries under relatively airless conditions. It is a highly valuable organic material for soil building.

Peat moss loosens heavy soils, binds light soils, holds vast amounts of water, increases aeration, aids root development, stops nutrients from leaching away. It can be added to the soil or used as a mulch.

When dry, it will absorb up to 15 times its weight of water. Its effect on soils is to make a "crumb" structure that holds much more water due to the increased surface area of the soil particles.

This fact becomes important when we realize that for every pound of dry matter or actual solids in a plant,

there must be taken from the soil from ¼ to ½ ton of water.

Soil-held moisture is not only vital in preventing drought damage, but it is also necessary to carry in solution the nutrients the plant must have to grow. Proper amounts of moisture also aid the soil organisms to break up the organic compounds into usable forms.

Peat moss has a very open, fibrous texture, permitting free development of even tiny hair roots. It improves aeration, too, letting the soil "breathe deeply." The ground is kept loose and friable, without crusting or compacting, and it does not dry out rapidly. Drainage is also improved in heavy clay soils, and in light, sandy ones, plant nutrients are prevented from leaching away. Peat moss contains no weed seeds, no plant disease organisms, no insect eggs or larvae. It is biologically sterile.

Like other organic materials, peat acts as a buffer against toxic substances. It will clear up unbalanced soil conditions, as when a soil is overloaded with alkalis or the residues of certain chemical fertilizers. Large applications of peat have restored many such soils to production.

Finally, its effects last many years.

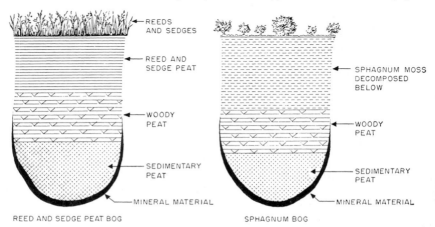

REEDS AND SEDGES

REED AND SEDGE PEAT

WOODY PEAT

SEDIMENTARY PEAT

MINERAL MATERIAL

REED AND SEDGE PEAT BOG

SPHAGNUM MOSS DECOMPOSED BELOW

WOODY PEAT

SEDIMENTARY PEAT

MINERAL MATERIAL

SPHAGNUM BOG

The above illustration, prepared by the United States Department of Agriculture, shows a typical profile of a peat formed mainly from sedges and reeds; another composed chiefly from sphagnum moss.

Tests at Pennsylvania State Agricultural College showed that 70 per cent of its organic content was still in the soil after ten years.

For all its good points, peat moss should not be regarded as a miracle soil amendment. While some sedge peats do contain as high as three per cent nitrogen, this is released slowly, over many years. Compost, or materials like leaf mold, are preferable to peat moss if easily procurable, because they have more nutrients and in a more readily available form.

ORIGIN OF PEAT: Peat is not a uniform substance. Its composition depends on the type of plants which make it up, its age, climate and other factors. It comes from swamps or bogs, hollows in the earth's surface where vegetative materials collected for hundreds of years under wet conditions. There are upwards of 12,000 square miles of such deposits in the United States, in some areas 30 feet deep.

By far the largest amounts of peat on the market come from bogs of sphagnum moss. Sedge peat is made from the rotting of grasses, sedge and reeds; it is finer in texture and darker than sphagnum because its decomposition is further advanced. Wood peat consists largely of decomposed forest litter, branches and the like, from swampy forested areas. Most peats are acid in reaction, although some sedge and wood peats are nearly neutral.

AMOUNT TO USE: The amount of peat moss to use depends on the physical condition of your soil. If it is already open and friable, it naturally will need less than a sandy or clayey soil. In general, if you are not incorporating any other organic materials, one part of peat to two of the soil is a good rule (for every three inches deep you dig, work in a one-inch layer of peat moss). Aim for a mixture that, when squeezed in the hand while damp, holds its form

when released but crumbles apart when lightly touched.

The acidity of an acid peat is not troublesome unless you are growing alkaline-loving plants or incorporating huge amounts of the peat, in which case add about a cupful of lime to each bushel of peat. *See also* ACIDITY-ALKALINITY.

The gardener who has no manure and who starts out the season without any compost can use peat humus, the black, completely decayed end-product of peat decomposition. It is sold under several trade names, it is an excellent soil builder and fertilizer when mixed with some animal matter like dried blood and bone meal.

Some recommendations for using peat: acid-loving plants thrive in a soil made up of 50 per cent loam, 50 per cent peat. In the wild garden, two parts of peat to one of loam is good. Established lawns can be top-dressed with a ½-inch of peat moss twice a year, and poor spots renovated by mixing in a like amount, plus organic fertilizer, before reseeding.

Shredded sphagnum is an ideal medium for starting seeds, but once the seedlings are up they need some feeding with a weak solution of compost or manure. Equal parts of sand and finely sifted peat moss are good for rooting cuttings. In the greenhouse, sedge peat makes a good substitute for leaf mold and can replace most of the manure in the soil mixture.

Peat moss is a fine mulching material. However, a summer mulch of peat moss alone should not be made more than an inch deep. A deeper mulch will soak up and hold water that falls on it rather than pass it down to the soil. A winter mulch three to four inches deep will stabilize underground temperatures and prevent heaving. The coarser grades of peat moss make good livestock bedding and poultry litter.

ORIGIN OF PEAT: In the U. S. Dept. of Agriculture report, "Peat and Muck in Agriculture," Drs. M. S. Anderson, S. F. Blake and A. L. Mehrling write the following:

Where evaporation is high, peat is formed in low spots on poorly drained lands that are submerged most of the time, or in shallow ponds and marshes. In very humid and cool regions it may be formed also on steep slopes. Some peat deposits cover wide areas—for instance, the Everglades in Florida. Organic matter decomposes very slowly under water. Thus the remains of vegetation growing in water, or falling into it, tend to accumulate more rapidly than they decompose, until the accumulation of deposits is exposed to the air at the surface during dry periods. At this stage decomposition of organic matter keeps pace with its accumulation. As the level of the bog is raised, new types of vegetation appear in response to the changing environment.

A vertical cut through a peat deposit often reveals a series of layers that have originated from different kinds of plant materials. When the surrounding hills contain calcareous deposits, the product formed may be essentially neutral or even alkaline in reaction.

The materials making up a peat bog form irregular patterns, sometimes rather definite layers, varying in depth in different parts of the bog. The depth of the layers depends on the history of the bog, particularly on the length of time each phase of vegetation lasted. In some sphagnum bogs studied, the surface layer of sphagnum moss peat varied from five to six inches to 25 feet in thickness often being six to eight feet; the bed of reed-sedge peat below it varied from two to 12 feet; the stratum of woody peat below, or often above, the reed-sedge peat, varied from four inches to 1½ feet or was lacking; and the sedimentary peat at base of the deposit varied from none to a layer of 3½ feet.

TYPES OF PEAT: The vegetation from which peat is formed varies widely as does also the character of each peat developed from it.

The physical and chemical properties of peat depend on the kinds of plants from which it was formed, on their degree of decomposition, and on the kind and quantity of mineral matter present. There is not yet general agreement on the classification of peats according to their botanical characteristics. For present purposes, peats may be divided according to gross botanical composition into the four following groups:

SPHAGNUM GROUP: Peat of this type is formed mainly of several species of sphagnum, usually intermixed with small quantities of various herbaceous plants and undershrubs, such as ferns and sedges, orchids, sundews, pitcherplants, and often cranberry. Also, these deposits occasionally contain lenses of wood or remains of shrubs, commonly of the heath family. This type of vegetation is similar to that of the European highmoor. Sphagnum-moss peat is usually loose, spongy, and often layered; it varies from light grayish brown to deep brown in color. It nearly always has a strongly acid reaction.

HYPNUM AND OTHER MOSSES GROUP: These peats are made up mostly of disintegrated plants of hypnum, often associated with other mosses and with intermingled rootlets of sedges and other flowering plants. They are formed chiefly in areas with a slightly acid, neutral, or alkaline reaction. The material is brownish or drab, light, spongy, and matted, and often laminated and porous.

REED-SEDGE GROUP: Deposits of the reed-sedge type are formed mainly in shallow areas around the border of water-filled depressions, of which they gradually take possession, or in boggy meadows. Important constituents of peats of this group are various plants of the sedge family (*Carex, Scirpus, Eleocharis, Rynchospora, Eriophorum,* and others), cattail (*Typha*), various grasses (particularly the reed *Phragmites;* also *Glyceria* and *Calamagrostis*), burreed (*Sparganium*), arrowhead (*Sagittaria*), and a miscellaneous assortment of shore and swamp-loving plants of other families. In their normal development, peats of this type are rather fibrous and somewhat felted or matted; they consist mainly, so far as recognizable vegetable matter goes, of roots and rootlets of the plants mentioned, but they often also contain the rootstocks or stems of the plants. They are light yellowish to reddish, rusty brown, or even blackish in color.

SHRUB-AND-TREE GROUP: An important plant group represented is the heaths, which are mainly plants of acid habitats. They include leatherleaf, bog-rosemary, Labrador-tea, huckleberry, and blueberry. Other plants often present are alder, dwarf birch, sumac, chokeberry, buttonbush, willow, and cornel. Among the trees that normally succeed the shrubs are red maple and elm, and, in more northern areas, birch, larch, black spruce, and, usually in more calcareous regions, arborvitae. The greater part of such peat consists of material derived from roots, trunks, branches, twigs, and bark, in a tangled mass and not highly decomposed, mixed with remains of leaves, ferns, rootlets, and often in a matrix of more finely divided material.

The terms "highmoor" and "lowmoor" designate two general classes of peat. Highmoor refers to a marshy, treeless area of relatively low evaporation, with low-lime soils. The peat formed there is normally of strongly acid reaction. Lowmoor includes a plant association dominated by grasses, sedges, reeds, and rushes, normally growing in environments better supplied with calcium and potassium than are highmoor areas. *See also* MULCH; HUMUS; MUCK SOILS.

PEA WASTES: Pea wastes are of several kinds, mainly available in quan-

tities in the cannery regions. Apart from the high feeding value of any legume crop, pea shells and vines should be returned to the land in some form. If they can be fed and thus be used as manure residue, they are best employed. If they show diseases, they can be burned and the ashes used for fertilizing. Pea pod ash contains almost three per cent phosphoric acid and 27 per cent potash. They can be composted with great ease since their nitrogen content, which is highest in green pods and vines, tends to produce a quick breakdown.

PECAN (*Carya pecan*) For years the odd mythology that the pecan will prosper only in the Deep South has stopped many northern gardeners from growing pecans. This belief in Cotton-Belt exclusiveness still persists despite the established fact that the pecan grows—and produces—in Ohio, in Iowa, in Toronto, and in British Columbia.

Originally, the pecan was native to Iowa and was found on the Ohio River spreading west and south to Texas. It reached into northwest Missouri and it lined the streams in Oklahoma and eastern Texas.

The pecan is native to North America. It has weathered and survived chilling, killing frosts for hundreds of thousands of years. It does this by sleeping late in the spring. Some bad years it has to sleep so late it doesn't get time to produce a crop.

The significance of this extensive range is obvious; the pecan is as much a northern as a southern tree!

CULTURE: Plenty of compost from the start around each tree and plenty of mulch.

Some growers plant the pecan trees 60 feet apart and interplant with other nut and fruit trees. *See also* NUT TREES; ORCHARD.

PEDICULARIS: A large genus of the figwort, *Scrophulareaceae,* family, commonly called lousewort or wood-betony. Native to North America, some species grow as far north as the Arctic circle. Annual or perennial herbs sometimes used in the rock garden for showy yellow, white, purplish, red, or rose spikes of tubular flowers, they are partially parasitic on roots of other plants. Propagated by seed or division, pedicularis needs native woods' loam to thrive. Leaves are finely divided and fern-like.

Wood-betony, *P. canadensis,* grows to 1½ feet, with soft, fern-like leaves and dull reddish or yellowish flowers in April to June. It is a common woodland flower. *P. lanceolata* grows to three feet, and has yellow flowers. *P. densiflora* is a crimson-flowered species, with flowers about one inch long, and is a native of California.

PELARGONIUM: The common garden geranium, sometimes known as Stork's bill geranium. *See also* GERANIUM.

PELICAN FLOWER (*Aristolochia grandiflora*) A species of the wild ginger family, closely related to Dutchman's pipe. A woody greenhouse vine, native of the West Indies, remarkable for its very large yellowish-green flower whose flattened outer rim of petals sometimes reaches eight inches in diameter, or in the variety *Sturtevantii,* 18 inches. The flowers arise from an inflated, purple-spotted tube, which is tailed, the tail measuring as much as three feet in *Sturtevantii.* Plants require rich soil and a warm, humid atmosphere. Propagation is by cuttings, layers, or seed.

PELLETT CLOVER: *see* HONEY PLANTS

PENICILLIN: *see* ANTIBIOTIC

PENNISETUM: *see* GRASS, ORNAMENTAL

PENNYROYAL: (*Hedeoma pulegioides*) An annual plant found in dry soils from Nova Scotia and Quebec to the Dakotas and southward. Both the dry herb and the oil obtained from it by steam distillation are marketable products.

Pennyroyal grows well on average soils and is frequently abundant on sandy or gravelly slopes. In field planting, the seed is sown in rows in fall and covered not to exceed ¼ of an inch, since it rarely germinates if planted at a greater depth. It must be sown thick to assure a full early-spring-stand, because much of it is lost in winter. For best results, clean cultivation and freedom from weeds are essential. In the garden, it prefers light shade.

The crop is harvested early in summer, when the plants are in full flower. The herb is dried, preferably in the shade, and the large stems are then removed to improve the quality of the product.

Pennyroyal grows to 1½ feet high, has a mint-like fragrance. It is often used to make tea.

There is also a prostrate perennial type, (*Mentha pulegium*), with a peppermint odor useful for a ground cover. It is not hardy. *See also* MINT.

PENTSTEMON: It is strange indeed that pentstemons are not more commonly found in gardens. These perennials, sometimes called beardtongue, are charming and beautiful, and very easy to grow. There are handsome pentstemons in a wide range of colors and sizes for beds, borders, rock gardens and backgrounds.

The flowers, ranging from white and yellow to pink, red, purple and deep blue, are borne in racemes through late spring and summer. Pentstemons vary in height from three inches to over six feet, with foliage from soft green or pale gray to a surprising bright blue. A few will bloom the first year from seed. Several species are important bee plants in the West.

They like sunny locations, and a light mulch during the winter. Good drainage is very important, and coarse gravel is recommended in the bottom of the planting hole. Standing moisture is especially bad in the winter.

Pentstemons will thrive in hotter, drier conditions than many other plants, given a porous, sandy loam soil that is not too rich. Peat moss, leaf mold or compost are better to use in preparing the soil than manure, which tends to make the plants short-lived.

Usually the seeds are sown in late November, but they can be planted in the cold frame as late as early March. The young plants are easily moved to their permanent locations. Pentstemons are not notably long-lived, so it's a good idea to start some new ones each year for replacements.

Some of the pentstemons especially good for sunny spots in the rock garden include *P. nitidus* and *P. angustifolius,* both growing about a foot high and crowded with spikes of glowing turquoise-blue flowers in early spring and later. *P. glaber* and *P. unilateralis* are somewhat taller, with large, bright blue or purplish flowers, while *P. heterophyllus* grows two to three feet tall and has opalescent pink or rose-purple blooms. The dwarf *P. rupicolus* is less than five inches high, with comparatively large, bright red flowers; it likes a gritty soil and shade during the hottest part of the day. *P. crandallia* is another little beauty that will spread into a mat two to three feet wide, with blooms in the entire range of pentstemon colors.

The shell-leaf pentstemon, *P. grandiflorus,* which grows from four to six feet high with numerous big lavender flowers, is a wonderful plant for the perennial border. There is a variety with pure white blooms. *P. cobaea* has large white, purple-veined flowers on two-foot stems, and soft green leaves that appear to have been sprinkled with frost crystals.

Two of the tallest pentstemons are *P. murrayanus* and *P. torreyi.* Both have brilliant scarlet honeysuckle-like blooms that open over a period of many weeks; they need staking. *P. gloxinoides* are hybrids in many sizes

and colors, and will usually bloom the first year from seed. There are many other gorgeous varieties, most of them quite hardy.

Pentstemons make fine cut flowers if the stem ends are burned or plunged in hot water for a minute or two to seal the sap. *See also* FLOWER GARDENING.

PEONY (*Paeonia*) A beautiful and outstanding perennial, producing a showy array of blooms during the months of May and June. Although the flowering season lasts only a short while, the peony retains its pretty green foliage until frost. Once started, this hardy perennial will produce blooms year after year with a minimum of attention.

CULTURE: Since the peony, once planted, is left undisturbed for many years, it is wise to prepare a deep bed and enrich the soil generously with compost and well-rotted manure. Bone meal is also frequently used.

Roots may be planted from late August until hard frost. The ground should be prepared one to two weeks ahead of planting time. If planted before the soil has settled, sinking or burial of the crown occurs. Select root divisions with at least three eyes for planting. Hollow out sufficiently large holes for each clump and place the growing points or eyes just below the soil surface so that the buds will be two to three inches deep. Planting too deep may be the reason for failure to bloom. Tamp the soil firmly around the root and water deeply. Place new clumps about three to five feet apart allowing room for full development of each plant. Peonies may be planted either in full sun or in partial shade, but not close to trees or shrubs. Mulching the first winter is usually desirable, but is not required thereafter.

Peonies often need support, which should be provided early in the spring. Barrel hoops and stakes will do, but welded iron rod supports are for sale reasonably and will last for years. If the size of the flower is important for cutting or for show, disbud by removing the two side buds as each group of three forms; otherwise don't disbud and the flowering period will last longer. In the fall cut off the foliage as soon as it is wilted by frost. This will avoid possible spread of disease. It is wise to enrich the soil around older plants from time to time with compost, well-rotted manure, and bone meal.

PROPAGATION: Peonies are propagated by root division. The clump need not be disturbed for as long as ten years, but if the flowers grow small and the stems are crowded it is best to divide the clump. Early fall is the preferred dividing time. Loosen the soil at least 18-20 inches around the plant and about 12 inches deep; lift the clump and let roots dry in the sun for two or three hours. Gently wash off surplus earth and cut the stems to two inches. Bend the large clump carefully to find weakest parts and divide there. Cut with a sharp knife. Then subdivide each section into strong roots leaving at least three eyes on each section for planting.

VARIETIES: The herbaceous peony that dies down in autumn is the type most commonly grown. It offers a wide range of colors from white to deep red. A few of the popular varieties and colors are: Baroness Schroeder—bluish to white; Enchanteresse—creamy white; Felix Crousse—rose red; Festiva Maxima—red-flecked white; La France—soft pink; Longfellow—bright red; Marie Crousse—salmon pink; Mary Brand—crimson; and Walter Faxon—pure rose.

Varieties include the Chinese peonies (*P. albiflora*), whose ancestors can still be found growing wild in Asia. Usually growing to about three feet high, this common peony has long flower stalks and smooth fruit. The variety *sinensis* has large crimson blooms.

The tree peony (*P. suffruticosa*)

makes an attractive shrub, reaching as high as six feet and producing blooms almost a foot across.—*Barbara J. Hardy.*

See also PERENNIALS.

PEPPER: (*Capsicum*) The garden pepper belongs to a different botanical family from that of the black pepper. Peppers are picturesque plants of bushy habit, generally treated as annuals in cold climates, though in warm places they are true perennials. Five or six pepper plants will supply the average family with plenty of peppers for table use, as well as add a decorative appearance to the garden. The colorful fruits are attractive when used with other vegetables for table arrangements, and in salads provide a touch of color as well as nutritive value. Peppers are a fine source of vitamin C.

CULTURE: Since the pepper is a very tender vegetable and one which requires a long growing season, the plants must be started inside about eight to 10 weeks before the outside planting date. One packet of any variety will provide more than enough plants for the average family. Seed can be started in a flat or flower pots in a sunny window, hotbed, or a cold frame.

Put a layer of pebbles or coarse material for drainage in the bottom of flats or flower pots, and fill to ½ inch of the top with a finely screened mixture of one part sand, one part loam, and one part compost.

Keep the containers evenly moist until germination has occurred and the seedlings are growing well. When the plants have at least their first pair of true leaves and are crowding, move to plant bands, or to flats, allowing each plant at least two inches in all directions. To prevent wilting and sudden death of young plants from fungus infections, be very careful not to overwater, especially during damp cloudy weather.

When the weather has become

warm, and absolutely all danger of frost is over, set the pepper plants in a sunny location in the garden in rows two to three feet apart, with 18-24 inches of space between the individual plants. They will grow in any well-prepared garden soil and do not require a great deal of fertility. During very dry weather give the plants an occasional thorough watering. Mulching the plants with grass clippings or hay will save work by smothering the weeds, and by holding moisture in the soil.

Because the pepper plant's requirements are so similar to those of the tomato, many gardeners when setting out a planting of tomatoes, substitute pepper plants for tomato plants here and there throughout the planting. Peppers are also often grown amid flowers and shrubs.

INSECTS AND DISEASES: Peppers are not especially susceptible to insect pests. Sometimes when the plants are first set out, cutworms cause damage, but they can be quite easily controlled by placing cardboard collars in the ground around the stems.

The most serious disease is mosaic, a virus infection. Leaves become malformed, mottled in color, and the plants are stunted and eventually die. Remove and destroy such plants at once. Wash hands (or tools) before touching healthy plants.

VARIETIES: Peppers are classed in two groups: the sweet, or mild, and the hot. The sweet-fleshed peppers are desirable for slicing, salad, and stuffing. World Beater, California Wonder and Merrimack Wonder are good sweet varieties. Long Red Cayenne, Red Chili, and Tabasco are good hot varieties. The hot varieties are fine for sauces, flavoring and pickling either fresh or dried.

HARVESTING: The sweet varieties are usually picked when they have reached sufficient size and are still green in color. However, if green peppers are allowed to turn red before picking, their vitamin C content will be higher. The hot varieties are picked when ripe and usually a bright red. All peppers should be cut from the plant with $\frac{1}{2}$ inch of stem, not pulled. —*Barbara J. Hardy.*

See also VEGETABLE GARDENING; PIPER.

PEPPER BUSH: *see* CLETHRA

PEPPER GRASS: *see* CRESS

PEPPERMINT: (*Mentha piperita*) A perennial herb frequently growing wild in moist situations throughout the eastern half of the United States. The volatile oil, which is widely used for flavoring chewing gum, confections, and dentifrices and in medicines, is the principal marketable product, but there is some demand in the crude-drug trade for the dried leaves and flowering tops. Its leaves are much used for tea also.

Peppermint can be grown on any land that will produce good crops of corn, but is most successful on the muck lands of reclaimed swamps. It is propagated by stolons, commonly called roots or runners, which are laid almost end to end in furrows about three feet apart and covered to a depth of about four inches. The first year the crop is grown as "row" mint, but in fall and the following year the plants spread all over the ground and thereafter for several years it is grown as "meadow" mint. It is essential that the ground be kept free from weeds, since their presence in the crop at harvest seriously reduces the quality of the oil.

The upright stems of peppermint grow over two feet high; the plant is propagated by cuttings or division. *See also* MINT.

PEPPER-TREE: *see* SCHINUS

PEPPERWORT: (*Marsilea*) These aquatic herbs do not have flowers, but are interesting for their floating, clover-shaped leaves. They are very easy to grow in pools or aquaria, *M. quadrifolia* being a hardy plant that may become a pest, completely choking a pool; *M. drummondi,* sometimes called nardoo, is grown outdoors only in the deep South, but is suited to greenhouse pools and aquaria elsewhere. Pepperworts are called fern allies, because they reproduce by spores.

PERENNIALS: Any plant which lives for more than two years is considered a perennial. This includes woody plants like trees, shrubs and many vines. But usually when the gardener speaks of perennials, he is referring to herbaceous perennials. The stems of these are not woody and die down to the ground annually (except for a few evergreen perennials), but the plant persists by means of its underground parts.

Perennials are adapted to a wide variety of conditions. Some are found growing wild in wet spots; others thrive on rocky hillsides or dusty, gravelly soils; some in rich bottomlands.

A few of them are practically "liveforevers." Others start to fail after the second year or die out after three or four years. But all of them have a place, whether it be in borders, grouped under shrubbery, in rock or wall gardens, or in naturalized settings or the wild garden.

Beautiful perennials for any setting are numerous, but even the most confirmed enthusiast will admit that you can't make a whole garden or even a whole border of perennials and get constant bloom through the season. Most perennials have comparatively short blooming periods. In England, where pure perennial gardens are quite common, the damper climate makes for longer bloom, but here the climate usually just won't allow it (except perhaps in the Pacific Northwest). It is necessary to fill in with annuals and bulbs.

But the often spectacular bloom and interesting foliage of perennials nevertheless makes them the mainstay of the flower garden. Next to trees and shrubs, they are the plants that most add stability and permanence. In every situation and climate, there are perennials that will thrive.

Among the most long-lived species are bleeding heart, peony, Japanese anemone, goldenrod, day-lilies, paniculate phlox, plantain lilies, dictamnus, and border chrysanthemums.

PROPAGATION: The perennials that are true to species are most easily propagated by seed. They may be sown in spring or midsummer, in a well-prepared seedbed or in pots or flats in a cold frame or greenhouse. These will give strong plants by fall, plants that will bloom the following year. Aquilegias and other strong-germinating seeds may be sown where the plants are to grow. Seeds of a few perennials, such as phlox, must be sown immediately after ripening or they will not germinate. It's a good idea to have a special propagating bed somewhere in your garden for starting new plants and storing surplus ones.

Many durable perennials may be propagated by division of their mature clumps, and some from late summer cuttings from main shoots. Most perennials should be divided and reset every three or four years.

SOIL: A rich soil, not too heavy, is best for practically all perennials. It should be light and crumbly, well-drained but moisture-retaining, amply supplied with humus.

The best way to provide this is to dig at least 18 inches deep and work in a three-inch layer of leaf mold or peat moss, plus a one-inch layer of rotted manure or compost; increase these amounts if your soil is poor to start with.

TRANSPLANTING: Thin your seedlings as soon as they have their first true leaves, and give them plenty of room at all times. Transplanting is best done in the fall, at least four to six weeks before freezing weather is expected. Eight or ten weeks before is even better in order to let the plants get well established. Always water thoroughly when transplanting.

MULCHING: Mulching in late fall is recommended, even though the plants are hardy. After frost has penetrated the ground an inch or so, apply a mulch three to six inches thick, depending on the severity of your winters. It should be a light mulch, such as strawy manure, pine needles, fresh or partly decayed leaves, peat moss or salt hay. Be careful not to smother any plants that have evergreen leaves. Mulch under these, and use evergreen boughs to protect their upper portions. Many growers believe in leaving a two- to three-inch mulch under their perennials all year round. *See also* FLOWER GARDENING (PERENNIALS); BORDER.

PERESKIA: A genus of the cactus family which bears true alternate leaves persistent to the extent that they may be said to be evergreen. Species, which may be shrubby, tree- or vine-like, are native to the West Indies, Central, and South America. Spines in the axils of the leaves but no barbs. White, yellow, pink or red flowers in small clusters on stems. Juicy fruit, which is edible in some species. Easily propagated by cuttings.

Barbados gooseberry (*P. aculeata*) also sometimes called lemon-vine, grows to a woody vine ten to 20 feet long, with thick leaves, two or three recurved spines, and edible fruit.

P. bleo grows to a 20-foot tree with a smooth trunk, with spines in clusters of five or six on mature wood, lance-shaped leaves to eight inches, flowers rose-red.

P. grandifolia is a shrubby tree to 15 feet with a spiny trunk, leaves six inches long, flower rose or white, and fruit pear-shaped and leafy. Spines are single or in pairs.

PERIWINKLE: (*Vinca minor*) Also known as creeping or running myrtle, periwinkle is a trailing, hardy evergreen often used as a ground cover

for shady areas. It is also a fine plant for edging a window box or for growing in hanging baskets or vases. Periwinkle makes a slender growth one to two feet long. A variegated form has leaves marked with yellow. *See also* GROUND COVERS; VINCA.

PERSEA AMERICANA: *see* AVOCADO

PERSIAN CLOVER: *see* GREEN MANURE

PERSIMMON: (*Diospyros*) Often used as an ornamental, the deciduous Japanese persimmon tree (*D. kaki*) grows as high as 40 feet, producing three-inch long orange-colored edible fruit. It can stand temperatures as low as 15°, but does best in warmer regions. Hachiya is a highly successful variety.

The common or American persimmon grows higher than the Japanese type, and is also hardier, being grown as far north as the Great Lakes. Ripening season is from the middle of summer through December. Recommended variety is Early Golden.

The date plum (*P. lotus*) is deciduous, grows to 40 feet and produces green or red blooms.

Persimmons do well in a wide range of soil types, being known to grow satisfactorily in poor soils. General procedures regarding planting, mulching and fertilizing persimmons are similar to other fruit trees. *See also* ORCHARD; FRUIT TREES.

PESTICIDE: Any one of a number of deadly chemical sprays which are used to kill insects and other harmful life in horticultural and agricultural areas. The use of pesticides is not condoned in the organic method because of the harm done to beneficial insects and soil life, and because of the potential threat to human health. *See also* INSECTICIDES.

PESTS: *see* INSECT CONTROL

PETAL: *see* FLOWER

PETALOSTEMON: Also known as prairie clover. A genus of herbs, mostly perennial, of the pea family, *Leguminosae,* native in North America and hardy in the lower Mississippi basin. Generally not cultivated, except for specimens transferred from the wild to rock or wild gardens. Flowers pea-like, in clusters, and colored white, pink, rose and purple.

White tassel-flowers (*P. candidum*) grows to two feet, with white flowers and compound leaves. Four-inch flower spikes followed by clusters of hairy legume pods.

P. decumbens is a semi-trailing form, with short spikes of pink flowers.

Red tassel-flower (*P. purpureum*) is one of the most hardy species, growing north into Saskatchewan. It grows three feet tall, and has two-inch spikes of violet or purple flowers.

Another hardy species is *P. villosum,* which grows as far north as Michigan. Its rose-purple spikes are four inches long, on two-foot semi-trailing stems.

PETASITES: Butterbur. Members of the daisy family, *Compositeae,* blooming early in spring when they send up spikes of fragrant lilac to white flower heads from fleshy perennial roots, followed by mats of low-lying wooly leaves. They spread quickly and easily by root runners, and are useful only as cover for barren spots where little else will grow. Increased by division, or by seeds.

Winter heliotrope or sweet coltsfoot (*P. fragrans*) has evergreen leaves, silky below, and small purple flower heads. Grows to one foot.

P. frigidus grows as far north as Alaska, with triangular or heart-shaped leaves.

A large species, *P. japonicus,* is useful as a food. Growing to six feet, the stems are used as a vegetable and the flower buds as a seasoning herb on its native island, off the coast of Siberia.

PE-TSAI: *see* Chinese Cabbage

PETUNIA: The genus of annuals of the nightshade family from which many garden varieties have been developed. Originally hybridized from two species, the hybrids are much more important now than their forbears. Original petunia species had straggling stems, sticky and weak leaves and flower stalks bearing fragrant white, purple, or reddish salver-shaped blossoms all summer. Two natives of Argentina were used to develop the hybrids found in modern gardens. They were the large white petunia (*P. axillaris*) with flowers about two inches long, and *P. violacea,* the violet-flowered petunia, whose 1½ inch flowers ranged through rose to reddish purple.

The common garden petunia, *P. hybrida,* comes in many varieties, colors, and sizes up to five inches across and 3½ inches long. Some of the named varieties are *alba, compacta, elegans, fimbriata, gigantea, grandiflora, kermesina, maculata, nana, pendula, purpurea, rosea,* and *superbissima.* Flowers are singles, doubles, ruffled, crisped, marked with stars, eyes, and margins, in white, pink, lavender, rose, blue, red, and purple. Two types of growth are compact and bushy, for bedding, or trailing (the balcony petunias), for window boxes.

CULTURE: Petunias are tender to frost, but can be carried over the winter if cuttings of young shoots are rooted in fall before the frost. The cuttings are kept cool in the greenhouse until February, when they are brought into the sun and cultivated for planting out when the weather is warm. Only the finer strains are handled in this way, the commoner sorts being grown from seed. The tiny seeds are planted indoors about ten weeks before planting out, and seedlings transplanted to individual pots before hardening off for the garden. Petunias will grow in partial shade, but blossom most freely in the sun. They like a moist, rich soil, but will grow also where the soil is dry.

VARIETIES: Hybridizers have had a keen interest in the simple petunia so a multitude of varieties have been developed. Seeds of the Giant varieties, double and hybrid should be started early, but the dwarf and bedding petunias are comparatively early flowering and therefore more successful for planting later in the season. Miniature or Gem petunias are dwarf varieties. The plants are neat and compact, about six inches tall. Rose Gem, Violet Gem, and White Gem are typical varieties. There is also a semi-dwarf group. These grow about a foot tall and flower very freely. Rosy Morn is one of the most popular varieties of this group. There are also Peach Red, Fire Chief, Blue Bird, and many others.

Bedding petunias branch and are more sprawling. They need to be sheared back occasionally in order to maintain continuous bloom. Snowstorm, Radiance and Flaming Velvet are good examples of this type.

The ruffled, fringed and double petunias are beyond description. Large blooms in a multitude of shades and shapes are available. It is best to consult the seed catalogs to see the large selection.

USES: Petunias are adaptable plants. They can be planted as an edging for a walk or terrace, as a cover for banks, in porch or window boxes, hanging baskets, and as a whole bed or clumps scattered throughout the border. *See also* ANNUALS; FLOWER GARDENING.

PFEIFFER, DR. EHRENFRIED E.: A foremost pioneer in biodynamics, Dr. Pfeiffer is world-known as an agricultural scientist, nutritionist and biological researcher. Starting with his studies of the biochemistry of plant growth in 1926, after his graduation from the University of Basle, Switzerland, he became active with gardeners and farmers in various parts of Europe who were making the first field tests of Dr. Rudolf Steiner's bio-dynamic method. Pfeiffer progressed to a scientific study of this system and of the relationship of plants to the humus-forming processes in the soil.

In Europe—principally Holland and Switzerland—he worked for several years, directing experimental farms. His agricultural advisory work and lecturing have taken him through all of this nation as well as to France, England, Egypt, East Africa and Dutch East Indies. Besides a considerable number of scientific books, Dr. Pfeiffer has written many articles on his research and the bio-dynamic method. From 1940 to 1944, he directed Kimberton Farms and Kimberton Agricultural School at Phoenixville, Pa. He now maintains his own farm at Chester, N. Y., is president of the English Bio-dynamic Association for Soil and Crop Improvement, a member of the American Association for the Advancement of Science, and scientific adviser to the Bio-dynamic Farming and Gardening Association in the U. S.

Since 1945, Dr. Pfeiffer has renewed his studies at the Biochemical Research Laboratory at Threefold Farm, Spring Valley, New York, of which he is director. *See also* BIODYNAMIC METHOD.

pH: The term pH is the method of expressing the amount of soil acidity or alkalinity.

The pH scale runs from 0 to 14. The 0 end of the scale is the acid end, while the 14 end of the scale is the alkaline end. A soil testing a pH of 7.0 will be exactly neutral. A soil testing any number greater than 7.0, for example, 8.5, will be an alkaline soil. Likewise, a soil testing less than 7.0, for example, 6.0, will be an acid soil.

In general, most common vegetables, field crops, and fruits, and flowers do best on soils that have a pH of 6.5 to 7.0, in other words, on a soil that is slightly acid to neutral. Especially if plenty of organic matter is present in the soil, most plants will generally do fairly well on soils that have a lower or higher pH. A few plants, such as azaleas, camellias, and gardenias do best on a quite acid soil.

For an extensive discussion of pH values, see ACIDITY-ALKALINITY; LIME.

PHACELIA: Also known as Bee's friend. A genus of annual or perennial herbs of the water-leaf family, *Hydrophyllaceae,* native to North America. Only a few are grown as ornamental plants. Blue, purple, or white flaring bell-shaped flowers grow in loose, one-sided clusters, often with decorative sterile white anthers protruding from the bells. Leaves are velvety and simple or compound on reddish stems; leaves also are reddish when young and attract many bees. Easily grown from seed where they are to grow, but do not transplant well. Often self-seed. Perennial species may be propagated by division, and thrive in any good garden soil.

California bluebell (*P. campanularia*) is an eight-inch annual with blue flowers and white anthers, used in masses as a low border. Blossoming period lasts about one month.

Also called California bluebell is *P. whitlavia,* which grows to 1½ feet, and has purple or blue flowers, with variety *gloxinoides* white with blue centers and *alba,* all white.

Fiddleneck (*P. tanacetifolia*) grows to three feet, with slender hairy leaves, and blue or lilac blossoms, both stamens and style protruding.

PHALARIS: *see* REED CANARY GRASS

PHASE: A *phase* or, more specifically, a *soil phase* is a subdivision in soil terminolgy, based on some important deviation such as erosion, slope, stoniness, or soluble salt content. It marks a departure from the normal, or key type, already established. Thus, a Cecil sandy loam, eroded phase, or a Hagerstown silt loam, stony phase, are examples of soils where distinctions are made in respect to the phase. *See also* SOILS.

PHASEOLUS: Genus of the pea family, *Leguminaceae,* which includes two important garden beans, snap beans and lima beans. Not included in the genus are broad beans, genus *vicia,* or soybeans, genus *glycine.* Also included in *Phaseolus* is the scarlet runner bean, grown for ornament. Mostly twining vines with three-part leaves and typical pea flowers, red, purple, or white, in clusters, followed by flat pods. Bush varieties of garden beans are horticultural developments.

Various species are grown in all parts of the world for food. Among those grown in India and Asia are the mat bean or moth bean (*P. aconitifolius*) with gray and black mottled seeds; Adzuki bean, (*P. angularis*) with variously colored seed; Mung bean (*P. aureus*) with small seed, sometimes blackish; rice bean (*P. calcaratus*) with yellow flowers and seed which is red, black, brown, or yellowish; and black gram (*P. mungo*) also called the urd or gram, with white-spotted black beans.

Two species are grown as ornament, though seeds are edible and are sometimes grown in other countries as food. They are snail-flower or corkscrew flower (*P. caracalla*), a fragrant yellowish or purplish flowered tender perennial vine, and scarlet runner bean (*P. coccineus*) also a tender perennial but grown as an annual, with showy red flowers. Scarlet runner is used as a quick-growing climber for screening or for covering unsightly fences and buildings.

Beans grown for food in this country belong chiefly to the species *P. vulgaris,* and include kidney beans, string beans, and several varieties dried and sold as navy beans and marrow beans. Variety *humulis* is the bush bean. Lima beans belong to species *Limensis,* and are perennial in tropical America. Bush limas are variety *limeanus. See also* BEANS; LIMA BEANS.

PHELLODENDRON. Known as the cork-tree, this is a genus of ornamental trees of the rue family, *Rutaceae.* (Not grown for cork, which is made from cork-oak, *Quercus suber.*) Cork trees are hardy, have attractive dark green foliage and rounded heads, growing to 50 feet in some species. Inconspicuous flowers, male in some trees and female in others, are followed by blackish clusters of berry-like fruits, which persist long after the leaves have turned yellow and fallen. Fruit and leaves are both aromatic.

Cork-tree thrives in almost any soil, and is easily grown. Propagation is by seed, root cuttings, or greenwood cuttings. Most commonly cultivated are Amur cork-tree (*P. amurense*) growing to 50 feet, with deeply furrowed gray bark; and *P. chinense,* 30 feet, with smoother brown bark.

PHILODENDRON: A genus of the arum family, *Araceae,* comprising woody climbers native in the tropics and grown in the United States mainly as house plants or greenhouse specimens. Many of the large-leaved varieties have recently become popular because of their suitability in modern interiors. Characterized by thick glossy leaves, more or less heart- or arrow-shaped, sometimes pinnately cut. In the tropics the vines climb by means of aerial roots produced from the leaf joints, which attach to tree trunks. As house plants, if they are given a mossy or roughly barked stake to climb on, they will make use of it provided it is kept damp.

The most commonly grown species is *P. cordatum,* with heart-shaped leaves which will grow as much as 16 inches long and six inches wide. It may be grown on a stake, as described above, or as a trailing vine.

The larger leaved varieties should be given support.

P. erubescens also has heart-shaped glossy leaves, whose undersurface is red. *Mandaianum* is similar, but redder; *hastatum* glossy, heart-shaped, and green; *sodiroi* heart-shaped gray, with green at margins and along midrib; *panduriforme,* called horse's head or fiddle philodendron, has three-lobed green leaves; *imbe* is like *hastatum* but has red-spotted leaf stalks; and *squamiferum* has five-lobed leaves, its stalks covered with red hairs.

Often mis-named *P. pertusum* is *Monstera deliciosa,* member of an allied genus, with deeply notched leaves, from which it gets its common name, Swiss cheese plant.

Philodendrons respond well to moderately good care, and make good decorative house plants because they thrive in situations where they do not get direct sunlight. They should be placed in a strong light, but not direct sun. They need rich soil and plenty of moisture. They will grow for long periods in water, but should be potted after roots have developed. Well-rooted plants should be given an occasional drink of manure water. Propagation is by cuttings. *See also* HOUSE PLANTS.

PHLOX: A perennial and annual genus of the *Polemoniaceae* family.

A very desirable feature of these flowers is their ability to produce blossoms over a long period. Their blossoms begin unfolding in early spring and provide a continuous array of beauty throughout the spring and summer season. Phlox can provide the "backbone" of the summer garden.

CULTURE: To grow it well, the soil should be well-drained, deeply spaded and have a goodly amount of compost added. It may be planted in the fall or spring in a sunny location, and it makes a beautiful foundation planting on the east and south side of a building, furnishing a beautiful color contrast to a white background.

The plants require very little, if any, protection during the winter. They should, however, be dug up and divided every three or four years or they will become too crowded and as a result will have poor, small

Phlox vary in height from a few inches to four feet. They blossom over a long period and make fine foundation plantings in a sunny location.

flowers. They should never be let go to seed, nor should they be watered overhead. When watering becomes necessary, let the hose run slowly on the ground and thus keep the blooms and foliage dry. This method will prevent mildew.

The natural growth of phlox is to produce a large main head of blossoms, but they can be topped in early spring, which causes them to branch out and produce more and smaller clusters.

Phlox are versatile and congenial as they lend themselves to many arrangements according to the individual desire. Their vivid colors are sure to make a lasting impression when arranged in individual beds on the lawn or in the garden. There are small varieties that lend themselves to the rock garden, or you may want to use them in conjunction with your rose bed.

VARIETIES: Phlox vary in size from a few inches to as high as four feet; there are crawling as well as upright types. The annual varieties can be sown in early spring in a cold frame, or outdoors when the weather becomes warmer. The seed should be planted very shallowly in fine soil. The perennial types are grown from cuttings or root division.

Phlox varieties include the annual phlox (*P. drummondi*)—an erect grower to 18 inches with white purple flowers; Blue phlox (*P. divaricata*)—an erect perennial to 18 inches with creeping stems; trailing phlox (*P. nivalis*)—prostrate perennial with white or pink flowers; wild sweet William (*P. maculata*) an erect perennial reaching three feet with purple or pink flowers; and garden phlox (*P. paniculata*) a perennial with stems to four feet high and large clusters of flowers in a variety of colors. *See also* FLOWER GARDENING.

PHOENIX DACTYLIFERA: *see* DATE

PHOSPHATE ROCK: An excellent natural source of phosphorus for fertilizer use. Phosphate rock varies somewhat in its composition dependent upon its source; however, the general constituents are as follows: Calcium Phosphate or bone phosphate of lime composes 65 per cent of the total (equivalent P_2O_5—30 per cent). Phosphate rock contains other compounds and mineral elements, many of which are essential for plant growth; included are calcium carbonate, calcium fluoride, iron oxide, iron sulphide, alumina, silica, manganese dioxide, titanium oxide, sodium, copper, chromium, magnesium, strontium, barium, lead, zinc, vanadium, boron, silver, and iodine.

The phosphate rock sold on the market today is different from that of a few decades ago. Phosphate rock today has been much more finely ground. In the old days the machinery for grinding the raw phosphate rock into a powder was quite crude so that ground-up particles were coarse and did not break down too easily in the soil. However, today there is such elaborate machinery available that the rock can be ground finer than talcum powder, thus a sufficient part of it is immediately available to the plant because the particles are so tiny that the organic acids and carbon dioxide produced by the plant roots and bacteria in the soil can break them down quickly.

Many of the minor elements found in phosphate rock are inactivated in the superphosphate process. Such elements as boron, zinc, nickel, iodine and others are available in rock phosphate but not in superphosphate.

Phosphorus may be added to the compost heap and to the soil in the form of raw pulverized phosphate rock or as bone meal. The soil acids will make these relatively inert forms of phosphorus soluble in sufficient amounts to meet the needs of the plants.

SUPERPHOSPHATE: The difference between superphosphate and rock phosphate is that the former has been treated with an equal amount of sulphuric acid to make it more soluble. This results in mono-calcium-phosphate, a slowly water soluble phosphate and calcium sulphate, a highly soluble neutral salt. One of the bad things about sulphur, of many others, is that it causes sulphur reducing bacteria to multiply which work on it to reduce it. But these sulphur reducing bacteria have to feed, and part of their diet is a certain fungus whose function is to break down cellulose in the soil. It becomes a vicious cycle. Sulphur multiplies a bacteria which destroys certain badly needed fungi. The use of superphosphate, therefore causes an imbalance in the micro-biological population of the soil.

Rock phosphate, on the other hand, is not highly water soluble and is lost in the soil only through cropping. The beneficial effects of rock phosphate far outlast those of superphosphate. Rock phosphate, when finely ground is available to the plant as it needs it. Plant roots give off carbon dioxide and certain organic acids, which in contact with the rock phosphate in the soil, make it available for plant use. Thus, that rock phosphate which is not made available by the action of plant roots remains unchanged in the soil until roots develop in its vicinity.

HUMUS AND PHOSPHATE: In his article, "Organic Matter . . . The Key to Phosphate Availability," Dale H. Sieling, Dean of the University of Massachusetts School of Agriculture, wrote that additions of chemical phosphate "usually have only a very temporary beneficial effect because the action of certain soil components changes the phosphate into forms not readily available to plants. In fact, some experiments with radio-active phosphorus have shown that only five to ten per cent of the phosphate added to acid soils reaches the crop for which it was intended."

He recommends following the procedure of "practical farmers (who) have long observed that loss of organic matter in soils caused phosphate deficiency and consequent crop failure. Others have found that management practices which traditionally included the addition of large amounts of barnyard manure were adequate for great crop production, even though the manure was known to be low in phosphate."

PROFITABLE: Reports also point out the added profit in using rock phosphate, since it is actually less expensive than superphosphate. A. L. Lang, professor of Agronomy at the University of Illinois, reports on the lasting quality of rock phosphate. "Laid down once in a rotation, rock phosphate will have plenty of reserve plant food at the end of four or five years." As an example of this permanence, he cites a demonstration plot in Urbana, Illinois, where 1,500 pounds of rock phosphate per acre were applied in 1935 on land which was continually cropped without the addition of any other fertilizer except limestone until 1949. At the end of these 15 years the gross returns over limestone amounted to $129.67 an acre or $8.65 for each dollar invested. In the same experiment an equal amount of money spent for superphosphate returned only $4.90 per dollar invested during the same period.

Professor Lang concludes: "This is the kind of return which makes us feel here in Illinois that rock phosphate is a good investment and that it will make a good investment in any part of the country where there is a phosphorus deficiency, particularly in the acid soils of the South."

In most grain growing areas, the limiting factors in production are poor physical structure and inadequate amounts of phosphate, nitrogen and water. Limestone and rock phosphate, states Professor Lang, have been used to eliminate these confining factors. This is done by applying them not to the grain crop but to the legume and grass in the rotation in large enough quantities to insure immediate response and maximum growth. The legumes supply the soil with nitrogen and, together with the grasses, add active organic matter which improves the physical structure of the soil and increases its water holding capacity. In many sections of the country rock phosphate use is on the recommended list of conservation practices for which the Production and Marketing Administration will contribute about half of the cost.

APPLICATION RATE: For vegetable and flower gardens, apply liberally around plants and mix with top inch of soil. Generally, one pound for ten square feet is enough for three to five years. The same application is usu-

ally recommended for lawns. *See also* FERTILIZER; ROCK FERTILIZER; MINERAL ROCK.

PHOSPHORUS: A major element in plant nutrition, which all plants need. It is essential for healthy growth, strong roots, fruit development, and greater resistance to diseases. When soils are first put under cultivation, there is a fast decay of organic matter. This decay produces carbonic and nitric acids within the soil that release the insoluble phosphates. As the humus decreases, so do the acids; soon there is a phosphate deficiency. This has commonly happened in midwestern soils of the United States, and phosphate deficiency is considered by many agronomists to be the limiting factor in crop production.

Rock phosphate is most commonly used as a source of phosphorus by organic growers. (See the previous entry). A discussion of other sources follows:

BONE MEAL

Bones have been used for centuries as a fertilizer, their value recognized first in England. They have long been recognized as an excellent source of phosphorus as well as nitrogen.

In the early days of farming in this country, great amounts of buffalo bones were collected on western plains for use as fertilizer. Now the main source of bone meal comes from the slaughter-houses. Consisting mostly of calcium phosphate, the phosphorus and nitrogen content in bone fertilizers depends mainly on the kind and age of the bone. According to Prof. G. H. Collings of Clemson Agricultural College, young bones generally contain less phosphorus and more nitrogen than older bones. The percentage of fluorine in older bones is considerably higher than in younger bones.

RAW BONE MEAL: This material generally contains between two to four per cent nitrogen, 22 to 25 per cent phosphoric acid. Because of the fatty materials found in raw bone meal, decomposition is somewhat delayed when it is applied to the soil.

STEAMED BONE MEAL: Most common of the bone meal fertilizers sold. This type is made from green bones that have been boiled or steamed at high pressure to remove the fats. Its removal causes a slight loss in nitrogen content, but a relative increase in phosphorus. When the bones are steamed, they can be ground more easily and are considered to be in better condition for the soil; steamed bone meal is almost always finer than raw bone meal. Steamed bone meal contains one to two per cent nitrogen, up to 30 per cent phosphorus.

BONE BLACK: Charred bone, with a nitrogen content of about 1.5 per cent, a phosphoric acid content over 30 per cent, and many traces.

Best results for bone meal are obtained when it is applied in conjunction with other organic materials. Its effectiveness is increased because of its nitrogen content. In general bone meal acts more quickly when applied to well-aerated soils. Because of its lime content, bone meal tends to reduce soil acidity.

OTHER PHOSPHATE SOURCES

MATERIAL	PHOSPHORIC ACID PER CENT
Marine Products	
Shrimp waste (dried)	10
Dried ground fish	7
Lobster refuse	3.5
Dried Blood	1 to 5
Tankage	2
Hoof and Horn Meal	2
Wool wastes	2-4
Cottonseed Meal	2-3
Raw Sugar wastes	8
Rape seed meal	1 to 2
Cocoa wastes	1.5
Castor Pomace	1 to 2
Silk Mill wastes	1.14
Activated sludge	2.5-4.0
Manure	
Poultry manure, fresh	1-1.5
dried	1.5-2.0

MATERIAL	PHOSPHORIC ACID PER CENT
Goat and Sheep Manure, fresh	0.6
dried	1.0-1.9
Hog Manure, fresh	0.45
Horse Manure, fresh	0.35
dried	1.0
Cow Manure, fresh	0.25
dried	1.0
Wood ashes	1-2
Pea Pod wastes (ashed)	3
Banana residue (ashed)	2.3-3.3
Apple pomace (ashed skin)	3
Citrus wastes (orange skins, ashed)	3

See also FERTILIZER; MINERAL ROCKS.

PHOTOSYNTHESIS: The process of forming starches and sugars that takes place in leaves in the presence of water and plant nutrients brought up from the roots, carbon dioxide from the air, chlorophyll in the leaf tissues, and light. Chloroplasts, microscopic bodies in the leaves which carry the green leaf coloring, manufacture carbohydrates using radiant energy from the sun for their power source. Thus leaves are the only known agents which are capable of transforming the sun's energy to food energy. *See also* LIGHT.

PHYLLANTHUS ACIDUS: *see* OTAHEITE GOOSEBERRY

PHYSALIS: Known as ground cherry, these are herbaceous annuals and perennials of the nightshade family, *Solanaceae.* Usually trailing or creeping, with small axillary flowers whose calyx often becomes large and papery to enclose fruits. Fruit cases keep for a number of weeks, and are used in dried flower arrangements. Some fruits are edible.

P. alkekengi, the winter cherry or Chinese lantern plant, is sometimes grown for its orange to yellow papery two-inch lanterns. It grows from long fleshy underground stems which spread rapidly, and become a nuisance in the garden if they are not planted in a confined area.

Tomatillo (*P. ixocarpa*) is a Mexican native which has been grown in northern gardens. It is a three to four-foot annual, with ¾ inch yellow flowers with black spots, and a fruit calyx veined with purple. Also called Mexican ground cherry.

Cape gooseberry (*P. peruviana*) is a tender perennial with an edible yellow berry enclosed in a long pointed calyx. It grows in the tropics.

Strawberry tomato, husk tomato, or dwarf cape-gooseberry (*P. pruinosa*) has fruit quite similar to *P. peruviana*, but it is distinguished by its hairy stems and fruit calyx. It is also edible.

Most species of the *physalis* like a warm, sunny bed, and need a long growing period to develop color in the calyxes, so seed should be sown early indoors. Perennials may also be propagated by root division.

PHYSOCARPUS: *see* NINEBARK

PHYSOSTEGIA: A genus of three species hardy perennials of the mint family, *Labiatae*, known as false dragonhead, American heather, obedient plant, Mexican heath, and accommodation flower. August blossoms are rose-purple, pink, or white, and resemble spikes of miniature snapdragons. The plants grow two to four feet tall, have neat lance-shaped leaves, toothed, and make compact clumps in a short time. They prefer a moist soil in either full sun or partial shade; are propagated by seed or division of clumps. Flowers last well as cut flowers.

P. virginiana is the most cultivated species, having flower spikes to eight inches long. The type has rose-pink to lilac flowers. Varieties are *alba*, white flowered; *gigantea*, to seven feet; *nana, rosea, rubra, splendens*, and *superba*.

PHYTOLACCA: *see* POKEWEED

PICEA: *see* SPRUCE

PIERIS FLORIBUNDA: *see* MOUNTAIN FETTER-BUSH

PIGEONS: Pigeons and squabs can be raised economically and profitably on the small homestead. Squabs increase in weight 40 times in 25 days over their weight at birth. They, like most domesticated birds, respond to good housing. A draft-free building is a prerequisite, though it needn't be pretentious.

Squabs are ready for market when they are fully feathered under the wing and just about ready to leave the nest—from 25 to 28 days old.

Pigeons mate at about six months age, in pairs, and stay that way. They lay two eggs which hatch in 18 days. The parent birds take regular shift turns at setting, and do all the feeding of their squabs. Squabs are ready for marketing or eating at 28 to 30 days of age—as soon as the body feathers under the wings have grown out.

Breeding pigeons may be kept up to 25 pairs in a pen and loft together. Their lofts must always be dry and without drafts. They may be raised anywhere. Pigeons need sunshine. Often their flying pen extends up over a small part of the loft roof, allowing them to perch and sun themselves. But they do not need a large fly pen. Make it six by ten by seven feet high, and of one inch mesh wire. Use two inches of fine gravel on the ground.

The loft floor should be smooth wood so as to be easily scraped. Use open front lofts in warmer climates, and closed fronts with a large, opening glass window in colder climates. Never give the pigeons nesting material. It is useless, messes up the floor, and prevents the accretion of valuable manure from remaining pure. Nest bowls will keep eggs and squabs together. After a few months use they may be discarded and fresh ones used.

Each breeding pair of pigeons will need two nests—one for the current squabs and the other for the start of a second nest when first squabs are some two weeks old.

Provide a drinking fountain so that the birds may drink without fouling the water. Pigeons are very clean by nature. They love to bathe. Place a large bath pan with three inches of water in it in their flying pen twice weekly on fine mornings for an hour. Then remove, wash, empty. Pigeons kept in a clean, dry loft and allowed to bathe regularly don't have insect pests.

It's generally cheaper to buy your grains unmixed, and feed that way. Use a whole, small, hard yellow corn. Instead of the very expensive Canadian pea use the small, brown Austrian peas. Cost two-thirds as much and birds like them much better.

Pigeons eat grain feeds in this ratio of preference: Corn, 40 per cent; Austrian peas, 30 per cent; kaffir or milo, 20 per cent; and lastly, hard red wheat, ten per cent.

White and silver kings, and homers are considered fine breeds for squab producing. The white and silver birds produce a fine white or golden-skinned squab. Generally pigeons with blackish beaks and purplish or blackish feet will produce dark-skinned squabs.

In the pigeon world the male helps with the "nesting" sitting on the nest from early morning to late afternoon, the female during the rest of the day. This fact may help in sexing the pairs to be kept for breeding. The male may also be more aggressive, with coarser appearance and larger size.

During incubation a substance forms in the crops of both male and female birds, called "pigeon milk or curd," on which the young are fed for the first five or six days, or until they can digest grain. At first the grain is given in the squabs' mouth from the crops of the parents, the same as the milk. The parents feed the young shortly after partaking of a meal themselves, and young birds are quickly affected if feed is moldy, sour or spoiled.

Squabs are ready to be killed when the feathers under the wings are just past pin feather stage and should not be kept longer. They will not have left the nest at this stage.

Soft, immature carcasses and beaks identify a squab rather than a tough pigeon and this means a difference of 50 cents or more in price. They are choice meat for home use, and can be kept in all parts of the United States. In addition to the food angle, pigeons give recreation through flying and exhibition projects, and perhaps this article will serve as a gentle reminder to those who would like a new addition to the poultry on the farm. —*Gordon L'Allemand.*

PIGS: Hickory-smoked bacon and ham, fresh tasty pork, lard and sausages for the whole family—that's what keeping a couple of pigs on your homestead can mean. A home-raised, 200-pound pig will dress out about 125 pounds, worth more than $50 to your larder. And a pig is one of the easiest animals to keep and feed.

One of the most popular of all lean-meat breeds of pigs is the Yorkshire. Other good ones are Duroc-Jersey, Berkshire, Hampshire, Poland-China, Chester White and Tamworth.

It's best to buy weaned, eight-weeks-old pigs, always choosing whenever possible the largest and huskiest-looking in the litter. Select barrows—castrated males—if possible, and look for animals that have short legs, compact shoulders and plump hams. They should weigh between 25 and 40 pounds. You can locate pigs for sale by watching the classified ads in your local paper, or buy them by mail from ads in regional farm magazines.

PEN: A sanitary pig pen is easy to build, and most experiment stations have plans for these. Pigs, by the way, are very clean animals, contrary to what most people believe. Given a large enough yard, they will always leave their droppings in one corner. Pig manure is a valuable fertilizer, and should be handled the same way as rabbit manure.

Under the confinement system, you can supply a large part of the feed for a couple of pigs from garden wastes— pea vines, cabbage leaves and the like —plus table scraps. Some grain and fresh greens or good cured hay fill out the diet. Skim milk and home-raised corncob meal is also excellent feed. A mineral mixture of two pounds of oyster shell or limestone flour to two of bone meal and one of salt, fed one pound to every five pounds of feed, will take care of mineral needs.

The thing to remember is that pigs need a balanced diet much like that of a human being as regards vitamins, proteins and so on. Garden wastes and clean kitchen or restaurant garbage are all the feed many a commercial piggery gives its pigs. There is no danger of overfeeding, for a pig will never overeat.

PASTURE: The pasture system is unbeatable for raising pigs. Good pasture can supply from 20 to 30 per cent of a pig's total feed requirements. Alfalfa, clover and rape, or a mixture of rape and oats produced the most pork per acre in Missouri Experiment Station tests. Sudan grass, sorghum and soybeans are good summer pastures, and rye, rye grass or winter barley for later in the season. An acre of good forage will handle up to 20 pigs weighing 100 pounds apiece, with their grain or garbage ration cut in half. A few pigs, incidentally, will root out quackgrass and eat the plants, roots and all, from a surprisingly big plot in a few days.

A movable, easily constructed house is used in the pasture system. Self-feeders, troughs and automatic waterers can also be home-built from experiment station bulletins. Natural or artificially-provided shade is also important.

You can buy young pigs for feeding either in spring or fall. Those kept over the winter need good shelter and adequate straw bedding. The shortage of green feed for wintering pigs, however, may mean a more substantial layout for vitamin and protein concentrates, unless you have a good source of legume hay and meat scraps.

Clean, fresh earth from a field where pigs have not been pastured for at least two years should always be available to pigs in confinement. A pig who cannot be outdoors to root in the ground still needs the trace elements it contains. Animal nutritionists believe soil may also contain other unknown substances vital to the assimilation of nutrients.

PIGWEED: *see* WEEDS

PILLBUG: *see* INSECT CONTROL

PIMPINELLA: *see* ANISE

PINCHING: Actually a method of pruning, since the tender growing tips of plants are nipped off with the nails of the first finger and thumb. The objective of pinching off the top bud is to develop the side buds in the axils of the leaves into side shoots. This gives the plant a stocky, well-branched appearance. The practice of pinching is often recommended over shearing, since shearing tends to cut into mature wood, while the cutting force of pinching is limited to thumb and fingernail strength, hence only tender, new growth can be cut.

House plants which are commonly pinched include English Ivy, fuschia, geranium and flowering maple; annuals include cosmos, marigold, verbena, ageratum and snapdragon; perennials include delphinium and phlox, while pinching is often done also to encourage sturdier growth in vegetable plants. *See also* PRUNING.

PINCUSHION CACTUS: This name is commonly applied to two groups of cacti, the *Mammillaria* and the *Coryphantha*. Both are favorite subjects for pot culture; a few of them are widely grown in desert gardens outdoors. Nearly all flower regularly, and many bear bright red fruits. They have spines in bunches at the end of each knob-like protuberance. Some of them have blooms that are enormous compared to the size of the plant.

Golden Stars (*M. elongata*) forms dense, erect clumps, each prominence tipped with long golden spines. Its big blooms are white and bell-shaped. Old lady (*M. hahniana*) is globular in shape, covered with snowy hair that gets thicker with age, and bears rose-carmine flowers. Snowball (*M. candida*) is neatly clustered, with dense white spines and rose flowers. Powder puff (*M. boscasana*) has single spines on each nipple, white silky hairs and white blooms. Grape cactus (*M. multiceps*) has reddish-yellow flowers, while bird's nest (*M. camptotricha*) carries as many as eight curving, yellow, papery spines on each nipple. The clusters of feather ball (*M. plumosa*) are completely hidden in the wooly hair and mass of short spines. There are many other varieties, some with lovely delicate pink flowers, and others that have as many as 60 spines per cluster. The *Coryphantha* are similar to *Mammillaria* in both habit and bloom. Both lend themselves well to miniature desert gardens in simple or ornate containers. *See also* CACTUS.

PINE: (*Pinus*) These gorgeous evergreen trees are widely cultivated as ornamentals and for timber. Over 50 species are grown in this country, varying from about 25 to over 150 feet in height.

Pines do best in a light soil, not too rich. Dry soil doesn't bother them because they have very deep-reaching roots, but exposure to dry, scorching winds will brown the needles; so will a warm late winter's sun, for which reason pines should not have a southern exposure. They are best planted on a northern slope. Pines are not easily moved except when quite young because of the long taproot.

Pruning a pine requires special knowledge. Cutting should be avoided. Examine the longest branches in fall, winter or spring for a cluster of buds and carefully remove the central bud. The remaining ones will develop into strong lateral branches.

SPECIES: Species pines are propagated by seed planted in late spring, varieties by veneer-grafting on closely related hardy species.

The white pine (*P. strobus*) is the most beautiful of our northeastern evergreens. Some of its forms are dwarf, others have variegated foliage, and one is columnar. The Swiss pine (*P. cembra*) is suitable for large specimen trees on estates; it is slow-growing and bears edible seeds. *P. nigra*, the Austrian pine, like *P. thunbergi*, the Japanese black pine, is planted throughout the country and is especially adapted to city growing; the latter is a very rapid grower. The rugged but not very handsome Jack pine (*P. banksiana*) is often grown on northern dunes. It has scraggly branches and twisted needles, but in the spring it bears oddly shaped flowers of great beauty that take 15 years to develop into the hard cones.

The Swiss mountain pine (*P. mugo*) and its many forms, which it assumes under different conditions of soil and climate, are widely cultivated. Occurring frequently as a prostrate shrub, in its native home it is a 60-foot tree with a girth of nine to ten feet. It is perfectly hardy, fine for low, massed plantings, and the foliage does not turn brown, as does that of many evergreens when they drop their old leaves.

The foliage of Norfolk Island pine (*Araucaria excelsa*) is a bright grass-green and the branches are produced in regular whorls of five at short but regular intervals, making a very pretty and symmetrical plant. It is one of the most popular house plants and is the best formal plant for house decoration. The Norfolk Island pine will stand a great deal of neglect, so long as it is in a cool place and the soil about its roots kept moist.

Some other valuable pines are *P. densiflora,* the Japanese red pine, a round-headed tree about 75 feet high, with a dwarf form, the tanyosho; *P. excelsa,* the Himalayan pine, a big, wide-spreading tree; *P. aleppo,* the aleppo pine, 50 feet tall, hardy only in the South and far West; *P. jeffreyi,* the huge Jeffrey pine; *P. ponderosa,* the ponderosa or yellow pine, an enormous tree planted mostly for timber; *P. resinosa,* the Norway or red pine, extremely hardy and growing rapidly to 80 feet or so tall; *P. rigida,* the picturesque pine of Atlantic coastal dunes; and *P. sylvestris,* the Scotch pine, which has many forms with white, yellow or variegated foliage, columnar form or hanging branches. The low Mexican stone pine or pinon, *P. cembroides,* is hardy only in the Southwest, but a variety, *P. edulis,* the nut pine, grows as far north as lower Nebraska.

Blister rust, a deadly disease of white pines, is spread by currant and gooseberry bushes. Don't plant pines near these. Blister rust cankers on pines should be cut out immediately and burned. *See also* CHRISTMAS TREE FARMING; FIR.

PINEAPPLE: (*Ananas*) The pineapple, a native of northern South America, was widely distributed throughout tropical regions of the world long before the discovery of America. This plant found its true home in Hawaii, but when it was first planted on this island is not known.

CULTURE: The plant is grown from slips taken from the base of the fruit, from the crown that issues from the top of the fruit, or from suckers

that grow from the lower part of the stem. It is not grown from seeds. Seed-producing varieties are avoided because the development of seeds in the flesh of the pineapple spoils it for canning. The varieties most commonly grown are Red Spanish and Smooth Cayenne. When fully grown, this plant is from three to four feet high and bears over a hundred long, somewhat spiny leaves arranged spirally on the central stem. The root system is comparatively small and must have its nutrient materials in the top few inches of the soil.

The first evidence of fruiting in a plant is the appearance of a "red bud" or flower cluster in the center of the plant where the new leaves have been forming. In this cluster are approximately 150 spirally arranged flowers which open when the cluster has reached a length of two or three inches. The petals are pale blue, and the flowers generally open progressively upward. Each flower blooms for a single day when the petals wither and drop off while the remainder of the flower develops into one unit of the multiple fruit.

The fruits are mature and ready for harvesting about 20 months after the plants are set out.

After the fruits are harvested, the old plants are pruned by removing superfluous suckers in preparation of the second or "ratoon" crop. Each of the one to two suckers which are allowed to remain on the old plant will produce a pineapple which will mature in about one year.

Soil must be given especial attention to insure a good crop of pineapples. Preparation begins six to eight months before planting. All vegetation is carefully worked in. To increase the rate of the composting of the vegetable matter in the soil, plowing and harrowing are repeated several times. Occasionally, subsoiling may be practiced to increase drainage, an important factor in the growth of pineapples. Erosion is minimized by contour planting. Terracing is practiced in fields having a considerable slope.

Pineapples are planted spring or fall, depending upon soil and weather conditions. The rows in the field are formed by strips of mulch paper which tends to prevent the growth of weeds, conserves moisture, and increases the temperature of the soil. The mulching paper is put down with a machine which covers both edges of the paper with soil to hold it down. The paper is marked to show the spots through which the slips are to be planted.

After the slips, which have been collected from old plants, have been distributed along the lines of paper, the planters begin their operations. A narrow steel trowel is plunged through the mulch paper at the spots marked. A hole is made with a deft twist of the wrist and a slip is thrust into the hole at the same time the trowel is being withdrawn in such manner as to let the soil pack around the base of the slip. An average of about 10,000 plants are planted to the acre. Sometimes shade is provided for certain varieties by means of lath strips.

PINEAPPLE GUAVA: *see* GUAVA

PINE BEETLE: A troublesome beetle which infests pine trees. The damage of the pine beetle is usually done in summer, and it has been found that the most serious attacks of beetles coincide with periods of low rainfall. Keeping pine stands properly thinned, and removing damaged, old, or unhealthy trees will help keep beetle damage to a minimum. *See also* INSECT CONTROL.

PINE NEEDLES: Like other leaves, pine needles are worth while for fertilizing and mulching purposes; they break down slowly, largely because resins and turpentines counteract attacks by bacteria as well as by water. Small quantities can be mixed in with fertilizers of other kinds, especially as part of the plant matter of the compost heap; larger quantities may be used for mulching trees; but considerable quantities had best be exposed in a separate pile to the influence of the weather so that they may gradually break up. The nitrogen content is estimated about half of one per cent. *See also* MULCH.

PINKROOT: (*Spigelia marilandica*) A native perennial herb occurring in rich open woods from North Carolina to Ohio and south to Florida and Texas. The root was at one time considered an important drug, but its use has declined in recent years. Although the plant is generally found under partial shade, it may be grown in the open in rich moist loamy soil. It is propagated either from seed or from divisions of old roots. The seed, which ripens in midsummer, should be sown immediately in drills six inches apart in a well-prepared seedbed or mixed with moist sand and kept in a cool place and sown in fall. In spring, when the young plants are a few inches high, they are set in their permanent location, spaced 18 inches apart in rows at least three feet apart. The old roots are divided when dormant, so that each division consists of a portion of the root with one or more buds and a number of the small rootlets. They are set in the same manner as the seedlings. Thorough cultivation to control weeds is necessary.

PINKS: Usually refers to the Dianthus, which are often used as low border perennials. These include sweet William (*D. barbatus*), clove pink (*D. caryophyllus*) and grass pink (*D. plumarius*) as well as many others. Pinks generally do best in a warm, well-drained, almost neutral soil. They all prefer full sun, but will not do well if soil is poor. Mulch will protect plants from weather extremes during both summer and winter. They are usually propagated from cuttings,

division and layering. *See also* DIAN-
THUS.

PIP: *see* LILY

PIPER: A large genus of the pepper
family, *Piperaceae,* of which only a few
are cultivated, one of them the plant
from which we get black pepper (*P.
nigrum*). All are tropical woody vines
which become tree-like in maturity in
some cases. A few are grown as greenhouse curiosities. Flowers are catkin-
like spikes, fruit in berries. Grown
in United States only in tropical
greenhouses with very moist atmosphere.

Cubeb (*P. cubeba*) a climbing or
tree-like vine, is grown in the East
Indies for medicinal use.

P. nigrum gives us our black or
white pepper, the dried berry of the
vine which is yellowish-red before
drying. Black pepper is the whole
seed, white pepper has the outer peri-
carp removed.

P. ornatum is a tropical vine grown
for its variegated leaves, which are
spotted pink when young and white
when mature.

PIPEVINE: (*Aristolochia durior*) A
woody vine of Eastern North America growing sometimes to 30 feet.
Common name is descriptive of yel-
lowish-greenish flowers with curved
tubes three inches long and three-
lobed spreading opening which is
brownish-purplish. Leaves are roundish, six to 14 inches wide. Will grow
rapidly in a moist, rich soil. Usually
grown from seed, it is often known
as Dutchman's Pipe.

PISTACHIO: (*Pistacia vera*) A species
of the sumac family, *Anacardiaceae,*
a spreading deciduous tree bearing
the yellow-green nut considered a
delicacy here and on the Mediterranean, where it is native. Leaves of
the pistachio are compound, alternate,
and the inconspicuous flowers, which
grow in terminal clusters, are male
on one tree, female on another.

The Chinese pistachio (*P. chinensis*) grows to 60 feet, and is grown
principally for ornament, or for rootstock on which is grafted *P. vera.*
Propagated mostly by budding or
grafting. Pistachios are grown only
in California in this country, where
they find the dry climate they need.

PISTIL: The ovule bearing organ of a
flower; becoming after fertilization by
pollen the seedbearing organ. The female reproductive body. The pistil
is composed of the *ovary* at the base,
a stalk-like *style,* and the cap of the
style, or *stigma,* which receives the
pollen. Each complete unit of ovary,
style, and stigma is called a *carpel.*
The pistil may be composed of one
carpel, or may be compound (composed of more than one carpel.) In
a compound pistil, the styles and stigmas may be fused to form what seems
to be one organ. *See also* POLLEN;
FLOWER.

PISTILLATE: Flowers bearing only pistils, and no stamens. Female flowers.

PIT: *see* COMPOST; STORAGE

PITCHER PLANT: (*Nepenthes*) Insectivorous semi-woody sometimes climbing plants native in the tropical Orient, grown here only under glass as
curios. Named because of the typical
pitchers formed by an extension of
the leaf midrib, which broadens into
a pitcher-shaped vessel with wings,
often brightly colored, and large or
small lid. The pitchers are suspended
from the tips of the leaves. Insects
are trapped in the pitchers, and eventually drown in a pool of viscous
liquid in the bottom, where they are
digested. Inconspicuous flowers, borne
in clusters, are male on some plants
and female on others. Unless seed is
required, the flowers are removed
from exhibition specimens. Seed is in
a leathery capsule.

Propagation is by cuttings or seed,
at a temperature of 80 to 85°, using
sphagnum and peat moss in a glass

jar or case. After thoroughly rooted, they may be removed to hanging baskets under the roof of the greenhouse, where they are shaded and kept constantly above 65°. Soil should be a mixture of peat fiber, sphagnum, and sharp sand.

Many hybrids were developed when pitcher-plants were in great vogue, with brightly colored pitchers and lids. Original species include: *N. distillatoria,* with five-inch pale green to dull red pitchers, wings fringed; *N. Hookeriana,* six-inch pitchers pale green marked with purple, lower pitchers doubly fringed wings; *N. khasiana,* green to reddish-green seven-inch pitchers with narrow fringed wings; *N. maxima,* highly colored free-flowering, pale green blotched purple, wings varying from top to bottom, funnel-shaped, cylindrical, and expanded; *N. phyllamphora,* six-inch pale to reddish-green or red pitchers, slender cord-like wings; *N. rafflesiana,* purple spotted seven-inch pale green pitchers, urn-shaped to funnel-shaped; *N. sanguinea,* ten-inch red to reddish-green pitchers; and *N. veitchii,* hairy yellowish-green to reddish eight-inch pitchers. *See also* CARNIVOROUS PLANTS; DARLINGTONIA.

PITTOSPORUM: Known as Australian laurel, this is a genus of evergreen trees and shrubs native to Asia and the South Pacific islands to Australia. Some used in California, Florida, and the Gulf states in hedges and windbreaks. One variety grown in greenhouses for its thick, leathery foliage. Small purple, red, or yellow flowers are sometimes fragrant. Propagated by seeds, greenwood cuttings, and grafting.

Karo (*P. crassifolium*) is used as a windbreak in California. It is a shrub or small tree, growing to 30 feet in New Zealand. Leathery leaves are three inches long, flowers red or purple in terminal clusters.

Tawhiwhi (*P. tenuifolium*) is a dense tree good for screening, because it will stand close clipping. Also called kohuhu and black mapau.

Japanese pittosporum (*P. Tobira*) is the species used for greenhouse culture. It has yellowish-white fragrant flowers in terminal clusters. Also used in warm climates as a hedge shrub.

Victorian box (*P. undulatum*) is used as an avenue tree in Southern California, and is also planted for its fragrant flowers. The tree grows to 40 feet, leaves to six inches.

Queensland pittosporum (*P. rhombifolium*) is also grown as an avenue tree, and has yellow-orange fruits which remain decorative for a long period. It grows to 80 feet, its toothed leaves about four inches long, flowers white.

The willow pittosporum (*P. phillyraeoides*) is an Australian desert tree that resembles the weeping willow.

Tarata (*P. eugenioides*) is used in clipped hedges and for ornamental plantings in California. It is a tall slender tree.

PITYROGRAMMA: Also known as Gymnogramma, Gold fern or silver fern. Evergreen American ferns, natives of the tropics, grown as house plants. Dark green fronds have powdery substance below. Easily grown in moderate temperatures, never below 55°. Propagated by spores kept warm and moist on peat moss, or by division in February.

Silver-fern (*P. calomelanos*) has frond to three feet, with toothed or cut segments, and white powdery lining.

Jamaica gold-fern (*P. sulphurea*) has fronds about a foot long, five inches wide at the base, powder sulphur-yellow.

California gold fern (*P. triangularis*) has fronds to seven inches, six inches wide, deep golden-yellow below, or sometimes white. Native from California to Alaska. *See also* FERNS.

PLANE TREE: (*Platanus*) Also known as buttonball tree. It belongs to the family *Platanaceae*, comprising six species of handsome deciduous trees, characterized by the large patches of bark that flake off, and dense maple-like foliage. The trees thrive in rich moist soil, and will stand severe pruning. Flowers are ball-like, with male and female separate, but on the same tree. Fruit is a ball-like mass.

London plane (*P. acerifolia*) grows to 140 feet, with a wide spread. Leaves blunt-tipped, three to five-lobed. Hardy except in coldest parts of the United States.

Buttonwood or sycamore (*P. occidentalis*) is a very large tree, growing to 150 feet, and with very thick trunk. Not as good for city planting as London plane, but hardy in the woodlands.

Oriental plane is not usually grown in this country, but it is thought that London plane was originally a hybrid of buttonwood and oriental plane.

PLANNING, GARDEN: You can expect three results from planning your garden properly: maximum beauty, maximum productiveness, and minimum maintenance.

Theoretically, if your soil is built up organically, you need only to plant sun-loving plants in the sun and shade-loving plants in the shade, and your garden should look well.

But there's a lot more to successful layout. The new home owner especially will achieve far more pleasing results if he works from a plan. It's almost unbelievable how much time, space and money a gardener can save if he has a complete plan to follow when he is ready to start planting.

First of all, take a good look at your house and its surroundings. Those parts of the grounds that are of primarily utilitarian character—the driveway and garage, service area and laundry area—can often be concealed, or at least have their less attractive features minimized, by plantings.

Foundation plantings in front of your house are equally important, and will often set the character of the whole place.

The boundary lines of your property should be considered at the same time, for good landscape design calls for harmony between all the elements, whether near or far from the house. This takes in fence and screen plantings and shade or fruit trees that will make the frame for the picture your home presents to passers-by, and shrub borders and specimen plants that will give emphasis or balance to other features of the picture. For other principles of good landscape design, *see also* LANDSCAPING.

Consider also the placement of your compost heap, and structures like the cold frame, arbors or a tool house. If you plan to have a greenhouse, it will, of course, be given first choice above all else for placement in regards to exposure to sunlight.

Where you place your flower beds and borders will probably be determined mainly by the sunlight available. The possibilities for the placing and design of these are so vast, it would be a good idea to carefully study the sections on BORDERS; FLOWER GARDENING; ANNUALS.

Many gardeners have a short hedgerow of lilacs, wild roses, or whatever is easily available, to serve as a nursery for young plants. Wild plants from the woods or meadows will be more likely to survive transplanting if they are acclimated to "civilized" living in the shelter of the hedgerow for a year before being set in permanent spots in the border. Rooting cuttings of choice shrubs can be set in the shade of the row, protected from strong sun and wind as well as from accidental damage from dogs and children. A propagating bed can be used in the spring for annuals which are to be transplanted to other locations, then for summer planting of perennials.

The size and layout of that all-important feature of the organic garden, the vegetable garden, is covered under VEGETABLE GARDENING. However, remember that many common vegetables have decorative value. They can be grouped informally among flowers, tucked in odd corners or even grown by themselves in borders. Many vegetables look well placed near small-growing perennials such as lavender and thyme; neat annuals—snapdragons and dwarf zinnias—also fit in nicely. A center garden walk, lined on both sides with growing vegetables, makes an attractive sight.

In every instance where it is at all possible, try to use double-purpose plants—those that are both decorative and sources of food—in your garden. These include dwarf and full-size fruit trees, the small fruits, nut trees, herbs, the rugosa rose and so on.

Maintenance is largely a matter of choosing plants that need little special care, and using methods that eliminate routine chores. Mulching naturally is a big maintenance-reducer, cutting down weeding, feeding and watering amazingly. Advice on achieving minimum maintenance will be found under all the headings on plant types, such as SHRUBS.

For wild gardens, rock gardens, lily pools and other specialized subjects you may decide to include in your garden, see the headings for these.

PLAN YOUR GARDEN ON PAPER: One of the best ways to plan a garden successfully is to use large sheets of paper ruled off into squares, using a scale of two feet to the inch. Remember to draw all large plants the size they will be at maturity. Locate first all the major fixtures, such as already existing trees, shrubs and hedges, and buildings and paths. Mark off north and south on your plan. Then add each item you want in your garden, considering them in order of their importance to you and your family and the space and time you can devote to them.

Finally, keep records. You'll probably want to modify your plan, including new features and discarding some old ones every season. How well certain plants did on certain sites, the effect of their form and color, the rotation of your vegetable crops— these are but a few of the factors which should be noted down conscientiously to make it easy to revise your plan for more efficiency and beauty. A camera can be a lot of help in this, giving you a record of your summer garden to work on during the winter months. Get in the habit of "taking inventory" every day you work in your garden.

In gardening as in so many other things, experience is the final and best teacher. Truly good gardeners get to know plants' likes and dislikes, they can spot just the right place in the garden for any plant, where it will do best.

HOMESTEAD PLANNING: If you have a larger place and plan to make it into an organic homestead, there will be many more factors to consider than in laying out a garden. Homestead planning calls for a great deal more thought and care, for the layout will determine both its productivity and the ease of running it.

Your vegetable garden, root cellar, cold frames and greenhouse should be given top priority in planning the place. The orchard is important, too, and you'll very likely want full-size trees rather than dwarfs to get the biggest possible crops of organic fruit. Locate your compost heaps or pits midway between the barn and the vegetable garden, to reduce the distance it will be necessary to carry manure and other compost materials.

Some of the other features to consider are your bee hives, a roadside stand for selling your surplus or cash crops, perhaps a fish pond for supplementary food. *See also* HOMESTEAD.

PLANTAIN-LILY: *see* HOSTA; LILY

PLANT BREEDING: New varieties are being produced in nature all the time. Every seed of a fruit which grows into a new plant results in a new variety. Most of them it is true, are of less value than what we already have but, now and then, there is one or two or more which have characteristics which are worth perpetuating. This method of finding new varieties is called "selection." You select the individual plant which shows improvement over others in the same bed or field.

Those varieties of plants, such as peas, beans, and corn, which are reproduced from seeds each year, quite frequently develop an individual plant which is different and better. If you select the *one* plant out of your garden which is better than all the others, plant the seeds from that plant and watch it next year and the year after —each year selecting seeds from the best plants—you may gradually develop a better variety.

CROSS POLLINATION: If, on the other hand, you wish to become a little more technical, you can produce new varieties more rapidly by cross pollination. By this method, you carry the pollen from one plant to another and the resulting seeds are a combination of the two plants—the plant on which the pollen grew and the plant on which the flower grew which was fertilized by the pollen you carried. One or more of the resulting seedlings may be better than either parent.

An easy way to do this is to simply pick a blossom when the pollen is ready, carry it to the other blossom and dust the pollen over that other blossom, as soon as the flower is open. If you wait too long, the bees may pollenize the blossom ahead of you and, after the pistil has once been covered with pollen, it cannot be pollenized again.

If you are interested in fruits of any kind, including the bush fruits as well as the tree fruits, you can get new varieties by simply planting the seeds, for every fruit seed grows into a new variety because there is no control of pollination.—*John Y. Beaty.*
See also POLLEN.

PLANT DEFICIENCIES: When plants do not receive the proper amounts, or the correct balance, of nutritive elements, they will begin to show signs of deterioration in many different ways. The expert gardener can often tell what elements are lacking in a plant by the nature of the "hunger signs." Soil testing is also important. *See also* DEFICIENCIES, SOIL; FERTILIZER; TRACE ELEMENTS.

PLANT DISEASE: *see* DISEASE

PLANT FAMILY: One of the divisions of the plant kingdom, a sub-division of a botanical order, and a grouping of genera. The plant kingdom is divided first into phyla (singular, phylum), which are divided into classes, composed of orders, which in turn are divided into families, the families divided into genera (singular, genus), the genera into species, and different varieties sometimes occurring in the species. The Latin name for a plant is given as its genus and species name, with variety indicated, if any. Thus, apple is *Malus pumila,* with numerous varieties, a genus of the rose family, *Rosaceae.*

Some of the hundreds of botanical families of interest to gardeners are: among the trees, pines, *Pinaceae;* maples, *Aceraceae;* beech or oak, *Fagaceae;* palms, *Palmaceae.* In the vegetable garden, peas and beans, *Leguminosae;* squash and cucumbers, *Cucurbitaceae;* potatoes and tomatoes, *Solanaceae;* mint, *Labiatae;* mustard and cabbage, *Crucifereae;* gooseberry, *Saxifragaceae;* grapes, *Vitaceae;* carrots, *Umbellifereae.* Among shrubs and flowers, iris *Iridaceae;* lily, *Liliaceae;* amaryllis, *Amaryllidaceae;* poppies, *Papaveraceae;* daisies, *Compositeae;* pinks, *Carophyllaceae;* buttercups, *Ranunculaceae;* roses, *Rosaceae;* violets, *Violaceae;* mallows, *Malva-*

ceae; myrtle, *Myrtaceae;* rhododendrons, azaleas, heath, *Ericaceae;* snapdragons, *Scrophulariaceae;* portulaca or purslane, *Portulacaceae.*

PLANT FOOD: *see* FERTILIZER; COMPOST

PLANTING: *see* VEGETABLE GARDENING; FLOWER GARDENING; GERMINATION; BRAMBLE FRUITS; SHRUBS; TREES; FRUIT TREES; NUT TREES; NAMES OF INDIVIDUAL PLANTS

PLANTING BY THE MOON: *see* MOON PLANTING

PLANTING, COMPANION: *see* COMPANION CROPS

PLANT MATTER: *see* ORGANIC MATTER; ORGANIC MATERIALS; HUMUS; COMPOST; GREEN MATTER

PLANTINGS, SECOND: A second planting is one which is grown in late spring or summer, when an early spring crop has been harvested.

Plan your garden to have a constant supply of a variety of vegetables throughout the season. There are vegetables for early planting, and vegetables for late planting. There are vegetables for summer harvesting and those for fall harvest. There are plants which get a vigorous start in early spring when temperatures are low and moisture high, and there are those that do better later on.

Although a little more care may be needed to realize a good uniform stand from summer-sown seeds compared with spring-sown seeds, weed control and pest control are far easier in summer-sown garden rows.

SUMMER SEEDING: Seeds should be sown just a trifle deeper and a little more thickly in summer fitted gardens.

Where water is available readily, it is a good idea to water new plantings frequently enough to prevent crusting of soil until seedlings have emerged. Where water may not be available readily by garden hose it is very helpful to carry enough water to soak the furrow bottom before seed is sown. A few gallons is sufficient for a 30- or 40-foot row. Seeds that are sown directly on the moistened furrow bottom and covered as usual respond more uniformly and more promptly than seed that is sown in rather dry soil.

PLANTING TIMES: Summer seeding time for any kind of variety of vegetable depends mostly upon three factors. These are:

the natural frost-hardiness or lack of hardiness of the vegetable;

the usual date of occurrence of the first killing frost in the area with relation to frost-tender vegetables like snap beans;

the usual onset of growth-stopping freezes that affect freeze-hardy vegetables like cabbages.

MATURITY DATES: In order to plan your successions, you'll have to know how many days will pass between planting and maturity. This information is listed in seed catalogs, on seed packets, and in many different garden books and pamphlets. Time of maturity often varies with the variety. For example, Sparkler radishes take about 25 days to mature, whereas White Chinese, another variety, takes about 60 days.

Keep in mind also those plants which may be planted before the last killing frost in spring. Some vegetables in this category are asparagus, cabbage, chives, garlic, onions, peas, potatoes, rhubarb, and turnips. By doing this, you will be able to harvest the first crop earlier, and, of course, plant the second one earlier as well.

NUTRIENT DEFICIENCIES: Try not to plant members of the same family in succession. Root crops, for example, take a great amount of potash from the soil. To follow radishes with turnips, both root crops, may undermine the soil's supply of potash and result in poor crops later on. The same is true of leaf crops (lettuce, cabbage, etc.) which absorb a great amount of nitrogen.

See also VEGETABLE GARDENING.

SUMMER PLANTING VARIETIES

Frost-Tender Crops

BUSH SNAP BEANS—Topcrop, Contender and **Wade** (45 to 50 days).

Plant during the first half of July for first harvests during the latter half of August and to allow a 3- to 4-week period of harvest before frost may occur. Remember that bush beans, due to their nature of sharply determined or limited period of flowering, will not continue to yield snap pods indefinitely.

POLE or CLIMBING SNAP BEANS: Kentucky Wonder and **McCaslan** (60 to 65 days).

Plant along in June for first harvests of snap pods along in August and for successive pickings until the plants are killed by frost. Unlike bush beans, pole beans continue indefinitely to send out new vegetative growth which gives rise to flowers and snap pods.

SWEET CORN. Golden Cross Bantam (80 to 85 days) should be planted by mid-June for late harvests before frost but **Golden Beauty** (65 to 70 days) may still be planted early in July.

CABBAGES and RELATED VEGETABLES.

These kinds are not only hardy against 20°F to 25°F and even lower temperatures but, well started, they survive and thrive through rather hot drouthy summer weather to yield the best of produce in autumn.

The delicate, leaf-covered heads of cauliflower survive quite a few degrees of frost unharmed, but cabbages and other kinds can be frozen in the garden without injury especially provided that harvesting and handling for storage is delayed until a return of moderate temperatures enables natural thawing and resumption of circulation of plant juices.

LATE CABBAGE. Hollander and **Danish Ballhead** (90 to 100 days) for late fall and winter use should be grown from seeds sown in June for transplants to set out early in July. **EARLY CABBAGE: Golden Acre** (round) and **Early Jersey Wakefield** (pointed) which are rated as 60 to 65-day varieties can be planted at the same time to furnish delicious tender new cabbage during late summer and early autumn.

CAULIFLOWER: Early Snowball (55 to 60 days from transplanting) can be timed in seeding and planting as above or even a little later for fall harvests.

BRUSSELS SPROUTS: Long Island Improved (80 to 90 days) and **SPROUTING BROCCOLI: Italian Green Sprouting** or **Calabrese** (70 to 80 days) can be timed with late cabbage. Both of these healthful vegetables provide successive harvests from each plant from the earliest date implied in parentheses until hard freezing weather puts a stop to gardening.

Root Crops

CARROTS: Red Cored Chantenay (60 to 70 days) and **BEET: Detroit Dark Red** (50 to 60 days to substantial harvests) may be planted during late June or early July to furnish crisp, richly colored vitamin-rich roots for immediate use throughout late summer and autumn and surpluses for storage.

RADISH: Early Scarlet Globe (25 to 30 days) and **White Icicle** (30 to 35 days) may be sown along in August for fall use; remain usable for a relatively long time in autumn without becoming pithy, compared with spring plantings.

TURNIPS: Early White Flat Dutch (40 to 45 days); **Snowball** (40 to 45 days) and **Purple Top White Globe** (50 to 55 days) may be sown along in August to furnish crisp little roots even earlier than indicated and usable larger roots throughout autumn months.

Salads and Greens

LETTUCE: Salad Bowl leaf lettuce (40 to 45 days to substantial harvests) and even **Great Lakes** head lettuce (75 to 80 days) have produced well in our mid-summer plantings. Head lettuce plants must be thinned early to 12 inches apart to induce heading.

Since lettuce seed not only prefers but demands a relatively cool (65° F to 75° F) temperature and moist but well drained soil conditions for prompt germination. It is a very good practice to make summer plantings in a cool evening, preferably during a reasonably coolish spell of weather that occurs quite often in summer.

Lettuce seeds that are sown during periods of 85° F to 90° F and higher temperatures are often induced thereby into a condition known as delayed dormancy, from which they may not emerge in time to germinate and produce the intended crop.

SPINACH: Seeds of America and **Bloomsdale** (about 45 days to plants of substantial size for use) can still be sown well along in August to yield the best of long-standing plants for immediate use throughout late fall and for quick freezing for winter use.

PLASTIC GREENHOUSE: see GREEN-
HOUSE

PLATANUS: see PLANE TREE

PLATYCERIUM: see STAGHORN FERN

PLATYCODON: see BALLOON FLOWER

PLOWING: An ancient soil practice
that in recent years has become a
controversial one.

Plows have been used since the
earliest days of history. From the days
before Christ to shortly after the
American Revolution plows were
made from a crooked branch of a
tree, with a little piece of metal fastened on the tip to stop excessive wear.
Improvements both in the development of steel and heavy-duty tractors
now enable farmers to cultivate their
fields with multiple bottom plows.

CRITICISM: Perhaps the most famous criticism of the harmful effects
of plowing on the soil was made by
Edward Faulkner in his book, *Plowman's Folly.* Here are the basic reasons for the growing anti-plowing
attitude:

The plow turns manure and crop
residue under and buries it where very
little decomposition takes place. Turning the soil "wrong side up" exposes
the bare, unprotected ground to the
hot rays of the sun in summer and
to unnecessary freezing in winter.
The soil is also subjected to wind
and water erosion. A hard, driving
rain soon loosens the bare soil particles
and seals over the surface of the land.

Another unwanted feature of the
moldboard plow is "plow sole." It is
a hard crust that forms at plow depth
and retards capillary action and water
penetration. Critics describe the plow
as a good tool with which to exploit
the land, but one of the poorest machines in the world to build back fertility. Rotary tillage, chisel plowing
and a system of mulch farming are
their recommendations to replace
plowing.

METHODS: In spite of all the argu-
ments, plowing continues to be a basic

farm practice, often done in the home
garden as well. Garden tractors are
effective plowing tools.

To do a neat job of plowing a small
garden, be sure that the sides of your
plot are parallel. Otherwise, you will
end up with short rows and will have
to do too much turning.

Plowing should not be done when
the ground is too wet or too dry. You
need good conditions to do a good
job with a small power unit.

You can either start your furrow at
the outside of your plot and work
in, or vice versa. But be sure to reverse the procedure every year. If you
start at the outside every year and
always work counterclockwise, after
several years you will develop a depression in the middle of your garden.
You will be constantly moving the
earth away from the center of your
plot.

By all means do your plowing in
the spring, so the soil is not left unprotected over the winter. If you do
have to plow in the fall, be sure to
mulch afterwards or plant a cover
crop.

After plowing, of course, you must
disk and/or harrow to break up the
clods and prepare a fine seedbed.
Oftentimes you can save time and
trouble by weighting your discs with
a rock to make them bite deeper.
Usually, several passes with disks are
necessary. Disks are always set at an
angle to make them move and disturb
more earth. See *also* NO-DIGGING
METHOD; VEGETABLE GARDENING;
ROTARY TILLAGE.

PLUG PLANTING: see LAWN

PLUM: (*Prunus*) The plum is one of
the easiest of the stone fruits to grow
—if you choose the right varieties.
There are four types of plums: American, European, Damson and Japanese. Some varieties in each type, or
hybrids, can without doubt be found
to suit your area and general conditions.

No matter where you live, you can

have dark red, royal purple, coral red or golden yellow plums. Many new hardy varieties have been developed, as well as early, mid-season and late-bearing strains. And the beauty of their masses of white flowers in the spring are an added inducement to growing them around the home.

CULTURE: Well-drained soil is especially important to plums. The European and Damsons do best in heavy loam soils, the Japanese on light, sandy loams, and the Americans on a wide range of soils, in general doing best on ground suited to peaches. With the use of compost and natural fertilizers, vigorous growth is made. Fertilizing too heavily, which is hardly possible with natural materials, will stimulate too much growth and delay bearing. On the home grounds, a mulch, renewed yearly, is of course the best practice. In orchards, late-summer-sown cover crops like clover, buckwheat, oats or barley, are recommended.

If you keep poultry, plant plum trees in your poultry yard and you'll never be troubled with the plum curculio, which causes wormy fruits. The chickens and ducks will eat the bugs wholesale. Dormant sprays and regular sanitation take care of other pests.

Two-year-old trees are usually planted. They should be set 20 feet apart, and at least two varieties of the same type should be planted for cross-pollination. Plum trees are generally trained around a central leader, three to five main branches being allowed to develop. After the first year, only interfering or superfluous branches or those making acute crotches should be pruned out. The Japanese and American types usually require the most pruning. Thinning is aimed at spacing the individual fruits one to three inches apart when mature.

Most plum trees are fruitful for 30 to 40 years. Well-cared-for mature

Besides the yield of fruit, the masses of lovely white flowers make plum trees even more valuable for the home grounds. A mulch around base of tree extending to drip line is known to improve fruit yield.

trees should yield from three to four bushels of fruit annually.

VARIETIES: Here are just a few of the best varieties:

American—Surprise and Wolf are large, highly productive trees bearing medium-sized red fruits. De Soto and Pottawattomie are small trees producing big red or yellow-red, sweet fruits. All of these are high-yielding and very hardy.

Damson—the best Damson is Shropshire, which produces terrific yields of dark purple fruits. A similar variety, with larger, better quality fruits in somewhat less abundance, is the French.

European—all the Europeans are medium or large trees, hardy eastward from the Great Lakes region. Stanley, Hall and Italian Prune give dark blue or purple fruits. Washington has sweet, delicious yellow fruit, as does Reine Claude; both are medium-sized trees. Imperial Epineuse has perhaps the sweetest fruit of all, borne on a big, vigorous tree.

Japanese—all the best Japanese have red or reddish-purple fruits, and most of the trees are quite large. Formosa, Burbank, Beauty and Santa Rosa are probably the all-around favorites. Abundance is also good, but its very juicy friuts do not store well.

The native beach plum (*P. maritima*) by the way, does well in gardens. It grows wild along the Atlantic Coast as far south as Virginia. When the beach plums are ripe, many a family drives out for a day of picking and frolicking on the beach. The fruit is rather astringent but makes delicious jam and jellies when made with honey. *See also* FRUIT TREES; ORCHARD.

PLUMBAGO: Also known as Leadwort. A genus of about a dozen species of small tender shrubs grown outdoors in the South, and in cool greenhouses North, for their phlox-like flowers borne all summer. For northern gardens, they may be grown

in pots which can be used on the terrace or patio, and returned to the greenhouse to dry and rest in the fall. About February the foliage is cut back severely, and brought into the light at about 65° to start their growth for the coming year. Grown outside in warm climates, the growth is cut back in spring to one inch of the ground. Old flower stalks must be removed to insure continued bloom. Propagated by seed, cuttings, or division. Young shoots are pinched back several times to promote bushy growth.

P. capensis has blue flowers with individual florets ¾ inch across. Will grow into a spreading eight-foot shrub.

P. indica has reddish-purple flowers, and is a partial climber, with support.

Toothwart (*P. scandens*) is white-flowered, a native of tropical America.

PLUM CURCULIO: A beetle which infests and damages plums and other fruits. The control of plum curculio may be accomplished by cleaning up all areas near the orchard that provide places where the beetle might winter. This is followed by discing under the trees to break up and kill the pupae in the ground. During early morning, trees may be jarred so that the beetle will drop on to sheets spread underneath. From here they may be gathered and destroyed. Finally, it is suggested that drops found beneath the trees be gathered and destroyed while the larvae are in them. *See also* INSECT CONTROL.

PLUME GRASS: *see* GRASS, ORNAMENTAL

PLUMERIA: Frangipani or temple tree. A genus of tropical American shrubs and trees of the dogbane family, *Apocynaceae*. Grown in warm climates for their large, funnel-shaped, waxy, and fragrant flowers. Branches are thick and soft, sap is milky, leaves narrow, oval, or blunt-ended, seven to 15 inches long.

Red jasmine (*P. rubra*) is a shrub or tree growing to 15 feet, with large leaves and pink, red, or purple flowers. Flowers in the variety *acutifolia* are white with yellow-tinged throats, sometimes flushed with rose. This variety is a favorite graveyard tree in the South.

P. alba has narrow leaves to ten inches long, small white flowers, and the tree grows to 35 feet.

PLUNGE: To sink a pot containing a plant in soil as deep as the soil within the pot. This may be done in the garden in a partially shaded and protected spot during the summer, or it may be done under the bench in the greenhouse during the winter, when the plant is in its resting stage. The reason for sinking the pot is to keep the soil cool and moist, without as frequent watering as is necessary when the pot is exposed to evaporation.

Plants which are to be propagated by cuttings in fall, and the old plant discarded, as geraniums or coleus, may be removed from the pots and planted directly in the border. Usually house plants which will be brought back indoors are left in the pots to avoid root-shock that follows re-potting after the roots have been allowed their freedom for the summer.

PODOCARPUS: A genus of evergreen trees and shrubs mostly native of the southern hemisphere, formerly included in the yew family, *Taxaceae,* but now for technical botanical reasons given a family of their own, *Podocarpaceae.* Grown outdoors in this country only in the warm parts of California and Florida, except for one species, *P. alpina,* which is somewhat hardier. Grown in tubs in greenhouses for their attractive foliage. Male and female flowers on separate trees, the male flowers catkin-like, the female flowers inconspicuous and followed by a plum-shaped red, purple, or yellow fruit on a fleshy stalk. Grow best in sandy peat or loam. Propagated by seeds or cuttings.

P. alpina grows to about 15 feet, as a dense small-leaved tree. Fruit is a small red berry. Will stand some frost.

P. andina grows about 30 feet tall, with small leaves striped white below, and yellowish-white plum-shaped fruit, about one inch in diameter.

P. elongata is grown in California as a shrub, and is also grown as a greenhouse plant, but in its native surroundings in Africa it attains 70 feet.

P. macrophylla is a slightly smaller tree, but with leaves three to four inches long. Half-inch fruit is greenish-purple, on a fleshy purple stalk.

PODZOL SOILS: This type of soil is a group which occurs in temperate, humid regions where once forests or heaths stood and where through the leaching of rain waters the soil has become acid. Although a typical podzol has a gray, bleached, strongly leached topsoil layer there is a much larger variation and extent of coloration, depending on the degree of podzolization. The word podzol is of Russian origin and means ash-colored soil. Usually where the climate is humid, where there has been plenty of rainfall, there naturally has sprung up forests, thus causing the gradual development of this type of soil. Almost half of the soil of the United States was in forest when Columbus came to America. In the prairies where high grasses grew there also occurs podzolization, but it is much milder than where forests stood.

To create podzol soils there should be a high rate of rainfall as the first requirement for podzolization is leaching, and excess rainfall will wash downward many of the substances that are in the topsoil. There must be such a relationship between temperature, rainfall and plant life that there will result an accumulation of organic matter on the surface of the soil. There must also be a type of decay of the organic matter which will give acidity, because one of the requirements for a soil to be a podzol is, that the acids yielded up in the process of decomposition of this organic matter, leach the iron and aluminum into the subsoil. Subsoils of podzols are always rich in iron and aluminum. But whether aluminum is in the topsoil or in the subsoil it does not affect the harm it can do in a condition of high acidity, which makes it soluble, and thus "available" to plant roots. Aluminum in more than trace quantities is toxic to plants. But the effect of the application of organic matter plus lime tends to "lock in" the aluminum in the soil, and prevent it from getting into plant roots.

PODZOL PROFILE: A profile of podzol soil indicates first that the soil on top is covered with a thin layer of organic litter. Then follows under it a layer of partially decomposed organic matter, about five times as thick as the litter. Underneath this is a thin layer of black well-decayed humus about the same thickness as the surface litter. Then comes the mineral soil, containing a large quantity of silica, which is a little less in thickness than the layer of partially decomposed organic matter described above. It could be about two or three inches in extent. This layer usually is high in organic matter. Of course there is a great deal of variation in the measurements of the different layers, depending on the abundance of organic matter and the amount of rainfall. If the organic matter is plentiful and the rainfall heavy there may be a thin layer of precipitated humus under the mineral-silica section just described. Below all this is the subsoil.

If drainage is poor, or there are large accumulations of organic matter, or torrential rainfalls occur, the iron podzol becomes a humus podzol and could become transformed into a bog. In sandy soils podzolization is more intense than in clays, because leaching is much easier, podzolization is a deteriorative process. Generally in a podzol, the soil structure is poor, the soil is low in organic matter, it erodes easily and makes for poor aeration. One of the trace elements, boron, is lacking in many podzolic soils. Overliming a soil further reduces the boron which is an important nutritional element. Boron aids the ability of the plant to get the most out the calcium it takes in. Without boron calcium will not go as far as it otherwise would.

ACIDITY: An essential requirement for podzolization is acidity, and the more advanced the podzolization the greater the acidity. Because of this condition, much of the organic matter decomposes readily and the soluble portions of it leach out. In winter and spring the acidity is the highest. Since podzols are related to forests and trees, their acidity is related to that fact. Trees do not take in much calcium and therefore give off very little in the leaves which fall and decay under them. The acidity is normally produced by the carbon dioxide absorbed by the rains, and the acids that come from the decomposing leaves. If there were sufficient calcium in the latter it would counteract this acidity.

With evergreen or coniferous forests, the acid condition is more pronounced than where there are broadleafed deciduous trees. There are varying conditions within groupings of trees which however may depart from pattern. A soil may be rich in calcium, and trees growing there would give the soil more than the average amount of calcium in their leaves, which could tend to keep the soil neutral rather than acid. This has been found to be true especially of maple and beech tree forests. There are some areas in zones of podzolization which contain large deposits of limestone which affects the rate of acidity. Poor drainage in some areas on the other hand is a factor the other way, contributing to increased acidity.

GEOGRAPHY: One-half of the soil of Russia is podzol. In the United

States, of a total of three million square miles, 614,400 are podzol, 149,100 of which are mature and 465,300 strong, medium to weak. There are mature podzols in the northern section of the Great Lakes region and in New England. In New York, New Jersey and some of the lands along the south coast, the sandy soil areas are mature podzols.

There is a group of brown podzol an imperfectly developed upland forest type, in New England and Eastern New York. These soils are sandy loams or stony sand. There are the gray-brown podzol soils of the middle west going from the Prairie region to the Atlantic and south to Tennessee. And of course the red and yellow podzols in the south, which go as far west as the eastern-central part of Texas. Your County Agent or State Agricultural College can give you the exact classification of your soil. *See also* SOILS.

POGONIA: Rose pogonia, or snake-mouth, the only cultivated species of the *pogonia,* a genus of orchids growing in North American bogs, and hardy to Newfoundland. Can be grown only in the bog garden, in strongly acid soil or in sphagnum moss, in a shady spot. Grows to 21 inches, with a single four-inch leaf on the stem, and flowers, usually single but occasionally two, pink or rose pink, nodding, with petals and sepals about equal, the lip fringed or crested with yellow-brown hairs. About one inch in diameter. Blooms in June or July. *See also* ORCHIDS.

POINCIANA: A most beautiful tropical flowering tree or shrub. It is easily and quickly grown and with its broad spreading crown and filmy foliage is well fitted for shade and ornament in yards and parks. It is and well deserves to be a general public favorite throughout the tropics of the world.

Botanists have changed its scientific name to *Delonix regia,* but it will always be known to the public at large as *Poinciana regia* or the Royal Poinciana. It is sometimes called the flame-flower, the royal-peacock-flower and the flamboyant. It came from far-off Madagascar and East Africa.

Some poincianas are brighter than others and some bloom at different times so there is a chance to have many color varieties and a longer blooming season.

Grown mostly in Florida, California and the Gulf States, they usually do well in a wide range of soils.

There are also several shrubs, *gilliesi, regia* and *pulcherrima,* that make attractive landscaping plants. Barbados pride or dwarf poinciana (*P. pulcherrima*) grows to ten feet high, produces yellow-orange flowers. Bird-of-paradise bush (*P. gilliesi*) has showy yellow blooms. *See also* FLAMBOYANT TREE.

POINSETTIA: Poinsettia with its large, red, flower-like bracts is one of the most favored Christmas flowers.

The poinsettia, although a tropical American species of *Euphorbia,* is most popular as a pot plant. It is suitable for garden culture in frost-free regions and is considered a shrub, growing to ten feet or sometimes twice that height under proper conditions.

CARE DURING BLOOMING: Protect the poinsettia from draft, keeping it in a temperature of 70° in the daytime and not lower than 63° at night. A sunny window, preferably protected by a storm sash to prevent cold drafts, is a good place to keep the potted poinsettia, as they require a lot of sun. Water every day from above with tepid or slightly warm water. Never let the soil dry out, yet do not keep it soggy. The utmost care must be taken in watering, as excess moisture is sure to shorten the period of the plant's attractive display.

Even if kept under perfect conditions, the plants will drop their leaves later in the winter until only the red bracts remain at the top. This is the natural behavior of the poinsettia which requires a resting period after it has bloomed. When the lowest leaves begin to drop, withhold water gradually, and finally keep altogether dry. When only the naked stems remain, store the pot in a warm, dry place until early May without applying any water.

SPRING AND SUMMER CARE: In May shake the old soil out of the pots and repot in fresh, rich soil. The soil should consist of garden loam, sand and leaf mold, to which a small quantity of dried sheep or cow manure may be added. Cut down the stems to within two or three eyes from the base. Water and sink the pot outdoors in a sunny spot level with the soil surface. Soon after placing outdoors new shoots will grow from the eyes. All during the summer the plants will grow into large, well-branched specimens. Plants must receive full light and sunshine throughout the day and require lots of moisture.

FALL CARE: In the fall, when the temperature drops to 45 or 50° at night, take the pots up and give them a sunny place indoors where the temperature does not fall below 65°. Plenty of sunshine is imperative, and with judicious watering the plants will again be a blaze of color at Christmas.

PROPAGATION: The propagation of poinsettias is accomplished by cuttings. The tops which are removed before the plants are repotted are suitable for cuttings. Divide them into four to six inch lengths and place in warm water for about 15 minutes. This stops the sap from flowing too freely. Dip the lower end into the powdered charcoal and insert the lower third into sharp sand for rooting. A temperature of 65° must be maintained during the rooting process; keep them in a sunny location. When roots have formed, set them in small pots, water and keep shaded for a week or two. As top growth increases, repot into larger containers. From now on they

are handled in the same manner as the mother plant.—*Barbara J. Hardy. See also* HOUSE PLANTS (GIFT PLANTS).

POISON IVY: (*Rhus radicans*) One of the most widespread and troublesome of all pest plants, this woody perennial inflicts a high toll of suffering every year, especially at summer camps, parks, bathing beaches and woodlands. Teamed with its similarly infectious relatives, the poison sumacs, it is also often responsible for reducing land values in these and other areas.

Poison ivy varies in growth habit from dwarf to climbing types producing aerial rootlets which anchor the vines to trees, as pointed out above.

The poisonous properties of this plant are attributed to urishiol, a yellow, slightly volatile oil, which occurs in resin ducts of leaves, flowers, fruits and the bark of stems and roots. The wood, pollen and leaf hairs are not poisonous.

Contact with poison ivy causes inflammation and swelling of the skin, followed by intense irritation and blisters. Often the skin breaks, the liquid escapes, and scabs or crusts form. Symptoms may appear from 12 to 24 hours after contact, although it varies from a few hours to several days. Some persons are apparently more susceptible at certain times than at others. Also, contact with the plant at different times during the season may result in varying degrees of infection and skin irritation.

It is generally advisable to consult a physician for treatment. If contact with poison ivy is known or suspected, immediate lathering with a strong alkali (laundry) soap with frequent rinsing can prevent inflammation and blistering. The alkali soap emulsifies the oil and, by thorough rinsing, this may be removed from the skin.

PLANT CHARACTERISTICS: Poison ivy varies in growth habit from dwarf and erect forms to straggling or climbing types that produce aerial rootlets which anchor the vines to fences, walls or trees. Slender, creeping rootstocks grow from the base of the stems and run underground for several yards. Short, leafy stems emerge from the soil from these rootstocks.

The leaves of poison ivy are alternate on the stem and are divided into three leaflets; each is oval-shaped, pointed at the tip and tapered to the base. The terminal leaflet is longer stalked than the two lateral ones. The leaf surface, contrary to popular notion, may be *either* glossy or dull green and smooth or somewhat hairy. Leaf margins may vary from entirely straight to toothed or somewhat lobed. In deep shade or in dry weather, leaves may be light green, yellowish-green, or even red. In autumn, they turn yellow and bright red before falling.

The greenish-yellow flowers, borne in clusters, often pass unnoticed. The grayish-white, berry-like fruit measures up to about $\frac{1}{4}$ inch in diameter and contains a one-seeded pit. Stripes make it look like the segments of a peeled orange. These fruits persist on the shrub through the winter and are eaten by some 55 different species

of birds in the U. S. In this way, seeds are readily dispersed from place to place. Because some plants produce only male flowers, fruits are not always found on a green plant.

Poison ivy, though often found in rich woods, also thrives in dry, rocky fields, pastures, fence rows, banks and waste places. In being cautious for its presence, one should not mistake Virginia creeper or moonseed for poison ivy. Virginia creeper has five leaflets and moonseed is only three-lobed. Hog peanut, another plant sometimes confused with the pesty ivy, does have three leaflets, but has pink or white flowers, produces a pod, and is a twining-type vine.

CONTROL: In large infestations, poison ivy can be controlled by mowing close to the ground in midsummer, followed by plowing and harrowing, or by grazing sheep or goats. For smaller patches, the roots may be grubbed out. If these plants are burned, one should be careful not to stand in the smoke of the fire because the infection-causing oil will stick to particles of soot and may thus be carried to the skin.

There is much helpful control information in the Farmer's Bulletin No. 1972, *Poison Ivy, Poison Oak and Poison Sumac,* which can be obtained from the Supt. of Documents, U. S. Government Printing Office, Washington, D. C., for 15 cents. Main methods described are cultivating, mowing or cutting, grubbing out roots, using spray, and smothering. A most effective way of eradicating new plants is to put on a long-sleeved jacket and leather gauntlet gloves and pull them out by hand, as fast as they appear, and destroying the roots.

Under trees where it may be difficult to mow regularly by machine, and where plowing is not feasible, try smothering the ivy with tar paper or cardboard. A deep mulch of straw or other organic material will also be effective as well as more attractive. Poison vines growing in the trees themselves can be handled most effectively by cutting all of the vines near the ground, and coming back a week or more later and pulling the dying, wilted plants from the trees. Be careful, however, as the vines are still virulent.

Aside from medicine available from physicians to foster immunity, some gardeners report that liberal applications of linseed oil give effective protection.

On the Pacific coast, poison oak (*R. diversiloba*) can be controlled by the same methods used to eradicate poison ivy.

POISON OAK: *see* POISON IVY

POISONOUS MUSHROOMS: There are more than 4,000 different species or kinds of wild mushrooms. Of these, some 40 to 50 are known or suspected to be more or less poisonous. The genus Amanita includes several of the most deadly kinds. This type is characterized by gills that are "free," that is, they come up close to the stem, but are not attached to it. The spores and gills are white. A ring is present and usually prominent on the stem just below the cap as it expands, but this ring later shrinks and becomes inconspicuous. The base of the stem is enlarged into a cuplike sheath or bulb—but this is often hidden in the soil and can easily be missed unless one suspects its presence and looks for it.

Although the genus Amanita contains the more deadly of the poisonous kinds of mushrooms, a number of others are known to be toxic in varying degrees. Common sense dictates that one should not eat wild mushrooms without knowing which are edible. It is not enough to learn the mushrooms of the Amanita genus, avoid them, and then eat all others. The only safe way is to learn to recognize some of the edible kinds and eat only those you know thoroughly. For example, the saddle fungus, *Gyromitra esculenta,* has long been eaten in quantity both in Europe and America, and is considered by many to be of the choicer edible fungi. However, this fungus has caused a number of cases of fatal poisoning.

OTHER POISONOUS PLANTS: It is well for the gardener to remember that certain other common plants are poisonous. For example, rhubarb leaves are poisonous; all parts above the stem should be removed before it is prepared for cooking. Even lily-of-the-valley can be poisonous if taken internally. Aconite (all parts), larkspur (foliage), Christmas rose (roots), foxglove (leaves), garland flower (berries), oxalis (leaves), oleander (leaves)—all can prove poisonous. Others include jimson weed, matrimony vine, meadow saffron, and English ivy.

POISON SUMAC: (*Rhus vernix*) A bog bush, known also as swamp sumac, poison dogwood, poison elder, poison ash or thunderwood, this pest plant can be more poisonous than its near relative, poison ivy. The conditions of poisoning and the toxic principles are the same as for poison ivy.

Bearing greenish-white berries, poison sumac can be distinguished from the harmless staghorn sumac and smooth sumac, both of which have red berries. Some confuse green ash with poison sumac; however, green ash has only one stem per plant and the leaf margin is toothed, while poison sumac produces a clump of stems and has leaves with unbroken margins.

A coarse shrub that grows from six to 20 feet tall, poison sumac has smooth, gray bark and smooth branches. There are from seven to 13 leaflets per leaf and the leaves are opposite. Autumn foliage is orange to scarlet in color. The greenish-yellow flowers may be male or female and are arranged in a spreading or pendulous branch arising from the point of leaf attachment to the stem. Flowers appear from May through July; the globular fruits ripen from August to November and are conspicuous all winter.

Poison sumacs are most common in wet places: in bogs and swamps or along streams and ditches. In contrast, the harmless sumacs grow only in well-drained soil or even in fairly dry soils. Control recommendations made for poison ivy are applicable to poison sumac, with the added caution that this plant is even more toxic. *See also* POISON IVY.

POKEROOT: (*Phytolacca americana*) A native perennial plant of frequent occurrence in moist rich soil along fences and in uncultivated land throughout the eastern half of the United States. The root and the berries are used in medicine. The seeds and the roots are poisonous.

Pokeroot thrives in deep rich soil well supplied with moisture and may be readily grown from seed sown early in spring in rows four feet apart and barely covered. The seedlings are thinned to stand about three feet apart in the row. Frequent shallow cultivation is required. The plant develops long, thick, fleshy roots. At the end of the first year these may be turned out without great difficulty by means of a deep-running plow, but when the plants are older they may have to be dug by hand.

POKEWEED: (*Phytolacca*) Also known as pokeberry and inkberry,

A poisonous wild shrub that grows to ten feet high, pokeweed or pokeberry produces white flowers. Its toxic root resembles horseradish.

pokeweed (*P. americana*) is a poisonous wild shrub growing to ten feet high; its highly toxic root resembles horse-radish. The plant produces white flowers and blackish-red berries. Another member of this plant family, umbra (*P. dioica*) is often grown as an ornamental evergreen tree in California, where it sometimes grows as high as 50 feet.

POLEMONIUM CAERULEUM: see JACOB'S LADDER

POLLEN: Without the tiny invisible seeds of life we call pollen, the world would become a bare, bleak place in a very few years. Borne by wing and wind, it is the vital link between old life and new life. Pollen grains are only one-100th of an inch thick— under the microscope they assume all sorts of shapes: burrs, dumbbells, Christmas tree ornaments, wicker baskets. Many are eight-sided, with spikes and knobs all over them and ribbed or checkered markings. Most are golden in color, but some are bright red, green, blue and brown. The anthers in which they nest resemble sea shells, hat boxes and cornucopias.

POLLINATION: Without pollen, no seed could set, fruit trees would bear no fruit and the earth's carpet of grass would wither. The beautiful flowers we cherish have but one purpose, to serve as carriers for the frail, yet enormously potent grains that are the plant's sole means of reproducing itself.

Many plants are self-fertile, carrying both the male (pollen) and female (ovules) organs within each flower. Gravity may achieve the necessary meeting of these, as when corn pollen drops from the tassel to the silks. Other plants, like the holly, are either male or female, depending on the wind and pollinating insects to bring the male pollen to the egg in the female plant.

The latter process is called crosspollination, and plants resulting from it, as Charles Darwin noted, are usually healthier and bigger than those resulting from self-pollination.

For this reason, many plants that carry both the male and female elements in the same flower have special contrivances to prevent inbreeding by their own pollen: the egg may be infertile to it, or the organs may mature at different times. Thus another plant of the same species must provide the pollen. The law of eugenics says that inbreeding weakens a race, while crossbreeding strengthens and perpetuates it.

Even ordinarily self-pollinated plants may benefit from cross-pollination: cotton yields are increased when bees are present in the fields. And many fruits have their size increased up to 75 per cent by insect pollination as compared to self-fertilization.

The long distances pollen grains may have to travel from one plant to another seem all the more incredible when we realize that they are more perishable than snowflakes. These microscopic grains, with a life of perhaps two to three hours, may be airborne several miles before alighting on a target smaller than the head of a pin. Hot sun can kill them, and too much moisture will make them swell up and burst.

Some pollen, like that of the conifers, has air sacs that keep it wonderfully buoyant—pine pollen, abundant in the spring, has been found on the snows of Greenland, although the nearest pine trees are several hundred miles away across open sea!

ROLE OF INSECTS: Because pollen is so delicate, however, 90 per cent of the world's plants depend on insects for pollination. Wild bees, fleas, moths, wasps, beetles and butterflies spend a large part of their lives transporting pollen. Hummingbirds, which winter in Central America and move northward as far as Alaska in warm weather, carry pollen thousands of miles from country to country. Even snails, bats and slugs help in the vital work. Some pollen, too, clings to animal's fur and man's clothing, helping to pollinate many forests and field crops.

The best all-around pollinator, however, is the common honeybee. Working from early spring to late fall, she wallows in pollen while hunting nectar, literally covering herself with it and turning gold. Unlike other pollinators, she sticks faithfully to one kind of flower at a time, never mixing the pollen of even very similar-looking plants.

FLOWERS: Nature has artfully designed every flower so that its color, shape and fragrance will attract the busy winged workers. Even flowers that open at night have a special heavy fragrance to catch the sense of smell of night-flying insects on breezeless nights. Many flowers close their petals when storms approach, using them as umbrellas to protect the precious pollen.

When a flower blooms, the anthers open and the pollen shakes out like talcum powder. Then the bee, searching for nectar, picks up some pollen on her feet, belly or back, meanwhile depositing pollen she has brought from another plant on the stigma, a tube leading to the flower's female element. Some flowers have mallet-like anthers that dust the bee liberally with pollen. To make sure she treads in just the right places to pick up and deposit pollen, the nectar is often hidden beneath the anthers, with bright streaks of color to lead the bee across them.

When pollen grains are deposited on the stigma, they begin to sprout, sending a long thread down toward the egg cells. This process is activated by a hormone that may make the grains "travel" 1,000 times their own diameter. If you have a microscope, you can watch this phenomena by placing a pollen grain on a moist slide, with a bit of ovary tissue from the same plant near it. A thread will grow from the pollen straight to the ovary, guided by the hormone which has spread in the moisture on the slide.

Many plants are adapted to pollination only by certain insects. The yucca moth, for instance, deliberately collects pollen from the yucca's anthers and places it on the stigma, so that her larvae will have yucca seeds to eat. And in Africa there is an orchid that carries its nectar at the bottom of a 12-inch-long pollen-lined tube: only the hawk moth, with a foot-long tongue, can reach the nectar, pollinating the plant in the process!

The luscious Calimyrna fig will not produce fruit without pollen from the wild Capri fig, brought in by a tiny wasp. The ancient Greeks knew this, and "planted" the wasps in their orchards. (See the discussion of Caprification under FIG.)

HISTORY: The ancients' knowledge of plant mating, however, was forgotten for many centuries. Then in 1717, Thomas Fairchild made the first plant hybrid by placing pollen from a carnation on the female flower of a sweet William. Since then the rose has been crossbred 15,000 times, tulips 8,000 and China asters over 4,000.

Gregor Mendel, the Austrian monk who spent his life pollinating peas in his cloister garden, proved that plant breeding can be an exact science, a tool that can combine the best characteristics of several plants, to give us a finer grain to feed a starving world or a more beautiful rose to grace our lives.

Artificial pollination to increase the yields of many crops has been tried recently. Quick-frozen apple pollen, sent from the Blue Ridge to New England, has succeeded in pollinating the stubborn McIntosh when carefully applied by hand. But dust and liquid mixtures of pollen, sprayed from the ground and air—and even in bombs and shotgun shells—have notably failed to increase "sets" of many fruits. All of which goes to show there is nothing like the bee.

Pollen is a very rich food. Fed to baby bees by the nurse bees in the hive, its high content of protein, vitamins and minerals makes them grow amazingly fast. Certain Indian tribes collected pollen for soups and gruel, and believed it gave them great vigor. And some modern doctors credit the health-giving properties of honey to the numerous pollen grains it contains.

Some scientists have recently discovered that soil fertility and plant fertility are inseparable: a rich soil, particularly one well supplied with trace elements, produces plants whose pollen has better germinating qualities. Thus more seed and fruit are set because the pollen is more "live." *See also* BEES.

POLLINATION: Referring to the distribution of pollen; more specifically, the transfer of pollen to the stigma. It may be accomplished by insects, gravity, wind, birds, water or by artificial methods. Following is a definition of terms relating to pollination, as prepared by Prof. W. H. Griggs of the California Experiment Station:

Self-pollination: the transfer of pollen from the anthers of a flower of one variety to the stigma of a flower of the same variety.

Cross-pollination: the transfer of pollen from the anthers of a flower of one variety to the stigma of a flower of a different variety.

Pollenizer: the variety (plant, tree) used to furnish pollen. The male parent.

Fertilization: the union of the male germ cell, contained in the pollen grain, with the female germ cell, or egg, in the ovule.

Fruitful: a plant or variety that sets and matures a commercial crop of fruit.

Unfruitful: a plant or variety that fails to set a commercial crop of fruit and mature it.

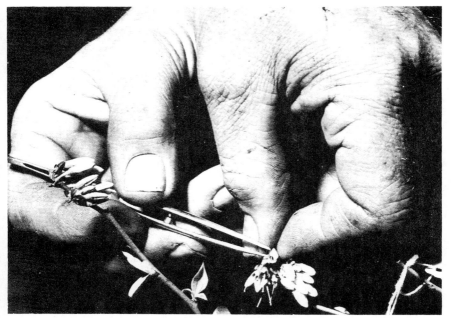

Artificial pollination is often tried in plant development tests. Above two blueberry varieties are crossed. The corolla and anthers are removed with tweezers from a flower on plant chosen as parent.

Fertility: the ability to set and mature fruit with viable seed.

Sterility: the inability to set and mature fruit with viable seed. This failure may be due to nonfunction of the pollen, the ovules, or both.

Compatible: ability of pollen to develop in the styles and reach the ovules in time to effect fertilization.

Incompatible: inability of viable pollen to develop in the styles rapidly enough to reach the ovule in time to effect fertilization.

Self-fruitful: a variety which sets and matures a commercial crop of fruit with its own pollen. This term would also describe plants which develop commercial crops of parthenocarpic fruit.

Parthenocarpy: the development of the edible fruit without fertilization. Parthenocarpic fruits are seedless.

Self-unfruitful: a variety which is unable to set and mature a commercial crop of fruit with its own pollen (or as a result of parthenocarpic fruit development).

Self-fertile: the ability of a variety to produce fruit with viable seed following self-pollination.

Self-sterile: the inability of a variety to produce fruit with viable seed following self-pollination. (Some varieties may be self-fruitful, even though they are self-sterile, because of their ability to produce parthenocarpic fruits.)

Self-compatible: a variety which produces pollen that is capable of developing in the styles and fertilizing ovules of the same variety.

Self-incompatible: a variety which produces functional sex cells but is self-unfruitful because the pollen tubes grow too slowly to reach the ovules in time to effect fertilization. Such a variety may, however, serve as an effective pollinizer for some other varieties. (Some varieties may be self-fruitful, even though they are self-incompatible, because of their ability to produce parthenocarpic fruits.)

Cross-fruitful: one variety, A, is used as a pollinizer for another variety, B, and B produces a commercial crop.

Cross-unfruitful: one variety, A, is used as a pollinizer for another variety, B, and B fails to produce a commercial crop.

Cross-fertile: one variety, A, is used as a pollinizer for another variety, B, and B produces fruit with viable seed.

Cross-sterile: one variety, A, is used as a pollinizer for another variety, B, and B fails to produce fruit with viable seed.

Cross-compatible: the pollen of one variety, A, is capable of functioning in the styles and fertilizing the ovules of variety B. (Variety B, however, may not be cross-compatible with A.)

Cross-incompatible: variety A produces functional sex cells, but its pollen tubes grow too slowly in the styles of variety B to effect fertilization. Variety A may, however, serve as an effective pollinizer for some other varieties. (Variety B may serve as an effective pollinizer for variety A.)

Interfruitful: varieties A and B both produce commercial crops when pollinated by each other.

Interunfruitful: varieties A and B both fail to produce commercial crops when pollinated by each other.

Interfertile: varieties A and B both produce fruit with viable seed when pollinated by each other.

Intersterile: varieties A and B both fail to produce fruit with viable seed when pollinated by each other.

Intercompatible: the pollen produced by either variety of a combination is capable of functioning in the styles and fertilizing the ovules of the other variety.

Interincompatible: varieties A and B are unfruitful when pollinated by each other because the pollen tubes of each variety grow too slowly in the styles of the other to effect fertilization. Either variety may serve as an

effective pollinizer for some other varieties.

Effective bloom: the length of time the tree is in conspicuous blossom.

See also POLLEN; ORCHARD (POLLINATION); BEES.

POLYGALA: Milkwort. A large genus of annual and perennial herbs, some shrubby, native in many parts of the world. Included in the genus are the principal cultivated species of the milkwort family. Some are grown for their flowers, which in some cases are showy clusters or spikes of various colors. At least one species, Seneca snakeroot (*P. senega*) is grown for its medicinal root. Some tropical species are grown as potted greenhouse plants. They are propagated by cuttings made in spring, and rooted in sandy loam in a cool greenhouse. Hardy species may be grown from seed or cuttings. All require sandy loam or sand peat.

Fringed polygala or flowering wintergreen (*P. paucifolia*) is a pretty native trailing perennial with light rosy-purple flowers. Also called gaywings, from the effect of its unequal petals. Grows in rich woods soil, from New Brunswick to Georgia, and may be grown as a wild garden subject.

P. dalmaisiana is a tender shrub growing to six feet, with rosy-purple flowers over a long period. Grown as a greenhouse plant.

Orange milkwort (*P. lutea*) is a showy annual which can be grown in bog gardens from Long Island south. Dense spike-clusters of yellow-orange flowers grow to about 1½ inches long.

POLYGONATUM: *see* SOLOMON'S SEAL

POLYGONUM: Knotweed or fleeceflower. A genus of the buckwheat family, *Polygonaceae,* of which most species are weed-pests, such as smartweed, knotweed, and black bindweed. A few are grown for ornament. Most are trailing or climbing, annual or perennial, sometimes woody, with alternate leaves, the stem swollen where the leaves clasp it. In cultivated species, flowers attract bees. Usually pink or white, the flowers are small and grow in terminal clusters or spikes. Annuals are started from seed. Perennials may be started from seed or may be propagated by woody cuttings or by division.

Silver lace-vine (*P. aubertii*) sometimes also called China fleece-vine, grows to 20 feet, with masses of fragrant white flowers in late summer. It is hardy to New York.

Prince's feather (*P. orientale*) is an annual which may also be grown under heat indoors. It grows to six feet, with large hairy leaves and pink or rose flower spikes 3½ inches long.

Japanese knotweed or Mexican bamboo (*P. cuspidatum*) is a perennial shrub which dies back to the root each year. Also a rampant grower that may easily become a pest.

Mountain fleece (*P. amplexicaule*) is a perennial growing to three feet with rose-red or white flower spikes up to six inches long, borne in fall. Recommended for the border.

POLYPODY: (*Polypodium*) A large genus of ferns, growing in all parts of the world. Many are native in North American woods; many are tropical. A few are cultivated as greenhouse or houseplants, and in the rock garden. Easy to grow, nearly all grow from a rhizome, or fleshy rootstock, and are shallow-rooting. Some are root-climbers. Propagation is by spores, by division of rootstocks or rhizomes.

Hares-foot fern or golden polypody (*P. aureum*) is a coarse tropical fern with fronds growing to four feet and a foot wide. A number of cutlivated forms were developed from this one.

Strap-fern (*P. phyllitidis*) is a native in southern Florida, and southward. Shining, leathery fronds to three feet, simple, sometimes with wavy margins.

Resurrection fern (*P. polypodi-* *oides*) grows in trees in the southern states and in tropical America. During the dry seasons the foliage curls up into a dry mass, and opens again to continue its growth when the weather is moist.

The common polypody (*P. vulgare* or *P. virginianum*) is common everywhere in the eastern and northern United States, growing on shaded rocky situations, on boulders and logs. Fronds are six to ten inches, with rounded pinnae, dark green, and evergreen. Easily transplanted to the rock garden, but should be cut, not torn, from its native woody bed. *See also* FERNS.

POLYSTICHUM: These ferns, growing from underground stems, are native in the temperate zone. Sometimes transplanted to the garden, and also grown in greenhouses. All are easily grown in sandy loam, and should be protected from strong light. Need plenty of water and a slightly acid soil. Most propagated from spores, a few by division. Fronds are usually evergreen, compoundly divided into sharp-toothed segments. Spores are in cases in rows on under side of vein.

Christmas fern or dagger fern (*P. acrosticoides*) somewhat resembles Boston fern. It grows from Nova Scotia to Texas, and is one of the most common American ferns. Fronds grow up to two feet.

East India holly-fern (*P. aristatum*) is more finely divided, being compound to three times. Variety *variegatum* has segments banded with whitish-green.

Shield fern (*P. brauni*) also called Broun's holly-fern, has rigid, shining fronds twice compound, the stem covered with chaff or scales.

Mountain holly-fern (*P. lonchitis*) has hardy evergreen fronds two feet long, native in the mountains of North America, Europe, and Asia.

Giant holly-fern (*P. munitum*) grows to 3½ feet, and is hardy as far north as Alaska.

Japanese holly-fern (*P. varium*) is an oriental species that grows from creeping stems. It is twice or thrice compound, fronds growing to two feet. *See also* FERNS.

POME: Fruit like the apple, pear, or quince, with seeds enclosed in parchment-like carpels which are encased in a fleshy fruit.

POMEGRANATE: (*Punica*) A fine fruiting shrub that has followed civilization around the world.

One of the most famous pomegranate hedges in the Southwest is the one which lines either side of the roadway leading to the Santa Ana Botanic Garden. In early summer the brilliant hibiscus-like flowers present a dazzling blaze of color, and the big crimson fall-ripening fruits weigh down the pliant branches with their heavy load. There are many varieties on the market, but Wonderful, Dwarf, and Sweet are most highly recommended.

CULTURE: Pomegranates are easily propagated from hardwood cuttings taken at the dormant period in midwinter when the leaves are off. They grow quickly into large eight-foot bushes and will thrive anywhere in the Southwest's mild climates from the cool seacoast to the hottest deserts. Heat develops the most luscious and juicy fruit.

The common variety of pomegranate (*P. granatum*) growing between ten to 20 feet high, is hardy as far north as Maryland on the eastern coast, although California and Florida are most suited. For fruit growing, plant the trees about 15 to 20 feet apart. Cut out shoots coming out of the base to keep the tree more compact.

The pomegranate grows well in many type soils and also makes a fine hedge. It blooms in spring and the attractive fruit ripens in summer.

POMEGRANATE MELON: *see* QUEEN ANNE'S POCKET MELON

PONDEROSA LEMON: *see* LEMON

PONDS, FISH: A homestead or farm fish pond can cost you from a few dollars to several hundred. It can return you thousands of dollars in fish crops, fun, and fire and drought insurance.

In fire protection alone, an adequate available source of water can save your home or barn. Using the pond for supplementary irrigation can mean higher yields or an entire crop saved from drought. Farmers have recognized these facts by building nearly a million ponds in the last two decades.

The average pond is from one-half to three acres in size. It's far from being just a hole scooped out of the ground just any old place. Don't try to build a pond without expert help, as nine out of ten ponds built by farmers alone fail. Only an expert can allow for all the conditions of rainfall, silting, seepage and so on a pond has to cope with.

Your county agent, the Soil Conservation Service, the Agricultural Extension Service and private pond contractors can help you. It would also pay to study Farmers Bulletin 1983, and USDA leaflet 259.

WATERSHED: The proper size watershed is very important. Five acres of cropland or ten acres of pasture or woodland are generally needed to "feed" an acre of pond of an eight-feet average depth. A much smaller watershed, of course, will do if you can find a brook or spring to supply some of the water.

Don't dam a stream—it usually has too big a watershed and will be sure to wash out your dam. You can divert part of a stream with pipe, tile or ditches to feed your pond on a by-pass basis, or use diversion ditches to channel runoff into it. Some naturally wet spots make ideal ponds, but dig them out sufficiently; a shallow pond breeds mosquitoes and makes for poor fishing because of weeds.

Water must never flow over your dam. You'll need a broad, well-sodded spillway about two to three feet below its top, to carry away heavy overflows.

You can also have a "trickle tube," a vertical drainage pipe with its open end six inches below the level of the spillway, and connected to a pipe running through the dam into the outside overflow. This will keep the spillway from being constantly wet, which would kill off the grass.

Fence your pond against stock, if you don't want the dam and banks trampled and broken in. A multiflora rose hedge makes an attractive barrier, and is also a fine bird refuge. You can turn in sheep during the day—they rarely break down the banks—and cows at night; they almost never go near the water after dark.

The Soil Conservation Service or state or commercial hatcheries will supply the proper kind of fish for your pond. One hundred to 300 fingerling bass to 1,000 bluegill fingerlings per acre is the usual ratio in many areas. The bass feed on the young bluegills, keeping their populations down. Crappies, sunfish and trout are used in other regions.

FEEDING: How you feed your pond will determine the quantity and quality of your fish harvest. One thousand pounds per acre of manure is good. Compost may be substituted for the manure, and 500 pounds finely ground rock phosphate is another good feeder. These fertilizers may be spread in equal amounts once a month from May to September. They go to feed, not the fish, but the minute organisms called algae and plankton which the fish eat. This microscopic plant life is the green scum which forms on a pond in summer. If the water in your pond is clear for more than a foot down, there are not enough algae—fertilize quickly.

But don't overfertilize. Too much will reduce the oxygen content of the water and injure the fish. Excessive feeding that makes very dark, scummy water can be overcome by spreading lime. Never use copper sulphate, as recommended by some experts, to clear the water. In more than a very minute two parts per million, it will kill everything living in the pond.

Silt, too, is an enemy of algae, so if there are cultivated fields or other erodible land in the watershed, use approved soil conservation methods on them to keep soil out of the pond.

Constant fishing is necessary to keep the pond from becoming overstocked. You can't overfish—most ponds, say authorities, would produce twice as heavily if their potential was realized by more fishing. *Fish are a farm crop.* You can harvest more than 300 pounds of fish per acre per year from a good pond (more than the amount of beef you could raise on the same area!). You should remove at least five pounds of fish per acre each week. That's a lot of vital protein for your whole family.

It takes 5,000 gallons of water to produce a bushel of corn. In drought, irrigation from a pond can rescue a parched crop. And a pond will help maintain the water table. Dry wells are rare in pond areas.

Around your pond you want to create the best possible conditions for wildlife. Fertilize your dam and plant it to grasses and a legume like the tall sericea lespedeza, which will provide cover and food for birds and small animals. Plant a willow or two, and other shrubs and trees nearby. Your pond will soon play host to all kinds of birds, plus insect-eating frogs and snakes, and perhaps even muskrats or raccoons.

A private swimming hole, a cool bank to picnic on, fat bass for the table, plus boating, skating and mallard shooting—that's what a pond can mean to your family. It can immeasurably increase your enjoyment of life, as well as the value of your organic farm or homestead.

POOLS, GARDEN: *see* LILY POND; WATER GARDEN

POPLAR: (*Populus*) Most species of poplars prefer rich, damp or even wet soils. They are quick-growing, hardy, relatively short-lived trees, sometimes called aspen or cottonwood. The poplar is an esteemed ornamental tree, and many hybrids have been developed for reforestation and farm woodlots. The flowers appear in early spring in hanging catkins.

Quick-growing hardy trees, Lombardy poplars are very often used for screen plantings along property lines. These trees prefer damp, even wet soils.

The white poplar or abele (*P. alba*) is the only species that does well on dry soils. It grows from 30 to 60 feet tall, and has a variety, the bolleana poplar, which is of a columnar habit. The lombardy poplar (*P. nigra italica*), is also columnar. Both are popular for screen plantings, but the lombardy poplar rarely lives more than 20 years. The black poplar (*P. nigra*), is a wide-growing tree from 40 to 80 feet tall, with twisted leaves that quake in the slightest breeze.

Others with quaking leaves are the quaking aspen (*P. tremuloides*), the European aspen (*P. tremula*), the large-toothed aspen (*P. grandidentata*), and the cottonwood or balsam poplar (*P. balsamifera*), and the Carolina poplar (*P. canadensis*). The certinensis poplar (*P. berolinensis*), is a columnar tree, very hardy and often used for windbreaks in the prairie states. *P. canadensis,* balm-of-Gilead, is not as hardy as the other poplars; its buds are made into cough medicine. All of these grow 50 feet tall or taller. *P. simoni,* the shortest poplar, grows 20 to 30 feet high. There are many other poplars, not as widespread as these, and several varieties with weeping forms.

Since their seed does not often come true, poplars are usually propagated by hardwood cuttings, buried in sand over the winter.

POPPY: (*Papaver*) The true poppies are annual or perennials growing from six inches to four feet high. Some of them are among the showiest plants in our gardens, having blooms of both magnificent coloring and huge size. Many poppies make long-lasting cut flowers if the bottom inch or two of the sappy stems is burnt before putting them in water.

A very showy plant, ranging from six inches to four feet high, poppies should have full sun, plenty of room to grow, and a humus-rich soil.

Poppies like light soils, sandy or even gritty in texture, with good drainage and lots of humus. Dig the bed at least 18 inches deep, and mix in manure, leaf mold and sand. Full sun and plenty of room to grow are also vital.

ANNUAL TYPES: The annuals include the free-flowering tulip poppy (*P. glaucum*), which especially likes loose soil and is a biennial in warm climates. The corn poppy (*P. rhoeas*), is the famous one that grows in Flanders fields. The Shirley poppy was developed from the corn poppy, and if given ample room, both of these will make handsome plants up to three feet across, with spectacularly lovely flowers. The opium poppy (*P. somniferum*) is a very tall, wide poppy that also needs plenty of space and a sandy loam soil. *P. pavoninum* is a one-foot-tall, hairy annual.

All the annual poppies suffer from transplanting, so sow the seed where they are to grow whenever possible. Unless the winters are very severe, sow in late summer or early fall; in very cold climates, in early spring.

PERENNIAL TYPES: The short Iceland poppy (*P. nudicaule*) and the tall oriental poppy (*P. orientale*) are favorite hardy perennials of great beauty. Like all the perennial poppies, they need a rich soil for superlative bloom. The Iceland poppy in particular requires perfect drainage, or it will rot off. It will bloom the first year from seed, and self-sows freely.

Oriental poppies want a mulch of rotted manure in the fall, removed in the spring, and need staking. They are long-lived and get more beautiful each year. Any transplanting should be done in August, just after the foliage dies down. Propagating can be done then, too, by cutting the taproots of mature plants into small pieces and planting them in sandy loam soil.

Another perennial is the alpine poppy (*P. alpinum*) a very low grower which is excellent for the rock garden. It self-sows freely, prefers a gritty soil, and may be treated as an annual. Two others are *P. pilosum,* very similar to the Iceland poppy, and *P. bracteatum,* which grows three feet tall and is an extremely hairy plant.

Sow the seed of perennial poppies under glass or in the cold frame, transplanted to a mixture of equal parts of loam, sand and leaf mold, and plant them in their permanent spots as early in the spring as possible. Or sow in summer where you want them to grow, covering the seed very lightly and sprinkling gently every other day. Always thin to provide ample room. *See also* FLOWER GARDENING.

PORTULACA: Often called Purslane, this low-growing, bright-flowered plant is a perennial—although widely grown as an annual in the North. Its single and double flowers are vari-colored, appearing in masses of yellow, pink and purple.

The plants will grow in almost any garden soil, but do best in well-drained loam. Seeds are usually sown in April, require ample moisture to germinate. Once started, however, these plants will survive almost desert dryness and provide generous blossoming if in the sun.

Portulaca is useful in rock gardens and for low borders and edgings. It's also a valuable plant to place between stones in paved areas, and makes a good grass substitute in hot, dry locations.

Most popular species is *P. grandiflora,* commonly known as Rose Moss, which has low, slender stems, short leaves and one-inch bright-colored blooms.

POTASH: One of the three major plant nutrients, potash is essential for the development of strong plants. Potash is the mineral that concerns itself chiefly with carbohydrate manufacture, whether starches or sugars. Although potash is not put into the carbohydrate molecules, all starch and sugar making stops when potash is not available.

Potash can do more than any other mineral to counteract excesses of nitrogen. While high nitrogen may cause plants to lose their resistance to disease, a good supply of potash will increase resistance. The plant can then readily construct cell walls to house extra protein with the increased starch and therefore cellulose. Fungi will have trouble boring through the firm outer tissues that are built up. Good

NATURAL SOURCES OF POTASH

MATERIAL	Potash Content (K₂O)
Wood ashes (broad leaf)	10.0%
Wood ashes (coniferous)	6.0
Molasses wastes (curbay)	3.0 to 4.0
Flyash	12.0
Tobacco stems	4.5 to 7.0
Garbage (NYC analysis)	2.3 to 4.3
Water Lily stems	3.4
Cocoa Shell residues	2.6
Potato tubers	2.5
Dry potato vines	1.6
Vegetable wastes	1.4
Castor pomace	1.0 to 2.0
Rapeseed meal	1.0 to 3.0
Cottonseed meal	1.8
Olive pomace	1.3
Beet wastes	0.7 to 4.1
Silk Mill wastes	1.0
Wool wastes	1.0 to 3.5

HAY MATERIALS

Vetch hay	2.3
Alfalfa hay	2.1
Kentucky blue grass hay	2.0
Red clover hay	2.1
Cowpea hay	2.3
Timothy hay	1.4
Soybean hay	1.2 to 2.3
Salt hay	0.6
Pea forage	1.4
Winter rye	1.0
Immature grass	1.2
Garden Pea Vines	0.7
Weeds	0.7

LEAVES

Apple leaves	0.4
Peach leaves	0.6
Pear leaves	0.4
Cherry leaves	0.7
Raspberry leaves	0.6
Grape leaves	0.4
Oak leaves	0.2

NATURAL MINERALS	Potash Content (K₂O)
Granite dust	3.0 to 5.5%
Greensand marl	7.0
Basalt rock	1.5

STRAW

Millet	3.2
Buckwheat	2.0
Oats	1.5
Barley	1.0
Rye	1.0
Sorghum	1.0
Wheat	0.8
Corn Stover	0.8

MANURE

Cow (fresh excrement)	0.1
(dried excrement)	1.5
(fresh urine)	0.5
Horse (fresh excrement)	0.3
(dried excrement)	1.6
(fresh urine)	1.5
Hog (fresh excrement)	0.5
(fresh urine)	0.8
Goat and Sheep (fresh excrement)	0.3
(dried excrement)	3.0
(fresh urine)	2.3
Chicken (fresh)	0.6 to 1.0
(dried)	1.2
Pigeon (fresh)	1.0
Duck (fresh)	0.6
Goose (fresh)	0.6
Dog (fresh)	0.3

ASHED MATERIAL

Banana residues (ash)	41.0 to 50.0
Pea pods (ash)	27.0
Cantaloupe rinds (ash)	12.0

potash supply will encourage sturdy plants and fruits will be richly colored.

DEFICIENCIES: Plants lacking potash do not resist heat, cold or disease well and their process of photosynthesis is slowed down. Weak stems often indicate potassium deficiency in grains. Deciduous fruit trees show firing of the leaves when potassium is lacking. Of course, a lack of this element reduces yields.

MURIATE OF POTASH: America's main source of chemical fertilizer potash is the vast deposit of potassium chloride salts in our southwestern desert. Some gardeners and farmers think this fertilizer is "natural" because it was deposited there by natural means. But this muriate of potash, as it is commonly called, is a deposit of an ancient ocean and has more in common with the salty environment of the seas than with productive natural soils.

Tobacco farmers have had much trouble with muriate of potash in recent years, because the residue of chlorine it leaves in the soil hurts the "burn" quality of the tobacco. Natural mineral and organic sources of potash do not carry this chlorine residue.

Potash supply has long been a problem for eastern and midwestern farmers, because many soils in temperate regions are inherently deficient in this element. On the other hand, many soils in arid regions have good natural potash reserves.

NATURAL SOURCES: There are three sources of potassium used by organic gardeners and farmers:

1. Plant residues
2. Manures and compost
3. Natural mineral sources, like granite dust and greensand.

Plant residues, manures and compost bring to the soil potash that is free and available. It is a known fact that even in highly fertile soils the supply of this free potassium is hardly ever enough to meet the needs of a growing crop. So during the growing season the roots of plants come in contact with potash "locked up" in the soil's minerals and make it available.

Following is an explanation from the book *Irrigated Soils,* by Thorne and Peterson:

"The supply of soluble potassium in the soil solution is inadequate to meet the requirements of growing crops even on highly fertile soil . . . At the present time, direct root absorption of potassium from clay and other minerals through contact exchange is considered more important than feeding from the soil solution."

What that means is that if your soil does not happen to have proper reserves of potash in its mineral structure, you are likely to have a potash deficiency. Natural mineral fertilizers —granite dust and greensand—are the ideal solution because they supply the mineral potash reserves that plants can draw on throughout the growing season. Natural minerals for potash are useful even if you use pretty much compost or manure, as the potash from these organic sources can be washed out of the soil or used up by plants. The best plan is to use both organic and mineral potash sources—organic for short term potash release and mineral for the long term. An added advantage of that plan is that the organic material you add will stimulate soil bacterial activity which makes it easier for the mineral potash to be released.

GRANITE DUST: Granite dust is now the most widely used natural potash mineral. Granites from different areas have varying potash contents, but the average is from three to five and one half per cent. Fineness of grind of the material should be considered when buying a potash mineral, because the more finely ground material will release its nutrients quicker.

See also FERTILIZER; GRANITE DUST; GLAUCONITE; GREENSAND.

POTASH ROCK: A naturally-occurring rock containing a high percentage of potassium. Potash rock is one of the most effective potassium fertilizers.

Modern machinery can pulverize rock materials to such fineness that nutrients become available for plant assimilation in relatively short periods of time, dependent upon the condition of the soil to be treated.

How to Use: Potash rock may be used in any quantity, usually one-half ton per acre, or about two and a third pounds per 100 square feet of garden area. It may be used on most any type of soil, contributing a wide variety of minerals without danger of overdosing. The mineral elements are readily available, when organic matter is added to soils, by multiplying the bacteria and also gives mild organic acids, which takes care of most deficiencies. Potash rock may be applied directly to the soil or may be added to the compost pile. *See also* Greensand; Glauconite; Granite Dust; Potash; Fertilizer.

POTASSIUM: One of the three essential elements (along with phosphorus and nitrogen) needed by growing plants. *See also* Potash; Fertilizer; Granite Dust; Glauconite; Greensand.

POTATO: (*Solanum tuberosum*) The home gardener with sufficient garden space and a cool, dark storage cellar may grow and store his family's potatoes by the organic method in almost any part of the country. Formerly a crop which could be successfully grown only in cool areas, potatoes are now grown in areas where summers are fairly hot if they are sufficiently mulched. Moreover, potatoes which are mulched seem to suffer less from insects and diseases than those grown by the older methods.

Seed potatoes certified free of disease may be purchased from seed dealers. Unless the gardener has been able to save some of his own which he knows were disease-free, certified seed potatoes are safest to plant. Varieties best for planting differ with each area; however, there are a few which are

outstanding and should be planted wherever possible.

VARIETIES: Kennebec is especially recommended as a late potato (110 days) which is resistant to late blight. Katahdin, also a late potato (110

Potatoes need plenty of moisture and an acid soil, between pH 5 and 6. Plant seed potatoes 12 inches apart in 3 to 5 inch deep furrows.

days) is partly resistant to virus diseases, and has a very high vitamin C content. Also high in vitamin C is Irish Cobbler, which takes 100 days to mature. Cherokee (107 days) is resistant to scab and late blight.

CULTURE: Potatoes need plenty of moisture and an acid soil. They should be planted in a different position each year, following a crop of a legume if possible. They should never follow tomatoes, which are of the same family and subject to many of the same diseases. Although they need calcium, they should not be planted on freshly limed soil, because lime favors the spread of scab. Ground limestone should have been applied to the soil at least a year before the potatoes are planted.

Soil for potatoes should have a pH factor of 5.0 to 6.0. This may be attained by a plentiful addition of green manure.

Fresh manure must never be used on potato land and even if well-rotted manure is used, it should be plowed or raked well under the topsoil in the autumn before the spring planting. For a hundred foot row, ten wheelbarrow loads of rotted manure will pay dividends. But never touch the planted tubers with it. It may burn them and thus ruin chances for a successful crop.

An excellent green manure crop to use before the potato crop is soybeans, according to R. G. Atkinson and J. W. Rouatt. They recommend that soybeans be sown for several years in soil heavily infested with scab, as a control measure. Scab, they discovered, can only live in neutral or slightly alkaline soil. Soybeans turned under as green manure acidifies it. It has long been an accepted fact that green manure, whether soybean or Japanese millet, which is also recommended, will help to control scab by rapidly decaying and fostering rival soil organisms, beneficial to the potatoes and antipithetic to scab.

Insufficient potash in soil can result in potatoes which become soggy when cooked. Ample potash produces mealy potatoes. A potash deficiency can be corrected by adding to the soil about ¼ pound per square foot of a natural potash mineral such as greensand, granite dust, or pulverized feldspar. These natural minerals also contain the trace elements which are so essential to normal healthy growth, and which may be lacking in the soil.

A good fertilizer for potatoes may be made by mixing one part cottonseed meal, one part dried fish meal, one part bone meal, two parts greensand, and two parts ground phosphate rock.

Best seed potatoes are small ones which do not need cutting. Each potato, or piece, should contain one or more eyes, and should weigh one to two ounces. Pieces should be cut with plenty of flesh around the eyes since the plants must live on this stored food while sprouting. Cut seed should be allowed to dry 24 hours before planting.

Depending on the size and the number of eyes, five to eight pounds of potatoes are needed to plant a hundred foot row. The trenches or drills are five inches deep and the pieces of tuber are placed every twelve or fourteen inches. Early varieties are planted about two weeks before the last killing frost. Late varieties may be planted to mature as late as the first fall frost. Early crops, growing while the weather is still cool, are less likely to be bothered by disease than late varieties. Seed for late crops should always be chosen from the disease-resistant strains.

As soon as planting is finished, a mulch of straw or hay ten to twelve inches deep should be applied. This will keep the soil moist and cool, and foster healthy potatoes.

One organic gardener has reported growing potatoes successfully on leaves with a cover of mulch, but without planting in soil. Leaves are piled over the potato patch the previous fall to a depth of three feet and left there for the winter. By spring they have packed down and earthworms are working through them. Potatoes are planted by laying the pieces directly on the leaves, in rows where they are to grow. The seed is then covered with 12 to 14 inches of hay or straw. More mulch is added later, if tubers appear through the first. When harvest time comes the mulch is pulled back, and potatoes are picked up and put into their sacks, with no digging necessary. No potato bugs have ever visited this bed, according to the grower.

HARVESTING: Potatoes are ready for harvest when the majority of the tops have withered. Early potatoes may be dug for table use at any time after they are large enough. But for storage, the potatoes should be fully mature. They may be left in the ground as much as four to six weeks if the weather is not too warm or too wet. After they are dug they should be allowed to dry as quickly as possible, and then should immediately be stored in a cool dark place. Stored in the light, they may "green," and greened potatoes are not fit for human consumption.

Potatoes are ready for harvest when the majority of the tops have withered. After they are dug, allow them to dry before storing in cool place.

In the garden, the insects and diseases injurious to potato plants can be controlled by removing insects as soon as they appear; give them no chance to breed. The Colorado potato beetle and the red slugs occur frequently. Sometimes blister beetles enter the garden and raise havoc among the potato plants. In the small garden, it is wise to place them in containers of kerosene.

There are about sixty diseases of potato plants, but many of them are local and unimportant. Where the air is particularly moist and cool, early blight may kill the vines. Late blight may also occur and cause tuber rot. Unusually warm, dry weather may result in tip-burn or hopper-burn which destroy the foliage. Common scab is disfiguring to the potato and can be avoided by keeping the soil acid. Applications of lime or wood ashes should not be used if this is to be accomplished.

Organic matter goes a long way in controlling plant disease. Several organic growers report they successfully controlled potato scab when their soil was treated with plenty of compost. After vines have already been infected with disease, one might pull them up and add them to the compost heap. *See also* VEGETABLE GARDENING; INSECT CONTROL; SWEET POTATOES.

POTATO BEETLE: *see* INSECT CONTROL

POTATO WASTES: The potash content of tubers is usually around 2.5 per cent. Dry potato vines contain approximately 1.6 per cent potash, 4.0 per cent calcium, 1.1 per cent magnesium, and considerable amounts of sulphur and other minerals.

Potato skins are usually put on the compost with other kitchen wastes. Their nitrogen content has been found, even when the skins were reduced to ashes, as high as .6 per cent. Tubers are storage organs and therefore abound with trace minerals. *See also* COMPOST; GARBAGE.

POTENTILLA: Also known as cinquefoil and five-finger. A genus of perennials of the rose family, native mostly in the north temperate to frigid zones. Stems are creeping, and plants somewhat resemble strawberry plants both in manner of growth and foliage. Flowers are mostly yellow or white in the species, with pink, red, orange both in doubles and single hybrids. Some are very showy, and are useful in beds and borders, and in rock gardens. Spread rapidly from rooted creeping stems. Thrive in any sunny spot, but prefer sandy soil. May be increased by seed or division. Hybrids flower from July to September. Some hybrids require a light covering of leaves in winter.

Best garden varieties are *P. argyrophylla,* with silvery foliage and amber-colored one-inch flowers in clusters; *P. fragiformis,* with velvety strawberry-like leaves and ¾ inch golden flowers; *P. fruticosa,* a four-foot shrub bearing yellow flowers from May to frost; *P. fulgens,* with yellow flowers, or scarlet in some varieties; *hybrida,* variety *Flambeau,* with double crimson flowers, or variety *Voleant,* single crimson flowers; *P. nepalensis,* with cherry-pink clusters on two-foot plants, and varieties *Roxana,* salmon-colored, *Miss Willmott,* magenta, or *recta,* pale yellow; *P. nitida,* growing silky mats one inch high, with one-inch apple-blossom pink flowers; *P. warrenii,* 2½ feet with showy yellow flowers.

POT LAYERING: *see* LAYERING

POT MARIGOLD: *see* CALENDULA

POTTING: *see* HOUSE PLANTS

POULTRY: There are many opportunities for the hobbyist, backyarder and homesteader to obtain pleasure and healthful food, and perhaps even reap a profit, from poultry.

Allowing poultry to range in field or yard is the recommended plan. Chickens in confinement have no way to correct deficiencies in feed formula.

Many people, for instance, who like fresh eggs daily at small cost, and who enjoy caring for animals, buy a half-dozen pullets in the fall and keep them through the winter. If such a pint-sized operation is properly managed, it can be quite profitable. Other opportunities include broilers, capons and turkeys, as well as ducks and geese. Then, too, there are many bantam and fancy breeds of poultry from which you can select an interesting hobby. The entire family can take part in any of these poultry enterprises.

But before you decide on any of these projects, be sure you understand what you are getting into. There are three things to consider in raising poultry:

1. Breeding
2. Housing and general management
3. Feeding

No matter what type of poultry you choose, you will be able to purchase birds which are the result of all the scientific advancements in breeding. The poultry division of your state agricultural college is the best authority to contact for data on good breeds.

You may find it helpful to know how long it takes to produce birds or products which are marketable:

Layers—it takes five to 5½ months before they produce their first eggs.

Broilers—Three to 3½ pounds in ten weeks.

Ducks—5½ pounds in ten weeks.

Geese (goslings)—12 pounds at 12 weeks of age.

Turkeys—toms average 26 pounds at 26 weeks of age and hens average 15 pounds at 24 weeks. Weights will vary depending on breed, feeding and management program used.

HOUSING: Housing for poultry need not be elaborate. There may be many instances where you can use a build-it-yourself program for housing and even equipment. Many feed companies have plans for nests, feeders, water stands, roosts and other equipment which can be homemade.

Plans for brooder houses and small poultry houses can be obtained from your local county agricultural agent, or from your state agricultural extension service. These agencies may also have information on plans for home-made equipment.

Floor space required per birds for various types of poultry is as follows:

Layers—Three to four square feet (depending on breed).

Broilers—¾ to one square foot.

Turkeys—Four square feet per hen, five square feet for mixed flocks of males and females, six square feet for toms.

Ducks—Four to six square feet for breeder flock.

If you plan to brood chicks, poults, ducks or geese, probably one of the simplest ways is to use an infrared brooder. This type of brooder can be set up in just a few seconds. Be sure to follow safety rules relative to type of sockets to use, reflector and protective devices.

FEEDING: Any bird or egg is only as good as the quality of the feed it gets. Only by building up your soil organically and producing your own poultry feed on it can you be sure of supplying your birds with all the vital elements they need. If you, as a poultry raiser, do nothing else to improve the condition of your flock but grow organic feed, you will be going a long way toward eliminating disease and production problems.

One tremendous advantage to growing your own feed is the fact that you can grind it frequently and in small batches. If ground feed is allowed to stand for two weeks or more without being used, a considerable portion of its vitamin content is lost. It is very difficult to tell how fresh a commercial mash is, and it is almost impossible for a layman to discover whether it is rich or deficient in essential vitamins and minerals.

Chickens in confinement have no chance to correct mistakes in the compounding of their feed formulas. Thus it is important to mix accurately a mash that will supply correct amounts of protein, fiber, calcium and phosphorus and vitamins. There is prac-

tically no limit to the number of ways in which different ingredients can be combined to form a satisfactory ration. In different regions, different crops can be used to compound a balanced poultry ration.

For that reason, it is important to take advantage of the excellent work done by the state experiment stations in analyzing and originating poultry mash and scratch formulas. Write to your own experiment station for their feed mixing recommendations. Here, for a start, is a simple formula devised by the Iowa Experiment station: ground yellow corn, 100 pounds; ground heavy oats, 100 pounds; ground wheat, 100 pounds; meat scrap, 80 pounds; dried milk, 20 pounds; salt, 4 pounds. Clean, warm water and fresh feed should be available from dawn to dark. Soluble and insoluble grit are also vital.

Feed requirements for the different classes of poultry vary:

Layers—need four to seven pounds of feed to produce a dozen eggs.

Broilers—2½ pounds of feed per pound of gain.

Ducks and turkeys—four to 4½ pounds of feed per pound of gain.

It takes about 30 pounds of feed to raise a pullet chick to laying age. Geese after the first few weeks can live largely on grass and other tender green feed and water. Geese make rapid growth, often gaining a pound a week for the first ten to 12 weeks.

RANGE: Allowing poultry to range on grass during the favorable seasons is the cheapest way to give them the advantages of fresh feed and of the organic method. Grass can supply as much as 20 per cent of their total feed intake. The bugs and worms they pick up are good fodder, too.

In late summer and fall when the grass dries up, you can feed fresh-cut alfalfa or clover, lawn clippings or greens like cabbage, kale, beet tops or Swiss chard. Poultrymen with no land for pastures do this regularly. Green pasture in the winter can be obtained by growing rye, oats or other suitable crop. Clean, mold-free legume hay is also good, and sprouted grains are especially valuable for winter feed.

Silage made from grasses, cereals or legumes while they are still immature and rich in proteins is excellent. Cut in half-inch lengths and pack tightly in 50-gallon barrels, with four gallons of blackstrap molasses diluted in about four times as much water added as a preservative. Two to five pounds per 100 laying hens and ten pounds per 100 turkeys is the recommended daily feeding rate.

LITTER: A practice that makes healthier and more productive chickens is deep litter, sometimes called built-up litter. Simply let the litter accumulate instead of cleaning out the poultry house every couple of weeks. Biological activity in the litter, just as in a compost heap, produces huge amounts of rich food.

Litter-reared chickens need no expensive animal proteins or mineral supplements, and if pastured or given ample green feed in addition, will need no vitamin A and D supplements. Antibiotics are also produced—litter-raised poultry is remarkably free from disease. Cannibalism, caused by imperfect diet, also disappears. The litter should always be at least six to eight inches deep, and it gets better with age. Peat moss, straw, ground corn cobs, wood chips, sawdust and peanut hulls are some good litter materials.

MANURE: Poultry manure is a valuable source of humus and nutrients for the soil. It exceeds all other farm manures in fertilizing value. Under average conditions, it is safe to estimate that in most flocks about 150 pounds of manure are produced per layer per year. Poultry manure is high in nitrogen but low in phosphoric acid and potash, so supplement it with natural ground phosphate and potash rock. Phosphate rock will also help fix the nitrogen in the manure, and deep litter will cut down on the nitrogen loss by absorbing the liquid portion of the droppings.—*Milton R. Dunk.*

BROODING PERIOD: Here is some expert advice from organic poultryman Thomas E. Johnston on starting out with chickens:

Housing and space: Set house for best exposure to sun—south or southeast.

Put 250 chicks in a ten by 12 house. Avoid the delusion that they appear lonesome and need a hundred or more companions. In a few weeks 250 will be crowding the house.

Cover litter with heavy paper, giving chicks a few days to learn the difference between starting mash and litter.

Devise a guard at each corner of the house to prevent crowding and smothering there.

Temperature: Start with a temperature of 90-95° F. at the edge of the hover of the fuel-burning brooder.

Effect gradual reduction of temperature to 80-85° F. at end of second week and 60-65° at sixth week.

Feed and feeder space: Begin with

Percentage composition of fresh and oven-dried poultry manure (U.S.D.A.)

Source of manure	Undried manure			Oven-dry manure		
	N	P_2O_5	K_2O	N	P_2O_3	K_2O
Laying hens, fresh	1.1	0.8	0.5	4.1	3.7	2.3
Laying hens, old litter	1.8	1.4	0.8	2.5	2.7	1.4
Growing chicks	1.6	0.9	0.6	5.4	3.6	2.4
Baby chicks	1.7	1.3	0.7	4.5	3.5	1.9
Turkey	2.0	1.4	0.6	—	—	—
Duck	1.1	1.4	0.5	—	—	—

starting mash in feeders before chicks all the time.

Allow one inch of space at the feeder for each chick at the start. This space should be doubled by the time chicks are six weeks old.

Make change to growing mash gradually at six weeks of age.

Start feeding cracked grains, such as a mixture of cracked corn and wheat to make up one quarter of the daily food intake, at eight weeks of age.

Water and water fountains: Provide one two-quart water fountain for every 50 chicks at the start. Give them water with the chill taken off.

Double the water fountain space by the age of six weeks.

Clean and disinfect water fountains every day.

Ventilation and humidity: The house should be equipped with a ventilating flue attached to a weather vane so that its opening turns away from the wind.

If air inside the house becomes dry, keep an open pan of water on the brooder stove.

Internal arrangement of house: Set feeders to get maximum light from all sides.

Set water fountains between hover and feeders so chicks will drink going to and coming from feed.

Allow no wet spots in litter by spilling of drinking fountains or other causes.

Train chicks to roost by the fifth week by providing them roosts, first on the floor and gradually raising them to a height of fifteen inches.

These rules are recognized as practices in chick raising which go far in preventing losses and promoting health in the flock of growing chicks. *See also* BANTAMS; DUCKS; GEESE.

POULTRY MANURE: *see* MANURE; POULTRY.

POWDER PUFF: *see* PINCUSHION CACTUS

POWDERY MILDEW: *see* DISEASE

PRAIRIE CLOVER: *see* PETALOSTEMON

PRAIRIE SMOKE: *see* GEUM

PRAYING MANTID: *see* MANTID, PRAYING

PRICKLY ASH: (*Zanthoxylum americanum*) A thorny-stemmed pest plant, this large shrub or small tree is a member of the citrus family. Measuring up to 12 to sometimes 25 feet in height, it has sharp, thorny stems. Branches, stems and twigs all have thorns up to ½ inch in length which occur in pairs at the bases of leaves.

The leaves are compound, bear from two to four pairs of leaflets plus an odd one. Young leaves are downy, becoming nearly smooth on the upper surface as they mature, but remaining hairy beneath. They are rather thick and are dotted with translucent oil glands. While the leaves and somewhat fleshy fruit (reddish-brown when ripe) are pleasantly aromatic, their taste is disagreeably pungent. Seeds are shiny black, about ⅛ inch long. Flowers are yellowish-green and open before the leaves appear.

Prickly ash inhabits rich, moist woods, thickets and river banks, besides thriving at edges of woodlands. Eradication of these thorny shrubs can be accomplished by grubbing out the roots.

PRICKLY GREENBRIER: (*Smilax hispida*) A thorny plant, the spines are black, very firm, and usually ¼ to ½ inch long. They may tear clothing or inflict wounds to unprotected skin. Even in winter the stem is a bright green which makes the plant readily identifiable.

Not too common, prickly greenbriers occur in scattered clumps which climb on other plants in woodlands of rich, moist soil. They attain lengths up to 20 feet. Several stems arise from a common rootstock. A pair of tendrils is at the base of each of the leaves, which are thin, vary from oval to heart-shaped, and generally have seven prominent veins each. Six to 20 flowers are clustered at the base of leaves. Berries are bluish-black in color.

The greenbrier may be controlled by grubbing out the rootstocks.

PRICKLY PEAR: (*Opuntia*) The prickly pear is one of the largest of the cactus families, some of which are called cholla or tuna. They may be flat or cylindrical in shape, a few inches high or over ten feet tall.

The hardiest opuntias are *O. compressa,* the common wild prickly pear of the northeast and central states, and *O. polyacantha,* the low, round-stemmed cholla, which thrives outdoors up to North Dakota. Both of these grow on sandy soils, often along shores, and have three-inch yellow flowers. They are easily transplanted from the wild or propagated from stem cuttings.

The outdoor culture of the rest is confined to the Southwest, but they are favorite greenhouse and house plants all over the country. Nearly all have extremely sharp spines arising from masses of short, barbed hairs, and white, yellow or red flowers. In some, the handsome berries are edible.

Some of the smaller ones for window gardens include the thimble tuna, *O. sphaerica,* a dwarf, red-flowered type that grows in clusters; cinnamon cactus, *O. rufida,* with green pads spotted with short spines, and yellow or orange flowers; fairy needles, *O. soehrensi,* grows in clusters with long spines and yellow flowers; *O. basilaris,* the rose tuna, has pretty rose-red pads and large pink blooms; and rabbit's ears, *O. microdasys,* is similar to cinnamon cactus but has plushy golden spines. Tuna, *O. tuna,* is a low, prostrate cactus with yellow, red-tinged flowers and pear-shaped berries nearly three inches long, a popularly eaten fruit in the West Indies.

There are also many big prickly pears, suited to greenhouse culture. They can be grown in tubs and put outdoors as garden accents in the sum-

mer. *O. cylindrica* grows up to ten feet tall and sometimes has no spines. *O. imbricata* is about the same height, but shrubby and with large purple blooms. *O. fulgida,* eight feet tall, has a woody trunk and pink flowers. Nopal, *O. lindheimeri,* sometimes called cacanapa, grows about 12 feet tall, with three-inch yellow blooms and two-inch purple fruits. The Indian fig, *O. ficus-indica,* is cultivated throughout the tropics for its big, juicy, edible red fruits. It is tree-like, often 15 feet high and usually spineless. The spineless prickly pears, incidentally, are sometimes used for cattle feed, particularly when the range grasses fail in drought. *See also* CACTUS.

PRICKLY PHLOX: *see* GILIA

PRIMROSE: (*Primula*) An increasingly popular perennial, with species suitable for flower borders, rock gardens, greenhouse or house plants, bog gardens, and for naturalizing in woody landscapes.

Popular perennials, primroses are grown both as a house plant and in the garden. This polyantha type is well suited for naturalizing under trees.

Growth habit is mostly low, the leafless flower stalks rising from a rosette of somewhat hairy leaves. Flowers are of many colors, growing solitary, in flat-topped clusters or umbels, sometimes one umbel above another on the stem; in loose clusters arising in whorls around the stem; and in dense round heads that resemble flowery popcorn balls. Individual florets have a slender tubular corolla with spreading lobes, the tip of the pistil sometimes showing in the corolla tube, called a pin-eye, or sometimes the stamens showing in the entrance of the tube, when it is called thrum-eyed.

Tender primroses are grown as greenhouse or house plants. Some hardy species are also grown indoors. Species treated in this way include *P. sinensis, obconica, malacoides, forbesi, japonica, kewensis, floribunda, verticulata, grandiflora,* and *stellata.*

All primroses need a moist situation, and must not be permitted to dry out even in the heat of summer. Where temperatures are high at midday, a northern or eastern exposure is best, with afternoon and midday shade. Some species prefer to grow under deciduous trees giving light shade, such as birches, where they will have shade all summer. The north side of a deciduous shrubbery border is also suitable for the earliest-flowering types. Especially suited for naturalizing under trees are *P. vulgaris, veris, eliator, acaulis,* and *polyantha.*

Although they must have moisture, most species must also have good drainage. Exceptions to this rule are the following, which grow well in the bog garden and will tolerate water around their roots, though never in their crowns: *P. pulverulenta, bulleyana, beesiana, florindae,* and *sikkimensis.*

Rock gardens or beds mulched with pebbles or stone chips are suitable situations for many types, which need coolness and at the same time exceptionally good drainage around the crowns. Many of the plants are small, and make good rock crevice plants. Suitable for rock gardens for one of these reasons are the following species: *P. auricula, bulleyana, capitata, clusiana, cortusoides, denticulata, elatior, farinosa, frondosa, japonica, juliae,*

marginata, spectabilis, vulgaris, veris, rosea, mistassinica, and *littoniana.*

Hardy and suited to the open border when they can be given enough moisture and partial shade are the following varieties: *P. auricula, capitata, elatior, farinosa, frondosa, vulgaris, veris, japonica,* and *sieboldi. P. florindae* and *sikkimensis,* also good rock garden or border specimens, are a little tender for northern gardens.

Outdoor Culture: Primroses grow best in a soil well supplied with organic matter which is retentive of moisture. A liberal addition of leaf mold or thoroughly rotted manure or well-decomposed compost should be spaded in where they are to be planted. Unlike many woods natives, primroses do not want too much acid. Their preference is a pH between 6.0 and 8.0. Yearly top-dressings of rotted manure may be lightly dug in around them.

Seed germinates best in cool weather, and may be sown in a cold-frame in fall, when germination will take place early in spring. Or seed may be started in a cool greenhouse in January, the seedlings transplanted to flats, then planted out in beds in May, and transplanted to their permanent sites in fall. Summer-sown seed does not seem to germinate as well, unless it has just ripened and been sown immediately. Some authorities believe that the tiny seeds become too hard to split open easily. They recommend rubbing the seed between two pieces of fine sandpaper before planting.

Plants are more frequently propagated by division than from seed, especially in the double varieties. When clumps have become large they should be lifted and divided, usually about every two or three years. If they are left too long, the divisions will become small and will not bloom the following season. The division should be done as soon after flowering as possible, except in the South, where it is done early in fall. When they are lifted, clumps will be found to have one large and possibly several smaller crowns. Each crown should be placed separately, and care should be exercised to prevent soil from remaining in the center of the crown, which seems to cause it to rot. Plants must be kept well watered until they are established.

INDOOR CULTURE: Winter is the natural blooming season of the Chinese primrose. The two most important factors essential to success with this primrose are a fair humidity and a cool temperature ranging between 45° and 55° F. However, it is quite hardy and will stand a temperature as low as 35° without showing any bad effects. Even if the plants have been frosted lightly they may be brought back if thawed out gradually in a dark room at a temperature of 35°. High temperatures of 70° or more, as are usual in living rooms, are not suitable for the Chinese primrose, and under such conditions the plants do not last long. A sunny window free from drafts is a good place for the plants. With the rising of the sun, as spring approaches, a little shade may be needed during the midday hours. If conditions are congenial the plants will bloom freely and continually for many weeks. Watering the plants requires both care and good judgment. Never let water touch any part of the plant.

Particular care should be taken never to pour water into the heart of the plant where the new flower spikes are forming. Always use water of room temperature. Apply it moderately whenever the soil shows signs of drying out. Hold the leaves together while carefully pouring the water on the soil. Do not splash it on, to prevent washing the soil away from the roots and wetting the stems and foliage. A small watering can with a long spout is almost indispensable, as the spout may be rested on the rim of the pot and by slightly tilting the can a thin stream of water will fall lightly on the soil. An hour or two after each watering, examine the saucers below

the pots and pour out any water that may have percolated through the soil. Sometimes older plants of the Chinese primrose bend over at the neck or base of the plant. If such is the case with any of your primroses, place three or four small sticks close to the stem to prop up the plant and hold it in an upright position. If because of too heavy watering the soil has been washed away from the base of the plant, add a little soil and press it moderately firm around the base to hold the plant up. Wilting leaves and flower stems should be cut out with a knife close to the base to prevent decay of the entire plant. While the plant can be carried over summer in a sheltered place in the garden, the results with the Chinese primrose are usually not worth the care they require.

The top primrose (*P. obconica*) is even more showy than the Chinese primrose, but the fact that contact with the leaves causes some people to contract a painful irritation of the skin is a point against its universal favor. If you are susceptible and by chance come in contact with the leaves, rub the affected parts briskly with clean sand, which is said to prevent the poisoning. *P. obconica* is easier to grow in the house than the Chinese. Its general cultural requirements and care do not differ materially from the points already outlined, but the temperature best suited ranges between 42° and 45° F. Present-day varieties of the Chinese primrose, particularly those of the variety *gigantea,* are marvels of size and color.

The Fairy primrose (*P. malacoides*) revels in the cooler temperature of 42° to 45°. The blooms are quite small but they are borne profusely and continuously. The discovery that the flowers will last some time after cutting has made this species valued also for bouquets. Its culture does not differ materially from that of *obconica.*

All the tender primroses can be grown from seed. The right time to start the seed is in April or May in order to have blooms the following Christmas. January-sown seed gives fall-blooming plants. They are not easy to grow without a greenhouse, but to those who have one, they present a good test of gardening skill. A leading grower of *obconicas* recommends that leaf mold, peat moss, and undecayed compost be avoided for these, as the cause of yellowing foliage. He recommends sowing the seed in pans or pots without covering it. Keep it dark, moist, and at a temperature of 54° to 58°. When germination takes place in from 14 to 21 days, a very thin layer of fine compost soil may be sifted over the young seedlings. Repeated transplantings are necessary. The plants should never be permitted to become pot-bound, and a moderately heavy loam should be used, free from freshly decaying materials, for re-potting. Weak liquid manure may be given once a week to established plants to increase the growth of foliage and flowers.

PRIMROSE WILLOWS: (*Jussiaea*) A genus of the *Onagraceae,* the evening primrose family, comprising mainly tropical creeping marsh or water plants, of which only two are under cultivation. They have alternate willow-like toothed leaves, and solitary yellow or white flowers. Grown in the aquatic garden, they are treated as annuals and planted from seed each year. Seed is planted in shallow pans or dishes and covered with sand; they are submerged below about an inch of water to germinate. After germination they may be potted to grow outdoors or in the greenhouse, and need to be kept very moist but not necessarily under water.

Cultivated species are *J. longifolia,* an erect two-foot herb from Brazil, with three to four inch leaves and yellow flowers. *J. repens* sends up three-inch oval leaves and small yellow flowers from creeping stems.

PRIVET: (*Ligustrum*) A genus of shrubs or occasionally trees of the olive family, *Oleaceae,* native in Asia, Australia, and the Mediterranean region. Several species are used in this country for hedges and wind-breaks. Many are very hardy, dense, glossy-leaved, and in some cases almost evergreen. Leaves are ovate, small, opposite. Flowers grow in white terminal clusters, sometimes fragrant and sometimes malodorous. They are easily grown in almost any soil, and are propagated by seeds, cuttings, or in the choice species by grafting.

Common privet (*L. vulgare*) will grow to 15 feet, with slender spreading branches and dense flower clusters followed by black berries.

California privet (*L. ovalifolium*) is upright and rather stiff, half-evergreen, with leaves to two and one-half inches long. Tender in the colder climates.

L. ibota or *L. obtusifolium* is a hardy Japanese form with wide-spreading branches, growing to six feet. Small nodding flower clusters bloom in June, and following are black bloomy berries that remain on the shrub most of the winter. Variety *regelianum* is a denser and lower-growing form which is good in front of higher shrubs.

Amur privet (*L. amurense*) is the hardiest, growing well in regions where other privet may be winter-killed. It will attain 15 feet, has light green foliage and berries.

L. indicum is an evergreen species, but can be grown only in southern California and Florida and the Gulf states. Wax privet (*L. japonicum*) is also evergreen, and grows slightly farther north. Oval leaves are about three inches long and leathery. *L. lucidum,* also evergreen, grows to a 30-foot tree in the far south. It is used frequently for street planting.

Striking for its midsummer flowers is *L. quihoui,* a six-foot Chinese shrub hardy in protected positions in the north. Flowers grow in clusters six to eight inches long in August and September. *See also* HEDGE; SHRUBS.

PROFILE: *see* SOIL

PROPAGATION: The great majority of plants can be propagated by seeds, cuttings, division and layering. For vegetables, annuals, biennials, and perennials, the most common reproducing method is by seeds.

Taken at the end of the growing season or during dormant period, hardwood cuttings are a fine method of reproducing many new plants.

Cuttings are an excellent way of reproducing new plants identical with the parent plants. Parts of plants cut from a parent plant, cuttings are usually inserted in water, sand, soil, peat moss or some other medium where they form roots and become new plants. This method is used for herbaceous perennials, trees and shrubs. Stem cuttings are obtained from softwood (when the stem breaks with a snap) and hardwood (taken at the end of the growing season or during the dormant period). The system of leaf cuttings is used with begonias and African violets, while root cuttings are used with such plants as oriental poppies.

Division is a type of cutting, often used with rhubarb, daylilies, peonies and iris. By this method, new plants are not grown from seeds or bulbs, but are separated from the parents.

Methods of division vary widely. Rough division consists of using a sharp spade to cut across large clumps of such plants as phlox and rhubarb. The pieces are then dug and replanted. Finer practices include digging and breaking the clumps apart with the hand or the fingers, or cutting them apart with a sharp knife. Suckers which develop from plants such as red raspberry and snowberry are dug individually. Crowns or rooted buds, which form (usually at the tips of rhizomes) toward the close of the growing season and push forward in the soil, are often severed and planted. The best example of this type is lily-of-the-valley, millions of whose "pips" are forced annually by florists. Tubers (short thickened parts of subterranean branches such as dahlia) are broken apart from the main stems and clumps and then planted separately.

Layering refers to the rooting of parts of a plant while it is still attached to the parent plant. This method is commonly employed with many bramble fruits and ornamental shrubs as forsythia, mock orange and junipers.

Still another way of plant propagation is by suckers or runners. Certain plants produce young shoots, called suckers, around the base of the parent plant. These suckers can be replanted and will develop quickly. Lilacs, snowberries and Japanese quince can be handled in this manner. With strawberries, propagation is by runners, on which new plants form at the nodes along the trailing branches. *See also* LAYERING; CUTTING; DIVISION; BUDDING; GRAFTING; VEGETABLE GARDENING; FLOWER GARDENING; HOUSE PLANTS; BRAMBLE FRUITS; COLD FRAME; FRUIT TREES.

PROSO MILLET: *see* PANIC GRASS

PROTECTING PLANTS: *see* MULCH; DRY WEATHER GARDENING; COMPOST; EVERGREENS; FRUIT TREES; ROSES; FLOWER GARDENING; VEGETABLE GARDENING; WINTER GARDEN CARE

PROTEIN: *see* HUMUS; NUTRITION

PRUNE: Any variety of plum which can be easily dried without spoiling. Italian plums are grown in the Northwest, and in California, where the bulk of the American prunes are dried, the varieties most grown are Sugar, French, and Imperial. Conditions in other parts of the country are too humid for sun-drying the fruit, and any that is dried elsewhere is done under artificial conditions.

Fruit is fully ripened on the trees until it drops, before drying. Sometimes the last of the crop is dislodged by shaking branches. The prunes are caught in a canvas frame, and are processed before drying. Commercially dried prunes are subjected to a lye bath, which splits the skin to make drying faster. They are rinsed, and then left in the sun for ten days or two weeks, after which they are stored for a period in air-tight containers to distribute evenly the remaining moisture.

Organically dried prunes are not subjected to the lye bath, and their skins are tougher after drying, but they are also free of the lye residue which is found on commercial fruit.

PRUNING: Trimming out unwanted or unhealthy portions of a plant in order to benefit the portions which remain. Pruning is done for one of the following seven reasons:

1. To remove dead or injured members. This work should be done whenever you see dead or injured parts of the plant.

2. To check the growth of plants where space is limited. This is not an ideal procedure but if you want to grow certain types of plants that tend to be too large for your grounds, you can do some intelligent pruning that will keep the plants within bounds for a limited time.

3. To thin plants that have become too dense to admit light and air to the area in which they are planted.

4. To encourage root growth by root pruning at the time of planting.

5. To alter intelligently the form and size of plants for design purposes. The pruned hedge and the sculptured plant are examples of this form of selective pruning.

6. To rehabilitate shrubs that suffer from neglect or poor growing conditions.

7. To encourage flower or fruit production, or to encourage the growth of larger flowers and fruit.

The time of pruning varies with the type of plant that you want to prune and with the results that you wish to achieve through pruning. Some pruning is done at any time suitable to the gardener's convenience; some pruning must be done at a specific season.

Pruning is not a mysterious process but a garden technique that requires an understanding of the growth habits of plants plus an intelligent program of plant care and an appreciation of the beauty of plant forms.

HOW TO PRUNE: Pruning heavy members of big trees is not a good job for the amateur, but if you want to undertake this work, the first requisite is a sharp saw. The first cut is made about a foot from the trunk. The branch is sawed about a third of the way through from top toward the bottom of the limb. Next an undercut is made an inch closer to the trunk from the bottom of the branch, until the branch drops off. This will leave a one-foot stub to be removed. Always remove stubs on trees and shrubs and cut back cleanly to the larger member. Paint large cuts with material which is made for the purpose.

This type of pruning cut should always be used for lateral branches above three-quarters inch in diameter.

Smaller laterals may be cut with a single cut of the pruning shears, always being slanted from flush above to slightly protruding below, in order to facilitate healing. No stub should ever be left. Lateral branches should not be cut half-way back, except in unusual cases, and then they should be cut to within one-quarter inch of a bud. It is better to cut them back all the way to the trunk.

PINCHING: There are many types of pruning tools, but one of the best and most convenient devices for small pruning is the combination of your thumb and forefinger. You can fashion many small plants to your bidding by constant and careful pinching back of soft growth with your thumb and forefinger. Terminal buds of conifers can be nipped out and the plant somewhat dwarfed. As you walk in your garden, nip off random growth, break out small twigs and branches that interfere with the form of the plant or with its size. This is a continuing operation to be done whenever the need arises.

Disbudding is usually done with the thumb and forefinger or can be done with a small sharp knife. The object is to produce fewer and handsomer blooms and is practised on roses, chrysanthemums and many other flowering plants. Disbudding is done early in the season before side buds have fully developed. When the side buds are removed the strength goes into the terminal bud which results in a finer, larger flower.

ORNAMENTALS: Since flowering shrubs and trees are grown in great part for their blossoms, one should strive to encourage and save the flowering wood. The best time to prune most flowering shrubs and trees, therefore, is shortly after flowering. Although it is not necessary to prune many of these shrubs throughout their lifetime, certain sorts benefit by removal of sucker growth, the occasional removal of old wood and a little heading back to control the general shape of

the plant. This is also true of flowering trees and the hawthorn is one that needs pruning more frequently than most of the others. The hawthorn sends out many "water sprouts" or suckers which are often sterile and just fill up the head of the tree. Crab-apples also benefit by removal of sucker growth. Remember that the natural form of the shrub or tree is usually beautiful and should be preserved.

Prune evergreen plants such as rhododendrons sparingly and for good reasons only such as removal of dead or injured parts, removal of an occasional random shoot that tends to spoil the fine form of the plant. Rhododendron, camellias, Pieris, skimmia and many other broad leaved evergreens require an absolute minimum of pruning, but if you prune them do so immediately after flowering. Early spring to mid-summer is the preferred time for pruning English laurels, hollies and other broad leaved plants that are used for hedges and screens and are kept to a rather regular width and height. Deciduous shade trees and fruit trees can be pruned (if they are used as shade trees) in the winter, but you may wish to do additional pruning in summer when the trees are in leaf. At that time the trees may be thinned if they require more light and air.

WHEN TO PRUNE SHRUBS: There are two types of shrubs; those blooming on buds formed the previous season, and others that bloom on buds of the current season's growth. Those that bloom from buds formed the previous season should be pruned immediately after flowering in late spring or summer. If pruning is done during the dormant season, much of the flowering wood will be removed. The second group should be pruned during the early spring or winter months before new growth starts.

Here is a list of shrubs that should be pruned immediately after flowering, since these shrubs bloom on the previous year's wood: azaleas; barberry;

bittersweet; dogwood; forsythia; lilac; hydrangea hortensus; climbing roses; Spirea prunifolia; snowball viburnum; wisteria; flowering almond; white fringe.

Here is a list of shrubs that should be pruned during the dormant period in winter or early spring: butterfly bush; clematis; rose of sharon; high-bush cranberry; bush roses; flowering raspberry; matrimony vine; clethra.

When shrubs have been neglected and are full of suckers, are ill-shapen, and a tangle of weak growth, you may need to do the most drastic type of pruning—to cut the entire plant right down to the ground. Leave just a few inches of growth. Do this type of pruning in the early spring. The result will be a new top for the shrub that has been cut back. As the young shoots grow they can be thinned or pruned to make a shapely shrub. This method is advised for deciduous plants such as forsythias, snowberries, weigelas and others that are vigorous growers.

The Japanese have brought the art of dwarfing and sculpturing plants to perfection, working for years to achieve the small gnarled plants that they grow in tubs and in rockeries. If you are interested in modifying and controlling the shape of trees and shrubs you must develop patience and an eye for form. Retain the main form that you wish the plant to take and then prune during the growing season, a little at a time to bring the plant to the desired shape. Young junipers and pines respond well to this treatment, but the results are not fully accomplished for many months, sometimes several years.

Hedges which grow rapidly may require more than one pruning in a season. You may need to prune them in spring and again in the middle of the summer. Keep the base of the hedge slightly broader than the top at all times. The hedge will look better and will suffer less from ice and snow loads if it is tapered from a broad base to a narrower top.

Roses: Except for the removal in the fall of the year of unusually long tips of unusually tall canes of any rose that would be in danger of breaking, due to wind, sleet or snow damage, all pruning of bush roses should be done in the spring as soon as the buds have begun to swell and all danger of severe freezing weather has passed. This time would vary from February in Georgia to mid-April in our most Northern States. The pruning of climbing roses should be done just after they have bloomed. The same rule applies to such shrub roses as Hugonis and the Rugosas. Ground covering types of roses such as Wichuraiana or Max Graf, require little or no pruning other than the removal of dead or offending branches so as to improve the appearance and neatness of the planting, and may be done at almost any time.

In all types of pruning—use a sharp pair of shears that will make a good clean cut. Ragged, crushed, or mutilated cuts discourage healing or callousing and encourage stem fungus and stem borers. Cut about one-fourth of an inch above a bud or "eye" and, if possible, one that points to the outside of the plant rather than the inside. Make a slightly slanting cut in a direction parallel to the slant of the bud above which you cut. A touch of antiseptic tree paint on the cut will aid greatly in discouraging stem fungus or stem borers from entering the wound before a callous is formed.

In pruning hybrid tea roses, the grower will be governed greatly by the space allotted to each plant, the effect desired, and the locality in which the roses are being grown. In extreme northern sections of the country, the severe winter temperatures often freeze back the canes of the rose to a point where removal of all damaged wood and lightly shaping the plant itself, is all that can be done. In any event, where the amount of live wood in spring will permit it, severe pruning of hybrid tea roses to canes shorter than eight inches from the ground should be discouraged. The food of the rose, as of all other plants, is produced in the foliage of the plant and the amount of foliage is dependent to a large degree on the amount of wood remaining after pruning. If we remove too much of the top of the rose, we will remove its ability to produce food and subsequently reduce the number of blooms that follow.

The space allotted to each rose and the effect desired greatly determine the type of pruning necessary to achieve that effect.

For the grower who has spaced his roses closely, or from 15 to 20 inches apart, pruning to eight to 12 inches is most practical. For spacings of 20 to 30 inches, medium pruning 12 to 18 inches. For 30 or more inches apart, high pruning, that is, 18 to 24 inches. The various heights of pruning also help to determine the size and number of blooms produced by the plant during the growing year. The larger we allow our roses to grow without spoiling the appearance of the garden, the stronger and more productive they will be.

When pruning, first remove all injured or diseased wood, next crossed, weak, or interfering branches, and lastly cut back to the desired height and shape the bush to a pleasing appearance. A weak cane or branch may be defined as one that is less than one-fourth inch in diameter. Varieties that produce a few tall, heavy canes from the bud should be permitted to retain more height than the varieties that break readily from the bud, if the maximum number of blooms is to be enjoyed.

FLORIBUNDAS: When buying Floribunda roses select carefully the varieties according to the height they attain in accordance with the effect desired, and then prune only that which is necessary to gain that effect. The Floribunda is a great producer of bloom if given the opportunity to grow in a normal manner. Heights of three to four and one-half feet with hundreds of blooms are not uncommon among the tall-growing Floribundas, while the low-growing ones may be kept at heights of two to two and one-half feet or less and flower quite heavily.

CLIMBERS: Climbing roses present a slightly different problem in pruning. First we must separate them into three different types, namely, ramblers or small flowered ones; large flowered climbers; and the everblooming or climbing hybrid teas. The ramblers are very vigorous growers and send up many shoots from the bud each year. Each cane which has produced blooms should be cut back as near to the ground as possible as soon as it has finished blooming. The young shoots which grow up in the spring and summer should be tied in a pleasing manner to a support of some type as they will produce blooms the following spring.

Large flowered climbers are handled in a slightly different manner from the ramblers. Inasmuch as they do not produce as many canes from the bud as the rambler each year, a proportionately smaller number of canes should be removed. A good rule to follow in pruning large flowered climbers is to remove as many old canes each year as there are new ones produced. Always remove the oldest canes in so doing. They will be the canes with the darkest and roughest bark. In removing them, cut as closely to the ground as possible without injuring the plant. The new canes should be tied to a support.

Everblooming and climbing hybrid tea roses are the most restricted growers of all climbing roses and need little or no pruning other than the removal of injured or diseased wood and the removal of spent or withered blooms immediately after blooming. The blooms should be cut off just above the first leaf below the withered bloom.

Pruning is one of the easiest and simplest of all rose maintenance problems and once the rose grower has found the procedure that suits his or her particular needs, it is a routine matter to maintain a rose garden with a minimum of labor.

FRUIT TREES: Generally, pruning fruit trees is considered as being a winter or early spring operation, when the tree is dormant and void of leaves. At this time of the year the framework of the tree and the branches are easily distinguished. The best time to prune a fruit tree is during the months of March and April. However, pruning can be done as late as blossoming without serious results. Summer pruning should be limited only to the removal of watersprouts and broken limbs, since pruning during this season of the year dwarfs the tree more than during the dormant period.

A watersprout is a vigorous shoot that develops from the older limbs, primarily in the center region of the tree. They grow straight up, resembling a whip. These sprouts harbor insects and if not removed may interfere with the framework of the tree.

Pruning is also done at the time of planting regardless of the season of the year. This pruning is largely a training operation and a very important one.

The central stem of a young tree is known as the main leader, or trunk in the case of an older tree. A stem possessing leaves is known as a shoot while a stem void of leaves is a twig. A branch is a group of connected shoots or twigs arising from a limb or another branch. A limb is an enlarged lateral branch of the main leader or trunk.

Pruning commences at the time a fruit tree is planted and continues annually until the tree is removed. During the first few years pruning is primarily a training operation directed toward establishing a strong tree

framework. Pruning during the bearing years consists of removing weak wood, thinning the branches, controlling height and width, and repairing damaged limbs.

The framework of a tree consists of several branches growing laterally from the main leader of the tree at more or less definite locations. Usually one or more of the lateral branches is chosen at planting with two or more years being necessary to complete the selection. In choosing the laterals, there are distinct procedures to follow. The main lateral branches should be spaced at definite intervals on, as well as around, the central leader. This is done for a precise reason: so that no one lateral is close to or directly above another. Under the bark of the tree is a system of pipes that carry water and nutrients from the roots to the leaves and food materials from the leaves down to the roots. Each branch has its own pipe system connecting the roots and the leaves. By arranging the lateral branches as has just been indicated, each branch will have its own unrestricted pipe system.

From a structural standpoint the weakest part of any tree is where the upper side of a limb joins with the trunk, which is known as the crotch. The smaller the angle between the branch and central leader, the weaker the crotch. Thus, by selecting only branches with wide angles (60 to 90 degrees), this crotch weakness is reduced, resulting in a stronger framework.

It is not uncommon to find a young tree that has had one of its branches develop into a leader similar to the central leader of the tree. If allowed to develop, this condition will result in a forked tree, structurally weak. Under the weight of a heavy crop of fruit, the tree is apt to split into two parts. This vigorous branch can be suppressed in growth by cutting off the branch just above the first good lateral branch growing toward the outside of the tree. This type of pruning is known as heading-back or suppressing growth, and may be applied to almost any branch. By cutting to an outside lateral, the limb is encouraged to spread out rather than to continue straight up, which would be the result of cutting to an inside lateral. If by heading-back, a branch is reduced in length to less than 30 inches, it should be removed in its entirety.

A condition may be found on a tree where several branches originate at the same point on a limb. This may appear as a fork or whorl. It is recommended that all the branches be removed but one. Usually the largest diameter limb is left.

A tree in its early years is like a young boy, very vigorous and a rapid grower. As the tree or boy ages, the rate of growth diminishes until the tree bears fruit or the boy reaches manhood. In succeeding years, growth is largely filling out, putting on a little weight. To a young tree, pruning is an invigorating process that tends to delay the time of fruiting. Consequently, prior to bearing as little wood as possible should be removed from the tree. By all means small branches and short stubby spur growth should be left. It is from this type of wood that the first fruit develops. Once the main lateral branches have been selected, pruning should be limited as much as possible, to removing broken limbs or correcting bad situations. The general tendency is always to over-prune a young tree.

When the fruit tree has come into commercial bearing, the tree should be pruned every year to encourage the development of good-sized, highly-colored fruit. The way to prune a bearing tree is to start on the top and sides of the tree and work in toward the trunk. Detailed pruning, cutting many small diameter branches one-fourth inch and down with a pair of handshears, is very time-consuming. Generally a saw, loppers, or pole pruners are used to make bigger cuts from one-half inch and up. Limbs

arising from the center of the tree that are smaller in diameter than the main lateral limbs and interfering with the branches on the main laterals should be removed or suppressed. It may be necessary to head-back some branches or eliminate whorls or forks as previously described.

The severity of pruning depends upon the kind of fruit. Very little wood if any should be pruned from pear trees, but considerable wood from peaches, to encourage annual terminal growth of from 15 to 24 inches.

GRAPES: Grapes must be pruned each year to keep the vines within reasonable limits, maintain vigor and assure fruit of good quality. Grapes bear only on new wood—the shoots which start in the spring from buds formed the previous summer on canes which themselves had developed during that year. The most productive buds are the fourth to tenth buds on a cane. Grapes have a tendency to overbear. A definite relationship exists between the leaf area of a vine and the amount of fruit that can ripen normally. The unpruned vine or too lightly pruned one will produce a large number of bunches, but it will not have enough leaves to mature the fruit properly, and the result will be small clusters of berries which tend to remain sour and green.

There are many systems of training grapes. Some varieties respond more favorably to certain systems than others, however, the system followed in most cases is largely dependent upon personal preference. The following classification can be made of habit of shoot growth and system of training: *Shoots upright* — Chautauqua; High Renewal; Fan. *Shoots drooping*— Single trunk, four-cane Kniffin; two-trunk four-cane Kniffin; single-trunk, six-cane Kniffin; Umbrella Kniffin; Y-trunk Kniffin; Munson; and Hudson River umbrella.

Detailed descriptions of all these systems would become voluminous, therefore, a brief résumé of one upright and one drooping shoot system will be made. In the Chautauqua system, more or less permanent arms are established and maintained. The canes are tied in an upright position on horizontal wires and the shoots are tied in the summer. Two wires are commonly used, but three are more desirable. A cane for the future trunk is tied to the lower wire. Shoots from this cane, extending horizontally right and left are tied to the wire. All others are removed. The number of canes left is regulated by the vigor of the vine, although three or four are most usually allowed to remain.

The single-trunk, four-cane Kniffin system consists of a vertical permanent trunk which is trained to the upper of two horizontal wires. Four canes, two to the right and left of the trunk, are selected and tied to wires. Usually 8-10 buds are allowed on each of the four canes. To allow for the development of new canes near the trunk for the following year, often two or three short spurs of two buds each are left at both the lower and upper wires. Unlike the previous system, the shoots that grow during the summer are allowed to droop, untied.

BRAMBLE FRUITS: Pruning most of the bramble fruits is relatively simple. Canes grow to full height one year, and the year following send out fruiting laterals and bear a crop, after which they die back to the ground level.

In pruning red raspberries, remove the dead canes; cut out those that are growing outside the "hedgerow" and those in the row that are too small and weak to produce a good crop. With certain varieties, if the plants are vigorous, it may be advisable to remove some of the large canes if they are crowded. The amount of thinning out will vary with conditions, but it is generally desirable to keep the hedgerow not more than 15 to 18 inches wide and with not more than four or five canes per row foot. Head back all remaining canes to a height of 24 to 30 inches (under eastern conditions) or higher if a trellis is used.

The new shoots of black and purple raspberries are ordinarily pinched off during the growing season when they are 18 to 24 inches high. This is done to induce lateral branches to grow from the main stem. At the dormant season, any canes not pinched should be cut back to 24 to 36 inches and all lateral shoots pruned back to about six inches; also remove all dead, weak, injured or diseased canes.

Bush blackberries usually have stronger, sturdier canes than raspberries and should be summer pinched at about 30 to 36 inches. The dormant pruning will consist of cutting out weak, dead or diseased canes, cutting back those which were not pinched, and shortening the laterals to eight to 12 inches.

Dewberries are essentially trailing blackberries which root at the tips and do not produce suckers at the base of the parent plant. They usually are not pinched during the summer. In the spring, remove the weak, dead or diseased canes. The usual practice is to collect the remaining canes in a bundle and tie them to a stake, cutting the canes at a height of about 26 inches. Dewberry canes are rather susceptible to frost injury, so it is best to wait until the buds start to grow before pruning and tying them up.

BLUEBERRIES: The blueberry produces fruit on wood of the previous season's growth. The largest berries are borne on the most vigorous wood. Most varieties tend to overbear and unless part of the buds are pruned off, the berries are small and there is little new growth for the next year's crop. Pruning is usually started at the end of the third season the plants have grown. The erect-growing varieties, such as Rubel, Rancocas, June, Concord and Scammell, need to be thinned at the center, whereas Cabot and Pioneer are especially spreading and are likely to need pruning of the lower drooping branches. The amount of pruning necessary depends on plant vigor; the more vigorous the plant the less pruning needed.

Pruning should consist of removing low spreading branches next to the ground, leaving only the erect branches or shoots. If the center of the bush is dense, the weak and the older branches should be removed.

RED CURRANTS: In pruning red currant bushes, the late fall, winter or very early spring are the best times. Remove canes four years old or older; low-growing canes that drop to the ground when heavy with fruit; broken or diseased canes; the weaker one-year shoots. After pruning, an ideal bush might consist of about five one-year shoots, four two-year canes, three three-year canes, and possibly two or more four-year canes, if they are vigorous.

GOOSEBERRIES: Gooseberries may be pruned at any time during the dormant season; that is, after the leaves fall and before growth starts in the spring. Remove dead or broken canes, then those branches that are borne around lower part of bush, low enough to touch ground when loaded with fruit. Canes more than four years old usually are too weak to be productive, so they should be cut out. This will usually be all the pruning needed, although it may be desirable to remove a few twigs here and there to shape up the bush, or open up a crowded part of it. *See also listings under individual plants;* SHRUBS; ROSES; BRAMBLE FRUITS; GRAPES; FRUIT TREES.

PRUNUS: The stone fruits, growing mostly on deciduous small trees or shrubs, a genus of the rose family, *Rosaceae.* About 200 species are included, many of them important fruit trees. Leaves are alternate and mostly simple, flowers are white or pink and fragrant. Fruit is a drupe, with a single pit or stone.

Most of the species are hardy in the North, though after a severe winter flower buds may be killed. They like limey, loamy soil, but are easily grown in almost any soil. Propagation is by seed, by wood cuttings under glass, or by budding. For further growing directions, see specific fruits under their common names. For principal species, see below.

PLUMS: *P. americana;* yellow or red fruit on a small twiggy or thorny tree.

P. maritima, beach plum; bitter red or purple fruit growing in sandy coastal areas, good for jellies and jam.

P. hortulana, native of Kentucky and surrounding area; red and yellow fruit, good cultivated varieties stem from it.

P. domestica, common plum; from which were developed many fruits, Bullace and Damson in the group.

P. cerasifera, cherry plum; stock used for grafting and for hedges.

P. spinosa, sloe or blackthorn; bush with blue-black acid fruit.

P. salicina, Japanese plum; very hardy, used to develop many fruit trees.

CHERRIES: *P. avium,* sweet cherry, Mazzard cherry; small fruit, used for stock.

P. cerasus, sour cherry; small cherry used for preserves and pies.

P. lannesiana, Japanese flowering cherry; many horticultural forms with pink, rose, red, and white flowers, single and double.

P. serrulata, Japanese flowering cherry; white flowers.

P. sieboldi, Japanese flowering cherry; flowers pink or white.

P. subhirtella, variety *pendula;* the weeping-form Japanese cherry.

P. mahaleb; used for stock.

P. tomentosa; ten-foot shrub with pink and white flowers.

P. glandulosa; ornamental shrub with double pink and white flowers.

P. besseyi, western sand cherry; small sweet cherry used for fruit, also for crosses to bring about dwarfing.

P. pennsylvanica, wild red cherry;

small white blossoms in umbels and light red fruit.

P. padus, European bird cherry; very hardy, clusters of white flowers followed by small dark fruit.

P. serotina, black cherry; timber tree to 100 feet, late flowers and purplish-black fruit.

P. virginiana, chokecherry; racemes of white flowers, red fruit.

CHERRY-LAUREL: *P. caroliniana,* 40 foot evergreen from N. Carolina south, also called wild-orange and mock-orange; creamy white flowers.

P. laurocerasus, English laurel; evergreen shrub with glossy leaves and clusters of white fragrant flowers, hardy in the south.

P. lusitanica, Portugal laurel; thick evergreen leaves and long clusters of white flowers, tender in the north.

ALMOND: *P. communis,* almond, also called *P. amygdalus;* not hardy, pink flowered tree, more or less edible nut.

P. nana, Russian almond; hardy pink-flowered bush.

P. triloba, flowering almond; hardy bush with pink flowers.

APRICOT: *P. armeniaca,* apricot; pinkish flowers, many varieties cultivated for fruits.

P. mume, Japanese apricot; hardy north on a plum stock, decorative double white and double pink flowers, called also flowering plums.

PEACH: *P. persica,* peach, and variety *nucipersica,* nectarine; grown for fruit in many named varieties.

P. davidiana, a less hardy peach whose buds are often winter-killed.

PSEDERA: *see* PARTHENOCISSUS

PSIDIUM: *see* GUAVA

PTERETIS NODULOSA: *see* OSTRICH FERN

PTERIS: *see* FERN

PULMONARIA: Lungwort. A genus of European herbs, perennials with creeping rootstocks, of the borage family, *Boraginaceae,* closely related to forget-me-nots. Flowers blue to purple

in flat clusters, florets with funnel-shaped corollas with fuzzy throats. Leaves large in basal clump, and long-stemmed, few smaller ones on leaf-stalk. Basal leaves sometimes mottled. Prefer partial shade, rich moist soil. Easily grown from seed or may be divided.

Bethlehem sage (*P. saccharata*) has basal leaves mottled white, flowers reddish-violet. Blossoms in April or May.

P. angustifolia has dark blue flowers, with varieties in gold, light blue, and red.

P. montana grows a little taller, to one and one-half feet, and has bright green leaves and violet flowers.

P. officinalis has spotted leaves and reddish flowers which turn to violet.

PULSATILLA: Known as pasque-flower. A genus of the buttercup family, *Ranunculaceae,* formerly grouped with genus *anemone,* and similar to anemone except in fruit. Hardy perennial growing to about one foot from long-stalked cluster of finely divided basal leaves. Flowers cup-shaped and purple, lilac, or white, two and one-half inches across. Silky clusters of seed-fruits showy. May be raised from seed planted immediately after ripening, or by division. Prefer shade.

American pasque-flower (*P. patens*) blooms in April or May before the leaves develop, the flower violet and raised above the low leaf-clump.

P. vernalis, the European pasque-flower, has flowers purple outside and white inside. *P. vulgaris,* the common pasque-flower, has blue to lilac flowers, and varieties have red flowers or variegated foliage. Both leaves and flowers grow to about one foot.

PUMPKIN: *see* SQUASH

PURPLE MOMBIN: *see* OTAHEITE APPLE

PURSLANE: *see* PORTULACA

PUSSY WILLOW: (*Salix discolor*) Pussy Willow, known also as Glaucous

Willow, is a shrub or small tree which is native to eastern United States. It seems to prefer wet places, but may easily be transplanted in dry situations. The leaves are lance-shaped and are dark green above but white with hairs beneath. The most distinguishing feature of this willow is the soft, silky catkin. These catkins or flower clusters appear in March before the leaves unfold. The male plants can be recognized by the yellow anthers of the stamens which give the male catkins a golden tone. The female catkins consist of a cluster of beaked pistils which produce seeds bearing long silky down.

Twigs of Pussy Willow may be forced into bloom in late winter by placing their bases in water indoors. Such twigs often form roots and, if set out in soil later, will grow into new plants.

PYCNANTHEMUM: *see* MOUNTAIN MINT

PYRACANTHA: A genus of evergreen thorny shrubs and climbers of the rose family, *Rosaceae,* having orange-red berries that remain on the plants all winter. Most species are tender to frost, except *P. coccinea,* which is fairly hardy to Massachusetts. White flowers in clusters during the summer, leaves simple, alternate. Propagated by seed, layering, cuttings, and grafting. Prefer sunny, well-drained position. Sometimes trained against walls, or used for hedges.

P. angustifolia grows to 12 feet, with branches sometimes prostrate, and matted dense flower cluster. Very tender.

P. coccinea, the hardiest firethorn, grows to 20 feet, with long toothed leaves. Its variety *lalandi* is hardier than the type. Both can be trained as vines.

P. crenulata is erect, growing into a small tree of 12 to 20 feet. Tender.

P. gibbsi has glossy leaves, and red berries that ripen later than the others. Hardy from Washington, D.C. southward.

P. koidzumi is an extremely tender species from Formosa. It has small leaves which are hairy, and flower clusters which are not.

PYRETHRUM: This name is given both to *Chrysanthemum coccineum* and to an insecticide derived from the flower heads of this very popular summer-blooming perennial herb. The plant grows one to two feet tall, with fern-like leaves and big, showy daisy-like flowers in white, pink, red or lilac, often double. Pyrethrum is a favorite border and pot plant with many named varieties, and is sometimes called painted daisy or painted lady. It is hardy, likes a rich soil and a compost or rotted manure mulch, and is best propagated by root division in the spring. Set the plants about six inches apart.

INSECTICIDE USE: The flower heads, dried and powdered, are used in insecticidal sprays and dusts. Pyrethrum insecticide is rather expensive, but it is not harmful to plants, and is regarded as the least toxic to man and animals of all insecticides. It is effective against a large number of soft-bodied insects that attack plants, man and animals.

Sometimes pyrethrum is mixed with a sesame oil by-product, with a substance called asarinin that occurs in the bark of the southern prickly ash tree, or with other plant extracts that enhance its effectiveness. But it is also mixed commercially with many other compounds, some of which may be quite toxic. Pyrethrum can be obtained pure only from veterinarians or pet shops. It kills pests by rapidly paralyzing them, but it has little residual effect and must be applied directly to the insects.

PYROXENE: Any of a common and important group of iron, magnesium, and calcium silicates found in many igneous rocks and molten lava.

PYRUS: *see* PEAR

Q

QUACKGRASS: (*Agropyron repens*) Like many other weeds, quackgrass has a "Jekyll-and-Hyde" personality. In certain situations, it can be extremely useful. It binds loose soil on banks and steep, sandy slopes very efficiently, preventing erosion and adding organic matter. Also, it will provide good forage where better grasses will not thrive, in some areas of the West.

However, quackgrass in general is a most troublesome pest. Gardeners and especially farmers in the north central states have good reason to hate it. Although it prefers acid, moist soil, it will do well under all sorts of conditions, and it increases by both seeds and rhizomes (underground stems).

Quackgrass grows 18 to 30 inches tall and produces great quantities of seed on straw-colored spikes above the hairy leaves. These seeds can retain their ability to germinate for four years or longer. They are difficult to separate from the seeds of many of our common grasses. Farmers who do not sow only certified seed, which is guaranteed to be free of quackgrass seed contamination, may be introducing the pest into their fields.

The rhizomes, often several feet long, spread laterally in the upper three to six inches of soil. New plants can be produced at each node (joint), so that the weed quickly honeycombs the soil with a dense, extremely tough sod.

Seeds or pieces of rhizome may be introduced into new areas in topsoil brought in to make new lawns, in manure, mud on the wheels of implements and on shoes or the feet of animals, and in hay or other forage.

Quackgrass infesting a vegetable garden often makes such prolific growth in the spring that seedlings are greatly handicapped. A badly infested plot should therefore be planted only to crops with vigorous seedlings, or to transplanted crops. Cabbage, corn, squash and tomatoes are good choices. Their roots can easily penetrate the mass of rhizomes, and because such plants are widely spaced, it is easy to hoe around them.

CONTROL MEASURES: Constantly removing new top growth will reduce the food reserves in the rhizomes, thus weakening them. So hoe or cultivate weekly during the growing season. Always use a sharp hoe or a cultivator with a sharp blade—tined tools will not completely sever the top growth from the underground parts.

Spading late in the fall will kill many of the rhizomes by exposing them to drying and freezing. (Sometimes in extreme cases, the rhizomes can be raked up and hauled away, but this means a loss of considerable valuable organic matter. Thereafter, pull stray shoots by hand to prevent re-infestation.

A mulch of plastic, boards or similar materials is also effective. Even better is a deep mulch of organic materials, which, at the same time it is smothering the quackgrass, will add organic matter and have other beneficial effects. A mulch should give a complete kill if left on the ground for one season.

Some crops make a dense shade that will smother quackgrass. Squash and pumpkins are excellent, particularly when planted closer together than usual. Until they make a heavy growth, hold down the quackgrass by frequent hoeing.

In making a new lawn or planting ornamentals or small fruits, heavy mulching or tilling is necessary for a season to eliminate serious infestations. If you choose the tillage method, use a tined cultivator that will lift the rhizomes to the surface and expose them to drying.

Always build up the soil for a new

lawn organically, so that the grass will quickly make a tight sod that will crowd out the weed. Keep the lawn watered well to prevent its being weakened by drought, and clip it weekly to a height of one and one-half inches to maintain good vigor.

Sometimes ryegrass, included in lawn seed mixtures to provide quick cover, is mistaken for quackgrass. However, you can recognize ryegrass by its fibrous roots instead of rhizomes, and smooth leaves rather than hairy.

On farms, frequent tillage throughout the season to kill top growth and expose the rhizomes to drying is again the rule. The weed must never be allowed to make abundant leaf growth, for this means abundant rhizome growth. Plowing it under deeply in the spring also helps by forcing the plant to send up a long shoot from way down, an easy way to weaken it. Late fall tillage can expose a goodly number of rhizomes to freezing, and close grazing will reduce the weed's vigor in pastures. In row crops, a cultivator fitted with sharp duckfoot shovels will cut the shoots and leaf growth without injuring crop roots. Good smother crops are buckwheat, millet, sudangrass and closely drilled soybeans.

QUAIL: *see* WILDLIFE

QUAIL-BRUSH: (*Atriplex breweri*) This low, gray-foliaged shrub is grown mainly in California. It is salt-tolerant, does well in almost pure sand, and will stand a high degree of heat and drought. The *Atriplex* genus also includes several troublesome weeds, notably the greasewood or saltbush of the West, and a garden vegetable, the orach.

QUAKE GRASS: *see* GRASS, ORNAMENTAL

QUAKER BONNETS: *see* LUPINE

QUAKER COMFREY: *see* COMFREY

QUAKER LADIES: (*Houstonia coerulea*) Sometimes called bluets and

innocence, this spring-blooming perennial suits the wild garden. It prefers a very moist spot, liking its roots in cool water, and can be found growing wild in mountain meadows and on flat, wet rocks along stream banks. The plant is delicate and tufted, about seven inches high, with little blue or white flowers. The clumps can be dug from the wild and increased by division. Star Violet (*H. serpyllifolia*) is similar but with creeping stems. Both are found in the eastern United States.

QUAKING ASPEN: *see* POPLAR

QUAKING GRASS: *see* GRASS, ORNAMENTAL

QUAMASH: *see* CAMASSIA

QUAMOCLIT: *see* STAR GLORY

QUARANTINES: The Plant Quarantine Act of 1912 is designed to prevent the spread of injurious insects and plant diseases. The Secretary of Agriculture is empowered to prohibit or regulate the importation and interstate movement of all plant materials that may harbor pests.

Ball and burlap nursery stock from foreign countries, for instance, is forbidden entry into the United States, because the soil around the roots might carry pests. Many other plant materials, including propagative parts, fruits, vegetables, cut flowers and plant products, are also regulated. An example of this is the prohibition against the importing of elm seeds from Europe, which might spread the Dutch elm disease. Certain other plant materials may be imported or moved across state lines only under permit and upon U. S. Department of Agriculture inspection.

The law is revised whenever a pest becomes controlled or a new disease or insect appears. Information on current regulations can be obtained from the Bureau of Entomology and Plant Quarantine, U. S. Department of Agriculture, Washington 25. D.C.

Most states have their own quarantine laws controlling the movement of suspect plant material across their borders. Your Experiment Station can inform you as to the latest regulations affecting any plants you may be contemplating carrying across state lines. *See also* INSECT CONTROL.

QUARTZ: A combination of silicon and oxygen, quartz is the most common of all solid minerals. It may be colorless and transparent, or colored. Many semi-precious gems are forms of quartz. The crystals usually vary from a fraction of an inch to several inches in length, but one three feet long weighing 500 pounds was found in Maine.

Although it is everywhere—in beach sand, granite, gravel and practically all soils—quartz is of no importance to the soil. It greatly resists weathering, remaining intact after all other rock components have disintegrated into soil materials. Tiny quartz crystals may dissolve over many years, but no plant nutrients are released and no clay is formed as they do.

The only effect quartz has on plants is when large masses of it underlie a soil, making it shallow. This usually occurs on steep slopes in mountainous regions. *See also* MINERAL ROCKS.

QUASSIA CHIPS: These shavings from the wood of a South American tree are sometimes recommended as a "safe" insecticide. The juice is extracted by boiling, and the liquid is occasionally used by hop growers as a contact spray to kill plant lice. In medicine, it is used as a bitter tonic and a worm remedy.

QUEEN ANNE'S LACE: The wild carrot is sometimes a nuisance weed, cropping up in gardens and crowding out useful grasses from fields and pastures. For this reason, it is often called, "devil's plague." Other common names are bird's-nest and crow's-nest weed, derived from its flat-topped

clusters or umbels of tiny white or yellow-green flowers. Queen Anne's lace is found throughout the United States, and grows one to three feet tall, with umbels up to five inches across. It is hardy and spreads rapidly. Serious infestations on farms are best controlled by plowing the weed under just before it blooms.

A garden annual, *Didiscus coerulea,* is also called Queen Anne's lace. It grows two feet tall, with charming umbels of pure blue flowers.

QUEEN ANNE'S POCKET MELON: This small, highly fragrant melon is inedible, and is grown only for ornamental purposes. Usually called the pomegranate melon, it is a decorative plant for banks and prefers a sandy, fertile soil.

QUEEN-OF-THE-MEADOW: (*Filipendula ulmaria*) Growing three to five feet high, this beautiful feathery white-flowered herb is very easy to grow. It prefers ordinary garden soil with ample moisture. Propagation is by division of the clumps in the spring. Queen - of - the - meadow is found throughout the north temperate zone.

QUEEN-OF-THE-PRAIRIE: (*Filipendula rubra*) A very easy perennial herb to grow, queen-of-the-prairie has numerous deep pink flowers and reaches a height of five to seven feet. Any good garden soil suits it. In early spring, it may be increased by division of the clumps. It is commonly grown in the eastern states.

QUEEN OLIVE: *see* OLIVE

QUEEN PALM: (*Arecastrum romanzoffianum*) This "feather palm" reaches a height of 50 feet or more when grown outdoors. It is used widely as a street and avenue tree in Florida and California. Elsewhere it is a popular subject for the warm greenhouse. In pots, its leaves do not reach the ten-foot length they often do when it is grown outdoors, but they are very thin and feathery and the fruits hang in large attractive clusters. In the greenhouse, queen palm does best with a soil high in humus and plenty of moisture in the air as well as in the soil.

QUEEN'S FLOWER: see LAGERSTRO-EMIA

QUEENSLAND NUT: (*Macadamia ternifolia*) This is one of the dual-purpose nut trees that deserves to be planted much more frequently than it now is. Recently introduced from Australia, it is a handsome evergreen semi-tropical tree growing about 50 feet tall. It does well in the southern and warmer central states, standing mild frosts.

The nuts are very good, about an inch in diameter, hard-shelled and with a mild and delicate flavor somewhat like that of Brazil nuts. The food value is said to be comparable.

Even if the tree did not bear valuable nuts, its beauty would merit more extensive planting of it in gardens, parks and elsewhere. The leaves are a deep, lustrous green with spiny margins, looking much like a big holly leaf. These contrast interestingly with the smooth gray trunk and lovely foot-long racemes of white flowers.

For farm woodlots and land not needed for other purposes, it has another value. Macadamia wood brings a good price, being close-grained and reddish, in demand for cabinet making.

The Queensland nut likes a deep, rich soil, with plenty of moisture. It is a somewhat slow grower, but is easily propagated by stratifying the nuts over the winter in sand, then planting them in separate pots of humusy soil with bottom heat. This will produce germination in about a month, whereas planting them outdoors will result in much slower sprouting. Water the seedlings sparingly to prevent damping-off, and transplant them outdoors when they are about 18 inches tall. Try to disturb the roots as little as possible when transplanting. See also NUT TREES.

QUEEN'S WREATH: (*Petrea volubilis*) This pretty tropical vine can be grown outdoors only in southern Florida, but is an excellent specimen for the warm-temperate greenhouse elsewhere. The stem is woody, reaching a height of 15 to 20 feet, and the evergreen leaves may be eight inches long. It blooms very heavily in early spring, with large clusters of beautiful blue flowers. Give it a humusy soil, plenty of water and high humidity.

QUENOUILLE: Used in France for centuries, this system of training ornamental trees and shrubs is rarely seen here. The idea is to produce a perfect cone shape by tying down the lower branches and pruning the upper ones. It involves considerable patience and work.

QUERCITRON: (*Quercus velutina*) Sometimes used as another common name for the black oak. See also OAK.

QUERCUS: see OAK

QUICK FREEZING: see FREEZING; STORAGE

QUICKLIME: see LIME

QUILLAJA: see SOAPBARK TREE

QUINCE (*Cydonia*) A beautiful tree bearing valuable fruit. Commercial quince orchards are rarely seen today, but the tree is easy to grow and a real addition to the home grounds.

The fruit of the quince cannot be eaten raw, having a sour, astringent taste. But when it is cooked, this changes to a piquant flavor that is quite pleasant. Quince preserves and jellies are delicious, and the fruit can also be used to give a guava-like flavor to apple and pear preserves and other cooked fruit dishes. By themselves, quinces are excellent stewed, or cored and baked with their centers filled with honey. The fruit is high in calcium, phosphorus and vitamins A and C, and contains appreciable amounts of potassium and iron.

CULTURE: The quince is a shrub-like tree that grows up to 25 feet high. It's best to plant two-year-old nursery trees, about 15 feet apart each way. They will yield best and live longest in a moist but well-drained, deep clay loam. Quinces do not require a high degree of fertility. Apply and maintain a ring mulch of well-rotted compost, hay or other suitable material after planting, and no further feeding should be necessary. The trees will begin to bear two to three years after they are set out, and should continue producing well for up to 40 years.

A little heading-back to correct straggly growth is usually the only pruning a young quince requires. Useless and interfering branches and twigs should also be cut out. Do all pruning in late winter or early spring. Some thinning may be needed if the tree overbears in any year.

The fruit must be picked and handled carefully to avoid bruising the delicate skin. Quinces can be stored two months or longer after harvesting, but do not keep them near apples or pears, which will absorb their strong odor.

FLOWERING QUINCE: Closely related to the garden quince is the shrub known as the flowering quince (*Chaenomeles*). Its fruit is small and only used occasionally for preserves. However, its showy spring bloom makes it a prized specimen plant, and it is also a favorite for hedges. The best known variety is the Japanese flowering quince (*C. lagenaria*) which has scarlet, pink or white blooms and spiny branches, and grows four to six feet tall. The dwarf Japanese quince (*C. japonica*) stays under three feet, has red flowers, and is valued for its ability to stand city conditions. Not as winter-hardy and not very commonly grown is the Chinese quince (*C. sinensis*) which grows up to 20 feet tall and has light pink flowers and no spines. All of these like full sun and a medium-fertile soil. *See also* SHRUBS; FRUIT TREES.

QUINCULA: These perennial herbs of the potato family are related to the ground cherry. The only common variety is *Q. lobata*, a prostrate plant found in the central and southwestern states. Well-suited to very hot, dry, sandy sites, it produces orange kidney-shaped fruits, but not profusely.

QUINCUNX: A method of spacing orchard trees to get more trees per acre. Four trees are planted in a square, with a fifth in the center. This takes advantage of all available sunlight, as well as leaving no areas of soil unused by the tree's roots. *See also* ORCHARD.

QUININE BUSH: (*Garrya eliptica*) Often called the silk-tassel tree, quinine bush bears silver-gray flowering tassels in hanging clusters that persist through the winter. The fruit is a round, velvety berry, not edible. The shrub grows six to 12 feet high and is hairy-leaved and evergreen. It is not considered especially pretty, and is grown mostly in the West, from California to Oregon. It will grow freely in any fairly fertile soil, but it needs some shelter from cold winds.

QUININE TREE: (*Cinchona*) The tropical trees whose bark produce quinine, a drug important in the treatment of malaria, are not grown in the United States, except for one variety of little ornamental value and suited only to the southernmost part of Florida.

QUIXOTE PLANT: *see* YUCCA

R

RABBIT MANURE: Rabbit manure is a fine source of nitrogen and other fertilizer values. The analyses differ according to the feeding practices, but an average sample is rich enough in nitrogen to produce good heating in a compost heap.

The manure can be applied to the soil as it is taken from the hutches, dug in or used on lawns, between vegetable rows or around trees and shrubs all through the year. A large doe and her four litters of about 28 to 32 young a year will produce approximately six to seven cubic feet of manure annually.

The manure can also be mixed with a small amount of soil, kept moist and used as needed, or composted with plant wastes to cut down the odor. Sawdust, straw, dry leaves, grass and the like are often used for litter in the hutch, producing an excellent compost as the droppings and urine are caught and absorbed by these materials.

Rabbit manure compost has been called one of the finest soil builders for the garden. Large applications of the fresh manure should not be used on crops like potatoes, sugar beets and cereals, or on young deciduous trees and shrubs. *See also* MANURE.

RABBITS: Rabbits are fun to raise and an excellent source of delicious, fine-grained white meat for the table or freezer. They need very little room and simple equipment, thus are ideal for the gardener or homesteader to raise.

Rabbits breed very prolifically, so don't make the mistake of getting too many to start with. Three or four does and one buck are plenty. Some of the most popular breeds are the New Zealand Red, New Zealand White and Flemish Giant. The last is a fast-growing animal, weighing seven or eight pounds at two months of age and dressing out to five to six pounds. The New Zealands are ready for use as fryers at two months (about four pounds) or as roasters at four months (eight pounds or so). There are also the fancier fur breeds like Angora, Dutch, Chinchilla, Imalayan and Havana. Buy only healthy-looking, unblemished, good-sized stock.

HOUSING: A roomy hutch on wooden legs is easy to build from scrap lumber and poultry netting. U. S. Department of Agriculture Farmers' Bulletin No. 1730, "Rabbit Production," gives detailed information on constructing all types of hutches. The usual size is four feet long by two to three feet wide and two feet high.

In northern climes, the hutches may be kept outside for perhaps six months of the year. In cold weather, put them in a corner of the barn or a shed where they will get a good supply of fresh air, and sunshine for part of the day. Further south, they are placed on the north side of a building or trees in summer, the south side in winter. Rabbits can stand a lot of cold, but wet, chilly weather is bad for them.

If the hutch is constructed with half the floor made of three-quarter-inch hardware cloth, the droppings will fall through to litter trays beneath containing sawdust or shavings. Or you can have a completely wooden floor and put a box of sawdust in a corner; the rabbits will quickly learn to use this as a bathroom. Feeding troughs for hay and grain, and a nesting box in each doe's hutch, complete the equipment. Sawdust, peat moss, dry leaves and straw or hay make good bedding. Clean this out whenever it gets dirty. With clean, dry hutches and proper feeding, there will be no disease problems. All the hutch cleanings are excellent fertilizer.

FEEDING: Rabbits are easy to feed. Good quality hay, preferably legume, should be kept in the hay racks at all times. Fresh green feed such as vegetables, weeds and grass, plus carrots and apples, is also fed daily, along with corn, wheat, barley, rye or oats. A little corn cob meal can be fed. Turnips or mangel-wurzels are good winter feed, and rabbits relish dried potato peelings, dry leaves and stale bread. Rolled oats and whole milk are commonly fed to pregnant animals. Experience will tell you if you are overfeeding. Mix a teaspoonful of salt in the grain box once a week, and provide clean, fresh water at all times.

A good way to provide green feed is to plant a small plot to a crop that can be cut back and will come up again during the growing season. Your experiment station will give you a list of such crops. Sudan grass is a good one, suitable to many parts of the country. It can be cut and fed each time it reaches a height of eight to ten inches. But do not feed it after it has been damaged by frost, for in that condition it is harmful.

BREEDING: Does can be bred from the age of eight months to four years. They will produce three or four litters a year. The gestation period is 31 days. Young rabbits will come out of the nest box to eat with the mother about three weeks after birth, and should get small amounts of grain and plenty of legume hay. It is important to withhold green feed from them for the first couple of weeks so they won't overfeed. They are weaned at eight weeks of age.

Conservation Bulletin No. 25, ten cents from the Superintendent of Documents, U. S. Government Printing Office, Washington 25, D. C., gives full details on breeding and managing rabbits.

PREVENTING RABBIT DAMAGE: Wild rabbits are often one of the gardener's worst headaches. They love to eat his vegetables and the young shoots of many plants.

One of the best rabbit repellents, perfectly safe to plants, is powdered rock phosphate. Sprinkle it gently on seedling leaves as soon as they emerge. Dried blood sprinkled around the roots is another tried-and-true solution. Others include powdered aloes dusted on the plants, and a solution of cow manure and water applied as a spray. Onions also seem to repel rabbits, and an occasional row of them interplanted with your other crops can be quite helpful.

A poultry fence is a more initially expensive but permanent solution. It must be at least 30 inches high and stoutly anchored on stakes or piping.

Fruit trees need a cloth or heavy paper wrapping, or a wire mesh cylinder, around their trunks to prevent rabbits from gnawing the bark in late winter and early spring. This is often necessary on ornamental trees and shrubs as well. Be sure that the guard extends about 18 inches above the expected maximum snowfall, so that cottontails standing on snow crusts can't reach over it.

Anchor wire guards firmly in the soil. If made large enough to allow for trunk growth, such a guard will protect the tree for many years. Some gardeners report animal lard smeared on the trunk is an effective repellent.

RABBIT'S-TAIL GRASS: *see* GRASS, ORNAMENTAL

RACEME: A raceme is a long flower cluster, with all the flowers on short stalks springing from a single main stalk. When the flower stalks are all on separate branches arising from the main stalk, the cluster is called a compound raceme or panicle. If each flower arises directly from the main stalk with no stalk of its own, the form is known as a spike.

RACHIS: The long main stalk of a flower cluster, or the main leafstalk from which two or more leaflets arise, is called a rachis.

RADISH: (*Raphanus sativus*) The name "radish" comes from the Latin, *radix,* meaning *a root.* The radish is one of the first recorded cultivated vegetables, dating back to earliest historical times. Radishes are generally grown and enjoyed as an appetizer or are used in salads. Although radishes do not supply a large amount of nutritive food in the diet, they are a good source of vitamin C.

Of all the vegetables, there is no group which is as easily cultivated as the root crops. All types of radishes can be grown in any part of the country if they are planted at the proper time. Radishes are a hardy, quick-growing, succession crop. It is simply a matter of sowing seed in the open ground, and the radishes will practically take care of themselves until they are ready to be eaten.

CULTURE: There are three types of radishes: the early or spring, the summer or midseason, and the winter.

Early or Spring: The spring, or forcing, radish requires the cool spring and fall months to develop advantageously. While they may be sown during the warm months, they seldom produce good, edible roots. The roots will either be very small and pungent, or they will shoot to seed. Radishes prefer a cool, moist, loose, and fertile soil. If planted in heavy soils, the roots are apt to be misshapen and have a number of lateral fibrous roots. Compost or well-rotted manure may be used in large amounts. The spring types will mature in 20 to 30 days. Succession plantings can be made a week apart during April and May, or as soon as the ground can be worked. For fall planting, succession plantings can be made during August and September.

Sow the seed in rows 12-18 inches apart, covering ½ inch deep. Thin the plants to about one to two inches in the row. Radishes grow so quickly they do not need much care. Cultivation is almost unnecessary. The roots are small and essentially surface feeders, so deep hoeing and raking does more harm than good. Radishes may be a

nuisance because they have to be planted so often for a continual supply, but they make up for this by not requiring much attention after planting.

Summer or Midseason: In general, the soil and fertilizer requirements of summer radishes are the same as those of the early spring types, but summer radishes are much more heat resistant than the other two types. Summer radishes should be sown about ¾ inch deep, in rows about ten to 15 inches apart, and thinned to three to five inches apart in the row. Since these roots require a longer period to develop (45 to 60 days) and they will withstand heat, they may be sown in successive plantings every week from May to the middle of August.

Winter: While winter radishes have the same general requirements as the other radishes, they seem to do well in the North only during the fall months. They are generally grown during the fall months to produce roots for the winter months. Winter radishes may be kept in storage for three months during the winter. Because of their extreme size, they must have a greater spacing then the other two types. Winter radishes are generally sown ¾ of an inch deep, in rows 18-20 inches, and six inches between plants in the row. Sixty to 70 days are required to mature a crop from seed.

HARVESTING: Harvesting consists of merely pulling the radishes from the ground. The early ones can be harvested when they are big enough to eat, usually in about 20-30 days. The summer radishes can be harvested in six to seven weeks, and the winter radishes either can be pulled in eight weeks for immediate use, or can stay in the ground until frost comes.

INSECT CONTROL: Radishes are fairly free from insect enemies. They are quite free from plant disease. However, they are sometimes affected by root maggots. For this reason, radishes are sometimes planted with onions as a trap crop, that is, they are planted for the sole purpose of attracting the maggots away from the onion roots. The maggot-infested roots are, of course, afterwards removed. But should root maggots, wire-worms, borers, etc., be excessively active in your garden, these may be controlled by the application of large quantities of unleached wood ashes. At the same time, it is worth noting that if the soil is improved by the use of liberal amounts of mature compost, these pests will soon become a thing of the past. *See also* INSECT CONTROL.

Because of their quick germination and rapid growth radishes are frequently used to mark rows in the garden. Radish seed is often mixed with beet seed so that the sprouting radishes will mark the row and make early cultivation possible.

Most of the winter radish crop is stored for future use. Since radish roots are very resistant to cold, their storage is easily arranged by placing them in a well drained, straw-lined trench and covering them with two or three alternating layers of straw and earth. This storage is best arranged after the first fall frosts have arrived. Leaves or dry litter may be used in place of straw.

RAGWEED: (*Ambrosia*) There are several causes of hayfever—and one major cause is plant pollen. In spring, pollens come primarily from trees; in summer, from grasses and plantains; and in autumn, from ragweeds, principally from the common ragweed (*A. artemisiifolia*) and the giant ragweed, or kinghead (*A. trifida*). Both species are native annuals which grow generally in moist, waste places.

Common ragweed grows from one to three feet tall, has mostly alternate leaves in the upper branches and opposite leaves on lower stems. Leaves are divided two or three times. The nut-like fruits are ⅜ inch long, have four to seven short, stout spines plus a beak at one end.

Because there are no ray flowers, it may appear that the plant is not in flower and so does not produce pollen. However, abundant pollen is produced on the petal-less flowers.

Giant ragweed is a robust grower, commonly six feet tall and sometimes as much as 15 feet. Leaves are all opposite and three parted, except for those near the top.

A good all-round soil improvement and weed control program can help keep ragweed in check. Regular mowing in midsummer prevents production of pollen and seed. *See also* WEEDS.

RAGWORT: (*Senecio*) There are over 1,000 ragworts or groundsels, a few of which are grown in the border. *S. cruentus* is a greenhouse plant, sold by florists as cineraria. Its many varieties have flowers of nearly all colors, and they are popular plants for the cool window garden or greenhouse.

S. cineraria is the dusty miller, a two-foot-high hardy perennial with cream or yellow flowers and very hairy foliage. Somewhat similar is *S. aureus*, golden ragwort, another good early-summer - blooming perennial. Two other favorites are tansy ragwort (*S. jacobea*) growing up to four feet high with red and yellow flowers good for cutting, and *S. pulcher,* a tender perennial with hairy leaves and big yellow flower heads.

German ivy (*S. mikanioides*) is a tender climbing perennial having shiny leaves and clusters of small yellow flowers, a fine house or window box plant. Leopard's-bane (*S. doronicum*) grows over two feet high, and its showy orange or yellow flower heads brighten the border in spring. Purple ragwort (*S. elegans*) is a tender annual for the border or cool greenhouse and resembles dusty miller, except that its flowers are yellow and red or purple.

RAIN: Rainfall is one of the most important factors in many areas in determining what may be grown. East of the Alleghenies there is an annual rainfall of from 35 to 50 inches, sufficient for most garden plants. Given organic treatment of the soil, any summer droughts that occur will have little or no effect on crops.

Moving westward, the average rainfall gradually lessens, the forest being replaced by grassland, until in the Southwest we find desert, where very few things will grow without irrigation. Along the upper Pacific Coast and through the Northwest, however, is the heaviest rainfall in the United States. Here can be grown as wide a range of plants as in England.

Deficiency of rainfall, the organic gardener knows, does not have to mean poor crops. How the rainfall is conserved is far more important. Organic methods hold runoff to a minimum, and water infiltration and storage are increased as the organic matter content of a soil is built up. The proper selection of plants, plus the organic method, is the only answer to drought. *See also* DRY WEATHER GARDENING; MULCH.

RAISIN: Raisins are the dried fruits of the small, extremely sweet vinifera grapes. The Black Corinth, Muscat and Thompson Seedless are raisin grapes. In the United States, raisin production is confined almost entirely to 11 counties in California. The grapes are harvested from August to November, and sun dried in the field. Proper drying requires hot, rainless weather, and the earliest picked grapes dry in ten days, the later ones take four weeks or longer. About three-fourths of the original weight of the grapes is lost in drying. Raisins are a very mineral-rich food.

RAKING: The gardener uses a rake to pulverize his soil in making a seedbed. It is necessary to have the soil finely textured so that small seeds, such as those of lawn grasses or flowers, will make maximum contact with the soil particles and thus be helped to germinate. Raking breaks up the clods and smooths the seedbed. It also conserves soil moisture by making a blanket of particles that prevents its escape, and

aids the decomposition of organic materials that supply plant food. Weed seedlings are killed. Finally, raking encourages roots to develop rapidly, strongly and deeply.

Soil in good tilth, amply supplied with organic matter, is the easiest to crumble and pulverize. Always keep your steel-tooth rake sharpened, and work backwards so that you do not walk over and compact the raked area. Never attempt to rake when the soil is wet, or its structure will be damaged. A harrow is merely a large rake and is used for bigger areas than the garden.

RANUNCULUS: *see* BUTTERCUP

RAPE: *see* GREEN MANURE

RAPESEED MEAL: Just as castor pomace is the residue of castor beans after extraction of the oil, rapeseed meal is the ground up rapeseed from which the oil has been extracted. The final product has between five and six per cent nitrogen and between one and two per cent phosphoric acid and potash. The material is fine for compost activation.

RASPBERRY: (*Rubus*) Belonging to the bramble fruits which are of American origin from wild species, raspberries have prickly stems; are intermediate between an herb and a shrub in that the root is perennial but the stems die back nearly to the crown the second season of their life after maturing a single crop of fruit. Exceptions to this are the everbearing species which bear terminally and continuously all summer.

Canes of the American red raspberry (*R. strigosus*) and European red raspberry (*R. idaeus*) grow upright throughout the season; those of the blackcap raspberry (*R. occidentalis*) grow more or less upright the first season but later droop down near the tip and may strike root.

The red raspberry is the most important species among the bramble fruits, being especially desirable for desserts, jams, freezing, etc. It can be grown as far north as any cultivated fruits. For complete planting, propagating, insect control, and cultural directions, *see also* BRAMBLE FRUITS.

RASPBERRY, TRAILING: (*Rubus parvifolius*) A native of Japan, trailing raspberry was first introduced into this country in 1929 by the Bureau of Plant Industry. The fruit closely resembles the darker-fruited strains of the dewberry. Organic growers have been especially interested in trailing raspberries, since it can spread rapidly and forms a dense cover for protection of soil and wildlife. Therefore it has been found effective in stopping erosion in small areas. Here are some general facts about the plant:

Trailing raspberry is not too particular about soil fertility and will grow on a wide range of soils east of the 24-inch rainfall line; initial plantings require some form of cultivation for at least two years in order to compete with other vegetation; the plant is moderately shade-tolerant and will grow underneath and along the edges of tree and shrub rows; established plantings provide excellent ground cover and are especially useful in wildlife areas in providing nesting and feeding places for birds and small game; the fruit is of acceptable quality and is suitable for making pie, jelly, jam, tarts, and fresh dessert; the plant is quite resistant to bramble diseases and is not greatly damaged by insects and rodents; new plants may be obtained from seed or from cane tips covered with soil in midsummer; old plantings, if renovated, may regain vigor and fruit production. Renovation is accomplished by cutting out old canes, thinning plants, applying fertilizer if needed, and frequent tillage after plowing between rows, up to the time canes start rooting.—*Fred Eshbaugh.*

See also BRAMBLE FRUITS.

RAVENNA GRASS: *see* GRASS, ORNAMENTAL

RECEPTACLE: The widened, flower-bearing end of a stem is called a receptacle. Rose hips and strawberries are receptacles, botanically speaking, and so are the fruits of many other plants, either wholly or in their early stages before they mature. In some plants, like the oleaster, the receptacle resembles a berry and is often mistaken for a true fruit.

RECORDS, GARDEN: *see* PLANNING, GARDEN

REDBUD: (*Cercis*) These handsome shrubs or small trees are especially valuable for their very early bloom. They bear small, showy rose-pink or rose-purple blooms in generous profusion before most other flowering shrubs come into bloom. Redbuds do not like heavy, clayey soils or much moisture, and do best in an open-textured, sandy loam.

The American redbud (*C. canadensis*) is hardy over most of the country, and rarely grows over 20 feet tall. Some of its varieties have double flowers or white flowers. The Asiatic redbud (*C. chinensis*) is hardy only to southern New England, and tends more to a shrubby form than the American species. Its flowers are bigger and even more numerous, and it begins to bloom when younger. *C. siliquastrum* is similar to American redbud, but is hardy only to southern Oklahoma and lower Maryland. Redbuds are propagated by seeds, greenwood cuttings or layers. *See also* SHRUBS.

RED SPIDER MITES: *see* INSECT CONTROL

REDWOOD: *see* SEQUOIA

REED CANARY GRASS: (*Phalaris arundinacea*) A vigorous, tall-growing grass useful for binding soil, preventing formation of gullies, because of its ability to take over on wet and waterlogged land. It is also a productive grass on upland soil, continuing its growth and remaining green during midsummer drought.

Because of its ability to flourish on water-logged land, reed canary grass is very effective in preventing gully formation and binding soil.

A rule-of-thumb guide states that the best time to use reed canary is when the gully is wet and will stay in that condition for at least three weeks. A large pickup truckload of green hay will treat 500 feet of gully bottom, five feet wide. Next tramp or poke the hay into the mud to get it in close contact with the moisture, thereby preventing its washing out while new sod is starting. Green shoots start in a week, while roots form in about two weeks.

Methods of establishing reed canary-grass are seed, sod and stems.

Seeding of shaped waterways is often desirable and successful. Germination of the seed should be tested, since it often is low. A minimum seeding rate should be eight pounds of live, pure seed per acre, on a well-firmed seedbed, with the seed covered not more than one-quarter to one-half inch.

Early spring and late summer are favorable dates for planting. Late spring seedings too often suffer from summer heat, while fall seedings are hit by winterkill. Competing vege-

tation should be kept down in the establishment year.

Canary grass in a waterway can be used for hay or grass silage if cut twice a year. It will also produce good pasture, although livestock generally do not like it as well as brome or bluegrass.

Reed canary is suited to a wide range of climate. In the United States, it is well adapted to the whole area north of Kentucky, Arkansas and Kansas and also in the higher areas further south and in the Pacific Coast states.

REED MEADOW GRASS: *see* Grass, Ornamental

REGAL LILY: *see* Lily

REPOTTING: *see* House Plants

RESTHARROW: (*Ononis*) The restharrows are hardy perennials with pretty white, pink, red, yellow and purple flowers, shaped like butterflies. They are very easily grown in a medium-rich soil and a sunny location in borders or the wild or rock garden. Three of the common varieties are *O. hircina, O. rotundifolia* and *O. spinosa,* all growing 18 to 24 inches high, their form somewhat shrubby. *O. cenisia* is about ten inches tall. The restharrows make good coverings for banks.

The seeds are sown in a cool place indoors or in the cold frame in March, or outdoors in April in a partly shaded spot. They should be barely covered. Transplant them to their permanent spots, and after flowering, prune the larger species lightly into a pleasing shape. In late fall, cut down the flower stems and give the plants a manure mulch for the winter. They should be taken up and divided every fourth year or so.

RESTING SOIL: *see* Fallow

RESURRECTION PLANTS: These interesting plants have the ability to curl up and appear dead, much like a hibernating animal, in dry periods.

However, when they get water, they quickly spring into growth again. They can repeat this "death-and-resurrection" cycle over and over again.

The one most commonly known as resurrection plant is *Anastatica hierochuntina,* a desert plant that folds up into a tight little ball until it receives moisture. Then it becomes a foot-wide, fern-like plant. It is easy to grow in a sunny, warm place and sandy soil, from seed sown in spring. It can be stored for many years in its resting state on a shelf. The resurrection fern (*Polypodium polypodioides*) is an epiphytic fern growing in the southeast, and *Selaginella lepidophylla* is a very small plant of the southwestern desert.

RETARDING: Retarding is the opposite of forcing, and is commonly used to slow up the growth of plants like hydrangeas, Easter lilies and azaleas so they will flower on a later date. Cold storage may be used to retard Easter lily bulbs, while deep, unheated but covered pits or special houses where light and temperature can be controlled are common for retarding other bulbs and many plants. Darkness and a temperature of around 40° are essential. Sometimes a cool greenhouse where these factors can be managed is suitable for retarding. These methods can often extend the dormancy of certain plants for several weeks.

REX BEGONIA: see Begonia

RHAMNUS: The hardy common buckthorn (*R. cathartica*) is a thorny shrub about 20 feet high, with inconspicuous spring flowers. It is not very ornamental, but is used in hedges occasionally. The evergreen *R. californica,* sometimes called coffeeberry, is planted in the South and Pacific Coast states as a bee plant; it grows four to six feet tall and has small umbels of long-lasting greenish flowers, and berry-like black fruits. *R. purshiana,* which grows only in the North-west, is a tall shrub whose dried bark is the source of the laxative, cascara sagrada. Alder buckthorn (*R. frangula*) grows about 15 feet tall, is very hardy and is esteemed for its brilliant yellow autumn foliage. The yellow bush or Indian cherry (*R. caroliniana*) grows somewhat taller, but is hardy only to Nebraska. All of them do best in medium-rich, moist soils.

RHAPIS: These tufted palms are popularly grown as pot or tub plants, and outdoors in Florida and southern California. *R. excelsa* grows to about five feet high, with several stems and fanlike leaves, while *R. humilis* is similar but not as big. They are handsome indoor or terrace plants, and prefer to be nearly pot-bound and kept at a winter night temperature of 55 to 60°. Their soil should be made up of equal parts of loam, sand and leaf mold or humus, with dried cow manure added. Give them very little water in the winter and feed once a month with liquid manure in the summer.

RHIZOME: A rhizome is an underground stem, a rootstock of many perennial plants. It is thick and fleshy, storing food gathered by the roots it sends out. Many rhizomes spread laterally, acting as an active means of vegetative reproduction and giving rise to new shoots. Rhizomes can be easily divided in spring or fall to make new plants.

RHODODENDRON: Rhododendrons are among the most magnificently beautiful spring-blooming plants for the garden. Several hundred varieties of these broad-leaved evergreen shrubs, from six inches to 40 feet high, are grown in temperate North America.

The native and named varieties of rhododendrons available from nurseries are legion. Practically all of the named varieties are hybrids of the native *R. catawbiense* or similar species with either Oriental or European species. The flowers come in every color and shade from white, cream and pink to yellow, orange, crimson, mauve, lavender, bright blue and deep purple. Most are bell-shaped, and some are spotted handsomely.

There are rhododendrons suitable for ground covers, many dwarfs especially fine for the rock garden, medium-low kinds for many sites on the home grounds, and bigger ones for background use or for bigger places. Rhododendron specialists may list 250 or more varieties in their catalogs, with new ones being added every year. Size and color are generally the factors to consider, most rhododendrons being hardy to near or below zero.

Rhododendrons can also be taken from the wild in many areas, if they are cut back and lifted when dormant. Only well-formed, bushy plants, no more than three feet high, should be selected, preferably with crowns having ten or more stems. Some nurseries that collect wild rhododendrons cut them all the way back to the ground, but this means four to five years delay before they reach blooming size. Dig a trench at least 15 inches deep around the plant, or thrust in a sharp spade to full depth in a circle around it. Then lift the plant carefully with a large ball of dirt and wrap the ball in burlap.

Site: Rhododendrons thrive best in a location that is sunny half the day, with protection from the hot afternoon sun. Exposure to winds should also be avoided. The north side of a house is good, or suitable protection can be provided by evergreens such as hemlock or spruce. They are especially magnificent planted against a backdrop of pine trees, which offer filtered shade and a constant mulch of needles. Shade is also important from the early morning sun in winter.

If not protected, the sun turns rhododendron leaves yellow and the wind injures the leaf tips, resulting in a brown, dead margin which mars the leaf. If it is not possible to plant them where they will get shade, it must still be provided for the first two or three years, by a lath screen set above them. Thereafter, they will probably be unharmed by all but the hottest sun, but will not do as spectacularly well as they would in partial shade.

Soil: One of the "musts" for these plants is a distinctly acid soil pH 4.5 to 5.5. It should be well-drained but supplied with ample moisture at all times, much like a forest floor. They definitely do not like a heavy clay soil or lime.

Do not attempt to acidify your soil with chemicals, such as aluminum sulphate—aluminum will injure the roots—or ammonium sulphate, which is changed quickly into a nitrate that yellows the leaves and causes poor growth.

A good planting mixture is one part decayed oak or other hardwood sawdust, leaf mold or acid peat to two parts of loam. Hardwood sawdust or leaf mold contains tannin, which is beneficial to rhododendrons. All these materials retain moisture in the soil, making a cool, moist environment the roots like.

Planting: Rhododendrons, like their relatives, azaleas, are surface feeders and should not be planted deep. Dig the hole two to three times the size of the root ball—at least two feet deep and two or three feet wide is right for good-sized plants. Put some of the soil mixture on the bottom and set the plants no deeper than they grew in the woods or nursery. Fill in slowly, tamping the soil, then soak thoroughly with water.

The final step is providing a permanent, deep, well-rotted acid humus mulch. Use three or four inches of decaying sawdust, pine needles or acid peat moss, or six to eight inches of oak or other acid leaves. Do not mound up the material but make a basin around the base of the plant. The feeder roots will spread into this mulch and find optimum living and feeding conditions there.

Pruning is not necessary at planting.

CARE: With proper soil preparation and a good mulch, watering will probably be rarely necessary. But if your rhododendrons should require watering in hot, droughty periods, soak the soil thoroughly rather than sprinkle it. Plenty of moisture is especially vital in the growing season after flowering. In extremely dry periods, soaking might be necessary once or even twice a week, but certainly no more frequently than this. Waterlogging the soil will injure the plants.

Fertilization is usually not needed, but if your plants do not seem to be growing at their best, five pounds per 100 square feet of tankage or cottonseed meal can be spread on the mulch and allowed to wash in. Fish meal, fish oil emulsion or blood meal are also good.

After the plants have finished blooming, it is wise to remove the flower heads before the seeds form. This will result in more blooms the following year. There is a knack to removing them: just the bloom cluster should be snapped off. Removing too much will mean no flowers the next season.

Pruning is done after the blooms fade, and is best limited to taking out weak and dead branches, and cutting old ones back lightly to make a well-shaped shrub. Heavy pruning should be avoided in any one season.

In the winter in areas that have weather approximating that of lower New England or colder, a covering of evergreen boughs or dried cornstalks is advisable.

PROPAGATION: Growing rhododendrons from seed is fairly simple, but few of the seedlings are apt to be as good as the parent plant. The seeds can be sown under glass in a finely sifted, peaty mixture that is acid in reaction. The seedlings usually take several years to reach flowering size after they are transplanted to pots.

Cuttings are difficult to root, requiring careful control of temperature and humidity. A slightly acid sand-peat mixture and an electric hotbed where the bottom temperature can be kept at 70 to 75°, are used by commercial growers. Ordinary layering or air layering are probably easier for the gardener. Both air layering and the taking of cuttings should be done with soft wood during the early part of the growing season. Grafting by side, saddle or veneer grafts on popular species in a propagating frame or greenhouse in spring is a method of propagation commonly used by commercial growers. *See also* LAYERING; GRAFTING; EVERGREENS.

RHUBARB: (*Rheum*) A hardy perennial which is easily grown. Rhubarb, interestingly enough, is the only vegetable that replaces fruit in our diet. It is delicious for sauces or stewed with other fruits, too. Remember, the stalks only are used for eating. The leaves contain large amounts of calcium oxylate, a poison which has been known to cause death. Rhubarb is good from a health standpoint also. It will help supply vitamins A and C, plus calcium and iron in your diet.

Seldom victim to insects or disease, rhubarb thrives in deeply-dug soil that has received generous applications of both compost and manure.

CULTURE: Several root divisions will be enough to start a good clump for the average family. You may obtain them from a seedsman or from anyone who has a large patch of rhubarb in his garden. Each division should have at least one bud. Rhubarb plants which have become old are improved by being divided. After about five years or more in one place the plants deteriorate and the stalks become thin and short. The clumps should then be dug up, divided and replanted. It is simply a matter of digging them up, cutting them into several good-sized divisions with a knife, and planting them again. New healthy growth will soon start.

One point to remember—rhubarb requires a good rich soil so the more compost and rotted manure you give them the better they like it. Before planting the divisions, enrich the ground; then regular feeding from year to year is required if good-sized stalks are to be grown. A good plan is to heap compost, manure, or both, around the plants in the fall and to dig it in when spring comes.

Fall or spring planting may be done. Many prefer fall planting in September as the plants are well established and in the spring you may have some to harvest. By the second and third years you can expect a full harvest. Dig the soil thoroughly and incorporate plenty of organic fertilizer before planting the rhubarb divisions. Set the roots three or four inches deep and allow three or four feet between plants. Be sure to firm the soil well around each crown.

For the most part, rhubarb is seldom troubled by insects and disease. There are a few leaf-eaters which can be easily checked by picking them off by hand. Cut out flowering growths as they take nourishment away from the plants and reduce their vigor.

Rhubarb can be forced by placing a bottomless bucket or nail keg over the crowns in the latter part of February. This forces the plant to seek the light and it grows tall more quickly than if left in the open.

VARIETIES: There are not many varieties of rhubarb from which to choose. Victoria is the perennial favorite and does well anywhere. Mac-Donald is extremely hardy and pro-

duces thick, sturdy stems of rich crimson color.

Rhubarb is not a finicky plant. You can grow it anywhere, although cool seasons and freezing winters are more to its liking. The cold produces the delicate pink shade on the stalks and makes it look so appetizing.

RHUS: *see* SUMAC

RIBBON-GRASS: (*Phalaris variegata* or *P. arundinacea picta*) Ribbon-grass is a relative of reed canary grass. A perennial, its pretty white- and yellow-striped leaves make it a popular border plant in the garden. It grows from about four to six feet tall, with narrow, foot-long leaves and a dense flower panicle. Ribbon-grass grows well in any medium-rich, fairly moist garden soil. It can be increased by division of the clumps. *See also* REED CANARY GRASS; GRASS, ORNAMENTAL.

RIBES: *see* CURRANT

RICE-FLOWER: (*Pimelea*) The rice flowers are low shrubs, generally grown as greenhouse plants. They grow two to three feet tall, with small but pretty white or rose-pink flowers in heads or clusters surrounded by red bracts. Given a cool, humid spot in the greenhouse, with shade in the summer, they make an attractive display. The seeds are sown in late winter or spring, one-eighth-inch deep in equal parts of loam, sand and leaf mold or compost. They may also be propagated by rooting cuttings of the young shoots in a sand-peat mixture in the spring, transplanting them often to slightly larger pots as they grow. Pinching back will make them bushy. After flowering, they are usually cut back and repotted.

RICE HULLS: Often considered a waste product, rice hulls have been found to be very rich in potash and decompose readily when worked into the soil, thereby increasing humus content. It makes an excellent soil conditioner. *See also* HULLS; MULCH.

RICE, WILD: (*Zizania aquatica*) Far more nutritious than ordinary rice, containing more protein and slightly more fat than its cultivated cousin. Too, wild rice is not polished, so its outermost and best layer of grain is intact. Its delicious flavor makes it a favorite of gourmets, particularly as a stuffing for wildfowl. It is even said to have some medicinal properties. The modern Indian and others boil it for dessert, grind it for porridge and mill it as flour. And many species of wild ducks are large consumers of wild rice —it is the main feed for waterfowl on the Mississippi flyway.

Wild rice grows on single stems, usually five to ten feet tall, with panicles about 24 inches long. The husks are an inch long, containing slender grains of a dark slate color when ripe. The plant is a reseeding annual.

It grows in lower Canada, our northern states and the Pacific Northwest, and down as far as Florida and Louisiana. Minnesota is the biggest producer, growing about 30,000 acres, or 500,000 pounds of processed rice a year (two-and-a-half pounds of the harvested rice is needed to make a pound of the processed rice).

CULTURE: Wild rice grows best in quiet, pure water from one to six feet deep, along the margins of streams, ponds, lakes or the flood plains of rivers with rich mud bottoms. It prefers a slow current of about a mile an hour and never grows in stagnant lakes or pools. The best soil is organic, six inches or deeper, preferably containing some calcareous material like snail shells. Most Minnesota stands are on mucky soil overlaying sand or gravel.

Two important points: the water must be *pure,* and its level should not fluctuate more than six inches during the growing season. An excessive rise in the water level, due to spring floods, will "drown out" the plant, preventing its reseeding.

If these requirements are fulfilled, wild rice will grow practically anywhere in the United States. Even small farm ponds, fairly shallow around the edges and fed by streams, can grow enough to provide the farm family with a goodly supply of this delicacy for their own enjoyment.

Wild rice may be planted by scattering the seed over the surface at the rate of a bushel per acre or a large handful to a six-by-six-foot area. Good seed will sink quickly. The best planting time is just before ice forms in the fall (but in non-freezing areas much seed planted then is lost to migrating ducks) or as soon as the ice breaks up in spring.

Don't try to plant the store product; only unhulled seed will sprout. Rice intended for planting must be sacked and kept wet. If allowed to dry out, the seed usually will not germinate until the second year.

The seeds lying in the soft, rich mud sprout early in spring, the first shoots appearing above the water in June. The first leaf is a "floater" which soon dies and is followed by the main stem. One seed can produce several flowering stems. A panicle then forms, its blossoms pollinated by the wind. Early in September in Minnesota, the seeds ripen on the heads and harvest begins. They ripen over a ten-day period, so a bed must be harvested three times to get most of the crop.

The plants are then frozen in for the winter. When the spring rains raise the water level, the old plants are torn up by the lifting ice. The straw is either cast up on shore or sinks, adding fertility. The pulling of the roots from the mud is Nature's method of cultivating the beds and aiding the germination of the seed.

COMMON RICE: The widely-grown cereal grass, *oryza sativa,* grows three to four feet high. Seed is generally sown in April in ground which is later inundated with about eight inches of water. When the plant is ready to be harvested the water is drained off.

RICINUS: *see* CASTOR BEAN

RIPE: Usually we think of a fruit as being ripe when it is ready to be eaten. Actually, the term is more correctly applied to fruit that has matured to the point where its seeds will germinate. Also, ripe wood is wood that will root easily or is in the proper condition for grafting.

ROCK: Beneath the earth's surface lies a hard covering, a layer of rock known as *bed rock*. This is covered by loose and unintegrated materials called *mantle rock,* found everywhere except in small, infrequent areas. The part of this *mantle rock* that sustains the growth of plants is, of course, the soil.

Mantle rock (a term which includes soft masses such as sand and clay as well as harder substances like granite) is classifiable into three divisions, based on their origin: *igneous* rocks (those cooled from a molten condition); *sedimentary* rocks (those moved from elsewhere and deposited by wind, water or ice); and *metamorphic* rocks (ones that underwent chemical and physical change). Chemically speaking, rocks are classified as either acidic (those with a high percentage of silica) or basic (those containing large amounts of iron, calcium, magnesium or sodium). In general, basic rocks condition soil better than siliceous, acidic ones.

Igneous rocks constitute the principal source of phosphorus, potash, lime and soda.

Sedimentary rocks are produced by the debris of other rocks and so are also called fragmentary, or clastic. From the viewpoint of soils they comprise the great soil-creating formations, and contain a very high percentage of silica, 58.38 per cent.

The process of metamorphism which transforms rocks originally of other types to that which are called *metamorphic* sometimes strengthens rather than weakens them; for example, marble is much harder than the more friable limestone from which it

was derived. Gneiss, schists, slates, quartzite and marble are the common types of metamorphic rocks.

For millions of years the earth's crust has been "weathering"—its rock structure decomposing through the action of heat and cold, winds, rains, fogs, glacier movement, climatic change, and the life and death cycles of plants and animals. The soil that is thus being formed represents only a thin skin, compared to the rock mass which is still weathering and shaping soil underground. This continuous addition of soil takes the place of some of the surface soils carried off by erosion. The underground mass of rock is the soil parent and plays an important role in the action and history of the soil's cultivation. *See also* MINERAL ROCKS; SOIL; PHOSPHATE ROCK; GRANITE DUST; GLAUCONITE.

ROCK FERTILIZERS: Rock dusts are potentially our most abundant source of plant nutrient materials. Soil is formed primarily by the action of organic matter on crumbling rock dust. The rock basis for soil produces a continuing supply of mineral-rich silt that keeps breaking down and in large part replaces the minerals that crops take from the soil.

BUILDING FERTILITY: According to Dr. W. D. Keller, professor of Geology at the University of Missouri, "the first step in the restoration of soil fertility is to ask ourselves from whence and how did the fertility originate. Then action must be taken to duplicate the process by which Mother Earth assembled such a wealth of richness in the topsoil.

"This procedure cannot be impossibly complicated, and need not be the least artificial, because the fertility came by natural means and not by the hand of man. This observation leaves a clue to the method to be proposed to utilize naturally available earth materials and to follow the paths of nature.

"The fertility of the virgin soil represented a long-time accumulation or concentration of nutrient elements which were derived from two main sources. One of these was the organic contribution from a long parade of previously growing plants. The other nutrient elements were liberated by the rocks which weathered to form the body of the soil and its accessories.

"Solid rocks in various parts of the earth contain all of the natural elements that have been found. They contain, over widespread areas, the main nutrient elements, except for nitrogen, upon which plants evolved their botanical kingdom," concludes Dr. Keller.

ADVANTAGES: Natural rock fertilizers provide a "balanced diet" to the soil, supply long-lasting nutrients that eliminate the need of frequent applications, improve the soil's physical structure and water-holding capacity, and do not leave harmful after-effects that slow down the activities of soil bacteria.

USING ROCK FERTILIZERS: One of the first things to learn is to be root conscious. The roots of crop plants literally wrap themselves around the grains of rock fertilizer, excrete their natural plant acids, and in that manner unlock the plant food that the fertilizer contains.

Legumes are ideally adapted to rock fertilization. Their roots are numerous and they are heavy feeders on the nutrient-rich silt particles in the soil. The fact that legume roots sometimes penetrate as deep as 30 feet indicates how great is the subsurface activity of those nitrogen gathering plants.

One of the most important points in favor of putting ground rocks on legumes is the fact that legumes are nitrogen producers. Rock fertilizers supply almost all the essential plant nutrients but nitrogen. Therefore, when they are used with legumes there is a balance achieved of food the plant needs.

It is generally agreed that fresh organic matter—raw manure and newly plowed down green manure—is more effective for releasing rock fertilizer nutrients than decayed organic matter. The reason is that it is the vital action of decaying organic matter that does the work of releasing soil and rock nutrients. Organic matter that has already decayed is rich in bacteria and nutrients in itself, but its period of intense decaying vitality has passed and it is of less use as a stimulant to rock fertilizer.

The combining of rock fertilizer with raw organic matter is also important when your soil has an alkaline tendency. Rock fertilizers become available more slowly on alkaline soil. But you can circumvent that difficulty by mixing the ground rock with fresh manure before applying it to the soil.

Farmers in acid soil regions will also want to mix ground rock fertilizer with their manure, especially if manure must accumulate for a while before being spread. The practice pays off in greater effectiveness of both the rock and the manure. Phosphate rock tends to prevent the escape of nitrogen when it is spread on manure.

Rock fertilizers should not be mixed or applied with lime, as the alkalinity of lime hinders its action. A final point—rock fertilizers should not be just broadcast on the surface of the soil and allowed to stay there. It should be disked or plowed into the ground.

Here are general recommendations for amounts of rock fertilizers to apply:

Gardens—(all vegetables) ten pounds per 100 square feet or apply directly in hills or rows, with plants and seeds;

Roses and bushes—one pound each;

Flower beds—five to ten pounds per 100 square feet;

Lawns—five pounds per 100 square feet;

Trees—(all kinds) 15 to 100 pounds per tree. Spread to edge of drip line;

House plants—one tablespoonful to five inch pot, one teaspoonful to smaller pots;

Corn, soybeans, oats, wheat and rye —250 to 400 pounds in drill or planter attachment, or an application of 500 to 1,000 pounds broadcast per acre;

Alfalfa and all clover crops—new seeding, or at time of planting, 500 to 1,000 pounds per acre.

CONVERTING TO ROCK: It is important to remember that natural rock fertilizers are insoluble, and one application will last for as long as five or ten years. Instead of feeding the plant by a hand-to-mouth method, when you use natural rocks you are in a way putting plant nutrients in the soil bank. When you put in a hundred pounds of rock phosphate you know it will be there until the plant has used it up.

Because natural rocks are permanent fertilizers it is somewhat unnecessary to rely on soil tests to tell you how much to use. You don't have to be afraid of putting too much on. But, since so much fertilizer of the chemical type is applied on the basis of information supplied by soil tests, it is helpful to know what the corresponding natural fertilizer applications are.

Most recommendations for phosphorus are given in terms of pounds of superphosphate per acre. A good rule of thumb for converting that to terms of natural rock is to merely double the application. In other words, instead of applying 200 pounds of superphosphate, apply 400 pounds of rock phosphate. Since rock phosphate is usually about half as expensive as superphosphate, your investment will be about the same.

Actually, a "normal" application of rock phosphate is 1,000 pounds per acre. Two thousand pounds per acre will suffice for probably five years. It is usually recommended that you apply a five year dose at one time to save application costs.

The problem of determining the proper application rate for rock potash fertilizers is somewhat more difficult, as their quality and degree of fineness varies. If a soil test shows that your soil is low in potash it is not unreasonable to apply as much as three or four tons of granite dust or two tons of greensand per acre.

For soils that need only a moderate amount of potash, an application of one or two tons of granite dust or one ton of greensand is considered normal.

When using the more mild sources of potash—like basalt and diabase dusts—it is necessary to make quite large applications. That is also true of rocks that you are contemplating using mainly for their trace element value—rocks that may not be particularly rich in the basic nutrients like phosphorus and potash. In many cases you can pick up those rocks from quarries that have the waste dusts on hand. You may get them for a few dollars a ton if you do the hauling.—*Raymond Whitelaw.*

See also FERTILIZER; PHOSPHATE ROCK; BASALT; GRANITE DUST; GREENSAND; GLAUCONITE; MINERAL ROCKS.

ROCK GARDEN: A rock garden is truly a thing of beauty. By combining the rough texture of stone with the delicate gems of alpine flowers it has become one of the most interesting garden forms devised to capture and hold the beauty of nature.

A place high on the upper slopes of a great mountain offers information about the purpose of rock gardening. There, above the line of trees, the soil is thin and mixed with rock chips and bits of moss. Rocks are everywhere. Even though at first glance the landscape looks desolate, it has certain aspects of a garden. The rigors of the climate have "weeded out" shrubs and vines and grasses, leaving only the rock plants anchored in the veins of soil between the boulders. Some plants, like the lichens, are growing on the bare faces of the rocks themselves.

Iceland poppies, saxifrages, campanulas and sempervivum are at home on these high mountain slopes. The short growing season and long months of dormancy are just what they like. Take these beautiful plants down to a lower altitude where there is plenty of warm soil and long months of sun and they will soon be crowded out by the far more fast-growing plants that like that environment.

Rock gardens and walls add variety to the garden landscape. Shade and a short growing season benefit rock plants like moss pink and armeria.

Long ago, skilled gardeners realized that if the beauty of the high mountain slopes was to be captured in a sea-level garden, it was not enough to just bring the plants—the sheltering rocks must be brought too. And they must be set into the ground in such a way as to re-create the compact fissures of soil, rock chips and humus that the alpine plants found so inviting in their original homes. A few rocks scattered on the surface of a bare bank would not do. Finally, if the most difficult mountain plants were to be grown, their roots should be able to reach down into moisture that was free to move—not a stagnant pool.

SITE: Although a slope is a natural place to build a rock garden, many successful ones have been made on flat ground that was scooped out to make a flowing contour. A slope simplifies drainage and, if facing north, will shade the garden. Shade and a short growing season are important to many rock garden plants. In their mountain home, alpine plants get only a month or so of warm weather and they are dormant the rest of the year. Although you can't give them the cold, damp weather they are used to, shade helps simulate dormant conditions. Many successful rock gardeners cover plants with a mulch during all but the summer months to stretch their dormant period.

Where a rock garden is to be made in full sun, it is best to plant with a northeast exposure, avoiding especially a southwestern exposure if the summer tends to be hot and dry. Where more rainfall occurs, with less sun and heat, use southern and western exposures more.

Rock plants are in general more resistant to drought than they are to excessive moisture. For this reason it is safer to lean toward the dry side when selecting a site for your rock garden. Don't locate it where the plants will be subject to the drip from trees. Good drainage down deep is also important, particularly for the larger plants which send their roots way down. Using a sprinkler or hose to water rock garden plants, by the way, is not a good idea—take the time to use a sprinkling can.

SOIL: A loam, sandy loam or peat soil is most suitable for a rock garden. Avoid a heavy clay soil at all costs, or be prepared to renovate it with large amounts of organic matter.

Usually it is a good idea to make your own soil mixture: dig out the site to a depth of 18 inches, and replace the existing soil with a mixture of equal parts of loam, sand and leaf mold or similar humus material. Where alkaline-loving plants are to be grown, add five to ten per cent of limestone chips, pulverized clean clam, oyster or eggshells, or ground limestone. To create acid conditions, use oak leaf or pine needle mold or acid peat.

Some rock gardeners cover the soil after planting with a stone mulch made of crushed rock the size of peas. This helps to keep the moisture in and the heat out, and also prevents winter heaving. Evergreen boughs, salt hay or leaves also make good winter protection for most rock garden plants.

SETTING THE ROCKS: Remember, it is the part of the rocks *below the soil* that is important. Actually, you should be more concerned about the *spaces between the rocks,* than about the rocks themselves. Here are some general rules to follow in doing rockwork:

1. Use quarried stone. Rounded rocks are too difficult to fit together tightly, and eventually they work loose.

2. Don't use a collection of different types of stone. You are making a garden, not a collection of geological specimens.

3. Every rock should be set firmly in the ground. It shouldn't move when walked on. At least one-third of the stone should be buried beneath the surface.

4. Slope the top surface of the rock back into the bank behind, so that water will flow back in where the roots of your plants are.

5. Don't let overhanging rocks keep rain off plants and roots below.

PLANTS FOR THE ROCK GARDEN: Here are some of the better known and more easily grown rock garden plants:

Allysum saxatile (basket of gold) with bright gold flowers. Its ten-inch-high clumps spread but it is nevertheless easy to control. There is also *A. s. flore-pleno* with double form flowers.

Phlox subulata, known both as mountain pink and moss pink. The

red one named Vivid and the lavender G. F. Wilson are excellent choices.

Arabis alpina (rock cress) with woolly gray leaves and sprays of white flowers. There are also single pink and double white forms.

Allysum, phlox subulata and *arabis* all bloom in April and May. Each requires several square feet of ground space and all should be kept cut back sharply after blooming.

The armerias (thrift) are cushion plants. *Armeria caespitosa* with pale pink flowers on one-inch stems is particularly attractive.

The *aubretias* (purple cress) are carpeting plants with red, pink, lilac or purple flowers. As it seldom comes true from seed the color of its flowers varies greatly. Plants may be difficult to find but it is easy to start from seed and, if an exceptional color appears, to increase by division in August and September.

Anemone pulsatilla, the pasque-flower, has a clump of ferny foliage supporting large cup-shaped purple flowers on eight-inch stems. Thrift, purple cress and the pasqueflower all bloom in April and May.

Aquilegia (columbine) blooms in May and June. The native plant *A. canadensis,* with red and yellow flowers on twelve-inch stems finds a suitable place in many gardens. *A. akitensis,* a Japanese dwarf, has large blue flowers with inner petals of pale yellow.

Aquilegia Jonesii is a native of the mountain peaks of Wyoming and Colorado. Only three or four inches high, its flowers have purple sepals and blue petals with short spurs. Although easily started from seed, few if any experts here or abroad have succeeded in inducing it to flower away from its natural habitat and few plants have been in cultivation due to scarcity of the seed, which now is available in ample supply.

The campanulas (bell flowers) should be in every rock garden. *C. carpatica* (the tussock bellflower) is the one most frequently available and from June to October has violet blue cups on ten-inch stems. *C. garganica* is smaller and fussier and a gritty lime soil with leaf mold not in full sun is recommended for best results. In June and July it has open violet flower stars above an attractive foliage of sharply notched leaves.

The dianthus (pink) family offers a large number of contributions to the rock garden. *D. neglectus* is not too difficult and in May and June has pink flowers on three-inch stems. It likes a gritty lime soil in full sun and insists on good drainage.

Dianthus deltoides is the readily available and super-invading maiden pink from which self-sown seedlings spring up everywhere.

Geranium sanguineum lancastriensis, originating on the Walney Island, is a delightful dwarf plant with rosy-veined pink flowers in May and June.

The helianthemums or sun roses provide mass color effects in June and July. These are hardy evergreen shrubs and for colors there are pink, carmine, red, copper, gold, white and bi-colors. A spread of 18 inches or more should be allowed for each plant.

Mertensia virginia, well-known as Virginia bluebell, has lavender blue flowers in April on 15-inch stems. It likes a rich acid soil with at least half shade, and after flowering the leaves disappear until the following spring.

Sanguinaria canadensis, better known as bloodroot, can be depended upon to produce its large white flowers in April before any of its leaves appear. It grows wild in rich acid soil and in shady spots but does not seem exacting in any rock garden. There is also a double flower form which is rare.

The sedums (stonecrops) are easy to grow and prefer poor soil. Those most readily available are fast invading creepers but others of a clump type with flowers of various colors will behave well in the rock garden. The interesting *sempervivums* or

houseleeks, popularly known as "hens and chickens," are available in large variety, with some blooming in June and others as late as October.

Thymus (thyme) offers a number of fast-spreading carpeters with purple or white flowers and a few which are not invading. The foliage is very aromatic and that of many of these plants is used for flavoring.

The veronicas (speedwell) include several invading plants such as *V. pectina* and *V. repens. V. incana* has a four-inch clump of silvery leaves with spikes of bright blue flowers in June and July.

The discussions of annuals, borders, miniature plants and flower gardening describe plants suitable to the rock garden. *See also listings of individual plants;* WALL GARDEN.

ROCK PHOSPHATE: *see* PHOSPHATE ROCK; FERTILIZER; ROCK FERTILIZERS

ROCK POTASH: *see* POTASH ROCK; GLAUCONITE; GREENSAND; GRANITE DUST; FERTILIZER; ROCK FERTILIZERS

ROCKROSE: (*Cistus*) These low evergreen, summer-blooming shrubs are generally hardy only in the South and along the Pacific Coast. They are handsome plants but need a sunny position and friable, well-drained soil on the slightly alkaline side. Rockroses do not like to be moved, so seedlings are generally raised in pots until they are planted in their permanent spots. They can also be propagated by layering or by rooting cuttings of side shoots in sand under glass during the fall.

C. crispus grows less than two feet high, with reddish-purple blooms, and is a charming shrub for the rock garden. *C. villosus* grows about a foot taller, with big rose-purple, yellow-centered blooms, while *C. landiferus* and *C. albidus* reach four feet and higher, the former with huge white flowers. The tallest rockrose is *C. laurifolius,* which grows six feet or so high and has white, yellow-centered flowers borne in showy clusters. There are many varieties and hybrids.

RODGERSIA: These hardy summer-blooming perennials have bronze leaves and showy, feathery flower clusters up to a foot long. They like a soil high in organic matter, plenty of moisture and partial shade. Give them plenty of room, for they have spreading root-stocks. A light covering in the winter is advised in the northern states. *R. tabularis* grows three feet tall, with white flowers, *R. podophylla* up to five feet with greenish or yellowish-white flowers. Both are propagated by division of the rootstocks in early spring.

ROLLING: Referring usually to the operation where a weighted roller is taken over a newly-planted lawn to firm seed or to smooth lawn surface in spring. *See also* LAWN.

ROMAINE LETTUCE: *see* LETTUCE

ROMNEYA: These tender perennials have beautiful, enormous white flowers, up to six inches across, and grow six to eight feet high from spreading root-stocks. The best known species is *R. coulteri,* the California tree poppy. Not too easy to grow, romneyas are best started in pots, the seeds sown as soon as they are ripe, barely covered in a sand-peat mixture. Putting them under a bell-jar will aid seedling growth, and the temperature should be kept at 60° or slightly less. When transplanting, disturb the roots as little as possible. Give them a soil high in sand and peat and a position in a sunny border with excellent drainage. Romneyas are occasionally grown in northern greenhouses.

ROOT: A plant root has two functions —gather and absorb food and moisture from the soil, and to store and trans-

Some crops that have only a small growth above ground may have deep roots that bring up minerals from the subsoil, ultimately enrich the topsoil.

port these materials to the upper parts of the plant. Actually, the first function is carried on by the tiny root hairs or tips, the second by the larger, more easily seen roots. The big roots also serve to anchor the plant in the soil.

ROOT CROPS: Any crop whose edible portion is taken from under the ground is commonly called a root crop. Popular garden ones are beets, carrots, onions, parsnips, potatoes, salsify, sweet potatoes and turnips. Actually, onions are bulbs, and potatoes are tubers, rather than true roots. *See also* VEGETABLE GARDENING.

ROOT CUTTING: *see* CUTTINGS; BRAMBLE FRUITS

ROOT DIVISION: *see* DIVISION

ROOT-KNOT: *see* NEMATODE

ROOT PRUNING: When fruit trees fail consistently to set fruit, and all other conditions are favorable, the grower may resort to root pruning. A trench about two feet deep is dug in the fall around the tree, at least six feet from the trunk, exposing the big anchor roots for cutting. If no big roots are found, there is very likely a wild tap root that must be located and cut. Any ornamental tree that has spread its roots out into areas where they are not wanted can be treated in the same way. A metal or cement barrier set in the trench will prevent subsequent spread.

When planning to move a deciduous shrub, it's a good idea to prune its roots by forcing a sharp spade into the soil close to the stems during the summer. The plant will then develop more fibrous roots and be easier to take up in the fall. Sometimes judicious root pruning will force a recalcitrant flowering shrub into bloom, and a system of root pruning and top pruning is often used to keep tub plants small.

In the nursery, trees and shrubs are either lifted several times or planted wide apart and root pruned regularly until they are sold. Both these methods force them to develop a mass of fibrous roots rather than a few heavy, widespreading ones that would make them difficult to move and establish successfully. Special machines are used to cut the roots under as well as around the plant. *See also* PRUNING.

ROSA RUGOSA: An attractive landscape plant that has been prized by gardeners for hundreds of years. It has large, attractive blooms almost every month of the growing season.

It is a rugged plant that requires no pampering or pruning. Rugosa roses grow up to six feet tall, thrive even in salt air and are not bothered by pests or diseases. The wrinkled, "rugose" foliage is much more beautiful than the foliage of the more sensitive, garden-variety roses.

In the early fall the large bushes are covered with the orange and red fruits.

It is a fact that rosa rugosa has hips that are more valuable than the hips of any other rose. Here is a list show-

In early fall, the large bushes of Rosa Rugosa are covered with orange and red berries, called hips (shown above) which are very high in vitamin C.

ing the vitamin C content of the hips of various roses:

MILLIGRAMS OF VITAMIN C PER 100 GRAMS OF ROSE HIPS	
Rosa rugosa	3000
Rosa laxa	3000-4000
Rosa acicularis	1800-3500
Rosa cinnamomea	3000
Rosa canina	711-1338
Rosa mollis	1260
Rosa nipponensis	1180
Rosa multiflora	250

Although there are three roses on that list that have hips with a vitamin C content equal to rugosa, their hips are not as large or as numerous.

Rosa rugosa is native of China, Korea and Japan and is one of about 200 different *species* of roses grown in the temperate and sub-tropical regions of North America. Because it is a distinct species, it can reproduce itself from seed. Modern floribunda and hybrid tea roses are just *varieties,* not distinct species, and cannot reproduce true from seed. They must be budded or propagated from cuttings, a hand process which increases the cost of nursery plants.

Over the years, horticulturists have selected and hybridized rugosa roses, seeking to produce plants with larger blooms and exotic colors. Although seedlings of rugosa are widely used for hedging and produce the typical, valuable rugosa hips, 15 or 20 of the improved varieties have been propagated extensively and are sold by some nurseries. The interesting thing about these improved varieties is that even though they were first produced for their superior flowers, several of them have hips which are considerably larger than the hips of the seedling rugosa. Some of these "super-hips" are as large as crab apples.

These are the varieties which produce the largest hips and the greatest number of hips:

Hansa—blossoms are violet-red and have a clove fragrance.

Frau Dagmar Hartopp—a low-growing rose with soft pink flowers.

Delicata—pink flowers bloom all season.

Rugosa magnifica—a spreading plant four to five feet tall with deep red flowers. *See also* ROSE HIP; ROSE.

ROSE: Roses have been known throughout the northern hemisphere as far back as literature records. Early poets of Greece, China, and Persia all sang praises of the rose. Dried roses have been found in Egyptian tombs. An indication of its antiquity is the fact that the name for a rose is almost the same in every European language.

Linnaeus, in 1762, described 14 rose species, a number which he soon increased to 21. After Linnaeus had pointed the way other botanists followed with more and more complete classifications. John Lindley in 1820 described 76 species and sub-species. In recent years Professor Alfred Rehder at Arnold Arboretum classified 296 species.

Species described by botanists are pure strains. They do not include crosses, hybrids, doubles, bud mutations, and sports. The latter varieties, though not recognized by academic botanists as separate species, account for 95 per cent of the roses listed in current catalogs. It has been estimated that through the latter half of the nineteenth and the first half of the twentieth century at least 16,000 varieties of roses were developed. Each year sees a new crop of hybrids presented to the gardener.

One of the first recorded hybrids was Champneys' Pink Cluster, a cross between a China rose and a musk rose developed in Charleston, S.C., in 1810 by John Champneys. A Charleston florist, Philippe Noisette, sent plants of the Champneys rose to his brother in Paris, where it became known as the Noisette.

In 1817 a rose named the Bourbon rose appeared in a planting of Chinas and Damasks in a garden on the Isle of Bourbon.

These two, the Noisette and Bourbon, were the chief varieties used by the hybridizers of the early 19th century. It is believed that in combination they produced the first of the modern hybrid perpetuals.

The Empress Josephine, in her celebrated gardens at Malmaison, collected all the varieties of roses obtainable in her day. It has been estimated that at the time of her death in 1814 Malmaison gardens contained approximately 250 varieties.

The first hybrid tea rose, La France, was developed in 1867, a cross between the hardy perpetual Mme. Victor Verdier and the tea rose, Mme. Bravy. But it was not until after 1911, when a hardy understock of the multiflora was used in its graft that the hybrid tea rose became popular. Thousands of hybrid teas are now listed in rose growers' catalogs.

With so many roses to choose from, the gardener may want help in planning his rose garden. Each year the American Rose Society, Harrisburg, Pa., issues "A Guide for Buying Rose

Plants." This leaflet is free upon request. It summarizes the Society's national reports on the most successfully grown varieties of the previous year. Newly developed hybrids as well as old favorites are listed.

CLASSES: For the practical gardener roses may be divided into four main classes, according to use. These classes are bedding roses, climbing roses, creeping roses, and shrub roses.

Bedding roses include teas, hybrid teas, hybrid perpetuals, and polyanthas or floribundas. They are used in free-standing beds and in low borders. Their average height is about 30 inches to three feet.

Tea roses were derived mainly from *R. odorata*. They are everblooming, but are not hardy enough to endure extreme winters of the northern states. Colors range from white through pink to rose, with some yellows, but no deep shades.

Hybrid perpetuals are the hardiest of the hybrids, and were most popular in the latter part of the 19th century. They range in color from white through pink to deep red, but there are no yellow shades. They bloom mainly in the spring, with a light secondary bloom in the fall if conditions are right. Principal ancestors of the hybrid perpetuals were *R. chinensis* and *R. damascena*.

Hybrid tea roses are very complex in origin, developed mainly from hardy perpetuals crossed with *R. odorata*. They have long pointed buds and large handsome flowers in all shades and combinations of colors. They are everblooming and hardy.

Polyantha hybrids, sometimes called floribundas, are derived from polyanthus, from which they take their clusters of flowers, and from hybrid perpetuals, whence comes great hardiness. Floribundas are becoming increasingly popular for their resistance to disease, their wide color range, and their abundance of blossoms throughout the season.

Climbing roses are of two types—those with flowers in clusters, called ramblers, and those with single large flowers, designated as large flowered climbers.

Climbers and bush roses are two common classes found in the garden. All types do best in a sunny location and a well-drained, slightly acid soil.

Ramblers are varieties of polyanthus, derived principally from *R. multiflora* and *R. wichuraiana*. They are generally hardy in latitudes where peaches can be grown commercially. They are rapid growers, making canes as long as 20 feet in one season. Many varieties are susceptible to mildew. Colors range from white through pink to deep red. Ramblers bloom only once each year.

Most large-flowered climbers were developed from hardy teas or hardy perpetuals, and are called climbing hardy teas or climbing hardy perpetuals, C.H.T., or C.H.P. Their color range includes yellows, deep shades, and bicolors. They may be hardy and everblooming or not, depending upon their parent stock. They grow less rapidly than ramblers, and bloom best when trained to low fences.

Shrub roses are species roses which may be planted in borders of deciduous shrubbery like forsythia and weigela. All are hardy, and many bear attractive hips in fall which are a valuable source of vitamin C. Chief among these are the rugosas (*R. rugosa*), which grows six to 15 feet tall, will endure heat, cold, dryness, sandy or clayey soil, and even salt sea air. Its flowers are single, double, or semi-double, in white, pink, and red.

Hybrid sweet-briers or Penzance briers were developed from common sweet-brier (*R. rubiginosa*). They are tall and graceful, and have scented foliage. Colors are pink, white, yellow, and copper.

Scotch roses, the burnet of northern Europe, are descended from *R. spinosissima*. They are very hardy, and are useful in hedges.

R. palustris may be naturalized in low, swampy locations where other roses will not grow. *R. rubrifolia* is useful chiefly for its interesting reddish foliage.

Creeping roses are climbers adapted to trailing along banks or walls. Their flowers are generally small, but they are hardy and provide an attractive ground cover.

Tree roses, or standard roses, are special adaptations of bush roses, and may be grafted from any bedding variety. They are used as accents or specimen plants in the garden, and require special winter care in cold areas.

CULTURE: Roses require sun, free circulation of air, and porous, well-drained, acid soil with a *p*H of five to six. Full sun for eight hours a day is best, but six hours' sun, provided they are morning hours, are sometimes sufficient.

Roses planted too close to buildings or fences where air does not circulate freely through their canes, are more subject to mildew. Climbers intended to decorate buildings or walls are best held away from the solid support with trellises. A three-foot space between vine and house will not only provide air space, but will facilitate painting the building.

Best plants to buy are two-year-old field grown budded stock. Roses may be planted in fall or spring. Most nurseries dig their roses in the fall, store them through the winter, and ship in spring. If they are purchased in fall and held over for spring planting they should be heeled in at the bottom of an 18-inch trench, covered with loose soil, and mulched after the ground is frozen.

Soil should be trenched and prepared to a depth of 24 inches for best results with roses. Experiments have proved that roses planted in more shallowly prepared soil will give equal results with those in deep beds during the first year, but after the second year the roses in 24-inch beds are superior.

In preparing a rose bed, the top spade's depth of soil is removed and saved, the lower spade's depth then removed and discarded. In its place, a mixture of ½ rotted manure and ½ humus is mixed with the top loam. The mixture is then returned to the bed and permitted to settle for two weeks before planting.

If drainage is a problem, a special drainage system may be installed in the rose bed. When the soil has been removed to a depth of 24 inches, the hardpan below is broken up with a pick or mattock. A four-inch layer of gravel, cinders, or rubble is placed in the bottom of the trench before the enriched top soil is returned to it. Where the ground is very badly drained, drainage tiles are laid from the rose bed to carry off seepage from the gravel layer at the bottom of the bed.

A hole slightly larger in diameter than the spread roots of the plant should be dug deep enough barely to bury the bud graft when planting. Soil is mounded cone shape in the center of the hole, and the plant seated upon it. If any of the roots are damaged, they should be pruned back of the damage. Long straggly roots also are cut back, and the tips of most others removed. The hole is half filled with soil, and a pail of water poured into it, to wash soil among the small rootlets. When the water has seeped away, the hole is filled to garden level and tamped around the plant. Canes are then pruned to six to eight inches above soil level.

CARE: Roses need plenty of water when the season is dry, but it should be supplied at weekly intervals in quantities large enough to reach the deepest roots rather than in small daily doses. Watering done in the morning of a sunny day will be less likely to cause mildew than if it is done in the evening, when foliage may remain wet over night. Recommended practice is to allow the water to dribble slowly from the hose under the bush, rather than from a spray which will wet the leaves.

Mulch may be spread around the plants when the weather becomes hot and dry, to conserve moisture. Compost, buckwheat hulls, ground corn cobs, straw, decayed or shredded leaves, or lawn clippings may be used. If peat moss is used, it should be moistened before application. It is advisable to mix a nitrogenous fertilizer with the mulch, particularly if corn cobs are used.

A formula developed especially for spring and summer rose feeding contains the following: two parts fishmeal, two parts dried blood, one part cottonseed meal, one part wood ashes (if soil is very acid), one part phosphate rock, and one part greensand. The first three ingredients supply nitrogen; wood ashes supply potash; and phosphate rock and greensand provide phosphorous. Application of this fertilizer may be repeated in monthly doses, ending August 1 in the North, September 1 in mid-sections, and October 1 in the South.

WINTER PROTECTION: Most bush roses need winter protection in areas where temperatures fall below 10°. It is standard practice to mound the soil

around the plants to a depth of at least eight inches Canes are drawn upright, and the longer ones trimmed to 30 inches. After the soil is thoroughly frozen and field mice have found their winter quarters elsewhere, a mulch of straw, leaves, or garden refuse mixed with manure may be filled in between mounds. Further protection is seldom necessary, unless the plants are exposed to drying winter winds. Burlap held by stakes may be used to shield the bed from strong winds.

To protect roses from extreme cold, mound the soil around plants about eight inches deep. After ground freezes, apply a mulch of straw or hay.

Winter cover should be removed before growth starts in the spring. Mulch should be raked away, and the winter's manure may be cultivated into the top layer of soil. The bed is then left to bake under the warm spring suns to kill spores of fungus diseases until the time arrives for covering with the summer mulch.

In sections where winters are extremely severe it may be necessary to protect climbing roses and ramblers. The only way to give them adequate cover is to take them down from their supports, gather the canes in a horizontal bundle on the ground, and cover them with soil. After the ground is thoroughly frozen a straw mulch may be spread over the soil.

Tree roses are difficult to protect in an upright position, because the drying winter winds, which do more damage than low temperatures, cannot be kept out of their cases. The best protection can be given only when the tree top is bent down to the ground and the canes are covered with soil. Straw and leaf mulch may be placed around the plants in an upright position if a burlap structure is built around it, but great damage may be done by field mice inside the cover.

PRUNING: Bedding roses are pruned in the spring when new shoots are about one-fourth inch long. Dead wood—all wood with brown, dried or shriveled bark—is trimmed off first. The plant is then inspected for injury, and any canes injured by the winter winds or ice are trimmed back. Next rough, gnarled branches with weak twigs, and thin weak shoots are removed. Then the remainder of the branches are shortened by one-third of their length if many flowers are desired, or two-thirds length for larger but fewer blossoms. For exhibition bloom the canes are cut back to six or eight inches.

Large flowered climbing roses are pruned in early spring in much the same way as bedding roses. Tree roses are also pruned in spring, being cut back more severely than bush types to control their shape. Species roses are pruned very little, except to remove dead wood in early spring and overgrown canes after blooming. These varieties are left to develop their own graceful shapes.

Ramblers are pruned in spring only to remove the dead wood. Their heaviest pruning is done immediately after blooming, when all canes that have flowered are cut back to the ground. Canes will grow as much as 20 feet before the end of the summer, and the following year's bloom will all be borne on wood developed after pruning.

Because of their more vigorous growth, ramblers are best suited for positions where a high vine is desired. They may be trained to overhead trellises and supports, or to high pillars for vertical accents. Climbing hybrid teas and climbing hybrid perpetuals do not make as much growth in one season and are better suited to lower supports, such as fences. Trained horizontally along a fence they will bloom more freely than on an upright support. Bloom buds will arise from almost every leaf joint of a horizontal cane.

CUTTING: Roses should be cut late in the day, unlike other flowers which last longer when cut early in the morning. It has been found by experiment that a rose cut after 4:30 p.m. will last ten hours longer than one cut at 8 a.m. The reason for this is thought to be the extra supply of sugar in the leaves late in the day. Sugar is manufactured in daylight by the chlorophyll. During the night it travels to the roots and other parts of the plant, but after long daylight hours the leaves are saturated with sugar, which is used for nourishment of the flowers after they are cut.

Everblooming roses should not be cut below the second leaf axil on the cane if the bush is expected to continue to bloom. Later blooms will arise from the lower leaf axils. The fewer leaves removed from the plant, the more flowers will follow. If the flowers are allowed to remain on the plant until the petals fall, the old bloom should be pinched off just above the top leaf.

PROPAGATION: Roses are seldom grown from seed because seed-grown plants will revert to species. It is possible to propagate species from seed, but requires more work than most gardeners are willing to do for the results achieved.

Several methods of handling rose seed are suggested. The seed is contained in a fruit called a hip, similar to an apple, to which it is closely related. Hips are collected when fully ripe—usually just before the first frost.

One method of growing roses from seed is the "ripening" method. Hips are mashed to make a pulpy mash, and this is permitted to ferment at about 40° for 60 to 120 days. "Ripening" takes place during this period, a process thought to aid in germination. After fermentation, seeds are washed and layered in humus in a flat or flower pot, and placed outdoors on the north side of a building to refrigerate.

A second method of handling seed is to remove it from the hips and, without fermenting, to place it in leaf mold or peat moss in a flat or pot outside. Weathering during the cold months seems to help the seed to germinate. A third, and simpler method, is to plant the seed directly in the garden in the fall. If this method is adopted, seed should be sown about an inch deep, and six inches apart. After germination plants may be moved to stand a foot apart and permitted to grow for two years before taking their place in the shrubbery border.

A practical method for propagating roses true to the parent is by cuttings or slips. Cuttings are taken from the most healthy plants, and are made at a point where the cane breaks with a snap. If it bends, the wood is too tough. If it crushes, it is too green. A point below the sixth set of leaves on a shoot that has just finished blooming usually has the right texture.

The two bottom sets of leaves are removed, leaving the two nodes. (Nodes are the joints on the stem from which the leaves grow.) The stem is cut off just below the two top sets of leaves, and the stem tip discarded.

Slips may be set directly into an existing rose bed, or may be started in a corner of the shrubbery where they will receive morning sun only. They are inserted in the ground up to the

remaining leaves, and the soil firmed. A light sprinkling of peat moss may be made around them, and they are covered with glass jars, which are pushed securely into the soil. They are then watered well with a light spray from the hose. It is not necessary to water them too often, because the moisture which condenses inside the glass jar will keep them sufficiently wet.

If the cutting forms roots, new shoots will appear within three or four weeks. Jars are not removed until the cuttings have roots enough to supply plenty of moisture to the leaves—possibly not until the following spring. Cuttings may be made any time from June until the first frosts. If they are made during July or August, it is well to shade them from the afternoon sun.

Some climbers and shrub roses spread through root runners, which send up shoots at a distance from the parent plant. When these shoots have made a root system of their own they may be severed from the parent and moved to a new situation. Many ramblers will root where the tip of a branch touches the ground. Thoroughly rooted tips may be cut from the parent canes, and the new plant moved.

ENEMIES AND DISEASES: Weakened roses are subject to many fungus and insect infestations. Whether rose plants are weak or strong they are always subject to some diseases and pests, but many organic gardeners find that their well-fed and properly mulched roses are no more subject to these disorders than are many more rugged garden specimens.

A few simple sanitary measures are recommended for gardeners who prefer not to use chemical sprays. Garden trash and mulches are removed from rose beds early in spring, and the bare soil is exposed to sun for at least a month. This drying process kills many spores and fungi which may have wintered in the mulch or soil.

Rose leaves that fall from the plants during the growing season may be assumed to be harboring an insect or disease, and should be removed to the compost pile as soon as possible. Leaves on the plants showing signs of disease or insects are best removed, also.

Fungus diseases which attack roses are:

Black spot. Irregular circular spots with radiating margins (mycelium) appear on the leaves and sometimes also on canes. The leaves turn yellow and fall.

Mildew. This appears as a white powdering over leaves and canes, causing buds and leaves to become dwarfed and gnarled. Ramblers are likely to show mildew in spring, bedding roses in late summer, especially after a prolonged period of wet weather. Full sun and adequate ventilation is the best preventive. Care should be taken never to wet foliage with the hose, especially late in the day when the sun will not have time to dry it before evening.

Rust. Orange-brown powdery spore masses appear on under leaf surfaces. Infested leaves should be destroyed.

Leaf spot, or anthracnose. Spots on leaves are ashy in the center, with red brown borders.

Chlorosis or mosaic. This is a virus disease that turns leaves yellow along the veins. It is more prevalent in greenhouses than outdoors. Plants attacked must be destroyed to prevent spreading.

Canker. Infection from fungus may occur in open wounds in the canes to prevent the wound's healing. This happens most often with wounds made during the winter, and when plants are covered. Canes should all be inspected in spring, and damaged tissue cut back. Prompt pruning of cankered canes is the best control.

Sucking insects which attack roses are aphids and rose leaf hoppers. Chewers that like rose flavor are rose saw-fly, whose slug-like larvae skeletonize the leaves; rose chafer or rose beetles which attack buds and flowers;

Japanese beetles, which eat the flowers; rose curculio and climbing cutworm, both of which bore holes in buds; leaf cutters that nip circular holes out of leaves; leaf rollers which tie up leaves; stem girdlers that tunnel in twigs to cause swellings; and rose midge, a small fly that lays eggs near flower buds, in order to supply its offspring with tender rose petals for sustenance.

Many of these insects may be hand-picked. According to organic gardeners, not many of them attack plants grown with proper sanitary control of soil, plenty of food and mulch, and a reasonable amount of year-round care. Where one disease or another is difficult to control, special varieties resistant to that disease may be planted. Many of the newer roses are being bred especially for their hardiness and disease resistance. Lists of them may be found in any grower's catalog. *See also* SHRUBS; PRUNING; MULTIFLORA ROSE.

ROSE ACACIA: *see* LOCUST

ROSE BAY: *see* OLEANDER

ROSE, CHRISTMAS: *see* CHRISTMAS ROSE

ROSE HIP: An extremely rich source of vitamin C, rose hips (sometimes called heps) are the fruit of the rose. After petals drop in the fall, the hips appear as pods of various sizes and colors. Most varieties of roses have hips the size of a pea or a marble. Many are green; some orange and red.

The great majority of American gardeners think that rose hips have no value, except possibly as an accent in flower arrangements. But concentrated in the hips of some varieties of roses is nature's richest source of vitamin C. Several common hips are as much as *60 times* richer in vitamin C than oranges, and oranges are generally recognized as just about the richest common food source of vitamin C. In Norway and Sweden, rose hips are collected in the fields and woods and made into soups, stews, preserves, sauces and juices to fortify vitamin-poor winter menus. Their pleasant flavor is both fruity and spicy. In the early fall the large bushes are covered

After the rose petals fall, the hips appear as pods of different sizes and colors. They can be collected, trimmed and prepared in many recipes.

with the orange and red fruits. Some people enjoy eating them fresh—right off the bush. Most often, though, they are collected, trimmed and cooked lightly before being used in a variety of recipes. No food that can be produced in a garden comes anywhere near having the concentrated food value of rose hips.

USING HIPS: Because the elusive vitamin C is difficult to hold through a drying process, rose hips are not easily prepared in powder form. If you grow your own roses or if you have access to roses whose hips you can use, the best idea is to make an extract or puree of them. This can then be stored with a minimum loss of food value, and used throughout the year by the tablespoonful or in fruit juices, salads, soups, sauces, etc.

ROSE HIP EXTRACT: One of the most practical recipes for rose hip extract comes from Adelle Davis' excellent cook book *Let's Cook It Right* (published by Harcourt, Brace and Company, N. Y.). Says Miss Davis: "Gather rose hips; chill. (This is

to inactivate the enzymes which might otherwise cause a loss of vitamin C.) Remove blossom ends, stems and leaves; wash quickly. For each cup of rose hips bring to a boil 1½ cups of water. Add one cup of rose hips. Cover utensil and simmer 15 minutes. Let stand in a pottery utensil for 24 hours. Strain off the extract, bring to a rolling boil, add two tablespoons lemon juice for each pint, pour into jars and seal. (Remember, don't make the mistake of using copper or aluminum utensils when you are cooking rose hips.)"

That cautioning note at the end of the recipe is there because copper destroys vitamin C on contact, and aluminum cookware also causes a considerable loss. Incidentally, researchers have found that the best time to gather the hips is when they are fully ripe, but not overripe. Rose hips are bright scarlet when ripe, orange when unripe and dark red when overripe. Location makes a difference in vitamin content, too, with roses farther north showing more vitamin C than those grown farther south.

Regardless of what you're making, follow these few rules:

1. Trim both ends of the rose hips with a pair of scissors before cooking.
2. Use stainless steel knives, wooden spoons, earthenware or china bowls and glass or enamel saucepans.
3. Cook quickly with the lid on so there will not be much loss of vitamin C.
4. After the hips have been cooked the required time, strain out the spines and seeds or break them down by rubbing the cooked pulp through a sieve.

ROSE HIP PUREE: Take two pounds of rose hips and two pints of water. Remove the stalk and remnants of the rose from the end of the berries and stew them in a saucepan until tender. This will take about 20 minutes and the lid should be kept on. Then press the mixture through a sieve and the result will be a brownish-tinted puree of about the same consistency and thickness as jam.

ROSE HIP SOUP: In Sweden, rose hip soup is a popular, healthful dish. It's easy to make: The hips are ground and boiled for ten minutes, then strained and again brought to a boil and thickened with four level teaspoonful of potato flour (you can use soybean or whole wheat flour) which has been prepared with two cups of cold water. This soup can be served hot or cold. *See also* ROSA RUGOSA.

ROSELLE: *see* HIBISCUS SABDARIFFA

ROSEMARY: (*Rosemarinus officinalis*) The spicy leaves of this perennial evergreen shrub are used dried or fresh in the kitchen. A member of the mint family, it grows three to five feet high and very dense, with light blue flowers. Both leaves and flowers are very aromatic.

Rosemary will do well in the North in a sheltered position; in the South, it is commonly used as a hedge plant. Propagate by cuttings about six inches long, taken in September and rooted in a sand-loam-leaf mold mixture in the cold frame or cool greenhouse. Set them out in the spring in the same type of soil. The growth can be pruned back several inches once or twice each season after the plants are large enough. *See also* HERBS.

ROSE MOSS: (*Portulaca grandiflora*) An annual flower that thrives under the most trying conditions of heat, drought and poor soil, rose moss has narrow, succulent leaves that are completely hidden in a blanket of gay colors in sunlight when the blooms open. For a summer edging, window box or rock garden plant, probably nothing surpasses the rose moss. It is sometimes called the garden portulaca or wax pink. The flowers are white, pink, yellow, red or purple, single or double and up to an inch and a half across, borne on trailing stems up to about four inches high.

Rose moss likes a dry, sunny situation. The seeds are best sown when the weather warms up, in late May or June. The young plants are easy to transplant. The blooming season is short, so it's a good idea to sow at monthly intervals through the summer. The plant self-sows freely, but volunteer seedlings should not be used because of the possibility of mixing in plants of the wild type which have inferior flowers. *See also* PORTULACA.

ROSE-OF-HEAVEN: *see* LYCHNIS

ROSE-OF-SHARON: (*Hibiscus syriacus*) Sometimes called shrubby althea, rose-of-sharon is a handsome, late-flowering (midsummer through October) deciduous shrub. It grows from six to 12 feet high or higher, and its lower branches can be pruned out to give a "tree" effect. A long-time favorite in gardens, it is hardy in most of the United States if given plenty of sun and moderately fertile soil, not too wet or dry.

Plant in spring and cut back all shoots to about two inches of their base to get the plant started growing vigorously. Prune each year in spring before growth starts, aiming at developing a shapely bush form. Cuttings of growing wood taken in July will root under glass in a few weeks, or you can take cuttings of mature wood in early winter, store them in a cold place covered with sand and plant them in the open as soon as the soil is dry enough to work freely.

There are many varieties and forms. Some of the best are the large-flowered single white Snowstorm; coelestis, blue-flowered; roseus, white flowers with carmine eyes; ruber, beautiful red flowers; Jeanne d'Arc, a spectacular double white; Lady Stanley, white with pink shading; Ardens, lavender; anemonaeflorus, bright pink; and Lucy, semi-double rose-pink. A few have variegated leaves, such as mee-hani, with lavender-blue flowers and leaves marked with yellow.

The name rose-of-sharon is also applied to *Hypericum calycium,* a Saint John's-wort. This is an evergreen shrubby plant growing a foot or less high, useful as a ground cover in shade and sandy soil.

ROSE PINK: (*Sabbatia dodecandra*) A useful plant for seaside gardens, rose pink grows in salty, moist sand. It is found in salt marshes all along the Atlantic coast, grows about a foot high, and has pretty pink blooms through the summer. Other names for it are sea pink and American centaury. It is not difficult to transplant, but must be given conditions very similar to those in its wild situation.

ROSE POGONIA: *see* POGONIA

ROSETTE: A rosette is a cluster of stalkless leaves that radiate from a single point on a stem, as in some palms, but more often from the base of the plant. The name comes from its resemblance to the form of a rose bloom. The houseleeks are notable examples, and many biennials have rosette forms their first year.

ROTARY MOWER: *see* MOWER, POWER

ROTARY TILLAGE: Rotary tillage methods have been developed because of a desire to simplify and speed up the process of preparing soil for planting. Ordinary tillage methods require the use of a plow, disk and a harrow before seed can be planted. Sometimes a field is also dragged to break up clods and firm the seedbed. Developers of rotary tillage equipment hoped to be able to build a machine that would do those three jobs in one operation. They have succeeded.

Rotary tillage has another advantage. It provides a better means of incorporating crop wastes and other organic matter into the soil than the plow-disk-harrow combination. Plowing tends to bury organic matter in a layer four to six inches deep, often too far below the surface to allow optimum decay and breakdown by microorganisms. Rotary tillage mixes such organic matter into the soil evenly through the full tillage depth.

Farm-scale rotary tillage is steadily growing in popularity, but it has so far failed to be adopted by the great majority of farmers. The major implement firms have not yet added rotary tillers to their lines. There are a number of reasons why farmers have tended to stay with their old practices. Larger tractors able to pull four and five bottom plows have become common and have made plowing more rapid an operation. Tillers are more difficult to operate in rocky ground. Perhaps most important, some farmers have felt that tillers require a larger initial investment and greater maintenance expense. By contrast, the plow is one of the simplest tools used by man and has been tested and proven in field use for thousands of years. Any new implement coming along to challenge the supremacy of the plow must undo those centuries of ingrained acceptance of a traditional tool.

In American gardens, tillers have made much more progress and have actually replaced the plow as the most common power tillage tool. The reason for the garden popularity of rotary tillers is easily explained. A plow requires the horsepower and traction of at least one real horse to work efficiently. To build such pulling power into a small garden tractor requires a fairly large expense. However, a very efficient tiller can be built using a small engine. It will be a small unit, but it will easily prepare a seedbed in the average small garden. For about $150 a gardener can purchase an efficient tiller. It would cost more to purchase a tractor, plow, disk and harrow that would do an equivalent job. In addition, the tiller can also be used as a cultivator without the purchase of an additional attachment.

Tillers have become extremely popular with organic gardeners and farmers, primarily because of their efficient handling of soils with heavy plant cover. Often a rotary cutter or heavy mower is first run over the land to chop up plant material before tilling. For farm-scale tilling, the rotary cutter is almost a necessity.

When using a tiller (especially on soil that is low in organic matter) it is necessary to be careful not to pulverize the soil too thoroughly. If that is done, the tilth of the soil can be harmed and packing will result. Pulverizing can be prevented by using the slowest efficient tine speed. Also, the soil should not be too wet or too dry when tilling is done. *See also* GREEN MANURE.

ROTATION: Crop rotation means a regular scheme of planting whereby different demands are made on the soil each year. A four-year rotation might be corn, oats, clover, wheat, in four fields of similar size. Each year the farmer has all four crops but in different places. The fifth year corn goes in where it was at first and the repetition starts. Depending on his needs, he may have a three, a five or an even longer rotation, sometimes leaving a perennial like alfalfa in each field in turn for two or more years. This requires careful planning concerning both time and place, and the right division of the farm into smaller units. It may take several years of trial and error to get just the right rotation for all the factors involved, each farm being an individual entity. But once rightly established, the rotation can go on indefinitely.

Crop rotation is one of the *essentials* of a good growing program. A legume (clovers, alfalfa, beans or peas) is advised at least once in four years, since it is a soil builder. Vegetable garden rotations have been worked out, too, and the same principles apply with flowers. Plants are classified, according to their needs and their groups. The *heavy feeders* (1),

needing generous fertilizing, include corn, tomatoes and cabbage. Next the *legumes* (2), to help the soil following the heavy demands of those crops, especially in poorer soils. In a live humus soil, legumes may go in third place if desired. The last group, *light feeders,* (3) include root vegetables, bulbs, herbs, etc. When in doubt about a plant, put it in this group.

FLOWERS: A flower garden probably contains both annuals and perennials, which complicates rotation, as we cannot shift perennials every year. However, we can keep these principles in mind when they do need moving, meanwhile treating them to the kind of fertilizing they like.

In *Group 1* belong flowers in the cabbage family—arabis, cheiranthus, rocket, aubrietia, alyssum, candytuft, etc. If cabbage is often followed by cabbage, the inevitable result is club foot (the immediate result of not rotating crops) and all such diseases, as well as the cabbage butterfly, cabbage worm and other pests. Here perennials as well as annuals need frequent change of location, besides good manuring. In this group is the ranunculus or buttercup family with many garden favorites—peony, delphinium, larkspur, monkshood, columbine, nigella, clematis, anemone, meadow rue, helleborus, adonis. All these give off from their roots a peculiar substance called ranunculin.

RANUNCULIN: Though produced in small amounts, ranunculin is said to direct soil fermentation processes toward acidity and sterility rather than towards humus. These garden plants are greedy. They like plenty of manure, but they use it up, leaving the soil sterile for other plants. Another "isolationist" family in Group 1 are the poppies. Wild poppies look beautiful in the grain fields of Europe, but they are bad companions. With plenty of manure they will do less damage. Carnations and mignonette are in this group too.

LEGUMES: The legumes in *Group*

2 form one of the largest and most important of plant families, distinguished by its ability to "breathe in nitrogen" whereas other plants "breathe it out" of the soil. Because they are so beneficial in or around a garden, we list here all the more commonly known, be they trees, shrubs or garden flowers—sweet peas, lupines, scarlet runner beans, kudzu vine, bush clovers, lotus, coral tree, baptisia, amorpha, false indigo, lead plant, pea tree, robinia, false acacia, yellow wood, Japanese pagoda tree, colutea, sainfoin, coronilla, licorice, wisteria, gorse, golden chain tree, laburnum, Scotch broom, red bud, cassia or senna, honey locust, mimosa, acacia. Although not in this family, all the flaxes are soil benefactors and for cultivation purposes may be classed here. Their fine root structure has an excellent soil-loosening effect.

COMPOST LOVERS: *Group 3,* the light feeders, include the lilies and all bulbous plants, those with fleshy roots such as iris, and plants with delicate growth and high aromatic quality like most herbs. Some of these may grow naturally under rather poor conditions, but remember that under cultivation unusual demands are made on them while they also give up their naturally chosen habitat and companions. Fertilizing, though lighter, is not less essential, with well-decayed compost. One family belonging here has special interest in that its members are helpful companions to delicate, warmth-loving plants. This spurge family has between 700 to 1,000 species, most having a milky juice, many being fleshy, desert plants or native in warm climates. Best known are snow-on-the-mountain, poinsettia, crown of thorns and castor bean. They seem to radiate a certain warmth into the soil around them that helps plants which need a little coddling, perhaps because they, too, are far away from their native tropics.—*Ehrenfried Pfeiffer.*

See also FLOWER GARDENING; VEGETABLE GARDENING.

ROTENONE: Rotenone, sometimes called derris, is an insecticide derived from certain tropical plants, derris, cube, barbasco, timbo and a few others. It is a contact and stomach poison, often mixed with pyrethrum, and is of very low toxicity to man and animals. Like pyrethrum, it can be obtained in the pure state only from pet shops and veterinarians. When purchased in commercial dusts and sprays, rotenone is often mixed with synthetic compounds that may be toxic in varying degrees. Devil's shoestring (*Tephrosia virginiana*) is the only native plant which contains rotenone. It is a common weed in the eastern and southern states, and its roots may contain as high as five per cent rotenone. Rotenone can be safely used on all crops and ornamentals. It kills many types of insects, and also certain external parasites of animals. However, it has little residual effect and the period of protection it offers is short. *See also* INSECTICIDES; INSECT CONTROL.

ROUGHAGE: A coarse bulky feed high in crude fiber and relatively low in percentage of digestibility, such as hay, straw, and stover.

ROUGHPEA: *see* GREEN MANURE

ROYAL FERN: *see* OSMUNDA

ROYAL LILY: *see* LILY

ROYAL PALM: (*Roystonea*) These big feather palms are very tender and are grown only in central and southern Florida. They make gorgeous specimen or street trees, and are extensively planted on boulevards in the great cities of the tropics. In Florida, the most popular species is the Cuban royal palm (*R. regia*), which grows 50 feet tall or taller, with leaves up to 15 feet long. The Barbados royal palm (*R. oleracea*) grows over 100 feet high on avenues, but the Puerto Rican royal palm (*R. borinquena*) is only 30 feet tall and best suited to lawn planting. Both of these last are very tender. Royal palms are rarely successful in the greenhouse.

RUBBER PLANT: (*Ficus elastica*) One of the most popular plants for house culture. It is usually grown as a single stem plant and in this shape is very pretty indeed for formal effects, but equally decorative specimens can be had by growing compact, branching plants. The leaves are anywhere from three to 12 inches long, about one-third as wide as they are long, and oblong to elliptical in shape with a small, abrupt point. The upper side of the leaf is very glossy and dark green, but the under side is dull and light green.

Compared with the palms, the rubber plant is a fast-growing subject, but a plant grown to a single stem will not become too tall for the living room for a couple or three years. A rubber plant six to eight feet tall always has a "leggy" look, for, as a rule, the bottom leaves drop off. When a rubber plant gets too tall for the house, don't cut off the top and throw it away, but root it and make a new plant.

If you have a greenhouse or a propagating box in which bottom heat and a humid atmosphere can be maintained, the stem can be cut up into short pieces —one leaf to a piece. The cuttings can then be put directly into the propagating box or the cuttings tied to small sticks so as to maintain the leaf in an upright position, and the whole planted in two and one-half inch pots and then plunged in a cutting bench. In order to make the cuttings root, a steady heat and humidity in the atmosphere must be maintained.

The rubber plant is a gross feeder so there is no danger of getting the soil too rich. Use an ordinary potting soil such as has already been described in the chapter on soils and when the pot has become filled with roots, manure water, or other plant food in liquid form may be given once or twice a week.

During the summer the rubber plant will receive much benefit from being put outdoors, but if the plant has grown much in the house, do not put it where it will get the full sunshine, for the leaves will be burned. Place them where they will get the early morning and late afternoon sun, but be shaded during the middle of the day. *See also* HOUSE PLANTS.

RUBIA: The common madder (*R. tinctorum*) is an interesting hardy perennial with fleshy roots from which a dye is obtained by grinding them. It grows about three feet high, with yellowish-green flowers in clusters and hairy leaves. It is not often grown in gardens, but given a sunny position, will do well in practically any soil.

RUBUS: Some 500 species, and almost countless hybrids, make up the *Rubus* or bramble genus of the rose family. Over 60 species are cultivated in the United States, the most important of these being the blackberry, dewberry, loganberry and raspberry. A few have worthless fruits but are ornamental. The flowering raspberry (*R. odoratus*), for example, has showy flowers and is useful for shrub borders in shade; the swamp dewberry (*R. hispidus*) is a trailing plant that makes a good ground cover in shady places; and the boulder raspberry (*R. deliciosus*), the cutleaf blackberry (*R. laciniatus*), and the balloon berry or strawberry-raspberry (*R. ilecebrosus*) are all used mainly for ornament. The wineberry (*R. phoenicolasius*) is a dense plant for thick hedges. There are also perhaps 100 species of native wild brambles. *See also listings under individual plants;* BRAMBLE FRUITS.

RUDBECKIA: *see* CONEFLOWER

RUGOSA ROSE: *see* ROSA RUGOSA; ROSE HIP; ROSE

RUMEX: *see* SORREL

RUMINANT: Any animal such as a cow or sheep which chews its cud, brings up its food and rechews it previous to swallowing a second time.

RUNNER: Referring to the prostrate shoots which root, such as strawberry runners. Runners are often used for propagation purposes, since all that is needed is to separate the rooted joints of the shoots.

RUSSIAN OLIVE: see OLEASTER

RUST DISEASE: see DISEASE

RUTABAGA: (*Brassica napobrassica*) This excellent late-season root crop is high in food value and can easily be stored in pits or in moist sand in the cellar for winter eating. Rutabagas are sometimes called winter, yellow or Swedish turnips, but they are bigger and hardier than the common turnip, and take longer to mature. They are best planted July 15 or later, in a moist, rich soil, and harvested after a frost. But they must not freeze or their keeping quality will be impaired.

Sow the seed in drills, one ounce being sufficient for 400 feet of drill. Space the plants 12 inches apart. The best yellow varieties are Perfection Swede, Golden Neckless, Golden Heart and Improved Purple-top. There are also several fine new white Macombers with especially sweet flesh. The latter can be planted several weeks earlier and will not develop tough flesh as will the yellow kinds if planted early.

Rutabagas are good winter stock feed, and are sown a month earlier so they will make big roots, about two pounds of seed per acre drilled or five pounds broadcast. Special varieties that yield heavy roots have been developed for this purpose. *See also* TURNIP.

RYE: (*Secale cereale*) For 2,000 years rye has been one of the most widely planted crops on earth. Besides its value to the farmer as a grain and, in many areas, as fall and spring pasture, it is a marvelous soil protector and builder. Its extensive root system—one rye plant was found to have a total root length of 385 miles—binds the soil and supplies enormous quantities of organic matter. Balbo, Rosen and Abruzzi are the most commonly planted varieties, but Tetra Petkus, a new giant-sized high-yielder, is fast gaining favor.

Rye is an annual grass, growing three to five feet tall. It is sown in the fall and plowed under in spring when about nine inches high for a green manure. It does well in either sandy or clay soils, mildly acid to mildly alkaline.

Italian rye grass (*Lolium multiflorum*) is a perennial that grows about two feet tall, and like its relative, *L. perenne*, commonly called perennial rye grass, is used for pastures and meadows. Italian rye grass is sometimes used for a spring-sown lawn, to be dug in before sowing a permanent lawn in the fall. Perennial rye grass, tough and quick-growing, is added to lawn seed mixtures to help keep out weeds until the other grasses make good growth. It yields to them in a few years. *See also* COVER CROP.

S

SAFFLOWER: (*Carthamus tinctorius*) An ancient oil-bearing crop from India that was first grown in the United States in 1925. It is now regularly grown in the western Great Plains and north-central California. Yield is as high as 2,500 pounds on dry land, up to 3,000 or even 4,000 pounds on irrigated land. In some areas, safflower is seeded with an airplane, and later the seed is disked into the soil. In California, safflower is often grown in rotation with rice on high water table land. Safflower oil is highly valued in cooking; in addition, it has many industrial uses.

SAFFRON CROCUS: *see* CROCUS

SAGE: *see* SALVIA

SAGITTARIA: Known as arrowhead, this is a genus of water or bog plants of the family *Alismaceae*. Most have arrow-shaped leaves; are perennials, growing from tuberous or gnarled rootstocks. Flowers are male or female, both growing on the same plant, three-petalled and growing in clusters of three. They can be grown from seed in boxes and sunk in ponds or aquaria, or from dividing the rootstock.

S. engelmanniana is a native of the central and northern Atlantic coast, grows to 1½ feet, with eight inch arrow-shaped leaves.

S. latifolia grows to four feet, with some linear and some arrow-shaped leaves. Roots were used as potatoes by the Indians.

Giant arrowhead (*S. montevidensis*) is a six-foot native of South America and the southern states. Flowers are two inches or more across, with brownish-purple spots at the base of the petals.

Old-world arrowhead (*S. sagittifolia*) grows to four feet, with arrow-shaped leaves and flowers spotted purple at the base. Roots eaten in the Orient.

SAGO PALM: (*Cycas revoluta*) The *cycas* has a short stem which is crowned with a whorl of leaves. Only one whorl is produced a year, but with care the old leaves may be made to persist for two or three years. The foliage is dark green; the individual leaf is long and flat, being composed of a long central stem to which the pinnae are attached in two rows. When the new leaves come out, they unroll just like the fiddle-head fern fronds, and are upright, but as they grow older, they gradually drop, until the following year, when it is time for the new set of leaves to come out, they are horizontal or slightly drooping.

The cycas is easy to grow, and succeeds well in the varying temperature of a living room and almost any well-drained soil. It grows six to ten feet high, does best in a rather warm greenhouse and should be given plenty of water. It is much used for funeral wreaths.

SAINT AUGUSTINE GRASS: *see* LAWN

SAINTFOIN: *see* ONONBRYCHIS

SAINT JOHN'S WORT: (*Hypericum*) Legend of the plant goes back to the days of witchcraft. It was said that if the plants were collected during St. John's Night (June 24th), protection against witches and evil spirits would be given. Though somewhat weedy, the plants are often grown in the rock garden and border. Rose-of-sharon (*H. calycinum*) grows about one foot high, is evergreen, makes a good ground cover in shady or sandy areas in the southern part of the country. Gold-flower (*H. moserianum*) grows less than two feet, has reddish stems, large flowers. Many of the species prefer part shade, and are simple to grow. They can be propagated by seeds or division. Bush broom or shrubby St. John's Wort

(*H. prolificum*) grows on dry, light soils, reaches as high as five feet.

SAINTPAULIA: *see* AFRICAN VIOLET

SALAL: (*Gaultheria shallon*) An evergreen shrub from one to five feet tall with long racemes of pink flowers. It grows from Washington south to central California in the redwood forests. Salal does best in an acid sandy soil and in a part-shady location.

Wintergreen (*G. procumbens*) is a low-growing evergreen, that produces red fruit. Also known as ground holly, teaberry and spiceberry.

SALINE SOIL: Under hot, arid conditions, soluble salts often accumulate in the surface of soils whenever the ground-water comes within a few feet of the surface. This can happen under natural conditions, in the flood plains of rivers, the low-lying shores of lakes, and in depressions in which drainage water accumulates—in any region where marsh, swamp or other ill-drained soil would be found in humid regions. During dry periods the surface of these soils is covered with a salt crust, which is dissolved in the soil water each time the soil is wetted.

Saline soils typically have an uneven surface, being covered with small puffed-up spots a few inches high that are enriched in salts. Salts congregate in the moist salty areas because these areas remain moist longest after the onset of drought.

Saline soils normally show no change of structure down the profile, implying that the soil is barely affected by soil weathering and soil-forming processes. Usually they are low in humus, because the natural vegetation cannot make much annual growth on them. The salts usually present in the soil are the sulphates and chlorides of sodium and calcium, though nitrates occur in a few places, and magnesium sometimes constitutes an appreciable proportion of the cations. Under these conditions, the pH of the soil is below 8.5 and the color

of the soil surface is light. In some saline soils the pH is nine or ten.

They may contain over 100 tons per acre of salt in the top four feet of soil, that is, the salts may constitute over one per cent by weight of the soil, though many saline soils contain less than this. *See also* SOIL.

SALIX: *see* WILLOW

SALPIGLOSSIS: *see* PAINTED-TONGUE

SALSIFY: *see* OYSTER PLANT

SALT HAY: Generally referring to hay used for mulching by gardeners living near coastal marshes. *See also* MULCH.

SALTY SOIL: *see* SALINE SOIL

SALVIA: Known also as sage, this is a large genus comprising more than 500 species of annuals, perennials, and sub-shrubs of the mint family, *Labiatae,* which are distributed all over the world. Leaves in pairs on square stems are usually oval or lance-shaped, toothed, and sometimes hairy or woolly. Flowers grow in spikes, red, blue, white, purple, and pale yellow, with a two-part corolla with five lobes, three below and two above. Usually those grown for their flowers are known as salvias or flowering sage, those for seasoning or medicine, sage. Many fine varieties are half-hardy, and can be carried over the winter by digging up roots and storing them frost-free. Some are hardy in most parts of the United States, others must be treated as annuals throughout the country. They are not particular as to soil, growing well in any good garden loam. Propagation is by seed, cuttings or division.

Best known as salvia is the scarlet sage (*S. splendens*) which is used as an annual in beds and borders. Its brilliant red blossoms are borne from early summer to frost. Seed is usually started indoors in February or March, and plants set outside when soil is warm.

Two species are grown in the north as blue salvia (*S. patens*) blue sage, a fine ultramarine half-hardy type which grows to two feet, and *S. farinaceae* or mealycup sage, growing to four feet with silvery foliage and lavender flowers.

S. azurea has light blue or white flowers on a hardy plant which grows to four feet. *S. pitcheri*, also a hardy blue growing about the same height or slightly taller, has brilliant blue flowers on slender stems which should be staked.

Silver salvia or silver sage (*S. argentea*) a biennial or perennial, sends up foor-foot stems of pink, blue, yellowish, or white flowers in August from rosettes of silver-woolly leaves. These too should be staked.

Spanish sage (*S. bicolor*) is a three-foot perennial or biennial with two-foot spikes of flowers which are bluish-violet and white.

Thistle salvia (*S. carduacea*) is a spiny two-foot plant with lavender flowers in two-inch roundish heads.

Texas sage (*S. coccinea*) is a two-foot variety with eight-inch scarlet flower spikes. Varieties are white or red and white.

Cardinal sage or Mexican red sage (*S. fulgens*) is a woolly three-foot shrub with scarlet flower spikes a foot long.

The sage used for seasoning (*S. officinalis*) is a hardy perennial or partly woody shrub with woolly white leaves and shorter spikes of purple, blue, or white flowers.

S. officinalis makes its best growth in a rich clay loam with a good supply of nitrogen, but it will grow in a wide range of soils of reasonable nitrogen content provided they are well drained. Excessive moisture in the soil during freezing weather results in winterkilling in the northern states. Sage will withstand below-zero temperatures if it is protected by snow or a mulch of leaves or straw.

Sage may be propagated by stem cuttings, which can be rooted easily in sand and then planted 12 to 18 inches apart in rows three feet apart. For larger plantings seed may be drilled directly in the field about three-fourths of an inch deep in rows three feet apart early in spring, as soon as the ground is warm. The plants are later thinned to the desired spacing. A few plants set in a corner of the garden or in a perennial flower bed will furnish sufficient leaves for ordinary family use. Six to eight inches of the top growth can be cut from the plant about twice during the season. The leaves should be harvested before the plant blooms.

The tops may be tied in small bundles or spread on screens and dried in a well-ventilated room away from direct sunlight. If the leaves are dusty or gritty, they should be washed in cold water before drying. When they are thoroughly dry remove the stems and pack the clean dry leaves in paper bags or some other closed container.

Use the leaves sparingly with onion for stuffing pork, ducks, or geese. The powdered leaves rubbed on the outside of fresh pork, ham, and loin gives a flavor resembling that of stuffed turkey. Crush the fresh leaves to blend with cottage or cream cheese. Steep the dried leaves for tea.

SAMBUCUS: *see* Elderberry

SANDBUR: (*Cenchrus pauciflorus*) Because this grass plant produces a bur with spines stout enough to penetrate the flesh of man and animals, which in turn can result in inflammation and infection, it is very obnoxious, especially at beaches. The burs mix with sand along the shore, ready to puncture the skin of swimmers or sun bathers. They are also annoying because they adhere to clothing or get entangled in the fur of domestic animals.

The grass flower is enclosed by a hairy, spiny bur which is composed of many bristles, each provided with recurved barbs. It is these barbs that enable the spines to work into the flesh. Seeds in the bur can live in soil for at least four years and probably longer.

Since it is an annual plant, reproduction occurs only from seeds contained in the burs. Infestation may be spread by burs carried on man or animals or floated along the shore from one place to another.

Sandbur eradication is possible by burning the burs with a flame burner directed at the tops of the plants. Because burs are produced so close to the ground, mowing is ineffective.

SANDY SOIL: A typical "light sandy" soil may be composed of approximately 70 per cent sand, 20 per cent silt, and 10 per cent clay. The particles in a sandy soil are comparatively large, permitting water to enter the soil and to pass through it so quickly that it dries out very rapidly, and often carries nutrients with it. Organic matter is especially important in improving the structure of sandy soils. *See also* SOILS; ORGANIC MATTER; SEASIDE GARDEN.

SANITATION: Sanitation in gardening means the destruction of diseased, injured or insect-infested plants or parts of plants, and certain other clean-up techniques that further aid in promoting the health and productivity of plants.

Promptly removing diseased or insect-damaged plants is the first rule of sanitation. It's a good idea to cultivate the habit of watching carefully for anything abnormal in the growth of your plants. Sometimes just removing a few sickly leaves or a single plant may prevent a bad infestation of bugs or the spread of a disease.

Many weeds serve as hosts for insects or diseases, either during the summer or sheltering them in their over-wintering stages. Cultivation, or better yet, mulching, will eliminate these. Fallen petals, foliage and old stalks of plants should be sent to the compost pile as soon as possible, too. The same applies to sickly branches or twigs pruned from ornamental trees and shrubs.

With house plants, removing yellowed, withered or dead foliage immediately, plus giving all but soft-leaved plants a weekly hosing with water, does wonders in removing dust, keeping down insects and promoting general health.

IN THE WOODLOT: Judicious pruning and the removal of badly damaged trees constitutes proper woodlot sanitation. Sometimes disease or insect injury can be prevented by harvesting certain trees. Recent forest experiments showed that weak or abnormally slow-growing pines, for example, were much more likely to be attacked by the pine bark beetle than healthy pines. Removing these for use or sale is called "sanitation salvage." It prevents not only their destruction and loss to the owner, but also their serving as a source of damage to other trees in the lot.

LIVESTOCK: With livestock, cleanliness is important to good growth. This does not mean using disinfectants all the time, or having floors spotless. Proper bedding, and deep litter for poultry, will tend to eliminate disease and insects because of their composting action. Manure should not be allowed to accumulate uncovered or unmixed with other organic materials, as this can cause insects like flies to multiply.

ORCHARD SANITATION: Probably in no other agricultural situation can sanitation pay off better than in fruit plantings.

Thoroughly scraping off all loose, rough bark in the spring will destroy almost half the overwintering codling moth larvae on a tree (the progeny of a single pair of these can damage 150 bushels of apples). You can make a good scraper from an old hoe, a piece of saw blade or a mower section, or a floor scraper. Use a gentle, even movement. The tool should not be too sharp, and don't scrape down to live bark, which might result in damage to the tree.

Put a sheet or canvas under the tree to catch all the scrapings, and immediately put them in a fresh compost pile. Scraping, by the way, will permit more thorough coverage with the dormant oil spray you apply to control scale insects, aphis, red mite and other pests.

Next, apply tanglefoot, or wrap and tack a two-to four-inch-wide band of corrugated paper or burlap around the trunk. This will trap a great many of the remaining larvae. But don't use chemically treated bands, which can injure the tree.

Old decaying wounds are a favorite habitat for codling moth larvae and other destructive pests. The cavities resulting from poor pruning cuts, split trunks and broken branches are filled with punky wood where they hibernate.

PRUNE TREES PROPERLY: Prune off all dead, split or broken branches and stubs cleanly at the point of origin, beveling the edges to encourage healing. Compost the prunings promptly —dumping them into a gully or brush heap means the larvae can continue to develop and eventually return to the tree as adult moths.

All running cavities and stubs that have rotted back into the tree should be cleaned out with a gouge chisel to solid live wood. This can be done in almost any season, except in wet weather. A straight chisel is best for finishing the edges of a cavity, trimming them back to live bark and bringing the cavity to a point at top and bottom. Cut all edges so they are at right angles to the bark to promote rapid healing.

All cuts over two inches in diameter should be painted with tree paint. It's not a good idea to fill cavities with cement—it may look neater, but you won't be able to see if more decay shows up in the cavity later.

Cutting out cankers and diseased limbs during the winter, and rubbing off suckers and watersprouts while they are still very small, will go a long way towards eliminating bacterial diseases like fireblight. Bitter rot, blister canker, black rot and blotch fungi also live in old cankers and attack the tree through new, open wounds. Remove the bark on old cankers to healthy tissue, and paint them and all new wounds promptly.

Certain pests require specific treatments. Black knot fungus of plum trees must be eradicated by cutting out the knotted tissue, removing it for an inch beyond the boundary of the knot. The plum curculio beetle, which attacks apples and stone fruits, can be shaken off the tree into a sheet by jarring it or hammering with a mallet.

Tree hoppers live on weeds, so keep your fruit plantings weed-free. Apple scab fungi overwinter on leaves on the ground—make sure these are incorporated well into your mulches.

KEEP MULCH FROM TREE: A mulch should be of fairly fine material: whole cobs, cornstalks and large weeds can harbor larvae and disease organisms. And keep it at least two feet from the trunk—not only rodents, but also such pests as the apple flea weevil, like to live in the cover there. A wire mesh guard, veneer bands or paper wrapped around the trunks of young trees will prevent mice and rabbits from girdling them.

A wire probe or knife is usually necessary to dig baby borers out of the trunk near the ground. You may have to hoe away the soil a few inches deep to be sure of getting those that have bored into the tree below ground level. Look for tiny holes, soft spots in the bark, and masses of amber, gummy material. Keeping the ground clean around the trunk will let the birds find the eggs and young worms before they start boring (we need more birdhouses in our gardens and orchards!). Tanglefoot, building paper, or a loose band of tin filled with tobacco dust around the trunk will also prevent borer damage.

During the growing season, pick off all wormy or diseased fruit as early as possible to reduce sources of infection. And pick up all dropped fruit every two or three days. Put the dried, shrivelled "mummies" in the compost heap. The rest can be used for fruit dishes or jelly, or fed to livestock.

GATHER RUBBISH PERIODICALLY: Keep your garden or orchard clear of rubbish, for old baskets, sacks and decaying prunings can harbor a surprising number of destructive organisms. Also, don't mow any tree sprouts or underbrush. The ragged stubs left by the mower are excellent hibernating places. Always grub them out. Weeds and fallen bark should likewise be promptly removed to the compost pile and buried therein.

Here's another point orchardists may slip up on: crates stored in an open packing shed provide a fine breeding ground for codling moths and other pests. Sheds should always be enclosed, or screened with heavy cloth in spring and early summer to prevent the adult insects from escaping to the orchard. A pan of kerosene in the shed, with a light left burning over it, will kill many of the bugs.

With berry fruits, sanitation usually consists merely of removing diseased or pest-attacked parts of the plants promptly. Watch particularly for swelling of the canes or wilted tips, signs of borer damage. If you have any wild brambles growing nearby, keep an eye on them, too, and destroy infested parts immediately.

One final suggestion: if you grow sweet clover in your orchard, always clip it at the proper time. The rank stem growth that results when it is allowed to reach maximum size the second year is a favored place for codling moth larvae to spin. *See also* INSECT CONTROL; FRUIT TREES; ORCHARD; TREE SURGERY.

SANSEVIERIA: Also called bow-string hemp and snake-plant. A genus of perennial herbs with thick stiff leaves and clustered flowers on slender stalks. Member of the lily family, *Liliaceae.* Grown outdoors in the South, and as house plants in the North. Easily propagated in rather heavy soil, they require little sun. Propagated by division of the fleshy root, or by leaf cuttings set in sand. When grown indoors leaves should be sponged frequently.

Most often cultivated is *S. zeylanica,* whose leaves grow to 2½ feet and are concave in the middle, transversely striped with light green, flowers greenish-white and 1½ inches long. Native of Ceylon.

S. trifasciata is a native of the Belgian Congo, with similar growth but the leaves are striped longitudinally with yellow.

A shorter species is *S. thyrsiflora,* whose 1½ foot leaves are almost four inches across and flat, margined with yellow and banded crosswise with lighter green. Flowers are greenish white, 1½ inches, and fragrant. Native of South Africa.

S. cylindrica, which comes from tropical Africa, is a five-foot species with thick cylindrical leaves 1¼ inches thick, striped and banded with dark green, flowers white or tinged pink.

SAP: The juices of a plant, specifically the liquid which circulates through its vascular tissues. The term may be used to designate liquid entering through the roots, composed principally of water with plant nutrients dissolved in it, which circulates upward to the leaves. It is also used to indicate the liquid returning from the leaves which contains the sugars and starches manufactured in them to roots, flowers or seed for storage.

SAPINDUS: *see* SOAPBERRY

SAPONARIA: Known also as soapwort, this is a genus of the pink family, *Carolphyllaceae,* whose crushed leaves and stems yield a soap-like lather. Lance-shaped leaves grow opposite, pink or white flowers in clusters have petals, sepals, and stamens in fives. Native of the north temperate zone, they are perennials or hardy annuals. Some are naturalized along roadsides, and are often transplanted to the garden in September or in early spring. They are useful for border or rock garden, and grow well in any good garden soil, preferably somewhat sandy.

Bouncing Bet or soapwort (*S. officinalis*) is an evening blooming flower, sending up dense clusters of pink or white blooms about three feet. They flower from May to September, are perennials.

Cowherb or cockle (*S. vaccaria*) is a three-foot annual with intense pink flowers, or sometimes white in loose clusters.

Best rock garden variety is the species *ocymoides,* a trailing nine-inch perennial. Bright pink flowers have a purple calyx, grow in open clusters. Blooms May to August.

SAPOTA: Known also as sapodilla, this is a species of the gutta-percha family, *Sapotaceae,* which yields chicle and a sweet plum-like fruit unknown in the North. Botanical name is *S. achras* or *Achras sapota,* depending upon the authority. Also sometimes *A. zapota.* A dense tropical American tree growing to 60 feet with leathery leaves growing to four or six inches. Flowers, borne throughout the year, are white, with cup-shaped corolla of six petals and six sterile stamens, followed by a red-brown sweet plum with shiny black seed. Grown only in frost-free climates, they are propagated by shield-budding or grafting.

SAPROPHYTE: A plant which lives upon dead and decaying plants. A saprophyte has no chlorophyll so cannot manufacture its own sugar and starch, and must obtain them from its host. This it does with the help of bacteria and fungi involved in the decomposition of decaying plant matter.

SASSAFRAS: Trees with aromatic bark and clusters of pale yellow flowers in early spring. Common sassafras (*S. albidum*) produces a beautiful scarlet foliage in fall, sometimes grows as high as 100 feet. It grows from Maine to Michigan and south to Florida and Texas.

SATIN-FLOWER: *see* GODETIA

SATINPOD: *see* HONESTY

SAVORY: Summer savory (*Satureja hortensis*). An annual plant belonging to the mint family, is native to southern Europe and generally cultivated in gardens in this country. It grows well under a wide range of soil and climatic conditions. The dried herb formerly came to this country from Austria.

It is grown easily from seeds sown early in spring in rows three feet apart. Drill the seeds to a depth of half an inch at the rate of ten to 12 to the foot. The plants will form a solid row if spaced three to four inches apart in the row. Only a few feet of row will furnish enough of the herb for family use. In good soil plants grow 16 to 18 inches high and require little cultivation.

The tender leaves and stems may be used any time during the season, but for drying six to eight inches of the top growth should be cut when blooming begins. Sometimes two or more crops can be harvested in one season.

The top growth as cut from the plants may be tied in small bunches or spread on screens or paper to dry. When thoroughly dry, the leaves should be stripped from the stems and stored in closed containers. Care should be taken to remove all small pieces of woody stems, as they interfere with the use of the leaves in flavoring foods.

Winter savory (*S. montana*) is a hardy perennial, with small white or purple flowers, that grows to two feet. It is often used as a low hedge or accent plant. The young shoots and leaves can be picked any time, are best dried for winter use. It grows best in light sandy soil. *See also* HERB.

SAWDUST: An organic material that is becoming more and more widely recommended for use in gardening and farming. It is a fine natural mulch and soil conditioner that can be used to bring about improvement in soil structure.

Sawdust is low in nitrogen, containing about 1/10 of one per cent nitrogen. One of the objections against using sawdust is that it may cause a nitrogen deficiency. However, many gardeners report fine results applying sawdust as a mulch to the *soil surface* without adding any supplementary nitrogen fertilizer. If your soil is of low fertility, watch plants carefully during the growing season. If they become light green or yellowish in color, side-dress with an organic nitrogen fertilizer as cottonseed meal, blood meal, compost, manure or tankage.

Some people are afraid that the continued application of sawdust will sour their soil, that is, make it too acid. A very comprehensive study of sawdust and wood chips made from 1949 to 1954 by the Connecticut Experiment Station reported no instance of sawdust making the soil more acid. It is possible, though, that sawdust used on the highly alkaline soils of the western U.S. would help to make the soil *neutral*. That would be a very welcome effect.

Plentiful quantities of wood chips are becoming available in many sections of the country and are being widely used by gardeners and farmers. In some ways wood chips are superior to sawdust. They contain a much greater percentage of bark, and have a higher nutrient content.

The general verdict on sawdust and wood chips is that both materials are safe and effective soil improvers. They do a fine job of aerating the soil and increasing its moisture-holding capacity.

As A MULCH: Sawdust is valuable as a mulch to the home gardener provided it is used intelligently. Raw sawdust is not a manure or compost and cannot be used as a substitute, that is, it should not be deeply worked into the soil.

Plant vegetable seeds in the usual way after the soil has been fertilized according to its needs. Then spread a band of sawdust about four inches wide and ¼ inch thick on top of the planted row. The mulch will help reduce crusting of the soil and allow the young seedlings to push through easily.

When the plants are about two inches high, apply a one-inch layer of sawdust over the entire area between the rows. Weeds more than one inch tall should be killed by cultivating or hoeing before the mulch is added. If weeds are less than an inch tall, the sawdust will smother them. Some weeds will continue to grow up through the mulch. These can easily be pulled out by hand when the ground is moist after a rain. Do not cultivate as this will mix the sawdust with the soil and destroy its value as a mulch. *See also* MULCH; FERTILIZER.

SAWFLY: *see* BRAMBLE FRUITS (Insects)

SAXIFRAGE: (*Saxifraga*) Genus of the *Saxifragaceae,* or gooseberry family, which includes about 400 species, mostly perennials, and many of them grown in the rock garden. Most common among their many growth habits is the rosette of basal leaves, either fleshy or sometimes tufted, sending up slender sprays of pink, white, purple, or yellow flowers whose sepals, petals, and stamens are in fives or multiples.

Seed may be sown in late summer

if it can be protected through the winter, and plants set in their permanent places in spring. Or the clumps may be increased from their offsets, or by division. After becoming established, they need little winter protection in most climates. They prefer a gritty, slightly gravelled soil with lime. Naturalize well among rocks either in rock garden or in terrace walls.

S. aizoon has small white flowers, speckled purple or crimson, on 20-inch stems from five-inch rosettes of silvery leaves. Many varieties with leaves and flowers variously colored.

S. apiculata is a hybrid forming a three-inch high mat with yellow flowers in clusters.

S. burseriana is densely tufted with a very early solitary white flower about one inch across. Continues to bloom until June.

S. camposi has glossy leaves to six inches long, and white flower sprays in May.

Crimson moss (*S. decipiens*) has mossy foliage that turns crimson in late fall. Flowers are white in May and June.

S. geranoides is a six-inch Alpine with many small white flowers in early summer.

Meadow saxifrage (*S. granulata*) has a stem that becomes bulbous at the base, and bulblets in the axils of kidney-shaped leaves. Drooping white blossoms are one inch across, bloom in May.

S. hostii grows to two feet, with four-inch leaves in rosettes and rimed. Flowers white with purple spots.

S. longifolia also grows to two feet, with thick three-inch leaves, flowers white with red spots in July.

S. macnabiana is a hybrid whose green leaves turn to brilliant colored rosettes in fall. White crimson-spotted flowers in spring.

Mountain saxifrage (*S. oppositifolia*) is a spreading plant to two inches which forms dense mats of tiny leaves, with rose and purple clusters of flowers.

S. pygmaea is one of the smallest Alpines growing from one to two inches, with very small yellow flowers.

S. retusa, a tufted Alpine to two inches, with ruby or purple-red flowers, one to four to a cluster.

Strawberry geranium (*S. sarmentosa*) is almost the only saxifrage grown as a house plant. Also called mother-of-thousands, Aaron's beard, and old man's beard. Kidney-shaped leaves up to four inches in diameter are marked white on top, red underneath, and grow from a low rosette that sends up two-foot white flower sprays in the summer. Propagated by strawberry-like runners.

London Pride (*S. umbrosa*) is a spreading saxifrage with one-foot sprays of white flowers sprinkled with red, in June and July.

A native of the northeast is *S. virginiensis,* which grows in the mountains from New Brunswick to Georgia, and blooms April to June.

SCABIOSA: Also known as Mourning Bride and Pincushion Flower, they are upright bushy plants, often weed-like in appearance. They should have full sun, usually do well in ordinary garden soil. Seed can be sown in the open in spring; may also be propagated by division. Cut flowers last well. *See also* MOURNING BRIDE.

SCALE: *see* LANDSCAPING

SCALE INSECTS: Sucking insects which appear in the female adult as tiny immovable brown, black, or cottony dots on plant stems. Under a magnifying glass these may look like overlapped mollusk shells. The young are born live or hatched from eggs which remain under the mother's shell until hatched. They move around for a time until they choose their own position, when they attach themselves to the plant by a sucking organ. Females remain attached throughout their lifespan. Males develop wings after several moults, and move about.

Most important commercially is the black or brown pinhead San Jose scale, which attacks orchard trees; brownish-gray oyster-shell scale, found on trees and shrubs including many grown in the garden, such as roses, lilacs, and peonies; black scale, a pest on citrus trees in California where it causes a sooty mold; terrapin scale, shiny and brown, living on shade and fruit trees; and the grayish-white scurfy scale, sometimes serious on elms, willows, or dogwood. For control, *see* INSECT CONTROL.

SCALLION: A name popularly used for young "bunch" or green onions, whether grown from sets or from seeds, sown thickly, and not thinned until of edible size. It is actually a

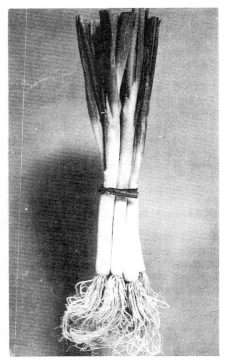

Actually young onions which are pulled before the bulb has formed, scallions can be easily grown by planting bottom sets in early spring.

young onion pulled before the bulb has formed.

CULTURE: Scallions can be grown from sets or from seeds. A simple way to grow green onions and the method employed by many home gardeners, is to plant bottom sets early in the spring and pull the green onions when they attain desired size. Fall sowing is also recommended. This plant is a perennial and can be overwintered, but some protection should be provided to insure that they overwinter comfortably. The sets may be set out in the fall before the ground freezes and preferably long enough for them to get fairly well established before the ground freezes hard. A loose mulch of leaves, straw, etc., will provide ample protection over winter.

Soil for scallions should be rich in available plant food, especially humus. The area in which they grow should be very heavily supplied with mature compost humus. Scallions will thrive in a moderately acid soil. The optimum soil reaction is 6.0-6.5. Only on soils more acid than pH 5.6 is it desirable to use lime.

Seed should be planted quite thickly and covered with ½ inch of sifted compost. Sets should be placed close together in rows. The usual spacing of rows is 12-18 inches apart. Scallions will tolerate a slight amount of shade, but prefer open, moist, sunny conditions.

During dry weather, sufficient water should be provided to supply the natural requirements of the plants. This is best done by a thorough, slow flooding of the area, during the cool of the evening.

HARVESTING: Green bunch onions are harvested as soon as they reach the edible stage. Several pullings are usually made, removing the largest plants each time and leaving the others to develop. The roots are trimmed and the outer skin is peeled off, leaving the stem clean and white.

VARIETIES: Southport White Globe is widely used for the production of green bunch onions from seed, as less skinning is required to produce the desired white bulb. Long Bunching, White Welsh, and Egyptian are other popular varieties. *See also* ONION.

SCARLET LIGHTNING: *see* LYCHNIS

SCHINUS: Known also as pepper-tree. A small genus of resinous trees of the *Anacardiaceae* family, mostly native in tropical and South America. They are grown mostly for their decorative fruits. Leaves are compound and alternate, flowers small white clusters, and fruit a small berry-like purple, pink, red, or white drupe. Male and female blossoms occur on different trees. Two species are grown in California south of San Francisco, the California pepper tree (*S. molle*) growing to 20 feet, with rose-red fruit; and Brazilian pepper tree (*S. terebinthifolius*) also called Christmas-berry tree for its bright red fruit.

SCHISANDRA: A genus of deciduous woody climbers of the magnolia family, *Magnoliaceae*. Simple leaves, red, pink, or white flowers in clusters from the leaf axils, male on one vine, female on another. Both must be planted to obtain the red berry-like decorative fruits. The only species hardy in the North is *S. chinensis,* which is useful for twining around trees or trailing on fences. Grows to 20 feet, with fragrant pink flowers and bright red berries. They are propagated by seed, greenwood cuttings under glass, layering, and suckers; prefer sandy soil and partial shade.

SCHIZANTHUS: *see* BUTTERFLY-FLOWER

SCHIZOCODON: *see* SHORTIA

SCILLA: Sometimes called squills. Few plants require less care than the scillas. They are especially adapted for borders and rockeries, and grow successfully out of cultivation. They are hardy adventurous plants, and are among the very first to bloom in

early spring. The leaves are grass-like, and the flowers are borne in clusters at the top of naked stems.

For garden purposes scillas may be grouped into squills which bloom with chinodoxa and crocus, and the bluebells or so-called wild hyacinths which bloom in May with Darwin tulips and lilacs, and are excellent for interplanting with tulips. They naturalize wonderfully and spread quickly. Scillas seed freely, and new plants may be grown from seeds without much trouble.

VARIETIES: Scilla varieties include the sea onion (*S. verna*)—to six inches high, blue flowers; Cuban lily (*S. peruviana*)—purple flowers; Spanish bluebell (*S. hispanica*)—to one foot or more high, blue flowers; star hyacinth (*S. amoena*)—to six inches, white or blue flowers. Scillas are best grown in humus-rich, sandy soil in a part-shady location. *See also* BULBS; BULB GARDEN; FLOWER GARDENING.

SCION: Also called cion. A detached shoot of a plant having one or more buds, prepared for use in grafting. The scion is inserted in a rootstock, and will reproduce the tree or shrub from which it was taken, rather than the tree or shrub whose root was used.

SCOTCH THISTLE: (*Onopordon acanthium*) The prickly Scotch thistle is occasionally planted in sunny borders where the soil is well-drained but not very rich. It grows five to eight feet high and needs plenty of room. The leaves may be as long as a foot, silvery and tipped with spines, and the purple flower heads are big and round-shaped. Two other varieties, *O. bracteatum* and *O. tauricum,* grow about six feet tall, with white or pale purple flowers and yellowish spines. All are biennials, propagated by sowing the seed ⅛-inch deep in spring.

SCREENS, PLANTS FOR: Screen planting is done for privacy, to screen out objectionable features of the landscape picture, or to serve as a windbreak.

Where space is limited, screening should be done by planting a single variety of tree or shrub. Where approximately three times as much depth is available, a screen planting of a variety of subjects will make a more interesting landscape picture.

Listed below are plants recommended for screen planting by E. L. Kammerer of the Morton Arboretum. Plants listed as narrow will require less trimming to keep them within bounds. Wider material should be used only where space is not limited. Figures indicate maximum height x width through the mature plant in feet. (For example, the Columnar Norway maple can be expected to reach as high as 25 feet and three feet around.)

NARROW DECIDUOUS TREES

Columnar Norway maple, 25 x 3
Erect Norway maple, 30 x 8-10
Sentry maple, 20 x 2
Pyramidal European white birch, 20 x 5-6
Columnar European hornbeam, 15-20 x 4-5
Pyramidal European hornbeam, 20 x 6
Pyramidal American hornbeam, 18 x 5
Pyramidal Washington hawthorn, 30 x 10
Columnar Siberian crabapple, 25 x 4-5
Pyramidal Simon poplar, 30 x 10
Pyramidal English oak, 40 x 10
Erect black locust, 25 x 5-20
Pyramidal bigleaf linden, 25 x 10

NARROW EVERGREEN TREES

Pyramidal white fir, 25 x 6
Columnar Chinese juniper, 25 x 6
Cypress spruce, 25 x 3½
Swiss stone pine, 30 x 8
Pyramidal white pine, 30 x 10
Compact Douglas fir, 15 x 10
Wintergreen pyramidal arborvitae, 20 x 5

NARROW DECIDUOUS SHRUBS

Erect border privet, 8 x 3
Tallhedge columnar buckthorn, 12 x 3-4

NARROW EVERGREEN SHRUBS

Hatfield Anglojap yew, 10 x 6-8
Hicks Anglojap yew, 10 x 6-8

WIDER DECIDUOUS TREES

Amur maple, 20 x 20
Pyramidal singleseed hawthorn, 20 x 12
Anise magnolia, 25 x 15

WIDER EVERGREEN TREES

Dwarf white pine, 6 x 6
Waterer Scotch pine, 8-10 x 12
Japanese yew, 10 x 10

WIDER SHRUBS
(Widths approximately equal to heights)

Five-leaf aralia, 6 ft.
Glossy chokeberry, 8 ft.
Mentor barberry, 6 ft.
Winged euonymus, 8-10 ft.
Compact winged euonymus, 6 ft.
European euonymus, 12 ft.
Winter honeysuckle, 8 ft.
Late honeysuckle, 15 ft.
Red flowered tatarian honeysuckle, 8 ft.
Mountain ninebark, 5 ft.
Glossy buckthorn, 12 ft.
Buckthorn species, 6 ft.
Chinese lilac, 12 ft.
Common lilac, 12-15 ft.
Arrowwood viburnum, 10-12 ft.
Wayfaringtree viburnum, 10-15 ft.
Lantanaphyllum viburnum, 10 ft.
See also SHRUBS; EVERGREENS.

SCREW PINE: see PANDANUS

SCROPHULARIACEAE: The figwort, snapdragon, or foxglove family, a large family which includes many garden ornamental plants, many hardy, and a few shrubs and trees, but no vegetables. Flowers are distinguished by their four or five petals generally joined to form two lips above a tubular calyx and united corolla, two long and two short stamens.

Beside foxglove and snapdragon, well-known representatives of the family are the houseplant, calceolaria; flower border plants, pentstemon, torenia, nemesia, linaria, mimulus, and veronica.

SCRUB PINE: *see* Pine

SCUM: *see* Algae

SCUTELLARIA: *see* Skullcap

SEA BUCKTHORN: (*Hippophae rhamnoides*) Brought into this country during colonial days, this shrub is noted for its silvery-coated foliage, for the showy color of its translucent berries, and for the abundance in which they are produced. Often the berries completely hide the branches. There are also small inconspicuous April borne flowers.

Most plants reach a height of almost 30 feet, are erect and spiny branched, with a rounded top. Sea buckthorn is often recommended for seashore planting because of its tolerance of wind and salt spray, and its ability to stabilize dunes. It does well in well-drained sandy sites, as well as heavier soils.

SEA DAHLIA: (*Coreopsis maritima*) A member of the sunflower family and a native California plant which is easily grown and which bears a large amount of large, bright flowers through the early spring. Often used for mass planting and for flower arranging indoors.

Sea dahlia is a bushy perennial, growing about two feet high, and dying back each year almost to the ground. Flower heads are bright yellow, to four inches in diameter; flowers are usually most abundant from February through May in California. The plant is usually treated as an annual; after flowering, the top is trimmed back; often the plant is replaced with a later-blooming annual. It grows readily from seed, sown directly in the garden or in flats for later transplanting. Plants grow well in sandy, well-drained soil, and are not usually troubled by insects. *See also* Coreopsis.

SEA FIG: *see* Mesembryanthemum

SEA GRAPE: (*Coccolobis uvifera*) Woody shrubs often found along the coast of southern Florida. The plants usually grow to about 25 feet high, produce small flowers in clusters. The purple fruit can be used for preserves.

SEA HOLLY: *see* Eryngium

SEA-KALE: (*Crambe maritima*) The only species of the genus *crambe* of the mustard family, *Crucifereae,* which is of interest to the gardener. Sea-kale is a large, coarse plant with blue-green leaves and clustered white flowers whose shoots are blanched early in spring and cut like asparagus as a vegetable. Grown in rich, well-manured soil in the perennial vegetable garden, beside the rhubarb, asparagus, and strawberries, where it will yield for six or more years. May be grown from seed, when the first cuttings are made in its third year, or from root cuttings, when it may be harvested the year after planting. Plants are set three or four feet apart in the row. When leaf shoots appear in spring, they are hilled for blanching, otherwise they become tough and stringy. Cut when 12 inches.

SEA LAVENDER: *see* Limonium

SEA MATERIALS: Approximately 8,000 kinds of plants and over 200,000 species of animals live in the sea. Every known element is found there. Acre for acre, the sea is probably as productive as the best soil on any farm. (This is not surprising when we consider that, instead of a few inches of topsoil, the sea's productive area is limited only by the depth that sunlight can reach—about 200 feet.)

Sea water covers 70 per cent of the earth. Marine experts say that half the world's photosynthetic fixation of carbon dioxide into organic matter is done by algae and plankton—a vast source of animal, human and soil food.

Seaweed makes up some 25 per cent of the Japanese diet, being made into flour, noodles and other products. In Hawaii, over 70 species of sea plants are eaten. In Holland, Belgium, Scotland and Norway, certain kinds of seaweed are consumed raw, cooked or made into bread.

In this country, industry has found that seaweeds yield substances valuable in the making of everything from ice cream and salad dressing to burn ointments and dental impressions.

Along the Pacific Coast, there are great beds of giant kelp, perhaps 100 million tons of it, along its shores. Coastlines of every country in the temperate zones boast like amounts. And this is only the floating type; non-buoyant seaweeds also exist in profusion.

A form of algae, these "aquatic alfalfas" are rich in fats, carbohydrates, proteins and vitamins. Twenty to 50 per cent of their dry weight may be minerals (some doctors say they make a fine diet supplement; seaweed tablets are marketed now.)

Kelp "farming" is a fascinating process. One Pacific Coast company harvests the seaweed in 125-ton-capacity boats, using a sickle bar much the same as the type used in grain harvesting. The cutter is lowered into the water, and a conveyor throws the cut seaweed back into the ship. The plants may be 150 feet long, and will grow faster, with bigger leaves, after cutting.

Huge amounts of kelp are also chopped up, dehydrated and ground for animal feed concentrates. Now sold in every state, they have been proven to strengthen disease resistance in stock, and improve milk production in cows and laying in hens. All types of stock benefit from having five to ten per cent of it in their feed rations. Kelp meal is said to stimulate the appetite, improve bone formation and coat growth, clear up breeding troubles and raise the butterfat content of milk. Seaweed-herb mixtures are achieving considerable success in England. Some concentrates are a blend of seaweeds from deep and shallow water, which insures getting a product that is not too high in any one element.

OTHER PRODUCTS: Fish meal today is recognized as a fertilizer and feed of great value. Almost 1/3 of a fish is recoverable waste after canning. Many canneries are equipped with conveyors under the floors, immediately moving the scraps to huge grinders and cookers. The fish meal is turned out so fast it's dry in the bag before the fish in the can is cool.

Another type of fish fertilizer is sold in emulsion form, actually "liquid fish." The company producing this plant food reports it gives better results than chemical fertilizers having higher analyses. *See also* ALGAE; SEAWEED; SEASIDE GARDENS.

SEA PINK: *see* ROSE PINK

SEASIDE GARDENS: The properly designed and managed seaside garden has many advantages over the inland garden. There is an abundance of sunshine and moist air; the sea lessens extremes of temperature; frosts usually come later and leave earlier. Snow rarely stays long; and poor drainage is never a problem. However, along with them, there is also salt, sand and wind. Because of them, organics is a desperate necessity.

WIND PROTECTION: First, it's vital to put up a barrier against wind, salt spray and blowing sand (the latter can literally scour the life out of tender leaves).

If you live on a shore that has frequent gale-force winds, this will likely have to be a temporary, artificial one until you can get a natural plant barrier established. A drift or snow fence will do the job, or you can erect a picket or solid wooden fence. Even better, if you have access to old grass or hay, you can pile this up and anchor it with brush or boards. The grass will decompose and start building the sand into soil.

In the lee of this barrier—or without any barrier, if yours is not a very windy shore—plant a soil-binding grass. Ordinary beachgrass is fine. You can't buy this grass, so you'll have to transplant clumps of it from where it grows along the beach. Other plants that can be used include sea-oats, Volga wildrye, sea panicgrass, Virginia creeper, broomsedge, seacoast bluestem, tall fescue, hairy vetch and purple beach pea (the last two are legumes, producing nitrogen that aids the growth of the others). Your state experiment station can tell you the best ones for your region.

TREES AND SHRUBS: The grass cover should be well established in a year or two. Then you can plant trees and shrubs for a real windbreak. Rugosa rose and Japanese black pine are two excellent choices. Others that will do well for landscaping purposes on the fully exposed front of your property are: many other pines, honey locust, tree of heaven, London plane tree, tupelo, sycamore maple, white spruce, red cedar, weeping willow, laurel willow, beach plum, wild cherry, Scotch broom, shadbush, Russian olive, inkberry, barberry, sumac, elderberry, California privet and many hollies, junipers and cotoneasters. The selection is bigger than you thought, isn't it?

Don't expect your plants to thrive in pure sand. Always make a planting hole at least twice the size and depth of the root ball, and fill it with a mixture of about four parts of topsoil to one part each of rotted manure and peat moss. Leaf mold and compost can be used if you have them. Water well at planting time, and stake young trees if the wind is strong.

Organic soil building over your whole place is a "must." Not only will ample organic matter act as a buffer against the poisoning effects of salt, but it will also give you rich, black earth, steadily improving in fertility. Thus you will be able to grow a much wider variety of plants than you would in the usual poor, sandy seaside soil.

Sheet composting is one of the easiest ways to build your soil. Take bushel baskets on every trip through the countryside and bring back leaves, forest leaf mold, old hay, corn cobs and the like. Dig them into your soil, then plant a green manure crop later for extra enrichment.

THE SEA IS ORGANIC: The sea itself will provide plenty of materials:

Seaweed is one of the finest fertilizers and soil conditioners. It contains as much nitrogen, half the phosphorus and twice as much potash as manure—plus 400 pounds of organic matter to the ton, an enormous variety of trace elements, and powerful antibiotics. From 20 to 50 per cent of some seaweeds is minerals.

If your soil is already fairly well supplied with humus, you needn't wash the seaweed to get rid of the salt. But if your soil is low in humus, hose it off thoroughly. Then dig it in fresh into the upper soil, bury it in trenches or leave it on the surface to be plowed in in the spring.

Seaweed composts easily if mixed with other materials (you can collect beach grasses and grasses from tidal flats for this). Allowed to dry in the sun, it becomes brittle and easy to chop or shred up. Incidentally, seaweed contains alginic acid, a bacteria stimulator which makes it an efficient compost accelerator.

SEAWEED FOR MULCH: One of the basic tenets of seaside gardening is to never leave the ground bare to the drying action of the wind. So use chopped seaweed as a mulch for your plants. It may be used alone or mixed with shredded leaves, ground corn cobs, compost and other mulch materials. Such a mulch will conserve water in the soil, carrying your plants through long droughts, and make them healthy and vigorous.

You can also dig finely chopped seaweed into the upper few inches of your soil at the rate of 50 to 200 pounds per 100 square feet in spring, well in advance of planting. Since it's low in phosphorus, it's good practice to mix in some rock phosphate or bonemeal.

Another good seaside material is oyster or clam shells. High in phosphorus, calcium and trace minerals, they are best used as a mulch or crushed for the compost heap. Mud from mud flats where rivers or streams drain into the sea is a mineral-rich soil amendment, too.

You'll want to use every bit of fish you can get your hands on. Flower and vegetable growers and greenskeepers say fish is an unbeatable fertilizer. It contains all the major and minor nutrient elements in abundance. Also, it is a fine bacteria stimulator, thus speeding up the breakdown of other organic matter into humus and improving soil structure. All kinds of fish scraps and "waste" (commercially unsaleable) fish can be yours, if you will visit fishing wharves and packing and canning plants. Fish scales, by the way, are the most valuable part, fertilizer-wise.

Raw fish should never come in contact with plant roots, so either bury it in trenches in the fall, put it under your mulches or compost it.

LAWN: To make a really beautiful lawn by the sea, first sheet-compost plenty of organic matter, then fertilize with manure or sludge and sow a green manure crop like rye grass or buckwheat. If the soil is almost pure sand, it may be necessary to do this twice. At the end of the second season, you can sow a permanent lawn that will be the envy of your neighbors. Fertilize this every fall with a ½ inch depth of cured compost or ground seaweed, with smaller amounts applied in spring.

Here is a list of trees and shrubs that will flourish on your seaside estate protected by a windbreak or grown farther back where the wind diminishes: red or scarlet maple, Norway maple, birch, silver poplar, mulberry, hawthorn, crabapple, hydrangeas, euonymus, highbush blueberry,

butterfly bush, honeysuckle, forsythia, mountain laurel and viburnum. In really protected areas, such as the lee of a house, broadleaf evergreens like American and Chinese hollies and scarlet firethorn thrive. Sedum is the best ground cover.

A GOOD ROSE PROGRAM: A good program for roses includes a heavy mulch and winter wrapping with salt hay, tied carefully in place. New roses should always have large amounts of humus material put in the planting holes. To make sturdy canes less apt to winterkill, don't prune your roses severely in the spring—merely cut back the good live canes only slightly.

Perennials that stand shore conditions well are daylilies, bearded iris, phlox, gaillardia, campanula and columbine. Annuals like zinnias, marigolds, ageratum, nasturtiums, scabiosa, petunias, California poppy and geraniums are fine if not planted where strong wind and spray hits them. *See also* SEA MATERIALS.

SEASONAL GARDENING: *see* GARDEN CALENDAR

SEA SQUILL: (*Urginea maritima*) This half-hardy bulb is not very commonly grown, although it has pretty pink or yellow flowers borne on racemes over a foot long, on a five-foot stalk. The leaves are shiny green, up to 18 inches in length and several inches wide. The big, scaly bulbs, however, are frequently gathered from the wild for medicinal uses.

SEAWEED: The use of seaweed or kelp as a fertilizer dates back many centuries. As long ago as 1681, a Royal decree regulated the conditions under which seaweed could be collected on the coast of France; the kinds that might be collected were specified as was the manner in which they should be used.

Seaweeds are always associated with a rocky formation of the sea bed and most weeds are found in shallow water. The land in such situations is usually a thin cover of sand, or a sandy loam, overlying rock and is exposed to the eroding action of winter gales. The use of seaweed over many generations has resulted in a deep black earth which defies the Atlantic gales.

The seaweeds used as fertilizers belong to two main groups which are distinguished by their habitat. These are the brown weeds which grow between high and low water on rocky situations, and those weeds, also brown, which also grow on a rock bottom below low water mark down to a depth of 60 feet. The first group, often called rockweeds, are relatively small plants, but their growth is usually dense and they are easily collected by pulling or cutting from the rocks; 200 pounds per hour can be gathered easily from a good site. While the number of rockweeds is legion, only two need be mentioned since they are very much more common than any other weeds; these are "knobbed wrack" and "bladder wrack." Both these plants are made conspicuous by the air-filled vesicles which enable the plant to reach the surface when the tide comes in; in this way the plants receive more light for photosynthesis.

The sublittoral brown weeds, variously known as Laminaria, oarweeds or tangles, are much larger plants and appear to have a root, a stem and a single large leaf; this similarity with land plants is very superficial and, in fact, these various parts do not function like their counterparts in land plants. Weed beds are often dense and growth is usually about 20-30 tons per acre and may approach 50 tons. All these plants have a frond, or leaf, which is replaced annually, usually about May; a new frond develops and the old growth is detached and cast on the beaches. Unfortunately these fronds soon rot and a decaying heap can be most unpleasant to collect. Stormy weather is usually associated with the fall and winter; during such storms, plants are broken and torn from the sea bed and cast high and dry by the storm. Thousands of tons may be cast on a beach by a single storm. The complete plant is much more resistant to decomposition and such heaps can be removed without qualms.

These two types are very widespread and flourish over most of the Northern Hemisphere. A third type, the giant kelp, grows off the coast of California. These are brown weeds and both annual and perennial types abound; their chief feature is their length which may exceed 200 feet. They shed their fronds between April and June and decay rapidly if the water temperature exceeds 76° F. Like other brown weeds they are cast by storms and drift weed may also be collected.

Lastly, some mention must be made of the "gulf weed" which gave notoriety to the Sargasso Sea. Although modern evidence refutes the tales of the medieval mariners, Sargassum species do exist, and cast weed is available on the beaches of the Gulf States.

COMPOSITION: The chemical constitution of seaweeds is markedly different from that of the land plants. In general, land plants owe their rigidity to cellulose whereas seaweeds contain only about five per cent cellulose and owe their mechanical strength to alginic acid. The food reserve of land plants is starch, that of marine plants is laminarin, while the place of sugar is taken by mannitol which is rarely found in land plants. Alginic acid, laminarin and fucoidin are found only in seaweeds.

A typical analysis of a commercial sample of rockweed is:

Moisture	13.5%
Fats	1.4%
Protein	10.5%
Carbohydrates	51.9%
Fibre	6.1%
Minerals	16.6%

The mineral matter contained:

Silica 1.48%
Copper 0.002%
Manganese 0.016%
Iron 0.01%
Sulphates 4.18%
Chlorine 1.72%
Magnesia 1.01%
Calcium 1.54%
Potassium 2.83%
Iodine 0.17%
Salt 3.65%
Bromine 0.68%
Aluminum 0.22%
Phosphorus 0.18%

The most interesting feature of seaweeds is their ability to concentrate the mineral matter in the sea, which results in the presence of substantial amounts of a large number of elements in all seaweeds.

Traces of arsenic, boron, cobalt, molybdenum and vanadium are also present. Silver, barium, chromium, lithium, nickel, lead, rubidium, strontium, tin and zinc have also been shown to be present in seaweed. The arsenic content of seaweed (13 parts per million) is less than the normal arsenic content of the soil. The chlorophyll content (0.25 per cent) of seaweed is almost as high as that of lucerne and vitamins A, B, E, F, G and K are present in a sample of the giant kelp. Research has shown that vitamin B12 is also present in seaweed and this is the first known plant source of this vitamin.

Seaweeds vary widely in composition from month to month and a typical analysis of a brown weed—*Laminaria cloustoni*—illustrate the extremes of this variation:

	Minimum	Maximum
Alginic acid ...	17.4%	25.3%
Mannitol	5.3%	17.3%
Iodine	0.6%	0.9%
Fucosterol	0.1%	0.1%
Minerals	25.2%	43.7%
Laminarin	nil	14.1%
Cellulose	4.3%	7.9%
Fucoidin	4.8%	7.6%
Protein	9.6%	12.7%

Such variations are common to all seaweeds and, in this respect seaweed varies more than other fertilizers; but as ordinarily obtained in the wet state, it contains slightly more nitrogen than stable manure, twice as much potash but only about half as much phosphates. A citation of the constituents of seaweed reveals a rich source of trace elements, vitamins and potash, and an ample source of nitrogen. A rather special constituent is alginic acid, whose sodium salt has been shown to be active as a soil conditioner. An organic manure containing 25 per cent of a soil conditioner along with mineral nutrients, trace elements and vitamins can be expected to be a good fertilizer; centuries of usage prove it beyond doubt.

Alginic acid is very susceptible to bacterial attack; this reduces its value as a soil conditioner, but it also means that the microbiological soil flora is correspondingly enriched. This property is undoubtedly the basis of seaweed's activity in a compost heap. When only limited quantities are available, the best use is as a compost accelerator. When chopped it rots readily, and a 200 pound heap will heat to 100° F. in two days—chopping is essential otherwise decomposition is slow. Such a heap should be made to form the core of a compost heap which will be ready for use in six weeks. When only small quantities are available, the weed should be chopped and soaked in hot water (one gallon to two pounds of weed) and the mixture poured over the compost heap after soaking overnight. With dry milled weed a temperature of 140° F. is sufficient, but fresh, chopped weed should be scalded and soaked initially at 160-180° F. Such extracts are good compost accelerators.—*Ernest Booth*.

See also SEASIDE GARDENING; SEA MATERIALS.

SECHIUM: A genus of the gourd family, *Cucurbitaceae*. The single species, *S. edule,* is a tropical American perennial vine of which almost every part is useful for food or forage. The fruit of the *sechium,* known as chayote, Christophine, chuchu, vegetable pear, or mirliton, is a squash-like vegetable, pear-shaped, and three or four inches long. Fifty to 100 may be produced in a single year. The vine grows from a tuber, which increases after the second year to produce additional tubers which may be harvested and used as a vegetable. The young shoots may be used as pot herbs, and the leaves are useful as forage.

Vines are hardy only in areas where the frost does not penetrate the ground deeper than one inch. They may be grown as annuals further north, but only where the growing season is long. Fruits are planted whole, with stem slightly protruding from rich, mellow soil where the vine is to grow. Support must be supplied. Because the flowers are male or female, occasionally it may be necessary to plant more than one vine, because both kinds of flowers are not always found on the same vine.

SECKEL: *see* PEAR

SEDGE PEAT: *see* PEAT

SEDIMENTARY: Designating rocks formed by simple precipitation from solution, as rock salt and rocks formed of organic materials, as limestones, coal and peat. *See also* MINERAL ROCKS; ROCKS.

SEDUM: Also known as stonecrop or live-forever. A genus of succulent perennials, most of the cultivated sedums are low, creeping plants with roots at the joints, used in rock gardens or in naturalistic rock wall plantings. They are native of the north temperate zone. Flowers are usually yellow or white, occasionally red or blue, solitary or in clusters. Leaves are fleshy, alternate, opposite, or in whorls. In a few species the stems are erect, the leaves are broad.

Primary requirements for successfully growing sedums are good drainage and sun. The fleshy varieties quickly rot when kept too wet or when they are in contact with rotting moist organic matter. If the soil is heavy or rich with humus, a layer of sand or fine gravel on top will help preserve the pulpy foliage. Propagation

Often grown in rock gardens, most sedums are low, creeping plants. A well-drained soil and sunny location are important for successful growth.

is by seed or cuttings, the stems with roots at their joints easily making new plants when moved. Cuttings may be made at any time in the year, though spring or summer during the period of greatest growth are best.

Many sedums are now under cultivation, due to the popularity of rock gardens, and more are becoming available each year. Some of the most popular species follow:

Wall pepper or mossy stonecrop (*S. acre*) also called golden moss and gold-dust. Small light green leaves with yellow flowers in June and July. Leaves have peppery flavor. To five inches, forms a carpet.

S. album, sometimes called wormgrass, is a dark green creeper that forms evergreen mats. White flowers in midsummer. Cylindrical leaves are alternate and fleshy.

S. anglicum is a biennial, self-sowing, which seems evergreen because of its new plants constantly coming up. Gray foliage, white flowers.

S. brevifolium has rows of tiny leaves on four sides of the crowded stem, with whitish flowers in July.

S. dasyphyllum is one of the best

sedums, making small evergreen tufts with leaves ⅛ inch long, tiny ¼ inch flesh-pink and yellow flowers rising on slender stems above the foliage in July.

S. ewersi is perennial, a somewhat tender evergreen which may die back but come up again from the roots. It is 12 inches tall, with pink to lavender flowers in late summer. May be used as a house plant.

S. hispanicum is an annual or biennial species used in the rock garden. It has gray-green foliage and pinkish flowers in midsummer. Variety *minus* is used for a low carpeting plant.

S. kamschaticum, orange stonecrop, grows erect to nine inches, with orange-yellow flowers growing from the strong glossy-green clumps in July and August.

S. lydium is low, with leaves tipped red and small pink flowers in late summer. Good for a carpet.

S. pulchellum, called widow's cross or flowering moss, grows to one foot with slender trailing branches crowded with narrow leaves, and rosy-purple flowers.

Yellow stonecrop or Jenny stonecrop, (*S. reflexum*) is a creeping evergreen which sends up one-foot flower stalks with golden ½-inch flowers.

S. rupestre is a gray-green creeper with yellow flowers in summer. In dry weather and in fall its leaves turn red.

Showy stonecrop (*S. spectabile*) is a common erect perennial growing one foot high with three-inch fleshy light green leaves, in whorls of three, and numerous ½-inch pink flowers in September.

S. spurium is a hardy evergreen, with pink or white flowers, or crimson in variety *splendens.*

Live-forever or orpine (*S. telephium*) is erect, to two feet, with three-inch leaves and red-purple flowers in late summer.

SEED: The body, usually small, produced by flowering plants which con-

tains an embryo capable of developing by germination. The fertilized and ripened ovule usually encased in a fruit, pod, or sometimes naked, as in the pine.

Some seed pods are constructed to explode like miniature bombs and shoot their seeds away from the mother plant. Included in the exploding varieties are: Violet, bluebonnet, phlox, touch-me-not, balsam, witchhazel and angel's trumpet.

The wind is the most powerful ally of all in the wide distribution of seeds. It carries the kite, balloon and parachute types through the air with the greatest of ease. Seeds sowed in this manner are many species of milkweeds, dandelions, thistles, floweringstraw, goat's beard, leather flower, oleander, nymph's comb, carrion plant, and many others. Seeds of the blue thistle have blown 1000 miles from where they grew.

There are also numerous varieties of seeds, such as the flutter-mill, rain lily, yucca, potato chip, basket grass, Russian thistle, and bluebells which never actually rise in the air but are blown along the ground at an amazing speed and for considerable distances, strewing seeds as they go.

Other types of heavier seeds, like pecans, walnuts, buckeyes, acorns, mountain laurel, sycamore balls, cypress and pine cones, and osage orange, travel by the water route and are sometimes carried for many miles before becoming embedded in soil.

Many of the berry-like seeds, such as lantana, Spanish mulberry, black and red haws, dogwood berries, honeysuckle fruit, pokeberry, screwbean, hackberries and mistletoe berries, are carried over wide areas by birds. In some instances the seeds are cleaned from feet or break on a limb and fall to the ground, or mistletoe seeds take root on the limb. In other instances the berries are eaten by the birds, but the seeds are impervious to the digestive tract and may be dropped far and wide.

Not every one is aware that some seeds actually depend upon the "hitch-hiking" method for getting from place to place! Among the most notorious hitch-hikers which cling to people's clothing, to the fur of animals or to wagons and plows, are: Devil's horns, beggar's lice, grass and cockle burs, Spanish needles, goat head's and burdock seeds.

Squirrels, chipmunks, gophers, rats and other small rodents are the chief agents in distributing many kinds of seeds, like corn, acorns, buckeyes, and all kinds of nuts. In some sections of the country, squirrels are credited with planting many more valuable trees than man has planted.

Then there are containers so constructed that they shake out their seeds a few at a time, much as a person shakes salt or pepper from a shaker. Poppies, sea urchins and American lotus are good examples of the "shaker" types of seedpods which, when shaken by the wind, spill out their seeds from time to time.

Some seeds have wings which help them travel by air for a short distance, and they can also travel by water for a little while, or until the wings get water-soaked. Seeds with wings are those of the elm tree, maple tree, boxelder, wafer ash, basswood. and ash.

Seeds of a certain kind of grass crawl along the ground. On the coverings of these seeds are stiff hairs, which when damp, move over the ground.

Then there are seeds that get away from the mother plant by coasting away. The seedpods of the locust tree remain on the tree until cold weather, and then when a pod falls off it coasts along on the snow or ice much like a miniature sled.—*Jewell Casey.*

SEED, SPROUTING: *see* SPROUTING SEED

SEEDS AND SEEDLINGS: Seed may be saved from any annual or perennial garden plant, and from any shrub or tree, to be planted at a later time. Some seed will keep well, and will produce plants exactly like the parent plant, year after year. Other plants produce seed that quickly deteriorates, or seed that will revert in time to the species from which highly improved horticultural varieties were developed. Also, some plants take a long time to mature from seed, and are more efficiently propagated from cuttings or division. A knowledge of the life history of the plant will help the beginning gardener to know which seed will be worth saving, and which should be purchased each year.

Generally, the seed from plants which bear the species name will come true to the parents from seed. Those which bear a variety or hybrid name may not. Thus, listed under lobelia in the seed catalog, we find gracilis blue, which is a lobelia species, and may be expected to self-seed true to type. Also listed is Mrs. Clibran improved, which might revert after a year or more to the species from which it was developed, or might give an assortment of colors and sizes after the first year.

Reversion and cross-pollination can also be expected of seed saved from vegetables. Almost all the vegetables grown in our gardens are greatly improved varieties, some carefully hybridized by professional seed growers. Where it may be possible to disbud flowers for a time, while specially selected specimens are setting seed, this is not practical in the vegetable garden, where seed from many of the vegetables is the crop, and very acceptable for food, even though the plants which grow them may be horticultural sports. Also, some vegetables, such as the root vegetables, parsley, cabbages and brussels sprouts are biennials and will not produce seed the first year. If we wish to save seed from these, the roots themselves must be saved in cool storage and planted out the second year to produce seed.

SAVING SEED: For the gardener who has a special variety of vegetable or flower which cannot be found in seed catalogs, the process of seed-saving may be worth while. If he wishes to maintain its quality, he must take the same precautions in growing his seed as are taken by professional seed growers. He must allow only his best plants to set seed. The plant which produces the largest seed-pod is not necessarily the one with the best seed. Plants which grow as the gardener wants his next year's crop to grow should be chosen for seed. Lettuce which is early to head and slow to bolt should be marked. Spinach which produces the most leaves and the latest seed should be used. Or if an early crop is wanted, as in plants like corn or tomatoes, then the first fruits should be saved.

Safest way to be sure of propagating seedlings true to the parent plant is to be sure that there are no other varieties of the same plant, sometimes of the same genus, growing in the neighborhood. If this is not possible, blossoms of the seed-producing plant must be protected, usually by a paper-bag cover, from pollination by stray insects. If paper bags are used, hand-pollinating is necessary. This is done with a small soft brush, which is brushed over the stamens and pistils of flower after flower, the paper bag being returned to each one. The cover is kept on the flower until fruit has begun to form. Sometimes it is necessary to cover again when the seed is almost ripe, to prevent birds from harvesting the crop.

Whenever possible seed should be allowed to dry on the plant. In this category are beans and peas, corn, root vegetables, cabbage, spinach, etc. Seed embedded in soft fruit should be left on the plant until the fruit is somewhat over-ripe before harvesting. Tomatoes, squash, cucumbers, and eggplant are done this way. When fruits are taken indoors, the seeds should be scraped out and soaked a day or more in water, until they start to ferment. Careful watching is necessary at this stage. The seed should not be permitted to begin sprouting. When it has fermented a little, the pulp may be loosened by rubbing it between the hands. Seeds then can be lifted out and dried on sheets of paper.

All seed should be thoroughly dry before it is stored. Drying should be done in a warm room which has good ventilation. As it dries, the seed should be stirred occasionally, to prevent moulding. After drying it should be stored in a warm, rather than a cold room, preferably one comfortable for human beings, and should be protected from rodents and weevils. Paper containers or glass jars are better storage receptacles than metal, but if the seed is kept in paper envelopes, the envelopes may be stored in a metal container for protection. Glass jars should be covered, or should be set in dark closets away from the light.

GERMINATION TEST: Some seed will deteriorate with age, and though it is carefully prepared, may refuse to germinate. Before planting home-grown seed and depending upon it in spring to produce a crop, it is wise to make a germination test. This is done by duplicating as far as possible the conditions of warmth and moisture that the plants need when growing in the garden.

Twenty or more seeds are counted out for the test, and the quantity noted. They are then placed on a layer of absorbent material in a saucer. Absorbent cotton, blotting paper, or heavy cloth may be used. Sterile cotton is recommended, because it will not mould as quickly. A second layer of the material is placed over the seeds, it is sprinkled with water and excess water is poured off. The seed may start to germinate in 24 hours, or it may take two or three weeks, but meanwhile the covering material should not be allowed to dry out. The top layer should be lifted from time to time to allow air to reach the seed. If mould appears near the seed, the covering layer may have to be removed entirely. Seed is germinated, for testing purposes, when it has swelled and put forth a sprout.

The germination tests will show whether the seed should be used at all, and how thickly it should be sown. Even if only a small number of seeds germinate, it may be wise to use the seed, because unusually strong plants are said to result from planting old seed.

The following is a list of vegetables with the number of years indicated during which their seeds can be expected to be viable. If the seed is older, it should be tested before using: corn, onion, parsnip, soy bean, salsify, two years; bean leek, parsley, peas, three years; carrot, mustard, pepper, tomatoes, four years; broccoli, cabbage, cauliflower, kohlrabi, lettuce, okra, pumpkin, radish, spinach, and turnip, five years; beets, eggplant, melons, squash, six years; celery, eight years; cucumber, endive, ten years. Whether the seed is purchased or home grown, tests should be made if it exceeds the above ages.

Few seeds will germinate as soon as they ripen. Most of them require a rest period of at least a month, and in some cases as much as a year. There are exceptions to this. Some grains, for instance, will sprout in the seed head if the weather is wet when they ripen. A few plants such as beans, sunflowers, lilies, and mustard, will start to sprout in a few days. Others, like carrots and parsnips, need a month or more before they are ready to grow. And some trees and shrubs will not germinate in less than a year.

STRATIFYING: This is the practice of handling those seeds which do not germinate quickly, but which need a period of "after-ripening" in order to break the rest period. In nature, seeds of nut trees, for example, are given this rest period as they are covered by the litter of the forest. To imitate this natural procedure, seedsmen practice cold stratification, where such seeds are mixed with sphagnum moss, put in a polyethylene bag in a refrigerator, and allowed to stay there from one to four months at a temperature of around 40°. Warm stratification is also done with certain seeds; most common, though, is soaking seeds in hot water, followed by cold stratification. Another method of stratifying is to place seeds in boxes of sand, then burying boxes about six inches deep. Wire cages are often placed over boxes to protect seeds from animal pests.

SOWING: Most seed may be planted indoors to give it an early start, or it may be started in a cold frame, or sown directly in the bed where it is to grow. A few exceptions to this rule are noted through the encyclopedia under specific plants. Usually the exceptions are those plants whose roots are so fine or brittle that transplanting will damage them, or are plants which require special conditions for germination.

Hardy and quick-growing annual flowers and vegetables are usually started in their bed in the garden. More tender plants, slow-growing plants, those which take a long time to germinate, and those with seed so fine that weeks are required to develop them into manageable plants, are usually planted indoors. Perennial flowers may be started in mid-winter indoors, if they may be expected to bloom the first year from seed. Or they may be sown in a special nursery bed outside in spring, to be transplanted in fall to their permanent garden positions. Biennials may be planted in midsummer, at about the time when seed normally ripens on the plants. Or they may be planted outdoors in spring, and when planted at this time, will make larger plants and produce more bloom the following year.

Early vegetables may be sown indoors and hardened early in a cold frame or in a sheltered place outside before they are set in the garden to yield early crops. The time for planting out is given under VEGETABLE GARDENING, which see. This may include such vegetables as corn and squash, normally planted directly in the garden. These may be sown in pots inside, or in paper containers, such as the bottoms of milk cartons. At the normal time for planting in the garden, these early plants may be set out without disturbing their roots, and earlier vegetables may be produced from them.

Seed planted outside will be planted into the soil in which it will grow during the entire season. So the soil must be properly prepared in advance, with added manure, compost, bone meal, or whatever that particular vegetable or flower will need for good growth. If the seed is to be planted in rows, a drill or trench may be made with the edge of a board which will keep the row straight.

Depth of planting depends upon the size of the seed, the consistency of the soil, and the season of the year. The usual rule is to plant a seed four times its diameter below the surface. This rule is modified by soil—heavy clay soil will be more damp and it will require less of it above the seed to maintain the proper amount of moisture necessary for germination. Sandy soil will dry out faster at the top, so the seed may need to be planted deeper in it. Seed should never be drowned during germination by too much moisture. Nor should it be kept too cold. If the soil is clay and wet, it will be cold beneath the surface early in spring. Later the same season, the same seed will be able to germinate from further down in the clay. But it also needs air during germination, so the tilth of the soil, while fine, should be granular, so that air may penetrate to the depth of the seed.

Fine seed should be sprinkled on top of the soil and firmed down with a board, the back of the hoe, or with the hand. A very slight sifting of sand or fine compost over it will help keep it moist. Soil should be firmed around newly planted seed only if the soil is of open texture and not too wet. Summer planted seed almost always needs to be firmed. Spring planted seed may or may not need it, depending upon soil and weather. Also, summer planted seed should be covered to protect it from drying until it germinates.

Seed sown indoors should be planted in soil that is not too rich, that is, of a texture which will hold moisture, but which will also drain well. The usual rule is half garden loam to half sand.

If the seed is planted in a pot, the bottom quarter of the pot should be filled with broken pieces of flower pot, or with gravel. In a flat, the bottom quarter to half of the flat should be sphagnum moss. Soil which is added to cover these layers should be moist, not wet or dry. Seed should be thinly sown in rows or in circles in the pot, and in rows in the flat. If more than one kind of seed is planted in a container, the seeds should be chosen to germinate in about the same length of time, and to grow at the same rate so that all will be ready for transplanting together. After the seed has been placed in its rows, sand or fine compost is sifted over it to the correct depth. The soil may then be firmed and watered, either with a very fine misty spray from above, or by plunging the container into water almost as deep as the soil. When wet patches begin to appear on top of the soil, the container should be removed from the water and drained.

Seed flats may be covered to preserve surface moisture until germination starts. Temperature for germination of seed may usually be somewhat higher than the plants will bear after growth has started. (Exceptions are the seeds which need a period of frost before they will germinate. These are specially noted under directions for growing specific plants.) Soil should be kept moist, but not wet, during this period. If the top of the container is covered with glass or paper, the cover should be lifted occasionally to permit air to circulate. At the first sign of fungus growth, the cover should be removed.

As soon as the first green begins to appear, covering should be removed from the seed pot and it should be placed in a southern window. Gradually, as the seedlings sprout and the roots stretch down into the pot, watering may be lighter and less frequent, but the container should never be permitted to become dry. If seedlings are too thick they must be thinned immediately. Occasionally when fine seed is planted it will come up unevenly, with thick patches in places in the pot. These patches should be thinned by means of tweezers, because crowding at this stage will almost inevitably result in damping-off.

TRANSPLANTING: When seedlings are large enough to handle they should be transplanted to stand two inches apart in a flat. The usual rule is to transplant when the first pair of true leaves has formed. By this time they will have developed roots that are long in proportion to their tops. The new flat may have a small amount of compost mixed with the loam and sand, but the mixture should be kept lean. If the roots must seek further for food, they will build a strong healthy root system, which is more important than height of stem at this point in their growth.

About two weeks before the seedlings are to be planted in the garden they should begin their hardening-off. At first they should be carried out to stand in the sun in a spot sheltered from the wind, in the middle of the day. Gradually the period when they are left outside may be lengthened into the cooler parts of the day. If a cold frame is available, they may be placed in the frame with the sash lifted at midday.

When planting in the garden, most plants are benefitted by being sunk lower than they were in their flats. Transplanting should be done when the sun will not directly shine on exposed roots—on a cloudy day, early in the morning, or in the evening. Plants should be protected from the direct rays of the sun for several days after transplanting, if possible. They should be watered as soon as they are placed in the ground, and the soil should be kept moist around them until they are established. If a deep mulch is used, a handful of it may be lightly spread across the tops of the plants for protection. A cutworm collar is necessary in most gardens to protect the young seedlings. This may be a piece of cardboard or stiff paper about 3 x 5 inches, which is wrapped loosely around the stem and sunk about an inch in the soil all round the plant. *See also* GERMINATION; VEGETABLE GARDENING; FLOWER GARDENING; HOUSE PLANTS; COLD FRAME.

SELAGINELLA: A genus of the family *Selaginellaceae* comprising a number of mossy or fern-like primitive herbs, flowerless, creeping, erect or climbing. Most are native of tropical climates, found in forests. Increase by spores. Grown largely in greenhouses for their decorative foliage. Sometimes grown to cover unsightly spots in the greenhouse, under benches, where they quickly increase in the warmth and moist shade to cover. New growth is started easily from old plants which are chopped up and scattered over the soil, covered with glass, and kept at 70°.

S. kraussiana is a bright green African mossy creeping perennial, used for cover. *S. emmeliana* is grown as a fern, with bright green leaves to one foot. *S. brauni* has straw-colored foliage over one foot, and is used in window boxes. *S. martensi* has fine pale green foliage used as cut foliage. Resurrection plant (*S. lepidophylla*), is a desert native of Texas and Central America, often sold in its dry state. When moisture is withheld from it, the leaves curl up into a dry brown ball. When it is again moistened it becomes a mossy plant about four inches tall. It may be potted and will continue to grow in this condition. *See also* FERNS.

SELENICEREUS: Climbing cactus plants which includes the night-blooming cereus (*S. pteranthus*). It is grown in the greenhouse or in the garden in the deep South. They produce fragrant white showy flowers. *See also* CACTUS.

SELF-POLLINATION: *see* POLLINATION; ORCHARD

SELF-STERILITY: *see* POLLINATION; ORCHARD

SEMPERVIVUM TECTORUM: *see* OLD-MAN-AND-WOMAN; HOUSELEEK

SENECIO: *see* RAGWORT

SENEGA: (*Polygala senega*) Known also as senega snakeroot and senega root, it is a small native perennial occurring in rocky woods in the eastern states and Canada. The root is used in medicine.

Senega can be grown in any soil that contains a fair proportion of leaf mold or similar humus. Shade is not essential, although the plant thrives in partial shade in open hardwood forests. To propagate from seed it is necessary to plant seed that has been stratified by mixing it with sand and burying it in boxes or flowerpots in moist soil until the following spring, when it may be sown in seedbeds or shallow boxes of loam and leaf mold. The seedlings when old enough to be handled safely can be readily transplanted to the permanent beds and set in rows to facilitate cultivation. The plant can also be propagated from roots, which may be obtained from dealers or collected from the wild plants in fall or early spring. In cold situations the plants will probably need protection during the first winter after transplanting. A light covering of straw or pine needles will be sufficient to protect them from severe frost.

SENNA: (*Cassia*) A genus of the pea family, which includes several hundred herbs, shrubs, and trees, mostly tropical. Leaves are compound, but flowers do not conform to the typical pea-like shape. Petals almost equal, with perhaps one a little larger than the others. Most are tender and can be grown only in the southernmost portions of the United States. They have attractive finely cut foliage, prefer sandy loam, and must have full sun. Propagated by seeds and division, or the woody species, by cuttings.

C. corymbosa is a half-hardy shrub from South America, with yellow flowers produced through the summer. Grown in greenhouses.

Golden shower (*C. fistula*) is a small tree from India whose fruits are the cassia pods of commerce. Long racemes of yellow flowers.

Pink shower (*C. grandis*) is a 50-foot tropical American tree which has drooping clusters of rose-pink flowers.

C. artemisoides is a shrub with silver narrow leaves and light yellow flowers which grows in dry places in California.

Wild senna (*C. marylandica*) is a hardy perennial that may be grown in the border from New England south. Growing to four feet, it has bright yellow flowers in summer.

SENSITIVE PLANT: *see* MIMOSA

SEPARATION: *see* DIVISION

SEPTEMBER GARDEN OPERATIONS: *see* GARDEN CALENDAR

SEQUOIA: Only two species of these enormous pre-historic trees, the redwood (*S. sempervirens*), and the giant sequoia (*S. gigantea*), still exist, mainly in California and Oregon. They are the biggest and probably the oldest evergreens in the world, some well over 300 feet tall and more than 2,500 years old. Occasionally much smaller specimens are found in the East, but the climate there is generally unsuitable—the sequoia is a mountain tree, the redwood likes a lot of rain and fog. Redwood is an important timber tree, and its burls, sold by florists for centerpieces, sprout quickly and freely when put in water. The most magnificent sequoia is the General Sherman tree, which has a trunk 35 feet wide, in Sequoia National Park.

SERICEA: A perennial lespedeza. It should be sown shallow on a firm seed bed.

A good stand should last indefinitely. When a plant is six inches tall, its roots will be a foot or more in the ground; when mature, some roots will have gone down as much as four feet in search of moisture. The roots penetrate tight, heavy clay subsoils. It is valuable in erosion control. The vigorous roots, heavy top growth, and the coating of fallen leaves bind the soil while depositing large quantities of organic material on eroded surfaces.

Sericea was introduced from an Asiatic climate much like that of Missouri, Kansas, Indiana, and Ohio. It seems to be well suited for the section of the United States about 100 miles north of the Ohio River to the Gulf of Mexico and from the Atlantic to central Kansas and Oklahoma. However, it has survived several seasons in southern Vermont and southern Michigan. A late spring freeze is likely to do more damage to sericea than excessively low winter temperatures.

Sericea seeds are relished by birds and the plants make an ideal cover for quail and other wildlife. Seeds hang on well into the winter and are high enough on the tall plants to provide food for birds when low-growing plants are covered with snow. It is not bothered much by insects or diseases. *See also* LESPEDEZA.

SERVICEBERRY: *see* AMELANCHIER; SHADBLOW

SESAME: (*Sesamum orientale*) One of the first oilseed crops ever to be cultivated by man. Recently a new type of sesame plant, a semi-shattering variety which matures uniformly along the stalk, has been developed, so that the crop can be harvested with conventional farm machinery. Known as Renner sesame No. 1, it replaces the ancient types which bore seed pods that shattered as they matured, thus requiring hand harvesting.

As harvest time approaches, the white blooms of sesame ripen into fat green pods and leaves fall off. Oil is rich in calcium and vitamin C.

FOOD VALUE: The oil yield from sesame's seed is about 50 per cent and is quite rich in calcium and vitamin C, even more so than sunflower seed. It has long provided the basic fats in place of butter and lard in the diets of citizens of the Near East, especially those of Turkey and Syria.

The seed contains a certain amount of lecithin, vitamins E and F (unsaturated fatty acids). A variety of delicious food products can be made from it, such as butters, vegetable milk, delicious oil, candies and dressings to mention a few. The hulled seeds may be chewed as they are; and they are often tender, easier to chew, and as tasty, as the sunflower seed.

Sesame is well adapted to the climatic and soil conditions throughout the cotton growing areas of Texas and other southern areas. Because it is very drought tolerant, it is a dependable crop. Besides having a relatively low cost of production, sesame is a short season crop which can be used very effectively in a diversified system of farming with other cash crops, grasses and legumes.

Here are details on the semi-shattering sesame type:

It is an erect annual plant which grows from 36 to 72 inches high and matures in 90 to 120 days, depending upon strain and growing conditions.

The plant contains small seed pods or capsules which are borne at each leaf axil.

The pod is about the size and shape of a peanut pod, and the sesame seed is similar in size and shape to a tomato seed.

A plant approximately 40 inches high will usually contain about 150 pods and each pod has from 75 to 100 seeds.

Sesame has a combination type root system consisting of a tap root and an extensive fibrous or secondary root system. This combination enables the plant to utilize subsoil and surface moisture very effectively.

It will grow well under a wide range of soil conditions but thrives best on well-drained fertile soils. Neutral soils are preferred, but good results can be expected on either acid or alkaline soils. Generally speaking, sesame will grow well on any land that will grow cotton and thrives under high temperatures and droughty conditions.

There's a very important "caution" that goes with growing sesame, one that organic growers will especially want to remember. Sesame is a soil-depleting crop that would tend to deprive the soil of essential minerals and destroy its physical structure unless incorporated into a rotation schedule with legumes and grasses.

Sesame should not be planted until all danger of cool weather is past. Planting dates may be as early as March 15 in the southern part of the adapted area and as late as June 15 toward the northern limit. Generally, sesame could be planted shortly after cotton in cotton-growing areas and after sorghum in sorghum-growing areas.

SESBANIA: *see* GREEN MANURE

SET: Term used to indicate successful pollination of fruit or vegetable, when ovary begins to swell to show beginning of fruit form, and the tree is said to have "set" fruit.

Also used to indicate a small dwarfed onion bulb grown from seed too thickly sown one season, and planted the following spring to provide early scallions.

Also sometimes applied to the rooted sprout of the sweet potato by which it is propagated.

SEWAGE SLUDGE: The use of sewage sludge by gardeners and farmers throughout the United States has been climbing upward in recent years. In cities where sludge has been sold, such as Boise, Chicago, Wichita, Grand Rapids, Duluth, Omaha, Santa Fe, Schenectady, Houston, Roanoke and Milwaukee, superintendents of sewage treatment plants report that demand for sludge has been increasing.

Most cities and towns don't sell their sludge, but make it available to local gardeners and farmers free at the plant site. In Illinois, for example, according to Sanitary Engineer Carl Gross, "virtually every city and sanitary district which operates a sewage treatment works makes the digested and air-dried sludge available at the treatment works to anyone. In a few instances, there is a nominal charge but in general, the sludge is available at no cost."

ACTIVATED OR DIGESTED: The fertilizer value of the sludge produced depends largely on which processing method is used.

Activated sludge: This kind is produced when the sewage is agitated by air rapidly bubbling through it. Certain types of very active bacteria coagulate the organic matter, which settles out, leaving a clear liquid that can be discharged into streams and rivers with a minimum amount of pollution.

Generally, activated sludge is heat-treated before being made available to gardeners and farmers; its nitrogen content is between five and six per cent, phosphorus from three to six per cent. Its plant food value is similar to cottonseed meal—a highly recommended organic fertilizer.

Digested sludge: This type of residue is formed when the sewage is allowed to settle (and liquid to drain off) by gravity without being agitated by air. The conventional anaerobic digestion system takes about ten to 14 days from the time the sewage reaches the sedimentation tank until the digested solids are pumped into filter beds, often sand and gravel, for drying. The final step is removal of the dry material, either to be incinerated or used for soil improvement.

A few medium-sized cities located in agricultural areas dispose of a part of their short-time activated and subsequently digested sludge in liquid form. This is delivered to farmers within a radius of about ten miles and is used for direct application to land.

Digested sludge has about the same fertilizer value as barnyard manure. Nitrogen varies from two to three per cent, phosphorus averaging about two per cent. It often has an offensive odor that persists for some time after application to a soil surface during cool weather. "This odor differs greatly in character, however, from that of raw sludge," Dr. Myron Anderson, senior chemist for the Agricultural Research Service at Beltsville, Maryland, states, "since drastic changes have taken place during digestion. The odor from digested sludges may be eliminated by storage in a heap during warm weather."

AMOUNTS TO USE: The city of Marion, Indiana, has printed an excellent little pamphlet which includes the following suggestions for using sludge as a fertilizer and soil builder:

A great many cities throughout the United States make their sewage sludge available free to gardeners and farmers. The sludge shown above at the Allentown, Pa. plant is a useful soil aid.

(1) *For starting new lawns*—prepare the seed bed by mixing the sludge with the soil. A minimum dosage of one part sludge to two parts soil may be used if the soil is of a heavy clay texture. Spade the ground to a depth of at least six inches, making sure the sludge is thoroughly intermixed with the soil. Never have layers of sludge and layers of soil in the seed bed.

(2) *For feeding well-established lawns*—the sludge should be applied in the winter and early spring months when the ground is frozen. The lawn may be covered with a layer of sludge one-half inch deep during the cold months of December, January and February. This cover will provide an insulation to protect the grass roots from the harmful effects of freezing and thawing during this time of the year. In addition, ample plant food will be made available for a luxuriant growth of grass in the spring.

(3) *For reconditioning old lawns*—on yards or portions of yards where the soil has been too poor to support an average growth of grass, it is recommended that the procedure under (1) above be followed. It should be remembered that grass roots grow into the soil to a depth of six or seven inches only when the ground is of such a composition that will permit this growth. To top-dress and seed a section of ground that has not been properly prepared is a waste of time and money.

(4) *For gardens and farm land*—sewage sludge provides an economical means of replenishing land with nitrogen, phosphorus, and humus material. It should be put on the land just previous to the fall or spring plowing and cultivated into the soil. The sludge cake may be applied as a manure to farm land at the rate of ten to 15 tons to the acre. The weight of the sludge is approximately one ton to the cubic yard.

Heat-dried activated sludge is generally acid, its pH averaging 5.0 to 6.0. Air-dried digested sludge after a short period of storage will normally show a drop in pH to about 6.0. Experience shows that the continued use of any type of sludge, unless previously conditioned with lime, requires the periodic addition of lime to the soil to prevent harmful acidity.

SLUDGE IS SAFE: In the U. S. Dept. of Agriculture report on sludge, Dr. Anderson writes:

"Activated sludges need heat-treatment before use as fertilizer. Such treatment is normally provided for material to be marketed. The heat used for drying normally accomplishes the destruction of dangerous organisms. This means that properly heat-dried activated sludges may be used with confidence regarding their safety from a sanitary standpoint. . . .

"It seems that states have generally accepted the conclusions of the Committee on Sewage Disposal of the American Public Health Association that heat-dried activated sludges are satisfactory from a sanitary standpoint, and that digested sludges are satisfactory except where vegetables are grown to be eaten raw. All danger is thought to be removed by action in the soil after a period of about three months during a growing season."

EXCELLENT FOR LAWNS AND TREES: What kind of results can you expect when you add sludge to the soil? LeRoy Van Kleek, Principal Sanitary Engineer of Connecticut's Dept. of Health and an experienced gardener, answers that question quite conclusively in his report, "Digested Sewage Sludge as a Soil Conditioner and Fertilizer."

" . . . Sludge is particularly adapted to lawns. Sludge deepens the green color of grass and stimulates a luxurious growth. Its benefits seem noticeable for several years. It should be applied late in March and again if desired early in September.

"The home owner may well use it for the flower garden. Here it provides a much needed humus for the hot summer months as well as a moderate but long-yielding nitrogen.

"Its use is also indicated for trees and shrubs. Trees fertilized with sludge frequently have a healthier foliage, both in amount and color, and retain their leaves for a longer time in the fall than nearby unfertilized trees.

"Soils repeatedly planted to growing crops are greatly benefited by the organic humus supplied by manures, peat moss, green cover crops or sludges. The value of sludge should not be judged solely by comparison of chemical analyses with artificial fertilizers, but by the results it produces in plant growth. Dependence exclusively upon commercial fertilizers without consideration for the maintenance of humus content and good soil structure is an unsound practice." *See also* FERTILIZER.

SHADBLOW: (*Amelanchier*) Also known as serviceberry and juneberry, these are small trees or shrubs that produce purple-red clusters of edible fruit.

There are about 25 species, three of them arborescent, of which the western *florida* and the eastern *laevis* supply most of the edible fruit. Besides their value for food, they are extraordinarily handsome, especially when seen in the earliest days of spring just before the landscape breaks into green. Then they raise a mass of snow-white blossoms that stand out even at great distances like tiny clouds anchored against the still grey-brown of the woods' edges and old fields that are their favorite haunts. Their lovely appearance is aided by the woolly white or red of the uncurling leaves, which later become a delicate green, and finally a clear yellow before they reach the ground in the fall. The bark is a soft ashy grey or reddish brown. The trunk is often branched at the ground, but in the dense forest will sometimes rise in a clear bole with little taper to heights of 70 feet. *See also* AMELANCHIERS.

SHADE-TOLERANT PLANTS: Many plants may be grown in partial shade, the number increasing the further south they are planted. Some annual and perennial flowers which thrive only in the full sun in the North require shade during the hottest parts of the day in the South. Similarly, some cool-climate plants may be grown where the summers are fairly warm if they are given moist but well-ventilated spots in the partial shade of trees or shrubs.

Along with the usual list of flowers which may be planted in shade more or less heavy, many of the annuals and perennials thought to be sun-border plants may be induced to grow and bloom if they are given more than their usual requirement of food and moisture. When they are deprived of sun, they seem to need more of their other requirements. This is particularly true when they are planted under trees whose roots are shallow, where they rapidly lose their allotment of food and water to the trees.

Many early spring bulbs and perennials will thrive under trees if their beds have sun when they bloom. Planted under trees which leaf out late in spring, they miss little of their normal share of the sun.

Plants growing in fairly heavy shade may thrive as to foliage, but put forth fewer blossoms than they would in the sun. Generally, heavily-blooming flowers may not be expected to do well under trees, but the more delicate light sprays will blossom almost as well as in sun. White flowers, too, will do better than the darker varieties. Wild flowers and ferns that are natives of woodland will thrive in the shady spots of the garden.

The following annuals may be expected to bloom in partial shade: sweet alyssum, snapdragon, sweet-sultan, cornflower, China aster, clarkia, cynoglossum, California poppy, godetia, balsam, lupine, mimulus, forget-me-not, nemophelia, flowering tobacco, pansy, petunia, and schizanthus.

The perennials which will bloom without full sun include: Japanese anemone, hardy aster, Chinese balloon-flower, beebalm, black-eyed-Susan, bleeding heart, ajuga, anchusa, candytuft, cardinal flower, columbine, cranesbill, coral bells, primrose, daylilies, evening primrose, foxglove, gasplant, cattail, gayfeather, harebell, joe-pye-weed, lily-of-the-valley, purple loosestrife, Maltese cross, meadow rue, monkshood, moss phlox, pansy, perennial sweet pea, adonis, plantain lily, rose campion, rose mallow, St. Johns wort, speedwell, pachysandra, sedum, wild sweet William, torchlily, violets, Virginia bluebell, and sweet woodruff. *See also* SHRUBS.

SHALLOT: (*Allium ascalonicum*) A small onion of the Multiplier type. In its requirements it is similar to other onions. The bulbs have a more delicate flavor than most onions. They seldom form seed and are propagated by means of the small cloves or divisions into which the plant splits during growth. The plant is hardy and may be left in the ground from year to year, but best results are to be had by replanting the smaller ones at the desired time. *See also* ONION.

SHASTA DAISY (*Chrysanthemum maximum*) Herbaceous perennials that

The white flowers of shasta daisies make excellent cut flowers, are as much as six inches in diameter. Shastas do best planted in full sun.

grow about two feet high, have single white daisy flowers. Shastas are often used in the border and make excellent cut flowers. They form bushy, upright plants, seldom branching. The white flowers with yellow centers are sometimes as much as six inches in diameter. Easy to grow, they do best planted in full sun, in a well-drained, moderately rich soil. Divide clumps every second year; replant about one foot apart. Shastas are winter hardy, should be frequently divided.

SHEEP: Sheep have always been the universal stock. Since earliest Biblical times, flocks have roamed every continent. From barren Arabia to lush Argentina, from the rigors of Iceland to the almost-desert of the Australian interior, breeds of every description have followed man.

They revitalize neglected land, grazing down and killing off even wild blackberries and poison ivy. They clean up brushy land: says one organic farmer, "Intermittent grazing on a brushy lot made it look like a golf course in two years—the clover came back beautifully."

Sheep can give as much or more net return above overhead as any other type of stock. A $300 beef cow, for instance, will produce a single $200 calf a year. Eight ewes for the same price will give you nearly $300 worth of wool and lambs. Too, a beef cow gets 75 per cent of its nourishment from forage—sheep get 90 per cent.

Sheep are not scavengers. True, they do better on poor land than any other stock (except perhaps goats). But you can't expect them to produce their best meat and wool—both high in protein—on a constant diet of brush or scraggly weeds (weeds, often deep-rooted and thus mineral-rich, can, however, make up a large part of their diet).

Top production calls for top pastures and hay, timed properly through the year. Fine, short, tender grass, plus good legume hay, are as necessary to them for good production as to other animals.

Early fall is usually the best time to start a flock. Most sheepmen recommend buying good grade western ewes. They carry some fine-wool blood and in general are healthier and better producers than native ewes. You'll find all breeds are just about equally good —health is the big point to watch out for in buying foundation stock.

Sheep equipment is simple and inexpensive. An open-front shed is ample protection even in the North if lambing takes place late in the season; for early lambing, a warm, ventilated barn is necessary in cold climates.

Sheep do best on rolling land with good fertility and good forage. Figure their pasture at the rate of eight ewes to the acreage needed to support one Jersey cow. They should always have a source of clean, running water.

A variety of grasses means good nourishment: orchard grass, timothy, alfalfa, ladino, bluegrass, brome and sweet clover are all excellent. For early-season grazing, permanent pasture of a mixture of grasses, is low cost feed that carries little bloat danger. The sheep will get rid of weeds and improve fertility—this is one of the cheapest, surest ways to improve permanent pasture. When the grass gets short, put them on temporary pasture. Sown forage crops of cereals or rape make fine temporary pasture.

A month or so before breeding, as well as towards lambing time, feed your ewes small amounts of grain. This will make them more likely to produce strong, healthy twin or triplet lambs. One-half bran and one-half oats is good; corn or barley may also be used.

The grain feeding that you start before lambing should be continued as long as the ewes are nursing, for milk makes the fastest, cheapest gains on the lambs. Keep the lambs housed for a week or two before putting them on pasture, and creep-feed them some grain. Keep legume hay in a rack next to the creep until they are on pasture constantly. Lambs kept for fall fattening should get some grain again in late summer when the grass is poor.

Good nutrition and management will prevent practically all sheep diseases. Anthrax, the worst killer, can be avoided by not letting your sheep graze closely on sparse late-summer pastures: anthrax germs live in the soil and can be picked up by the animals on short grass.

Many sheepmen never dip their sheep these days, believing it too dangerous. Most dips contain arsenic or DDT, neither of which are safe for the animals. Stay away from phenothiazine, too — this powerful worm-killer affects the sheep's body growth and metabolism, and may well be responsible for today's big lamb losses and the increase in "mystery" diseases. Pasture rotation is a better preventive of worms and parasites. And make sure your sheep never have to drink stagnant water: it holds the larvae of the land snail, host to liver fluke.

Sheep like affection. One reason for the renown of the Basque shepherds is their constant attention to each and every sheep in their flock. Soothing talk, removing briers from their ears, and occasionally rubbing their noses and chins keep them contented and good producers.

SHEEP ON THE HOMESTEAD: A ewe with a lamb needs at least 15 square feet of space in the barn, maybe 25 square feet in the lot. She'll need two gallons of water a day. If you have good pasture that's all you need for sheep in the grazing season, but off pasture, figure four pounds of alfalfa or clover hay per ewe. If you just have grass hay, add one-half pound of supplement to supply protein so the lamb will be born strong and vigorous. A ewe will make nearly a ton of sheep manure a year. Like the cow, the sheep is a ruminant, has four stomachs instead of one. Lately we are learning some astounding things about the rumen; it can take bulky forage and roughness, even ground corn cobs and stalks, and make nutrition out of them. The college researchers have perfected supplements out of soybean meal, molasses, bone meal, salt and codliver oil, which you sprinkle on the roughage—not to feed the sheep, but to feed the bacteria which thrive on that warm, soupy medium in the rumen. They break down the coarse forage into highly nutrient elements.

SHEEP MANURE: *see* MANURE

SHEEP'S FESCUE: *see* ORCHARD GRASS

SHEET COMPOSTING: By this method, leaves, weeds, manure, and other waste organic materials are spread over the garden or field and worked into the soil to decompose. It's recommended to make several passes with a rotary mower over this material as cut-up material breaks down faster. Also add any lime, nitrogen fertilizers, bone meal, tankage, or dried blood, phosphate or potash rock at this time. *See also* COMPOST.

SHELL-FLOWER: Common name sometimes applied to at least four different flowers belonging to different families, *Alpinia speciosa,* one of the ginger family species; *Molucella laevis,* or Molucca balm, an annual of the mint family; *Chelone glabra,* also called turtlehead, one of the snapdragon family; and *Tigridia pavonia,* a bulbous plant of the iris family.

SHE-OAK: *see* AUSTRALIAN PINE

SHEPHERDIA: Also known as buffaloberry. A genus of the oleaster family, consisting of three species, two of which are cultivated. Both are extremely hardy, growing far into the North and standing winds and soils that no other plant could survive. They have opposite leaves, inconspicuous small yellow flowers, and fruit which is a small drupe. *S. argentea,* commonly called buffaloberry,

wild oleaster, and silverleaf, is a prickly shrub or tree to 18 feet, with silvery foliage and edible yellow or red fruit used for jelly. *S. canadensis,* also called buffaloberry, grows to about eight feet, its leaves green above and silvery below, and its fruit flat-tasting but edible.

SHOOT: A very young and vigorously growing stem or branch of a plant.

SHORTIA: (*Schizocodon*) A genus of stemless evergreen shrubs, growing from creeping rootstocks, with solitary, white bell-shaped flowers in early spring. Leaves are roundish and leathery. Useful in rock gardens and for planting under acid-loving shrubs, such as rhododendron. They need acid soil rich in humus, and should be regularly mulched with oak leaf mold. Propagated by division or runners.

Oconee bells (*S. galacifolia*), is native only in the mountains of North Carolina, and has never been found elsewhere. It grows to eight inches, with roundish wavy-margined leaves. White flowers, or rose in the variety *rosea.*

Fringed galax or fringe-bell (*S. soldanelloides*), is a Japanese species, with rose flowers, white or light pink at the edges.

Nippon-bells (*S. uniflora*), is similar to oconee bells except that the leaves are more heart-shaped, and margins are wavy. *See also* OCONEE BELLS.

SHREDDERS: Compost shredders enable the home gardener to make compost in as little time as ten days. They actually ease the task of preparing compost and mulches. It is now recognized that cut-up leaves, weeds and other similar material make better mulch than the rough raw product because they hold moisture better and form a thicker blanket which chokes off weeds. Breakdown of shredded materials is faster, since the heap heats up more quickly. The machines are also used to grind and pulverize fin-

Hay is one of the many organic materials that will break down faster in a compost heap, after passing through a shredder or grinder.

ished compost, which is ideal for lawns and potting soil, flower beds and in greenhouses. *See also* COMPOST.

SHRIMP PLANT: *see* HOUSE PLANTS

SHRUBS: Shrubs are woody plants growing from a cluster of main stems, as distinguished from trees whicn grow from a single stem or trunk. Some small trees branch so close to the ground that for practical garden uses they may be grouped with shrubs. Some of these will be found among the lists which follow.

Both evergreen and deciduous varieties of shrubs are useful in the home grounds, and should be mixed for the best year-round landscape picture. Other characteristics which should be taken into account in planning shrubbery plantings are: 1. *flowering*—blooming period, color and fragrance of blooms; 2. *foliage*—color, texture, fine or coarseness, evergreen or brilliant in autumn; 3. *fruiting*—decorative, attractive to birds, or food for the family; 4. *location*—suitability of shrubs chosen for problem spots that are wet, dry, or shady.

Besides horticultural considerations, the landscape picture should be consulted. Shrubs break up views that are too broad in a garden and make vistas between them, where the vision takes in too much of the garden at a sweep. It leaves nothing to hunt for and one is not drawn out into the garden to become acquainted with it. This may be corrected by well-placed groups of shrubs or single specimens so arranged that vistas are formed.

PLANTING: Most shrubs can be planted in either spring or fall. One safe rule to follow in either spring or fall planting of leaf-dropping species is that they be set out while dormant; that is, at least a week before the leaves appear in spring or after they have fallen in autumn.

If you are not ready to set the shrubs in their permanent place when they arrive, you will have to heel them in. In other words, dig a trench and place the stock with the roots down and then throw soil over them and water them well. They can be kept in this manner for a long time. If you are going to plant them in a few days, you can coat the roots with thick, soup-like mud and stand them in the shade, covered with wet burlap. This is called "puddling," or "mudding." It can also be used to protect the roots from drying out if they are planted on hot windy days.

Dig holes large enough so that the roots will not be cramped. Fill the bottom of the hole to the desired height with topsoil and firm it down well. Then place your plant in the hole, with the roots puddled if necessary, and after making certain that the roots are well spread, and that any broken ones are cut off, fill in with soil and tramp it down well. Leave a shallow depression around the newly planted shrub, so that water will collect there and provide plenty of moisture.

Unless you have done so previously, shape your shrub. Cut it back at least ⅓ of its height. This applies to all woody plants except evergreens. Few shrubs require staking.

The following shrubs are difficult to move, and should always be purchased balled and burlapped: abelia,

SUGGESTED SHRUBS FOR PLANTING HOME GROUNDS
DECIDUOUS—2 TO 15 FEET

Common Name	Scientific Name	Height (Ft.)	Time of Bloom	Color
FIVE-LEAVED ARALIA	Aralia dentaphyllum	8–10	May	
RED CHOKEBERRY	Aronia arbutifolia	8	May	White
FLAME AZALEA	Azalea calendulaceum	6–8	May	Yellow
BUTTON BUSH	Cephalanthus occidentalis	8–10	July August	White
WHITE FRINGE	Chionanthus virginica	10–20	May	White
SWEET PEPPERBUSH	Clethra alnifolia	6–10	May	White
GRAY DOGWOOD	Cornus paniculata	10–15	May	White
RUSSIAN OLIVE	Eleagnus angustifolia	10–20		
WAHOO	Euonymus atropurpureus	10–15	May	
GOLDEN BELL	Forsythia spectabilis	6–10	April May	Yellow
BEAUTY BUSH	Kolkwitzia amabilis	8	May	White Pink
AMUR HONEYSUCKLE	Lonicera maacki	10	May	
MOCK ORANGE	Philadelphus virginalis	8	May	White
COMMON NINEBARK	Physocarpus opulifolius	10	May	White
URAL FALSE SPIREA	Sorbaria sorbifolia	6	May	White
VANHOUTTE SPIREA	Spirea vanhouttei	10	May	White
HIGHBUSH CRANBERRY	Viburnum opulus	12	May	White
BLACK CHOKEBERRY	Aronia melanocarpa	4–6	May	White
SWAMP AZALEA	Azalea viscosa	4–6	June	White
SNOW AZALEA	Azalea ledifolia alba	4–6	May	White
BUDDLEIA (In Variety)		3–4	June July	Various
PURPLE BEAUTYBERRY	Callicarpa purpurea	4–6	May	White
SWEET SHRUB	Calycanthus floridus	6	May June	Purple
LEMOINE DEUTZIA	Deutzia lemoinea	4–5	May	White
LEATHERWOOD	Dirca palustris	4–6	May	
REGEL PRIVET	Ligustrum obtusifolium regelianum	6	May	White
BAYBERRY	Myrica pennsylvanica	5		
FRAGRANT SUMAC	Rhus aromatica	6	May	
FATHER HUGO ROSE	Rosa hugonis	6	May	Yellow
GLOSSY ABELIA	Abelia grandiflora	3	June to October	White to Pink
JAPANESE BARBERRY	Berberis thunbergi	4	May	Light Yellow
BLACK HUCKLEBERRY	Gaylussacia baccata	3	May	White
OAKLEAF HYDRANGEA	Hydrangea quercifolia	4	August	White
GLOBE FLOWER	Hypericum moserianum	3	June	Yellow
DWARF SWEET MOCK ORANGE	Philadelphus coronarius nanus	4	May	White
ALPINE CURRANT	Ribes alpinum	4	May	Yellow
POLYANTHA ROSES (In Variety)		2–4	All Summer	Various
FROEBEL'S SPIREA	Spirea froebeli	4	May	Pink
CARL'S VIBURNUM	Viburnum carlesi	4	May	White

SUGGESTED SHRUBS FOR PLANTING HOME GROUNDS

EVERGREENS—TALL—6 FEET OR MORE

COMMON NAME	SCIENTIFIC NAME	HEIGHT (FT.)	SPREAD (FT.)	FORM
*TREE BOX	Buxus sempervirens	8–12	8–10	Upright
*JAPANESE HOLLY	Ilex crenata	8–10	6	Upright
*INKBERRY	Ilex glabra	8	6	
CONVEXLEAF HOLLY	Ilex convexa	10	4–6	Rounded
SPINY GREEK JUNIPER	Juniperus excelsa stricts	8	3	Columnar
VON EHRON JUNIPER	Juniperus sabina von ehron	10	6–8	Vase shaped
ROCKY MT. JUNIPER	Juniperus scopulorum	30	3–4	Cone
CANAERT RED CEDAR	Juniperus virginiana canaerti	25	8–10	Cone
*FIRETHORN	Pyracantha coccinea lalandi	10	8	Spreading
*PURPLE RHODODENDRON	Rhododendron catawbiense	8	6	Spreading
*GIANT LAUREL	Rhododendron maximum	12	8	Spreading
JAPANESE YEW	Taxus cuspidata	10	8	Spreading
UPRIGHT YEW	Taxus cuspidata capitata	25	8	Cone
PYRAMIDAL ARBOR-VITAE	Thuja occidentalis pyramidalis	25	3	Cone

EVERGREENS—4 TO 6 FEET

PFITZER'S JUNIPER	Juniperus chinensis pfitzeriana	6	6	Spreading
*MOUNTAIN LAUREL	Kalmia latifolia	6	6	Pink-white
*MOUNTAIN FETTER-BUSH	Pieris floribunda	5	4	White

EVERGREENS—2 TO 4 FEET

ANDORRA JUNIPER	Juniperus horizontalis plumosa	3	4	Spreading
MYER JUNIPER	J. squamata meyeri	4	2½	Vase
*OREGON GRAPE	Mahonia aquifolium	4	3	Upright
MUGHO PINE	Pinus mugo mughus	4	4	Globe
GLOBE ARBORVITAE	Thuja occidentalis	3	2½	Globe

*Broad-leaved evergreen

—*T. D. Gray*, West Virginia University

northern bayberry, buckthorn, cotoneaster, holly grape, inkberry, magnolia, shrub-althea, smoketree, Japanese snowball, sweetfern, Canadian yew.

PRUNING: Unless shrubs are intended to be used as hedges, their pruning will be light and will consist mainly of cutting back dead wood, removing faded flowers before fruit forms which might too greatly tax the strength of the plant, or cutting back overgrown specimens which have become leggy.

Any shrub which will bloom early in spring on wood grown the previous year should not be pruned until after the blooming period. If an attractive fruit is expected to follow the flowers, pruning should be limited to cutting out leggy growth, removing old wood, and shaping. If the shrub is a slow-grower like lilac, pruning should be very light. If it grows rapidly like Forsythia, it may be cut back drastically each year to produce a more graceful growth for the following year.

The following shrubs are pruned immediately after blossoming: deutzia, dogwood, except berried varieties, fringetree, Forsythia, golden currant, bush honeysuckle, except fruited varieties, lilac, magnolia, mountain laurel, pearlbush, mockorange, flowering quince, unless fruit is desired, rhododendron, climbing roses except those which produce edible hips, snowball, spring-flowering spiraea, and weigela.

Shrubs that bloom in summer and fall, and spring blossoming varieties that bear desirable fruit, are pruned just before growth starts in spring. A partial list of these follows: barberry, bladdernut, bladder-senna, hibiscus, coralberry, false-indigo, fruited bush honeysuckle, hydrangea, bedding roses, snowberry, summer blooming spiraea, and fruited viburnum.

Pruning should be done primarily to keep shrubs in good health, rather than to restrain their growth. If small plants are required, specimens which naturally remain small should be planted. Large growing species should not be barbered to small sizes and shapes. A natural-growing shrub will be more graceful, and will blend itself in to the landscape picture much better than one that has been too drastically shaped except in special cases where sculptured forms are required in formal gardens.

Most shrubs will be improved by the removal of old wood from their centers. Many shrubs send up suckers which should be removed, from their roots. Before pruning is begun, it is necessary to study the individual growth habit of each shrub, and to encourage it rather than to place it under restraint.

If shrubbery has become too thick and too high, as may happen in foundation groupings where ill-advised plantings of large-growing varieties were made, it is better to remove some of the old shrubs which interfere with light inside the home, and to replace them with lower-growing species. The following deciduous shrubs will grow no higher than three feet: *Azalea mollis* and *A. pontica,* leadplant, Jersey-tea, *deutzia gracilis,* bush-honeysuckle, golden and shrubby St. Johns wort, kerria, shrub cinquefoil, golden mockorange, fragrant sumac, Scotch brier rose, *bumalda* and Anthony Waterer *spirea,* stephanandra, dwarf cranberrybush, shrub yellowroot. Some of the dwarf species of evergreens are also useful for such planting, but extreme care must be taken to obtain dwarf, not tall-growing varieties.

CULTIVATION: Soil requirements differ with various shrubs, but generally evergreens need an acid soil rich in humus, but with not too high a nitrogen content, while deciduous shrubs need richer soil, and may be given top dressings of compost or rotted manure. A leaf mulch under most shrubs will replenish organic matter in the soil. Unless fungus disease is a problem, leaves should be left where they fall, and should be supplemented by liberal mulching with grass clippings, peat, corncobs, straw, composted sawdust, or leaf mold. Bone meal may be added, and wood ashes are also beneficial if extreme acidity is not necessary to the species. Evergreens which are overfed become weak and spindly, and do not bloom too well. Most deciduous shrubs are grateful for nitrogen, and the more rapidly they grow, the more hungry they are for it.

FLOWERING SHRUBS: Some of the most spectacular of the flowering shrubs are also tender, and cannot be grown in the North. However, in southern states the following are successful: *elaeagnus angustifolia,* or oleaster; gardenias, in many varieties; lantana, grown as an annual flower in the North; the showy pineapple guava, and other guavas; royal poinciana, or the flamboyant tree; camellias; and many tender varieties of azalea.

Hundreds of varieties of rhododendron and azaleas make a dazzling spring showing further north, a few being hardy as far north as New England. Other hardy shrubs which bloom where winters are extreme are: spiraea, both spring and summer blooming varieties; *buddleia,* or butterfly

Butterfly bush or buddleia is a very hardy shrub that can withstand great cold. Its fragrant lilac spikes spread out about five feet.

bush, whose fragrant lilac spikes attract butterflies; forsythia; Japanese quince or japonica, *chaenomeles lagenaria;* various dogwoods; the haw-

thornes; redbud, or *cercis;* mockorange; the flowering crabs and cherries; bush-honeysuckles; the long-blooming weigela; rose-of-Sharon, *hibiscus syriacus;* also calycanthus, daphne, deutzia, hydrangea, magnolias in some varieties, snowball or cranberry bush, snowberry, and flowering quince. Hardy vines which can be grown in the colder half of the country include wisteria, clematis, celastrus or bittersweet, and bignonia, or trumpet vine.

FOR DRY SOUTHERN GARDENS: Some corners of southern gardens are sunny and dry out quickly, and for these locations shrubs are required that will grow with a moderate amount of water. These include rock-roses (*Cistus*), correa, Australian bluebells, plumbago, and *Fremontia mexicana.*

FOR EXTREME NORTHERN WINTERS: In severe climates, such as in northern Minnesota, the native shrubs are more reliable than many of the standard cultivated kinds because they are sure to be hardy. A less extensive variety of native shrubs is found than farther south, but proper selection makes available bloom from earliest spring to midsummer, and colorful fruit and foliage from then on to late fall and early winter.

These include: leatherwood, fly-honeysuckle, shadblow (*Amelanchier*), red-berried elder (*Sambucus pubens*), red osier (*Cornus stonifera*), pagoda dogwood, (*C. alternifolia*), high-bush cranberry (*Viburnum trilogum*), arrowwood (*V. dentatum*), mountain maple (*Acer spicatum*), black chokeberry (*Aronia melanocarpa*), winterberry or swamp holly (*Ilex verticillata*), dwarf or low birch (*Betula pumila*), comon hazelnut (*Corylus americana*), hawthorn, meadowsweet (*Spirea alba*), buckthorn, sumac and northern sandcherry.

Most hardy species rose for northern gardens is the meadow or smooth rose, *Rosa blanda,* so-called because it is often without prickles. It will grow to six feet in a sunny location, and bears pink blossoms in spring.

SHRUBS FOR WET PLACES: In low, swampy areas where the soil may be quite acid only a few selected shrubs can be grown. Among the most attractive of these are: many varieties of alder (*Alnus*) with their early spring catkins; red and black chokeberry (*Aronia arbutifolia* and *A. melanocarpa*); swamp azalea; spicebush, (*Benzoin aestivale*); buttonbush, blossoming in mid-summer; St. John's Wort, (*Hypericum densiflorum*); inkberry; winterberry; swamp rose (*Rosa palustris*); pussywillow (*Salix discolor*); blueberry; and several viburnums—the arrowwood and nannyberry.

SHRUBS FOR SHADY PLACES: Among the shrubs already mentioned are some that will stand shade for more than half the day. They are: chokeberry, Chinese and pontic azalea, spicebush, Thunberg barberry, Jersey-tea, buttonbush, coral, panicle, and gray dogwood, *Hydrangea arborescens*, regel and California privet, holly grape, rhododendron, fragrant sumac, snowberry, coralberry, arrowwood, nannyberry, and weigela.

Others which will stand partial shade are: *Acanthopanax pentaphyllus;* box (*Buxus sempervirens*); sweetshrub (*Calycanthus floridus*); summersweet (*Clethra alnifolia*); white fringetree (*Chionocanthus virginica*); winter-hazel (*Corylopsis spicata*); witch-hazel (*Hamamelis virginica*); rose-of-Sharon (*Hypericum calycinum*); goldflower (*H. moserianum*); Japanese hypericum (*H. patulum*); morrow and tartar honeysuckle; southern wax myrtle (*Myrica cerifera*); stagger-bush (*Pieris mariana*); jetbead (*Rhodotypos kerrioides*); mountain currant (*Ribes alpinum*); flowering raspberry (*Rubus odoratus*); maple-leaf viburnum (*Viburnum acerifolium*); and prickly ash (*Zanthoxylum americanum*).

SHRUBS WITH EDIBLE FRUIT:

Shrubs which serve as ornamentals and can also supply food for the family make themselves doubly valuable. Many bush-fruits supply large quantities of vitamin C, particularly some of the lesser known and used berries and haws.

High on the vitamin C list is the fruit of *Rosa rugosa,* a hardy species rose that may be grown in hot dry places, in severe winter latitudes, in rich or poor soil, and even near the sea. A well-grown plant will attain 15 feet, with glassy somewhat crumpled foliage and white, pink, or purple flowers in spring. Rugosa hips are useful for their extract, which may be added to fruit juices, jellies, or other foods for additional vitamin C. *See also* ROSA RUGOSA.

Nanking cherry produces another vitamin C-rich fruit. This tall, rounded shrub, also called tomentosa cherry, (*Prunus tomentosa*) is an early flowering species which opens its pink-white blossoms early in April. The cherries, which develop in June, are sweet and may be juiced to make a delicious drink.

The fruit of the Nanking cherry (Prunus tomentosa) develops in June. The cherries are sweet, and will make a tasty, nutritious summer drink.

Japanese quince is an early flowering border shrub useful in any sunny location. It is especially good because it blooms and fruits well despite clipping.

For a taller growing variety, common garden quince may be planted. While it lacks the glossy foliage of the Japanese forms, it offers larger pinkish-white flowers and larger fruit.

Two cornelian-cherry dogwoods rate high on the list of edible-fruited shrubs. Besides their yellow spring flowers and green summer foliage, they produce large quantities of attractive oblong red fruit in fall. Fine-flavored jelly may be made from the tart fruit.

Purpleleaf sandcherry is a medium-sized plant with reddish-purplish foliage that remains unchanged throughout the growing season; edible purplish-black fruit in fall.

European and Asian Blackthorn are tall bushes of twiggy growth bearing white flowers in May and good sized blue fruit in fall.

Beach plum (found mostly on the Atlantic coast), sand cherry (Great Lakes Shore), western sand cherry—these three shrubby plants, often used to hold sandy soil in place, have whitish flowers with berries $\frac{1}{2}$ to $\frac{3}{4}$ of an inch wide, which are wonderful for jam and jelly.

Some years ago, Prof. A. J. Riker of the Univeristy of Wisconsin developed the viking currant which makes a very suitable clipped hedge. It's especially recommended, not only for the red fruit, but also because it is rust-resistant.

The elderberry or American elder with its summertime fragrance has long been a favorite roadside shrub. The juicy, purplish-black berries ripen in August. Since they are coarse growers, elders are not recommended where space is limited.

If your soil is acid, consider the highbush blueberry as a shrub. Its sizable, frosty-blue fruits are both attractive and flavorful, and the small bell-shaped white flowers make a pretty picture. Highbush blueberries save their finest appearance for later on in the season, when the autumn foliage takes on a brilliant scarlet.

Even the viburnum family has something to offer in the way of fruit. Several years ago, the United States Department of Agriculture chose three seedling forms of the American cranberry bush viburnum because of the size, quality, flavor and high pectin content of their fruit. They were Wentworth, with large red berries ripening in August; Hahs, a midseason variety growing more erect; and Andrews with large, late-maturing fruit. All three are first-class ornamentals that are attractive in flower and have good foliage. Another viburnum whose fruit is rated valuable for jelly and jam is the native blackhaw. This makes a tall bush, with oval blue-black berries.

The Rosezalea, tall, broad-growing shrub develops a covering of crab-apple blooms in May and June, followed in late summer by attractive red fruit.

The European or Asiatic blackthorn or sloe (*Prunus spinosa*) is a tall twiggy bush whose white flowers open early before it leafs out. Berries in fall are bright blue.

Clove currant (*Ribes odoratum*) opens its spicy yellow blossoms in May. Its large black fruit which ripens in late summer is somewhat like a gooseberry in shape and flavor.

A little-used shrub, the only member of the custard apple family hardy in the north, is the pawpaw (*Asimina triloba*). Purplish three-parted blossoms open in spring when the leaves unfold, to be followed later in the fall by a sweet-flavored three to five inch banana-shaped fruit.—*E. L. Kammerer.*

FORCING SHRUB BLOSSOMS: Many early spring-flowering shrubs will provide flowers during the late winter months if branches are cut and brought into the house. Especially good for forcing are varieties which open their blossoms before their leaves.

At any time after its leaves have dropped in the fall forsythia will open its flowers indoors. Branches cut in December may take four or five weeks to bloom. Those cut nearer to the natural outdoor blossoming period will open more quickly in the house. Bloom may be hastened if the branches are sprayed with warm water daily.

Other shrubs which may be forced indoors include Japanese quince, pussywillow, redbud or Judastree, cornelian cherry, spiraea (*Thunbergia* species), Juneberry, goldenberry, magnolia, and filbert. Color is completely lacking in some of the more delicately tinted blossoms when they are forced. In others, the color will grow stronger the closer to normal flowering time the forcing is done. *See also names of individual shrubs;* LAYERING; PRUNING; EVERGREEN; FORCING.

SIDALCEA: Known also as false mallow. A genus of annual and perennial flowers of the mallow family, growing to three feet, and resembling small hollyhocks. Flowers are white, pink, red, and purple. Leaves are alternate, palmate. Only the perennial species are cultivated, but they are not reliably perennial and are better treated as biennials. Require rich sandy soil. May be propagated by seed or division, but if the latter, should be lifted and divided about every other year.

Checkerbloom or wild hollyhock (*S. malvaeflora*) has rose flowers, or in varieties purple or pink; *S. candida,* a native of the Rocky mountains, has pure white flowers; and a number of attractive hybrids are offered in pink or satiny rose flowers as *S. hybrida.*

SILAGE: A succulent forage such as corn, alfalfa, grass, or sorghum which is cut into short lengths and preserved by compaction and fermentation in the absence of oxygen.

A silo is any building or other storage receptacle for preserving cut green feed in the absence of air. It may have wood, stone, metal, glass or earth as its air-excluding walls, or the silage itself may serve as a barrier. *See also* HAY.

SILENE: *see* LYCHNIS

SILICA: *see* LATERITE

SILK MILL WASTES: Silk is the thread spun by the silkworm and a material comparable to wool or feathers, substances very rich in protein and easy to break up in composting. The main value of these substances is their nitrogen and phosphorus content. Silkworm cocoons contain about ten per cent nitrogen, 1.8 per cent phosphoric acid and over one per cent potassium. By-products from silk mills vary in their composition, but are frequently among the most useful wastes obtainable. The nitrogen content of one sample was 8.37 per cent and the phosphoric acid value 1.14 per cent.

SILK-TASSEL TREE: *see* QUININE BUSH

SILK TREE: (*Albizzia julibrissin rosea*) The silk tree belongs to the Legume family. Although *Albizzia* is a large genus of tropical shrubs and trees, the Silk Tree is hardy as far north as Boston. It is a small tree with a broad spreading crown with much compounded leaves having the appearance of the feathery leaves of acacia or mimosa. It produces exotic-looking, light-pink feathery flowers in slender-stalked, compact heads. The fruits are flat pods about five inches long and one inch wide.

The Silk Tree is highly ornamental, and tends to create a distinctly tropical atmosphere in a northern garden. New plants can be easily propagated from seed under glass. It may be planted as a specimen tree in a lawn.

SILT: A primary source of plant nutrients.

Silt particles are microscopic pieces of rock—much smaller than sand—

that help make up soil. Silt of the non-quartz minerals is rich in plant food.

SIMPLE LAYERING: *see* LAYERING

SISYRINCHIUM: Known also as blue-eyed grass or satinflower. A genus of small half-hardy to hardy perennials of the iris family, with grass-like leaves and flowers with sepals, petals, and stamens in threes, in blue, yellow, or reddish-purple flat-topped clusters. They grow wild in rich meadows and swamps, may be grown in the border where they make attractive clumps. Easily grown in any garden soil, they prefer rich moist places, and may be naturalized in the wild garden. Propagated from seed or division of fibrous roots.

S. angustifolium grows to two feet, with violet-blue flowers.

S. californicum, native to Oregon and California, is called golden-eyed grass for its bright yellow flowers; to one foot.

S. graminoides has light green leaves and blue flowers.

SKIMMIA: Tender shrubs native in Asia which may be grown, where the climate suits them, in cities. They are slow-growing evergreens, belonging to the rue family. Hardy south of Washington, D. C., and on the west coast. Alternate dotted leaves, aromatic when crushed. Small white flowers and red berry-like fruits which persists. *S. japonica* has male and female flowers, the staminate fragrant and larger, and usually though not always on separate plants. Grows to five feet. *S. reevsiana* is a smaller plant, and its flowers all contain both stamens and pistils. Also somewhat more tender than *S. japonica.*

SKULLCAP: (*Scutellaria*) A genus of herbs, usually perennial and sometimes shrubby of the mint family, *Labiatae.* Small plants, growing no more than one foot, they are useful in the rock garden or border for their often silvery foliage and spikes of

scarlet, yellow, blue, or violet flowers. Herbaceous species are propagated by seed or division. Shrubby species increased by cuttings of half-tender wood in spring. One kind, *S. ventenati,* which has long racemes of scarlet flowers, is a greenhouse annual. *S. indica* variety *japonica* has intense blue flowers in dense four-inch clusters. *S. orientalis* has gray-green foliage and yellowish flowers. *S. alpina,* with clusters of purple and white flowers, is a rapid spreader. *S. angustifolia* has large solitary violet-blue flowers.

SKUNK: Many investigators have made detailed food studies of skunks and have shown that their principal food is insects and most of the insects taken are injurious to plant life. When fruits are ripe and plentiful, they constitute an important part of skunk diet. Most of these are gathered from the surface of the ground, so represent waste as far as man is concerned. Mice constitute another important food item and their destruction is favorable to man. An occasional bird is taken and not infrequently they were previously injured or already dead when taken by the skunk. Under these circumstances, this too is a service to man.

Skunks deserve much credit for digging out the June bug or May beetle in both the larval and adult stages.

The species is definitely more helpful than harmful in the long run. However, skunks do cause damage later in the fall, invading and sometimes breaking hives in their search for food. Damage can be prevented if hives are placed on benches or stands, since skunks are ground feeders mainly.—*LeRoy Stegeman.*

SLAG: *see* BASIC SLAG

SLIP: Referring to a cutting taken from a plant for propagation purposes. *See also* CUTTING.

SLIPPERWORT: *see* CALCEOLARIA

SLUDGE: *see* SEWAGE SLUDGE

SLUGS AND SNAILS: Grayish insects with worm-like legless bodies. Each snail and slug builds its own highway by secreting a slimy material which hardens into a silvery trail. This material not only smooths the way for these creatures, but it forces them to stick to the trail whether it be right side up or upside down. Slugs can even form mucous ropes for suspending themselves from supports or for going from one level to another. When snails decide to move it takes them about 15 days to travel one mile, while slugs can cover the same distance in about eight days. Slugs differ from snails by having no shell or a mere rudiment of a shell.

These animals cannot stand dry conditions. During periods of drought, snails place a pane of "glass" over the entrance to their shell house. A film of mucous is stretched across the entrance to the shell. This quickly hardens into a transparent "window pane." In the same way, they close their house for the winter. But in winter the door is barred with a heavy pane that is not transparent.

Mulched gardens are always so moist that snails and slugs direct their silvery highways toward them. Under the mulch they find welcome relief from the drying effects of the noonday sun. The organic gardener must use common sense and understanding in dealing with them. A thoughtless few will throw up their hands and yell for help, but not so with the nature student.

F. C. King of Cumberland, England, an unusually observant gardener and writer suggests that the lack of earthworms and consequently of worm casts on the land today is giving rise to the terrible slug menace. Worm casts are alkaline and thus inimical to slugs which seek a more acid soil for their abode. Mr. L. Ford, another Englishman, says that slugs prefer wilted weeds to growing plants. According to Mr. Ford, slugs will (1) attack seedlings mercilessly if the soil is clean cultivated and lacks humus, (2) attack seedlings on clean cultivated soil dressed with ripe compost, but (3) will not touch seedlings if there is a top-dressing of (a) unripe compost, or (b) ripe compost plus chaff, straw, or wilted vegetable matter.

CONTROL: Snails and slugs tend to be nocturnal, *i.e.* they move about and feed at night but rest in a dark, cool, moist place by day. Advantage may be taken of this habit to eliminate them from your garden if they are troublesome. Place shingles or other similar materials in the garden to serve as traps. Each morning destroy the individuals which have hidden away under the traps for the day.

The body of snails and slugs is soft and highly sensitive to such sharp objects as sand and slag and to such dry and slightly corrosive substances as slaked lime and wood ashes. A narrow border of sharp sand or cinders around a bed or border will serve as an effective barrier against them. A sprinkling of slaked lime or wood ashes along a row of tender plants will keep the snails and slugs away because their soft bodies are sensitive to these materials.

Snails and slugs may prove to be at times mortal enemies of such perennials as delphiniums, foxgloves, and primroses. "A strong man armed keepeth his palace in peace." Instead of battling with these creatures which are always ready to wage destruction upon your plants, it will be the wiser part of valor to build a defense against them.

Winter is the time when snails and slugs feed on the roots of the perennial plants, and January is the month when they appear in the largest numbers and cause the greatest damage to the unprotected crowns of the plants. The defense against these creatures should be built in the fall. Before the first frost stiffens the ground, remove all soil from above the crowns of the plants. Watch carefully for any slugs which may be in this, and destroy them immediately. Then cover the whole top of the plant and fill the entire excavation up to the surface of the ground with coarse river sand. This rough sand is sharp and painful to the tender bodies of the slugs, and will act efficiently in keeping them away from the roots. In the spring when the plants are cultivated and humus is added to the earth, the sand will become mixed with the soil and assist with the needed drainage of the soil.—*Dr. William Eyster.*

See also INSECT CONTROL.

SMALL FRUITS: *see names of individual fruits;* BRAMBLE FRUITS

SMARTWEED: (*Polygonum*) There are many species of this pest plant (46 in northeastern North America). A number of these contain juices that are bitterly pungent or peppery and cause smarting or irritation when in contact with the eyes and nostrils. Occasionally a skin rash occurs among people who are particularly sensitive.

The common smartweed (*P. hydropiper*) is probably the most irritating. Found primarily in damp or wet places, it has weak, reddish stems, willow-shaped alternate leaves and greenish flowers. Another widely found species is the Lady's thumb smartweed (*P. persicaria*). This differs from the common smartweed by the presence of a somewhat triangular, purple blotch on each leaf, which gives it the popular name "Lady's thumb."

Frequent mowing will prevent seed set and thus eliminate plants. By improving drainage, these plants will not thrive. *See also* POLYGONUM.

SMILACINA: *see* VAGNERA

SMILAX: Known also as greenbrier. A genus of tendril-climbing vines of the lily family. Smilax is the common name for *Asparagus asparagoides,* used by florists for ornamental purposes, and grown almost entirely in greenhouses.

Greenbriers are sometimes cut and used decoratively, and when sold by florists are usually called "southern smilax." Not many of the greenbriers are cultivated, and at least one, *S. glauca,* or cat-brier, is a viciously barbed vine, having stout, hooked thorns. It grows in dry places from Massachusetts to Florida. Genus also includes carrion-flower (*S. herbacea*) which is less barbed than the others, with stems and leaves that usually die down in the fall, after producing flat clusters of bluish-black fruit.

The smilax of the florists also belongs to the lily family, and is a graceful branching vine with spade-shaped leaves about an inch long, small white flowers from the leaf axils followed by dark purple berries. In the greenhouse, it is grown in beds kept at 60 to 65°, and trained on strings to climb upward. It is kept shaded in spring and summer. Soil must be rich and porous in order to keep the vines producing sprays for cutting over a period of three or four years. Propagation is by seed sown in February, and later potted before being transferred to the bench, where they are spaced seven by ten inches.

SMOTHER CROP: Referring to plants, such as buckwheat, that are sometimes thickly sown in a field or yard that has become overrun with weeds. As the term implies, the purpose of the seeded crop is to smother the weeds. Later all the vegetation can be worked into the soil, similar to any green manure crop.

SNAILS: *see* SLUGS AND SNAILS

SNAKE-MOUTH: *see* POGONIA

SNAKE PLANT: *see* SANSEVIERIA

SNAKES: Snakes consume enormous numbers of harmful rodents and insects.

There are about 220 distinct kinds of snakes extant on the North American continent, all working for man's continued existence. The United

States has only four families of snakes with defense mechanisms which sometimes prove hazardous to man: the rattlesnake (of which there are 13 main species), the copperhead, the cotton-mouth moccasin, and the coral snake.

SNAP BEANS: *see* BEANS, BUSH

SNAPDRAGON: Hardy, late-blooming perennial or annual flowers that can be divided into three groups: tall —to four feet; intermediate—to 1½ feet; and dwarf—to under one foot. Popular for the color they add to the flower garden, snapdragons are also fine for cut flowers.

CULTURE: For early bloom start seeds indoors at least six to eight weeks before the last severe spring frost in your locality. Plant the seed in flats, or in pots if you prefer, in regular garden soil. Either scatter the seed or plant in rows on the surface, covering them lightly with approximately ⅛ inch of soil. Tamp the soil lightly to make good soil-seed contact, but be careful not to pack the soil. Keep the soil moist and place the container in a warm, sunny location. The seed may be rather slow in germinating, but after the true leaves have formed, the growth is usually pretty rapid. When sunny spring days come along, set the flat of young seedlings outdoors, bringing them in at night. The plants will develop and grow faster in the open ground if they are permitted to "harden" or "cure off" for at least a week outdoors before transplanting to the permanent garden location.

Seeds may also be planted directly outside when the soil has warmed up, but an early start indoors lengthens the flowering season.

Snapdragons prefer a sunny location and a well-drained soil that is moderately rich. Before planting the seedlings or seed, add some compost or leaf mold to the soil, mixing it well. Water the seedlings for several days until their roots are well established.

Water throughout the season during dry spells. Set the seedlings about eight to ten inches apart in rows or in groups as you prefer. To encourage the growth of flower-bearing side branches, pinch out the central bud. By keeping faded flowers cut, you will also encourage more blooming.

VARIETIES: The dwarf varieties are generally used for edgings, the intermediate for massing in beds, and the taller types for use in groups in the border. All of them may be used as cut flowers.

Plant breeders have done much work on the snapdragon, perfecting bigger blooms, longer spikes, double flowers, and rust-resistant strains. It is important to select the rust-resistant varieties because this disease can be a serious handicap. Some good varieties are: tall—Loveliness, Copper Shades, and Snow Giant; intermediate —Pink Shades, Rosalie, and Velvet Beauty; dwarf—Ruby, Apple Blossom, and Gypsy Girl.

SNOW: Although snow does not contain any appreciable quantity of plant nutrients, it often acts as a natural buffer or mulch, helping to protect the soil and plants it covers from severe freezing and heaving. In some cases, it has been said that the gradual thawing of snow improves the soil's texture.

SNOWBERRY: Common name applied to two different plants, *Symphoricarpos albus,* the snowberry bush, and *Chiogenes hispidula,* snowberry vine.

Snowberry bush is a member of the honeysuckle family which makes a hardy slender shrub easily grown in any soil in North American gardens. It has oval leaves, pinkish flowers, and fat white berries which attract birds in early winter. Propagated by seeds, cuttings, suckers, and division.

Snowberry vine is a creeping evergreen of the heath family, which grows in cold wet places in the wild in the northern part of the United States. Can be grown only in wild garden or rock garden under ever-

The oval leaves, pinkish flowers and fat white berries make the snowberry bush (Symphoricarpos albus) a very attractive shrub in the landscape.

greens where the summers are not too hot. Flowers are white small bells, followed by white berries of the same size. Propagated by cuttings and division.

SNOWDRIFT: *see* SWEET ALYSSUM

SNOWDROP: (*Galanthus*) Attractive flowering plants that bloom for weeks in early spring. Common snowdrop (*G. nivalis*) grows to about one foot high; flowers are green inside, white outside. They do best in light, humus-rich soil, preferring partial shade. Giant snowdrop (*G. elwesi*), growing to about 1½ feet, does best in sandy soil, should have more sun. Mulch with compost in fall.

For best effect, mass plantings should be made. Plant bulbs around Labor Day, placing them three inches deep and apart. *See also* FLOWER GARDENING; BULBS.

SNOWDROP TREE: (*Halesia*) Also known as Silverbell tree. Growing on the banks of streams from Virginia and Illinois south to Florida is the beautiful Snowdrop or Silverbell tree. This small tree bears clusters of white bell-shaped flowers which appear with the leaves but on the twigs of the previous season. The pendant white

flowers which clothe the branches in spring make the Silverbell one of the loveliest of small hardy trees. The fruit is an oblong, rather fleshless dry drupe. By proper pruning, this small tree can be kept small in the home grounds.

SNOWFLAKE: (*Leucojum*) A genus of bulbous plants of the amaryllis family, having drooping white flowers at the top of the hollow stalks, with narrow basal leaves which do not appear until after the flowers in the fall-flowering species, but with the flowers in the spring-flowering. Bulbs are planted four to five inches deep in sandy soil, and left undisturbed.

Spring snowflake (*L. vernum*), also called St. Agnes flower, has solitary flowers that appear about a month after snowdrops, white, tipped with green, and on stalks nine to 12 inches high.

Summer snowflake (*L. aestivum*) grows a little taller, with its blossoms in clusters of two to eight on a stalk.

Autumn snowflake (*L. autumnale*) has very slender stalks on which one to three blossoms open. This species is more tender than the others, needing winter protection in the North.

SOAPBARK TREE: (*Quillaja saponaria*) Occasionally grown in Florida and southern California, this evergreen tree comes from South America. About 60 feet tall, it is fairly ornamental, but the chief interest lies in its bark, from which a lather can be worked up.

SOAPBERRY: (*Sapindus*) A tropical American genus of trees and shrubs, with berries rich in saponin, which lathers like soap and is used for cleansing. Pinnate leaves, small flowers in clusters. It grows in dry sandy or rocky soil, can be propagated by seed or cuttings made in spring. Grown in the south of Florida for ornament.

S. drummondii is a deciduous tree growing to 50 feet, with ten-inch clusters of yellowish-white flowers followed by yellow berries which turn black.

S. saponaria is an evergreen that grows to 30 feet, flowers in ten-inch white clusters, fruit shiny and yellow-brown.

SOAPWORT: *see* SAPONARIA

SOD: A thick stand of grass or other vegetation forming a compact layer of herbage on the surface of the soil.

SOIL: The loose top layer of the earth's surface that supports the growth of plants. A soil consists mainly of four parts—minerals, organic matter, water and air.

An average topsoil of an active garden or farm might consist of about 25 per cent air, 25 per cent water, 49 per cent minerals and only one per cent organic matter. In a virgin prairie soil the organic matter could go to more than ten per cent. There are some soils that might contain up to 20 per cent of organic matter. The amount of organic matter in the subsoil gradually goes down until, at a depth of about 30 feet it may amount to only 1/8 of one per cent.

PROFILE: In discussing soil, the word profile means a side view of a vertical section of earth. If we could slice away a section of it we could then regard the profile and see the various layers down to bed-rock. A soil profile is often visible at a place, where a road has been cut through a hill. An average profile might consist of five or six layers beginning with the rock below, and going through the various stages of sub-soil, to the uppermost layer, or topsoil. These layers, called horizons, are extremely significant in their effect on the processes of plant growth.

How SOIL IS FORMED: Originally the entire earth was one mass of rock and the only living things were microbes—single-celled organisms. These bacteria and fungi through their activities liberated carbon dioxide and certain organic and inorganic acids which have a solvent action upon rocks, beginning the process of their breakdown into soil. The dead bodies of these organisms were the beginnings of the organic matter which was

This side view of a vertical section of earth shows the soil profile which comprises several layers, which are known as A, B and C horizons.

mixed with the tiny fragments of rocks to form soil. The action of heat and cold wind and rain, glacier movement and other influences and biological factors soon took a hand in the procedure. The difference in temperature between day and night caused expansion and contraction which produced open seams in the rock and detachment of fragments, permitting water to enter deeper into the rock.

Part of the process of soil formation consisted of the decaying remains of the low forms of plants such as lichens and mosses which soon began to cover the exposed rocks, digging their tiny tentacles into the rock. This slowly formed a film of soil over them. This bit of soil provided the foothold for the plants which are the next step up the evolutionary scale—the ferns, and gradually as the soil thickened other higher plants and trees began to grow, until there came into being overgrown jungles.

We must remember that without the soil organisms—the bacteria, fungi, actynomycetes, yeasts, etc., no soil formation could take place. The making of soil is a biological process, meaning that living forces take a prominent part in it. We might say, therefore, that the process of soil formation consists of physical, chemical, and biological elements. The physical part is accomplished by the wind and the rain, the chemical by the excretions and respirations of the microbes, and the biological by the other activities of these organisms.

Soil has formed not only from the original bedrock, but also by rock that has been moved by glacial and other forces. And soil formation is still going on. Soil is constantly being created by the same forces which formed it originally—that is, climate, decaying plant matter, etc. Deep down at bedrock, some of the rock is still gradually turning to sub-soil. It takes these processes perhaps 500 years to make one inch of soil, but man with his destructive farming practices can destroy an inch in only a few years of soil mining—that is, farming that only takes out, putting nothing back that has staying power. It has been estimated that in about 200 years of farming in the United States, over 60 per cent of the topsoil has been destroyed.

Soils are classified into groups, series, and types. The groups are based largely on climatic factors and associated vegetation, the series on parent material, and the soil types on the texture of the soil. The following information is based on government agricultural reports:

TEXTURE: By texture is meant the relative amounts of the various sizes of particles making up the soil. These particles range in size from stones and gravel, through sand and silt to clay, the particles of which may be too small to be seen under the strongest microscope.

STRUCTURE: Refers to the grouping of individual particles into larger pieces, or granules. Good granulation or crumb structure of the heavier soils is essential to good results. Sandy soils show little if any granulation, due to the coarseness of their component particles. With soils containing a substantial percentage of clay, working them when wet results in destruction of the granular structure. Excessive tramping by livestock under like conditions is likely to have a similar effect. See also COMPACTION.

Alternate freezing and thawing, or wetting and drying, and penetration of the soil mass by plant roots, are natural forces which favor the formation of soil granules, or aggregates. Such aggregation is most highly developed in soils near neutrality in their reaction: both strongly acid and strongly alkaline soils tend to "run together" and lose their structural character. Tillage also tends to break down the structure of many soils.

POROSITY: Associated with both texture and structure is pore space, or porosity. These spaces may be large, in the case of coarse, sandy soils or those with well-developed granulation. In heavy soils, containing mostly finer clay particles, the pore spaces may be too small for plant roots or soil water to penetrate readily. Good soils have 40 to 60 per cent of their bulk occupied with pore space, which may be filled with either water or air, neither of which can truly be said to be more important than the other.

Here, as in all other soil relationships, a satisfactory balance is important for productivity. Too much water slows the release of soil nitrogen, depletes mineral nutrients, and otherwise hinders proper plant growth. Too much air speeds nitrogen release beyond the capacity of plants to utilize it, and much of it is lost. The stored water in an overly-aerated soil evaporates into the atmosphere and is lost to plants.

WATER: Soil water occurs in three forms, designated as hygroscopic, capillary and gravitational. The hygroscopic soil water is chemically bound in the soil constituents and is unavailable to plants. Gravitational water is that which normally drains out of the pore spaces of the soil after a rain. If drainage is poor, it is this water which causes the soil to be soggy and unproductive. Excessive drainage hastens the time when capillary water runs short and plants suffer from drought.

It is the capillary water upon which plants depend very largely for their supply of moisture. Hence the capacity of a soil to hold water against the pull of gravity is of great importance in ordinary agriculture. Organic matter and good structure add to this supply of water in soils.

But plants cannot extract the last drop of capillary water from a soil, since the attraction of soil materials for it is greater than the pull exerted by the plant roots. The point at which these two forces are just equal is called the "wilting coefficient" of a soil. This term is used to express the percentage of water in a soil at the time the loss from transpiration exceeds the renewal of the water by capillary means. Medium-textured loams and silt loams, because of their faster rate of movement of moisture from lower depths to the root zone, and the fact that they can bring up moisture from greater depths than either sands or clays, provide the best conditions of available but not excessive soil moisture for best plant growth.

EROSION: Generally erosion works this way: first, the main loss is by sheet erosion; each time it rains, the runoff water removes a thin layer of surface soil. Then as the topsoil becomes thinner, miniature gullies appear. After most of the surface soil

is gone, gullies become the main problem.

Usually there's a clear difference between the topsoil and subsoil. The subsoil is finer-textured, more plastic, and lighter in color than the topsoil. Here's how erosion is classified:

No apparent erosion. All or nearly all the surface soil is present. Depth to subsoil is 14 inches or more. The surface may have received some recent deposits as the result of erosion from higher ground.

Slight. Depth to subsoil varies from seven to 14 inches. Plowing at usual depths will not expose the subsoil.

Moderate. Depth to subsoil varies from three to seven inches. Some subsoil is mixed with the surface soil in plowing.

Severe. Depth to subsoil is less than three inches. Surface soil is mixed with subsoil when the land is plowed. Gullies are beginning to be a problem.

Very severe. Subsoil is exposed. Gullies are frequent.

Very severe gullies. Deep gullies or blowouts have ruined the land for agricultural purposes.

There is a direct relationship between erosion and a soil's ability for intake of air and water. For example, when the soil surface becomes compacted, the danger of erosion increases, while the intake of water and air decreases.

SOIL SERIES: This refers to a subdivision of soil groups. A series is often given the name of a town, river or other geographical feature near which the soil was first identified. Since many soils in this country are young, the original geological characteristics of the soil materials is still evident. Thus members of the same soil series, or subdivisions, signify soils which have developed from the same kind of parent material and by the same processes.

A soil phase is a subdivision on the basis of some important deviation such as erosion, slope or stoniness. It indicates the departure or difference from the overall soil description.

SOIL GROUPS: All soils are composed of particles varying greatly in size and shape. In order to classify them by texture as well as physical properties, four fundamental soil groups are recognized: gravels, sands, loams and clays. (The last three make up most of the world's arable lands.)

The sand group includes all soils of which the silt and clay make up less than 20 per cent by weight. Its mineral particles are visible to the naked eye and are irregular in shape. Because of this, their water-holding capacity is low, but they possess good drainage and aeration, and are usually in a loose, friable condition.

In contrast, particles in a clay soil are very fine (invisible under ordinary microscope), become sticky and cement-like.

Texture of the loam class cannot be as clearly defined, since its mechanical composition is about midway between sand and clay. Professors T. Lyon and Harry Buckman in their book, *The Nature and Properties of Soils,* (Macmillan, New York) describe loams "as such a mixture of sand, silt and clay particles as to exhibit light and heavy properties in about equal proportions. . . . Because of this intermixture of coarse, medium and fine particles, usually they possess the desirable qualities both of sand and clay without exhibiting those undesirable properties, as extreme looseness and low water capacity on the one hand and stickiness, compactness, and very slow air and water movement on the other."

Fortunately for the gardeners and farmers in the United States, most soils are in the loam classification. The majority of soils are mixtures; the more common class names appear below: (Combinations are given when one size of particles is evident enough to affect the texture of the loam. For example, a loam in which sand is dominant will be classified as a sandy loam of some kind).

Sandy Soils

Gravelly sands	Fine sands
Coarse sands	Loamy sands
Medium sands	

Loamy Soils

Coarse sandy loams
Medium sandy loams
Fine sandy loams
Silty loams and stony silt loams
Clay loams

Clayey Soils

Stony clays	Silty clays
Gravelly clays	Clays
Sandy clays	

You can get a good idea of your soil's texture and class by rubbing it between the thumb and the fingers or in the palm of the hand. Sand particles are gritty; silt has a floury or talcum-powder feel when dry, and is only moderately plastic when moist, while the clayey material is harsh when dry and very plastic and sticky when wet.

Observe Profs. Lyon and Buckman: "This method is used in all field operations, especially in soil survey, land classification and the like. Accuracy . . . can be acquired by the careful study of known samples." If you're interested in developing an ability to classify soils, contact the local county agent for soil samples that are correctly classified.

The ideal structure is granular, where the rounded aggregates (or clusters) of soil lie loosely and readily shake apart. When the granules are especially porous, the term crumb is applied.

SOIL CLASSIFICATIONS: Descriptions of soil classifications for podzol, chernozem and laterite soils have been discussed under those entries, which see. Following is a discussion of other types:

TUNDRA: The word Tundra

comes from the Finnish word Tunturi which means a flat, barren plateau. The Tundra lacks hills, and there is poor growth. There is much marsh and swamp. It consists of treeless plains, and is closely related to the bog soils. The land is a mat of grass, moss, sedges and lichen. Some berries, herbs and dwarf shrubs grow. There is a tendency for the land to form peat. Cultivated crops are leafy vegetables which thrive under cool-growing conditions and potatoes which are grown from sprouts. There is a limited amount of dairying, and in some sheltered areas, hay and grain.

The soil is very shallow which is termed a lithosol type of soil. The topsoil is somewhat on the peaty side, under which is a thin layer of humus. Below that is about two or three inches of yellow-brown soil, beneath which is six inches of gray, sticky clay. Underneath the entire tundra region is a frozen layer that in some places extends downward for a thousand feet. This is called the permafrost. Only a few surface feet thaw out in the summer.

The Tundra soils are in the Greenland, Siberia, Arctic Ocean and Bering Sea regions. In some protected areas, alpine vegetation and forests will flourish. The activity of bacteria and fungi are at low ebb, and the soil is not necessarily acid.

PRAIRIE SOILS: This is a semi-podzolic type of soil, but differs from the latter in that no trees grew in this region in the formative period. The organic matter is high. There is only one prairie soil region in the world and it is in the United States, covering an area of close to 300,000 square miles. This soil type includes most of Iowa, about three-fourths of Illinois, the southeast of Minnesota, the eastern half of Oklahoma and Missouri, a part of eastern Kansas, and some of central Texas. Soils somewhat similar to prairies are located in Oregon, Washington, California and Idaho.

Prairie soils have a good granular structure and a high fertility. Some of the best farm land in the U. S. is of this type. It is a rich dark-brown, but as it goes southward it becomes more reddish. There is a heavy accumulation of humus, from the native grass residues and due to the hot dry summers which deterred the activities of the decay-producing microorganisms. In the formative period the grasses were more than six feet high. In some sections the humus layer is 20 inches deep.

The rainfall is from about 30 to 45 inches, spaced out nicely in the growing season, but there is usually a midsummer dry period. There is not the heavy rainfall of the podzol areas which cause a leaching of the minerals out of the top layer. The soil is not excessively acid.

Crops consist of the small grains, hay, corn, and soybeans. The farms are big and highly mechanized. Cattle raising and dairying are done on a big scale. This is the best soil in the country for growing the small grains and hay crops.

PLANOSOLS: These are soils of the poorly drained prairie lands located in southern Illinois and Iowa and northern Missouri and in a few places in the humid forest regions. They are relatively flat lands where under natural conditions there is little erosion but in cultivation, with poor management, they may suffer badly from the worst forms of soil destruction. There is always a hardpan or clay pan in the subsoil. The surface soil is acid and leached.

These are not very productive soils, and the practices of the organic method would be a must. The soils in the spring are often too wet to work. Because of the hardpan roots remain shallow. Crops suffer from extremes of climatic changes.

DESERT SOILS: Desert soils are in arid regions where grasses will not grow and are divided into three groups: (1) Desert, (2) Serozem

(Gray Desert), and (3) Red Desert. The Serozem and Red Desert soils are known as semi-desert soils. The desert soils have the lowest rainfall, the serozem having between eight to 11 inches of precipitation. On desert soils water is critically scarce and there is usually a death struggle for it. Erosion is a serious factor. In some years in desert areas there is no rainfall at all. In the red and serozem soils rainfall comes with more regularity.

TEMPERATURE: The serozems have the lowest temperature of the three types of desert soils, the average being between 45 and 50° F. The red soils will go up to about 60°, but the desert soils, as the name indicates, have the highest temperatures. An unusual feature pertaining to the latter is that there is wide variation between day and night temperature, being in many cases about 50°. This has been a factor in the process of soil formation in these areas in connection with the rock weathering, and due to the condensation of moisture, because of such fluctuating temperatures, there has developed more clay in the soils.

COLOR: Desert soils are usually gray in color, an indication of low organic matter which is the result of the sparse vegetation of this type of soil. The red soils have a variation in color from a light pink-gray to red-browns and red. The serozems are a gray to a light-gray brown. In Russian the name serozem means gray earth, in contrast to chernozem which means black earth.

The red color of the red soils was no doubt due to earlier conditions hundreds of thousands of years ago when the climate was more humidly tropical or subtropical and the weathering of rocks released iron into the soil.

GEOGRAPHY: The gray desert soils are located in Nevada, Utah, Oregon, Idaho and Washington in the Great Basin intermountain desert plains and plateaus. The red soils are in the hot arid areas from Texas to southeastern California, which includes southern Nevada, western Arizona and parts of New Mexico. The serozems are in the drier parts of the Great Basin areas in western Colorado, eastern Utah and smaller portions of Oregon and Idaho.

In the desert there grow shrubs like the horsebrush, white sage, Indian rice grass, rabbitbrush, and cactus. On the red soils there are the creosote bush, prickly pear, yucca, Mormon tea, wolfberry and mesquite. On the serozem there are black sagebrush, crested wheat grass, juniper, blue grama, etc.

Unless there is irrigation these lands are good only for cattle grazing, sheep raising being the main activity in some parts of these areas. When water is supplied in the form of irrigation the land becomes extremely fertile and a large variety of crops can be grown such as the grains, vegetables, fruits, beets and pasture crops. There is evidence, however, that the nutritional value of irrigated crops is inferior to crops grown in the conventional manner.

THE DESERT SOILS: In desert soils the humus content is very low, and there is an accumulation of salts in the surface. Under conditions of irrigation the soil suffers from alkali disease. These soils usually form a thin hard crust on the surface. Under the surface horizon there is a layer of calcium carbonate (lime) which in many cases becomes a hardpan. Underneath that the soil may be loose and crumbly.

In some places the blowing of the wind clears off sufficient soil to leave an accumulation of pebbles and stones which are referred to as desert pavement, a hard rocklike formation. Sometimes this covers large areas. As a general rule desert soils are sandy and gravelly. The content of organic matter is between 1/2 and 1 1/2 per cent, and conditions are usually on the alkaline side. See also ALKALI SOILS.

ADOBE SOILS: These soils should not be confused with desert soils. The terms are not synonymous. Adobe can occur any place where the rainfall is less than 20 inches, and there must be clearly defined wet and dry seasons. The word adobe is of Spanish origin and has reference to sun-dried bricks. This kind of soil varies from fine sand to heavy loam, and clay. Usually, however, it refers to heavy clay soils only. These soils occur in Nevada, Colorado, Wyoming, Utah, California, Oregon, Idaho, New Mexico, Arizona and Texas.

This type of soil cracks when dry into irregular but roughly cubical blocks. Many gardeners and farmers obtain poor results in adobe soils unless they furnish it with an abundance of organic matter. The latter spectacularly destroys the adobe quality which makes it so difficult to cultivate. Sensational results are obtained on adobe soils when the organic method is practiced. *See also* ADOBE SOILS.

CHESTNUT AND BROWN SOILS: These soils are closely related to the chernozems which see. They take in parts of the following states—Kansas, Texas, Oklahoma, Colorado, New Mexico, Idaho, Utah, Montana, Wyoming, Washington, Oregon and Arizona. Just as the chernozem, it has developed under grass, but due to the lower rainfall, the grasses were shorter than the chernozem and the amount of organic matter less. The natural vegetation in this region is shorter and more sparse than in the chernozem regions, the growth being of the steppe type.

Due to the small amount of rain and therefore a lack of leaching, a great deal of calcium carbonate (lime) accumulates in the subsoil. Where rainfall is very low, the calcium carbonate will be found nearer the surface. Usually gypsum will also be found in the subsoil (calcium sulphate). Under certain conditions the soil becomes powdery because of lack of rain, giving rise to dust-bowl blow-ing. There is a loss of crumb structure in the topsoil.

The chestnut soils are brown, reddish brown and red in color because they contain less organic matter than the chernozem, and sometimes because of oxidation of iron, due to higher temperatures. There are also grey and yellow chestnut soils.

These soils are referred to as the spring wheat belt. Cotton, corn, small grains and sorghum are the principal crops. Cattle grazing is done on a larger scale than in the chernozems. Under irrigation a much larger variety of crops are grown including orcharding and sugar beets. The pasturage consists mainly of dried buffalo and grama grasses.

The rainfall in these regions is only between ten to 15 inches, and dry farming therefore has to be practiced on irrigated land in order to conserve the moisture. A grain is grown one year followed by fallowing the next, a type of fallow in which no crop is grown, the land merely being cultivated. This eventually leads to dust-bowl conditions when an exceptionally dry period comes. The dust-bowl region is in New Mexico, Texas, Kansas, Oklahoma and Colorado.

RENDZINA: Rendzinas represent dark soils on certain kinds of limestone formation, with a very high humus content, sometimes up to ten per cent, and is found in humid regions. The color ranges from black to gray and sometimes brown. There are some rendzinas in Texas. The black belt of Alabama, and Mississippi are rendzinas. The chalk cliffs of Dover, overlooking the English channel are rendzinas. There is a wide range of fertility to these soils, being rich or poor depending on what kind of limestone they originated from.

WIESENBODEN AND BOG SOILS: This type of soil is usually associated with the podzols. They are found in Illinois, Wisconsin, Ohio, Iowa, Indiana, and Florida, and especially in the area of prairie soils. They are very rich in organic matter. The bog soils are those that contain 18 inches or more of it. These are peat soils. Where well-drained, exceptionally good crops may be obtained. The Everglades of Florida are an example of bog soil. *See also* AERATION; CARBON-NITROGEN RATIO; CARBON; A HORIZON; B HORIZON; C HORIZON; HUMUS; ORGANIC MATTER; MINERAL ROCKS; CHERNOZEMS; PODZOLS; LATERITES; COLLOIDS; MUCK SOILS.

SOIL AND HEALTH FOUNDATION: A non-profit organization, incorporated under the laws of Pennsylvania, established in 1947 by J. I. Rodale and supported solely by contributions from those interested in organiculture and investigations leading to better health, foods and soil conservation.

The Foundation's formation stems from the work of Sir Albert Howard, who over a period of more than 30 years proved that the use of artificial fertilizers was producing food with lower nutritional and vitamin content than foods produced in soils where organic matter enriched the land. In addition to testing at the Organic Experimental Farm in Emmaus, Pa., it has established research branches at Antioch College, Yellow Springs, Ohio; the University of Missouri, Columbia, Missouri; the National Agricultural College at Farm School, Pennsylvania; Laval University, Quebec, Canada; and the School of Horticulture at Ambler, Pennsylvania. Under these grants, impartial research has been conducted to establish irrefutable, scientific evidence as to the value of organic methods and principles.

The purposes of the Foundation have been to show, through this continuing experimentation and research, that good crops, produced organically and without poisonous sprays and chemical fertilizers, will: (1) keep the soil fertile, (2) offset erosion, (3) make available more nutritious food, both for humans and animals which

give us meat, milk and eggs, and (4) these foods, being free of contaminating products, will markedly effect a decrease in degenerative diseases and make for a healthier nation.

SOIL ASSOCIATION: *see* HAUGHLEY EXPERIMENT

SOIL IMPROVEMENT: *see* AERATION; COMPOST; MULCH; GREEN MANURE; COVER CROPS; CONSERVATION; VEGETABLE GARDENING; FLOWER GARDENING; MANURE; ROTARY TILLAGE; ACIDITY-ALKALINITY; FERTILIZER

SOIL TEMPERATURE: Soil temperatures vary just as much as air temperatures. The difference, however, is that soils don't change in the same degree as air; one part of the garden is probably hotter (or colder) than another depending upon its location, chemical and physical make-up.

Here are some examples of how soil temperatures influence your gardening results:

1. Germination of seeds depends upon warmth of soil below as well as upon air above;

2. Planting your first crop as soon as soil has warmed up enough in spring can mean that you'll have time to have a late planting in the same spot;

3. A mulch or cover crop regulates your soil's temperature to your advantage;

4. Small animals, such as rabbits, pick certain sites in your garden to dig their burrows because they know that surface conditions above will protect them from winter's cold;

5. You'll learn how to save plants from frost damage;

6. You can aid the work of helpful soil bacteria, if you know at what soil temperatures they work best.

BACTERIA: Organic gardeners are well aware that their soil is alive—providing a home for millions of beneficial bacteria. These bacteria require special conditions of warmth, moisture and free aeration of soil to do their best job. These conditions are found only in the upper cultivated layers of the soil, and are more easily obtained in sandy loams than in clays where the moisture content is too high and the supply of oxygen is lacking.

According to T. Bedford Franklin, author of *Climates in Miniature,* "Fields of corn turn yellow, especially on the clay lands, when cold and drying east winds cool the soil in the spring, because the bacteria produce too little nitrates in a cold soil to feed the crop; it is only when warmer conditions arrive and the bacteria resume activity that the bright green color returns to the crop." He points out that during the summer months a light, well-warmed soil, kept well-cultivated, may produce eight times as much nitrates as the same soil left to itself and never stirred with a hoe.

EFFECT OF MULCH: Soil bacteria like heat and, Mr. Franklin believes, work best at about 100° F.; they stop work below 41° and above 130°. Mulch is an effective way to keep soil in that 41 to 130° range. In effect, a two-inch mulch can give soil a seven degree boost.

Many soil scientists have found that an organic mulch acts both directly and indirectly to decrease the fluctuations in soil temperature. Directly, a mulch makes the soil warmer in winter and cooler in summer. Indirectly, a mulch retains more snow, which further protects the soil against temperature extremes.

Prof. Roy Donahue of New Hampshire writes, in his latest book on soils that: "The greatest direct influence is shown on a hot summer day when the sun is shining. Oak leaves in New Jersey during a hot summer day kept the soil 15 degrees cooler than in an adjoining plot with no oak leaves.

The transfer of heat within the soil depends on the ease with which the heat can be conducted from particle to particle of the soil across the gaps which contain air when the soil is dry and water when wet. Briefly, the temperatures of the top three inches of very dark soils warm up much faster than light colored soils. Sandy soils heat up the fastest, clay soils the slowest.

Clay is a cold soil in summer, partly due to its high specific heat and partly due to the constant evaporation from its surface where it seldom gets dry. From May to September clay is colder than loam or sand at the four-inch depth by as much as five degrees, but is warmer than loam or sand from October to April by about the same amount. So it is generally considered a slow starter but a good finisher in the autumn.

WHEN TO WATER: Mr. Franklin has this advice for gardeners with sandy soil: On a hot day in summer, plants on a sandy plot may give off more water from their leaves than their roots can absorb from the soil. The result is that these plants wilt.

The natural reaction by most gardeners is to rush for the watering can or hose and water the wilting plants, and then be surprised and disappointed that the plants do not recover but only wilt all the more. "The reason," Mr. Franklin writes, "is really obvious, for on a hot day, the soil may be at a temperature of 80 to 90°, while the water is at 55 to 60°.

"Since absorption of water by the plant slows down as the temperature of the soil falls, we have now made it impossible for the roots to supply the plant with as much water as they did before. The wise gardener avoids this trouble by always having a can full of water in the sun all day ready for use." The same reasoning also suggests that the best time to water your garden would be in the evening, when the soil has had a chance to cool off. *See also* MULCH; FROST.

SOIL TESTING: A good gardener wants to know as much about his soil as possible. He wants to know what general type of soil it is, what plants will grow best on it, and how to fertilize it. It is easy to see that many benefits can be gained by learning more about the composition and capabilities of your soil.

There are two ways to find out what nutrients your soil is hungry for. You can send a sample of your soil to a laboratory or to your state college, or you can buy a testing kit and make many of the necessary tests yourself. It doesn't hurt to use both methods, because you will be able to double check your results. A home testing kit is valuable because it enables you to make frequent periodic tests of your soil. Most people don't realize that the nutrient supply in the soil varies greatly from one season to another.

A soil test will tell you what nutrients are "available" or soluble in your soil. There are also "unavailable" or insoluble nutrients in your soil which plants can feed on, but the supply of soluble and insoluble nutrients is usually quite similar. If your soil is low in soluble phosphorus, it will probably be low in insoluble phosphorus, etc.

The best place to start your soil analysis is with its pH. Is it alkaline or acid or neutral? This is important, because correcting the pH will often release supplies of major and minor plant foods. A soil that is too acid will not release "unavailable" nutrients properly, and the same is true of a soil that is too alkaline.

Soil Samples: Collecting the soil sample is the first step in making a test. In fact, collecting the sample could be considered the most important and critical part of the testing procedure. There is often a great variation in soil condition nutrients in various parts of a garden or field, so it is important to collect a number of samples from different locations. These samples can be tested individually and the results averaged, or you can mix all the samples together and use a portion of this "homogenized"

sample for your test. Always be careful to make sure that your collecting shovel or container is not contaminated by a fertilizer. That might throw off the results.

The test is made by putting a small portion of the sample in a test tube and then introducing one or two "reagents." A reagent is a chemical which reacts with the nutrient being tested and shows the quantity of the nutrient available by changing color. Color charts are supplied with the test kits, and the final analysis is made by checking the color of the solution in the tube with the test chart for the nutrient being tested. *See also* FERTILIZER; LIME; ACIDITY-ALKALINITY; DEFICIENCIES, SOIL; TRACE ELEMENTS; COMPOST.

SOLANUM: An extremely large genus that includes the potato, tomato, eggplant, nightshade, bittersweet as well as many other shrubs, vines and sometimes trees. *See listings of individual plants.*

SOLOMON'S-SEAL: (*Polygonatum*) A genus of hardy perennials of the lily family. Often grow in bogs and marshy places from fleshy rootstocks buried about two inches below the surface. Common name alludes to the scars on the creeping rootstocks left from each year's growth. Graceful leafy stems arise from the rootstocks, with small white or greenish bell-shaped flowers growing from the leaf axils. Fruits blue or black berries. Easily propagated by seed or division, and may be grown in moist situations among shrubs and ferns, or on the shady side of the house. Native North American solomon's-seals are *P. bi-florum,* which grows to three feet with four-inch leaves, and *P. commutatum,* an eight-foot species whose leaves are six inches long. *P. multi-florum,* to three feet, and *P. latifolium,* to four feet, are natives of Europe and Asia.

SORBARIA: Known also as false

spirea, this is a genus of deciduous shrubs, some tender and some hardy of the rose family. Leaves are compound, pinnate, and flowers are white, in small clusters, similar to those of spirea. Thrive in moist, rich soil, where they will spread rapidly by runner, by which they may be propagated. Also may be grown from seeds and cuttings.

S. aitchisoni is hardy from Long Island Sound south; grows to ten feet, and blooms in July and August. *S. arborea,* just about as hardy, grows to 18 feet. A shorter species, *S. sorbifolia,* which grows to six feet, is hardy throughout the United States and much of Canada.

SORBUS: *see* MOUNTAIN ASH

SORGHUM: (*Holcus sorghum*) A native of the tropics that grows from three to six feet high, grain sorghums are an important grain and feed crop. They replace corn in many drier sections of the country. They need a good soil, growing well in sandy soil, generally doing better on alkaline lands than corn. Sorghum is a relatively drought-resistant crop. Best known varieties are Kafir, Milo and Blackhull.

SORREL: (*Rumex*) Most of the sorrels or docks are vigorous-rooted perennial weeds, but some are cultivated for their edible leaves. They have long panicles of tiny greenish-white flowers, and are easily grown from seed sown in early spring. *R. acetosa,* common sorrel, grows up to three feet tall; its basal leaves are eaten as greens. Herb patience or spinach dock (*R. patientia*) is twice as big and also bears leaves fine for salads or to add tang to soups and drinks. The spinach-rhubarb (*R. abyssinicus*) grows eight feet tall; its leaves are used like spinach and the stalks like rhubarb in pies.

Curled dock (*R. crispus*) and sheep sorrel (*R. acetosella*) are both very weedy and may spread if planted in gardens. Curled dock is one of the best and most widely found wild greens, cooked like spinach, and its roots are highly prized as a blood medicine. The leaves of sheep sorrel are somewhat bitter, but may be used in salads or cooked until tender and made into pies. French gardeners would not consider their vegetable gardens complete without some sorrels grown for the table. *See also* WILD GREENS.

The tuberous roots of *R. hymenosepalus,* canaigre, are an excellent source of tannin. This three-foot-tall, spring-blooming perennial, propagated by seeds, roots or root crowns planted in the fall, may be a new crop for sandy soils in the Southwest. The roots are harvested in the summer and dried. They have been used for centuries by the Indians for tanning leather. Yields of ten tons per acre of fresh roots are common. *See also* OXALIS.

SOTOL: (*Dasylirion*) Desert plants growing from central Texas to Arizona and south into Mexico. They produce flowers resembling those of the lily, on stalks usually growing about 20 feet high. Sotol does best in full sun, can stand intense summer heat, and a small amount of frost. The species (*D. texanum*) is known as Bear grass.

SOURCLOVER: *see* GREEN MANURE

SOUR GUM: *see* NYSSA

SOUTHERNWOOD: (*Artemisia abrotanum*) Semi-shrubby plant from two to five feet tall, with finely divided, grayish-green leaves.

Southernwood is a hardy perennial most easily propagated by division; endures city conditions well; does best in full sun. *See also* ARTEMISIA.

SOW: To broadcast or drill seeds, generally resulting in a rather dense population. *See also* SEEDS AND SEEDLINGS; FLOWER GARDENING; VEGETABLE GARDENING.

SOW BUGS: *see* INSECT CONTROL

SOYBEAN: (*Glycine max*) An ancient legume that can easily be grown in the garden. Culture is simply that of a warm weather crop, such as corn or string beans. Plant after all danger of frost is past. Soybeans grow sturdily upright and are very prolific in yield.

In addition to adding nitrogen to the soil like other legume plants, soybeans are rich in protein, are sometimes used as a meat substitute.

In other parts of the world the soybean, being very high in protein, takes the place of meat. Soy cheese, soy milk, soyburgs, soy flour are among the many foods developed from this nutritionally-rich plant.

Here we are primarily concerned with three, the green bean, dried bean and sprouted bean.

In the green bean stage they look like baby limas, can be cooked the same way, but have a certain nutty flavor and a firm texture. After stripping pods from plant, blanch five minutes. This enables beans to be easily popped from shell. Cook in boiling salted water approximately 15 minutes. Serve with butter or a thin cream sauce.

Leaving some plants to mature will provide dried beans for seed and for making baked beans and bean sprouts.

For baked beans soak dried beans overnight, add salt and cook till almost done; drain. Now treat beans as you would for your own baked bean recipe.

Soy sprouts are really a fascinating dish to make. Any container with drainage holes such as large flower pot can be used. Soak a cupful of dried beans overnight, then place in container and cover with cloth to exclude light which makes beans green. Four times or more daily flush and rinse beans and place back in a warm spot, such as the top of a cabinet. A spray is handy for the flushing and rinsing. In four to six days sprouts will be from two to three inches long. Sprouts can then be removed, freed from loose skins and stored in refrigerator. *See also* SPROUTING SEEDS; BEANS, SPROUTING.

Vitamin C is developed during this sprouting, which places bean sprouts in the fresh vegetable category. Unlike other vegetables, though, Vitamin C continues to increase for as long as a week during refrigeration.

Use the sprouts with the bean attached. Saute, by placing butter in pan plus a small amount of water. Cover and cook ten to 15 minutes. Beans are chewy but crisp. Sprouts can also be added to soups, stews, salads or included in scrambled eggs and omelets.

Edible soybeans have proven to be one of the best sources of high quality protein combined with minerals and vitamins.—*Robert Lemp.*

CULTURE: Like other legumes, soybeans will return nitrogen to the soil. After the beans are picked, turn the tops and roots into the soil. Soybeans prefer a well-limed, well-drained soil. Give plants plenty of room; allow about three feet between rows. They require a long growing season, about 100 days of warm weather; do not plant seed early.

SPADING: *see* Vegetable Gardening; Flower Gardening; Cultivation

SPANISH MOSS: (*Tillandsia usneoides*) An epiphyte, requiring support from other plants, sometimes thriving on electric wires. It has long slender gray mosslike stems covered with tiny leaves and very small inconspicuous flowers. In native southern states, its long strands hanging gracefully from the branches of trees are a characteristic feature of the landscape.

When used as a mulch, Spanish moss will form a good covering without packing excessively, and will prevent the growth of weeds; it will conserve moisture also.

It has been reported that this mulch does not decompose and it must be removed for cultivation. Unlike leaves and straw, the plants will not grow through it.

SPATHE: A hood-like bract which covers a flower or inflorescence, which is usually a spadix. The spathe may be leaf-like, or fleshy and colored like a petal, as in the case of calla lily, whose large white or yellow cornucopia-shaped outer sheath is the spathe. Most of the members of the iris family have spathes, which are the papery covering over the flower buds, which dry and curl up on the stem below the flower after it has opened.

SPEARMINT: (*Mentha spicata*) A well-known mint frequently found growing wild throughout the eastern half of the United States. The leaves and flowering tops are widely used for seasoning meats and beverages, and the volatile oil distilled from the whole herb is used for flavoring chewing gum and dentifrices and in medicine.

Spearmint is easily grown in any fertile soil that is fairly moist and, like peppermint, is well adapted to reclaimed swamplands.

Fresh leaves and leafy stem tips may be picked any time. For drying, it is best cut just as flowering begins and carefully dried in the shade. Spearmint can be propagated by cuttings or divisions. *See also* Herb.

SPEAR NEEDLE: *see* Grass, Ornamental

SPECIES: A group of plants which are subdivisions of a genus, resembling each other to such an extent that they might all have had a common parent. Small differences within the species such as differences of color or size of flower or foliage are varieties. The latin name for a plant gives first the genus name, followed by the species. Thus *Lilium tigrinum* is a tiger lily, as distinguished from other lilies of the *lilium* genus.

SPHAGNUM MOSS: *see* Peat Moss

SPICEBUSH: (*Lindera benzoin*) Also called spicewood and Benjamin bush. One of a group of 60 species of *Lindera,* a genus of aromatic trees and shrubs of the laurel family.

Spicebush is hardy throughout the United States. It grows from eight to 15 feet high, and starts and ends its season in a blaze of yellow. Early in spring the bush is covered with small yellow blossoms, and in fall the foliage turns bright yellow. Originally a swamp shrub, it prefers a moist, partially shaded site, but will grow in almost any soil or location. It may be propagated by seeds sown as soon as they ripen, or by cuttings rooted in sand.

SPICE TREE: *see* Umbellularia

SPIDER FERN: *see* Fern

SPIDER-FLOWER: (*Cleome spinosa*) A tall garden annual, tropical American in origin. As a background in a flower border where height is needed, spiderflower is very satisfactory. Seeds may be sown in the open ground during autumn. Volunteer seedlings usually are numerous where old plants have grown.

When it is grown in front of shrubs as a landscape plant, spider-flower will succeed with a generous mulch of leaves or rotted manure.

SPIDER-LILY: (*Hymenocallis*) Popular in southern tropical gardens or in northern greenhouses. Basket flower (*H. calathina*) produces leaves almost two feet long and eight inch flowers. This is sometimes called the Peruvian daffodil. Another species, *H. caribaea,* is a summer-bloomer, with one to 1½ foot leaves.

SPIDERWORT: (*Tradescantia*) Weak-stemmed and sometimes trailing genus of the spiderwort family, natives in America, many from the tropical portions. Leaves are long and narrow, and grow directly from the stem without stalks. Flowers are blue and white or pink, lasting a short time.

Best known species is one of the plants called wandering jew (*T. fluminensis*) the other which goes by that name being another genus of the same family, *Zebrina pendula.* It is a tender species, grown mostly in greenhouses, and used in hanging baskets. A variety has white-striped leaves.

Two hardy species are *T. bracteata* and *T. virginiana,* which can be grown in the flower border. They grow better in moist than in dry places, and like some shade. Propagation is by cuttings.

SPIGELIA MARILANDICA: *see* PINK-ROOT

SPIKE GRASS: *see* GRASS, ORNAMENTAL

SPINACH: (*Spinacia oleracea*) One of the most important potherbs cultivated; rich in vitamins and minerals. Potherbs or pot-greens are leafy plants grown solely for their foliage.

CULTURE: Spinach is a cool season crop. It should be planted in the open ground as early in the spring as possible. It can also be planted in the fall (September, October, or just before

the ground freezes). Protect it by a mulch of hay, straw, or leaves. This crop will be ready to use very early the following spring. You may also be able to plant during an early February or March thaw. For spring planting, weekly sowings can be made, the last one 50-60 days before hot weather of summer is expected.

Any good, well-drained garden soil will suit spinach provided it is not acid, the desirable reaction being a pH of 6.0 to 7.0. More acid soils should be limed at whatever rate is indicated by the soil test. Spinach requires an abundance of plant food, especially nitrogen. The soil should be well prepared by spading to a depth of six inches with well-rotted manure or compost. Lime should not be applied in direct contact with the manure, but after the manure has been spaded in.

One packet of seeds plants 25 feet or one ounce of seed plants 100 feet. Cover the seeds with ½ inch sifted compost and firm well. Rows should be 12-15 inches apart and plants one to two inches apart in the row.

Spinach is a quick-growing, leafy plant and requires adequate moisture. If the season is dry, this should be accomplished by thoroughly soaking the area late in the day. During the growing period the soil should be kept well loosened and weeds kept down.

Spinach matures in 40-50 days, and can be picked only once. The best method is to cut individual plants by the roots and wash.

VARIETIES: There are two types: one with crumpled leaves, of which Bloomsdale Savoy Long Standing is the most popular; the other has thicker, smoother leaves, as typified by Nobel. Both of these are relatively long standing, that is, they are less prone than others to shoot seedstalk and become inedible. Another smooth leaf variety, long standing, is King of Denmark.

Varieties recommended for freezing are: Giant Noble, King of Denmark,

Long Standing Bloomsdale and Old Dominion.

For all sowing the disease-resistant Virginia Savoy and Old Dominion are recommended.

New Zealand spinach is not true spinach and does not resemble it in the garden, but when cooked and served there is little difference between them. It has the great merit of flourishing in summer heat, and as its leaves are picked, others grow to replace them.

DISEASES: Spinach blight shows as a yellowing and mottling of the leaves. It is a virus disease transmitted from one plant to another by insects and it stops growth. Where it is known to be in the neighborhood, the resistant varieties should be planted. *See also* VEGETABLE GARDENING.

SPINDLE-TREE: *see* EUONYMUS

SPIREA: (*Spiraea*) A genus of mostly hardy deciduous flowering shrubs of the rose family, including many of our most widely grown garden species. Many hybrids have been developed with great hardiness as to climate, soil, and culture. Most species will grow well in almost any site, doing best where there is a reasonable amount of moisture and a large amount of sun.

Leaves are alternate, usually toothed, and with stalks; florets are small but arranged in large showy clusters, sometimes flat-topped, sometimes in large showy clusters, sometimes flat-topped, sometimes in dense spikes. Colors of the early-flowering varieties are mostly white, but the summer-flowering ones tend toward pink and red.

Propagation is by seed, by green wood cuttings under glass, by rooted branch tips, by layering. Early-flowering species are pruned, mostly only to remove dead wood, after blooming. Later-flowering kinds are more severely pruned early in spring.

Meadowsweet (*S. alba*) is a four

to six-foot shrub with leafy clusters of white flowers. Summer-blooming.

S. bumalda is a hybrid whose variety *Anthony Waterer* is one of the best known of all shrubs. It is a late-blooming variety with crimson flowers.

Also called Bridal wreath, Spirea vanhouttei is an early flowering white variety, producing heavy masses of blossoms and growing well in the city.

S. cantoniensis is not quite hardy in the northern sections. It is a bushy shrub to five feet, with early masses of white umbels.

A late bloomer, native of the Pacific coast, is *S. douglasi,* growing five to eight feet high with deep rose long dense flower clusters.

S. japonica is a four to six foot vase-shaped shrub, bearing loose clusters of pink flowers in the summer.

S. margarita is a smallish hybrid, which bears bright pink flowers from July through September.

Bridal wreath is the name applied both to *S. prunifolia* and *S. vanhouttei,* both early-flowering white species, the former with double blossoms, and the latter single but flowering in heavy masses of blossoms. *Vanhouttei* is a good shrub for city culture, and very showy.

S. thunbergi is a handsome shrub growing to five feet, with foliage that turns red in fall. Small clusters of early flowers are quite white and very prolific.

Hardhack (*S. tomentosa*) also called steeple-bush for the steeple shape of its flower clusters, is low, grows in moist places, and bears rosy-purple flowers in late summer.

S. trilobata resembles *vanhouttei* but is smaller in all its dimensions. Grows to four feet, and its leaves are usually three-lobed.

SPONDIAS: *see* OTAHEITE APPLE

SPORE: Any of various primitive reproductive bodies produced by some of the lower orders of plant life, notably ferns, common mosses, lichens, fungi, algae, and some unicellular forms of plant and animal life. Unlike seeds, spores contain no embryo, but they take the place of seeds among the plants in which the occur. Among unicellular bacteria, yeasts, and molds, they represent a resting stage, during which the microorganism is armed against destruction by heat, acid, or dryness. In this stage, disease caused by spore-bearers may be spread among plants, as, for instance, anthracnose among beans handled while wet. Spores are also important to the gardener as means of propagation of ferns. *See also* DISEASE; MICROORGANISM; FERNS.

SPORT: Mutation. A sudden variation by which the offspring differs from its parents in some marked characteristic due to an alteration of genes or chromosomes. This variation may occur in a seedling, or it may occur in one branch of a plant such as a rose, apple, or dahlia, where flowers or fruit may differ from those borne on other branches of the same plant. In the case of a differing branch, the mutation is known as a bud sport.

Until recently horticulturists waited for mutations to occur by accidents among their plants, and cultivated any such accidents which produced improvements. Mutations which occurred by accident producing monsters were "rogued" by seedsmen—that is, the monsters in their seed-beds were pulled out and destroyed to preserve the purity of seed strains.

In 1957 British seedsmen found that their "rogues" suddenly increased five-fold. Reports poured in to the press from all parts of the country reporting odd "monsters" throughout England. These monsters were not true sports themselves, having grown from seed which proved the purity of its strains in other plantings, but they occurred mostly in gardens with a certain common exposure. A study made by the Henry Doubleday Research Association indicated that radioactive fallout might be responsible for the odd growths. Seed from some of these "rogues" proved to give sports in 20 to 60 per cent of the cases.

The U. S. Atomic Energy Commission, recognizing the possibilities of producing mutations at will with gamma radiation, established a garden in 1953 at the Brookhaven National Laboratories in Upton, N. Y. Experiments are still going forward there on the effect of gamma radiation from cobalt-60 on higher plant life. By exposing certain plants to the cobalt isotope it has been found there that evolution might be speeded up many times, with innumerable sports produced each year.

SPRAYS: *see* INSECTICIDES

SPRAYS, DORMANT OIL: Used properly, a three per cent miscible oil dormant spray is effective against a host of chewing and sucking insects, organic gardeners report. Aphids, red spider, thrips, mealybugs, whiteflies, pear psylla, all kinds of scale insects and mites fall before it. The eggs of codling moth, oriental fruit moth, various leaf rollers and cankerworms are destroyed.

A dormant spray is applied to orchard trees before any of the buds open. Some gardeners make it a practice to use it on all dormant trees, shrubs and evergreens every spring, but this is rarely necessary if the plants have been organically grown for a number of years. Fruit trees, however, have many enemies and dormant spraying should be a regular practice for them, along with a strict program of sanitation.

In early spring insects that hatch from eggs laid on plants the previous fall can be readily killed because the shells of the eggs and the protective covering of hibernating scales become softer and more porous at this time. The dormant spray penetrates and makes a tight, continuous film over these, literally suffocating the organism to death.

It will, of course, form a similar film over leaves and injure them, which is why it is applied only while the trees are in a leafless state. Citrus trees, which do not shed their leaves, are given a very dilute spray, usually made with "white oils," highly refined oils that present the least chance of foliage injury.

Dormant oil sprays have a residual effect, too. An oil film covering the plant interferes with the successful establishment of any young insects that may hatch for several days after spraying.

Stock preparations of miscible oil sprays are sold by all garden supply stores, with instructions for dilution and use. You can also make your own, using a gallon of light grade oil and a pound of fish-oil soap (an emulsifier) to a half-gallon. These ingredients are mixed together, brought to a boil and poured back and forth from one container to another until emulsified (thoroughly blended). Since all oil emulsions tend to separate into oil and water again, the mixture should be used as soon as possible after it is prepared. Dilute it with 20 or more times its volume of water for use.

Sometimes miscible oils are combined with Bordeaux mixture, arsenate of lead or other strong chemicals, to increase their insecticidal power. These are definitely harmful to plants and dangerous to handle, and should never be used. Lime-sulphur is also employed as a dormant spray, but it is intensely poisonous, will discolor paint and harm the soil and plants, and is generally less effective than an oil spray.

It is difficult to apply harmful amounts of a miscible oil spray. If too much of the emulsion is applied, the excess simply runs off. A tree should for this reason be sprayed all at once, not one-half first (as when a sprayer goes down an orchard row), the other half later, after the first has dried. Almost twice as much oil would in this case be deposited where the coverages overlap, and this could conceivably cause damage on citrus trees, especially in arid areas. The drier and warmer the air, it seems, the more likelihood of damage, though probably quite slight. Always cover a tree thoroughly in one spraying.

Sometimes oil sprays are recommended for summer use, when the trees are in leaf. This is not a good practice—it can cause leaf burn and heavy leaf and fruit drop, as well as changes in the flavor of the fruit. The insects are destroyed just as effectively, or in some cases, more effectively, in the spring.

In recent years, fruit growers in the Northeast have been using "superior dormant spray oils." These are highly refined oils which are safer to use later than the regular ones, after some new growth has appeared in the buds.

This later application is said to give a higher kill of, for example, European red mites, whose eggs become increasingly more susceptible to oil as their hatching period approaches. More mite eggs are killed with a two per cent superior oil spray applied in the delayed-dormant stage than by a four per cent spray when the trees are still dormant. The delayed dormant stage of apples is said to be when about a ½-inch of leaf tissue is exposed in the blossom buds. A three per cent superior oil concentration will destroy many oil-resistant pests. *See also* FRUIT TREES; ORCHARD; INSECT CONTROL.

SPROUTING SEEDS: The ancient practice of sprouting seeds is still a very valuable one. Sprouting converts the dried seed into a fresh vegetable, and increases its food elements greatly.

A seed, someone once said, is the stored-up "vital life force" of a plant. It is the pampered baby of the plant, getting only the best of the soil nutrients. Nature makes sure the plant saves up the best for the seed so it will have the concentrated germinating energy which is the only force that insures the plant's reproduction.

Give the seed the proper conditions, and it will almost literally "explode," releasing the vital life force within it. A tiny, crisp sprout appears. And as this sprout grows, vitamins are formed in it. Its nutritional content jumps overnight:

The most spectacular rise is in vitamin C. Dried peas that contain no vitamin C have 86 milligrams of this vitamin after they have sprouted four days. Sprouted soybeans are so rich in vitamin C that a two-ounce serving supplies half an adult's daily requirement. The 11-milligrams of C contained in 100 grams of whole oats becomes 42 milligrams after five days of sprouting.

The same happens with the other vitamins. B-2 increases 1350 per cent in oats. Folic acid, the B vitamin which prevents pernicious anemia, rises from 28 parts in dry wheat to 106 parts in the sprouted grain. The niacin content of Mung bean sprouts quadruples over that of the dry beans. Seven parts of thiamine become nine parts in sprouted wheat. The riboflavin content of corn, barley and wheat rises four times. Pyridoxine and pantothenic acid triple. Other vitamins, notably E and K, also rise.

In addition, sprouted seeds also contain fats and carbohydrates, calcium, iron, phosphorus, potassium and other minerals. The carbohydrate content, incidentally, is quite low, making sprouts fine for dieters.

SEEDS TO SPROUT: The list is practically endless: lentils, soybeans, sweet corn, barley, wheat, rye, alfalfa, lima beans, sunflowers, oats, navy beans, clover, parsley and millet are all excellent.

One important point: whenever you can, purchase certified organically grown seeds, or use seeds you have grown yourself. Ordinary commercial seeds are often treated with chemicals—wheat seed, for instance, is usually doused with mercury poisons to kill rust and smut disease organisms, and other grains are treated to prevent weevil infestation in storage. Seeds should always be of the current crop to insure full germinating power. Keep them stored in a cool, dry place.

Sprouting is easy. You can use any wide-mouthed container, such as a large fruit jar, flower pot or colander. Plug the drainage hole of a flower pot with a piece of crockery.

Soak about a cupful of your seeds overnight in plenty of water. Then drain and wash them several times, discarding any broken or imperfect seeds. Put them in your container, covering it with a double layer of cheesecloth fastened with rubber bands. This will hold in the humidity, and by cutting down the light, prevent undesirable leaf growth.

If you are using a container with no drainage hole, stand it upside down on two small pieces of wood to get rid of excess water that would cause molding.

Keep the container in a warm spot (near a radiator is good), and flush and rinse the seeds three or four times daily. A spray is handy for this.

In three to five days, sprouts are ready to be removed and stored in the refrigerator. You can discard the loose skins if you wish, but they are fine roughage.

JAPANESE METHOD: A variation on this is the Japanese method. A series of shallow trays with small holes drilled in their bases are mounted one on top of the other. This set-up makes it easy to pour water over the top tray and let it seep down to moisten the whole unit. Other methods involve using strawberry boxes, or rolling the seeds in a damp towel and moistening it occasionally.

Catharyn Elwood, author of *Feel Like a Million* (Better Nutrition Institute, Washington 10, D.C.), makes these suggestions on when to use your sprouts:

"Wheat sprouts are most delicious when the sprout is the length of the seed. Mung bean sprouts are best when 1½ to three inches long. Alfalfa sprouts are best when one to two inches long. Pea and soybean sprouts are good short or long. Lentil sprouts mold quickly so must be used when about one inch long. Sunflower seed sprouts are best when no longer than the seed. If longer they develop a strange objectionable sting in the throat after eating." In general, she says, "the longer the sprout, the more nourishment. When the green appears, vitamin A and chlorophyll are developing. However, most sprouts are less delicious if too long."

Seed sprouts are very versatile. Use the whole sprout with the seed attached. You may want to keep some frozen for quick salads or to use in Chinese dishes, chicken a la king and the like. Alfalfa sprouts make an unusual breakfast food, while soybean sprouts and others are luscious in a vegetable casserole with sliced onions and green peppers.

Some people find it hard to develop a taste for soybean and certain other sprouts raw, so try steaming them over very low heat in a tiny bit of water, no longer than ten to 15 minutes. Or saute them in a little butter and water in a covered pan about ten minutes.

They're delicious roasted, too, or included in various egg dishes. *See also* BEANS, SPROUTING.

SPRUCE: (*Picea*) Trees of the pine family, with a single trunk, whorled branched, four-sided needles, cones pendant or berry-like, and catkin-like flowers. Natives of the northern hemisphere. Genus includes many fine ornamental trees as well as timber trees, and some used for paper pulp. Growth habit pyramidal. Propagated from seed and cuttings, and rare varieties grafted. Mostly hardy, they will also tolerate some shade. Grown in almost any well-drained soil with sufficient moisture. Shallow rooted and easily transplanted. Dense foliage makes them useful as hedges and windbreaks.

Norway spruce (*P. abies*) grows to 150 feet, pyramidal, with horizontal branches and drooping branchlets. Needles shiny and dark green, cones drooping and to seven inches long. Many varieties, one with variegated needles, several dwarf forms, and one prostrate form.

Alcock spruce (*P. bicolor*) grows to 75 feet, and is distinguished by two white bands on the upper side of the needles.

Engelmann's spruce (*P. engelmanni*) grow to 150 feet with close-set branches, with needles one inch long and bluish-green. Very hardy. Varieties have more silvery needle, bluer needles, and drooping branches.

White or skunk spruce (*P. glauca*) grows to 100 feet, with raised branches and drooping branchlets. Cones 1½ to two inches long. Many varieties with different colored needles or dwarf.

P. mariana, black spruce, is one of the few that will grow in moist places, being sometimes found in bogs. To 50 feet, very hardy.

Blue spruce (*P. pungens*) also called Colorado blue spruce grows to 140 feet in the wild, with 1¼ inch blue-green needles, and cones to four inches. In the variety *kosteriana* branches are drooping and needles are more blue.

Red spruce (*P. rubens*) is used chiefly for paper pulp, and rarely cultivated.

Sitka spruce (*P. sitchensis*) is a beautiful tall tree with needles silver above and glossy green below. Not hardy along the Atlantic coast. *See also* TREES.

SPURGE: (*Euphorbia*) A group of pest plants containing a highly acrid milky-juice in the stems, leaves and roots. This juice may produce severe skin irritation and blistering. If eaten, spurges often cause vomiting. There is also swelling about the eyes and mouth accompanied by abdominal pains.

The common spurges include:

Snow-on-the-mountain (*E. marginata*), a native annual often planted in gardens because the leaf margins are white and petal-like.

Cypress spurge (*E. cyparissias*) a weedy perennial herb, introduced from Europe; sometimes called graveyard spurge because of its frequent occurrence in cemeteries; usually inhabits dry, gravelly or sandy soils.

Flowering spurge (*E. corolata*), known also as poison milkweed, is a native perennial found mostly in dry, sandy areas; each stem has from 25 to 75 or more leaves along it; showy, flower-like parts are actually appendages below the petal-like flower.

Leafy spurge (*E. esula*), a noxious perennial herb, reputedly brought here in oats from Russia near the end of the last century; a deep-rooted weed (some grow 16 feet deep), it bears cuplike structures near the top which contain the greenish-yellow flowers.

The spurges may be controlled by digging scattered plants if the infestation is small. Continous mowing will prevent seed formation and exhaust food reserves in roots or underground stems. Close grazing by sheep in spring can eliminate leafy spurge. *See also* EUPHORBIA.

SQUAB: *see* PIGEON

SQUASH: (*Cucurbita*) A member of the large family of annual, trailing or climbing vines, which also includes pumpkins and gourds.

The squash flourishes in practically every part of the country where enough moisture is available. It is a truly native American plant.

Squashes are divided into two types, summer squash and winter squash. Both types succeed in reasonably rich soil, although they favor a sandy loam. You will find both types easy to cultivate.

SOIL PREPARATION: Regardless of the condition of the garden, greater success will be assured if you dig in a few shovelfuls of compost per hill. Any spot in the garden where more than one plant is to grow in a group is called a hill.

The soil should not only be enriched by the addition of good humus, it should be as carefully prepared as you can make it.

It will pay you to keep in mind the idea that the squash plants will have to be so vigorous that they will succeed in reaching maturity and developing their fruits before insect enemies and diseases can cut them down.

Squash seed should not be planted until all danger of frost has passed and the ground has warmed up. This is about the same time that sweet corn is being planted in your locality.

SEED PLANTING: The seeds should be planted an inch deep, not more than six seeds to the hill, and the hills spaced four feet apart each way. Depending upon the type of summer squash you select a half ounce of seed should plant from ten to 15 hills.

Avoid planting seed too thickly. With squashes it is a waste of seed to plant thickly and thin out afterwards. It is better to save any extra seed. Properly stored it will remain viable up to four years.

Although squash plants grown in rich, deep soil will usually succeed with no more attention than moderate cultivation to keep down weeds and to insure sufficient moisture, it is best to get them off to a good start.

One of the best ways to protect young squash seedlings aginst the attacks of disease-carrying striped-beetles is by the box method. For each hill, take a box of wood, or heavy fiberboard, about 18 inches square and 12 inches deep from which both the top and bottom have been removed. Press the box firmly over the hill and bank a little earth up around it. Over the open top a piece of cheesecloth is stretched and held in place with tacks or some similar method.

BARREL STAVE METHOD: A very old method was to place two barrel staves in the form of a cross over each hill. Tie the staves at the point where they cross, then cover them with a piece of cheesecloth. A little earth drawn up over the edges of the cloth will hold it in place against winds.

Lacking boxes or barrel staves, it is quite practicable to drive three or four stakes into the ground close around each hill so that the stakes stand about a foot high. Cover the stakes with about a yard of cheesecloth to form a small tent and secure the edges with heaped earth.

Besides defending the seedlings against beetles and other insect pests, this protection speeds up their growth. It should be removed promptly when the plants outgrow it. This is best done on a dull, clouded day.

USING WOOD ASHES: As soon as the protection is removed, the plants should be dusted with finely powdered wood ashes, care being taken to cover the stems and the area around their bases.

Dusting with wood ashes has a tendency to discourage insect pests, and the material, when it finally washes down to the roots of the plants, is beneficial to their growth.

Squash bugs attack foliage. These bugs live by sucking the juices from the plant. They can be trapped by placing pieces of board and the like on the ground near the plant. The traps should be emptied early each morning.

If you notice patches of the shiny brown eggs of the squash bugs grouped on the underside of the leaves, crush them by hand.

During the warmer weather a few inches of compost applied as a summer mulch around the hills greatly assists also in maintaining the moisture content of the hills.

BORERS AND WILTING: When the squash plants are fully grown and developing their fruits, you may find that some of them have suddenly wilted.

If you examine the stem of one of the wilted plants closely, there may be a large white grub (the squash borer) living inside the stem. These grubs can be removed by slitting the stem lengthwise at the points where external signs indicate their presence. If the slit stem is afterwards placed in close contact with the ground and a little earth heaped over it, new roots will form at the nearest nodes.

SUMMER AND WINTER VARIETIES: Summer squashes, including the marrows and zucchini types, should be harvested as needed during the summer and early fall. They should be used while the rind is still soft enough to be easily marred by pressure with the edge of the thumb nail. The zucchinis are best used while extremely young.

For this reason it is advisable to plant only enough hills of summer squash to meet the home demands of this vegetable. But you can secure a succession of ripening and thus a longer period of summer harvesting by selecting two types of summer squash. You can plant one that matures in 55 days and another that matures in 85 days (one of the Acorn types).

The bulk of the hills, however, should be given over to winter squash, the rugged Blue Hubbards, the Buttercups, and the Delicious types. These are planted and cared for in the same manner as the summer squashes except that the hills should be about ten feet apart each way.

Winter squashes require from 125 to 160 days to mature. They should be harvested for storage before frost touches them.

STORING: Select for storage only hard-shelled, sound squashes. You will find that the shell of a well-ripened winter squash is almost unmarked by pressure with the edge of the thumb nail.

They should be washed quite clean, special care being taken with that part which rested upon the ground. They should be dried carefully and examined closely for marks of injury.

A dry place in the cellar or basement where the temperature remains between 40 and 50° is the best place for their storage. It is feasible to store squashes at much higher temperatures (between 60 and 65°) but they will dry out more rapidly at higher temperatures and thus will not remain edible for as long.

You will find it best not to stack squashes but to place them in single layers of rows on shelves well off the floor.

During the winter it pays to wipe and examine stored squashes occasionally to prevent condensed moisture from encouraging superficial moulds. These moulds, if neglected, can eventually become deep-rooted. They will penetrate and destroy large parts of the inside of the squash without greatly marring its surface if not cleaned away. Properly stored squashes will keep until the following spring.

SAVING SEED: If you have grown several varieties, you will find it interesting to dry out a few seeds and save them for planting the following spring. Few garden experiences are more instructive than to watch the different shaped and variously colored squashes these seeds will produce.

Planting a hill with a few cross-bred squash seeds might serve as your pleasant introduction to the vast and complicated subject of plant hybrids and plant variation.

If you have a few squashes left over at the close of the winter, these can be put to good use. If a small disk is cut in the side of the squash and the squash placed near a stove, it will soon dry out. Most of the seeds can then be shaken out of it.

BIRD NESTING HOUSES: Long before the arrival of the white man, Indians suspended these dried squashes for the wrens and martins to use for nesting houses. While the ground is still hard frozen and the trees are bare, you might like to place a few in position near your garden.

PUMPKIN: The common pumpkin is also a member of the *Cucurbita* family, and its culture is very similar to squash. They should be planted in hills four to six feet apart and the ground should be sufficiently warm. Some large-scale gardeners, and many farmers, interplant pumpkin with corn. Sometimes it's necessary to pinch back vines to encourage further development of fruit.

SQUILL: *see* SCILLA

STACHYS: Also known as betony. A genus of coarse herbs or shrubs of the mint family, *Labitae,* also called woundwort. Annuals and perennials, mostly growing in moist places, with white, yellow, purplish, or scarlet flowers in spiked or whorled clusters. Roots generally fibrous, but Japanese artichoke, (*S. sieboldi*), has an edible tuber, and thrives in sandy loam. Another garden species is *S. lanata,* lamb's-ears, a hardy perennial coated with a thick silvery wool which makes it valuable as a foliage plant. *S. grandiflora* is a three-foot perennial with violet flowers, or in varieties, purple, white, or rose flowers. *S. ciliata* is a perennial with reddish purple flowers that grows to six feet.

STAGGER-BUSH: *see* LYONIA

STAGHORN FERN: (*Platycerium*) A genus of ferns with typical fronds shaped like a stag's antlers. Native of tropical Africa and Asia, where they grow on tree trunks and branches or on rocks. Grown principally in warm greenhouses in this country, though a few will thrive with good care as house plants. There are two kinds of fronds—fertile erect antler-shaped segments on fronds growing 1½ to five feet, and sterile circular or shield-shaped fronds which enclose the roots and embrace the trunk or branch on which the plant lives. Roots are embedded in a mass of decayed sterile fronds, and sometimes pierce the bark of the tree.

Common staghorn fern grown as a house plant is *P. bifurcatum,* with grayish-green one to three foot drooping fertile fronds clustered, and the sterile fronds wavy-margined. These are grown usually as basket fern or attached to pieces of charred wood or cork. They should have plenty of indirect light and frequent syringing, but should be watered directly only if they droop. Division of plants is accomplished by attaching a piece to a new branch or piece of wood with wire, keeping it shaded and damp until roots form. Can be done only in a humid warm greenhouse.

A large form with five-foot fronds, much divided, is the *P. biforme,* growing in Java. *P. grande,* which comes from Australia, has six-foot fronds almost free of the hairs common to others. A deep green species is *P. hillii,* with short erect fertile fronds about 1½ feet. Triangle staghorn (*P. stemaria*) has graceful drooping three-foot fronds which are twice forked. Another attractive form is the Java staghorn (*P. willinckii*) whose fertile fronds are clustered in threes, and segments are long and narrow.

STAKING PLANTS: Ornamental plants are staked to protect their naturally upright growth from breaking under special stress, as heavy winds or top-heaviness, or they may be staked to curb a natural tendency to sprawl. Vegetables are staked or are given climbing supports to protect the fruit from dirt and damage on the bare ground, or in order to save space.

Some upright shrubs with slender stems which have been bred for large flowers, such as some of the roses, require stakes. Tall perennials—delphiniums, foxglove, hollyhocks, lilies, and others, may be grown more compactly when they are given support so that each stem remains perfectly upright. A more dense mass of bloom will result from such treatment. With both shrubs and perennials, stakes may be placed near the center of the plant and left there year after year. Or if the stakes are unsightly when the plants die back, or are pruned, shorter stakes may be substituted in the same holes, both to mark their positions and to prevent fresh root damage which might occur when a stake is thrust into the ground.

Many annual flowers profit by stakes, some short and stocky, others tall and slender. Tall snapdragons, calendulas, annual campanulas—all have a tendency to sprawl unless they are given some support. If their main stalks are tied to an upright support when they are about six to eight inches tall, the later growth will be much more erect.

Some perennials, such as peonies, which put forth many stalks, must be supported as a mass, rather than with individual stakes for each stem. Four stakes set into the ground around them in the form of a square with a wire, wooden, or heavy twine connection between the tops of the stakes will usually be sufficient. In the case of peonies, this support should be placed when the leaves are no more than a foot high, and the growth should be trained up through the support. When they have attained their full growth the leaves and flowers will lie over the top wire or twine and will hide it from view. A similar support is useful for tall-growing oriental poppies.

Materials used for staking may be purchased or may be culled from material pruned from the garden. Since a large variety of sizes, thicknesses, and strengths are needed in a border, it is sometimes easier to find just the right sized stake in a collection made from prunings from the shrubbery than in fresh new dowel sticks or bamboo stakes purchased in the garden store. Moreover, a twig with its grey bark will disappear from view much more readily in the border than will a new peeled dowel. Short stakes for smaller annuals need not be more than half to three-quarters of an inch thick. Corner stakes for peonies, which may have quite a sizable load when rain-filled blossoms lean on them, should be at least as thick as a broomstick. Dahlias and hollyhocks need stakes at least an inch through. Some of the shorter annuals and perennials do best when permitted to grow up through a twiggy stake, untrimmed. Others need to be tied to the stakes.

String or twine for tying should be colored, if possible green, tan, or grey, rather than white. Until a white string has weathered, it is sometimes the only thing visible in a border which otherwise is quite tidy and well planted. Wire is sometimes used, but only when it is covered with a paper or string coating which will prevent its burning the stem when it gets hot under a midsummer sun. Wires used to support small trees and shrubs are sometimes inserted in old lengths of rubber hose where they will contact the bark, to prevent chafing.

Twine or wire is first securely tied to the stake at the desired height. It is then tied around the stem of the plant, leaving a loop large enough to permit later growth, but not large enough to allow the plant to blow around inside its support.

Chicken-wire fencing in one to three-foot widths may be used for some supports, where the lateral growth of the plants may be expected to grow through the wire and hide it, as around chrysanthemums, dahlias, and other bushy plants. The fencing may be formed into a circle or irregular shape to contain a clump, or it may be used as a double-row fence, with the row of plants between two lengths of chicken-wire. A similar support, though less likely to remain visible, may be made by spacing stakes about a foot apart on each side of the row, and tying a continuous piece of twine diagonally through the bed, as well as along the outside, from stake to stake. Either of these supports should be placed early in the season so that the plant growth through and around them will be perfectly natural.

Supports used for bulbs, such as gladiolas, or for tubers, such as begonias, should be placed before the soil is filled in above the corm or tuber when it is planted. If the stake is not placed until the shoot emerges from the ground, the gardener runs a risk of piercing the bulb with it, and perhaps killing a valuable plant. Short temporary markers which go deep into the ground may be used here, also, if tall stakes would be unsightly.

In the vegetable garden stakes are always placed before the plants or seeds are in the ground. Supports for tomatoes may be stout stakes, two by two inches; square supports similar to those used for peonies; or the plants may be tied to successive wires of a fence as they grow taller. Peas are usually supported on chicken-wire fencing, or they may be supported by twigs pruned from shrubbery. A dual purpose may be served by such a support, if the twigs are freshly pruned from spring-flowering shrubs and immediately thrust into the ground near the peas, because some of the twigs may root, affording a supply of new young shrubs.

Poles for pole beans are usually young sapling trunks, cut during the winter and trimmed for the purpose.

They may be set erect at each hill, or three poles may be tied together at the top, tripod style, and the seeds planted in the center between them. Poles for beans should be sunk two to three feet in the ground before seeds are planted.

STALK BORER: The common stalk borer is a very active, slender, brown worm commonly found within the stems of weeds and cultivated plants. Its back and sides are striped with white. The stalk borer is a chewing insect. It burrows in the stems of corn, potatoes, tomatoes, eggplant, cabbage, and other crops. Young corn is most liable to injury. Infested plants wilt, break down, and die at the top. The worms often travel from one plant to another, and thus increase their destructiveness.

Little trouble from the common stalk borer is to be expected if weeds are kept down in the vicinity of the garden or on the farm. *See also* INSECT CONTROL.

STAND: The density of population of crop plants.

STAR-APPLE: (*Chrysophyllum cainito*) A tropical evergreen tree of the sapodilla family, which is grown both as an ornamental and for its fruit. Leaves are alternate, leathery, with golden hairs underneath. Flowers are small, in inconspicuous clusters, purplish-white. Fruit smooth, light green or light purple, to four inches across, with white edible pulp, its seeds arranged star-shape in cross-section. Can be grown only in frost-free sections of Florida, and is sometimes grown in greenhouses. Soil should be sandy and rich for best growth. Propagated by seed or cuttings of ripe wood over heat.

STARCH HYACINTH: *see* GRAPE-HYACINTH

STAR GLORY: (*Quamoclit*) These vigorous, handsome climbing vines are good for screening porches and trellises, or for growing in window boxes or tubs. They are big favorites in the South and California. Only one, *Q. lobata,* is a perennial. It grows 15 to 20 feet high, with crimson and yellow flowers in racemes. Cardinal climber (*Q. sloteri*) grows ten feet tall and has striking bright red, white-throated flowers that appear all season. Cypress vine (*Q. pennata*) is distinguished by its feathery foliage and starry orange, scarlet or white flowers. It blooms very freely in full sun, and reaches a height of 20 feet. Star ipomoea (*Q. coccinea*) reaches ten feet and has heart-shaped leaves and scarlet, yellow-throated flowers.

Seeds should be sown early indoors or in a cold frame or cool greenhouse. Transplant them outdoors, 12 inches apart, when frost is definitely over. They like a fertile soil, well supplied with humus. But avoid nitrogenous fertilizers, which will produce too much foliage and few flowers.

STAR-OF-BETHLEHEM: *see* ORNITHOGALUM

STAR VIOLET: *see* QUAKER LADIES

STATICE: *see* LIMONIUM; ARMERIA

STEEPLE-BUSH: *see* SPIREA

STEM: The main axis of a plant which bears buds and shoots instead of roots. The stem is usually above ground, though some stems may also be found below ground in perennials, when they are called rootstocks, and are an important source of new plants for the gardener. Being a continuation of the root, the stem has an internal structure similar to that found in the root, but also has layers of cells whose function is to stiffen the plant and raise it above ground. In woody plants, this tissue has the ability to persist through the winter and bear buds which will develop the following year. In herbs the stem dies to the ground each year. A trunk is the stem of a tree. A stalk is the stem of a leaf or flower. A bulb, tuber, corm, or rootstock is a specialized stem.

STEPHANANDRA: A genus of Asiatic shrubs of graceful growth belonging to the rose family, closely related to and not so showy as spirea. They are valuable for plantings on rocky slopes. Leaves are small and alternate. Flower clusters, usually white, are at the tips of the stems. Easily grown in any garden soil. Propagated by seed, cuttings, or division. *S. incisa* grows to eight feet, with dense masses of slender branches, sometimes drooping, deeply lobed leaves which turn reddish-purple in autumn. Hardy to Long Island Sound. *S. tanakae* is slightly hardier, with larger leaves which turn yellow, orange, and scarlet in autumn.

STERILITY: *see* POLLINATION; ORCHARD

STERNBERGIA: Also known as winter daffodil and lily-of-the-field. A genus of bulbous herbs of the amaryllis family which bloom in autumn. Basal leaves grass-like, 3/4 inch wide and eight to 12 inches long. Three or four flowers from each bulb, on separate stems six to eight inches long. Flowers yellow, crocus-like. Bulbs are planted in August, four to six inches deep in an exposed site in full sun, or on the south side of a wall or building, where roots may bake in summer sun, and be thoroughly drained in winter. After planting they should be left undisturbed for years, and will develop into clumps through bulblets which are formed near the bulbs. Foliage persists through the winter, dying back in spring. If the bulbs must be lifted for any reason, they may be moved when leaves have completely died. *S. lutea,* which grows in Palestine, is thought to have been the biblical "lilies of the field". *S. colchiciflora* and *S. fischeriana,* a spring bloomer, are good rock garden subjects.

STEWARTIA: Also known as *Stuartia.* A genus of deciduous trees and shrubs of the tea family, native on the southern Atlantic coast and in Asia. Although native from North Carolina southward, *S. pentagyna* and *S. pseudo-camellia* may be grown as far north as Massachusetts. Flowers resemble single roses, three to four inches across, white, with anthers orange or blue-violet. *S. pentagyna* grows to 15 feet, *pseudo-camellia* to 50 feet, and its foliage turns brilliant scarlet to yellow in autumn. Silky camellia, (*S. malachodendron*) is a 12-foot shrub which is not hardy north of Virginia. Mountain camellia (*S. ovata*) is also a 10-15 foot shrub, hardy to Long Island Sound.

STILBESTROL: *see* HORMONE

STINGING NETTLES: There are two principal kinds of stinging nettles. One is wood nettle (*Laportea canadensis*) which grows mostly in rich, moist woods in deep shade or in shade along streams or lakes. The other is the stinging nettle (*Urtica dioica*) which is common on higher ground, often in full sunlight. The stinging nettle is a perennial plant and is usually found in dense patches.

Nettles are not generally poisonous, but are irritating. The leaves are covered with hairs which have broad bases, tapering toward the tip. At the slightest touch, the globular tip is knocked off, leaving a sharp point which easily penetrates the skin. At the same time, a noxious liquid oozes out of the hair into the skin, causing a burning sensation of short duration.

The wood nettle, also a perennial, produces itching similar to that caused by stinging nettles. Both kinds have strongly developed root systems and a network of underground creeping rootstocks. One visible difference is in leaf arrangement, the wood nettle having alternate leaves and the stinging nettle opposite ones. Also, those of the wood nettle are more often heart-shaped.

Nettles can be controlled by grubbing out the rootstocks and killing by drying, if this is feasible. Mowing frequently, close to the ground, will prevent seed formation as well as exhaust food reserves stored in the roots and rootstocks.

STIPA: *see* GRASS, ORNAMENTAL

STOCK: (*Mathiola incana*) Stocks, also called gillyflowers, are biennial or perennial plants, usually treated as half-hardy annuals. They grow from one to two feet high, and the beautiful, fragrant flowers are single or double, in many shades of yellow, white, red, blue and purple, borne in racemes. Stock has soft, gray foliage that makes an attractive effect in beds and borders. The flowers last well in the garden or cut. In areas of mild winters, stock may live over and bloom again in the spring.

Start the seeds in February or early March in a moderately rich, well-drained soil in a cool spot indoors or in the cold frame. Cover them very lightly and water sparingly. When the seedlings are large enough to handle, prick them out into flats about three inches apart each way. Harden them off and plant them in their permanent positions as soon as the night temperature doesn't fall much below 50°. Always save the seed of stock, for it will germinate very well after several years if kept in an airtight container. Ten weeks stock is the most commonly grown strain, but there are many others.

Stocks can also be grown in the greenhouse, started anytime. They will usually bloom in about 14 weeks after sowing. However, remember that they are essentially cool-weather plants, and bloom may be delayed by hot weather. For winter house plants, sow the seeds in July, transplanting each plant to a six-inch pot. Feed weekly with liquid manure after they are established.

Evening stock (*M. bicornis*) has small lilac-colored flowers that open at night, filling the garden with fragrance. Its foliage is inconspicuous, so the plants should be surrounded by more showy flowers. Sow the seeds in April outdoors, thinning to six inches apart.

STOLON: An above-ground spreading stem, rooting and sending up new shoots from each node, as white clover does.

STONECROP: *see* SEDUM

STONE MULCHING: A practice which consists of placing rocks between and around growing plants. The stones are placed close together so that very little soil is exposed to the sun. This method greatly aids weed control without cultivation. The elimination of cultivation in itself is of considerable value in that cultivating tools can sometimes cut into lateral-growing roots near the surface.

Stone mulching is an effective way of controlling weeds in the vegetable garden. Stones are placed closely so that little soil is exposed.

Recent studies have shown that stone mulching provides such beneficial conditions as the conservation of moisture; good soil aeration, reduction of wind and water erosion on slopes; maintenance of ideal conditions for soil bacteria, earthworms and burrowing insects; enrichment of the soil by the gradual disintegration of the stone bottoms because of the erosive action of organic acids, and moisture, in the soil; the protection of the soil from the direct rays of the sun; the prevention of the growth of weeds and other plants in competition with food plants; and acts as a temperature regulator.

To follow the stone mulching procedure in your vegetable garden, first cultivate the soil thoroughly. After the stone mulch has been applied, cultivation will be discontinued, so do a good job of it. Apply a generous dressing of compost and then build up the level of the soil in the rows only by bringing additional soil there and repeating with some more compost. In laying the stones, dig into the ground a bit so that the flat surfaces show up. *See also* Mulch; Vegetable Gardening.

STOOL LAYERING: *see* Layering

STORAGE: The health benefits of organic foods can be yours every month of the year, if you know how to store them after harvesting. Organic crops are good keepers, and it's very easy to save even the bulkiest ones for winter use.

Cross-section of a potato storage pit. Hay is laid around and over the potatoes, firmed and shaped into a tepee. Soil is then placed on top.

Canning and freezing, of course, are the chief methods for the quickly perishable crops, such as vegetables like green peas, limas, corn, asparagus and broccoli, and the berry fruits. While much work has been done on drying green vegetables, even under skilled technical control the resulting products make poor food; the amateur had best leave the process alone. *See also* Canning; Freezing.

Drying Fruits: A hot, dry attic is a fine place to dry peaches, apples, cherries and other small fruits. So is a rack above the kitchen range, or any sunny, dry place outdoors. Simply wash and pit the fruits, place them on trays and cover with mosquito netting or window screens. After drying, they can be put in containers and stored in a cool, dry place. Dried fruits take up little space, and this method preserves their food values naturally. (Commercially dried fruits have been treated with all sorts of chemicals.)

Storing Vegetables and Fruits: The good keepers—the root crops and cabbage, onions, pumpkins, late squashes and many fruits—can often be held fresh through the whole winter. Parsnips, salsify, leeks and Brussels sprouts may be left in the ground in areas of not too severe winters, the first two with a straw mulch to make it easier to dig them when wanted. But generally taking them up in late fall and storing them in a cool but frost-free cellar, pit or cold frame is the better practice.

Briefly, root crops, cabbage and celery need cold (not freezing) and moisture, while pumpkins, squash and sweet potatoes need warmth (not heat) and dryness. The last three will keep all winter in a comparatively dry atmosphere at 50 to 60°. Squashes must be handled very carefully to avoid the slightest scratch or scrape that would invite decay.

Pits, Barrels and Cold Frames: Most root crops keep best at close to 32°. They can be stored in a two-foot-deep hole in the ground that is provided with drainage and lined with straw and leaves. Top it with several inches of soil and a heavy mulch. Or a cold frame makes an excellent cover for a storage mound. You can easily fill your cold frame with root crops packed in leaves or straw. The sides and cover protect the contents from wandering animals and the ravages of a northern winter.

CHART OF HOME STORAGE OF FRUITS AND VEGETABLES

(Department of Agriculture)

COMMODITY	PLACE TO STORE [1]	STORAGE PERIOD	TEMPERA- TURE [2]	HUMID- ITY
VEGETABLES:				
DRY BEANS AND PEAS	Any cool, dry place	As long as desired	Cool	Dry
LATE CABBAGE	Pit, trench, or outdoor cellar	Through late fall and winter	"	Moderately moist
CAULIFLOWER AND BROCCOLI	Any cold place	2 to 3 weeks	32° F	"
LATE CELERY	Pit or trench; roots in soil in storage cellar	Through late fall and winter	Cool	Moist
ENDIVE	Roots in soil in storage cellar	2 to 3 months	"	"
ONIONS	Any cool, dry place	Through fall and winter	"	Dry
PARSNIPS	Where they grew, or in storage cellar	"	Cold; freezing in soil does not injure.	Moist
VARIOUS ROOT CROPS	Pit or in storage cellar	"	Cool	"
POTATOES	"	"	See text	"
PUMPKINS AND SQUASHES	Moderately dry cellar or basement	"	50° to 60° F.	Moderately dry
SWEET POTATOES	"	"	55° to 60° F.	"
TOMATOES (mature green)	"	4 to 6 weeks	"	"
FRUITS:				
APPLES	Storage cellar, pit, or basement	Through fall and winter	Cool	Moderately moist
PEARS	Storage cellar	Depending on variety	"	"
GRAPES	Basement or storage cellar	1 to 2 months	"	"
PEACHES	"	2 to 4 weeks	31° to 32° F.	"
PLUMS	"	4 to 6 weeks	Cool	"

[1] Always avoid contact with free water that may condense and drip from ceilings.

[2] Cool indicates a temperature of 32° to 40° F.; avoid freezing.

Ordinary barrels of any size make fine storage containers for many fruits and vegetables. Put them in the garage, a cold spot in the cellar or on the back porch. *See also* BARREL ROOT CELLAR.

A tile buried upright in the soil is recommended by Purdue University. Three bushel baskets of fruit or vegetables can be stored in a tile 18 inches in diameter and 30 inches high. The more porous field tile is best, although the hard burned vitrified or concrete tile may be used. It should be located in a well-drained area, away from possible overflow from downspouts and eaves, and where it will be shaded. Cover with a deep mulch of straw, hay or leaves. A tight barrel could be buried in the same way.

CELLAR STORAGE: The old-time cool, moist, dirt-floor cellar was ideal for fruit and vegetable storage. But even hot, dry cellars can be used if you follow this plan:

Build a small, shelf-lined storage room in a corner away from the furnace, using building paper and matched boards to cover the partition studs. This will leave a four-inch insulating space between the boards. Concrete or cinder block partitions are also good. Put in a heavy, tight door.

Two windows, shaded to keep out light, are necessary to provide free air circulation (to dissipate the gases given off by fruit, which hasten ripening). Ventilate regularly and carefully. The ideal storage temperature for most fruits, like root crops, is close to 32°—apples and Bartlett pears will ripen three times as fast at 40° as at 32°; neither will freeze until it drops below 30°. Many of the root crops keep best buried in boxes of soil and dug as needed.

Humidity should be around 80 per cent. To insure this, sprinkle the floor whenever the humidity gets too low. A three-inch layer of gravel will evaporate much more water, and is therefore better for preventing dryness, than a bare floor because it has a greater surface area. An inexpensive instrument called a psychrometer will tell you both humidity and temperature. Most late varieties of apples, as well as some pears, will keep until April or longer in your storage room or in a well-insulated shed or garage. Always pick them while still very hard. Some varieties of fruits are better preserved in other ways—your experiment station will give you data on those grown in your area.

Remember, it always pays to keep your best-quality produce for storage. Eat during the season anything that is marked or blemished, because the top quality fruit and vegetables are the best keepers.

Farmers' Bulletin No. 1939, available for ten cents from the Superintendent of Documents, U. S. Government Printing Office, Washington 25, D. C., gives a great deal of excellent information on storing crops.

STORAX: (*Styrax*) Ornamental shrubs, mostly native in tropical climates. Leaves are oval or elliptical, alternate, and toothed. Flowers are white, fragrant, growing in loose drooping clusters, and followed by egg-shaped more or less dry drupes. They grow well in warm sandy loam, in full sun. Propagation is by seeds, layers, or by grafting. *S. japonica,* which makes a graceful growth to 30 feet, is hardy as far north as Massachusetts, as is *S. obassia.* Both are showy specimen plants. *S. americana* is somewhat less hardy, growing to ten feet, and tender north of New York City. *S. grandifolia* is a showy 12-foot shrub, hardy only to Philadelphia.

STOVER: Dried stalks of corn or sorghum from which the seed or grain has been removed.

STRAIN: A group of plants differing less than varieties of a species differ from each other, with little or no morphological difference, but with a quality of strength, weakness, color, or texture which persists through all generations of the plants. Strain is a horticultural term, rather than a botanist's term. It is used most often by seedsmen who develop slight improvements in plants through selection, and name the improved seed a strain of that variety.

STRAMONIUM: (*Datura stramonium*). A poisonous annual that occurs as a common barnyard weed in most sections of the United States. The leaves and flowering tops are used medicinally and as a source of atropine, an important medicinal alkaloid. There is also a limited use for the seed for the same purpose.

Although stramonium grows wild on a variety of soils, it thrives best under cultivation on those that are rich and rather heavy. The plant is readily propagated from seed, which is sown directly in the field with a seed drill in spring in rows three feet apart. Germination is usually good. When the plants are several inches high they are thinned to stand six to ten inches apart in the row.

STRATIFY: *see* SEEDS AND SEEDLINGS

STRAW: The stalks or stems of farm crops, commonly used as a mulch and compost material. The fertilizer value of straw is, like that of all organic matter, twofold: first, carbon material is added to the compost; second, plant food is added. The carbon serves the soil bacteria as energy food, while the plant food becomes released for growing crops. Where much straw is available, it is advisable to incorporate considerable amounts of nitrogen, preferably in form of manures, so that the

bacteria which break down the straw into humus do not deplete the soil of the nitrogen that is needed by growing plants.

It is also recommended that the straw be cut up if used in quantities. If mixed with other materials that hold water, or if composted with goodly amounts of barnyard manure, long straw offers no trouble, though heaps cannot be turned easily. Straw compost must therefore be allowed to stand longer. Quicker action is secured by weighing down the material with a thicker layer of earth. This also preserves the moisture inside the heap.

If a large straw pile is allowed to stay outside in the field where deposited by the thresher, it will, with the help of rain and snow, in time decay at its bottom into a slimy mass rich in fungi, while the inside will be broken up by fungi into a crumbly substance. Such predigested material is excellent for compost-making and mulching. Some of the fungi are of the types that form mycorrhizal relations with the roots of fruit trees, evergreens, grapes, roses, etc., and a straw mulch will therefore benefit these plants not only as a moisture preserver but as an inoculant for mycorrhizae.

The nitrogen value of straw is not negligible, but so small that it need not be accounted for in composting. The mineral value of straw depends on the soils where the crops were grown. Typical analyses of straws, computed by Kenneth C. Beeson of the Dept. of Agriculture, are in per cent:

	Calcium	Potash	Magnesium	Phosphorus	Sulfur
Barley	.4	1.0	.1	.1–.5	.1
Buckwheat	2.0	2.0	.3	.4	?
Corn stover	.3	.8	.2	.2	.2
Millet	1.0	3.2	.4	.2	.2
Oats	.2	1.5	.2	.1	.2
Rye	.3	1.0	.07	.1	.1
Sorghum	.2	1.0	.1	.1	.2
Wheat	.2	.8	.1	.08	.1

See also MULCH; COMPOST.

STRAWBERRY: Common name for genus *Fragaria* comprising about 20 species of the rose family. Hardy perennial herbs grown throughout the United States and in most parts of Canada and in Alaska. Best growing areas are the cool, moist states, though with special treatment strawberries can be grown even in the hot Gulf states. Cultivated since about the 15th or 16th century in European gardens, the strawberry was not as popular a fruit as it is today until the advent of the Hovey seedlings, grown in the vicinity of Boston about 1840. These are thought to have been developed from the species *F. vesca,* which is responsible for the late bearing qualities of many of today's everbearings. Also used in developing modern varieties were the following species: *F. chiloensis, F. moschata,* and *F. virginiana.*

Strawberries grow best in a light, humus-rich soil with a pH between 5 and 6. Mulching with sawdust or wood shavings is useful around plants.

Present-day varieties are in constant process of improvement. The following are recommended for various sections of the United States:

Hardy varieties, to be planted in sections where cold is extreme in winter, or where temperatures go below 10° without accompanying snow: Howard 17, Dunlap, Pocomoke, Crescent, and Dakota.

Varieties for northern states and

North Atlantic coastal states: Howard 17, Clermont, Dorsett, Fairfax, Catskill, Glen Mary, Big Joe, Chesapeake, Gandy, and Late Stevens.

Specially recommended for Pacific coastal states: Clark, Dollar, Magoon, Marshall, Oregon, Wilson, Nick Ohmer.

For Florida, the Gulf states, and the hottest part of California: Klondike, Missionary, Aroma, Blakemore, and Southland.

Everbearings: Progressive, Gem, Green Mountain, Mastodon.

SOIL: Strawberries may be grown in any soil which is not too alkaline, too dry, or in need of drainage. Best soil is a light rich loam with plenty of humus and a pH factor between 5.0 and 6.0.

If strawberries are to be planted in the spring, they will profit by being put into a bed which was prepared the previous fall. Site for the plot should be soil which has been cultivated preferably two years before strawberries are planted. This will be free of the beetle grubs and wire worms which may infest soil in which sod has recently been turned.

A site which slopes slightly, toward the south if possible, is best for perfect drainage. Water must never be allowed to stand on a strawberry patch during the winter. A southern slope will encourage earlier blossoming and earlier fruit. This may not be desirable in areas where late frosts often nip the flower buds, unless protection can be given the beds during such emergencies. (Frost-bitten blossoms may be distinguished by their darkened centers.)

Barnyard manure may be turned under in fall at the rate of 500 pounds to each 1000 square feet of proposed strawberry patch. At the same time compost or leaf mold may be stirred into the top layer of soil. Or if no manure is available, leaves and lawn clippings may be worked in to the soil at the rate of five or six bushels to each hundred square feet, accompanied by liberal dressings of cottonseed or dried blood meal, ground phosphate rock, and bone meal. Limestone should be avoided unless the soil is very acid—below pH 5.0.

PLANTING: As soon as the soil is workable in spring the plants may be set. Young plants with vigorous roots should be used. Damaged or diseased leaves or roots are first cut out. The hole dug for each plant should be large enough to permit spreading the roots without crowding. A mound of soil is heaped in the center of the hole, and the plant seated on the mound with roots pressed firmly into the soil all around the base of the mound. Each plant should be set so that the soil level will naturally cover all the roots, but will not cover any of the small leaves which are beginning to develop in the crown. The hole should be half-filled with soil, and water poured in to wash the soil around the roots. Then the balance of the hole is filled, and the soil firmed around the plant. A berry box or basket may be inverted over the newly set plant, to prevent drying during the first few days. From beginning to end of the planting operation, the roots should never be exposed to sun or drying winds. If the day is sunny the plants should at all times be shaded. A damp layer of sphagnum moss or a piece of wet burlap may be placed over the receptacle containing the plants to prevent drying, and one plant removed at a time. Soil should be kept moist for several days after the plants are set.

Several systems of planting are in use throughout the country, all described below. The number of plants needed, provided space is not limited, may be calculated by the family capacity for strawberries, figured at the rate of 50 to 75 quarts of spring berries or 75 to 100 quarts of everbearing from 100 feet of row.

Strawberries may be grown by the matted-row system, the spaced-row system, the hill system, by the stone-mulch system, or by a combination of some of the above systems with the permanently-mulched garden system.

Many commercial growers in the northern and eastern states use matted rows. With this system they plant entire fields each spring for the following spring's production, after which the plants are plowed under and new plantings are made again the following year. Plants are set 18 to 42 inches apart in rows of three to $4\frac{1}{2}$ feet apart, depending upon how many runners the particular variety can be expected to make, and what type of cultivation will be used. Most of the runners are permitted to grow during the first season, only the fruit buds being removed to strengthen the plants. A mat is formed which may be straightened and maintained at the desired width by cultivation. For ease in harvesting, best width is three feet or less. Twin matted rows are sometimes made six to 24 inches apart, with wider paths between one pair of twins and the next.

SPACED ROW: The spaced row system is most often used for varieties which are moderate to weak in sending out runners and producing daughter plants, or when especially fancy fruit is desired. Because of the extra work involved the system is not widely practiced. The daughter plants are spaced at definite distances by covering selected runners with soil until the desired number of daughter plants is obtained for each mother plant. Later formed runners are either removed as they appear or all surplus runners are removed at one time.

In the Cape Cod, Massachusetts region, spacing is used rather extensively. Mother plants are set about 12 inches apart, and two runner series are allowed to form, one with three and the other with four daughter plants.

HILL SYSTEM: In the Hill system plants are set 12 to 18 inches apart, where a small garden tractor or a field tractor can be used for tillage between the rows. In the home garden where hand weeding is necessary, the rows can be spaced closer, or about 18 inches apart.

No daughter plants are allowed to develop in the hill system. Fruit production is entirely dependent upon the yield of the mother plants. Individual plants become quite large and bear more than those in the matted row system.

The matted-row and Hill systems are both temporary, the plants being plowed under after their year, or at most two or three years' production is finished. The spaced-row system may be carried on indefinitely. A variation of the spaced-row system is used in a stone-mulched bed.

STONE MULCHED-BED: To prepare the stone-mulched bed, the ground should first be well plowed or spaded, for this will be the last treatment of the soil in this way as long as the program is continued. Apply a generous dressing of compost. Rows of stone about two feet wide should then be laid with a soil space of about ten inches width in between. The stones should be dug into the ground a little so that wherever possible a flat surface is up. The level of the soil should be built up even with the stones by bringing additional soil and compost there. The labor involved in handling and laying the rocks is not small, but after once established, the labor will be greatly reduced. One can work it on an extended basis, putting in one section each year until the desired number of sections have been established.

The strawberry plants are planted in the soil rows about two or three feet apart. The blossoms should be removed the first year to enable the plants to become established and produce runner plants.

The stone-mulch plot should be a "permanent" plot. To relocate it every couple of years would entail a great deal of work. By keeping the plants well nourished and properly spaced, and seeing that every plant that has produced a crop is replaced by a runner plant, a vigorous, heavy-bearing strawberry patch can be maintained for many years.

A self-perpetuating bed under permanent mulch may be started from an already established strawberry patch, or it may be freshly planted. Soil should be prepared as described earlier. Plants are set 12 inches apart in rows 2½ feet apart. As soon as they are set, the soil in the rows and in the paths between is covered with a six-inch layer of mulch. Grass clippings, straw, ground corncobs, pine needles, or chopped leaves may be used for mulch. Plants are well watered, and are left to develop runners freely throughout their growing season. If new plants have been set, all fruit buds should be removed, to permit all the strength to go into runner development. If runners seem to sit on top of the mulch, they will send roots down through it to the soil below. As the mulch decomposes during the summer, the layer will shrink from six to about two inches, and newly rooted plants will be only slightly above soil level.

If an old strawberry patch is being used to prepare a permanent mulched bed, the procedure is the same as that followed during the second year of a bed set as above. Preparation of the bed for the following year begins with harvest of this year's strawberries. As the picker harvests, he marks with pegs or plant markers the best bearing plants in each row, trying to space markers about 10 to 12 inches apart down the row. When all berries have been harvested, all the unmarked plants are pulled out and mulch is removed. The strawberry patch now contains single rows of plants spaced 10 to 12 inches apart. Well rotted manure, compost, decomposed sawdust plus cottonseed meal, or enriched leaf mold are now worked into the top layer of soil. If the soil is too alkaline, a generous handful of peat moss is worked in around each plant. The soil is smoothed out, and a six-inch mulch is again placed around plants, ready now to form runners which will supply young plants for next year's bearing.

By careful selection of the best bearers each year, a strawberry patch may be made to bear a larger crop with each succeeding year. The heavy mulch during the summer will preserve soil moisture for the young rooted runners, and the decomposed layer of mulch on top of the bed will enrich the soil, which becomes blacker and more mellow with each succeeding year.

IRRIGATION: Strawberries need plenty of water, especially during their bearing period. Everbearing berries should be kept moist during the entire summer in order to produce. A heavy mulch will help preserve soil moisture, but during periods of extreme drought it may be necessary to irrigate plants. A test for soil moisture may be made by digging down six to twelve inches, taking a handful of soil, and forming a ball with it. If the soil will form a moist ball, no water is needed. If it breaks up and crumbles, the strawberries need additional water.

WINTER MULCH: Strawberries grown in the North must be mulched over the winter in order to prevent heaving or drying. The mulch should not be applied until the ground is frozen. If plants are covered too early, while the soil is still warm, they may be stimulated into new growth and will be more vulnerable to the cold when it comes. In the latitude of New York state the mulch should be placed over the bed during the latter part of November.

Straw or pine needles make the best winter mulch. A layer about four inches deep should be placed over the entire bed. If the area is not usually covered with snow, it may be necessary to anchor the mulch with cornstalks or twigs. Where snow may be expected to cover the bed, only the mulch will be necessary.

When the weather begins to turn warm, and the ground thaws in March, the winter mulch should be first loosened, and then removed entirely. It may be stacked beside the garden to use later as summer mulch after the bed has been renovated, if the permanent mulch system is being used.

STRAWBERRY BARREL: Strawberries may be grown in holes in the sides of a barrel, if garden space is limited, although the yield will naturally be small.

Everbearing berries are usually used for a strawberry barrel. Two inch holes are drilled in the sides of the barrel, spaced about six inches apart each way. The barrel is then placed where it will stand, giving it as much sun as possible. Rich garden loam is placed inside, to the level of the first row of holes. Plants are inserted through the holes, and their roots spread. Another layer of soil is filled in on top of the roots, to the level of the next row of holes, and plants are inserted through the second row. This is continued until the barrel is filled.

Various improvements on the strawberry barrel may be added. A perforated pipe may be incorporated down the center of the barrel, through which water or liquid manure may be fed to the plants. The whole barrel may be mounted on a small wheeled platform, to permit it to be turned so that plants on all sides will get sun. A perforated pipe filled with manure may be placed in the center of the barrel, and water applied through the manure, to leach out its nutrients into the barrel.

A variation on the strawberry barrel is the tiered hoop strawberry bed. This is built up above the garden level with successively smaller hoops, each about six inches deep, made of metal. Soil is filled in the hoops, and a water pipe is incorporated in the center as in the barrel. Plants are set in the setbacks between the hoops. The advantage of this arrangement over the barrel is that all the plants may receive their share of sun. *See also* VEGETABLE GARDENING.

STRAWBERRY TOMATO: *see* PHYSALIS

STRAWBERRY TREE: (*Arbutus unedo*) An ornamental large evergreen shrub. It has handsome dark-green leaves and clusters of small white flowers, which resemble lily-of-the-valley, and red strawberry-like fruit which gives the shrub its common name. The flowers and fruit appear simultaneously during the winter months and the fruit is edible. The ultimate height of this shrub is about ten feet. It does best in well-drained soil, and in a wind-protected location. The fruit is edible. *See also* SHRUBS; UNEDO.

STRAWFLOWER: (*Helichrysum bracteatum*). Tall robust annuals which may attain a height of three feet if well grown, strawflowers supply attractive material for dried bouquets. Cut the flowers when they are about half open, strip off the leaves and hang in bundles, blossom end down, in a shady, well-ventilated place until dry. The plants will stand some cold but are best set out after the danger of frost has passed.

STRELITZIA REGINAE: *see* BIRD-OF-PARADISE

STRING BEAN: *see* BEAN

STUARTIA: *see* STEWARTIA

STUBBLE MULCH: Under this system, a continuous cover of crop residues or other organic materials is maintained on the land during the period between harvest and the establishment of new crops as well as during the cultivation of row crops. The basic idea is to till the soil without inverting or burying the residue.

In the arid parts of the country, mulch tillage or stubble mulching has been proven definitely successful. Erosion and water runoff has decreased, and yields are at least as high as those under soil-depleting clean cultivation. Currently soil scientists are debating the advantages of mulch tillage in the eastern half of the nation, where the chief problem is how to keep yields up while preserving the soil and water conservation benefits of the mulch.

Stubble mulching creates an environment of moisture, temperature, aeration and position of food for microorganisms that is similar to the one that nature creates in grassland and forest, where a protective cover of living and dead residues is maintained on the soil surface.

At the Nebraska Agricultural Experiment Station, T. M. McCalla made a comparative study of the effects of stubble mulch on the types, numbers and location of microbial populations. Here are the results:

The earthworm population in the surface eight inches of soil was two to five times as great in plots mulched with crop residues as in plots in which the residue was plowed under. As much as 41 tons of worm casts per acre per year were produced under eight-ton straw mulch.

Where crop residues were left on the surface, a greater number of fungi, aerobic bacteria, and actinomycetes developed in the surface inch of soil than when such residues were plowed under. In the one- to 6-inch depth there was no significant difference.

The number of denitrifying organisms was slightly greater where stubble mulch was practiced than where the land was plowed. When very large amounts of straw mulch (four and eight tons per acre) were used, the numbers were increased greatly.

In answer to the question of how much crop residue it takes to control wind erosion, scientists working in South Dakota have found that it takes about 1,000 pounds per acre on heavy soils, 1,500 pounds on medium-textured soils, and 2,500 pounds on sandy soils. A ten bushel per acre wheat crop will produce approximately 1,000 pounds of crop residue. This amount, if properly managed, is sufficient to afford protection to crops planted on heavy textured soils.

STUMP REMOVAL: Occasionally the problem arises of how to remove tree stumps: Here is a discussion of methods to be considered:

1. Pulling the stump out with heavy tractors or mechanical equipment.

2. Blasting with explosives (not practical near buildings or landscaped areas).

3. Use of chemicals commonly sold for killing and disintegrating stumps.

4. Cut the stump at the ground level, cover it with soil and keep the soil moist. To hasten decay, bore several vertical holes in the stump before covering it with soil.

5. Stumps can be burned out fairly quickly with charcoal, coke, or coal in a "stove" made of a metal container such as a five-gallon paint can. Remove the top and bottom of the can and punch draft holes in the sides near the bottom. Put the stove on top of the stump, or down over it, and build the fire, starting with kindling wood. Add charcoal, coke, or coal and move the stove (if on a large stump) as it burns one part.

6. Using a grub hoe, a mattock, an axe, a shovel, and some muscle power, dig a trench about two feet deep around the stump where the roots enter the ground, cut the roots as close as possible to the stumps, and roll or slide the stump out of the hole. This is least difficult if the stump was cut high, so that leverage is good when a tow chain or something similar is used. Instead of taking the stump out, you can dig a very deep hole beside and under it and let it drop down. Be sure the hole is deep enough to bury the stump with several inches of soil over it, and pack the soil well, preferably watering it in tight.—*David Stry.*

STYRAX: *see* STORAX

SUBSOIL: *see* SOIL; C HORIZON

SUBSOILING: The basic idea of subsoil tillage or chisel plowing is to get more water and organic matter down deeper into the soil and to disturb the land's surface as little as possible. Generally, the word "subsoiling" has come to mean working or cutting up the land with a subsoil chisel to a depth of from 16 to 30 inches and with heavy single chisel implements to over five feet. Power requirements for these heavy deep-working tools are high. Sometimes the combined power of three of the biggest tracklayer tractors is needed. But for the lighter tools, with a single chisel, penetrating up to 30 inches deep, the power of the ordinary wheeled two to three plow farm tractor is usually sufficient.

Subsoiling can be carried out at any time when the land is not frozen or covered with a growing crop. It generally is advisable to subsoil at the driest time of the year, during the late summer or early fall months, so that the cuts may be open to receive the water of the fall rains and winter snows.

Since subsoiling leaves residues on top of the soil, it serves to reduce runoff. Tests at the University of Nebraska Experiment Station have shown that the runoff from plowed land is from two to three times as great as where subsoiling was carried on.

Research at the Idaho Experiment Station has revealed that four per cent more of the moisture received was retained under subtillage methods compared to one-way discing and moldboard plowing.

Besides controlling erosion, the subsoiling practice most times boosts yields. In southern Idaho, where the annual rainfall is about 15 inches, experiments have clearly shown yield advantages of three to four bushels of wheat per acre gained from subtillage. In areas of greater rainfall, subsoiling has not made appreciable differences in the yield figures, but here it is well to remember that the practice saves the soil and helps insure continued high yields.

The idea of subsoil improvement by means of plant growth can well be regarded as an accompaniment to other methods of subsoil treatment. Growing deep-rooting legumes, supplements the mechanical steps and can make an effective combination to prevent water runoff and erosion. As the roots of these plants decompose, they put organic matter down deep into the subsoil and leave channels to facilitate water intake. Alfalfa and sweet clover have long been the standard plants for this soil conditioning service and other legumes are also being tested. *See also* AERATION; HARDPAN.

SUCCESSION PLANTING: *see* PLANTINGS, SECOND; VEGETABLE GARDENING

SUCCULENT FEEDS: Those feeds high in water content such as pasturage and silage.

SUCCULENTS: Plants with juicy tissues. The term succulent is used to include many kinds of plants from a large number of families whose tissues have been specialized through the needs of their climatic conditions to store large quantities of moisture.

Besides possessing spongy storage tissues, succulents are enabled to survive in their desert homes by a variety of water-saving devices. Leaves, when present, have leathery surfaces which permit little evaporation. In some cases the leaves turn to present only their edges to the sun. In others, the leaves contain thick sponges which are storage vessels. Some of the succulents are leafless, their leaves having become thorns or spines attached to the stems. Leaves appear on some succulents only during their growing season, a brief period representing the rainy season in their native deserts. Few, if any, leaves persist on these plants during the resting period.

Many succulents are grown in window gardens, rock gardens, or in the Southwest in desert gardens, for their surprising, odd, or sometimes sculpturesque shapes. Cacti, round or barrel-shaped, with disjointed shoots piled on each other are popular forms. Some of the stone plants from South Africa, which resemble green pebbles partly sunk in the soil, and the *fenestrarias,* window plants whose growth is underground and only seen through its translucent flat tissue at ground level, are grown as curiosities.

Brilliant flowers may be found in some succulents, as in some of the cacti, kalanchoes, rocheas, mesembryanthemums, and echeverias. Others, such as sedums, put forth masses of tiny delicate flowers. Flowers of the century plant are rare, occurring traditionally only after the plant has grown 100 years but actually in less time than that. But because of the rarity of the bloom, century plant flowers are prized more as a horticultural feat than as blooms of spectacular beauty. Their flowers are large and colorful, but not more so than many which bloom in a year.

While most succulents are native to desert or arid areas of tropical and semi-tropical America and Africa, some are at home in climates where the temperatures drop far below zero. Sedums, for instance, come from such frigid spots as Greenland, Alaska, Siberia, and Mongolia. Sedums are also to be found in areas where the climate is predominantly humid, as are kalanchoes, rochea, and other members of the *Crassulaceae.* These succulents require more moisture during their growing season than do some of the drier desert natives, but like cacti, need an almost dry resting period.

Members of the cactus family, while certainly succulents, are not included among those grown by some of the succulent specialists. Among amateurs, however, the following species are grown in succulent collections: *echinocereus,* with its low, sometimes trailing growth; *cereus* and *echinocactus,* each often large in growth; round or spherical *ferocactus; neomammillaria,* cylindrical or globular and covered with tubercles; *opuntias* or prickly pears; *epiphyllum,* airplants with branches which are flat and leafy in appearance.

Aloes, apicras, gasterias, haworthias, and yuccas are all succulents belonging to the lily family. Sansevieria, a well-known house plant, is probably the most wide-spread lily succulent. The century plant is one of the agaves, a member of the amaryllis family which is closely allied to the lilies.

Stapelia, hoodia, huernia and *trichocaulon* are succulent members of the milkweed family, many of them with beautiful flowers which have offensive odors.

Some of our most familiar succulents are members of the orpine family, the *Crassulaceae.* Among them are sedums and sempervivums, commonly known as stonecrop and hens-and-chickens. Among the succulents with handsome and fragrant flowers are the cotyledons, crassulas, kalanchoes, and rocheas, also of this family.

Some of the most fantastic forms are found among the spurge family members. Crown-of-thorns, *Euphorbia splendens; E. caput-medusae,* or Medusa-head, with its writhing leafless stems; *E. obesa,* the fat, and *E. meloformis,* the melon-shaped, are all from this group.

From the *Compositeae,* the daisy family, come kleinia, senecio, and othonna, each of which is represented among the succulents.

A large group of fig-marigolds, or mesembryanthemums, are from the *Aizoaceae,* and are mostly native in South Africa. These include the stone plants, window plants, and a variety of other small species with tiny brilliant flowers, which carpet the ground in warm areas where they may be naturalized. Many of them make interesting window garden specimens.

CULTURE: Though temperature requirements for succulents may widely differ, all have one common cultural requirement. They must all be grown in well-drained soil. Even the most rugged species, which will stand many degrees of frost, will not tolerate water standing around their roots and stems, especially in winter.

Outdoors, the best soil for most varieties is sandy to gravelly, in a location which slopes and receives full sun. If a completely sunny spot is not available, the less sun the plants get, the less moisture they want.

The same principle holds for plants in the succulent class grown indoors. With full sun and plenty of air circulating around them they will tolerate a moderate amount of moisture and higher temperatures than if they receive little sun. If they are grown with little or no sun, they should be kept cool and watered only when they begin to show thirst by shrinking.

Soil required by most succulents grown indoors should consist of at least 50 per cent sand, with light loam, broken brick, and broken flower pot filling the balance of the pot. Soil should be more alkaline than acid, and may be sweetened with ground limestone and bone meal. Fresh or decaying organic matter should be avoided. To avoid nematodes in such soil, which is devoid of fungus, the nematodes' natural enemy, it may be necessary to sterilize the soil with boiling water before potting. Or the soil may be potted and the pots left out in freezing weather for a period to kill some of the more vulnerable soil pests.

Some authorities advise watering succulents only from the bottom. Others recommend weekly spraying of the tops of plants. The individual succulent may require one or the other treatment—experience will quickly tell which.

During the growing period, succulents should be watered well, though not until soggy, at least once each week. Excess water must be allowed to drain away immediately. Watering should continue, and the plants should be given as much sun as possible, as long as growth continues. Small new shoots at the growing tip of the plants will indicate when this period begins, and when it ends.

Some succulents may be propagated by seed. More frequently they are propagated by suckers, or by cuttings. Suckers may be removed from the parent plant and potted in similar soil with little loss of growth. Cuttings should be made during the growing period, if possible. If woody tissue is present in the plant, it should be avoided. Cutting should be done with a sharp knife through the green tissue. Before planting the cutting in sand, the cut surface should be allowed to heal, or at least to dry in the sun.

House-grown succulents will usually profit from a summer outdoors. Pots should be sunk to the rims in a sandy bed in full sun, or it may be sunk in a bed of ashes. They should be protected from heavy rains while outside. *See also listings for individual plants;* CACTUS.

SUCKER: A shoot from the root or lower stem of the plant, especially applied to shoots arising on trunks of trees below the main branches. In some cases, as in lilacs, the suckers arising from the roots may be used to propagate the plant. In other plants, where an improved variety has been grafted on an unimproved rootstock, a sucker arising from the root or stem below the graft will produce an unimproved variety plant, and should be immediately removed. Suckers on fruit or ornamental trees are thought to rob the top of the tree of food. Sucker is sometimes also applied to water sprouts, that is, atypical vertical shoots which arise on the branches of trees, especially where the root-branch balance has been upset by too severe pruning or by injury to a branch.

SUCKERING: *see* BRAMBLE FRUITS; PROPAGATION

SUDAN GRASS: *see* GREEN MANURE

SUGAR WASTES: In sugar manufacturing, several wastes accumulate; the greatest quantity is the filter material, often made of bone transferred into charcoal, which is filled with residues from the sugar and sold as bone black. Its phosphorus content is above 30 per cent, its nitrogen value around two per cent, its potassium content variable.

Raw sugar wastes show a content of over one per cent nitrogen and over eight per cent phosphoric acid.

SUMAC: (*Rhus*) The sumacs are especially valued for their magnificent brilliant red autumn foliage and hairy red fruits. They are shrubs or small trees that do well in a large variety of soils, near neutral and not wet. Sumacs will tolerate even very dry, sandy sites or rocky hillsides. They can be grown easily from seed, and are hardy over most of the United States.

Fragrant sumac (*R. canadensis*) is a low shrub growing at most three feet high. Its flowers, appearing in spikes in early spring, are greenish-yellow, and the foliage is quite fragrant. White sumac (*R. glabra*) grows from ten to 20 feet tall, while staghorn sumac (*R. typhina*) may grow taller. Both have dense clusters of green flowers in early summer and very showy fall fruits and foliage. Dwarf sumac (*R. copallina*) grows as a shrub or small tree up to about 12 feet tall, and stands city smoke and dry soil very well. *R. trilobata,* the lemonade sumac or squaw-bush, resembles fragrant sumac, but it is neither as beautiful nor as aromatic as that species.

Some other members of the sumac family are the sourberry (*R. integrifolia*), a shrub or small tree with pink flowers, hardy only in the southernmost parts of the country; and the smoke trees, *R. cotinus* and *R. americanus,* which grow ten to 15 feet tall. Both of these last have handsome fruiting clusters with long plumes, and are hardy in the lower central, southern and Pacific states, as far as lower New England in the East.

The leaves and flowers of the sumacs are high in tannin, and their shallow, spreading roots are valuable for preventing erosion. *See also* POISON SUMAC.

SUNFLOWER: (*Helianthus*) Members of the daisy family. Included in the genus, beside sunflowers, are *H. tuberosus,* or Jerusalem artichoke, which see.

Sunflowers are often grown for ornament, as well as for the purpose of harvesting their valuable seed. They do best in a moist, rich, deeply cultivated soil. In the home garden, seed can be planted about a foot or more apart and ½ inch deep.

Native throughout America, sunflowers were grown here by the Indians who used the seed for food. Seed was ground to provide meal, and oil was extracted by the Indians. Seed has long been a delicacy of some of the Old World countries, where it is munched as a between-meals snack, much as we might eat peanuts.

Sunflower seeds are an important ingredient in many of the best poultry feeds. It has been known for years that poultry fed on this seed were healthier. It is extremely high in protein, calcium, phosphorus, thiamin, riboflavin and niacin. Its oil is an important source of linoleic acid, and lecithin is also present in it. However, it was not until the Second World War, when fats were in short supply, that mills were set up in the midwest and in Canada to extract sunflower-seed oil. Experimental work carried out by Texas, Massachusetts, Manitoba, and other agricultural agencies and departments has encouraged the planting of sunflowers as a farm crop. But because harvesting was largely a manual operation, farmers have been reluctant to plant them. New smaller varieties are now being developed, of a size which may

be harvested by existing farm machinery.

LARGE SCALE GROWING: Sunflowers will grow successfully on any land which will produce field corn. A light loam is preferable to a heavy wet soil. The field should be prepared by plowing, disking, and smooth harrowing, similar to the seed bed preparation made for corn planting.

A green manure crop should be planted in the field the previous fall. Soil should be tested for acidity, and ground limestone applied if necessary to bring it to pH 6.0 to 8.0. Manure may be applied at the rate of ten tons per acre, sunflowers being heavy feeders. Also, 1,000 pounds of phosphate rock and 500 pounds of granite dust per acre should be applied.

Seed is planted at the rate of three pounds per acre, using a two-row corn planter, dropping seeds at 24-inch intervals. Rows are spaced 36 to 42 inches to allow a cultivator to pass between them. Plants are cultivated twice and thinned at six inches to stand three or four feet apart in the row. Crowding causes plants to fall in heavy winds, and become a total crop loss. Allow a growing period of 120 days before the first frosts. Sunflowers are hardy to light spring frost, and may be planted when it is safe to plant field corn. The plants are much more resistant when they come up than at the four to six-leaf stage.

As heads grow heavy the stalks may need support of some kind. Sometimes gently looping two or three stalks together will help them to withstand heavy winds.

Sunflower plants grown close together have been found effective as a weed smotherer. In fields badly infested with weeds they may be grown about 12 inches apart in the row, with the rows 12 inches apart. Their leaves are so broad that weeds cannot get any sun, and wither away. Such sunflower plants are cut before maturity, and the leaves fed to cows, pigs, steers, and chickens.

HARVESTING: Sunflowers are ready for harvest as soon as birds begin to pick at the outer rows of seed. At this time the outer rows are completely ripe, the next rows are ripe but not dry, and the center seeds are still somewhat green. Heads are cut off the flowers with about a foot of stalk attached. Stalks are tied together, and the heads hung in an airy barn or loft to dry. When thoroughly dry, the seeds may be removed by rubbing them lightly. Stored in airtight containers, their food content and vitamins will remain in good condition for a long time.

Varieties include the river sunflower (*H. decapetalus*)—a perennial growing to five feet; giant sunflower (*H. giganteus*)—also known as Indian potato, strong-growing perennial to 12 feet high; common sunflower (*H. annus*)—the annual type growing about 12 feet, with one foot yellow flower heads; swamp sunflower (*H. angustifolius*)—perennial to eight feet.

SUNSCALD: A burning or browning of plant tissue as a result of intense heat or exposure to sun, which is followed by an infection becoming cankerous. This may happen in summer, but is more serious when it occurs during the winter on tree bark. Winter sunscald is a result of extreme cold, and should be treated by being cleaned out and coated to prevent infection.

SUPERPHOSPHATE: *see* ROCK PHOSPHATE

SWAINSONA: Also known as poison bush and darling pea. A genus of herbs of the pea family, native to Australia, and grown only in warmest sections of the species being pests in Australia, Only two species are cultivated, some of the species being pests in Australia, where they poison grazing cattle.

Winter sweet pea (*S. galegifora*)

is a sprawling or partly climbing shrub with clusters of red, pea-like flowers. Varieties have white, pink, rose, or violet flowers. *S. greyana* has whitish woolly young foliage, with erect stalks of pink flower clusters.

SWATH: A row of hay or grain left by the mower.

SWEET ALYSSUM: (*Lobularia*) Often grown in straight rows along the edge of beds, it is equally as effective in masses in informal beds. Seed may be planted in the tulip bed or other spring bulb beds, and after the bulbs have finished blooming the Sweet Alyssum will act as a camouflage hiding the ripening leaves of the bulbs.

Other common names for Sweet Alyssum are Snowdrift and Sweet Alison. Sweet Alyssum's greatest assets are its easy culture, profuse bloom over a long period, and general pest-resistance.

For early bloom, sweet alyssum seed should be sown as soon as ground is workable. It is often grown as edging in straight rows or masses.

CULTURE: Seed should be sown in the open ground as soon as it is workable for early bloom. Sweet Alyssum, like many other hardy annuals, may also be sown late in the fall. They will sprout, grow and bloom long before the plants raised from spring-sown seed. Sweet Alyssum will self-sow. Sometimes germination may take place the following spring; but if they start growth in the fall, the plants are likely to live through the winter if they are given protection with a loose mulch.

A well-prepared soil, rich in compost, will insure a strong growth and fine blooms, but Sweet Alyssum seems to thrive in soil and under conditions where something fussier fails. Prepare the soil for planting and cover the seed with about ⅛ inch soil. Sow thinly as germination is high. Seedlings can be thinned out or transplanted. During the summer, shearing the plant tops every few weeks will remove some fading flowers and stimulate the plants to produce more flowers.

WINTER BLOOMING: Sweet Alyssum may be easily grown in pots for winter blooming. It will bloom within a month after sowing in pots. Some plants from the garden may be brought indoors in the fall before severe weather sets in. Carefully lift the plants and reset with as much earth as possible adhering to the roots. Set in pots large enough to accommodate the roots conveniently. Flower buds should be pinched out. It is also important to keep the plants pinched back to force them into a bushy and well-branched form.

VARIETIES: Carpet of Snow with its dainty, pure white flowers give the impression of a white carpet. Fine for wide edgings, the plants grow about four inches high and spread considerably. Little Gem, which is also white, is a favorite for narrow edgings. Royal Carpet has rich royal purple flowers and grows low and spreading. Violet Queen is a deep shade of violet and keeps its color throughout the season.—*Barbara Hardy.*

See also ALYSSUM.

SWEET BASIL: see BASIL, SWEET

SWEET BELLS: see LEUCOTHOE

SWEET CICELY: (*Myrrhis odorata*) Decorative perennial with fern-like leaves and umbels of white flowers. It grows two to three feet tall. The delicate leaves and flowers are attractive and have a light airy appearance. Grows best in partial shade. Seeds are planted in fall of the year or stratified.

The green seeds have a spicy taste and are mixed with other herbs. They are used in certain liqueurs. Seeds are picked green and used fresh.

SWEET CLOVER: see CLOVER

SWEET COLTSFOOT: see PETASITES

SWEET FLAG: (*Acorus calamus*) A native plant having slender, lily-like leaves as much as six feet long. Best grown in clumps and kept in background. Will grow in damp spots. Thrives in wet soil and full sun, can be grown in drier places. Sweet flag is a hardy perennial, propagated by division.

Leaves and rootstalks often used for flavoring and sachets; plant has lemony fragrance.

SWEET GUM: (*Liquidambar*) The native sweet gum tree (*L. styraciflua*) grows as high as 125 feet; is most noted for its lovely scarlet foliage in fall. Grown from Massachusetts southward along the Atlantic Coast and in many midwestern states and further south to Mexico, the sweet gum prefers moist, rich soil. It produces small flowers, shiny brown fruit.

SWEET MARJORAM: see MARJORAM

SWEET PEA: (*Lathyrus odoratus*) An annual which seems to do well when planted in the fall. The one great obstacle to the successful growing of sweet peas is a hot, dry climate. Sweet peas love cool, moist weather. In regions where climatic conditions make fall sowing feasible it is much preferred to spring planting. The objective is to plant so late that the seeds will not germinate until spring. If you try both methods, you will find that the fall-sown seed will have sprouted and begun to make vigorous roots before it is possible to start planting in the spring.

CULTURE: The planting time is very important. In the southern states where there is only a very slight amount of winter freezing, seeds are sown during October. In the northern and central states where winters are severe, the seeds are planted late in the fall, just before the ground is expected to freeze.

To be sure of a good stand, sow the seeds one to two inches apart and three inches deep in rows three feet apart. Mound the soil slightly over the rows to prevent water from remaining there. As soon as the ground freezes hard, mulch the planting with about three inches of straw, hay or evergreen boughs. Remove this covering early in the spring.

In preparing the soil for planting, dig a trench 1½ to two feet deep, fill the bottom foot with good soil and well rotted manure, or compost, and the remainder with fertile top soil to which has been added one pound of bone meal to 15 feet of row. If the soil is acid, apply lime at the rate of ½ pound to 15 feet of row.

SUMMER CARE: After the plants get a good start, continued growth will depend largely upon the supply of moisture. Don't wait until they begin to lose vigor before supplying water. An effective method is to open a trench a few inches deep about a foot each side of the row and occasionally flood this with water. Mulching will also help to conserve the moisture, and especially important with sweet peas, keeps the soil several degrees cooler than when it is exposed directly to hot sun.

Whatever type of support is to be used, it should be put in place while the plants are only a few inches or at planting time. Wire is least desirable to use as a support as in the hot summer sun it may become hot enough to injure the stems.

A common cause of short flowering season with sweet peas, even when weather and other conditions are favorable, is neglect to prevent the forming of seed pods. Keep your sweet peas cut. This is a very important point, for once seed has set, the plant will have accomplished its purpose and will not continue to bloom.—*Barbara Hardy.*

See also LATHYRUS.

SWEET POTATOES: (*Ipomoea batatas*) One of the best food sources of vitamin A and vitamin C. One ordinary sweet potato will supply 33 per cent of the minimum daily requirement of vitamin C and 150 per cent of the adult requirement for vitamin A.

CULTURE: Sweet potatoes can be grown as a garden plant over a wide area of the U.S. They prefer a sandy soil, but can be grown in a heavier soil if it is worked five or six inches deep. Ridging is also necessary if optimum size and quality are to be produced.

An acre of sweet potatoes requires 10,000 to 12,000 plants, but 100 or 200 plants will produce an ample supply for the average family. Plants can be purchased from a nursery, or can be grown at home from four or five sweet potatoes placed in a shallow pan of water in your house. In about a month the plants will be large enough to separate and plant outdoors. The trick of this method is to get the right variety of potato.

Start preparing ground for sweet potatoes during April. Make a furrow long enough to accommodate the plants you need (they should be spaced 12 to 18 inches). Place an inch or two of well-rotted compost or manure in the furrow. Then ridge up the soil on top of this band of humus. Ridge height is important—it should be at least ten inches to prevent roots from growing too deep for easy growth and harvesting.

Don't set out the plants until about a month after the average date of the last frost in your area, or until ten days after the "frost free" date. Sweet potatoes are a tropical plant (of the morning glory family) and are very sensitive to frost. Use a rounded stick, like a broom handle, to push the roots of the plants four or five inches deep. Water them after planting to settle the roots.

The area around the plants should be kept free of weed growth until the vines shade out weeds themselves. Don't worry too much about drought, because sweet potatoes like hot, dry weather.

Dig the potatoes with a pitchfork before frost hits the vines. Frost on the vines can damage the tubers below. Be careful not to damage the potatoes during digging, as marked potatoes spoil more easily. Let them "cure" on the surface of the ground for several hours after digging. Curing helps yams keep better in storage.

An important point in favor of growing sweet potatoes is that they are a garden crop that can be stored and enjoyed all winter long. They make an excellent contribution to your year-round organic food supply.

VARIETIES: The Oklahoma Experiment Station has recently developed a sweet potato that has far better vitamin values than Porto Rico, the type that is presently used by many sweet potato growers. Called Allgold, the new potato contains 50 per cent more vitamin C and three times as much vitamin A as Porto Rico.

In addition to these remarkable vitamin qualities, Allgold has produced nearly double the yield of Porto Rico in extensive field trials. Over a four year period Allgold averaged 271 bushels of roots to the acre, while Porto Rico produced only 172. In taste and internal quality it is at least equal, if not superior, to Porto Rico. The fact that Allgold starts yielding in August makes it more suitable for areas with shorter growing seasons.

STORAGE: Sweet potatoes should be well cured before storage. This can be done easily by placing the harvested roots in a well-ventilated place where temperatures are fairly high. For best results the temperature should be around 80 to 85° and should be held in that range for ten to 15 days.

Following the curing period, the sweet potatoes should be stored at a temperature of about 50° and humidity between 75 and 80 per cent. During the storage period the sweet potatoes should not be handled or moved until time for use. Storage temperatures below 50° usually will favor decay, according to Purdue University agricultural reports. *See also* PO-TATO.

SWEET VIOLET: (*Viola odorata*) Hardy perennial with creeping rootstalks and heart-shaped leaves. Of the more than 600 kinds of violets known, this species is considered the most fragrant. Blossoms are deep violet and single.

It makes beautiful edging or border plantings; also useful in partially shaded spots. Thrives in poor soils especially in partial shade. Raised from seed or propagated by division. The flowers are occasionally candied and can be used in salads.

SWEET WILLIAM: (*Dianthus barbatus*) This herbaceous perennial or biennial is one of the oldest known garden flowers. Often used for borders and in flower arrangements because of its lasting quality. Sweet William grows to one to two feet high, topped with rounded clusters of flowers. Flowers come in many shades, from red to white, are fringed, single or double.

Plants can be easily grown from seed, started in June or July which will give blooms the following year. In the North plants can be wintered in cold frame or should be given some protection if left outdoors. They do best in full sun, well-drained, fairly rich soil. *See also* DIANTHUS.

SWEET WOODRUFF: (*Asperula odorata*) Low, spreading plant forming clumps about eight inches high. The slender leaves are borne in starry whorls; the flowers are very small and white, in loose clusters.

Woodruff makes a charming ground cover under taller plants. Can be grown as a perennial if winters are not too severe. In cold climates plants may be kept indoors or in cold frame over winter. Will thrive in half-shaded places.

SWISS CHARD: A variety of the common beet, variety *cicla* of *Beta vulgaris*. Chard grows without the enlarged red root used as a vegetable in the beet, and has finer textured leaves which are used as a cooked green, like spinach. A red-veined variety which is the older type has been supplanted by a white-veined variety, the vein sometimes being cooked alone like asparagus. Like beets and clover, chard is a very deep-rooted plant which is useful in a garden where the subsoil requires aeration. Roots are known to penetrate as deeply as six feet in a single season.

Chard will grow in any good garden soil in which lettuce thrives. It will do well in soil amply supplied with humus, in an open, sunny, well-drained location. Chard is a warm-weather plant, often grown to replace spinach as a green during the hot weather.

Plants should be spaced 12 inches apart in the row. Outer leaves are harvested, the inner ones developing within a week to harvest size. A row 15 to 25 feet long is usually sufficient for a family of four, and may be expected to supply greens for cooking from July until frost. In very hot sections plants may show a tendency to become exhausted, that is, to produce smaller leaves after a period of growth. When this happens, new seed may be planted to be ready for harvesting after a month or six weeks. Chard may be kept producing through all but the most severe winters by covering the plants with a deep layer of straw or similar mulch.

SWITCH GRASS: *see* PANIC GRASS

SYCAMORE: *see* PLANE TREE

SYKES, FRIEND: The well-known English farmer-author who has done an effective job of emphasizing the practicality of organic farming. Both his books (as *Humus and The Farmer*) and his 750 acre farm called Chantry support his belief that "I am humus-farming, because, after more than 40 years on the land, I am satisfied that there is more profit in it than in the use of artificial fertilizers. Farming is essentially a long-term policy, and if I would farm at a profit, I must see to it that I have some land to farm in the long years ahead."

SYMPHORICARPOS: Hardy shrubs of the honeysuckle family, mostly natives of China. Leaves opposite, usually entire, flowers inconspicuous, bell-shaped or tubular, occurring in small clusters. Fruits pairs or clusters of berries, for which the shrubs are usually planted. Easily grown in al-

The outer leaves of this Swiss chard are ready for harvest. A warm-weather plant, chard grows well in an open, sunny, well-drained location.

most any soil, and will thrive in part shade, or even in urban areas. Most widely grown species is the snowberry (*S. albus*).

Indian currant or coralberry (*S. orbiculatus*), is also a popular species, grown for its reddish-purple fruit and for its attractive crimson autumn foliage. It grows to five to seven feet, and is hardy even in cities, and as far north as New Jersey to South Dakota. More hardy northward is wolfberry (*S. occidentalis*), a stiffer five-foot bush with pinkish flowers and white berries. Most handsome fruit is that of *S. chenaulti,* a hybrid with white dotted red berries. *See also* SNOW-BERRY.

SYMPHYTUM: *see* COMFREY

T

TABERNAEMONTANA: The crape jasmine (*T. coronaria*) is a lovely shrub hardy only in Florida and southern California, and in protected parts of the deep South. Very fragrant, it grows six to eight feet high with shiny leaves and clusters of single or double white flowers. It wants a fertile, sandy soil high in humus, and full sun. Propagate by cuttings grown in pots and set out in the fall when the young plants are no less than a foot tall. In areas where there is frost, they must be protected the first winter by having soil banked up around them.

T. grandiflora is a slightly smaller shrub with yellow flowers that have no fragrance, and is not very popular except in southern Florida.

TAGETES: *see* Marigold

TAHITI ORANGE: *see* Otaheite Orange

TAIL-FLOWER: *see* Anthurium

TAMARACK: *see* Larch

TAMARISK: There are over 70 species of tamarisk, trees and shrubs highly tolerant of salt and sand and therefore good plants for seaside gardens. They have feathery foliage, the leaves extremely tiny, and similarly small flowers borne in panicles in summer.

The salt cedar (*T. gallica*) grows widely through most of the country, especially in the West. It has bluish foliage and white or yellow blooms, and grows about 20 feet tall. The salt tree (*T. aphylla*) is slightly taller and very tolerant of desert and alkali conditions. It is hardy only in the South and Far West, where it is often planted as a windbreak. *T. pentranda* grows ten feet or so tall, has big clusters of pink blooms, and is as hardy as the salt cedar. *T. odessana*, a small shrub up to five feet high, is similarly hardy. In the West, many of the tamarisks are important bee plants. Propagate by cuttings.

TANBARK: A waste material of the leather industry that is now being composted by some companies. Tanbark consists of waste materials from wattle, mangrove, myrobalans and valonia—plants used in modern tanning methods and imported from South America, Africa, India and Asia Minor. The composted material is a recommended organic fertilizer.

TANGERINE: (*Citrus nobilis deliciosa*) Also known as mandarin orange, this citrus fruit reaches the peak of its popularity around the Christmas season since it ripens somewhat earlier than most oranges and also because they are attractive to use for decorative purposes. The rich, red color of their medium-size fruit and the dark green, glossy foliage makes the tangerine trees one of the most beautiful of citrus trees. The flesh of their fruit is easily separated from the peel. *See also* Citrus Fruits; Orange.

TANGLEBERRY: *see* Huckleberry

TANIA: *see* Xanthosoma

TANKAGE: Refuse from slaughterhouses and butcher shops other than blood freed from the fats by processing. Depending on the amount of bone present, the phosphorus content varies greatly. The nitrogen content varies usually between five and 12.5 per cent, the phosphoric acid content is usually around two per cent, but may be much higher.

TANSY: (*Tanacetum vulgare*) A tall, hardy perennial growing to three or four feet high, with dark green, fernlike foliage and bright yellow, button-like flowers in flat clusters. It often occurs as a weed along roadsides. Said to be quite poisonous.

A good background plant, both foliage and flowers being attractive. Has a tendency to become weedy and sprawl. Grows in almost any good soil. Propagated by root divisions; seed can be sown in early spring.

TAPIOCA PLANT: *see* MANIHOT

TAPROOT: A root system in which the primary root continues prominent, in contrast to a fibrous root system. Because the larger taproot often goes down fairly deep into the soil, it makes moving of such plants difficult.

TARNISHED PLANT BUG: One of the most common insects found in vegetable gardens, the adult of the tarnished plant bug is brown mottled with various shades of reddish and yellowish brown and is about $\frac{1}{4}$ inch long. The young nymph is small, colored with various shades of green, and has four black spots on its back. As it becomes older, the fore part of its body becomes mottled with brown.

Both young and adults of this insect damage celery, cabbage, cauliflower, turnips, potatoes, tomatoes, and beans by sucking out the juices. The insect causes what is known as "black joint."

The tarnished plant bug spends the winter as a full-grown adult under trash and rubbish, such as leaves, stone piles, and garden refuse. It emerges during early spring and feeds on the twigs of trees or other vegetation that may be available. The bugs become full-grown in about a month. An effective preventive method is to keep garden clear of refuse. *See also* INSECT CONTROL.

TARRAGON: (*Artemisia dracunculus*) Quite different in appearance and use from other *Artemisias,* tarragon is an herbaceous perennial about two feet tall, much branched with narrow somewhat twisted green leaves. It is commonly used for flavoring foods and vinegar.

Tarragon grows in full sun, but seems to do better with a little shade. Propagated from root cuttings or by division. Protect in winter in cold climates.

Root divisions should be set early in spring in rows three feet apart and one foot apart in the row. Leaves and tops can be harvested throughout the growing season.

TARWEED: (*Madia elegans*) Tarweed is not a popular annual, although its flowers are very fragrant. It grows 18 to 24 inches tall, with small yellow flowers and long, narrow leaves. *M. sativa* (the Chilean tarweed) is about twice as tall, with much smaller leaves and tiny yellow flower heads. The tarweeds grow wild in the West. Seeds are sown where they are wanted, in any ordinary garden soil.

The name tarweed is also given to *Grindelia robusta,* a perennial that grows one to two feet high with yellow flowers and small, sticky leaves. It likes a dry situation and does not do well where the winters are cold and wet.

TAWHIWHI: *see* PITTOSPORUM

TAXODIUM: The three trees of this genus are usually known as cypresses, although they are not related to the true cypress. *T. distichum,* the magnificent southern or bald cypress, grows well over 100 feet tall and is an important ornamental and timber tree. It has graceful, feathery foliage that turns orange in autumn. In wild swamps it produces buttresses or "knees," thick woody root projections rising several feet above the water. It is hardy up to lower New England (but much smaller in the North) and will grow well on any fairly moist soil.

The pond cypress (*T. ascendans*) is similar but less tall and full-foliaged. *T. mucronatum,* the Montezuma cypress or atuehuete, is an enormous, very long-lived Mexican evergreen, some 120-foot specimens having a trunk diameter of over 50 feet and an age equalling or perhaps exceeding that of our giant sequoias. It is occasionally grown in southern California and Florida, but is not hardy elsewhere in this country.

TAXUS: *see* YEW

T-BUDDING: *see* BUDDING

TEA: (*Thea sinensis*) The tea shrub is grown mainly as a curiosity in the United States rather than for ornament or the commercial production of tea. It grows as a shrub or small tree with leathery leaves and fragrant white flowers. Give it a moist, friable, humusy soil and manure as a fertilizer.

TEABERRY: (*Gaultheria procumbens*) Teaberry is a name often given to the common wintergreen, an evergreen woody ground cover. It grows about four inches tall with tiny white or pink flowers in late spring and early summer and red berries. It is very hardy and prefers a definitely acid, sandy soil and partial shade. This teaberry is a very good rock garden plant. It is difficult to transplant from the wild and is best propagated by seed or by cuttings of half-ripe wood. *See also* GROUND COVER.

The name teaberry is also sometimes given to partridge berry (*Mitchella repens*) a prostrate wild garden and terrarium plant. Its stems root at the joints to make a mat, and it bears small white flowers and pretty red berries. Give it a rich, humusy soil and shade.

TEA GROUNDS: Useful as a mulch or for adding to compost heap. One analysis of tea leaves showed the relatively high content of 4.15 per cent nitrogen, which seems to be exceptional. Both phosphorus and potash were present in amounts below one per cent.

TEA OLIVE: (*Osmanthus*) These evergreen shrubs or small trees have fragrant flowers borne in clusters, and are favorite landscaping plants throughout the south and Pacific Coast states. They thrive in almost any soil that is not too wet or acid. Some of the ten species do well in a cool greenhouse, given a soil mixture of equal parts of loam, sand and leaf mold or compost, plus some dried cow manure and a little bone meal.

O. fragrans, the most popular species, grows ten to 20 feet high, with white flowers appearing in April. *O. ilicifolius* is a little taller and blooms in early summer. It is somewhat hardier than *O. fragrans,* useful as a hedge plant, and has forms with gold, purple and variegated leaves. Devilwood (*T. americanus*) is a small tree with fragrant greenish flowers, blooming in late spring.

The tea olives are propagated by seed (very slow germinating) or by cuttings of half-ripe wood taken in late summer and rooted under glass.

TEA ROSE: *see* ROSE

TEASEL: (*Dipsacus*) Stout, coarse perennials, two to four feet tall with prickly stems and toothed, prickly leaves, and blue flowers in dense heads. It blooms in early summer.

TEA TREE: *see* LEPTOSPERMUM

TELEGRAPH PLANT: (*Desmodium motorium*) This odd perennial herb is usually grown in the warm greenhouse as an annual raised from seed. It grows about three feet high with very small lavender flowers and inch-long pods. It has a large terminal leaf and smaller lateral leaves which constantly move in all directions as regularly as a telegraph.

TEMPERATURE: *see* SOIL TEMPERATURE; HOUSE PLANTS; FROST; VEGETABLE GARDENING

TEMPLE TREE: *see* PLUMERIA

TEMPORARY MEADOW: Hayfields used for a short time, not more than one crop season.

TENDER: Tender plants are those susceptible to killing by freezing temperatures. Some plants that are hardy in areas of dry winters must be considered tender in regions where the winters are wet and slushy. Tender annuals are those which cannot be sown early enough to bloom outdoors north of a line from upper Virginia to Nevada. *See also* HARDINESS; VEGETABLE GARDENING; FROST; SOIL TEMPERATURE.

TENDRIL: Tendrils are thin, wiry extensions of a leaf or stem, used usually to help a vine cling to a support. Some plants have very prickly tendrils to help them hold on to smooth surfaces, while others have thread-like coiling ones which grip a blank wall or rock face with amazing tenacity.

TENT CATERPILLARS: The larvae of any number of moths and butterflies which construct on trees large silken webs; especially applied to *Malacosoma americanum*.

Tent caterpillars, which thrive on the tender leaves of plants, multiply rapidly and can defoliate many deciduous trees and shrubs in a short time, over a wide area. In recent years, mass spraying operations have failed to stop the multiplication of the tent caterpillars. At the present time a biological control is being sought.

NATURAL ENEMIES: Soon after the female moth of the tent caterpillars lays her eggs, these are attacked by a minute wasplike insect known as *Tetrastichus*. This parasite measures only 1/16 inch in length and is of a shiny dark-green color with red eyes and iridescent wings. She lays one of her eggs in each tent caterpillar egg and the tiny white grub which soon hatches proceeds to devour the egg of the pest. When the grub is full grown, it entirely fills the hard caterpillar egg shell and spends the winter in this snug retreat. These egg parasites emerge from hibernation much later in the spring than do the caterpillars in the same egg mass.

The tent caterpillar moth lays an average of 156 eggs in each mass which she attaches to the terminal twigs of the trees or shrubs. These egg masses may therefore be readily gathered in large quantities throughout the winter months.

The most spectacular insect enemy of the Rocky Mountain Tent Caterpillar is a new species of digger wasp which has been labeled *Podalonia occidentalis*. This insect is somewhat less than an inch in length and is entirely black with the exception of the abdomen which is mostly a gleaming red-orange with a black tip. This wasp selects the full grown caterpillar, which is two and a half times her own size as her prey. Although the parasite feeds entirely upon the nectar of wild flowers, her young are carnivorous and must have living flesh for food. To provide this, the wasp engages in numerous battles with her oversize antagonists and paralyzes them by means of an anesthetic which she injects into the central nervous system. The wasp then drags the caterpillar to an underground burrow which she has previously prepared, lays an egg on the skin of the pest, covers up the entrance to the chamber and hurries off to seek a new victim.

The parasite grub which soon hatches drills into the body of the caterpillar and proceeds to feed upon the slumbering host. It first devours the non-vital tissues so that it may continue to have fresh food to eat. It keeps from fouling its food supply by delaying the evacuation of waste products until it attains full size and emerges from the host carcass. Then it constructs a very tough parchment-like cocoon about itself and remains underground until the following spring when it quickly transforms into an adult wasp which works its way up through the soil.

Full grown caterpillars which have escaped the digger wasps are often attacked by another important parasite which the layman may mistake for the common house fly. It is, however, twice the size of the latter and is known as *Sarcophaga aldrichi.* The light-grey thorax bears three longitudinal black stripes and the abdomen is divided into alternating light and dark squares.

These extremely beneficial flies which, incidentally, keep in the open fields and do not bother man, insert their living maggots beneath the skin of the caterpillars. The pest usually lives long enough to spin its cocoon and transform to the pupa before it succumbs. When the maggot reaches its full growth, it emerges from the caterpillar cocoon and drops to the ground. Digging quickly beneath the surface to escape its natural enemies, it rounds up and the outer skin hardens into a dark brown seed-like shell inside which it transforms to a pupa. With the advent of spring, the pupa changes to a fly which pushes the cap off its puparium and emerges from the soil.

See also INSECT CONTROL; INSECT CONTROL, BIOLOGICAL.

—*Norman Appleton.*

TERMINAL: A flower, leaf or other structure growing at the end of a branch or stem is said to be terminal. The term is generally used to distinguish such forms from those located elsewhere, such as on the sides of stems or branches (lateral), or flower clusters which rise from the leaf axils.

TERMINALIA: The Indian or tropical almond (*T. catappa*) is the only ornamental species of this genus. It is a very popular street tree in southern Florida and the tropics. The foot-long leaves cast a heavy shade and turn a beautiful red before falling. It grows about 70 feet high and bears two-inch-long pods with edible seeds much like almonds. Other species of *Terminalia* are commercially valuable plants yielding various resins, tannin extracts and other products.

TERRARIUMS: *see* HOUSE PLANTS

TERRESTRIAL: Referring to plants growing in soil, in contrast to epiphytic plants which grow in the air (supporting themselves on trees or wires).

TESTING SOILS: *see* SOIL TESTING; ACIDITY - ALKALINITY; FERTILIZER; LIME

TETTERWORT: (*Sanguinaria canadensis*) This beautiful spring-blooming wild perennial is often called bloodroot because of its red root and sap. It has one large leaf six inches wide, a waxy, pink, many-petalled flower and a small fruit pod. Tetterwort prefers part shade and well-drained, rich woods soil, near neutral. It is easily transplanted from the wild or increased by seed or root division.

TEUCRIUM: The best known teucrium or germander is the hardy perennial, *T. chamaedrys,* used for medicinal purposes since ancient times. It grows one to two feet tall and makes an excellent low hedge for a flower border. The shiny green leaves and spikes of white-spotted, red or red-purple blooms are very attractive in August. It is not, however, hardy outside of the South without winter protection. Propagate by seed or by cuttings or root division in spring, and space the plants a foot apart.

Of the other germanders, wood sage (*T. canadense*), is about the same size, purple-flowered and grows throughout the East. *T. marum* is a small shrub with very fragrant foliage and flowers, and *T. orientale* is a perennial herb that grows less than a foot tall, with feathery foliage and lavender or blue flowers.

THALICTRUM: The pretty meadow rues are good perennials for sunny spots in the border, rock and wild garden. About 20 species are grown in the United States, all blooming in early summer with big, showy panicles of flowers in a wide range of colors. They like a moist, loamy soil, and are propagated by division in spring, each plant often yielding a half-dozen new ones.

T. kuisianum is an especially pretty little one, growing prostrate or nearly so and producing a mass of mauve-lavender blooms for up to two months. Its leaves are interesting, resembling the delicate foliage of a maidenhair fern. This variety prefers shade and good drainage.

T. dipterocarpum grows a foot or so tall with pale red or lilac flowers. *T. minus* and *T. dioicum* are about the same size but have yellowish-green blooms. The handsome *T. aquilegium* grows two to three feet tall, with flowers ranging from white and pink to orange and purple in its forms. The yellow-flowered *T. glaucum* is three feet high, while *T. polyganum* has white flowers and grows up to six or seven feet.

THAWS: Early spring thaws followed by re-freezing of the soil results in heaving, which can damage many plants. Those most affected are lawn grasses and shallow-rooted perennials. Heaving most frequently occurs on moist soils with considerable clay or silt. The roots of the plants, thrown up out of the soil, may die from exposure to cold and dryness.

A winter mulch is the best preventive, but it must be removed early in the spring if the soil gets very wet from spring rain, to prevent rotting the plants. Perennials should also be planted firmly in heavy soils, in the spring when possible to get strongly established. Lawns should be rolled to correct heaving, but not immediately after a heavy rain if the soil is very moisture-retentive, as this would cause serious packing.

Another effect of an extra-early thaw is sudden unseasonable growth of many plants. If a hard freeze follows, the new growth and even the plant itself can be killed. Early warm spells can also damage evergreens, by making them need moisture which the roots cannot supply. The plants then

"burn." For these plants, a winter mulch to keep the ground cool and prevent early growth, plus a covering of burlap, evergreen boughs or similar material, is essential. *See also* FROST; MULCH; VEGETABLE GARDENING; FLOWER GARDENING.

THERMOPSIS: These showy, early-summer-blooming perennials are good border plants, given somewhat light, well-drained soil and full sun. They have yellow flowers borne on long spikes and hairy pods two to four inches long. Sow fresh seed, or propagate by dividing the rootstocks in spring. All the varieties will do well in dry, exposed locations, being highly tolerant of drought. *T. fabacea* grows a foot or so high, *T. mollis* two to three feet, and *T. caroliniana* up to five feet.

THINNING: Thinning consists of pulling up certain seedlings in a row to give room to those that are left. Sometimes the pulled seedlings are kept and replanted, in which case the procedure is called pricking out. *See also* SEEDS AND SEEDLINGS.

Disbudding, the removal of some flower buds to make the remaining ones grow larger blooms, is also a form of thinning, and in fruit growing thinning consists of pruning out some of the fruitlets as soon as they are set to prevent too many small fruits being produced. *See also* PRUNING; VEGETABLE GARDENING.

THISTLE: Thistles are found in many plant genera. All of them are characterized by prickly leaves and spiny, often lovely flower heads. Usually they are weeds: Russian thistle (*Salsola pestifer*), for example, is a dense plant that must be cultivated out of gardens and mowed out of roadsides and fence rows to prevent its profuse seeding. Canada thistle (*Cirsium arvense*) is one of the worst weeds in America. It has showy blue-purple flowers, and a deep root that cannot be destroyed by cultivation so must be dug out. Any little pieces left in the ground will produce new plants.

A number of thistles, however, are good garden plants. The blue-flowered globe thistles of the genus *Echinops* are handsome plants with species growing from one to over six feet tall, popular for the hardy border. The blessed thistle (*Cnicum benedictus*) grows up to two feet tall with yellow blooms, and the biennial or perennial *Carduus kerneri* is a little taller and has rose-purple flower heads.

An edible thistle is *Silybum marianum*, the milk thistle, sometimes grown as a vegetable. The roots, leaves and flower heads can be eaten. It grows three feet or so tall, with glossy leaves over two feet long and big red-purple flower heads. Sow the seeds one-eighth-inch deep in spring in any fertile soil.

THRIPS: *see* HOUSE PLANTS; INSECT CONTROL

THUJA: *see* ARBORVITAE; EVERGREENS

THUNBERGIA: These tender shrubs and vines have spectacular flowers and are very popular ornamentals in the South and California. Their lush growth makes them excellent for covering porches, trellises or small buildings. A number of them will thrive in the warm greenhouse in the North, in a loamy soil high in humus. They are propagated by layers or cuttings.

The black-eyed Susan vine (*T. alata*) has showy white, lavender-throated flowers from late July through September and is a rapid climber. Mountain creeper (*T. fragrans*) is evergreen with pure white flowers, and is hardy only to central Florida and lower California. *T. erecta* rarely grows over five feet tall with a somewhat shrubby habit and big purple blooms. The sky-flower (*T. grandiflora*), is a great favorite, having very beautiful flowers in drooping clusters, and big evergreen leaves. It will grow throughout the South and

along the Pacific Coast with winter protection. Another popular variety is *T. gibsonia,* which has hairy foliage and orange flowers.

THYME: (*Thymus vulgaris*) A small shrubby, sometimes prostrate, hardy perennial plant native to southeastern Europe. The herb is widely used for flavoring foods, and the volatile oil obtained from the herb by steam distillation is used for medicinal purposes, for flavoring medicinal preparations and dentifrices, and to a minor extent in perfumes. A number of varieties of this species, also other species, especially *T. serpyllum,* are likewise used as savory herbs.

Thyme prefers a mild climate and a mellow upland soil but will persist to a marked degree on poor dry soils. It may be propagated from seed or cuttings. Seed is drilled in the field early in spring in rows about three feet apart, or the seedlings may be started in the greenhouse or an outdoor seed bed and later set in the field spaced 18 inches apart in the row. Crown divisions and cuttings rooted under glass in sand are additional means of propagation. The plants require cultivation throughout the growing season. Since they have a tendency to become woody, it is good practice to renew the planting in two or three years.

Thyme herb is harvested when the plant is in bloom. Cut with hand shears so that several inches of the tender stems are included.

Thyme appears to be well adapted to the milder sections of the North and to some localities on the west coast. *See also* HERB.

TIGERFLOWER: (*Tigridia pavonia*) The very pretty summer-blooming Mexican tigerflower or shellflower is easy to grow. The bulbs (actually corms) are generally considered tender, although they have been successfully carried over the winter outdoors under a mulch. The big, brilliantly colored dramatic flowers are not very long-lasting, but several appear from the stem in succession. It will bloom from July to frost, giving fine cut flowers. The sword-shaped leaves grow up to 18 inches high, and the flowers range in color from deep red to yellow, buff and lavender, with magnificently spotted centers.

Tigridias like sandy, well-drained soil and are fine accent plants for a sunny border. Well-rotted manure worked into the soil, plus an occasional feeding of liquid manure, will insure large, spectacular blooms. Plant them three to four inches deep in groups. Usually the bulbs are dug up after first frost and stored in a cool, dry place over the winter. Seed can be saved and sown in late winter under glass or outdoors when the soil has warmed up. The bulbs are often eaten by Mexican Indians.

TIGER LILY: see LILY

TILIA: see LINDEN

TILLAGE: see ROTARY TILLAGE; CULTIVATION; VEGETABLE GARDENING; STUBBLE MULCH; SUBSOILING

TILLANDSIA: Only a few of the many epiphytic plants in this genus are found in the United States. One of them is the well-known Spanish moss (*T. usneoides*) that drapes cypress and oak trees so picturesquely in the southeastern states. Its threadlike stems and numerous tiny leaves get their sustenance from the air and rain, and the gardener need only drape some strands of the moss over a suitable tree to get dense garlands of it.

Most of the tillandsias are tropical plants. The other species are grown in the warm greenhouse, wired by their roots to a board to which some osmunda fiber is attached. They need plenty of moisture in the spring and summer, much less in winter. One of the prettiest is *T. lindeneana,* which has a basal rosette of foot-long leaves and big spikes of purple blooms with brilliant scarlet bracts. The leaves

of *T. fasciculata* grow up to 18 inches long and it bears a six-inch spike of blue flowers. *See also* SPANISH MOSS.

TILTH: As ordinarily understood, tilth refers to the physical condition of the soil; good soil tilth means one that is loosened to the depth necessary for root penetration and plant growth. A friable soil is one that has good tilth. In addition, soil tilth is also used to mean cultivation. *See also* SOIL.

TIMOTHY: (*Phleum pratense*) Timothy is a perennial grass extensively grown for hay. It grows as high as five feet, depending on soil and climatic conditions. Timothy thrives in sandy loam to poorly drained clay, neutral to acid. *See also* HAY.

TIP LAYERING: *see* BRAMBLE FRUITS; LAYERING

TISSWOOD: (*Halesia monticola*) Tisswood is usually a southern tree but is hardy along the coast as far north as lower New England. It grows about 50 feet tall with pretty white or pink flower clusters in spring. Give it a sheltered location and fertile, well-drained soil. Propagate by layers, root cuttings or stratified seed. Tisswood is a good shade tree and blooms profusely.

TITHONIA: Sunflower-like shrubs that are native to Mexico, often grown in Florida. In those tropical sections, large seeds may be sown in the open garden in March, then seedlings thinned later to stand three feet apart. In full sun and a fertile soil the plants will surpass six feet in height during the rainy season. Deep orange-yellow, daisy-like flowers on long stiff stems are available for cutting through most of the summer.

TOAD: Name applied to any of a genus (*Bufo* and allied genera, especially of the family *Bufonidae*) of tailless, leaping amphibians.

The toad is a true friend of the gardener. It was found that nearly

90 per cent of a toad's food consists of insects and other small creatures, most of which are harmful to the garden. In three months a toad will eat up to 10,000 insects, 16 per cent of which are cutworms. In capturing various forms of animal life it shows that dead or motionless food is of little interest. Only moving objects, apparently, make any impression on its sensory apparatus. A toad's tongue is attached at the front end of the mouth, and is free behind. It is thus an organ especially adapted for flinging forward and capturing insects and other active forms of animal life.

LIFE OF THE TOAD: The time of appearance of the toad in spring varies with locality and temperature. In the northern states toads have emerged from their winter hibernation retreats as early as the middle of March, but the majority of the individuals appear after April 1. When the toad emerges in spring it proceeds to some shallow pool or overflow of a stream. The males usually precede the females to the water, but do not commence to sing until about the third week in April, or as late as May, according to latitude.

It is not unusual to find hundreds of toads congregated in a small pond during the spawning season. Under normal conditions, if mated in the water, the female begins laying at once, and may lay from 4,000 to 15,000 eggs, the process being usually completed within one day unless there should be a sudden drop in temperature. The eggs are laid in long spiral strings of jelly. The hatching period depends upon the temperature. Below 65° it requires eight to 12 days, and above that temperature three to eight days. Toads are thus born in the water and in it spend their early life in a larval, fish-like state, breathing by means of gills. The transformation of a tadpole to a young toad takes place sometime between 50 and 65 days after birth and under abnormal conditions it has required 200 days.

If the weather is moderate, toads may remain active from March to the middle of November. During the winter months they hibernate in the ground, and statements regarding their being found under leaves, boards or stones probably refer to temporary refuges sought after a too hasty emergence in spring or before beginning their real hibernation in fall. The toad makes its burrow with its hind legs and always goes down backwards; the hind feet possess a spur which is of assistance in digging. As the animal descends, the dirt fills in over its head. It was formerly thought that toads burrowed down into the mud around ponds and became encysted in balls of clay. It has been found that those toads which fail to burrow below the frost line perish. Newton has found also by a series of well-conducted experiments that the toad usually digs deeper as the frost level comes nearer to it. Terrestrial amphibians can tolerate high temperature with moisture, but they quickly succumb to cold and drought. Toads, which possess drier skins than frogs, habitually avoid the sunshine, and conceal themselves during the day in holes or crevices. *See also* FROG.

TOADFLAX: *see* MOROCCAN TOADFLAX; LINARIA

TOBACCO: (*Nicotiana tabacum*) An annual growing six feet tall, tobacco is a handsome garden plant. Its broad leaves may be a foot or more in length, and the stem is covered with sticky hairs. The two-inch flowers are white, rose or rose-purple, borne in racemes.

Tobacco is grown commercially on a large scale in the southern states, and also in Connecticut and Pennsylvania. There are special varieties for cigarettes, cigars and pipe tobacco. All require approximately the same culture.

The seeds are sown in a very rich and friable soil under glass in late winter. The minimum temperature of the hotbed must be 70°. Some varieties require shading. Probably no crop needs a rich organic soil more than tobacco—fine tilth is of the greatest importance to good growth and health. The plants are set out in rows three feet apart and 12 inches apart in the row, and cultivated until they cover the soil. The tops are picked off to prevent the plants going to seed, just before flowering. Drying is a process which must be done very carefully in a special curing house. All the numerous pests and diseases of tobacco are easier prevented than cured, by means of proper soil building with lots of humus, insuring good drainage, and practicing rotations. *See also* NICOTIANA.

TOBACCO WASTES: Tobacco stems, leaf waste and dust are good organic fertilizer, especially high in potash. The nutrients contained in 100 pounds of tobacco wastes are 2.5 to 3.7 pounds of nitrogen, almost a pound of phosphoric acid, and from 4.5 to seven pounds of potassium.

These wastes can be used anywhere barnyard manure is recommended, except on tobacco, tomatoes and other members of the tobacco or potato family, because they may carry some of the virus diseases of these crops, especially tobacco mosaic virus.

Compost tobacco wastes, or use them in moderation in mulching or sheet composting mixed with other organic materials. They should not be applied alone in concentrated amounts as a mulch—the nicotine will eliminate beneficial insects as well as harmful ones, and earthworms and other soil organisms. For the same reason, nicotine insecticides are not recommended, and in addition they may contain even more harmful hydrated lime and sulfur compounds which can damage foliage.

TOMATILLO: *see* PHYSALIS

TOMATO: (*Lyopersicum esculentum commune*) A fine source of the vita-

mins A, B, and C, the common tomato is easily grown in almost every back yard. Because of its food value and ease of culture, it ranks amongst the most important plants available to the home gardener.

When setting out tomato or other plants, allow the soil clinging around roots to remain. Insert seedlings in properly-spaced holes and firm soil.

The origin of the tomato is obscure. Its name came from the Mexican word "Tomatl," but until a comparatively recent date the tomato was grown as an ornamental known by such a name as the "Cancer Apple." In olden times it was believed to be poisonous and disease-producing.

STARTING FROM SEED: One ounce of seed can produce about 2,000 plants. If you buy a couple of generous packages of good quality seed, you should be able to produce about 300 plants.

In February or March in a sunny, southern window, arrange some sort of window box. Almost any small, wooden box filled with fine, loose soil and having reasonable drainage will serve as a seed bed. Tomato seed germinates best at about 70°—approximately house temperature. The seed should be evenly spaced and not planted deeper than one-half inch.

The young plants should appear in from eight to ten days and for the next two weeks they should be watered from the bottom. The surface of the soil in the seed bed should remain as dry and sunny as possible to reduce the danger of damping off, a condition fatal to seedlings and brought about by the growth of soil-born organisms flourishing because of excess moisture.

To water from the bottom, place the box containing the seedlings in a pan containing shallow water and allow it to remain there until the soil has absorbed the moisture it requires.

As soon as the seedlings form one or two true leaves in addition to their seed-leaves, they should be transplanted. The tray into which they are transplanted should be capable of holding individual containers about three inches deep. These individual containers may be berry boxes, paper cups with the bottoms removed, paper boxes, small flower pots, cans with holes in the bottom, etc. Each plant should be moved to its own container and the containers packed in the tray with soil to prevent too rapid drying out.

The objective is to give each seedling about three inches space each way and to keep them growing rapidly. When the time comes for moving the young plants into the garden (about seven weeks from the time the seed was sown), this can be done in such a way as to cause the least possible disturbance to the roots and the soil surrounding them.

The tray containing the young plants should be kept at a rather low temperature in a cold frame or unheated room in order that the seedlings may become stocky rather than spindly.

SOIL: Although tomato plants will bear fruit in from 48 to 86 days after they are planted in the garden, they are essentially a warm weather plant. They require an open, sunny, well-drained location.

The soil should be porous, fairly light, and contain a fair amount of humus. If the soil in your garden is quite heavy, that is, containing a large percentage of clay, you will find that you can improve its texture by the addition of peat moss or sand. But for plant food it is necessary to apply a generous quantity of humus from a well-made compost heap. The addition of composted material will also bring very sandy soil to a satisfactory condition.

Avoid choosing a poorly-drained spot. Any part of the garden where rain water tends to form a pond is a very poor place for tomatoes. Many diseases of tomatoes are associated with poor drainage, including bacterial wilt, stunting, and fruit rots.

You will find also that air drainage is quite important. Tomatoes thrive in open locations where the free movement of the air is not hampered by the surroundings. Most leaf-blighting fungus diseases and fruit decay are prevalent in locations where poor air drainage exists.

STAKING: Perhaps the most desirable method of growing tomatoes for the home gardener is the pruned, stake method. More plants can occupy a given space by this method and the difficulties of cultivation are greatly reduced.

After all danger of frost is past, set the tomato plants deeply and about two feet apart each way. Drive a five-foot long stake into the ground alongside each plant. Tie the plant to the stake with soft yarn or small strips of old cotton clothing. It is best to make the tie tight around the stake and loop it loosely around the stem of the plant just beneath a leaf node. This prevents injury to the rapidly growing stem.

If paper containers have been used, the plants can be set in the prepared place without removing the containers. The less shock the plant has to endure, the more quickly it will continue its rapid growth.

However, you will find that the plants will overcome the shock of transplanting more quickly if supplied with a good starter solution. This is easily made. Mix two parts of water with one part of sifted compost. Allow the mixture to settle. Apply this solution to the hole in which the plant is to be set and again after the plant has been firmed and settled in place.

Because of the necessity of hurrying the growth of the young plants, they are set out as early as possible so that it is sometimes necessary to give them protection against the damage of late frost. This is easily done by using inverted baskets or paper bags over the plants during unusually cold nights.

Using the pruned, stake method, it is necessary to pinch out the side shoots so as to produce two main shoots which are tied to the stake. If you follow this method, you will have larger tomatoes and will have no trouble keeping them off the ground.

Recent research at Ohio State University has indicated that both yield and quality of tomatoes are improved if more foliage is allowed to develop on the plant. Working with early maturing varieties, as Valient and Queens, the experimenters found that fruit cracking was reduced as much as 60 per cent by this method of modified pruning. Extra foliage is obtained by allowing growth of axillary shoots or suckers. One suggested practice is to remove the suckers developing below the first fruit cluster. Then suckers developing later should be carefully tied to the stake.

NON-STAKING METHOD: Many gardeners grow tomatoes without staking or training. If you do this, your total crop will likely be about the same although the individual fruits will be smaller.

It is best, if you decide to use this method, to set the plants about four feet apart each way. And before the many sprawling branches bend down to the ground, spread a layer of clean straw, dried grass or similar material around each plant to keep the fruits from coming into direct contact with the ground.

Cutworm damage can be prevented by placing a paper collar around the stem. This collar should extend about an inch above and below the level of the ground.

Mulching with a layer of straw or similar material has been found effective in controlling blossom-end rot.

VARIETIES: Generally speaking, it is best to use only wilt-free certified varieties. In this way you eliminate one of the chief enemies, tomato wilt.

Early strains are usually more satisfactory for the gardener than the late kind. But if the summer is long in your locality you might use the late varieties to advantage.

The late varieties can be grown from seed planted in a cold frame and then transplanted directly to the garden, instead of using the seedbed-container-garden routine.

In some localities it is practicable to plant the seed directly into drills in the garden. The seedlings are then thinned until they stand the necessary distance apart. The advantages claimed by the adherents of this method are that the plants are much stronger because they root naturally in the place in which they are to grow, that the work of transplanting is avoided, that the plants undergo no shock and its following set-back caused by transplanting.

The disadvantages of this method seem to be that the seedlings, being very tiny are difficult to weed and cultivate and are a particularly easy prey to insects and disease and extremes of weather. This method is also quite wasteful of seed.

HARVESTING: During the summer the vines should provide a steady supply of fresh fruit for the family use. Later, when the crop reaches its peak, you will find it best to preserve much of it for future use. Tomatoes and tomato juice can be preserved in a number of ways. Whichever way you choose, you may be confident that the material will be a valuable addition to your family diet.

After most of the tomatoes have been gathered, but before the first killing frost, you will find a large number of green and still growing tomatoes on the vines. This not inconsiderable crop should be gathered and stored. The smaller green tomatoes may be used for the making of relishes, etc.

The larger green tomatoes may be wrapped individually in newspaper and placed about three layers deep in open crates or boxes. These crates of wrapped tomatoes may be stored in any warm place and will ripen without the aid of light.

SAVING SEED: Perhaps, as the vines grow and their fruits hang heavily on them, you will notice several plants which produce fruit that especially appeals to you—some striking difference, better flavor, thicker flesh, finer color, larger vine—some quality you admire. You wonder about the possibility of saving seed from these special plants for use next year. This is easily done.

But before you begin you will find it best to consider the individual plant as a unit rather than the individual fruit. The seed of an occasional large fruit found upon a vine which produces only inferior fruit will, as a rule, produce plants bearing fruit equal only to the inferior fruit. But if the vines you select show vigorous growth, good leaf color, and heavy sets of uniform fruit, then the chances are that the seed will produce plants having these superior qualities.

You will find it convenient to mark any plant selected for seed. Tomatoes are self-fertile and do not cross to any great extent, so you will not have to worry much about the distance of the selected plant from some inferior one.

The tomatoes selected for seed should be allowed to remain on the vine beyond the edible stage, but not so long that decay has set in. If only a few seeds are to be collected it is a simple matter to halve the fruits, re-move the seeds with the thumb, then wash and dry them.

For large quantities, the fruit is picked, placed in a wood or earthenware vessel and mashed. Water is added in a quantity equal to the mash and stirred vigorously. The resulting pulp should be held at about 70° and allowed to ferment for three or four days, being stirred now and then.

This fermentation will cause the good, heavy seed to settle to the bottom where it will remain while the pulp, inferior seed, and water, are poured off. This fermentation is also Nature's method of eliminating many seed-born bacterial diseases.

The heavy seed should then be washed in clean water and spread out thinly on paper. It should be kept out of direct sunlight but in a place where it will dry rapidly. When dry, the seed should be stored in envelopes or paper bags in a cool, dry place.— *Roger Smith.*

EARLY TOMATOES: To grow early tomatoes some gardeners give the young plant the cold treatment recommended by Michigan State University researchers.

The cold treatment consists in growing the plants for three weeks at night temperatures of about 50° F. to 55° F., beginning after the seed leaves have unfolded. This can be done before seedlings are picked off, during this operation and afterward.

Such cold treatment has been shown conclusively year after year to precondition the blossoming closer to the ground level on sturdier plants that have stronger side shoots and which are hardier against the hazards of transplanting and early growth than those transplants which have been grown indoors continuously as usual at higher temperatures.—*Gordon Morrison.*

To encourage early bearing, some gardeners prepare their soil deeply, adding much compost, and plant sturdy foot-long tomato seedlings from which they have taken off every leaf and branch except on the top. The plant is set with only three inches of the growth above ground. It is then mulched. Under this method, tomatoes have ripened by the first week in July.

VITAMIN-RICH VARIETIES: The Doublerich tomato, developed at the University of New Hampshire's Experiment Station by Dr. A. F. Yeager, has twice the principal nutritive content of all other regularly grown types.

Starting with an extremely small Peruvian wild tomato (*Lycopersicon peruvianum*), a cross was made first with the *Michigan State* forcing tomato. The tiny, greenish-white Peruvian strain, bearing fruits about an inch in diameter, was selected for its one outstanding characteristic: its vitamin C content is nearly four times as great as that of common tomatoes. The final development was a plant that produced larger-sized fruits, improved disease resistance, and a 100 per cent increase in vitamin C content.

Another new tomato, Caro-Red, is ten times richer in vitamin A than ordinary tomatoes; has been developed by agricultural experiment station research men at Purdue University.

In outside appearance, the new tomato is more orange in color than the usual garden tomato. However, the inside flesh color is orange-red, differing from existing varieties. Caro-Red has an internal color that is intermediate between the orange of certain garden types and the red of standard varieties. *See also* VEGETABLE GARDENING.

TOP DRESSING: The application of compost, lime, manure, and fertilizers to the surface of the soil. Usually the material is lightly raked into the ground around growing plants and along rows. *See also* COMPOST; FERTILIZER.

TOPIARY: Examples of topiary are not often seen today. It is the pruning and training of shrubs into ornamental figures, usually either animals, people

or geometric designs. The Romans practiced it, and old English and American estates still use it for decoration. Topiary work takes a high degree of skill and knowledge. In this country the best subjects are arborvitae, privet and yew.

TOPSOIL: *see* SOIL

TORREYA: Three of these handsome evergreen trees, relatives of yew, are grown in parts of the United States. The stinking cedar (*T. taxifolia*) is hardy only in the deep South and lower California. It grows about 25 feet tall, and its shiny dark green narrow leaves have a disagreeable odor when crushed. *T. nucifera* is somewhat taller and is hardy through most of the country. The biggest one, *T. californica,* the California nutmeg, grows as high as 70 feet and has approximately the same hardiness range as the stinking cedar. All of them have single-seeded green or purple fruits, and do well in medium-fertile, reasonably moist soils with a mulch.

TOUCH-ME-NOT: *see* IMPATIENS

TOYON: (*Heteromeles arbutifolia*) This lovely shrub, an important bee plant sometimes called the Christmas berry or California holly, grows ten to 15 feet high with leathery, pointed leaves. The tiny white flowers are borne in heavy panicles in summer, followed by bright red or occasionally yellow berries, often used for holiday decorations. It is hardy from the deep South to central California. Increase by seed, layers or cuttings.

TRACE ELEMENTS: Trace elements are minor mineral nutrients needed by all plants, animals and humans in extremely small or "trace" amounts. In order to be present, these micronutrients must be available in the soil in which the plants and foods are grown. Too little of one or more of these produces deficiencies, resulting in plant and animal disease. On the other hand, an excessive quantity of any trace element similarly brings about a host of toxic conditions in plants and sicknesses in animals and people.

Just how important these elements are can be seen by the fact that although trace elements may constitute less than one per cent of the total dry matter of a plant, they are often the factor that determines the vigor of the plant. Even where good crops have been thought to be produced, trace element additions to the soil have raised yields and improved crop quality, often amazingly.

Most soils originally contained a sufficient supply of these elements to sustain good plant growth. But intensive cropping, erosion, chemical fertilization and the replacement of manure-producing animals with machines, have caused widespread deficiencies to occur.

HOW TO SUPPLY TRACE ELEMENTS: The most reliable, safe method for assuring an adequate supply of the minor elements is by thorough organic fertilizing, plus using certain plants which accumulate these minerals.

Compost, mulch, leaf mold, natural ground rock fertilizers and lime help provide a complete, balanced ration of both major and minor nutrients. The soil, like human beings, should have a varied diet. Some other good sources are seaweed and fish fertilizers, weeds that bring up minerals from deep in the subsoil, and garbage compost and sewage sludge which contain wastes from all over the world.

Besides supplying trace elements themselves, these materials, upon decomposing, release acids that make elements already present in the soil available.

ACCUMULATOR PLANTS: Recently it has been discovered that certain crop plants, weeds and trees have the ability to *collect trace minerals from the soil.* They can store up in their tissues up to several hundred times the

amount contained in an equal weight of soil.

The gardener or farmer will find this a definite advantage. He can use these plants as green manures, or compost, sheet-compost or mulch with them to overcome or insure against minor element deficiencies.

AGRICULTURAL FRIT: Another valuable source of trace elements is the recently developed *agricultural frit.* It is a product made much like glass, the raw materials being mixed and melted at a very high temperature. The molten mass, flowed into cold running water, is cooled immediately and breaks into many small pieces, which are ground up.

By coming into contact with the frit particles, plant roots absorb essential amounts of iron, manganese, boron, copper, zinc and molybdenum. Soil acids slowly disintegrate the frit, making the elements available in a gradually soluble form. Thus a constant source of trace elements is provided over a long period of time. Plant responses to applications of frit are excellent, including generally better growth and less disease, bigger flowers and increased crop yields.

OTHER FORMS OF TRACE ELEMENTS: Adding trace minerals in chemical forms such as borax, manganese sulfate, zinc sulfate and the like, can be highly dangerous. It's far too easy to use too much—more than an ounce of molybdenum to the acre, for instance, will make pasture plants so toxic they poison animals eating them. In some soils, only 20 pounds of boron can ruin a potato crop. Each species of plant has its own requirements and tolerances.

Too, a tiny bit too much of one element can make it "displace" another. Some need others to work—cobalt must have copper and iron present if it is to prevent certain cattle ailments. Dozens of these relationships have already been discovered. The subject is too enormously complex to permit

TRACE MINERALS

Trace Minerals	Where Deficient	Hunger Signs	Accumulator Plants and Other Sources
BORON	Widespread	Dwarfing of alfalfa, heart rot of beets, corking of apples, stem cracking in celery, discoloration of cauliflower	Vetch Sweet clover Muskmelon leaves Granite dust Agricultural frit
COBALT	East and North Central States	Anemia, muscular atrophy, depraved appetite, poor growth	Vetch Most legumes Kentucky bluegrass Peach tree refuse Basic rocks
COPPER	Atlantic Coast States	Paralysis, anemia, falling in animals; poor growth, dwarfing of tomatoes, dieback of citrus trees in plants	Redtop Bromegrass Spinach Tobacco Dandelions Kentucky bluegrass Lignin (wood shavings, sawdust) Agricultural frit
IRON	Southeast	Anemia, salt sickness in animals; chlorosis in plants	Many weeds
MANGANESE	Many varied soils	Poor milk production, deformity of hogs, poultry; poor growth, chlorosis of tomatoes, gray speck of oats and peas, poor leaf color in plants	Forest leaf mold (especially hickory, white oak) Alfalfa Carrot tops Redtop Bromegrass
MOLYBDENUM	Many varied soils	Necrosis of leaf edges	Vetch Alfalfa Agricultural frit Rock phosphate
ZINC	West Coast and South	Hair loss, skin thickening in animals; poor fruiting, dieback in citrus, white bud in corn, top blight of some nut trees	Cornstalks Vetch Ragweed, Horsetail Poplar and hickory leaves Peach tree clippings Agricultural frit

"shotgun" treatments with chemicals that cannot help but be unbalanced.

Also, chemical forms leach out rapidly, can "burn" plants because they are overconcentrated, or react chemically with soil compounds to become fixed and unavailable to plants. These effects do not occur with frit and organic materials.

Many minor elements once considered non-essential are today being found to play definite roles in plant and animal nutrition. Barium, vanadium, strontium, silver, titanium and several others have shown indications of being important. Some day even the rare earths like yttrium, lanthanum and dysprosium may prove to be necessary to good growth and health. A lack of these might be almost impossible to recognize—another good reason for using all available organic materials in variety to build up your soil.

Complete soil tests are available through some laboratories which will include a report on the trace elements, indicating which of the vital micro-nutrients are deficient. By using organic matter rich in these elements, by applications of rock fertilizers, and by using agricultural frit and accumulator plants, the grower can overcome these deficiencies naturally and inexpensively.

The chart lists the principal trace minerals, the areas where they are deficient, some of the deficiency symptoms, and the accumulator plants and other sources of supply recommended.

See also listings of specific elements; DEFICIENCIES, SOIL; FERTILIZER.

TRADESCANTIA: *see* SPIDERWORT

TRAGOPOGON: *see* OYSTER PLANT

TRAILING ARBUTUS: (*Epigaea repens*) Sometimes called winter pink or ground laurel, trailing arbutus is one of the most fragrant of all wild flowers. It is a prostrate, hardy evergreen plant with tiny pink or white blooms appearing in spring. It must have an extremely acid soil containing lots of leaf mold. Perfect drainage and full shade are also vital. It can be propagated by very fresh seed or by cuttings in pots (it is very difficult to transplant).

TRAILING PLANTS: *see* VINES

TRAINING PLANTS: *see* ESPALIER; PRUNING; PINCHING; BONSAI

TRANSPIRATION: Transpiration is not simple evaporation of water, but a complex process whereby moisture is "exhaled" from the leaves of plants. The water needs of the plant, its stage of growth and the weather all affect the rate of transpiration. It has a very direct effect on wilting and growth. Some plants have special mechanisms for controlling transpiration, such as the resurrection plant, which curls up

into a tight ball in drought to reduce the moisture loss. *See also* SOIL.

TRANSPLANTING: When seedlings are about a half inch high or have their true leaves (those resembling the species, instead of the ones known as "seed leaves" which appear first), they have reached the proper stage for transplanting to other containers.

Generally it's a good practice to trim back evergreens and shrubs at time of planting, so that the roots will be able to provide for top growth.

The containers for transplanting purposes are practically the same as those used for sowing. Use a somewhat richer potting mixture, so that the seedlings will have plenty of available plant food. Dampen the soil and fill the containers loosely, smooth it off and press it down with a flat board. Make holes, in which to set the young seedlings, with a small round stick. Be sure these holes are wide and deep enough to accommodate the roots in their natural position without crowding. Lift the seedlings carefully from their old flat, hold them in your fingers at the proper depth in the hole, and with the other hand press the soil firmly around the roots. The proper depth is to see that the plant receives support, with the roots thoroughly covered. Air spaces around the roots, as there might be with loose planting, are fatal. Those fine feeder roots which do not come in close contact with the soil will dry out and the seedling dies for lack of food. Water thoroughly and shade them from direct sun until the seedlings begin active growth.

Plants which are grown in the house are usually too tender to transplant directly into the garden. They must be "hardened off"; that is, gradually accustomed to outdoor conditions, so that there will not be any shock to check active growth. If they are very tender, they may be placed for a week or two in the hotbed or cold frame. Always transplant, if possible, on a damp, cloudy day.

The soil in your seedbed must be well-fertilized and finely raked. Make small holes, deep enough to care for the seedling's roots without bending them up. Remove the plants from the cold frame with a ball of earth at the roots and trim off any uneven or broken roots. This is easily done, as the thorough watering given the plants a few hours previous will make earth cling to the roots. Insert the seedlings in the hole and firm the earth around the roots as well as around the stem. Both thumbs can be used to press the soil down properly. This leaves no air pocket to dry out the roots.

Space holes at the proper distance for the mature plants. Small ones, such as pansies, will be from six to eight inches, and large ones, such as some cosmos, about two feet apart in the row. After planting, water thoroughly. Shade the seedlings until they become established, with paper, slats, cheesecloth, or berry boxes turned over them. Many annuals and perennials can be transplanted even in full bloom, if a very large ball of earth is kept around the roots.

In planting be sure to dig the holes large enough so that the roots will not be bent. The stock should be set not more than an inch deeper than it grew in the nursery. This can be determined by the soil ring around the stems, and there is usually a difference in color above and below the old ground line.

Keep the topsoil in a separate pile and the subsoil in another. Loosen the earth at the bottom of the hole and if the subsoil is very poor, dig deeper and place a layer of well-rotted manure or compost in the bottom. Cover this over with some good loam so that the manure will not burn the roots and then set the tree or shrub. If the ground is very dry, fill the holes with water and allow it to drain away before planting. Fill in as much topsoil as possible around the roots and then finish off with the poorer soil, which can be enriched later with a top dressing of fertilizer. Tramp the earth down around the plant with your foot, so that no air pockets are left, and water again. A shallow depression around each specimen will hold water until the roots take a firm hold. Later fill in with good soil, and keep it loose to hold the moisture in the ground.

After the tree or shrub is planted, it must be pruned at once, so that the shortened roots will be able to provide adequately for the top growth. Evergreens and other plants which are received with a large solid ball of earth in burlap bags need no pruning, but all deciduous stock (trees which lose their leaves in winter) must have the branches cut back at least fifty per cent. Prune weak shoots first, then thin out those badly placed and shorten the others. Do not clip them all back to the same length, as this makes an ugly-looking tree or bush.

Tall trees and shrubs may need to be staked until they are well established. The best way is "guying"; that is, placing three stakes in the form of a triangle around the tree, about eight feet from the trunk. Fasten three strands of wire or heavy twine around the trunk about five feet from the ground. Run these to the stakes, leaving a little slack to allow for some play of the tree during a heavy wind. Wrap the thin-barked trees with burlap from the ground to the first limb to prevent sun scald (sunburn or blistering), or too rapid loss of moisture.

If for any reason you are moving established trees or shrubs, the method will vary somewhat with the variety and the season. Should the specimens be large, it is wiser to have them cared for by professional tree movers. The main thing is never to let the roots be exposed to either sun or air. Tiny root hairs through which the specimens feed are very sensitive and cannot stand exposure. Plants moved with a ball of earth large enough to include most of the roots will suffer little shock on transplanting. Evergreens, especially, should have the additional protection of burlap wrapped around this earth ball. This keeps their roots free from dry air and wind.

Water copiously before and after transplanting. A light mulch around newly planted stock will help to keep moisture in the soil so that the dormant (inactive) plants may be well nourished. *See also* SEEDS AND SEEDLINGS; COLD FRAME; VEGETABLE GARDENING; FLOWER GARDENING.

TRAPS: *see* INSECT CONTROL; GOPHERS; MOLE.

TREBIZOND DATE: *see* OLEASTER

TREE ASTER: (*Olearia*) About 20 species of tree asters are grown in the Far West and deep South. Some are bushy shrubs four to eight feet high while others grow as small trees up to 20 feet. *O. haasti* is a little hardier than most and grows about six feet tall with small clusters of white flowers that resemble asters. Other species have panicles of showy lavender blooms. They do well in any medium-fertile garden soil and are increased by seed or cuttings of half-ripe wood.

TREE CYPRESS: *see* GILIA

TREE-OF-HEAVEN: (*Ailanthus altissima*) Also known as stinkweed. Asiatic trees up to 60 feet tall with great, pyramidal clusters of pale greenish flowers on male and female trees, and winged fruits that last all winter. Tree-of-heaven thrives in crowded city lots under the most unfavorable con-

ditions. The staminate flowers and the leaves have a very unpleasant odor.

TREES: Trees serve many different purposes, and the trees selected should be architecturally adapted to these purposes. Between the living exclamation points, like Lombardy poplars and tall narrow evergreens, and wide-spreading growths such as untrammeled oaks or black walnuts, one finds a host of trees that differ in size and shape and structure and texture of bark and seed containers, and so on. Trees truly do afford a vast variety of ornamental forms that the homeowner may well take into consideration. For more and more, this is the age of the picture window; and it is wise to make sure that the picture is pleasing.

If, as is often the case, trees are already growing on a home site, these are by no means to be sacrificed, even though they are not exactly the trees that one would prefer. Being already established, trees give an atmosphere that can be achieved on a bare site only after years of patient nursing of new trees. But they can be supplemented, and, after new trees are grown, the old ones can be removed if it is desirable.

Before selecting trees for home grounds, be sure to study trees in the open, and trees in close stands. Grown under differing conditions, the same tree will assume very different forms. Where trees are grown too close to one another, they reach upward for the sunlight, and so assume one form. Grown in the open, with no near competitors, they expand uninterruptedly on all sides and assume their natural forms.

PLANTING: The planting of trees with specific recommendations for soil enrichment has been given under FRUIT TREES and NUT TREES, which see. The same treatment applies to all types of trees.

Be sure when planting your tree to set each root carefully in the topsoil, straightening it out and working the topsoil in around it carefully. Do not

HOW A TREE GROWS

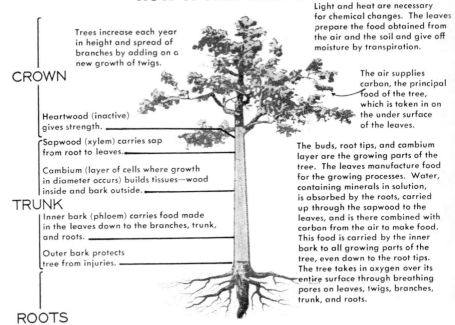

CROWN

Trees increase each year in height and spread of branches by adding on a new growth of twigs.

Light and heat are necessary for chemical changes. The leaves prepare the food obtained from the air and the soil and give off moisture by transpiration.

The air supplies carbon, the principal food of the tree, which is taken in on the under surface of the leaves.

Heartwood (inactive) gives strength.

Sapwood (xylem) carries sap from root to leaves.

Cambium (layer of cells where growth in diameter occurs) builds tissues—wood inside and bark outside.

TRUNK

Inner bark (phloem) carries food made in the leaves down to the branches, trunk, and roots.

Outer bark protects tree from injuries.

The buds, root tips, and cambium layer are the growing parts of the tree. The leaves manufacture food for the growing processes. Water, containing minerals in solution, is absorbed by the roots, carried up through the sapwood to the leaves, and is there combined with carbon from the air to make food. This food is carried by the inner bark to all growing parts of the tree, even down to the root tips. The tree takes in oxygen over its entire surface through breathing pores on leaves, twigs, branches, trunk, and roots.

ROOTS

leave the roots in a compact ball, merely covering it with topsoil—this will defeat your purpose by slowing down the roots in their search for food.

In many cases, this will mean a hole about three feet or more in diameter and at least two feet deep. The soil should be enriched with organic fertilizers, as compost and the rock dusts before planting is begun. Sand, leaf mold, peat moss—these are some of the materials that will improve drainage in a clay soil.

Transplanting of any tree involves injury and shock. It's your job to keep these to a minimum and you can—if you know what you are doing and then do it quickly. Tender roots are damaged, the entire organism is suffering from undue loss of water through the exposed areas. Plan everything in advance and get your tree into the protective soil as fast as you can.

Be sure to trim off all injured roots and limbs. Keep the tree in balance while doing so, trimming the roots to keep their volume and extent in line with the branch system—and vice versa. The importance of maintaining this balance cannot be overstressed if you want truly top-flight performance from your trees. However, do not cut back the central leader of the tree.

Trees with delicate roots should be transplanted only in the spring. These include mountain ash, beech, birch, franklinia, dogwood, magnolia, grafted cherry and yellow wood.

Hardy varieties may be planted in the fall as well as the spring because of their greater vigor. Among these are the elm, linden, pin oak, poplar, most fruit trees, also the Norway, silver and American red maples.

SIZE OF TREES: Small trees can be transplanted more easily and will adjust themselves more quickly to their new environment than large trees. This is readily understood when one considers that a large proportion of the root system of a tree is destroyed in digging, according to Landscape Architect T. D. Gray of West Virginia University. This is particularly true of trees that are dug from the wild (trees growing along fence rows, in open fields, or in woods). The tree must build up its root system to balance the top before it will continue to grow.

A small tree, six to eight feet tall, will adjust itself more quickly than a tree 16 to 18 feet tall. At the end of four or five years the eight-foot tree probably will be as tall as the 16-foot tree and more vigorous. Large trees can be transplanted with proper equipment, if you are willing to pay the added cost of handling the larger trees. The general advice is not to attempt it without the assistance of someone skilled in this type of work.

Deciduous trees may be collected and moved with bare roots. Preserve as much of the root system in digging as possible. As soon as the tree is dug, wrap the roots with wet burlap and protect from the sun and wind.

Evergreens should be moved with a ball of dirt and the ball wrapped in burlap and tied securely. The limbs should be pulled together in a bunch and tied. This will prevent them from breaking as the tree is handled.

Nursery-grown trees are prepared for transplanting by pruning both the roots and tops. This increases the chances of success when they are planted. For those who can afford it, the best source of supply is a nursery.

DEPTH TO PLANT: Trees should be set approximately the same depth or slightly deeper than they grew in the field or nursery. Spread out the roots of deciduous trees and work good soil in around them to eliminate air pockets. As soil is added it should be tamped with the feet. When the hole is about three-fourths full, add water until the soil is thoroughly soaked. After the water has been absorbed, the remainder of the soil should be added. Dish the soil slightly toward the center

HOW A TRUNK GROWS

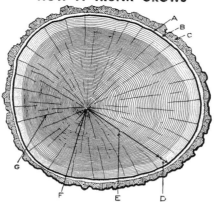

How the tree trunk grows. All growth takes place in the cambium, lying between the inner bark and sapwood. This is a very thin layer of living cells which divide and subdivide, forming on the outside bark and on the inside wood (A). The inner bark, or last tissue, is soft and moist. Its function is to carry the food prepared in the leaves to all growing parts of the tree (B). By a gradual change the inner bark passes into outer bark, a corky layer composed of dry, dead cells. This serves to protect the living stem against evaporation and mechanical injury (C). The woody growth during one season is called an annual ring. In the spring the newly formed cells are thin-walled and spongy, while in mid-summer and fall the walls of the cells become thicker and denser. This difference can be distinguished in many kinds of trees as light-colored spring wood and darker colored summer wood. Sapwood (D) is the lighter colored band of wood beneath the bark, often from 1 to 2 inches thick. It carries the sap from the roots to the leaves. Heartwood (E) is formed by a gradual change in the sapwood by which it becomes darker, heavier, and often more lasting. Most of the trees, but not all, form heartwood. Pith is the soft tissue on the innermost part of the stem, about which the first woody growth takes place in the newly formed twig (F). From it extend the pith rays (G). These are flat, vertical bands of tissue which connect the pith with the various layers of wood and the inner bark. They transfer and store up food. (Prepared by the U. S. Dept. of Agriculture.)

to bring the water to the tree around the trunk.

TIME TO PLANT: Evergreens may be planted in the fall or spring. In the fall, the best season is September and October. March and April are the best months for spring planting. When balled and burlapped, however, evergreens may be moved at any time, except when the young growth is coming out. Boxwood requires shading for a period of six weeks or more after transplanting.

Deciduous trees may be planted in spring or fall. Fall planting may be done any time after the middle of October for as long as the weather permits. Spring planting may be done between February 15 and April 15. Thin-barked trees, such as the birches, beeches, dogwood, yellow poplar, and magnolias, transplant best in the spring.

WRAPPING: Hardwood trees, such as the sugar maple, red oak, and dogwood, are subject to sun scalding which results in the bark cracking. This is common at the base of the tree. Wrapping the trunk when the tree is planted will prevent this type of injury. Burlap, cut into six-inch strips, or specially prepared wrapping paper can be used. The trunk should be wrapped up into the branches. The wrapping may be left on until it falls off.

STAKING: Stake the transplanted tree to prevent it from being whipped around by strong winds. One stake may be used and the tree trunk tied to it with some material that will not injure the tree. Wire, with an old bicycle tire between it and the trunk, is good. A triangle of three stakes also can be used with ties from each stake to hold the trunk of the tree. If the tree is likely to be rubbed by cattle or hogs, a wire enclosure should be provided around the stakes.

EDIBLE-FRUITED TREES: Following is a partial listing of ornamental trees that also produce edible fruit, according to officials at The Morton Arboretum:

The Persimmon (*Diospyoros virginiana*) produces plump orange fruit ripening late in the fall. Frost action is necessary to make it palatable. The persimmon is always an attractive medium-sized shade tree of pyramidal habit while young, round-headed later.

The foliage somewhat resembles Magnolia.

A number of the Flowering Crabapples supply in addition to attractive floral displays, usable fruit as well. The profuse white flowered Dolgo Crab (*Malus* "Dolgo") is one, a handsome tree of Russian origin introduced by Dr. Niels E. Hansen, formerly of the South Dakota Agricultural Experiment Station. Coloring early— in August, the interestingly shaped 1¼ inch diameter miniature apples change during the ripening process from yellow (red cheeked) to glowing scarlet. Of good flavor, they may be eaten directly from the tree or made into jelly. Pink flowered Hopa Crab (*Malus* "Hopa"), another floriferous Hansen origination, also bears showy orange to bright red apples of culinary value. Although not as large, the pretty, mealy fleshed soft yellow fruit of *Malus* "Gibbs Golden Gage," an English selection originating at Aldenham House Gardens in Hertfordshire, are quite pleasing in flavor. Pink budded white flowers provide the trees' spring effect. One of the so-called Rosybloom Crabapples deserves mention also; first, because it is an annual bearer, producing its 1½ inch diameter purplish red apples regularly; secondly, because of the effectiveness of its early appearing light pink flowers. A word for the foliage, too, which has a bronzy green cast changing to brilliant orange red in autumn. The Red-flesh Crabapple has still deeper and very fragrant rose pink blooms (early-midseason) and large (1½ inch diam.) bright red apples. They are red fleshed and useful for jellies and preserves. This is another Hansen introduction.

Although susceptible to climatic extremes, the picturesque Asiatic Ansu Apricot (*Prunus armeniaca ansu*) is most certainly a tree for consideration. Its plump deep pink flower buds are among the first of the *Prunus* to open and if the winter has been mild the resultant pink floral display is lovely to see. Yellowish, red cheeked apricots follow in summer, small but flavorsome. There are several larger fruited clones in cultivation. Several trees are necessary to insure proper pollination. Not to be overlooked either, is the Wild Plum (*P. americana*), native species occurring in undulating thickets along fence rows and woodland margins. It not only dominates the early spring landscape with its foamy, honey-scented white blossoms, but provides a rich harvest of edible red plums in the fall as well. Small red plums—cherry-like in size, shape and coloring—are the unusual fruits of the Hortulana Plum (*P. hortulana*), single trunked arborescent species of limited distribution in the central midwest. Too tart in flavor to be eaten raw, the fruit's only economic value is for jellies. From the standpoint of lateness and attractiveness, however, they are unequalled. Their exfoliating bark and long narrow leaves are further distinctions.

Mulberries, so often avoided because of the litter resulting from the fallen fruit, should not be ignored entirely. Some forms such as the Everbearing Mulberry produce berries of excellent flavor, and most species are fast growing round headed trees with dense bright green variably shaped leaves. Birds find their fruit irresistible. Although childhood memories of redhaws may be altered by time, the fact remains that the Downy Hawthorn (*Crataegus mollis*) producing them is the earliest flowering (early May) and one of the tallest of the hawthorns. Unusually large leaves are also typical of the tree and its fruits often reach an inch in diameter. Another small tree group contributing generously to the beauty and bounty of the landscape are the Juneberries or Shadblows. Misty white flowers in early spring, large and often surprisingly sweet flavored fruit in June, orange to terra cotta and old gold foliage color in the fall and distinctive gray bark in winter assure no lagging of interest whatever

the season. The Allegheny Shadblow (*Amelanchier laevis*), a multiple trunked small tree is one of the best, although the Apple or Snowy Shadblow (*A. grandiflora*), has a picturesque spreading growth habit and larger, white flowers in loose pendulous racemes.—*E. L. Kammerer.*

TREES, FLOWERING: Among the larger shade trees are a few with flowers so lovely that they are considered among the handsomest of our ornamentals. The horse-chestnut especially has gorgeous white blossoms faintly tinged with red, and is a favorite street tree in Paris, where it is commonly called chestnut. Catalpa, locust, tulip-tree, and the Japanese pagoda tree (*Sophora japonica*) are all good shade trees with conspicuous flowers.

Many of the smaller trees, however, are more beautiful still and in many cases more suitable for the small place. Among these are included the magnolia, which see, as well as the following:

Japanese Cherries. One of the best known of the Japanese cherries is *Prunus yedoensis,* known as Yoshino. The flowers are delicate pink or white, fragrant, and borne in short clusters of five or six. It blooms about April 10 in Washington. *Prunus subhirtella,* often the first to bloom, is a large tree-like bush, 15 feet or more in height and as much across, literally covered with thousands of tiny soft rose-pink flowers. A fine form of this so-called rosebud cherry is the weeping or pendulous type; another variety blooms in the autumn, in late October or early November. The double-flowered forms, also seen in Washington, sometimes bloom a few days later than *P. yedoensis.*

Crabapples. The crabapples vary in size, color of flower and fruit, and season of flower and fruit. Sargent's crabapple is very slow-growing, and one of the best of all for a small yard. It seldom reaches a height of more than eight feet, and has a spread of approximately 12 feet when mature. The blossoms are pure white, and the fruits dark crimson with a soft purplish bloom. The Chinese crabapple (*Malus floribunda*) and its many forms are among the first to blossom. The flowers of this type are rose fading to white, borne on a large tree-like bush with wide-spreading branches. Fruits are red or yellow-red. *Astrosanguinea,* the carmine crab, has rose-purple flowers not fading to white. *Purpurea* has wine-red flowers and foliage that opens a deep purple. Two other scarlet-flowered types are *aldenhamensis* and *eleyi.* The Betchel crab is a double-flowered form of *M. ioensis,* with white or rose-tinted blooms.

The double-flowering peaches, in red, pink, and white, occasionally striped forms, with foliage ranging from pale green to purple, flower early and stay in blossom longer than any other flowering fruit trees. They bloom the third year and reach a height of eight to ten feet. Some of the seedlings, which sprout from the fruits that drop on the ground, produce single flowers instead of double. The apricot, although hardy only to New York or perhaps to Boston, has such beautiful flowers in delicate pinkish yellow tones that it is cultivated in spite of tenderness. It blooms very early in the spring but seldom sets fruit in the North. Also the dwarf fruits, as peaches, apples and apricots, produce gorgeous flowers in spring. *See also names of individual trees;* FRUIT TREES; NUT TREES; ORCHARD; INSECT CONTROL; FERTILIZER; MULCH; PRUNING; SANITATION; STAKING; TREE SURGERY.

TREES, TRAINING: *see* ESPALIER

TREE STUMP: *see* STUMP REMOVAL

TREE SURGERY: The care of damaged trees consists of the proper removal of all injured wood. All broken places must be cut back to solid wood to prevent decay and the eventual death of the limb or tree itself.

First, remove all hopelessly broken limbs. If a limb is merely split down and most of the heart wood and bark is in good condition, cut back severely to relieve tension. When cutting back branches, always make a slanted, smooth cut leaving no stub, so that the cambium layer (just beneath the bark) will grow over the wound.

Split crotches should be secured by a cable held by bolts through each branch, not by a chain or wire around them, which will girdle and kill the tree.

All but the smallest tree wounds should always be shaped and painted. Cankered or decayed areas must be cut away or scraped out to clean, sound wood and pointed at top and bottom to facilitate callus growth. Any good white, black or gray house paint may be used. However, a paint containing creosote (as do many roof and waterproofing paints) will injure and may even kill the tree. Or you can use the composition filler called "elastic cement," and concrete for very large cavities near the base of the tree where extra strength is needed. Leave the filling just a tiny bit below the edge of the cambium layer to encourage the tissue to grow over it slightly and make a perfect seal. *See also* PRUNING; SANITATION; INSECT CONTROL.

TREFOIL, BIRD'S-FOOT: (*Lotus corniculatus*) Perennial legume which has been extensively planted in New York, Vermont and other eastern states where it has spread freely. Grows to two feet, blooms from June to August. St. James trefoil (*L. jacobaeus*) grows to three feet, is used widely as an ornamental. *See also* LOTUS.

TRELLIS: Trellises can be simple structures or highly ornate ones. When used to support ornamental or grape vines on the side of a house or wall, they are usually strictly utilitarian and designed to be inconspicuous so as not to detract from the beauty of the vine. Lattice trellises or grills are free-standing structures, generally closely woven and perhaps interworked with designs. Treillage, a very fancy system of trellising, was once used to construct elaborate garden structures, but is rarely seen today. The name is now more commonly given to the wires on which espalier or other trained fruits are attached. *See also* ARBOR; ESPALIER.

TRENCHING: Trenching might be called a "soil exchange" process. Its aim is to exchange enriched surface soil with soil from lower depths. This puts fertile soil down deep, and brings about better structure, drainage and root development.

Usually a trench is dug 12 to 18 inches deep, and the soil removed from it is hauled to the other end of the area to be trenched. Then a layer half as deep is taken off from the next strip, enriched with rotted manure, compost, rock fertilizers and other organic materials, and dumped into the first trench. This is then filled to its original level with the remaining soil from the lower part of the second trench.

This process is repeated until the last strip is reached, and this is filled with the soil previously carried there from the first trench. Some gardeners bring up an inch or so of the subsoil in each trench and mix it thoroughly with the upper soil, thus making their soil fertile and friable to a greater depth each time they trench it.

TRENCH LAYERING: *see* LAYERING

TRICHOGRAMMA: A tiny insect that may become increasingly important in biological insect control. The female Trichogramma lays her eggs inside the eggs of harmful insects by the use of her pointed egg laying apparatus. When the Trichogramma egg hatches, the young parasite proceeds to eat out the contents of the egg in which it lives, causing the egg to become black and preventing it from producing a harmful insect. Primarily, the Trichogramma attacks worms of the Lepidoptera order. Some of these are the cotton boll-worm (corn earworm), European corn borer, looper, Oriental fruit moth, pecan nut case bearer, greenhouse leaf tier, imported cabbage worm, and tomato worm.

TRICHOSPORUM: These two shrubby trailing plants are often called blushwort. In the tropics they grow rampantly on trees and dead logs. They are occasionally grown in greenhouses having a winter temperature of 60 to 70°, with shade from strong sun. Both *T. lobbianum* and *T. pulchrum* have showy crimson, yellow-throated flowers in clusters. The best way to propagate them is to insert three-inch-long cuttings in an osmunda-sphagnum moss-charcoal mixture and keep them at a temperature of 75 to 85° until rooted.

TRILLIUM: The trilliums or wakerobins are hardy perennials, very well suited to the wild garden. They bloom in early spring, the flower stalks rising from heavy rootstocks. Sow the seeds in a mixture of sand and acid peat in the cold frame and transplant to shady spots with a similar soil with ample moisture. The roots can be divided in late fall or early spring.

The snow trillium (*T. nivale*) grows about six inches high with white flowers, while *T. erectum,* the purple trillium or birthroot is a foot tall with pink or purplish, disagreeably scented blooms. The red trillium or nosebleed (*T. sessile*) also grows a foot tall and has green or purple flowers. The best of the large trilliums are *T. grandiflora,* the great white trillium, a vigorous grower to 18 inches and very hardy, with pink blooms; and painted trillium (*T. undulatum*) which has beautiful white, crimson-striped flowers. There are many other varieties and forms of trilliums, some hardy only in the South.

TRIOSETUM: The horse gentians or feverworts are occasionally grown in the wild garden. They are somewhat weedy, about three feet tall, with stalkless leaves up to ten inches long and small, not very pretty red or brown flowers in summer. Propagate by division and give them a woodsy, moist soil.

TRIPHASIA TRIFOLIA: *see* ORANGE-BERRY

TRITICUM: *see* WHEAT

TRITOMA: (*Kniphofia*) Perennial plants of the *Liliaceae* family, often called torch lily and flame flower. They begin growing in early spring and by June make thick clumps of long grassy leaves. Out of these masses of leaves grow bare slender stems topped by long clusters of tiny tube-shaped flowers. This helps explain why they are called red-hot-poker or torch lily. The flowers at the bottom of the cluster open first. Sometimes they fade to a lighter color so that the cluster has a two-tone effect. Tritomas are good for cutting and come in shades of red, orange, yellow, or white. They vary in height too. The long clusters are very effective when cut and used with yellow callas, or other flowers of a similar color but a very different shape.

CULTURE: Tritomas are easy to grow. Plant them in spring and let them have plenty of room. They like a rather rich soil, a fair amount of water, and full sun. About all the feeding they need is a yearly mulch of strawy manure. They should be mulched with straw in winter.

Springtime is one of the best hardy varieties. It is of medium height and blooms in July. The spike is red at the tip and the older flowers fade through orange and yellow to almost white, giving the clusters a sky-rocket effect. White Fairy is an almost white one, quite small and blooming in June. Vanilla is another June bloomer, pale yellow, long-stemmed, and one which sends up spikes again in the fall. Gold-mine is a deep yellow tinted with gold and amber, blooming in August and on into the fall. The clusters are large, but the plant is not extremely tall.

Coral Sea has this same characteristic. It is a deep coral-red, not bright, but very beautiful. It blooms in late July and August. All of these tritomas are hardy with a light mulch where the temperature goes below zero. Plants usually grow from two to four feet.

TRITONIA: These South African bulbs are often called montbretia or blazing star. The beautiful yellow or orange flowers are borne on spikes two to three feet tall in summer. There are many named varieties that have blooms in varying shades from peach and bronze gold to purple. All have narrow, sword-shaped leaves.

The corms are planted about three inches deep and five inches apart when the weather has warmed up. Below Pennsylvania they are hardy without protection, and north of this can sometimes be carried over the winter in the garden by mulching with strawy manure before the ground freezes hard. But usually it is safer to take them up and store them in a cool cellar. Tritonias like a fertile, friable soil with good drainage, and light shade. Work in a good feeding of well-rotted manure and bone meal before planting, and water well in dry weather.

T. crocata grows only a foot tall and is good for the front of a border, or it can be forced for winter bloom indoors.

TROLLIUS: *see* GLOBE-FLOWER

TRUMPET CREEPER: (*Campsis radicans*) This beautiful sturdy vine may climb as high as 30 feet, with many aerial rootlets. It has hairy leaves and red or orange flowers in summer, and will stand city conditions well. Trumpet creeper is hardy through most of the United States and likes open situations and rich soil. Its vigorous growth makes it a fine cover for sheds and poultry houses. The Chinese trumpet creeper (*C. grandiflora*) does not grow as high, but its scarlet blooms are bigger and more showy. This species blooms in late summer and is hardy only in the South and along the Pacific Coast. Both are easy to increase by seed, cuttings or layers.

TUBER: Tubers are short, thick, fleshy stems, usually underground and bearing buds or "eyes." The potato and Jerusalem artichoke are common examples. Tubers should not be confused with tuberous roots, such as are found in dahlias and are merely swollen, food-storing roots. A few plants have tubers borne on their aboveground parts.

TUBEROSE: (*Polianthes tuberosa*) The tuberose is one of the most fragrant of all summer garden flowers. A tender bulb, it bears gorgeous spikes of waxy white blooms on three to four-foot stems. There are double and single forms, all with bright green basal leaves up to 18 inches long.

Plant them as soon as all danger of frost is past, three inches deep and six inches apart in fertile, friable soil and full sun. Or start them in pots indoors and set them out in early June. Be sure they get ample moisture. The bulbs are taken up before the first frost, and stored at 65 to 70° for the winter. Propagate by offsets, which will bloom late the second year.

TUFTED: A plant with many stems growing in close clusters or very tight clumps is said to be tufted. Many grasses are tufted, as well as some sedums and the like. Sometimes the plant is very densely tufted, in which case it is called a cushion plant. This tight-growing habit, commonly found in plants that grow in dry or high altitude locations, helps them to survive by reducing transpiration.

TULIP: (*Tulipa*) Bulbous plants which are natives of the Old World where they occur in an area extending from the Mediterranean region to Japan. There are some 60 species and several thousand horticultural forms. They are doubtless the most popular bulbous

plants of the garden in spring. The satiny textured flowers in a wide range of colors and color combinations appear in the spring from bulbs planted in the fall.

"SPECIES" TULIPS: These tulips have been derived from wild species, and generally breed true from seeds. "Species" tulips, also known as botanical tulips, are not generally grown in quantity as are the garden tulips. They are planted in groups in the border, or rock garden. Among the best species are *T. suaveolens,* the type of the Duc van Thol. Tulips of today which may be recognized by their fragrance and their pointed petals and sepals: *T. clausiana,* the Candy-stick or Lady Tulip, has cherry-red sepals and white petals; *T. kaufmanniana,* a tulip from Turkestan with colors ranging from yellow to red; *T. eichleri,* with flowers that are bluish black at the base but scarlet above; *T. dasystemon,* a small early-flowering yellow tulip; *T. acuminata,* having light yellow flowers streaked with red; *T. biflora,* a species with small tinted white flowers on branching flower stalks; *T. praestans,* a variety with hairy leaves and light scarlet flowers, and *T. fosteriana,* a species with brilliant red flowers.

All species of tulip grow well in the rock garden, but the dwarf and semi-dwarf ones are especially fitted for rock garden planting. Especially good species for the rock garden are *T. dasystemon* which hardly ever grows taller than five inches; *T. fosteriana,* a stout plant with broad leaves and bright crimson flowers; *T. kaufmanniana,* a showy species of plants varying from five to ten inches high; *T. montana,* a dark crimson flowered species which hardly ever exceeds eight inches in height; and *T. persica,* a low plant with fragrant, whitish or pale yellow flowers in clusters of three.

GARDEN TULIPS: The Turks appear to have been the first to develop the garden tulip, and spread them over

Europe. Since then the Dutch have been the great breeders of tulips. Most garden tulips were derived from innumerable crosses with the species *T. gesneriana* and *T. suaveolens,* and the thousands of named forms which have since arisen. Garden tulips are divided into groups as follows:

1. *Early Tulips.* These are the first of the tulips to bloom and follow close behind crocuses. They are chiefly dwarf in habit and may have single or double flowers in a variety of colors. Typical of the early tulips is the Duc van Thol.

2. *Breeders Tulips.* These are tall-stemmed tulips which bloom in May. The flowers are distinctive in that they have a rounded base, while the sepals and petals have square ends. The Dutch varieties have oval or cup-shaped flowers mostly in shades of brown, purple, bronze, or red, but the base of the flower is white or yellow, often stained blue, green or bluish-black. The English varieties have ball-like flowers, the base of which is yellow or white but not stained with any other color.

3. *Cottage Tulips.* These are tall-stemmed, May-blooming tulips with self-colored, mostly pointed or rounded sepals and petals. The flowers in general have a square or somewhat rounded base and pointed or rounded tip.

4. *Darwin Tulips.* These are the tallest of the self-colored May-flowering tulips. They may be recognized by the flower which has a somewhat rectangular base, while the sepals and petals are square-tipped or rounded.

5. *Lily-flowered Tulips.* These are tall-stemmed, May-flowering tulips with the sepals and petals distinctly long-tipped.

6. *Triumph Tulips.* These are tall, early flowering tulips, blooming just after the Early Tulips.

7. *Mendel Tulips.* These are medium-early flowering tulips derived from crossing the Duc van Thol with the Darwin varieties.

8. *Special Tulips.* This is a heterogeneous group, including such tulips as the Bizarres having yellow flowers streaked with scarlet or brown, Bybloems with flowers that are white splashed with red or purple, Rembrandt or Darwins in which the color is broken, Retroflexa in which the sepals are recurved, Parrot tulips with feathered petals.

SELECTING TULIPS: In selecting tulips for the garden, the background must be considered. For instance, a yellow cottage tulip would seem to be an intruder in front of a pink-flowered dogwood or a flowering crabapple tree, but would be superb and glorious near the violet-blue racemes of *Wisteria floribunda.* Matching the flowers of tulips with those of flowering shrubs and trees can be an intensely interesting garden function.

Tulips are companionable flowers and never look better than when holding up their shapely flowers of some color shading, seemingly selected by nature for this glorious festival of spring. They may be planted in groups in a bed or border to produce striking color schemes because they get along together. But they seem to be at their best in the garden growing with other plants, such as pansies, bluebells, forget-me-nots, rock cress, lungwort, Jacob's ladder, English wallflower, bleeding heart, doronicum, and the often so harsh *Alyssum Saxatile.—Dr. William Eyster.*

PLANTING: The bulbs grow best in well-drained, light loam. The soil should be deep and enriched with plenty of well-rotted manure or compost to insure good plant growth and large flowers over a period of several years. Fertilizers such as bone meal, dried and shredded cow or sheep manure or compost are excellent dressings. The best time to plant the bulbs is two to four weeks before the ground freezes or from October 1st to November 1st; later planting may result in short stems and smaller flowers. Tulips will usually do better and bloom earlier in the sun than in half shade. Large bulbs may be planted deeper than small ones; the ideal depth from four to six inches, and four to nine inches apart. The rule is: planting too deep will waste much strength of the bulb pushing through the soil; planting too shallow, the bulbs may be pushed or heaved out of the soil, or possibly freeze. When setting the bulbs in the soil, give a half twist as though screwing the bulb into the soil; it assures that the base of the bulb is in solid contact with the soil.

Never cut the green leaves at any time; these leaves feed the bulb with new food to be stored for the next season. When the leaves begin to turn yellowish at the base and have a withered appearance, they can be pulled out easily from the soil. The bulbs are then more or less cured and may remain in the ground for at least two more seasons or even a third if the flowers have appeared well the last season. Lack of flower development is a sign that the bulbs should be lifted and reset. Lifted bulbs may be reset in a new bed immediately, or they may be stored for the fall planting. If stored, the lifted bulbs should never be exposed directly to the sun, but stored immediately in an airy, shady, cool place. Exposure to the sun of only 30 minutes may crack the coats of the bulbs and thus expose them to damaging influences.

DISEASES OF THE TULIP: Tulips are subject to a few diseases. If the blossoms blister with brown or water-soaked spots on the petals, and if the leaves have greenish spots which gradually increase in size, the plants have "fire blight." If this disease occurs in your tulips, cut off all the blooms and diseased leaves immediately to prevent its spread to the bulb. If the fungus has invaded the bulb, place it in the compost heap.

Insects such as the Green Peach or Spinach aphid, the Narcissus Bulb fly may attack tulips grown in soils of low fertility. Another animal pest which attacks tulips grown in depleted soils is the milliped. The best remedial measure is to enrich the soil with composts and pulverized rock minerals.—*G. Wittrock.*

SAVING TULIP BULBS: Tulip bulbs will not last for years in the ground without special care. Either they will rot during the summer from too much moisture, or they will be eaten by rodents who love the juicy pulp. To save bulbs, most gardeners have found that it is necessary to lift them every spring.

WHEN TO REMOVE BULBS: The first or second week in June is a good time to remove tulip bulbs from the soil. By this time the late Darwins have finished blooming. If you are too busy at the time, the bulbs may be removed as late as the middle of the month. But, the sooner the better, as the stems will be firmer, and there will be less chance of their breaking off from the bulbs. Stem and bulb must remain intact for proper curing.

Use a garden spade for lifting the bulbs from the ground. A garden fork does not give the necessary protection during the lift. Insert the spade at least four inches from each tulip stem. Force the spade straight down to a depth of six inches. Then, gently press down upon the handle, outwardly, until the ground heaves and the plant moves. Bring the bulb to the surface and carefully shake free of dirt, taking care not to snap off the stem. The new bulbs need the nourishment stored in the stem, now that their soil food supply has been cut off.

Place your stemmed bulbs neatly in a pile until all have been taken up. If a bright, hot sun is shining, protect the tender bulbs with a damp sack or heavy paper. Never expose tulip bulbs to the direct rays of the sun, as they are quick to bake.

HILLING IN: After your bulbs have been dug and each variety placed upon a separate pile, remove them to your garden. Dig a trench in a vacant spot, long and deep enough to accommodate all the bulbs. Lay the bulbs in carefully. Then, before hilling in, stake or number each variety so you will know which is which when you take them up later.

Cover the bulbs with at least six inches of soil, but allow the green stems to remain exposed to the hot sun. As the sun dries the stalks, the food supply gradually trickles down to the bulbs. There, it is stored for next year's growth.

REMOVING FROM TRENCH: In about a week or two, as soon as the stems have turned yellow, take up the bulbs from the trench. Never allow them to remain hilled in more than three weeks, or they will rot. Run your fingers through the loose dirt after lifting, to get all the tiny bulblets that might have broken off. Spread the bulbs out on a flat surface in a heavy shade to dry for about an hour. Then proceed in removing the bulbs from the stems and casings.

As you begin your work you will notice that the bulbs are encased in a thick, brown pouch of cloth-like fiber. Tear this apart, and remove all bulbs found among the different layers. No bulblet is too small to save. Even the tiniest grows to a reasonable size in one year. Besides the parent bulb, you will find as high as four or five bulblets with each stem. These smaller bulbs should be planted separately in the fall.

When the pouch is completely empty, throw it on a pile with the discarded stems. Later, this can be added to your compost heap or mulching material.

As the bulbs are removed from their casings, it is wise to place them immediately into trays specially built for tulip bulbs. They are nothing more than large squares with two-inch high sides, and bottomed with heavy window screening to prevent the loss of tiny bulblets. If you have several different varieties, you might partition off the squares, and save room. Some sort of legs, in the form of one-inch blocks should be nailed under each corner to allow a good circulation of air through the moist bulbs.

Don't forget to tag the trays if you have several varieties of tulips. This information will enable you to plant different arrangements in your beds next fall to create striking color effects in spring.

PROPER STORAGE CARE: As soon as you have finished this phase of work, take the bulbs immediately indoors. Never expose, even for a minute, to the hot sun. Set the filled trays in a warm, dry place. The attic floor of your home or garage is excellent. Place the trays on the floor individually. That is, don't pile one on top of the other. And don't worry about the heat concentrating too heavily over the bulbs during the hot summer. It won't hurt them a bit. The hotter it is, the drier the air will remain. Tulip bulbs must be kept completely dry to prevent rotting.

With your hands, roll the bulbs back and forth in the trays several times during the first two weeks of curing. This is to prevent moisture from gathering among the bulbs. One roll a week for the following month will finish the job. It is best to allow the bulbs to remain in their trays until planting time.

If you are bothered with mice, be sure to set traps. Mice love the taste of tulip bulbs, and can put away quite a few by fall. If you are afraid to take a chance with traps, you might tack another sheet of window screening across the tops of the trays.

OTHER TYPE OF BULBS: If you grow hyacinths, they definitely should be lifted. If there are any meadow mice or moles in your garden or lawn, they will soon find the sweet bulbs and eat out the centers. Snip off the stems as soon as you dig them up. Do not hill in as you did the tulips, for hyacinths rot quickly. Slip off the outer skins and store immediately in the dry attic. They should be rolled frequently until properly dried. If a few show signs of rotting after a few weeks, simply rub off the rotted part with your thumb and put back in the tray. The bulb will usually heal the wound quickly, and dry up nicely.

Such bulbs as daffodils, crocus, and day lilies need not be taken up from their permanent growing spots. They do not rot from excessive moisture, and rodents detest their bitter flavor. But, if you wish to use the beds for deep-rooting tubers or annuela, it is best to remove them, and reset in the fall after killing frost. After digging, hill in for a week, snip off, and store along with the tulip bulbs.—*Betty Brinhart.*

See also BULB; BULB GARDEN; BULBS, FORCING; FLOWER GARDENING.

TULIP POPPY: *see* HUNNEMANIA

TULIP TREE: (*Liriodendron tulipifera*) This stately, handsome tree, also called tulip poplar or whitewood, grows up to 200 feet high with nearly square leaves and big, showy greenish-yellow, orange-banded flowers. In several eastern states, tulip tree is valued as the best honey plant. It blooms in May and produces large quantities of dark red honey with a fine distinctive flavor. For the large place, it is one of the finest lawn trees available, and thrives on a rich, moisture-retentive soil. There is a variety with a pyramidal habit. Tulip tree is hardy up to Massachusetts and Wisconsin, and can be increased by stratified seeds and grafting.

TUNG-OIL TREE: (*Aleurites fordi*) In this country, the tung-oil tree is grown only in a narrow belt along the Gulf Coast and upper Florida. The oil from its seed is used in making paint, varnish and similar products. The fruits fall to the ground in autumn and the oil is pressed out after they dry.

The tung-oil tree prefers a somewhat acid loam soil with excellent drainage and a mulch rich in nitrogen. Growers commonly plant legumes as summer cover crops. It is a very fast-growing tree, seeds planted in February germinating in two months and growing as high as five feet the first year. The tree begins fruiting at a young age and reaches full size in ten years. It should be given good feedings of ground rock fertilizers every few years, and supplementary organic nitrogen as needed. The trees are generally planted from 20 to 30 feet apart. Some high-yielding varieties bear their fruits in clusters.

TUPELO: *see* NYSSA

TURF: Turf of sod can be cut from any good lawn planting and used to repair poor spots in lawns or lay on steep banks, the edges of paths and similar places. Usually sods are cut in strips about 12 by 15 inches for easy handling. These can be kept if necessary for a couple of days stacked in shade, face to face. The soil on which the turf is to be laid should be organically prepared just as it would be for seeding a lawn, and the sods carefully set down with their edges tight together. Thorough watering, plus rolling or heavy tamping completes the job. Be sure to fill in any holes or ragged edges with soil. On steep banks, pegging may be necessary to prevent the sods washing down in a heavy rain.

TURKEY: Turkeys can be a profitable sideline for the organic homesteader, particularly if he can grow the large amounts of green feed they thrive on, and if he sells his birds at retail.

Some of the most popular breeds are the White Holland, Bronze, Bourbon Red and Narragansett. The new smaller Beltsville turkeys developed by the Department of Agriculture Research Center at Beltsville, Md., are steadily gaining in popularity and find a good market all through the year. Always buy quality stock from a reputable hatchery or breeder.

HOUSING AND FEEDING: The usual advice given by experts is to start with 100 to 200 day-old poults. A pen approximately 20 by 20 feet in a barn or poultry house will handle 100 to 150 poults until they are put on range at 16 weeks of age. A raised wire porch the same size is also necessary to keep the young birds off the ground and reduce the danger of the highly infectious, fatal blackhead disease.

A good-sized electric brooder plus waterers and feed hoppers are other needs. Sand and shavings are usually used for litter in the house. The poults can go out on the porch if the weather is good when about two weeks old.

Grains are fed in addition to the mash after the birds are about two months old. Good commercial feeds for starting all the way through rearing and fattening are available. If the birds' entire lives are spent on wire, however, they should have fresh green feed, such as rape, oats or ladino clover brought to them.

Turkeys on range will eat great quantities of succulent forage, as well as pick up waste grain, weed seeds and insects. An acre of good range is generally sufficient for each 100 birds. Oats and rape make fine pasture. For permanent pastures, a good mixture is red, ladino and alsike clover with timothy and Kentucky blue grass. In the last five weeks or so the birds need plenty of whole corn to make plump flesh.

Turkeys should never be run with chickens, which harbor the dread blackhead organism.

Turkey manure is an excellent fertilizer and soil conditioner. The droppings which fall through the wire floors of the porches should be cleaned up and applied to the soil or composted weekly.

For more details on brooding, rearing and other aspects of turkey production, get some of the excellent bulletins available from your experiment station or state college. A very useful one is "Turkey Raising," Bulletin No. 1109, ten cents from the Superintendent of Documents, U. S. Government Printing Office, Washington 25, D. C. *See also* POULTRY.

TURKEY BEARD: *see* XEROPHYLLUM

TURNIP: (*Brassica rapa*) Turnips are treated in the home garden very much the same as any other underground garden crop. One of the secrets of their good flavor is the rapid growing of this vegetable. For this rapid growth, a good soil with a heavy supply of organic matter and phosphate rock is essential.

A loose friable soil will prove satisfactory for raising this short season crop. Mulching the garden with grass clippings, hay and other organic mulches will further benefit the crop.

The types and varieties are many and take on various sizes and shapes. Some are flat, some are round and still others are cylindrical. When grown under the same conditions though, they all taste practically the same. Included in the more common varieties are the Extra Early Purple Top, Golden Ball, Large White and Large Yellow Globes, Snowball, White Egg, Yellow Aberdeen, Early White Dutch (a flat type) and Cowhorn, which is cylindrical and grown mostly for cattle feed.

Turnip tops are richer in vitamin A, B_1, and B_2 than the white or yellow turnip roots, and the vitamin C content is the same for both tops and roots. There are several extra early types which are planted in the spring and harvested in early summer, but most gardeners favor the fall and winter varieties. For the main crop, Purple Top is usually grown.

WINTER TURNIPS: Keeping in mind that the average home grower likes a good crop of winter turnips, he should be ready to sow the seed during the latter part of July or early in August. Never cover turnip seed with more than a quarter inch of soil as they are very small and the tender young plants are easily buried when there is a thicker layer of soil on top. Seed sown in August will produce a good fall or winter crop. The seed is sown in rows which should be 12 to 15 inches apart. These late plants, left in the garden all winter, will bloom and set seed in the following spring.

That part of the garden which is reserved for turnips should have a good supply of rotted manure or compost worked in. Turnips should be dug before the first light frost. In the case of a mild winter, they can be left in the ground until after Thanksgiving Day.

Although rapid growth is needed for this crop, it bears watching. The turnips should not be allowed to grow too large. If they are permitted to do so, they will become woody and stringy, and will be bitter-tasting if held in the ground too long. If the soil is apt to be on the acid side, it might be best to apply lime at the rate of half to one pound to each ten square feet.

After pulling up, the turnips should then be lifted, topped and stored in the basement. The Swede or rutabaga turnip is generally conceded to be the best variety for winter storage. If yellow turnips are preferred, plant American Purple Top.—*Charles E. Booth.*

See also VEGETABLE GARDENING.

TWINFLOWER: (*Linnaea borealis* and *L. americana*) Trailing plants of the honeysuckle family, with glossy evergreen leaves and pink bell-shaped fragrant flowers which grow one inch and one-half inch long, respectively. *L. borealis* is the Eurasian species, being found in the northern woods of Europe, Asia, and into Alaska. The American species is grown in the United States as far south as the latitude of Philadelphia, the mountains of West Virginia, and across to the northern California coast.

Twinflower may be grown in the rock garden in an acid, moist, peaty soil, in a cool, partially shaded situation. Soil must be well-drained for it to survive. The species was named after Linnaeus, whose favorite flower it was said to be.

U

UDO: (*Aralia cordata*) This perennial herb, growing six feet tall, is cultivated mainly for its young shoots, which are edible. They have a bitter, turpentine-like odor which largely disappears when they are blanched by earthing up. A turpentine flavor, however, persists until the shoots are boiled in salty water. Udo needs a fertile, humusy woods soil, and is best planted in semi-shade in the wild garden. Propagate by division in the spring. Most people use it in salads or like asparagus.

ULE: (*Castilla elastica*) Ule or Mexican rubber tree is a source of rubber in Central America. Here it is grown only in the southernmost part of Florida, where it produces no rubber due to insufficient heat.

ULMUS: *see* ELM

UMBEL: A cluster of flowers whose stalks arise from a single point on a stem is called an umbel. Sometimes several umbels are grouped together into one large one, which is called a compound umbel. Many herbs and flowers, as well as vegetables of the carrot family (including parsnips and celery) are characterized by umbels, hence are called *Umbelliferae*.

UMBELLULARIA: The spice tree (*U. californica*) a handsome, aromatic evergreen, is also called bay tree, balm-of-heaven and California laurel. Growing 20 feet or so tall, it bears dense clusters of greenish-yellow flowers in late winter and early spring, followed by interesting berry-like fruits. It is hardy in the South and along the Pacific Coast, and likes medium fertile, moist soils. Propagation is by seeds.

UMBRA: (*Phytolacca dioica*) This striking evergreen tree is hardy only in lower California and central Florida. It is one of the most vigorous-growing trees known, 50-foot specimens often having a trunk six feet or more in diameter. Umbra is a highly popular ornamental in areas where it is hardy, and bears small white flowers in racemes.

UMBRELLA LEAF: (*Diphylleia cymosa*) A perennial for wild gardens in the southeastern states, umbrella leaf likes woodsy soil and shade. It bears small white flowers in clusters and blue berries a half-inch in diameter, and a huge leaf up to 18 inches wide arising from its base, complemented by two smaller, shorter-stalked leaves. Give it a cool spot, lots of shade and woods humus as a mulch.

UMBRELLA PALM: (*Hedyscepe canterburyana*) The umbrella palm grows 25 feet high outdoors in Florida and lower California. The beautiful feathery leaves appear in a dense cluster at the top of the trunk, along with the handsome flower panicles. It is also a popular greenhouse and tub plant, growing much lower under these conditions. Give it a sand-humus soil mixture, ample water during its growing season, and shade from hot sun.

UMBRELLA PINE: (*Sciadopitys verticillata*) A tall evergreen, the umbrella pine or parasol fir is pyramidal in shape, and grows over 100 feet high. Its dark, glossy six-inch-long leaves—really stems assuming the functions of leaves—are arranged in umbrella-like whorls on the branches. It is a slow grower, hardy up to lower New England, and likes fairly moist, protected spots. Propagate by stratified seeds, preferably in the cold frame, or by cuttings taken in the fall. A very handsome ornamental.

UMBRELLA PLANT: (*Cyperus alternifolius*) This is a popular pot plant needing wet soil and a temperature of 55 to 65°. The many stems grow to about three feet tall, with umbrella-like arching leaves at the top. The flower spikes rise prettily above these. It can be propagated by cutting off the leaf crown and rooting it in sand. *See also* MOISTURE-LOVING PLANTS.

Another species, *C. papyrus,* is an eight-foot-tall aquatic plant with stems clothed in sheaths which the ancient Egyptians used to make paper. It is a fine plant for a greenhouse pool.

UMBRELLA TREE: (*Magnolia tripetala*) The umbrella tree gets its name from the huge leaves, two feet long and half as wide, that radiate from the ends of the branches like an umbrella. It grows 30 to 40 feet tall, with big, creamy, cup-shaped flowers up to ten inches across, that appear in late spring and have a disagreeable odor. Sometimes planted for ornament, it is hardy from southern New England west to Nebraska, and likes a deep, fairly rich loam soil. Two other magnolias, *M. fraseri* and *M. macrophylla,* have a similar habit and are sometimes called umbrella trees, but both have fragrant flowers. *Melia azedrach* is the Texas umbrella tree or Chinaberry.

UMKOKOLO: (*Dovyalis caffra*) Also called kei-apple, umkokolo is a shrub growing from ten to 20 feet high, with sharp thorns and tiny greenish flowers. It does well on sandy soils in Florida and California. The pulpy yellow fruits, about an inch in diameter, are edible cooked and taste much like cranberries. The Ceylon gooseberry or kitambilla (*D. hebecarpa*) is a similar plant hardy throughout the deep South, with purplish fruits somewhat sweeter than those of umkokolo. Both species are unisexual and must have both male and female specimens planted together to produce fruit. They are generally propagated by seeds.

UNEDO: (*Arbutus unedo*) Also known as strawberry tree. A broad-leaved evergreen, hardy in the South and along the Pacific Coast. It bears

orange-red, edible but tasteless fruits that look like strawberries. The tiny pink or white flowers are borne in small, drooping clusters. Another species, *A. menziesi,* the madrona or laurelwood, has the same hardiness range but slightly bigger flowers, and is an important honey plant in California. Both species like well-drained soil and shelter from wind. They are propagated by layers or by cuttings of ripe wood in the fall under glass.

UNICORN PLANT: (*Proboscidea louisianica*) The unicorn plant or devil's claw is a sprawling tender annual with leaves up to ten inches across. It bears big bell-shaped yellowish-purple blooms in clusters and odd three-inch-long fruits that are used like pickling cucumbers while still green. It can be started indoors and the seedlings hardened off and set out, about five feet apart each way, in any medium fertile, near-neutral soil. A mulch is beneficial until the plants blanket the soil.

UNIOLA: *see* GRASS, ORNAMENTAL

UNISEXUAL: A flower containing only one organ of reproduction—either the male (stamen) or female (pistil) is said to be unisexual. Plants that have separate male and female flowers on the same plant are called monoecious, while those having male and female flowers on separate plants are dioecious. Flowers that contain both male and female organs are called perfect.

UPLAND CRESS: (*Barbarea vulgaris*) Upland cress is a tangy salad herb, used alone or in mixed green salads. It resembles water cress in appearance and flavor, but the plant is much bigger, up to 18 inches tall, with large leaves. A hardy biennial, its seeds are sown in early spring in a medium-fertile soil. Cut the leaves often—the more you shear them, the faster the new, tender leaves spring up. Upland cress will live over the winter with a covering of salt hay, providing fresh leaves for spring salads until the plant flowers and goes to seed.

Pepper grass (*Lepidium sativum*) is also sometimes called upland cress. It has lacy, curled leaves and a sharp pepper flavor, and is used with other greens in salads or as a flavoring for soups and blender drinks. *See also* Herbs; Weeds, Edible.

URBINEA: (*Echeveria agavoides*) This low succulent, grown in cool greenhouses and used often as a summer bedding plant, has pretty red flowers that rise on leafy stalks above its rosettes. Outdoors, it is grown mainly in the Southwest and other areas of dry winters.

URD: (*Phaseolus mungo*) Also called black gram, urd is a bean grown for food in India and other hot countries, but rarely here. It is a spreading annual legume growing about two feet tall, with tiny yellow flowers and two-inch-long pods that bear the black beans.

UREA: *see* Nitrogen

URGINEA: *see* Sea Squill

URINE: The fertilizer value of liquid animal manure is not as well recognized by gardeners and especially farmers as it should be. Urine is high in nitrogen and potassium, containing two-thirds of the nitrogen and four-fifths of the potassium voided by the animal.

The following amounts of urine are given by livestock animals yearly: a horse, 3,300 pounds; sheep, 4,200; a cow, 8,000; and a pig, 12,200. The urine of an average 1,000-pound cow provides 92 pounds of nitrogen and a similar amount of potassium annually. This is highly valuable plant food that is all too often wasted.

The wise farmer or homesteader uses plenty of bedding to capture this precious substance. In barns, a pipe arrangement can be employed to carry it from the gutters to a storage tank or pit. Either the bedding or the liquid can be applied then at will to his garden or field crops and pastures.

Since liquid manure is relatively concentrated, it should be applied sparingly when used alone, and only in damp weather, to prevent "burning" plants.

The Washington Experiment Station found that fertilization with liquid manure alone produced extra fine growth of grasses and clover much earlier in the spring than other types of feeding (the elements in urine being in solution, they are quickly available). Urine is also an especially fine activator for converting crop residues to humus. *See also* Manure.

URSINIA: Ursinias are handsome, bushy tender annuals growing eight inches to two feet high, with yellow or orange, purple-based flowers resembling daisies. They are particularly good annuals for droughty conditions. Seeds can also be sown in January in the greenhouse to produce pot plants that bloom in early spring.

U. S. DEPARTMENT OF AGRICULTURE: *see* Government Services

UTRICLE: Any small, one-seeded fruit that ripens without bursting its outer sheath, is called a utricle. Examples are the fruit of the buttercup and the beet.

UTRICULARIA: The bladderwort (*U. vulgaris*) is found in swampy waters or the inlets of lakes, and can be grown in aquariums. It floats submerged near the surface, sending up clusters of pretty yellow flowers rising above the water on stiff stems. On its delicate underwater branches are tiny sacs, less than an eighth of an inch long, that catch insects.

Each sac or bladder is provided with a trap door, triggered by bristles which make it spring open and suck in minute water bugs or larvae who touch them. Once inside, these organisms cannot escape and are digested by the plant. The bristle-trap door mechanism is so sensitive even a microscopic paramecium can spring it. A single plant may have hundreds of these sacs, each of which can digest several insects at once.

Bladderwort is very hardy, and propagates itself by seeds or by winter buds which rest on the mud during the cold season and develop into new plants in spring. There are some 230 species of bladderwort; some tropical ones have blooms as lovely as orchids. *See also* CARNIVOROUS PLANTS.

UVA-URSI: (*Arctostaphyllos uva-ursi*) Commonly called bearberry or kinnikinnick, uva-ursi is a handsome, hardy evergreen ground cover. The sprawling stems are often six feet long and root at the joints to make a dense mat. It has white or pinkish flowers, and the foliage turns bronze in winter. Plant in early spring or late summer in the North. Give it a light, acid soil containing lots of sand and humus. Frozen clumps can also be taken up from the wild in winter and planted. *See also* GROUND COVERS.

UVULARIA: Also called bellwort, these perennials belong to the lily family, are spring-blooming. Strawflower or corn flower (*U. grandiflora*) is a hardy 1½ foot high perennial with yellow flowers. It is also known as wood daffodil. Wild oats (*U. sessifolia*) grows to one foot, while Mohawkweed (*U. perfoliata*) is about six inches taller.

Plants grow best in light, humus-rich soil and some shade. They are often used in the border or wild garden.

V

VACCINIUM: A genus of shrubs, erect and prostrate, of the heath family, native from the tropics to the Arctic, and including two of great commercial importance, the blueberry and cranberry. Both require an extremely acid soil, between pH 4.0 and 5.0, and cranberry must have bog conditions, such as obtained in its native habitat. These two, with the cowberry which is sometimes planted in a cultivated "wild" garden are the only species of *Vaccinium* under cultivation. A few others are sometimes transplanted from the wild, such as the whortleberry (*V. myrtillus*); dwarf bilberry (*V. caespitosum*); bog bilberry (*V. uliginosum*); and the sparkleberry or farkleberry (*V. arboreum*).

Blueberries should be grown in an acid soil. Although they are spoken of as bog plants, blueberries will not tolerate a water table within one foot of the surface of the soil during the growing season. In the home garden, sufficient moisture will usually be available if the plants are mulched with a thick layer of chopped oak leaves, pine needles, or sawdust.

Cranberries cannot ordinarily be grown in the home garden, nor in most parts of the country. In order to grow them at all, one must have a plentiful supply of acid water, a bog with a pH factor of 4.5, and a dam which will enable the gardener to flood his bog during the season when temperatures drop below 26°. Because of these stringent requirements, cranberries are grown in only a few sections—in Massachusetts on Cape Cod, in New Jersey in the pine barren area, and in Wisconsin.

Blueberry species include high-bush blueberry (*V. corymbosum*), a shrub growing to 12 feet with fruit ⅓ inch in diameter. Hardy north into Canada. *V. virgatum,* a similar shrub, is hardy only in the southern states. Cranberry species include *V. macrocarpon* and *V. oxycoccus. See also* BLUEBERRY; CRANBERRY.

VAGNERA: (*Smilacina*) Also known as False Solomon's Seal. A genus of the lily family. These are perennial herbs growing from rhizomes, a few useful for naturalizing in partly shady corners of the garden, with ferns and semi-wild garden plants. They grow well in any moderately rich garden soil with plenty of moisture. Propagated by division. Pale greenish-white flower clusters at top of plant, followed by berries similar to that of Smilax. Leaves are simple, alternate, with parallel veins. The most frequently cultivated species are *S. racemosa,* commonly called spikenard or treacleberry, and *S. stellata,* starry Solomon's seal. Spikenard grows to three feet, with individual leaves six inches long, and bears red berries. *S. stellata* grows to about half that size.

VALERIAN: (*Valeriana officinalis*) A hardy perennial, often called garden heliotrope. It has heavy spreading rootstocks that are strong-smelling and used dried for medicinal purposes. The plant grows four to five feet tall, with broad leaves and fragrant white, pink or pale violet flowers borne in clusters.

Valerian thrives best in a rich and rather heavy loam, well supplied with water. Propagate by seeds sown in a well-protected, sunny seedbed as soon as they are ripe, or by division of the roots in fall or spring. Roots to be sold to drug houses are sliced lengthwise and dried, generally by artificial heat.

A perennial sometimes called red valerian is *Centranthus ruber,* a two-foot-high plant with crimson flowers. The African valerian (*Fedia cornucopiae*) grows a foot tall, with dense clusters of red blooms; it is grown as a hardy annual and is sometimes used as a salad plant. The blue-flowered perennial Jacob's-ladder (*Polemium caeruleum*) is sometimes called green valerian.

VALERIANELIA: The leaves and stems of the valerianellas are used for salads, especially in the winter, for which the seed is sown in September. The Italian corn salad (*V. eriocarpa*) and the field salad (*V. olitoria*) both have rounded five-inch leaves and grow about a foot tall, with pale blue flowers. The seeds are sown a half-inch deep in medium-fertile, friable soil, from April to September, and the plants thinned to three inches apart.

VALLARIS: These woody climbing vines are grown only in the deep South. The most commonly cultivated species, *V. heynei,* grows very tall with hairy leaves and clusters of fragrant white flowers. The one-celled fruits are four to six inches long. It does well in any medium-rich soil with good drainage.

VALLOTA: The vallota or Scarborough lily is a member of the amaryllis family and resembles amaryllis (*Hippeastrum*) in every respect, except that the long strap-like leaves appear at the same time as the flower stalk, instead of later. The blooms are deep scarlet and the stalks rise up to three feet high. For culture, *see also* AMARYLLIS.

VALVE: Each segment or piece into which a pod splits is called a valve. An example is the pea pod, which has two valves.

VANCOUVERIA: The vancouverias are evergreen shrubs growing less than two feet tall with heavy creeping rootstocks. Their small white or yellow flowers are borne in drooping panicles. The best species is *V. hexandra,* which is a fine ground cover or border plant, hardy in the South and along the Pacific Coast. It needs a deep, highly fertile soil and shade from hot sun. It is easily increased by division of the rootstocks.

VANDA: Few orchids surpass vandas in the beauty of their foliage and flowers. The often extremely fragrant, medium-sized blooms are borne in sprays. With plenty of sun, they will usually bloom two or three times a year.

Vandas have a monopodial growth habit, which means their single stem grows higher each year, with new leaves springing from its tip. The flower stalk arises from the axils of the leaves, and aerial roots appear on the older portions of the plant. Should it become too tall, the top part with some aerial roots attached may be cut off and repotted. They can also be propagated by taking off the young growths which spring from near the base of the stem.

The strap-leaf vandas have evergreen leaves and are very popular house and greenhouse plants. The best varieties are *V. coerulea, V. rothschildiana* and *V. sanderiana.* The first two have magnificent blue flowers, while *V. sanderiana* is the largest-flowered—up to five inches—of the species and is used to produce many hybrids, giving them distinct and spectacularly beautiful color patterns.

Terete and semi-terete vandas are grown outdoors in full sun in tropical and semi-tropical areas. They have cylindrical, pencil-like leaves. None of them are suitable for indoor growing. In many parts of Florida and other warm southern states, lovely beds of these kinds of vandas can be seen in backyards. *V. teres* is one of the most popular of the terete vandas, with blooms shaded from white to rose. *See also* ORCHIDS.

VANILLA: The vanilla orchid (*V. planifolia*) is a big-leaved climbing vine needing a trellis. It blooms in the spring with numerous clustered three-inch green flowers, which usually are rather dull in color and last only a few days. Its chief value in the tropics lies in its dried seed pods, which are the source of the flavoring extract vanilla.

In this country, several of the vines planted in a pot in osmunda fiber make a handsome display for the window garden or greenhouse. They produce roots freely from their climbing stems, hence are readily propagated by cuttings. No pods, however, are formed without artificial pollination.

Other species include *V. lutescens,* a climber that has very showy greenish-yellow flowers, six inches across, with a brilliant yellow lip; *V. phalaenopsis,* an interesting climber, produces long leafless stems and large orange and blue flowers; *V. walkeriae* is also leafless and has delicately transparent pure white flowers streaked with deep green.

VANILLA GRASS: (*Hierochloe odorata*) Vanilla grass is a perennial sweet-smelling grass that grows wild in the Northeast. It is not often cultivated in the garden, although its creeping rootstocks can be easily divided and transplanted from the wild. The leaves and brownish panicle grow about a foot high and are not especially ornamental.

VANILLA LEAF: (*Trilisa odoratissima*) This spring-sown perennial grows two to three feet high and has tongue-shaped leaves that smell like vanilla when crushed. The flower heads are white or rose-purple and appear in late summer and fall. Vanilla leaf is a good border or wild garden plant. Sow the seed ⅛ inch deep in any fertile soil. The roots can be divided in early spring.

VARIATION: Divergence in character of offspring from the character of the parent. A variation may be temporary, the third generation returning to the character of the original parent, or it may be permanent, a sport (which see), with all future offspring retaining the variation which appeared in the second generation, passed on to them by a change of genes or chromosomes in the seed.

Temporary variations may be caused by growing conditions—unusual conditions of moisture, plant nutrients, sun or shade, soil acidity, or temperature. Most common instance of this is the dwarf nature of many plants grown in the North, which may be killed to the soil and appear as two or three foot perennials where winters are cold. In the South where they are not killed back in the winter, the same plants will become tall woody shrubs or trees. Cuttings taken from the northern plant and rooted in the South will develop into woody shrubs or trees.

Permanent or hereditary variation, in which the genes or chromosomes are changed, is a sport or mutation. These permanent changes are now thought to be caused by gamma radiation.

VARIEGATED: Any leaf which has stripes, bars, blotches or other markings of a different color from its ground-color is said to be variegated. Most variegated leaves have green for their ground-color, but many handsome foliage plants, such as caladium, may have practically any ground-color.

These are often irregular markings, and are due to the presence of two or more colors, caused by special pigments or, in the case of yellow or white foliage, to their absence. Variegation, or the diversity of colors in individual plants, generally heightens their attractive appearance and adds to their usefulness in landscaping and garden or house plant arrangement.

VARIETIES: *see listings of individual plants;* VEGETABLE GARDENING; DISEASE (Resistant Varieties); FRUIT TREES (Resistant Varieties)

VARIETY: A group of plants whose difference from others of its type is too trivial or too inconstant to warrant giving it a separate species' name. Thus in a species whose flowers are small, single, and red, varieties with the same characteristics except in the flower may be white, pink, or lavender, double, large, or frilled. When the character cannot be transmitted through the seeds, but must be propagated by cuttings from the plant which first showed the variation, called the clone, the offspring are called clonal varieties. *See also* STRAIN; SPECIES; GENUS.

VARNISH TREE: (*Koelreuteria paniculata*) The varnish or golden-rain tree grows about 25 feet tall. It is a round-headed, feathery-leaved tree that bears beautiful yellow flower clusters up to 18 inches long in summer, and papery pods. It is hardy in all but the northernmost states. Give it an open position and fairly moist soil. *K. formosana* is somewhat taller with bigger leaves, but is hardy only in central Florida and southern California. Both are propagated by root cuttings or stratified seeds.

VEGETABLE BRAIN: (*Blighia sapida*) Tropical African tree of the *Sapindaceae* family, cultivated in southern Florida for its fruit, or akee, called vegetable brain. Leaves are compound pinnate, flowers grow in fragrant clusters. Fruit is a three-celled capsule surrounded by a thick coating, or aril, which is the part used for food. Over- or under-ripe arils are said to be poisonous. They can be eaten only at one stage in their ripening. The tree can be grown only in frost-free climates. Propagation is by seeds or shield-budding.

VEGETABLE GARDENING: Most gardeners who have turned to the organic method have done so primarily because of their vegetable gardens. Organically grown vegetables not only contain more vitamins and minerals, but are also free of poison sprays, artificial colorings, and preservatives often found on vegetables purchased in the market.

In order to eat foods from his own vegetable garden for as many months of the year as possible, the gardener must plan his garden program carefully before he puts a single seed into the ground. His first concern will be a plan of the main source of his produce, the garden plot itself.

LOCATION: On a small suburban lot the vegetable garden is placed at the end of the plot where it will receive the least shade from buildings and trees, and where it may be screened by plantings or fences from the landscaped areas.

Where limited space is not a factor in placing the vegetable garden, it is usually located near compost heaps, tool sheds, and barns, and is not too far removed from the kitchen. If the vegetable plot must be distant from the house, a supplemental herb and salad plot near the kitchen door is useful.

Ideal situation for a vegetable garden is on a plot that slopes gently toward the east, southeast, or south. Good drainage is essential, and a slope is likely to be well-drained. Also, a southern slope is warm—warms up early in spring and can be kept warm, with moderate protection, into late fall. This type of situation may be made to prolong the growing season from four to eight weeks. With judicious use of cold frames and hotbeds, the season may be prolonged another four to eight weeks, making it possible for the gardener to grow his own table greens about three months longer than is average in his climate, without the use of a greenhouse.

In addition to a favorable exposure, the vegetable garden should be placed where it will get as much sun as possible—from sunrise to sunset, if such an exposure is available. It should be removed from shallow-rooted trees, such as elms, maples, poplars, and willows. Such trees not only rob the soil of food and moisture, but as soon as they find the fine, rich soil which will be developed in an organic vegetable plot, they seem to send out all their roots to dwell there.

SIZE AND SHAPE: Where space is limited by the size of a lot, the size

VEGETABLE PLANTING TABLE AND REQUIREMENTS

| Vegetable | Nutrient Requirements EH = Extra Heavy H = Heavy M = Moderate L = Light | | | | Planting Directions | | | | |
	Nit.	Phos.	Pot.	pH factor	Time to plant	Distance between plants (inches)	Distance between rows (inches)	Amount of seed per 100 row-feet	Yield per 100 row-feet
Asparagus	EH	H	EH	6.0-7.0	Spring	18	48-60	Roots	12-24 lb.
Beans, bush	L	M	M	6.0-7.5	1-8 weeks after last spring frost	4-6	18-24	1 lb.	50 lb.
lima	L	M	M	5.5-6.5	2-6 weeks after last spring frost	6-10	24	1 lb.	60-75 lb.
Beets, early	EH	EH	EH	5.8-7.0	2-4 weeks before last spring frost	3	12-18	2 oz.	100 lb.
late	H	EH	H	same	6-8 weeks before first fall freeze	3	12-18	2 oz.	100 lb.
Broccoli	H	H	H	6.0-7.0	4-6 weeks before last spring frost	18-24	24-30	Plants	50 lb.
Cabbage, early	EH	EH	EH	6.0-7.0	4-6 weeks before last spring frost	15-18	24-30	Plants	100 lb.
late	H	H	H	same	3 months before first fall freeze	24-30	24-30	1 pkt.	175 lb.
Carrots, early	H	H	H	5.5-6.5	2-4 weeks before last spring frost	3	12-18	1 oz.	100 lb.
late	M	M	M	same	10 weeks before first fall freeze	3	12-18	1 oz.	150 lb.
Cauliflower, early	EH	EH	EH	6.0-7.0	2-4 weeks before last spring frost	18-24	24-30	Plants	45 heads
late	H	H	EH	same	3½ months before first fall freeze	18-24	24-30	1 pkt.	45 heads
Corn, early	H	H	H	6.0-7.0	On frost-free date	12-18	24-36	4 oz.	100 ears
late	M	M	M	same	10 weeks before first fall frost	12-18	24-36	4 oz.	100 ears
Cucumbers	H	H	H	6.0-8.0	1 week after last spring frost	36-60	36-60	½ oz.	150 lb.
Eggplant	H	H	H	6.0-7.0	1 week after last spring frost	24-30	24-30	Plants	125 fruit
Lettuce, head	EH	EH	EH	6.0-7.0	4-6 weeks before last spring frost	6-12	12-18	½ oz.	50 lb.
leaf	H	EH	EH	same	6 weeks before first fall freeze	6-12	12-18	½ oz.	50 lb.

Nutrient Requirements: EH = Extra Heavy, H = Heavy, M = Moderate, L = Light

Vegetable	Nit.	Phos.	Pot.	pH factor	Time to plant	Distance between plants (inches)	Distance between rows (inches)	Amount of seed per 100 row-feet	Yield per 100 row-feet
Muskmelons	H	H	H	6.0-7.0	1-2 weeks after last spring frost	48-72	48-72	½ oz.	50 fruit
Onions	H	H	H	6.0-7.0	4-6 weeks before last spring frost	2-3	12-18	1 oz. 300 pl.	75-100 lb.
Parsnips	M	M	M	6.0-8.0	2-4 weeks before last spring frost	3-6	18-24	¼ oz.	100 lb.
Parsley	H	H	H	5.0-7.0	2-4 weeks before last spring frost	3-6	12-18	¼ oz.	50 lb.
Peas	M	H	H	6.0-8.0	4-6 weeks before last spring frost	1-3	18-36	1 lb.	40 lb.
Potatoes, white	EH	EH	EH	4.8-6.5	4-6 weeks before last spring frost	12-15	24-30	6-10 lb.	75 lb.
sweet	L	M	H	5.0-6.0 or 6.0-7.0	1-2 weeks after last spring frost	12-18	30-48	Plants	100 lb.
Radishes	H	EH	EH	6.0-8.0	2-4 weeks before last spring frost	1	12-18	1 oz.	1200
Rutabaga	M	H	M	6.0-8.0	3 months before first fall freeze	6-10	18-24	¼ oz.	150 lb.
Soybeans	L	M	M	6.0-7.0	On frost-free date	6-10	24	½ lb.	50 lb.
Spinach	EH	EH	EH	6.5-7.0	4-6 weeks before last spring frost	2-6	15-24	1 oz.	50 lb.
Squash, summer	H	H	H	6.0-8.0	On frost-free date	36-80	36-80	½ oz.	100 fruits
winter	M	M	M	6.0-8.0	1-2 weeks after last spring frost	48-120	60-120	½ oz.	100 fruits
Strawberries	M	M	L	5.0-6.0	Spring	12-18	36	Plants	Varies
Tomatoes	M	H	H	6.0-7.0	On frost-free date	24-48	24-48	Plants	200 lb.
Turnips	L	H	M	6.0-8.0	4-6 weeks before last spring frost	3	12-18	½ oz.	100 lb.

and shape of the vegetable plot is determined for the gardener. But where space is almost unlimited, as it may be in a small country place, or on a farm, it is easy for a gardener to become over-ambitious, and to make his plot larger than he can handle.

The size of the vegetable garden must ultimately be determined by what it is expected to yield—the quantity of food that the family can eat during the growing season, plus the amount that can be stored in freezer, cold cellar, or can be canned. This can be estimated fairly well in most families. The estimate should take into account the tastes of the family, methods of preparing foods, and the available labor during peak harvest season when preserving food may be a problem. Approximate yields are indicated on accompanying chart.

Having estimated his needs, the gardener must now figure how much space will be necessary to grow that amount of food. The accompanying chart gives spacing between plants in a row which can be used to calculate the row-feet that will be needed.

In his calculations, the gardener must take into account the fact that some crops can be expected to share the same space during the growing season. Early peas, for example, may be followed by the late planting of beets, corn, cabbage, or pole beans. *See* PLANTINGS, SECOND. This is called succession planting. Radishes do not need a space in the garden plan. They mature so quickly that they may be sown in rows with slowly germinating seed, like carrots, and the radishes will mature and be pulled before the carrots feel any crowding. This is called companion cropping or intercropping. Muskmelons and pumpkins may be started in the early corn, and will be grateful for a little shade in the hottest weather. By the time their fruits are ready for full sun to help them ripen, the early corn stalks may be pulled out, to leave the melons alone

in the patch. *See also* COMPANION CROPS.

Garden space may also be saved by doubling rows of narrow-growing crops. Thus onions, which take only as much space as the diameter of the bulb, may be grown in double rows six inches apart. Mulch may be arranged between the two rows when the plants are large enough, to cut down the amount of hand-weeding necessary. Carrots, beets, parsnips, and turnips may be handled in the same way.

Plants which may be expected to occupy their plots during the entire summer include all the perennials, such as asparagus, chives, horseradish, perennial onions, rhubarb, perennial herbs, and berries. These must be given a situation where they will grow for two to ten years without being disturbed. They must also be located where power tillage or cultivating tools will not be inconvenienced by them. If necessary, they may be given a plot of their own, removed from the rest of the vegetable garden.

Annual vegetables that like sole possession of their garden space for the summer include lima beans, Swiss chard, cucumbers, eggplant, okra, onions, parsley, parsnips, peppers, sweet potatoes, late white potatoes, salsify, squash, both summer and winter, New Zealand spinach, tomatoes, and watermelon.

TIMING OF PLANTINGS: Some plants which may be grown as early vegetables, to be out of the ground in time to be supplanted by late crops are: bush beans, beets, cabbage, cauliflower, carrots, corn, kale, kohlrabi, lettuce, mustard, green onions, peas, early potatoes, radishes, spinach, turnips, and rutabaga. Seed for early varieties of many of these vegetables will be different from that planted for later varieties. Or a short season crop may be planted in spring, and replanted later in the year for a yield just before frost.

Later sowings may be made of almost all the plants on the foregoing list, with the exception of a few which thrive only in cool weather. This includes peas, which become too dry when the weather gets hot; kohlrabi which gets tough in hot weather; lettuce which bolts in the heat; and spinach, which needs cool weather of spring or fall.

Hot-weather varieties are offered by seedsmen for most of these crops. Wando summer peas can be planted to make most of their growth in August, but will yield best if they do not mature until cool weather. Early planted heading lettuce may be followed in summer by heat-resistant leafing varieties, with curly endive and escarole planted in August to carry on after the first light frosts. Seed catalogs indicate which vegetables are best for spring sowing, for fall crops, for storage, or for freezing.

It is easy to calculate the number or row-feet needed to grow vegetables like onions, beets, kohlrabi, or carrots where the whole plant is uprooted and used at once. Others that grow fruits or pods which are picked, while the plant is left to yield more, are not so easy to calculate. This is especially true in an organic garden, where increasingly rich soil and improved growing conditions sometimes bring about phenomenal yields. At the outset, however, the organic gardener will not be able to expect much better results than are common to his area. This will be limited by length of growing period, rainfall, and temperature, as well as by soil fertility and culture. Only experience can dictate the quantities of many vegetables that can be grown in a given locality and garden. However, there are some rules which will guide the beginner.

Snap beans and wax beans bear abundantly at the peak of the crop. A small number of seeds, or a few feet of row—15 to 50—must be planted several times to bear continuously through the summer. But lima beans and peas, though much the same type plant, do not bear the same way. Lima

beans will bear their main crop shortly after the first beans are large enough to pick, but they will continue to bear, if given abundant water and a good mulch, until frost. Lima bean seed

Seeds of many vegetable plants, such as lima beans, should be sown about two to three inches. Later thin plants approximately one foot apart.

should be planted late—two to four weeks after the first snap beans—and the seed should be spaced fairly close, two to three inches, and plants thinned later. Peas, like snap beans, bear their main crop and are through bearing. But peas should be planted thickly. A trench hoe-width can be liberally sprinkled with seed about two inches apart each way, to give the most abundant pea crop. To plant this thickly will require a pound of seed to 100 feet of row. Two or three pounds of seed will grow peas for the table and freezer for the average family.

Tomatoes may be grown in several different ways, and each type of culture will produce a different number of tomatoes per plant. If the plants are allowed to sprawl on the ground, they will need the largest amount of space—approximately nine to 16 square feet per plant, and will bear the largest amount of fruit each. But some of the lowest fruit on the plant may be lost because of slugs, or because the lush foliage hides it until it becomes over-ripe. If plants are tied to a stake, they will bear less fruit because the cords tend to crowd the middle branches, but less will be lost. If the branches are kept pinched out at the leaf nodes, and only the main stalk is allowed to grow tall, tomato plants may be spaced 30 inches apart along a fence, and will yield the least per plant, but the most for the space. Depending on cultural methods, two to four dozen plants will grow all the tomatoes that most families will be able to use fresh in summer and canned in winter.

Swiss chard is an easily grown vegetable that is sometimes over-planted by the beginner. A row 15 to 20 feet long is sufficient for the average family. Leaves are cut from the outside of the plants, and are replaced quickly by the plant to be ready for the next cutting.

Only a few plants of several other vegetables will be needed for the tables of most families. Besides chard, parsley, horseradish, peppers, rhubarb, and most herbs can be planted in small quantities.

SPACING OF ROWS: By calculating the number of plants he will need to supply his family with vegetables, the gardener has now arrived at a figure telling him how many row-feet he will need in his garden. In order to calculate the dimension of the garden he must know in addition how close together his rows can be planted. Before he can arrive at this figure he must decide how his garden is to be cultivated, or if it is to be under mulch, either during the summer or permanently.

A vegetable plot kept under a dust mulch during the summer months, that is, a plot which is hoed by hand, by a rotary tiller, or by a tractor to keep down the weeds will need more space between rows than a garden under an organic mulch. Each plant, however it is cared for, needs a certain amount of space to make its growth. In addition, if a machine is to pass between plants without damaging them, an open path must be left down the center of the space between rows. On the accompanying chart spaces between rows are indicated giving a maximum

needed for power tool cultivation, and a minimum for crops under straw mulch, where no cultivation is needed except hand-weeding around young plants. A stone-mulched vegetable garden (see below) cannot be spaced as a cultivated or straw-mulched plot can be, because stone mulching is permanent. In order to make provision for rotating crops in a stone-mulched area, a stone path two feet wide is left between rows, which are themselves about a foot wide. With this much space, almost any crop may be placed in any row.

By calculating the space between rows, and the row-feet needed the gardener is now able to compute the size of his plot. One other dimension must be added. This is the space needed at each end of the rows, if it is to be plowed in spring by tractor or cub tractor, for the machine to turn in. This space can be used for nothing except grass, because the plow will not turn the soil satisfactorily while the tractor is turning around, and the weight of the tractor will pack the soil too hard for anything except grass.

LAYOUT: If the garden is on a slope, rows are usually planned to follow the contour to avoid erosion. However, if the slope is very gentle and the garden will have a permanent straw or hay mulch, erosion will present no problem, and rows can be made up and down hill, to make irrigation easier.

Permanent fixtures of the garden should be placed at one end where the power tools that may be used for tillage or cultivation will not be inconvenienced by them. These fixtures include, besides the perennial vegetable and berry plots, cold frames, stone mulched beds, and hotbeds. These may be placed at either end of the garden, but are best near the water supply.

In laying out the vegetable row plan, the only rule that is invariable is that the tallest vegetables are planted on the north end, or where they will not shade shorter ones. When crops are rotated yearly to cut down disease or to balance nutrient demands on the soil, it is not always possible to place corn, for instance, in the top rows. In that case it may be placed on the south side of a vegetable which will stand some shade, such as lettuce, peas, cucumbers, kohlrabi, or scallions, or it may be placed beside plants which will grow moderately tall by the end of the corn's growth, such as peppers, staked tomatoes, or mustard.

Disease and insect infestation may be kept to a minimum if plants subject to the same ones are not allowed to follow each other in the same bed. This applies to the cabbage family— kale, kohlrabi, radishes, cauliflower, and cabbage; to the beans—snap beans, limas, and soybeans; and to squash, cucumbers and melons.

MULCH: Gardening experts have come to agree that a mulch during the hot summer months will produce the best results in a home vegetable garden. Besides conserving moisture and cutting down labor required for weeding, an organic mulch breaks down gradually through the summer to add humus to the soil. Even if the mulch is raked away in fall or spring for plowing, a certain amount of it will have broken down into particles too small for the rake to remove, and will be plowed in. Also, earthworms thrive in the layer of soil just below the mulch, and carry on their work of aerating and enriching the soil, and of carrying broken-down bits of mulch below the surface, to increase the amount of humus around roots.

Materials used for the mulch will depend upon what the gardener can get in his own neighborhood. Hay or straw are most commonly used. Spoiled hay may sometimes be purchased cheaply. Leaves which have been shredded and stored from the previous fall make excellent vegetable garden mulch. Sawdust can be used around some of the acid-loving berries and vegetables. Ground corncobs make a good mulch where a granular texture is required for shoots to push through, as in an asparagus bed.

If the mulch is fine textured, as is shredded leaf mold or ground corn cobs, it may be plowed under the following spring to increase the organic content of the soil. A coarse mulch, such as straw or hay, breaks down slowly and should not be used in this way unless a large amount of nitrogenous supplement is plowed under with it. If it is turned under alone, it can rob the soil of its existing supply of nitrogen. So a coarse mulch is either left on the soil year round, and no plowing is done, or it is raked away while the soil is being turned, disked, or harrowed, and then immediately pulled back over the soil to protect it from drying out.

A permanent year-round mulch has been used successfully in some gardens. The soil is permanently covered with a six-inch blanket of straw or other material, and is never turned or harrowed. Mulch is separated in rows or spots for planting. This type of culture has been most successful where the original soil was porous, either sandy or gravelly, or where it had been cultivated for several years previously, and a large amount of humus had been incorporated with it. Before beginning to grow a garden under mulch, without benefit of a yearly stirring of the soil, it is necessary to attain a certain openness of soil texture. A heavy clay soil will react favorably during the first year, after it has had its deep plowing preparatory to applying the mulch. It may even remain in condition to plant the second year. But eventually the clay will pack, and a condition like that in a forest will be obtained where a thin top layer of rich organic material will rest on a solid clay subsoil, with only a thin layer of topsoil between.

If conditions are right for it, the garden is thoroughly plowed and harrowed before permanent mulch is applied. As much organic material as is available—manure, leaf mold, compost

—is stirred into the top layer of soil with a disk or harrow. The soil should be tested, and rock phosphate and potash, ground limestone, bone meal, or other needed supplements should be spread before the mulch is applied.

A six-inch layer of straw or hay will protect soil moisture and prevent weeds from growing during a period of about three months. Additional mulch may be spread whenever it is needed, but the mulch should be allowed to become somewhat thinner in the fall, so that when spring comes, the spring warmth can penetrate it. It should not be allowed to disintegrate entirely, at this or any other time, because it is an excellent protection against drying fall winds and heavy fall and spring rain erosion.

A combination of permanent mulch and tillage has been used successfully on some gardens where the soil is too heavy for the mulch alone. The mulch is spread, and separated in spring where rows are to be planted. The soil is then stirred with a fork, and compost or manure dug in, on a foot-wide strip along the planting line. Where single plants are to be set, such as tomatoes or peppers, or where squash, melon, or cucumber hills are to be planted, the mulch is pushed back and a circular area a foot wider than the planting site is similarly prepared.

STONE MULCHING: Stone mulching is similar to permanent straw mulching in that the bed is prepared deeply, fertilizers and supplements are added, and the stones are set in place to remain there for years. Stone mulch has one great advantage over straw mulch—a stone mulched garden warms up earlier in spring than any other. While the soil is still frozen in most of the garden, soil between and around large rocks will be found thawed in early spring. The rocks soak up heat from the sun, and remain warmer than the air during the night hours.

The bed is prepared deeply, and organic matter is disked into the top layer of soil, along with any other needed supplements. If they are available, a thick layer of leaves are then spread over the soil, and the rocks set on top of the leaves.

The rocks are set in paths two feet wide, leaving a foot for planting between. Rocks are placed with flat surfaces up, and made as level as possible. Spaces between them are then filled with compost or with garden loam, and the planting channel is filled with compost. A layer of gravel over the soil between rocks will help to keep down weeds in that area, or the rock paths may be covered with a layer of straw mulch after the soil has become thoroughly warm in spring.

If the whole vegetable garden is not stone mulched, a few stone mulched rows at one end of the garden are useful for growing early vegetables, and for the last outdoor salad greens in the fall. Two or three such rows will prolong the use of the garden as much as six weeks altogether. Seed may be planted in fall for hardy herbs, such as parsley, dill, and scallions, to come up early in the stone mulch. And early in spring lettuce may be transplanted from indoor flats to grow under hotcaps in a stone-mulched bed long before seed can be sown outdoors.

In autumn hardy greens, such as endive and escarole, may be protected and kept growing in the stone mulched beds until after Thanksgiving. Broccoli and brussels sprouts will yield into the winter in stone mulch. Root vegetables can be left out until much later in a stone mulch, and in some cases their flavor will be much improved.

If a permanent mulch cannot be used in the vegetable garden for any reason, a seasonal mulch may be spread between rows and around plants. In spite of the old belief that such plants as corn and tomatoes needed to bake their roots, mulch has been shown to improve the yield even of these crops. Because the soil does not dry out as rapidly, plants are better fed, and the general health of the garden is improved. Less watering is needed during periods of drought, and weeding is cut to a minimum.

FERTILIZING VEGETABLES: Nutrient needs of different vegetables vary, and sometimes the needs of the same vegetable vary from season to season. Cauliflower, for instance, needs more nitrogen and phosphorus to yield early heads than it will need later in the fall. Squash plants which will produce summer fruit need heavier feeding throughout their season than squash which ripens its fruit in fall. Acid or lime requirements of various plants also differ.

Fast-growing, heavy-feeding vegetables require large amounts of organic fertilizers. Above compost is placed around young cabbage plants.

In order to do an intelligent job of feeding his vegetables, the gardener must know what his soil lacks, and must supply the lack for each of the plants he grows. Soil testing kits are offered on the market containing materials and information for tests which are quick and easy to perform. Until he is thoroughly familiar with his garden, the gardener should make frequent and thorough tests. *See also* SOIL TESTING.

From the accompanying chart, it will be seen that most vegetables will grow well in a soil whose pH factor is between 6 and 8. Potatoes, parsley, and a few others prefer a more acid soil, and will not grow well in the presence of lime. In rotating crops from year to year, this must be taken into account. Limestone should be spread on portions of the garden where lime-loving vegetables are to be planted, and acid-preference plants should not be put in these areas until two or three years have elapsed, and the lime has had time to leach away.

Vegetables whose need for nitrogen is high may profitably be planted in the rows previously occupied by beans, peas, soybeans, or limas—legumes whose roots harbor nitrogen-fixing bacteria. Fast-growing vegetables which make a heavy growth in a season should be enriched with compost, rotted manure, cottonseed or blood meal. These same heavy feeders usually need more water than do the plants which make a smaller growth. For that reason, soil about their roots should be especially rich in humus which holds the water.

Just as a plant's need for food varies at different periods, its need for water will also vary. Usually during the

At planting time, seedlings should be "watered in." Firmly press soil around roots in order to avoid air pockets and insure proper feeding.

period when it is producing its heaviest crop, the vegetable will need the most water. This will show in the disease and insect resistance of the plants. Tomatoes, if given all the water they need while ripening, will bear a healthy, blight-free crop. As soon as they begin to feel a drought, brown blight spots will begin to appear on the bottom of the fruit. Squash plants seem to be freer of squash beetles in a wet than in a dry year. Many organic gardeners report that as the moisture-holding humus content of their soils increase, Mexican bean beetle infestations wane.

Muskmelons and celery are two crops which need abundant water and at the same time, very well-drained soil. Celery cannot be grown successfully in heavy clay soils. It must have light, friable, but very rich loam, with plenty of moisture. Until his soil has attained this quality, it is not advisable for the gardener to try to plant celery. Good melons may be grown, however, if the hills are well composted and kept moist. Two or three spades full of rich compost or rotted manure should be dug in where each hill, or group of melon seeds, will be planted. A six-inch flower pot may be sunk in the center of the hill, if desired, and kept filled with water. This may be filled once each week with manure water, when the melons are forming on the vines.

Manure water or side dressings of cottonseed or blood meal may be given to any of the heavy-feeding vegetables during their fruiting period. Lima beans will bear longer and produce better beans if given plenty of food and water while pods are forming. Tomatoes should not be fed too heavily until after they begin to give an abundance of ripe fruit, because a large amount of nitrogen fed early will slow the ripening process. When size of the fruit begins to drop off, manure water will help to make larger tomatoes.

Eggplant is another vegetable that may be grown in a hill composed chiefly of manure and compost. Crookneck squash and zucchini are both heavy feeders, and need plenty of compost to start the season, and water to form their large watery fruits.

TRENCHING: The European method of garbage trenching may be used to advantage where more garbage is available than is used in the compost heaps, or where compost heaps cannot be built, as in some towns.

A trench about a foot deep is dug across the garden in spring, and the soil left heaped up beside it. (The trench and heap of soil may both be temporarily covered with mulch, to prevent drying.) As the trench is filled with garbage, starting at one end and working toward the other, the heap of soil is pulled over it, and again mulched. The entire row is left unplanted during the whole season, to permit bacterial action below ground to be completed. *See also* TRENCHING.

STARTING SEED: Early produce from the garden is the aim of every gardener. One way to hasten early crops is by starting many of them indoors, before outdoor planting is possible. A few vegetables dislike transplanting, and must be sown directly in the garden for best results. Among these are peas, corn, carrots, and beans. Melons and squash may be started inside with special techniques, but they grow so rapidly outdoors that the early start seems to make little difference.

Onions, tomatoes, peppers, eggplant, cabbage, cauliflower, and celery are usually started under glass. Seed for the larger varieties of onions may be started as early as January, and planted in the garden before the last spring frost. Cabbage, cauliflower, and celery may also be hardened off to plant out early, but their seeds develop more quickly inside, so they are started about six to eight weeks before time to transfer to the garden. Tomatoes, peppers, and eggplant cannot be planted in the garden until the soil is thoroughly warm, so their seed is started indoors about four weeks after the cabbage.

Seed is usually started in small pots, in a mixture of sand and garden loam. Seedlings are transferred to flats after the first true leaves have appeared, where they are allowed a space one by two inches per plant. The soil in the flat should not be rich, to encourage good root growth and discourage legginess. Soil can be sterilized by an hour in the oven, or with boiling water. Flats should be kept in full sun during the day, and should have a temperature at night of no more than

60°. If the plants grow too fast for the advancing spring, they may be held back and further prepared for planting out if they are transplanted once more, this time to individual pots.

PLANTING: At least a week before being planted out, the seedlings should be hardened off. This may be done in a cold frame, where they should be ventilated with the sash open during the day, or they may be set outdoors in the daytime and brought in to a cool room at night.

Plants are set out in the garden in the evening, or on a cloudy day. Every effort should be made to prevent the roots from becoming dry while the seedlings are in transit from flat to garden bed. The soil should be prepared in advance, a trench or series of holes dug for the plants, and a watering can or hose kept at hand to wet the soil as the small plants are placed. If they are being planted out very early in spring, when frosts might still be in the offing, a protection of some sort should be provided.

In deep mulch, protection will be afforded the seedlings by the mulch which is heaped up beside them. If a pane of glass is laid over the hole in the mulch that was made for the plant, a miniature cold frame is formed for each plant. If this is not possible, a hot cap or a basket may be inverted over the plants and left there until danger of frost is past. It is best to shade the newly set seedlings for several days, even though the weather is warm. Plants set out in the middle of the summer may need protection from the sun for as long as two weeks, until their roots have spread into the garden bed.

Seed which is sown directly in the garden is scattered in a drill, or trench, which is shallow or deep depending upon the size of the seed. The usual rule is to cover the seed to four times its diameter. Finely sifted compost makes the best cover because it will not cake as clayey soil may do. Late crop seed which is sown in the garden may

need to be covered to prevent drying while it is germinating. A light layer of mulch, burlap, or cardboard may be used. The cover must be promptly removed when the seedlings begin to push through the soil.

If late crops are started in flats for transfer later to garden rows, the midsummer flats can be left outside in the shade to germinate. These flats may require a large percentage of humus to maintain a sufficient degree of moisture. More uniform moisture may be supplied them if a wick arrangement is set up when the flats are filled. To prepare a wick flat, a piece of muslin or burlap is cut to fit the bottom of the flat, with about a foot overhang at each end. The flat is then filled with soil, covering the wick. Seeds are planted in the flat in the usual way, and the flat is then placed over a large pan of water, with the wick hanging over each end into the water. If the pan is not allowed to go dry, the soil in the flat will remain uniformly moist until seeds germinate.

INSECT PESTS: As has already been mentioned, many insect pests seem to disappear when healthy plants are grown organically. Plants given enough food, water, and humus are comparatively free of such pests as squash bugs, Mexican bean beetles, and aphids. A few of the larger pests, such as tomato worms and Japanese beetle can be picked off by hand. Cutworm damage can be minimized if plants are set out with paper collars.

A 3 x 5 file card makes a collar of about the right size for most plants. As the plant is firmed into the soil, the collar is loosely wrapped around its stem, and thrust into the soil, to make a fence against cutworms.

Slugs are pests that come with mulch or loose debris in any garden. Actually, the slug makes most of his living from the dead plant material, and is one of the soil creatures who helps to break down organic material and to turn it into humus. But he also feeds to some extent on growing leaves and vegetables. Slug damage is always greatest in wet weather, because he must keep his skin damp to survive, and unless the top of the mulch is damp, he must stay underneath it.

If slugs seem to cause more trouble than their services are worth, they can be killed by a light sprinkle of ordinary table salt on their backs. Or plants may be protected from them in bad cases of infestation by pulling the mulch away a few inches, to permit a circle of soil at the base of the plants to become dry on top. *See also* SLUGS AND SNAILS.

A novel cure for cucumber beetles is suggested by one organic gardener, who claims that marigolds with odorous foliage planted near her cucumbers chased the beetles away.

Birds are of great assistance in ridding the garden of many insects. But there are times when such birds as starlings and pheasants may do more harm than good to strawberries or peas. To keep birds away from such plants, or to keep rabbits and woodchucks out of newly sprouted succulent greens, portable wire covers that may be moved from row to row are convenient. These may be made of three-foot wire fencing with 2 x 4-inch mesh, cut slightly longer than the rows. The fencing is folded down the middle to form a right angle, the ends folded over to make a triangular wall at each end, and the tent-like protectors are then placed over the rows where they are most needed. These wire covers are also useful in early spring or late fall, when they may be covered at night with plastic, burlap, or newspaper to protect the plants from frost.

GARDEN RECORDS: A complete record of space used and treated in a vegetable garden is an invaluable aid to the gardener in planning his next year's garden. It is not enough to place the high vegetables on the north, the corn in blocks, and the asparagus where the tractor will not run it down. A map showing the pH factor in vari-

ous garden areas should be made and kept up to date. Application dates of slowly available materials, such as rock phosphates, should be recorded. With such a record before him, the gardener can make a long-range plan of his garden that will be of inestimable help.

VITAMINS AND HARVESTING: Government studies have indicated that there is a wide variation in nutrient content of vegetables, particularly of vitamin C, depending on how old the vegetables are when picked, the time of day when picked, and whether the prevailing weather is cloudy or sunny. Light has a remarkable effect upon the accumulation of vitamin C. Seedlings sprouted in light contained, after seven days, more than four times as much vitamin C as seedlings of the same age grown in darkness. Plants grown in the greenhouse during May and June in the neighborhood of Washington, D. C., contained twice as much vitamin C as plants grown during December and January. In more northerly latitudes it might be expected that the differences at the two seasons would be even greater. However, tests with tomatoes conducted at the U. S. Department of Agriculture's Regional Laboratory at Ithaca, New York, yielded differences in vitamin C values in the summer and winter months similar to those which had been found with other types of plants at Washington, D. C.

Fruit from the shaded side of a tree has been shown by other workers to have a lower vitamin C content than that from the sunny side, and even in individual fruits the sunny side has been found to have more than the shaded side. The changes in the amount of vitamin C in a plant under varying conditions of sunlight as compared to shade are noticed first in the leaves, though later differences may be observed in other parts, even in the roots.

When the time comes to harvest fruits and vegetables, particularly vegetables of the leafy type, due consideration should be given to variations in the amount of light. Test results suggest that for good vitamin C values the harvesting of vegetables should not be done before mid-forenoon, say 10 o'clock, after generally clear weather. It is preferable to harvest, if possible, after a spell of clear weather, or, if it must be done following cloudy days, collection should be made late in the day. Because of the tendency of vegetables, especially those of the leafy type, to lose vitamin C on standing, it would follow that when weather conditions permit, vegetables from the home garden should be freshly picked each day. *See also names of individual vegetables;* COLD FRAMES; COMPOST; FERTILIZER; SEEDS AND SEEDLINGS; MULCH; SOIL; INSECT CONTROL; DISEASE; PLANTINGS, SECOND; COMPANION CROPS; STORAGE; STAKING; GARDEN, CALENDAR; NUTRITION; TRANSPLANTING; NO-DIGGING METHOD.

VEGETABLE GOLD: (*Crocus sativus*) *see* CROCUS

VEGETABLE OYSTER: *see* OYSTER PLANT

VEGETABLE PEACH: *see* SECHIUM

VEGETABLE SILK: (*Beaumontia grandiflora*) A tall woody vine or small tree of the family *Apocynaceae,* native in India. Leaves are six to nine inches, flower trumpets fragrant, white, five inches long and five inches across. Fruit is a long cylinder lined with silk, which is used as vegetable silk in India. May be grown in a warm moist greenhouse, but cannot be confined to a pot. It is grown outside only in frost-free climate. Also known as herald's trumpet.

VEGETABLE SPONGE: *see* LUFFA

VEGETABLE STORAGE: *see* STORAGE

VEGETABLE TALLOW: (*Sapium sebiferum*) One of a genus of poisonous-juiced trees of the spurge family, native to China and Japan. Grows to 50 feet in native surroundings, but somewhat smaller in the southeastern United States. Inconspicuous flowers in terminal clusters followed by half-inch seed capsules, whose waxy coating is used in the Orient for candles and soap. Easily grown in almost any soil. Propagated by seeds, cuttings, or grafting. Also known as Chinese Tallow Tree.

VEGETATIVE REPRODUCTION: *see* PROPAGATION

VELAMEN: The roots of tree-perching orchids and certain other epiphytes are covered with a whitish or greenish coating called a velamen. This "skin" absorbs moisture and minerals from humus material and the air and also anchors the plant to the surface it is living on. The velamen serves the same food-gathering purpose as the root hairs of plants that live in soil.

VELVET BEAN: (*Stizolobium*) These annual leguminous vines are suited only to hot regions with long growing seasons. The Florida velvet bean (*S. deeringianum*) sends its vines sprawling 50 feet or more along the ground or up supports and has lovely drooping clusters of purple flowers. The Yokohama bean (*S. hasjoo*) grows about 20 feet long, and there are other species with white or brown flowers. All the velvet beans bear thick, sharp, hairy pods. They make a good forage or green manure crop for warm regions and are becoming increasingly popular throughout the South. Give them a sandy soil of medium fertility.

VELVET BENT: *see* LAWN

VELVET GRASS: (*Notholcus lanatus*) This perennial grass grows two to three feet high and is covered with velvety hairs. It is a good ornamental grass, with leaves six inches long and clusters of green spikelets. Grow it in clumps, propagating by division of the rootstocks in spring or fall. It likes a fairly moist, not-too-rich soil. There is also a variety with white-striped leaves.

VENIDIUM: A genus of annuals and perennials of the daisy family, native in South Africa. Leaves are hairy, gray-green, and deeply cut. Flowers are solitary, four inches across, with yellow or orange rays banded purple at the base, and purple centers. Usually grown as annuals outdoors, and sometimes as perennials in the greenhouse. Can be used for cut flowers, though flowers close at night. For outdoor plants, seed is started early inside. They thrive in any well-drained, sunny location. *V. decurrens* is a perennial species growing to two feet, with yellow flowers with dark centers, about 2½ inches in diameter. Flowers of *V. fastuosum,* a 1½-foot annual, grow to four inches across, are bright orange with a purple-brown base.

VENUS FLY-TRAP: (*Dionaea muscipula*) Each leaf of this curious plant has two rounded halves which are hinged together like the shells of a clam. Both are covered with tiny sensitive hairs and the edges have rows of tough bristles. When an insect touches one of the hairs, it triggers the closing of the trap, and the bug is soon digested.

Venus fly-trap grows best in a very moist, acid soil, and is often planted in wet sphagnum moss or a sand-acid peat mixture. It is a favorite oddity for the cool greenhouse or cool window garden. The leaves are borne in basal rosettes and the small white flowers in clusters at the end of the ten-inch stalk. It can be grown as a wild garden or bog plant in the Southeast. *See also* CARNIVOROUS PLANTS.

VENUS HAIR: (*Adiantum capillus-veneris*) The true black maidenhair fern of Europe. Slender, erect, delicate fern growing to 1½ feet, with blackish stipes and two-three pinnate segments. Grows in the temperate and tropical parts of this country, and in the warmer parts of Europe. Found

sometimes along the Pacific coast. May be planted in partial shade, in a moist situation, and given protection over its roots in winter. Sometimes called southern maidenhair.

VENUS LOOKING-GLASS: (*Specularia speculum-veneris*) An easily cultivated annual of the Canterbury-bell family, growing to 18 inches, with blue or white flowers growing one to three in a cluster, each tubular ¾ inch across, with reflexed lobes. Grows in any good garden soil, and is useful in rock gardens. Seed usually started early indoors.

VERATRUM: Also known as false hellebore. A genus of hardy perennial herbs of the lily family, growing four to nine feet tall, with white, yellow, or purple flower clusters at the tops of the stems. Sometimes grown in the border, in the wild garden, or naturalized along streams. Propagated by seed or division of the fleshy rootstock.

European white hellebore (*V. album*) grows to four feet, with leaves to one foot long and flower clusters two feet long.

California hellebore (*V. californicum*) grows to six feet, with 20-inch leaves and 1½-foot flower clusters.

V. nigrum is a four-foot species with narrow clusters of blackish-purple flowers.

American white hellebore (*V. viride*) grows to eight feet, with greenish-yellow flowers in two-foot clusters. This is the most hardy species, growing from Georgia to Minnesota and New Brunswick.

VERBASCUM: Also known as mullein. Biennial and perennial herbs of the snapdragon family, native around the Mediterranean but naturalized all through the northern hemisphere. Some species are used as ornamentals, but many are weeds which spread rapidly and may become a nuisance. Grown easily in any soil except cold or wet. Propagated by cuttings, division, or seed. Usually treated as a biennial in the border. Foliage gray-green, with large basal leaves and smaller ones ascending the main stalk, which is topped by a columnar yellow, red, purple, or white flower spike.

Moth mullein (*V. blattaria*) is a six-foot species with smooth dark green leaves, and yellow flowers in a loose cluster. Purple mullein (*V. phoeniceum*) has dark green wrinkled leaves in its basal rosette, and woolly purplish flowers in a cluster sometimes branched. Common mullein (*V. thapsus*) which is also called velvet plant, candlewick, and flannel-leaf, is a six-foot perennial, covered with a yellowish felt, with yellow flower spikes.

VERBENA: (*Verbena hortensis*) A tender perennial, garden verbena or vervain is usually treated as an annual. It is a trailing plant growing about a foot tall, with white, yellow, pink or red flowers in clusters. There are many named varieties, several of which are often grown indoors or in the greenhouse.

Sow the seeds in March in a sand-soil mixture in the cold frame or cool

A tender, trailing plant about one foot high, with clusters of flowers, verbena can be sown in March, planted outside after danger of frost.

greenhouse, and plant outdoors after all frost is over. Those with choice colors should be propagated by cuttings, made by shearing off the plants in late summer and cutting the young shoots which then spring up. Root these under glass and plant them outdoors in the spring.

Among the other verbenas are *V. hastata*, four feet tall with blue flowers; *V. canadensis*, about a foot high with creeping rootstocks and white, red or lavender flowers; *V. lanciniata*, a spreading, lilac-flowered species; and *V. rigida*, blue-flowered and 18 inches tall. All require the same culture as the garden verbena. *See also* ANNUALS; LEMON VERBENA; MOSS VERBENA.

VERBESINA: A genus of annual and perennial American herbs of the daisy family, grown as shrubs in warmer climates and sometimes in wild gardens for their yellow, orange, or white flower clusters. *V. crocata* grows to a 15-foot shrub, with opposite, sometimes deeply cut leaves to nine inches, and one-inch orange-red flower heads. Too tender to grow north of Mexico. An annual which is sometimes grown in Florida is *V. encelioides*, three feet high, with golden-yellow flower heads two inches across. Hardy to southern Illinois is the perennial species, *V. virginica*, which grows to six feet, and has clusters of three to five one-inch white flowers.

VERMICULITE: A mineral of the mica family, rapidly gaining acceptance as a medium for starting seedlings and rooting cuttings. When vermiculite ore is heated to about 2,000° F. in processing, moisture within turns to steam, popping the granules to many times their original size. Countless tiny air cells thus produced provide high air- and water-holding capacity, which is an aid to germination and the development of dense root systems. Several times its own weight of water can be contained in vermiculite. Even when thoroughly wet, ample air circulates about plant roots, helping to avoid damping off.

Vermiculite is also used for mulching or as a soil conditioner to lighten and aerate heavy clay soils and help sandy soils to retain moisture. However, it does not do this job as well as organic matter, which in addition feeds plants and exerts many other beneficial effects.

Vermiculite can also be used to store bulbs and winter vegetables, and as a base for floral arrangements.

VERNONIA: Also known as ironweed. A genus of shrubs, trees, and perennial herbs from all over the world, belonging to the daisy family. Simple alternate leaves, pink, purple, or white flower clusters composed of disk flowers only, sometimes surrounded by bristly bracts. Fall bloom makes some species valuable in the border. *V. altissima* grows from five to nine feet, with leaves to one foot, and purple flowers. *V. novaboracensis* grows to about seven feet, with bristles surrounding purple flower heads. Both are hardy to Massachusetts.

VERONICA: The veronicas or speedwells are pretty perennials for the border or rock garden. They are easy to grow in rich organic soil and can be propagated by division after bloom. Give them full sun and perfect drainage.

V. filiformis is a good ground cover, two inches high, fast-growing and producing light-blue flowers. *V. pectinata, V. repens* and *V. fruticulosa* grow a little taller, with white, pink or blue flowers and are fine for the rock garden. The wooly speedwell (*V. incana*) is best for edgings and the crevices of rock walls.

V. latifolia, the germander speedwell, is probably the most popular of the veronicas, growing 15 to 18 inches tall with very handsome white, pink or blue flowers. Some of its varieties are smaller and suitable for ground covers and the rock garden. There are a number of other species in the one-

foot or slightly taller group. Of the tall veronicas, the best is *V. virginica,* the blackroot, a wild garden plant growing up to five feet tall with big flower clusters. *V. officinalis* is a low-growing weed that is sometimes a nuisance in lawns. The veronicas boast almost total disease and insect resistance.

In the *Veronica* genus are also found many shrubs grown in the South and California. Some make good hedges, and a few are suitable for the temperate greenhouse. They range in size from one to 20 feet, with white, blue or purple flowers. *V. traversi* is the best for greenhouse culture, while those with the finest bloom are *V. andersoni,* about six feet tall; *V. elliptica,* 15 feet tall or taller; and *V. hulkeana,* two or three feet.

VERTICAL MULCHING: *see* MULCH

VERVAIN: *see* VERBENA

VERVEINE JOLIE: *see* MOSS VERBENA

VESICARIA: Also known as bladderpod. A genus of perennial herbs of the mustard family, native in central Europe and the Mediterranean. Similar to lunaria and alyssum, to which they are closely related, but have inflated fruit pods which are decorative. Most frequently grown species, *V. utriculata,* is a perennial in warm climates, but is grown as an annual in the North. Seeds are sown early in spring where the plant is to bloom. Grows 18 inches tall, with yellow flower racemes.

VETCH: (*Vicia*) The vetches are annual or biennial legumes widely used for green manures and forage. They add large amounts of organic matter and nitrogen to the soil when plowed down. Especially recommended for poor soils, they grow with great vigor on good land, producing up to 20 tons of green matter per acre and a dense, sod-like mat of deep roots laden with nitrogen-gathering nodules. Slender, viny plants, they are often sown with rye, oats, wheat or some other erect crop to provide support.

Vetch can be planted in spring or fall. If sown in the fall, by winter the land will be completely covered and protected from wind and water erosion. If spring planted, it can be plowed under the same year. When planted alone, use about 50 pounds of seed to the acre, or 40 pounds with a half-bushel of rye or wheat. About 35 pounds is sufficient if planted in corn.

Vetch makes a palatable and luxuriant pasture, but stock should be removed when the seeds begin to form early in July. The seeds are then permitted to ripen and shatter, which re-seeds the plant. It is also a good hay and silage crop.

Winter or hairy vetch, *V. villosa,* is extremely hardy in the northern states. Common vetch (*V. sativa*) is half-hardy and is sometimes called spring vetch. Some of the other valuable vetches are monantha vetch (*V. monantha*); Hungarian vetch (*V. pannonica*); bitter vetch (*V. ervilea*); and purple vetch (*V. atropurpurea*). Several of these will survive temperatures down to 20°. New varieties of considerable merit have been developed in recent years.

V. faba, the broad bean, is an erect annual growing three to five feet tall and produces edible seeds. The cow vetch (*V. cracca*) is a handsome ornamental, a perennial that climbs up to five feet and has showy white or lavender flowers in big racemes. The seeds are sown in early spring. *See also* Cover Crops.

VETIVER: (*Vetiveria zizanioides*) Vetiver is a perennial grass growing six to eight feet tall, the thick roots spreading out wide and binding the soil. It is grown in the South and the heavy rootstocks are harvested in late fall for use in making medicines, perfume and mats and screens.

Vetiver will grow in almost any soil, but light, sandy soils are preferred because they make harvesting the roots

easier. It is propagated by divisions of the old clumps, planted in spring or fall, about five feet apart each way.

VETKOUSIE: *see* Mesembryanthemum

VIABLE: Seeds which are alive and capable of growing are said to be viable. Some seeds remain viable for only a matter of months, while others have kept their germinating power for 20 years or longer. Two to three years is the average for many vegetable seeds. *See also* Germination.

VI-APPLE: *see* Otaheite Apple

VIBURNUM: A large genus of popular ornamental shrubs and trees of the honeysuckle family, native throughout the northern hemisphere. Many of the viburnums are brilliantly colored in autumn, and carry over into the winter ornamental fruits which attract the birds. The evergreen species are hardy only in warmer climates, but the deciduous ones are hardy north to Massachusetts. Leaves opposite and simple, small pink or white flowers in flat terminal clusters, fruit a drupe or haw.

An attractive ornamental shrub growing to five feet, Viburnum carlesii produces fragrant pink and white flower clusters opening in early spring.

Viburnums will grow in almost any soil. They are propagated by stratified seed, hardwood cuttings, greenwood cuttings under glass, or by grafting. Snowballs, as many viburnums are called, are sometimes grown in the greenhouse for forcing.

Dockmackie (*V. acerifolium*) grows

to six feet, with three-lobed maple-like leaves, and three-inch clusters of white flowers followed by purple-black fruit. Leaves rose-colored in fall. Does well in dry places.

American wayfaring-tree (*V. alnifolium*) also called hobble-bush, grows to ten feet, with wrinkled leaves that turn purplish in fall, and persistent purple-black berries. White flowers in five-inch clusters. Prefers moist and half-shaded position.

V. carlesii has fragrant pink and white flower clusters opening early in spring, along with the leaves. It grows to about five feet, with a rounded habit.

Withe-rod (*V. cassinoides*) also called Appalachian tea, makes a compact, round-headed growth to 12 feet, with clusters of creamy-white flowers in June, succeeded by green to pink to blue-black fruit in fall. Grows well in moist situations.

Arrow-wood (*V. dentatum*) grows to 15 feet, with coarsely toothed leaves and clusters of white flowers, later blue-black berries. Good for shady moist spots, even flourishing under trees.

V. dilatatum is a free-flowering ten-foot shrub which bears many red berries which remain well into winter.

V. fragrans has pink and white flowers which open in early spring, even before the leaves begin to unfold. Fruit is blue-black.

V. hupehense is a rounded six-foot shrub, which bears an abundant crop of scarlet berries into the winter.

V. lantana is the species commonly called viburnum, also known as the way-faring tree. It thrives in drier locations than most viburnums, and grows to a vigorous 15 feet. White flower clusters followed by red berries which turn black in winter, and foliage which is light green and wrinkled, turning deep red in fall.

Nanny-berry or sheep-berry (*V. lentago*) grows to a 30-foot tree with lustrous leaves, creamy-white flowers, and black berries. It may be dis-

tinguished in winter by its long pointed buds.

V. lobophyllum grows to 15 feet, and has heavy clusters of scarlet berries in fall.

V. molle makes a dense 12-foot growth. Bark in winter appears flaky with light gray young stems. Berries dark blue.

European cranberry-bush (*V. opulus*) has three-lobed leaves that turn crimson and orange in fall. Flowers are showy and white, berries scarlet. Variety *nanum* is dwarf; variety *roseum,* the common snowball-bush, has round heads of sterile flowers; and variety *xanthocarpum* has yellow berries.

Black-haw (*V. prunifolium*) is a wide-spreading shrub or small tree growing to 15 feet, with handsome foliage, white flowers, and blue-black fruit. It is native on rocky hillsides from Connecticut to Florida.

V. pubescens, probably a form of arrow-wood, has many white flower clusters in early summer, followed by blue-black fruit. Hairier than arrow-wood.

V. rhytidophyllum is a ten-foot evergreen species, with dark green wrinkled leaves and yellowish-white flowers, fruit turning from blue to black. Must be planted in a protected position, but hardy in the North where temperatures do not go below zero.

Southern black-haw (*V. rufidulum*) grows to a 40-foot tree in the South, but is a shrub in the North. It has shiny dark green leaves, with brown rusty-appearing hairs on the leaf and flower stalks. Flowers are white, fruit blue.

V. sargentii is the Asiatic form of *V. opulus,* and is also like the American *V. trilobum,* but has the handsomest flowers of the three.

Laurestinus (*V. tinus*) is evergreen, and hardy only in the South. It grows to ten feet, with flowers pink to white, and black fruit. Sometimes grown in northern greenhouses.

V. tomentosum is one of the handsomest viburnums. It has wide-spreading horizontal branches with clusters of conspicuous white flowers and fruit which is scarlet, turning black. Not hardy in the coldest parts of the United States, but may be grown all along the Atlantic seaboard to Maine.

American cranberry-bush (*V. trilobum*) is very much like *V. opulus*. Its large three-lobed leaves turn scarlet in fall, and clusters of scarlet berries that remain until spring.

V. wrightii is similar to *V. dilatatum,* but it bears so many scarlet berries that branches are often weighed down to the ground. *See also* SHRUBS.

VICTORIA: The enormous leaves of these water lilies grow up to six feet across with up-turned margins that make them look like giant floating pans. *V. regia* is found only in the tropics, but *V. cruziana* is a spectacular plant for water gardens in the North. Its fragrant white flowers, up to 18 inches wide, turn deep pink the second day after blooming. The leaves have handsome radiating colored veins, which so reinforce the leaf that it can support weights of 100 pounds or more. Sharp red spines cover the leaves, stems and flowers.

For best growth, victoria needs a very rich soil and a large pool, for as many as ten huge leaves may be produced from one plant. The seeds are sown in pans containing a sand-soil mixture early in March, and the pans are submerged in a tank of water several inches deeper than the pan. In a few weeks, two floating leaves will appear. Then the seedlings are potted up in three-inch pots in three parts of rich soil to one of sand, and transplanted to six- or eight-inch pots after they make dense root growth. Keep the water in the tank fresh.

When the water temperature of the pool is about 75°, work about a two-inch depth of manure into the bottom, plus a few handfuls of bone meal, and plant the lily. It will reach giant size in about two months.

The seed pods will not ripen on the plant except in the long growing season of the South, so cut them off at the first light frost. Put them in a tub of water in the greenhouse, being careful of the sharp spines, and in a month or so the seeds will come free from the pods. They can then be buried in moist sand and kept at approximately 60° until they ripen, at which time they are very dark in color. To induce the seeds to germinate, they are filed or cut to puncture the hard shells before planting.

VICTORIAN BOX: (*Pittosporum undulatum*) Also called cheesewood. Evergreen tree growing to 40 feet, native to Australia. Cultivated in California and the southern states as an ornamental. Shiny green leaves oblong, four to six inches long. Fragrant white flowers in terminal clusters. Seed capsule about ½ inch long. Propagated principally by grafting, also by seed sown in cool greenhouse, and by half-ripened wood cuttings. *See also* PITTOSPORUM.

VICTORIAN HAZEL: (*Pomaderris apetala*) Called tainui in Australia and New Zealand, where it is native. A small tree, to 20 feet, belonging to the buckthorn family, *Rhamnaceae.* Leaves white-woolly, oval three to four inches, small greenish-white flowers in three to seven inch loose clusters. Grown in warmest parts of the United States as an ornamental. Propagated by cuttings of half-ripened wood in early summer. *P. edgerleyi,* a four-foot shrub of the same genus, is also grown in California.

VIGNA: These tropical vines are legumes used commonly for forage or green manuring in the southern states. *V. sesquipedalis,* the yard-long or asparagus bean, is a long trailing vine with yellow or lavender flowers and fleshy pods up to three feet long. The catjang (*V. catjang*) is similar but has much smaller pods. *V. sinensis* is the cowpea. All of them are grown as annuals and should be inoculated. *See also* COWPEA.

VINCA: One of the most popular evergreen ground covers, vinca is also called periwinkle or myrtle. *V. minor* is a hardy trailing plant with wiry stems, shiny leaves and small blue flowers. There are varieties with white flowers. It is an excellent ground cover for moist, shady places. *V. major* has larger flowers and in some varieties, leaves variegated creamy yellow. Not hardy in the North, it is generally used for window boxes, and will stand more sun than *V. minor*. *V. rosea* is grown as an annual and has showy rose-purple, pink or white flowers. The last is usually propagated by seed and treated as a tender annual, the other two by division or by cuttings of young shoots rooted in a sand-soil mixture in the cold frame in summer. Pinch the tips of young plants to make them grow bushy. *See also* GROUND COVER; PERIWINKLE.

VINCETOXICUM: (*Cynanchum acuminatifolium*) Often called the mosquito-trap, this hardy perennial has hairy leaves and fruit like that of the milkweed. The white flowers trap small bugs. It is easily grown in a variety of soils. *See also* CARNIVOROUS PLANTS.

VINE: There are many species and varieties of climbing plants that are beautiful and useful in the garden. Vines soften hard surfaces of garden walls and houses, while adding great decorative value.

There are evergreen and deciduous vines. Some climb by adhesive disks, such as Boston Ivy; others attach themselves to supports by means of tendrils, while some twine around any support they contact.

In selecting vines for any position it is well to consider their means of support. Those planted against the walls of a house should have the support of hinged trellises, which can be unhooked and let down when the house has to be painted. This will cause less damage to the vines than any other method of support. The group is a large one which climbs by the turning of stems. Honeysuckles and Morning Glories are some of those in this class.

Some vines are grown for their handsome foliage and others for their beautiful and fragant flowers. All climbing plants are not suitable material for planting against a house. Some, like the Wisteria, make too heavy growth; but there are vines for all positions in the garden, those that will cover large wall spaces or make light, slender growth.

Vines are decorative on garden walls and make fine backgrounds in the garden for shrubs and flowering plants. The position vines are to occupy should be well thought out before planting time.

Incidentally, if you have a compost bin, you can make it more picturesque by having vines grow up its sides.

In starting a new garden use both perennial and annual vines. The perennials will be permanent and remain year after year, while the annuals will make a quick covering and may be taken out when the perennials have made good headway.

SPECIAL PURPOSES: *Flowering vines* —various bignonias, tecomas, bougainvilleas, jasmines, honeysuckles and many others.

For covering brick and masonry— Boston and English ivy (*Bignonia tweediana*), creeping fig, climbing euonymus.

High climbers—*Bignonia cherere* and *B. tweediana,* bougainvilleas, wisteria, *Solanum wendlandi,* and cup-of-gold.

Quick-growing annuals — gourds, moon vine, morning glory, scarlet runner bean, cup-and-saucer vine.

PLANTING VINES: In planting, careful preparation of the soil is rewarding. The plants will make quicker and healthier growth if planted in ground that is well prepared. The soil around the foundation of buildings is often of poor quality. Make the hole three times deeper and wider than the ball of roots, and open up the bottom of the hole to ensure good drainage, for this is important to the future well-being of the plant.

Then put in two or three spadefuls of well-decayed composted material, and two of top soil; mix thoroughly together. Mix compost with soil to fill in around the ball of roots. Tamp down the soil mixture in the hole, putting in enough so that when the plant is placed on it, the top of the ball of roots will be level with the ground. In time it will settle a little. Fill in with soil around the roots. When the hole is nearly filled, run a slow stream of water in from the hose, letting it run until the water is down below the roots. This will settle the soil and fill up any air pockets. Fill in with soil and finish planting by making a well around the vine to hold water. Tie the vine to its support.

The decayed vegetable matter in the soil will make a soft run for the roots to penetrate, and will put humus in the soil, so necessary for healthy growth. During the summer months cover the ground over the roots with a good mulch, which always has to be renewed every little while, as it breaks down and gets washed into the ground.

Vines should not be planted close to the foundation wall of a house when there are wide, overhanging eaves, but placed 12 to 15 inches out from the wall.

Autumn is a good time to plant vines, as they have the benefit of winter rains to help them get established and strong growth starts in spring.

After vines are planted, they are tied neatly to trellis or whatever the support is to be. Climbing plants often suffer from neglect after they are planted and yet a little routine care of pruning, tying, and feeding will keep them neat and healthy looking.

Perennial vines need feeding in early spring. Work some compost and a little rotted manure lightly into the ground around them and water well to carry nourishment down to the roots, then mulch.

SOME DESIRABLE VINES: Perhaps the most popular vine is the Wisteria. A well-grown specimen when in bloom is a beautiful and graceful feature in the garden, which it dominates during the flowering season; and when that is over, rich green foliage covers the vine for the remainder of the summer. No diseases trouble it and it is hardy and long-lived. Grafted plants flower sooner than those grown from seed.

The Chinese variety (*W. sinensis*) in purple and white, is the most popular. The Japanese Wisteria flowers two or three weeks later and is fine for succession of bloom. Its flowers are in long racemes, sometimes twenty-four inches long. The Chinese variety flowers before the leaves appear, but the Japanese is in full leaf at the time of flowering. The Wisteria is too heavy a vine to have on a house. It is charming on an arbor or growing up an old tree.

A vine that is beautiful in foliage as well as in flowers is the Easter lily vine (*Beaumontia grandiflora*), a native of India. The white lily-like flowers are fragrant and the vine is decidedly ornamental in appearance even when not in flower. It should be planted in a frost-free area. It makes splendid growth in seaside gardens. It begins to flower in April and continues till June. This is a quick-growing vine and will cover a large space of wall.

The various Bignonias are useful for screening or for shade, as they flower for a long time. They thrive in a deep, rich soil and good watering once a week if the weather is hot and dry. *B. cherere,* one of the trumpet vines, is a splendid climber that will cover a large space on fence or wall. The reddish trumpet flowers with yellow throats have a long flowering season, and the rich green leaves make an effective background for them.

Gelsemium sempervirens, the Carolina Jessamine, is a fine winter flowering climber for a mild climate. It has bright green foliage and begins to flower at the end of December, its golden yellow trumpet-shaped flowers continuing to April. Plant in a sunny position. It may be trained on a trellis to flank the front door of a house, or on an arch over a garden gate.

Where a vine is needed to cover a large surface, the Cup-of-Gold or *Solandra guttata* will do it. On the side of a garage it will climb to the roof. It grows luxuriantly in a mild climate, but is sensitive to frost. Give it a warm position. The large, yellow cup-shaped flowers measure six to eight inches across and the still larger, bright green leaves make a fine background for them.

A choice and lovely evergreen vine from Madagascar is *Stephanotis floribunda.* The clusters of waxy white tubular flowers are delightfully fragrant. This climber needs light shade during the hottest hours of the day. Plant it on the north side of the house.

The Moonflower vine, sometimes listed as *Ipomoea grandiflora alba* or *Calonyction aculeatum,* has large fragrant white flowers, which open in the evening and close before noon next day. It makes quick growth. The seeds should be soaked for twenty-four hours before sowing, and some gardeners puncture the seeds to hasten germination.

The morning glory family has many fine members. Scarlette O'Hara has flowers of a brilliant and unusual shade of red. These plants grow quickly and produce flowers in a short time from seed. Plant in good ground in full sun.

Trachelospermum jasminoides, also known as the Star or Malay Jasmine, comes from the Malay Peninsula. The fragrance of the white flowers is exquisite. It may be grown as a shrub if carefully pruned and will form a strong framework of branches. It may be used as a ground cover on a low, sloping bank, or on level ground. The star jasmine may be trained up either side of a group of windows or over a door.

Solanum wendlandi and *Bignonia violacea* are two good vines to plant side by side. One is deciduous and the other evergreen. They both have lilac flowers and will decorate a wire fence or wall for a long time. The Bignonia will start to flower in April and continue through May into June, while the *Solanum* will flower during summer and early autumn.

Hibbertia volubilis, Guinea Gold Vine, is an attractive one from western Australia. Its branches are densely covered with handsome dark green leaves. In summer it is covered with quantities of brilliant yellow flowers that resemble a single rose. It is one of the finest evergreen vines. *See also names of individual vines;* FOLIAGE PLANTS.

VINE BOWER: *see* CLEMATIS

VINE CACTUS: (*Fouquieria splendens*) This huge cactus, growing ten to 15 feet tall or taller, is sometimes called ocotillo, coach-whip or Jacob's staff. It has many prickly rigid stems and bears small crimson flowers in beautiful ten-inch clusters in spring. It is hardy only in the Southwest and very popular in desert gardens there, and also a favorite subject for large greenhouses in the North.

VINEGARWEED: (*Trichostema lanceolatum*) An herb of the mint family, native to California and Oregon but too tender for the East, belonging to genus commonly called blue curls for its arched protruding flower stamens. Leaves are opposite, blue flowers in the leaf axils are two-lipped, and attract many bees. The plant likes to bake in hot, dry, sandy sites in full sun. Used in wild or rock gardens in the West.

VIOLA: The violas or violets are popular bedding, edging and rock garden plants. Very free-blooming in spring and into summer, they have long-lasting flowers, good for cutting. The colors range from white through many shades of yellow, red and blue.

There are many named varieties of violas. Most of them are crosses of *V. cornuta, V. gracilis, V. lutea* and *V. tricolor*. Jersey Gem has purple or white flowers; Arkwright Ruby is wine-red; Blue and White Perfection have large flowers. Purple Heart has big royal purple flowers with yellow eyes. Gardeners report they have picked bouquets of Purple Heart violas from mid-March until after the plants were covered by winter snows.

Violas like rich, moist, humusy soil and full sun, but will tolerate some shade, especially during hot weather. Plenty of compost, leaf mold or rotted manure should be incorporated into the soil. Usually they are treated as biennials, the seed sown in summer. Or you can sow it in September or early in the spring in the cold frame or greenhouse. The rootstocks may also be divided at these times, and cuttings of young shoots a few inches long can be taken in late summer and rooted in a shaded cold frame, to be transplanted outdoors in early spring.

Numerous varieties of sweet violet (*V. odorata*) are grown for winter bloom, the seeds sown outdoors in spring and the plants moved to the cool greenhouse or cold frame in late summer. If they are brought into a warm place, they may be attacked by red spider unless the atmosphere is kept moist. They need a deep, rich soil, plenty of moisture, and semi-shade while grown outdoors. Freezing when in the cold frame will damage them. The long-flowering hybrid strains are particularly good for window boxes.

The native violets, such as *V. blanda, V. canadensis, V. cucullata, V. priceana* and others, are often planted in the wild garden. They are hardy and are planted outdoors or in the open cold frame in autumn. They have runners which can be easily rooted to make new plants. *V. pedata* likes open, dry locations. Some of these violets can be transplanted from the wild, and a number of them make good ground covers in semi-shade. Give them a woodsy soil. They will do especially well where they can get their roots under rocks or stones to keep them moist and cool.

A mulch of compost and leaf mold is always a good practice with all types of violets. *See also* BORDER; PANSY; FLOWER GARDENING.

VIOLET: *see* VIOLA

VIPER'S-BUGLOSS: (*Echium*) A genus of herbs and shrubs of the borage family. The genus is native to Europe and Asia, but the common viper's-bugloss has become naturalized throughout eastern United States. Plants bristly, with alternate simple leaves, flowers blue, pink, purple, or white, in spikes blooming on one side, some quite showy and cultivated outdoors or under glass. They become shrubs in warm climates, and are grown in California as ornamentals. *E. fastuosum,* a four-foot shrub, and *E. wildpreti,* grown as a biennial, are encountered only in California in the open. Blueweed, blue thistle, and blue devil are some of the names given common bugloss, *E. vulgare,* a weedy biennial growing to about two feet with pink flowers, turning blue in maturity, along eastern roads.

VIRGINIA COWSLIP: *see* MERTENSIA

VIRGINIA CREEPER: *see* PARTHENO-CISSUS

VIRGINIA SNAKEROOT: (*Aristolochia serpentaria*) A hardy herb of the birthwort family cultivated in some places for its root, which is thought to have medicinal value. Grows to about 18 inches, with wiry stem, heart-shaped leaves, small s-shaped flowers. A woodland plant, it must be grown in a sheltered, partly shaded spot, with rich soil which has plenty of humus. Propagated by seed.

VIRGINIA STOCK: (*Malcomia*) A genus of annual and perennial herbs of the mustard family, grown for their profuse lilac, pinkish, or white flowers. Not scented, as are many stocks. Properly known as Virginia stock is the species *M. maritima,* an annual growing to 12 inches, with spreading habit, having oval leaves and lilac and reddish to white flowers, followed by erect seed pods. They flourish in ordinary garden soil, and may be planted where they are to bloom in early spring.

VIRGINIA WILLOW: (*Itea virginica*) A shrub of the saxifrage family grown along the Atlantic coast from New Jersey to Florida for its fragrant, showy white flower clusters that open in June and July. Usually a moderate sized three to five-foot plant, it sometimes reaches eight feet. Oval leaves turn red in autumn. Prefers moist, rich soil. Propagated by division.

VIRUS DISEASE: *see* Disease

VITAMINS: *see* Nutrition

VITEX: (*Vitex negundo*) This ten-feet-tall deciduous shrub bears lovely spikes of tiny blue flowers in late summer and fall and is hardy to lower New England and southern Illinois. It is often grown as a bee plant. The stems may die out over the winter but new vigorous shoots will come up in spring. The chaste tree (*V. agnus-castus*) grows somewhat smaller and has scented leaves and showy spikes of white or blue flowers. There are also varieties with yellow or red blooms. Propagate by seeds or by cuttings of young shoots under glass. Vitex does not need an especially rich soil.

VITIS: *see* Grape

VITTADINIA: Woody perennials of the daisy family growing in both north and south temperate Pacific islands. Only cultivated species is *V. australis,* a somewhat hairy one-foot plant growing from a thick rootstock. Alternate leaves are lanceolate, sometimes with three lobes. Solitary flowers have white rays, yellow disks, the heads surrounded by rows of overlapping bracts. Grown only in warm climates. Propagated by seed or division.

VRIESIA: A genus of tropical air plants of the pineapple family, grown in greenhouses for their striking foliage rosettes and exotic flowers. Native in tropical America, but can be grown outdoors in southern Florida. Outdoors their dense clusters of stiff, spiny, sometimes variegated leaves often spring from the trunks of living trees. In the greenhouse they are rooted in rich, fibrous soil, and watered heavily during their summer growing season. They are shaded during the warm months, and are kept in a cool greenhouse and only lightly watered through the winter.

V. duvaliana grows to one foot, with leaves that are tinged with red below. Flowers are yellow tipped with green in spikes, set in the axil of scarlet and green bracts.

V. fenestralis has 1½-foot green leaves with dark veins and brown tips, pale yellow flower spikes growing from spotted green bracts.

V. hieroglyphica has yellowish flowers, leaves banded and irregularly marked with dark green above and brown-purple below.

V. saundersi, also with yellow flowers, has stiff fleshy grayish leaves dotted with white above and red-brown below.

V. speciosa has yellowish-white flowers enclosed in bright red bracts, to three feet, with one-foot leaves banded with brown.

W

WALKS: The various paving materials available to most gardeners provide a wide choice of effects for the garden

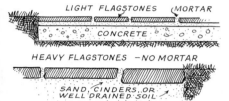

Cross-sections of heavy and light flagstones show typical structure. Thin flagstone needs mortar support between stones. Heavy flagstone may be set into a coarse material such as sand.

walk. Bricks, slates, and flagstones are the most popular of all the paving materials, although scrap materials can be used very effectively in many cases. Bricks may be laid in various interesting patterns. Most materials require a mortar base to keep them in place. An exception to this rule is in the case of thick flagstones and slates, which are heavy enough to require no supporting base. In the case of irregularly shaped stones, mortar should be applied between the stones as well as beneath.

WALLFLOWER (*Cheiranthus cheiri*) A perennial of the mustard family, grown in England and through Europe in fences where the foliage and rather weak stems are supported by having them grow up through the fence. Not so successful in this country, where the winters are too wet and the springs too hot for best bloom. Grows to 2½ feet, slightly hairy, narrow simple leaves, flowers in fragrant clusters somewhat like stocks, with four-clawed petals, in yellow, yellow and brown, and new varieties in red to black. Blooms early in spring, and must be planted early the previous spring to make a good growth before hot weather. Plants may be wintered in the cold frame in pots,

and planted out in spring as soon as the ground is open. A few types will give flowers the first year if sown early enough under glass, and may be treated as annuals. New colors do not always come true from seed, but may be propagated by cuttings.

WALL GARDEN: A planting involving a free-standing wall or the wall of a building. A wall garden may be: (1) A planting against a wall of a building, a free-standing wall, or a terrace retaining wall with vines, espaliered trees, or shrubs trained to decorate the wall; (2) A masonry wall built with niches or planters incorporated in its surface but isolated from the ground, intended to hold potted plants; (3) A dry wall with soil pockets in place of mortar, the pockets planted with rock garden material or vines which are permanently planted in the wall.

Plants suitable for wall gardens as shown above include sempervivum, aubrietia, veronica and campanula—ones also used for rock gardens.

For the first type of planting, the following shrubs, trees, and vines are especially recommended: for espalier—fruit trees, such as peach, apple, and pear; shrubs such as forsythia, cotoneaster, buddleia, euonymus, Japanese snowball, winter jasmine, *Pyracantha coccinea lalandi*. Good vines for training against buildings include many roses, wisteria, ivy, clematis, matrimony vine, bittersweet, grape, trumpet vine, and innumerable annuals and perennials.

Niches or planters incorporated in walls usually have an architectural purpose, and must be planted in harmony with that purpose. If the niche is isolated from the ground, plants which may be used will be temporary, probably replaced every year, and chosen from greenhouse or window box material. Provision is made in some modern patio architecture for permanent plantings in set-back sections of masonry walls. Soil in such set-backs must be well-drained, with a thick layer of rubble 18 to 24 inches below the surface, and tiles laid from the base of the planting to open ground. Planting material must be chosen with the architectural style in mind.

Dry wall planting is usually done in a wall which is used as a retaining wall on a steep terrace, with a bank of soil behind the wall to its top. This wall should be planted as it is constructed.

A foundation trench 12 to 18 inches deep must be dug at the base of the dry wall. Largest stones are set in the trench, flat side down. Soil is packed in and around each succeeding course of stones as it is laid. Stones should be placed as they are in a rock garden, with the narrowest faces on the surface and the deepest dimension running back into the wall. At the same time, the flat surfaces of the rocks are slanted downward on the inside of the wall, to help carry moisture into the roots of wall plants. The face of the wall should slant back two inches to the foot, to provide a shelf at the front edge of each rack for catching water. Thickness of the wall at the base should be approximately half the height.

As the stones are laid in the wall, rock plants may be placed upon them, roots spread and covered with well-enriched sandy loam. Occasional pebbles should be placed between the courses of stone to take the weight of the wall off the roots of the plants.

Plants suitable for this type of garden will be the same as those which may be used in a rock garden. The following are especially recommended: adonis, *Alyssum saxitile,* rockcress, poppy-mallow, *Campanula carpatica, Cerastium tomentosum,* glory-of-the snow, cheddar pink, maidenhair fern, Christmas fern, common polypody, snowdrops, creeping gypsophila, hepatica, coralbells, candytuft, dwarf iris, sea-lavender, grape hyacinth, moss phlox, rock soapwort, *Scilla sibirica,* various sedums, thyme, *Veronica rupestris,* Ajuga, and Kenilworth Ivy.

A free-standing dry rock wall may be built like the terrace-facing wall, if it is made double, with a core between its two sides filled with soil. Great care must be taken when constructing such a wall to provide drainage at the base of the wall, so that water entering at the top will not find its way out through the rocks at the side. The vertical soil layer through the wall may be planted with trailing vines, with perennial or annual flowers, rock plants, or with hedges or dwarf evergreens. *See also* ROCK GARDEN; ESPALIER; VINES.

WALNUT: (*Juglans*) Important nut trees found mostly in North America. Also includes the butternut. English walnuts, or more properly Persian walnuts (*J. regia*), have previously been limited by lack of hardiness, to a line about through Maryland and southern Pennsylvania on west, as their northern limit. Or more specifically to regions where winter temperatures do not go lower than ten degrees below zero, and only the more hardy ones would stand that low. But even in the regions of the United States that are warm enough, they have not thrived well enough to be grown commercially except in some parts of California and Oregon. English walnut trees grow to 100 feet high.

A hardy strain of Persian walnuts

has been introduced into the United States and Canada from the Carpathian Mountains of Poland. This was accomplished primarily through the work of the late Reverend Paul C. Crath. This strain of Persian walnut is known in this country as the Crath Carpathian walnut.

The Crath Carpathian walnuts have been grown in this country long enough so that it is safe to say that they will succeed in many locations from Virginia northward far into Canada. They may succeed in some locations father south but their greatest weakness is that they leaf-out early in the spring and a late spring frost will kill back the new growth and the nut crop for that year. Secondary buds will come on later and produce leaves and new growth, but no nuts. This is much more serious in the South than in the North, but frost pockets should be avoided as a location for the trees in all regions.

The trees make beautiful ornamentals, growing somewhat the shape of apple trees but eventually much larger. They are quite rapid growing under good conditions. Nuts mature in a comparatively short season. At North Latitude 45° they ripen from mid-September to early October.

The Carpathians are quite free of serious diseases and insect enemies. In some regions there is some trouble with leaf spot or walnut anthracnose with some varieties. They are more resistant to the "brooming-disease" than the other walnut species. The most serious insect pest is the "butternut curculio." The larva infests both the terminals of the new growth and the nuts. Apple and plum curculio may also attack them. Husk maggots are serious in some locations. The only injury they do is to darken the nuts and the affected shucks do not open up normally, making the harvesting more difficult.

It has now been definitely proven that the Crath Carpathian walnuts are hardy enough to succeed in most regions of the northern half of the United States and many regions in Canada, that they will thrive in many of our soils and in size of nuts and quality of kernel they compare favorably with the best of the California-grown nuts.

In doubtful regions, the planting of seed nuts or seedling trees is to be recommended as they are much cheaper than grafted trees, and most of them will produce good nuts.

Some of the best varieties are Metcalfe, McKinster, Colby, Weng, Orth, Morris, Deming. Also, one that should be included in this list is Hanson. Although it is not a Carpathian it is very hardy and is one of the best quality nuts.

Seed nuts or seedling trees from these named varieties will not prove true to variety. The only way to secure a Metcalfe or other named variety tree is to purchase a grafted tree or to graft or bud a tree with wood from one of them.

Grafted trees will usually produce pistillate blossoms in three to five years from transplanting. They will usually not produce pollen until seven or eight years old. If pollen from larger trees is present, nuts will be produced at the younger age but if not, it will take the longer period.— *Gilbert Smith.*

BLACK WALNUTS: These tall trees grow as high as 150 feet, make fine ornamental trees, besides producing rich, oily nuts.

Dr. L. H. MacDaniels of Cornell University, a past president of the Northern Nut Growers' Association, has worked out a list of the most desirable varieties of *J. nigra.* He rated Thomas first, and then Snyder, Cornell, Tasterite, Wiard, Huber and Cochran as best for conditions in his area where the growing season is about 150 days in length.—*Dr. Lewis Theiss.*

See also NUT TREES; BUTTERNUT; HEARTNUT.

WANDERING JEW: *see* SPIDERWORT

WASTES: Waste products—industrial, agricultural and "natural"—may develop into the fertilizer of the future, since they offer an almost limitless and inexpensive supply of raw materials, and are available throughout the nation so that shipping costs can be kept to a minimum.

Research is turning up more and more waste products that have properties of value to the soil. For some years, a number of companies producing organic wastes have catered to the garden market. Buckwheat hulls, cocoa bean wastes, peanut shells, plus several others, have been available commercially for many years. But now a great many others are being "discovered." Some represent potential sources of organic matter; others can furnish needed minerals to the soil.

A list of the wastes that are being or should be tested for use in soil improvement include apple pomace, banana residues, basic slag, beet wastes, brewery wastes, castor pomace, citrus wastes, coffee wastes, cotton gin waste, feathers, fish products, felt wastes, garbage, grape pomace, leather dust, nut shells, peanut hulls, pea wastes, potato wastes, rice hulls, seaweed, sewage sludge, silk mill wastes, tobacco wastes, and wood wastes. *See also listings of specific wastes;* ORGANIC MATERIALS; COMPOST; FERTILIZER; SEWAGE SLUDGE.

WATER: From the time a seed is planted until the carcass of the plant goes to compost, every growing thing depends upon water. Each molecule of nourishment taken in through the roots is transported by water, dissolved in water, while the plant body maintains the proper temperature and rate of growth by transpiration of water through the leaves. Elements in the soil are immobile unless carried by ground water from one locality to another. Roots reach outward and downward for one reason: to find water and the plant foods that accompany it. *See also* IRRIGATION; MULCH; DRY WEATHER GARDENING; SOIL TEMPERATURE (WATERING); LAWN; HOUSE PLANTS; VEGETABLE GARDENING; SOIL; AERATION.

WATERCRESS: (*Nasturtium officinale*) A member of the *Cruciferae* or mustard family, which includes the turnip, mustard and cabbage. It is a hardy perennial that grows best in gently flowing water. Watercress is adapted to the northern United States, since it does better in cool water than warm. (Winter is its best season in the South.)

An average bunch of watercress contains about 50 milligrams of vitamin C. It is also high in iron and iodine.

Watercress can be grown in pots as long as the soil mixture is kept wet, and therefore the pots in which cress is planted must be set in a tray of water.

You can also plant it outdoors in a miniature sunken garden, for example, in pots placed in a sunken bird bath or some other container sunk in the ground. (The water stays cooler that way.) The water should be changed often.

To start plants, place seeds thinly in pots filled with a mixture of earth, some ground limestone, and sifted woods humus. In its native habitat, watercress thrives on bits of leaf mold that become entangled in its mesh of roots and stems after being sifted over the sands and stones of the creek bed. It has a preference for water that issues from limestone, since it thrives on calcium. Keep seedlings wet at all times, and be sure the window sill tray, or other container, is set in a cool, only partially sun-lit spot.

If you have a stream, start plants as mentioned above. As soon as the plants are large enough to handle, set them out in a convenient elbow along the banks of the stream. The best time to do so is during April and May. An established bed will provide cuttings each spring and fall. Care must be taken that the water is clean; otherwise the cress is not fit to use. The window sill method is excellent for a winter crop. Seedlings mature in about 50 days.

Plants can also be obtained by rooting sprigs from a bunch. Sprigs will sprout in a glass of water, provided the water is changed daily.—*Clee Williams.*

WATER GARDEN: Besides lily ponds, there are several other types of water gardens, including natural and artificial brooks, large ponds and bogs.

If you are lucky enough to have a natural brook on your place, you can make it one of the loveliest spots in your garden. Or you can construct an artificial brook, using the same methods as for making a lily pond. If your brook, whether natural or artificial, has places in it at least 18 inches deep, it can, of course, grow water lilies and other handsome floating plants.

Other suitable plants for a brook— and also for shallow parts of a sizable pond—include lotus, papyrus, hardy water iris, sweet flag, rushes and cattails, water poppy, water snowflake and water hyacinths. In general, all the details which apply to a lily pond are applicable here. *See also* LILY POND.

However, where bog conditions prevail, a somewhat different approach is necessary. Boggy sites are usually found on the sides of lakes, streams and ponds, or in marshy hollows where the ground is of a distinctly peaty character. The soil is rich and acid, fibrous and full of decayed humus material.

MAKING A BOG GARDEN: Usually such sites need only clearing to get rid of unwanted plants, with no soil work other than digging. However, it is a good idea to prepare a compost for use in building mounds throughout the bog, and for mulching. Use pine needles, oak leaves, hardwood sawdust, manure and similar materials.

Bogs generally have low banks, not much more than a foot high at most.

These can be planted to a large number of acid- and moisture-loving plants. Some of the best are: marsh marigold, horsetail (*Equisetum*), moisture-loving primroses such as *Primula japonica, P. bulleyana, P. chionantha* and *P. helodoxa, Iris sibirica, I. laevigata* and others, eulalia (*Miscanthus sinensis*), purple loosestrife (*Lythrum salicaria*), and willow herbs (*Epilobium*). Suitable shrubs are *Ilex verticillata, Myrica gale, Andromeda potifolia* and *Kalmia potifolia.* Birches, alders and willows fit in well with these.

On the mounds you may want to plant native orchids, the cypripediums or showy orchis. The leapoard, meadow and turk's cap lilies do well here, too, along with many of the trilliums and ferns that like boggy situations.

The ferns also do well in the wet depressions, along with bogbean (*Menyanthes trifoliata*), forget-me-nots, gentians, arrowheads (*Sagittaria*), pickerelweed (*Pontederia cordata*), flowering rush (*Butomus umbellatus*), wild rice, and the bog arum (*Calla palustris*). *See also* MOISTURE-LOVING PLANTS.

Remember that a bog garden should have a natural, informal look, whether it is large or small. Given the right conditions—you may even be able to produce them artificially in a low spot in your garden if they do not occur naturally—you can have bog plants, shallow water aquatics and deep water plants all in one setting. A cascade or waterfall can be built if your water garden includes a brook. Imagination is perhaps a more important ingredient in making water gardens than any other kind of garden. A cool, serene, entirely naturalistic setting should be the result of good planning.

WATER HYACINTH: (*Eichhornia*) Floating water plants that grow abundantly in fresh-water streams and lakes in the deep South. It is rated as a weed pest in areas, as Florida, where it is very difficult to control, and even more so to eradicate. In those areas, it can make waterways unnavigable. *E. crassipes,* the common water hyacinth, has fine feathery roots, makes an attractive plant for shallow pools.

Since the water hyacinth is so plentiful, it can be an important source of organic matter to southern gardeners. When almost free of moisture, it contains about one per cent nitrogen, four per cent potash. It is fine for adding to the compost heap or for use as mulch.

WATERLEAF: (*Hydrophyllum*) Perennial herbs one to three feet tall with large compound leaves and clusters of bell-shaped flowers. Waterleaf blooms in May or June from South Dakota and Quebec south to Kansas and South Carolina.

H. canadense grows about 1½ feet high, has white flowers; *H. virginianum,* also known as Indian salad, reaches the same height, has white or violet flowers.

WATER LILY: *see* Nymphaea

WATERMELON: (*Citrullus vulgaris*) A member of the cucumber family, native in tropical Africa. *C. citroides,* citron melon, is the only other species of the genus which is cultivated. The citron melon is eaten only cooked, and is called the preserving melon. It is not the fruit sold as candied citron, which is *Citrus medica.*

Watermelon requires a long hot growing season, so is best cultivated in the hot areas of the United States. It may be grown most successfully in the North when seed is started in the cold frame or greenhouse about a month before the last frost, and planted out in the garden six weeks later. Or early maturing varieties may be planted outside when the last frost is past and the ground is warm.

Watermelon vines require at least six feet in each direction, so may be grown only when garden space is not limited. To keep soil moist, a heavy layer of mulch is helpful after the spring suns have warmed the site. Seed

should be planted in hills enriched with several large forks full of compost or rotted manure. A slightly acid to neutral soil is best, pH factor 6.0 to 7.0. Water-holding humus is more important to best growth than heavy feeding. Moisture may be supplied as it is for cantaloupes, if needed.

Melons are most flavorful when permitted to ripen on the vines. Since it does not change color upon ripening, experience is necessary to judge a ripe melon. According to Mark Twain, a green melon says "pink" or "pank" when thumped with the knuckles. A ripe one says "punk." White skin on the under side of a ripe melon is slightly pebbly and leathery in appearance. Tendrils on the vine near the ripened fruit turn dry and dark. *See also* Vegetable Gardening.

WATERSHED: All the land and water within a natural drainage area is called a watershed. For example, the Mississippi River - Missouri River valley is a watershed; each river has a watershed, and streams feeding either of these drain watersheds.

In many cases, by carefully studying the topography of an area, the Soil Conservation Service can establish a manageable section called a "small watershed" in their efforts for better water management.

WATSONIA: A genus of strong-growing summer blooming bulbs of the iris family similar to gladiolus, to which they are closely related, and native in South Africa. Sword-shaped leaves and flowers in racemes which will open after cutting, making it a valuable cut flower. Flowers are more trumpet-shaped than gladiolus, giving it its common name of bugle-lily. Grown widely in California for hot-weather bloom.

Species differ principally in height and color. Best ones are *W. angusta,* four feet, scarlet; *W. beatricis,* three feet, apricot-red; *W. brevifolia,* 1½ feet, rose-red; *W. coccinea,* one foot, scarlet; *W. densiflora,* three feet, rose-red; *W. iridifolia,* four feet, pink, variety *O'Brienii* white; *W. longifolia,* five feet, white to deep rose; *W. marginata,* five feet, rose, with small bugle; *W. pillansii,* six feet, brick red; *W. wilmaniæ,* five feet, purplish rose, 20-inch leaves with green midrib and yellow margins; *W. wordsworthiana,* five feet, purplish-lilac.

WATTLE: *see* ACACIA

WAX FLOWER: (*Stephanotis floribunda*) Also called Madagascar jasmine. A twining woody vine of the milkweed family, native to Madagascar and Malaya, and grown in a cool greenhouse as a specimen plant. Thick leathery leaves four inches long, flowers white, waxy, fragrant, in umbels. Propagated by cuttings of half-ripened wood. Must be shaded and kept moist in greenhouse between 55° and 65° in winter, 70° to 90° in summer. Should be cut back and re-potted each year. Should be sprayed with water often to discourage mealy bug, who consider it a delicacy.

WEATHERED: Referring to rocks whose appearance is changed by exposure to the atmosphere. *See also* MINERAL ROCK; ROCK.

WEAVER'S BROOM: (*Spartium junceum*) Also called Spanish broom. An almost leafless shrub, to ten feet, of the pea family, native in southern Europe, and grown along the Pacific coast for its profuse yellow fragrant pea-like flowers through the summer. Flower clusters are often 15 inches long, and may be borne most of the year in California. Will grow in any soil in warm sections. Propagated by seed and cuttings.

WEBWORM: *see* INSECT CONTROL

WEEDS: It is true that we should eliminate weeds from our cultivated grounds. But we should also understand why we do it and what we do. Nature has a reason for allowing weeds to grow where we do not want them. If this reason becomes clear to us, we have learned from Nature how to deprive weeds of their "weedy" character, that is, how to exclude them from cultivated land, or rather, how to improve our methods of cultivation so that we are no more troubled by weeds.

Declining soil fertility is a prime cause of weed growth. Fertile soil, especially soil well conditioned with organic matter, is not naturally conducive to weed growth. Many types of weeds appear to thrive only on soil that is low in some minerals and has an excess of others. As many farmers have learned, declining fertility lets such weeds as broomsedge and ticklegrass invade fields and pastures. Building up a soil organically, therefore, is one of the best ways to lick the weed problem.

Also, it is a fact that a soil rich in organic matter is more easily worked, and cultivation and tillage can be timed most advantageously. Such soil is in good shape after a rain and can be worked without causing clods to form. Spring tillage on a good organic soil can prepare a fine seedbed.

Young plants in organic soil grow rapidly; their root systems tend to crowd out those of weeds, and their rapid vegetative growth often makes thick shade that helps suppress weeds. Too, weed seeds lose their viability sooner in a bacteria-rich soil than in one poor in bacterial life. With organics, ordinary crop tillage operations will usually go a long way toward controlling weeds.

NEW METHODS OF TILLAGE: The use of rotary tillers and chisel plows, some farmers believe, does a lot more to eliminate weed problems than the plow. Moldboard plowing, they say, buries weed seeds deep, where they lie dormant for long periods. These seeds when plowed up and exposed to sunlight and warm air, sprout and grow.

Rotary tillage and chisel plowing keep weed seeds closer to the soil surface, where they either rot or grow. And the mulch-making effect accomplished by the rotary tiller, chisel plow and field chopper on crop residues is almost as destructive of weeds as is the heavy mulch the gardener uses.

CHEMICAL WEED CONTROL: Chemical weedicides, a recent development, have proven to do more harm than good. Not only are they expensive and dangerous to both man and domesticated animals, but they damage crops, either directly or by causing the accumulation of toxic substances in the soil. They kill off bees and other beneficial wildlife. Many of them are non-selective and kill vegetables, flowers, shrubs and lawns through mishandled or drifting spray.

BIOLOGICAL CONTROL: The introduction of insects and fungus organisms that destroy weeds is a new and promising science. The prickly pear cactus, a pest on rangeland, has been controlled by a moth that tunnels through the weed. Klamath weed, a poisonous Western pest, is falling to a tiny beetle who lives on nothing else. A moth has been found that controls ragwort, another poisonous range plant. Leaf beetles are being employed against the American lotus, an aquatic plant that crowds out duck-food plants in many waterfowl areas.

The artificial spreading of organisms that control weeds has certain indisputable advantages: it is cheap, it is natural, and it restores nature's balance.

WEEDS AS INDICATORS: Weeds can tell you a lot about your soil—whether it is acid or alkaline, its soil type, how well it is drained, and so on. The following lists of soil conditions and the weeds that favor them can be helpful both to the gardener and the farmer:

Acid soils—sheep sorrel, swamp horsetail, cinquefoil, low star grass, hawkweed, corn spurrey and knapweed.

Slightly acid soil—daisy, horsetail, field sorrel, doorstep weed.

Alkali soil—salt grass, tussock weed, pickleweed, saltbushes, nitrophila, yerba mansa, common spikeweed, goldenrod, kochia, saltwort, samphia and sesuvium.

Sandy soil — goldenrod, many-flowered aster, wild lettuce, onions, partridge pea, broom bush, yellow toadflax.

Limestone soil—penny cress, field peppergrass, wormseed, Canada blue grass, field madder, mountain bluet, yellow camomile.

Poor drainage—smartweed, hedge bindweed, silverweed, swamp horsetail, meadow pink, hedge nettle, stinking willie, March foxtail, tradescantia, rice cut grass, Joe-Pye weed and many of the sedges.

Hardpans — field mustard, horse nettle, penny cress, morning glory, quackgrass, camomiles and pine-apple weed. *See also* DEFICIENCY, SOIL.

WEEDS CAN BE VALUABLE: Weeds are not always to be considered nuisances. Many of them perform useful services:

1—Deep-rooted weeds bring up minerals from the subsoil and make them available to plants. Many of them are trace element accumulators.

2—Weeds with powerful roots break up hardpans, letting crop plants feed on the lower depths of the soil.

3—Weeds conserve nutrients that otherwise would be washed, leached or blown away from bare ground.

4—They add organic matter that is rich in a large variety of elements because of their diverse nutritional requirements.

5—They fiberize the soil and make room for the roots of crop plants to spread out, as well as improving aeration and water-soaking capacity, both important to the microorganisms that give life to the soil.

6—Weeds can actually *contribute*

water to a crop—water which rises along the outer wall of a weed's roots can be taken up by the crop's roots.

For more information on controlling or using weeds, *see also the names of specific weeds;* MULCH; CRABGRASS; COMPOST.

WEEDS, EDIBLE: The use of edible wild plants for a "spring tonic" has been practiced for centuries in many lands. In early spring when cultivated greens are scarce, nature provides the wise seeker with a bountiful harvest from field and wood.

Many other wild plants can be eaten at other times of the year, and quite a few are worth growing in a small garden patch near the kitchen door to insure a certain supply. They will do well if their wild environment is duplicated fairly closely.

Edible weeds are often among the best of natural foods. It seems the struggle for survival in the wild gives these plants vigorous root systems that seek out more elements in greater variety than are taken up by garden crops. Consequently, they have higher vitamin, mineral and trace element content than do a lot of their domesticated cousins.

Here are some of the best edible weeds (if you are in doubt about any strange ones you come across, check with your county agent or state college):

BURDOCK (*Arctium lappa*)—the young stems are peeled and eaten raw or cooked; the pith of the roots is boiled like parsnips or used in soups.

CARELESS WEEDS, also called PIG-WEED (*Amaranthus*)—the leaves and stems can be cooked like spinach.

CARRION FLOWER (*Stapelia*)—cook the young asparagus-like shoots, found in late spring, until tender.

CATTAIL (*Typha latifolia*)—the rootstock can be used as a salad or cooked vegetable, the young flower heads for soup; eat the early shoots raw or cooked.

CURLY DOCK, also called sour or yellow dock (*Rumex crispus*)—cut off the leaves close to the ground and cook them alone or with other greens.

DANDELION (*Taxacum officinale*)—one of the earliest greens, with leaves useful for salads or cooked like spinach, and roots that are good roasted. Pull up the plants while the bud is still tiny and furry.

FERNS (several species)—pick when the shoots, called fiddleheads, are still tightly curled and six to eight inches high; cut them up like string beans and boil them, or cook whole and serve on toast like asparagus. The rootstocks of some ferns can be eaten raw or boiled.

GROUND CHERRY OR HUSK TOMATO (*Physalis*)—the berries, ripening in late summer and fall, are edible raw or used in preserves or pies.

GROUNDNUT (*Apios americana*)—the starchy underground tubers, available all year, can be parboiled and roasted or sliced and fried with butter; the seed pods may be cooked like beans.

JACK - IN - THE - PULPIT (*Arisaema triphyllum*)—the starchy corms are baked or boiled in several waters to remove the extremely bitter juice.

LADY'S THUMB (*Polygonum persicaria*)—the leaves add an interesting flavor to salads.

LAMB'S QUARTER (*Chenopodium album*)—the young shoots are cooked like spinach (delicious creamed) or boiled with meat.

MARSH MARIGOLD OR COWSLIP (*Caltha palustris*)—the young spring growth is used as a pot herb, picked just as the first flower buds begin to burst into golden bloom.

MILKWEED (*Asclepias*) — young sprouts are cooked like asparagus or braised; a little later, the young stems and furry leaves are delicious, and finally, the roots and young pods are eaten raw or cooked.

PEPPERGRASS (*Lepidium*) — the young greens have a hot, biting flavor and are often used in salads with other wild plants, or as a flavoring for soups and blender drinks.

POKEWEED (*Phytolacca decandra*) —the tender spring stalks are treated like asparagus, the leaves cooked as greens. The roots are poisonous and the mature plant may also be dangerous.

This mature milkweed plant is ready for picking. The seeds are brown, but the pods have not started to open, releasing the floss inside.

PURSLANE OR PUSSLEY (*Portulaca oleracea*)—a decorative garnish for many dishes, or fine in salads with other wild or cultivated greens; the stems and leaves can be cooked and used like okra.

SKUNK CABBAGE (*Symplocarpus foetidus*)—boiled in several waters, the leaves lose their acridity and make tasty greens. The Indians also ate the underground parts.

SOLOMON'S SEAL (*Polygonatum biflorum*)—the rootstocks are boiled as a vegetable.

SORRELS (*Oxalis*) — good sours that add an interesting tang to soups, salads and drinks; sometimes used like rhubarb in pies.

SOW THISTLE AND RUSSIAN THISTLE (*Sonchus oleraceus* and *Salsola pestifer*)—the young shoots of these are good raw or cooked.

SPATTERDOCK (*Nuphar advenum*) —the seeds or starchy underwater

roots are dried and ground into meal; the roots can also be eaten whole.

SPRING BEAUTY (*Claytonia virginica*)—the small tubers, boiled for ten minutes, taste like potatoes.

TOOTHWORT (*Plumbago scandens*) —very fiery, the crinkly brown tubers clinging to the roots fortify a salad better than the hottest radish.

TURK'S CAP LILY (*Lilium superbum*)—the bulbs are used in soups.

WATERCRESS (*Nasturtium officinale*)—a favorite very early spring green eaten raw in sandwiches or salads, or cooked as greens.

WILD GARLIC (*Allium vineale*)— eaten raw, or used as a flavoring for poultry and meat.

WILD LEEK (*Allium moly*)—fine in salads or use in the blender, or eat with bread and butter like green onions.

WILD LETTUCE (*Lactuca*)—young leaves are good used sparingly in salads, or cooked like spinach.

WILD ONION (*Allium canadense*) —eaten raw or used to flavor meats and poultry.

WILD PRIMROSE (*Primula*)—when cooked like spinach, these are so flavorful they are called "butter weeds."

WOOD LILY (*Lilium philadelphicum*) — the bulbs are used like potatoes.

In addition to these, there are literally hundreds of other wild plants whose edibility is not commonly known. Many of them are regularly sold in the foreign markets of large cities. Some garden plants also yield edible parts.

The leaves of young violets, for instance, add a delicate taste to salads. In late summer, elderberry flowers are fine added to scrambled eggs or pancake batter. The leaves of white clover are delicious raw or cooked. Wild ginger, the leaves of horseradish and sweet potato, plantain, chickweed, pumpkin vines and young blackberry plants—these are but a few of the many useful in the kitchen.

How to Use Edible Weeds: Always pick your wild plants when young and small for best flavor. Remember to mix your weeds whenever possible; variety enhances their flavors. Introduce them gradually, adding increasing amounts to dishes using the familiar garden greens. And don't hesitate to put them in the blender when making those healthful raw vegetable concoctions.

Never overcook wild plants, or use soda. A tasty way to prepare many wild greens is to add them to lean, well-cooked salt pork, and cook no longer than ten minutes. Try flavoring them, too, with lemon juice, butter or vinegar. *See also listings of individual weeds.*

WEEPING TREES: A term for all kinds of trees, sometimes including shrubs, which have pendulous branches. Weeping trees may be natural, as exemplified by the weeping willow, or may be artificially produced by grafting, as is often done with flowering crab or flowering almond. The latter are produced by grafting prostrate varieties on upright forms of the same species. They may be produced to "weep" from any height, according to the trunk upon which they are grafted, and branches may be made to touch the ground, to hang loose above ground, or to trail, as desired. Weeping trees are usually not planted among other trees or shrubs, but are featured as accents in the garden, standing free and alone, or are used in a row to form an alley.

Naturally weeping trees may occur as freaks in many families, though there are several whose natural form is pendulous. Three species of willows are among these: *Salix babylonica,* the common weeping willow which grows to 40 feet; *S. blanda,* Wisconsin weeping willow, a hybrid variety, and *S. elegantissima,* Thurlow's weeping willow, a handsome medium-sized tree.

Another naturally pendulous tree familiar east of the Rockies is the weeping American elm (*Ulmus americana pendula*) a stately ornamental growing to 120 feet, and much used as a street tree. The Camperdown elm (*U. glabra camperdowni*), also with pendulous branches, is often grafted to make a small tree for the garden.

Weeping beech (*Fagus sylvatica pendula*) may grow to a height of 80 to 90 feet, with pendulous branches which completely hide the trunk. The purple form grows to about half that height.

Weeping mulberry is a grafted tree for which *Morus alba* is used as the standard. Weeping cherry (*Prunus subhirtella pendula*) is naturally a weeping tree, but is often grafted to keep its height at the desired height for the garden.

Weeping birch (*Betula alba pendula*) has white bark, and is especially handsome planted in groups near water.

A weeping maple, Wier's cut-leaf maple (*Acer saccharinum*) is a freak when it occurs with pendulous branches.

WEIGELA: A genus of handsome flowering shrubs of the honeysuckle family, native in Asia. Tubular blossoms about 1½ inches long and pink, red, or white, open in spring and early summer. There are many hybrids among the cultivated species, which are widely grown because they thrive in most gardens throughout the country. Any moderately moist garden soil and partially protected site will grow healthy specimens. They require little pruning, and should never be pruned until after the blooming period, because flowers are produced on the growth made the previous year.

W. florida grows to six feet with rose-pink flowers. In some varieties the leaves are variegated with yellow markings. This is the most commonly grown weigela. Variety *venusta* is the earliest to bloom, and the hardiest. *W. praecox* is similar to *florida,* and is also early.

W. coraeensis is not so profuse a bloomer as *florida,* but grows often to 15 feet, with large flowers in pink to carmine.

W. floribunda is distinguished by its dark crimson blossoms. It grows to ten feet.

W. hybrida is a name under which many of the crosses between the above species are placed. Some of the best hybrids are Avalanche, Dame Blanche, Vestale, Mme. Lemoine, Candida, and Mont Blanc, with white flowers; Abel Carriere, Andre Thouin, Esperance, Gustave Mallot, Seduction, and Styraica, with pink to rose blossoms; Congo, Eva Rathke, Henderson, Incarnata, and Lavalle, with red to crimson flowers. *See also* SHRUBS.

WHEAT: (*Triticum*) An important food plant, wheat belongs to the *Gramineae* or grass family, and has been cultivated since before the recorded history of man. Specimens of wheat have been found amid the ruins of the Stone Age in Switzerland. It was one of the five crops used by the Emperor of China as early as 2700 B.C. in a certain ceremonial demonstration of how to plant. It is said that at least somewhere in the world, wheat is being planted and harvested every day in the year.

CLASSIFICATIONS: There are two general types of wheat that are grown in the United States—one that loses its chaff, and another type of grain to which the chaff clings in the threshing process. The former is considered our true wheat, while the latter is used for stock feed, and includes emmer, splets and einkorn which are adapted to regions of limited rainfall.

The free threshing type comprises several groups which vary as to their climatic adaptation, time of seeding, and their use:

The *hard red winter* class is seeded in the fall and is capable of standing more severe winter temperatures than any other class. It is grown chiefly in Kansas, Nebraska, Oklahoma, and Texas, with smaller acreages to be found in the states lying to the north of this region.

A basic food plant and a member of the grass family, wheat becomes a thing of beauty, as it flows rhythmically across fields in golden waves.

The *soft red winter* class is less tolerant of extremely low temperatures and requires more moisture than the hard red winter class. This class also is seeded in the fall and is to be found growing in the more humid region of the country, extending from the Mississippi River to the Atlantic Coast, and in some parts of the Pacific Northwest.

The *hard red spring* class is seeded in the spring in the section of the country where the winter temperatures are too low for even the hard red winter class to survive. It is found in the Dakotas, Minnesota, western Nebraska, and Wyoming.

Durum class is found growing in quite the same region as the hard red spring class. Durum wheat is more drought resistant than any of the other classes of wheat.

The *club wheat* class, grown chiefly in Washington, Oregon, Idaho, and upper California, has very stiff straw, is resistant to shattering.

WHIP: A year-old shoot or stem of a woody plant, usually grafted, without branches. Also called a maiden.

WHISPERING BELLS: (*Emmenanthe penduliflora*) Also called yellow bells and golden bells. An annual of the water-leaf family native in California and Mexico. Grows 12 to 18 inches high, with segmented slightly sticky leaves and branched clusters of drooping cream-white bells. May be grown as a hardy annual, or seed may be planted indoors for early bloom.

WHITE GRUBS: The white grub that lives in the soil is a soft-bodied worm with a brown head and a distinctly curved body. A full-grown grub is $1/2$ to one inch long.

Potatoes, sweet corn, turnips, beets, and almost all garden crops are subject to injury by white grubs. Crops planted on land that was in sod during the preceding season are most likely to be attacked. These insects feed entirely underground on the roots or tubers of the crops they attack. This destruction of the root system causes infested plants to wilt and die prematurely or else it results in reduced yields and in vegetables of inferior quality and poor appearance.

Garden crops should not be planted on sodland or in gardens that grew up to weeds and grass during the preceding season. However, if it is necessary to plant a garden on sodland, the sod should be plowed early in the fall and kept free of weeds and grass until winter. Repeated plowing and disking until late in the spring also help to reduce grub damage. *See also* INSECT CONTROL.

WHITEWASHING: It is claimed that whitewashing the trunks of trees reduces insects and disease organisms that burrow in the bark tissues; insect eggs are also supposedly killed by the whitewashing substance. Whitewashing prevents some scald and heat injury of the bark tissues of very young trees.

The general practice of whitewashing is to make an application over the trunk and main supportings of the tree.

WHITLAVIA: *see* PHACELIA

WHORL: Three or more leaves or flowers rising in a circle around the stem.

WIGANDIA: Stout perennial herbs in tropical parts of America, a genus of the water-leaf family, planted in California for its large leaves which are covered with shining stinging hairs. Flowers grow in terminal clusters. *W. caracasana* grows to ten feet or more, as a shrub or small tree, and is sometimes planted in beds for its striking foliage. Propagated by seeds sown in winter under glass, or by root cuttings in spring.

WILD GARDEN: A garden which duplicates, as far as possible, natural untouched landscape and provides a sanctuary for native wild plants. Materials used in a wild garden should be native to surroundings similar to those in which the garden is set, and unimproved varieties and species should be planted, rather than cultivated strains, double flowers, grafted woody plants.

Planting design of the wild garden is always naturalistic rather than formal. Material is placed in clumps, irregular masses, and drifts, rather than in lines, squares, and circles. Repetition and symmetry are avoided.

It is a temptation to plant in the wild garden all border plants which like surroundings such as the wild garden provides. Such cultivated natives of Europe and Asia as primroses, daffodils and narcissus are charming in a woody setting, but the garden becomes a naturalistic rather than a wild one when they are planted in it. A successful wild garden is a challenge to the gardener's skill, and it is also a place where wildflowers which are becoming increasingly rare

WILD GARDEN MATERIAL FOR A THICKET OR RICH MOIST WOODS

Small trees and shrubs: American hornbeam, American crab, dogwood, snowdrop or silver bell tree, mountain laurel, American yew or ground hemlock, witchhazel, rose acacia, American bladder-nut, rhododendron.

NAME	DESCRIPTION	PROPAGATION	SPECIAL NEEDS
Shield fern — *Aspidium spinulosum dilatatum*	1-3 feet, 3 times pinnate. Bottom pinnae 3 times length of top.	Transplant—division	Very acid rocky soil, does well in mountains
Royal fern—*Osmunda regalis*	2-5 feet. Young fronds pink or yellow. Top pinnae fertile fronds brown.	Transplant	Moist acid soil—partial shade
Partridge berry—*Mitchella repens*	Evergreen trailing herb, scarlet berries	Transplant	Acid soil, sun or shade
Gaywings or flowering wintergreen —*Polygala paucifolia*	Perennial trailer. Rose-purple or white flowers	Root division	Very acid leaf mold, moist or dry soil. Shade
Bloodroot—*Sanguinaria canadensis*	1½ in. white flowers on 8 in. stalk from rosette of palmate leaves	Seed. Root division. To transplant dig root ball 5x5x6 in.	Acid to neutral well-drained soil. Shade to ¾ sun
Rattlesnake plantain—*Epipactis pubescens*	6-12 inches. Flower a white orchid. Blue-green leaves veined white	Rootstock near surface. Transplant with three inches soil.	Acid soil. Plant under evergreens
Maidenhair fern—*Adiantum pedatum*	8-20 in. Shiny black stem divided into 2 branches—pinnae on outer side	Root division	Neutral soil. Moist rich woods. Mulch
Rue anemone—*Anemonella thalictroides*	5-9 in. Flower white, pink tinged	Root division in fall	pH 5.0—8.0. Moist woods. Thin shade
Foam Flower—*Tiarella cordifolia*	6-10 in. white flower, orange anthers. Forms ground cover	Division or seed. Increases rapidly	Indifferent to acidity. Rich moist soil
Common blue violet—*Viola papilionaceae*	3-7 in. violet purple flower	Transplant or seed	Indifferent to acidity. Moist soil in sun or part shade

NAME	DESCRIPTION	PROPAGATION	SPECIAL NEEDS
False Solomon's seal — *Smilacina racemosa*	24-30 in. white flowers. Berries white speckled brown, changing to red.	Division	Neutral moist soil. Sun or shade
Wake-robin (Red trillium)—*Trillium erectum*	7-12 in. Flower dull purple-red or maroon	Tuber. Plant 6 in. deep	Neutral rich moist woodland soil
Trillium—*Trillium grandiflorum*	10-18 in. Flower white changing to pink	Transplant when dormant. Plant tubers 6-8 in. deep	Neutral moist but well-drained woodland soil
Dutchman's pipe—*Aristolochia macrophylla*	Vine 10-25 feet high. Dull green to purple-brown "pipes".	Cuttings. Seed	Neutral soil, rich and moist
Pipsissewa—*Chimaphila umbellata, C. maculata*	10 in. half woody evergreen. White to pale pink flowers.	Division of creeping stems	Acid soil with leaf mold. Well-drained. Shade
Bunchberry—*Cornus canadensis*	9 in. Purplish-white flowers—scarlet berries	Seed. Transplant	Acid rich woods soil, well-drained. Shade. Cool
Pink ladyslipper—*Cypripedium acaule*	Pink woods orchid	Buy plants. Seed	Very acid woods soil, well-drained. Full shade. Pine needle mulch
Yellow ladyslipper—*Cypripedium parviflorum pubescens*	Yellow woods orchid	Buy plants. Seed	Moderately acid to neutral well-drained soil. Half shade
Hepatica (Liverwort)—*Hepatica americana*	Delicate 4-in. high blue-violet blossoms from rosette of red-backed round leaves	Division. Seed. Transplant with 3x3x3 in. ball	Acid woods soil. Full shade. Good drainage
Twinflower—*Linnaea borealis, L. americana*	Evergreen creeper, fragrant rose to white flowers	Cuttings	Rich acid soil. Full shade
Trout lily (Dogtooth violet)—*Erythronium americanum*	4-8 in. Yellow	Bulbs. Set 6-8 in. deep. Transplant when in bloom with 6x6x8 in. ball	Neutral moist wood or brook banks
Showy orchis—*Orchis spectabilis*	5-10 in. rosy lavender and white flowers in clusters	Buy plants	Neutral moist stony woods
Wild ginger—*Asarum canadensis*	6-10 in. spreading plant with brownish blossoms underneath, lying on the ground	Rootstock near surface. Transplant with 3 inches soil	Neutral moist rich soil
Celandine poppy—*Stylophorum diphyllum*	12-16 in. Gold yellow flowers	Transplant	Neutral soil, moist shaded spots

WILD GARDEN MATERIAL FOR ROCKY HILLSIDES AND OPEN UPLANDS

Small trees and shrubs: Paper or canoe birch, mountain ash, bird cherry, striped maple, juniper, ninebark, shadbush, hop tree, Stewartia, bush honeysuckle, snowberry, azalea, mountain laurel, blueberries, huckleberries, pinxter-flower.

NAME	DESCRIPTION	PROPAGATION	SPECIAL NEEDS
Canada mayflower—*Maianthemum canadense*	3-6 in. white flower	Division	Acid dry or well-drained soil. Shade
Christmas fern—*Polystichum acrostichoides*	8 in. to 3 feet. Thick evergreen fronds in circular clump	Transplant with crown half above surface	Any soil. Rocky or shady hillside, moist or dry.
Baneberry—*Actea rubra*	1-2 ft. White flower, bright red berries	Seed sown in fall or root division in spring	Acid to neutral soil. Open, well-drained woods
Polypody fern—*Polypodium vulgare*	4-15 in. Simple deeply pinnate fronds	Root division or transplant in sods	Neutral soil on rocky, shady hillsides
Shinleaf—*Pyrola elliptica*	6-10 in. White flower	Root division	Acid soil in dry woods
Fire pink (Catchfly)—*Silene virginica*	12-18 in. Crimson flower	Seed sown in fall	No soil preference. Dry open woods, well-drained. Half shade
Violet wood sorrel—*Oxalis violacea*	4-6 in. Rosy-purple flowers	Transplant bulbs	Any rocky soil, sun or shade
Yellow violet—*Viola scabriuscula*	6-16 in. Golden yellow	Transplant. Seed	No soil preference. Dry shady woods
Solomon's seal—*Polygonatum biflorum*	18-30 in. Greenish-white flowers, berries blue-black.	Division	Neutral soil. Dryish wooded slopes. Shade or half sun
Large twayblade—*Liparis liliifolia*	4-5 in. Madder-purple flowers	Plant roots	Neutral soil, dry shaded hillside
Columbine—*Aquilegia canadensis*	6-10 in. Showy red and yellow flowers shaped like jester's cap	Seed in summer	Acid to neutral poor dry soil. Sun to ¾ shade
Dutchman's breeches—*Dicentra cucullaria*	5-9 inches. White yellow tipped flowers shaped like breeches	Transplant in flower with 4x4x5 in. ball of earth	Neutral soil in thin woods—dry slope
Early saxifrage—*Saxafraga virginiensis*	4-10 in. white flowers	Rhizome division. Seed	Neutral soil in rock crevices. Sun or shade
Sweet white violet—*Viola blanda*	3-5 inches. Fragrant white flowers with purple veins	Transplant. Seed	Neutral soil, moist or dry

WILD GARDEN MATERIAL FOR SWAMPS OR RICH BOTTOM LAND

Small trees and shrubs: Hemlock, arborvitae, sumac, viburnums, red maple, yellow wood, tupelo, magnolia, swamp honeysuckle, rhodora, spice bush, sweet bay, red chokeberry, black alder, buttonbush, meadow sweet, steeplebush, shrubby cinquefoil, azalea.

NAME	DESCRIPTION	PROPAGATION	SPECIAL NEEDS
Cinnamon fern—*Osmunda cinnamomea*	4-6 ft. Once pinnate. Tuft of rust-brown wool at base of each pinnae. Black half-exposed rootstock	Cut rootstock with axe a few inches from growing tip and transplant	Acid marshy soil. Low wet woods. Shade
Virginia bluebell (Virginia cowslip) —*Mertensia virginica*	1-2 ft. Buds pink, opening to blue bell-shaped flowers	Self-sown seed	Neutral. Moist meadows, banks of stream, sun or half-shade
Job's tears—*Tradescantia virginiana*	12-15 in. Blue flower	Seed or division	Neutral soil
Pitcher plant—*Sarracenia purpurea*	4-12 in. Dark red "pitchers"	Seed	Very acid soil. Bog
Creeping buttercup—*Ranunculus repens*	Trailing golden-yellow flowers	Division	No soil preference. Swamp or bog
Anemone—*Anemone canadensis*	1-2 ft. White flower	Seed or division	Neutral. Low moist soil
Tall meadow rue—*Thalictrum polyganum*	3-10 ft. White flower	Transplants easily in spring. Seed or division	Any soil, any exposure in wet meadow
May apple—*Podophyllum peltatum*	12-18 in. White flower under pair of umbrella-shaped palmate leaves	Division or seed	Any exposure. No soil pH preference, but must be rich and damp
Turtlehead—*Chelone glabra*	1-3 feet, white flower tinted pink	Seed or division	No soil preference. Bog or beside brook
Joe-pye-weed—*Eupatorium purpureum*	3-12 ft. Flower pink	Division. Seed	No soil preference
Fringed gentian—*Gentiana crinita*	3 ft. bright blue fringed flower	Sow fresh seed every fall. Protect until April with burlap	Neutral heavy or sandy muck with abundant sub-soil moisture. Sun to half shade
Jack-in-the-pulpit—*Arisaema triphyllum*	12-30 in. Yellow-green and purple-brown striped flower bract. Scarlet berries	Transplant in fall when berries are red. Corm 6-8 in. deep. Easily grown from seed	Neutral soil. Better color in the shade

WILD GARDEN MATERIAL FOR PLANTING ALONG BANKS OF STREAMS OR PONDS

Small trees and shrubs: Sweet gale, speckled alder, wild hydrangea, yellowroot, false indigo, holly, white alder, fringe tree (south only), viburnums, birch, willows.

NAME	DESCRIPTION	PROPAGATION	SPECIAL NEEDS
Loosestrife—*Lysimachia terrestris*	8-20 in. Golden yellow	Transplant	No pH preference. Sandy soil
Jacob's ladder—*Polemonium van-bruntiae*	2-3 ft. Blue-violet flowers	Division or seed sown in fall	No soil preference. Open place along stream
Forget-me-not—*Myosotis scorpoides*	6-12 in. Light blue	Seed or division	No soil preference. Sun or shade in moist spot
Bee balm—*Monarda didyma*	24-30 in. Scarlet flowers	Division in spring	Any soil along stream or moist woodland border
Pickerel weed—*Pontederia cordata*	18-30 in. Violet-blue flowers	Division	Neutral soil in shallow water
Large blue flag—*Iris versicolor*	15-30 in. Violet-blue iris	Division	Margins of water, pond or stream
Crested iris—*Iris cristata*	3-6 in. Violet iris, orange crest	Set roots 10-12 in. apart. Will form mats	Neutral soil on hillsides or along streams. Some sun
Marsh marigold—*Caltha palustris*	8-24 in. Golden yellow	Transplant. Fibrous root may be pulled out of muck by hand	Neutral soil. Moist open spot. Or shallow water

WILD GARDEN MATERIAL FOR SANDY SITES

Trees and shrubs: White pine, Jersey pine, gray pine, white spruce, red cedar, bayberry, sweet fern, beach plum, inkberry, New Jersey tea.

NAME	DESCRIPTION	PROPAGATION	SPECIAL NEEDS
Bluebell—*Campanula rotundifolia*	6-18 in. Light purple flowers	Seed or division	Neutral soil on rocky cliffs or sandy fields. Sun or shade
Cattail gayfeather—*Liatris pycnostachya*	3-4 ft. Spikes of thistle-like pinkish lavender flowers	Seed or division	Rich light well-drained soil—full sun or part shade
Sand myrtle—*Leiophyllum buxifolium*	2 ft. evergreen shrub	Cuttings	Acid sandy soil. Half sun
Mountain cranberry—*Vaccinium vitis-idaea minus*	Evergreen ground cover	Seed or cuttings	Acid gritty soil. Sun to half shade
Bird's foot violet—*Viola pedata*	Dark violet and pale lilac flowers	Division or seed	Acid sandy well-drained soil in full sun
Blue lupine—*Lupinnus perennis*	1-2 ft. Violet blue spikes of pea flowers	Seed sown where plant is to stand	No pH preference. Poor sandy soil in full sun
Bearberry—*Arctosta phylos uva-ursi*	Evergeen trailer. Scarlet berries	Hard to transplant. Fall or winter cuttings under glass. Seed slow, needs winter exposure	Acid to neutral sandy well-drained soil. Sun to part shade
Trailing arbutus—*Epigaea repens*	Fragrant pink-white blossoms, leathery leaves	Do not dig. Take cuttings with sharp knife. May be grown from fresh seed	Very acid sandy leaf mold—good drainage. Full shade

WILD GARDEN MATERIAL FOR ROADSIDES AND HEDGEROWS

Small trees and shrubs: Red cedar, sassafras, redbud, hazlenut, lead plant, burning bush, species roses, elders.

NAME	DESCRIPTION	PROPAGATION	SPECIAL NEEDS
New England aster — *Aster novae-angliae*	2-5 ft. Rosy lilac to deep purple flowers	Division or seed	Neutral soil. Sun
Virgin's bower—*Clematis virginiana*	12 ft. vine. Green-white delicate flowers. Fluffy seed pods	Division or cuttings	No soil preference. Sun or half-shade. Roadside fences
Wild geranium—*Geranium maculatum*	12-18 in. Magenta to pink flowers	Transplant	No soil preference. Thin shade or full sun
Bittersweet—*Celastrus scandens*	6-25 ft. vine. Orange berries in fall	Cuttings, root cuttings, seed sown in fall	No soil preference. Hedgerow, fences, stone walls
Butterfly weed—*Asclepias tuberosa*	12-30 in. Orange flower	Division or seed	No pH preference. Dry poor soil in full sun
Blue vervain—*Verbena hastata*	3-6 ft. Purple	Seed	No soil preference. Full sun, open site
Wild bergamot—*Monarda fistulosa*	2-3 ft. Pale lilac	Division in spring	No pH preference. Dry sunny site
Purple cone-flower—*Brauneria purpurea*	2-3 ft. Magenta pink	Division or seed. Do not divide too often	No pH preference. Rich soil in open site
Goldenrod—*Solidago speciosa*	3-5 ft. Yellow	Seed or division	Neutral soil. Sun
Black-eyed Susan—*Rudbeckia hirta*	1-2 ft. Deep yellow rays, purple-brown cone	Seed or division	Acid or neutral soil in dry sunny spots

in their native habitat may be perpetuated.

Because they are so rare, many wild flowers should not be dug out of their few remaining hideouts for transplanting to the garden. It is difficult to move many of the scarcer plants, because they may have roots which go down four or five feet into the soil, or have delicate stems, or fine feeding roots which must not be disturbed. Before going into the woods to dig up specimens for the wild garden, the gardener should have some knowledge of the growth habits of the material he will dig. He should also have a place prepared for it in his garden, with location, soil, and exposure to suit its needs. Unless he knows exactly what he is doing, he will do better to leave the plants untouched, and to mark their position for transplanting or taking cuttings at a later time.

Some wild flowers, ferns, shrubs, and trees are adaptable, and will make the move from part shade to full sun, or from a bog to a moist wood, without losing much of their original vigor. Woody plants, with the exception of the heaths, are usually more adaptable than herbaceous ones. Roots of trees and shrubs go deep into the soil, and if they do not find conditions to their liking at one level, they may find them at another. Moreover, when woody plants are relieved of the competition of the wilds and are placed in surroundings where they have room to grow, and where weedy growth has been removed, they may accept a little more sun, or a little more moisture than they are used to.

Herbaceous plants are not so adaptable, as a rule. Before they were able to germinate and grow at all in their native surroundings, conditions had to be nearly perfect for them. With a few exceptions, they will not do well unless they are transplanted to positions and soil almost exactly duplicating that which they had.

After a wild garden is started and plants have found comfortable living quarters in it, very little maintenance work is required. Occasional thinning of the more rampant growers and removal of undesirable volunteers is all that should be necessary. If the proper combinations of plants are brought together, they will provide their own mulch and plant nutrients, and will maintain soil conditions to the liking of all. A really successful wild garden is one that can perpetuate itself.

SOIL: Some of the rarest wild flowers require very acid soil, with a pH of 4.0 to 5.0. Unless the garden site is in a pine woods, the chances are against its having soil near this extreme of acidity. Many other wild plants need slight acidity, and a still larger number, among them the commonest wild flowers, will grow in neutral soil, or are indifferent to slight acidity or alkalinity.

Very acid soil is composed largely of partially decomposed leaves, bits of bark and branches, and toppled dead trees rich in tannic acid. These are most commonly hemlock, pine, or oak. Forests in which these trees predominate will have a floor of extremely acid soil. On the other hand, woods which are made up of maples and other sweet-wooded trees will be carpeted with soil which is neutral or nearly so. Native vegetation which may be found growing under these two types of forests may be used as an index of the acidity. In the acid soil blueberries, wood anemone, and star grass may grow. Poison ivy and goldenrod are an indication of little or no acidity in the soil.

By mixing soil from a very acid area with neutral soil, a slightly acid layer may be produced in which some of the plants needing only slight acidity may grow. But to achieve a very acid soil in a neutral soil area, it may be necessary to plant some of the acid-producing trees first. Temporary soil acidity may be manufactured by use of acid mulch and humus, but unless a permanent supply of such mulch and humus is planted on the spot, the wildlings dependent on it will eventually die out.

Before he can determine the needs and possibilities of his wild garden, the gardener must test the soil for acidity. A soil testing kit is one of the best tools of wild gardening. A plan of the area should be drawn, with tests made at frequent intervals both of soil and waterways. With this information, the gardener is ready to plan his planting, and to dig material from nearby woods suitable for his soil, with some certainty that they will succeed after being transplanted.

Soil texture may be altered more easily than the pH factor to suit specific plants. Plants like alpines which require a gritty soil may be accommodated by spreading a fine rock-chip mulch over the soil surface. Damp meadow conditions may be simulated by laying perforated water pipes below the surface of the soil. A chopped leaf compost mixed with plenty of rotted manure or cottonseed meal has approximately the texture and nutrients of rich woods soil. If acid spring water is available on the site, a planting of sphagnum moss in it will make a fine bed for pitcher plants or bog orchids.

PROCURING PLANTS: Plants of some species may be found easily in woods and fields, and may be transplanted to the wild garden. But some of the choicest plants are scarce, and even if found, should not be dug. Specialists may be found who raise many of the wild plants for sale, and some will also supply seed. If plants can be purchased from local nurseries they will probably succeed better than if they were raised in a distant locality.

Wild flower seed is often hard to germinate, but when it does grow it probably produces the most healthy plants for the wild garden. Not much is known about many wild flowers and their propagation. Some seed grows quickly if it is fresh, some needs to ripen until the following year, and still other seed may need a freezing winter before it will germinate. Because of the uncertainty of growing plants from seed, it is best to plant in containers which may be sunk in a moist, protected spot where they may stay for a year or more. Good labels and patience produce fine results in a wild garden.

Wild ferns are fairly easy to transplant if they are kept moist throughout the process. They may be dug with balls of earth, or the soil may be carefully washed from the roots, which are then packed in wet moss until they can be replanted.

Material which may be planted in various wild garden sites is listed in the accompanying chart. *See also* ROCK GARDEN.

WILDLIFE: An abundance of beneficial wildlife is essential in the garden and on the farm. The animals and birds that eat insects, weed seeds, small animal pests and other harmful organisms should be protected as a vital resource.

On the farm especially, a sizable wildlife population can often mean the saving of a whole crop from insects or disease. Perhaps even more important is the prevention of "hidden" crop damage, the lowering of yields which may not be obvious to the farmer because he is still getting a fair amount of profit from the crop. Numerous studies have shown that yields which are considered good can often be surprisingly raised by putting into practice measures specifically designed to foster wildlife.

In New York State, for example, one study showed that pastures which were considered good yielders were having more of their grass and clover eaten by insects than by the cattle. In another in Michigan, meadow mice were consuming half again as much alfalfa in a hay meadow as the grazing sheep. A goodly population of birds, skunks, weasels, foxes, owls and the like would have prevented this loss.

HARMFUL PRACTICES: Often wildlife can be increased simply by eliminating certain practices detrimental to them. Burning vegetation, clean fall plowing, overgrazing, clear cutting and early clean mowing of pastures and watercourses destroy the food and habitats of a vast number of helpful birds and animals. And of course, the use of chemicals, insecticides and weed killers accounts for fantastic numbers.

THE SOIL AND WILDLIFE: Just as poor soil will not produce good crops, neither will it support large amounts of wildlife. The importance of having a fertile soil amply supplied with all the major and minor elements is something which wildlife experts are increasingly emphasizing.

They have found, for instance, that pheasants are usually abundant in areas where corn and small grains are grown. But in addition to these foods they must have plenty of calcium, and if the soil is lacking in this element, few pheasants will live in the area, no matter how plentiful the grain food. A study in Missouri showed that raccoons in areas with very fertile soil were often twice as big as those in regions where the soil was poor. Deer have also been shown to avoid areas where the browse is low in cobalt.

Building up the soil, therefore, is one of the best ways to increase the numbers and variety of beneficial wildlife on your place.

WILDLIFE NEEDS: All wildlife has three requirements—water, food and shelter. Water may be obtained from succulent foods, dew or surface sources. Any wet land—streams, marshes and ponds—not suitable for crop production should have their depths, margins and banks planted to suitable vegetation. Here as in most wildlife plantings, a variety of cover and food plants is essential: grasses, thickets and woods.

Establishing good wildlife situations also includes the planting of hedges, windbreaks, fence rows, waste areas and borders to suitable plants. A list of some of the best of these follows.

Check with your experiment station for others suited to your area.

WILDLIFE PLANTS: For hedges, fence rows and borders (of woodland, shelterbelts, ditches, roadsides, etc.): thick-growing shrubs such as multiflora rose, coralberry, viburnums, Tartarian honeysuckle, red cedar, gray dogwood, American hazelnut, bayberry, high bush cranberry, Russian olive, wild plum; legumes and grasses.

For windbreaks and shelterbelts: shrubs such as bush honeysuckle, autumn olive, privets, chokecherry, wild plum, Russian olive, squawbush, multiflora rose; trees like American elm, box elder, green ash, black locust, hackberry, mulberry, catalpa, honey locust, cottonwood and willow. Evergreen shelterbelts can be made with Norway or white spruce and many of the pines.

For waste areas: grasses and legumes, evergreens, trees in variety, and fruit-producing shrubs like multiflora rose, high bush cranberry, thornapple, blackberry, Russian olive, gray and silky dogwoods, bush honeysuckle, bayberry, wild plum and chokecherry.

Brushpiles are an excellent means of getting quick cover in locations where it is needed. A good brushpile is at least 15 feet wide and six feet high. It can be made in an unused fence corner, around a rock pile, or at the head of a gully. The droppings of birds and animals will deposit seeds which will soon make a thicket of vines and berry bushes. You can also plant some sprouts of wild grape, Virginia creeper or bittersweet around the edges to speed up the process.

WATERFOWL: The best plants to supply food and/or cover for waterfowl include muskgrasses, sago pondweed, wild rice, wild celery, duckpotatoes, wild millet, duckweeds, chufa, bulrushes, watercress and coontail water lilies. Information on these and other marsh and water plants, as well as a list of dealers who sell them, can be obtained from the Fish and

Wildlife Service, U. S. Department of the Interior, Washington 25, D. C.

Two excellent booklets on increasing beneficial wildlife are "The Farmer and Wildlife," available from the Wildlife Management Institute, Washington 5, D. C.; and Farmers' Bulletin No. 2035, "Making Land Produce Useful Wildlife," 15 cents from the Superintendent of Documents, U. S. Government Printing Office, Washington 25, D. C. *See also* BIRDS; CONSERVATION; WINDBREAK.

WILD RICE: *see* RICE, WILD

WILLOW: (*Salix*) A genus of rapid-growing trees of the *Salicaceae* family, mostly native to the northern hemisphere. Leaves deciduous and lance-shaped, flowers male on one plant, female on another, in erect catkins. Distinguished from poplars, to which they are closely related, by having erect, as opposed to drooping, catkins. In Louisiana the black willow (*S. nigra*), yields tons of light-colored honey. The common osier (*S. viminalis*), is grown in this country and abroad for their twigs, which are used in basket-making. Large species, which grow very fast, are sometimes planted beside more durable slow-growing trees which need shade to protect them until they are well started. For the weeping willows (*S. babylonica, S. blanda,* and *S. elegantissima*), see WEEPING TREES. Grow near water in moist places, or sometimes in dry spots. Easily propagated by cuttings or seed.

White willow (*S. alba*), grows to 60 feet, with finely toothed leaves lined with silky hairs.

Goat willow or sallow (*S. caprea*), is a shrub or small tree to 25 feet. Conspicuous catkins are bright yellow.

Pussy willow (*S. discolor*), is a shrub or small tree which grows to 18 feet. Catkins used for cutting grow on female plants.

Black willow (*S. nigra*), has dark purple or black bark, grows to 35 feet throughout North America.

Laurel or bay willow (*S. pentandra*), also has showy yellow catkins on a tree that grows to 60 feet.

Golden osier (*S. vitellina*), has bright yellow twigs in winter. Hardy everywhere.

Common osier or osier willow (*S. viminalis*), is the species grown for basketry, and where the tops of European specimens have been repeatedly cut back it becomes the familiar "pollarded" willow of Continental countryside.

WILT: *see* DISEASE

WILTING: A loss of turgidity in plants caused by poor conditions of moisture, heat or wind.

When plant cells are filled with water, they are swelled up like so many tiny balloons. This makes celery and lettuce crisp, and corn stand tall and straight. It makes leaves appear wide and lush, and flowers lift up their heads. Loss of turgidity means droopy plants, leaves that are curled up tight or folded, and twisted or wrinkled stalks.

TEMPORARY WILTING: Unless gardens have plenty of organic matter in the soil that is capable of taking up excess water and then releasing it to thirsty plants, and unless tender plants are shielded from the direct rays of a hot summer sun, and hot, dry winds, there will be some wilting. This is called temporary wilting. It is a result of loss of water in the plant cells. As soon as the conditions are removed that caused the wilting, as with the coming of night, the plant cells immediately regain their turgidity, and are bright and fresh and crisp looking again.

Temporary wilting does not necessarily mean a loss of vital activity. If water is restored to the plant soon enough, turgidity is re-established and the plant resumes its vital activity. However, temporary wilting does slow down growth because photosynthetic activity is retarded. Also yields may be somewhat reduced.

PERMANENT WILTING: If plants don't get water soon enough to recover from temporary wilting, plant physiologists say that the plants are permanently wilted. Permanent wilting is very injurious to plants. New root hairs must grow to replace the ones that died from lack of water. If wilting has progressed to the stage where water is withdrawn from the green cells of the plant, the photosynthetic ability of the cell is injured for a long time, or even permanently. This means that permanent wilting retards, or completely stops, the growth of new organs, and if at seeding or fruiting time, it results in reduced yields of poor quality.

REVIVING PLANTS: Putting potted plants into a moist atmosphere is a simple way of reviving temporary wilted ones. This can be done by enclosing them in plastic or glass (as in the case of a greenhouse). Stand the plant on a pail of water inside the plastic enclosure.

Flooding wilted vegetable plants or flowers will not work, as excess water hinders capillary action. When watering wilted plants, use water that is about air temperature. (Many gardeners keep a barrel filled with water near the garden for this purpose.) Shading the plants will also help.

With wilting in the case of cut flowers, it is often helpful to make a fresh cut without taking the stem out of the water. *See also* SOIL TEMPERATURE (WATERING).

WINDBREAK: A screen of living trees will help hold down soil against heavy winds, keep snow from drifting over driveways, and in many cases, reduce fuel bills. The U. S. Department of Agriculture reports the following on the value of windbreaks:

The influence of forests on local climate is nowhere better illustrated than in the shelterbelt plantings of the prairie-plains region. Through literally hundreds of varied observations, it has been established that shelterbelts, placed at right angles to prevailing winds, afford a protection on the leeward side to 20 times the height of the trees—that is, with a belt 50 feet high, to a horizontal distance of 1000 feet.

The report further makes the point that a chain of such belts of trees will check movement of air in a marked way and that there is a slowing down in wind velocity even before the windbreak is reached. The effect of such retardation of the wind starts a whole chain of favorable climatic influences, such as the reduction of evaporation, lowering of temperature, increasing relative humidity of the air—all of which result in an increase of crops grown under the protective influence of shelterbelts.

Aside from their influences on crops, tree belts reduce soil blowing. The ability of wind to move and pick up soil particles is cut considerably although as little as a ten per cent reduction may mean the difference between considerable soil blowing and very little. A 50 per cent reduction should practically keep the wind from moving soil particles.

PLANTING: Make every effort to plant your windbreak where it will do the most good. Study the location and relationship of your buildings and the grounds you want protected. Windbreaks are usually planted across the west and north sides of property. But there can be many exceptions to this rule depending on local conditions and land configuration.

Try not to plant the screen too close to the garden or plants it is designed to protect to avoid its robbing plants of moisture and nutrients. Out on the Great Plains where the winds blow free in the wide-open spaces, they plant their windbreaks at least 50 feet from the field crops.

While you probably don't have this kind of space to spare, it is good to be generous in leaving air and growing room between the screen and the garden area. Since a windbreak has a

EVERGREENS RECOMMENDED FOR WINDBREAKS

These varieties should do well in these areas with ordinary planting procedures and maintenance. Characteristics, soil and moisture preferences should be carefully considered.

NORTHEAST

Canada Hemlock; any good soil; don't plant near house.

Eastern Red Cedar; slow-growing; alkaline soil.

*Douglas Fir; average garden soil; any exposure.

Hinoki False-Cypress; slow-growing; hardy.

*Red Pine; sandy soil; extremely hardy.

Serbian Spruce; any good garden soil; likes sun.

Western Arborvitae; any good soil; not too far north.

White Fir; stands drought well; any good soil.

*White Pine; any good soil; likes sun.

NORTHWEST

*American Arborvitae; slightly acid soil; needs sun.

California-Laurel; slightly acid soil; tolerates sea air.

Hick's Yew; slightly acid soil; likes sun.

Hinoki False-Cypress; acid soil; sun or shade.

Madrona; moist, slightly acid soil; sun or shade.

SOUTHERN

American Holly; acid to neutral soil; sun or shade.

*Canaert-Cedar; good for small place; likes sun.

*Cherry-Laurel; makes good tall hedge; sun or shade; slightly acid soil; very tolerant.

Deodar Cedar; for small grounds; neutral soil; likes sun.

Loblolly Pine; neutral to slightly acid soil; sun or shade.

Sweet Bay; for small place; acid soil; sun or shade.

NORTH PLAINS

*American Arborvitae; rich, moist soil.

Canada Hemlock; needs protection when young.

Colorado Spruce; ordinary garden soil, likes sun.

*Norway Spruce; ordinary soil; likes sun.

*Red Pine; fast-growing; any soil; likes sun.

Swiss Stone Pine; very slow-growing; ordinary soil.

White Fir; any garden soil; needs sun.

White Pine; fast-growing; prefers sun but shade tolerant.

*White Spruce; any garden soil; needs sun.

CENTRAL STATES

American Holly; well-drained, acid soil; part shade.

Canada Hemlock; rich, moist soil; part shade.

*Douglas Fir; moist, well-drained soil; likes sun.

Japanese White Pine; moist, well-drained soil; likes sun.

*Red Pine; moist, well-drained soil; likes sun.

*White Pine; moist, well-drained soil; likes sun.

SOUTHWEST

Bailey Acacia; average soil; needs full sun.

Carob; deep-rooted; tolerates alkaline soil; needs sun.

Common Olive; for patios; drought-resistant; needs sun.

Deodar Cedar; needs room and sunlight; average soil.

Particularly recommended variety.

protective factor of 20 times its height, a ten-foot screen will give you wind protection up to 200 feet. It will also give you protection for a score of feet in front of the tree belt; the trees cause the air to back up and act as an invisible wall before the main stockade of tree is actually reached.

SOIL PREFERENCE: The following trees, useful for windbreak plantings, have been listed according to soil preferences:

Acid: Pink Oak, Strawberry-tree.

Dry: Chinaberry, Carob, Acacia, Boxelder, Eucalyptus, Eastern Redcedar, Mimosa, Chestnut Oak, White Poplar, Ponderosa Pine, Fremont Cottonwood, Virginia Pine, Scrub Pine, Pitch Pine, Russian Olive.

Wet: Alders, Eastern Larch, Red Maple, Pin Oak, Water Elm.

Gravel: Mordmann Fir, Mimosa, Oregon White Oak, Mugho Pine.

Alkaline-West: Fremont Cottonwood, Jujube, Velvet Ash.

Alkaline-East: Eastern Red Cedar, Beech.

Sandy: Ailanthus, Pfitzer Juniper, Savin Juniper, Mimosa, Pitch Pine, Scotch Pine.

Most windbreaks out on the Great Plains where conditions are most rugged are composed of five distinct classes of plants:

1. Tall, fast-growing trees provide the backbone of quick protection.
2. Tall, slower-growing trees are on each side of the middle rows.
3. Short, fast-growing trees are on the outer edges to the leeward.
4. Shrubs are in outside rows on the windward side.
5. Conifers are used between the shrubs and the taller rows.

See also TREES; SCREENS, PLANTS FOR.

WINDOW GARDENING: One type of gardening that may be enjoyed by all. It matters not whether you live in the country where you can invite the choice plants of your summer garden indoors to spend the winter season in your windows or in an apartment high above the street in a metropolis. The window box or the pot filled with soil represents your "garden bed."

In planning a window garden, make a careful survey of your windows and sun porches to determine day and night temperatures, amount and kind of light including direct sunlight, source and kind of heat, and presence or absence of air currents. In selecting plants for your window garden you will doubtless give first consideration to those which you like. But before you definitely decide to include any specific kind of plant, make sure that you can provide it with the conditions it requires for vigorous growth and profuse flowering. Study its suitability for a place in a particular window. Some plants will give a good account of themselves in a south window but will fail miserably in a window having a northern exposure. Some plants will do well if they receive only two hours' sunlight per day, while still others are happy in a north window where they get no direct sunlight. Before accepting a plant for your window garden, learn its requirements as to light, humidity, temperature, soil sensitivity to any fumes that may be present in the house, and other conditions that may affect its growth and well being.

GENERAL REQUIREMENTS: The first requirement of a plant is a suitable soil. A soil that is suitable for most plants consists of a mixture of two parts good garden loam, one part compost (or leaf mold), and one part clean sharp sand. This mixture may be enriched by adding bone meal at the rate of one teaspoonful for a five-inch pot, more for larger pots and less for smaller ones. For azaleas, camellias and other acid-loving plants include one part acid peat to the soil mixture. For cacti and other plants which live in sandy soils in nature, add more sand. For African violets, primroses, and other plants which are at home in woodlands, add more compost.

See to it that your plants have plenty of light for growing, and sun for flowering. Many plants may be grown in an up-stairs, unheated room but must be brought to a sunny window later for the blooming period. Also plants may be used on the dining table or the buffet for decorative purposes but should be moved to the window for the light they need. Remember that a green plant is a solar machine, and can live only by utilizing energy in the form of light. Some plants, as the wax begonia, require little or no direct sunlight for blooming while others, as the geranium require all the sunlight a south window can afford.

Keep your plants cool, as the florist does. You will be surprised to learn that most plants definitely require a temperature far below that of the average home. The Christmas cherry thrives at 55° F. and dies at 70° F. Even the southern gardenia is happier at 60° F. than at 70° F. Plants grow better when the night temperature is from 5 to 10° F. lower than day temperatures as occurs in nature after the sun sets. In extremely cold weather window plants should be protected by drawing the curtains or shades or by placing paper between the plants and the window panes.

LIGHT REQUIREMENTS: As a rule flowering plants are more difficult to grow satisfactorily in the window garden than foliage plants. It is only in full sunlight that flowering plants come into their own. Many window gardeners grow flowering plants in windows with little or no direct sunlight, but move them from window to window and finally into south windows where they burst into profuse flowering.

LIGHT BUT NO SUNLIGHT: Many foliage plants thrive in windows without direct sunlight. The following plants will give a good account of themselves under such light conditions: Aloe, Baby's Tears, Boston Fern, Chinese Evergreen (*Aglaone-*

ma), Chinese rubber plant (*Crassula arborescens*), English ivy, grape ivy, kangaroo vine (*Cissus antartica*), Nephthytis, Pandanus, Philodendron, Pothos, Sedums, Sansevieria, and Wandering Jew, African violet, primroses, Cyclamen, Anthurium, and bulbiferous plants.

TWO HOURS OF SUNLIGHT: In a window which enjoys at least two hours of sunlight, it would not be difficult for even the amateur to grow the following plants successfully: Asparagus "fern", Begonias, Flowering maple, House iris (*Marica*), Maranta, Osmanthus, Pick-a-Back (*Tolmiea*), Peperomia, Pittosporum, Strawberry begonia, and spider plant (*Anthericum*).

FULL SUNLIGHT: A window with full sunlight is the choice window for house plants, especially those which produce flowers. Those which enjoy or really demand a place in full sunlight include Abutilon, Astilbe, Azalea, Cactus, Calceolaria, Cineraria, Crown of Thorns, Gardenia, Geranium, Heliotrope, Hydrangea, Jerusalem cherry, Kalanchoe, Lantana, Oxalis, Passion vine, Plumbago, Poinsettia, Shrimp plant, Sweet olive, wax plant (*Hoya carnosa*), and Eucharis.

PLANTS FOR BRIGHT NORTH LIGHT: Certain hardy ferns and Caladiums with their large ornamental leaves marked with white or pink or crimson, conspicuously veined, are well worth trying in your north windows. Caladiums should be planted in bulb fiber in August and changed to small pots of rich soil in compost when roots have developed. They should be repotted twice during the period of rapid growth, each time in a pot one size larger. They must be warm and moist at all times. In brass bowls on a modern Chinese chest, with the light shining through their leaves, these bicolored members of the Arum Family are a breath-taking sight.—*Dr. William Eyster.*

See also HOUSE PLANTS.

WINDROW: A row of harvested crops raked up to dry, such as hay. *See also* HAY.

WINE: Wine making is an art that requires a great deal of patience and skill. Making your own wine insures you of its quality and purity, especially if you raise your own grapes. A cool, dark cellar—not warmer than 50°—is an ideal place to store your home-made wine.

It is very important to pick over the grapes, removing all the green, rotten and dried berries, leaving only the healthy purple ones adhering to the bunch. Crush the grapes, and place everything, juice and pulp into a wooden receptacle, preferably a barrel. Make sure it is no more than two-thirds full. Also important is that the container be absolutely free from offensive odors. It is a good idea, if doubtful, to burn the inside of the barrel, and then cleanse it thoroughly with salt water. This barrel should be open at the top, and have a hole on the bottom from which you can later remove the juice.

All this should remain undisturbed until it begins to rise. When it has risen about two or three inches, it must be pushed down with a wooden handle, and mixed thoroughly. It will rise again after about 12 hours during the next 48 hours, and this process should be repeated about four times.

The wine will then begin to color. Then it is time to uncork the hole on the bottom of the container and run the juice out. This is now placed in the barrel in which it is to remain until used and placed in its permanent storing place. About a gallon of juice for each 50 gallons of wine being made should be kept aside in a glass jug to be used for refilling the barrel when it ferments. The residue, that is, the skins and pulp remaining in the first barrel, is now pressed in a wine press, and that juice added to the other. If it seems a little dirty, it does not matter, for whatever dirt there may be in it, is expelled by the process of fermentation.

This second barrel must be filled to the top. It should be placed on its side, and it must have a hole on the top, for the foam of fermenting to escape. A spigot should be at the bottom where the wine will be taken when ready for use.

This will likely begin to ferment within 24 hours or so, but if it does not, then ten to 15 pounds of sugar for every 50 gallons of wine should be added. However, real Italian wine is just pure grape juice. Fermentation is noted by foam that comes out of the hole at the top of the barrel. When the foam is expelled it is noted that wine recedes, and then the juice in the jug should be used in order that the barrel may be completely full at all times. If the barrel is not full, the dirt is retained in the wine, making it cloudy, instead of the ruby clear color it should have. When it stops fermenting, it should be left open for a few more days, and then should be lightly corked for three or four days. By listening closely, one can hear slight noises. As long as these continue, the barrel should not be tightly corked, but when they are no longer evident, then the cork can be sealed, and the wine is left to age for several months. Once the barrel is tapped, it is best to continue drawing from it. Some people like to bottle it, although it is preferable to let it remain undisturbed in the barrel.

To make a sweet wine, like muscatelle, smash the grapes, and press immediately without letting it stand in the pulp. Strain the juice, add three pounds of sugar and enough water to make a full gallon. This can be put in jugs and left uncorked to ferment, a process which takes about two or three months. When it no longer ferments, it can be sealed until used.— *Jennie Romano.*

WINEBERRY: (*Rubus phoenicolasius*) A bramble native to Japan and China but naturalized in Eastern United States. Arching canes which may root at tips covered with red sticky hairs and weak thorns, leaves three-parted, flowers small pink or white, berries bright red surrounded until ripe by orange bracts. Grown sometimes for ornament, but berries also very good for freezing and for jelly, though of somewhat insipid flavor when freshly picked. Fruit on canes of previous year's growth. Easily grown on any good garden soil, with some shade, and less likely to winter-kill in a northern exposure. Propagated by root cuttings, suckers or seeds.

WINTERBERRY: Popular shrubs of the holly family (*Ilex*), including the native winterberry (*I. verticillata*), smooth winterberry (*I. laevigata*) and also *I. glabra,* more commonly known as inkberry. Like other hollies, the winterberry does best in a north or northeast exposure. The more sunlight, the bushier the plant, although a richer green foliage is developed in shade. They thrive best in a neutral or acid soil. A continuous mulch of oak leaves or peat moss will be helpful, as well as regular fertilizing with decomposed manure, especially poultry droppings. The plants benefit from watering during dry periods in both summer and winter. *See also* HOLLY.

WINTER GARDEN: Evergreens are generally considered the backbone of the winter garden design. However, there are many deciduous trees and shrubs with valuable winter characteristics, which offer beauty, color and interest during the colder months.

These include the hardy crabapples, many willows, the hawthorns, the striped maple or moosewood (*Acer pennsylvanicum*), the birches and dogwoods. Many shrubs also produce attractive berries, as the hollies, snowberry, viburnums and Japanese barberry. Colorful foliage during winter is offered by the cotoneasters, bonny heather, lavender-cotton and some

honeysuckles, especially *Lonicera fragantissima.*

Some plants even produce blooms in cold weather as rosebud cherry (*Prunus subhirtella autumnalis*), Christmas rose, spring or winter heath, and some of the witch-hazels. *See also listings of specific plants;* EVERGREENS; BULBS; BULB GARDEN; FLOWER GARDENING.

WINTER GARDEN CARE: Since many if not most of the plants in your garden and home grounds are natives of other regions and other countries, some winter protection is necessary for many of them. In growing plants every effort and every cultural practice should be used which will insure early growth and proper hardening of the twigs before cold weather sets in. This is true of the everblooming roses, and other plants which are natives of a warmer climate.

Burlap screens are an effective way of protecting rhododendrons against biting winter winds, while permitting plants to get plenty of air.

Unless the autumn is especially dry, watering should be discontinued early enough to permit proper hardening of the new growths. In a dry autumn, the wood ripens well and yet, if it should be unseasonably dry just after the first heavy killing frost, good watering is advisable to get the normal amount of sap in the plants.

Often evergreens planted near buildings, where they get rainfall from one direction, receive serious winter damage. If such plantings are well soaked before the ground freezes, there is seldom much damage. During most years, foundation plantings need watering as a preparation for winter.

Snow is one of the best winter protective mulches, but over a large part of this country it cannot be depended on to give continuous protection during all the really cold months. Frequently a mid-winter thaw is followed by a cold spell and frost sinks deep into the ground.

MULCHES: By far the best kind of winter protection for plants is a mulch which must vary according to the kind of plant. With a suitable mulch on the surface, the ground freezes little or not at all and the roots of plants and the soil organisms remain reasonably active and can start functioning in the early spring when bright, sunny and windy days, followed by sharp frosts at night, have a drying effect on vegetation. Under such conditions, many choice coniferous and broad-leaved evergreens lose so much water through their leaves that cannot be replaced from the frozen soil that they turn brown and often die as a result. No method of winter protection, however elaborate, can equal the value of a proper mulch on the ground. This prevents the ground from freezing and keeps the roots active so that the water needed by the plants in winter can be absorbed by the roots and sent up the stem to the leaves.

Mulching biennial and perennial flowers, shrubs, and trees is the last and most important job of the year so far as the garden and home grounds are concerned. It may make the difference between beautiful flowers and healthy shrubs and trees as compared with flowers that are badly frozen and sickly and insect-ravaged shrubs and trees.

Prepare your mulching material during the autumn months, but do not apply it until the ground has been frozen slightly. If snow falls in the meantime, mulch over the snow.

This will insure complete dormancy of the plants under the mulch. Do not be in a hurry in the spring to remove the mulch. Mulches should be removed gradually and only as plants have begun the renewal of growth in spring.

BURYING PLANTS: Climbing roses can be protected most satisfactorily by laying them on the ground and covering them with about three inches of soil. As soon as the soil has frozen, cover the soil over the roses with a winter mulch. Deciduous shrubs and trees overwinter well if buried in the soil.

Hybrid tea roses are partially buried by heaping the ground around the base of the plant to form a mound a foot or more high. As soon as the soil in this mound has frozen slightly, a mulch or plant materials should be put over it.

COVERING PLANTS: Some plants and especially the biennials which have a rosette of leaves near the surface of the ground must be protected during the winter, but cannot endure a mulch which packs and thus excludes a proper supply of oxygen. As examples of such plants may be mentioned delphinium, fox-glove, Canterbury bells, violas, and pansies. A suitable protection for such plants consists of an inverted box large enough to cover the plant with six or eight inches of plant mulch over and around the box. If leaves are used for mulching, wire screening over them, weighted down with stones or bricks, will keep the leaves in place.

Most plants are sufficiently protected if covered with a layer of autumnal leaves, especially dry oak leaves which are less apt to pack into a tight, compact layer. Of course, any leaves that are available may be used. Boughs of hemlock, spruce, or other coniferous trees may be used as a winter protective cove. of biennial and perennial herbaceous plants. Any material which will not pack may be used for a winter mulch as salt hay, straw, excelsior, wood shavings, rock or mineral wool.

BRIGHT SUN AND BITING WINDS: When southern plants are grown near or beyond their northern limits, some protection against wind and weather is necessary. Magnolias of the *soulangeana* type and sweet cherries should have their trunks wrapped with burlap, to prevent trunk damage by cracking and sunscald. The same may be said for English walnuts and other trees which tend to have a succulent bark. Magnolias in such northern localities are far more successful if grown as large shrubs with branches near the ground rather than as trees. Sweet cherries should be allowed to branch low to begin with, even if, when the trees get larger, a few of the lower limbs have to be removed.

Tender shrubs can be protected by wrapping them with rye straw. This protective covering should not be applied until the weather has become quite cold and the plants are completely dormant. For protecting such plants as boxwood and rhododendron against the biting winter winds, burlap screens or covers may be used. This breaks the force of the wind and still permits sufficient air to keep the plants in a healthy condition. Windbreaks may also be made of other materials as bamboo or fiber matting, boards, poultry wire covered with heavy paper, a barrel with both ends removed, and hedges of such hardy plants as spruce or hemlock. These top coverings are to be regarded as additional protective measures to be taken after the ground has been well mulched for the winter.

Foundation plantings also need to be protected against snow slides from the roofs of buildings, against the formation of ice on the plants from water which drips from the roof, and against falling ice which accumulates on buildings and later falls to the ground.

VEGETABLES: The vegetables which are to be left in the garden soil over winter should be mulched to prevent excessive freezing of the soil. With proper mulching, almost any of the fleshy-rooted vegetables may be overwintered right in the garden. Following is a discussion of cool-temperature vegetables and their care:

Asparagus seems to do best in locations having winters sufficiently cold to freeze the ground to a depth of at least a few inches. The latitude of southern Georgia is about the southern limit of its profitable culture. The plants should be cut off at the ground level in the fall and the tops allowed to remain on the soil as a winter mulch.

Horseradish is perfectly hardy and is well adapted for growing in the north temperate regions of the United States. It requires no particular winter care. It might be well to stake the plants so that roots can be dug in early spring before new growth begins.

The *dandelion* is hardy and adapted for growing in almost any garden soil. In colder parts of the country it is desirable to mulch slightly during the winter using leaves, straw, strawy manure, or any mulching material which will not pack. Before putting down the winter mulch, apply a thin layer of compost between the rows and work it into the soil lightly. Early the following spring the plants will be ready for use as greens.

Kale, or *borecole*, is hardy and lives over winter in latitudes as far north as Pennsylvania and in other locations where similar winter conditions prevail. In northern regions where it lives over winter the last sowing should be about six weeks before frost in order that the plants may become well established. A light winter mulch applied after the ground is frozen will help keep the plants vigorous and insure a good growth in early spring.

Spinach is a reasonably hardy cool-weather plant that withstands winter conditions throughout most portions of the South. In colder portions of the southern states it may need some protection during the winter, for, like cabbage and other hardy crops, it is sometimes severely injured or even killed by low temperatures. With some protection, as cold frames, spinach can be grown in winter even in the North. Also cloches are ideal for keeping spinach and other greens in production throughout all or most of the winter.

In the south *endive* is mainly a winter crop. For winter use in the North, plants should be removed from the garden with a ball of earth, placed in a cellar or cold frame where they will not freeze, and tied and blanched as needed.

Lettuce is a cool-weather crop, being as sensitive to heat as any vegetable grown. In the South, lettuce culture is confined to late fall, winter, and spring. For northern gardens, sow a variety of winter lettuce which is highly resistant to low temperatures.

Another winter vegetable is *parsley* which is hardy to cold but sensitive to heat. If given a little protection it may be carried over winter throughout most of the North.—*Dr. William Eyster.*

See also MULCH; EVERGREENS; ROSES.

WINTERGREEN: (*Gaultheria procumbens*) A low-growing evergreen plant with a creeping stem. It is found in scattered localities in woods and clearings from eastern Canada southward to the Gulf States, especially at elevations of 2,000 feet or more.

Like other woodland plants, wintergreen thrives only in partial shade and plantings should be made in a grove or under a specially constructed shade, such as is used for ginseng or goldenseal. A fairly good growth may be expected in soil that is thoroughly mixed with leaf mold to a depth of four inches or more. For propagation, divisions of wild plants can be used, set in fall or spring about six inches apart each way in their permanent location. Wintergreen is usually gathered in October, at the end of the growing season. *See also* TEABERRY.

WINTER HELIOTROPE: *see* PETASITES

WINTER-KILL: Kill by exposure to extreme cold, or cold greater than the hardiness of the plant is able to take. Some tender plants will winter-kill at temperatures 10 to 20 degrees below freezing, others will not winter-kill above 20 below zero. Twigs and immature wood may be winter-killed, while the mature older wood remains untouched. Or the top of a plant may be winter-killed to the ground, and may sprout again from the roots. A sudden drop in temperature early in winter is more likely to winter-kill than the same drop late in the season when new growth has become hardened.

WINTER SAVORY: (*Satureja montana*) A perennial herb of the mint family, with an odor and flavor similar to that of the annual-type summer savory, but stronger. The plants grow to a height of 16 to 18 inches and are very branching and woody.

Seeds can be sown directly in the garden early in spring or in a cold frame or window box and the plants transplanted to the garden when two or three inches high. Several plants set 16 to 18 inches apart either in a row or in a bed with other perennials will be decorative and also will supply ample leaves for flavoring.

The tender tops and branches can be cut for use during the season in the same manner as summer savory or thyme. The leaves and flowering tops for winter use should be cut at the beginning of the flowering period. The herb can be hung in small bunches or spread on screens. When the leaves are dry remove them from the stems and store for use as needed. *See also* SAVORY.

WIREWORMS: Slender, jointed, usually hard-shelled worms. They are light to dark brown, clumsy in action, and range in length up to 1½ inches.

Chewing insects, they feed entirely underground, attacking germinating seeds and the roots, underground stems, and tubers of growing plants. Potatoes, beets, beans, cabbage, carrots, corn, lettuce, onions, and turnips, as well as other crops, are subject to injury. Damage is most likely to occur on poorly drained soil or on land that has been grass sod.

The best control measures to use against wireworms are those that will destroy the conditions under which the insects usually develop.

Good drainage tends to reduce wireworm damage. Newly broken sodland should not be used for the garden if other soil is available. If sodland must be used, it should be thoroughly plowed and stirred once a week for four to six weeks in the early fall preceding spring planting. Stirring the soil exposes many of the insects and crushes many others. Enriching soil with humus will also improve aeration and reduce wireworm attacks. *See also* INSECT CONTROL.

WISTARIA: Also spelled wisteria. A genus of flowering ornamental vines of the pea family, *Leguminosae,* hardy in the North, and native in Asia, Australia, and the United States. Some of the wistarias are vigorous growers which may cover an entire house. It is well to keep them under control by pruning, which will also make them bloom more freely.

Stems or trunks of mature specimens twining, leaves velvety and compound, flowers in large drooping clusters, some before the leaves open. Colors are purple, lavender, white, and yellow.

Thriving in deeply prepared rich soil, they are hard to transplant after making any appreciable growth. Plant in full sun. Because the seedlings take years to begin blooming, it is best to buy grafted potted plants from local nurseries. Soil should be prepared three feet deep, with a third of its bulk rotted manure. Manure should

also be used to mulch each year. Young plants should be tied to a support until they begin to twine.

W. floribunda or Japanese wistaria has 18-inch clusters of blue-violet flowers, followed by velvety pods. Variety *macrobotrys* or *multijuga* has flower clusters to three feet. There is also a white variety.

Chinese wistaria (*W. sinensis*), grows taller than the Japanese, though the flower clusters are not so large. Both these species blossom before the leaves open, and are very showy.

W. macrostachya is a native American species with lilac-purple flowers in one-foot clusters, but less showy than the above because the leaves open before the flowers. *W. frutescens,* also native here, has flower clusters no more than four inches long.

W. venusta, one of the hardiest, is a Chinese silky wistaria with white flower clusters six inches long. *See also* VINES.

WITCH-ALDER: (*Fothergilla*) A genus of the witch-hazel family, similar to witch-hazel but lacking petals. Grow in rich, moist places in the garden or wild garden. *F. gardeni,* dwarf alder, grows only south of Philadelphia, a three-foot shrub used as an ornamental. *F. monticola,* four to six feet, and *F. major,* which grows to ten feet, are not much more hardy, though their flower clusters are somewhat more conspicuous, being white spikes three to four inches long.

WITCH-HAZEL: (*Hamamelis*) A small genus of shrubs sometimes called winter-bloom, due to their blooming period which is between October and April. Leaves alternate, oblique at the base. Crumpled flower buds open to yellow bloom, seed in capsule. Foliage yellow or orange in fall.

Easily cultivated in the garden, or on the bank of a stream or other moist site. Propagated by seed, which is slow to germinate, or by layers.

H. virginiana is a shrub or tree to

25 feet, hardy from Canada southward. Light yellow flowers bloom
while leaves are falling.

H. vernalis, hardy from Philadelphia south, grows to six feet, and opens
its yellow flowers with dark red calyx
during the winter.

H. japonica, hardy through most of
the United States, blooms between
January and March. It grows to a
small tree 10-25 feet tall. Flowers are
bright yellow, or in variety *arborea,*
golden yellow.

H. mollis is the showiest species,
with leaves grayish-white beneath and
golden yellow flowers with red calyx
in February or March.

WOLFBERRY: *see* SYMPHORICARPOS

WOMAN'S TONGUE TREE: *see* LEB-
BEK

WOOD ASHES: A valuable source of
potash in the garden. Hardwood ashes
generally contain from one to ten per
cent potash, in addition to 1½ per
cent phosphorus. Wood ashes should
never be allowed to stand in the rain,
as the potash would leach away. They
can be mixed with other fertilizing
materials, side-dressed around growing plants, or used as a mulch. Apply
about five to ten pounds per 100 square
feet. Avoid contact between freshly
spread ashes and germinating seeds or
new plant roots by spreading ashes a
few inches from plants. It is not recommended to use wood ashes around
blueberries or other acid-loving plants,
since they are alkaline. *See also*
POTASH; FERTILIZER.

WOOD-BETONY: *see* PEDICULARIS

WOODBINE: *see* PARTHENOCISSUS

WOOD CHIPS: Like sawdust and
other wood wastes, wood chips are
useful in the garden. They have a
higher nutrient content than sawdust,
and do a fine job of aerating the soil
and increasing its moisture-holding
capacity.

Following is a summary report by

Herbert A. Lunt of the Connecticut
Agricultural Experiment Station on
the use of wood chips:

Studies were conducted over a five-
year period to determine the effectiveness of wood chips (and sawdust) for
soil improvement. In most cases the
chips were applied only once and
worked into the soil, with and without
extra nitrogen. Crop yields or plant
growth was measured and various
tests made on the soils. The work was
done in greenhouse pots, in outdoor
soil frames, and on field plots.

These studies show that wood chips
(or sawdust): (1) had no appreciable
effect on soil acidity nor were they
toxic to plants aside from the temporary nitrogen deficiency. (2) Chips
had a modest but generally favorable
effect on soil structure, organic matter
content, and associated soil properties
(3) When fresh, chips almost invariably reduced first crop growth, and
were not consistent in their effect on
succeeding crops. (4) When supplemented with sufficient nitrogen or
when composted before applying, chips
did not decrease first crop yields, and
they generally increased yields of succeeding crops. (5) Chips are probably
more effective on sandy soils than on
loams, although very coarse-textured
soils may become excessively loose and
open the first year or two, unless the
chips are first composted. (6) Birch
chips decomposed more rapidly than
either oak or pine and would require
the most nitrogen to prevent deficiencies. Pine decomposition was slowest of the three and required the least
amount of nitrogen. In general, pine
chips were more effective than oak or
birch in improving the soil.

It is concluded that wood chips,
sawdust, or other types of wood fragments are beneficial to the soil, particularly where the texture is sandy
loam or coarser. (Their effects on fine-
textured soils have not been studied
in this work but there is evidence from
the literature of marked improvement
in porosity and friability as a result

of sawdust or shavings applications.) Repeated use of chips every few years, in conjunction with good soil management, would undoubtedly result in appreciable and permanent soil improvement.

Generally the incorporation of fresh chips has no detrimental effect on the crop if sufficient nitrogen is present or provided. A safer practice, however, is to apply the chips ahead of a green manure crop, preferably a legume, or in any event to allow about a year interval between application and seeding or planting of the main crop. Other good ways to use wood fragments which may be preferable under some conditions are: (a) as bedding in the barn followed by field application of the manure; (b) as a mulch on row crops, eventually working the partially decomposed material into the soil; or (c) after adequately composting the chips with other organic materials. Naturally well-rotted pure chips or sawdust is safe material to use under almost any condition. *See also* MULCH; SAWDUST.

WOOD DAFFODIL: *see* UVULARIA

WOOD ROT: Decay of the wood of a living or dead tree by fungus, which enters the tree through a wound in the bark. If the injury goes only into the outer layers of bark, fungus may gain a foothold there and penetrate much more deeply into the wood. Wood rot of the heartwood of an old tree may be dangerous, causing the tree to lose its mechanical support. Best remedy for tree rot is prompt attention to injuries, removing injured branches, and filling cavities left by cleaning out dead tissue. *See also* PRUNING; TREE SURGERY.

WOODSIA: A genus of small rock ferns of the *Polypodiaceae* family, native of the northern regions of the northern hemisphere. Once or twice compound fronds grow abundantly from heavy rootstocks, with tufted stalks. Prefer rocky, shady spots, though some are found growing on sandstone or granite ledges in full sun. Peat and charcoal should be mixed in rock garden soil to accommodate them, and sandstone chips on the surface will benefit them.

Smooth woodsia (*W. glabella*), has once-pinnate fronds and straw colored stipes. Easy to grow, but found usually only in northern mountains.

Rusty woodsia (*W. ilvensis*), has two- to six-inch woolly fronds with fine hairs below which turn rusty by midsummer.

Common woodsia (*W. obtusa*), found in the Appalachians, grows six to 14 inches tall with rounded pinnae. Evergreen in the southern parts. A similar and slightly smaller species, *W. scopulina,* is found in the Northwest.

WOOD SORREL: *see* OXALIS

WOOD WASTES: More and more soil scientists have come to agree that wood wastes represent a large source of organic matter, which could and should be returned to the soil. Some firms, in fact, have already begun marketing composted bark as a soil conditioner. Like other organic matter, wood wastes serve to loosen the soil and improve structure; can be used as a base for fertilizer; and help to control the rate at which plants obtain food from the soil. Even paper mill sludge has been found beneficial; Wisconsin farmers have used it as a substitute for lime on acid soils. *See also* LIGNIN; WOOD CHIPS; SAWDUST; MULCH.

WOODY PLANTS: Shrubs, trees, or vines which do not die to the ground during the winter, and have buds above ground. Herbaceous plants, as opposed to woody plants, die to the ground each year, and have only underground buds.

WOOL WASTES: Also known as shoddy. Used by British farmers living in the vicinity of wool textile mills since the industrial revolution in the early 19th Century. The wool fiber decomposes when in contact with moisture in the soil, and in the process, produces available nitrogen for plant growth. Generally, the moisture content of the wool wastes is between 15 and 20 per cent. It analyzes from 3.5 to 6.0 per cent nitrogen, 2.0 to 4.0 per cent phosphoric acid, and 1.0 to 3.5 per cent potash.

WORM: *see* EARTHWORM; INSECT PESTS

WORMSEED: (*Chenopodium ambrosioides*) A coarse, usually annual weed, occurring commonly in waste places and often in cultivated ground throughout the eastern and southern parts of the United States. The seeds (fruits) and the volatile oil distilled from the fruiting tops of the plant are employed in medicine in the control of intestinal worms, especially in veterinary practice. American wormseed grows well under cultivation in almost any soil, but a good sandy loam is preferred.

WORMWOOD: (*Artemisia absinthium*) A hardy herbaceous Old World perennial that has escaped from cultivation in this country and now occurs as a weed in many localities in the southern states. It is grown commercially on a small scale in Michigan and Oregon. The volatile oil, which is used medicinally, is distilled from the herb and is the principal marketable product, but the dried leaves and tops also have some medicinal use. It is an ingredient of Absinthe.

Wormwood will grow in almost any soil, but it gives best results in deep, rich, moderately moist loams and muck soils, and it is on these that much of the commercial acreage is grown. The seed is small and should be sown on the surface of the soil in cold frames or seedbeds and lightly covered with very fine sandy soil. The plants are easily lifted when about five to six inches high and can be transplanted in moist weather with good results at almost any time during the growing season.

The plant grows two to four feet high; does best in a sunny location in the home garden; provides a gray accent. *See also* ARTEMISIA.

WYETHIA: A genus of western American perennials of the daisy family which has long slender leaves and yellow flowers. Sometimes transplanted to the wild garden. They need full sun, and are easily propagated by seed or division. *W. amplexicaulis* is a glossy-leaved two-foot plant with yellow flowers to four inches across. *W. angustifolia* has similar flowers, but its foliage is hairy.

X

XANTHISMA: This three-foot annual thrives in full sun and poor soil, and will withstand a great deal of drought and wind. It bears yellow flowers, about three inches wide, and sometimes grows as a biennial, but more usually blooms the first year. Xanthisma is best suited to dry, open spots in the wild garden.

XANTHOCERAS: The popular *X. sorbifolia* is a shrub growing ten feet or so tall and bearing beautiful ten-inch racemes of white, yellow-based flowers in spring. It is hardy in most of the United States and grows well in any medium-fertile, well-drained soil. The leaves are feathery and stay green long into autumn. Propagate by means of stratified seed or root cuttings.

XANTHOSOMA: The rootstocks of these pretty foliage plants are much used for food in the tropics. Here they are popular ornamental and indoor plants. *X. lindeni* is a fine plant for a warm window garden or greenhouse, and has 12-inch leaves veined with white and a six-inch white spathe. Like *X. violaceum,* which has larger, purple-veined leaves, it should be handled like caladium. Both of these make good summer bedding plants. *X. atrovirens,* the West Indian kale, and *x. sagittaefolium,* called yautia or tania, have even bigger leaves—up to three feet long and two feet wide—and can be grown outdoors in extreme southern Florida. Give these two full sun, very rich, moist soil, and heavy dressings of compost or rotted manure.

XERANTHEMUM: The xeranthemums or everlastings are annuals which are often grown for dried flowers. Immortelle (*X. annum*), is the best known and grows two to three feet tall, with white, pink or lavender flower heads. Some of the varieties are double. They are not particular as to soil and can be grown as tender annuals to give very early bloom.

Everlastings should be dried slowly by hanging them upside down in the shade, preferably without artificial heat. Some gardeners dry them by burying the flowers completely in pots of dry sand, which are left in a warm room for several weeks. Then the sand is poured off very slowly and the petals carefully cleaned off with a camel's-hair brush. Both these methods may be used to dry many other garden and wild flowers.

The name everlasting is given to many other plants whose flowers (or seed pods) last long when dried. Some of these are the globe amaranth (*Gomphrena globosa*), thrift (*Armeria*), cockscomb (*Celosia*), honesty (*Lunaria*), strawflower (*Helichrysum bracteatum*), winged everlasting (*Ammobium alatum*), and garden immortelle (*Helipterum*).

XEROPHYLLUM: The turkeybeards, wild garden plants, have very narrow grass-like leaves and bear dense racemes of tiny white flowers in early summer. *X. asphodeloides* grows four or five feet tall in moist, acid, sandy soil and is usually found along the borders of pine-barren bogs on the Atlantic Coast. *X. tenax,* sometimes called the fire-lily, grows on the Pacific Coast in similar soils, and has leaves two feet long and an 18-inch flower cluster. Both can be transplanted fairly easily to suitable spots in the wild garden.

XEROPHYTE: Plants which have special mechanisms to help them survive occasional or frequent long droughts are called xerophytes. Some plants like the cacti store water in their tissues, while others have foliage that rolls up tightly into a ball, has a varnish-like coating, or becomes very ashy-dry or actually falls—all means of reducing transpiration. *See also* RESURRECTION PLANT; SUCCULENTS.

XOLISMA: *see* LYONIA

XYLOPHYLLA: These tropical shrubs are sometimes grown as a curiosity in the greenhouse. They have odd branches that flatten out to resemble leaves, but no true leaves. *X. angustifolia* grows eight feet tall with clusters of small red flowers borne on the edges of the four-inch-long leaf-like branches. *X. speciosa,* sometimes called the seaside laurel, is 15 feet tall with white flowers. Both need a well-drained humusy soil in the warm greenhouse. Propagate by cuttings of the leaf-like branches.

Y

YAM: (*Dioscorea*) Yams are vines cultivated for ornament or for their edible tubers. The Chinese yam or cinnamon vine (*D. batatas*), bears cinnamon-scented white flowers and aerial tubers which are used for propagation. It is grown for ornament and is hardy as far north as New York. The underground tubers may be as long as three feet. The air potato (*D. bulbiferas*), has no big underground tubers, but is grown in the South and in greenhouses for the odd tubers borne in the axils of the leaves. These may weigh over two pounds, and are sometimes eaten like potatoes.

The yampee (*D. trifida*), is another Southern vine with small underground tubers, prized for their flavor, while the wild yam, *D. villosa*, grows along the Atlantic and Gulf Coast and has a woody rootstock. There are many other edible species, mostly tropical, some which have tubers weighing up to 100 pounds. The sweet potato is sometimes called a yam, but is of an entirely different genus (*Ipomoea*). *See also* SWEET POTATO.

YAM BEAN: (*Pachyrhizus erosus*) This tropical vine bears edible tubers and pods, but is rarely grown in this country. Its stems, which often reach a length of 20 feet, need support on a fence or trellis, and bear six-inch leaves and clusters of lavender or deep pink flowers. The hairy red pods are up to six inches long, each containing a half-dozen or more seeds. *P. tuberosus* is a variety with white flowers and huge pods. Neither species will stand the slightest frost.

YARROW: (*Achillea millefolium*) A hardy perennial growing two to three feet tall, yarrow has soft, feathery leaves and small white flowers in flat heads. There is a variety with showy red blooms. The entire plant is aromatic, and has long been used in medicine for bladder disorders, ulcers and the like. Yarrow's pretty flowers and delicate grayish foliage (*millefolium* means "thousand-leaved") make it an attractive border plant. It will grow in very poor soil, given full sun, and is easily propagated by division in spring or fall. Space the plants ten inches apart. It has a tendency to become weedy and must be kept in bounds.

A. filipendulina grows four feet tall, with numerous long leaves and showy yellow blooms, and *A. ageratum,* about half as tall, has dense clusters of yellow flowers. *A. ptarmica* grows two feet high with white flowers and has many named varieties good for the border and cutting.

In very sandy, droughty soils where ordinary lawn grasses do not thrive, the low yarrows can be used as interesting grass substitutes. *A. ageratifolia, A. argentea, A. nana* and *A. tomentosa* all grow less than six inches high, with white or yellow flowers in summer, and are also fine rock garden plants.

YAUTIA: *see* XANTHOSOMA

YAW-WEED: (*Morinda royoc*) A small shrub about three feet high, the yaw-weed or wild mulberry is hardy only through central Florida and southern California. It bears small white flowers in dense heads and fleshy yellow fruits an inch in diameter. The Indian mulberry (*M. citrifolia*), grows as a small tree in the same areas, and has big shiny leaves, small flowers and two-inch yellow fruits.

YEAR-ROUND MULCH: *see* MULCH; NO-DIGGING METHOD

YEAST: *see* MICROORGANISM

YEDDO HAWTHORN: (*Raphiolepis umbellata*). Yeddo hawthorn is a popular shrub in the deep South and up to central California. It usually grows low and spreading, and has stout evergreen leaves and beautiful, fragrant white flowers in clusters. The Indian hawthorn (*R. indica*), is a similar shrub with pink blooms, and *R. delacouri* is a hybrid of the two, with a very compact growth habit. All three varieties do well in any medium-fertile soil that is not too wet or acid, and *R. delacouri* is a favorite for patio and terrace plantings. They are also good shrubs for cool greenhouses in the North, given a humusy, well-drained soil. Propagate by seeds, or by cuttings of ripe wood under glass.

YELLOW BELL: *see* ALLAMANDA

YELLOW MOMBIN: *see* OTAHEITE APPLE

YELLOWROOT: *see* ZANTHORHIZA

YELLOW STAR: *see* HELENIUM

YELLOWWOOD: (*Cladastris lutea*) The yellowwood or gopherwood tree grows 30 to 40 feet tall, and is hardy to lower New England and southern Illinois. Its wood has a pronounced yellow color, and it bears drooping 18-inch clusters of white flowers and flat five-inch pods. The showy blooms and feathery foliage make it a popular tree, and it will thrive in practically any fairly moist soil. It is propagated by seeds in spring.

YERBA SANTA: (*Eriodictyon californicum*). A shrubby perennial commonly grown only on the West Coast, yerba santa is three to six feet high and has aromatic, shiny leaves, hairy beneath. The lavender flowers appear in late spring and early summer. It thrives in any fairly moist soil of medium fertility. The Indians chewed and smoked the bitter leaves and used them for medicine.

YEW: (*Taxus*) Yews are among the the most beautiful and popular of the evergreens. They range from small shrubs to 60-foot trees, and bear odd, lovely scarlet berries that have small holes in them through which the tiny gray seeds can be seen. The wood is very strong and flexible and has been used for centuries to make bows. Both the leaves and fruit contain a poison that is highly dangerous if eaten.

The Japanese yews will thrive on sandy slopes buffeted by driving storms. They keep their clean, fresh look, with thick velvety needles that stay beautiful even through the rigors of a New England winter. *T. cuspidata* is a more rapid grower than most evergreens and may reach a height of 35 to 40 feet, but is usually grown as a bushy shrub. A variety, *T. cuspidata nana,* makes an excellent hedge, as is easy to keep within bounds. It is equally perfect as a specimen plant.

The English yew (*T. baccata*), is a slow-growing, tall tree, not often planted here. But its varieties, though not as hardy as the Japanese yews, come in many forms from low spreading shrubs to columnar or wide trees. Some have golden or variegated foliage. There are varieties to suit every use in the garden.

Ground hemlock (*T. canadensis*), generally grows less than three feet high and is hardy throughout most of the United States. It is often used as a ground cover under evergreen trees, but does not do well in exposed positions.

Yews are propagated by seeds (very slow to germinate) or by cuttings taken in spring or fall. *See also* EVERGREENS.

YLANG-YLANG: (*Cananga odorata*) This pretty evergreen tree grows about 30 feet tall in the southernmost parts of Florida, and is hardy nowhere else in this country. It bears yellowish-green flowers which are highly fragrant and used to make perfume in some tropical lands.

Another plant called ylang-ylang is *Artabotrys odoratissimus,* a woody vine with the same hardiness range, but also suitable for growing in the warm greenhouse. The flowers are similarly colored and fragrant, and it bears yellow, fragrant fruits that resemble grape clusters. Outdoors it needs full sun and very fertile soil, preferably with a mulch of rotted manure or rich compost.

YORK AND LANCASTER ROSE:

(*Rosa damascena versicolor*) This is a variety of the damask rose that bears both white and pink flowers on the same bush, as well as white-striped red flowers. The name is derived from the Wars of the Roses, in which the houses of York and Lancaster each wore one of the colors. Like the damask rose, it is hardy to southern New England and grows as a shrub up to six feet high. *See also* ROSE.

YOUNGBERRY:

This comparatively new bramble fruit is a form of dewberry. It bears abundant maroon-colored, nearly seedless fruits tasting much like raspberries. They are prized for juice, jams and dessert. Hardy varieties have been developed, one of which is especially high-yielding and thornless. *See also* BRAMBLE FRUITS.

YOUTH-AND-OLD-AGE: *see* ZINNIA

YUCCA:

Yucca is usually thought of as a desert or semi-desert plant, confined to dry areas of the South and the southwestern desert, but several yuccas are surprisingly hardy in the North.

They are very handsome plants. Nearly all of the 30-odd species have stiff, sword-like silver-green leaves, growing in a clump at ground level. A single leafless stalk rises out of this, bearing a magnificent spike of highly fragrant, waxy flowers, in many species opening only at night.

Two species have trunks. *Y. brevifolia,* the Joshua tree, grows up to 40 feet high, its branches twisting into grotesque shapes. *V. aloifolia,* the Spanish dagger, about 20 feet tall, has very sharp-pointed long leaves and spectacular white or purple-tinged

flowers. Both of these will not stand wet winters and grow only in the South, *Y. brevifolia* up to Utah.

Quixote plant (*Y. whipplei*) has short basal leaves but sends up great creamy spikes, bearing as many as 15,000 blooms, as high as 18 feet. It will not stand frost or wet soil.

Very handsome plants, most yuccas have stiff, sword-like leaves growing at ground level, and one strong stalk that bears fragrant flowers.

Northern gardeners who have never grown the hardy yuccas are missing plants that add great beauty and architectural interest to gardens. One of the best is the Adam's needle (*Y. filamentosa*), sometimes called Spanish bayonet or candles-of-the-Lord. It is a deep-rooted, tough-fibered, handsome plant that has no trouble surviving rigorous New England winters. Its flower stalk may rise eight feet or higher. *Y. flaccida* is a similar species.

Other yuccas for the North are *Y. glauca,* bear grass or soap weed, and *Y. elata,* both good as far north as southern Minnesota if excellent drainage and shelter against harsh winds are provided. *Y. gloriosa* is reportedly even able to stand city smog. *V. recurvifolia* is much the same as *Y.*

gloriosa, except that its leaves droop over.

All yuccas want a sunny location—the sunniest and driest you have—plus a light sandy or gritty soil and perfect drainage. Digging a deep hole and filling it with a sand-humus mixture will take care of this. (In the West, incidentally, yuccas are valued for their ability to bind sandy soil.) A handful or two of compost, bone meal and dried manure once a year is all the feeding they require. Watering should rarely if ever be necessary—drought induces a lovely foliage and stem patina on desert-type plants.

Yuccas generally flower only in alternate years, so it is necessary to grow at least three plants to be sure of yearly blooming. But the flowers last four to six weeks.

Yuccas blend handsomely in borders, contrast beautifully with the shapes of both evergreen and deciduous shrubs, or can be planted to stand as majestic sentinels on each side of an entrance gate or door. Also good is a line of them along a driveway, fence or terrace, or as a dramatic picture against low, craggy rocks or clumped on a hillside. Finally, yuccas can be grown in tubs and moved around for special effects.

Yucca is obligingly easy to propagate. They can be increased by seeds, rhizome or stem cuttings, or by digging offsets from the side of an established plant.

In nature, yucca is propagated by a small white moth, the pronuba. This night-flying insect deposits her eggs in the seed vessel of a blooming yucca, then fertilizes the plant with pollen from another yucca. Thus when the infant grubs hatch out, they find a goodly supply of seeds to eat. Some seeds, of course, are left to produce more yuccas. Scientists call the yucca-pronuba relationship a perfect example of symbiosis, the mutual interdependence of two things in nature.

YULAN: *see* MAGNOLIA

YUQUILLA: *see* MANIHOT

Z

ZALUZIANSKYA: The charming, magnificently fragrant night phloxes are tender annuals. *Z. capensis* grows 15 inches high, with white flowers, purplish on the outside, while *Z. villosa* is about ten inches high, the insides of the blooms white or pale lavender. They bloom all summer, the flower spikes opening only at night. *See also* ANNUALS.

ZAMAN: (*Samanea saman*) The zaman or raintree can be grown here only in southernmost Florida, although it is a very popular shade tree everywhere in the tropics. It grows 50 to 60 feet tall and very wide, often spreading to 100 feet. Its vast number of leaflets fold up at night or just before rain. The showy yellow flowers are borne in heavy round clusters, with the crimson stamens protruding far out of these. The pulpy fruit pods may be eight inches long, and in some regions give the tree the name of monkey-pod.

ZAMBAC: (*Jasminum sambac*) Zambac or Arabian jasmine has shiny leaves and hairy branches and is an extremely tender climbing shrub, standing no frost. An excellent conservatory plant, it bears clusters of white flowers that are extremely fragrant and turn lavender with age. Like the other jasmines, it prefers full sun, and a fertile, friable soil.

ZAMIA: The zamias are suitable for outdoor culture only in absolutely frost-free sections of Florida. They are curious plants, having stiff evergreen leaves at the top of a trunk, resembling a palm. In *Z. floridana* the trunk is almost completely underground, but in *Z. integrifolia* it rises to a height of almost a foot. Both species bear six-inch-long woody cones. They can be grown in a moist, warm greenhouse, given a sandy soil mixture and ample water while growing.

ZANTEDESCHIA: *see* CALLA LILY

ZANTHORHIZA: Yellowroot is a low-growing shrub, up to two feet high, that thrives on moist, shady banks. It is hardy through most of the United States. The tiny brown-purple flowers are borne in drooping racemes in spring and the plant has interesting yellow roots. It can be easily increased by division, and is a useful shrub for suitable places in the wild or rock garden.

ZANTHOXYLUM: *see* PRICKLY ASH

ZAUSCHNERIA: This pretty perennial, often called the hummingbird's trumpet, has small hairy leaves and brilliant crimson flowers that resemble fuschias but bloom much later. It likes dry conditions and may not be hardy in eastern areas with wet winters. The plant grows about a foot tall, and does not like too rich a soil. Propagate by seeds or division.

ZEBRA GRASS: *see* GRASS, ORNAMENTAL

ZEBRA PLANT: (*Calathea zebrina*) The zebra plant is a popular indoor foliage plant, resembling caladium. It grows about two feet tall with leaves up to 18 inches long and ten inches wide. The foliage is usually a handsome green striped with light yellow-green and reddish-purple on the undersides.

Zebra plant can be grown outdoors in a moist rich soil in Florida and southern California, and should be fed heavily with compost or rotted manure. In the greenhouse it needs a temperature between 75° and 85° with a very moist atmosphere, shading from hot sun, and bi-weekly feedings of liquid manure. If the same warm, moist conditions can be provided in the home, it will make a fine house plant. Give it a sand-humus soil mixture and keep it close to pot-bound. There are many other varieties of *Calathea* growing from eight inches to over three feet tall, with variously colored and striped leaves.

ZEBRINA: A form of wandering Jew, *Z. pendula* is a prostrate spreading plant very similar to the common wandering Jew, *Tradescantia fluminensis.* The stems root freely at the joints and it has leaves striped white, light green or red. The flowers are reddish-purple. Zebrina is a popular subject for window boxes or hanging baskets indoors and in the greenhouse. It is very tender.

ZELKOVA: These trees resemble elms and grow to about 50 feet high. *Z. carpinifolia* is a round-headed tree hardy to lower New England and southern Missouri, while *Z. serrata* is a similar species hardy throughout most of the country. Neither is especially hardy. They do well in a variety of soils.

ZENOBIA: A nearly-evergreen shrub grown in the southeastern states, *Z. pulverulenta* reaches a height of five feet and bears bluish-green leaves and racemes of small white flowers in late spring. Give it a humusy, slightly acid soil, and mulch heavily with leaves. It is occasionally forced in the greenhouse.

ZEPHYRANTHES: The zephyr or fairy lilies are summer- or fall-blooming bulbs with dainty, funnel-shaped white, yellow, pink or red flowers. They are planted in spring in a sandy soil with ample humus, two inches apart and with the tips of the bulbs just under the soil surface.

Z. candida and *Z. atamasco* are the hardiest species and can be left in the ground as far north as Washington, D. C. All other species must be lifted before frost and stored in dry sand, except in the deep South. They can be forced for indoor bloom by potting a half-dozen in a five-inch bulb pan in equal parts of loam, sand and peat moss. A short cooling period before bringing them indoors—but not freezing—is beneficial. If they are allowed to dry off for a couple of months after bloom, they will flower again and perhaps even a third time in one year.

ZIGADENUS: A perennial for the wild or bog garden, zigadenus has one-foot-long, grass-like leaves and a flowering stalk two to three feet tall, bearing a panicle of tiny white or yellow-green flowers. It needs a moist, humusy, acid soil. Most species are quite hardy. Both the foliage and rootstock contain a dangerous alkaloid, which sometimes causes serious livestock poisoning in the West. Some of the other names for species of zigadenus are soap plant, alkaligrass, death camass and poison sego.

ZIGZAG CLOVER: (*Trifolium medium*). Like all the clovers, this is a legume useful for soil improvement. It is a one-foot-high perennial with zigzag stems and creeping rootstocks. The flowers are deep purple. *See also* CLOVER.

ZINC: *see* DEFICIENCY, SOIL; FRUIT TREES, DEFICIENCY; TRACE ELEMENTS

ZINGIBER: *see* GINGER

ZINNIA: Zinnias have become one of the favorite and best all-purpose annuals. Their use in the garden is almost without limit. They may form a flowering hedge or serve as a mixed border. Smaller varieties are excellent for edgings or the rock garden. Zinnias of all varieties are fine for cut flowers.

The development of the zinnia is one of the most impressive examples of improvement in a flower by hybridizing. When the zinnia, a native of Mexico, was first introduced, it was a small-flowered, coarse and unattractive plant. Today there are so many varieties of different heights, sizes of flowers and range of colors (every hue except blue) that it is best to consult seed catalogs for full descriptions.

CULTURE: Zinnias are easily grown in almost any soil and seem to survive in the hottest weather. The seeds are large and germinate quickly, often in four or five days. They are warm weather plants, so should never be sown until both the days and nights are warm and there is no danger of frost. Sow seed in the open ground and cover the seeds with about ¼ inch of soil. As practically every seed will sprout, they may be planted ½ inch to one inch apart. If the ground is very dry, soak the soil to hasten germination.

After the seedlings have their second or true leaves, they may be thinned to four or five inches apart. A final thinning should leave the plants 10-12 inches for dwarf varieties, 16-18 inches between those of medium growth and up to 20-22 inches apart for the tall varieties. Zinnias transplant readily so plants thinned out may be used elsewhere. Although they stand transplanting at almost any stage, you will have stronger well-branched plants if you transplant or thin when the plants are small.

Once the young plants are given enough room to grow, you can forget about them the rest of the summer if you wish. If you wish to cultivate, it is best to do a shallow cultivation so as not to risk disturbing the roots. Do not over-water them since this seems to help the foliage rather than the flowers.

Pinching is not important with zinnias. When the first center bloom has been cut they will branch freely. The dead flowers look unattractive, so keep them picked. *See also* ANNUALS; FLOWER GARDENING.

ZIT-KWA: (*Benincasa hispida*) Called here the wax gourd, in China this tender annual vine bears the Chinese preserving melon. It grows as a long trailing vine with big leaves and handsome yellow flowers. The fruit is about a foot long and does not have a hard rind. Give it the same culture as melons or cucumbers. It is a good ornamental for a sunny southern slope.

ZIZANIA: *see* RICE, WILD

ZIZYPHUS: *see* JUJUBE

ZOYSIA: Two species of these creeping Asiatic grasses have long been used for lawns to some extent in the deep South. But only a few years ago a new hardy strain, named Meyer Zoysia or Z-52, was developed from a Korean species, and is proving of value in many areas.

Zoysia is not seeded as are most grasses, but planted in small round plugs, or in sprigs which are strips of root and leaves pulled from these plugs. The plug method calls for the lawn-maker to dig holes two inches deep and about the same in diameter, spaced approximately one foot apart each way in a checkerboard pattern. The plugs are set firmly into place in these holes. Special plugging tools are available to speed up the job.

Zoysia generally needs two seasons to become thoroughly established, and it turns brown soon after frost and becomes green slowly in the spring. However, it does well on most types of soil, and maintains a dense, green turf despite long stretches of dry weather. *See also* LAWN.

ZUCCHINI: Zucchini is a summer squash, dark green and smooth-skinned. It grows as a compact, bushy plant, and the squashes are greatly liked by Italian people. *See also* SQUASH.

ZYGOCACTUS: The popular crab or Christmas cactus (*Z. truncatus*) is a hanging plant with fleshy stems that serve as leaves, very handsome three-inch crimson flowers and red berry-like fruits. It is an excellent house plant. *See also* CACTUS; EPIPHYLLUM.

ZYGOPETALUM: Handsome epiphytic orchids bearing spikes of large and showy, long-lasting flowers in fall and winter. They can be grown under the same or slightly cooler conditions than cattleyas. There are about 20 species, all with distinctive frilly, ruffled lips and long, strap-like leaves resembling those of an amaryllis. *Z. mackayii,* a most popular variety, is stunning, bearing up to a dozen three-inch blooms on each 18-inch stem, often with pure green or spotted petals and a white, crimson-striped lip.